BIRDS OF KENYA
AND NORTHERN TANZANIA

HELM IDENTIFICATION GUIDES

HELM IDENTIFICATION GUIDES

BIRDS OF KENYA
AND NORTHERN TANZANIA

Dale A. Zimmerman, Donald A. Turner, David J. Pearson

Illustrated by Dale A. Zimmerman, Ian Willis, H. Douglas Pratt

CHRISTOPHER HELM

A & C Black • London

© 1996 Text and maps: Dale A. Zimmerman, Donald A. Turner, David J. Pearson
© 1996 Illustrations: Dale A. Zimmerman, Ian Willis and H. Douglas Pratt

Christopher Helm (Publishers) Ltd, a subsidiary of
A & C Black (Publishers) Ltd, 35 Bedford Row, London WC1R 4JH

0-7136-3968-7

A CIP catalogue record for this book is available from the British Library

Printed in Singapore

Dedicated to the memories of:

Sir Frederick John Jackson (1860–1928), whose notes and collected specimens spanned a thirty-year period from the 1880s into the early years of the present century and provided a sound basis for development of regional ornithology,

Victor Gurner Logan van Someren (1886–1976), prodigious collector yet compassionate observer of East African birds, and the leading contributor to ornithology in the region for half of the 20th century,

AND

Reginald E. Moreau (1897–1970), unparalleled authority on northern Tanzanian birds, an extraordinary man who profoundly influenced and greatly enriched ornithology for the entire African continent.

KENYA AND NORTHERN TANZANIA
TOWNS, PHYSICAL FEATURES, NATIONAL PARKS AND GAME RESERVES

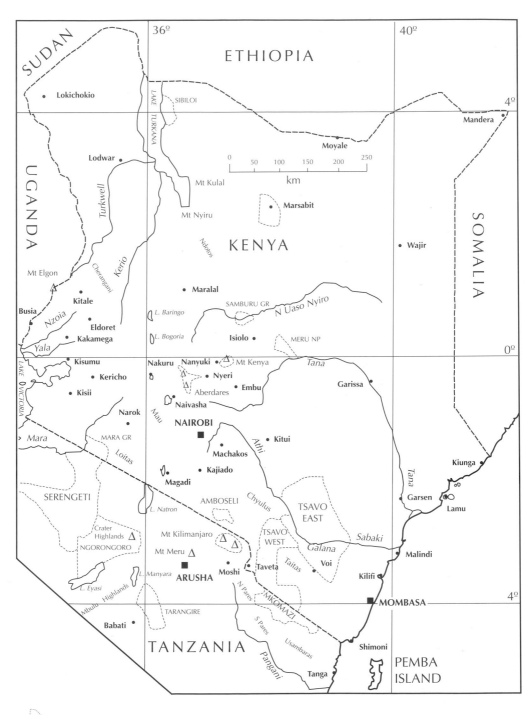

Boundaries of main National Parks, National Reserves and Game Reserves

Peaks above 3500 m

CONTENTS

ACKNOWLEDGEMENTS

For assisting us in the field, supplying information on certain birds, evaluating records, and/or offering specific suggestions we extend our thanks to A. L. Archer, G. C. Backhurst, Mark Beaman, P. A. Clancey, William S. Clark, Miles Coverdale, Robert Dowsett, Françoise Dowsett-Lemaire, John Fanshaw, Brian Finch, David Fisher, Alec Forbes-Watson, P. J. Frere, John Goodman, M. and P. Hemphill, Philip S. Humphrey, M. P. S. Irwin, Stuart Keith, Robert Lewis, Steve Madge, Y. Malcolm-Coe, D. Moyer, F. Ng'weno, Ian Parker, Robert B. Payne, Nigel Redman, Iain Robertson, Steve Rooke, Will Russell, Lester Short, Ian Sinclair, Peter Stettenheim, Terry Stevenson, Stephen Turner, J. P. Vande weghe, Claudia Wilds, Malcolm Wright, Pierre Yésou and Richard L. Zusi. Especially valuable have been constructive comments from Robert Behrstock and Kenn Kaufmann, who used portions of the early manuscript in the field. Our raptor species accounts have benefited materially from the critical perusal and detailed comments of Ian Willis. He and H. Douglas Pratt have transcended their illustrative tasks by providing scores of helpful hints which have improved the text.

Gail and Doug Cheeseman, Jennifer Horne and Iain Robertson kindly responded to our requests for tape recordings of selected species, and tapes generously supplied by Robert Behrstock, Brian Finch, David Fisher, Louis Hansen, Jens Svendsen and David Wolf have substantially improved our sections on voice. These were also aided by the Library of Natural Sounds at Cornell University, which, through Gregory Budney and Andrea L. Priori, made available recordings of Peter Kaestner, Stuart Keith, David Moyer, Myles North and Theodore H. Parker III. Richard Ranft generously provided sonagrams and additional tapes from the British Library National Sound Archive. Roy Gregory played for us selected recordings made by himself and R. A. McVicker. Neil Baker, Robert Behrstock, Aldo Berruti, Howard P. Brokaw, Peter Davey, William Drew, John H. Hoffman, Dustin Huntington, Dave Richards, Don Roberson, Lester Short, Malcolm Swinbank, Claudia Wilds and M. C. Wilkes kindly made available reference photographs of various birds, for which the artists are most grateful. Guy Anderson, Tom Evans and Laura Watson generously supplied photographs and important data pertaining to certain Usambara Mountains birds. Simon Tonge, Senior Curator of Birds at the London Zoo, allowed us access to the Usambara Eagle-Owl under his care, and provided extensive details concerning the bird's origins. David Blanton of Voyagers International, and Richard Mills and Craig R. Sholley of International Expeditions, Inc., have been helpful in arranging for couriers to carry manuscripts and photographs back and forth between Kenya and the United States. Mark Erickson efficiently prepared 4 X 5-inch transparencies of Zimmerman's colour plates, and printed the habitat photographs.

Study of specimens in various important collections, and nearly 100 specimen loans during the past decade, have been essential to the development of this book. These were made possible by ever-helpful curators, dedicated collection managers and assistants. (Asterisks mark those institutions which supplied most of the specimens for the artists' paintings.) Mary LeCroy, American Museum of Natural History*; Robert Prŷs-Jones and Peter Colston, Natural History Museum, Tring, UK; Frank Gill and Mark Robbins, Academy of Natural Sciences at Philadelphia; Kenneth C. Parkes and Robin Panza, Carnegie Museum of Natural History; Scott Lanyon, Melvin Traylor, Jr, and David Willard, Field Museum of Natural History*; Leon Bennun and Cecelia Gichuki, National Museums of Kenya; Kimball Garrett, Los Angeles County Museum of Natural History*; R. McGowan, Natural History Dept, National Museums of Scotland; Fred G. Sibley, Peabody Museum of Natural History (Yale University), J. Van Remsen and Steven Cardiff, Louisiana State University Museum of Natural History*; Bruce Beehler and Richard L. Zusi, United States National Museum of Natural History; Robert B. Payne, University of Michigan Museum of Zoology; Lloyd Kiff, Western Foundation of Vertebrate Zoology. Several of these individuals devoted considerable time to selecting well-prepared specimens with adequate data on bare-part colours, and otherwise catered to the specialized requests of bird artists.

Christian Erard of the Natural History Museum, Paris, and Michel Louette of the Koninklijk Museum, Tervuren, kindly provided data on specimens under their care. At the American Museum, Mary LeCroy searched James Chapin's files for information on certain specimens and on early African collectors, and photographed numerous bird skins that could not be loaned. Linda Macaulay efficiently responded to our requests for information concerning individual specimens. Special thanks must be extended to David Willard for his extraordinary assistance in supplying needed specimens, often at short notice, for providing extensive data from the Field Museum collections and for locating pertinent literature.

Robert Kirk, of A & C Black, deserves particular thanks for his skillful handling of many details relating to the book's design, and for accommodating certain editorial preferences of the authors.

Turner wishes to thank his wife and family for their considerable patience and understanding throughout the entire period.

Zimmerman is grateful to Dustin Huntington for continued assistance with computer operations, and to Sara Jo Anderson and Ann Walker of Western New Mexico University's Office of Business Affairs for transmitting and receiving hundreds of facsimile messages which greatly facilitated the involved operations of authors residing in three continents. Terry Heiner, Chairman of that university's Department of Natural Science, provided essential working space and facilities for housing specimens. Rosalie Rael, of the same department, was most helpful in assisting with specimen loans and in providing various secretarial services. Zimmerman also owes much to those persons who contributed directly to his operations in East Africa over the years: Dean Amadon, J. W. Boettcher, W. G. Dixson, John Karmali, Robert Lewis, the late Myles E. W. North, F. G. Seed, Robin D. Seed, David Sillu,

ACKNOWLEDGEMENTS

Antony Start, John and Helen Start, the late Pat and Mary Walker-Munro, John G. Williams and, particularly, the late Dr L. M. and Leta Pearl Zimmerman, who encouraged and partially supported their son's African research. Marian Zimmerman did extensive tape-recording of birds in the field, and took many of the habitat photographs reproduced in the Introduction. She deserves special thanks for valued advice and cogent criticism throughout the preparation of both text and colour plates, for the weeks devoted to typing and editing text revisions, for the long days of tedious proof-reading, and, most importantly, for enthusiastically sharing as well as tolerating her husband's decades-long preoccupation with African birds.

White-crested Helmet-shrike

11

FOREWORD by Roger Tory Peterson

In East Africa, where Kenya alone boasts nearly 1,100 species, scarcely more than half are figured in John Williams's widely used field guide. Because there has been so much guesswork by travelling birders about the hundreds of unfigured species, a superb team has finally done something about it and filled the gap. There will be no more guesswork.

Although other regions of our planet may boast of high avian diversity, few offer the combination of a large tropical avifauna and the opportunity to see much of it with relative ease and comfort. Kenya and adjacent Tanzania comprise just such a region, one whose popularity among world birders is reflected in the numbers of people seeking birds either on their own or with organized birding tours. Many of these visitors return again and again, attesting to the appeal of the diverse birdlife and attractive environments. Resident observers, ranging from serious students and ornithologists to casual backyard birdwatchers, are attuned to the wealth of species in their gardens, in the numerous national parks and reserves, and in other places throughout the countryside.

Kenya has a bird list of 1,080 species—the main thrust of this book—and there are 800 or so in northern Tanzania. Any bird-oriented visitor to the Serengeti, for example, is likely to encounter Grey-breasted Spurfowl and Rufous-tailed Weaver, so these and 32 other Tanzanian birds that do not quite make it into Kenya are also covered.

Coming to Kenya annually since 1961, Dale Zimmerman of New Mexico had long been conscious of the need for a fully illustrated guide that included *every* species and provided enough information for positive identifications. Although preparation for such a volume began years ago, active work on the project started in 1985 when two local experts joined Zimmerman in the undertaking: Don Turner, Kenya's foremost bird-tour leader and founder of East African Ornithological Safaris Ltd, and David Pearson, an authority on the many palearctic species which further diversify the Kenyan–Tanzanian avifauna during the northern winter. The authors know the entire region intimately, and each of them has enjoyed field experience with well over 1,000 of the local species. They also know birds in the hand as well as in the field, not only from their ringing projects and preparing bird skins, but also through diligently documenting specimen records and working out supplementary identification characters in the museums of three continents.

Zimmerman designed the 124 colour plates and painted nearly 80 of these, including all of the passerine birds, but his original plan for completing the entire series was thwarted by retinal deterioration which precluded long sessions at the drawing-board. Seeking assistance for the remaining plates, he engaged two of the world's leading bird artists, Ian Willis of Scotland and H. Douglas Pratt of the USA, both of whom travelled to East Africa to acquaint themselves with the avifauna.

Kenya and northern Tanzania have been the mecca of wildlife-oriented tourism for the past quarter-century. Here, in addition to the birdlife, vast herds of mammals still survive, and the wild vistas, extensive coastal beaches and coral reefs rank among the best in the world. Little wonder that tourism has become one of the outstanding regional economic success stories. Ecotourism, as it is now known, has expanded from a few thousand visitors per year in the 1960s to almost a million in the late 1980s, a development of paramount importance to both countries, creating employment in hotels, lodges, tour companies and national parks, and, most importantly, constituting the largest foreign-exchange earner.

Of growing concern, however, is the impact of tourist pressure on these sometimes fragile ecosystems which lure people to Africa. The ecological impact of off-road driving, for example, is rarely considered, yet vegetation loss in some areas is irreparable, directly and indirectly affecting wildlife. Over-use of certain areas already projects a somewhat negative image to the rest of the world and must be addressed at governmental levels, before wildlife populations and tourism revenues begin to decline.

At the same time, population and development pressures on forest, grasslands and wetlands, particularly in Kenya, are a major concern, as is the export of hundreds of thousands of wild birds each year from Tanzania for the overseas cage-bird trade. Although the continent of Africa has not yet lost a bird species in historic times, many are in decline and populations of some are severely threatened. A few may already have been extirpated from Kenya.

For many users of bird books identification constitutes an end in itself, but it is also a basic step essential to bird conservation. The present volume provides a superlative instrument for this purpose. It should be hailed not only by birders, but also by conservationists aware of the urgent need for African governments to establish strong strategies to preserve their rich natural heritage.

INTRODUCTION

This volume describes and illustrates the 1,080 bird species definitely recorded from the Republic of Kenya—whose avifauna is second in Africa only to that of Zaïre, a country with four times Kenya's land area. Our coverage extends south to latitude 5°30′ South in Tanzania, embracing an additional 34 bird species not found in Kenyan territory. Tanzania's most popular national parks and game reserves lie in this northern sector, whose inclusion in this book was influenced by requests from tour operators and bird students who frequently travel back and forth across a purely political boundary of no biological or ecological reality. Including the additional northern Tanzanian specialities therefore seemed practical. These birds are shown on three separate colour plates (122–124), although the text treats them in taxonomic sequence alongside their Kenyan relatives.

We do not cover the birds of extreme northwestern Tanzania, or those found only west of a line southward from Mwanza on the southern shore of Lake Victoria. These western species are more typical of the Ugandan/central African fauna and beyond the scope of this book (see Appendices 1 and 2). Our admittedly arbitrary southern boundary has been dictated by practical considerations, including limited access to areas of particular ornithological interest south of our limits where the additional montane endemics and southern miombo-woodland birds alone would materially swell our species list. Bird species new to science continue to be discovered in Tanzania—several during preparation of this book—reflecting the limited knowledge of the avifauna just beyond our boundary. However, many of the book's included species are widespread in eastern Africa, so that our coverage effectively embraces some 90 per cent of the 1,040 birds known from Tanzania, 85 per cent of Uganda's 1,004 species, and a majority of those in southern Ethiopia, Somalia and Sudan as well.

Various books have treated East Africa's birds over the years, but none has been devoted entirely to the region here considered, and those stressing identification of living birds have done so selectively, neither illustrating nor discussing many regularly seen species. John Williams's pioneering *Field Guide to the Birds of East and Central Africa*, and its successor by Williams and Norman Arlott, dealt with the vast area from the Red Sea to southern Mozambique, yet described and illustrated only 665 species, leaving field students with many uncertainties. The more inclusive, two-volume Mackworth-Praed and Grant 'handbook' for eastern and northeastern Africa filled a special need. A standard work for several decades, it nevertheless was deficient in illustrations, cumbersome for field use, and is now badly outdated. The multi-volume, large-format *Birds of Africa*, not yet complete, treats the entire continent but is inconvenient for field use in any one region. Our book is designed for use on safari, not for bookshelf decoration at home. Its primary aim is field recognition. Extensive experience the world over convinces us that a single field guide is unlikely to serve any one level of users equally well. Beginners learning to differentiate between swifts and swallows expect less of an identification manual than do intermediate or advanced students seeking fine points of distinction between puzzling waders or confusing larks. Realizing this, we have tried to adopt as broad an approach as possible, and the colour plates are designed to serve everyone's needs.

Our text, however, caters less to the casual viewer interested only in obvious species than to serious observers (at any level of expertise) and to ornithologists who desire practical descriptions of all of the region's birds, something about their vocalizations, and detailed treatment of their habitats and ranges. The East African avifauna is so large, so diverse and complex that it cannot, we feel, receive truly adequate treatment in a small, pocket-sized guide where an abbreviated text devotes only a few lines to each species. We typically provide a concise descriptive initial line or two designed to conjure up an overall image or impression of each bird, or to point out geographical or ecological restrictions that eliminate similar species. We then elaborate to a degree consistent with the complexity of the group, attempting to set forth all essential information. We have tried to err on the side of too much, rather than too little, descriptive material while avoiding delineation of every feather tract.

Although each of the three authors knows virtually all of the included species in life, many of them quite intimately, we are keenly aware that field identification of Afrotropical birds has not achieved the level of refinement now expected by advanced European and American students for their avifaunas. We try to stress 'field marks', bare-part colours, postures, voices and mannerisms useful in identification, although for a considerable number of our species such information remains incomplete and in some cases minimal. We provide supplementary material for in-hand identification of species in some groups where distinctions are particularly difficult. All subspecies known in the region and recognized by us are mentioned, and most are briefly described. Few are treated in detail, although distinctive ones are discussed more fully.

Zimmerman prepared the line drawings, designed the colour plates and painted 79 of them. He was not able to complete the series and we were fortunate in enlisting Ian Willis and H. Douglas Pratt, who executed the all-important final designs and painting of the remaining plates. Willis produced 25 plates, Pratt 20. Zimmerman prepared the introductory pages, including all illustrative material, and had primary responsibility for the facing-page notes accompanying the colour plates. The main species accounts section was the product of all three authors. Turner and Pearson prepared the distribution maps, and Turner assembled the gazetteer. We and others (see Acknowledgements) field-tested much of the text, revisions of which continued into 1995. The closing date for consideration of bird records was 31 December 1994.

THE ILLUSTRATIONS

Experienced observers know that positive species identification often involves more than matching an unfamiliar bird with a book illustration, but in most cases a person will first consult the colour plates. The brief notes opposite each of these emphasize diagnostic features that may not be obvious on the plates themselves, and they include a distributional or ecological statement to facilitate identification. Similar species are grouped together among the plates wherever practical, but there may be additional birds to consider before deciding on a species' identity. This is particularly true in certain challenging groups such as larks, cisticolas and greenbuls with numerous confusingly similar species. Sometimes, too, quite unrelated birds resemble one another. Notes accompanying the plates provide condensed information for quick reference, but it is always best to consult the text.

Except for nine birds shown as text figures, all of the region's 1,114 species are illustrated in colour. (Six additional species, to date undocumented but which may later be admitted to the Kenyan list, are also figured in the text.) The family sequence of the plates does not attempt to parallel that of the text, in some cases differing significantly. Within the non-passerines, 'waterbirds' precede 'landbirds'. Otherwise we have kept related groups together when practical, but there are exceptions. Plates 1 and 2, for example, depict pelagic species regardless of their taxonomic affinities. Optimal space utilization, an overriding consideration in plate design, has resulted in unconventional placement of some small families. Ostriches thus appear with other large ground birds, far from their traditional lead position. Sequence of passerine families also is at variance with the text. Some superficially similar but rather distantly related groups are placed near one another for easier comparison in the field: pipits are near the larks, and penduline tits, white-eyes and Little Yellow Flycatcher are with the warblers. The pitta and the broadbill follow the motacillids, as near the beginning of the Passeriformes as available space permitted. Several groups, notably starlings, corvids, orioles, drongos and the various shrike-like families, all come earlier in the plate sequence than might be expected. The 34 species restricted (in our region) to northern Tanzania are depicted on the three final plates. Only Kenyan birds are shown on plates 1–121. All plates and text are conspicuously cross-referenced to avoid location problems.

We have endeavoured to illustrate birds in typical postures for the species, yet still show essential field marks. Where space has permitted, we have included additional figures of flying birds or spread tails if these aid identification. Subspecific differences sometimes are important enough to be illustrated. We have preferred to depict these full-size (as with the various races of Yellow Wagtail), but at times smaller inset figures have had to suffice (e.g. White-headed Barbets). Most figures of flying birds also have been drawn to a smaller scale. A dividing line across a plate indicates two different size scales, and usually family separation.

Wherever practical, we have illustrated poorly known and less commonly seen adult and subadult plumages which can be puzzling in the field. Pictures of distinctive juveniles are infrequently published and we have included as many of these as practicable. Some noteworthy young birds could not be figured for lack of space on appropriate plates, and in other cases because no suitable reference specimens were available. We offer no apology for crowded plates; purely aesthetic considerations sometimes have been sacrificed in favour of illustrating additional plumages or subspecies. For a few species, we have shown both worn and freshly plumaged birds as feather abrasion and fading can profoundly alter basic appearance.

All figures of passerines and most non-passerines have been painted from specific museum specimens, often supplemented by photographs of living birds. For polytypic species, the bird figured usually represents a particular race and is so identified in the notes opposite the plates.

Our original water-colour paintings were prepared with strict attention to colour details of the important bare parts (irides, orbital rings, bills, feet, etc.). Despite this, even the finest printing invariably results in some shifting of colour values, so that tonal subtleties in the originals may not appear in the reproductions. As with plumage, considerable variation exists in bare-part coloration of many species; the bird seen through your binocular may therefore not look exactly like the picture in the book. We have illustrated typical individuals, but not all birds of a given age or sex, or of a particular population, appear precisely the same—another reason to consult the text, where attention is called to variation within each species.

FORMAT OF THE SPECIES ACCOUNTS

Species are treated following a brief family summary with emphasis on East African representatives. Occasionally, introductory paragraphs are also provided for subfamilies or genera. These contain information relating to the group as a whole, usually not repeated under the various species headings.

Each species account begins with the bird's English name (see below) followed by its scientific name—trinomial if only one subspecies of a polytypic species is present in the region, binomial if (a) no subspecies are recognized or (b) two or more are present here (in which case they are named later). A notation of metric length is followed by an approximate equivalent in inches. (Measurements are taken from dead birds in the flesh or, more often, from *well-prepared* museum specimens, in most cases by ourselves. They should be considered maximal; birds in life usually appear smaller than study skins. Many erroneous length figures in the literature are based on excessively stretched specimens. Measurements alone can be grossly inadequate for indicating a bird's size, or apparent size, in the field, but they serve as a general guide.)

Initial descriptive remarks concern important recognition features, mainly relating to the **adult** bird's appearance. Amount of subsequent detail varies with the complexity of the group or variation within the species. Little-known birds, and those difficult to identify, tend to be treated more fully. Noteworthy features or unique combinations important to identification are printed in *italics*. The sexes should be assumed to be alike or nearly so unless **male** and **female** are discussed separately, as, where applicable, are **breeding** and **non-breeding** adult plumages and those of immatures. The term **juvenile** refers to the bird's first real plumage following the natal down. **Immature** is used for any subsequent stage preceding adult plumage, although we may use **subadult** for certain intermediate plumages, and we often refer specifically to the **first-winter plumage**. (See discussion of plumages and moults on p. 44.) Where appropriate, different **morphs** or colour phases are mentioned. Significant subspecific differences are briefly covered in the identification section, with ranges of the named forms outlined later under **Status and Distribution**. Terms used in species descriptions are identified on the bird-topography drawings and in the glossary.

Voice includes an interpretation or description of vocalizations based wherever possible on our own tape recordings and field notes, supplemented by those of our colleagues. Bird voices often differ geographically, and where information from extralimital populations is presented the region is indicated. Interpretation of bird sounds may also vary markedly from one listener to another, so where transcriptions of others are included these are credited (full names given under Acknowledgements or Literature Cited), whether published or not. A **Habits** section (occasionally combined with **Voice**) is included for most species, but for more or less uniform groups such information may instead be covered only in the family introductions. In general, we mention only behaviour that may have some bearing on identification or may otherwise be of special interest.

Likely sources of confusion for a particular bird are discussed under a **Similar Species** heading, omitted for accounts of unique, unmistakable birds or if a closely similar species has been compared in the opening remarks.

The combined **Status and Distribution** section includes information on abundance, migratory status, habitat, and geographic range within Kenya and northern Tanzania. Numerical status references usually are expressed in the relative terms *abundant, common, fairly common, uncommon, scarce,* or *rare*. Such designations are intended only as a guide; a bird may be common, even abundant, in one season and scarce or absent in the next. Furthermore, numbers may vary greatly from one area to another. The terms also differ in numerical meaning between groups: a 'common' weaver or dove is far more numerous than a 'common' buzzard or eagle. Actual abundance may be quite different from the *frequency* with which a species is recorded. A low-density bird such as Red-chested Cuckoo, seldom truly common numerically, is nevertheless frequently recorded in the rainy season owing to its loud and distinctive call. Conversely, some species are locally numerous within their habitat but so secretive as to be rarely listed unless one knows their voices. Many forest birds are in this category. Unless stated otherwise, our designations refer to abundance *per se*.

A species termed *casual* is one recorded five to ten times in the region, but, considering its normal range, is one that can be expected to turn up again. *Occasional* species are recorded every few years, but not regularly. *Vagrant* birds or '*accidentals*' are those recorded only once or twice and which are not likely to be be seen again. Some pelagic species, currently so considered, may prove to be casual or regular with increased offshore observation.

Many of our birds are permanent *residents*, but the presence of a species within the region throughout the year does not necessarily imply that all individuals or populations are strictly sedentary. Many migratory (and other) movements are poorly known and may differ between subspecies (e.g. those of Grey-headed Kingfisher). Numerous *palearctic migrants* visit East Africa during the northern autumn and winter following breeding in Eurasia. Some remain here for a few months, but others move through as *passage migrants* to 'winter' quarters farther south. There are also *intra-African migrants* whose movements are not all alike. African Pittas move northward into our region after breeding farther south. Standard-winged Nightjars disperse southeastward into Kenya following nesting in central Africa. Some Black-and-white Cuckoos may be visitors from areas north of Kenya, but others are post-breeding visitors from south of our limits. The southern race of African Golden Oriole spends the April–August season in our area after breeding in the southern tropics, whereas some individuals of the northern nominate race visit western Kenya as non-breeders from the northern tropics. A few *Malagasy migrants*, such as Madagascar Pratincole, Madagascar Squacco Heron and Madagascar Lesser Cuckoo, breed on Indian Ocean islands before spending a significant portion of their year in Africa. Some Asian Lesser Cuckoos likewise visit our area.

Distributions are elucidated in terms of cities, major towns, districts, physiographic regions (e.g. the western or central Kenyan highlands), major topographic features (such as lakes, major rivers, mountains or the Rift Valley), and well-known national parks or game reserves. All of these are named and located in the gazetteer (p. 710). Spelling of Kenyan geographic names conforms to the *Atlas of Kenya* (Survey of Kenya 1962), and the *Kenya and Northern Tanzania Route Map* (Survey of Kenya 1978).

Terminology employed for habitat references is given below under MAJOR BIRD HABITATS. Elevation limits (in metres) are often provided, but may be omitted for altitudinally widespread species. *Highlands* are considered to be those areas above 1500 m (5000 ft), lowlands those below 500 m (1640 ft), and *medium elevations* everything between. The *western Kenyan highlands* are those west of the Rift Valley. The so-called *central Kenyan highlands* lie to the east of the Rift; they do not occupy a truly central position within the country. The *eastern Kenyan plateau* is not a discrete topographic feature, nor is it a plateau in the usual sense. Following Britton (1980), we use it as a convenient term to delimit the generally dry sections north, east and south of the highlands, including parts of the *Rift Valley*. The Rift itself in many cases separates related species or subspecies. This great trough, extending from Asia Minor to Mozambique, intersects Kenya from the north, and within it lie the important lakes of Turkana (Rudolf), Baringo, Bogoria, Nakuru, Elmenteita, Naivasha and Magadi in Kenya and Natron and Manyara in northern Tanzania. The *Masai Steppe* is an extensive shelf of dry country extending from

Tanzania's Rift wall east to the Pangani River valley below the Pare Mts, in most places *c.* 1200 m (4000 ft) above sea level, and covering some 23,310 sq. km (9000 sq. miles). References to the Pare Mts include both northern and southern ranges unless otherwise stated. Likewise, unmodified references to the Usambara Mts include both eastern and western ranges.

Occasional species require an additional **Note**, usually for taxonomic reasons, particularly if our treatment differs from that of other recent authors.

ENGLISH NAMES

In an effort to suppress synonyms and avoid ambiguity, numerous English bird names have undergone recent changes in an attempt to conform with international usage. A spate of publications has introduced names differing from those in earlier, widely used, East African bird books, and includes some novel appellations. The names in the present volume are largely those of the revised *Birds of East Africa* (East Africa Natural History Society, in prep.). We have introduced fewer than five wholly new names in this book, although numerous familiar ones now have modifiers so as to readily distinguish them from related species elsewhere, conforming to established practice.

It is always difficult to adapt to a new name for a familiar bird. Changes designed to promote uniformity or reflect taxonomic changes can be confusing and frustrating to laymen and to workers in allied fields, who are seldom aware of (and usually unsympathetic with) the nomenclatural manipulations of ornithologists. No official international code, such as that required for scientific nomenclature, exists for English bird names. These latter, after all, tend to evolve over time and (until recently, at least) have been determined by usage, not by decree. In this age of international birding a degree of uniformity is desirable, and we endorse some of the significant recent moves in that direction. Nevertheless, we have endeavoured to minimize our changes, and where little or no problem of ambiguity exists we have elected to retain certain long-familiar group names widely used in East Africa (e.g. mannikin instead of munia), although to conform with established usage elsewhere on the continent we have adopted some names which are unfamiliar to residents of East Africa (such as saw-wing to replace rough-wing for swallows of the genus *Psalidoprocne*).

Certain globally widespread species are widely known by names different from those traditionally used in East Africa or other parts of the continent, Striated Heron and Green-backed Heron being one example. Some birds are known by one name in one or a few other countries, and by another in East Africa, e.g. Malagasy Pond Heron and Madagascar Squacco Heron. The Thrush-Nightingale has long been known as Sprosser in East Africa, the White-throated Robin as Irania. In these and a few other cases we have attempted to give 'equal billing' to the standard European name and the one in local use. We have rejected many innovative names used by Sibley and Monroe (1990), Short *et al.* (1990) and Dowsett and Forbes-Watson (1993) as being unnecessary, often contrived, and in the aggregate needlessly and thoroughly confusing to many workers. Despite our desire to minimize changes, our English nomenclature will be seen to differ markedly from that of Mackworth-Praed and Grant (1952, 1955) and Williams and Arlott (1980). It more closely follows *The Birds of Africa* (Brown *et al.* 1982, *et seq.*) and, for primarily palearctic species, Beaman (1994). In virtually all cases, the differing names used in those works are included among the alternative names in the headings of our species accounts.

Despite attempts to promote uniformity, regional differences will continue to exist between eastern and southern Africa where many shared species have long been known by entirely different names, Harrier-Hawk and Gymnogene and turacos and louries being familiar examples. Likewise, some New-World names, such as jaeger for the smaller skua species, are foreign to most East African residents. Here, too, we include the better-known variations in the species-account headings, although we have been selective in our synonymy.

Spelling of names, like the names themselves, changes over the years. To correct long-standing inaccuracies, and to agree with southern African spelling, we use *Ovambo* (not 'Ovampo') Sparrowhawk, *Diederik* (instead of 'Didric') Cuckoo, and *Marico* (instead of Mariqua) Sunbird. We prefer to follow accepted rules and practices of English grammar in use of possessives (thus *Ayres's*, not Ayres'), and we tend to be conservative in hyphenation, avoiding many unnecessary contributions to what Kenn Kaufman describes as the "recent trend toward awkwardness and ugliness in bird names". Double-noun compound names reflecting *resemblance* of one bird by another are written with a hyphen, e.g. Oriole-Finch and sparrow-weaver (designating an oriole-like finch and sparrow-like weaver, respectively). These differ from unhyphenated names such as Bat Hawk, Honey Buzzard, Lizard Buzzard or Brown Snake Eagle implying food preferences and such. They likewise differ from those unhyphenated names reflecting a bird's habitat or features thereof (reed warbler, scrub robin, cliff chat and others). We also avoid the peculiar and unnecessary hyphenation of a noun and its modifying adjective (e.g. Golden Plover) except in two cases where there is need to clarify otherwise ambiguous taxonomic status: painted-snipe (only distantly related to the true snipes) and Egyptian-plover (a glareolid, not a plover). For capitalization of words in compound species names, we follow Sibley and Monroe (*op. cit.*), Dowsett and Forbes-Watson (*op. cit.*) and other recent authors in distinguishing names such as African Hawk-Eagle (which *is* an eagle) or Cuckoo-Hawk (which *is* a hawk) from those such as Lühder's Bush-shrike, Black Cuckoo-shrike or Grey-crested Helmet-shrike (birds in families distinct from the true shrikes, Laniidae).

TAXONOMY AND SCIENTIFIC NOMENCLATURE

At present, avian classification is being profoundly influenced by various recent and current investigations, especially those by Sibley *et al.* into DNA–DNA hybridization, a biochemical method that measures the degree of genetic similarity between the DNA of different species. Some interpretations of accumulated evidence as set forth by Sibley and Monroe (*op. cit.*) and Sibley and Ahlquist (1990), represent significant departures from the taxonomy familiar to most workers. The classification followed in this book takes into account some of these findings, and our nomenclature reflects a few changes proposed by those authors. However, DNA–DNA hybridization is not necessarily conclusive, and it remains, after all, only one of several approaches to bird classification. It would be inappropriate and premature to diverge markedly from more traditional treatment in this book.

Users of East African bird books and check-lists published prior to the 1990s will notice some unfamiliar generic and specific names, plus a few changes at the family level. We transfer paradise flycatchers and other monarchs from Muscicapidae to their own family, Monarchidae, following Traylor (1986d) and others. The batises and wattle-eyes, also formerly considered muscicapids, we place in Platysteiridae, again following Traylor, and we position them adjacent to the somewhat similar helmet-shrikes. Our family sequence is basically that of Voous (1977, 1985), but there have been several modifications, especially in arrangement of the passeriform families.

In general, our taxonomic treatment parallels that of the recent volumes of *The Birds of Africa* (*op. cit.*), although there are some important exceptions at both generic and specific levels. Various authorities differ in their treatment of certain allopatric forms as species or subspecies, and standard zoological nomenclature provides no convenient intermediate category to designate populations believed to be evolutionarily between mere subspecific standing and 'full' species status. In East Africa, a few taxonomically puzzling birds have in our opinion diverged sufficiently from their near relatives to be very strong candidates for species status, yet are not universally recognized as such. For such cases we treat the bird under a separate heading (and English name), and indicate in parentheses after the generic name the species to which it seems most closely related and/or under which it is treated by other authors, e.g.: *Struthio* (*camelus*) *molybdophanes*, Somali Ostrich; *Egretta* (*garzetta*) *dimorpha*, Dimorphic Egret; and *Turdus* (*olivaceus*) *helleri*, Taita Thrush. Where our use of a particular name is likely to be confusing, resulting from change in spelling under the International Code of Zoological Nomenclature, use of a different binomial or other deviation from recent standard African literature, we call this to the reader's attention.

Where applicable, trinomial designations are used throughout, as we have felt obliged to treat subspecies in greater detail than in typical field guides or handbooks. Although many subspecies differ only in minor ways from one another, and are of little or no concern to the average observer, basic knowledge of known races is of interest to ornithologists, to conservation workers and to persons handling birds for ringing. This is particularly true in a complex avifauna such as ours, with much yet to be learned of movements and distribution of bird populations. Additionally, numerous subspecies are readily recognizable under field conditions, and others are potentially so given the excellence of modern optics and the advanced knowledge of today's serious bird students.

THE MAPS

Distribution maps accompany the text for all but 56 species (mainly pelagics, vagrants and a few of very restricted range). The maps show at a glance broad aspects of a species' current range (from *c.* 1980 to date), but they cannot reflect details, for which one must consult the 'Status and Distribution' section.

Most well-known species have their mapped ranges enclosed within a shaded area. *Solid black* portions of the maps indicate the distribution of breeding and presumed breeding residents; *open hatching* (with diagonal lines) shows the non-breeding range of both East African resident species and those migratory birds breeding elsewhere but migrating through and/or spending most of their non-breeding season within our borders. For both of the preceding, it is understood that the map reflects distribution of a species only in areas of suitable habitat within the broadly designated range. *Solid black dots* indicate isolated breeding records outside the species' main range, or (for colonial waterbirds) mark breeding sites. *Open dots* show sites of isolated non-breeding records, both early (i.e. first half of the 20th century) and recent (to 1994). For a few species (e.g. Black Heron), open dots may also indicate former breeding sites. Not reflected in the maps is former distribution of species which have suffered a major decline in range. Such details are discussed in the text. Open dots are also used for all records of rare or little-known migrants (e.g. Spotted Crake); such records are likewise mentioned in the text. On the maps, international boundaries are represented by dashed lines. The only physical features depicted are Lake Turkana, the eastern edge of Lake Victoria, and the Tana and Athi–Galana–Sabaki Rivers.

BASIS FOR INCLUSION OF SPECIES IN THE BOOK

The important publications of Jackson (1938), van Someren (1922, 1932) and Britton (1980) have provided a firm foundation for preparing an accurate compilation of Kenyan and northern Tanzanian birds, but we have not accepted every species attributed to our territory by those or more recent authors. In the present book, inclusion of the vast majority of species is based on the existence of at least one specimen from the area in question preserved in a public museum and examined by us. Specimen evidence once provided the only basis for admittance of a species to official national lists, but, except for salvage of birds found dead, there is now little collecting in East Africa, particularly in Kenya. This is unfortunate, as various taxonomic and distributional questions can be answered with certainty only through judicious collecting.

Photography, although no substitute for preserving specimens, has substantiated numerous observations in recent years, and is increasingly important in validating sight records, which increase annually, requiring consideration by authors and check-list compilers. As members of the East African Rarities Committee in recent years, the three authors of this book have evaluated all submitted reports. We also have re-evaluated all species historically attributed to Kenya on the basis of sight records or limited specimen evidence. Our rejection of certain records as inadequate or inconclusive has resulted in deletion of several species from earlier published lists. We have accepted several species on the basis of photographs which we (and others) have examined, and one species (Green Crombec) based on tape recordings that supplement sight records made by experienced observers. We admit 27 species solely on the basis of sight records, i.e. observations supported only by observers' written reports and lacking in photographic or tape-recorded evidence. Names of these are preceded by an asterisk (*) in the species accounts.

Species attributed to our region by other authors, but rejected by us for lack of convincing evidence, are mentioned in the text under a related species. All names appear in the index. Several of these have long been considered part of Kenya's avifauna solely on the basis of specimens which may not have been taken here despite unquestioned acceptance of the reports for a half-century or longer. We have not been able to trace specimens of a few other birds, almost certainly collected in Kenya early in the century. Some of these were perhaps destroyed in Europe during World War II, and literature references to the skins now appear to constitute the only evidence for existence of the specimens in question. We include and illustrate those species, realizing that some, such as Speckled Tinkerbird and Forest Wood-hoopoe, are now most unlikely to be found again in Kenya, whatever the basis for early specimen reports, because of widespread forest destruction in the west.

A special problem for ornithologists was created by the deliberate falsification of data, involving substitution of labels, on significant numbers of stolen Kenya-collected specimens distributed from Nairobi to several European museums during the late 1960s and 1970s. Workers must interpret with caution information based on birdskins from that period allegedly collected by the fictitious 'R. D. Charles'.

We wish to stress the importance of detailed documentation of sight records and the need for photographing the subjects wherever possible. Pictures of living birds, and of those found dead but unfit for preservation, are of great value. Also, a wing or tail removed from a carcass can provide positive identification if the entire bird cannot be salvaged. Ringers can enhance the value of their efforts by photographing unusual birds handled, and by removing a rectrix or two to confirm identifications of rarities. In-hand misidentifications of living birds are frequent, and *ringing a bird does not in itself constitute a scientific record*. (Worldwide, too many individual birds ringed as one species have proven, upon recovery and preservation of a specimen, to represent another. Some intriguing inclusions on East African ringing schedules could have provided highly significant distributional information had they been supported by tangible evidence.) Evidence in support of records should be sent to the Ornithological Sub-Committee, East Africa Natural History Society, P. O. Box 48019, Nairobi. Transparencies can be properly preserved at Visual Resources for Ornithology [VIREO], Academy of Natural Sciences of Philadelphia, PA, USA. Photographs, like specimens, are often misidentified, but, *if published or preserved in a public collection for future re-evaluation*, they can make the difference between acceptance and rejection of a record. Copies of most of the record-supporting photographs referred to in the following pages are on file with the authors and/or National Museums of Kenya.

Completion of the book has been prolonged well beyond our original expectations, as preparation of the accounts for species after species developed into involved research exercises in library, field and museum. Even so, more questions remain unanswered than we would like. Further study is needed to settle some taxonomic issues. Still lacking are basic descriptions of vocalizations for East African populations of several birds, and for others only minimal information exists. Gaps remain in knowledge of distributional details, habitat preferences and migratory behaviour for numerous species, and for some we would prefer delineation of more sophisticated field-identification criteria than we have been able to provide. Recognizing these limitations, we believe that we have established a reliable basis for future work, and we hope that we have introduced no significant errors of our own. If such are found, we ask that they be brought to the authors' attention.

CLIMATE OF THE REGION

Although astride the Equator, Kenya is anything but uniformly 'tropical' in terms of the average temperate-zone resident's concept of the word. Much of that country, and significant parts of northern Tanzania, are over 1200 m (4000 ft) above sea level, and during the rains may be chilly to cool for exended periods. Above 2400 m (8000 ft) it becomes truly cold at times. Whereas all coastal areas are warm to hot with perpetually high humidity, the northern and eastern lowlands away from the coast are hot and generally dry. Still, there are periods of cloudy overcast weather when even the low bush country and semi-desert can be surprisingly cool. As in many tropical regions, the alternation of wet and dry seasons is perhaps the single most prominent climatic phenomenon in East Africa. Brown and Britton (1980) based their major eco-climatic regimes largely on precipitation, following in part the

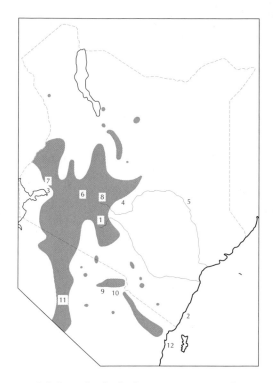

Relief map showing land over 1500 m (c. 5000 ft)

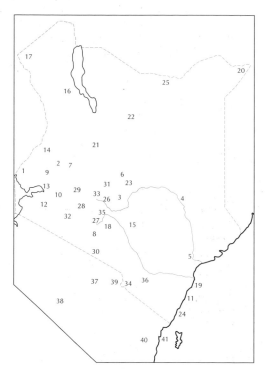

Political map showing all principal towns in the region

KENYA PROVINCIAL CENTRES

1 Nairobi
2 Mombasa
3 Kisumu
4 Embu
5 Garissa
6 Nakuru
7 Kakamega
8 Nyeri

REGIONAL AND DISTRICT CENTRES IN N TANZANIA

9 Arusha
10 Moshi
11 Mbulu
12 Tanga

KENYA (in alphabetical order)

1 Busia	13 Kisumu	25 Moyale
2 Eldoret	14 Kitale	26 Murang'a
3 Embu	15 Kitui	27 Nairobi
4 Garissa	16 Lodwar	28 Naivasha
5 Garsen	17 Lokichokio	29 Nakuru
6 Isiolo	18 Machakos	30 Namanga
7 Kabarnet	19 Malindi	31 Nanyuki
8 Kajiado	20 Mandera	32 Narok
9 Kakamega	21 Maralal	33 Nyeri
10 Kericho	22 Marsabit	34 Taveta
11 Kilifi	23 Meru	35 Thika
12 Kisii	24 Mombasa	36 Voi

N TANZANIA

37 Arusha	39 Moshi	41 Tanga
38 Mbulu	40 Korogwe	

rainfall regimes proposed by Griffiths (1958). Together with elevation, rainfall bears directly on the distribution of different vegetation types and their associated birds. Although detailed treatment is impractical here, some information on the seasonal distribution of rainfall may be useful.

East Africa is influenced by different air masses at different times of year. A northeasterly one originates over Arabia and the Horn of Africa, and tends to dominate from November to March, typically bringing hot and generally dry weather to much of Kenya in January and February. Warm, moist southeasterly air (the southeast trade-wind) brings rainfall from the Indian Ocean to coastal areas from April to July. Another relatively moist, westerly air mass originates over the Atlantic Ocean and the Zaïre Basin, bringing rain to western Kenya, especially in August (Nyamweru 1986). To some degree, local conditions can modify this general pattern.

Within East Africa, precipitation varies greatly in quantity, as well as seasonally. Large sections of arid northern and northeastern Kenya annually receive as little as 255 mm (10 in.) of rainfall, and this often erratically—although Moyale, on the Ethiopian border, has some 660 mm (26 in.) in two distinct seasons: April–May and October–November. In the northwest, Lodwar averages only 178 mm (7 in.). At the other extreme, the higher reaches of Mt Kenya and Kakamega Forest, like parts of Tanzania's Usambara Mountains, average over 2000 mm

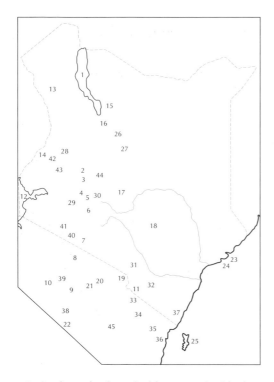

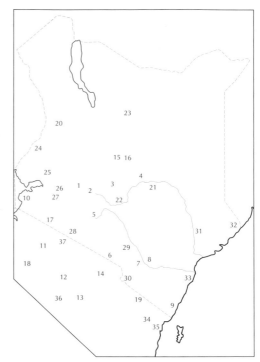

Regional map showing major lakes, mountains, islands, hills/highland areas, plateaux and other topographic areas mentioned in the text

Regional map showing national parks, game reserves, national reserves and major forest areas outside national parks

LAKES

1 Turkana	5 Elmenteita	9 Manyara
2 Baringo	6 Naivasha	10 Eyasi
3 Bogoria	7 Magadi	11 Jipe
4 Nakuru	8 Natron	12 Victoria

MOUNTAINS

13 Mt Loima	17 Mt Kenya	20 Mt Meru
14 Mt Elgon	18 Mt Endau	21 Mt Monduli
15 Mt Kulal	19 Mt Kiliman-	22 Mt Hanang
16 Mt Nyiru	jaro	

ISLANDS

23 Manda Island	24 Lamu Island	25 Pemba Island

HILLS/HIGHLANDS

26 The Ndotos	32 Taita Hills	38 Mbulu
27 Mathews	33 North Pares	Highlands
Range	34 South Pares	39 Crater
28 Cherangani	35 West	Highlands
Hills	Usambaras	40 Nguruman
29 The Mau	36 East	Hills
30 The Aberdares	Usambaras	41 Loita Hills
31 Chyulu Hills	37 Shimba Hills	

OTHER TOPOGRAPHIC AREAS MENTIONED IN THE TEXT

42 Trans-Nzoia	44 Laikipia
43 Uasin Gishu	45 Masai Steppe

NATIONAL PARKS

1 Lake Nakuru	6 Amboseli NP	10 Ruma NP
NP	7 Tsavo West	11 Serengeti NP
2 Aberdare NP	NP	12 Lake Manyara
3 Mt Kenya NP	8 Tsavo East NP	NP
4 Meru NP	9 Shimba Hills	13 Tarangire NP
5 Nairobi NP	NP	14 Arusha NP

GAME RESERVES

15 Samburu	16 Shaba GR	18 Maswa GR
/Buffalo	17 Masai Mara	19 Mkomazi GR
Springs	GR	

NATIONAL RESERVES

20 Nasolot NR	22 Mwea NR
21 Kora NR	23 Marsabit NR

MAJOR FOREST AREAS OUTSIDE NATIONAL PARKS

24 Mt Elgon (par-	29 Kibwezi Forest	34 West
tially in NP)	30 Kitovu Forest	Usambaras
25 Kakamega,	31 Tana River	35 East
North and	Primate	Usambaras
South Nandi	Reserve	36 Nou Forest
Forests	32 Boni Forest	(Mbulu
26 The Mau	33 Arabuko-	Highlands)
27 Trans-Mara	Sokoke	37 Loliondo
28 Ngurumans		

(80 in.) per year, and most highland forest areas receive in excess of 1000 mm (40 in.) annually. Parts of the western Kenyan highlands (e.g. Eldoret, Kitale) are rather uniformly wet from April to September. The tropical coastal belt likewise receives heavy precipitation: over 800 mm (32 in.) at Shimoni and more than 1200 mm (47 in.) at Mombasa, much of it between April and July, with May the wettest month. The Masai Mara Game Reserve in southwestern Kenya, and much of adjacent interior Tanzania, receive most of their rainfall between December and May, with northern Tanzania experiencing a long dry season. At Seronera, in the Serengeti Plains, the mean annual rainfall is over 1000 mm (40 in.). The rainfall pattern in Kenya's Narok District is similar, with most of the year's 725 mm (29 in.) usually falling from November to May, whereas in adjacent Kericho District the rains normally come between April and October. Nearby Kisumu, on Lake Victoria, receives rain throughout the year but is wettest from March to May.

Much of Kenya east of the Rift Valley experiences two distinct annual rainy seasons. Nyeri, Nairobi and Kajiado, for example, traditionally receive most of their precipitation between March and May (the so-called 'long rains'), and lesser amounts (the 'short rains') in November and December. This pattern is also true of the Usambara Mountains, where about half of the annual rain comes between March and June and much of the remainder in November. At some Kenyan localities, e.g. Marsabit, Isiolo and Meru, this is modified to a pattern of two almost equally wet seasons—March or April to May, and October to December—separated by a decidedly dry three- or four-month period. Garissa, on the Tana River in eastern Kenya, receives 329 mm (13 in.), the main part typically in November and December, with a less certain wet season from March to May; the pattern is similar for the Tsavo region. However, precipitation regimes are not always predictable and in some years the rains are delayed or fail altogether, producing widespread drought with noticeable effects on bird populations and movements. When they do arrive, breaking long dry spells, the countryside undergoes a transformation nearly as dramatic as the change from winter to spring in northern climes. In much of East Africa, bird reproduction is conspicuously geared to the rains and the resultant sudden flush of green foliage, flowers and invertebrate food sources.

VEGETATION AND MAJOR BIRD HABITATS

Kenya and northern Tanzania contain a broad spectrum of environmental types, with **desert** and **semi-desert** occupying extensive areas in the north, and various types of **grassland** and **bush** prevalent in many areas. The widely used term 'bush' refers to a broad range of shrub or low tree growth, with open or closed canopy, mainly under 5 m in height. Bush grades into **bushed grassland** with widely spaced thickets of shrubby growth, or into more open **shrub savanna**, characteristic of many hillsides and lower mountain slopes. It also occupies flat terrain adjacent to patches of grassland in western Kenya and merges in places with littoral grassland near the coast. Where more water is available, there can be extensive grassy areas with scattered trees for which we use the term **savanna**, following Moreau (1935, 1966), Chapin (1932) and others dealing with African bird distribution, as well as Shantz and Marbut (1923); it is the equivalent of the 'tree grassland' of Greenway (1968) and Pratt and Gwynne (1977). Widespread savanna tree genera include *Acacia*, *Terminalia*, *Combretum*, *Erythrina* and *Euphorbia*. **Scrub**, following Greenway (*op. cit.*), is a convenient term for the open assemblage of low shrubs or coarse perennial herbs (e.g. *Barleria* and other Acanthaceae) up to 2–3 m in height. Bush and scrub may be deciduous (e.g. *Acacia*) or evergreen (*Euclea* and others), thorny or unarmed.

In regions of higher rainfall, bush and savanna merge into denser **woodland** with trees attaining heights of 17 or 18 m; in semi-desert areas this is confined to riparian strips. Woodland differs from savanna in its more nearly continuous tree canopy (over 20 per cent coverage). Vast expanses of 'thorn-bush' and woodland are dominated by various species of *Acacia* on the heavier soils and *Commiphora*, usually on red soils, the trees leafless for much of the year. Locally, there are conspicuous baobab trees (*Adansonia digitata*) or tall succulent *Euphorbia* species. Limited *Brachystegia* woodland exists locally near the coast on white sandy soils. With increasing water, both bush and woodland become thicker and more floristically diversified, in places forming dense thickets with closely interwoven branches, and up to 15 m in height. Elsewhere, woodland merges almost imperceptibly into forest.

Forest, with a closed upper tree canopy of interlaced crowns, is categorized as **riparian** (along watercourses), **lowland** (below 1000 m) and **highland** or **montane** (above 1500 m). In riparian forest and woodland at various elevations, *Acacia xanthophloea* (fevertree), *Populus* (poplar), *Trichilia* and *Ficus* (fig) often are dominant or conspicuous. Montane forests are of two general types, both evergreen, one dominated by *Juniperus* (juniper or cedar) and *Podocarpus*, with *Olea* (wild olive), *Teclea*, *Celtis* and many other genera in areas receiving in the neighbourhood of 1000 mm (40 in.) of rainfall per year. The second type, less extensive and on wetter sites (with rainfall of 2000 mm or more), lacks *Juniperus*, and *Podocarpus*, *Ocotea* (camphor), *Cassipourea* (pillarwood) and *Croton* are among the important trees. Some anomalous major tracts such as the western Kakamega and Nandi Forests, are 'highland' in terms of elevation yet support many 'lowland' bird species.

Red coastal soils may support a low, often dense, mainly evergreen forest of *Afzelia*, *Brachylaena*, *Combretum*, *Terminalia* and other broad-leaved trees. Locally, as in Gedi National Monument, a different, semi-deciduous forest contains *Adansonia* (baobab), *Sterculia* and *Gyrocarpus*, as well as more widespread trees. Although some coastal Kenyan forests, and that in the Shimba Hills, have been designated **lowland rainforest** (Greenway *op. cit.*), our region contains almost no forest that can be so considered. Except for small, remnant coastal patches, most of it is in narrow riparian strips or other sites where trees are maintained by ground-water, not rainfall. Examples are the Kibwezi and former Kitovu Forests and parts of the Mara River Forest in Kenya, and the Lake

Manyara Forest in Tanzania. Our nearest approach to the well-developed lowland rainforest so typical of western and central Africa in recent times is the high-rainfall **temperate** or **intermediate rainforest** near Kakamega (cf. Zimmerman 1972), at elevations of 1520–1820 m (5000–6000 ft), and the somewhat different Amani Forest as low as 900 m (*c.* 3000 ft) in the Usambara Mountains. Although structurally and floristically distinct from that at Kakamega, other montane wooded areas on the Mau, Mt Elgon, Mt Kenya, the Aberdares and Mt Kilimanjaro also are high-rainfall forests. (The eastern slopes of Mt Kenya support a much wetter type than those on the western side.) Less well-developed but species-rich '**dry' forests**, with annual precipitation in the region of 750 mm (30 in.), exist on the lower slopes of some mountains, in the Taita and Chyulu Hills, and near Nairobi. These species-rich forests are essentially evergreen.

More localized habitat types include **moorland**, above 3000 m (*c.* 10,000 ft), and thickets of montane **bamboo** (*Arundinaria*), both similar to those on high tropical mountains elsewhere. Between the bamboo and moorland zones there may be intermediate belts of scrubby *Hagenia* and *Hypericum* and of giant heath (*Erica arborea*, *Philippa* spp.), forming a dwarf subalpine forest or shrub association. The moorlands themselves are characterized by coarse tussock grasses (especially *Festuca* and *Agrostis* spp.) with impressive giant species of *Lobelia* and *Senecio*. Above the moors, on the highest mountains, is an **alpine zone** where vegetation is reduced to scattered low plants in sheltered sites and birds are few.

In swamps or along rivers, **palms** of several kinds form belts of specialized habitat. Picturesque doum palms (*Hyphaene coriacea*) are widespread near and along watercourses in northern and eastern Kenya. **Papyrus swamps**, consisting of nearly pure stands of the sedge *Cyperus papyrus*, are prominent around Lake Victoria and scattered elsewhere. **Mangrove swamps**, dominated by *Rhizophora*, form an important coastal environment, *R. mucronata* becoming an 80-foot tree in well-developed forests, occupying sites landward from the *Sonneratia* and *Avicennia* on the water's edge.

Throughout our region, increasingly large areas of human-modified or -created habitats are superimposed on the original vegetational pattern. Locally attractive to birds are the often well-wooded **gardens** associated with rural or suburban residences and frequently supporting a few remnant indigenous trees. The more widespread croplands, pastures and cultivated fields, some in various stages of abandonment and regrowth, we consider under the term **cultivation**. Much indigenous highland forest has given way to farms and to stands of introduced *Eucalyptus* or exotic conifers. For most birds, adapted to African forest types, these **plantations** have little to offer. (Most sylvicultural practices continue to ignore indigenous trees in replanting efforts, to the detriment of native birds.)

Strictly aquatic habitats of importance are the large alkaline bodies of water known in East Africa as **soda lakes**, exemplified by Nakuru, Magadi and Natron. Their biota differs greatly from that of **freshwater lakes**, such as Naivasha. Lakes Turkana and Baringo, though alkaline, are fresh enough to support rich fish populations. Smaller freshwater ponds and artificial impoundments behind dams are numerous, and in recent years **sewage treatment ponds** have provided new resting and feeding areas near the larger cities and towns. Regularly **irrigated fields**, as in the Mwea and Ahero rice schemes, now cover significant acreage and have become important feeding areas for waterbirds and waders. **Temporarily flooded land** in low-lying places, inundated after heavy rains, may persist for months as marsh, swamp or open water, providing important breeding and feeding areas for many species.

Open coastal habitats which warrant mention are sand and coral-rock **beaches**, and the **tidal estuaries** and **mudflats** so essential to palearctic-breeding shorebirds on passage and during their winter sojourn in East Africa.

1 Extreme lava-rock desert. Dida Galgalu Desert *c.* 160 km (100 miles) north of Marsabit, n. Kenya. Elevation *c.* 600 m. Among the very few birds are Masked Lark, Thekla Lark and Williams's Lark.

2 Semi-desert scrub on rocky substrate. Dominant plant at the site photographed is *Barleria* sp. Shaba GR, n. Kenya. Elevation *c.* 670 m. Habitat of Lichtenstein's Sandgrouse and Masked and Williams's Larks.

3 Grassland with widely scattered *Acacia drepanolobium* (whistling thorn). Crater Highlands, n. Tanzania. Elevation *c.* 1500 m. Birds include Common Ostrich, Secretary Bird, Tawny Eagle, Kori Bustard, Yellow-throated Sandgrouse, Lilac-breasted Roller, Southern Ground Hornbill, Rufous-naped Lark, Grassland Pipit and Yellow-throated Longclaw.

4 Moorland/heath vegetation on Mt Kenya, Sirimon Track. Elevation *c.* 3800 m. The few birds include Jackson's Francolin, Hill Chat and Scarlet-tufted Malachite Sunbird.

5 High montane grassland with distant moorland, montane forest and patches of bamboo. Aberdare NP, Kenya. Elevation *c.* 3000 m. Birds include Jackson's Francolin, Common Stonechat, and Wing-snapping and Aberdare Cisticolas.

6 Wet montane grassland with *Kniphofia thomsonii* (red-hot poker) in foreground; *Hagenia abyssinica* woodland in background. Aberdare NP, Kenya. Elevation *c.* 3000 m. Grassland birds include Red-capped Lark, Sharpe's Longclaw, Common Stonechat, Wing-snapping and Levaillant's Cisticolas and Long-tailed Widowbird.

7 Bamboo (*Arundinaria alpina*) surrounding moorland and patches of *Hagenia abyssinica* woodland. Aberdare Range, Kenya. Elevation *c.* 3100 m. Typical birds are Mountain Buzzard, Jackson's Francolin, Abyssinian Ground Thrush, White-starred Robin, Brown Woodland Warbler, Hunter's Cisticola, Doherty's Bush-shrike, Golden-winged Sunbird and Abyssinian Crimsonwing.

8 Bamboo thicket interior.

9 Moist grassland, Kakamega District, w. Kenya. Elevation 1600 m. Birds include Blue-headed Coucal, African White-tailed Nightjar, White-headed Saw-wing, Mackinnon's Fiscal (forest edge), Broad-tailed Warbler and Stout Cisticola. (Similar habitat farther west in Busia District, at 1150 m, supports Blue Swallow and Marsh Tchagra; in thickets, Yellow-fronted Tinkerbird, Green Crombec, Olive-bellied Sunbird and Bar-breasted Firefinch.)

10 Low tree and shrub savanna on lower slope of Mt Elgon. Elevation 1800 m. Trees include *Terminalia* and *Erythrina*. Typical birds are Green-backed Eremomela, Yellow-bellied Hyliota, Foxy Cisticola, Black-crowned Tchagra and Yellow-fronted Canary. White-breasted Cuckoo-shrike is scarce.

11 Short-grass plains, **open broad-leaved bush and forest strips,** Mara GR, sw. Kenya. Elevation 1675 m on plains. Grassland birds include Coqui Francolin, Crowned Plover, Capped Wheatear, Northern Wheatear (winter), Pectoral-patch Cisticola, Grassland Pipit and Plain-backed Pipit.

12 *Combretum–Terminalia–Acacia* bush/low woodland, Kongelai Escarpment, w. Kenya. Elevation 1670 m. A rich habitat, with Brown-backed Woodpecker, African Paradise Flycatcher, African Penduline Tit, Black-headed Batis, Green-backed Eremomela, Lesser Blue-eared Starling, Chestnut-crowned Sparrow-Weaver, Jameson's Firefinch, Stripe-breasted Seedeater and Brimstone Canary.

13 *Erythrina–Cussonia–Acacia* savanna/bush, Chyulu Hills, se. Kenya. Elevation *c.* 1500 m. Low broad-leaved forest on hill in background. Birds include Lesser Honeyguide, Flappet Lark, Northern Pied Babbler, Common Bulbul, Pale Flycatcher, Chin-spot Batis, Common Stonechat, Yellow-bellied Eremomela, Broad-tailed Warbler, Siffling Cisticola, White-bellied Tit, Variable Sunbird and Black-faced Waxbill. In the forest are Scaly Francolin, Black-backed Puffback, Stripe-cheeked Greenbul and others.

14 Moist doum palm (*Hyphaene coriacea*) savanna with acacias in background, Tsavo West NP, se. Kenya. Elevation *c.* 915 m. Typical birds are Hartlaub's Bustard, Quail-plover, Violet Wood-hoopoe, Pangani Longclaw, Black-headed (Village) Weaver and Cardinal Quelea.

15 *Acacia tortilis–A. clavigera* **savanna**, Serengeti NP, Tanzania. Elevation 1450 m. Birds include d'Arnaud's Barbet, Pearl-spotted Owlet, Blue-naped Mousebird, Hoopoe, Silverbird, Buff-bellied Warbler, Banded Parisoma, Brubru, Common Drongo, Superb Starling, Red-billed Oxpecker and Rufous-tailed Weaver.

16 Open thorn-scrub north of Isiolo, n. Kenya. Elevation 610 m. Representative birds are Eastern Pale Chanting Goshawk, Somali and Heuglin's Coursers, Somali Bee-eater, d'Arnaud's Barbet, Common Rock Thrush (winter), Pied and Isabelline Wheatears (winter), Somali Long-billed Crombec, Red-fronted Warbler, Pale Prinia and Fischer's Starling.

17 Open *Acacia* thorn-bush, Buffalo Springs GR, n. Kenya. Elevation 610 m. Typical birds are Northern Grey Tit, Mouse-coloured Penduline Tit, White-browed Scrub Robin, Rufous Bush Chat (winter), Pygmy Batis, Fan-tailed Raven, Magpie-Starling and Donaldson-Smith's Sparrow-Weaver.

18 Well-developed thorn-bush/savanna with *Acacia* spp. and (low areas in background) doum palms (*Hyphaene*), Samburu GR, n. Kenya. Elevation 610 m. Birds include Somali Ostrich, African Harrier-Hawk, Gabar Goshawk, Vulturine and Helmeted Guineafowl, Ring-necked Dove, Emerald-spotted Wood Dove, Von der Decken's and Yellow-billed Hornbills, Slate-coloured Boubou, Pringle's Puffback, Spotted Morning Thrush, Eastern Violet-backed Sunbird, Green-winged Pytilia, Black-capped Social Weaver, White-browed Sparrow-Weaver and Vitelline Masked Weaver.

19 Heavily grazed dense thorn-bush, near Iltalal, s. Kenya. Elevation *c*. 1000 m. Nests are those of Grey-capped Social-Weaver. Other species here are Namaqua Dove, Grey Hornbill, Red-and-yellow Barbet, Grey Flycatcher, White-browed Scrub Robin, Blue-capped Cordon-bleu, Taita Fiscal, African Silverbill and Southern Grosbeak-Canary.

20 *Commiphora* bush with baobab trees (*Adansonia digitata*) near Mtito Andei, se. Kenya. Elevation *c*. 700 m. Dry-season aspect. Birds include African Orange-bellied Parrot, Red-billed Hornbill, White-bellied Go-away-bird, Böhm's and Mottled Spinetails, White-browed Scrub Robin, White-crowned Shrike, Golden-breasted Starling, Hunter's Sunbird, Lesser Masked Weaver and Somali Golden-breasted Bunting.

21 *Commiphora* bush near Kibwezi, s. Kenya. Elevation *c.* 750 m. Dry-season aspect. Abundant birdlife includes Von der Decken's Hornbill, d'Arnaud's Barbet, Green Wood-hoopoe, Nubian Woodpecker, Bare-eyed Thrush, Grey-headed Bush-shrike, Grey Wren-Warbler, Red-faced Crombec, Superb Starling and Red-billed and White-headed Buffalo-Weavers.

22 Tall, dense *Acacia* woodland, Kerio Valley, nw. Kenya. Elevation 1460 m. Typical birds: Diederik Cuckoo, Red-fronted Barbet, Greater and Scaly-throated Honeyguides, Grey Woodpecker, Black Flycatcher, Tawny-flanked Prinia, Yellow-breasted Apalis, Rattling Cisticola, Brubru, Chin-spot Batis, Black-headed Oriole, Marico Sunbird and Little Weaver.

23 Open fevertree (*Acacia xanthophloea*) savanna near Seronera River, Serengeti NP, Tanzania. Elevation 1480 m. Representative birds: Grey-breasted Spurfowl, Blue-naped Mousebird, Grey Woodpecker, Abyssinian Scimitarbill, Greater (Black-throated) Honeyguide, Brown Parisoma, Buff-bellied Warbler, Red-throated Tit, Brubru, Sulphur-breasted Bush-shrike, Magpie-Shrike, Rüppell's Long-tailed Starling and Red-headed Weaver.

24 Lacustrine fevertree (*Acacia xanthophloea*) woodland with tall herbaceous understorey, Lake Nakuru NP, Kenya. Elevation 1850 m. Typical birds are Verreaux's Eagle-Owl, Green Wood-hoopoe, Black Cuckoo, Red-throated Wryneck, Bearded Woodpecker, Grey-backed Fiscal, Arrow-marked Babbler, White-browed Robin-Chat, Black-headed Oriole, Black Cuckoo-shrike, Rattling Cisticola, Yellow-breasted Apalis and Brown Parisoma. Grey-crested Helmet-shrike is scarce.

25 ***Brachystegia*** **woodland**, Arabuko-Sokoke Forest northwest of Kilifi, coastal Kenya. Elevation 20 m. Birds include Crested Guineafowl, Barred Owlet, Brown-hooded Kingfisher, Common Scimitarbill, Green Barbet, Mombasa Woodpecker, Pale Batis, Ashy Flycatcher, Sokoke Pipit, Retz's and Chestnut-fronted Helmet-shrikes, Amani Sunbird, and Dark-backed and Clarke's Weavers.

26 Coastal evergreen forest, Arabuko-Sokoke Forest, northwest of Kilifi, coastal Kenya. Elevation 15 m. Birds include Crested Guineafowl, Tambourine Dove, Fischer's Turaco, Sokoke Scops Owl, Narina Trogon, Eastern Green Tinkerbird, Tiny, Fischer's and Yellow-bellied Greenbuls, East Coast Akalat, Red-tailed Ant Thrush, Little Yellow Flycatcher, Blue-mantled Crested Flycatcher, Forest Batis, Green-headed Oriole and Plain-backed Sunbird.

27 Tall riparian forest with *Diospyros*, *Ficus*, *Podocarpus*, *Olea et al.* Mara River, sw. Kenya. Elevation 1675 m. Conspicuous birds include African Green Pigeon, Klaas's Cuckoo, Ross's and Schalow's Turacos, Narina Trogon, Black-and-white-casqued Hornbill, Grey-throated Barbet, Woodland and African Pygmy Kingfishers, Cinnamon-chested Bee-eater, Common Wattle-eye, Blue Flycatcher and Black-backed Puffback.

28 Interior of same forest as in Fig. 27. Among the undergrowth birds are Yellow-whiskered and Placid Greenbuls, Red-capped and White-browed Robin-Chats, Grey-capped Warbler, Red-headed Bluebill and Black-and-white Mannikin.

29 Intermediate rainforest (with *c.* 125 tree species), Kakamega Forest, w. Kenya. Elevation 1600 m. The 130 true forest birds (excluding many 'edge' species) include Buff-spotted Crake, Great Blue and Black-billed Turacos, Blue-headed Bee-eater, Bar-tailed Trogon, three honeyguides, four barbets, four woodpeckers, six babblers, 12 bulbuls, Dusky Tit, four wattle-eyes, six thrushes, 13 warblers, three cuckoo-shrikes, four bush-shrikes, Western Black-headed Oriole, four starlings, eight sunbirds and six weavers.

30 Intermediate rainforest interior, Kakamega Forest. Birds at such sites include African Broadbill, Equatorial Akalat, Brown-chested Alethe, Red-tailed Bristlebill, Pale-breasted and Scaly-breasted Illadopses, Jameson's and Yellow-bellied Wattle-eyes and Dusky Crested Flycatcher.

31 *Juniperus–Podocarpus* montane forest near Molo, sw. Kenyan highlands. Elevation 2350 m. Tall trees in cleared area are *Juniperus procera* encased by 'strangler' figs (*Ficus* sp.). Typical birds are Black-and-white-casqued Hornbill, Lemon Dove, Olive Pigeon, Hartlaub's Turaco, African Black Swift, Double-toothed Barbet, Red-throated Wryneck, Moustached Green Tinkerbird, Fine-banded Woodpecker, Olive Thrush, Abyssinian Ground Thrush, Grey and Black-collared Apalises, White-eyed Slaty and White-tailed Crested Flycatchers, Montane White-eye, Eastern Double-collared Sunbird, Waller's, Sharpe's and Blue-eared Starlings and Abyssinian Crimsonwing.

32 Montane Forest with *Cassipourea malosana* (pillarwood), Crater Highlands, Tanzania. Elevation 2400 m. Habitat of Cinnamon-chested Bee-eater, Mountain Greenbul, African Hill Babbler, Brown-headed and Chestnut-throated Apalises, White-eyed Slaty and White-tailed Blue Flycatchers and Red-faced Crimsonwing.

33 Montane forest of *Podocarpus, Olea, Cassipourea, Polyscias et al.* Mt Kenya. Elevation 2200 m. Birds include most species cited for Fig. 31, plus Scaly Francolin, Bronze-naped Pigeon, Red-fronted Parrot, Slender-billed and Mountain Greenbuls, White-starred Robin, Rüppell's Robin-Chat, Purple-throated and Grey Cuckoo-shrikes, Chestnut-throated and Black-throated Apalises, White-browed Crombec, Brown-backed Scrub Robin, Black-fronted Bush-shrike, Montane Oriole, Tacazze Sunbird and Oriole-Finch.

34 Farmland on lower slopes of Mt Kenya, near Nyeri. Elevation *c.* 1800 m. Typical birds are Augur Buzzard, Red-eyed and Dusky Turtle Doves, Speckled Mousebird, Common Bulbul, Common Fiscal, Pied Crow, Blue-eared Starling, Bronze Sunbird, Baglafecht (Reichenow's) Weaver and Rufous Sparrow.

35 Alkaline lake (with flock of Lesser Flamingos), Lake Bogoria, cent. Rift Valley, Kenya. Elevation 970 m. Other birds include Black-necked Grebe, Greater Flamingo, African Fish Eagle, various ducks and shorebirds.

36 Freshwater pond (with Great White Pelicans, Black-winged Stilt), Amboseli NP, s. Kenya. Elevation 1340 m. Habitat of numerous herons, waterfowl and waders, Kittlitz's Plover and Collared Pratincole.

37 Papyrus (*Cyperus papyrus*) along Lake Victoria, Kenya. Elevation 1100 m. Habitat of Swamp Flycatcher, Greater Swamp Warbler, Carruthers's Cisticola, Papyrus Gonolek and Papyrus Canary.

38 Fringing mangroves along tidal estuary near Kilifi, Kenya. Sea level. Hill in background supports dense ever-green thicket at base, and higher patches of disturbed semi-deciduous forest. Birds utilizing the habitat include Tambourine Dove, Mangrove Kingfisher, Trumpeter Hornbill, Zanzibar Sombre Greenbul, Winding Cisticola, Grey-backed Camaroptera, Black-headed Batis, Mouse-coloured and Amethyst Sunbirds, Black-bellied Starling and African Golden Weaver.

CONSERVATION

Various East African habitats and their wildlife components face increasing pressure from deforestation, over-grazing, expanding agriculture, urbanization, pollution, and other consequences of an exploding human population—in Kenya increasing at an annual rate of some 3–4 per cent. (When the senior author began studying Kenyan birds in 1961, there were 7.5 million people in the country; in 1991 the figure was 22 million. At the present rate of increase, the prediction for the year 2025 is 83 million.) Within the past decade or so, at least two bird species appear to have vanished from Kenya, coinciding with accelerated habitat destruction in the west. Several others have become disturbingly scarce. Some are now much restricted in range, hence exceedingly vulnerable. Unless present trends are reversed, others surely will disappear. Several montane forest species in northern Tanzania are also at risk. In both countries, the artificial fragmentation of essential habitat, constricting animal populations into isolated and often biologically inviable units, is of increasing concern. This applies particularly to forest birds, for, as wooded corridors linking forest areas are severed, essential movement of sylvan animals is curtailed. Greatly restricted gene flow between fragmented populations is the precursor of local exterminations, hence reduced species diversity. Such problems are not confined to forested areas. Drainage of wetlands and agricultural conversion of native grasslands are effectively reducing birds of those habitats, and some once widespread species are now hard to find. Use of destructive pesticides, including some that are banned in other countries, provides another insidious region-wide threat, and may be involved in the great decline of raptorial birds in recent years. Some Kenyan lakes, world-famous only a few years ago for their astounding avian diversity, have experienced great losses of birdlife from pollution, unrestricted gill-netting and introduction of exotic animals and plants.

If East Africa is to retain its ecological integrity, and maintain its attraction to world naturalists, significant new action on the conservation front must be forthcoming. It is our hope that this volume will be of service not only to birdwatching tourists but also to the residents of Kenya and Tanzania, who, through their governments, will determine the future of their incomparable wildlife resources.

BIRD-FINDING

With literally hundreds of fine birding sites available in our region, detailed treatment of this subject would necessitate a separate volume. In **Kenya**, fortunate residents and long-term visitors can enjoy the luxury of seeking birds at leisure in a wide array of choice habitats at all seasons. Even individuals with only two or three weeks at their disposal can, after diligent homework or with proper guidance, easily see 500 species here—with a little effort, over 600. Some well-organized birding tours now regularly record over 700, and some have reached the astonishing total of 785 species in three weeks. Clearly, a list of 800 is possible. On carefully planned efforts, birding continuously for 24 hours, we have individually recorded over 330 species in a single day, and 350 would be attainable by one with sufficient knowledge and stamina, and with nothing better to do. We cite such figures not to stress listing *per se* but to demonstrate the enormous birding potential of the country.

Visitors with only a short time in Nairobi can find a great variety of open-country and savanna birds, plus a few forest species, in Nairobi National Park, 30 minutes from the city centre, or by spending a day along the Magadi Road which skirts the Park to the west before descending into the Rift Valley. Nearly all of Kenya's famous national parks and game reserves are exceptional places to look for birds. Mt Kenya National Park, with peaks rising above 5000 m, includes moorland and montane forest. Lower-elevation favourites are Lake Nakuru, Amboseli, Masai Mara, Tsavo (East and West), Meru, Shaba and Samburu, each with bird lists of several hundred species. Around most lodges and campsites in these extraordinary places, birds are not only abundant but also accustomed to people and therefore easily observed.

For those who would seek birds without the restrictions associated with birding in parks and reserves, Kenya abounds in rewarding localities. Easily visited from Nairobi are Olorgesaille, lakes Magadi, Elmenteita and Naivasha, the Kinangop Plateau and the Kieni Forest, to name a few highly productive sites. Farther afield, the Kibwezi bush country, Naro Moru, Meru Forest and Lake Baringo are traditional favourites of residents and visitors alike. In the west, the remnants of the Kakamega Forest hold numerous unique species, as do Saiwa Swamp and the Kongelai Escarpment near Kitale. The varied habitats around Kisumu, Homa Bay and Usengi along Lake Victoria are worth several days of any birder's time, as are the Uganda-border areas in Busia District. At the coast, perhaps the two most popular places are Mida Creek, renowned for its waders, and the intriguing Arabuko–Sokoke Forest with its 145 bird species of which several are rare and restricted. Other rewarding areas include the Sabaki River estuary, Gede National Monument and Shimba Hills National Park, all easily reached and readily worked. For the more adventurous there are innumerable remote sites in the north, at times subject to closure for security reasons.

In the portion of **northern Tanzania** covered in this book is the world-famous Serengeti National Park, covering 14,504 square kilometres (5600 sq. miles) of savanna, grassland and woodland supporting nearly 400 bird species (including two endemics). Northern Tanzania also embraces four other national parks: small (46 sq. miles) but well-forested Arusha; arid Tarangire, whose nearly 2600 square kilometres (1000 sq. miles) host a vast assortment of bush and open-country birds; Lake Manyara, with its waterbirds, tall forest and spectacular view of the Rift Valley; and Mt Kilimanjaro, rising to 19,430 feet and sheltering species typical of montane forest and moorland. There are in addition Maswa and Mkomazi Game Reserves, the latter essentially an extension of Tsavo

West National Park across the border in Kenya. Other outstanding areas for birds are the scenic Crater Highlands (including the Ngorongoro Conservation Area) and the Usambara Mountains (East and West), whose 69 forest birds include three endemics and no fewer than 17 endangered species. Pemba Island, off the coast just south of the Kenyan/Tanzanian border, has a depauperate bird fauna but five endemic species.

Of special interest to students of migration is Ngulia Lodge in Tsavo West NP, where impressive nocturnal 'falls' of thousands of migrant passerines occur in misty periods between late October and early January.

FIELD IDENTIFICATION

To the tyro, some of today's experts possess seemingly incredible bird-recognition powers. The ability of experienced birders quickly to take in the many features of a bird in a brief glimpse and come up with its correct name is directly proportional to the amount of time spent in the field, training both eye and ear. Typically it relates to years of study in library and museum as well. It is important for the novice, especially in a bird-rich region like East Africa, to realize that acquiring identification skills takes time and effort and does not come automatically. There may seem to be a bewildering array of birds at first, but after learning the common ones the others become progressively easier. Identification challenges will, of course, always remain, enhancing the enjoyment of field work as well as contributing to its frustrations. (Even skilled experts cannot name every bird they see.) For beginners, some basic hints may prove useful.

Learn to observe *carefully*, noticing more than the bird's general colours and impression. Its *size*, obviously important, can be surprisingly difficult to judge correctly, even after considerable experience. Various factors such as distance, lighting and presence or absence of comparative objects affect size impressions. Nevertheless, it usually is possible to determine approximate length relative to a few well-known birds such as Pied Crow, Ring-necked Dove, Olive Thrush or Superb Starling. Note overall *shape*. Is the bird plump like a quail or slender like a bee-eater or swallow? Is its *tail* short or long, square-tipped, rounded, pointed or forked? The *bill* can be especially diagnostic. In finches, sparrows and many weavers it is thick and heavy, adapted to seed-cracking, thus very different from the fine-pointed small bills of insectivorous foliage-gleaners such as warblers. Waders' bills may be short and swollen towards the tip (as in a plover), long and decurved (curlew), slender and upturned (avocet), long and straight (snipe) or almost needle-like (Marsh Sandpiper). There is great variation.

General *behaviour* such as swimming, diving, wading or tree-climbing is obvious, but, in addition, does the bird pump its tail, flick its wings, bob its head or exhibit other unusual actions? Useful to note is manner of *flight*—direct, undulating, erratic, soaring or fluttering.

Colour and *pattern* are important, and one should automatically check for eye-rings, superciliary stripes ('eyebrows'), wing-bars, pale tail corners, patches on either rump or upper tail-coverts and any other field marks. Open wings and spread tails often reveal patterns not visible on a resting bird. Some species (or plumages) are boldly marked and easy to track down in the book, but many birds are sombrely clad, quite plain or with subtle and intricate designs of bars, streaks, spots, speckles, vermiculations and other marks.

Most birds have brown eyes (often appearing black), so any deviation from this is noteworthy. One must often look closely to distinguish dark red from brown, or white from pale yellow, on the limited area of a bird's irides. Colour details of other bare parts can also be useful, so the bill, orbital skin, tarsi and toes should be studied.

The importance of taking field notes cannot be overstated. Writing descriptions while a bird is under observation teaches one to look at everything. Key points will be forgotten or confused if note-taking is done later. Always write impressions before consulting the book.

The variety of optical equipment now available to birders is limited only by the size of one's budget. Binocular style is a personal choice, but important considerations are magnification, size of field, close-focusing ability (at least down to 5 m) and humidity resistance. Perhaps most popular are 8X, 40 or, for open-country use, 10X, 40 binoculars. In forest or in low-light situations, wide field and greater light-gathering power are more important than increased magnification. Spotting scopes of 20X or 30X are necessary for effective viewing over lakes, vast grasslands and seashores. Higher magnification is rarely necessary, and the resulting increase in atmospheric distortion, reduced field of view and unsteadiness offset the advantage of larger image size.

Vocalizations of birds are almost as varied as plumage patterns and are equally intriguing and important. Expert birders rely as much on their ears as on their eyes; in familiar territory, they may do 80 or 90 per cent of their identification by ear alone. Despite variation in songs and calls, some species are much easier to name by voice than by appearance, and knowledge of vocalizations permits many poorly viewed or unseen birds to be recognized. In forest or papyrus swamp, where one bird is seen (and often fleetingly) for every dozen or more heard, the tape recorder is as indispensable as the binocular. Commercially available recordings exist for many common species, although they may not sound quite the same as the local birds owing to regional differences in dialect. Making one's own recordings, now feasible with inexpensive portable recorders and lightweight directional microphones, can be more satisfying and educational.

TERMINOLOGY RELATING TO BIRD IDENTIFICATION

Serious identification of any group of organisms involves some acquaintance with an appropriate vocabulary familiar to most biologists but not always to laymen. As bird study has become more popular, birders and authors have sometimes taken liberties with definitions of certain ornithological terms, creating a degree of confusion and inaccuracy. Whereas adequate supplementary literature is readily available to students elsewhere in the world, users of this book in East Africa may not have convenient access to ornithological texts, hence our extensive glossary and extra detail in the accompanying drawings.

Plumage Terminology. Birds replace their plumage periodically through the process of moulting, which involves shedding and renewal of the feathers. Each species normally exhibits a definite pattern of moult and a characteristic plumage sequence. Although detailed treatment of the moult process is beyond the scope of this book, a brief resume of terms used is in order.

Traditional moult and plumage terminology, developed to describe holarctic birds, is often inappropriate for tropical species whose reproductive cycles and moults are correlated with rainy and dry seasons, not 'summer' or 'winter', and for other species which may have very protracted moulting periods. 'First breeding' plumage is a further misnomer for those species which do not breed in the feather generation of that name. In the system of Humphrey and Parkes (1959), now widely used in the Americas, 'basic' describes the plumage when there is no feather change in the annual cycle, i.e. when one feather coat is worn throughout the year. It also applies to the duller non-breeding plumage when there is more than one feather coat per cycle, 'alternate' being used for the often brighter second, alternating plumage. (In birds which have three plumages per cycle, the third may be referred to as **supplemental**.) Despite the advantages of the Humphrey/Parkes system, Old World ornithology remains geared to the more conventional terminology which we employ here. Americans also customarily use 'juvenal' instead of 'juvenile' with reference to a bird's first plumaceous plumage. In this book, **juvenile** refers to the bird with its first true contour feathers, usually worn for only a short time before being lost during the often incomplete *post-juvenile* (or *first prebasic*) moult and replaced by the **first-winter** (or **first basic**) **plumage**. This dress is in turn lost by the *first prenuptial* (*first prealternate*) moult, resulting in the **first-breeding** (or **first alternate**) **plumage**, itself lost through the complete *first post-nuptial* (*second prebasic*) moult that produces the **second-winter** or **non-breeding** (or **second basic**) **plumage**. This is followed by another *prenuptial* (or *prealternate*) moult for the **second-breeding** (**second alternate**) **plumage**, and so on. The 'full' **adult** or **definitive plumage** (either **basic** or **alternate**) is that which does not change to a different pattern or coloration as the bird ages. In some species, there is no obvious difference between the first basic and definitive basic plumages.

Throughout the book, numbering of primaries is from the innermost outwards, following the usual sequence of moult and for comparisons between different groups of birds. (Homologous primaries bear the same number if the count is done in this way, for as primaries are lost during the course of evolution they are always lost from the outer end of the series.)

Nape

Occiput

Crown

Forehead

Eye-ring

Central crown stripe

Lateral crown stripe

Superciliary stripe

Eye-line (eye-stripe)

Upper back (mantle)

Scapulars

Rump

Inner secondaries

Upper tail-coverts

Rectrices (tail feathers)

Primaries

Belly

Under tail-coverts   Vent region

Crissum

Leg (tibia)

Tarsus

Hind toe or hallux (I)

Lore

Maxilla (upper mandible)

Commissure

Mandible (lower mandible)

Malar stripe

Submoustachial stripe

Moustachial stripe

Bend of wing ('shoulder')

Lesser coverts

Side

Greater coverts   Median coverts

Flank

Inner toe (II)   Primary coverts

Middle toe (III)

Outer toe (IV)

Superciliary stripe

Iris (eye)

Lore

Filoplume

Maxilliary tomium

Mandibular tomium

Rictus (gape)

Rictal bristle

Ear-coverts (auriculars)

Eye-wattle

Supraloral stripe

Chin

Throat

Breast band

Primaries

Posthumerals ('tertials')

Scapulars

Hindneck

Nape

Eye-ring

Lore

Nostril

Rectrices

Under tail-coverts

Secondaries

Greater coverts

Flank

Median coverts

Lesser coverts

Tibia

Tibiotarsal joint

Tarsus

Throat

Foreneck

Breast

Side

45

Cere

Crest

Cere

Gape flange

Operculum

Ear-tuft

Facial dis

Facial wattles incl. lappets

Nail

Lamellae

Orbital ring

Casque

Nasal tuft

Gonydeal angle

Lappet

Frontal shield

Casque

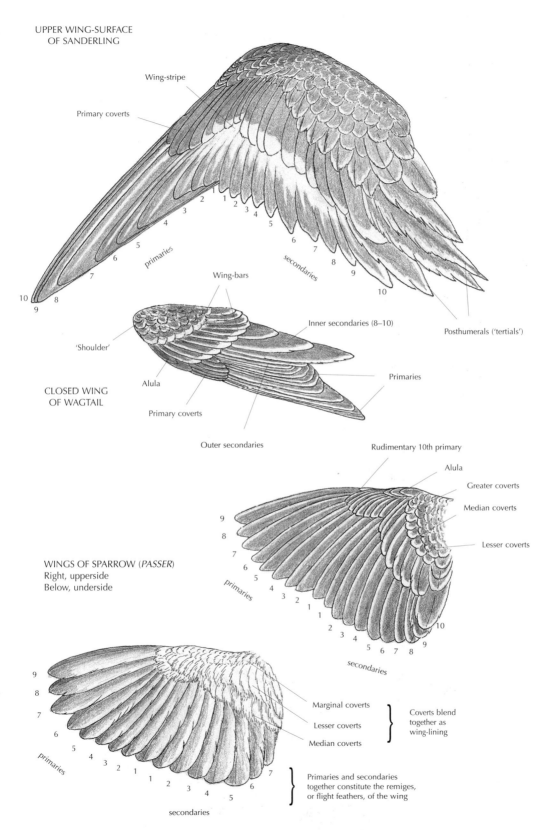

UPPER WING-SURFACE
OF SANDERLING

Wing-stripe

Primary coverts

1
2 1
3 2
3 4
4 5
5 6
primaries 7
6 8
7 9
8
10 10
9

Wing-bars

Inner secondaries (8–10)

secondaries

Posthumerals ('tertials')

CLOSED WING
OF WAGTAIL

'Shoulder'

Alula

Primary coverts

Primaries

Outer secondaries

Rudimentary 10th primary

Alula

Greater coverts

Median coverts

Lesser coverts

9
8
7
6
5
primaries 4 3 2 1
1
2
3
4 10
5 6 7 8 9

secondaries

WINGS OF SPARROW (*PASSER*)
Right, upperside
Below, underside

9
8
7
6
5
primaries 4 3 2 1
1
2
3 7
4 6
5

secondaries

Marginal coverts

Lesser coverts

Median coverts

} Coverts blend
together as
wing-lining

} Primaries and secondaries
together constitute the remiges,
or flight feathers, of the wing

GLOSSARY OF TERMS USED IN THE TEXT

Air sacs: components of the bird's respiratory system; extensions from the lungs to several areas of the body cavity, into certain large bones and under the skin.

Allopatric: relating to two or more congeneric forms whose breeding ranges do not overlap.

Alula: the feathered 'thumb' lying along the outer edge of the wing; contains a few stiffened feathers resembling abbreviated primaries.

Anterior: relating to the front part of a bird or other animal; opposite of posterior.

Aquatic: Living in water.

Auriculars (**ear-coverts**): the feathers covering the external ear opening; often referred to as the cheek.

Avian: pertaining to birds.

Axillars (**axillaries**): elongate inner wing-lining feathers of the subhumeral tract, lying between wing and body.

Booted: referring to an undivided tarsal sheath, i.e. one not consisting of separate scales or scutes.

Brood parasite: a bird which lays its eggs in the nest of another species (the **host** species) and plays no parental role in raising the young, e.g. Old-World cuckoos and the New-World cowbirds.

Carpal: pertaining to the wrist area at the bend of the wing.

Casque: in hornbills, a conspicuous raised corneous (horny) excrescence extending upward from the culmen; in guineafowl, the bony 'helmet' arising from the top of the head.

Cere: in hawks, owls and parrots, the soft basal covering on the maxilla. The nostrils open in or at the edge of this structure, which may be swollen and/or distinctively coloured.

Cheek: technically the side of the jaw (i.e. the malar region), but loosely considered to be the general auricular region.

Circumorbital: around the eye.

Commissure: the line of closure of the two mandibles.

Congeneric: belonging to the same genus.

Conspecific: belonging to the same species.

Contour feathers: all outer feathers of the head, neck, body, wings (including remiges) and tail.

Coverts: when used here without modifiers, refers to the wing-coverts in general, particularly the median and greater secondary coverts. Cf. **shoulder**, **primary coverts**, **secondary coverts**, **upper tail-coverts**, **under tail-coverts**.

Crissum: the under tail-coverts together with the feathers in the vent region; sometimes contrastingly coloured, as in d'Arnaud's Barbet.

Cryptic: aiding in concealment.

Culmen: the dorsal ridge of the maxilla.

Decurved: curved downward, as the bill of a curlew.

Dichotomous key: a device for identification consisting of pairs of contrasting morphological characters.

Dimorphic: having two distinct morphs or colour phases. See **Polymorphic**.

Distal: farthest from the body, pertaining to the tip of an appendage; opposite of proximal.

Diurnal: active by day.

DNA: standard abbreviation for deoxyribonucleic acid.

Dorsal: pertaining to the upper surface; opposite of ventral.

Down: a small soft feather with short (or vestigial) rachis and no vane.

Ear-tuft: a group of modified erectile feathers originating on the head, especially in the so-called horned or eared owls. They are not related to the ears and serve no auditory function.

Eclipse plumage: a dull plumage worn by males of certain brightly coloured birds (e.g. some sunbirds and male ducks) following breeding.

Emarginate: pertaining to a primary feather that is notched or abruptly narrowed along the edge, usually near the tip. Also refers to a slightly forked or notched tail.

Endemic: confined to a particular region. Turacos and mousebirds are endemic to Africa.

Erythrism (adj. **erythristic**): relating to excess reddish-brown pigment in feathers, as in the so-called red morph of Common Quail.

Eye-line: a dark line through the eye; distinct from the superciliary stripe *above* the eye.

Facial disc: a circular area of radiating feathers on the face, surrounding the eyes, as in an owl.

Family: a taxonomic category immediately above the genus in rank, composed of a genus or several genera. Family names of birds and other animals invariably end in -*idae*.

Feather tract (**pteryla**): a tract or area of skin to which contour feathers are restricted.

Filoplume: an inconspicuous, specialized, hair-like feather, usually most noticeable on the hindneck.

Flight feathers: as used here, the long wing feathers or remiges (primaries and secondaries); strictly, the remiges and rectrices taken collectively.

Foot: the tarsus and toes, collectively.

Forked: referring to a tail with the outer feathers distinctly longer than the innermost, as in most swallows.

Form: as used here, a deliberately non-committal term applied to species or subdivisions thereof when more specific taxonomic designation is not desirable or practical.

Frontal shield: a flattened horny basal extension of the maxilla covering much of the forehead, as in a gallinule.

Frugivorous: fruit-eating.

Gallinaceous: pertaining to galliform or 'chicken-like' birds (quail, francolins and others).

Gape: the mouth opening; sometimes used to refer to the rictus (*q.v.*).

Gape flange: expanded soft tissue of the rictus (or rictal commissure), as in young birds and adults of some cuckoo-shrikes; in raptors, may be extended far back to below eye.

Genus (pl. **genera**): a taxonomic category between family and species; a group of closely related species.

Gonys: the lower median ridge of the mandible; usually smoothly curved, but forms a distinct **gonydeal angle** in gulls and some other birds.

Graduated: referring to a tail in which the innermost rectrices are longest, the others becoming progressively shorter toward the sides.

Granivorous: seed-eating.

Greater coverts: see **Secondary coverts**.

Gregarious: commonly assembling or moving in flocks.

Gular: pertaining to the throat.

Hackles: long slender feathers on the neck, as in a Vulturine Guineafowl.

Half-collar: a distinctively coloured band of feathers around much of the hindneck in certain birds; sometimes merely termed 'collar', though rarely completely encircling.

Hawking: as used here, flight behaviour involving pursuit and capture of flying insects, with the mouth open, as by flycatchers or nightjars.

Heterodactyl: with toes nos. 1 and 4 turned backwards, as in trogons; see **Zygodactyl**.

Holarctic: referring to the Holarctic region, i.e. the combined Nearctic and Palearctic biogeographical regions, *q.v.*

Homologous: deriving from a common ancestor and having the same structure (though not necessarily the same appearance or function).

Host: the individual, or species, which incubates the eggs and raises the young of avian **brood parasites**, *q.v.*

Humerus: the upper arm bone.

Immature: in this volume, used to refer to the plumage(s) replacing juvenile feathering and preceding adult plumage. See **Juvenile** and **Subadult**.

Indigenous: native to a particular country or region. See **Endemic**.

Insectivorous: insect-eating.

Invertebrate: an animal lacking a spinal column or 'backbone'; insects, molluscs, worms, and others.

Iridescence: a type of shiny or 'metallic' structural coloration, essentially independent of feather pigments; well developed in sunbirds and glossy starlings.

Iris (pl. **irides**): the coloured contractile diaphragm of the eye, surrounding the pupil.

Juvenile: a young bird in its first true plumage following the natal down.

Lacustrine: pertaining to lakes.

Lamellate: possessing numerous thin plates or lamellae, as along the sides of a duck's bill.

Lanceolate: long, slender and pointed; lance-shaped.

Lappet: a wattle, especially at the corner of the mouth.

Lateral: pertaining to the side.

Lesser coverts: see **Secondary coverts**.

Lore (pl. **lores**; adj. **loral**): the space between bill and eyelid; may be bare or feathered.

Malar region: the side of the jaw, posterior to the bill. At times marked by a **malar stripe** bordering the upper edge of the throat.

Mandible: the lower part of the bill (often called 'lower mandible'); the plural is used with reference to both upper and lower portions.

Mandibular ramus (pl. **rami**): the projection of the mandible extending posteriorly on each side of the jaw.

Mantle: the interscapular region. This term, which we generally avoid, is used for the **upper back** by British writers, but is applied to back, scapulars and wing-coverts, collectively, by Americans.

Maxilla: the upper half of the bill; often termed 'upper mandible'.

Median coverts: see **Secondary coverts**.

Melanism (adj. **melanistic**): dark plumage resulting from an excess of black pigments, sometimes genetically determined. May be regular, as in the dark morphs of some raptors, or of rare and sporadic occurrence in various species.

Monotypic: containing only one type or representative. A monotypic species includes no recognized subspecies.

Morph: a plumage 'colour phase' of a polymorphic or dimorphic species.

Morphological: pertaining to form or structure.

Moult: the process of shedding old feathers and replacing these with new ones. See p. 44.

Moustachial stripe: a line originating behind the soft tissue of the rictus; below it there may be a **submoustachial stripe**.

Nasal tuft: an erect tuft of bristles or bristle-like feathers near the nostrils at base of the maxilla, as in Helmeted Guineafowl and Grey-throated Barbet.

Nearctic region: the biogeographical region comprising North America south to the tropics.

Neotropical region: the New World tropics; one of the world's six major biogeographical regions.

Nestling: a young bird which has not left the nest.

Nidicolous: refers to bird species in which young remain in the nest for some time following hatching.

Nidification: nest-building.

Nidifugous: refers to bird species in which young leave the nest soon after hatching.

49

Nocturnal: active at night.

Nominate subspecies (race): the first population of a polytypic species to be described. Designated by repetition of the specific epithet, e.g. *Amadina fasciata fasciata*.

Nuchal: pertaining to the nape.

Obsolete: indistinct or lacking.

Occipital plumes: the ornamental feathers originating from the **occiput**, between crown and nape, e.g. the long breeding plumes on the heads of egrets.

Operculum (adj. **operculate**): a flap-like membrane, sometimes swollen, above the nostril.

Orbital ring: a circle of bare skin surrounding the eye, as opposed to the feathered eye-ring.

Order: in the taxonomic hierarchy, one of the higher categories, between family and class. The Class Aves is usually considered to comprise 27 or 28 living orders. Ordinal bird names end in the suffix -*iformes*.

Palearctic region: one of the world's six major biogeographical regions, comprising Eurasia south to the Himalayas and North Africa.

Panel: term used for an elongated wing-patch formed by more or less contrasting feather edges, as in the primaries of various cisticolas. Cf. wing edgings.

Passerine: pertaining to the Order Passeriformes, the 'perching birds'.

Patagium (adj. **patagial**): the fold of skin between the carpal area of the wing and the body.

Pectinate: comb-like, i.e. bearing numerous tooth-like projections, as the middle claw of herons or nightjars.

Pectoral patch: a clearly defined dark area of plumage on either side of the breast.

Pelagic: pertaining to the open sea.

Pileum: the entire top of the head, including forehead, crown and occiput.

Plumaceous: feather-like, as opposed to a downy (plumulaceous) covering.

Plumage: a bird's feathers, collectively. Also used more specifically for a feather coat or feather generation between moults. See p. 44.

Polyandry (adj. **polyandrous**): mating of one female with two or more males.

Polygyny (adj. **polygynous**): mating of one male with two or more females.

Polymorphic: having two (then often called dimorphic) or more distinct, genetically determined colour morphs within a species, independent of age, sexual, seasonal or subspecific variation.

Polytypic: having two or more taxonomic divisions within the category referred to. Usually applied to those species divisible into subspecies.

Posterior: pertaining to the rear parts of a bird or other animal; opposite of anterior.

Posthumerals (posthumeral quills): in some birds, the large, often long, inner wing feathers, usually lacking the rigidity of remiges, lying along or near the trailing edge of the humerus (though not pressed against it). Sometimes confusingly called tertiaries or tertials (*q.v.*), but not a series comparable with secondaries or primaries, and distinct from the true tertiaries which arise from the humerus in certain very large birds.

Postocular stripe: a (usually dark) line behind the eye; the posterior part of an **eye-line**.

Powder-down feathers: highly modified body feathers, short, silky and disintegrating at the tips into a very fine powder that produces a characteristic bloom on the bird's plumage. Usually in short compact tracts, and best developed in herons (among East African birds), but also scattered around the body in parrots.

Precocial: referring to birds whose young at hatching are well developed, downy and capable of moving away from the nest and feeding themselves.

Primary extension: the length of that portion of the primaries visible beyond the ends of the secondaries in a folded wing.

Primary coverts: small feathers concealing the bases of the primaries.

Primaries: the outermost flight feathers of the wing, those attached to the bird's hand bones and digits. Most non-passerine birds have 10 primaries (grebes, storks and flamingos, 11; Ostrich 16). Most passerines have only nine, or the outermost (10th) is much reduced. (See p. 44.)

Proximal: nearest to the body, pertaining to the innermost part of an appendage; opposite of distal.

Race: see **Subspecies**.

Rachis: the shaft of a feather, bearing the vane.

Raptor: a bird with strong claws and sharp talons for tearing prey. Usually used with reference to the diurnal Falconiformes (hawks and relatives), but applies also to owls.

Raptorial: referring to birds of prey.

Ratite: having a flat sternum without the keel for pectoral-muscle attachment present in most birds.

Rectrices (sg. **rectrix**): the tail feathers. Viewing the folded tail from above, the central pair conceals all but the edges of the others. The two outermost dominate the often very different appearance of the underside. (Thus, a perched Narina Trogon appears green-tailed from above or behind, white-tailed from the front; and in flight, as the rectrices are spread, the bird shows a white-sided tail.)

Recurved: curved upwards, as an avocet's bill.

Remiges (sg. **remex**): the flight feathers of the wing; the primaries and secondaries collectively.

Rictus: the soft, rather fleshy extension of the tomium at the angle of the mouth opening or commissural point, often referred to as the gape (*q.v.*).

Rump: that portion of the upperparts between the lower back and upper tail-coverts.

Scapulars: distinct tracts of feathers between the wings and the back.

Scute(s): the horny plates or scales, as in a scutellate tarsus.

Secondaries: the series of flight feathers (remiges) arising from, and attached to, the ulna, in our species varying in number from eight (some swifts) to 37 (albatrosses). The more or less differentiated proximal (inner) secondaries are sometimes called **tertials** (*q.v.*).

Secondary coverts: partially overlapping feathers covering the bases of the secondaries, including a conspicuous row of **greater coverts**, a row of shorter **median coverts**, and several rows of still shorter **lesser coverts**; usually refers to the upper surface of the wing, but a comparable series of feathers exists on the under surface (cf. **wing-lining**).

Serrate: saw-toothed.

Shaft streak: a narrow longitudinal mark along the rachis, or central axis, of a feather.

Shoulder: commonly refers to the bend of the wing where the lesser coverts (and often some median coverts) may be coloured differently from adjacent feathers, as in the Red-shouldered Cuckoo-shrike.

Sibling species: two or more very closely related species, nearly identical morphologically but each usually distinct vocally or behaviourally.

Species (sg. & pl.): in the vernacular, a 'kind' of bird (or other organism). As defined by Mayr (1942), a group of "actually or potentially interbreeding populations which are reproductively isolated from other such groups". Unlike subspecies (*q.v.*), 'good' biological species do not freely interbreed with one another in nature. Distinctions are not always clear-cut, but species are separated from one another by significant reproductive barriers (even if these are not, in every case, quite complete). As birds continue to evolve, there will be at any given time some populations which have passed beyond what we think of as 'ordinary' subspecies without having yet attained 'full' species status (e.g. Somali Ostrich).

Speculum: A bright, sharply contrasting patch near the rear edge of a wing, especially the iridescent areas on the secondaries of waterfowl; conspicuous in flight.

Spur: a sharp projection (corneous modified skin over a bony core), as on the tarsus of a spurfowl or from near the carpal joint on the wing (as in Spur-winged Plover).

Square: referring to the tip of a tail in which all rectrices are of nearly equal length.

Streamer: exceptionally long, slender outermost or innermost rectrices, as in a tern or tropicbird.

Subadult: applies to the later (older) stages of immature birds (i.e. those two or three years old) in those species which require more than one year to reach full maturity. (See p. 44.)

Sub-eclipse plumage: see **Supplemental plumage**.

Subspecies (sg. & pl.): a geographic **race** of a species; a population (or group of populations) morphologically and geographically defined. The subspecies of a species interbreed freely where (and if) their ranges overlap, thereby producing intermediate populations sharing characteristics of each form but readily assignable to neither. Designated trinomially in scientific nomenclature. See **Species**.

Supercilium: that part of the head immediately above the eye; in many birds marked by a **superciliary stripe**.

Supra-: a prefix meaning 'above'. Supraloral lines are above the lores.

Supplemental (supplementary) plumage: a third feather coat in the annual cycle, e.g. the sub-eclipse plumage of some ducks. (See p. 44.)

Sympatric: applied to two congeneric species whose breeding ranges overlap; the opposite of allopatric.

Tarsus (pl. **tarsi**): technically, the **tarsometatarsus**, typically featherless, and covered with a series of smooth scales, but feathered in sandgrouse, most owls and some other birds; together with the tibia, loosely termed 'leg' (though the tarsus and toes together really constitute a bird's *foot*).

Taxon: any taxonomic unit—order, family, genus, species, etc.

Taxonomy (adj. **taxonomic**): the science of classification of plants and animals according to their natural relationships.

Terrestrial: ground-frequenting.

Tertials: "a term preferably treated as obsolete" (Thomson 1964; Campbell and Lack 1985), now generally avoided by ornithologists but perpetuated by birders to apply to a few differently coloured or patterned inner secondaries, as well as to strongly differentiated proximal secondaries or adjacent specialized posthumeral feathers (usually markedly elongated and pointed) in such groups as shorebirds, larks or motacillids. True tertiaries or tertials, originating on the humerus, are found only in certain large, long-winged birds such as albatrosses.

Thigh: see **Tibia**

Tibia (pl. **tibiae**): the **tibiotarsus** ('drumstick') of the leg; partly bare in numerous birds such as herons, but largely feathered in most passerines and other small birds (the entire tibia featherless in Golden Pipit). Often casually designated as the 'thigh' (especially if the feathering is contrastingly coloured), but the true thighs are seldom visible on a living bird.

Tomia (sg. **tomium**): the hard cutting edges of the bill. There are maxillary tomia (one on each side) and comparable mandibular tomia, mutually apposed in the closed bill.

Tribe: in taxonomy, a group of closely related genera within a subfamily or family.

Trinomial: designation of a bird's scientific name by a generic name and both specific and subspecific epithets, e.g. *Anthreptes collaris elachior*; in other words, the name of a subspecies.

Ulna: the posterior and heavier forearm bone to which a bird's secondaries are attached.

Underparts: the feathers from chin to under tail-coverts, usually not including the underside of the tail.

Upperparts: the feathered dorsal surface from forehead to upper tail-coverts, usually including the scapulars and wing-coverts, sometimes also the upper surface of the tail.

Upper tail-coverts: the feathers concealing the rectrix bases, posterior to the rump; sometimes contrastingly coloured and conspicuous in flight (e.g. the often miscalled white 'rump' of a harrier or chanting goshawk).

Vane: the flattened part of a feather, attached to the rachis; divided into outer and inner **webs**.

Vent: the opening of the cloaca to the surface of the body. Sometimes applied to the feathers of this region, between the lower belly and under tail-coverts.

Ventral: pertaining to the underside of the body; opposite of dorsal.

Vertebrate: any 'backboned' animal (Subphylum Vertebrata) supporting a vertebral column—bony fish, amphibian, reptile, bird or mammal.

Wattle: a fleshy, largely unfeathered appendage of the head or neck, usually more or less wrinkled and often brightly coloured, as the **eye-wattles** of paradise flycatchers or wattle-eyes. Facial wattles, sometimes called **lappets**, are more pendent structures originating elsewhere on the face, as in African Wattled Plover, Helmeted Guineafowl and Wattled Starling.

Web: of feather, see **Vane**. Of toes, a thin flexible membrane attached to the sides of (and often connecting) the toes of various waterbirds.

Wing-bar: a usually light-coloured band across the wing, formed by the contrasting tips of the greater and/or median coverts. Distinct from wing-stripe, *q.v.*

Wing edgings: contrastingly coloured edges of the flight feathers, becoming less conspicuous as the outer web of the feather wears away.

Wing formula: the relative lengths of the primaries, reflecting differences in shape or appearance of the wing tip.

Wing-lining: the under wing-coverts considered collectively.

Wing-stripe: a contrasting, narrow, *longitudinal* area on the closed wing (as opposed to a wing-*bar* which is across the long axis); usually formed by the outer edges of certain secondaries, sometimes with similarly coloured greater coverts, as in a Common Wattle-eye. On the spread wing, a line formed by pale (usually basal) portions of some primaries and secondaries, and sometimes the adjacent tips of their coverts.

Xanthochroism (adj. **xanthochroic**): abnormal yellow plumage coloration.

Zygodactyl: two toes (nos. 2 and 3) in front and two (1st and 4th) directed backwards, as in woodpeckers, cuckoos and some others.

PLATES 1–124

PLATE 1: PELAGIC BIRDS (FRIGATEBIRDS, TUBENOSES AND BOOBIES)

1 GREATER FRIGATEBIRD *Fregata minor*   **Page 314**
Usually far from shore. Long, pointed wings and long, forked (when spread) tail. The most likely frigatebird in our area. (Vagrant Lesser Frigatebird. shown in figure on p. 314)
1a. Adult female. Grey chin and throat merge with white breast (throat black in Lesser).
1b. Immature. White or pale chestnut head.
1c. Adult male. Entirely black underparts. (Lesser shows small white flank/wing-lining patches.)

2 BLACK-BROWED ALBATROSS *Diomedea melanophris*   **Page 305**
Rare north to latitude of Mombasa. Underside of wings with white centre, black borders.
2a. Adult. Upperside.
2b. Adult. Underside.

3 SHY ALBATROSS *Diomedea cauta*   **Page 305**
Wanderer to Pemba Channel, possibly regular August–September. Black mark at junction of underside of wing and body, and black notch near carpal joint.

4 WEDGE-TAILED SHEARWATER *Puffinus pacificus*   **Page 307**
Scarce; recorded between Shimoni and Lamu. Wings held forward, slightly bowed and angled. Long wedge-shaped tail with even sides. Smaller Jouanin's Petrel (see figure on. p. 306 and text) shows different tail outline.
4a. Adult. Upperside.
4b. Adult. Underside.

5 AUDUBON'S SHEARWATER *Puffinus lherminieri*   **Page 307**
Uncommon but regular offshore, mainly north of Kilifi. Fluttering flight. Dark brown cap extends below eyes; under tail-coverts dark. (Flanks and sides also brown in *P. l. persicus*. See text. Mascarene Shearwater, *P. atrodorsalis*, is black, not dark brown, above and has white under tail-coverts. See figure on p. 306 and text.)

6 BROWN BOOBY *Sula leucogaster*   **Page 312**
Vagrant. Smaller and longer-tailed than Masked Booby. White confined to lower breast, belly and under-tail-coverts and central part of underwing. Female illustrated.

7 MASKED BOOBY *Sula dactylatra melanops*   **Page 311**
Uncommon but regular in Pemba Channel.
7a. Immature. Whitish collar more or less conspicuous; white area on underside of wing encloses dark stripe parallel to leading edge. (Similar to rare Brown Booby; see text.)
7b. Adult. Black tail and yellow bill distinguish this species from similar Red-footed Booby. (Extralimital Cape Gannet, possible in Tanzanian waters, has pale blue-grey bill and yellow wash on head.)

8 RED-FOOTED BOOBY *Sula sula rubripes*   **Page 312**
Casual, August–March. Plumage variable. Feet red.
8a. Brown morph.
8b. White morph. White tail distinctive.

PLATE 2: PELAGIC BIRDS (STORM-PETRELS, TROPICBIRD AND MARINE TERNS)

1 **BLACK-BELLIED STORM-PETREL** *Fregetta tropica* Page 309
Vagrant. Black mid-ventral line on white belly.

2 **WILSON'S STORM-PETREL** *Oceanites oceanicus* Page 309
Uncommon, but probably annual, April–December. Small and dark. Flight fluttery, usually just above water, the feet often pattering on the surface. Feet project beyond tail in flight.

3 **LEACH'S STORM-PETREL** *Oceanodroma leucorhoa* Page 309
Vagrant. Feet do not project beyond forked tail in flight.

4 **BROWN NODDY** *Anous stolidus pileatus* Page 419
Uncommon offshore throughout the year. Numerous near breeding islands, June–September. Wedge-shaped tail.
4a. Adult. Tail darker than the back. Whitish cap contrasts sharply with dark loral area.
4b. Immature. White restricted to forehead. Feathers of upperparts and wings pale-tipped.

5 **LESSER NODDY** *Anous t. tenuirostris* Page 419
Rare, but perhaps regular off s. Kenya and in Pemba Channel. Tail of adult appears greyish, paler than the back. Whitish cap often extends below eye, not contrasting with loral area; bill longer and thinner than in Brown Noddy.

6 **WHITE-TAILED TROPICBIRD** *Phaethon l. lepturus* Page 310
Uncommon but regular in Pemba Channel, August–March. Occasional farther north at other times. (Immature has different pattern and lacks tail streamers; see text.)

7 **WHITE-CHEEKED TERN** *Sterna repressa* Page 416
Locally common, sometimes in large flocks north of Mombasa, uncommon farther south. Occasionally seen from shore.
7a. Non-breeding plumage. Darker, and narrower-winged than similar Common Tern, and with broader dark area on forewing.
7b. Breeding plumage. Grey above, including rump; black cap separated from dark grey underparts by broad white facial streak.

8 **SOOTY TERN** *Sterna fuscata nubilosa* Page 417
Regular and sometimes common at sea; rarely seen from shore. Breeds erratically in Lamu area. Feeds by daintily dipping or hovering near surface.
8a. Juvenile. Pale lower belly/crissum and forked tail separate it from noddies.
8b. Adult. White on forehead and underparts.

9 **BRIDLED TERN** *Sterna anaethetus antarctica* Page 416
Fairly common at sea; rare inshore. Associates with Brown Noddy and Sooty Tern.
9a. Juvenile. Paler than young Sooty Tern; whitish collar on hindneck.
9b. Adult. Back brownish grey, usually separated from black cap by whitish collar. White of forehead extends back above eyes.

PLATE 3: SMALLER TERNS IN FLIGHT (See also Plates 2 and 5)

1 BLACK TERN *Chlidonias n. niger* **Page 418**
Rare inland migrant.
1a. Breeding adult (rare in East Africa).
1b. Non-breeding adult. Rump and tail grey. Dark grey patches on sides of breast.

2 WHITE-WINGED TERN *Chlidonias leucopterus* **Page 418**
Common migrant on large inland lakes. Scarce at coast. Some present all year.
2a. Non-breeding adult.
2b. Juvenile. Dark back patch, pale wings.
2c. Breeding adult.

3 GULL-BILLED TERN *Sterna n. nilotica* **Page 414**
Locally common migrant, August–April, on large inland lakes. Smaller numbers along coast. Stocky, thick-billed.
3a and 3d. Spring adults. Pale grey above.
3b. Juvenile.
3c. Winter adult.

4 WHISKERED TERN *Chlidonias hybridus delalandii* **Page 418**
Widespread inland. Breeds in small colonies on freshwater lakes. Suggests short-tailed *Sterna*.
4a. Non-breeding adult. Back and tail uniformly grey.
4b. Juvenile. Brown back with buff feather edges.
4c. Breeding adult. White facial stripe separates black cap from dark underparts; bill dark red.

5 ROSEATE TERN *Sterna dougallii bangsi* **Page 415**
Coastal. Present all year; locally abundant, May–October. More slender and appears whiter than other terns. Bill long and narrow.
5a. Juvenile. Narrow whitish forehead band, mottled back, white collar and pale grey rump, dark carpal bar. Bill black.
5b and 5d. Breeding adults. All-red bill and feet, very long outer rectrices.
5c. Non-breeding adult. Narrow black bill may show some dull red at base; white forehead.

6 COMMON TERN *Sterna h. hirundo* **Page 416**
Common/abundant along coast, August–December and in April. Scarce on Rift Valley lakes. Shorter, greyer than Roseate Tern.
6a. First-winter bird (some juvenile feathers). Dark-edged outer rectrices; base of bill orange.
6b and 6d. Spring adults. Dark trailing primary edge; outer rectrices darker-edged and shorter than in Roseate Tern. Bill usually black (becomes largely red after birds leave East Africa).
6c. Non-breeding adult. White forehead and forecrown.

7 LITTLE TERN *Sterna a. albifrons* **Page 417**
Status uncertain (April specimens from coast and Lake Naivasha).
7a. Juvenile. First-winter birds may retain many juvenile feathers.
7b and 7d. Breeding adults. Black only on outer two or three primaries (outer three or four in Saunders's); tail white (not pale grey).
7c. Non-breeding adult. Usually inseparable from Saunders's Tern. See text.

8 SAUNDERS'S TERN *Sterna (albifrons) saundersi* **Page 417**
Abundant coastal migrant, most numerous October–April. Status at Lake Turkana uncertain (one Oct. specimen record).
Breeding adult. White forehead patch less elongate than in Little Tern.

PLATE 4: LARGER TERNS AND SKIMMER IN FLIGHT (See also Plate 5)

1 CASPIAN TERN *Sterna caspia*   **Page 414**
Annual winter migrant to Lake Turkana and the coast north of Mombasa. Size may suggest gull, but tern-like bill and habits distinctive.
1a. Juvenile acquiring first-winter plumage.
1b. Winter adult.
1c. Spring adult.

2 SANDWICH TERN *Sterna s. sandvicensis*   **Page 415**
Uncommon migrant to n. Kenyan coast. Vagrant to Rift Valley lakes.
2a. Juvenile.
2b. Winter adult.
2c. Spring adult.

3 LESSER CRESTED TERN *Sterna b. bengalensis*   **Page 415**
Present along coast throughout the year. Vagrant to Rift Valley lakes.
3a. Breeding adult.
3b. Non-breeding adult.
3c. First-year bird.

4 GREATER CRESTED TERN *Sterna bergii*   **Page 414**
Coastal. Less common than Lesser Crested Tern. *S. b. velox*, with darker grey upperparts, on n. Kenyan coast. Birds along south coast and Pemba Channel are the paler race *thalassina*.
4a. *S. b. velox*, breeding adult.
4b. *S. b. velox*, juvenile.
4c. *S. b. velox*, non-breeding adult.
4d. *S. b. thalassina*, breeding adult.
4e. *S. b. thalassina*, non-breeding adult.

5 AFRICAN SKIMMER *Rynchops flavirostris*   **Page 419**
Resident at Lake Turkana; uncommon and irregular elsewhere.
5a. Newly fledged juvenile.
5b. Non-breeding adult.
5c and 5d. Breeding adults.

PLATE 5: SMALL GULLS, TERNS AND SKIMMER (See also Plates 3, 4, 7 and 8)

1 GREY-HEADED GULL *Larus cirrocephalus poiocephalus* **Page 412**
Common on inland lakes; rare at coast. Larger, stouter, longer tarsi and thicker bill than Nos. 2 and 3.
1a. Non-breeding adult. Suggestion of breeding pattern; sometimes faint ear spot. **1b. Juvenile**. Broad white collar. **1c. Breeding adult**. Dove-grey hood, pale eye. **1d. First-year**. Fainter head markings and tail band than 3c; primaries dark.

2 SLENDER-BILLED GULL *Larus genei* **Page 413**
Scarce palearctic migrant to lakes Turkana and Nakuru; rare elsewhere. Long-billed; shallow sweeping forehead. **2a. Spring adult**. **2b. Winter adult**. **2c. First-winter**. From 2b by two-toned bill, dark band across wing, dark tail tip.

3 BLACK-HEADED GULL *Larus ridibundus* **Page 412**
Uncommon palearctic migrant, inland and coastal. Slender bill of medium length. **3a. Spring adult**.
3b. Winter adult. **3c. First-winter**. Two-toned bill.

4 WHITE-CHEEKED TERN *Sterna repressa* **Page 416**
Coastal, mainly beyond the reef; present all year. **4a. Breeding adult**. White facial streak; grey underparts.
4b. Non-breeding adult. Suggests Common Tern, but darker grey and bill shorter.

5 ROSEATE TERN *Sterna dougallii bangsi* **Page 415**
Coastal; present all year. Elegant pearl-white appearance. **5a. Breeding-plumaged adult**. Long outer tail feathers; pink bloom on underparts; bill becomes red when breeding (See Plate 3). **5b. Non-breeding adult**. White forehead and crown, shorter outer tail feathers, narrow black carpal bar.

6 LESSER CRESTED TERN *Sterna b. bengalensis* **Page 415**
Common all year along coast; regular on lower Tana River, and vagrant to Rift Valley lakes. Crested, with slender orange or orange-yellow bill. **6a. Breeding adult**. Entire top of head black. **6b. Non-breeding adult**. Extensive white on crown.

7 COMMON TERN *Sterna h. hirundo* **Page 416**
Common palearctic migrant along coast; large offshore flocks. Many immatures oversummer. Scarce on Rift Valley lakes. **7a. Late-spring adult**. (Bill usually black in our region, becoming red after leaving East African waters.) **7b. Winter adult**. Broader black carpal bar than in non-breeding Roseate Tern.

8 GREATER CRESTED TERN *Sterna bergii* **Page 414**
Coastal. Large, with heavy, pale yellow or greenish-yellow bill drooping at tip. **8a. S. b. velox, breeding adult**. Visitor north of Malindi. **8b. S. b. velox, post-breeding adult**. **8c. S. b. thalassina, non-breeding adult**. South of Mombasa and in Pemba Channel.

9 SAUNDERS'S TERN *Sterna (albifrons) saundersi* **Page 417**
Common migrant along coast, October–April; also on lower Tana River and Lake Turkana. Small size, rapid wingbeats. See text and Plate 3. **9a. Non-breeding adult**. Differs from 5b and 7b in size and wing action. See text. **9b. Breeding adult**. Black-tipped yellow bill. 'Square' white forehead patch does not extend behind eyes as in Little Tern.

10 CASPIAN TERN *Sterna caspia* **Page 414**
Uncommon migrant along coast and at Lake Turkana. Large and crested, with heavy red bill. **10a. Winter adult**. **10b. Spring adult**.

11 SANDWICH TERN *Sterna s. sandvicensis* **Page 415**
Uncommon palearctic migrant on n. Kenyan coast; accidental inland. Pale and crested. Yellow bill tip inconspicuous at distance. **11a. Winter adult. 11b. Spring adult**.

12 AFRICAN SKIMMER *Rynchops flavirostris* **Page 419**
Locally common at Lake Turkana; sporadic elsewhere; rare along coast. Appears less elongate than shown.

13 GULL-BILLED TERN *Sterna n. nilotica* **Page 414**
Migrant, August–April, locally common on large inland lakes; less numerous along coast. Stockier, greyer above than Sandwich Tern, with heavier bill. **13a. Winter adult. 13b. Spring adult**.

PLATE 6: LARGE GULLS (See also Plates 7 and 8)

1 SOOTY GULL *Larus hemprichii*   **Page 410**
Coastal resident, at times common; some breed north of Lamu. Long-winged and long-billed.
1a. Juvenile (acquiring first-winter plumage). Pale head and dorsal feather edgings.
1b. Non-breeding adult. Head/neck pattern less well defined than in breeding plumage.
1c. Breeding adult. White neck patch separates dark hood from grey-brown breast. Bill pale, with black band and red tip.

2 LESSER BLACK-BACKED GULL *Larus fuscus*   **Page 411**
Palearctic migrant, common October–April along coast and on larger inland lakes; some oversummer. Somewhat smaller and lighter in build than Heuglin's Gull.
2a. *L. f. fuscus*, second-winter. Bill largely pale yellowish.
2b. *L. f. fuscus*, first-winter. Bill blackish.
2c. *L. f. fuscus*, winter adult. Black of back same shade as primaries.
2d. *L. f. graellsii*, second-winter. Dense streaking on back and neck; medium grey on back.
2e. *L. f. graellsii*, winter adult. Medium grey.

3 HEUGLIN'S GULL *Larus heuglini*   **Page 411**
Regular along n. Kenyan coast, November–March; sometimes fairly common (but no Kenyan specimens). Flocks with Lesser Black-backed Gulls. See text.
3a. (Presumed) *L. h. taimyrensis*, pale adult. (Illustration from bird photographed at Malindi, Dec. 1992.)
3b. (Presumed) *L. h. taimyrensis*, darker adult. (From bird photographed at Malindi, Jan. 1983.)
3c. *L. h. heuglini*, second-winter. Bill blackish.
3d. *L. h. heuglini*, winter adult. Bill yellow with red or black-and-red spot. Black primaries slightly darker than back. Bill somewhat larger than in *L. f. fuscus*; head and neck usually with some dark streaking.

4 KELP GULL *Larus dominicanus vetula*   **Page 412**
Vagrant from s. Africa.
4a. Juvenile/first-winter. Bill blackish.
4b. Non-breeding adult.

5 GREAT BLACK-HEADED GULL *Larus ichthyaetus*   **Page 413**
Uncommon palearctic migrant, December–March, mainly along coast and at Lake Turkana. Large, with long sloping forehead and thick bill drooping at tip.
5a. Late-spring adult.
5b. First-winter. Dusky eye patch extends over hindcrown. Nape and often side of breast densely dark-streaked or spotted; pale greyish patch on wing; broad blackish tail tip.
5c. Winter adult.

1a 1b 1c 2a 2b 2c 2d 2e 3a 3b 3c 3d 4a 4b 5a 5b 5c

DALE A. ZIMMERMAN
1995

PLATE 7: SUBADULT GULLS IN FLIGHT (See also Plates 5, 6 and 8)

1 **HEUGLIN'S GULL** *Larus heuglini taimyrensis* **Page 411**
Birds apparently representing this form regular along Kenyan coast, from Tana River delta south to Malindi, November–March. See text.
1a. First-winter.
1b. Second-winter.

2 **LESSER BLACK-BACKED GULL** *Larus f. fuscus* **Page 411**
Common migrant along coast, October–April, less numerous on inland lakes. A few oversummer. Slightly smaller and lighter in build than Heuglin's Gull.
2a. First-winter.
2b. Second-winter.

3 **SOOTY GULL** *Larus hemprichii* **Page 410**
Present along coast throughout year, some breeding in the north. Long-winged and long-billed.
3a. First-winter.
3b. Second-winter.

4 **BLACK-HEADED GULL** *Larus ridibundus* **Page 412**
Locally common palearctic migrant. Shorter-billed and shorter-tailed than Slender-billed Gull.
4a. First-winter. More sharply marked than Slender-billed Gull.
4b. Non-breeding adult.

5 **SLENDER-BILLED GULL** *Larus genei* **Page 413**
Scarce to uncommon migrant. **First-winter** bird is longer-tailed and has less distinct postocular spot than more numerous Black-headed Gull.

6 **GREY-HEADED GULL** *Larus cirrocephalus poiocephalus* **Page 412**
Common on inland lakes; rare at coast. Heavier and thicker-billed than Black-headed and Slender-billed Gulls. **Juvenile/first-year** bird also darker on head and with less white in primaries.

7 **GREAT BLACK-HEADED GULL,** *Larus ichthyaetus* **Page 413**
Uncommon migrant, December–March, mainly along coast and at Lake Turkana. Appears longer and more 'front-heavy' than other large gulls, owing to long bill and long sloping forehead.
7a. First-winter.
7b. Second-winter.

PLATE 8: SKUAS AND ADULT GULLS (See Plates 5, 6 and 7 for other gull plumages)

1 POMARINE SKUA *Stercorarius pomarinus*   **Page 408**
Scarce, October–March, along coast and on Rift Valley lakes. Size of large gull, thick-necked, deep-chested. Bill long, deep, with prominent gonydeal angle. Harries gulls and terns. Immatures and adults lacking typical central tail feathers difficult to identify. See text.
1a. Spring adult, light morph. Rounded and twisted central tail feathers; black cap.
1b. Adult, dark morph. Uncommon. Identify by size, build, shape of central tail feathers.
1c. Immature (and similar non-breeding adult). Barred upper tail-coverts and rump. Best distinguished from Arctic Skua by size and heavy build.

2 LONG-TAILED SKUA *Stercorarius longicaudus*   **Page 409**
Vagrant. Less massive than larger species, flight more buoyant and tern-like; wings long and narrow, showing less white on upperside of primaries (only two shafts white). **Immature** variable, wing-linings more barred than in non-breeding adult. See text. (Adult has long, pointed central tail feathers.)

3 ARCTIC SKUA or PARASITIC JAEGER *Stercorarius parasiticus*   **Page 409**
Rare migrant along coast and on Rift Valley lakes. Smaller, less massive than Pomarine; more falcon-like in flight. Pursues gulls and terns. See text.
3a. Immature. Upper tail-covert barring more buff and brown, less black and white than in young Pomarine.
3b. Adult, pale morph. Central tail feathers straight and pointed. Dark breast band, if present, evenly grey, not mottled or barred.

4 GREY-HEADED GULL *Larus cirrocephalus poiocephalus*   **Page 412**
The common gull of inland lakes; rare along coast. **Breeding bird** has pale grey hood with dark rear margin, more dark in primaries than Black-headed and Slender-billed Gulls. Eye yellowish white.

5 SOOTY GULL *Larus hemprichii*   **Page 410**
Common along the coast (less numerous south of Malindi, June–Sept.). Long wings and long bill. **Breeding adult**. (Non-breeding adult has paler hood and duller bill. See Plate 6.)

6 LESSER BLACK-BACKED GULL *Larus f. fuscus*   **Page 411**
Present and sometimes common along coast and on some inland lakes (especially Turkana), October–April. Closely resembles dark Heuglin's Gull, *L. h. heuglini*. See text.

7 BLACK-HEADED GULL *Larus ridibundus*   **Page 412**
Regular palearctic migrant on Rift Valley lakes; less regular elsewhere, including coastal areas. Dark brown hood, dark eye and different wing pattern distinguish **spring adult** from common Grey-headed Gull.

8 SLENDER-BILLED GULL *Larus genei*   **Page 413**
Scarce but regular palearctic migrant on lakes Turkana and Nakuru; rare elsewhere. Occasional in summer. Appears more elongate than Black-headed Gull, with longer bill and longer, slimmer neck. Bill dark dusky red to bright orange.

9 GREAT BLACK-HEADED GULL *Larus ichthyaetus*   **Page 413**
Uncommon, December–March; most regular around Sabaki River mouth and Malindi, less so at Lake Turkana. Rare elsewhere. Large size and long bill. **Spring adult** has black hood, with conspicuous white crescents around eyes.

PLATE 9: STORKS AND CRANES

1 WHITE STORK *Ciconia c. ciconia*   **Page 323**
Common palearctic migrant in grasslands and grain fields, November–April; a few oversummer in Kenyan highlands. In high flight, white tail diagnostic.
1a and 1b. Adults.

2 YELLOW-BILLED STORK *Mycteria ibis*   **Page 324**
Common and widespread along shallow rivers and lakeshores. Breeding adult has pink wing-coverts. In high flight shows black tail, unlike White Stork.
2a and 2b. Breeding adults.

3 WOOLLY-NECKED STORK *Ciconia episcopus microscelis*   **Page 323**
Fairly common on coastal lagoons; local and uncommon elsewhere. Dark back and wings contrast with white posterior underparts.
3a and 3b. Adults.

4 ABDIM'S STORK *Ciconia abdimii*   **Page 323**
Intra-African migrant, October–April, often in large flocks with White Storks. White belly and (in flight) white back; bill and legs dull greenish grey.
4a and 4b. Adults.

5 SADDLE-BILLED STORK *Ephippiorhynchus senegalensis*   **Page 323**
Local and uncommon in swamps, marshes and flooded grassland.
5a and 5c. Adult females. Eye yellow.
5b. Juvenile. Dark bill, dark plumage areas grey-brown.
5d. Adult male. Eye dark brown.

6 AFRICAN OPEN-BILLED STORK *Anastomus l. lamelligerus*   **Page 324**
Widespread; locally common in Lake Victoria basin. Large flocks frequent in se. Kenya/ne. Tanzania. Glossy plumage; unique bill. (Juvenile is duller and browner; bill shorter, with narrow tomial gap.)

7 BLACK STORK *Ciconia nigra*   **Page 323**
Regular palearctic migrant, October–April; uncommon in and near wetlands.
7a and 7b. Adults. White belly, red bill and legs; back and rump dark. (Immature has dull olive-green bill and legs.)

8 MARABOU STORK *Leptoptilus crumeniferus*   **Page 324**
Widespread; locally common on town and village outskirts. Joins vultures at carcasses.
8a and 8b. Breeding adults.
8c. Non-breeding adult.

9 DEMOISELLE CRANE *Anthropoides virgo*   **Page 379**
Palearctic vagrant. Grey, with black foreneck and long breast feathers. Elongated secondaries droop over tail.

10 GREY CROWNED CRANE *Balearica regulorum gibbericeps*   **Page 379**
Fairly common and widespread in wetlands above 1300 m. Rare at Lake Turkana and in coastal lowlands.
10a and 10b. Adults. Largely grey neck; white cheek patch scarlet at top. (Juvenile more rufous, with smaller crest.)

11 BLACK CROWNED CRANE *Balearica pavonina ceciliae*   **Page 380**
Vagrant to Lake Turkana. Neck blackish; cheek patch white above, pink below; short pinkish throat-wattle.

1a

1b

3a

3b

2a

4a

4b

2b

5a

7a

6

5b

5c

7b

9

5d

8b

10a

8a

10b

11

8c

A. ZIMMERMAN
1989

PLATE 10: IBISES, SPOONBILLS AND FLAMINGOS

1 GLOSSY IBIS *Plegadis f. falcinellus* **Page 326**
Widespread in permanent wetlands. Appears all black at a distance. Feet project beyond tail in flight.
1a and 1c. Adults.
1b. Juvenile.

2 AFRICAN GREEN or OLIVE IBIS *Bostrychia olivacea akeleyorum* **Page 325**
Scarce in montane forests. Feeds on forest floor and in clearings. Rarely seen, except when flying to and from roosts at dusk and dawn. Little or no overlap of range with Hadada Ibis.

3 HADADA IBIS *Bostrychia hagedash brevirostris* **Page 325**
Common and widespread in wet areas, along forest borders, in cultivation, Nairobi city parks and suburbs. Feet do not project beyond tail in flight.
3a and 3b. Adults. (Juvenile similar but duller.)

4 AFRICAN SPOONBILL *Platalea alba* **Page 326**
Widespread on inland waters; local in coastal lowlands. Forehead unfeathered.
4a. Immature. Dull yellowish bill and facial skin.
4b. Adult.
4c. Subadult.

5 SACRED IBIS *Threskiornis a. aethiopicus* **Page 325**
Widespread in wetlands, including coastal estuaries.
5a. Juvenile.
5b. Breeding adult.
5c. Non-breeding adult.

6 EURASIAN SPOONBILL *Platalea leucorodia* **Page 326**
Fairly regular at Lake Turkana, scarce elsewhere. Forehead entirely feathered; bill largely black.
6a. First-winter. No yellow on bill tip; facial skin dark.
6b. Spring male acquiring breeding plumage. (Non-breeding adult lacks crest and the yellow on lower neck.)

7 GREATER FLAMINGO *Phoenicopterus (ruber) roseus* **Page 326**
Largely confined to brackish and soda lakes in Rift Valley, where locally common. Uncommon at coast.
7a, 7c and 7d. Adults. Bill pink with black tip.
7b. Immature. Greyer plumage; black-tipped grey bill.

8 LESSER FLAMINGO *Phoeniconaias minor* **Page 327**
Abundant on Rift Valley soda lakes.
8a. Immature.
8b. Juvenile.
8c, 8d and 8e. Adults.

PLATE 11: LARGE HERONS AND HAMERKOP (See also Plates 12 and 13)

1 PURPLE HERON *Ardea p. purpurea*　　　　　　　　　　**Page 321**
Widespread and locally common in wetlands with extensive reedbeds. Colourful, slender. Less chestnut on wings than much larger Goliath Heron. Bill long and slim.
1a. Juvenile.
1b and 1c. Adults.

2 BLACK-HEADED HERON *Ardea melanocephala*　　　　　**Page 322**
Commonest heron; widespread in open grassland, cultivation. Often on dry ground.
2a and 2b. Adults. Black crown, nape and hindneck; underside of wings strongly two-toned (unlike Grey Heron).
2c. Juvenile. Appears largely grey above, whitish to pale grey below.

3 GOLIATH HERON *Ardea goliath*　　　　　　　　　　　**Page 321**
Uncommon and local, mainly around larger lakes and swamps. Very large with massive bill.
3a, 3b and 3c. Adults.
3d. Juvenile.

4 GREY HERON *Ardea c. cinerea*　　　　　　　　　　　**Page 321**
Widespread and uncommon in wetlands.
4a, 4b and 4c. Adults. Blackish flight feathers contrast with grey wing-coverts above; wings more uniformly grey below.
4d. Juvenile.

5 HAMERKOP *Scopus u. umbretta*　　　　　　　　　　　**Page 322**
Widespread and fairly common at swamp edges, lakesides and along rivers.
5a, 5b and 5c. Adults. (Juvenile similar.)

Nest of Hamerkop.

1a

1c

2a

2c

1b

2b

3c

4b

4c

3a

3b

4a

4d

3d

5c

5a

5b

HDP

PLATE 12: SMALL HERONS (See also Plates 11 and 13)

1 DWARF BITTERN *Ixobrychus sturmii*   **Page 316**
Widespread but uncommon in reedbeds and seasonal swamps. Secretive.
1a. Juvenile.
1b. Adult.

2 LITTLE BITTERN *Ixobrychus minutus*   **Page 316**
Widespread in permanent marshes. Skulks in reeds. Nominate race present October–May.
2a. *I. m. minutus*, first-winter.
2b. *I. m. minutus*, adult male.
2c. *I. m. payesii*, adult female.
2d. *I. m. payesii*, juvenile.
2e and 2f. *I. m. payesii*, adult males.

3 SQUACCO HERON *Ardeola ralloides*   **Page 319**
Widespread in wetlands. White wings may be largely concealed by body feathers.
Non-breeding adult. (See Plate 13 for breeding plumage.)

4 MADAGASCAR SQUACCO or MALAGASY POND HERON *Ardeola idae*   **Page 320**
Uncommon non-breeding migrant, May–October, inland to Mwea NR and Ngorongoro Crater.
Non-breeding adult. (See Plate 13 for breeding plumage.)

5 RUFOUS-BELLIED HERON *Ardea rufiventris*   **Page 320**
Uncommon and local; regular in nw. Mara GR and Tarangire NP.
5a and 5c. Adult males.
5b. Adult female.

6 GREEN-BACKED or STRIATED HERON *Butorides striatus atricapillus*   **Page 320**
Fairly common along coastal creeks, well-vegetated lakes and rivers.
6a and 6c. Adults.
6b. Juvenile.

7 BLACK-CROWNED NIGHT-HERON *Nycticorax n. nycticorax*   **Page 317**
Locally common in permanent wetlands. Nocturnal.
7a. Juvenile.
7b. Subadult.
7c and 7d. Adults.

8 WHITE-BACKED NIGHT-HERON *Gorsachius leuconotus*   **Page 316**
Scarce along shaded river banks, mangroves. Nocturnal.
8a. Juvenile.
8b and 8c. Adults.

PLATE 13: HERONS and EGRETS (See also Plates 11 and 12)

1 GREAT EGRET *Casmerodius albus melanorhynchos*   **Page 321**
Widespread in wetlands. Large size; dark line from base of bill extends beyond eye; bill colour variable. Legs and feet black.
1a. Non-breeding adult.
1b. Courting adult. (Amount of yellow at base of bill varies. Eyes may be briefly red.)
1c. Immature.

2 YELLOW-BILLED or INTERMEDIATE EGRET *Mesophoyx intermedia brachyrhyncha*
    Page 320
Less common than Great Egret; smaller, with shorter neck and bill; black gape line from bill does not extend past eye; legs and feet black.
2a. Non-breeding adult.
2b. Immature.
2c. Breeding adult.

3 CATTLE EGRET *Bubulcus i. ibis*   **Page 317**
Common and widespread; not restricted to wet places. Small, stocky, heavy-jowled.
3a. Breeding adult.
3b. Juvenile. (Tarsus colour varies; see text.)
3c. Non-breeding adult.

4 MADAGASCAR SQUACCO or MALAGASY POND HERON *Ardeola idae*   **Page 320**
Breeding-plumaged adult rare in East Africa. (Non-breeding plumage on Plate 12.)

5 SQUACCO HERON *Ardeola ralloides*   **Page 319**
Fairly common and widespread in wetlands.
5a and 5b. Breeding adult. White wings obscured in perched bird. (See Plate 12 for non-breeding plumage.)

6 WESTERN REEF HERON *Egretta gularis schistacea*   **Page 318**
Uncommon along coast (Mida Creek) and at Lake Turkana; rare at other Rift Valley lakes. Bill longer, heavier and deeper than in Little or Dimorphic Egrets, never black. (Caution: Little Egrets feeding in some Rift Valley lakes may have pale, soda-encrusted bills.) Legs and feet largely greenish olive, the toes, and often front of tarsi, yellow.
6a. White morph.
6b and 6c. Dark morph. (Amount of white in wing varies individually.)

7 LITTLE EGRET *Egretta g. garzetta*   **Page 317**
Common and widespread except along open coastal areas, where scarce. Toes greenish yellow (partly black in very rare dark morph). Largely black bill (pale on basal half of gonys).
7a. White morph, **non-breeding.** Lore usually grey.
7b. Dark morph, breeding.
7c. White morph, breeding. Lore yellow, or dull peach colour at onset of breeding season (orange during peak courtship activity; see text).

8 DIMORPHIC EGRET *Egretta (garzetta) dimorpha*   **Page 318**
Strictly marine. Strongly dimorphic; dark birds common, as are pied intermediates. May show yellow spot on mandible. Legs variable: tibiae always dark (unless whitewashed with excrement); tarsi black, often with yellowish or greenish 'anklets' extending up front of tarsus. Saddle at base of maxilla more prominent than in Little Egret. See text.
8a. White morph, non-breeding. Facial skin grey; toes and parts of tarsus yellow or greenish.
8b. White morph, courting. Toes, lore and base of bill bright rose-pink.
8c and 8d. Dark morph, breeding. Toes (and part of tarsus) bright yellow or orange-yellow; base of bill bright yellow; lore and orbital ring yellow-green. White in wing variable in extent or lacking. (Bare parts of non-breeding dark morph as in 8a.)
8e. Dark morph, courting. Facial skin and bill base bright rose-pink.
8f. Juvenile/immature. Largely grey, greyish blue or nearly lavender; some pale brown and white on wings and neck. *E. (g.) dimorpha* not known inland; similar grey birds seen on Rift Valley lakes may be young of dark-morph *E. g. garzetta*. (Grey immature of *E. gularis schistacea* has larger, paler bill.)

9 BLACK HERON *Egretta ardesiaca*   **Page 319**
Local, mainly at coast, Lake Jipe and Rift Valley lakes.
Adult shaggy-crested. Eye dark; toes orange or orange-yellow. (Juvenile duller and greyer, lacks long plumes; toes lemon-yellow or greenish yellow.)

1b

2b

2c

1a

1c

2a

3a

3b

4

3c

5a

6b

5b

7a

6a

6c

9

8d

8b

8c

7b

8a

7c

8e

8f

DALE A. ZIMMERMAN
1994

PLATE 14: PELICANS, CORMORANTS AND DARTER

1 GREAT WHITE PELICAN *Pelecanus onocrotalus* **Page 310**
Common on alkaline lakes in Rift Valley. Secondaries largely black.
1a. Breeding adult. Pinkish-orange face (briefly shows swollen orange-red knob at base of culmen at peak of courtship activity).
1b, 1c and 1d. Non-breeding adults.
1e. Immature. Mottled plumage replaces uniform dark brown of juvenile.

2 PINK-BACKED PELICAN *Pelecanus rufescens* **Page 311**
Widespread on lakes, rivers and coastal saltpans. Secondaries brownish grey.
2a and 2b. Adults. Greyish white. Pinkish back and rump visible only in flight.
Develops shaggy crest, and pouch becomes deep yellow, when breeding.
2c. Juvenile.

3 LONG-TAILED CORMORANT *Phalacrocorax a. africanus* **Page 312**
Widespread on freshwater lakes, ponds and swamps with ample fringing vegetation. Long-tailed, with small bill. Adults red-eyed.
3a. Immature. (Juvenile similar but brown-eyed, and may be paler below.)
3b. Post-breeding adult.
3c. Breeding adult. (Non-breeding adult may have white underparts, but eyes are red. See figure below.)

4 GREAT CORMORANT *Phalacrocorax carbo lucidus* **Page 312**
Locally common, often in large flocks on Rift Valley lakes. Wanders to coastal estuaries. Heavy-billed and short-tailed.
4a. Immature. Brownish, with whitish underparts, darkening with age.
4b and 4c. Breeding adults. White flank/thigh patch.

5 AFRICAN DARTER *Anhinga rufa* **Page 313**
Formerly fairly common in freshwater areas with fringing trees. Now scarce in Kenyan highlands. Long, broad tail, sinuous neck, sharp-pointed bill.
5a. Female.
5b. and 5c. Adult males.

Non-breeding adult Long-tailed Cormorant.

PLATE 15: GREBES, GEESE AND DUCKS (See also Plate 16)

1 WHITE-FACED WHISTLING DUCK *Dendrocygna viduata*   **Page 328**
Common and widespread in wetlands below 1500 m. White face, long black neck, black belly and tail.
1a and 1b. Adults.

2 FULVOUS WHISTLING DUCK *Dendrocygna bicolor*   **Page 327**
Widespread visitor (rarely breeds) on lakes and wetlands below 1500 m, often in large flocks. Broad black line on hindneck, whitish U-shaped patch on upper tail-coverts.
2a and 2b. Adults.

3 GREAT CRESTED GREBE *Podiceps cristatus infuscatus*   **Page 304**
Increasingly scarce and local resident on lakes of cent. Rift Valley, Arusha NP and Ngorongoro Crater. Rare wanderer to Laikipia Plateau.
3a. Breeding adult.
3b. Juvenile.

4 LITTLE GREBE *Tachybaptus ruficollis capensis*   **Page 304**
Widespread. Most numerous on larger Rift Valley lakes and in Arusha NP.
4a. Breeding adult.
4b. Non-breeding adult.

5 BLACK-NECKED or EARED GREBE *Podiceps nigricollis gurneyi*   **Page 304**
Local on Rift Valley lakes, sometimes common July–November. Wanders elsewhere; sporadic in n. Tanzania.
5a. Breeding adult.
5b. Worn, post-breeding adult. (No black-and-white non-breeding plumage in East African birds.)

6 EGYPTIAN GOOSE *Alopochen aegyptiacus*   **Page 328**
Common on freshwater lakes, ponds, river banks (sometimes fields) below 3000 m. May perch on trees.
6a. Juvenile. Forewing patch grey.
6b, 6c and 6d. Adults. Variable; forewing patch white.
6e. Gosling.

7 WHITE-BACKED DUCK *Thalassornis l. leuconotus*   **Page 328**
Locally common on lakes and ponds with emergent vegetation. Avoids open water.
7a and 7b. Adults.

8 AFRICAN PYGMY GOOSE *Nettapus auritus*   **Page 329**
Local on secluded, well-vegetated lakes and swampy pools near coast. Occasionally wanders.
8a and 8c. Males.
8b. Female.

9 SPUR-WINGED GOOSE *Plectropterus g. gambensis*   **Page 328**
Locally common in freshwater wetlands below 3000 m.
9a. Female. No forehead caruncles.
9b. Male.
9c. Juvenile.

10 KNOB-BILLED or COMB DUCK *Sarkidiornis m. melanotos*   **Page 329**
Widespread on freshwater lakes, ponds, flooded grassland below 3000 m. Perches in trees.
10a. Breeding male.
10b. Non-breeding male.
10c. Juvenile.
10d. Female. Grey rump/lower back.

PLATE 16: DUCKS (See also Plate 15)

1 MACCOA DUCK *Oxyura maccoa* Page 335
Uncommon in Kenyan highlands; more numerous in n. Tanzania. Only East African stiff-tail. Squat, thick-set, large head and bill; swims low in water. **1a. Male. 1b. Female.**

2 HOTTENTOT TEAL *Anas hottentota* Page 333
Widespread on alkaline and freshwater lakes. Often common inland; rare on coast. Dark crown and blue-grey bill diagnostic. **2a. Female.** Exposed secondaries brown. **2b. Male.** Secondaries green.

3 RED-BILLED TEAL *Anas erythrorhyncha* Page 333
Common and widespread inland; local on coast.

4 COMMON TEAL *Anas c. crecca* Page 331
Regular, November–March, in highlands and Rift Valley. Small, compact. **4a. Female.** Sometimes has paler loral area than shown, never as pale as 6b. **4b. Male.** Head looks dark at distance; yellowish-buff patch on sides of black under tail-coverts.

5 CAPE TEAL *Anas capensis* Page 330
Largely confined to alkaline Rift Valley lakes; common.

6 GARGANEY *Anas querquedula* Page 332
Widespread, October–April. Common in Kenya, less so in n. Tanzania. **6a. Male. 6b. Female.** Sharper head pattern than 4a; pale loral spot.

7 YELLOW-BILLED DUCK *Anas u. undulata* Page 332
Common in Kenyan highlands, much less so in n. Tanzania. Green speculum (blue in northern *A. u. rueppelli*) conspicuous in flight.

8 AFRICAN BLACK DUCK *Anas sparsa leucostigma* Page 330
Uncommon on mountain streams, mainly above 1850 m. Shy and wary. White-bordered blue or purple speculum conspicuous in flight.

9 EURASIAN WIGEON *Anas penelope* Page 330
Uncommon on fresh water, November–March, typically above 1800 m. No recent Tanzanian records. **9a. Female, rufous morph.** Very plain (also grey and intermediate colour morphs). **9b. Male.**

10 MALLARD *Anas p. platyrhynchos* Page 329
Vagrant. No definite recent records of wild birds. **10a. Male. 10b. Female.** Bill orange with dusky markings; no white patch in secondaries. See text.

11 GADWALL *Anas s. strepera* Page 331
Rare on freshwater Kenyan lakes. Small white patch in secondaries distinctive in flight, sometimes visible on water. **11a. Female.** Grey-brown; orange-sided bill. **11b. Male.** Grey with black rear end.

12 NORTHERN SHOVELER *Anas clypeata* Page 333
Locally common, November–March. Long spatulate bill. **12a. Female. 12b. Sub-eclipse male** (autumn, early winter). **12c. Male** (breeding plumage, late December-early April).

13 NORTHERN PINTAIL *Anas a. acuta* Page 332
Fairly common and widespread, November–early April. **13a. Male. 13b. Female.** Somewhat streamlined; plain head on long neck.

14 FERRUGINOUS DUCK *Aythya nyroca* Page 335
Scarce and local, December–March. Usually with Southern Pochards. **14a. Female.** Duller than male; brown-eyed. **14b. Male.** White-eyed. Appears black at distance, with white rear end.

15 COMMON POCHARD *Aythya ferina* Page 334
Rare on open water (six records, December–March). Long bill, peaked forehead. **15a. Female.** Hoary face patches, sooty rear. **15b. Male.**

16 SOUTHERN POCHARD *Netta erythrophthalma brunnea* Page 334
Locally common on highland waters, mainly November–February. **16a. Female.** Pied face, white rear end. **16b. Male.** Dark, with long pale grey bill.

17 TUFTED DUCK *Aythya fuligula* Page 335
Scarce on highland waters and Lake Turkana, November–March. Short crest on hindcrown usually evident. **17a. Male. 17b. Female.** White loral patch often lacking; can show white under tail-coverts.

PLATE 17: COURSERS, PRATINCOLES AND THICK-KNEES

1 **MADAGASCAR PRATINCOLE** *Glareola ocularis*   **Page 391**
Malagasy migrant to East African coast, April–September; locally abundant north of Kilifi (especially Sabaki River estuary Aug.–Sept.). **1a and 1b. Non-breeding plumage**. Shorter, shallower tail than in Collared Pratincole; dark brown upperparts, throat and breast; rufous belly patch. White subocular streak.

2 **ROCK PRATINCOLE** *Glareola n. nuchalis*   **Page 391**
Local on rocks in Nzoia River, w. Kenya. White postocular stripe joins hindneck collar. Short white stripe on wing-linings; feet red. **2a and 2c. Adults. 2b. Juvenile.**

3 **COLLARED PRATINCOLE** *Glareola pratincola fuelleborni*   **Page 390**
Locally common along Rift Valley lakes and coastal estuaries. Long pointed wings, deeply forked tail. **3a and 3d. Breeding adults**. Creamy-buff throat with black border; belly white. **3b. Immature**. Throat border blurred, breast mottled. **3c. Juvenile**. Buff feather edges, short tail.

4 **BLACK-WINGED PRATINCOLE** *Glareola nordmanni*   **Page 391**
Rare palearctic passage migrant; associates with Collared Pratincole. Underside of wing entirely black; no white trailing edge.

5 **VIOLET-TIPPED COURSER** *Rhinoptilus chalcopterus*   **Page 389**
Local in se. Kenya/n. Tanzania. May–November. Uncommon in open bush and woodland. Nocturnal. Shape and head pattern suggest Crowned Plover.

6 **TWO-BANDED COURSER** *Rhinoptilus africanus gracilis*   **Page 389**
Local and uncommon on short-grass plains and alkaline flats in s. Kenya/n. Tanzania. Two black breast bands; white superciliary stripe.

7 **HEUGLIN'S COURSER** *Rhinoptilus cinctus*   **Page 389**
Uncommon in dry bush and semi-desert scrub. Largely nocturnal. Cryptic pattern, chestnut neck and breast bands.

8 **CREAM-COLOURED COURSER** *Cursorius cursor*   **Page 390**
Vagrant to Lake Turkana. Larger and sandier-coloured than Somali Courser, with different tail and under wing pattern, relatively shorter bill and tarsi. **8a and 8b. Adults.**

9 **TEMMINCK'S COURSER** *Cursorius temminckii*   **Page 390**
The commonest courser; widespread on short-grass plains south of the Equator. Dark brown above; rufous belly with black central patch.

10 **SOMALI COURSER** *Cursorius somalensis littoralis*   **Page 389**
Locally common on short-grass plains and semi-desert in n. and e. Kenya. Pale, with distinctive head pattern, creamy-white legs and feet. **10a and 10b. Adults.**

11 **SPOTTED THICK-KNEE** *Burhinus capensis*   **Page 388**
Locally common in dry bush country. Largely nocturnal. Boldly spotted upperparts; relatively unpatterned closed wing. **11a and 11b. Adults.**

12 **EURASIAN THICK-KNEE or STONE-CURLEW** *Burhinus o. oedicnemus*   **Page 387**
Scarce palearctic migrant, October–March, regular in n. Kenya; scarce elsewhere. Narrow white wing-bar bordered above and below by black. **12a and 12b. Adults.**

13 **SENEGAL THICK-KNEE** *Burhinus senegalensis inornatus*   **Page 387**
Local near rivers and lakeshores in n. and nw. Kenya (e.g. lakes Turkana and Baringo). Nocturnal. Finely streaked; no white bar on closed wing. Bill large, mostly black, yellow at base; legs and feet yellowish. **13a and 13b. Adults.**

14 **WATER THICK-KNEE** *Burhinus v. vermiculatus*   **Page 387**
Widespread along river banks and lakeshores. Broad grey wing panel, narrowly streaked with black. Base of bill greenish; legs and feet olive. **14a and 14b. Adults.**

15 **EGYPTIAN-PLOVER** *Pluvianus aegyptius*   **Page 388**
Vagrant to northern shores of Lake Turkana. **15a and 15b. Adults.**

PLATE 18: LARGE PLOVERS

1 BROWN-CHESTED PLOVER *Vanellus superciliosus*   Page 394
Vagrant, mainly in Lake Victoria basin and w. Serengeti NP.
1a and 1b. Adults. Broad chestnut breast band, black crown.
1c. Juvenile. Brownish crown, yellow on face.

2 BLACK-WINGED PLOVER *Vanellus melanopterus minor*   Page 393
Locally common above 1500 m on short-grass plains, cultivated fields. Broader breast band and larger, less
sharply defined white forehead patch than smaller Senegal Plover; legs and feet dull red; orbital ring purplish red. Broad diagonal white wing-stripe in flight. **2a and 2b. Adults**.

3 SENEGAL PLOVER *Vanellus lugubris*   Page 393
Local and nomadic, mainly below 1500 m, on open or bushed grassland in the Lake Victoria basin, Mara
GR, Tsavo, Arusha NP and the coastal lowlands. Small. Sharply defined white forehead patch, white trail-
ing wing edge; legs and feet dark slate-grey; faint orbital ring dull yellow. **3a and 3b. Adults**.

4 BLACKSMITH PLOVER *Vanellus armatus*   Page 392
Common on highland and Rift Valley wetlands north to lakes Bogoria and Baringo. White cap and hindneck patch; black flight feathers. **4a and 4b. Adults**.

5 BLACK-HEADED PLOVER *Vanellus tectus*   Page 392
Locally common in dry thorn-bush. Long crest; wing pattern as in Crowned Plover.
5a and 5b. V. t. latifrons. Ne. Kenya, Meru and Tsavo East NPs. Large white forehead patch.
5c. V. t. tectus. Nw. Kenya south to lakes Baringo and Bogoria. Small forehead patch.

6 CROWNED PLOVER *Vanellus c. coronatus*   Page 393
Widespread. Fairly common on dry plains and cultivated land. White-ringed black crown; broad diagonal
white wing stripe includes primary coverts. Highly vocal.
6a, 6b and 6c. Adults.
6d. Juvenile

7 AFRICAN WATTLED PLOVER *Vanellus senegallus lateralis*   Page 394
Western. Local on moist short-grass plains. **7a and 7b. Adults**. Long yellow wattles.

8 SPUR-WINGED PLOVER *Vanellus spinosus*   Page 392
Common on northern river banks and lakeshores; uncommon at coast; rare on southern Rift Valley lakes,
where replaced by Blacksmith Plover. **8a and 8b. Adults**.

9 LONG-TOED PLOVER *Vanellus c. crassirostris*   Page 392
Local in marshes and swamps. Forewing (incl. primary coverts) white. **9a and 9b. Adults**.

10 PACIFIC GOLDEN PLOVER *Pluvialis fulva*   Page 394
Uncommon coastal migrant, scarce inland.
10a. Adult in nearly full breeding plumage.
10b. Immature. (Winter adult similar, but less yellowish.)

11 GREY PLOVER *Pluvialis squatarola*   Page 395
Common migrant along coast; some oversummer. Occasional inland. Black axillaries (grey in Pacific
Golden Plover).
11a and 11b. Adults in non-breeding plumage.
11c. Adult in nearly full breeding plumage.

Dale A. Zimmerman
1994

PLATE 19: SMALL PLOVERS

1 KITTLITZ'S PLOVER *Charadrius pecuarius* Page 395
Common around Rift Valley lakes.
1a. Adult. Rich buff underparts.
1b. Juvenile. Buff superciliary stripe and collar.

2 WHITE-FRONTED PLOVER *Charadrius marginatus tenellus* Page 396
Locally common on sandy n. Kenyan coast and on sandbars in Galana/Athi Rivers. Sporadic at Lake Turkana. Thin black eye-line; white of forehead extends behind eye.
2a. Adult.
2b. Juvenile.

3 LITTLE RINGED PLOVER *Charadrius dubius curonicus* Page 395
Regular, October–April, along rivers, lakeshores and saltpans. Much less common than larger Ringed Plover. Yellow orbital ring; no orange on bill; legs and feet pinkish or yellowish.
3a. Spring adult.
3b. Winter adult.

4 CHESTNUT-BANDED PLOVER *Charadrius pallidus venustus* Page 397
Locally common on Rift Valley soda lakes. Small, with narrow chestnut breast band, long-legged appearance.
4a. Adult male. Black frontal bar and eye-line.
4b. Juvenile. Narrow, broken greyish breast band.
4c. Adult female. Broader breast band than male; no black on head.

5 KENTISH PLOVER *Charadrius a. alexandrinus* Page 396
Migrant in small numbers, regular at Lake Turkana, October–April; rare elsewhere. Small, slim. Pale, with dark bill, dark patch or bar at side of breast.
5a. Spring male. Rufous nape.
5b. Spring female.

6 RINGED PLOVER *Charadrius hiaticula tundrae* Page 395
Common and widespread along coast and inland waters, September to early May; some oversummer. Portly, with stubby bill, orange legs and feet. No prominent orbital ring (unlike l ittle Ringed Plover).
6a. Spring adult. Dense black facial area and breast band; base of bill orange.
6b. Juvenile. Paler, incomplete breast band.
6c. Winter adult. Bill largely dark.

7 THREE-BANDED PLOVER *Charadrius t. tricollaris* Page 396
Widespread on inland waterways. Pale-eyed, with red orbital ring and bill base; double breast band.
7a. Juvenile. Greyish forehead.
7b. Adult. White forehead.

8 GREATER SANDPLOVER *Charadrius leschenaultii crassirostris* Page 397
Common along coast, mainly August to early May; many first-year birds oversummer. Scarce inland. Bill larger and tarsi longer than in Lesser Sandplover.
8a. Spring male. Chestnut breast band, black ear-coverts.
8b. Winter adult. Grey-brown breast band and ear-coverts.
8c. Spring female. Trace of rufous breast band, grey-brown ear-coverts.

9 CASPIAN PLOVER *Charadrius asiaticus* Page 398
Regular, August–April, on short-grass plains in Mara GR/Serengeti NP, where large numbers winter; mainly passage migrant elsewhere (often common on muddy shores at Lake Turkana; also short-grass areas in Tsavo East NP). Tall, slim, with small head; slender bill.
9a. Spring male. (Female usually has grey-brown breast band.)
9b. Winter adult.

10 LESSER or MONGOLIAN SANDPLOVER *Charadrius mongolus pamirensis* Page 397
Common along coast, August to early May; many first-year birds remain all year. Scarce but regular inland, especially along Rift Valley Lakes. A smaller, shorter-legged and smaller-billed version of Greater Sandplover.
10a. Spring female. Sooty-brown mask, trace of rufous on nape and breast.
10b. Winter adult. Same pattern as 8b, but with different proportions.
10c. Spring male.

PLATE 20: SMALL SANDPIPERS (See also Plate 21)

1 TEMMINCK'S STINT *Calidris temminckii* **Page 399**
Local and uncommon in freshwater wetlands, October–April. Rare along coast; accidental in n. Tanzania. Legs and feet yellowish or olive; tail tip projects beyond primary tips (unlike in other resting stints).
1a. Spring adult.
1b. Winter adult.

2 RED-NECKED STINT *Calidris ruficollis* **Page 399**
Vagrant.
2a. Pale spring adult. Wing-coverts grey (rufous-edged in spring Little Stint).
2b. Bright spring adult.
2c. Pale winter adult. From 3c by paler feather centres above. See text.

3 LITTLE STINT *Calidris minuta* **Page 398**
Common and widespread, August–May. Bill, legs and feet black. See text.
3a. Spring adult.
3b. Juvenile.
3c. Winter adult.

4 LONG-TOED STINT *Calidris subminuta* **Page 399**
Rare migrant on coast and inland lakeshores. Smaller-headed, longer-necked than Little Stint. Oversized toes often obscured by mud; legs and feet yellow or greenish; bill fine, slightly decurved.
4a. Spring adult. Often shows obscure whitish V on back (as do some Little Stints).
4b. Winter adult.

5 BROAD-BILLED SANDPIPER *Limicola falcinellus* **Page 401**
Annual at Sabaki estuary, August–April; rare elsewhere; usually on mudflats. Long, dark bill kinked downwards at tip; double (forked) superciliary stripe.
5a. Spring adult.
5b. Winter adult. Greyer above than in spring; dark patch may be visible at bend of wing.

6 SANDERLING *Calidris alba* **Page 401**
Widespread along coast, August–April; some oversummer. Scarce on inland lakes. Feeds at water's edge, running ahead of breaking waves. Compact, with short, stout black bill.
6a. Winter adult. Pale, with black 'shoulder' mark.
6b. Juvenile.
6c. Spring adult.

7 CURLEW SANDPIPER *Calidris ferruginea* **Page 400**
Common and widespread, August–May; some young birds oversummer. Evenly decurved bill, long-legged appearance.
7a. Juvenile.
7b. Winter adult.
7c. Spring adult.

8 DUNLIN *Calidris alpina* **Page 400**
Vagrant. Similar to Curlew Sandpiper but more compact, with shorter neck, shorter tarsi, bill decurved only at tip.
8a. Winter adult.
8b. Spring adult.

9 RUFF *Philomachus pugnax* **Page 402**
Common migrant, August–May; some oversummer. **Spring female** ('Reeve') shown. Portly, small-headed, short-billed; plumage strongly 'scaled'; legs and feet pinkish red or orange; slow, deliberate movements. (See also Plate 23.)

10 PECTORAL SANDPIPER, *Calidris melanotos* **Page 400**
Vagrant. Streaked breast sharply demarcated; short bill.
10a. Juvenile female.
10b. Winter adult.

11 BUFF-BREASTED SANDPIPER *Tryngites subruficollis* **Page 402**
Vagrant. Plump, plover-like, short-billed; yellow legs and feet. (Some individuals more whitish, less buff, than adult illustrated.)

PLATE 21: FLYING SANDPIPERS AND PLOVERS (Winter adults, except as indicated)

PLATE 22: SANDPIPERS, SHANKS AND PHALAROPES (Adults)

1 TEREK SANDPIPER *Xenus cinereus*　　　　　　　　　　　**Page 406**
Common coastal migrant, August–April; scarce inland. Long upcurved bill and bright yellow-orange legs and feet.
1a and 1b. Winter.

2 COMMON SANDPIPER *Actitis hypoleucos*　　　　　　　　　**Page 406**
Common and widespread, August–April.
2a and 2b. Winter. Tail extends well beyond primary tips. Bobbing motion on land. In stiff-winged low flight, wings remain below the horizontal.

3 COMMON GREENSHANK *Tringa nebularia*　　　　　　　　　**Page 405**
Common and widespread, September–April.
3a and 3b. Winter. Bill slightly upturned. Hoary head/neck; in flight, long white wedge on back, but wing pattern different from that of No. 4.

4 COMMON REDSHANK *Tringa totanus ussuriensis*　　　　　　**Page 405**
Uncommon; largely coastal.
4a and 4b. Winter. Shorter, bulkier than Spotted Redshank; forehead dark. In flight, large white wing patches, unlike Common Greenshank and Marsh Sandpiper.

5 SPOTTED REDSHANK *Tringa erythropus*　　　　　　　　　**Page 404**
Widespread on inland waters, November–May. More slender than Common Redshank, with longer tarsi and longer, thinner bill.
5a and 5c. Winter. Forehead white. In flight, lacks strong contrast; white wing patches marbled.
5b. Spring. Plumage mostly blackish. Legs and feet dark red.

6 MARSH SANDPIPER *Tringa stagnatilis*　　　　　　　　　　**Page 405**
Common and widespread on wetlands (scarce at coast). Some oversummer. Suggests diminutive Common Greenshank with straight, needle-thin bill. Legs and feet pale greenish or yellow-green.
6a and 6c. Winter. In flight, toes project well beyond tail.
6b. Spring.

7 WOOD SANDPIPER *Tringa glareola*　　　　　　　　　　　**Page 406**
Common and widespread on freshwater wetlands. Bold white superciliary stripe. Slim and long-necked compared with more compact Green Sandpiper.
7a and 7b. Winter. Prominently spangled above. Tail finely barred.

8 GREEN SANDPIPER *Tringa ochropus*　　　　　　　　　　　**Page 406**
Common along rivers, streams and roadside pools. Stockier than Wood Sandpiper, with narrow superciliary stripe, dark olive legs and feet.
8a and 8b. Winter. Dark olive-brown, with faint pale speckling. In flight, shows bold tail bars and strong contrast between white rump and dark wings/back.

9 GREY PHALAROPE *Phalaropus fulicarius*　　　　　　　　　**Page 407**
Vagrant. Bill shorter and thicker than in Red-necked Phalarope.
9a and 9c. Winter. Paler grey above than Red-necked Phalarope.
9b. Spring female.

10 RED-NECKED PHALAROPE *Phalaropus lobatus*　　　　　　**Page 407**
Regular offshore, October–April, at times in large flocks. Scarce inland on Rift Valley lakes. Needle-like bill.
10a. Spring female.
10b. Spring male.
10c and 10d. Winter.

11 RED KNOT *Calidris c. canutus*　　　　　　　　　　　　**Page 401**
Vagrant. Stocky, with short neck and bill; tarsi short and greenish.
11a and 11c. Winter. May show traces of red spring plumage.
11b. Spring.

PLATE 23: GODWITS, CURLEWS, RUFF AND TURNSTONE

1 RUDDY TURNSTONE *Arenaria i. interpres*   **Page 407**
Common along coast, September–April; rare inland.
1a and 1b. Spring Adults.
1c. Winter Adult.

2 RUFF *Philomachus pugnax*   **Page 402**
Common and widespread inland, August–May; rare at coast. Legs and feet pink, pinkish red or orange in adults. Movements sluggish, deliberate. See Plate 20 for spring female.
2a. Spring male. Flight pattern same for both sexes at all ages; conspicuous white oval patches straddling upper tail-coverts.
2b. Winter female.
2c. Winter male. White-necked individual (variable; most show bright orange-red legs and yellow, orange or pink bill base).
2d. Juvenile female. 2e. Juvenile male. Buff face and underparts, scaly upperparts; legs and feet greenish or olive-brown.

3 WHIMBREL *Numenius p. phaeopus*   **Page 404**
Common along coast, especially August–April; rare inland. Bill kinked downward near tip, crown boldly striped.
3a and 3b. Winter. Adults in flight appear compact and dark, with white rump narrowing to point. (Immature similar.)

4 EURASIAN CURLEW *Numenius arquata orientalis*   **Page 404**
Uncommon but regular on coast, mainly August–April; a few in summer. Occasional inland. Larger, slightly paler than Whimbrel, with longer bill evenly decurved throughout its length.
4a and 4b. Winter adults. Paler flight feathers than Whimbrel; no head stripes. (Immature similar.)

5 BAR-TAILED GODWIT *Limosa l. lapponica*   **Page 404**
Uncommon migrant on coast, mainly August–October; rare inland. Lacks white in wing; tail finely barred; legs much shorter than in Black-tailed Godwit.
5a. Spring female. Bright individual.
5b and 5c. Winter adults. Upperparts noticeably streaked; white extends up back; toes barely project beyond tail.
5d. Spring male. Russet extends to under tail-coverts.

6 BLACK-TAILED GODWIT *Limosa l. limosa*   **Page 403**
Fairly common, mainly October–April, in wetlands. Broad black tail band and large white wing-stripe.
6a and 6b. Winter adults. Feet project well beyond tail in flight.
6c. Spring adult. Barred flanks, white posterior underparts.

1a

1b

1c

2a

2b

2c

2d

2e

3a

3b

4a

4b

5a

5b

5c

5d

6a

6b

6c

IW

PLATE 24: LARGE PIED WADERS, SNIPE AND PAINTED-SNIPE

1 CRAB-PLOVER *Dromas ardeola*   Page 385
Present on coast all months, most numerous August–April.
1a and 1b. Adults.

2 EURASIAN OYSTERCATCHER *Haematopus ostralegus longipes*   Page 386
Uncommon on coast. Sporadic at lakes Turkana, Baringo and Nakuru.
2a. Winter. White on lower throat.
2b. Spring. All-black head and neck.

3 BLACK-WINGED STILT *Himantopus h. himantopus*   Page 386
Widespread resident of wetlands, including coastal creeks and saltpans. Dusky head markings variable.
3a and 3b. Adults.

4 PIED AVOCET *Recurvirostra avosetta*   Page 386
Fairly common on alkaline Rift Valley lakes; scarce elsewhere.
4a and 4b. Adults.

5 GREATER PAINTED-SNIPE *Rostratula b. benghalensis*   Page 385
Uncommon. Widespread in marshy areas and recently inundated grassland.
5a. Adult female.
5b and 5c. Adult males.

6 PINTAIL SNIPE *Gallinago stenura*   Page 403
Vagrant from Asia (three Kenyan records, Oct.–Jan.). Possibly overlooked. Very similar to Common Snipe.
Bill averages shorter; less contrasting pale back lines, plainer breast, paler and faded-looking wing-coverts
especially noticeable in flight, along with virtual lack of pale rear edge to secondaries.
6a. Adult and first-winter.
6b. Unique tail shape, with ultra-narrow outer tail feathers (unlikely to be seen in the field).

7 AFRICAN SNIPE *Gallinago nigripennis aequatorialis*   Page 403
Local resident of *high-elevation* marshes and bogs (w. and cent. Kenyan highlands; common on moorlands
of Mt Elgon, Mt Kenya; also Kilimanjaro and Crater Highlands in Tanzania.) Longer-billed, darker-breasted
than Common Snipe.
7a. and 7c. Adult and first-year.
7b. Much white in tail.

8 JACK SNIPE *Lymnocryptes minimus*   Page 402
Scarce and sporadic palearctic migrant, mainly November–February. Small size, short bill. On ground,
shows all-dark crown, double buff facial stripes, no flank bars.
8a. Adult and first-winter.
8b. Tail dark, with no white or chestnut.

9 GREAT SNIPE *Gallinago media*   Page 403
Uncommon palearctic migrant, October–December and April–May. Lake edges, flooded grasslands, dry
fields. Flight mode and shape distinct. Barred belly, white wing-bars. See text.
9a. Adult and first-winter.
9b. Broad white tail sides.

10 COMMON SNIPE *Gallinago g. gallinago*   Page 402
Palearctic migrant, October–March, when the commonest snipe below 2000 m in marshes, along lake
edges and in wet fields.
10a. Adult and first-winter.
10b. Tail mostly rufous, with little white.

PLATE 25: GALLINULES, RAILS, JACANAS AND FINFOOT (See also Plate 26)

1 **AFRICAN WATER RAIL** *Rallus caerulescens*   **Page 376**
Widespread in cent. Kenyan highlands south to Mara GR, Amboseli and Arusha NPs; scarce elsewhere.
1a. Adult.
1b. Juvenile.

2 **BLACK CRAKE** *Amaurornis flavirostris*   **Page 377**
Common and widespread.
2a. Juvenile. White on throat variable.
2b. Adult.

3 **AFRICAN JACANA** *Actophilornis africanus*   **Page 384**
Common and widespread on waters with floating vegetation.
3a. Juvenile.
3b and 3c. Adults.

4 **LESSER MOORHEN** *Gallinula angulata*   **Page 378**
Local intra-African migrant, mainly April–August. Largely yellow bill; no red on legs.
4a. Adult.
4b. Immature.
4c. Juvenile.

5 **LESSER JACANA** *Microparra capensis*   **Page 384**
Scarce. In flight, white trailing edge on secondaries and pale wing-coverts distinctive.
5a and 5b. Adults.

6 **COMMON MOORHEN** *Gallinula chloropus meridionalis*   **Page 378**
Common and widespread above 1400 m. Scarce in coastal lowlands. Largely red bill/frontal shield and red tibial 'garters'.
6a. Juvenile.
6b and 6c. Adults.
6d. Downy young.

7 **ALLEN'S GALLINULE** *Porphyrio alleni*   **Page 377**
Local and uncommon on cent. Rift Valley lakes (mainly Naivasha and Baringo), June–September. Rare in n. Tanzania.
7a. Juvenile. Rail-like, with streaked upperparts.
7b. Adult. Bluish frontal shield.

8 **PURPLE SWAMPHEN** *Porphyrio porphyrio madagascariensis*   **Page 378**
Local and uncommon.
8a. Adult. Large; all-red bill and frontal shield
8b. Subadult. Underparts pale purplish grey, shading to buffy white on belly.

9 **RED-KNOBBED COOT** *Fulica cristata*   **Page 379**
Locally abundant (especially on Lake Naivasha and some n. Tanzanian lakes).
9a. Non-breeding adult. Inconspicuous knobs at base of frontal shield.
9b. Breeding adult.
9c. Downy young.

10 **AFRICAN FINFOOT** *Podica senegalensis somereni*   **Page 380**
Scarce and local on well-shaded streams and rivers with overhanging vegetation. Shy and elusive.
10a. Female.
10b. Male.

PLATE 26: CRAKES AND FLUFFTAILS (See also Plate 25)

1 **WHITE-SPOTTED FLUFFTAIL** *Sarothrura pulchra centralis* Page 374
Locally common along wooded streams in w. Kenya.
1a. Female. Rear body tiger-striped between rufous foreparts and tail.
1b and 1c. Males. Scattered large white body spots.

2 **STRIPED FLUFFTAIL** *Sarothrura affinis antonii* Page 375
Confined to tussock grass at high elevations. Few recent records.
2a. Female. Rich buff; heavily spotted breast/belly, barred back and flanks.
2b and 2c. Males. White-striped back; scaly/streaky pattern below.

3 **STREAKY-BREASTED FLUFFTAIL** *Sarothrura boehmi* Page 375
Rare intra-African migrant, April–May, in flooded grasslands. Very short black tail.
3a. Female. Dusky breast, barred flanks and under tail-coverts.
3b and 3c. Males. White-striped back, narrowly streaked lower breast and sides.

4 **RED-CHESTED FLUFFTAIL** *Sarothrura rufa* Page 374
Common in w. Kenyan marshes and swamps, less so elsewhere. Rarely seen on dry ground.
4a. Female. Barred flanks, pale breast.
4b and 4c. Males. Body and wings black with fine white markings.

5 **BUFF-SPOTTED FLUFFTAIL** *Sarothrura e. elegans* Page 374
Uncommon in w. Kenyan forests. Occasional elsewhere during rains.
5a. Female. Large dark eye on pale face. Buff spots above, spot-barring below.
5b and 5c. Males. Buff-spangled above, white-spotted below.

6 **BAILLON'S CRAKE** *Porzana pusilla obscura* Page 376
Uncommon and local in wetlands. Irregular black and white marks on brown upperparts.
6a. Juvenile. Buff face and breast; barring on flanks, sides and breast.
6b. Adult male. Blue-grey face and breast, strongly barred flanks, all-green bill, red eye.

7 **SPOTTED CRAKE** *Porzana porzana* Page 376
Scarce palearctic migrant in wet places, November–April.
7a and 7b. Males. Stocky; yellow chicken-like bill, reddish at base; spotted white foreparts, buff under tail-coverts. (Female browner on neck/breast.)

8 **STRIPED CRAKE** *Aenigmatolimnas marginalis* Page 377
Scarce intra-African migrant, May–November, in wetlands. Bill heavy.
8a. Juvenile. Plain light brown back, buffy-brown foreparts, dull white belly and crissum.
8b. Male. Rufous-brown head, neck and flanks, tawny or buff crissum.
8c. Female. Grey foreparts, tawny or buff crissum.

9 **CORNCRAKE** *Crex crex* Page 375
Scarce palearctic migrant in savanna/grassland; regular, mid-April, in Mara GR.
9a and 9b. Adults. Buffy brown, with barred flanks and pale flesh-brown bill, grey superciliary stripe and foreneck. (Female may show little or no grey.) In flight, has large orange-rufous wing patches.

10 **AFRICAN CRAKE** *Crex egregia* Page 375
Uncommon in wet grassy places; regular intra-African migrant, April–September.
10a. Juvenile. Brownish-buff foreparts, obscure brown flank barring.
10b and 10c. Adults. Grey foreparts, narrow white superciliary stripes.

PLATE 27: TURNICIDS, QUAIL, STONE PARTRIDGE AND FRANCOLINS
(See also Plate 28)

1 BLUE QUAIL *Coturnix adansonii* **Page 365**
Rare intra-African 'rains migrant' in wet grassland; may breed on Pemba Island.
1a and 1b. Males.
1c. Female. Heavily barred underparts.

2 HARLEQUIN QUAIL *Coturnix d. delegorguei* **Page 365**
Common and widespread in grassland and savanna. Concentrations coincide with periods of heavy rain.
2a and 2b. Females. Sides of breast spotted; primaries plain brown.
2c and 2d. Males. Bold face pattern; underparts appear dark in flight.

3 COMMON QUAIL *Coturnix coturnix erlangeri* **Page 364**
Fairly common local resident of highland grain fields and grassland. Inconspicuous, but trisyllabic call frequently heard.
3a and 3b. Females. Streaked sides, spots across breast, buff bars on primaries.
3c. Male. Chestnut face, striped crown. (Some birds have chestnut underparts. Paler migrant *C. c. coturnix* has whitish cheeks in both sexes.)

4 QUAIL-PLOVER *Ortyxelos meiffrenii* **Page 372**
Local and uncommon in dry grassland. Somewhat nocturnal; solitary. Suggests small courser. On bare ground, employs slow, chameleon-like locomotion. Wing pattern unique; flight lark-like.
4a. Female.
4b and 4c. Males.

5 COMMON BUTTON-QUAIL *Turnix sylvatica lepurana* **Page 373**
Locally common in grassland, savanna, abandoned cultivation. Solitary (or in small loose groups during rainy season). Pale buff wing-coverts contrast with dark flight feathers.
5a. Adult male.
5b. Adult female.
5c. Immature male.

6 BLACK-RUMPED BUTTON-QUAIL *Turnix hottentotta nana* **Page 373**
Rare in moist grassland and marsh edges. Secretive.
6a and 6b. Adult females. Black rump and tail; long buff streak on scapulars. Wings lack contrast of Common Button-quail. (Male has black or pale rufous crown, speckled malar area, whitish or buff throat.)

7 RING-NECKED FRANCOLIN *Francolinus streptophorus* **Page 366**
Rare and local on grassy escarpments in w. Kenya (Mt Elgon, Samia Hills and the Maragoli Escarpment).
Male illustrated. (Female similar.)

8 CRESTED FRANCOLIN *Francolinus sephaena* **Page 368**
Locally common in lowland bush, dry scrub, open riverine woodland, dense thickets. Small; runs with tail erect; frequently in small groups.
8a and 8c. *F. s. grantii*. Widespread, except in coastal lowlands and extreme ne. Kenya.
8b. *F. s. rovuma*. Coastal. Short brown streaks on underparts.

9 HILDEBRANDT'S FRANCOLIN *Francolinus hildebrandti* **Page 369**
Locally common in scrub and thickets near wooded areas, especially in cent. Rift Valley. Sexes distinct.
9a. *F. h. altumi*, male.
9b. *F. h. altumi*, female.
9c. *F. h. hildebrandti*, female.

10 STONE PARTRIDGE *Ptilopachus p. petrosus* **Page 366**
Local on rocky slopes and in gorges in n. and nw. Kenya. Shy and elusive. Runs and hops among boulders, tail erect. May perch in trees. Vocal at dawn and dusk.

11 COQUI FRANCOLIN *Francolinus coqui* **Page 366**
Widespread in savanna, grassy bush and thicket borders. *F. c. coqui* uncommon in coastal lowlands; *F. c. hubbardi* locally common in cent. Rift Valley, w. Kenyan highlands, Mara GR south to Serengeti NP. (*F. c. maharao* uncommon and local east of Rift Valley.)
11a. *F. c. hubbardi*, female.
11b. *F. c. hubbardi*, male.
11c. *F. c. coqui*, female.
11d. *F. c. coqui*, male.

DALE A.
ZIMMERMAN
1995

PLATE 28: FRANCOLINS AND GUINEAFOWL (Adults, except as indicated. See also Plate 27)

1 ORANGE RIVER FRANCOLIN *Francolinus levaillantoides archeri* **Page 368**
Local and rare in n. Kenya (Mt Kulal and Huri Hills). Underparts with short fine streaks. See text.

2 MOORLAND FRANCOLIN *Francolinus psilolaemus elgonensis* **Page 367**
Local; high elevations on Mt Elgon and (similar *F. p. psilolaemus*) on Mt Kenya and the Aberdares.

3 SHELLEY'S FRANCOLIN *Francolinus shelleyi uluensis* **Page 367**
Locally common in grassland/open savanna in cent. and s. Kenya; uncommon in n. Tanzania. (Similar *F. s. macarthuri* uncommon in Chyulu Hills.) Belly heavily barred with black; wings show much rufous in flight.
3a and 3b. Adults.

4 CHESTNUT-NAPED FRANCOLIN *Francolinus castaneicollis atrifrons* **Page 369**
Vagrant (?) along edge of s. Ethiopian highlands near Moyale, in forest edge and juniper woods. Underparts nearly plain creamy buff (unlike well-marked Ethiopian races).

5 RED-WINGED FRANCOLIN *Francolinus levaillantii kikuyuensis* **Page 367**
Scarce in remnant grasslands in w. and sw. Kenyan highlands. Ochre or orangey band between throat and black-and-white neck ring. Wings extensively rufous.
5a and 5b. Adults.

6 SCALY FRANCOLIN *Francolinus squamatus maranensis* **Page 368**
Locally fairly common in forest, bamboo and dense forest-edge bush. Bill entirely red or vermilion (brown above and orange below in presumed immatures). (*F. s. schuetti*, west of Rift Valley, similar but paler.)

7 JACKSON'S FRANCOLIN *Francolinus jacksoni* **Page 369**
Common along montane-forest edges on Mt Kenya and in the Aberdares; rare on Mt. Elgon.

8 RED-NECKED SPURFOWL *Francolinus afer* **Page 369**
8a. *F. a. cranchii*. Locally common in Lake Victoria basin, Mara GR and Serengeti NP.
8b. *F. a. cranchii*, juvenile.
8c. *F. a. leucoparaeus*. Local in Kenyan coastal lowlands. (Eastern Tanzanian birds may be the similar *F. a. melanogaster*; species also present in Tarangire NP.)

9 YELLOW-NECKED SPURFOWL *Francolinus leucoscepus* **Page 370**
Locally common in open light bush and savanna. Numerous in most national parks and game reserves. Pale buff wing patch conspicuous in flight. In n. Tanzania, hybridizes with Grey-breasted Spurfowl (see Plate 122). **9a and 9b. Adults.**

10 HELMETED GUINEAFOWL *Numida meleagris* **Page 371**
Widespread in bush, woodland, savanna and shrubby grassland: *N. m. reichenowi* common south of the Equator, *N. m. meleagris* uncommon in n. Kenya; *N. m. somaliensis* in northeast south to Wajir. (*N. m. mitrata* in coastal lowlands.)
10a. *N. m. reichenowi*, adult.
10b. *N. m. reichenowi*, immature.
10c. *N. m. reichenowi*, juvenile.
10d. *N. m. reichenowi*, downy young.
10e and 10f. *N. m. meleagris*, adults.
10g. *N. m. somaliensis*, adult.

11 CRESTED GUINEAFOWL *Guttera pucherani* **Page 371**
Local in forest and dense woodland: *G. p. pucherani* coastal, inland to eastern edge of Kenyan highlands and to Lake Manyara; *G. p. verreauxi* in w. Kenyan highlands (incl. Mau, Nandi and Kakamega Forests) east to southern Aberdares, isolated populations in Mara GR and Serengeti NP.
11a. *G. p. verreauxi*, adult. Unspotted purplish-black collar; dark brown eyes; no red on face.
11b. *G. p. verreauxi*, downy young.
11c. *G. p. pucherani*, adult. Bluish dots extend up to throat skin; red eyes and much red on face.

12 VULTURINE GUINEAFOWL *Acryllium vulturinum* **Page 371**
Locally common in dry bush and savanna in n. and e. Kenya, south to Tsavo West NP, Mkomazi GR and the Masai Steppe.
12a. Adult.
12b. Downy young.

DALE A. ZIMMERMAN 1995

PLATE 29: BUSTARDS (See also Plate 30)

1 WHITE-BELLIED BUSTARD *Eupodotis senegalensis canicollis* **Page 383**
Widespread in shrubby grassland.
1a. Male.
1b. Female.
1c. Subadult male.

2 CRESTED BUSTARD *Eupodotis ruficrista gindiana* **Page 382**
Widespread in northern and eastern areas, in dry bush and scrub below 1250 m.
2a. Female.
2b. Male.

3 BLACK-BELLIED BUSTARD *Eupodotis m. melanogaster* **Page 383**
Local in moist grassland. Slightly smaller, slimmer, longer-legged and with slightly thinner bill than Hartlaub's.
3a, 3b and 3c. Adult males. Head pattern less bold and with less white in wing than Hartlaub's Bustard; hindneck buffy brown, lower back to tail brown. In display, shows black bands on brown tail.
3d. Adult female. Neck pale buffy brown or tan and finely vermiculated; appears plain. Lower back to tail brownish.
3e. Juvenile male. Neck brownish.

4 HARTLAUB'S BUSTARD *Eupodotis hartlaubii* **Page 383**
Locally common, mostly below 1500 m. Prefers drier habitat than Black-bellied, but the two sympatric in places (e.g. Nairobi and Meru NPs).
4a, 4b and 4c. Adult males. Sharper face pattern than Black-bellied; broader black postocular line and dark line from eye to throat bordering bright white ear-coverts. Neck greyish, not buffy brown. Much white in wings; rump and tail appear black.
4d. Immature male. Neck grey.
4e. Female. Neck finely streaked or speckled, not vermiculated, with cream central line down front. Upper breast with blackish marks. Lower back and tail grey.

5 HEUGLIN'S BUSTARD *Neotis heuglinii* **Page 381**
Northern Kenya. Uncommon in lava desert, bush and shrubby grassland. Blue-grey neck, chestnut band on lower breast.
5a and 5b. Adult males. Black crown and face. (Some males, and many females, show white line on centre of crown.) Some primaries white along most of their length.
5c. Juvenile male.

6 DENHAM'S BUSTARD *Neotis denhami jacksoni* **Page 381**
Local and uncommon in grassland above 1500 m.
6a and 6b. Females. Rufous on hindneck; white patch at base of primaries. (Male similar but larger; see Plate 30.)

PLATE 30: LARGE GROUND BIRDS (See also Plate 29)

1 **ABYSSINIAN GROUND HORNBILL** *Bucorvus abyssinicus*   Page 474
Scarce and local in nw. Kenya, mainly in short-grass areas below 1000 m.
1a and 1c. Males.
1b. Female.

2 **SOUTHERN GROUND HORNBILL** *Bucorvus leadbeateri*   Page 474
Widespread but uncommon and local in grassland and savanna.
2a. Female. Chin/upper throat violet-blue.
2b and 2c. Males. Chin and throat red.
2d. Juvenile.

3 **SECRETARY BIRD** *Sagittarius serpentarius*   Page 336
Uncommon but widespread in grassland, open savanna and cultivation.
3a and 3b. Adults.

4 **KORI BUSTARD** *Ardeotis kori struthiunculus*   Page 382
Widespread. Uncommon in grassland and savanna.
4a and 4b. Adults.
4c. Male in display.

5 **ARABIAN BUSTARD** *Ardeotis arabs*   Page 382
Rare in far-northern Kenya. Smaller than Kori Bustard; no black on wing-coverts.

6 **DENHAM'S BUSTARD** *Neotis denhami jacksoni*   Page 381
Uncommon and local in grassland above 1500 m.
Male in courtship display. (See also Plate 29.)

7 **SOMALI OSTRICH** *Struthio (camelus) molybdophanes*   Page 303
Eastern and ne. Kenya.
7a. Breeding male.
7b. Non-breeding female.
7c. Juvenile.

8 **COMMON OSTRICH** *Struthio camelus massaicus*   Page 303
Widespread in s. Kenya and n. Tanzania.
8a. Breeding male.
8b. Downy young.
8c. Non-breeding female.
8d. Non-breeding male.
8e. Breeding female.

Dale A. Zimmerman
1989

PLATE 31: VULTURES AND PALM-NUT VULTURE

1 **LAMMERGEIER** *Gypaetus barbatus meridionalis*   **Page 340**
Scarce around mountains and inselbergs, mainly alpine areas of mts Elgon, Kenya, Meru and Kilimanjaro.
1a. Adult. Rusty-tinged head and underparts, black mask and beard.
1b. Juvenile. Pale face, hooded appearance; black secondaries. Head whitens with age.

2 **PALM-NUT VULTURE** *Gypohierax angolensis*   **Page 352**
Local in coastal lowlands, evergreen forest; usually near water. Heavy bill.
2a. Adult. White plumage areas often earth-stained; bare face pinkish or pale orange.
2b. Juvenile. Dark brown, with pale face; feathered head and neck.

3 **HOODED VULTURE** *Necrosyrtes monachus pileatus*   **Page 340**
Widespread, but urban only in w. Kenya; elsewhere, now confined to national parks and game reserves.
Compact, short-tailed, slender-billed.
3a. Juvenile. Greyish-white face; sepia down on head.
3b. Adult. Pink or red face; 'woolly' head.

4 **EGYPTIAN VULTURE** *Neophron p. percnopterus*   **Page 340**
Widespread but uncommon. Breeds on cliffs, forages in open country.
4a. Adult. Shaggy neck, yellow face.
4b. Juvenile. Pale face and foreneck. Dark hood blends into rest of plumage. Bases of secondaries grey
(black in juvenile Lammergeier).

5 **RÜPPELL'S GRIFFON VULTURE** *Gyps r. rueppellii*   **Page 341**
Locally common in dry open country; roosts and nests on cliffs. Long-necked; slightly larger and heavier-
billed than White-backed Vulture.
5a. Juvenile. From adult White-backed by darker neck/head down and slightly paler bill.
5b. Adult. Scaly pattern and yellowish-horn bill unique.

6 **AFRICAN WHITE-BACKED VULTURE** *Gyps africanus*   **Page 341**
Commonest vulture. Nests in trees. Bill blackish at all ages.
6a. Juvenile. Head/neck with pale down; underparts buff-streaked. No white on back.
6b and 6c. Adults. Bill, head and neck blackish; white back patch visible when wings spread.

7 **WHITE-HEADED VULTURE** *Trigonoceps occipitalis*   **Page 342**
Widespread but uncommon in open/semi-open country. Pink bill with blue cere at all ages.
7a. Juvenile. Bill colour and angular head distinctive.
7b. Adult female. (Male has grey secondaries.)

8 **LAPPET-FACED VULTURE** *Torgos t. tracheliotus*   **Page 341**
Uncommon to fairly common and widespread in national parks and game reserves. Huge size and massive
bill.
8a and 8c. Adults.
8b. Juvenile.

PLATE 32: VULTURES AND EAGLES OVERHEAD (See plates of perched birds for status and habitat notations)

1 LAPPET-FACED VULTURE *Torgos t. tracheliotus* **Page 341**
1a. Juvenile. Long, broad wings with pinched-in inner primaries. No contrast on wings, or forewing slightly paler with some obscure pale lines. **1b. Adult**. Whitish leg feathers and forewing line.

2 RÜPPELL'S GRIFFON VULTURE *Gyps r. rueppellii* **Page 341**
2a. Adult. Pale-mottled body, lines of crescent-shaped marks on wing-linings. **2b. Juvenile**. Ochre-brown, buff-streaked body and wing-linings contrast with blackish flight feathers. Single white forewing line in youngest birds makes separation from young African White-backed Vulture difficult or impossible. See text.

3 AFRICAN WHITE-BACKED VULTURE *Gyps africanus* **Page 341**
3a. Adult. Pale wing-linings and body. **3b. Juvenile**. Plumage identical to 2b, but wing tips often more tapering. See text.

4 HOODED VULTURE *Necrosyrtes monachus pileatus* **Page 340**
4a. Adult. Whitish down showing through the tibial feathers (not depicted on plate) may suggest miniature Lappet-faced Vulture, but no white line on wing-linings. **4b. Juvenile**. Dark, except for paler feet and head.

5 WHITE-HEADED VULTURE *Trigonoceps occipitalis* **Page 342**
5a. Adult female. Inner secondaries all white (greyish, and separated from dark forewing by white line, in male). **5b. Juvenile**. White line on wing; from adult male by all-brown body.

6 LAMMERGEIER *Gypaetus barbatus meridionalis* **Page 340**
Narrow pointed wing tips and long, wedge-shaped tail. **6a. Adult. 6b. Juvenile**.

7 EGYPTIAN VULTURE *Neophron p. percnopterus* **Page 340**
7a. Adult. Wedge-shaped white tail. **7b. Juvenile**. Dark, with paler tail; body and wings lighten with each moult.

8 VERREAUX'S EAGLE *Aquila verreauxii* **Page 355**
Adult. Pinched-in wing base, white primary patch.

9 BATELEUR *Terathopius ecaudatus* **Page 344**
Juvenile. Protruding head, short tail (longer than in adult), narrow wing tips.

10 LONG-CRESTED EAGLE *Lophaetus occipitalis* **Page 357**
Adult. Blunt, broad wings; long, two-banded tail; white primary patches.

11 LESSER SPOTTED EAGLE *Aquila p. pomarina* **Page 353**
This species and No. 14 slightly shorter-winged and shorter-tailed than larger *Aquila* spp. **11a. Adult**. Wing-coverts paler than remiges; pale carpal crescents. **11b. Juvenile**. Greater coverts and flight feathers pale-tipped in fresh plumage.

12 STEPPE EAGLE *Aquila nipalensis orientalis* **Page 354**
12a. Juvenile. White central wing band, trailing wing edges and tail tip; pale inner primaries, barred flight feathers. **12b. Pale subadult**. Body darker than wing-coverts; pale throat. **12c. Adult**. Body and wing-coverts darker than flight feathers.

13 TAWNY EAGLE *Aquila r. rapax* **Page 354**
Shape as in Steppe Eagle; plumage variable as in that species. **13a. Adult**. (Typical, untidily mottled bird.) Faint barring on flight feathers. **13b. Juvenile**. Cinnamon-brown (fading to yellowish tawny, then blond); pale inner primaries; obscure pale grey mid-wing line. As warm tones wear away, more difficult to separate from immature plumages of Steppe Eagle, but Tawny lacks pale tips to under primary coverts.

14 GREATER SPOTTED EAGLE *Aquila clanga* **Page 353**
Shape differs slightly from that of Lesser Spotted Eagle, the wings broader and tail shorter. Both soar and glide with flat or slightly drooping wings. **14a. Adult**. Coverts and body darker than flight feathers and tail; pale carpal crescents as in Lesser Spotted. **14b. Juvenile**. Buff spotting on belly; streaks on breast (evident at close range); pale tips on remiges and tail feathers.

15 IMPERIAL EAGLE *Aquila heliaca* **Page 355**
Longest wings of any East African *Aquila*. **15a. Juvenile**. Buff-streaked body and wing-coverts, dark secondaries, pale inner primaries; greater coverts all grey. **15b. Adult**. Coverts and body darker than remiges, tail broadly black-banded.

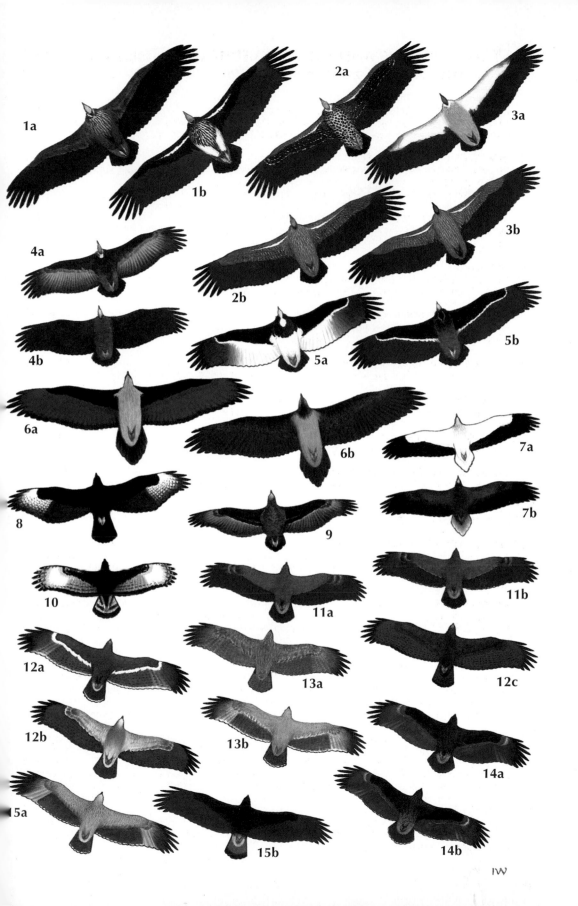

IW

PLATE 33: BUZZARDS, ACCIPITERS AND CHANTING GOSHAWKS

OVERHEAD (See plates of perched birds for status and habitat notations)

1 AUGUR BUZZARD *Buteo a. augur* **Page 352**
Very broad wings, short tail; black carpal marks shared by pale adult and juvenile. **1a. Pale adult**. Black band at rear wing edge, rufous tail. **1b. Dark adult**. Blackish body and wing-coverts, rufous tail. **1c. Juvenile**. Pale buff body and wing-coverts; dull brown tail with darker subterminal band; rear edge of wing grey.

2 MOUNTAIN BUZZARD *Buteo oreophilus* **Page 351**
Suggests Common Buzzard, but body and wing-linings densely spotted; no rufous, except for tibial barring.

3 COMMON (STEPPE) BUZZARD *Buteo buteo vulpinus* **Page 350**
Variable. (Common brown morph resembles Mountain Buzzard, but lacks spots. Dark morph identical to 4b.) Usually a pale breast patch on all morphs. **3a. Juvenile, rufous morph**. Rear edge of wing obscurely grey, barred tail, streaked body (not barred as in adult). **3b. Adult, rufous morph**. Like 4a, but has dark hood; black band on rear edge of wing. Some have uniformly rufous or chestnut body/wing-coverts (barred at close range).

4 LONG-LEGGED BUZZARD *Buteo r. rufinus* **Page 351**
More aquiline proportions than Common Buzzard. **4a. Typical adult**. Warm brown wing-linings and body, whitish head, black belly patches; very pale rufous tail (some almost whitish) with no discernible barring. **4b. Dark adult**. Black-banded grey tail. Identical to dark morph of Common Buzzard. **4c. Juvenile**. Paler, buffier than adult, barred tail, suffused grey band on wings.

5 EURASIAN HONEY BUZZARD *Pernis apivorus* **Page 338**
Differs from *Buteo* spp. in flat-winged soaring, slimmer and more protruding head; polymorphic adults have bands across primaries and unique tail pattern (two dark basal bands, one at tip). For juvenile, see Plate 39. **5a. Typical adult. 5b. Dark adult. 5c. Light adult.**

6 GRASSHOPPER BUZZARD *Butastur rufipennis* **Page 350**
Slim silhouette suggests harrier. Whitish underwing, rufous body.

7 EASTERN PALE CHANTING GOSHAWK *Melierax poliopterus* **Page 346**
Outer wings of both *Melierax* fuller than in sparrowhawks, and tail tip strongly rounded. Grey hood and black wing tips common to **adults** of both chanting goshawks, the two impossible to separate with view of underparts only.

8 GREAT SPARROWHAWK *Accipiter m. melanoleucus* **Page 350**
Large; pinched-in outer wing and long tail typical of all sparrowhawks. **8a. Rufous-breasted juvenile. 8b. White-breasted juvenile**.

9 DARK CHANTING GOSHAWK *Melierax m. metabates* **Page 346**
Juvenile. No known criteria for separating juveniles of the two *Melierax* species in ventral view.

10 RUFOUS-BREASTED SPARROWHAWK *Accipiter r. rufiventris* **Page 349**
Plain rufous wing-linings and body; throat and under tail-coverts whitish. (For juvenile, see Plate 42.)

11 LIZARD BUZZARD *Kaupifalco m. monogrammicus* **Page 350**
Stocky proportions, black throat streak, single white tail band. (From above, shows white upper tail-coverts.)

12 LEVANT SPARROWHAWK *Accipiter brevipes* **Page 348**
Pointed wings (less so when primaries spread in soaring). **12a. Juvenile**. Black-spotted on white; more banded on wing-linings. **12b. Adult female**. Black-tipped pale wing, chestnut barring. (Male has more contrasting black wing tips, paler body barring.)

13 SHIKRA *Accipiter badius sphenurus* **Page 347**
Small and compact, with blunt wings. **13a. Juvenile**. Brown-spotted buff body/wing-linings; faint flight-feather barring. **13b. Adult**. Dusky-tipped pale wings; body/wing-linings faintly barred pinkish brown.

14 EURASIAN SPARROWHAWK *Accipiter n. nisus* **Page 349**
Pale superciliary stripe in female and juvenile. **14a. Juvenile**. Ragged barring on body. **14b. Adult female**. Neat grey body barring (smaller male has chestnut barring).

15 GABAR GOSHAWK *Micronisus gabar aequatorius* **Page 346**
15a. Dark morph. Grey barring on flight feathers and tail; red cere, legs and feet distinguish it from dark Ovambo and much larger Great Sparrowhawks. **15b. Pale morph**.

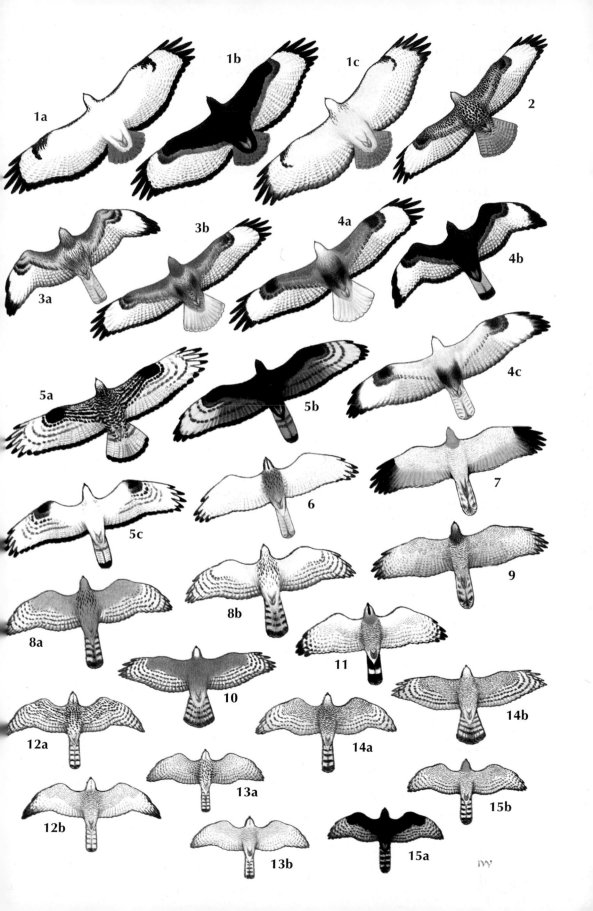

ivy

PLATE 34: MISCELLANEOUS LARGE RAPTORS OVERHEAD

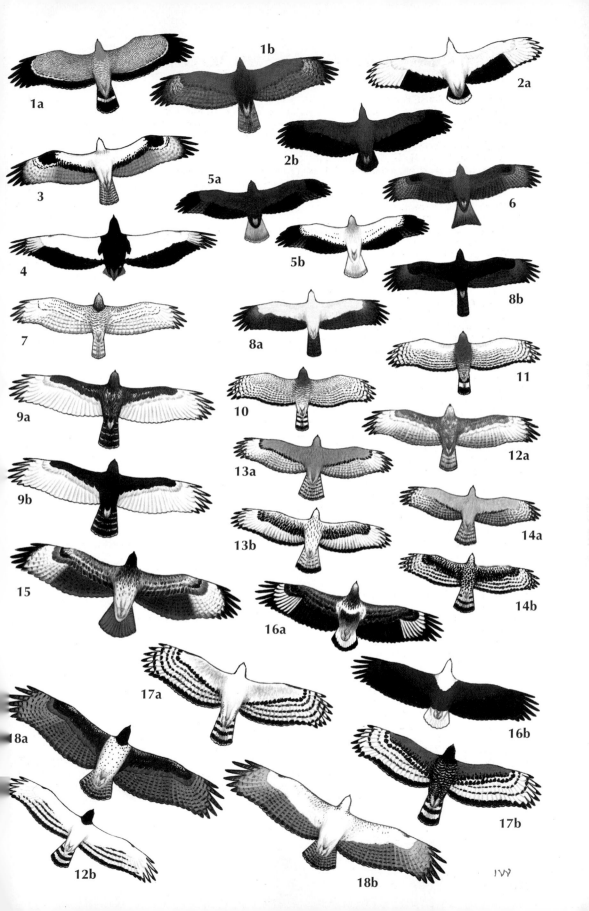

1a

1b

2a

2b

3

5a

6

4

5b

8b

7

8a

11

9a

10

12a

9b

13a

14a

13b

15

14b

16a

17a

16b

18a

17b

12b

18b

١٧٧

PLATE 35: EAGLES, BUZZARDS, AND OTHER RAPTORS IN FLIGHT (See plates of perched birds for status and habitat notations)

1 VERREAUX'S EAGLE *Aquila verreauxii* **Page 355**
Wings very narrow basally. **1a. Adult**. Black, with white rump and primary patches and white lines on back. **1b. Juvenile**. Pale upper tail-coverts and primary patches; rufous nape, cream crown.

2 GREATER SPOTTED EAGLE *Aquila clanga* **Page 353**
2a. Pale juvenile (rare). Whitish mid-wing line, pale primary panel and rump/tail-coverts; fulvous-buff forewing and body. **2b. Adult**. Very dark, with pale area on primary bases and upper tail-coverts. **2c. Dark juvenile**. White upper tail-coverts; pale spots on wing-coverts and back.

3 STEPPE EAGLE *Aquila nipalensis orientalis* **Page 354**
3a. Juvenile. From 6a by dull earth-brown body and wing-coverts, wider, brighter rear edges to secondaries and tail in fresh plumage, and brighter white primary patch; rump dark. **3b. Adult**. Pale back mark, tawny nape (usually), whitish primary patch; flight feathers and tail sometimes barred.

4 LESSER SPOTTED EAGLE *Aquila p. pomarina* **Page 353**
Slimmer wings and longer tail than Greater Spotted Eagle. **4a. Adult**. Dull brown, palest on smaller wing-coverts, with white inner primary flash and U on tail-coverts. **4b. Juvenile**. Warm brown wing-coverts and body; outer median coverts tipped with white; white patches on back, tail-coverts and primaries.

5 IMPERIAL EAGLE *Aquila heliaca* **Page 355**
Proportions as in Steppe and Tawny Eagles. **5a. Adult**. Large cream nape patch, grey tail with black tip, white lines on back. **5b. Juvenile**. Probably inseparable from 2a at distance except for proportions, although buff rather than fulvous-buff hue on body and wing-coverts.

6 TAWNY EAGLE *Aquila r. rapax* **Page 354**
Proportioned like Steppe Eagle. **6a. Juvenile**. Pale fulvous-brown body and wing-coverts in fresh plumage. **6b. Tawny adult**. Highly variable, depending on degree of wear and fading. Roughly streaked and mottled tawny and blackish brown. **6c. Immature**. Pale, worn and bleached individual.

7 COMMON (STEPPE) BUZZARD *Buteo buteo vulpinus* **Page 350**
Wings and tail less attenuated than in Long-legged Buzzard. **7a. Brown juvenile**. Brown head/wing-coverts, pale greater-covert tips in fresh plumage, and finely barred grey-brown tail. **7b. Rufous adult**. Red-brown wing-coverts and head; orange-rufous tail may have terminal barring.

8 LONG-LEGGED BUZZARD *Buteo r. rufinus* **Page 351**
More aquiline proportions than other *Buteo* spp. **8a. Pale adult**. Creamy-brown wing-coverts merge with white of head and neck; pale rufous-orange tail almost white at base. **8b. Juvenile**. Dark barring on pale grey-brown tail. **8c. Dark adult**. Sooty head, body and wing-coverts, grey tail with broad black band at tip. Indistinguishable in field from dark morph of Common Buzzard.

9 AFRICAN FISH EAGLE *Haliaeetus vocifer* **Page 352**
Adult. All-white tail, head and neck.

10 PALM-NUT VULTURE *Gypohierax angolensis* **Page 352**
Adult. Distinctive wing and tail patterns, but sometimes confused with African Fish Eagle.

11 GRASSHOPPER BUZZARD *Butastur rufipennis* **Page 350**
Slender; prominent rufous wing patches.

12 AFRICAN CUCKOO-HAWK *Aviceda cuculoides verreauxii* **Page 337**
Cuckoo-like shape, grey head, boldly banded tail.

13 AFRICAN HARRIER-HAWK *Polyboroides t. typus* **Page 344**
Broad black rear band and tips to wings; whitish band on mid-tail.

14 LONG-CRESTED EAGLE *Lophaetus occipitalis* **Page 357**
Broad-tipped wings with striking white primary patches; bold tail bands.

15 BOOTED EAGLE *Hieraaetus pennatus* **Page 356**
Buteo-like shape; flight feathers and tail wholly dark. **15a and 15b. Pale adults**. Cream middle wing-coverts and scapular patches and U on tail-coverts; small white 'headlights' at forewing bases (in all plumages.)

16 LIZARD BUZZARD *Kaupifalco m. monogrammicus* **Page 350**
Stout and compact; white rear edge to secondaries, white tail-coverts and tail band.

PLATE 36: FLYING SPARROWHAWKS, CHANTING GOSHAWKS, PYGMY FALCON AND HARRIERS (See plates of perched birds for status and habitat notations)

PLATE 37: FALCONS and KITES OVERHEAD (Adults except as indicated)

1 LANNER FALCON *Falco b. biarmicus* Page 358
Large, with long wings and tail. **1a. Adult**. Pale, lightly spotted body and wing-linings. **1b. Juvenile**. Heavily blotch-streaked body; wing-linings dark.

2 PEREGRINE FALCON *Falco peregrinus minor* Page 359
More compact than Lanner. (For migrant *F. p. calidus*, see text.) **2a. Adult**. Broad black 'moustache'; finely barred body and wing-linings not contrasting with flight feathers. **2b. Juvenile**. Resembles adult, except for bold streaks on rustier body.

3 TAITA FALCON *Falco fasciinucha* Page 360
Small, compact, short-tailed. Stiff shallow, 'parrot-like' wingbeats. White throat/cheeks shade into rufous body; wing-linings also rufous.

4 EURASIAN HOBBY *Falco s. subbuteo* Page 360
Slim, elegant shape; dashing flight. Boldly streaked underparts, chestnut crissum (lacking in juvenile).

5 BAT HAWK *Macheiramphus alcinus anderssoni* Page 338
Crepuscular. Suggests dark, broad-winged falcon. Variable amount of white on throat, small white eye marks. (See plate 44 for juvenile.)

6 SOOTY FALCON *Falco concolor* Page 362
Grey, with sooty wing tips and pale throat; no barring; tail tip wedge-shaped.

7 GREY KESTREL *Falco ardosiacus* Page 363
Grey body and wing-linings as in Sooty Falcon, but flight feathers and tail finely barred.

8 DICKINSON'S KESTREL *Falco dickinsoni* Page 362
Greyish-white head and upper tail-coverts, ladder-like tail pattern.

9 AFRICAN HOBBY *Falco cuvieri* Page 360
Shape and flight style of Eurasian Hobby, but faintly streaked underparts and wing-linings deep rufous.

10 ELEONORA'S FALCON *Falco eleonorae* Page 362
Rakish, with very elongated wings and tail. Dark wing-linings contrast with pale flight-feather bases and heavily streaked rufous body.

11 AMUR FALCON *Falco amurensis* Page 361
Somewhat more compact than kestrels; usually gregarious. **11a. Male**. White wing-linings; otherwise like Red-footed Falcon. **11b. Female**. Pale body heavily blotched with black; white wing-linings finely spotted away from edge; crissum pale tawny-buff.

12 RED-FOOTED FALCON *Falco vespertinus* Page 361
Shape and flight action as in Amur Falcon. **12a. Male**. Blackish wing-linings show minimal contrast with dark grey flight feathers, tail and body; crissum deep chestnut. **12b. Female**. Rich buff wing-linings and body; flight feathers and tail barred.

13 RED-NECKED FALCON *Falco chiquera ruficollis* Page 361
Finely barred body, wings and tail appear grey at a distance; throat white; tail tip broadly black-banded; rusty cap/nape. (For juvenile, see Plate 45.)

14 LESSER KESTREL *Falco naumanni* Page 363
Lighter in build than Common Kestrel; tail tip often strongly wedge-shaped. **14a. Male**. White wings, lightly speckled pale buff body, dark primary tips; no moustachial marks. **14b. Female**. Virtually identical to Common Kestrel. See text.

15 COMMON KESTREL *Falco t. tinnunculus* Page 364
Regularly hovers. (For resident race, see Plate 46.) **15a. Male**. Black band at tip of pale tail; dark-streaked buff body and pale buff wing-linings; crown and cheeks grey, lightly streaked with brown. **15b. Female**. Tail wholly barred; body and wing-linings boldly streaked.

16 BLACK-SHOULDERED KITE *Elanus c. caeruleus* Page 338
Habitually hovers. White underparts, with contrasting black primary tips and upper leading wing edges. (For juvenile, see Plate 43.)

17 AFRICAN SWALLOW-TAILED KITE *Chelictinia riocourii* Page 339
Tern-like, with black carpal patches. (Juvenile has much shallower tail fork.)

18 FOX KESTREL *Falco alopex* Page 363
Tawny-buff wing-linings and whitish flight feathers; finely barred tail.

19 GREATER KESTREL *Falco rupicoloides arthuri* Page 363
Black-edged whitish under wing-surface, tawny body, bold tail barring. (Flank bars lacking, or almost so, in juvenile; see Plate 46.)

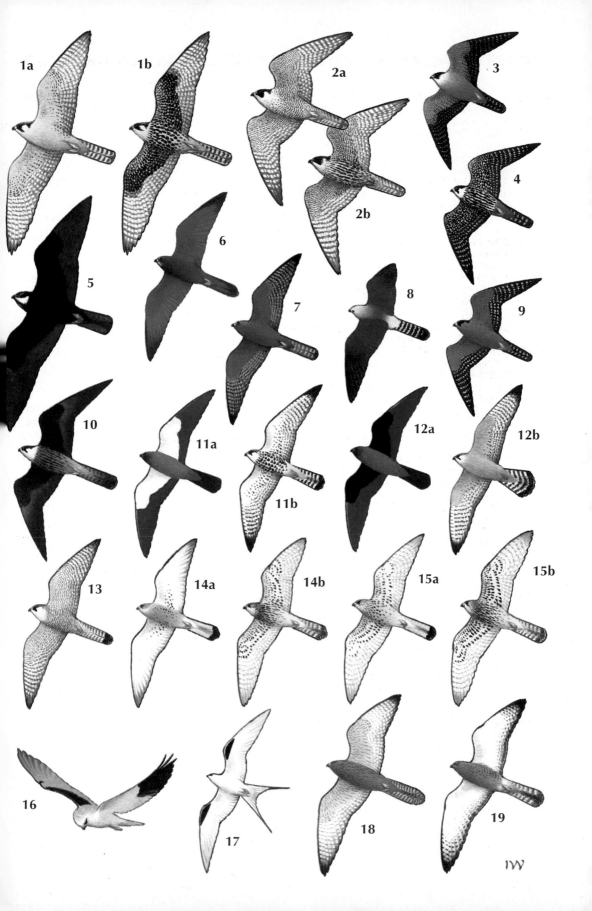

PLATE 38: *AQUILA* EAGLES (For flight figures, see Plates 32 and 35)

1 VERREAUX'S EAGLE *A. verreauxii*   Page 355
Uncommon/scarce around rocky hills, gorges, mountains.
1a. Adult. Coal-black plumage relieved by white lines on back.
1b. Juvenile. Black from face to belly; rufous-buff on upperparts.

2 GREATER SPOTTED EAGLE *A. clanga*   Page 353
Rare palearctic migrant, mainly near Rift Valley soda lakes. Like commoner Lesser Spotted Eagle, lacks
'baggy' leg feathering typical of larger *Aquila* spp.
2a. Typical adult. Dusky brown, with pale under tail-coverts.
2b. Typical juvenile. Blackish brown; whitish spots most evident on wing-coverts; buff-streaked breast.
2c. Pale juvenile (rare). Similar to Tawny Eagle, but with white rear edges on greater wing-coverts and secondaries. See text.

3 IMPERIAL EAGLE *A. heliaca*   Page 355
Scarce migrant, November–March.
3a. Adult. Pale 'mane', white 'braces', black-tipped grey tail.
3b. Juvenile. Buff-streaked body, plain buff head and leg feathering. (See text for separation from juvenile
Steppe Eagle.)

4 LESSER SPOTTED EAGLE *A. p. pomarina*   Page 353
Regular palearctic migrant, November/early December; a few remain to March in Rift Valley and nearby
highlands, mainly in savanna, open woodland and farmland. At close range nostrils seen as circular, not
oval as in Tawny and Steppe Eagles; yellow gape skin extends to below middle of eye.
4a. Juvenile. Warm brown, with white spots on greater (and sometimes median) wing-coverts; buff nape
patch, faint streaks on body and leg feathers.
4b. Adult. Dull brown; feathered tarsi narrow.

5 TAWNY EAGLE *A. r. rapax*   Page 354
Common and widespread in open country. Solitary or in pairs. Yellow of gape extends to below middle of
eye. Plumage variable; darker birds often scruffy.
5a. Dark adult. Tawny-brown, varying from very dark to lighter ginger-brown; mixture of dark or dark-centred feathers typical.
5b. Juvenile (fresh plumage). Pale tawny, with narrow white wing bands.
5c. Pale adult. Pale buff to whitish blond. Whitish upper tail-coverts but no white on wings. (This plumage,
common in bleached and worn juveniles and subadults, also occurs regularly in adults.)

6 STEPPE EAGLE *A. nipalensis orientalis*   Page 354
Common palearctic migrant in interior highlands and open plateau country, often in small to large groups.
Yellow skin of gape extends to below rear edge of eye (unique among *Aquila*).
6a. Adult. Dark brown; barred secondaries evident only at close range.
6b. Juvenile. Medium brown; greater wing-coverts and secondaries edged with broad white bands.

7 WAHLBERG'S EAGLE *A. wahlbergi*   Page 355
Most numerous August–April. Widespread in dry wooded, bushed or cultivated country. Little larger than
Black Kite, from which distinguished by short crest (often difficult to see) and long feathered tarsi.
7a. Paler adult. Medium-brown body contrasts with black flight feathers and tail. (See Plate 34 for rare pale
extreme.)
7b. Typical dark adult. Uniform dark brown.

PLATE 39: BUZZARDS, HONEY BUZZARD, OSPREY AND EAGLES

1 COMMON (STEPPE) BUZZARD *Buteo buteo vulpinus* **Page 350**
Fairly common palearctic migrant, October–November and March; some winter, mainly in lightly wooded country. Variable. (See also Plates 33, 35 and 44.)
1a. Rufous adult. White breast band barred; pale pinkish-rufous tail plain or barred, with broader subterminal band.
1b. Rufous juvenile. Streaked breast; all tail bars narrow; pale-edged greater coverts.

2 MOUNTAIN BUZZARD *Buteo oreophilus* **Page 351**
Resident of montane forest, adjacent moorlands and fields. Little plumage variation. Highly vocal, unlike Common Buzzard.
2a. Adult. Heavily blotched/spotted underparts; wide subterminal tail band.
2b. Juvenile. Buffier below, with fewer spots than adult; finer tibial barring; tail bars equal.

3 AUGUR BUZZARD *Buteo a. augur* **Page 352**
Common and widespread in highlands. Bulky, with very short tail, especially adult. (For dark morph, see Plate 44.)
3a. Light adult. Black above, pure white below, with rufous tail (often a narrow black subterminal band); secondaries barred.
3b. Light juvenile. Brown above, with pale-edged feathers; dull brown or red-brown tail longer than in adult, barred and with wider subterminal band.

4 LONG-LEGGED BUZZARD *Buteo r. rufinus* **Page 351**
Rare palearctic migrant in open country. Aquiline size and proportions.
4a. Adult. Pale head, dusky belly and leg feathers; plain tail very pale rufous to whitish orange.
4b. Juvenile. Streaked below, with dull, barred tail; head, body and wing-coverts paler than on young Common Buzzard.

5 OSPREY *Pandion h. haliaetus* **Page 337**
Palearctic migrant along large lakes, estuaries, coastal creeks. Perches in open, plunges for fish. Black facial mask on white head; bushy crest.

6 EURASIAN HONEY BUZZARD *Pernis apivorus* **Page 338**
Uncommon palearctic migrant in wooded areas, October–April. Sluggish, soars on flat, not upward-angled wings; small head. Adult yellow-eyed; three bands on tail.
6a. Typical adult. Heavily barred below.
6b. Rufous/cinnamon adult. Pale-barred below.
6c. Pale juvenile. Black eye patch on white head; dark-eyed; dark-streaked underparts, four tail bands.

7 AFRICAN CROWNED EAGLE *Stephanoaetus coronatus* **Page 357**
Uncommon in montane forest and woodland. Large, with short erectile crest.
7a. Adult. Banded/mottled underparts, pale yellow eyes, bright yellow cere and toes.
7b. Juvenile. Pale buff or whitish head and underparts, banded tail, black-spotted leg and tarsal feathers; grey eyes, light yellow toes.

8 MARTIAL EAGLE *Polemaetus bellicosus* **Page 357**
Widespread in open country. Impressive, crested, large-footed.
8a. Adult. Dark grey-brown hood, spotted underparts; blue-grey cere and toes.
8b. Juvenile. White face, underparts and tarsi; brown eye, whitish or grey cere and toes.

PLATE 40: SNAKE EAGLES, FISH EAGLE AND BATELEUR (For flight figures see Plates 32, 34 and 35)

1 SHORT-TOED SNAKE EAGLE *Circaetus gallicus*   Page 342
Bulky head, owl-like yellow eyes. *C. g. gallicus* a vagrant; *C. g. beaudouini* of uncertain status, possible in the west.
1a. *C. g. gallicus*, typical adult. Breast streaked grey-brown; short crescentic bars on white belly.
1b. *C. g. gallicus*, adult (dark-hooded form). Heavily marked below; dark head and breast.
1c. *C. g. beaudouini*, juvenile. Buffy-white head and underparts; separation from post juvenile Black-chested Snake Eagle difficult (see text).
1d. *C. g. beaudouini*, adult. Darker than 1a, with narrow barring below.

2 BROWN SNAKE EAGLE *Circaetus cinereus*   Page 343
Fairly common in bush, savanna, open country with baobabs. Upright posture, owl-like head, bright yellow eyes.
2a. Adult. Sooty brown, with banded tail, yellow eyes and bare whitish tarsi.
2b. Juvenile. Usually shows whitish markings on underparts and face.

3 BLACK-CHESTED SNAKE EAGLE *Circaetus pectoralis*   Page 342
Thinly distributed in open or lightly wooded country.
3a. Adult. Sharp separation between dark and light areas below.
3b. Juvenile. Mottled rufous and white underparts (may show rufous on face), scaly-patterned wing-coverts, plain grey tail.

4 BANDED SNAKE EAGLE *Circaetus cinerascens*   Page 343
Scarce and local in riverine or moist woodland. Stocky; similar to No. 5, but tail shorter and differently patterned. Brown extends from throat to lower breast, barring restricted to lower belly; single white tail band. (Juvenile resembles 5b, but tail as adult.)

5 SOUTHERN BANDED SNAKE EAGLE *Circaetus fasciolatus*   Page 343
Coastal and near-coastal forests; uncommon.
5a. Adult. White barring up to chest; banded grey and dark brown tail shows two or three white bands below.
5b. Juvenile. Pale-mottled head and breast (some almost whitish-headed); belly white; tail as adult.

6 AFRICAN FISH EAGLE *Haliaeetus vocifer*   Page 352
Widespread along coastal and fresh waters. Wing tips project well beyond short tail.
6a. Adult. White head, back, bib and tail.
6b. Juvenile. Whitish-mottled head and leg feathers; black eye-line.

7 BATELEUR *Terathopius ecaudatus*   Page 344
Widespread in dry bush and grassland. Extremely short tail.
7a. Juvenile. Grey face, buff head contrasting with blackish-brown body; tail longer than adult's.
7b. Adult female (cream-backed morph). Partly grey secondaries and pale grey forewing; feet project beyond chestnut tail.
7c. Adult male (chestnut-backed morph). All-black secondaries (grey-centred in female), red face and feet, pale grey forewing.

PLATE 41: CHANTING GOSHAWKS, *HIERAAETUS* AND GREAT SPARROWHAWK (See also Plates 33, 36 and 42)

1 DARK CHANTING GOSHAWK *Melierax m. metabates*　　　　　　　　　**Page 346**
Northwestern Kenya and Mara/Serengeti; fairly common.
1a. Juvenile. Wholly dark-barred upper tail-coverts only safe way to separate from 2a, but these usually concealed in perched bird. Breast sometimes slightly mottled or plain grey-brown, but see comments under 2a.; no white greater-covert tips.
1b. Adult. Red or coral-pink cere instantly separates from 2b. Tarsi usually pinkish red; grey wing-coverts and back washed with brownish; upper and under tail-coverts barred.

2 EASTERN PALE CHANTING GOSHAWK *Melierax poliopterus*　　　　　**Page 346**
Common in dry country north, east and south of the Kenyan highlands, in and (mainly) east of the Rift Valley; west of Rift only on Loita Plains. Nowhere alongside Dark Chanting Goshawk. Tarsi longer than in that species.
2a. Juvenile. Plumage often identical to 1a, except for less barred (appearing white) upper tail-coverts, (always?) white-tipped greater coverts in fresh plumage, and finer, fainter, more widely spaced dark under-tail-covert barring. Breast streaking and mottling equally variable in young birds of both species.
2b. Adult. Readily distinguished from 1b by yellow cere and longer, typically orange-red tarsi; upper tail-coverts white or occasionally partly barred; under tail-coverts plain white; darker 'saddle' on back contrasts with pure grey wing-coverts; greater coverts white-tipped (unless worn).

3 BOOTED EAGLE *Hieraaetus pennatus*　　　　　　　　　　　　　　**Page 356**
Uncommon palearctic migrant, October–April, especially in dry woodland and bush. Buzzard-sized, with striking pale wing-coverts and scapular patches and smoky mask.
3a. Rufous adult. Dull cinnamon/rufous head and underparts.
3b. Light adult. White or off-white underparts, variably dark-streaked. (For dark morph, see Plate 44.)

4 AYRES'S HAWK-EAGLE *Hieraaetus ayresii*　　　　　　　　　　　**Page 356**
Scarce and local in moister, more wooded habitats than African Hawk-Eagle. Stocky and long-legged.
4a and 4b. Adults. (Males may be much whiter about face than shown, and females entirely black-headed except for white throat.) All-dark wings, densely black-blotched underparts and leg feathers. Tail pattern as in 5b.
4c. Juvenile. Buff or pale rufous underparts (may be very narrowly dark-streaked) and sides of face; pale scaly upperparts.

5 AFRICAN HAWK-EAGLE *Hieraaetus spilogaster*　　　　　　　　　　**Page 356**
Uncommon and local in open woodland and scrub, usually in drier areas. More attenuated, lankier appearance than Ayres's Hawk-Eagle.
5a. Juvenile. Rich rufous with dark streaks below; wings and back plain dark brown, as cheeks; lacks pale eyebrow of juvenile Ayres's.
5b and 5c. Adults. Silvery-grey secondary bases; plain white underparts (including leg feathers), not splotched as in Ayres's. In flight, whitish primary panel and broad black rear border to pale grey (dark-barred) secondaries.

6 GREAT SPARROWHAWK *Accipiter m. melanoleucus*　　　　　　　　**Page 350**
Widespread in forest, woodland, wooded suburbs. Largest accipiter.
6a. Typical adult. (For dark morph, see Plate 44.)
6b. Rufous-breasted juvenile. Cinnamon-rufous underparts dark-streaked down to belly, streaks heaviest across breast. Similar to juvenile Ayres's Hawk-Eagle in same habitat, except for dense streaking.
6c. White-breasted juvenile. White ground-colour only difference from 6b.

PLATE 42: ACCIPITERS (See also Plates 33, 36, 41 and 44)

1 LITTLE SPARROWHAWK *Accipiter m. minullus*   Page 348
Local and uncommon in woodland. Very small and compact, especially male.
1a. Adult female. Dark grey above, with two white central tail spots and white upper tail-coverts.
1b. Juvenile female. Narrow white band on upper tail-coverts; two or three white spots on central tail; heavy dark spotting and barring below.

2 SHIKRA *A. badius sphenurus*   Page 347
Uncommon but widespread in dry country.
2a. Adult male. Faintly barred with pinkish rufous below, except for unmarked white leg feathering; closed tail plain grey; eye red.
2b. Juvenile. Breast heavily spotted, rest of underparts barred with brown; dark central throat stripe.
2c. Adult female. Darker subterminal tail band than in male; eye orange.

3 OVAMBO SPARROWHAWK *A. ovampensis*   Page 348
Rare in woodland; few confirmed records. Long, slender and small-headed. In very close view, long, slender middle toe diagnostic.
3a. Typical adult. Grey barring extends onto throat and chin. (Other adult accipiters are white-throated.) White shaft marks between dark bands on upper tail-surface. (For dark morph, see Plate 44.)
3b. Rufous-breasted juvenile. Broad white superciliary stripe, finely streaked breast.
3c. Light-breasted juvenile.

4 RUFOUS-BREASTED SPARROWHAWK *A. r. rufiventris*   Page 349
Widespread in montane forest and plantations; shy, unobtrusive.
4a. Adult. Bright rusty underparts and cheeks; white throat; slaty-black upperparts, with dark-capped appearance.
4b. Juvenile. Well marked with dull rufous below; leg feathers plain.

5 GABAR GOSHAWK *Micronisus gabar aequatorius*   Page 346
Widespread in woodland and bush. White upper tail-coverts (all ages).
5a. Juvenile. Streaked breast, rest of underparts barred; no pale superciliary stripe; white rear border on secondaries.
5b. Adult. Red cere, tarsi and toes; grey hood. (Dark morph on Plate 44.)

6 LEVANT SPARROWHAWK *A. brevipes*   Page 348
Rare palearctic migrant in bush or open savanna.
6a. Adult male. Pure dove-grey above, including cheeks (cf. 7b); resembles large Shikra, with similar red eye and rufous-pink barring, but leg feathers also barred and often rufous wash on breast.
6b. Adult female. Larger and browner than male, with stronger barring; narrow dark central throat stripe.
6c. Juvenile. Rows of large blackish-brown spots and black central throat stripe.

7 EURASIAN SPARROWHAWK *A. n. nisus*   Page 349
Scarce palearctic migrant in wooded or bushed country. Conspicuous white superciliary stripe in female and juvenile. Adults yellow-eyed (unlike Levant Sparrowhawk).
7a. Adult female. Dark grey or grey-brown above, including cheeks; white throat; dark brown barring below.
7b. Adult male. Dark slate-grey above, chestnut barring on cheeks and underparts.
7c. Juvenile female. Browner than adult female, with narrower, more jagged barring on underparts (including leg feathers).

8 AFRICAN GOSHAWK *A. tachiro sparsimfasciatus*   Page 347
Widespread in wooded areas, including Nairobi suburbs.
8a. Juvenile female (male smaller). White superciliary stripes; blackish lines of spots on underparts, except for barred leg feathering.
8b. Adult male. Slaty black above, including cheeks, which contrast with white throat; chestnut barring below. (Female is larger, sometimes greatly so; browner above and with coarser brown barring below.)

9 GREAT SPARROWHAWK *A. m. melanoleucus*   Page 350
Large size. **Typical adult** shown. (For other plumages, see Plates 41 and 44.)

PLATE 43: CUCKOO-HAWK, KITES, HARRIERS, AND GRASSHOPPER AND LIZARD BUZZARDS (For flight figures, see Plates 33–37)

1 AFRICAN CUCKOO-HAWK *Aviceda cuculoides verreauxii* **Page 337**
Uncommon in wooded areas. Shy, retiring. Crested; long wings (tips reach end of tail); adult suggests large Eurasian Cuckoo. **1a. Juvenile.** Short whitish superciliary stripe; sometimes sparsely spotted/blotched underparts. **1b. Adult male.** Grey breast sharply demarcated from boldly rufous-barred belly and flanks. (Female larger, browner, with broader paler barring.)

2 AFRICAN SWALLOW-TAILED KITE *Chelictinia riocourii* **Page 339**
Local and uncommon; mainly northern; a few breed near Longonot in cent. Rift Valley. **Adult** figured. (Juvenile has much shorter tail and rufous-edged feathers on back and wings.)

3 GRASSHOPPER BUZZARD *Butastur rufipennis* **Page 350**
Intra-African migrant in eastern bush country, November–March. Shape suggests both *Buteo* and harrier. Rufous wing patches distinctive. **3a. Adult.** Dark-streaked pale tawny underparts, dark throat stripe, yellow eye. **3b. Juvenile.** Faint throat stripe, dark moustache on tawny-buff head; pale rufous feather edging above, tail plain apart from dark terminal band; brown eye.

4 AFRICAN MARSH HARRIER *Circus ranivorus* **Page 345**
Local and uncommon, mainly near wet areas in highlands. See No. 7. **4a. Adult.** Cream/buff 'frosting' on face, breast, leading wing edge; no grey in wings, and barred brown tail. **4b. Juvenile.** Buff patch on nape and throat, ragged band across breast and wing edge; buff speckling on coverts and back.

5 BLACK-SHOULDERED KITE *Elanus c. caeruleus* **Page 338**
Widespread in open areas. Stocky, short-tailed, large-headed. **5a. Juvenile.** Cinnamon wash on breast; white-edged feathers above. **5b. Adult.** Pale grey above; black epaulettes on wings.

6 LIZARD BUZZARD *Kaupifalco m. monogrammicus* **Page 350**
Common in coastal lowlands, where conspicuous on roadside poles, wires; scarce elsewhere. Stocky; broad black central throat stripe, red cere and tarsi. (Juvenile similar.)

7 EURASIAN MARSH HARRIER *Circus a. aeruginosus* **Page 345**
Fairly common, October–April, in wetlands, moist grassland. Long-legged and long-tailed. **7a. Adult male.** Plain grey tail and wing patch; more buff on head and breast than African Marsh Harrier. **7b. Juvenile.** Creamy-white crown and throat, sometimes all-dark head. (Female similar, but usually with cream-edged forewing and yellowish-buff breast patch.)

8 BLACK KITE *Milvus m. migrans* **Page 339**
Adult nominate *migrans*, present October–March. Black bill contrasts with yellow cere; black-streaked head and neck greyer than in resident *parasitus* or migrant *aegyptius*, both yellow-billed. (*M. m. parasitus* on Plate 44.)

9 AFRICAN HARRIER-HAWK *Polyboroides t. typus* **Page 344**
Uncommon but widespread in wooded areas, including Nairobi suburbs. Bare face, small head, shaggy 'mane,' long legs and long tail. **9a. Dark juvenile.** Generally chocolate-brown, with pale face; paler feather edges form large patch on wing-coverts. **9b. Pale juvenile.** Large pale wing patch; mottled/streaked head and underparts. **9c. Non-breeding adult.** Yellow face; black spots above, white band across tail. **9d. Breeding adult.** Bare face flushes red or pink with excitement.

10 PALLID HARRIER *Circus macrourus* **Page 344**
Locally fairly common, October to early April, especially in se. Kenya, n. Tanzania. **10a. Adult female.** Darker face than 11a, giving a masked appearance; darker cap and eye-line, paler, broader collar. Generally inseparable from 11a in the field. **10b. Juvenile.** Darker, more extensive dark facial areas and shoulder patch, pale collar; underparts often paler and buffier than 11b.

11 MONTAGU'S HARRIER *Circus pygargus* **Page 345**
Locally common, October to early April, in open high plateau areas, including agricultural lands. Brown 'ring-tailed' birds as shown here require care and close views to separate from 10a. (For males of both species, see Plate 36.) **11a. Adult female.** Black rear border of ear-coverts and whitish face; vague collar. **11b. Juvenile.** Face and collar pattern similar to female; pale rufous-brown underparts with variable faint dark streaking.

PLATE 44: DARK-PLUMAGED RAPTORS (Adults, except as noted)

1 LONG-CRESTED EAGLE *Lophaetus occipitalis*　　　　　　　　　**Page 357**
Widespread in wooded and cultivated country.

2 AUGUR BUZZARD *Buteo a. augur*　　　　　　　　　　　　　　**Page 352**
Dark morph. Locally common in highlands. Short, reddish tail, pale-barred secondaries.

3 BROWN SNAKE EAGLE *Circaetus cinereus*　　　　　　　　　　**Page 343**
Fairly common resident in bush, woodland. Large owl-like head and yellow eyes. (See Plate 40.)

4 BOOTED EAGLE *Hieraaetus pennatus*　　　　　　　　　　　　**Page 356**
Dark morph. Duller above than light morph (Plate 41); under tail-coverts may be darkly mottled or all dark.

5 AYRES'S HAWK-EAGLE *Hieraaetus ayresii*　　　　　　　　　　**Page 356**
Dark morph. This plumage not recorded in East Africa. Tail pattern as in light morph (Plates 34 and 41); may show some white breast markings.

6 WAHLBERG'S EAGLE *Aquila wahlbergi*　　　　　　　　　　　　**Page 355**
Dark extreme. (For lighter plumage, see Plate 34.)

7 BLACK KITE *Milvus migrans parasitus*　　　　　　　　　　　**Page 339**
Common, especially near water and human settlements. Forked tail. *M. m. aegyptius* also yellow-billed. (For racial differences see text, and Plate 43 for migrant nominate race.)

8 BAT HAWK *Macheiramphus alcinus anderssoni*　　　　　　　**Page 338**
Uncommon and local in woodland, forest edge, villages. Crepuscular; roosts by day within canopy. Suggests bulky, broad-winged falcon in flight.
8a. Adult. White throat and eye marks; short crest.
8b. Juvenile. White or whitish on belly.

9 COMMON (STEPPE) BUZZARD *Buteo buteo vulpinus*　　　　　**Page 350**
Dark morph. Mainly grey tail with broad black subterminal band.

10 AFRICAN GOSHAWK *Accipiter tachiro sparsimfasciatus*　　　**Page 347**
Dark morph. Fairly common in wooded areas. Indistinct pale spots on tail; eye yellow.

11 GABAR GOSHAWK *Micronisus gabar aequatorius*　　　　　　**Page 346**
Dark morph. Locally common in woodland and bush. Red bill base, legs and feet.

12 OVAMBO SPARROWHAWK *Accipiter ovampensis*　　　　　　**Page 348**
Dark morph. Rare and local in woodland and riparian trees. White arrowheads in centre of tail; red eye.

13 GREAT SPARROWHAWK *Accipiter m. melanoleucus*　　　　　**Page 350**
Dark morph. Rare in wooded areas. *Accipiter* shape, plain tail, white throat.

14 EURASIAN MARSH HARRIER *Circus a. aeruginosus*　　　　　**Page 345**
Dark morph. Very rare. Typical harrier shape; pale grey tail.

15 EURASIAN HONEY BUZZARD *Pernis apivorus*　　　　　　　**Page 338**
Dark morph. Uncommon in woodland, forest edge, October–April. Black terminal and two narrower basal tail bands.

16 RED-FOOTED FALCON *Falco vespertinus*　　　　　　　　　**Page 361**
Male. Palearctic vagrant. Orange-red bare parts.

17 ELEONORA'S FALCON *Falco eleonorae*　　　　　　　　　　**Page 362**
Male, dark morph. Scarce palearctic migrant. Larger, with more attenuated shape than Red-footed Falcon, and yellow bare parts.

PLATE 45: FALCONS (See also Plates 37 and 44)

1 LANNER FALCON *Falco biarmicus*   **Page 358**
Commonest large falcon; widespread. Longer-tailed than Peregrine.
1a. *F. b. abyssinicus*, adult. N. Kenya. Underparts streaked and barred.
1b. *F. b. biarmicus*, adult. Cent./se. Kenya, n. Tanzania. Rufous crown/nape with black forecrown; largely pale buff below with sparse spotting; tail evenly barred.
1c. *F. b. biarmicus*, Juvenile. Tawny crown/nape, heavily streaked below; plain tail.

2 BARBARY FALCON *Falco p. pelegrinoides*   **Page 359**
Rare in rough arid country.
2a. Adult. Fine barring below; dusky-tipped tail with indistinct barring.
2b. Juvenile. Sandy crown, nape and underparts, finely streaked below; tail barred.

3 SAKER FALCON *Falco c. cherrug*   **Page 359**
Rare palearctic migrant, mainly in Rift Valley, October–March. Heavily built; often pale-headed, with white superciliary stripe.
3a. Adult. Grey-brown, more easterly bird shown.
3b. Juvenile. Densely streaked head and body, tail almost plain above.

4 PEREGRINE FALCON *Falco peregrinus minor*   **Page 359**
Scarce resident of open country with cliffs and crags; also in Nairobi city centre. Pale migrant race *calidus* present October–March.
4a. Adult. Blackish crown/nape and broad moustachial marks; densely barred body.
4b. Juvenile. Rusty-washed body heavily streaked; tail evenly buff-barred.

5 EURASIAN HOBBY *Falco s. subbuteo*   **Page 360**
Migrant in open country (Oct.–Dec., March–May); some winter in highlands.
5a. Adult. Black cap, narrow moustachial marks; rufous leg feathers and crissum.
5b. Juvenile. Buff scaling on brown upperparts and crown; heavily streaked underparts, the leg feathers and crissum buffy white.

6 AFRICAN HOBBY *Falco cuvieri*   **Page 360**
Uncommon in Lake Victoria basin and w. Kenyan highlands. Small, slender and dark.
6a. Adult. Underparts deep rufous; upperparts darker than in Eurasian Hobby.
6b. Juvenile. More heavily marked below than adult; upperparts browner.

7 TAITA FALCON *Falco fasciinucha*   **Page 360**
Rare near cliffs and gorges, typically in dry areas. Chunky, rather short-tailed.
7a. Juvenile. Pale feather edges above; more heavily streaked below than adult.
7b. Adult. Rufous nape patches diagnostic; head pattern otherwise suggests Peregrine; upperparts plain slate-grey, rufous below with contrasting white throat.

8 RED-NECKED FALCON *Falco chiquera ruficollis*   **Page 361**
Uncommon in coastal lowlands south of Mombasa; elsewhere, scarce in open country with palms. Kestrel-sized, finely barred above and with broad black tail band.
8a. Adult. Bright rufous crown and nape; broad black-and-white barring below.
8b. Juvenile. Head pattern blackish brown; dull rufous underparts barred with black.

9 ELEONORA'S FALCON *Falco eleonorae*   **Page 362**
Palearctic migrant, scarce in autumn, rarer in spring, mainly in cent. Kenyan highlands; rare in n. Tanzania. Very long primaries reach tip of long tail.
9a. Light adult. Streaked rufous underparts contrast with white throat/cheeks.
9b. Juvenile. Pale-edged feathers above, pale buff below with heavy streaking.

PLATE 46: SMALLER FALCONS (See also Plates 37 and 45)

1 FOX KESTREL *Falco alopex*   Page 363
Northern Kenya; uncommon near cliffs in arid areas. Rich chestnut, streaked above and below; indistinctly marked tail.

2 GREATER KESTREL *Falco rupicoloides arthuri*   Page 363
Cent. and s. Kenya, n. Tanzania; fairly common in savanna, grassland. Stocky, with large head; pale rufous throat; barred above, finely streaked pale cinnamon underparts.
2a. Juvenile. Entirely streaked below, cinnamon tail bands, dark eye.
2b. Adult. Barred flanks, grey tail bands, pale eye.

3 COMMON KESTREL *Falco tinnunculus*   Page 364
F. t. tinnunculus a widespread palearctic migrant in open country and farmland. More rufous *rufescens* a resident of rocky hills in and near Rift Valley.
3a. F. t. tinnunculus, female. Spotted/barred above; buff with dark streaks below.
3b. F. t. tinnunculus, male. Grey head and banded tail; spotted back.
3c. F. t. rufescens, female. Dark, heavily marked throughout.
3d. F. t. rufescens, male. Darker than 3b, back heavily spotted, tail finely barred.

4 DICKINSON'S KESTREL *Falco dickinsoni*   Page 362
Vagrant to Kenya; rare in n. Tanzania except on Pemba Island, where common in open wooded areas and palm groves. Small and stocky.
4a. Adult. Slate-grey, chunky greyish white head, barred tail.
4b. Juvenile. Narrower, duskier tail barring, barred on flanks.

5 GREY KESTREL *Falco ardosiacus*   Page 363
Local in Serengeti and w. Kenya in savanna and bushed grassland. Wing tips fall short of tail tip. All grey, with yellow bill base, orbital skin and feet.

6 LESSER KESTREL *Falco naumanni*   Page 363
Locally common palearctic migrant in open or wooded country, October–May.
6a. Female. Usually smaller than Common Kestrel, with slighter build, finer breast streaks, longer central tail feathers.
6b. Male. Grey wing patch, no moustachial marks; lightly spotted underparts.

7 PYGMY FALCON *Polihierax semitorquatus castanonotus*   Page 358
Common in dry thorn-bush. Very small; large dark eye on white face, red feet.
7a. Juvenile male. Rusty-buff streaks below, scaly rufous edges above. (Juvenile female chestnut on back.)
7b. Adult female. Chestnut back.
7c. Adult male. All grey above.

8 RED-FOOTED FALCON *Falco vespertinus*   Page 361
Palearctic vagrant in open country.
8a. Male. Slate-grey, with chestnut crissum; red on bill and feet.
8b. Female. Unmarked rusty-buff crown and underparts.
8c. Juvenile. Rufous crown, white collar, streaked underparts, barred black-and-cream tail.

9 SOOTY FALCON *Falco concolor*   Page 362
Uncommon migrant in bush and grassland, late October to November, sporadic March to early May.
9a. Adult. Wings reach or extend slightly beyond tail tip (much shorter in Grey Kestrel); dark moustachial streaks contrast with pale chin.
9b. Juvenile. Buffy yellow below with slate-grey streaks, darkest (often dense) on breast; buff cheeks and throat, with dark moustachial streaks; blue-green orbital ring and cere.

10 AMUR FALCON *Falco amurensis*   Page 361
Palearctic passage migrant in open country (Nov.–Dec., late March to early May).
10a. Male. White wing-linings; somewhat paler than Red-footed Falcon.
10b. Female. Heavily marked white underparts with barred leg feathers, warm buff crissum.
10c. Juvenile. Dark grey crown, heavily streaked buff underparts; grey tail narrowly barred with black.

PLATE 47: PARROTS AND SANDGROUSE

PLATE 48: *STREPTOPELIA* DOVES

1 LAUGHING DOVE *S. s. senegalensis*   **Page 427**
Common and widespread below 1800 m. Greyish-blue wing-coverts; white confined to corners of tail.
(Juvenile lacks band of spots on chest, entire breast is paler than in adult; head more rufous.)
1a and 1b. Adults.

2 EUROPEAN TURTLE DOVE *Streptopelia turtur*   **Page 426**
Casual in our region. Note black-and-white patch on side of neck, broad rufous margins on wing-coverts.
2a and 2b. Adults.

3 AFRICAN WHITE-WINGED DOVE *Streptopelia reichenowi*   **Page 426**
Restricted to Daua River in extreme ne. Kenya.
3a and 3b. Adults.

4 DUSKY TURTLE DOVE *Streptopelia l. lugens*   **Page 427**
Locally common in highlands. Large solid black patch on side of neck. (Juvenile paler and browner, with
more extensive rufous feather edging.)
4a and 4b. Adults.

5 RING-NECKED DOVE *Streptopelia capicola somalica*   **Page 426**
Common and widespread from sea level to 2000 m. Eye almost black. This eastern race, ranging west to
Samburu GR, Lake Baringo, Kibwezi, Namanga and Arusha, is paler and greyer than the browner western
tropica. (Juvenile has much buff feather edging above.)
5a, 5b and 5c. Adults.

6 AFRICAN MOURNING DOVE *Streptopelia d. perspicillata*   **Page 425**
Common below 1400 m. Eye yellow (may be pale creamy orange); bare orbital ring orange-red. (*S. d. elegans* of ne. Kenya south to Malindi is paler, with white lower belly and breast. Juveniles of both races
brownish on crown and breast; eye pale brown.)
6a, 6b and 6c. Adults.

7 RED-EYED DOVE *Streptopelia semitorquata*   **Page 425**
Widespread from sea level up to 3000 m. Eye dark red, appearing black at a distance. Tail tip pale grey, not
white. (Juvenile brown-eyed, with many pale rufous feather edges above, and obscure blackish band on
nape.)
7a, 7b and 7c. Adults.

African Mourning Dove.

PLATE 49: PIGEONS AND DOVES (See also Plate 48)

PLATE 50: TURACOS

1 EASTERN GREY PLANTAIN-EATER *Crinifer zonurus* **Page 432**
Western. Large rounded head with shaggy nuchal crest; brown face. In flight, white band near tip of wing; long tail grey basally.
1a and 1b. All plumages.

2 WHITE-BELLIED GO-AWAY-BIRD *Corythaixoides leucogaster* **Page 432**
Widespread below 1500 m. Pointed crest; much white in wings and tail. In flight, white on primary bases, not near wing tip. Bill of **female (2a)** pea-green, that of **male (2b)** black.

3 BARE-FACED GO-AWAY-BIRD *Corythaixoides personata leopoldi* **Page 432**
Locally common in Mara GR, Serengeti and Tarangire NPs. (*C. p. personata*, with more extensive green breast patch, a vagrant in extreme northern Kenya.) Black face contrasts with otherwise white neck, bushy crest arising from forehead. In flight, wings and tail plain greyish.
3a and 3b. Adults.

4 GREAT BLUE TURACO *Corythaeola cristata* **Page 430**
Local in w. Kenyan forests. Large size, black-tipped tail (basally yellowish below); no red in wings.
4a, 4b and 4c. Adults.

5 ROSS'S TURACO *Musophaga rossae* **Page 430**
Western riverine forests and forest edge. Violet-blue with red crest and yellow bill; much red in wings.
5a and 5b. Adults.

6 HARTLAUB'S TURACO *Tauraco hartlaubi* **Page 431**
Common and widespread in highland forests. Dark bushy crest and white facial markings; much red in wings.
6a, 6b and 6c. Adults.

7 PURPLE-CRESTED TURACO *Tauraco porphyreolophus chlorochlamys* **Page 430**
Scarce and local in Thika and Machakos Districts. Dark crest like Hartlaub's, but no white on face. Bill black; much red in wings.
7a and 7b. Adults.

8 WHITE-CRESTED TURACO *Tauraco leucolophus* **Page 431**
Local in w. and nw. Kenya. Head largely white, bill yellowish; much red in wings.

9 SCHALOW'S TURACO *Tauraco schalowi* **Page 431**
Riparian woodland in Mara GR, forest in Mbulu and Crater Highlands. Long pointed crest, dark red bill; much red in wings.

10 BLACK-BILLED TURACO *Tauraco schuetti emini* **Page 431**
Scarce and local in w. Kenyan forests. Short green crest, small black bill; much red in wings.

11 FISCHER'S TURACO *Tauraco f. fischeri* **Page 431**
Coastal forests and dense woodland inland along the Tana River and in Usambara Mts. White-tipped reddish crest, bright red bill; much red in wings.

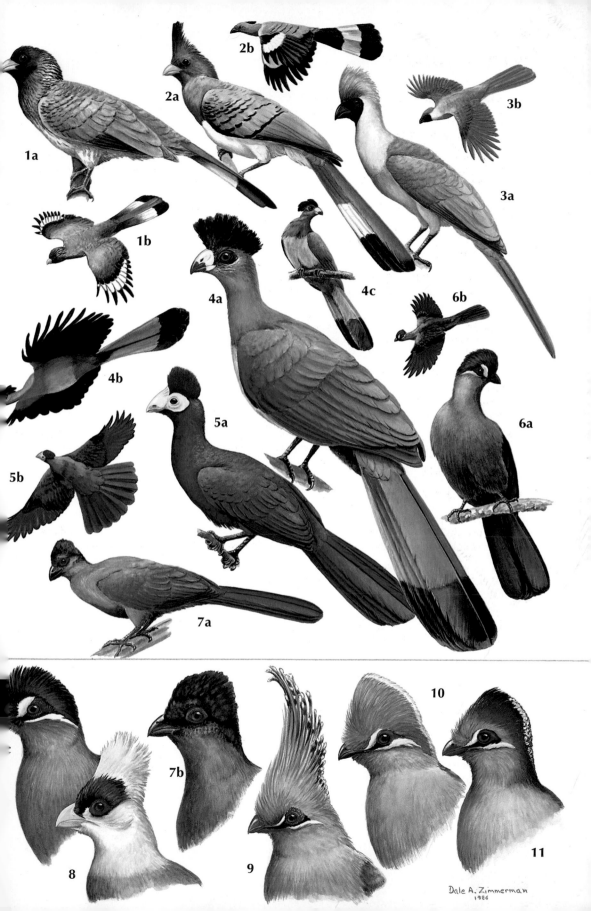

1a

1b

2a

2b

3a

3b

4a

4b

4c

5a

5b

6a

6b

7a

7b

8

9

10

11

Dale A. Zimmerman
1986

PLATE 51: CUCKOOS (See also Plate 52)

1 KLAAS'S CUCKOO *Chrysococcyx klaas* **Page 437**
Common and widespread in woodland and forest edge. White outer tail feathers obvious in flight.
1a. Juvenile.
1b. Adult female.
1c. Adult male.

2 DIEDERIK CUCKOO *Chrysococcyx caprius* **Page 437**
Common and widespread in dry woodland, savanna and bush. White spots on wings and on sides of tail.
2a. 'Rufous' juvenile.
2b. 'Green' juvenile. (Some birds are intermediate between 2a and 2b.)
2c. Adult female.
2d. Adult male.

3 AFRICAN EMERALD CUCKOO *Chrysococcyx c. cupreus* **Page 436**
Local in highland-forest canopy. Vocal, but seldom seen.
3a. Adult female. Wings rufous-barred; white underparts barred with iridescent green.
3b. Juvenile. Crown and nape barred.
3c. Adult male. Brilliant green above, bright yellow lower breast and belly.
3d. Immature male. Barred with white and iridescent green below.

4 MADAGASCAR LESSER CUCKOO *Cuculus rochii* **Page 436**
Present April–September. Nearly identical to No. 5. Under tail-coverts may be nearly plain, as shown, but often barred in centre and at tip, occasionally throughout. Flying bird, as in 5b, shows blackish upper tail-coverts contrasting with grey back (unlike Eurasian and African cuckoos).

5 ASIAN LESSER CUCKOO *Cuculus poliocephalus* **Page 435**
Asian migrant, present November–December and March–April in coastal areas, some inland to Tsavo NP late November–December. Winter records from West Usambara Mts. Buff under tail-coverts boldly barred with black.
5a and 5b. Adults.

6 EURASIAN or COMMON CUCKOO *Cuculus c. canorus* **Page 435**
Widespread palearctic migrant, uncommon in autumn, numerous March–April. Bill blackish with yellow or greenish-yellow base.
6a. Female, rufous morph.
6b. Juvenile/immature. Plain grey rump/upper tail-coverts; crown incompletely barred.
6c. Adult male. Limited yellow on bill base; outer rectrices incompletely barred.
6d. Adult female, grey morph. Some rufous-brown on breast (may extend to hindneck and crown).

7 AFRICAN CUCKOO *Cuculus gularis* **Page 435**
Intra-African 'rains migrant.' Uncommon in savanna, bush and acacia woodlands. Bill mainly yellow, with black tip.
7a. Juvenile. Barred rump/upper tail-coverts; crown barred throughout.
7b. Adult male. Much bright yellow or orange-yellow on bill; tail bars complete. (Female shows rufous-brown on sides of breast, as in female Eurasian Cuckoo.)
7c. Adult female. Grey upper tail-coverts as in Eurasian Cuckoo (not blackish as in No. 4 and No. 5).

8 BLACK CUCKOO *Cuculus clamosus* **Page 434**
Widespread and fairly common in woodland, savanna and forest edge.
8a. *C. c. clamosus*, juvenile. Dull sooty brown throughout.
8b. *C. c. clamosus*, adult. Glossy blue-black; may show faint buff bars on underparts.
8c. *C. c. clamosus/gabonensis* intergrade ('*jacksoni*'). Western Kenyan forests.

9 RED-CHESTED CUCKOO *Cuculus s. solitarius* **Page 434**
Common and widespread in wooded areas and suburban gardens. Highly vocal before and during rains.
9a. Juvenile.
9b. Adult male. Throat grey. Upper breast variable: russet with dark bars, as shown, or brighter rufous and unbarred. Many males similar to female (9c), but with grey throat.
9c. Adult female. Throat whitish to pale buff. Upper breast never barred, usually pale in centre.

PLATE 52: CUCKOOS AND COUCALS

1 **BLACK AND WHITE or JACOBIN CUCKOO** *Oxylophus jacobinus* **Page 433**
Widespread 'rains migrant' in dry bush and thickets, mostly below 1500 m.
1a. *O. j. serratus*, dark morph. Rare; migrant from s. Africa. (Light morph, uncommon in rainy season, April–September, similar to that of *O. j. pica*.)
1b. *O. j. pica*, light morph. Fairly common migrant. Breeds in Rift Valley and in west (March–August) and in se. Kenya (Nov.–Dec.).

2 **LEVAILLANT'S CUCKOO** *Oxylophus levaillantii* **Page 433**
Uncommon intra-African migrant; few breeding records. Most numerous west of Rift Valley, May–September. Disjunct coastal population.
2a. Dark morph. Large size; shows white in tail. Mainly coastal.
2b. Light morph. Some individuals more heavily streaked than shown.

3 **GREAT SPOTTED CUCKOO** *Clamator glandarius* **Page 434**
Uncommon in open wooded areas, savannas and cultivation. Most numerous October–March.
3a. Adult. (First-year birds have some black in crown and rufous in primaries.)
3b. Juvenile. Rufous primaries evident in flight.

4 **YELLOWBILL** *Ceuthmochares a. aereus* **Page 438**
Uncommon in forest thickets and tangles. Shy and secretive. Western ***C. a. aereus*** is dark, with blue tail iridescence. (Eastern *C. a. australis* is paler below, with strongly green-glossed tail.)

5 **BARRED LONG-TAILED CUCKOO** *Cercococcyx montanus patulus* **Page 436**
Local in montane forests on e. Mt Kenya and s. Aberdares; common in Usambara Mts. Shy; seldom seen, but highly vocal October–March. Vagrant to coastal forests.

6 **THICK-BILLED CUCKOO** *Pachycoccyx audeberti validus* **Page 434**
Uncommon in coastal woods (especially Brachystegia). Perches in tall treetops; displays in flight above forest canopy. Hawk-like in flight.
6a. Adult.
6b. Juvenile.

7 **SENEGAL COUCAL** *Centropus s. senegalensis* **Page 439**
Locally common in thickets and sugarcane in w. Kenya, mainly near Ugandan border. Smaller than Blue-headed Coucal of wetter areas.
7a. Juvenile. Dark-crowned, primaries plain except at tips. Tail blackish.
7b. Adult. Black on head lacks blue gloss.

8 **BLACK COUCAL** *Centropus grillii* **Page 438**
Widespread in moist and wet habitats. Smaller than other coucals. Seasonally dimorphic.
8a. Breeding adult.
8b. Non-breeding adult. No superciliary stripe, strongly barred tail. (Grey-eyed juvenile similar.)

9 **BLUE-HEADED COUCAL** *Centropus monachus fischeri* **Page 439**
Local in papyrus swamps, wet thickets and tea plantations.
9a. Adult. Large. Resembles Senegal Coucal, but head glossed with blue.
9b. Juvenile. Primaries barred throughout. Tail dark brown.

10 **WHITE-BROWED COUCAL** *Centropus s. superciliosus* **Page 438**
The common coucal. Widespread in bush and moist thickets, often near water. Superciliary stripe in all plumages.
10a. Juvenile.
10b. Adult. Crown dark brown in fresh plumage (black in darker race *loandae* of n. Tanzania and sw. Kenya).

1a 1b

2a 2b

3a 3b

4

5

6a 6b

7a 7b

8a 8b

9a 9b

10a 10b

DALE A. ZIMMERMAN
1995

PLATE 53: NIGHTJARS (See also Plate 54)

1 DONALDSON-SMITH'S NIGHTJAR *Caprimulgus donaldsoni*   **Page 448**
Common in dry e. and se. Kenya, west to Horr Valley and Lake Baringo; also Mkomazi GR and Masai steppe in n. Tanzania. Small size, small white tail corners; yellowish-edged scapulars. Short whistling song.
1a. Brown female.
1b and 1d. Grey-brown female.
1c and 1e. Rufous male.

2 NUBIAN NIGHTJAR *Caprimulgus nubicus torridus*   **Page 448**
Fairly common in e. and se. Kenya, mainly November–March, but some may be present all year. Most birds silvery grey and rufous. Not vocal in our region.
2a. Dark-tailed male.
2b. Grey-tailed male.
2c. Grey-tailed female.

3 GABON NIGHTJAR, *Caprimulgus ossii welwitschii*   **Page 451**
Resident on Pemba Island; local non-breeding visitor in se. and coastal Kenya, also Serengeti/Mara region. Pale trailing secondary edges; central rectrices not extending beyond others. Churring song.
3a and 3c. Males. Dark, with contrasting whitish wing bands and trailing edge, much like male Slender-tailed Nightjar, except for tail tip.
3b and 3d. Females. Wings paler, less contrasting than in male, pale areas buff or cinnamon-buff (including patch on primaries).

4 SLENDER-TAILED NIGHTJAR *Caprimulgus clarus apatelius*   **Page 451**
Common and widespread in dry areas below 2000 m. Similar to Gabon Nightjar, but tail often paler and greyer, central rectrices extending beyond the others. Churring song.
4a and 4b. Males.
4c and 4d. Females.

5 MONTANE NIGHTJAR *Caprimulgus p. poliocephalus*   **Page 447**
Common in highlands (including Nairobi suburbs). Generally dark, with prominent half-collar on hindneck. Shrill whistling song.
5a, 5b and 5c. Males. Broad white tail sides (usually concealed at rest).
5d. Female. Somewhat browner, less dusky; reduced white in tail. (See Plate 123 for Tanzanian *C. p. guttifer.*)

6 AFRICAN WHITE-TAILED NIGHTJAR *Caprimulgus n. natalensis*   **Page 450**
Western Kenya. Uncommon in wet grassy swamp and forest edges. Buff, with dark side of face. Stocky, rather short-tailed. Monotonous 'tocking' song.
6a and 6c. Males. Tail sides broadly white (as in much darker Montane Nightjar).
6b and 6d. Females. Tail narrowly buff-edged. Lacks wing-covert bands of darker Gabon Nightjar.

7 FIERY-NECKED NIGHTJAR *Caprimulgus pectoralis*   **Page 447**
7a and 7b. *C. p. nigriscapularis*, males. Local and uncommon in w. Kenyan forest remnants, moist thickets and riparian woods. Shrill whistling song. (Female has buff-tinged wing and tail spots.)
7c, 7d and 7e. *C. p. fervidus*, females. Fairly common in wooded areas of coastal lowlands, inland along lower Tana River and in Shimba Hills. Richly coloured. (Male has brighter white wing patches, no buff in white tail corners.)

8 DUSKY NIGHTJAR *Caprimulgus fraenatus*   **Page 450**
Common and widespread in dry country (between 650 and 2000 m). Generally dark, with black and creamy-buff scapulars. Churring song.
8a and 8b. Females. Greyer than male; tail corners dingy buffy grey.
8c and 8d. Males. Blacker than female; lacks warm tones of Fiery-necked Nightjar. White tail spots larger than in Donaldson-Smith's Nightjar.

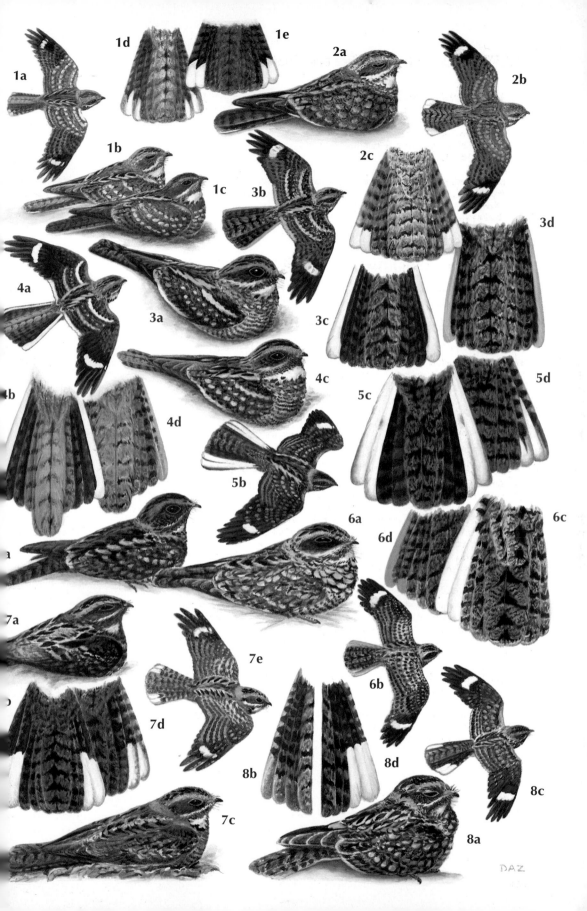

PLATE 54: NIGHTJARS (See also Plate 53)

1 PLAIN NIGHTJAR *Caprimulgus inornatus*   **Page 449**
Widespread in dry bush, mainly October–April. Possibly breeds in nw. Kenya. Rather plain above; no white throat patch. Silent in most of our region.
1a and 1b. Brown males.
1c and 1d. Rufous males.
1e. Brown female.

2 EURASIAN NIGHTJAR *Caprimulgus europaeus*   **Page 451**
Widespread migrant in wooded and cultivated areas, October–November and March–April. Blackish 'shoulder'; no half-collar on hindneck. Typically rests on tree branches. Does not sing in East Africa.
2a. *C. e. unwini*, female.
2b. *C. e. unwini*, male.
2c. *C. e. europaeus*, female.

3 STAR-SPOTTED NIGHTJAR *Caprimulgus stellatus simplex*   **Page 449**
Locally common on lava-rock deserts in n. Kenya (south to Lake Baringo). Plain; much white on throat. Clear yelping *hweu* or *pew* call.
3a and 3b. Brown males.
3c. Rufous female.
3d. Rufous-and-grey female.

4 FRECKLED NIGHTJAR *Caprimulgus t. tristigma*   **Page 449**
Local on rocky outcrops and escarpments. Finely marked above; no half-collar. Barking or yelping *ow-wow* song.
4a and 4b. Males.
4c and 4d. Females.

5 STANDARD-WINGED NIGHTJAR *Macrodipteryx longipennis*   **Page 452**
Rare migrant in nw. Kenya, vagrant south to Lake Baringo. Possibly breeds in nw. border areas. Rarely vocal in our region.
5a. Breeding male.
5b, 5c and 5d. Females.

6 PENNANT-WINGED NIGHTJAR *Macrodipteryx vexillarius*   **Page 452**
Locally common migrant in western areas July to early September and January–February; casual east to Nairobi. Flies immediately after sunset. Largely silent in our region.
6a and 6b. Breeding males.
6c, 6d and 6e. Females.

7 LONG-TAILED NIGHTJAR *Caprimulgus climacurus sclateri*   **Page 452**
Northwestern Kenya. Scarce and local in savanna and bush south to the Turkwell River. Birds moulting central rectrices resemble Slender-tailed Nightjars. Song a low rapid churring or purring.
7a and 7b. Brown females.
7c. Rufous male. (Some individuals more chestnut.)

1a 1b 1c 1d 1e
2a 2b 2c
3a 3b 3c 3d
4a 4b 4c 4d
5a 5b 5c 5d
6a 6b 6c 6d 6e
7a 7b 7c

DAZIMMERMAN
1994

PLATE 55: LARGER OWLS

1 BARN OWL *Tyto alba affinis* **Page 440**
Uncommon in and near towns, cliffs, kopjes. Pale, with white, heart-shaped face.

2 AFRICAN GRASS OWL *Tyto capensis* **Page 440**
Terrestrial. Scarce in highland marshes, grassland, moorlands. Dark-backed. Smaller buff wing patches than
Marsh Owl; white sides of tail show in flight.
2a and 2b. Adults. (Juvenile has darker facial disc.)

3 SHORT-EARED OWL *Asio f. flammeus* **Page 446**
Palearctic vagrant. Typically in open grassy marshes. Pale and heavily streaked; eyes yellow.
3a and 3b. Adults.

4 MARSH OWL *Asio c. capensis* **Page 446**
Locally common in highland grassland. Large buff patch in primaries, pale trailing edge to secondaries; eyes
dark.
4a and 4b. Adults.

5 AFRICAN LONG-EARED OWL *Asio abyssinicus graueri* **Page 446**
Mt Kenya: rare in *Hagenia* forest and adjacent giant-heath zone. Slender; tawny face; 'ear-tufts' near centre
of forehead.

6 AFRICAN WOOD OWL *Strix woodfordii nigricantior* **Page 446**
Fairly common in forest and woodland. Round-headed; dark eyes; barred underparts.

7 CAPE EAGLE-OWL *Bubo capensis mackinderi* **Page 443**
Local near highland cliffs and ravines, on alpine peaks and moorlands. Richly-coloured with bold blotching on breast; yellow-orange eyes.

8 SPOTTED EAGLE-OWL *Bubo africanus* **Page 443**
Fairly common; widespread in varied habitats. Dull grey or brownish, with dark blotching on breast.
8a. *B. a. africanus*: w. and s. Kenya to n. Tanzania. Smaller, less richly coloured than Cape Eagle-Owl; eyes
yellow.
8b. *B. a. cinerascens*: n. Kenya south to Kerio Valley, Baringo and Meru Districts. Eyes brown; smaller, more
boldly marked than Verreaux's Eagle-Owl.

9 VERREAUX'S EAGLE-OWL *Bubo lacteus* **Page 444**
Common and widespread in wooded areas. Uniformly pale, except for black facial-disc margins. Dark eyes
and pink eyelids conspicuous by day. 'Ear-tufts' often inconspicuous at night.

10 PEL'S FISHING OWL *Scotopelia peli* **Page 444**
Tana and Mara Rivers, rare and local in dense riparian trees. **Male**. Round head may appear smaller in resting bird. Markings variable. (Female and young are paler.)

DALE A. ZIMMERMAN
1994

PLATE 56: SMALLER OWLS

When active at night, the four scops owls usually compress their 'ear-tufts' and appear quite round-headed; they are shorter-tailed than the *Glaucidium species*.

1 SOKOKE SCOPS OWL *Otus ireneae* **Page 441**
Locally common in Arabuko–Sokoke Forest and East Usambara foothills. Nocturnal.
1a. Rufous morph (some individuals much paler than shown).
1b. Brown morph.
1c. Grey morph.

2 AFRICAN SCOPS OWL *Otus s. senegalensis* **Page 442**
Common in savanna, bush, acacia scrub. Nocturnal. Similar to Eurasian Scops Owl, but slightly smaller and highly vocal. See text.
2a. Grey morph.
2b. Grey-brown morph.

3 WHITE-FACED SCOPS OWL *Otus l. leucotis* **Page 442**
Uncommon in dry-country acacia bush and woodland.
3a. Juvenile.
3b. Adult.

4 EURASIAN SCOPS OWL *Otus s. scops* **Page 442**
Scarce palearctic migrant. Silent in East Africa. See text.
4a. Rufous-brown morph.
4b. Brownish grey morph.

5 AFRICAN BARRED OWLET *Glaucidium capense scheffleri* **Page 445**
Uncommon in Kenyan coastal forest and woodland; scarce inland to Kibwezi and Iltalal; rare in n. Tanzania. Partly diurnal.

6 RED-CHESTED OWLET *Glaucidium tephronotum elgonense* **Page 445**
Western Kenya. Uncommon in highland forest. Mainly nocturnal. Individuals vary in density of ventral spotting and in wing colour.

7 PEARL-SPOTTED OWLET *Glaucidium perlatum licua* **Page 445**
Common in dry woodland, savanna, riparian trees, except in Lake Victoria basin and coastal lowlands. Often wags tail or pumps it up and down. Shows large 'eye spots' on back of head. Partly diurnal; especially vocal at dusk.

1a

1b

2a

2b

1c

3b

3a

4a

5

6

7

4b

DALE A. ZIMMERMAN
1993

PLATE 57: SWIFTS

1 LITTLE SWIFT *Apus a. affinis*   **Page 458**
Widespread. Common in towns and around buildings, bridges. Square-tipped tail; white rump patch extends to sides.
1a, 1b and 1c. Adults.

2 MOTTLED SPINETAIL *Telacanthura ussheri stictilaema*   **Page 455**
Uncommon in eastern areas, especially in bush with baobab trees; local around se. Mt Kenya. Resembles Little Swift, but flight more fluttery and shows narrow white band across lower belly.
2a and 2b. Adults.

3 HORUS SWIFT *Apus h. horus*   **Page 458**
Locally common, March–September, mainly in cent. Rift Valley and Arusha District. Absent October–February. Shallowly forked tail; outer feathers not elongated as in White-rumped Swift.
3a and 3b. Adults.

4 WHITE-RUMPED SWIFT *Apus caffer*   **Page 458**
Widespread (except n. and ne. Kenya), but uncommon. More slender, with narrower white rump band than Horus Swift; deeply forked tail often appears pointed.
4a and 4b. Adults.

5 SCARCE SWIFT *Schoutedenapus m. myoptilus*   **Page 455**
Local, typically over highland forest, but also over adjacent plains. Slender, with pointed or long-forked tail; throat slightly paler than body.
5a and 5b. Adults.

6 BÖHM'S SPINETAIL *Neafrapus boehmi sheppardi*   **Page 455**
Uncommon; eastern and coastal; often around baobab trees. Tiny; wings narrower near body; looks tail-less; flight fluttery and bat-like. Sympatric in places with Mottled Spinetail.
6a and 6b. Adults.

7 SABINE'S SPINETAIL *Rhaphidura sabini*   **Page 454**
Rare over and near Kakamega Forest and Mt Elgon. Few recent records.

8 AFRICAN PALM SWIFT *Cypsiurus parvus laemostigma*   **Page 456**
Low-flying; common below 1400 m, typically around palm trees. Pale grey with grey throat; slender.
8a and 8b. Adults.

9 FORBES-WATSON'S SWIFT *Apus berliozi bensoni*   **Page 457**
Coastal; scarce migrant, October–February. In flocks. Large white throat patch and often whitish forehead. Resembles immature Eurasian Swift. See text.

10 AFRICAN BLACK SWIFT *Apus barbatus roehli*   **Page 456**
Locally common in highland-forest areas, and ranges far over plains and bush. Resembles Eurasian Swift, but from above body darker than inner wing feathers. Breeds and roosts in trees, sometimes in cliffs. See text.
10a and 10b. Adults.

11 ALPINE SWIFT *Apus melba africanus*   **Page 458**
High-flying; typically near major mountains, but also over distant open areas.

12 MOTTLED SWIFT *Apus a. aequatorialis*   **Page 457**
Widespread, often with other swifts. Breeds in cliffs (e.g. Hell's Gate NP), but ranges widely over open country. Large size, pale body, mottled underparts.

13 NYANZA SWIFT *Apus niansae*   **Page 456**
13a and 13b. *A. n. niansae*. Common to abundant in Rift Valley highlands. Breeds in cliffs (e.g. in Hell's Gate NP) and quarries. Browner than other swifts; body/inner-wing contrast as in darker African Black Swift.
13c. *A. n. somalicus*. Collected once near Mt Kenya. Status uncertain. See text.

14 EURASIAN or COMMON SWIFT *Apus a. apus*   **Page 456**
Common in large flocks, autumn and spring; less numerous in winter. Lacks strong body/inner-wing contrast of Nos. 10 and 13. (Immature shows much whitish about the face, resembling Forbes-Watson's Swift. *A. a. pekinensis*, common near coast November–December, is browner, less blackish; more like Nyanza Swift, but pale-faced.)

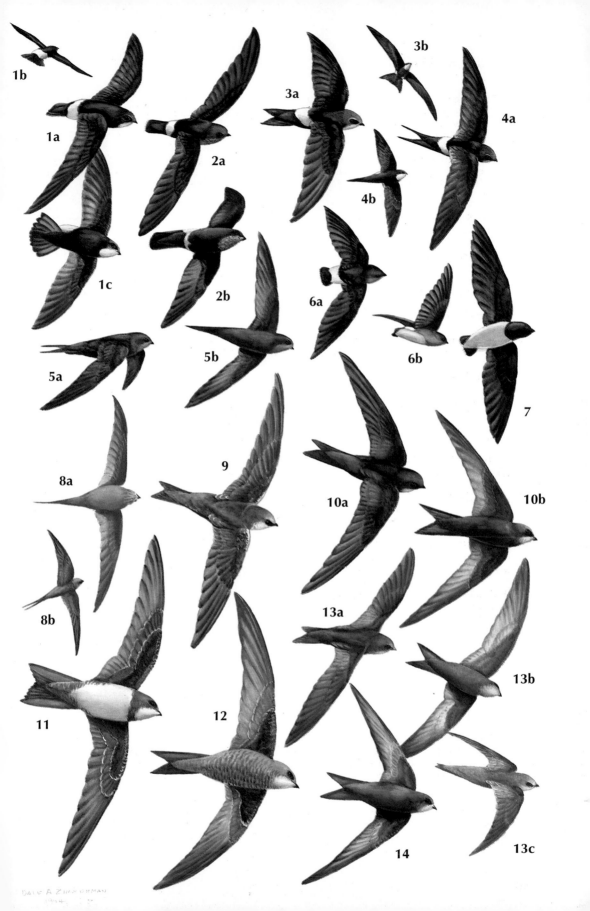

1b

1a

2a

3a

3b

4a

1c

2b

6a

4b

5a

5b

6b

7

8a

9

10a

10b

8b

13a

11

12

13b

14

13c

DALE A ZIMMERMAN

PLATE 58: MOUSEBIRDS AND TROGONS

1 BLUE-NAPED MOUSEBIRD *Urocolius macrourus pulcher* **Page 459**
This and two similar races common and widespread in dry bush and thorn-scrub, usually in small groups. (Juvenile lacks blue nape, has pink facial skin and greenish bill.)

2 SPECKLED MOUSEBIRD *Colius striatus kikuyuensis* **Page 459**
Common and widespread in various moist habitats, including towns and gardens, from sea level to over 2500 m. Avoids arid regions. Eye colour variable. (Similar coastal race *mombassicus* slightly paler and brown-eyed.)

3 WHITE-HEADED MOUSEBIRD *Colius leucocephalus turneri* **Page 459**
Local in dry bush below 1400 m from Samburu and Shaba GRs northward. (Southern nominate race uncommon in and near Amboseli and Tsavo West NPs and other Kenyan/Tanzanian border areas.)

4 NARINA TROGON *Apaloderma n. narina* **Page 460**
Uncommon in forest and rich woodland, mainly at lower elevations, but also on montane 'islands' in n. Kenya.
4a and 4d. Males.
4b. Female.
4c. Immature.

5 BAR-TAILED TROGON *Apaloderma vittatum* **Page 460**
Uncommon in highland forest, mainly above 1600 m; overlaps with Narina Trogon in Kakamega Forest and Arusha NP.
5a and 5c. Males.
5b. Female.

Blue-naped Mousebirds.

1

2

3

4a

4b

4c

5a

5b

5c

4d

DALE A. ZIMMERMAN
1994

PLATE 59: KINGFISHERS (Most juveniles have dusky or blackish bills and duller plumage)

1 **SHINING-BLUE KINGFISHER** *Alcedo quadribrachys guentheri*   **Page 463**
Vagrant, w. Kenya. Lustrous blue above, chestnut below; long black bill.

2 **HALF-COLLARED KINGFISHER** *Alcedo semitorquata tephria*   **Page 463**
Uncommon on wooded streams, mainly in Tanzania; casual se. Kenya. Turquoise-blue above, pale cinnamon or tawny below. Bill blackish.

3 **AFRICAN PYGMY KINGFISHER** *Ispidina p. picta*   **Page 463**
Widespread in forest, thickets, dense bush, often far from water.
3a. Adult. Lilac on orange-rufous face. Bill red.
3b. Juvenile. Black bill; indication of lilac ear-coverts. (*I. p. natalensis* is mainly coastal. See text.)

4 **MALACHITE KINGFISHER** *Alcedo cristata galerita*   **Page 463**
Widespread. Fairly common near water.
4a. Adult. Paler blue than African Pygmy Kingfisher. Floppy crest; no lilac ear-coverts.
4b. Juvenile. Black-billed, less crested; face duller than in juvenile African Pygmy.

5 **WOODLAND KINGFISHER** *Halcyon s. senegalensis*   **Page 462**
Fairly common in western wooded areas. Black-and-red bill. (Migrant race *cyanoleuca* has black postocular mark and blue wash on crown.)

6 **STRIPED KINGFISHER** *Halcyon c. chelicuti*   **Page 462**
Widespread, fairly common in savanna, bush, open woodland. Dull-coloured, but rump and tail flash cobalt or greenish blue in flight.

7 **GREY-HEADED KINGFISHER** *Halcyon l. leucocephala*   **Page 461**
Fairly common in wooded areas, often near water. (See text for other races.)
7a. Male. Chestnut belly and crissum, red bill. (Female duller.)
7b. Juvenile. Chestnut lacking or reduced to wash on flanks. Bill blackish, sometimes dull reddish below.

8 **MANGROVE KINGFISHER** *Halcyon senegaloides*   **Page 462**
Coastal; not restricted to mangroves. Fairly common. Bill entirely red; back greyish blue; no buff on underparts; feet blackish.

9 **BROWN-HOODED KINGFISHER** *Halcyon albiventris orientalis*   **Page 461**
Common in woodland, savanna, forest edge, sometimes near water. This race mainly in coastal lowlands. (*H. a. prentissgrayi*, interior e. Kenya and Tanzania, similar but with darker, often unstreaked crown.) Bill red, becoming dark brown at tip. Black back often separated from brownish-grey head by faint buff collar; feet reddish. (Female has sooty-brown back.)

10 **GIANT KINGFISHER** *Megaceryle m. maxima*   **Page 464**
Uncommon on wooded rivers, streams and lakes. Widespread in w. and cent. Kenyan highlands; very local in n. Tanzania.
10a. Male. Entire breast chestnut; throat and wing-linings largely white.
10b. Female. Upper breast slaty and white; rest of underparts and wing-linings chestnut.

11 **PIED KINGFISHER** *Ceryle r. rudis*   **Page 464**
Common and widespread on lakes, rivers, coastal estuaries. Often hovers.
11a. Male. Two black breast bands.
11b and 11c. Females. One breast band, often incomplete.

2

3a

3b

4a

4b

5

6

7a

7b

8

9

10a

10b

11a

11b

11c

ale A. Zimmerman
1987

PLATE 60: BEE-EATERS

1 BLUE-BREASTED BEE-EATER *Merops variegatus loringi*   **Page 467**
Local in moist grassland, marshes, papyrus swamps near Lake Victoria. Whitish cheeks below black mask; throat patch dark purplish blue. (Juvenile much like that of juvenile of Little Bee-eater, but slightly larger.)

2 LITTLE BEE-EATER *Merops pusillus cyanostictus*   **Page 466**
Common and widespread. Black throat patch bordered with bright blue; no white on side of face.
2a. Adult.
2b. Juvenile.

3 CINNAMON-CHESTED BEE-EATER *Merops oreobates*   **Page 467**
Locally common in wooded highlands. Larger and darker than Nos. 1 and 2.
3a. Juvenile. Greener below than Little Bee-eater.
3b. Adult. Underparts cinnamon-chestnut.

4 SOMALI BEE-EATER *Merops revoilii*   **Page 468**
Local in arid/semi-arid parts of n. and e. Kenya. Pale; lower back, rump and tail-coverts bright cobalt-blue.

5 CARMINE BEE-EATER *Merops nubicus*   **Page 465**
5a. M. n. nubicus. Migrant from northern tropics, September–March, common along coast and locally inland in se. Kenya, scarce in Rift Valley. Some breed in far north.
5b. M. n. nubicoides. Rare vagrant.

6 MADAGASCAR BEE-EATER *Merops s. superciliosus*   **Page 465**
Fairly common non-breeding migrant, May–September. Also breeds locally in coastal lowlands (especially Lamu and Pemba Islands). Distinguished from No. 7 by duller green upperparts, dark olive-brown crown, white forehead, chin and cheek stripe. Superciliary white, yellow or blue; underside of wings ochreous. (Juvenile short-tailed, with greenish crown, cinnamon-buff throat, pale blue breast.)

7 BLUE-CHEEKED BEE-EATER *Merops p. persicus*   **Page 465**
Locally common palearctic migrant, late October to early April, often along lake edges. Bright green above. Whitish forehead merges with pale blue above eyes; cheeks usually pale blue, but may be greenish or white; chin (and sometimes upper throat) yellow; underside of wings cinnamon or coppery rufous.
7a and 7b. Adults.

8 BLUE-HEADED BEE-EATER *Merops m. muelleri*   **Page 466**
Kakamega and South Nandi Forests; uncommon. (Juvenile has little or no red on chin.)

9 WHITE-THROATED BEE-EATER *Merops albicollis*   **Page 466**
Non-breeding migrant from northern tropics, September–April. A few breed in extreme north and near Lake Magadi in the south, April–May.
9a and 9b. Adults. (Juvenile has pale yellowish throat.)

10 EURASIAN BEE-EATER *Merops apiaster*   **Page 464**
Common and widespread palearctic migrant in autumn and March–April. Some winter.
10a and 10c. Spring males. (Female paler below, with greener scapulars.)
10b. Autumn male (Aug.–Oct.). Crown variably green-tinged.

11 WHITE-FRONTED BEE-EATER *Merops b. bullockoides*   **Page 466**
Locally common in cent. Kenyan Rift Valley, on lower slopes of Kilimanjaro and Mt Meru. Local in Kerio Valley and n. Mara GR.
11a. Male. (Female similar; juvenile paler, bluer above, little or no red on throat.)
11b. Yellow-throated variant. Rare.

DALE A. ZIMMERMAN
1994

PLATE 61: ROLLERS AND HOOPOE

1 BROAD-BILLED ROLLER *Eurystomus glaucurus suahelicus*   Page 470
Uncommon in wooded areas with tall trees. Perches high. Dark plumage, short yellow bill.
1a. Juvenile.
1b and 1c. Adults.

2 ABYSSINIAN ROLLER *Coracias abyssinica*   Page 468
Locally common in dry country west of Lake Turkana; occasional south to Mara GR. Irregular in ne. Kenya.
2a and 2b. Adults. Bright azure underparts; long tail.

3 EURASIAN ROLLER *Coracias g. garrulus*   Page 468
Common, October–April, in open woodland and bush in eastern areas. Uncommon autumn migrant in and
west of Rift Valley. Short, stocky; flight feathers black.
3a. First-winter.
3b and 3c. Spring adults.

4 LILAC-BREASTED ROLLER *Coracias caudata*   Page 469
Fairly common in open bush, woodland and cultivation.
4a and 4d. *C. c. caudata*, adults. Widespread resident.
4b. *C. c. caudata*, juvenile.
4c. *C. c. lorti*, adult. Migrant from Somalia; west to Marsabit, south to Tsavo.

5 RUFOUS-CROWNED or PURPLE ROLLER *Coracias n. naevia*   Page 469
Uncommon in dry bush and woodland.
5a. Juvenile.
5b and 5c. Adults.

6 HOOPOE *Upupa epops*   Page 470
U. e. africana a widespread resident in savanna, bush and other open habitats; in all plumages primaries
entirely black. Migrant *U. e. epops*, regular October–March in same habitats, has white band across primaries (as do races *waibeli* and *senegalensis*).
6a and 6d. *U. e. africana*, males. Secondaries largely white basally.
6b. *U. e. africana*, female. Secondaries similar to *U. e. epops*.
6c. *U. e. epops*, male.

PRATT

PLATE 62: WOOD-HOOPOES AND SCIMITARBILLS

1 **GREEN WOOD-HOOPOE** *Phoeniculus purpureus*   **Page 471**
The common wood-hoopoe, widespread in acacia woodland and savanna.
1a. *P. p. marwitzi,* **juvenile.**
1b. *P. p. niloticus,* **adult**. (Northwestern Kenya.)
1c. *P. p. marwitzi,* **adult male.**
1d and 1e. *P. p. marwitzi,* **adult female.**

2 **BLACK-BILLED WOOD-HOOPOE** *Phoeniculus s. somaliensis*   **Page 472**
Fairly common in ne. Kenya (where it replaces Green Wood-hoopoe).
2a. Female.
2b. Male.

3 **VIOLET WOOD-HOOPOE** *Phoeniculus damarensis granti*   **Page 472**
Local in riverine woodland east of the Rift Valley, typically associated with doum palms, mainly below 1000
m. Violet-blue on body, green on lower throat.

4 **FOREST WOOD-HOOPOE** *Phoeniculus castaneiceps brunneiceps*   **Page 471**
Formerly along Ugandan border in w. Kenya. Probably extirpated.
4a, 4b, 4c and 4d. Male, variations.
4e. Female.

5 **WHITE-HEADED WOOD-HOOPOE** *Phoeniculus bollei jacksoni*   **Page 471**
Fairly common in highland forests of w. and cent. Kenya.
5a. Immature.
5b. Adult.

6 **COMMON SCIMITARBILL** *Rhinopomastus cyanomelas schalowi*   **Page 473**
Fairly common in open woodland, savanna and bush, except in arid areas.
6a. Female.
6b and 6c. Males.

7 **ABYSSINIAN SCIMITARBILL** *Rhinopomastus minor cabanisi*   **Page 473**
Uncommon in dry bush. No white in wings or tail.
7a and 7c. Adults.
7b. Juvenile.

1a 1b 2a 2b

1c

1d

3

1e

4a 4e

4b

4c 4d

5a

6a

6b

7a

5b

7b

6c 7c

PRATT

PLATE 63: HORNBILLS (*Tockus* and *Bycanistes*) (All adults except as noted. See Plate 30 for ground hornbills)

PLATE 64: BARBETS

1 **WHITE-HEADED BARBET** *Lybius leucocephalus* **Page 482**
Local in open wooded areas and suburban gardens. **1a.** *L. l. leucocephalus,* **adult**. Western Kenya. Black tail and upper back; dark-streaked belly; white varies on breast and wings. **1b.** *L. l. albicauda,* **juvenile**. S. Kenya/n. Tanzania. Lower breast and abdomen brownish in both adults and young. **1c.** *L. l. senex,* **adult**. Cent. Kenya south to Chyulu Hills. Largely white, with blackish wings and upper back.

2 **GREEN BARBET** *Stactolaema o. olivacea* **Page 478**
Common in coastal forests and in the East Usambaras. Dull greenish olive, with dark brown head, large black bill.

3 **GREY-THROATED BARBET** *Gymnobucco bonapartei cinereiceps* **Page 478**
Fairly common in western forests. Small groups perch in tall dead trees. Drab brown, with greyer head, pale yellowish eye; erectile straw-coloured tufts at bill base.

4 **WHITE-EARED BARBET** *Stactolaema leucotis kilimensis* **Page 478**
Local in se. Kenya and ne. Tanzania. White belly, rump and flaring postocular streak. **4a and 4b. Adults**.

5 **RED-FRONTED BARBET** *Tricholaema diademata* **Page 481**
Uncommon but widespread in dry woodland. **5a. Juvenile**. Forehead black. **5b. Adult**. Scarlet forehead; yellow superciliary stripe. Pattern similar to that of smaller Red-fronted Tinkerbird (Plate 65).

6 **BLACK-THROATED BARBET** *Tricholaema melanocephala stigmatothorax* **Page 482**
Fairly common and widespread in dry thorn-bush and scrub below 1500 m. Largely immaculate sides; dark line from brown throat to lower breast or belly.

7 **SPOT-FLANKED BARBET** *Tricholaema lachrymosa radcliffei* **Page 482**
Locally common in moist acacia woods and tall riverine forest. Adults have spotted sides; black of throat reaches only to upper breast. **7a. Female**. Brown eye. **7b. Male**. Yellow eye; rounded spots. (Eastern and northern nominate race has teardrop-shaped spots.)

8 **HAIRY-BREASTED BARBET** *Tricholaema hirsuta ansorgii* **Page 481**
Kakamega Forest. Rare. Black polka-dots on yellowish underparts, white superciliary and whisker marks, yellowish speckling above. (Female has yellow speckling on crown, is brighter yellow below.)

9 **BROWN-BREASTED BARBET** *Lybius melanopterus* **Page 483**
Uncommon in eastern riverine woodland and coastal forest. Red head, brownish breast band, white belly.

10 **BLACK-COLLARED BARBET** *Lybius torquatus irroratus* **Page 483**
Local in coastal woodland. **10a. Adult male**. Black band separates yellow belly and red throat. **10b. Juvenile**. Largely dark head and breast.

11 **BLACK-BILLED BARBET** *Lybius guifsobalito* **Page 483**
Local in Lake Victoria basin and western border areas. Black belly and bill.

12 **DOUBLE-TOOTHED BARBET** *Lybius bidentatus aequatorialis* **Page 484**
Fairly common in western forests, woodlands, cultivation. White flank patch; ivory bill.

13 **YELLOW-SPOTTED BARBET** *Buccanodon d. duchaillui* **Page 481**
Local in w. Kenyan forests. Yellow superciliary stripe; no whisker mark.

14 **YELLOW-BILLED BARBET** *Trachylaemus purpuratus elgonensis* **Page 484**
Western Kenyan forests. Only barbet in this habitat with bright yellow bill.

15 **RED-AND-YELLOW BARBET** *Trachyphonus erythrocephalus* **Page 485**
Widespread in open woodland, savanna, thorn-bush and scrub. **15a.** *T. e. versicolor,* **male**. Blackish crown, limited red on face. **15b.** *T. e. versicolor,* **female**. Largely yellow crown, red-and-white ear-coverts. **15c.** *T. e. erythrocephalus,* **male**. Black crown, throat patch; much red on sides of face. **15d.** *T. e. erythrocephalus,* **female**. Crown and face mostly red.

16 **D'ARNAUD'S BARBET** *Trachyphonus darnaudii* **Page 485**
Common and widespread in dry habitats. Smaller than Red-and-yellow Barbet. May show some orange on head. **16a.** *T. d. usambiro,* **male**. (Mara GR to Serengeti NP). Largest race. Bill blackish. **16b.** *T. d. darnaudii,* **male**. Blackish brown above; crown orange-red, yellow and black. **16c.** *T. d. boehmi,* **male**. Blackish brown above; forehead and crown black. **16d.** *T. d. darnaudii,* **female**. Pale brownish above; crown orange and black.

1a

1c

1b

3

4a

4b

5b

7a

6

7b

8

10a

11

12

13

14

15a

15c

16a

15b

16b

16c

15d

16d

DALE A. ZIMMERMAN
1986

PLATE 65: TINKERBIRDS, SMALL WOODPECKERS AND WRYNECKS

1 **EASTERN GREEN TINKERBIRD** *Pogoniulus simplex*   Page 479
Uncommon in coastal forest, inland to foothills of East Usambara Mts.
1a. Adult.
1b. Immature.

2 **MOUSTACHED GREEN TINKERBIRD** *Pogoniulus leucomystax*   Page 479
Fairly common in highland forests. White moustachial mark, golden-yellow rump.

3 **SPECKLED TINKERBIRD** *Pogoniulus scolopaceus flavisquamatus*   Page 479
Extirpated. Formerly rare in w. Kenyan forests. Large bill, pale eye.

4 **YELLOW-RUMPED TINKERBIRD** *Pogoniulus bilineatus*   Page 480
Common in forest canopy, riparian woods, tall suburban trees.
4a. *P. b. jacksoni*, adult (highlands).
4b. *P. b. fischeri*, juvenile (coastal woods).

5 **YELLOW-FRONTED TINKERBIRD** *Pogoniulus c. chrysoconus*   Page 480
Fairly common in moist areas of w. Kenya below 1500 m, in savanna, riparian thickets and suburban trees.
Yellow forehead (black in juvenile).

6 **RED-FRONTED TINKERBIRD** *Pogoniulus pusillus affinis*   Page 480
Common in dry country below 2000 m. Vocally similar to No. 5, but no range overlap.
6a. Adult. Red forehead.
6b. Juvenile. Black forehead.

7 **CARDINAL WOODPECKER** *Dendropicos fuscescens*   Page 493
Common and widespread, the races *hartlaubii* and *hemprichii* in savanna and bush, *lepidus* in forest.
7a. *D. f. hartlaubii*, female. Pale; heavily barred above.
7b. *D. f. hartlaubii*, male.
7c. *D. f. hemprichii*, male. Darker, heavily barred.
7d. *D. f. lepidus*, male. Olive-yellow above, obscurely barred.
7e. *D. f. lepidus*, female.

8 **SPECKLE-BREASTED or UGANDA SPOTTED WOODPECKER** *Dendropicos poecilolaemus*
          Page 492
Local in w. Kenya.
8a. Male. Breast and neck finely spotted.
8b. Female. Fine speckling on breast.

9 **EURASIAN WRYNECK** *Jynx t. torquilla*   Page 489
Scarce palearctic migrant. Feeds in trees and on ground.

10 **RED-THROATED WRYNECK** *Jynx r. ruficollis*   Page 489
Uncommon in cent. and w. Kenya above 1500 m. Regular in Lake Nakuru NP. Often on dead trees, fenceposts.

Dale A. Zimmerman
1986

PLATE 66: WOODPECKERS

1 GREY WOODPECKER *Dendropicos goertae rhodeogaster*   **Page 494**
Fairly common in open wooded areas.
1a. Male. Red on belly centre, crown, rump and upper tail-coverts. Some western birds show little or no red below.
1b. Female.

2 BROWN-BACKED WOODPECKER *Picoides obsoletus ingens*   **Page 494**
Uncommon in woodland, forest edge, wooded suburbs. Brown above, with whitish wing and tail spots; variably streaked below.
2a. Female. No red on hindcrown.
2b. Male. Large red hindcrown patch. Eyes grey, dark red or red-brown.

3 FINE-BANDED or TULLBERG'S WOODPECKER *Campethera tullbergi taeniolaema*   **Page 491**
Kenyan highland forests. Heavily barred below. Face appears plain grey at distance.
3a. Male.
3b. Female.

4 BUFF-SPOTTED WOODPECKER *Campethera nivosa herberti*   **Page 492**
Small. Forages low in w. Kenyan forest undergrowth. Face and throat streaked.
4a. Male.
4b. Female.

5 BROWN-EARED WOODPECKER *Campethera c. caroli*   **Page 492**
Western Kenyan forests. Underparts spotted, and dark patch on side of head.
Female. (Male has crimson on hindcrown and nape.)

6 BEARDED WOODPECKER *Dendropicos namaquus schoensis*   **Page 493**
Widespread but uncommon in open wooded areas. Large, rather variable, but pattern diagnostic. (For other races, see text.)
6a. Male.
6b. Female.

7 YELLOW-CRESTED WOODPECKER *Dendropicos xantholophus*   **Page 493**
Western Kenyan forests. Large; golden yellow on head often indistinct in male, lacking in female. Facial pattern suggests Bearded Woodpecker, but back dull brownish-olive and habitats differ.

8 GREEN-BACKED or LITTLE SPOTTED WOODPECKER *Campethera c. cailliautii*   **Page 491**
Local and uncommon in eastern woods. (Greener western race *nyansae* from South Nyanza and Mara GR south to Serengeti NP.)
8a. Male. Greenish above with yellowish-white spots; no prominent malar stripes; throat and breast spotted.
8b. Female. Crown black with pale spots.

9 NUBIAN WOODPECKER *Campethera nubica*   **Page 490**
Common and widespread in acacia woodland, bush and savanna.
9a. *C. n. nubica*, male. Red malar stripe.
9b. *C. n. pallida*, female. Blackish malar stripe.

10 GOLDEN-TAILED WOODPECKER *Campethera abingoni kavirondensis*   **Page 491**
Local in riverine woodland in Mara GR and Serengeti NP (*C. a. suahelica* in n. Tanzania).
Male. Dense black streaking from chin to upper breast.

11 MOMBASA WOODPECKER *Campethera mombassica*   **Page 491**
Locally common in coastal and Tana River forests and the Usambaras.
Female. Heavily streaked below. (Male similar, but with red nape.)

Dale A. Zimmerman
1986

PLATE 67: HONEYGUIDES AND HONEYBIRDS

1 **WAHLBERG'S HONEYBIRD** *Prodotiscus r. regulus*   Page 488
Acacia woodland. Brown back; small, sharp-pointed bill.
1a. Juvenile. Three lateral pairs of rectrices all white.
1b. Adult. Dark T-pattern on tail.

2 **CASSIN'S HONEYBIRD** *Prodotiscus i. insignis*   Page 488
Forest edges and clearings in w. Kenya. Bright golden olive above; underparts dingy olive-grey; side of face greyish-olive.

3 **PALLID HONEYGUIDE** *Indicator meliphilus*   Page 488
Acacia woodland and forest edge. Stubby bill, no dark malar stripe, nearly plain golden-olive back.
3a. Juvenile. Olive extreme.
3b. Adult. Greyer individual.

4 **EASTERN HONEYBIRD** *Prodotiscus zambesiae ellenbecki*   Page 489
Open woodland, forest edge and suburban gardens east of Rift Valley.
4a and 4b. Adults. Face grey, with narrow white eye-ring. Underparts pale grey and whitish (buffier in juvenile), outer rectrices sometimes with small dusky tips.

5 **LEAST HONEYGUIDE** *Indicator exilis pachyrhynchus*   Page 487
Forests in w. Kenya. Small and dark.
5a. Juvenile. Facial marks less prominent, underparts darker than adult. Smaller and stubbier-billed than Thick-billed Honeyguide; lore olive.
5b. Adult. Small white loral spot, pale mandible base, dark malar stripe.

6 **LESSER HONEYGUIDE** *Indicator minor teitensis*   Page 487
Forest edge, savanna and acacia woodland. Paler, less well marked than Least Honeyguide; dark malar stripe sometimes faint.
6a and 6b. Adults.

7 **THICK-BILLED HONEYGUIDE** *Indicator c. conirostris*   Page 487
Western Kenyan forests. Dark olive-grey below, with no obvious facial markings.

8 **SCALY-THROATED HONEYGUIDE** *Indicator variegatus*   Page 486
Forest edge, savanna, riverine woodland. Large, with scaly breast and streaked throat.

9 **GREATER or BLACK-THROATED HONEYGUIDE** *Indicator indicator*   Page 486
Widespread in woodland, savanna and forest edge.
9a. Juvenile. Brownish olive above, yellow throat and breast, white rump.
9b and 9d. Adult males. Black throat, white cheeks; bill usually pinkish, but may be dull brown; golden yellow on wing often concealed.
9c. Adult female. Drab; streaked upper tail-coverts and yellow near bend of wing usually concealed; indistinct barring on chin and upper throat, pale wing-covert edges.

1a 1b 2 3a 3b 4a 4b 5a 5b 6a 6b 7 8 9a 9b 9c 9d

DALE A. ZIMMERMAN
1986

PLATE 68: GOLDEN PIPIT, LONGCLAWS, PITTA AND BROADBILL

1 GOLDEN PIPIT *Tmetothylacus tenellus*   **Page 510**
Widespread in dry country below 1000 m; locally common.
1a and 1b. Adult males. Large yellow wing patches.
1c. Subadult male. Similar but duller, less yellow on face.
1d. Adult female. Slim, brownish buff, some yellow on belly, wings and tail.

2 ROSY-BREASTED LONGCLAW *Macronyx ameliae wintoni*   **Page 511**
Local and uncommon in wet grasslands.
2a. Adult male. Red throat.
2b. Adult female. Pinkish throat.
2c. Juvenile. Brownish, with necklace of dark streaks; hint of pink on belly.

3 YELLOW-THROATED LONGCLAW *Macronyx c. croceus*   **Page 510**
Widespread and locally common in grassland and cultivation.
3a and 3b. Adult males. Yellow throat and breast.
3c. Adult female. Resembles male; black sometimes less extensive than shown; sides of upper breast more
streaked.
3d. Juvenile. Rich buffy brown, with yellow confined to lower breast and belly. Necklace of short streaks
on upper breast.

4 SHARPE'S LONGCLAW *Macronyx sharpei*   **Page 511**
Uncommon and local at high elevations. **Male** bright yellow below, with necklace of streaks in all
plumages. (Female similar.)

5 PANGANI LONGCLAW *Macronyx aurantiigula*   **Page 510**
Common in e. and se. Kenyan grassland. In n. Tanzania west to Lake Manyara and Tarangire NPs.
5a. Male.
5b. Female.

6 AFRICAN PITTA *Pitta angolensis longipennis*   **Page 495**
Rare southern migrant, mainly April–October; primarily coastal.
6a, 6b and 6c. Adults.

7 AFRICAN BROADBILL *Smithornis capensis meinertzhageni*   **Page 495**
Scarce in w. Kenyan forests. (Other races rare and declining.)
7a, 7b and 7c. Adults. White back patch visible in circular display flight from subcanopy perch.

PLATE 69: WAGTAILS

1 YELLOW WAGTAIL *Motacilla flava*   **Page 506**
Common and widespread palearctic migrant, September–April, mainly in moist areas below 2000 m.
Variable; males greenish-backed; females and young birds often brownish above. Most birds yellow below.
Autumn/winter adult males much duller than in spring, but, unlike females, have yellow throats. Some races
have bold superciliary stripes.
1a. *M. f. beema,* **male, spring**.
1b. *M. f. beema,* **male, winter**.
1c. *M. f. thunbergi,* **male, spring**.
1d. *M. f. thunbergi,* **female, spring**.
1e. *M. f. lutea,* **male, winter**.
1f. *M. f. leucocephala,* **male, spring**.
1g. *M. f. feldegg,* **female, spring**.
1h. *M. f. feldegg,* **male, spring**.
1i. *M. f. feldegg,* **male, winter**.
1j. *M. f. lutea,* **yellow-headed male, spring**.
1k. *M. f. lutea,* **first-winter female**.
1l. *M. f. flava,* **male, spring**. (Some individuals paler.)
1m. *M. f. flava,* **adult male, winter**.
1n. *M. f. flava,* **first-winter female**.

2 GREY WAGTAIL *Motacilla c. cinerea*   **Page 505**
Widespread palearctic migrant, October–March, especially along highland-forest streams. Very long tail;
yellowish-green rump; white superciliary stripe; wing-stripe obvious in flight.
2a. Adult male, spring.
2b. Adult female, winter.
2c. Adult male, winter.
2d. First-winter male. (Spring female similar.)

3 WHITE WAGTAIL *Motacilla a. alba*   **Page 505**
Uncommon palearctic migrant, November–March (common at Lake Turkana). Regular at sewage works,
oxidation ponds. Sides of head white.
3a. Adult male, winter.
3b. First-winter male.
3c. Adult male, spring.

4 MOUNTAIN WAGTAIL *Motacilla clara torrentium*   **Page 505**
Local along highland streams. **Adult male** slender; light bluish grey; narrow breast band.

5 AFRICAN PIED WAGTAIL *Motacilla aguimp vidua*   **Page 504**
Common and widespread, often around towns and villages.
5a. Adult male. Black and white above; white superciliary stripe.
5b. Juvenile. Brownish grey above; flanks washed with brown. Much white on wings.

6 CAPE WAGTAIL *Motacilla capensis wellsi*   **Page 505**
Uncommon around lakes and swamps, in other moist areas and cultivation. **Adult male** olive-grey or olive-
brown above; narrow breast band on buff-tinged underparts. Wing-coverts largely brown.

1a 1b 1c 1d 1e 1g 1h 1i 1j 1k 1l 1m 1n 2a 2b 2c 2d 3a 3b 3c 4 5a 5b 6

Dale Zimmerman
1987

PLATE 70: PIPITS

1 RED-THROATED PIPIT *Anthus cervinus*   **Page 508**
Palearctic migrant, late October–April. Adults heavily streaked (including rump), buff and blackish above;
short tail, fine bill, boldly streaked underparts. Usually in groups on wet ground.
1a. Adult male, winter. Some pink on face/throat.
1b. Adult male, spring. Bright tawny-pink from face to breast.
1c. First-winter female. (Oct.–Dec.)
1d. Adult male, autumn. Buff throat.

2 BUSH PIPIT *Anthus caffer blayneyi*   **Page 509**
Scarce and partly nomadic in bushed grassland. Small; no malar stripe.
2a. Adult, worn plumage. Breast streaks narrow and sharp.
2b. Adult, fresh plumage. Rich rufous-buff wing edgings.

3 SOKOKE PIPIT *Anthus sokokensis*   **Page 509**
Scarce and local in coastal forests. Small; heavy black breast streaks.

4 TREE PIPIT *Anthus trivialis*   **Page 508**
Palearctic migrant, October–April. Heavily streaked; olive-tinged upperparts; dark malar stripe. Bill heavier
than in Red-throated Pipit.

5 GRASSLAND PIPIT *Anthus cinnamomeus lacuum*   **Page 507**
The common East African pipit.
5a. 'Jackson's Pipit', *A. (c.) latistriatus*. Possibly a form of Grassland Pipit. Status unclear; see text.
5b. Juvenile. Dark; flanks streaked; mandible pinkish.
5c. Adult, fresh plumage. Flanks unstreaked; bright buff feather edges above; mandible yellowish, tarsi
pinkish.
5d. Adult, worn plumage.

6 MALINDI PIPIT *Anthus melindae*   **Page 508**
North Kenyan coast and lower Tana River Valley. Dull, not contrastingly streaked above; mandible and tarsi
orange-yellow.
6a. Immature(?). Narrowly streaked individual.
6b. Breeding adult. Heavily streaked individual.

7 PLAIN-BACKED PIPIT *Anthus leucophrys*   **Page 507**
Locally common on short-grass plains. Slim; unstreaked back, limited breast streaking, buff outer tail feathers.
7a. Adult *A. l. goodsoni*. Laikipia Plateau/ cent. Rift Valley. Pale; indistinct breast streaks.
7b. Immature *A. l. goodsoni*. Sharper breast streaks.
7c. Adult *A. l. zenkeri*. Western: Mt. Elgon south to w. Serengeti NP.

8 TAWNY PIPIT *Anthus c. campestris*   **Page 506**
Rare palearctic migrant. **Adult** slender, pale and faintly marked. Wagtail-like.

9 LONG-BILLED PIPIT *Anthus similis hararensis*   **Page 507**
Rift Valley scarps and Arusha NP. Locally common on rough ground. Large; long-billed and long-tailed.
Lightly streaked below.
9a. Juvenile. Streaks extend onto flanks; wing edgings tawny-buff or light rufous; long tail edged with rich
buff.
9b. Adult, fresh plumage. (Some birds greyer, more diffusely streaked than shown; worn individuals darker and more uniform above.)

10 STRIPED PIPIT *Anthus lineiventris*   **Page 509**
Rocky, grassy slopes in se. Kenya (rare) and ne. Tanzania. Large and well streaked; greenish-yellow wing
edgings.

1a

1b

1c

2a

1d

2b

3

5a

5b

5c

5d

4

6b

7a

7c

8

7b

9a

9b

10

DALE
ZIMMERMAN
1987

PLATE 71: LARKS (See also Plate 72)

1 FISCHER'S SPARROW-LARK *Eremopterix leucopareia* Page 503
Common, widespread; often in flocks on dry short-grass plains. **1a. Immature male.** Resembles adult male, but cheeks duller. **1b. Adult male.** Black mid-ventral line; whitish cheeks. **1c. Juvenile female.** Scaly or speckled above; mottled on breast. **1d. Adult female.** Rufous face, buff throat and upper breast.

2 CHESTNUT-HEADED SPARROW-LARK *Eremopterix signata* Page 504
Locally common on dry northern and southeastern plains; some wander to coast. **2a. Juvenile female.** Tawny about eyes. **2b. Juvenile male.** Buffy brown; diffusely streaked below. **2c and 2d. Adult males.** White crown and cheek patch; black or chestnut on face and throat. **2e. Immature male.** Reddish face with large whitish cheek patch. **2f. Adult female.** Crown darker than in immature male; face and throat buff.

3 CHESTNUT-BACKED SPARROW-LARK *Eremopterix leucotis madaraszi* Page 503
Scarce and local wanderer, favouring black 'cotton' soils. **3a. Immature female.** Chestnut wing-coverts, black belly. **3b. Adult male.** Chestnut back, white cheeks and nape band. **3c. Adult female.** Darkly streaked; chestnut wing-coverts.

4 SINGING BUSH LARK *Mirafra cantillans* Page 496
Widespread in grassland, open bush. Well patterned in fresh plumage, with dark spot on side of lower neck; rufous primary edgings often show as conspicuous patch in flight; outer rectrices white. See text. **4a. Presumed *M. c. chadensis*** (Kenyan–Sudanese border), **adult in fresh plumage. 4b. *M. c. marginata*, adult male in fresh plumage.** Dark inner secondaries ('tertials') with broad cream edges; bill mainly dark brown above. **4c. *M. c. marginata*, adult male in worn breeding plumage.** Duller; dark foreneck patches reduced or absent. **4d. *M. c. marginata*, juvenile.** Scaly-looking above; suggestion of dark submarginal lines on secondaries; bill mainly pinkish.

5 SOMALI SHORT-TOED LARK *Calandrella somalica* Page 501
Locally fairly common on dry plains, mostly in south. Prominent facial pattern; dark area at sides of lower neck; white tail edges obvious in flight. **5a. *C. s. athensis*.** S. Kenya, n. Tanzania. Whitish orbital/postocular areas contrast with dark ear-coverts. **5b. *C. s. megaensis*.** N. Kenya. Buffier than *athensis*.

6 GREATER SHORT-TOED LARK *Calandrella brachydactyla longipennis* Page 501
Palearctic vagrant. Pale, with small yellowish bill.

7 MASKED LARK *Spizocorys personata* Page 502
Locally common in northern Kenyan deserts. **7a. *S. p. yavelloensis*.** South to Dida Galgalu Desert. **7b. *S. p. intensa*.** Northeast of Isiolo.

8 FRIEDMANN'S LARK *Mirafra pulpa* Page 497
Scarce and irregular in dry grassland with scattered shrubs. Sporadic in the Tsavo parks. See text.

9 SHORT-TAILED LARK *Pseudalaemon fremantlii delamerei* Page 502
Local on short-grass plains and in dry open bush.

10 RED-CAPPED LARK *Calandrella cinerea* Page 501
Widespread in highlands, south to n. Tanzania. Common on short-grass plains. **10a. *C. c. williamsi*** (Kenyan highlands), **juvenile.** Dark crown with fine speckling, scaly back pattern; large blotches at sides of mottled breast. **10b. *C. c. williamsi*, adult male** (with crest erected). Darker and more heavily streaked than *saturatior*. **10c. *C. c. saturatior*, adult male** (sw. Kenya, n. Tanzania).

11 CRESTED LARK *Galerida cristata somaliensis* Page 502
Common in sandy deserts of n. Kenya. **11a. Juvenile female. 11b. Adult female.** (Male similar.)

12 THEKLA LARK *Galerida theklae huriensis* Page 503
Local on rocky substrate in n. Kenyan deserts. Darker, less sandy-coloured, than Crested Lark.

DALE A. ZIMMERMAN
1992

PLATE 72: LARKS (*Mirafra*) (See also Plate 71)

1 RED-WINGED LARK *Mirafra h. hypermetra*   **Page 498**
Locally common in bushed grassland below 1300 m and east of Rift Valley. Large, with rufous primaries; black neck patches conspicuous in adult (lacking in Rufous-naped Lark).
1a. Rufous adult.
1b. Pale adult in worn plumage.
1c. Pale juvenile.
1d. Rufous juvenile.
1e. Pale adult in fresh plumage.

2 RUFOUS-NAPED LARK *M. africana*   **Page 498**
Widespread and common in grassland above 1300 m east to Emali Plains and Arusha District. Stocky, short tailed, with rufous primaries. No black neck patches.
2a. *M. a. harterti*, adult. Emali Plains.
2b. *M. a. tropicalis*, adult. Crater and Mbulu Highlands of n. Tanzania north to Mt Elgon.
2c. *M. a. athi*, adult. Cent. Kenyan highlands south to Kilimanjaro.
2d. *M. a. athi*, juvenile. Darker, duskier than juvenile Red-winged Lark.

3 FLAPPET LARK *M. rufocinnamomea*   **Page 499**
Widespread. Uncommon in shrubby grassland, savanna and bush clearings. Outer rectrices tawny, buff or rufous. More slender, bill smaller, tail longer, back more scaly or spotted than in Rufous-naped Lark.
3a. *M. r. torrida*, adult. Central; Huri Hills south to interior n. Tanzania.
3b. *M. r. fischeri*, juvenile. Coastal; juveniles of other races similar. Darker, more uniform than young of other *Mirafra* species.
3c. *M. r. kawirondensis*, adult. Western. Buff outer rectrices.
3d. *M. r. fischeri*, adult. Coastal.

4 FAWN-COLOURED LARK *M. africanoides intercedens*   **Page 499**
Fairly common in dry open bush and shrubby grassland. Slender-billed; blackish lore and distinct white superciliary stripe.
4a. Rufous adult.
4b. Brown adult.
4c. Juvenile.

5 GILLETT'S LARK *M. gilletti*   **Page 500**
Rare in open thorn-scrub in extreme northeastern Kenya. Resembles Fawn-coloured Lark, but rump and upper tail-coverts grey; breast streaks brownish rufous.

6 PINK-BREASTED LARK *M. poecilosterna*   **Page 500**
Widespread; locally common in dry open *Acacia* and *Commiphora* bush below 1500 m. Perches in trees. Pipit-like; no white in tail.
6a. Light extreme.
6b. Dark extreme.
6c. Juvenile. Paler than Rufous-naped and Flappet Larks; no dark loral area.

7 WILLIAMS'S LARK *M. williamsi*   **Page 497**
Locally common in northern lava deserts, often with Masked Lark. Obscurely streaked to nearly plain above; heavy-billed. Variable. (Cf. Friedmann's Lark and Singing Bush Lark on Plate 71.)
7a. Worn adult female.
7b. Freshly plumaged adult female, dark morph. More uniform above and with darker ear-coverts than White-tailed Lark.
7c. Freshly plumaged adult male, rufous morph. Upperparts red- or orange-brown with sparse pale streaking; wing-coverts broadly edged with pale rufous; whitish semi-collar behind ear-coverts.

8 WHITE-TAILED LARK *M. albicauda*   **Page 496**
Uncommon in open grassland on black 'cotton' soils. **Unworn adult** blackish above.

9 COLLARED LARK *M. collaris*   **Page 499**
Uncommon/scarce on red desert soils in n. and ne. Kenya.

DALE A. ZIMMERMAN
1992

PLATE 73: SWALLOWS (See Plate 74 for flying birds)

1 **ROCK MARTIN** *Hirundo fuligula fusciventris*   Page 515
Common around rocky sites and near tall buildings. Cinnamon throat/upper breast. White tail spots concealed when at rest.

2 **BANDED MARTIN** *Riparia cincta suahelica*   Page 511
Locally common in open grassland. Large size; broad breast band; white supraloral line.

3 **MASCARENE MARTIN** *Phedina borbonica madagascariensis*   Page 516
Vagrant to coastal areas. Possibly more regular at Lake Jipe in June.

4 **PLAIN MARTIN or AFRICAN SAND MARTIN** *Riparia paludicola ducis*   Page 512
Common in open country in highlands. Dull brownish throat and breast.

5 **BLUE SWALLOW** *Hirundo atrocaerulea*   Page 513
Scarce in w. Kenya, April–September. White at sides usually concealed.

6 **SAND MARTIN or BANK SWALLOW** *Riparia r. riparia*   Page 512
Common migrant, September–May, mainly in the west. Small size, large breast band; no white above lore.

7 **RED-RUMPED SWALLOW** *Hirundo daurica emini*   Page 514
Fairly common in the highlands. Blue-black under tail-coverts.

8 **MOSQUE SWALLOW** *Hirundo senegalensis saturatior*   Page 515
Uncommon but widespread; most numerous in west. Large size, pale cheeks.

9 **RUFOUS-CHESTED SWALLOW** *Hirundo semirufa gordoni*   Page 515
Uncommon in Lake Victoria basin and Mara GR, especially near wet areas. Dark blue of crown extends below eyes; under tail-coverts and rump rufous.

10 **LESSER STRIPED SWALLOW** *Hirundo abyssinica unitatis*   Page 515
Locally common. Widespread, often around buildings. Largely rufous head and rump; striped underparts.

11 **GREY-RUMPED SWALLOW** *Pseudhirundo g. griseopyga*   Page 512
Uncommon in w. and cent. Kenya, mainly in grassland and cultivation. Rump grey or brownish grey. **11a.**
***P. g. griseopyga*, adult. 11b. *P. g. 'andrewi'*.**

12 **WIRE-TAILED SWALLOW** *Hirundo s. smithii*   Page 513
Widespread and fairly common, especially near water. **12a. Adult**. Chestnut cap; pure white underparts.
12b. Juvenile. Dull brown cap; buff-tinged underparts.

13 **BARN SWALLOW** *Hirundo r. rustica*   Page 513
Widespread migrant. Common to abundant, August to early May; some present all year. **13a. Adult**.
Chestnut throat and blue breast band. **13b. Juvenile**. Dull blue upperparts; brownish breast band.

14 **COMMON HOUSE MARTIN** *Delichon u. urbica*   Page 516
Common passage migrant. Winters locally in highlands. White rump and underparts may be buff-tinged in winter.

15 **BLACK SAW-WING or ROUGH-WING** *Psalidoprocne holomelas massaicus*   Page 516
Common and widespread near forests, high-elevation grasslands. (Smaller nominate race uncommon in coastal forests.)

16 **WHITE-HEADED SAW-WING or ROUGH-WING** *Psalidoprocne a. albiceps*   Page 517
Locally common in the west; scarce elsewhere. **16a. Juvenile**. Stockier and browner than Black Saw-wing, tail fork less deep. **16b. Adult male**. Head largely white. **16c. Adult female**. Throat white; may show some white on crown.

17 **ANGOLA SWALLOW** *Hirundo angolensis*   Page 514
Widespread in w. Kenya. Locally fairly common east to Nyahururu and Nanyuki. Underparts dingy grey-brown; breast band incomplete.

18 **ETHIOPIAN SWALLOW** *Hirundo aethiopica*   Page 514
Common in coastal areas and n. Kenya. Resembles small Barn Swallow, but breast band narrow and incomplete, tail less forked. **18a. *H. a. aethiopica*, adult. 18b. *H. a. aethiopica*, juvenile. 18c. *H. a. amadoni*, adult.**

DALE A. ZIMMERMAN
1993

PLATE 74: SWALLOWS IN FLIGHT

(Adults unless otherwise stated; young are similar, duller, often with shorter outer rectrices. Perched birds on Plate 73)

1 **MASCARENE MARTIN** *Phedina borbonica madagascariensis*   **Page 516**
Vagrant to coastal lowlands, inland to Lake Jipe. Dark wing-linings, streaked underparts, square tail.

2 **ROCK MARTIN** *Hirundo fuligula fusciventris*   **Page 515**
Widespread near gorges, cliffs, kopjes, tall buildings. Brown-backed; white tail spots evident in spread tail.

3 **SAND MARTIN or BANK SWALLOW** *Riparia r. riparia*   **Page 512**
Common and widespread migrant, mainly in the west. Small size, brown wing-linings distinguish it from Banded Martin.

4 **BANDED MARTIN** *Riparia cincta suahelica*   **Page 511**
Locally common in grassland. Flight leisurely, often low. Brown upperparts, white wing-linings.

5 **PLAIN MARTIN or AFRICAN SAND MARTIN** *Riparia paludicola ducis*   **Page 512**
Widespread and common, especially in the highlands. No breast band; dingy grey-brown throat, breast and sides.

6 **BLACK SAW-WING or ROUGH-WING** *Psalidoprocne holomelas massaicus*   **Page 516**
Common in wooded areas and grassland in highlands; often flies just above ground. (Uncommon coastal race, *P. h. holomelas*, is smaller and shorter-tailed.)

7 **BLUE SWALLOW** *Hirundo atrocaerulea*   **Page 513**
Scarce in shrubby grassland in w. Kenya, April–September. Appears all black at distance; outer rectrices vary in length.

8 **WHITE-HEADED SAW-WING or ROUGH-WING** *Psalidoprocne a. albiceps*   **Page 517**
Locally common in shrubby grassland and forest edge in w. Kenya; uncommon/scarce elsewhere. **Adult male** has largely white head. (Female differs from No. 6 in having shallow tail fork.)

9 **RED-RUMPED SWALLOW** *Hirundo daurica emini*   **Page 514**
Fairly common in the highlands, often near buildings. Rufous rump, blue-black under tail-coverts; no white in tail. Flight relatively slow and leisurely.

10 **RUFOUS-CHESTED SWALLOW** *Hirundo semirufa gordoni*   **Page 515**
Western. Uncommon in open areas below 1700 m. Rufous rump, under tail-coverts and wing-linings; dark blue of head extends below eyes; white tail spots. Flight swift and dashing.

11 **MOSQUE SWALLOW** *Hirundo senegalensis saturatior*   **Page 515**
Uncommon but widespread in open woodland, cultivation, clearings, mainly below 2600 m. Large, with white wing-linings, pale cheeks, rufous rump and under tail-coverts; no white tail spots in this race, but present in eastern *H. s. monteiri*.

12 **LESSER STRIPED SWALLOW** *Hirundo abyssinica unitatis*   **Page 515**
Widespread below 2000 m, usually near buildings. Streaked underparts; rufous on rump and head.

13 **BARN SWALLOW** *Hirundo r. rustica*   **Page 513**
Common and widespread migrant, late August to early May; scarce other months. **13a. Adult male.** Glossy blue-black upperparts and breast band; white tail spots. (Female has shorter outer rectrices.) **13b. Juvenile.** Duller above with faint gloss; dusky brown breast band; forehead and throat buff.

14 **WIRE-TAILED SWALLOW** *Hirundo s. smithii*   **Page 513**
Widespread and common, often near water. Shining blue above with chestnut cap; white below. Wire-like outer rectrices often broken or missing (or difficult to discern). (Juvenile on Plate 73.)

15 **COMMON HOUSE MARTIN** *Delichon u. urbica*   **Page 516**
Palearctic migrant, mainly in highlands. Small, high-flying; fluttery flight; white rump.

16 **ANGOLA SWALLOW** *Hirundo angolensis*   **Page 514**
Widespread in w. Kenya. Locally fairly common east to Nyahururu and Nanyuki. Dingy underparts and wing-linings. (Juvenile duller, with buff throat, smaller tail spots.)

17 **ETHIOPIAN SWALLOW** *Hirundo a. aethiopica*   **Page 514**
Common along coast; widespread in n. Kenya. Steel-blue above, with chestnut forehead; blue-black breast band; throat buff in this race, white in *H. a. amadoni* (cf. Plate 73).

18 **GREY-RUMPED SWALLOW** *Pseudhirundo g. griseopyga*   **Page 512**
Uncommon in grassland, open cultivation. Flight fluttery, slow, usually low; nests in holes in ground. Glossy blue-black on back.

DALE ZIMMERMAN
1993

PLATE 75: BULBUL, BRISTLEBILL, LEAF-LOVE AND LARGER GREENBULS

1 COMMON BULBUL *Pycnonotus barbatus*   **Page 525**
1a. *P. b. tricolor.* Widespread, except in n. and e. Kenya.
1b. *P. b. dodsoni.* Common in dry country of n. and e. Kenya. White ear patch.

2 HONEYGUIDE GREENBUL *Baeopogon i. indicator*   **Page 524**
Uncommon in canopy of w. Kenyan forests. Dark, with much white in tail; eye white in male (greyish in female).

3 EASTERN NICATOR *Nicator gularis*   **Page 527**
Secretive. Fairly common in eastern forest undergrowth (especially near coast). **Male** large; pale yellow or white spots; stout hooked bill. (Female smaller, with spot in front of eye white, not yellow.)

4 SHELLEY'S GREENBUL *Andropadus masukuensis kakamegae*   **Page 520**
Fairly common in some w. Kenyan forests. Forages at all levels; clings to tree trunks. Grey head, pale eyelids; small bill. (See Plate 123 for ne. Tanzanian race.)

5 RED-TAILED BRISTLEBILL *Bleda syndactyla woosnami*   **Page 526**
Fairly common near ground in western forests.
5a. Adult male. Yellowish below; pale blue orbital skin; eye red (brown in female).
5b. Juvenile. Rufous wash on flanks; orbital skin yellow or yellowish green.

6 MOUNTAIN GREENBUL *Andropadus nigriceps*   **Page 520**
Widespread and conspicuous in highland forest and forest edge.
6a. *A. n. nigriceps.* Nguruman Hills and n. Tanzania. Greyish head and breast, blackish crown; grey eyelids.
6b. *A. n. kikuyuensis.* W. and cent. Kenyan highlands. Grey head, white eyelids; yellow belly.
(For *A. n. usambarae* of ne. Tanzania, see Plate 123.)

7 ZANZIBAR SOMBRE GREENBUL *Andropadus importunus*   **Page 521**
Common and conspicuous in coastal scrub and thickets.
7a. *A. i. insularis,* adult. Eastern lowlands. Plain; eye pale.
7b. *A. i. insularis,* juvenile. Yellow eyelids and gape; eye brown.
7c. *A. i. fricki.* Local in cent. Kenyan highlands. Slightly darker, heavier-billed than 7a; juvenile also with yellowish eyelids.

8 STRIPE-CHEEKED GREENBUL *Andropadus milanjensis striifacies*   **Page 520**
Locally common in Taita and Chyulu Hills forests south into n. Tanzania. Robust; striped cheeks; eye pale grey.

9 JOYFUL GREENBUL *Chlorocichla laetissima*   **Page 525**
Uncommon in canopy of w. Kenyan forests. Vocal, conspicuous. Large size, bright yellow underparts.

10 YELLOW-BELLIED GREENBUL *Chlorocichla flaviventris centralis*   **Page 525**
Eastern. Common in coastal forest, dense bush; less numerous inland; scarce in cent. Kenyan highlands. Large; dull yellowish below; white on eyelid.

11 YELLOW-THROATED LEAF-LOVE *Chlorocichla flavicollis pallidigula*   **Page 525**
Locally common in w. Kenya. Retiring, but highly vocal. Large; pale throat feathers often raised. Eye dull yellow to pale brown.

PLATE 76: GREENBULS AND BROWNBULS

1 ANSORGE'S GREENBUL *Andropadus ansorgei kavirondensis*   Page 518
Common in subcanopy of Kakamega Forest. Small; olive-grey below; narrow light eye-ring.

2 LITTLE GREY GREENBUL *Andropadus gracilis ugandae*   Page 518
Scarce. Subcanopy of Kakamega Forest. Yellowish belly; bright tawny flanks and sides.

3 YELLOW-WHISKERED GREENBUL *Andropadus l. latirostris*   Page 519
Commonest highland greenbul in forest and riparian undergrowth.
3a and 3b. Adults. Yellow throat feathers.
3c. Juvenile. Blackish malar streak; mottled orange-and-black bill.

4 SLENDER-BILLED GREENBUL *Andropadus gracilirostris*   Page 519
Fairly common and conspicuous in highland-forest treetops. Olive-green above, plain grey below; slender black bill.

5 CAMEROON SOMBRE GREENBUL *Andropadus c. curvirostris*   Page 517
W. Kenyan forests; uncommon in tall shrubbery and creepers. Dark olive-grey throat contrasts with darker breast; small dark bill; greyish-white eyelids.

6 LITTLE GREENBUL *Andropadus v. virens*   Page 518
Fairly common in w. Kenyan forest undergrowth. Small and dark, with short bill; throat, breast and flanks uniformly olive; feet orange to yellowish brown. (Similar race *zombensis* common in Shimba Hills and ne. Tanzania.)

7 TORO OLIVE GREENBUL *Phyllastrephus hypochloris*   Page 521
Dense undergrowth in Kakamega Forest. Uncommon and shy. Slender-billed; mainly plain olive, paler than Little Greenbul; suggestion of yellow-and-grey streaking below; tail dark rufous. Feet bluish or olive.

8 CABANIS'S GREENBUL *Phyllastrephus cabanisi*   Page 522
Widespread and common in forest undergrowth, usually in small noisy groups; flicks wings.
8a. *P. c. placidus*. East of Rift Valley. Olive-brown with rufous tail; whitish or cream throat; eye usually grey.
8b. *P. c. sucosus*. West of Rift Valley. Yellower below than *placidus*; iris usually greyish tan. (Immature has still brighter yellow underparts.)

9 NORTHERN BROWNBUL *Phyllastrephus strepitans*   Page 523
Widespread, fairly common in forest undergrowth and thickets, often in noisy family groups. Rump and upper tail-coverts bright rufous-brown; narrow whitish eye-ring; eye red-brown.

10 TERRESTRIAL BROWNBUL *Phyllastrephus terrestris suahelicus*   Page 523
Uncommon in coastal forest undergrowth, often on ground; shy and secretive. Duller, slightly more olive-brown than Northern Brownbul, intermediate in colour between that species and Fischer's Greenbul; rump and tail-coverts not rufous; white throat contrasts rather sharply with breast. Eye dark red-brown.

11 FISCHER'S GREENBUL *Phyllastrephus fischeri*   Page 522
Common in coastal forest undergrowth; secretive. Olive-brown above with whitish throat, rufous-tinged tail; eye cream. Bill long and slender in **male**, much shorter in female, resembling bill of Cabanis's Greenbul.

12 GREY-OLIVE GREENBUL *Phyllastrephus cerviniventris*   Page 521
Kiambu, Thika, Taveta, Arusha and Moshi Districts. Local in forest undergrowth and riverine thickets. Pale eye-ring; feet pale straw colour or pinkish white.

13 YELLOW-STREAKED GREENBUL *Phyllastrephus flavostriatus tenuirostris*   Page 524
Rare in Kenya (two records). More numerous in Usambara and South Pare forests in nc. Tanzania. Crown grey; yellow streaks on greyish-white underparts; long, slim, dark brown bill; eye grey.

14 TINY GREENBUL *Phyllastrephus debilis rabai*   Page 524
Uncommon in coastal forest undergrowth. Small size; grey crown and face; eye pale yellow; underparts yellow-streaked. (*P. d. albigula* of Tanzania's Usambara Mts has olive crown.)

DALE A. ZIMMERMAN
1987

PLATE 77: GLOSSY STARLINGS

Highly iridescent, the colours appearing markedly different with changing light conditions: brilliant in strong sunlight, darker and often largely black in shade or when viewed against the light.

1 RÜPPELL'S LONG-TAILED STARLING *Lamprotornis purpuropterus* Page 632
Common in lightly wooded and open country. Long purple or bronze-purple tail.

2 HILDEBRANDT'S STARLING *Lamprotornis hildebrandti* Page 632
Locally common in bush and woodland. Often on ground with Superb Starlings.
2a. Juvenile. Brown or blackish-brown head; faint spotting on underparts.
2b. Adult. Eye red; breast paler than belly.

3 SHELLEY'S STARLING *Lamprotornis shelleyi* Page 633
Local and uncommon. Mostly a non-breeding visitor in dry e. and se. Kenya; possibly resident in far north. Typically in *Commiphora* bush. Underparts uniformly dark chestnut; eye orange.

4 SUPERB STARLING *Lamprotornis superbus* Page 633
Common and widespread. Feeds on ground.
4a. Adult. White band separating dark breast and rufous-orange belly; eye cream.
4b. Juvenile. White breast band faint or lacking; eye brown, soon turning greyish.

5 GOLDEN-BREASTED STARLING *Cosmopsarus regius* Page 633
Locally common in dry n. and e. Kenya and ne. Tanzania. Yellow underparts; long narrow tail.
5a. Adult. Upperparts mostly iridescent blue; wings often show purple; head green.
5b. Juvenile. Brownish head and breast; much duller and shorter-tailed than adult.

6 SPLENDID STARLING *Lamprotornis s. splendidus* Page 630
Scarce in Mt Elgon forests. Mostly arboreal. Large and broad-tailed; coppery patch on side of neck; velvety-black wing band; wings noisy in flight.
6a. Female. Underparts more blue, less purple, with less coppery iridescence.
6b. Male. Throat and breast violet, with band of brassy or coppery iridescence.

7 PURPLE STARLING *Lamprotornis purpureus amethystinus* Page 631
Scarce in w. Kenya. On ground or in trees, at times with other starlings. Large, bright yellow eye; relatively short-tailed and long-billed; purplish head and underparts.

8 BRONZE-TAILED STARLING *Lamprotornis chalcurus emini* Page 632
Nw. Kenya. Local and uncommon in trees or on ground, often with Blue-eared Starling; wings noisy in flight.
8a and 8b. Adults. Purple-and-blue tail may appear bronze as bird flies against the light.

9 BLUE-EARED STARLING *Lamprotornis chalybaeus* Page 631
9a. L. c. cyaniventris, adult. Common in the highlands; also east and west of Lake Turkana. Larger and bluer than *L. c. sycobius*.
9b. L. c. cyaniventris, juvenile. Sooty brown, washed with green or blue, belly dull black; eye grey-brown.
9c. L. c. sycobius, adult. Uncommon in n. Tanzania, also seasonally in Kenyan coastal lowlands inland to Tsavo and Kibwezi. Smaller and greener than *L. c. cyaniventris*, with bright magenta-violet flanks and belly. Closely resembles Lesser Blue-eared Starling.

10 BLACK-BELLIED STARLING *Lamprotornis corruscus mandanus* Page 630
Common in coastal forests and woods, inland along Tana River to Kora NR. (Larger race *jombeni* scarce/uncommon in Meru Forest and Nyambeni Hills.) **Male**. No black spots on wing-coverts; belly and crissum black (dark sooty in female).

11 LESSER BLUE-EARED STARLING *Lamprotornis c. chloropterus* Page 631
Western Kenya. Locally common in bush and woodland.
11a. Juvenile. Dark brownish head, dull brown or brownish-grey underparts; dark eye. (Juvenile *L. c. elisabeth* of ne. Tanzania has rufous-brown underparts.)
11b. Adult. Smaller, greener than Blue-eared Starling, with narrower dark ear-covert patch, shorter tail.

DALE ZIMMERMAN
1992

PLATE 78: STARLINGS AND OXPECKERS

1 **SHARPE'S STARLING** *Cinnyricinclus sharpii*   **Page 635**
Highland forests. Small-billed; upperparts blue-black.
1a. Juvenile. Arrowhead-shaped spots on underparts; duller above than adult; orange-brown eye.
1b. Adult male. Pale tawny-buff belly and flanks; yellow eye. Female slightly duller.

2 **ABBOTT'S STARLING** *Cinnyricinclus femoralis*   **Page 634**
Uncommon in montane-forest canopy. Dark above and on breast; eye yellow.
2a. Male. Blue-black of breast extends to point on upper belly.
2b. Female. Upperparts and breast brown, heavily streaked below.

3 **VIOLET-BACKED STARLING** *Cinnyricinclus leucogaster verreauxi*   **Page 634**
Flocks widespread in forested areas, riverine woods, fruiting trees.
3a. Female. Rufous-tawny feather edges in fresh plumage; shows rufous primary patch in flight.
3b. Male. Magenta-violet to blue iridescence above, white below.

4 **MAGPIE-STARLING** *Speculipastor bicolor*   **Page 635**
Flocks in northern semi-deserts, scrub, dry woodland; nomadic. White patch at base of primaries in all plumages; eye red in adults.
4a. Female. Less glossy than male; black band across breast.
4b. Male. Head and upperparts glossy blue-black.
4c. Juvenile. Dark brown above, on throat and on breast; eye brown. (Rare immature plumage shown on p. 636.)

5 **FISCHER'S STARLING** *Spreo fischeri*   **Page 635**
Locally common in dry bush country below 1400 m. Greyish or brownish grey above; crown much paler; lore blackish.
5a. Juvenile. Brownish on back and breast; eye dark brown; bill largely yellow.
5b. Adult. Greyer; eye white; bill black.

6 **WATTLED STARLING** *Creatophora cinerea*   **Page 636**
Widespread. Commonly in large flocks, often with ungulates. Plumage and bare parts variable, but rump whitish in all plumages.
6a. Non-breeding male. No wattles; head largely feathered.
6b. Male in full breeding plumage. Bare yellow facial skin; long black wattles.
6c. Male acquiring breeding plumage. Head well feathered; greenish-and-yellow skin near eyes; wattles variable.
6d. Juvenile. Brownish, with darker wings; yellow or greenish skin along sides of throat and behind eye.
6e. Adult female (and some non-breeding males). Dark malar streak; bare postocular skin.

7 **WHITE-CROWNED STARLING** *Spreo albicapillus horrensis*   **Page 635**
Uncommon in flocks in arid n. Kenya. White or whitish crown, wing patches, wing-linings and belly; underparts variably streaked.
7a, 7b and 7c. Adults. Upperparts shining olive-green, showing much gloss in strong light; wings and tail bluer. Eye creamy white.
7d. Juvenile. Browner, less glossy; pale tawny-white crown. Eye brown, becoming paler with age. Bill mostly yellow.

8 **RED-BILLED OXPECKER** *Buphagus erythrorhynchus*   **Page 636**
Common near large wild mammals, locally with livestock. No rump/back contrast.
8a. Adult. Yellow eye-wattle; all-red bill.
8b. Immature. Darker than adult; bill, eye and orbital skin dark.
8c. Juvenile. Similar to 8b, but bill yellow.

9 **YELLOW-BILLED OXPECKER** *Buphagus a. africanus*   **Page 637**
Locally common, but less widespread than Red-billed Oxpecker. Prefers buffalo and rhino. Larger than Red-billed, with pale creamy-buff rump; no eye-wattle.
9a. Adult. Expanded base of bill yellow, tip red.
9b. Juvenile. Bill dark; plumage duskier than adult's.

1a 1b 2a 2b 3a 3b 4a 4b 4c 5a 5b 6a 6b 6c 6d 6e 7a 7c 7d 8a 8b 8c 9a 9b

DALE A. ZIMMERMAN
1992

PLATE 79: CHESTNUT-WINGED STARLINGS (As seen in strong sunlight)

1 RED-WINGED STARLING *Onychognathus morio*   **Page 629**
Widespread around cliffs, city buildings. Long pointed tail less extreme than in Bristle-crowned Starling. Bill heavy.
1a and 1c. Males.
1b. Female. Head and neck grey with dark streaks.

2 BRISTLE-CROWNED STARLING *Onychognathus salvadorii*   **Page 630**
Local in n. Kenya near cliffs, rocky gorges. Velvety 'cushion' on head; very long, pointed tail. Much chestnut in primaries. **Male** illustrated. Female smaller, with greyer head, smaller 'cushion'.

3 SLENDER-BILLED STARLING *Onychognathus tenuirostris theresae*   **Page 629**
Locally common in cent. Kenyan highlands, at higher elevations than Red-winged Starling and typically around waterfalls. Chestnut primaries conspicuous in flight. Bill relatively long and slender.
3a. Female. Glossy blue-black, with many grey-tipped feathers.
3b. Male.

4 WALLER'S STARLING *Onychognathus w. walleri*   **Page 629**
Locally common in highland forests. Short-tailed. Primaries largely chestnut.
4a and 4c. Males.
4b. Female. (Western race *elgonensis* shows less grey on head.)

5 STUHLMANN'S STARLING *Poeoptera stuhlmanni*   **Page 628**
Common in w. Kenyan forest treetops. Iris brown, with narrow yellow peripheral ring.
5a and 5b. Males. Appear all black at distance, glossed blue in strong light. No chestnut in wings.
5c and 5d. Females. Dark grey with bluish gloss; chestnut primaries show in flight.

6 KENRICK'S STARLING *Poeoptera kenricki bensoni*   **Page 628**
Local in montane forests on Mt Kenya and Nyambeni Hills (smaller *P. k. kenricki* in ne. Tanzanian mountains). Eye grey.
6a. Male. Black with faint bronzy gloss. No chestnut in wings.
6b. Female. Slate-grey. Primaries largely chestnut, as in female Stuhlmann's Starling.

PLATE 80: ORIOLES AND CORVIDS

1 **EURASIAN GOLDEN ORIOLE** *Oriolus o. oriolus*   **Page 625**
Regular palearctic migrant, October-December and March–April, common in spring in coastal lowlands. Scarce, January to early March.
1a. Older adult female. Yellow underparts with faint olive streaks.
1b. Adult male. Black on lore, none behind eye; wings largely black.
1c. First-winter male (younger female similar). Bend of wing darker than side of neck; no grey postocular stripe; wing feathers not obviousy yellow-edged. Some immatures of both sexes more heavily streaked. Bill brown, pinkish later.

2 **AFRICAN GOLDEN ORIOLE** *Oriolus auratus notatus*   **Page 625**
Regular intra-African migrant, April–August, in wooded habitats, especially coastal forest; less common inland.
2a. Adult male. Much yellow wing edging; black stripe through eye.
2b. Adult female. Grey eye-line.
2c. Immature male. Resembles 1c, but bend of wing little darker than back and neck; grey eye-line extends behind eye; bold yellow wing edging. Bill black.

3 **GREEN-HEADED ORIOLE** *Oriolus chlorocephalus amani*   **Page 625**
Local and uncommon in Kenyan coastal forest north to Arabuko–Sokoke; more numerous in the Usambara Mts, ne. Tanzania. Greenish head, yellow collar. (Juvenile streaked with olive-green below the yellowish throat.)

4 **BLACK-HEADED ORIOLE** *Oriolus larvatus rolleti*   **Page 624**
Common in open woods, acacia savanna, forest edge; locally in mangroves.
4a. Adult. Central tail feathers olive; inner secondaries ('tertials') edged with pale yellow, outer secondaries with whitish; greater coverts mainly grey.
4b. Juvenile. Throat and breast densely streaked.

5 **WESTERN BLACK-HEADED ORIOLE** *Oriolus brachyrhynchus laetior*   **Page 624**
Only in Kakamega Forest, w. Kenya.
5a. Adult. Outer secondaries edged with slate-grey, not whitish; inner secondaries ('tertials') mainly olive-, not yellow-edged. Central rectrices yellow-olive.
5b. Juvenile. Head dusky olive; breast faintly streaked.

6 **MONTANE ORIOLE** *Oriolus percivali*   **Page 624**
Locally common in Kenyan highland forests. Some hybridization with Black-headed Oriole (see text).
6a. Adult. Central tail feathers black; wings with more black than in Nos. 4 and 5.
6b. Juvenile. Faintly streaked below the dark throat.

7 **PIAPIAC** *Ptilostomus afer*   **Page 626**
Scarce in w. Kenya near Ugandan border; often with large mammals.
7a, 7b and 7c. Adults. Eye purple or red-violet; bill black.
7d. Juvenile. Eye brown; bill largely pink.

8 **CAPE ROOK** *Corvus capensis*   **Page 628**
Local in grassland, semi-desert and cultivation. Slender bill; plumage browner when worn.
8a and 8b. Adults.

9 **FAN-TAILED RAVEN** *Corvus rhipidurus*   **Page 627**
Locally common near cliffs, rocky hills in n. Kenya. Very short tail exceeded by wing tips in perched bird.
9a and 9b. Adults.

10 **BROWN-NECKED or DWARF RAVEN** *Corvus (ruficollis) edithae*   **Page 626**
Common in arid n. Kenya. Ruffled feathers of nape, neck and breast show white bases (grey in other forms). Plumage browner when worn.
10a, 10b and 10c. Adults.

11 **HOUSE CROW** *Corvus s. splendens*   **Page 626**
Common along coast north to Malindi. Grey neck, sooty-grey underparts. Tail extends well beyond wing tips in perched bird.
11a and 11b. Adults.

12 **PIED CROW** *Corvus albus*   **Page 627**
Widespread up to 3000 m, including all urban areas.
12a and 12b. Adults.

13 **WHITE-NAPED RAVEN** *Corvus albicollis*   **Page 627**
Locally common around mountains, escarpments and rocky hills. Wing tips extend beyond tail tip. In flight, appears short-tailed, broad-winged.
13a and 13b. Adults. (Juvenile duller and browner; some black streaks on nape.)

LALE A. ZIMMERMAN
1993

PLATE 81: CUCKOO-SHRIKES AND DRONGOS

1 RED-SHOULDERED CUCKOO-SHRIKE *Campephaga phoenicea* Page 620
Scarce in canopy of open wooded habitats near Ugandan border in w. Kenya.
1a. Male.
1b. Female. Upperparts greyish or grey-brown with no olive tinge.

2 BLACK CUCKOO-SHRIKE *Campephaga flava* Page 620
Largely an intra-African migrant, May–October, when common and widespread in bush, woodland and forest edge.
2a. Female. Upperparts greyish olive; underside of tail largely yellow.
2b. Male, all-black morph.
2c. Male, yellow-shouldered morph.

3 PURPLE-THROATED CUCKOO-SHRIKE *Campephaga quiscalina martini* Page 621
Uncommon in forest and forest edge in the highlands.
3a and 3b. Males. Throat/breast glossed with purple. Mouth red or orange-red.
3c. Female. Upperparts plain olive; head mostly grey.

4 PETIT'S CUCKOO-SHRIKE *Campephaga petiti* Page 621
Fairly common in Kakamega and Nandi Forests, w. Kenya.
4a and 4b. Males. Prominent skin at gape and mouth-lining bright orange-yellow.
4c. Female. Upperparts barred with black; underparts plain except for bars on sides of lower throat and upper breast.
4d. Immature male. Plain above, barred below (sometimes more heavily than shown). (Juvenile heavily black-spotted below.)

5 WHITE-BREASTED CUCKOO-SHRIKE *Coracina pectoralis* Page 622
Rare in savanna and open woodland in w. Kenya and n. Tanzania.
5a. Female.
5b. Male.

6 GREY CUCKOO-SHRIKE *Coracina caesia pura* Page 622
Local in highland forests.
6a. Female.
6b. Juvenile male.
6c. Adult male. Blackish lores and chin.

7 SQUARE-TAILED DRONGO *Dicrurus ludwigii sharpei* Page 623
Local in w. Kenyan forests and (similar nominate race) in Tana River, Witu and Boni Forests; also in Usambara Mts, ne. Tanzania. Tail slightly notched, not splayed. Highly vocal.
7a. Adult. Eye red.
7b. Juvenile. Eye brown.

8 VELVET-MANTLED DRONGO *Dicrurus modestus coracinus* Page 623
Scarce in Kakamega Forest, w. Kenya. Less glossy than Common Drongo; back and rump velvety black; no pale wing flash in flight.

9 COMMON DRONGO *Dicrurus a. adsimilis* Page 622
Widespread and common in varied habitats, including forest edge. Shows pale silvery wing flash in flight.
9a. Adult. Eye red.
9b. Immature. Eye brown; skin at corners of mouth pale; less 'fork-tailed' than adult.
9c. Juvenile. Eye variable from amber or grey-brown to yellowish grey; underparts mottled grey-brown, with varying amounts of buff on feather tips.

PLATE 82: BUSH-SHRIKES (See also Plate 83)

1 **MARSH TCHAGRA** *Tchagra m. minuta* **Page 614**
Uncommon and local in wet grasslands, marsh edges. Solid black crown. Black V on back (obsolete in rare coastal/Usambara race *T. m. reichenowi*). **1a. Male. 1b. Female. 1c. Juvenile.**

2 **BRUBRU** *Nilaus afer minor* **Page 612**
Widespread in savanna, open woodland and bush. **Male** illustrated. (Female has black replaced by brown or blackish brown. Western *N. a. massaicus* has dark brownish-chestnut sides and flanks.)

3 **BROWN-CROWNED TCHAGRA** *Tchagra australis emini* **Page 613**
Widespread. Common in moist bush, woodland, bushed grassland, on or near ground in dense shrubbery. Skulking; sings from bushtops and in flight. **3a and 3b. Adults.** (Coastal *T. a. littoralis* smaller and paler.)

4 **BLACK-CROWNED TCHAGRA** *Tchagra s. senegala* **Page 613**
Locally common in shrubbery of wooded and bushed habitats. Skulking; conspicuous only in song-flight. Sympatric with No. 3 in many areas. **Male** illustrated (female similar).

5 **THREE-STREAKED TCHAGRA** *Tchagra j. jamesi* **Page 613**
Local and uncommon in dry bush below 1000 m. Sings on the wing like No. 4. Skulking. Some birds have narrow and incomplete central crown stripe. (Eastern *T. j. mandana* more sandy buff, less grey, than *jamesi*.)

6 **BOCAGE'S or GREY-GREEN BUSH-SHRIKE** *Malaconotus bocagei jacksoni* **Page 614**
Nandi and Kakamega Forests only. Arboreal, usually in canopy. **Male** illustrated (female similar).

7 **PINK-FOOTED PUFFBACK** *Dryoscopus angolensis* **Page 619**
Uncommon in w. Kenyan forest canopy (Nandi, Kakamega). **7a. Male. 7b. Female**.

8 **PRINGLE'S PUFFBACK** *Dryoscopus pringlii* **Page 619**
Local and uncommon in dry northern and eastern *Acacia* and *Commiphora* bush, often with mixed-species flocks in low trees, shrubbery. Eye crimson; basal half of mandible pale. **8a. Male.** Tail edged and tipped with dull white in fresh plumage. **8b. Female**. Dull, with narrow white eye-ring and white loral area.

9 **NORTHERN PUFFBACK** *Dryoscopus gambensis malzacii* **Page 618**
North of the Equator in lightly wooded areas. Arboreal. **9a. Male.** Rump grey (as in female Black-backed Puffback); scapulars grey or dull whitish, underparts dull white. **9b. Female.** Tawny-buff underparts, buff wing edgings, orange eye.

10 **BLACK-BACKED PUFFBACK** *Dryoscopus cubla* **Page 619**
Male clean-cut, bright white below, with white rump. Female has grey rump, white supraloral stripe. Coastal race *affinis* has all-black wings. **10a. D. c. affinis, immature female. 10b. D. c. affinis, male. 10c. D. c. hamatus, male. 10d. D. c. hamatus, female.**

11 **SLATE-COLOURED BOUBOU** *Laniarius funebris* **Page 618**
Common and widespread in scrub, bush and thickets below 2000 m. Dark bluish slate. **11a. Adult male. 11b. Juvenile male.**

12 **TROPICAL BOUBOU** *Laniarius aethiopicus* **Page 617**
12a. L. f. major. West of Rift Valley. **12b. L. f. ambiguus.** Highlands east of Rift Valley. **12c. L. f. sublacteus, normal morph.** Coastal, inland to Garissa, Taita Hills, Lake Jipe, East Usambara and North Pare Mts. **12d. L. f. sublacteus, black morph.** Coastal only; glossy black, not dull slate as in Slate-coloured Boubou.

13 **SOOTY BOUBOU** *Laniarius leucorhynchus* **Page 618**
Accidental in our region. Wholly sooty black or brownish black. Bill heavy; black in adults, ivory-white in young birds. **Adult female** illustrated. (Male slightly glossier.)

1b

2

3b

3a

4

5

6

7b

7a

8a

9b

8b

9a

11a

10c

10b

11b

10d

12a

12d

10b

12b

12c

13

DALE A. ZIMMERMAN
1997

PLATE 83: BUSH-SHRIKES (See also Plate 82)

1 LÜHDER'S BUSH-SHRIKE *Laniarius l. luehderi* **Page 617**
Western Kenyan forest undergrowth, forest-edge tangles. Shy and skulking.
1a. Juvenile. Buffy yellow on breast and sides; olive above, with rufous upper tail-coverts (barred with black) and tail.
1b. Adult.

2 RED-NAPED BUSH-SHRIKE, *Laniarius ruficeps rufinuchalis* **Page 617**
Eastern. Locally common in thickets in dry bush country; long white wing-stripe, white-sided tail. Shy and skulking.
2a. Juvenile. Olive-grey above, with suggestion of black mask.
2b. Adult. Forecrown black (orange-red in *L. r. kismayensis* around Kiunga).

3 PAPYRUS GONOLEK *Laniarius mufumbiri* **Page 616**
Papyrus swamps around Lake Victoria. Locally common.
3a. Immature. Yellowish-buff throat; pinkish or brick-red breast; crown greyish olive mixed with black.
3b. Adult. Golden-yellow crown; white in wing and on under tail-coverts.

4 BLACK-HEADED GONOLEK *Laniarius erythrogaster* **Page 616**
Western Kenya. Fairly common in dense shrubbery, brushy cultivation and thickets.
4a. Adult. Entirely black above; lower belly and crissum yellowish buff.
4b. Juvenile. Barred yellowish buff and black below; flecked with red when moulting into adult plumage.

5 FOUR-COLOURED BUSH-SHRIKE *Malaconotus quadricolor nigricauda* **Page 615**
Uncommon in eastern lowland-forest undergrowth and thickets. Skulking. Supraloral region orange or yellow; some red below black breast band. Tail black (olive-green in female).

6 DOHERTY'S BUSH-SHRIKE *Malaconotus dohertyi* **Page 615**
Uncommon in Kenyan highland-forest undergrowth, dense thickets with bamboo above 2200 m. Shy and skulking.
6a. Adult. Red forehead and under tail-coverts; no red below the black breast band.
6b. Adult, yellow morph. Rare. No red pigment. (Juvenile olive-yellow, finely barred above and below; under tail-coverts dull pink; tail dusky olive.)

7 SULPHUR-BREASTED BUSH-SHRIKE *Malaconotus sulfureopectus similis* **Page 614**
Widespread in dry woodland, acacia savanna, forest edge; arboreal. Small bill.
7a. Immature. Grey head, upper back; suggestion of white superciliary stripe.
7b. Adult. Bright yellow superciliary stripe; black facial mask; broad orange breast band.

8 GREY-HEADED BUSH-SHRIKE *Malaconotus blanchoti approximans* **Page 615**
Widespread but uncommon in bush and woodland; arboreal. Large, with heavy bill, grey head, white tips to wing feathers; yellow eye. Chestnut on breast variable; may extend to flanks, but lacking in northwestern race *catharoxanthus*. (Juvenile mottled brown on head, pale yellow below; bill brownish horn.)

9 ROSY-PATCHED BUSH-SHRIKE *Rhodophoneus cruentus* **Page 616**
Locally common. Near or on ground in dry bush and semi-desert. Long, white-cornered tail and rosy-red rump patch conspicuous in flight.
9a and 9d. *R. c. hilgerti*, male. North of Equator. Red throat/breast patch with no black border. (Female has black-bordered white throat similar to 9c.)
9b. *R. c. cathemagmenus*, male. South of Equator. Black border to red throat/breast patch.
9c. *R. c. cathemagmenus*, female. White throat, with black border expanded to form patch on upper breast.

10 BLACK-FRONTED BUSH-SHRIKE *Malaconotus nigrifrons* **Page 614**
Fairly common in highland forest; arboreal. Black forehead and mask. Underparts variable.
10a. Golden-breasted morph. Widespread.
10b. Red-breasted morph. Western and cent. Kenyan highlands and Mt Kilimanjaro. Some individuals duller red below.
10c. Buff-breasted morph. Mt Kenya, Taita Hills, Usambara Mts.

DALE A. ZIMMERMAN
1987

PLATE 84: SHRIKES (See also Plate 85)

1 YELLOW-BILLED SHRIKE *Corvinella corvina affinis* **Page 607**
Uncommon and local in w. and nw. Kenya, now mainly on and near ne. slopes of Mt Elgon. **Adult**. Brown, long tail, yellow bill. Wings show much rufous in flight.

2 MAGPIE SHRIKE *Urolestes melanoleucus aequatorialis* **Page 608**
Local in acacia savanna/bush in e. Mara GR and n. Tanzania. **Adult**. Large and long-tailed; tail length and amount of white in wings variable. Only shrike with black underparts.

3 LONG-TAILED FISCAL *Lanius cabanisi* **Page 610**
Common in dry open savanna/bush mainly east of the Rift Valley; also in coastal lowlands. Larger than Common Fiscal, with longer, broader tail.
3a. Adult male. Back dark grey; no white on scapulars.
3b. Juvenile. Large; closely barred above.

4 GREY-BACKED FISCAL *Lanius e. excubitoroides* **Page 610**
Common in moist bush and cultivation, mainly in w. and cent. Rift Valley. **Adult male**. Pale grey on back, much white at tail base. (Female has rufous on flanks.)

5 COMMON FISCAL *Lanius collaris humeralis* **Page 611**
Widespread in highlands above 1500 m; often common in open country, cultivation, towns and gardens. Slender, with long narrow tail.
5a. Juvenile. Heavily barred.
5b. Adult male. Back black, scapulars pure white. (Female shows trace of chestnut on flanks.)

6 MACKINNON'S FISCAL *Lanius mackinnoni* **Page 610**
Uncommon along forest edge and in cultivation in w. Kenyan highlands. **Adult female**. Grey above, with white scapulars, black facial mask. (Male lacks chestnut flank patch.)

7 LESSER GREY SHRIKE *Lanius minor* **Page 609**
Widespread palearctic migrant, common late March to early May in open country. Occasional in autumn.
7a. Spring adult. Grey above, with black forehead; in fresh plumage, shows pink tinge on breast and sides.
7b. Autumn adult (Oct.–Nov.). Some dark barring on forehead.
7c. First-autumn (Oct.–Nov.). Upperparts tinged brownish; no black on forehead; bill pale at base.

8 SOMALI FISCAL *Lanius somalicus* **Page 611**
Uncommon and local in semi-desert areas of n. Kenya. Short-tailed. **Adult male**. Crown, nape and hind-neck black; centre of back pale grey; white on scapulars and secondary tips. (Female lacks chestnut flanks.)

9 TAITA FISCAL *Lanius dorsalis* **Page 611**
Common in dry bush and savanna below 1500 m. **Adult male**. Lacks white secondary tips of Somali Fiscal. (Female usually has trace of chestnut on flanks.)

10 MASKED SHRIKE *Lanius nubicus* **Page 612**
Scarce palearctic migrant; most records from Lake Baringo. Favours acacias near water. Dainty, with slender bill.
10a. First-autumn female. Brownish grey above; extent of barring variable. By December, resembles adult.
10b. Adult male. (Female similar but duller: back and nape feathers tipped with brownish, lower back greyer, all white areas buffier.)

11 WOODCHAT SHRIKE *Lanius senator niloticus* **Page 611**
Uncommon palearctic migrant in w. and nw. Kenya, November–March.
11a. First-autumn bird with remnant juvenile plumage. More rufous than young Masked Shrike. Similar to Juvenile Red-tailed and Red-backed Shrikes (Plate 85), but scapulars and bend of wing paler and head markings less contrasting. Variable.
11b. Adult male. Rufous on head; white scapulars and upper tail-coverts.
11c. Adult female. Duller and often much smaller than male.
11d. First-winter female. Still duller; face pattern more obscure.

2

3a

4

3b

5a

5b

7c

8

3b

7b

9

7a

10a

10b

11c

11a

11b

11d

DALE A.
ZIMMERMAN
1988

PLATE 85: SHRIKES AND HELMET-SHRIKES (See also Plate 84)

1 RED-BACKED SHRIKE *Lanius collurio*   **Page 608**
Palearctic passage migrant (Nov.–Dec. and April) in open habitats. Some winter in se. Kenya, ne. Tanzania.
1a. *L. c. kobylini*, adult male. Rufous on back very restricted.
1b. *L. c. collurio*, adult male. Back more extensively rufous than in 1a.
1c. *L. c. pallidifrons*, adult female. Pale grey crown, whitish forehead.
1d and 1e. *L. c. collurio*, first-winter females. Variable barring; underside of tail greyish.

2 RED-TAILED or ISABELLINE SHRIKE *Lanius isabellinus*   **Page 609**
Common migrant and winter resident Nov.-early April in open habitats mainly east of the Rift Valley.
2a. *L. i. phoenicuroides*, adult female. Brown above; underside of tail rufous or cinnamon. Ear patch brown or black.
2b. *L. i. phoenicuroides*, typical adult male. Brown above, more rufous on crown; often white patch on primary bases.
2c. *L. i. phoenicuroides*, first-winter. (Oct.–Dec.). Barring fainter than on young Red-backed; underside of tail rufous.
2d. *L. i. phoenicuroides*, pale adult male. Pale greyish above, with paler crown; white below.
2e. *L. i. speculigerus*, adult male. Sandy grey above, tail pale rufous. White patch in primaries; pale cinnamon wash below.

3 HYBRID RED-BACKED X RED-TAILED SHRIKE *Lanius collurio* X *L. isabellinus*
3a. Male. Greyish upperparts, black-and-white tail.
3b. Male. Back rufous; tail rufous or rufous-edged, no white.

4 GREY-CRESTED HELMET-SHRIKE *Prionops poliolophus*   **Page 606**
Uncommon from Serengeti NP and Mara GR north to lakes Elmenteita, Naivasha and Nakuru. Conspicuous grey crest. No eye-wattle. Flight pattern similar to that of No. 5.

5 WHITE-CRESTED HELMET-SHRIKE *Prionops plumatus*   **Page 605**
Uncommon in woodland and bush below 1650 m. Restless, nomadic, noisy and gregarious. Yellow eye-wattle; crest whitish to pale grey.
5a. *P. p. cristatus*. Northwestern. Large. Curly-crested; closed wings largely black.
5b. *P. p. vinaceigularis*. Eastern. Moderate crest; little or no white in closed wing.
5c and 5d. *P. p. poliocephalus*. Southern. Small. Short-crested; long white wing-stripe.

6 CHESTNUT-FRONTED HELMET-SHRIKE *Prionops scopifrons kirki*   **Page 606**
Locally common in coastal Kenyan woods (replaced by similar *P. s. scopifrons* in East Usambara foothills). Slate-grey; much white in tail. Blue-grey eye-wattle inconspicuous. (Rare interior Kenyan race *keniensis* lacks whitish on crown and shows more white in tail.)

7 RETZ'S HELMET-SHRIKE *Prionops retzii graculina*   **Page 606**
Fairly common in coastal woods; uncommon inland to Kibwezi, upper Tana River, Mkomazi GR and Arusha NP. Gregarious.
7a and 7b. Adults. Black and grey-brown, with much white in tail. May show white spots on inner webs of primaries in flight.
7c. Juvenile/immature. Lightly scalloped first plumage becomes more evenly brown.

8 NORTHERN WHITE-CROWNED SHRIKE *Eurocephalus rueppelli*   **Page 607**
Common in dry bush and open woodland below 1600 m. Conspicuous; sometimes in small groups.
8a and 8b. Adults.
8c. Juvenile. Brownish crown, dark face.

1b
1d
2a
2b
1e
2c
2d
2e
3a
3b
4
5a
5b
5c
5d
6
7a
7b
7c
8a
8b
8c

Dale A Zimmerman
1987

PLATE 86: WATTLE-EYES AND BATISES

1 YELLOW-BELLIED WATTLE-EYE *Dyaphorophyia concreta graueri* **Page 604**
Kakamega and Nandi Forests; scarce in high undergrowth. Yellow belly, apple-green eye-wattle. **1a. Male.**
Yellow throat. **1b. Female.** Chestnut throat.

2 JAMESON'S WATTLE-EYE *Dyaphorophyia jamesoni* **Page 604**
Kakamega and Nandi Forests; fairly common in low undergrowth. White belly, blue eye-wattle. **2a. Adult male.** Glossy greenish black above and on throat. **2b. Juvenile.** Pale rufous throat.

3 CHESTNUT WATTLE-EYE *Dyaphorophyia c. castanea* **Page 604**
Kakamega and South Nandi Forests; fairly common in high undergrowth, low trees. Plum-coloured eye-wattle. **3a. Female.** Chestnut above and on breast. **3b. Male.** White collar and back, broad black breast band.

4 COMMON WATTLE-EYE *Platysteira cyanea nyansae* **Page 603**
Western. Widespread in woodland, forest edge, riparian trees. Scarlet eye-wattle, long white wing-stripe. **4a. Immature female.** Pale rufous wing stripe; rufous-tinged white throat; suggestion of adult's pattern. **4b. Adult female.** Maroon-chestnut throat. **4c. Adult male.** White throat bordered by broad black breast band.

5 BLACK-THROATED WATTLE-EYE *Platysteira p. peltata* **Page 604**
Local and uncommon in forest and riparian trees, this race east of Rift Valley to the coast. (West of the Rift, *P. p. mentalis* has greener gloss, lacks white in wings.) **5a. Male.** Narrow breast band across white underparts; eye dark brown. **5b. Female.** Throat and upper breast glossy black.

6 PYGMY BATIS *Batis perkeo* **Page 602**
Northern and eastern; fairly common in semi-arid regions, mostly in low *Acacia* scrub-savanna. Small, short-tailed and with white supraloral stripe not extending behind eye. **6a. Female.** Pale line from bill to above front of eye only; orange-tawny breast band; throat usually washed with buff. **6b. Male.** Pattern suggests commoner Chin-spot Batis, but white supraloral line does not extend as a superciliary stripe, breast band narrower and tail shorter.

7 GREY-HEADED BATIS *Batis o. orientalis* **Page 603**
Rare in far-northern dry country; known with certainty only from Ethiopian border. Complete superciliary stripe typically extending behind eye in both sexes (may be shorter in worn birds). See text. **7a. Male. 7b. Female.** Breast band broad, deep chestnut, not cinnamon or tawny; in hand, shows trace of rufous on white nuchal spot.

8 BLACK-HEADED BATIS *Batis minor* **Page 601**
Uncommon to fairly common in savanna and open wooded habitats in the west (*B. m. erlangeri*) and southeast (*B. m. minor*). See text. **8a. *B. m. erlangeri*, female.** Like female Chin-spot Batis, but lacks throat spot and crown usually darker (often as black as side of face). **8b. *B. m. erlangeri*, male.** Typically blackish-crowned; some individuals greyer. (Worn Chin-spot Batis similar.) **8c. *B. m. minor*, male.** Crown medium grey to blackish; breast-band width variable (typically narrower than in male Chin-spot). **8d. *B. m. minor*, female.** Crown grey to blackish; breast band often very narrow, but can be quite broad at sides. Commonly mistaken for Grey-headed Batis, and some individuals seem intermediate with that species. See text.

9 CHIN-SPOT BATIS *Batis molitor* **Page 601**
The commonest batis; widespread in various wooded habitats except in arid regions, Lake Victoria basin and along the coast. With wear, grey crown becomes darker and white superciliary stripe narrower. **9a. Male.** Breast band broad (especially in centre). **9b. Female.** Chestnut throat spot and chestnut breast band. (*Cf.* female Pale Batis.)

10 FOREST BATIS *Batis mixta ultima* **Page 602**
Coastal forest and evergreen thickets; fairly common in undergrowth. (Nominate Tanzanian race, on Plate 124, may be in montane-forest canopy). Short-tailed; eye red or orange. **10a. Female.** Tawny wing patch; frosty light cinnamon throat and breast. **10b. Male.** Eye colour distinctive.

11 PALE BATIS *Batis soror* **Page 602**
Coastal. In Kenya, primarily in *Brachystegia*; in the Usambara Mts, below1000 m in other open woodland. Paler and shorter-tailed than Chin-spot Batis. **11a. Male.** Yellow eye, narrow breast band. **11b. Female.** Pale tawny or cinnamon (not chestnut) throat spot and breast band; superciliary stripe faintly rufous-tinged (subject to wear).

DALE A. ZIMMERMAN
1986

PLATE 87: FLYCATCHERS AND SHRIKE-FLYCATCHER

1 SILVERBIRD *Empidornis semipartitus*   Page 555
Western acacia savanna, mainly below 1600 m.
1a. Juvenile.
1b. Adult.

2 PALE FLYCATCHER *Bradornis pallidus murinus*   Page 554
Widespread; typically in moister habitats than African Grey Flycatcher.
2a. Juvenile. Dorsal pale areas buff or tawny; throat streaked.
2b. Adult. Pale grey-brown above, with plain unstreaked crown. (Coastal race *B. p. subalaris* paler, with almost no trace of breast band.)

3 AFRICAN GREY FLYCATCHER *Bradornis m. microrhynchus*   Page 554
Common and widespread, except in coastal lowlands and Lake Victoria basin.
3a. Adult. Greyer than Pale Flycatcher, with streaked forecrown and smaller bill.
3b. Juvenile. Paler than juvenile Pale Flycatcher; throat unstreaked.

4 ASHY FLYCATCHER *Muscicapa caerulescens cinereola*   Page 553
Local; forest borders and acacia woodland. Ashy blue-grey, with white supraloral streak and eye-ring; tail grey. (Western *M. c. brevicaudata* more bluish-tinged above.)

5 LEAD-COLOURED FLYCATCHER *Myioparus plumbeus orientalis*   Page 555
Uncommon in riverine and acacia woods. Darker than Ashy Flycatcher, with white-edged black tail, this often raised and actively flirted.

6 AFRICAN DUSKY FLYCATCHER *Muscicapa adusta interposita*   Page 552
Common and widespread in highlands. Small; plain except for lighter wing-feather edges and tips, which wear away to leave more uniformly brown plumage.

7 SWAMP FLYCATCHER *Muscicapa aquatica infulata*   Page 553
Lake Victoria basin. Fairly common in papyrus swamps.

8 WHITE-EYED SLATY FLYCATCHER *Melaenornis fischeri*   Page 553
Common and widespread in highlands. (See Plate 124 for Tanzanian *M. f. nyikensis*.)
8a. Adult.
8b. Juvenile.

9 CHAPIN'S FLYCATCHER *Muscicapa lendu*   Page 552
Only in Kakamega and North Nandi Forests, where uncommon. Short, dark bill with yellow gape; narrow greyish supraloral line.

10 SPOTTED FLYCATCHER *Muscicapa striata neumanni*   Page 551
Widespread palearctic migrant, October–April. Variable streaks on crown, throat and breast, faint in some birds. Bill entirely black.

11 GAMBAGA FLYCATCHER *Muscicapa gambagae*   Page 552
Local and uncommon in n. and e. Kenyan thorn-scrub and savanna. Shorter-winged than Spotted Flycatcher; head smaller, rounder; bill shorter, with buff or yellowish mandible.

12 AFRICAN SHRIKE-FLYCATCHER *Bias flammulatus aequatorialis*   Page 605
West Kenyan forest canopy. Sideways wagging of tail diagnostic.
12a. Female. Rufous rump, crissum and wing-feather edgings.
12b. Male. Rump and underparts white.

13 SEMI-COLLARED FLYCATCHER *Ficedula semitorquata*   Page 555
Uncommon migrant in w. Kenya.
13a. Spring male (first year). Suggestion of white half-collar.
13b. Adult male, autumn/winter. Brownish, with bold black-and-white wing pattern.
13c. Female. Duller than autumn male.

14 COLLARED FLYCATCHER *Ficedula albicollis*   Page 556
Vagrant. See text.
14a. Male, spring. Complete white collar.
14b. Female. Somewhat darker and browner than female Semi-collared. May show vague pale nuchal collar or suggestion of dark breast band.

Dale A. Zimmerman
1987

PLATE 88: MONARCH FLYCATCHERS, BLACK-AND-WHITE FLYCATCHER AND BLACK FLYCATCHERS

1 RED-BELLIED PARADISE FLYCATCHER *Terpsiphone rufiventer emini* **Page 600**
Kakamega Forest interior; scarce. Interbreeds with No. 3. **Adult male**. Black head sharply defined from body; solid rufous underparts. (Female greyer on throat.)

2 HYBRID RED-BELLIED X AFRICAN PARADISE FLYCATCHER **Page 600**
T. r. emini X T. viridis ferreti. Kakamega Forest. Now more numerous than typical *T. rufiventer.*
2a. Female, rufous-breasted type. Paler on belly than 'pure' *rufiventer;* black or grey of throat extends onto breast.
2b. Male, grey-and-rufous type.

3 AFRICAN PARADISE FLYCATCHER *Terpsiphone viridis* **Page 600**
Common and widespread in wooded areas and gardens.
3a. *T. v. ferreti*, male, white morph.
3b. *T. v. plumbeiceps*, male, rufous morph. Coastal, no white in wing.
3c. *T. v. ferreti*, male. Rufous above, grey below, glossy black head with blue eye-wattle; central rectrices sometimes short.
3d. *T. v. ferreti*, female, rufous morph.

4 BLACK-AND-WHITE FLYCATCHER *Bias musicus* **Page 605**
Scarce or rare in Meru, Ngaia (and formerly coastal) forests; also in Usambara Mts. Stocky, long crest, yellow eye. Highly vocal.
4a. Female.
4b. Male.

5 BLUE-MANTLED CRESTED FLYCATCHER *Trochocercus cyanomelas bivittatus* **Page 599**
Uncommon in forest undergrowth throughout coastal lowlands, inland to the Chyulu Hills and Kitovu Forest, North Pare Mts, Arusha and Moshi Districts.
5a. Male. White wing patch.
5b. Female. Grey above, with white eye-ring and wing-bars.

6 NORTHERN BLACK FLYCATCHER *Melaenornis edolioides* **Page 553**
Locally common west of the Rift Valley near wooded areas and cultivation. Dull black. **Adult** figured. (Juvenile like 7b, but dull black.)

7 SOUTHERN BLACK FLYCATCHER *Melaenornis pammelaina* **Page 554**
Locally common in dry woodland east of the Rift Valley. No overlap with No. 6.
7a. Adult. Glossy blue-black.
7b. Juvenile. Duller, with tawny-buff spots.

8 DUSKY CRESTED FLYCATCHER *Trochocercus nigromitratus* **Page 599**
W. Kenya: uncommon in Kakamega and Chemoni forest undergrowth. Dull bluish slate, with black face and crest.

9 AFRICAN BLUE FLYCATCHER *Elminia longicauda teresita* **Page 598**
W. Kenya: locally common in woodland, forest edge and gardens. Pale blue; active and confiding.

10 WHITE-TAILED CRESTED FLYCATCHER *Trochocercus albonotatus* **Page 599**
Fairly common in montane forests of the w. and cent. Kenyan highlands and Usambara Mts. Much white in frequently fanned tail.

DALE A. ZIMMERMAN
1986

PLATE 89: BABBLERS AND CHATTERERS (*Turdoides*)

1 SCALY CHATTERER *T. aylmeri kenianus* **Page 530**
Uncommon in dry *Commiphora* scrub. Brown, not rufous; scaly throat and breast. Pale bluish-grey or whitish skin surrounding pale eye.

2 RUFOUS CHATTERER *T. r. rubiginosus* **Page 529**
Widespread in dense bush and thickets below 1500 m. Pale bill; eye usually pale.

3 SCALY BABBLER *T. s. squamulatus* **Page 528**
Uncommon in coastal forest and thickets, along Tana River and in extreme ne. Kenya. Dark face and ear-coverts, orange-yellow eye, scaly breast, whitish chin.

4 ARROW-MARKED BABBLER *T. jardineii emini* **Page 528**
Locally common north to Lake Nakuru NP, in thickets, forest edge and shrubby woodland. Orange-yellow eye, sharp-pointed white feather tips, dark lore.

5 BLACK-LORED BABBLER *T. sharpei* **Page 527**
Locally common in forest edge, thickets and dense bush. White eye, black lore.
5a. *T. s. vepres*. White throat patch, but ventral plumage variable. (See text.) Nanyuki and Timau Districts.
5b. *T. s. sharpei*. Mottled throughout below. Common around lakes Naivasha and Elmenteita.

6 BROWN BABBLER *T. plebejus cinereus* **Page 528**
Uncommon in nw. Kenya, south to the Equator. Yellow eye, pale lore and chin; white feather tips on breast.

7 NORTHERN PIED BABBLER *T. h. hypoleucus* **Page 529**
Cent. Kenya and n. Tanzania. Common in some Nairobi suburbs. White eye, dark flanks and patch on side of breast.

8 HINDE'S BABBLER *T. hindei* **Page 529**
Local in cent. Kenyan highlands. Variable. White feather edgings, tawny-cinnamon rump/upper tail-coverts. Red or orange-red eye.
8a. Light variation.
8b. Dark variation.

PLATE 90: ILLADOPSES, HILL BABBLER AND THRUSHES (Part)

1 **MOUNTAIN ILLADOPSIS** *Illadopsis p. pyrrhoptera* **Page 531**
On or near ground in montane Kenyan forests. Grey below, with brownish flanks and crissum; throat whitish.

2 **AFRICAN HILL BABBLER** *Pseudoalcippe a. abyssinica* **Page 530**
Arboreal in highland forest. Grey head sharply defined from tawny-rufous back; throat and breast grey.

3 **BROWN ILLADOPSIS** *Illadopsis fulvescens ugandae* **Page 531**
Western Kenyan forests (notably Kakamega). On ground and in undergrowth. Tawny below, with white throat; may show faint malar streak; tail fairly long.

4 **SCALY-BREASTED ILLADOPSIS** *Illadopsis albipectus barakae* **Page 532**
Terrestrial in Kakamega and Nandi Forests, w. Kenya. Dull olive-brown above, mottled below. Tarsi long and pale (usually whitish grey to greyish pink).
4a. Typical adult. Prominent scaly breast markings.
4b. Juvenile. Some orange-rufous on face; bill largely dark.
4c. Less scaly adult. Faint to very faint breast markings.

5 **PALE-BREASTED ILLADOPSIS** *Illadopsis r. rufipennis* **Page 532**
Terrestrial in w. Kenyan forests only. (See Plate 124 for Tanzanian *I. r. distans*.)
5a. Adult. Plain below, throat and belly whitish. Tarsi blue-grey or brownish grey.
5b. Juvenile. Base of mandible bright yellow to orange.

6 **GREY-CHESTED ILLADOPSIS** *Kakamega poliothorax* **Page 531**
Uncommon on ground in Kakamega and Nandi Forests, w. Kenya. Rufous-brown upperparts, grey breast and flanks.

7 **BROWN-TAILED ROCK CHAT** *Cercomela scotocerca turkana* **Page 547**
Dry, rocky bush country south to Baringo District. Plain; large eye and narrow eye-ring.

8 **RED-TAILED or FAMILIAR CHAT** *Cercomela familiaris falkensteini* **Page 546**
Rocky hillsides and escarpments. Rufous rump and sides of tail; lateral rectrices darker at tips.

9 **COMMON REDSTART** *Phoenicurus p. phoenicurus* **Page 543**
Palearctic migrant in w. and nw. Kenya. **Female** has lateral rectrices entirely rufous. (Male on Plate 93.)

10 **BROWN-CHESTED ALETHE** *Alethe poliocephalus carruthersi* **Page 538**
Forests in w. and cent. Kenya; terrestrial.
10a. Adult. Brownish breast band, white superciliary stripe.
10b. Juvenile. Densely rufous-spotted; tail dark. (Young robin-chats show rufous in tail.)

11 **ALPINE CHAT** *Cercomela sordida ernesti* **Page 547**
High montane grassland and moorland. Upright posture.

12 **SOOTY CHAT** *Myrmecocichla nigra* **Page 547**
Western grasslands (Mara/n. Serengeti Plains).
12a. Female. Plain dark brown.
12b. Male. Black, with white 'shoulders'.

13 **NORTHERN ANTEATER CHAT** *Myrmecocichla aethiops cryptoleuca* **Page 547**
Widespread in eroded dry grassland. Both sexes brownish black, with large white patches in primaries (usually concealed at rest).
13a and 13b. Adults.

DALE A ZIMMERMAN
1988

PLATE 91: THRUSHES (*Turdus, Monticola, Zoothera, Neocossyphus*)

1 LITTLE ROCK THRUSH *Monticola r. rufocinereus* **Page 548**
Local and uncommon in highlands, mainly on cliffs, rocky slopes and in forested ravines. Rufous rump and tail (except dark central feathers and tips); grey throat and breast. Crepuscular.
1a. Male.
1b. Female.

2 COMMON ROCK THRUSH *Monticola saxatilis* **Page 548**
Fairly common palearctic migrant, October–April, in largely open country.
2a and 2b. Spring males. Greyish-blue head, largely rufous underparts, white on back.
2c. Autumn male. Restricted rufous; much light feather edging. (Various intermediates between b and c relate to degree of feather wear plus a complete gradual moult, Dec.–Feb.)
2d. Winter female.

3 RED-TAILED ANT THRUSH *Neocossyphus r. rufus* **Page 539**
On and near ground in coastal forests, Shimba Hills and East Usambara Mts. Shy; attends ant swarms. Plain brown and rufous, tail brighter; flicks tail.

4 WHITE-TAILED ANT THRUSH *Neocossyphus poensis praepectoralis* **Page 539**
Uncommon in Kakamega and Nandi Forests. Usually near ground; follows ant columns. Flicks tail. White tail corners conspicuous in flight.

5 SPOTTED GROUND THRUSH *Zoothera guttata fischeri* **Page 549**
Migrant from southern tropics. Scarce in coastal forests, April–October. Shy; forages in leaf litter.

6 ORANGE GROUND THRUSH *Zoothera gurneyi chuka* **Page 549**
Uncommon in highland forests. Shy and skulking. Feeds on ground, sings from canopy trees or undergrowth. Eye-ring broken (unlike adult of No. 7); pale band across ear-coverts, large bill. See text for racial differences.

7 ABYSSINIAN GROUND THRUSH *Zoothera piaggiae kilimensis* **Page 549**
At higher elevations than Orange Ground Thrush, the two largely allopatric. Shy.
7a. Juvenile. Eye-ring small and broken; ear-coverts and crown mostly rufous-brown, latter spotted with buff. (Juvenile Orange Ground Thrush has dark crown and light band across ear-coverts, as in adult.)
7b. Adult. Eye-ring large and complete; ear-coverts plain, head rufous-tinged.

8 TAITA THRUSH *Turdus (olivaceus) helleri* **Page 550**
Taita Hills forests (se. Kenya); rare and shy.

9 BARE-EYED THRUSH *Turdus tephronotus* **Page 551**
Uncommon in eastern *Commiphora* bush and scrub. Forages on ground inside thickets; shy. Extensive bare orbital skin; throat heavily streaked; bill yellow.

10 OLIVE THRUSH *Turdus olivaceus abyssinicus* **Page 550**
Common in wooded highlands (including city suburbs and gardens, where it forages on lawns).
10a. Juvenile. Heavily spotted below; orange or yellow-orange eye-ring and bill.
10b. Adult. Breast dark; orange eye-ring bright and conspicuous; bill orange. (See Plate 124 for n. Tanzanian races.)

11 AFRICAN THRUSH *Turdus pelios centralis* **Page 550**
Western Kenya, east locally to Lake Nakuru NP and Laikipia Plateau. Fairly common in woodland, cultivation, forest edge. Resembles pale Olive Thrush.

DALE A. ZIMMERMAN
1988

PLATE 92: THRUSHES (robin-chats, scrub robins, chats)

1 **WHITE-BROWED SCRUB ROBIN** *Cercotrichas leucophrys* **Page 541**
Common and widespread in bush and scrub. Lower back and tail bright rufous, tail tipped black and white. Prominent superciliary stripe; variable white in wing.
1a. *C. l. zambesiana*. West and south of Kenyan highlands to Mara GR and Serengeti NP; also coastal. Broad white wing-bars, reddish back.
1b. *C. l. brunneiceps*. Southern Kenya, the Rift Valley highlands and Crater Highlands, and Mt Meru. White in wing extends to inner secondaries. Back darker and browner than 1a.
1c. *C. l. vulpina*. Dry interior se. Kenya. Lightly streaked below, much white in wing. Head grey-brown, contrasting with back. (Other races include the greyer-headed *C. l. leucoptera*, Turkana to Magadi, and paler northeastern *C. l. eluta* ranging south to the Tana River.)

2 **RUFOUS BUSH CHAT** *Cercotrichas galactotes familiaris* **Page 543**
Fairly common palearctic migrant in dry bush and scrub, November to early April. Pumps tail like scrub robin. Pale grey-brown, with largely rufous rump and tail, latter white-tipped with black subterminal band.

3 **BROWN-BACKED SCRUB ROBIN** *Cercotrichas hartlaubi* **Page 542**
Western and cent. Kenyan highlands, uncommon in wooded areas, thickets, gardens. Terminal half of tail black with white tips; narrow white wing-bars.

4 **CAPE ROBIN-CHAT** *Cossypha caffra iolaema* **Page 538**
Widespread in highland towns, cultivation and wooded habitats.
4a. Juvenile. Mottled and spotted, tail as adult's but duller. (See text for distinctions from other juvenile robin-chats.)
4b. Adult. Lower breast and sides grey.

5 **EASTERN BEARDED SCRUB ROBIN** *Cercotrichas q. quadrivirgata* **Page 542**
Common in dense moist thickets and wooded areas in coastal lowlands, inland to Mt Endau, Kibwezi, Taveta and North Pare Mts. Chestnut on rump, but none on tail.

6 **RED-CAPPED ROBIN-CHAT** *Cossypha natalensis intensa* **Page 536**
Common in coastal forests, April–November. (Similar *C. n. hylophona* breeds in thickets and riverine forest at Taveta and in sw Kenya.) Shy. No head stripes, wings bluish.

7 **BLUE-SHOULDERED ROBIN-CHAT** *Cossypha cyanocampter bartteloti* **Page 537**
Local in Kakamega, Kaimosi and Nandi Forests. Skulks in undergrowth; very shy. Pale blue at bend of wing sometimes concealed. Rump buffy olive; underparts mostly rich tawny-buff; outer rectrices narrowly black-edged.

8 **SNOWY-HEADED ROBIN-CHAT** *Cossypha niveicapilla melanota* **Page 538**
Local in remnant forest, riverine thickets and forest edge in w. Kenya. Black back, white crown, no superciliary stripe.

9 **SPOTTED MORNING THRUSH** *Cichladusa g. guttata* **Page 540**
Common in dry thickets and dense bush below 1600 m, especially along watercourses. Chestnut tail with no dark central feathers; heavily spotted below.

10 **COLLARED PALM THRUSH** *Cichladusa arquata* **Page 540**
Local in coastal lowlands, usually near palms. Forages low, in or near thickets. Chestnut tail; narrow black band around throat/breast.

11 **RÜPPELL'S ROBIN-CHAT** *Cossypha semirufa intercedens* **Page 537**
Common in Kenyan highland forest east of the Rift Valley, south to n. Tanzanian mountains. Blackish central rectrices, prominent superciliary stripe. Smaller than White-browed Robin-Chat, and vocally distinct.

12 **WHITE-BROWED ROBIN-CHAT** *Cossypha h. heuglini* **Page 537**
Common in woodland, forest edge and gardens. Avoids arid country and most highland areas occupied by Rüppell's Robin-Chat. Central rectrices light brown. Slightly larger than Rüppell's, with broader superciliary stripe. (Some birds more olive above.)

13 **CLIFF CHAT** *Thamnolaea cinnamomeiventris subrufipennis* **Page 548**
Locally fairly common on Rift Valley scarps, cliffs and rocky gorges.
13a. Male. Glossy black above, with white wing patches.
13b. Female. Dark grey, with chestnut belly.

PLATE 93: THRUSHES (akalats, Irania, chats *et al.*)

1 COMMON STONECHAT *Saxicola torquata axillaris* **Page 543**
Fairly common and widespread in open country above 1800 m.
1a. Female. Indistinct superciliary stripe; white stripe in wing.
1b. Male. White wing-stripe and collar; chestnut bib.

2 WHINCHAT *Saxicola rubetra* **Page 544**
Uncommon/fairly common in cent. Rift Valley, western grasslands and cultivation, October–March. White
superciliary stripe, dark cheek.
2a. Male.
2b. Female.

3 WHITE-STARRED ROBIN *Pogonocichla stellata intensa* **Page 533**
Widespread in highland forests. Black-and-yellow tail pattern diagnostic (except in Mt Elgon race).
3a. Juvenile. Strongly patterned below; base of bill yellow.
3b. Adult. Blue-grey head and wings; white spot above eye. (See Plate 124 for immature plumage of *P. s.
orientalis*.)

4 EQUATORIAL AKALAT *Sheppardia a. aequatorialis* **Page 535**
Fairly common in w. Kenyan forest undergrowth. Robin-like; orange below.
4a. Adult. Russet on rump and upper tail-coverts; tail brown; face greyish.
4b. Juvenile. Duller; mottled and spotted.

5 FOREST ROBIN *Stiphrornis erythrothorax* **Page 534**
Vagrant in w. Kenya. Yellow-orange throat and breast; white supraloral spot.

6 COMMON REDSTART *Phoenicurus p. phoenicurus* **Page 543**
Uncommon palearctic migrant, October–March. Local in w. and nw. Kenya. **Male** has tail largely bright
rufous; throat black, heavily veiled with white in early winter; breast rufous, veiled with white. (For female,
see Plate 90.)

7 GREY-WINGED ROBIN *Sheppardia p. polioptera* **Page 535**
Local in w. Kenyan forests. Rufous tail, rufous-orange underparts; blue-grey on wing-coverts.
7a. Immature. Variable white supraloral spot.
7b. Adult. Robin-chat-like pattern; crown dark slate-grey.

8 EAST COAST AKALAT *Sheppardia gunningi sokokensis* **Page 535**
Tana River and coastal forests, East Usambara lowland forest.
8a. Adult male. Underparts yellow-orange and white. (Female similar.)
8b. Adult male in display (showing erectile white loral feathers).

9 NIGHTINGALE *Luscinia megarhynchos hafizi* **Page 540**
Skulking palearctic migrant, November–March. Brown above, with rufous tail; breast plain greyish white.

10 SPROSSER or THRUSH-NIGHTINGALE *Luscinia luscinia* **Page 541**
Skulking palearctic migrant. Abundant in Tsavo region November/December. Slightly darker than
Nightingale, with mottled breast.

11 IRANIA or WHITE-THROATED ROBIN *Irania gutturalis* **Page 543**
Locally common palearctic migrant, November–March, in dry thickets along watercourses. Long black tail
in both sexes. Shy and secretive.
11a. Autumn male.
11b. Spring male.
11c. Female. Traces of orange on sides and flanks; ear-coverts often tawny.

1a

1b

2a

2b

5

3a

4a

6

3b

4b

7a

8a

7b

8b

9

10

11a

11b

11c

DALE A. ZIMMERMAN
1989

PLATE 94: THRUSHES (Wheatears)

1 ISABELLINE WHEATEAR *Oenanthe isabellina*   **Page 545**
Common and widespread, October–March. Paler, more uniform in colour, larger-billed than Northern Wheatear; superciliary stripe broader. Wings contrast little with body; wing-linings white. (Lores black in spring male, greyer in female and autumn birds.)

2 NORTHERN WHEATEAR *Oenanthe o. oenanthe*   **Page 544**
Common and widespread, late September–March. Smaller-billed than Isabelline Wheatear; wing-linings dusky.
2a. Winter female. Wing noticeably darker than body. (Unworn autumn birds have broader, pale buff feather edges, resembling Isabelline.)
2b. Autumn/winter male. Dark face patch, pale buff throat/breast, grey or brownish-grey back.

3 DESERT WHEATEAR *Oenanthe deserti*   **Page 545**
Palearctic vagrant. Black tail, white only at extreme base.
3a. Male. Black of face and throat connected to black wings.
3b. Female. Pale sandy or greyish-buff head and breast.

4 PIED WHEATEAR *Oenanthe p. pleschanka*   **Page 544**
Common and widespread in dry bushed grassland, October–March. Small-billed; black band at tail tip narrow (may be incomplete); white of rump extends to lower back; wing-linings black.
4a. Female. Darker than Northern or Isabelline; throat and breast often dusky.
4b. First-winter male. Brown crown and back; throat feathers pale-tipped.
4c. Adult winter male. Crown and nape feathers grey-tipped; black body feathers brownish-tipped.
4d. Spring male. Clean-cut black-and-white pattern.

5 HEUGLIN'S WHEATEAR *Oenanthe (bottae) heuglini*   **Page 546**
Extreme nw. Kenya. Brick-red below, black facial stripe, narrow white superciliary stripe; black tail band very broad.
5a. Male.
5b. Female. Breast feathers white-tipped in fresh plumage.

6 BLACK-EARED WHEATEAR *Oenanthe hispanica melanoleuca*   **Page 545**
Palearctic vagrant. Facial mask (sometimes throat also) blackish, separated from black wings by pale body plumage. Black tail band incomplete (occasionally so in Pied Wheatear). Variable sandy-buff wash above and below; some very pale.
6a. Spring male, black-throated form. Largely white or creamy white above and below.
6b. Spring male, white-throated form. Much paler than Northern Wheatear.
6c. Female. Variable; ear patch typically darker than in female Pied Wheatear.

7 ABYSSINIAN BLACK or SCHALOW'S WHEATEAR *Oenanthe lugubris schalowi*   **Page 545**
Locally common near eroded gullies in cent. Rift Valley, around Mt Meru and in Crater Highlands of n. Tanzania. Orange-buff or rufous rump, crissum and tail base.
7a. Juvenile. Dark dusky brown, variably speckled with pale buff; belly paler; rump and tail as in adult; no superciliary stripe.
7b. Adult female. Dusky brown above; streaked from chin to breast.
7c. Adult male. Streaked, pale brown crown; white belly.

8 CAPPED WHEATEAR *Oenanthe pileata livingstonii*   **Page 546**
Locally common on open grassland above 1400 m. Upright posture. Sexes alike, with broad black breast band connected to facial mask.
8a. Adult.
8b. Juvenile. Brown, heavily spotted with pale buff; pale superciliary stripe.

PLATE 95: WARBLERS (*Acrocephalus, Bradypterus et al.*)

1 LESSER SWAMP WARBLER *Acrocephalus gracilirostris* **Page 561**
Common wetland resident.
1a. Adult *A. g. parvus*. Blackish tarsi, orange gape.
1b. Immature *A. g. jacksoni*. Rufescent on breast and flanks.

2 BASRA REED WARBLER *Acrocephalus griseldis* **Page 559**
Palearctic migrant, November–April, in moist thickets, rank grass and wet places. Common in winter in lower Tana River valley. Regular autumn migrant through the Tsavo region. Large, long-billed; olive-brown, with no rufescent or bright buff tones.

3 GREAT REED WARBLER *Acrocephalus a. arundinaceus* **Page 558**
Palearctic migrant, November–April, in tall grass, green thickets and reedbeds, often near lakes and rivers. Large, heavy-billed, bright buff below. Usually has faint streaks on throat.

4 AFRICAN REED WARBLER *Acrocephalus baeticatus cinnamomeus* **Page 559**
Local wetland resident in Lake Victoria basin, cent. Rift Valley; occasional farther east. Small; bright buff below, rufous above; legs and feet brown or grey. (*A. b. suahelicus* is a common resident on Pemba Island.)

5 EURASIAN REED WARBLER *Acrocephalus scirpaceus fuscus* **Page 559**
Palearctic migrant, October–May, in scrub and cultivation, as well as moist thickets and reedbeds. Common in Lake Victoria basin. Slight rufous tinge to rump, broken eye-ring. Tarsi variable. See text.

6 GREATER SWAMP WARBLER *Acrocephalus rufescens ansorgei* **Page 560**
Locally common resident of papyrus swamps around Lake Victoria. Large, long-billed; drab brown above, brownish grey below; feet large.

7 BROAD-TAILED WARBLER *Schoenicola brevirostris alexinae* **Page 569**
Uncommon in wet grassland, moist meadows. Skulking. Tail large and graduated.

8 MARSH WARBLER *Acrocephalus palustris* **Page 560**
Palearctic migrant, common November to early January in bush and scrub. Less numerous April–May. Some winter. Rare west of Rift Valley. More olive-brown than Eurasian Reed Warbler, seldom with rufescent tones. Pale throat may contrast with buffier breast. Tarsi pinkish brown, usually paler than in No. 5.

9 CINNAMON BRACKEN WARBLER *Bradypterus cinnamomeus* **Page 568**
Locally common in undergrowth of highland-forest clearings, brushy edges, bracken and bamboo. Rufous-brown above, on flanks and on breast. Superciliary stripe prominent.

10 AFRICAN MOUSTACHED WARBLER *Melocichla m. mentalis* **Page 568**
Uncommon in rank streamside vegetation. Skulking except when singing. Shy. Pale eye, black malar mark, heavy bill.

11 LITTLE RUSH WARBLER *Bradypterus baboecala* **Page 566**
Fairly common in reedbeds, swamps and along streams. Variable streaks on throat and upper breast; tail broad. Two populations, with different songs (see text).
11a. Adult *B. b. elgonensis*. Whitish below, streaks few, restricted. (Adult *B. b. moreaui* darker, duller brown, less rufous, above.)
11b. Juvenile *B. b. moreaui*. Yellowish wash below, streaking heavier.

12 EVERGREEN FOREST WARBLER *Bradypterus lopezi mariae* **Page 567**
Skulking resident of montane-forest undergrowth. (Somewhat brighter race *usambarae* in Taita Hills, the Pare and Usambara Mts.) Creeps through low vegetation with tail elevated. Difficult to see, but quite vocal. Dark breast/throat streaking often obsolete. Tail generally worn, the feathers pointed.

13 WHITE-WINGED WARBLER *Bradypterus carpalis* **Page 567**
Locally common in interior of papyrus swamps around Lake Victoria. Forages low.

DALE A. ZIMMERMAN
1988

PLATE 96: WARBLERS (palearctic migrants except Nos. 1–3)

1 BROWN WOODLAND WARBLER *Phylloscopus umbrovirons mackenzianus* **Page 566**
Fairly common in montane forest, bamboo, giant heath. Arboreal and in undergrowth. Warm brown, with yellow-olive wing and tail edgings.

2 UGANDA WOODLAND WARBLER *Phylloscopus budongoensis* **Page 565**
Fairly common in Kakamega and Nandi Forests, w. Kenya. Arboreal. Striped face.

3 GREEN HYLIA *Hylia p. prasina* **Page 566**
Uncommon in Kakamega and Nandi Forests, w. Kenya. In low trees and undergrowth. Heavier, darker than Uganda Woodland Warbler, but similar head pattern.

4 WILLOW WARBLER *Phylloscopus trochilus* **Page 565**
Common September to early May, in woodland, forest edge and tall bush. Most numerous March–April. Often in acacias. Superciliary stripe conspicuous. Tarsus colour varies, but usually pale yellowish brown. Commonly pumps tail up and down. **4a.** *P. t. yakutensis*. Greyish above, dull white below. **4b.** *P. t. acredula*, **spring male**. Brownish olive (some individuals green) above, dull yellow or yellowish of throat/breast blends with dull white of belly. **4c.** *P. t. acredula*, **first-winter**. Brighter yellow below than adult, often brighter olive-brown above.

5 CHIFFCHAFF *Phylloscopus collybita abietinus* **Page 564**
Uncommon November to early March, in montane forest. Browner and buffier, somewhat shorter and rounder-headed than Willow Warbler. Tarsi typically dark.

6 WOOD WARBLER *Phylloscopus sibilatrix* **Page 564**
Scarce, November–April, in wooded areas at moderate elevations. Larger than Willow Warbler and Chiffchaff; bright yellowish green above; yellow of face and breast sharply separated from clear white belly. Wings longer, tail shorter than in Willow Warbler.

7 ICTERINE WARBLER *Hippolais icterina* **Page 563**
Uncommon, October–April, in open woodland, bush and gardens, mainly in or west of Rift Valley. Prominent wing panel in fresh plumage; long-winged. **7a. Spring male**. Yellow superciliary stripe and underparts. **7b. First-winter male**. Greyish; faint yellowish tinge on most birds.

8 UPCHER'S WARBLER *Hippolais languida* **Page 561**
Uncommon, November–April, mainly in dry bush east of Rift Valley. Larger, paler and greyer than Olivaceous Warbler, with heavier blackish tail; prominent wing panel in fresh plumage. Tarsi pinkish grey.

9 OLIVACEOUS WARBLER *Hippolais pallida elaeica* **Page 561**
Common, late October to April, in bush, woodland and trees along dry watercourses. Grey-brown above, no wing panel, often cream on breast. Long bill pinkish or pale orange below. **9a. Adult winter. 9b. First-winter** (Oct.–Dec.).

10 OLIVE-TREE WARBLER *Hippolais olivetorum* **Page 562**
Uncommon, October to early December and March–April, in dry open woodland and bush. A few winter. Large; very long bill bright orange or yellow towards base below; feet grey. Superciliary stripe shorter, cheeks darker than in Upcher's and Olivaceous Warblers.

11 GARDEN WARBLER *Sylvia borin woodwardi* **Page 564**
Fairly common, late October–April, in moist bush, woodland and forest edge. Plain brownish, with stubby bill, faint superciliary stripe and narrow pale eye-ring.

12 COMMON WHITETHROAT *Sylvia communis icterops* **Page 563**
Locally common, October–April, in dry woodland and bush. **12a. Female**. Sandy wing edgings, white eye-ring; tail white-edged. Iris colour varies from pale yellowish to brown. **12b. Male**. White throat and eye-ring. Iris yellow, ochre or red-brown.

13 BARRED WARBLER *Sylvia n. nisoria* **Page 563**
Common, October–April, in dry scrub, woodland and thickets. **13a. Male**. Large; variably barred; iris yellow. Some birds paler than figured. **13b. Female**. Large; brownish grey with light feather edges; yellowish iris. Barring distinct or lacking (as in immature, which may be brown-eyed).

14 BLACKCAP *Sylvia atricapilla dammholzi* **Page 564**
Common, late October to early April, in woodland, forest edge and cultivation. **14a. Male**. Grey or olive-grey, with solid black cap. **14b. Female**. Olive-brown above, with rufous-brown cap, white lower eyelid.

15 GRASSHOPPER WARBLER *Locustella naevia* **Page 558**
Vagrant. Streaky brown skulker with broad tail, slim pointed bill; very long, narrowly streaked under tail-coverts.

16 RIVER WARBLER *Locustella fluviatilis* **Page 557**
Fairly common in e. Kenya, Nov.–Jan. and late March to April, in green bush and thickets. Skulking. Plain brown above, with broad rounded tail; long dark under tail-coverts pale tipped; throat streaked.

17 SAVI'S WARBLER *Locustella luscinioides fusca* **Page 558**
Vagrant. Darker and warmer brown than River Warbler. Plain throat often bordered by necklace of faint spots; superciliary stripe indistinct.

18 SEDGE WARBLER *Acrocephalus schoenobaenus* **Page 558**
Common, November to early May, in scrub and low vegetation along lake edges or (especially spring) in drier habitats. Streaked above; bold cream-coloured superciliary stripe.

Dale A. Zimmerman
1988

PLATE 97: UNSTREAKED CISTICOLAS

1 SINGING CISTICOLA *Cisticola cantans pictipennis*   **Page 571**
Common in leafy vegetation, gardens and hedges in the highlands. Rufous wing panel and crown contrast with greyish back; loral spot dark. (Juvenile has greyer loral area, largely ochre-yellow bill.)

2 RED-PATE CISTICOLA *Cisticola ruficeps mongalla*   **Page 574**
Nw. Kenya only. Local in grassy bush near Lokichokio. Larger and longer-tailed than Tiny Cisticola, with relatively larger bill. **Breeding plumage** figured. (See Plate 98 for non-breeding adult.)

3 TINY CISTICOLA *Cisticola nanus*   **Page 574**
Uncommon in dry bush country in and east of Rift Valley. Very small and short-tailed. **3a. Adult male**. Rufous cap, white loral line; back streaks fainter with wear. **3b. Juvenile**. Rufous-tinted throughout; bill ochre.

4 LONG-TAILED or TABORA CISTICOLA *Cisticola angusticaudus*   **Page 574**
Sw. Kenya and n. Serengeti NP. Uncommon and local in open *Acacia* woodland. Prinia-like, with long slender tail, rufous cap.

5 RED-FACED CISTICOLA *Cisticola erythrops sylvia*   **Page 571**
Widespread; locally common in rank undergrowth in moist hollows and near water. **5a. Adult male**. Resembles Singing Cisticola, but face reddish, no rufous wing panel. **5b. Adult female, rufous extreme**. Rufous below, with whitish throat. **5c. Juvenile**. Some ochre on bill; tail spots distinct from below.

6 RATTLING CISTICOLA *Cisticola chiniana heterophrys*   **Page 577**
Common along coast and inland to East Usambara Mts, in varied habitats. (See Plate 98 for heavily streaked inland races.) Nearly plain above, the back with narrow dark shaft streaks; wing edgings and crown more rufous than back.

7 HUNTER'S CISTICOLA *Cisticola hunteri*   **Page 573**
Common at high elevations (typically above 2400 m) in brushy places, bracken, forest edge. Dark and drab, with obscurely streaked back, often very grey below; dark-lored. Indulges in animated duet or group singing. **7a. Adult**. Loral spot dark grey, not black as in Chubb's Cisticola; crown dull. **7b. Juvenile**. Duller and rustier above, paler below than adult; bill yellow-ochre; tail spots well defined (unlike Chubb's).

8 CHUBB'S CISTICOLA *Cisticola c. chubbi*   **Page 573**
Locally common in w. Kenya, in shrubbery and thickets near forest edge. **8a. Adult**. Reddish-brown cap, black loral spot, plain back, long tail. **8b. Juvenile**. More uniformly coloured above; bill yellowish.

9 TRILLING CISTICOLA *Cisticola w. woosnami*   **Page 572**
Sw. Kenya, southeast in Tanzania to Lake Manyara NP, Arusha and Moshi Districts. Locally common in grassy bush and savanna. Stocky and dull. **9a. Adult female**. Plain except for tail spots, conspicuous in flight; crown dull chestnut-brown. Bill heavy and well curved, greyish pink below. **9b. Adult male**. Bill rather large, greyish below; little contrast between back and dull chestnut crown, wing edgings. Trilling song. **9c. Juvenile**. Rufous, with grey eyes, yellow-ochre bill (smaller than that of juvenile Whistling Cisticola); crown can be rufous.

10 SIFFLING CISTICOLA *Cisticola b. brachypterus*   **Page 579**
Fairly common and widespread in bush, savanna, woodland clearings. **Breeding adult** is small, drab, a few obscure back streaks, sometimes nearly plain. (See also Plate 99.)

11 FOXY CISTICOLA *Cisticola troglodytes*   **Page 573**
Northwestern Kenya; rare and local. Small and rufous, similar to larger juvenile Whistling Cisticola, including grey eye, but bill brownish pink. (Juvenile Foxy is duller above, yellowish below.)

12 WHISTLING CISTICOLA *Cisticola lateralis antinorii*   **Page 572**
W. Kenya. Scarce and local in forest edge, woodland and bush. **12a. Adult male**. Large, bulky, plain. Like Trilling Cisticola, but darker, duller, dusky-crowned, larger-billed; clear whistling song. **12b. Adult female**. Plain, smaller than male; bill pinkish with brown culmen. **12c. Juvenile female** (male similar but much larger). Rufous, with grey eye. Bill heavy, yellowish.

13 ROCK CISTICOLA *Cisticola aberrans*   **Page 572**
Very local on rock outcrops, boulder-strewn hillsides in se. and sw. Kenya, n. Tanzania. Runs mouse-like over bare rock surfaces, around boulders in sparse vegetation; tail often elevated or in motion. Rufous pileum, prominent creamy-white superciliary stripe. **13a. *C. a. teitensis*, presumed non-breeding plumage** (type specimen figured). Se. Kenya, ne. Tanzania. Upperparts uniformly rufous-tinted, underparts rich buff. (Undescribed breeding dress may more closely resemble 13b.) **13b. *C. a. emini*, fresh breeding plumage** (presumably this race; no Kenyan specimen; illustration from photographs). Bill and loral spot blackish; noticeable eye-ring; rufous crown and nape contrast with brown back, rump and upper tail-coverts; underparts white or buff, greyish on sides.

Dale A. Zimmerman
1986

PLATE 98: LARGER STREAKED CISTICOLAS

1 RATTLING CISTICOLA *Cisticola chiniana*   **Page 577**
Common and widespread in dry shrubby habitats. Sexes similar in plumage, but males larger than females. Heavily streaked above, usually including crown (but see *C. c. heterophrys* on Plate 97); bill strong. **1a. *C. c. ukamba*, male**. Kenyan highlands and Rift Valley north of Nairobi. **1b. *C. c. humilis*, female**. Southern Kenyan/n.Tanzanian highlands; duller, but boldly marked. **1c. *C. c. victoria*, female**. W. Kenya to Serengeti NP. Less patterned; crown nearly plain. **1d. *C. c. victoria*, male**. **1e. *C. c. humilis*, juvenile**. Yellowish below. Bill smaller than that of Croaking Cisticola. Back less boldly streaked than in young Winding and Levaillant's Cisticolas.

2 WINDING CISTICOLA *Cisticola galactotes*   **Page 575**
Common and widespread. Slimmer, smaller billed than Rattling Cisticola; boldly streaked. **2a. *C. g. haematocephalus*, adult female**. Coastal race; in varied habitats; pale lores, rufous wing panel, dull crown. **2b. *C. g. amphilectus*, breeding adult**. Inland, typically near water or in low damp areas. Bright crown and nape, grey-and-black or rufous-and-black tail. Breeding adult, with black-streaked grey back, plain rufous crown and wing patch; tail greyish centrally. **2c. *C. g. amphilectus*, non-breeding adult**. As 2b, but buff-and-black streaks, streaked crown, rufous-and-black tail. **2d. *C. g. amphilectus*, juvenile**. Similar to 2c, but faintly yellow below; tail colour intermediate between 2b and 2c.

3 CARRUTHERS'S CISTICOLA *Cisticola carruthersi*   **Page 575**
Lake Victoria papyrus swamps. Like Winding Cisticola (*C. g. amphilectus*), but tail blackish, bill smaller, and wing edgings brown, not rufous.

4 LYNES'S or WAILING CISTICOLA *Cisticola (lais) distinctus*   **Page 577**
Locally common on rocky brushy hillsides and in ravines from Laikipia Plateau and cent. Rift Valley to e. Serengeti. Underparts and face rufous-tinted.

5 BORAN CISTICOLA *Cisticola b. bodessa*   **Page 578**
Locally common in n. Kenya in scrub and on rocky, grassy hillsides and slopes. Duller than Rattling Cisticola and crown essentially unstreaked.

6 LEVAILLANT'S CISTICOLA *Cisticola tinniens*   **Page 575**
Local in highland swamps and marshes. Slim; bright rufous-and-black upperparts. **6a. Adult**. Head unstreaked; back heavily streaked (sometimes nearly solid black). **6b. Juvenile**. Yellowish below; crown and nape streaked.

7 STOUT CISTICOLA *Cisticola robustus*   **Page 576**
Common in grassland. Stocky build, boldly streaked back, unstreaked bright rufous nape; pronounced sexual size difference. **7a. Adult male**. Heavy-bodied; rather short tail. **7b. Juvenile**. Bright yellow below, crown and forehead greenish-tinted; upperparts decidedly rufous. **7c. Adult female**. Much smaller than male.

8 ABERDARE CISTICOLA *Cisticola aberdare*   **Page 576**
Locally common in moist highland grassland (above 2300 m) near Molo, Mau Narok and Aberdare Mts. Like Stout Cisticola, but somewhat darker, with streaked nape. **Adult male** figured. (Female similar but much smaller, rufous of nape may not extend onto back.)

9 RED-PATE CISTICOLA *Cisticola ruficeps mongalla*   **Page 574**
Local in grassy bush near Lokichokio in nw. Kenya. **Non-breeding female** figured. (Male similar, slightly larger.) Top of head and nape rufous; distinct white superciliary stripe; bill relatively long. (For breeding adult, see Plate 97.)

10 CROAKING CISTICOLA *Cisticola natalensis*   **Page 576**
Uncommon and local in open wooded habitats and tall grass with shrubs. Heavy bill. Some birds have plumages intermediate between those figured. **10a. *C. n. kapitensis*, adult male, perennial plumage**. Tail relatively short; suggestion of rufous on nape. **10b. *C. n. kapitensis*, immature female**. Buff-and-black streaks; long tail; bill and feet yellowish. (Adults in non-breeding plumage similar but paler, with pinkish bill and feet.) **10c. *C. n. strangei*, adult male, perennial plumage**. Dull; lores grey or dusky; short-tailed. Some individuals paler and greyer on sides of crown, neck and back.

DALE A ZIMMERMAN
1987

PLATE 99: SMALLER STREAKED CISTICOLAS

1 SIFFLING CISTICOLA *Cisticola brachypterus*   **Page 579**
Fairly common in shrubby grassland savanna and bush. Dull, often indistinctly streaked.
1a. *C. b. brachypterus*, non-breeding. W. Kenya. Heavily streaked back; crown mottled; nape not streaked. (Breeding plumage on Plate 97.)
1b. *C. b. katonae*. Widespread in highlands. Nape not streaked. (*C. b. kericho* is similar but less heavily streaked.)
1c. *C. b. reichenowi*. Coastal. Plainer, slightly reddish, unstreaked crown; back faintly streaked.
1d. *C. b. katonae*, juvenile. Similar to adult, but washed yellowish below and grey-eyed; bill more yellowish; tail longer than in adults.

2 TANA RIVER CISTICOLA *Cisticola restrictus*   **Page 578**
Rare; lower Tana River only. Suggests Lynes's and Ashy Cisticolas. Sides grey; tail-feather tips red-brown or buff (not white); crown more reddish brown. See text.

3 ASHY CISTICOLA *Cisticola cinereolus*   **Page 579**
Common in low scrub and bush in dry areas, mainly east of Rift Valley.
3a. Juvenile. Faintly yellow on face and breast; grey-eyed, ochre-billed.
3b. Adult. Pale, generally greyish, uniformly streaked above.

4 ZITTING CISTICOLA *Cisticola juncidis uropygialis*   **Page 580**
Local in low grassy areas, especially near lakes. Bright rump, pale collar contrasts with back and crown.
4a. Female. Less contrast above, more whitish below than male.
4b. Non-breeding adult. Plumage acquired by some birds in south-cent. Kenya. Longer-tailed, brighter above.
4c. Juvenile. Rufous-tinged above, yellowish below.

5 BLACK-BACKED CISTICOLA *Cisticola e. eximius*   **Page 580**
Formerly in low grasslands in w. Kenya. Now very rare or extirpated.
5a. Juvenile. Yellowish below; similar to juvenile *ayresii* but paler, with dark subloral spot.
5b. Breeding male. Stub-tailed, bright rufous on rump and flanks; back boldly streaked; crown plain, lores dark.
5c. Non-breeding adult. Streaked crown, pale loral area. (Male longer-tailed.)

6 PECTORAL-PATCH CISTICOLA *Cisticola brunnescens*   **Page 581**
Widespread and locally common in grasslands from 1400 to 2000 m in Kenya, up to 2500 in n. Tanzania. Heavily streaked above; white-tipped short tail obvious in flight.
6a. *C. b. hindei*, non-breeding male.
6b. *C. b. nakuruensis*, breeding male. Plain rufous crown centre, black subloral spot; often has dark smudge on side of breast.
6c. *C. b. nakuruensis*, non-breeding male. Uniformly streaked above (may show faint collar); pectoral patch often lacking; no subloral spot. (For juvenile, see text.)

7 DESERT CISTICOLA *Cisticola aridulus tanganyika*   **Page 580**
Widespread, often common on dry, short-grass plains.
7a. Juvenile. White below, unlike Pectoral-patch and Wing-snapping Cisticolas.
7b and 7c. Adults. Similar to non-breeding Pectoral-patch Cisticola, but tail longer, rump unstreaked rusty buff.

8 WING-SNAPPING CISTICOLA *Cisticola ayresii mauensis*   **Page 581**
Locally common in Kenyan grassland above 2150 m. Replaces Pectoral-patch at high elevations. (Formerly rare down to 1700 m on Ngong Hills.) Much darker and brighter above; rump rustier than rest of upper parts.
8a. Juvenile.
8b. Breeding male. Often black-crowned.
8c. Non-breeding male. More uniformly streaked; resembles Pectoral-patch, but rump reddish.
8d. Adult female. Generally darker above.

1a
1b
1c
2
1d
4c
3a
3b
4b
4a
5a
5b
5c
6a
8a
7a
7b
7c
6b
6c
8b
8c
8d

DALE ZIMMERMAN
1987

PLATE 100: AFRICAN WARBLERS (*Apalis* and relatives)

1 GREY APALIS *Apalis c. cinerea*   Page 585
Widespread and common in forest and forest-edge trees. **1a. Adult**. Back grey, outer rectrices white, tail appears all white from below. **1b. Juvenile**. Olive-brown above; dull yellow below, darker on throat.

2 BUFF-THROATED APALIS *Apalis rufogularis nigrescens*   Page 585
Locally common in w. Kenyan forests. In canopy, often with mixed-species flocks. **2a. Female**. Buff or pale tawny on throat, upper breast; tail all white from below. **2b. Male**. Blackish brown above, creamy white below; underside of tail white.

3 BAR-THROATED APALIS *Apalis thoracica*   Page 587
Local in forest trees and undergrowth. **3a. *A. t. fuscigularis***. Taita Hills. Dark throat, grey back. **3b. *A. t. griseiceps***. Chyulu Hills and n. Tanzania. White throat, narrow breast band; yellow-green back.

4 CHESTNUT-THROATED APALIS *Apalis p. porphyrolaema*   Page 585
Fairly common in forest trees at high elevations. Chestnut throat, underside of tail largely dark.

5 BLACK-HEADED APALIS *Apalis melanocephala*   Page 586
Common in forest trees in e. and cent. Kenya and n. Tanzania. Dark above; tail long, most feathers white-tipped. **5a. Male *A. m. nigrodorsalis***. Uncommon in cent. Kenyan highlands. **5b. Female *A. m. melanocephala***. Common in coastal forest and along lower Tana River. (*A. m. moschi* common in n. Tanzanian forests.)

6 BROWN-HEADED APALIS *Apalis alticola*   Page 586
Fairly common in forest edges of the Nguruman Hills in se. Kenya, also at Loliondo, Crater and Mbulu Highlands of n. Tanzania. Resembles Grey Apalis, but underside of tail grey with white feather tips.

7 WHITE-WINGED APALIS *Apalis c. chariessa*   Page 587
Very rare in riparian trees along lower Tana River. **7a. Male**. Glossy blue-black, with white wing panel; throat white. **7b. Female**. Olive-backed, with white wing panel; throat grey.

8 BLACK-THROATED APALIS *Apalis j. jacksoni*   Page 586
Fairly common in Kenyan highlands, mostly in forest-edge trees. **8a. Male**. Black face and throat, with bold white stripes from bill. **8b. Female**. Largely grey head with white facial stripes.

9 BLACK-COLLARED APALIS *Apalis p. pulchra*   Page 587
Fairly common in Kenyan highland-forest undergrowth and at edges. Wags tail constantly.

10 YELLOW-BREASTED APALIS *Apalis flavida*   Page 584
Common and widespread in open wooded habitats. **10a. Male *A. f. golzi***. Distinct black breast spot (lacking or faint in female). **10b. Female *A. f. pugnax***. Longer-tailed than *golzi*; breast spot indistinct or lacking in female (but pronounced in male); broad yellow tail-feather tips. **10c. Juvenile *A. f. flavocincta***. N. Kenya. Upperside of tail brown, not olive-green as in southern races; no black on breast; head may be brownish. (For other races, see text.)

11 BUFF-BELLIED WARBLER *Phyllolais pulchella*   Page 592
Fairly common in savanna and open woodland; partial to acacia trees. Pale buff underparts; white outer tail feathers; bill yellowish below.

12 RED-FRONTED WARBLER *Spiloptila rufifrons*   Page 588
Near ground in dry bush country. *Apalis*-like; wags long, often erect tail. **12a. Male *S. r. rufodorsalis***. Tsavo East NP. Rufous wash on back. **12b. Female *S. r. rufifrons***: N. Kenya to n. Tanzania, except in range of 12. Rufous crown contrasts with dull grey-brown back. **12c. Male *S. r. rufifrons***. Much like female, but blackish breast band in some adults.

13 GREY WREN-WARBLER *Calamonastes simplex*   Page 583
Widespread in low-elevation bush and dry woods, except in sw. Kenya and adjacent Tanzania. Constantly flirts tail. Tarsi and toes dark grey or blackish. Barring on underparts indistinct.

14 PALE WREN-WARBLER *Calamonastes undosus*   Page 583
Local in north-cent. Tanzania and north to Serengeti NP, Loliondo and Mara GR. Tarsi and toes pinkish orange; ventral barring conspicuous; limited tail action.

1a

2a

1b

2b

3a

4

5a

3b

6

5b

7a

8a

9

10a

10b

7b

8b

11

10c

12c

13

12a

12b

14

ALE A. ZIMMERMAN
1988

PLATE 101: AFRICAN WARBLERS (*Prinia, Parisoma et al.*)

1 BROWN PARISOMA *Parisoma lugens jacksoni* **Page 592**
Uncommon in Kenyan highlands and Crater Highlands of n. Tanzania. Favours acacia trees. Narrow white tail-feather edges and tips.

2 BANDED PARISOMA *Parisoma boehmi* **Page 592**
Fairly common in acacia trees. **2a. *P. b. boehmi*, adult male**. Black breast band, white wing-stripe; throat spots variable; eyes yellowish. **2b. *P. b. boehmi*, juvenile**. No breast band. Buff on sides, wing-bars; white-edged tail, dark eyes. **2c. *P. b. marsabit*, adult female**. Breast band incomplete. Paler than southern birds, very little buff below.

3 WHITE-CHINNED PRINIA *Prinia leucopogon reichenowi* **Page 583**
Common in undergrowth in w. Kenyan woodland and forest edge. Long-tailed; creamy-white throat contrasts with dark face.

4 TAWNY-FLANKED PRINIA *Prinia subflava melanorhyncha* **Page 582**
Common in scrub, woodland and brushy edge habitats. Tawny brown, with long slim tail; white superciliary stripe, dark loral spot. **4a. Breeding male**. Bill black. (Non-breeding birds have horn-coloured bill, longer tail, are darker above.) **4b. Juvenile**. Like non-breeding adult, but faintly yellowish below, more rufescent above.

5 PALE PRINIA *Prinia somalica* **Page 582**
Fairly common in semi-arid n. Kenya; scarce south to Tsavo East NP. Pale brownish-grey upperparts. **5a. Adult**. Creamy white below. **5b. Juvenile**. Pale buff on breast, more sandy brown above.

6 BANDED PRINIA *Prinia bairdii melanops* **Page 582**
Locally common in w. Kenyan forest undergrowth. **6a. Adult**. Barred below, long tail, yellowish eyes; white wing spots. **6b. Juvenile**. Browner, less blackish than adult, buff wing spots; only suggestion of bars below.

7 RED-WINGED WARBLER *Heliolais erythroptera rhodoptera* **Page 583**
Scarce and local in w. Kenya, fairly common in e. Tanzania; feeds in undergrowth, sings from trees. Prinia-like, with large bill, maroon-rufous wings. **7a. Breeding adult**. Greyish to grey-brown above; bill black. **7b. Non-breeding adult**. More rufous above; bill pale, tail longer.

8 BLACK-FACED RUFOUS WARBLER *Bathmocercus rufus vulpinus* **Page 568**
Common in forest undergrowth in w. Kenya. Skulking, but highly vocal. **8a. Adult female**. Olive-grey back, black face and throat. **8b. Adult male**. Largely rufous, with black face and line to belly. **8c. Juvenile male. 8d. Juvenile female**.

9 YELLOW-BELLIED HYLIOTA *Hyliota f. flavigaster* **Page 593**
Western: Mt Elgon/Kongelai Escarpment; Fort Ternan to Mara GR. Uncommon in savanna, woodland and tall bush. Arboreal. **9a. Male**. Glossy blue-black above, yellowish tawny below. **9b. Female**. Dark grey above, with faint bluish gloss on back and tail.

10 SOUTHERN HYLIOTA *Hyliota australis slatini* **Page 592**
Uncommon in Kakamega and Nandi Forests, w. Kenya. Arboreal. **10a. Male**. Dull black above; belly white. **10b. Female**. Brownish above. (Darker *H. a. usambarae* scarce in Usambara Mts, ne. Tanzania.)

11 KRETSCHMER'S LONGBILL *Macrosphenus k. kretschmeri* **Page 589**
Formerly in Kitovu Forest near Taveta, se. Kenya. Now apparently restricted to Usambara Mts in ne. Tanzania. Greenbul-like. Long slender bill black above, pale below.

12 GREY-CAPPED WARBLER *Eminia lepida* **Page 588**
Fairly common in dense tangled vegetation on river banks, in moist ravines, forest edges and cultivation. **Adult** bright olive-yellow above, with grey head, black eye-line and chestnut throat. Chestnut on bend of wing often concealed.

1

2a

2b

2c

3

4b

4a

5a

5b

6a

7a

7b

8a

9a

9b

8b

10a

11

10b

12

DALE ZIMMERMAN
1987

PLATE 102: AFRICAN WARBLERS, LITTLE YELLOW FLYCATCHER AND WHITE-EYES

1 YELLOW-BELLIED EREMOMELA *Eremomela icteropygialis abdominalis* **Page 590**
Uncommon in open woodland and bush. Avoids arid habitats. Yellow extends from middle underparts to vent. (Western *E. i. griseoflava* has yellow only on lower belly.)

2 YELLOW-VENTED EREMOMELA *Eremomela flavicrissalis* **Page 590**
Uncommon in arid scrub and semi-desert in n. and e. Kenya. In more extreme habitats than Yellow-bellied Eremomela. **2a. Adult**. Yellow (often pale) confined to extreme lower belly and vent region. No olive on lower back as in *E. i. griseoflava*. **2b. Juvenile**. Buff wing edgings. Yellow very faint and restricted.

3 GREEN-BACKED EREMOMELA *Eremomela pusilla canescens* **Page 591**
Western Kenya. Uncommon and local in savanna, open woodland and on shrubby slopes. Bright yellow belly, grey crown, narrow blackish face mask.

4 GREEN-CAPPED EREMOMELA *Eremomela scotops kikuyuensis* **Page 591**
Uncommon and local in wooded habitats. Arboreal. Greenish-olive forecrown, yellow throat and breast. (Entire underside pale yellow in coastal race *occipitalis*. *E. s. citriniceps* of sw. Kenya to Serengeti NP is brighter, but has greyish-white belly.)

5 TURNER'S EREMOMELA *Eremomela turneri* **Page 591**
Uncommon in canopy of Kakamega Forest, w. Kenya. **5a. Adult**. Black breast band, rufous forecrown. **5b. Juvenile**. Hint of breast band or none, pale yellow below, olive above, sometimes with rufous forehead. Tarsi and toes pink.

6 YELLOW-THROATED WOODLAND WARBLER *Phylloscopus ruficapillus minullus* **Page 566**
Common in forest remnants on Taita Hills and in ne. Tanzanian mountains. Tawny-brown crown, yellow face and under tail-coverts.

7 DARK-CAPPED YELLOW WARBLER *Chloropeta natalensis massaica* **Page 569**
Uncommon in low leafy vegetation in moist places from 1100 to 2300 m. Suggests flycatcher, with broad bill and rictal bristles, often upright posture. **7a. Adult**. Blackish crown, yellow underparts. **7b. Juvenile**. Blackish-brown crown; tawny-buff throughout.

8 MOUNTAIN YELLOW WARBLER *Chloropeta similis* **Page 570**
Largely replaces No. 7 at higher elevations (1850–3000+ m) mainly in forest-edge vegetation. Less fly-catcher-like and lacks dark crown of preceding species.

9 PAPYRUS YELLOW WARBLER *Chloropeta gracilirostris* **Page 569**
Scarce in papyrus swamps around Lake Victoria. Flanks russet brown, rump tinged rufous; toes and claws large and dark.

10 LITTLE YELLOW FLYCATCHER *Erythrocercus holochlorus* **Page 598**
Common in coastal Kenyan lowlands, Shimba Hills and East Usambara Mts. Arboreal. Tiny, warbler-like; bright yellow underparts, narrow yellowish eye-ring.

11 MONTANE WHITE-EYE *Zosterops poliogaster* **Page 594**
Common in highland forest. Polytypic; eye-ring broad in all races. **11a. Z. p. silvanus**. Taita Hills and Mt Kasigau. Much grey below (female paler). **11b. Z. p. kulalensis**, **male**. Mt Kulal, n. Kenya. Yellow mid-ventral streak. **11c. Z. p. mbuluensis**. Mostly Tanzanian. In Kenya only in Chyulu Hills and Ol Doinyo Orok. Yellow forehead blends with yellowish-green crown. **11d and 11e. Z. p. kikuyuensis**. Cent. Kenyan highlands. Yellow forehead contrasts with crown. (For Tanzanian *Z. p. eurycricotus*, see Plate 124.)

12 YELLOW WHITE-EYE *Zosterops senegalensis* **Page 594**
Common in wooded habitats above 1500 m (to 3400 m on Mt Elgon in moorland). Narrow eye-ring and restricted yellow forehead band. Darker than Abyssinian White-eye, and greenish on sides and flanks. **12a. Z. s. jacksoni**. Widespread in Kenyan highlands. **12b. Z. s. jacksoni/stuhlmanni intergrade**. Kakamega Forest, w. Kenya. Plumage variable. (*Z. s. stierlingi* of Usambara Mts is darker on flanks, deeper yellow on belly.)

13 ABYSSINIAN WHITE-EYE *Zosterops abyssinicus flavilateralis* **Page 593**
Locally common in bush, savanna, forest edge and gardens. Widespread in and east of Rift Valley (common in Nairobi suburbs). Small and pale; eye-ring narrow; no obvious black loral area, no greenish wash on sides. (Far-northern *Z. a. jubaensis* is greyer above.)

DALE A. ZIMMERMAN

PLATE 103: AFRICAN WARBLERS (crombecs, camaropteras), TITS AND CREEPER

1 SOMALI LONG-BILLED CROMBEC *Sylvietta isabellina*　　　**Page 589**
Uncommon in dry scrub and bush in n. and e. Kenya. Pale coloration; bill nearly as long as head.

2 RED-FACED CROMBEC *Sylvietta whytii jacksoni*　　　**Page 589**
Fairly common in open woodland, bush and savanna, in moister areas than No. 3. No facial stripes; face and underparts uniform buffy rufous. (Coastal *S. w. minima* and northwestern *S. w. abayensis* more olive-brown above.)

3 NORTHERN CROMBEC *Sylvietta brachyura leucopsis*　　　**Page 589**
Fairly common in dry open woodland and bush, less so in the highlands. Facial stripes; throat and much of face whitish. (Superciliary stripe pale tawny in western *S. b. carnapi*.)

4 WHITE-BROWED CROMBEC *Sylvietta l. leucophrys*　　　**Page 590**
Local and uncommon in forest and bamboo in the Kenyan highlands. Greenish wings, brown cap, bold white superciliary stripe. **4a. Adult**. Throat and breast whitish to pale grey. **4b. Immature**. Throat, breast and sides olive-brown; belly yellow; eyebrow tinged greenish yellow.

5 GREEN CROMBEC *Sylvietta virens baraka*　　　**Page 590**
Locally common in dense bush and second-growth riparian woods near Ugandan border in Busia and Mumias Districts. Dull greyish-olive back, olive wings, grey-brown breast band and narrow whitish superciliary stripe.

6 GREY-BACKED CAMAROPTERA *Camaroptera brachyura*　　　**Page 584**
Common in forest, dense bush, garden shrubbery. Bright yellow-green wings; back usually grey or brownish, sometimes olive; underparts vary. **6a. Adult, *C. b. tincta***. W. Kenya. Throat, breast and back grey. (Some birds paler grey on throat and breast.) **6b. Immature, *C. b. erlangeri***. Coastal Kenya and interior ne. Tanzania. Upperparts olive, breast pale yellowish. **6c. Immature, *C. b. abessinica***. N. Kenya. Brownish above and on breast; flanks faintly barred. (Adult greyer, lacks barring.)

7 OLIVE-GREEN CAMAROPTERA *Camaroptera chloronota toroensis*　　　**Page 584**
Common in forest undergrowth and vines in Kakamega and Nandi Forests, w. Kenya. **7a. Immature**. Dark-chested extreme figured; some birds paler, more yellowish. **7b. Adult**. Pale tawny about face and on breast; throat white.

8 AFRICAN PENDULINE TIT *Anthoscopus caroli*　　　**Page 597**
Uncommon in open woodland, savanna and forest edge in areas of moderate to high rainfall. Tiny; bill sharp and conical; tail short. Darker than No. 9, forehead paler than crown. Variable. **8a. *A. c. sylviella***. Interior e. Kenya to Longido and Kibaya in n. Tanzania. Grey above, buff or rusty below; forehead usually buff, sometimes whitish. (*A. c. sharpei* near Lake Victoria similar, but darker below, with whitish forehead.) **8b. *A. c. robertsi***. Se. Kenya to Masai Steppe in Tanzania. Greyish olive above, pale yellowish to pale ochre-buff on belly and crissum. **8c. *A. c. roccattii***. W. Kenya. Olive above, with yellow forehead, dull yellow below.

9 MOUSE-COLOURED PENDULINE TIT *Anthoscopus musculus*　　　**Page 596**
Uncommon in bush, savanna and open woodland in semi-arid areas. Bill conical, sharp. Bright extreme shown; some birds nearly white below.

10 WHITE-BELLIED TIT *Parus albiventris*　　　**Page 596**
Fairly common in wooded habitats, including suburban gardens. Black, with white belly and wing markings. **10a. Juvenile**. Dull greyish black. **10b. Adult**. Glossy black.

11 NORTHERN GREY TIT *Parus thruppi barakae*　　　**Page 595**
Fairly common in dry n. and e. savanna and scrub. Black cap and bib contrast with whitish cheek.

12 RED-THROATED TIT *Parus fringillinus*　　　**Page 596**
Locally common in acacias in s. Kenya/n. Tanzania. Rufous-buff face and throat; much white in wing.

13 NORTHERN BLACK TIT *Parus leucomelas guineensis*　　　**Page 595**
Rare and sporadic in moist wooded areas of w. Kenya. Black, with white wing patch, yellow eye.

14 DUSKY TIT *Parus funereus*　　　**Page 596**
Fairly common in Kakamega and Nandi Forests, w. Kenya. Arboreal. Usually with mixed-species flocks. Dull blackish throughout; eye red.

15 SPOTTED CREEPER *Salpornis spilonota salvadori*　　　**Page 598**
Rare and local in acacias near Kapenguria, nw. Kenya. Plumage spotted and barred; creeps on tree trunks.

PLATE 104: LONG-TAILED SUNBIRDS (mostly males; for females, see Plate 107) (Pectoral tufts often wholly or partly concealed)

1 **MALACHITE SUNBIRD** *Nectarinia famosa cupreonitens*   **Page 649**
Highland-forest edge, open areas; mostly above 1800 m.
1a. Non-breeding male. (Birds in moult may show dark mid-ventral line, scattered shiny feathers.)
1b. Breeding male. Yellow pectoral tufts.

2 **SCARLET-TUFTED MALACHITE SUNBIRD** *Nectarinia j. johnstoni*   **Page 649**
Mainly on moorlands (above 3000 m), lower in cool wet seasons. Darker, bluer green than Malachite Sunbird, with scarlet pectoral tufts; very long central rectrices.
2a. Breeding male.
2b. Immature male. Variable; mostly greyish brown with limited green iridescence. Tail short.

3 **BRONZE SUNBIRD** *Nectarinia k. kilimensis*   **Page 648**
Common above 1200 m in gardens, cultivation, forest edge. **Adult male** with iridescent green head and breast, bronzy or brassy gloss.

4 **GOLDEN-WINGED SUNBIRD** *Nectarinia r. reichenowi*   **Page 649**
Highland-forest edge, cultivation; mostly above 1800 m, lower in wet season. Yellow wing and tail patches in all plumages.
4a. Breeding male. Velvety black with bronzy and coppery iridescence (lacking in non-breeding plumage).
4b. Adult female. Yellowish below, blackish face mask, short tail.

5 **TACAZZE SUNBIRD** *Nectarinia tacazze jacksoni*   **Page 648**
Highland forest, giant heath and gardens above 1800 m.
5a. Breeding male. Green to brassy-green head; ruby-violet iridescence on body.
5b. Non-breeding male. Mostly greyish, with black belly, dark face; shoulders, rump and upper tail-coverts metallic red-purple. Iridescence increases on head and body as moult progresses.

6 **BEAUTIFUL SUNBIRD** *Nectarinia pulchella*   **Page 650**
Common in dry acacia country.
6a. Juvenile male, *N. p. pulchella*. Nw. Kenya
6b. Non-breeding male, *N. p. pulchella*.
6c. Breeding male, *N. p. pulchella*. Green belly, yellow sides to breast.
6d. Breeding male, *N. p. melanogastra*. E. and s. Kenya, n. Tanzania. Black belly, yellow on breast.

7 **RED-CHESTED SUNBIRD** *Nectarinia erythrocerca*   **Page 650**
Lake Victoria basin. Fairly common.
7a. Adult male. Breast band darker, deeper red than in male Beautiful or Black-bellied Sunbirds; also larger, heavier.
7b. Juvenile male. Extent of black throat patch variable. Older immatures may show red or green feathers below.

8 **BLACK-BELLIED SUNBIRD** *Nectarinia nectarinioides*   **Page 650**
Locally common in dry eastern areas south to ne. Tanzania. Favours riverine acacias.
8a. Adult male, *N. n. nectarinioides*. Southern. Orange-red breast band. (Beautiful Sunbird shows much more yellow.) Intergrades with 8b along Northern Uaso Nyiro River.
8b. Adult male, *N. n. erlangeri*. N. Kenya. Lacks yellow pectoral tufts; breast band pure red.

DALE A. ZIMMERMAN
1991

PLATE 105: SUNBIRDS (See also Plates 104, 106 and 107)

1 PYGMY SUNBIRD *Anthreptes p. platurus* **Page 640**
Northwestern Kenya. Irregular in arid and semi-arid bush country. **Adult male**. (Female on Plate 107.)

2 COLLARED SUNBIRD *Anthreptes collaris garguensis* **Page 640**
Common in forest and forest edges. **2a. Male. 2b. Female.**

3 VARIABLE SUNBIRD *Nectarinia venusta* **Page 643**
Widespread in bush, forest edge, cultivation and gardens. **3a. *N. v. falkensteini*, breeding male.** Common throughout except in ne. Kenya; intensity of yellow varies. **3b. *N. v. albiventris*, breeding male.** Common in arid ne. Kenya. **3c. *N. v. falkensteini*, immature male**. (Juvenile male also black-throated but lacks iridescence.)

4 ORANGE-TUFTED SUNBIRD *Nectarinia bouvieri* **Page 647**
Scarce at forest edge and in moist scrub in w. Kenya. **4a. Adult male.** Orange pectoral tufts (not always visible), violet forehead, blue chin. **4b. Immature male.** Long bill, coppery/green wing- and upper tail-coverts.

5 MARICO SUNBIRD *Nectarinia mariquensis suahelica* **Page 645**
Common and widespread in bush, savanna, open woodland. **5a. Adult male.** Broad maroon breast band; larger bill than Purple-banded Sunbird. **5b. Juvenile male.** Yellow primary edges; mottled breast and sides.

6 PURPLE-BANDED SUNBIRD *Nectarinia bifasciata* **Page 645**
N. b. tsavoensis. Common in dry se. bush, but not the coastal strip. **6a. Immature male.**
6b. Adult male. Much narrower maroon breast band than in *N. b. microrhyncha*. Also smaller and smaller-billed than Violet-breasted Sunbird. **6c. Female.** (Some lack black throat; see Plate 107.) *N. b. microrhyncha*. Common along coast north to Malindi; scarce in west (Lake Victoria basin south to w. Serengeti NP). **6d. Breeding male.** Bill smaller than in Marico Sunbird. **6e. Non-breeding male.** Like black-throated female, but with green wing-coverts and dark wings. May show green throat feathers.

7 VIOLET-BREASTED SUNBIRD *Nectarinia chalcomelas* **Page 646**
Uncommon on n. Kenyan coast; scarce (seasonal?) inland to Tsavo, Bura, Galana Ranch. **Adult male** larger, heavier, longer-billed than Purple-banded Sunbird; large violet breast patch with no maroon along lower edge.

8 GREEN-HEADED SUNBIRD *Nectarinia verticalis viridisplendens* **Page 641**
Fairly common in w. and cent. Kenyan highlands in forest, riparian woods and gardens. Long, curved bill; iridescent head usually appears more blue than green. **8a. Adult male. 8b. Adult female. 8c. Juvenile male.** Blackish forehead, face and throat.

9 HUNTER'S SUNBIRD *Nectarinia hunteri* **Page 643**
Common in drier country than Scarlet-chested Sunbird. **9a. Immature male.** Throat and chin black (some metallic green at sides). **9b. Adult male.** Vivid scarlet breast with little blue iridescence; throat and chin black (shining green at sides); violet iridescence on 'shoulders' and rump. **9c. Juvenile female.** Yellowish below, with dark barring; pale throat, short eyebrow.

10 AMETHYST SUNBIRD *Nectarinia amethystina kalckreuthi* **Page 642**
Fairly common. Widespread in wooded habitats and gardens. **10a. Juvenile male.** Streaked yellowish underparts; black throat; long superciliary. **10b. Adult male.** Throat and 'shoulder' patch iridescent ruby, rose-violet or amethyst; forecrown green or turquoise. (Inland *N. a. kirkii* lacks metallic purple on upper tail-coverts.)

11 SCARLET-CHESTED SUNBIRD *Nectarinia senegalensis lamperti* **Page 642**
Common in gardens and open wooded habitats in moister areas than Hunter's Sunbird. **11a. Adult male.** Green chin and throat; red patch suffused with shining blue (visible at close range). **11b. Juvenile male.** Variable; usually whitish below and heavily barred; throat blackish; no superciliary stripe. **11c. Immature male.** Glittering green chin and throat; red patch shows more blue than in comparable plumage of Hunter's Sunbird.

12 GREEN-THROATED SUNBIRD *Nectarinia rubescens kakamegae* **Page 642**
Kakamega and Nandi Forests only; in canopy, often with mixed-species flocks. **Adult male** has narrow violet band below green gorget often not visible. (Female figured on Plate 107.)

ALE A. ZIMMERMAN
1992

PLATE 106: SUNBIRDS (adults, except as indicated) (See also Plates 104, 105 and 107)

1 AMANI SUNBIRD *Anthreptes pallidigaster* **Page 639**
Local in coastal *Brachystegia* woodland and East Usambara Mts. **1a. Female**. Plain, with blue-black tail. **1b. Male**. (Orange pectoral tufts not always visible.)

2 PLAIN-BACKED SUNBIRD *Anthreptes reichenowi yokanae* **Page 638**
Uncommon in coastal forest, Shimba Hills NP and East Usambara Mts. **2a. Male**. Black forehead and throat show blue gloss in bright light. **2b. Female**. Faint pale superciliary stripe; white eyelid feathering.

3 SUPERB SUNBIRD *Nectarinia superba buvuma* **Page 647**
Rare in Mumias and Busia Districts near Ugandan border. **3a. Female**. Large bill; long yellow superciliary stripe; belly and under tail-coverts yellow or yellow-orange. **3b. Male**. Blue crown; violet-blue and maroon underparts.

4 MOUSE-COLOURED SUNBIRD *Nectarinia veroxii fischeri* **Page 641**
Uncommon in coastal bush, thickets, mangroves and gardens. **Female**. Sexes similar. (Scarlet pectoral tufts not always visible).

5 OLIVE SUNBIRD *Nectarinia olivacea changamwensis* **Page 641**
Fairly common in forest, other wooded habitats. Yellow pectoral tufts in both sexes (lacking in females of inland race). **5a. Female. 5b. Male**.

6 GREEN SUNBIRD *Anthreptes rectirostris tephrolaemus* **Page 640**
Western Kenya. Uncommon in canopy of Kakamega, Nandi and Kericho Forests. **Male**. (Female on Plate 107.)

7 COPPER SUNBIRD *Nectarinia cuprea* **Page 647**
Common resident in bush, cultivation and forest edges in and near Lake Victoria basin. **Male**. (Female on Plate 107.)

8 SHINING SUNBIRD *Nectarinia habessinica turkanae* **Page 651**
Uncommon in dry northern Kenya; partial to acacias and flowering aloes. **Male**. Only far-northern sunbird with bright scarlet breast band. (Female on Plate 107.)

9 OLIVE-BELLIED SUNBIRD *Nectarinia chloropygia orphogaster* **Page 644**
Uncommon in w. Kenya below 1550 m, in bush, forest edge and cultivation. **Male**. Belly dark olive-brown; yellow tufts not always evident. (Female on Plate 107.)

10 EASTERN DOUBLE-COLLARED SUNBIRD *Nectarinia mediocris* **Page 644**
Fairly common in highland forest, gardens, bamboo and giant heath, 1850–3700 m. **Male**. Narrow scarlet breast band; longer tail, longer bill and slightly more golden-green than Northern Double-collared Sunbird; upper tail-coverts blue. (Female on Plate 107.)

11 NORTHERN DOUBLE-COLLARED SUNBIRD *Nectarinia preussi kikuyuensis* **Page 644**
Common in highlands, 1700–2800 m. Overlaps range of preceding species above 1800 m. **Male**. Broad scarlet breast band; tail and bill shorter than in Eastern Double-collared Sunbird; bluer green above; upper tail-coverts violet. (Female on Plate 107.)

12 EASTERN VIOLET-BACKED SUNBIRD *Anthreptes orientalis* **Page 639**
Widespread in dry bush and savanna below 1300 m. **12a. Male**. Rump blue-green; underparts snow-white. **12b. Female**. Underparts entirely white; tail dark blue with white feather tips. (Juvenile, not figured, similar, but belly faintly yellowish.)

13 ULUGURU VIOLET-BACKED SUNBIRD *Anthreptes neglectus* **Page 639**
Rare in coastal and Tana riverine forest, also in Shimba Hills. Fairly common in East Usambara Mts. **13a. Male**. Grey below; dull brown sides of face and collar. **13b. Female**. Iridescent violet crown and back; grey throat/breast, olive-yellow belly.

14 WESTERN VIOLET-BACKED SUNBIRD *Anthreptes l. longuemarei* **Page 638**
Scarce and local in w. Kenyan gardens, cultivation and forest edge in high-rainfall areas. **14a. Juvenile**. Underparts entirely pale yellow. **14b. Female**. Yellow belly; violet tail and upper tail-coverts. **14c. Male**. Upperparts uniformly violet.

1a

1b

2a

2b

3a

4

5a

3b

5b

6

7

8

9

10

12a

11

12b

13a

14a

13b

14b

14c

DALE A. ZIMMERMAN
1992

PLATE 107: DULL-PLUMAGED SUNBIRDS (Adult females except as indicated)

1 **OLIVE-BELLIED SUNBIRD** *Nectarinia chloropygia orphogaster* **Page 644**
Western Kenya. Local below 1550 m in bush and forest edge. Narrow pale superciliary stripes; obscure breast streaking; chin whitish.

2 **VARIABLE SUNBIRD** *Nectarinia venusta falkensteini* **Page 643**
Common, widespread below 3000 m in gardens, bush and cultivation. Olive-brown above; tail blue-black. (Female *N. v. albiventris* is grey-brown above, white below, with greyer breast.)

3 **NORTHERN DOUBLE-COLLARED SUNBIRD** *Nectarinia preussi kikuyuensis* **Page 644**
Common in Kenyan highlands, 1700–2800 m, in forest edge and gardens. Shorter bill and somewhat shorter tail than Eastern Double-collared Sunbird.

4 **EASTERN DOUBLE-COLLARED SUNBIRD** *Nectarinia m. mediocris* **Page 644**
Fairly common between 1850 and 3700 m in forest, subalpine vegetation, gardens. Similar to Northern Double-collared, but bill longer, more curved. (*N. m. usambarica* greener above, throat more streaked.)

5 **SHINING SUNBIRD** *Nectarinia habessinica turkanae* **Page 651**
Uncommon in arid n. Kenya. **5a. Female**. Pale brownish grey above; long bill. **5b. Juvenile male**. Like female, but with blackish throat patch.

6 **PYGMY SUNBIRD** *Anthreptes p. platurus* **Page 640**
Irregular in dry bush in nw. Kenya. Small size, short bill, yellow underparts.

7 **ORANGE-TUFTED SUNBIRD** *Nectarinia bouvieri* **Page 647**
Western Kenya. Scarce and local in forest edge in Busia/Kakamega Districts. Long, moderately curved bill; faint superciliary stripe.

8 **GREEN SUNBIRD** *Anthreptes rectirostris tephrolaemus* **Page 640**
Western Kenya. Mainly forest treetops. Plain, with yellowish superciliary stripe and faint pale mark under eye.

9 **VIOLET-BREASTED SUNBIRD** *Nectarinia chalcomelas* **Page 646**
Mainly in coastal shrub-savanna and thickets, inland to Galana Ranch and lower Tana River. Brownish grey above, plain below; primaries pale-edged.

10 **BEAUTIFUL SUNBIRD** *Nectarinia p. pulchella* **Page 650**
Common in dry country. Plain creamy-yellow underparts; dark lores and ear-coverts.

11 **BLACK-BELLIED SUNBIRD** *Nectarinia nectarinioides* **Page 650**
Locally common in dry country, especially in riverine acacias. **11a. Juvenile male**. Dusky throat bordered by pale yellowish stripes; breast and sides darkly mottled. **11b. Female**. Finely streaked underparts, often with trace of red or orange.

12 **PURPLE-BANDED SUNBIRD** *Nectarinia bifasciata* **Page 645**
Common in bush, scrub and gardens. Grey-brown above, well streaked below. **12a. N. b. tsavoensis**. Southeastern (but not coastal). **12b. N. b. microrhyncha**. Common along coast north to Malindi; scarce in Lake Victoria basin.

13 **RED-CHESTED SUNBIRD** *Nectarinia erythrocerca* **Page 650**
Lake Victoria shores and islands, east to Ruma NP, Ahero and Migori. Blue-black tail with slightly longer central feathers; mottled dusky below.

14 **GREEN-THROATED SUNBIRD** *Nectarinia rubescens kakamegae* **Page 642**
W. Kenya in Kakamega and Nandi forest canopy. Streaked underparts; dark brown back.

15 **COPPER SUNBIRD** *Nectarinia cuprea* **Page 647**
Fairly common in bush and cultivation in and near Lake Victoria basin. Faintly streaked breast; tail blue-black.

16 **MARICO SUNBIRD** *Nectarinia mariquensis osiris* **Page 645**
Widespread in open bush and savanna. Dark-streaked yellow underparts; throat pale yellow.

17 **AMETHYST SUNBIRD** *Nectarinia amethystina* **Page 642**
Widespread, fairly common in gardens, wooded habitats. Paler, less streaked below than Green-throated Sunbird; unlikely in western forests. **17a. N. a. kirkii**. Highlands. Throat streaked; superciliary short. **17b. N. a. kalckreuthi**. Coastal. Paler, with unstreaked throat, long superciliary stripe.

18 **HUNTER'S SUNBIRD** *Nectarinia hunteri* **Page 643**
Common in dry areas of n. and e. Kenya, ne. Tanzania. Underparts dull white, darkly mottled and barred.

19 **SCARLET-CHESTED SUNBIRD** *Nectarinia senegalensis lamperti* **Page 642**
Fairly common and widespread, except in dry areas; avoids forest. Underparts dull yellow, heavily marked. Throat darkly mottled or barred in fresh plumage.

20 **OLIVE SUNBIRD** *Nectarinia olivacea vincenti* **Page 641**
Fairly common in forest west of Rift Valley. Large bill; plain olive plumage. (This race lacks yellow pectoral tufts.)

21 **SCARLET-TUFTED MALACHITE SUNBIRD** *Nectarinia j. johnstoni* **Page 649**
Alpine moorlands above 3000 m. Brown; orange-red pectoral tufts; tail tips square, lacking white.

22 **TACAZZE SUNBIRD** *Nectarinia tacazze jacksoni* **Page 648**
Fairly common in wooded highlands above 1800 m. Dark facial mask bordered by pale stripe; greyish olive below.

23 **BRONZE SUNBIRD** *Nectarinia k. kilimensis* **Page 648**
Common and widespread in highland gardens, cultivation and forest edge. Resembles female Tacazze, but yellow below with diffuse dark streaks. **23a. Adult female**. **23b. Juvenile male**.

24 **MALACHITE SUNBIRD** *Nectarinia famosa cupreonitens* **Page 649**
Local in open areas and forest edge in highlands above 1800 m. **24a. Female**. Less yellow than Bronze Sunbird. Bill long, relatively straight. **24b. Juvenile**. More yellow below than adult; juvenile male may show blackish throat.

266

DALE A. ZIMMERMAN
1992

PLATE 108: SPARROWS, PETRONIA, SPECKLE-FRONTED WEAVER

1 CHESTNUT SPARROW *Passer eminibey*   Page 653
Locally common in bush and open wooded habitats.
1a. Male acquiring adult plumage. Largely chestnut. (Adult on Plate 115.)
1b. Female. Trace of chestnut above eye and on throat.

2 SOMALI SPARROW *Passer castanopterus fulgens*   Page 653
Locally common in villages and along watercourses in n. Kenya.
2a. Juvenile. Resembles female House Sparrow, but brighter above, darker below.
2b. Female. Bright rufous on scapulars and wings, pale yellowish below.
2c. Male. Bright rufous crown and nape, yellow cheeks and underparts.

3 HOUSE SPARROW *Passer domesticus indicus*   Page 653
Local and uncommon; spreading inland from coastal towns along highways and railroads in se. Kenya/ne. Tanzania.
3a. Female. Buff superciliary stripe and wing-bars.
3b. Male. Black face and throat, white cheeks and sides of neck.

4 RUFOUS SPARROW *Passer r. rufocinctus*   Page 652
Common in cultivation and open habitats in and near Rift Valley highlands. Pale eyes.
4a. Female. Dusky throat.
4b. Male. Black throat patch, grey-and-rufous head.

5 GREY-HEADED SPARROW *Passer griseus*   Page 651
Common and widespread in varied habitats. Polytypic, with noticeable intergradation between at least some forms. Bill black in breeding season, otherwise dull grey or brown above, dull yellowish below.
5a. *P. g. ugandae*, adult. West of Rift Valley. Grey head, dull rufous or rufous-brown back, white throat.
5b. *P. g. ugandae*, juvenile. Browner, short dark streaks on back.
5c. *P. g. gongonensis*, breeding male. 'Parrot-billed Sparrow'. In and east of Rift Valley from Lake Turkana, south to ne. Tanzania. Larger than *ugandae*; underparts evenly grey; bill stout.
5d. *P. g. gongonensis*, non-breeding female.
**5e. *P. g. swainsoni*. 'Swainson's Sparrow'. Ethiopian border areas. Back dull brown; dark grey below, with white belly, whitish throat.
**5f. *P. g. suahelicus*. 'Swahili Sparrow'. Sw. Kenya, n. Tanzania. Back and head uniformly coloured.

6 YELLOW-SPOTTED PETRONIA *Petronia pyrgita*   Page 653
Uncommon in bush, savanna and dry woodland.
6a. Juvenile. Brownish. Recalls House Sparrow, but with prominent eye-ring; bill pale.
6b. Adult. Greyish or brownish above, with white eye-ring. Small yellow throat spot sometimes visible.

7 SPECKLE-FRONTED WEAVER *Sporopipes frontalis emini*   Page 659
Uncommon in dry bush and open savanna. Black forehead and crown with white speckling; tawny-rufous nape, bold moustachial stripe.

DALE A. ZIMMERMAN
1990

PLATE 109: SPARROW-WEAVERS, BUFFALO-WEAVERS, SOCIAL WEAVERS *et al.*

1 GROSBEAK-WEAVER *Amblyospiza albifrons melanota* **Page 659**
Locally common near marshes, swamps; also visits woodland and forest.
1a. Female. Heavy bill; bold streaking.
1b. Male. Heavy bill; dark, with white forehead (variable), white wing patches. (Eastern races are black-headed.)

2 BLACK-CAPPED SOCIAL WEAVER *Pseudonigrita cabanisi* **Page 658**
Locally common in dry open savanna and bush.
2a. Adult. Black cap; large pale bill.
2b. Juvenile. Brown head, dull horn-coloured bill.

3 GREY-CAPPED SOCIAL WEAVER *Pseudonigrita arnaudi* **Page 658**
Locally common in bush and open woodland. Short tail with pale tip.
3a. Juvenile. Brownish-grey cap, dark cheeks, blackish lores.
3b. *P. a. dorsalis*, adult. Sw. Kenya, Serengeti NP. Pale cap; centre of back grey.
3c. *P. a. arnaudi*, adult. Mainly in and east of Rift Valley. Grey-brown back.

4 DONALDSON-SMITH'S SPARROW-WEAVER *Plocepasser donaldsoni* **Page 655**
Locally common in n. Kenya. Conspicuous in Isiolo District game reserves. Scaly, mottled plumage, buff cheeks, black whisker mark; white rump.

5 CHESTNUT-CROWNED SPARROW-WEAVER *Plocepasser superciliosus* **Page 658**
Local and uncommon in nw. Kenya. Chestnut cap; bold head pattern.

6 WHITE-BROWED SPARROW-WEAVER *Plocepasser mahali melanorhynchus* **Page 655**
Common in *Acacia* bush, savanna and dry woodland below 1400 m. White superciliary stripe, much white in wings, white rump and upper tail-coverts.
6a and 6b. Adults.

7 RED-HEADED WEAVER *Anaplectes rubriceps* **Page 672**
Uncommon in lightly wooded areas.
7a. Male *A. r. leuconotus*. Red and white, with black face, red bill.
7b. Female. Orange-red bill, wing and tail edgings (rarely yellow). (Juvenile on Plate 114.)
7c. Male *A. r. jubaensis*. All red.

8 WHITE-HEADED BUFFALO-WEAVER *Dinemellia dinemelli boehmi* **Page 654**
Common in dry bush and savanna below 1400 m. Orange-red on rump, tail-coverts and bend of wing; white head and wing patches.
8a and 8b. Adults.

9 WHITE-BILLED BUFFALO-WEAVER *Bubalornis albirostris* **Page 655**
Locally common in nw. Kenya, south to lakes Baringo and Bogoria.
9a. Adult male. Mostly black, bill ivory-white (blackish in female and non-breeding male).
9b. Juvenile. White mottling below; bill black.

10 RED-BILLED BUFFALO-WEAVER *Bubalornis niger intermedius* **Page 654**
10a. Adult female. Dark brown above, spotted and streaked below; bill brown or horn colour, pinkish at base.
10b. Juvenile. Generally tan above, cheeks grey; bill largely yellowish orange or yellowish pink; throat and breast barred.
10c. Adult male. Mostly black, with reddish bill.

1a

1b

2a

3a

2b

3b

4

5

3c

6a

6b

7c

7a

7b

8b

8a

9a

10a

9b

10b

10c

DALE A. ZIMMERMAN
1990

PLATE 110: WHYDAHS, INDIGOBIRDS AND QUELEAS

1 PARADISE WHYDAH *Vidua paradisaea*   **Page 695**
Fairly common in dry country.
1a. Breeding male. Buff nape; unusual tail, with two long tapering feathers.
1b. Breeding female. Larger than female indigobirds; dark marks on side of head; large dark bill; breast plain or with necklace of fine streaks.
1c. Juvenile. Plain; like juvenile Pin-tailed Whydah, but bill larger.

2 BROAD-TAILED PARADISE WHYDAH *Vidua obtusa*   **Page 695**
Rare. (Possibly extirpated from Kenya.)
2a. Breeding male. Similar to *V. paradisaea,* but long tail feathers much wider, equally broad almost to tips.
2b. Female. Paler bill than female of No. 1; less distinct face pattern. See text.

3 STRAW-TAILED WHYDAH *Vidua fischeri*   **Page 695**
Uncommon/fairly common in dry areas.
3a. Breeding male. Buff and black, with four long straw-like central tail feathers; bill red.
3b. Female and non-breeding male. Crown rufous-tinged; bill and feet red.
3c. Juvenile. Dull rusty brown.

4 STEEL-BLUE WHYDAH *Vidua hypocherina*   **Page 694**
Uncommon and local in dry areas.
4a. Breeding male. Dark shiny blue, with four long, slender dark tail feathers; white tufts beside rump often concealed.
4b. Female and non-breeding male. In fresh plumage, brightly patterned; wing feathers edged buffy rufous, upper tail-coverts and black tail feathers white-edged and -tipped (but much duller when worn). Tiny bill pale grey.

5 PIN-TAILED WHYDAH *Vidua macroura*   **Page 694**
Common and widespread, mainly in moist areas, including cultivation.
5a. Breeding male. Black and white, with long, slender floppy tail; red bill.
5b. Non-breeding male. Black-and-white head stripes; red bill. Tail variable.
5c. Adult female. Buff-and-brown head stripes; bill dusky or blackish above, reddish below (becoming all red after breeding). Much white on inner webs of rectrices.
5d. Juvenile. Plain, with suggestion of superciliary stripe; blackish bill (becoming red in a few weeks).

6 VILLAGE or COMMON INDIGOBIRD *Vidua chalybeata*   **Page 693**
Widespread, especially in moist areas, often in cultivation and gardens.
6a. *V. c. centralis,* breeding male. Dark blue-black, wings browner; bill whitish; feet orange, red or salmon-pink.
6b. *V. c. amauropteryx,* breeding male. Bill and feet red or orange; plumage slightly more blue-green than in 6a.
6c. *V. c. centralis,* juvenile. Suggests small female House Sparrow; no central crown stripe; bill pale.
6d. *V. c. centralis,* adult female. Patterned like female Pin-tailed and Paradise Whydahs, but breast plain, usually dingy greyish buff; bill greyish pink, paler below.

7 PURPLE INDIGOBIRD *Vidua purpurascens*   **Page 693**
Uncommon and local in bush and shrubby woodland. **Breeding male** black with dull purple sheen; bill and feet white. Plumage indistinguishable from that of male Variable Indigobird. (See text.)

8 RED-BILLED QUELEA *Quelea quelea aethiopica*   **Page 673**
Common in dry savanna, bushed grassland and cultivation.
8a. Non-breeding female. Heavy red bill; yellow wing edgings.
8b. Breeding male. Red bill; black face and throat.

9 CARDINAL QUELEA *Quelea cardinalis rhodesiae*   **Page 673**
Locally common in tall moist grassland. **Breeding male** with brownish hindcrown and nape, rest of head to upper breast red.

10 RED-HEADED QUELEA *Quelea erythrops*   **Page 674**
Scarce and sporadic in Lake Victoria basin and coastal lowlands. **Breeding male** has entire head red; barred blackish on throat; bill large, grey. (Female Red-headed and Cardinal Queleas on Plate 112.)

1a 2a 3a 4a 5a 6a 1b 2b 3b 4b 5b 6b 3c 1c 4b 5c 6c 7 8a 5d 6d 8b 9 10

DALE A. ZIMMERMAN
1990

PLATE 111: BREEDING MALE BISHOPS AND WIDOWBIRDS (*Euplectes*)

1 RED-COLLARED WIDOWBIRD *Euplectes ardens*   **Page 678**
Locally common in grassland, cultivation, moist brushy habitats.
1a. *E. a. suahelica*. Highlands of Kenya and n. Tanzania. Crown and nape red.
1b. *E. a. tropicus*. E. Tanzania north to Taita Hills and lower Tana River. Crown and nape black.

2 WHITE-WINGED WIDOWBIRD *E. albonotatus eques*   **Page 677**
Common in bushed grassland and cultivation. White wing patch.

3 LONG-TAILED WIDOWBIRD *E. progne delamerei*   **Page 678**
Locally fairly common in Kenyan highland grasslands.
3a. At rest, scarlet and buff wing-coverts may be partially concealed.
3b. Courtship flight slow and erratic, with bustle-like dangling tail.

4 JACKSON'S WIDOWBIRD *E. jacksoni*   **Page 679**
Locally common in grasslands of Kenyan and n. Tanzanian highlands. Long curved tail, tawny 'shoulders.'

5 YELLOW-MANTLED WIDOWBIRD *E. macrourus*   **Page 677**
Locally common in moist grasslands of w. Kenya and adjacent areas of n. Tanzania.
5a. *E. m. macrourus*, yellow-backed form. High grasslands, Mara GR to n. Serengeti NP.
5b. *E. m. macrocercus*, yellow-shouldered form. Widespread at lower elevations in w. Kenya.

6 HARTLAUB'S MARSH WIDOWBIRD *E. hartlaubi humeralis*   **Page 678**
Uncommon and local in w. Kenyan marshes and moist grassland, often alongside Fan-tailed Widowbird.
Buffy-orange 'shoulder' patch; long tail.

7 FAN-TAILED WIDOWBIRD *E. axillaris phoeniceus*   **Page 677**
Common in w. Kenyan marshes, local in n. Tanzanian and cent. Kenyan highlands. Short tail often fanned.
(Coastal race *E. a. zanzibaricus* is larger-billed and may show black tips to wing-coverts.)

8 NORTHERN RED BISHOP *E. f. franciscanus*   **Page 676**
Local in Rift Valley around lakes Baringo and Bogoria, in marshes and tall wet grassland. Head extensively black; tail-coverts largely conceal tail.

9 ZANZIBAR RED BISHOP *E. nigroventris*   **Page 675**
Southeastern; most numerous in coastal lowlands. Top of head entirely red; throat to belly black.

10 BLACK-WINGED RED BISHOP *E. h. hordeaceus*   **Page 675**
Species widespread; this race locally common in moist grassland and cultivation in coastal lowlands. Wings black, not brown. (Western *E. h. craspedopterus* has white under tail-coverts.)

11 SOUTHERN RED BISHOP *E. orix nigrifrons*   **Page 676**
Local in western marshes, rice fields and tall grass. Forehead and belly black, breast scarlet; tail-coverts do not conceal tail.

12 YELLOW BISHOP *E. capensis crassirostris*   **Page 676**
Fairly common, mainly above 1400 m, in cultivation, moist scrub, forest edge and roadsides. Lower back and 'shoulders' largely yellow.

13 YELLOW-CROWNED BISHOP *E. afer ladoensis*   **Page 674**
Local and uncommon in marshes, rice fields and moist grassland, mainly in w. and cent. Kenyan highlands and Arusha District. Top of head and most of back yellow.

14 FIRE-FRONTED BISHOP *E. diadematus*   **Page 674**
Seasonally abundant in east and southeast following heavy rains. Scarlet or orange forehead patch.

15 BLACK BISHOP *E. gierowii ansorgei*   **Page 675**
Western Kenya. Uncommon in moist grassland, sugarcane and scrub. Scarlet hindcrown, neck and breast band; yellowish upper back. (Mainly Tanzanian *E. g. friederichseni* is smaller, with broader breast band.)

DALE A. ZIMMERMAN
1990

PLATE 112: DULL-PLUMAGED BISHOPS, WIDOWBIRDS, QUELEAS, AND PARASITIC WEAVER

1 PARASITIC WEAVER *Anomalospiza imberbis*   **Page 680**
Local and uncommon in moist grassland. Stocky, heavy-billed. **1a. Breeding female, somewhat worn plumage.** Yellowish buff, sides streaked. **1b. Juvenile male.** Rich tawny-buff or orange-buff; may show streaks on flanks. **1c. Non-breeding female, fresh plumage.** More contrasting head pattern, throat whitish; few or no streaks below.

2 RED-HEADED QUELEA *Quelea erythrops*   **Page 674**
Scarce and sporadic, mainly in Lake Victoria basin and coastal lowlands. **Female.** Large bill; yellowish face, superciliary stripe and primary edges; throat white; heavy dark mark near base of bill.

3 CARDINAL QUELEA *Quelea cardinalis*   **Page 673**
Common in open moist places, especially tall grassland. **Female.** Yellowish face, throat, superciliary and flight-feather edges.

4 RED-BILLED QUELEA *Quelea quelea aethiopica*   **Page 673**
Common in dry savanna, bushed grassland and cultivation. **Juvenile male.** No yellow on face or throat; crown and nape brownish.

5 ZANZIBAR RED BISHOP *Euplectes nigroventris*   **Page 675**
Southeastern, mostly near coast. **Female.** Very small, no yellow flight-feather edges; postocular line and auriculars darker than in Nos. 6 and 7.

6 NORTHERN RED BISHOP *Euplectes franciscanus*   **Page 676**
(**Southern Red Bishop** *E. orix*, nearly identical)
Local, uncommon in Rift Valley at lakes Baringo/Bogoria; in marshes and wet grassland. **Female.** Face and auriculars paler than in No. 5; flight-feather edges pale brown.

7 FIRE-FRONTED BISHOP *Euplectes diadematus*   **Page 674**
Local in *Acacia* and *Commiphora* bush north to Meru NP and Laisamis. **Female.** Similar to female red bishops, but flight-feather edges yellow.

8 BLACK-WINGED RED BISHOP *Euplectes hordeaceus craspedopterus*   **Page 675**
Western. Widespread in wet grassland and cultivation north to Mt Elgon. **Female.** Larger than other bishops; rich tawny-buff breast band with fine streaks; dark cheeks and auriculars.

9 YELLOW-CROWNED BISHOP *Euplectes afer ladoensis*   **Page 674**
Local in marshes in w. and cent. Kenyan highlands and Arusha District. **Female.** Less buff below than other bishops; more boldly streaked; dark auriculars.

10 RED-COLLARED WIDOWBIRD *Euplectes ardens suahelica*   **Page 678**
Locally common in grassland, open grassy bush and cultivation in the highlands. Gregarious. Larger, longer-tailed than bishops; dark 'whisker' mark. **10a. Female.** Tail moderate, brownish; no yellow on 'shoulders'. **10b. Non-breeding male.** Wings and variably long tail blackish.

11 YELLOW-MANTLED WIDOWBIRD *Euplectes m. macrourus*   **Page 677**
Local in moist grasslands in Mara/Serengeti. Virtually identical *E. m. macrocercus* local in w. Kenyan scrub and grassy bush. **Female.** Yellow-margined 'shoulder' feathers (sometimes concealed).

12 WHITE-WINGED WIDOWBIRD *Euplectes albonotatus eques*   **Page 677**
Locally common in tall grass, bush, brushy habitats. **12a. Non-breeding male.** Rufous and white in wing; bluish bill. **12b. Female.** Some rufous at bend of wing, often concealed. Bill horn-brown above, flesh-white below; yellowish wash on cheeks, throat and breast.

13 YELLOW BISHOP *Euplectes capensis crassirostris*   **Page 676**
Widespread in moist bush and cultivation in highlands. **13a. Non-breeding male.** Bright yellow 'shoulders' and rump. **13b. Adult female.** Rump yellow or olive-yellow. (Juvenile like female, but rump brown and streaked.)

14 BLACK BISHOP *Euplectes gierowii ansorgei*   **Page 675**
Western. Uncommon in moist scrub, shrubby tall grass, sugarcane. Large and dark. Crissum feathers dark-centred, sides of breast spotted. **14a. Female.** Auriculars darkly mottled; breast light buff. **14b. Non-breeding male.** Wings and tail blackish, face and breast rich buff; superciliary stripe and chin yellowish.

15 FAN-TAILED WIDOWBIRD *Euplectes axillaris phoeniceus*   **Page 677**
Western Kenya in marshes, low wet places. (Similar *E. a. zanzibaricus* local in coastal lowlands.) **Female/juvenile.** Stocky, short-tailed; ochre at bend of wing (semi-concealed).

16 LONG-TAILED WIDOWBIRD *Euplectes progne delamerei*   **Page 678**
Local in Kenyan highland grasslands. **16a. Non-breeding male.** Bill bluish white; wings black, with buff and orange-red coverts (often concealed); tail feathers slightly to markedly long and pointed. **16b. Female.** Large size; whitish below, with buffy wash on streaked breast and flanks.

17 HARTLAUB'S MARSH WIDOWBIRD *Euplectes hartlaubi humeralis*   **Page 678**
Western Kenya. Local, uncommon in marshes and wet grasslands, often with Fan-tailed Widowbird. **Female/juvenile.** Underparts uniformly buff, with streaks on breast, sides and flanks; under wing-coverts dusky. (Non-breeding male similar, but wings as in breeding plumage; see Plate 111.)

18 JACKSON'S WIDOWBIRD *Euplectes jacksoni*   **Page 679**
Locally common in highland grasslands. **Female.** Pale buff to bright orange-buff below and on face; variably streaked. (Non-breeding male larger, darker and browner, breast streaks mostly at sides; wings as in breeding male, but with broad tawny feather edges.)

DALE A. ZIMMERMAN
1990

PLATE 113: *PLOCEUS* WEAVERS (part) AND PARASITIC WEAVER

1 PARASITIC WEAVER *Anomalospiza imberbis*   **Page 680**
Local and uncommon in moist grassland. Canary-like; short-tailed, heavy-billed.
1a. Breeding male. Underparts bright yellow, unstreaked; bill black.
1b. Immature male. Variably streaked on sides and crown; paler bill. (Females and juvenile on Plate 112.)

2 SLENDER-BILLED WEAVER *Ploceus pelzelni*   **Page 661**
Lake Victoria basin in marshes and swamps. Small size, slim bill.
2a. Juvenile. Pale bill.
2b. Adult female. Black bill. (Adult male on Plate 115.)

3 AFRICAN GOLDEN WEAVER *P. subaureus aureoflavus*   **Page 663**
Eastern, usually near water. Common at coast, local inland.
3a. Breeding male. Iris orange or pink; bill black; rufous-orange on face.
3b. Non-breeding female. Iris pink; bill pale buffy brown; underparts yellow and white.
3c. Juvenile female. Iris brown; underparts largely white.
3d. Breeding female. Iris orange or pink; bill black; underparts yellow.

4 GOLDEN PALM WEAVER *P. bojeri*   **Page 666**
Fairly common at Kenyan coast, inland to Kibwezi, Meru NP and Samburu GR.
4a. Breeding male. Brilliant orange-yellow head; orange-rufous on upper breast; iris dark brown, bill black.
4b. Immature male. Duller yellow; bill light below.
4c. Adult female. Lightly streaked back, underparts yellow; two-toned bill.

5 TAVETA GOLDEN WEAVER *P. castaneiceps*   **Page 666**
Locally common in Amboseli–Taveta region, Arusha and Moshi Districts and Lake Jipe.
5a. Adult male. Rufous on hindcrown and upper breast; iris dark brown.
5b. Adult female. Heavily streaked back, yellow underparts; two-toned bill; iris dark brown. (Juvenile on
Plate 116.)

6 NORTHERN BROWN-THROATED WEAVER *P. castanops*   **Page 666**
Uncommon around Lake Victoria in papyrus and lakeside trees. **Subadult male**. Rufous-brown throat, pale
eyes. (Adult male on Plate 115; female and juvenile on Plate 116.)

7 ORANGE WEAVER *P. aurantius rex*   **Page 663**
Rare along Lake Victoria shore and islands. **Male**. Bright orange-yellow; iris pale grey; bill pale, slender.
(Female on Plate 116.)

8 JACKSON'S GOLDEN-BACKED WEAVER *P. jacksoni*   **Page 667**
Locally common near water. **Adult female**. Heavily streaked back, bright yellow superciliary stripe; breast
and sides orange-buff. (Male on Plate 115.)

9 BAGLAFECHT WEAVER *P. baglafecht*   **Page 660**
Race *reichenowi* (**Reichenow's Weaver**) common in highland towns, forest edge, cultivation.
9a. *P. b. reichenowi*, juvenile. Olive head, buff-and-brown-streaked back, buffy yellow below.
9b. *P. b. reichenowi/stuhlmanni* intergrade, juvenile female. Head blackish (more extensively black in
male). W. Kenya (Bungoma–Siaya area). (Other plumages on Plates 114 and 116.)

10 HOLUB'S GOLDEN WEAVER *P. xanthops*   **Page 663**
Fairly common in gardens, cultivation, wet areas and edges of woodland in the highlands. Large, with heavy
black bill; iris pale yellow.
10a. Adult male. Orange wash on throat and upper breast.
10b. Adult female. Duller, more olive above; no orange on throat.

DALE A. ZIMMERMAN
1989

PLATE 114: *PLOCEUS* WEAVERS (part) AND MALIMBE (Adults, except as indicated)

1 RED-HEADED WEAVER *Anaplectes rubriceps leuconotus*
Uncommon in savanna and other open habitats. **Juvenile**. (other plumages on Plate 109.)

2 CLARKE'S WEAVER *Ploceus golandi* Page 671
Kenyan coastal-forest endemic.
2a. Female. Bright yellow on wings, yellow streaks on belly.
2b. Male. Black head and upperparts; yellow on wings.

3 DARK-BACKED WEAVER *P. bicolor* Page 672
Forest species; fairly common.
3a. *P. b. kersteni*. Black back. (East of Rift Valley; mainly coastal and in Usambara Mts.)
3b. *P. b. mentalis*. Grey back. (W. Kenyan forests.)

4 BROWN-CAPPED WEAVER *P. insignis* Page 662
Highland forest. Forages nuthatch-like on trunks and large branches.
4a. Male. Chestnut crown.
4b. Female. Black crown.

5 BAGLAFECHT WEAVER *P. baglafecht* Page 660
Widespread. Race *reichenowi* common in various highland habitats, including towns.
5a. *P. b. emini*, non-breeding female. Black-streaked grey back, white lower breast and belly.
5b. *P. b. reichenowi* (Reichenow's Weaver), adult male. Black face patch, pale eyes.
5c. *P. b. reichenowi*, adult female. Black head, pale eyes. (Other plumages on Plates 113 and 116.)

6 COMPACT WEAVER *P. superciliosus* Page 660
Western Kenya. Uncommon in moist grassy areas, woodland edge. Solitary. Heavy, deep-based bill; black face and throat.
6a. Breeding female. Dark crown.
6b. Breeding male. Yellow crown, grading to chestnut on forehead. (Non-breeding male on Plate 116.)

7 YELLOW-MANTLED WEAVER *P. tricolor interscapularis* Page 671
Rare. Solitary canopy species of w. Kenyan forests (possibly extirpated).
7a. Female. Black, with yellow band on upper back.
7b. Juvenile. Rufous-brown crown and upper back.
7c. Male. Yellow band on upper back; chestnut underparts.

8 RED-HEADED MALIMBE *Malimbus r. rubricollis* Page 672
Kakamega Forest treetops. Nuthatch-like in habits; in pairs.
8a. Female. Black forehead and forecrown.
8b. Male. Scarlet from forehead to nape.

9 VIEILLOT'S BLACK WEAVER *Ploceus nigerrimus* Page 670
Western Kenyan forests and forest edge. Gregarious.
9a. Male. All black, with yellow eyes.
9b. Female. Dark olive, with heavily streaked back; pale eyes.

10 BLACK-NECKED WEAVER *P. nigricollis melanoxanthus* Page 662
Widespread but uncommon. In pairs in dry bush and open woodland.
10a. Female. Yellow superciliary stripe, black bill.
10b. Male. Rich golden-yellow head, black bib.
10c. Juvenile male. Resembles female, but with pale bill.

11 BLACK-BILLED WEAVER *P. melanogaster stephanophorus* Page 662
Western Kenyan forests. Solitary or in pairs, usually low in undergrowth or vine tangles. Black, with yellow face, narrow black mask.
11a. Female. Yellow throat.
11b. Male. Black throat.

DALE A. ZIMMERMAN
1989

PLATE 115: *PLOCEUS* WEAVERS (part) AND CHESTNUT SPARROW
(Breeding males except as indicated)

1 **JACKSON'S GOLDEN-BACKED WEAVER** *Ploceus jacksoni* **Page 667**
Locally common in acacia woodland and scrub near water, cultivation, tall sedges. Back golden yellow, underparts rich chestnut. (Female on Plate 113.)

2 **YELLOW-BACKED WEAVER** *P. melanocephalus fischeri* **Page 667**
Confined to swamps and reedbeds in the Lake Victoria basin. Yellow collar separating black head from yellow-olive back. (Female on Plate 116.)

3 **JUBA WEAVER** *P. dichrocephalus* **Page 667**
Locally common in riverine bush in Daua River Valley near Mandera in ne. Kenya. **3a. Chestnut-headed individual. 3b. Black-headed individual.** (Female on Plate 116.)

4 **NORTHERN BROWN-THROATED WEAVER** *P. castanops* **Page 666**
Uncommon in papyrus and lakeside trees around Lake Victoria. Chestnut throat; white eye. (Subadult male on Plate 113, female and juvenile on Plate 116.)

5 **RÜPPELL'S WEAVER** *P. galbula* **Page 667**
Vagrant (?) along ne. Kenyan border areas. Chestnut face and throat; orange or orange-red eye. (Female on Plate 116.)

6 **LITTLE WEAVER** *P. l. luteolus* **Page 661**
Fairly common in acacia bush and woodland in nw. Kenya south to Baringo. Small bill; black face, forecrown, throat. (Female on Plate 116.) (Similar *P. l. kavirondensis* scarce and local in Lake Victoria basin and Mara GR.)

7 **SLENDER-BILLED WEAVER** *P. pelzelni* **Page 661**
Fairly common in swamps, marshes, waterside trees around Lake Victoria. Small size, slender bill. (Female and juvenile on Plate 113.)

8 **BLACK-HEADED or VILLAGE WEAVER** *P. cucullatus* **Page 670**
Locally common. Highly gregarious when breeding. **8a. *P. c. bohndorffi.*** Western. Large bill, black scapulars. **8b. *P. c. paroptus.*** N. and e. Kenya, ne. Tanzania. Black-and-yellow back; large bill; red eyes. (Females and juvenile on Plate 116.)

9 **SPEKE'S WEAVER** *P. spekei* **Page 669**
Widespread. Common in savanna, bush, cultivation, towns and villages, 1400–2200 m. Black-and-yellow back, no black on crown; creamy eyes. (Female on Plate 116.)

10 **LESSER MASKED WEAVER** *P. i. intermedius* **Page 669**
Local in savanna, bush and cultivation, in both dry and humid areas below 1500 m. Pale eyes, grey feet, black crown. (Female and juvenile on Plate 116.)

11 **NORTHERN MASKED WEAVER** *P. t. taeniopterus* **Page 669**
Local in Lake Baringo area and n. Lake Turkana, near water. Dark brown eyes, pinkish feet; crown deep chestnut; black of throat extends to upper breast. (Female and juvenile on Plate 116.)

12 **VITELLINE MASKED WEAVER** *P. velatus uluensis* **Page 668**
Widespread in dry savanna and thorn-bush. Black confined to throat, face; eye red. (Female on Plate 116.)

13 **HEUGLIN'S MASKED WEAVER** *P. heuglini* **Page 668**
Scarce and local in nw. Kenya, south to Kitale and Bungoma areas. Black face and throat extending to point on breast; back nearly plain; pale eyes. (Female on Plate 116.)

14 **SPECTACLED WEAVER** *P. ocularis suahelicus* **Page 661**
Widespread. Uncommon in tangled vegetation along forest and swamp edges. **14a. Female.** No black on throat. (Western *P. o. crocatus* has less rufous on face.) **14b. Male.** Black throat patch.

15 **CHESTNUT WEAVER** *P. r. rubiginosus* **Page 671**
Seasonally abundant, mainly in dry areas. Highly gregarious when breeding. **15a. Non-breeding male.** Rufous-buff and black back stripes, chestnut breast; eye red, bill heavy. **15b. Breeding male.** Mostly rufous-chestnut, with black head; eye red. **15c. Adult female.** Rufous wash on sides of breast, whitish wing edging; heavy bill; eye brown. **15d. Immature male.** Eye red; bill dusky above, paler below.

16 **CHESTNUT SPARROW** *Passer eminibey* (for comparison) **Page 653**
Locally common in dry country. Much smaller than Chestnut Weaver. Small bill, brown eye, wing edging not white, no black on head. (Female on Plate 108.)

DALE A. ZIMMERMAN
1989

PLATE 116: *PLOCEUS* WEAVERS (mostly females and juveniles)

1 LITTLE WEAVER *Ploceus l. luteolus* **Page 661**
Fairly common in acacia bush and woodland in nw. Kenya south to Baringo. **Female**. Small size, small bill. (Male on Plate 115.)

2 ORANGE WEAVER *P. aurantius rex* **Page 663**
Female. Rare along Lake Victoria shores and islands. Pale slender bill; eye pale. (Male on Plate 113.)

3 NORTHERN BROWN-THROATED WEAVER *P. castanops* **Page 666**
Uncommon in papyrus and lakeside trees around Lake Victoria. Usually near water. **3a. Female**. Slender black bill; short black eye-line; pale eye. **3b. Juvenile male**. Slender bicoloured bill; brown-and-buff-streaked back, brown eye. (Subadult and adult males on Plates 113 and 115 respectively.)

4 COMPACT WEAVER *P. superciliosus* **Page 660**
W. Kenya. Local in moist bush, cultivation and wet grassland. **Non-breeding adult**. Largely brown, with blackish-brown crown and eye-line.

5 RÜPPELL'S WEAVER *P. galbula* **Page 667**
Vagrant (?) in ne. Kenyan border areas. **Female**. Bright yellow wing edgings, usually trace of chestnut on face; bill short and thick; iris chestnut. (Male on Plate 115.)

6 YELLOW-BACKED WEAVER *P. melanocephalus fischeri* **Page 667**
Confined to swamps and reedbeds in the Lake Victoria basin. **Female**. Tawny-buff breast, yellow superciliary stripe, brown-and-black streaked back. (Male on Plate 115.)

7 TAVETA GOLDEN WEAVER *P. castaneiceps* **Page 666**
Locally common in Amboseli–Taveta region, Lake Jipe, Arusha and Moshi Districts. **Juvenile**. Bicoloured bill (as in Golden Palm Weaver), dark eye-line and yellow superciliary stripe, strongly streaked back. (Adults on Plate 113.)

8 LESSER MASKED WEAVER *P. i. intermedius* **Page 669**
Local in savanna, bush and cultivation, in dry and humid areas below 1500 m. Blue-grey feet, rather slender bill. (Male on Plate 115.) **8a. Juvenile male**. Pale bill; iris brown. **8b. Breeding female**. Grey bill; iris pale tan or cream.

9 JUBA WEAVER *P. dichrocephalus* **Page 667**
Locally common in riverine bush in Daua River Valley near Mandera, ne. Kenya. **Female**. Small bicoloured bill. (Males on Plate 115.)

10 NORTHERN MASKED WEAVER *P. t. taeniopterus* **Page 669**
Local in Lake Baringo area and northern Lake Turkana; near water. **10a. Juvenile**. Tan or buff; yellow superciliary stripe; white eye; bill mostly blue-grey; feet pinkish. **10b. Adult female**. Similar, but brown-eyed; breast, head and wing-linings more yellowish. (Male on Plate 115.)

11 VITELLINE MASKED WEAVER *P. velatus uluensis* **Page 668**
Widespread in dry savanna and thorn-bush. Similar to No. 9, but adults orange- or red-eyed; feet pinkish flesh; bill smaller; superciliary stripe duller. **11a. Non-breeding female**. Sides pinkish buff, back tan or buff with black streaks; iris dull red. (Young similar, but iris brown.) **11b. Breeding female**. Side and back more olive, breast more yellow; iris bright orange-red. (Male on Plate 115.)

12 SPEKE'S WEAVER *P. spekei* **Page 669**
Common in savanna, bush, cultivation, towns and villages. Large; bill heavy and long; superciliary stripe indistinct or lacking; back well streaked. **12a. Adult female**. Dull olive and yellow; iris pale; bill dark or partly dark. **12b. Juvenile**. Paler olive-yellow; iris brown; bill pale; whiter below (Male on Plate 115.)

13 HEUGLIN'S MASKED WEAVER *P. heuglini* **Page 668**
Scarce and local in nw. Kenya, south to Kitale and Bungoma areas. **Adult female**. Bill short, dark; back faintly streaked; iris pale (Male on Plate 115.)

14 BAGLAFECHT (EMIN'S) WEAVER *P. baglafecht emini* **Page 660**
Mt Loima and Kongelai Escarpment. **Juvenile male**. Head blackish; back streaked grey and black. (Other plumages and races on Plates 113 and 114.)

15 BLACK-HEADED (VILLAGE) WEAVER *P. cucullatus* **Page 670**
Locally common. Highly gregarious when breeding. Large and large-billed. **15a. *P. c. bohndorffi*, breeding female**. Western. Largely yellow; bill black; iris red. **15b. *P. c. paroptus*, non-breeding female**. N. and e. Kenya, ne. Tanzania. Grey-backed, yellow and white underparts, prominent yellow superciliary stripe; iris red. **15c. *P. c. paroptus*, early immature male**. Similar to female, but brown-eyed and sides more pinkish buff, less grey. (Adult males on Plate 115.)

PLATE 117: WAXBILLS AND RELATIVES

1 QUAIL-FINCH *Ortygospiza atricollis muelleri* **Page 689**
On ground in open grassland. Tiny, short-tailed, heavily barred. **1a. Male**. Black throat band; contrasting face pattern. **1b. Female**. Duller; lacks black on face and throat.

2 LOCUST-FINCH *Ortygospiza locustella uelensis* **Page 690**
Accidental in w. Kenya. Red-orange in wings and on upper tail-coverts. **2a. Male. 2b. Female**. Whitish underparts, barred flanks.

3 CUT-THROAT FINCH *Amadina fasciata alexanderi* **Page 692**
Fairly common in dry areas; on ground or in trees around water holes. Heavily barred; large pinkish-grey bill, chestnut belly patch. **3a. Female**. Sides of face strongly barred. **3b. Male**. Red band across throat.

4 ZEBRA WAXBILL *Amandava subflava* **Page 689**
Uncommon in moist grassland, rice fields. Yellow or orange underparts, orange or red upper tail-coverts, strongly barred sides. **4a. *A. s. subflava*, male**. Western. Orange below; red superciliary stripe. **4b. *A. s. clarkei*, male**. Eastern. Yellow below; orange confined to breast and crissum. **4c. *A. s. clarkei*, female**. Pale yellowish below; orange tail-coverts.

5 COMMON WAXBILL *Estrilda astrild* **Page 688**
Common, widespread in grassy and shrubby places, near ground. Brown rump and tail, red eye-line. **5a. *E. a. massaica*, male**. Southern and central areas east of Rift Valley. Pinkish below, including throat. **5b. *E. a. minor* male**. Coastal. Browner, less pink, below; throat whitish. **5c. *E. a. massaica*, juvenile**. Bill grey, eye-line orange, faint barring below.

6 BLACK-CROWNED WAXBILL *Estrilda n. nonnula* **Page 688**
W. Kenya, at lower elevations than No. 7. Fairly common near ground in cultivation, grassy forest edge, brush. Under tail-coverts white, black of head confined to crown. **6a. Juvenile**. Whitish to pale buffy brown below, no red on flanks; bill blackish. **6b. Male**. Underparts whitish; flanks tinged with pink. (Female paler grey above.)

7 BLACK-HEADED WAXBILL *Estrilda atricapilla graueri* **Page 688**
W. and cent. Kenya. Fairly common along edges of montane forest. Lower belly and crissum black; generally duller than No. 6, and black of head more extensive. **7a. Male**. Flanks red, some pink on bill. **7b. Juvenile**. Dusky below, no red on flanks, bill all black.

8 CRIMSON-RUMPED WAXBILL *Estrilda rhodopyga centralis* **Page 687**
Widespread; fairly common in bush, grassy areas, cultivation, often in dry areas. Upper tail-coverts red. **8a. Juvenile**. Face plain or with suggestion of eye-line. **8b. Adult**. Red line through eye, as in Common and Black-rumped Waxbills.

9 BLACK-RUMPED WAXBILL *Estrilda troglodytes* **Page 687**
W. Kenya only. Uncommon in scrub, thickets, rice fields. Pale, with black upper tail-coverts and tail. (Juvenile lacks red eye-line, has black bill.)

10 YELLOW-BELLIED WAXBILL *Estrilda quartinia kilimensis* **Page 687**
Fairly common in gardens, grassy clearings, forest edge in highlands. Olive back. **10a. Adult**. Bicoloured bill. **10b. Juvenile**. All-black bill.

11 FAWN-BREASTED WAXBILL *Estrilda p. paludicola* **Page 687**
Uncommon, local in moist grassland in w. Kenya. Tawny-brown back, red bill. (Juvenile has black bill.)

12 BLACK-FACED WAXBILL *Estrilda erythronotus delamerei* **Page 689**
Lake Victoria basin; Thika and Nairobi Districts south to Tanzania. Local in *Acacia* woods and bushed grassland; in undergrowth or trees. **12a. Male**. Black of face extends to chin and upper throat; belly and crissum black. **12b. Female**. Chin black; belly/crissum pinkish grey.

13 BLACK-CHEEKED WAXBILL *Estrilda charmosyna* **Page 689**
Locally common in dry n. and e. Kenya, south to Tsavo East NP. Wanders to eastern edge of highlands during droughts. **Male**. Chin whitish, crissum pale pink.

14 AFRICAN SILVERBILL *Lonchura cantans orientalis* **Page 690**
Small flocks in dry bush and scrub, on ground or in trees. **Adult**. Blue-grey bill, black rump and tail.

15 GREY-HEADED SILVERBILL *Lonchura griseicapilla* **Page 690**
Widespread, typically in less arid country than No. 14. Usually on or near ground. White rump, black tail. **15a. Adult**. Blue-grey head with black-and-white-speckled face. **15b. Juvenile**. Duller, with no speckling on face.

DALE A. ZIMMERMAN
1990

PLATE 118: ESTRILDIDS (cordon-bleus, pytilias and firefinches)

1 **RED-CHEEKED CORDON-BLEU** *Uraeginthus b. bengalus* Page 685
Widespread. Common in wooded areas, bush and gardens.
1a. Male. Red facial patch.
1b. Female. Like male, but no red.
1c. Juvenile. Brownish head, dusky bill. (Some birds may have blue cheeks.)

2 **BLUE-CAPPED CORDON-BLEU** *Uraeginthus cyanocephalus* Page 686
Fairly common in arid and semi-arid country. Paler and brighter blue than Red-cheeked, with longer tail.
2a. Male.
2b. Immature female.
2c. Adult female.

3 **PURPLE GRENADIER** *Uraeginthus ianthinogaster* Page 686
Fairly common in bush and thickets. Widespread except in north and east. Blue or purplish-blue rump, black tail; adults red-billed.
3a. Juvenile. Mostly tawny.
3b. Female. Silvery blue around eyes.
3c. Male. Largely violet-blue below (extent of rufous variable); blue on face.

4 **ORANGE-WINGED PYTILIA** *Pytilia afra* Page 681
Rare and very local in dense bush. Formerly more widespread. See text. Skulks in dense cover. Orange in wings separates it from Green-winged Pytilia.
4a. Male.
4b. Female.

5 **GREEN-WINGED PYTILIA** *Pytilia melba* Page 681
Common on or near ground in dense bush, thickets and scrub. Olive-green wings, red bill.
5a. Female.
5b. Male.

6 **BLACK-BELLIED FIREFINCH** *Lagonosticta r. rara* Page 685
Western. Uncommon, local in tall grass, overgrown cultivation. Black belly and crissum, pink patch on bill.
6a. Male. Body plumage deep wine-red.
6b. Female. Red loral spot, rosy-pink breast, grey throat.

7 **AFRICAN FIREFINCH** *Lagonosticta rubricata hildebrandti* Page 684
Widespread but uncommon and shy. On or near ground in dense cover at forest edge or in thickets. Bill grey or bluish; belly and crissum black.
7a. Female. Brown, with pale throat.
7b. Male. Bright rose-red on head and underparts; back dark brown.
7c. Juvenile. Pale, with black crissum.

8 **JAMESON'S FIREFINCH** *Lagonosticta rhodopareia taruensis* Page 685
Local in dry bush country; avoids towns. On and near ground.
8a. Male. Largely pink, including back; bill and feet bluish.
8b. Female. Red loral spot; more rose-pink than 7a. Under tail-coverts barred.

9 **RED-BILLED FIREFINCH** *Lagonosticta senegala ruberrima* Page 684
Common ground feeder in towns, villages, cultivation, bush.
9a. Female. Dusky brown; loral spot and mandible red; under tail-coverts barred/spotted.
9b. Male. Wine-red, with dusky brown belly and crissum; bill largely red; eye-ring yellow.
9c. Juvenile. Brown, with pale belly; red loral spot small or lacking; bill brown above, pink below.

10 **BAR-BREASTED FIREFINCH** *Lagonosticta rufopicta* Page 684
Western. Local on ground in cultivation, grassy thicket borders. Sexes alike. Large red bill, blue-grey eye-ring, faint white bars on sides and breast.

DALE A. ZIMMERMAN
1990

PLATE 119: ESTRILDIDS (mannikins, twinspots *et al.*)

1 BLACK-AND-WHITE MANNIKIN *Lonchura bicolor* **Page 691**
Local in forest clearings, forest edge, moist bush and cultivation.
1a. *L. b. nigriceps*. 'Rufous-backed Mannikin'. Kenyan highlands and coastal lowlands, inland to Usambara and Pare Mts, Arusha and Moshi Districts.
1b. *L. b. poensis*, adult. Widespread below 2000 m. west of Rift Valley.
1c. *L. b. poensis*, juvenile.

2 BRONZE MANNIKIN *Lonchura cucullata scutata* **Page 691**
Common, widespread. Feeds on ground in open habitats, cultivation and gardens.
2a. Adult.
2b. Juvenile.

3 MAGPIE-MANNIKIN *Lonchura fringilloides* **Page 691**
Rare in se. Kenya and Usambara Mts in moist thickets, forest edge, bush. One record from Alupe on Kenyan-Ugandan border.

4 WHITE-BREASTED NEGROFINCH *Nigrita f. fusconota* **Page 681**
Uncommon in Kakamega Forest canopy.

5 GREY-HEADED NEGROFINCH *Nigrita canicapilla schistacea* **Page 680**
Fairly common in highland forests, in canopy and undergrowth.
5a. Adult. White-edged grey crown and nape; white wing dots.
5b. Juvenile. Dull grey-brown, with suggestion of grey stripe on head and neck.

6 BLACK-BELLIED SEED-CRACKER *Pyrenestes o. ostrinus* **Page 683**
Rare in Busia District, w. Kenya, in moist grassy bush, forest edge.
6a. Female. Brown, with much red in tail.
6b. Male. Red tail, no red on bill.

7 RED-HEADED BLUEBILL *Spermophaga r. ruficapilla* **Page 683**
Common in w. Kenyan forest undergrowth; scarce in cent. Kenyan highlands. (Paler-backed *S. r. cana* uncommon in East Usambara Mts.) No red on tail. Adults with bright red-and-blue bill.
7a. Juvenile. Brown, with only trace of red on bill.
7b. Male.
7c. Female.

8 ABYSSINIAN CRIMSONWING *Cryptospiza salvadorii kilimensis* **Page 682**
Highland-forest clearings and edges; terrestrial. (In n. Tanzania, see also Red-faced Crimsonwing on Plate 124.) Variably red on wings, upper tail-coverts.
8a. Juvenile male.
8b. Adult male (Female similar, with less red, none on eyelids.)

9 PETERS'S TWINSPOT *Hypargos niveoguttatus macrospilotus* **Page 682**
Eastern, especially coastal lowlands. On or near ground in damp bush, thickets.
9a. Juvenile. Tawny-brown, with grey bill; trace of white spotting.
9b. Male.
9c. Female.

10 GREEN-BACKED TWINSPOT *Mandingoa nitidula chubbi* **Page 681**
Uncommon in coastal lowlands, Usambara and Pare Mts; scarce in cent. and se. Kenyan highlands, in damp forest undergrowth and moist thickets.
10a. Juvenile male. Tawny-buff face, olive on wings.
10b. Adult male. Red face (pale orange-tawny in female).

11 BROWN TWINSPOT *Clytospiza monteiri* **Page 683**
Scarce in w. Kenya, on or near ground in moist bushed grassland and thickets.
11a Juvenile. Grey head, red upper tail-coverts; no white spots below.
11b Male. Small red throat patch.
11c Female. Whitish throat.

Dale A. Zimmerman
1991

PLATE 120: CANARIES (*Serinus*)

1 AFRICAN CITRIL *Serinus citrinelloides*   Page 698
Widespread in highlands along forest borders, roadsides, in gardens.
1a. *S. c. kikuyuensis*, male (Kenyan highlands west to Kakamega). Black face.
1b. *S. c. kikuyuensis*, female. Streaked below; bold superciliary stripe.
1c. *S. c. brittoni*, adult (w. Kenya). Both sexes like female *kikuyuensis,* but face greyer; slightly more yellow-green below.
1d. *S. c. brittoni*, juvenile. Browner and buffier than adult.
1e. *S. c. hypostictus*, female (Kenya and Tanzania). Face greyer than in other races, superciliary stripe less bold.
1f. *S. c. hypostictus*, male. Less heavily streaked than female.

2 PAPYRUS CANARY *S. koliensis*   Page 699
Lake Victoria basin, in and near papyrus. Resembles streaked plumages of African Citril, but bill shorter, stubbier, with more curved culmen.
2a. Female. Mask greyish, extends onto forehead; heavy ventral streaking.
2b. Male. Brighter yellow; less streaked; mask dusky, not reaching forehead.

3 YELLOW-FRONTED CANARY *S. mozambicus*   Page 699
Fairly common at coast and in the west, in second growth, scrub and bush. Mainly in moist habitats. Bold facial pattern. Forehead and underparts entirely yellow.
3a. Juvenile. Pale, spotted breast.
3b. *S. m. barbatus*, male (western). Bright olive-green above.
3c. *S. m. mozambicus*, female (coastal; East Usambara foothills). Brownish olive above.

4 WHITE-BELLIED CANARY *S. dorsostriatus*   Page 700
Widespread in dry country. White belly; streaked on sides and flanks.
4a. *S. d. maculicollis*, female. White extends from belly to under tail-coverts.
4b. *S. d. dorsostriatus*, male (southern). Less white; crissum yellowish.
4c. *S. d. dorsostriatus*, female. Duller than male, short breast streaks.

5 YELLOW-CROWNED CANARY *S. canicollis flavivertex*   Page 698
Common in highlands. Often in tall trees.
5a. Male. Yellow crown, much yellow in wings and tail.
5b. Female. Variably streaked below, yellow wing edgings, white belly.

6 BRIMSTONE CANARY *S. sulphuratus sharpii*   Page 700
Widespread in bush, cultivation, north to Mt Elgon, Maralal and the Nyambenis. Large; heavy-billed; olive 'whisker' marks.
6a. Female. Often dull; faintly streaked below.
6b. Male. Plain bright yellow below.
6c. Both sexes in flight. Little contrast between rump and back.

7 NORTHERN GROSBEAK-CANARY *S. donaldsoni*   Page 701
Scarce in dry bush and semi-desert north of Equator.
7a and 7b. Males. Large, with very large bill; underparts bright yellow, with some white on belly. Yellow rump contrasts with back. (Female on Plate 121.)

8 SOUTHERN GROSBEAK-CANARY *S. buchanani*   Page 700
Uncommon in dry bush south of Equator. Large and large-billed; dull; rump slightly more yellow than back.
8a. Female.
8b. Male.

1a

1b

1c

2a

2b

1d

1e

3a

3b

3c

1f

4a

4b

5a

5b

6a

6b

8a

6c

7a

7b

8b

DALE A. ZIMMERMAN
1989

PLATE 121: SEEDEATERS, BUNTINGS AND ORIOLE-FINCH

1 **YELLOW-RUMPED SEEDEATER** *Serinus reichenowi* **Page 697**
Widespread in open bushed habitats. Common in roadside weeds, brush, woodland. Siskin-sized; yellow rump evident in flight. **1a and 1b. Adults.**

2 **BLACK-THROATED SEEDEATER** *Serinus atrogularis somereni* **Page 697**
Kakamega–Ukwala area of w. Kenya. Status uncertain. Throat heavily mottled with black; superciliary stripe less distinct than in Yellow-rumped Seedeater.

3 **STREAKY SEEDEATER** *Serinus s. striolatus* **Page 697**
Common in gardens, scrub, woodland openings and cultivation in the highlands. Feeds on ground. Boldly and sharply streaked below; broad facial streaks.

4 **THICK-BILLED SEEDEATER** *Serinus burtoni* **Page 698**
Fairly common in highland-forest undergrowth, low trees. Large, dull, heavy-billed; olive wing and tail edgings. **4a. S. b. albifrons** (east of Rift Valley). White forehead. **4b. S. b. tanganjicae** (west of Rift Valley). Dark forehead.

5 **NORTHERN GROSBEAK-CANARY** *Serinus donaldsoni* **Page 701**
Scarce in open bush, semi-desert, north of Equator. **Female.** Brown and streaky, large pale bill, yellow rump. (Sexually dimorphic; male shown on Plate 120.)

6 **STRIPE-BREASTED SEEDEATER** *Serinus (reichardi) striatipectus* **Page 696**
Local and uncommon on shrub-covered slopes with scattered trees. Dark cheek contrasts with white superciliary stripe; crown finely streaked black and white; broad diffuse streaking below.

7 **STREAKY-HEADED SEEDEATER** *Serinus (gularis) elgonensis* **Page 696**
Rare on scrub-covered slopes in Mt. Elgon/Kongelai area. Black-and-white crown streaks; largely plain underparts, with white throat.

8 **HOUSE BUNTING** *Emberiza striolata saturatior* **Page 702**
Scarce in rocky deserts of n. Kenya. **8a. Male.** Rufous/tawny, with dusky throat streaks. **8b. Female.** Pale sandy rufous; throat faintly streaked.

9 **CINNAMON-BREASTED ROCK BUNTING** *Emberiza t. tahapisi* **Page 702**
Uncommon/fairly common on ground in rocky places and on dry slopes. **9a. Female.** Head streaked brown and buff. **9b. Male.** Head streaked with black and white.

10 **GOLDEN-BREASTED BUNTING** *Emberiza flaviventris kalaharica* **Page 703**
Common in highland gardens, open woods, forest edge. Feeds on ground; sings from high trees. **10a. Adult male.** Golden yellow below, with white flanks and belly; back may appear solid rufous as grey feather edges wear; rump grey. **10b. Juvenile.** Pale yellow below; brown-and-buff head stripes.

11 **SOMALI GOLDEN-BREASTED BUNTING** *Emberiza poliopleura* **Page 703**
Common in dry bush and scrub in e. and n. Kenya. **11a. Juvenile.** Similar to young Golden-breasted, but less yellow below, usually fewer breast streaks. **11b. Adult male.** Resembles Golden-breasted, but brighter above, with white-edged feathers; rump largely pale grey; flanks and outer rectrices with more white.

12 **BROWN-RUMPED BUNTING** *Emberiza affinis forbesi* **Page 704**
Rare and local in nw. Kenya. On or near ground in bush, on brushy slopes or escarpments. Yellow extends to flanks and belly; rump brown.

13 **ORTOLAN BUNTING** *Emberiza hortulana* **Page 702**
Palearctic vagrant. On ground in open areas. **13a. Adult female, winter.** Pale yellow throat/upper breast; large whitish eye-ring; white outer tail feathers. **13b and 13c. First-winter.** Bold white eye-ring; white tail sides conspicuous in flight.

14 **ORIOLE-FINCH** *Linurgus olivaceus* **Page 701**
Uncommon in highland-forest undergrowth. **14a. Adult male.** Short yellow-orange bill. **14b. Immature (?) female.** Short, dull orange bill; wing edgings yellow and white. Some individuals obscurely streaked below.

DALE A. ZIMMERMAN
1989

PLATE 122: NORTHERN TANZANIAN BIRDS (See also Plates 123 and 124)

1 WHITE-THROATED SWALLOW *Hirundo albigularis*   **Page 514**
Widespread in southern Africa; vagrant to Lake Jipe. Breast band narrow in centre (not of equal width throughout as in Barn Swallow); throat white. **1a and 1b. Adults**. (Immature has brown breast band, lacks chestnut on forehead.)

2 SOUTHERN CORDON-BLEU or BLUE WAXBILL *Uraeginthus angolensis*   **Page 686**
Vagrant from south of our region. (Normally north to Handeni and Naberera.) Both sexes pale brown from forehead to lower back; bill slate-grey or pinkish, with black cutting edges. (Female Red-cheeked Cordon-bleu has less blue on sides of head and neck. Female Blue-capped Cordon-bleu is paler; male is blue from forehead to nape; juvenile has tan breast.)

3. SPIKE-HEELED LARK *Chersomanes albofasciata beesleyi*   **Page 500**
Confined to treeless short-grass plains 30–50 km north of Arusha. Upright posture; short, white-tipped tail.

4 SWALLOW-TAILED BEE-EATER *Merops h. hirundineus*   **Page 467**
Ranges north to Tanga, possibly wanders farther. (Similar northern race *heuglini* approaches Kenyan border in Uganda and Sudan.) Deeply forked bluish tail in adults and young.

5 ASHY STARLING *Cosmopsarus unicolor*   **Page 634**
Locally common in dry bush, savanna and acacia woodland. Feeds on ground. Common in Tarangire NP.

6 OLIVE-FLANKED ROBIN-CHAT *Cossypha anomala mbuluensis*   **Page 536**
Only in Nou Forest, Mbulu Highlands. Forages in forest undergrowth and on ground. Flicks wings; slowly raises and lowers tail. Other robin-chats have rufous on breast.

7 BENNETT'S WOODPECKER *Campethera bennettii scriptoricauda*   **Page 490**
Reportedly uncommon in Kilimanjaro area, North Pare Mts, and from Handeni southward. (Formerly on Kenyan coast.) Throat speckled in centre (unlike Nubian Woodpecker) and bill extensively yellow below.
7a. Male.
7b. Female.

8 RUFOUS-TAILED WEAVER *Histurgops ruficaudus*   **Page 658**
Locally common and conspicuous in acacia savanna in Ngorongoro Crater and se. Serengeti NP. Gregarious; feeds on ground; nests colonially in trees.

9 GREY-BREASTED SPURFOWL *Francolinus rufopictus*   **Page 370**
Locally common in Serengeti NP. Tarsi and toes dark brown (red in Red-necked Spurfowl); sides of breast grey. Some hybridization with Yellow-necked Spurfowl in area of overlap in se. Serengeti.

10 DUSKY LARK *Pinarocorys n. nigricans*   **Page 500**
Somewhat thrush-like. Flicks wings constantly. A miombo-woodland bird of w. Tanzania, accidental in our region. Favours recently burnt ground.

11 CRESTED BARBET *Trachyphonus vaillantii suahelicus*   **Page 484**
Uncommon at Lake Manyara and Tarangire NPs; scarce in cultivation in West Usambara Mts. Forages on ground in dry areas, especially in vicinity of termitaria.

1a 1b 2 3 4 5 6 7a 7b 8 9 10 11

DALE A. ZIMMERMAN
1995

PLATE 123: NORTHERN TANZANIAN BIRDS (Usambara Mts) (See also Plate 124)

1 **BANDED GREEN SUNBIRD** *Anthreptes rubritorques*   **Page 640**
Fairly common in forest canopy of both Usambara ranges. Short-tailed.
1a. Female. Olive-green above, pale greyish yellow below, with faint yellowish streaks.
1b. Male.

2 **RED-CAPPED FOREST WARBLER** *Orthotomus m. metopias*   **Page 588**
Common in West Usambaras, rare in East Usambaras (formerly at Amani). Skulks in forest undergrowth.

3 **LONG-BILLED APALIS** *Apalis m. moreaui*   **Page 587**
Rare and local in East Usambaras only. Forages in dense vine tangles at forest edge.

4 **FÜLLEBORN'S BOUBOU** *Laniarius fuelleborni*   **Page 618**
Common in undergrowth and low trees in West Usambara forests. **Female** figured; male deeper black, especially on head.

5 **SHELLEY'S GREENBUL** *Andropadus masukuensis roehli*   **Page 520**
Fairly common in Usambara and South Pare mountain forests. (Kenyan *A. m. kakamegae* shown on Plate 75.)

6 **CABANIS'S BUNTING** *Emberiza cabanisi orientalis*   **Page 703**
Fairly common in open areas of East Usambaras and around Ambangulu in the Western range. No white subocular streak, unlike other yellow-breasted buntings.
6a. Male.
6b. Female.

7 **USAMBARA WEAVER** *Ploceus n. nicolli*   **Page 672**
Rare; apparently now restricted to forest and forest edge in West Usambaras.
7a. Male. Forehead dull yellow; brownish-yellow wash on nape.
7b. Female. Head brownish black.

8 **MOUNTAIN GREENBUL** *Andropadus nigriceps usambarae*   **Page 520**
Common in forests of West Usambaras and South Pare Mts; scarce or rare north to Taita Hills in se. Kenya. Black superciliary stripe diagnostic. (Black-crowned *A. n. nigriceps*, also in n. Tanzania, on Plate 75.)

9 **WHITE-CHESTED ALETHE** *Alethe fuelleborni*   **Page 539**
Common in Usambara forest undergrowth. Accidental or casual in South Pare Mts.

10 **DAPPLED MOUNTAIN ROBIN** *Modulatrix orostruthus amani*   **Page 531**
Rare in East Usambara montane forest. Forages low, often in streamside undergrowth.

11 **USAMBARA GROUND ROBIN** *Sheppardia montana*   **Page 534**
Fairly common in West Usambara forests above 1650 m.

12 **SPOT-THROAT** *Modulatrix s. stictigula*   **Page 530**
Rare in montane-forest undergrowth in both Usambara ranges; most numerous above 1500 m. Actively forages on ground; shy.

13 **SHARPE'S AKALAT** *Sheppardia sharpei usambarae*   **Page 535**
Fairly common in both Usambara ranges. Forages on or near ground.

14 **SWYNNERTON'S ROBIN** *Swynnertonia swynnertoni*   **Page 534**
Rare in East Usambara lowland-forest undergrowth; feeds on ground. (Female duller, head more olive.) Usambara birds may represent an undescribed subspecies.

15 **USAMBARA EAGLE-OWL** *Bubo vosseleri*   **Page 444**
Rare in forest and wooded borders of tea plantations in both Usambara ranges.

16 **MONTANE NIGHTJAR** *Caprimulgus poliocephalus guttifer*   **Page 447**
Local and uncommon at forest edge and grassland between 1075 and 1700 m.

DALE A. ZIMMERMAN
1995

PLATE 124: NORTHERN TANZANIAN BIRDS (including Pemba Island specialities)

1 PEMBA WHITE-EYE *Zosterops vaughani* — **Page 595**
Only white-eye on Pemba Island.

2 FOREST BATIS *Batis m. mixta* — **Page 602**
Locally common above 900 m in the Pare and Usambara Mts, on Kilimanjaro and Mt Meru. **Female** is brown-eyed, darker, less hoary and with shorter superciliary stripe than female *B. m. ultima* of coastal forests (see Plate 86). Male resembles that of *ultima*.

3 PEMBA SUNBIRD *Nectarinia pembae* — **Page 646**
Common on Pemba Island. **3a. Female. 3b. Adult male. 3c. Immature male.**

4 MONTANE WHITE-EYE *Zosterops poliogaster eurycricotus* — **Page 594**
Common in montane areas of Arusha NP, Kilimanjaro, Mt Meru, Essimingor, Lossogonoi Plateau and Lolkissale. No yellow on forehead, little on underparts. (*Z. p. mbuluensis*, present in other Tanzanian mountains, on Plate 102.)

5 WHITE-TAILED BLUE FLYCATCHER *Elminia albicauda* — **Page 599**
Locally common in forest edge and riverine forest in the Mbulu and Crater Highlands. Active; twists, drops wings and fans tail.

6 ZITTING CISTICOLA *Cisticola juncidis uropygialis* — **Page 580**
Erythristic morph (restricted to Pemba Island).

7 PALE-BREASTED ILLADOPSIS *Illadopsis rufipennis distans* — **Page 532**
Common in East Usambaras, less so at Ambangulu in West Usambaras. Shy. Forages on and near ground in dense forest undergrowth. (Kenyan *I. r. rufipennis* on Plate 90.)

8 OLIVE WOODPECKER *Dendropicos griseocephalus kilimensis* — **Page 494**
Local in montane forests. Dark olive on breast; unbarred blackish tail. **8a. Male. 8b. Female.**

9 WHITE-STARRED ROBIN *Pogonocichla stellata orientalis* — **Page 553**
This subspecies only in Usambara Mts. Other races elsewhere in n. Tanzania. **Immature** shown. (See Plate 93 for adult and juvenile of this species.)

10 RED-FACED CRIMSONWING *Cryptospiza reichenovi australis* — **Page 682**
Fairly common in highland-forest undergrowth and along forest borders. As low as 300 m in East Usambara foothills. **10a. Male.** Broad red orbital/loral area (unlike Abyssinian Crimsonwing). **10b. Female.** Diffuse pale orbital area.

11 SOUTHERN GREY-HEADED SPARROW *Passer diffusus mosambicus* — **Page 652**
The only *Passer* on Pemba Island. Replaced on adjacent mainland by *P. griseus*.

12 JAVA SPARROW *Padda oryzivora* — **Page 692**
Uncommon and local on Pemba Island. **12a. Adult male. 12b. Juvenile.**

13 WHITE-EYED SLATY FLYCATCHER *Melaenornis fischeri nyikensis* — **Page 553**
Mbulu and Crater Highlands. Eye-ring narrower and body plumage duller than more widespread *M. f. fischeri* (on Plate 87).

14 PEMBA GREEN PIGEON *Treron pembaensis* — **Page 422**
Only green pigeon on Pemba Island; grey head and underparts.

15 KURRICHANE THRUSH *Turdus libonyanus* — **Page 551**
Coastal lowlands and formerly East Usambara foothills. Present status uncertain. White throat bordered by dark streaks.

16 PEMBA SCOPS OWL *Otus pembaensis* — **Page 441**
Only small owl on Pemba Island. **16a.** Orange-rufous morph. **16b.** Pale rufous morph.

17 OLIVE THRUSH *Turdus olivaceus* — **Page 550**
Common in wooded highlands. **17a. T. o. deckeni, male.** Mt Kilimanjaro, Monduli, Kitumbeine, Longido and in extreme s. Kenya at Ol Doinyo Orok. (Still darker and duller *T. o. oldeani* of the Crater and Mbulu Highlands not illustrated.) **17b. T. o. roehli, male.** North Pare and Usambara Mts. (See Plate 91 for *T. o. abyssinicus*.)

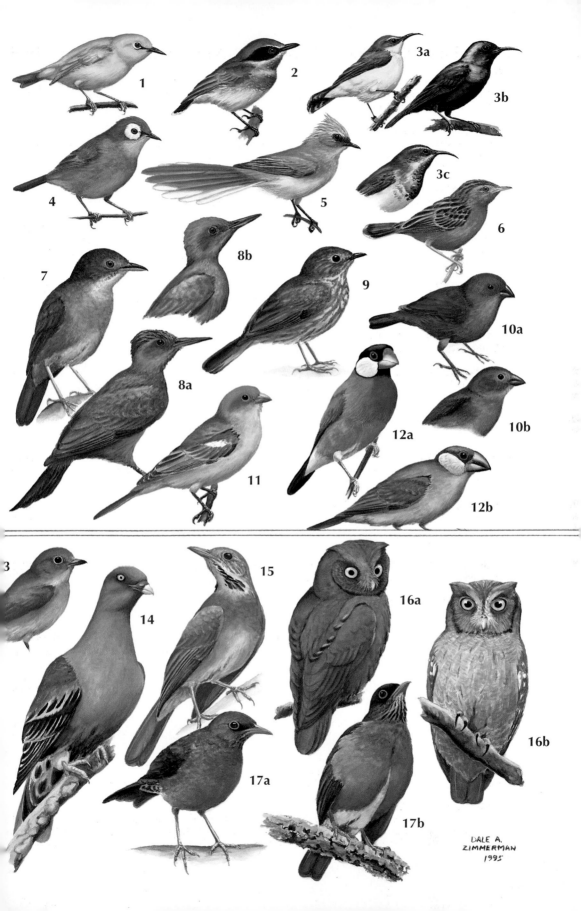

DALE A.
ZIMMERMAN
1995

OSTRICHES, FAMILY STRUTHIONIDAE
(1 or 2 species, now confined to Africa)

Flightless ratite birds, the largest of living species, weighing up to 136 kilos (300 lbs). They are powerful runners, with long sturdy legs, the thick thighs essentially featherless. There are only two toes on each foot. The head is very small, it and the long neck unfeathered except for fine bristles. The bill is short, flat and blunt-tipped; long eyelashes protect the large eyes. Sometimes evident in breeding males is the long (to 20 cm) grooved penis, an organ present in few bird species. Ostriches are gregarious, but single individuals are often encountered. Although mainly vegetarian, they readily feed on large insects. Males are sometimes polygynous and several females may lay eggs (totalling two dozen or more) in one nest, a large shallow scrape in the ground. The male usually incubates at night, the female by day. The nidifugous downy young are cared for by both sexes.

Freitag and Robinson (1993) believe that the Somali form may have diverged from the ancestor of other ostriches 3.6–4.1 million years ago. Their investigations show considerable mitochondrial DNA divergence between it and the other forms. This, especially in combination with morphological and ecological differences and reported interbreeding difficulties, suggests that separate species status is probably warranted for *molybdophanes*.

COMMON OSTRICH *Struthio camelus*   Plate 30

Length 2–2.5 m; *height of male up to 2.4 m (8 ft)*. **Adult male** brownish black with white (often stained) wings, tail and neck ring. In southern *S. c. massaicus*, parts of head and neck are thickly covered with woolly white down, and the pileum supports short, bristle-like feathers. *Pinkish skin of neck, sides of body and legs* becomes much brighter in breeding season (flushing red in sexual encounters), when the dark-tipped greyish-pink bill also becomes bright pink and the pink anterior tarsal scutes turn red; eyes dark brown; orbital ring yellowish. Male of nominate *camelus* has the head, most of neck, bare sides of body and legs pinkish, the bald crown ringed with short, stiff brown feathers extending down hindneck, and a collar of white feathers at base of bare portion of neck. Bill yellowish above, pink to red below; eyes brown. **Female** *massaicus* is grey-brown with pale feather edges; neck and legs pale pinkish, pinkish tan or creamy grey-brown. Dull grey-brown or pinkish-horn bill (darker at tip) becomes reddish or black with pink base when breeding; eyes brown. **Immature** similar. **Female** *S. c. camelus* has darker brown body feathers with pale edges; bill largely as in *massaicus*; neck and legs dirty grey-brown, changing to pink in breeding season, when tarsal scutes become brighter red. **Downy young** of both races *c*. 30 cm tall at hatching, striped buff and black on head and neck; body dappled black, buff and whitish above, whitish below. In *massaicus*, the stiff down gives way to feathers in about three months. **Juvenile** darker than adult female, with creamy-grey neck and legs. Males acquire whitish wing and tail feathers in their second year. Bill horn-brown; hazel-brown iris has buff outer ring. **VOICE**: Breeding male utters a deep booming *ooom, ooom, booo-ooooo*, descending in pitch, sometimes with an extra terminal *ooom*. Otherwise silent, except for an occasional loud hiss or bill-snapping. **HABITS**: Those of the family. **STATUS AND DISTRIBUTION**: Locally fairly common in dry open grassland and savanna. *S. c. massaicus* ranges from Serengeti NP east to Ngorongoro Crater and Arusha District, north across much of s. Kenya to Kilgoris, Nairobi and Tsavo West NP. A largely disjunct population present around Naro Moru, Timau and on the Laikipia Plateau, extends west to Baringo District and Maralal. *S. c. camelus* is known from border areas near Lokichokio on the Lotikipi Plains, where seasonally common prior to the mid-1960s. Now largely extirpated by local tribesmen for feathers. Occasional records of ostriches below the Kongelai Escarpment not racially assigned. **NOTE**: Some Kenyan ostrich populations may include in their ancestry birds representing extralimital subspecies from North Africa and Namibia that were part of the extensive stock of domesticated birds set free following collapse of early ostrich-farming operations. Atypical males (without the white neck ring) in Nairobi NP may also reflect limited interbreeding between *massaicus* and *molybdophanes* following introduction of the latter in the early 1970s. (Although male *molybdophanes* were initially rejected by local female *massaicus*, successful breeding eventually occurred, but in the absence of records it is not known if the resulting offspring were fertile.)

SOMALI OSTRICH *Struthio (camelus) molybdophanes*   Plate 30

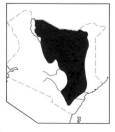

Length 2–2.5 m; height of male up to 2.4 m (8 ft.). **Adult male** differs from the preceding forms in its deeper black plumage, *blue-grey neck and legs*, black scutes on the lower tarsus and toes, those on *upper tarsus deep pink*, turning bright red when breeding (at which time thighs and neck become bluer). Bill pink above and whitish below, with horn-yellow or brownish tip, becoming bright pink when breeding. *Eyes pale brownish grey*. In both sexes the bare crown has a raised, dull yellow-brown horny hump surrounded by dense hair-like feathers; there is also sparse down elsewhere on the head and neck. Plumage of **adult female** and **immature** browner than in *massaicus*; eyes of female pale blue-grey. **VOICE**: Similar to that of other ostriches. **HABITS**: More of a browser than *massaicus*, often in bush and scrub. Usually solitary or in pairs. **STATUS AND DISTRIBUTION**: Uncommon to locally fairly common in savanna, bush and thorn-scrub in e. and ne. Kenya from the east side of Lake Turkana south to Samburu and Shaba Game Reserves, and from Isiolo, Garba Tula and Wajir Districts south to Meru NP, Galana Ranch and Tsavo East NP. Formerly sympatric with *S. c. massaicus* near Maralal.

GREBES, FAMILY PODICIPEDIDAE
(World, 19 species; Africa, 5; Kenya and n. Tanzania, 3)

Strictly aquatic birds with short wings, long neck, pointed bill and rudimentary tail. The legs are set far back on the body, the tarsi are laterally flattened, and the toes are lobed. Plumage is mainly grey, brown, chestnut and glistening satiny white; the head may have lateral tufts of feathers. Sexes are alike. Expert divers, grebes feed mainly on aquatic molluscs and fish. Flight is fast and direct with rapid wingbeats, the bird pattering across the water surface on take-off, and landing on its belly (not feet-first like ducks). Gregarious much of the year, they separate into pairs for breeding. The nest is a floating mound of plant material, usually hidden in vegetation. The three to six white eggs are typically stained brown. Young grebes are nidifugous and downy, the head and neck usually streaked or spotted.

GREAT CRESTED GREBE *Podiceps cristatus infuscatus* Plate 15

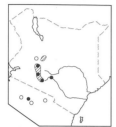

Length 46–56 cm (18–22"). Large, with a long thin neck typically held erect, and a long greyish bill. Upperparts dark brown; underparts, face and sides of neck white; crown and eye-stripe black. In flight, shows white bars on rear and front edges of inner part of wing. **Adult** has conspicuous black and chestnut frills on face and black 'ear-tufts' at sides of hindcrown. Eyes red; bill grey or brownish grey. Apparently no distinct non-breeding plumage in East African birds. **Juvenile** lacks frills and is paler, with striped head and neck. **Downy young** striped blackish and white; crown and lores partly bare and red; bill white with two vertical black stripes. **VOICE:** Harsh barking and honking calls when breeding; otherwise silent. **SIMILAR SPECIES:** Much smaller and shorter-necked Black-necked Grebe has shorter bill. **STATUS AND DISTRIBUTION:** Scarce and local resident on freshwater and alkaline lakes in the central Rift Valley; wanders to ponds on nearby Laikipia Plateau. Numbers greatly reduced in recent years through extensive use of gill nets by local fishermen. No breeding records 1979–92, and total Kenyan population probably under 50 individuals by 1995. In n. Tanzania a scarce resident on freshwater lakes in Arusha NP and Ngorongoro Crater.

BLACK-NECKED GREBE *Podiceps nigricollis gurneyi* Plate 15
(Eared Grebe)

Length 28–33 cm (11–13"). A small grebe with a *short, slender, slightly upturned* bill. **Breeding plumage** blackish above and on head and neck; white below with rufous band along flanks, *golden tufts behind eyes.* Shows small white patch on rear of wing in flight. Iris red, the pupil encircled by narrow white ring. No separate black-and-white non-breeding plumage, unlike northern races, but post-breeding birds become worn and faded. **Downy young** less sharply streaked than those of other grebes; bare parts of head pink; bill pink with black stripes. **VOICE:** A soft *preeip.* **SIMILAR SPECIES:** Little Grebe is smaller, more compact, with shorter neck, differently shaped head and bill, and chestnut foreneck. **STATUS AND DISTRIBUTION:** Local, breeding erratically in small numbers on permanent and seasonal Rift Valley lakes, mainly Bogoria, Elmenteita and (formerly) Nakuru, where hundreds may concentrate July–November. Occasionally wanders to Lake Turkana, Marsabit, Nairobi and the Tsavo region. Apparently moves in response to rainfall. In n. Tanzania a sporadic visitor, occasionally in large numbers, to Lake Lygarja (Serengeti NP); less frequent in the Crater Highlands and Arusha NP.

LITTLE GREBE *Tachybaptus ruficollis capensis* Plate 15
(Dabchick)

Length 23–29 cm (9–11.5"). A small dark grebe with rounded head, short neck and stubby bill. **Breeding plumage** dark brown above and dusky below, with *chestnut throat and foreneck.* Eyes brown; bill black, greenish at base, with conspicuous *pale yellow spot near rictus.* **Non-breeding plumage** dark brown above; sides of head, neck and breast brownish buff; throat whitish. **Juvenile** resembles non-breeding adult, but head and neck streaked with dull black. **Downy young** lacks bare head patches of other grebe chicks. Bill pale with vertical black band near base of mandible. **VOICE:** Common call a whinnying trill; alarm note *whit, whit.* **HABITS:** Usually in pairs or small groups. Territorial pursuits involve running across water with flapping wings. Frequently raises body from water and flaps wings. Attaches nest to submerged vegetation. **STATUS AND DISTRIBUTION:** Widespread and common on most permanent and seasonal waters below 3000 m. Most numerous on larger lakes of the Rift Valley highlands and in Arusha NP. Appears quickly on newly formed flood pools.

ALBATROSSES, FAMILY DIOMEDEIDAE
(World, 14 species; Africa, 9; Kenya, 2; n. Tanzania, 1)

Large web-toed seabirds with a strong hooked bill covered by horny plates and with tubular nostrils positioned laterally on the bill. Superficially somewhat gull-like, but considerably larger and with proportionately much longer wings. They feed largely on squid taken from the surface of the sea, and soar on stiff wings for extended periods, only rarely coming near land in our region. Most species nest on islands in southern oceans. They are long-lived and take several years to reach maturity. Status of these birds in East African waters is poorly known. Underwing pattern together with colours of head, bill and upperparts are important in identification.

*BLACK-BROWED ALBATROSS *Diomedea melanophris*   Plate 1

Length 81–95 cm (32–37″); wingspan *c.* 8′. **Adult** suggests a very long-winged, dark-backed gull with a white rump. Black upper wing-surface and back contrast with white head, which at close range shows *narrow black eye-lines and dusky lores.* Underparts white; *underside of wings typically white centrally with broad black tip and border* (the white central area broadest in older birds). Tail grey with blackish tip. Bill bright yellow or orange-yellow, red at tip, narrowly black at base; eyes brown in nominate *melanophris*, yellow in *D. m. impavida*; feet bluish white. **Juvenile** has grey or dusky bill, largely white head with a dark mark through the eye, grey nape and collar; underside of wings much darker than in adult, the pale central area reduced in extent. **Immature** has white head and *black-tipped, dull yellowish bill*; pale areas on underside of wings greyer than in adult. **Habits:** Soars in sweeping glides with wings bowed. Follows ships. Usually rests on sea when winds light or calm. **Similar Species:** See Shy Albatross. **Status and Distribution:** Rare visitor from southern oceans. Several sight records in Kenyan waters north to Mombasa (1955–90). Subspecies uncertain.

SHY ALBATROSS *Diomedea cauta*   Plate 1
(White-capped Albatross)

Length 89–99 cm (35–39″); wingspan 6.5-8′. Slightly larger than Black-browed Albatross, the longer bill much thicker basally. Readily identified by *black spot near body at base of leading edge on underside of black-bordered, black-tipped wing.* **Adult** grey-brown on upper back, shading to darker brown on lower back, which contrasts with white rump. Blackish around eyes. General head colour varies racially: white with grey cheeks in nominate *cauta*, white forehead and forecrown contrasting with otherwise grey-brown head in *salvini*, all grey and darker in *eremita*. Bill yellow with black spot at tip of mandible in *eremita*, yellowish grey with yellow tip in other races; no black spot in *cauta*. Eyes brown; feet pinkish, bluish at joints. **Immature** has greyish bill (sometimes with black mandible tip in nominate race; entire bill black-tipped in *salvini*). Grey nape (whitish in nominate race) and partial collar similar to young Black-browed Albatross. **Status and Distribution:** A wanderer from southern oceans, possibly regular August/September in the Pemba Channel (14 sightings plus photographs, 1989 and 1990). Specimen from Mombasa (Oct. 1986). To date, only nominate *cauta* recorded from East African waters.

PETRELS AND SHEARWATERS, FAMILY PROCELLARIIDAE
(World, 76 species; Africa, 32; Kenya, 7)

Web-toed 'tube-nosed' birds rarely seen from shore. As with other pelagic species, they are little known in East African waters, and some are admitted to our list only on the basis of wave-cast carcasses found on beaches. The distinctive flight of larger species consists of bursts of quick wingbeats alternating with banking and gliding on long, narrow, rigidly held wings. The smaller prions have a more erratic flight, typically just above the waves. In all species the hooked bill is covered with horny plates; the nostrils are separated by a partition but lie in a common tube at the base of the culmen. Most have pale underparts, but a few are uniformly dark. General build and flight characteristics are important in identification, as are various more subtle features. The birds breed in a burrow or scrape, mainly on oceanic islands. Most species are highly migratory.

*PINTADO PETREL *Daption capense*   Figure p. 306
(Cape Petrel, Cape Pigeon)

Length 36–40 cm (14–16″); wingspan *c.* 3′. A stocky medium-sized petrel with distinctively *pied upperparts*: back and rump white with bold black chevrons, wings with large white patches; tail white with broad black terminal band; head black. Underparts white, except for black wing borders and tail tip. Bill and feet black; eyes brown. **Voice:** A high *chichichichi* when feeding. **Habits:** Flies with stiff-winged flapping interspersed with glides, often high. Pecks pigeon-like at food organisms on water surface. Follows ships. **Status and Distribution:** Southern vagrant. One sight record off Mombasa, September 1974.

Vagrant procellariiform birds: 1. White-chinned Petrel 2. Jouanin's Petrel 3. Pintado or Cape Petrel 4. Matsudaira's Storm-petrel 5. Antarctic Prion 6. Slender-billed Prion.

WHITE-CHINNED PETREL *Procellaria aequinoctialis* Figure p. 306
(Cape Hen)

Length 51–59 cm (20–23"); wingspan 4–5'. A large, *dark brown* petrel with a conspicuous *greenish white or ivory-coloured bill* (culmen and mandibular groove blackish). The *small white chin patch* is difficult to see, and not always present. Eyes brown; feet black. Young resemble adults. *P. a. conspicillata* has more white on sides of face than the nominate race. **HABITS:** Flight powerful, with slow wingbeats and long glides. Sometimes soars high. Follows ships. **SIMILAR SPECIES:** Dark Wedge-tailed Shearwater is smaller, has dark bill and pale feet, and lacks contrasting white chin patch. **STATUS AND DISTRIBUTION:** Vagrant from southern waters. One photographed off Shimoni, September 1990, was apparently *P. a. aequinoctialis*, the only record from East Africa.

*WEDGE-TAILED SHEARWATER *Puffinus pacificus* Plate 1

Length 41–46 cm (16–18"); wingspan *c.* 3'. Fairly large and with a *long wedge-shaped tail. Holds wings forward, slightly bowed, and angled.* Bill slender, dark grey; feet flesh-white; eyes brown. **Dark morph** is wholly blackish brown with darker primaries and tail; sometimes shows paler bands across upper wing-coverts. Rare **pale morph**, not yet reported in East African waters, is lighter brown above, white below except for brown-margined wings. Juvenile resembles adult. **HABITS:** Under normal conditions flaps slowly, then glides upwards and banks. Does not follow ships. **SIMILAR SPECIES:** Smaller Jouanin's Petrel has shorter, thicker bill, sides of tail uneven owing to shorter outer feathers; flies rapidly. Flesh-footed Shearwater, *P. carneipes*, not yet recorded here, has pale bill, pale bases to underside of primaries, and holds wings straighter in flight. See White-chinned Petrel. **STATUS AND DISTRIBUTION:** Scarce. Several acceptable sight records from Shimoni to Lamu, with maximum of 12 birds observed off Mtwapa, early December 1991. Breeds in western Indian Ocean.

AUDUBON'S SHEARWATER *Puffinus lherminieri* Plate 1

Length 30 cm (12"); wingspan 27". A small, stocky shearwater with distinctive fluttering flight. *Upperparts dark brown, including cap, which extends to below eyes;* underparts white except for *brown under tail-coverts.* In Persian Gulf race *persicus*, brown extends to axillaries, sides of breast and flanks; wings appear dark beneath with a restricted pale central area. Bill narrow and blackish; eyes brown; *feet flesh-pink,* tarsi dusky on outer sides. **HABITS:** Solitary or in small flocks. Flight involves *bursts of rapid wing-flapping interspersed with short glides.* Sometimes rests on the water with wings partly raised. **SIMILAR SPECIES:** Little and Mascarene Shearwaters, *P. assimilis* and *P. atrodorsalis* (see Note below), are *black,* not brown, above, have white under tail-coverts, and in Little white of face extends to just *above* eyes; feet bluish. **STATUS AND DISTRIBUTION:** Uncommon, but recorded offshore most months, mainly north of Kilifi. One found dead inland at Limuru (Oct. 1963) was *P. l. bailloni,* which breeds on Mascarene islands, but *persicus* and *nicolae* could also reach East African waters. **NOTE:** Single birds seen 90 km east of Mombasa, 29 May 1991, and 500 km east, 2 June 1991, are believed to have been the recently described Mascarene Shearwater, *P. atrodorsalis* (Shirihai *et al.* 1995). See **Figure p. 308.** Unlike the slightly larger Audubon's, this is a *black*-and-white bird, whose long wings and tail and slender bill are reminiscent of extralimital Manx Shearwater, *Puffinus puffinus.* It is larger and slimmer than Little Shearwater, which like Mascarene, has been collected in s. Africa. The uniformly black upperparts are relieved only by narrow indistinct whitish greater-covert tips; a wedge of black extends down from rump to thigh, separating the white flank and crissum; narrow dark brown margin on leading edge of wing, remainder of wing-linings (including axillaries) pure white, remiges mostly dusky grey to blackish below, indistinctly whitish on basal outer webs of outer primaries. Tarsi and toes blue-grey and black (flesh-pink in Audubon's).

ANTARCTIC PRION *Pachyptila desolata* Figure p. 306
(Dove Prion)

Length 27 cm (10.5"); wingspan 61 cm (24"); bill length 24.7–29.5 mm; bill width 12–15 mm. On the basis of present evidence, the most likely prion in East African waters. A small petrel with *blue-grey* upperparts and a *bold, dark, open M-shaped band across wings and back.* Tail wedge-shaped, with black tip above and below. Crown dark blue-grey; side of face well marked with blackish eye-line, white superciliary stripe. Blue-grey of nape and hindneck extends downward to form a *dark smudge or patch on each side of lower neck and breast,* contrasting with white cheeks and throat (but this feature is difficult to evaluate without practice, as it is present to a lesser degree in other prions). Underside of wings whitish with dusky tips and trailing edges. Bill and feet pale blue. **HABITS:** Flight rapid and twisting, close to waves; rapid flapping alternates with short glides on slightly bowed wings. Higher flight erratic, almost bat-like, as bird flutters up and over a ship. **SIMILAR SPECIES:** Broad-billed and Salvin's Prions, *P. vittata* and *P. salvini,* neither known from East African waters, have less extensive grey patches at sides of lower neck and breast (posterior edge of patch more sharply defined in *salvini*). *P. vittata* has black bill. Fairy Prion, *P. turtur,* not recorded here, has more black on tail, a paler, less contrasting head

Mascarene Shearwater. Recorded at sea east of Mombasa and likely within our territory.

ta has black bill. Fairy Prion, *P. turtur*, not recorded here, has more black on tail, a paler, less contrasting head pattern, and smaller smudges at sides of breast. See Slender-billed Prion. **STATUS AND DISTRIBUTION**: Vagrant from southern oceans. Two heads, found on the beach at Watamu in August 1988, constitute the only specimen evidence from our region. A prion seen off Ras Ngomeni (near Malindi), 10 September 1983, and one photographed off Shimoni, September 1990, appeared to be *desolata*. Numerous dead Antarctic Prions were found on the coast of se. Somalia in August 1979 (Ash, 1983). **NOTE**: *Pachyptila* taxonomy is in flux, the forms variously treated as six species (Harper 1980) or only three (Cox 1980).

SLENDER-BILLED PRION *Pachyptila belcheri*
(Thin-billed Prion)

Figure p. 306

Length 26 cm (10"); wingspan 56 cm (22"); bill length 23–27.3 mm, bill width 10.2–12.5 mm. Very similar to the preceding species, but dark *patches on sides of lower neck/breast smaller, shorter and less conspicuous*; upperparts *paler* blue-grey, the *M-mark less bold*; underparts (including underside of wings) paler; *black of tail tip more restricted*; *outer tail feathers noticeably pale* above. Diagnostic *slender bill* is evident only under optimum conditions. **HABITS**: As for Antarctic Prion. **STATUS AND DISTRIBUTION**: Vagrant from southern oceans. One found dead at Watamu, 16 August 1984 (reported in earlier publications as *P. vittata desolata*).

JOUANIN'S PETREL *Bulweria fallax*

Figure p. 306

Length 30–32 cm (12–12.5"); wingspan 76–83 cm (30–32.5"). A blackish-brown petrel with rather heavy head and bill, long slender wings, and *long wedge-shaped tail*. A close view reveals grey tips to feathers of chin and forehead. Often shows pale brown diagonal band or series of pale spots on upper wing-coverts, presumably varying with moult. Bill black, or with the plates pale horn, held slightly downward, suggesting a high forehead; eyes brown; feet pinkish. **HABITS**: Flies fast in *swooping zigzagging arcs, with bowed wings held slightly forward*, and 'towers' 15-20 m above the water in *Pterodroma* fashion (Harrison 1983). In calm weather, swooping flight with low bows said to be characteristic; seldom follows ships, but flies alongside, mostly between and along the waves (Van den Berg *et al.* 1991). **SIMILAR SPECIES**: Wedge-tailed Shearwater is much larger, with slower wingbeats, and slender, dark grey bill held more horizontally. Flesh-footed Shearwater, *Puffinus carneipes*, also larger, has slender pale bill. Rare Mascarene Petrel, *Pterodroma aterrima*, is slightly larger, with shorter, more square-tipped tail. Bulwer's Petrel, *B. bulwerii*, is smaller, slimmer, with proportionately smaller head and bill. Of these four species, only Wedge-tailed is known in East African waters. **STATUS AND DISTRIBUTION**: Vagrant from nw. Indian Ocean. Three Kenyan specimen records from Malindi (Dec. 1953 and Dec. 1985) and off

STORM-PETRELS, FAMILY HYDROBATIDAE
(World, 20 species; Africa, 9; Kenya, 4)

Small, dark pelagic birds with erratic and often fluttering flight low over the water. The slender bill is short with a terminal hook, and the nostrils are united in a tube on the culmen. Storm-petrels are often in flocks, feeding on small fish and invertebrates picked from the surface of the sea. They nest in holes and burrows on distant oceanic islands. As with other procellariiform birds, they discharge oil from mouth and nostrils when disturbed. Some species are highly migratory. Identification is difficult, and relies in part on feeding action and flight characteristics. The family is also known as Oceanitidae.

*WILSON'S STORM-PETREL *Oceanites oceanicus*   **Plate 2**

Length 150–190 mm (6–7.5"); wingspan 38–42 cm (15–16.5"). A small *sooty-black* bird with *white rump, square or slightly rounded tail tip,* and a *pale band across the upper wing-coverts.* Sides of tail white below; wings rather short and rounded. Legs long and slender; the black toes, often projecting beyond the tail in flight, are joined by *yellow webs* (difficult to see). **HABITS:** Flight swallow-like with rapid shallow wingbeats and brief glides, wings held rather straight. When feeding, skips across water with wings raised, feet pattering the surface. Gregarious, and often follows ships. **SIMILAR SPECIES:** Leach's Storm-petrel is larger, with forked tail, shorter legs and different habits. **STATUS AND DISTRIBUTION:** Uncommon visitor to offshore waters from subantarctic breeding areas. Almost annual, April to December, from Shimoni north to Kiunga. Subspecies uncertain.

LEACH'S STORM-PETREL *Oceanodroma leucorhoa*   **Plate 2**

Length 190–230 mm (7.5–9"); wingspan 45–48 cm (18–19"). Sooty or brownish black with *forked tail,* and *white rump divided by greyish centre* (difficult to see in the field); pale bar across upper wing-coverts. Appears more slender and longer-winged than Wilson's Storm-petrel. Feet dark, *not projecting beyond tail.* **HABITS:** Flight erratic and buoyant, the deep wingbeats alternating with swooping glides. Often solitary. Does not follow ships. **SIMILAR SPECIES:** See Wilson's Storm petrel. **STATUS AND DISTRIBUTION:** Vagrant. A beached specimen (presumably of nominate race; not seen by us) south of Mombasa (Feb. 1967). Three sight records (Kilifi, Dec. 1973; Watamu, April 1978; Mtwapa, Oct. 1981).

*MATSUDAIRA'S STORM-PETREL *Oceanodroma matsudairae*   **Figure p. 306**

Length 240–250 mm (9–10"); wingspan 56 cm (22"). The only *dark-rumped* storm-petrel recorded to date from East African waters. Larger than Leach's and entirely *dark brown,* except for *paler diagonal bar on upper wing-coverts* and *small white patch* formed by bases of outer primary shafts; tail forked. **HABITS:** Normal flight heavier and more lethargic than that of Leach's Storm-petrel, with slower wingbeats and glides, but sometimes indulges in low twisting flight. **STATUS AND DISTRIBUTION:** Vagrant. Two sight records off Mombasa, July and August 1981. The species is known to migrate to the western Indian Ocean from breeding areas south of Japan.

BLACK-BELLIED STORM-PETREL *Fregetta tropica*   **Plate 2**

Length 200 mm (8"); wingspan 46 cm (18"). A vagrant *white-rumped* storm-petrel, larger than Wilson's, black above, and with a *dark central line on the white belly; wing-linings also white.* **HABITS:** Flies low and foot-patters like other storm-petrels. Seldom follows ships, more frequently flying beside or ahead of them. **SIMILAR SPECIES:** White-bellied Storm-petrel, *F. grallaria* (not recorded here, but known in southern African waters), is much paler, with all-white belly and crissum. **STATUS AND DISTRIBUTION:** Two records of beached birds, a specimen found dead at Watamu, June 1988, and another found dead but not preserved near Malindi, June 1994.

TROPICBIRDS, FAMILY PHAETHONTIDAE
(World, 3 species; Africa, 3; Kenya and n. Tanzania, 1)

Medium-sized aerial pelagic birds with stout pointed bills, very short tarsi, long tern-like wings, and a wedge-shaped tail with greatly elongated narrow central feathers. Adult plumage is white with black markings. Tropicbirds fly high above the sea, the fluttering wingbeats alternating with soaring glides. They hover and plunge for fish and squid. Nesting is colonial on tropical and subtropical oceanic islands. The single brownish egg is laid in a hole or among rocks on the ground, sometimes in a tree cavity. The nidicolous young are covered with white down at hatching.

WHITE-TAILED TROPICBIRD *Phaethon l. lepturus*

Plate 2

Length *c.* 81 cm (32") including tail streamers; wingspan 3'. **Adult** mostly white, with black diagonal bar on wing-coverts and black primary bases forming patch on forewing; long white tail feathers have black shafts, and there is a black crescent-shaped mark through eye. Bill and feet yellow; eyes brown. **Juvenile** has black wing tips and heavy black barring on upperparts; lacks large black bar on wings and has no tail streamers; yellow bill dark-tipped. **SIMILAR SPECIES**: Adult Red-tailed Tropicbird, *P. rubricauda,* lacks black bar and patch on wing, has red bill and tail streamers; juvenile lacks black wing tips, and the bill is black (becoming yellowish in immature). Extralimital Red-billed Tropicbird, *P. aethereus* (which could wander to Kenya from breeding areas in northern Somalia), has red bill, white tail streamers, heavily barred back, much black in wing tips; flying overhead, it shows distinct barring on inner secondaries; juvenile has yellow or orange bill, complete black nuchal collar, and much more black in primaries than young White-tailed Tropicbird. **STATUS AND DISTRIBUTION**: Generally uncommon, but regular in the Pemba Channel off Shimoni, August to March; recorded occasionally between Malindi and Kiunga, September to November. **NOTE**: The Red-tailed Tropicbird is included in some check-lists on the basis of an undated and unsubstantiated sight record from near Kiunga in

Red-tailed Tropicbird. Probable in Kenyan and n. Tanzanian waters, but no substantiated records.

1961. Reports from deep-sea fishermen suggest that the species is occasional in Kenyan waters. See Figure below.

PELICANS, FAMILY PELECANIDAE
(World, 8 species; Africa, 3; Kenya and n. Tanzania, 2)

Very large piscivorous swimming birds with short tarsi and fully webbed toes. The hook-tipped bill is long and straight, and between its tip and the throat is a large extensible gular pouch, suspended from the mandible. The wings are long and broad, the tail short. Males are larger than females, but no different in plumage. Pelicans are gregarious throughout the year. Flocks soar effortlessly for long periods and may fly considerable distances between breeding sites and fishing areas. The flight is ponderous, with the long neck retracted. They build large nests of sticks in trees or bushes or on the ground, generally laying two unmarked eggs that are incubated by both sexes. The nidicolous chicks are naked and pink on hatching; they are tended by both parents.

GREAT WHITE PELICAN *Pelecanus onocrotalus*

Plate 14

(Eastern White Pelican)

Length 140–178 cm (55–70"); wingspan 8–10'. Huge. **Adult** appears generally white on land or water; *in flight, tip and rear half of wing largely black.* **Breeding** bird tinged pinkish and with small occipital crest. Bare facial skin pinkish yellow in male, bright orange in female; bill greyish and pink, becoming bright yellow and bluish with red nail in breeding season, when both sexes develop a swollen orange-red knob at base of culmen. This turns pink and shrinks after the eggs are laid. Pouch usually yellow; *feet yellowish or orange*; eyes dark red-brown. Naked pink skin of newly hatched **downy young** becomes black, later develops dark brown down. At age of about four weeks brown **juvenile** feathers erupt, and by six weeks the plumage mainly grey-brown except for blackish flight feath pouch black but later mottled with ochre-yellow; feet grey. **VOICE**: Practically silent except in breeding colonies, where mooing sounds, a deep grunting *hunh-hunh-hunh-hunh*, and a continuous humming are evident, the latter continuing through the night. **HABITS**: Highly gregarious, often loafing in dense concentrations on lakeshores. Feeds in tightly packed co-ordinated flotillas, all birds submerging heads and necks in unison. Flies in V-formations and commonly soars. Nests colonially on ground, usually on inaccessible islands. Sometimes active at night. **SIMILAR SPECIES**: Pink-backed Pelican is smaller and greyer, with pale pinkish-grey bill and pouch; in flight, trailing edge of wings is grey, not black. **STATUS AND DISTRIBUTION**: Thousands inhabit alkaline Rift Valley lakes. Up to 5,000 pairs breed at Lake Elmenteita and smaller numbers occasionally nest on lakes Natron and Manyara. Wanders to other lakes, rivers and coastal estuaries. Movements between Rift Valley lakes in Ethiopia, Kenya and Tanzania are not clearly defined.

PINK-BACKED PELICAN *Pelecanus rufescens*   Plate 14

Length 135–152 cm (53–60"); wingspan 7–8'. Smaller and duller than the preceding species. **Adult** *greyish white*, with small black loral spot; *head tufted* and developing a dark *shaggy crest* when breeding. Wing tips dark above and below, but *secondaries brownish grey*, not black as in Great White Pelican. Bill, pouch and small bare orbital ring yellowish or pinkish grey, mandible more pink; eyes brown; *feet grey or pinkish*. When breeding, pouch deep yellow with many fine dusky vertical lines; orbital skin pink or orange above eye, yellow below; feet deep pink. *Pinkish back and rump may show in flight*; belly also washed with pink. **Juvenile** brownish grey on back and wings; head and back of neck brownish; rump, back and belly white; tail brown. Bill pale dull yellow; pouch grey (to greenish yellow?); feet greyish pink. **VOICE**: Almost silent. Utters guttural notes in breeding colonies. **HABITS**: Gregarious, usually in small parties, but dozens may rest on lakeshores, often with Great White Pelicans. Forages singly, catching fish with heron-like snapping action. Nests colonially in tall trees. **SIMILAR SPECIES**: See Great White Pelican. **STATUS AND DISTRIBUTION**: Widespread on lakes, rivers, seasonal flood waters, also coastal estuaries and saltpans. Colonies often small, widely scattered, and may be some distance from water. Occasionally breeds on islands in Lake Turkana.

BOOBIES, FAMILY SULIDAE
(World, 9 species; Africa, 6; Kenya, 3; n. Tanzania, 1)

Large, short-legged, web-toed seabirds. The long, stout, conical bill, pointed wing tips and wedge-shaped tail impart a streamlined appearance. Plumage is black and white or brown; the sexes are similar. Boobies catch fish and squid by diving head-first with partly folded wings, sometimes from considerable heights. Breeding is colonial, on islands or cliffs. The one to three eggs are laid in nests built on the ground or in trees. The nidicolous chicks are naked at hatching, downy later. Incubation and care of the young are by both sexes.

MASKED BOOBY *Sula dactylatra melanops*   Plate 1
Blue-faced Booby)

Length 81–92 cm (32–36"). **Adult** *white* with *black flight feathers and tail*. Bill yellowish, bare facial and gular skin blackish; legs and feet grey, eyes yellow. **Juvenile** dark grey-brown above, with dark brown head (including throat) and, on *some* individuals, a narrow white hindneck collar; *underside of wing shows dark stripe parallel to leading edge*, plus *broad dark trailing edge and tip*; bill dull olive. **Immature** retains dark plumage, but white hindneck collar becomes wider. Bill gradually turns pale greenish yellow. With moult, upperparts whiten from rump forwards; greater coverts are the first wing feathers to change. Some individuals breed in immature plumage. **VOICE**: A high double honk sometimes heard at sea. **HABITS**: Usually solitary except on nesting islands. Flies quite high and impressively plunge-dives almost vertically. **SIMILAR SPECIES**: Brown Booby differs from young Masked in having dark brown of neck extending to upper breast and continuous with upperparts; never shows hindneck collar (present on *some* juvenile Masked Boobies); underwing pattern also differs (see above). White morph of Red-footed Booby is smaller, with blue-grey bill, red feet, black carpal patch on underside of wing, and usually an all-white tail. Extralimital Cape Gannet, *Morus capensis*, has pale blue-grey bill and yellow wash on crown and nape; difficult to distinguish from Masked Booby at a distance. **STATUS AND DISTRIBUTION**: Uncommon but regular in the Pemba Channel August–February, presumably from breeding colony on Latham Island, Tanzania. **NOTE**: Report of Cape Gannet off Pemba Island, referred to by Pakenham (1979), was based on hearsay. The species is not known to range north of Zanzibar.

*BROWN BOOBY *Sula leucogaster*   Plate 1

Length 64–74 cm (25–29"). Appears smaller, more lightly built and longer-tailed than Masked Booby. Quicker wing action is reminiscent of a large cormorant. **Adult** brown, with lower breast, belly and under tail-coverts white; underside of wings white with dark tips and borders. Bill yellow (occasionally greenish grey with paler tip), slim and tapering. Bare facial and gular skin yellow or whitish with blue or green tinge in female, dark blue in male; eyes dark; legs and feet yellow. **Immature** resembles adult, but bill and facial skin grey, underparts and *underside of wings sullied with brown*. **Voice:** Mostly silent, but male utters a high *schweee*; female gives a loud honking *aar* (Brown et al. 1982). **Habits:** Usually flies close to water, diving at an angle, but at times plunges vertically from a greater height. Pursues flying-fish in the air. **Similar Species:** See juvenile Masked Booby. **Status and Distribution:** Rare. Sight records from Pemba Channel, August/September, and from Kilifi northwards mainly January/February. No specimens or photographs from Kenyan or Tanzanian waters. (Alleged specimens from Latham Island are immature Masked Boobies.)

RED-FOOTED BOOBY *Sula sula rubripes*   Plate 1

Length 66–77 cm (26–30"). A small, polymorphic booby, usually with *red feet* and *white tail*. Bill and facial skin bluish grey; eyes brown. **Adult** plumage variable: (1) white with black flight feathers and *black patch on underside of carpal area*; (2) white with dark brown back and upper wing surface; (3) brown with white rump, belly and tail; (4) wholly brownish. **Juvenile/immature** wholly brown with yellowish-grey legs and feet; bill dark. **Habits:** Those of the family. Readily approaches ships and fishing boats, often perching on rigging. **Similar Species:** Adult Masked Booby is larger, with yellow bill and black tail. Extralimital Cape Gannet also larger and with black tail. **Status and Distribution:** Casual. Seven records, August–March, including specimens from Kilifi (Oct. 1976), near Mombasa (March 1978) and Watamu (Sept. 1988). Brown morph reported off Shimoni (Aug. 1988) and at Latham Island, Tanzania (Nov. 1993).

CORMORANTS, FAMILY PHALACROCORACIDAE
(World, 32 species; Africa, 7; Kenya and n. Tanzania, 2)

Large, upright-perching, short-legged aquatic birds with fully webbed toes. The neck is long, the bill strong and hooked, with a small bare gular pouch at the base. The tail is stiff and rounded. The plumage is not entirely waterproof, and the short wings are often held outstretched to dry (and for thermoregulation) when at rest. Cormorants swim low in the water, with the bill tilted upward. They dive from the surface for fish and frogs, pursuing them underwater, and using the feet, not the wings, in swimming. The flapping flight is strong and direct, with outstretched neck. The bluish or greenish eggs are laid in nests of sticks on the ground or in trees. The young are nidicolous, naked at hatching, but later developing dense dark down. Incubation and care of the young are undertaken by both sexes.

GREAT CORMORANT *Phalacrocorax carbo lucidus*   Plate 14
(White-breasted Cormorant)

Length 80–100 cm (31.5–40"). A large heavy cormorant with a *short tail*, our race black with *white cheeks, foreneck and upper breast*. **Breeding adult** has white thigh patches, and the black plumage is glossed with green; lores orange (or scarlet in female). Bill grey; eyes emerald-green; gular pouch dark olive; feet black. Rare all-black individuals are known from Lake Victoria and west of our region. **Non-breeding** birds are duller, lack white thigh patches, and the greyish bill is white at base; gular pouch and skin below eyes yellow or olive; eyes and feet as in breeding plumage. **Juvenile/immature** brownish above and entirely dull white below, darkening with successive moults. Bill greyish above, dull greyish yellow below; gular pouch pale yellow. **Voice:** A rare guttural *korrrrk*, but usually silent away from breeding colonies, where birds utter a variety of growling, purring and snoring sounds. **Habits:** Gregarious. Roosts and nests in colonies in trees or on rocky islands. In water, often submerges until only head and neck are visible; patters across surface when taking flight. Hops awkwardly on ground. **Similar Species:** See Long-tailed Cormorant. **Status and Distribution:** Locally common resident, mainly restricted to large lakes with rocky or open shores, and especially numerous at lakes Victoria, Naivasha, Nakuru and Turkana. Some wander to smaller bodies of water including coastal estuaries. Generally scarce in n. Tanzania.

LONG-TAILED CORMORANT *Phalacrocorax a. africanus*   Plate 14
(Reed Cormorant)

Length 51–56 cm (20–22"). Much smaller than Great Cormorant, with *relatively long tail* and *small bill*. **Breeding adult** generally black with faint greenish gloss; feathers of back, rump and upper tail-coverts prominently

whitish-edged; wing-coverts and scapulars bronzy grey with black tips. Bristly feathers of short frontal crest white basally; ephemeral tufts of white filoplumes behind eyes. Bill yellow with brown culmen and some dark bars on mandible; bare facial skin yellow-orange or red early in breeding season; *eyes red*; feet black. Seasonal variation poorly understood in East Africa. Some non-breeding birds, red-eyed and probably adult, are white below, some with dark feathers on breast, as said to be true of non-breeding adults in southern Africa. **Juvenile** birds, whitish or buff and white below, are brown-eyed. **Voice**: A bleating *kakakakakoh* at roost; soft croaking, hissing and cackling at nest. Otherwise silent. **Habits**: Less gregarious than Great Cormorant, typically solitary or in small groups. Partial to reedy lakeshores, commonly perching on stumps and dead trees. Roosts and nests colonially in reeds or trees, often with other waterbirds. **Similar Species**: Great Cormorant is larger, with relatively larger bill and shorter tail. **Status and Distribution**: Widespread resident. Although ranging to the coast, generally prefers rivers, lakes, swamps and flooded areas with fringing vegetation and dead trees.

DARTERS, FAMILY ANHINGIDAE
(World, 4 species; Africa, Kenya and n. Tanzania, 1)

Large, slender, cormorant-like birds with a serrated dagger-like bill for spearing fish, and a long stiff tail. The distinctive outer rectrices and longest scapulars are laterally grooved or fluted. Darters swim low, often with only the small head and part of the long neck above water. The nest is a stick platform lined with reeds or twigs, constructed by the male. Both sexes incubate the two to six pale greenish or bluish eggs, which are markedly elongate. The young are naked at hatching, later developing down.

AFRICAN DARTER *Anhinga rufa* **Plate 14**

Length 71–79 cm (28–31″). Somewhat larger and with longer tail than Long-tailed Cormorant, with small head, *pointed bill*, and *long snaky neck*. **Adult male** largely black above and below, with oil-green gloss, but neck chestnut with white lateral stripes beginning below eyes; a narrow white eye-ring borders the bare orbital skin; scapulars, inner secondaries and wing-coverts narrowly streaked with white. Outer webs of innermost secondaries and median areas of the black tail feathers conspicuously transversely ridged. Bill yellow, ivory, greenish brown or dark grey; bare gular skin cream; feet brownish grey; eyes orange-red. **Female** differs in having the neck entirely brownish, with faint or no lateral white stripe; bill dark grey above, pinkish or horn below and towards tip; eyes orange-red. **Juvenile** *much paler* than adult, brownish above with some buff feather edges, later developing *long buff streaks on scapulars and inner secondaries*; wing-coverts broadly margined and streaked with buff; chin, throat and foreneck whitish, deepening to pale buff on breast; belly buffy white to buffy brown, becoming blackish in immature. **Voice**: Usually silent; gives a harsh croak at nest. **Habits**: Usually solitary, perching upright with wings outstretched or swimming unobtrusively. Flies strongly, with characteristically kinked neck. Nests in loose colonies in trees or shrubs over water, usually with cormorants and herons. **Status and Distribution**: Formerly a widespread resident of lakes, rivers, swamps and flooded areas with abundant fringing vegetation, including coastal creeks and estuaries. Kenyan highland population drastically declined in late 1980s (perhaps from increased use of pesticides and/or gill nets). Numbers survive along the lower Tana River, but now absent from many previously known sites. Scarce throughout n. Tanzania. **Note**: Considered conspecific with the Asian *A. melanogaster* by some authors.

FRIGATEBIRDS, FAMILY FREGATIDAE
(World, 5 species; Africa, 4; Kenya, 2)

Large aerial seabirds with a slender hooked bill, exceptionally long pointed wings, and a long, deeply forked tail. The legs are very short, the feet small and weak, the toes partially webbed. Highly manoeuvrable, frigatebirds soar for long periods with only occasional deep wingbeats. They habitually pursue and harass other seabirds, stealing the latter's newly caught food. They neither walk nor swim, but snatch food from sea surface or beach while on the wing. Although they can produce a harsh croak, they are practically silent. Adult males are blackish with a scarlet throat sac, inflated and balloon-like when breeding, even in flying birds, but neither species nests in East Africa. Females show conspicuous white areas on the underparts.

GREATER FRIGATEBIRD *Fregata minor* (*aldabrensis?*)   Plate 1
(Great Frigatebird)

Length 86–100 cm (34–40"); wingspan 6–7'. The most likely frigatebird in Kenyan waters. **Adult male** black with scarlet throat patch (seldom visible) and pale brownish bar on upperside of wing. Legs and feet red or reddish brown. **Female** differs in having grey chin and throat merging into white upper breast. Feet pink or reddish pink. **Juvenile** blackish brown above with paler wing-bar; white or pale chestnut head and throat separated from white belly patch by a rufous band; rest of underparts and underside of wings dark. The breast band is lost through moult, and **immature** is at first largely white below; upperparts paler brown than adult and the wing-bar paler. **Subadult female** is white from chin to upper breast, and with white belly patch. Transition to adult plumage takes several years. SIMILAR SPECIES: See Lesser Frigatebird. STATUS AND DISTRIBUTION: Frigatebirds are recorded almost annually off the Kenyan coast, but usually far out at sea, or in plumages rendering specific identification difficult or impossible. Accepted records include a specimen from Kipini, Tana River mouth (31 Aug. 1951); a skull from Kiunga (Aug. 1971); and sight records of adult males from Watamu (Aug. 1981) and near Lamu (early Sept. 1988).

*LESSER FRIGATEBIRD *Fregata ariel*   Figure below

Length 71–81 cm (28–32"); wingspan 5.5–6'. Only slightly smaller than Greater Frigatebird, but **adult male** easily identified by *small white patches on upper flanks extending onto the wing-linings*; also *lacks pale bar on upperside of wing*. Feet reddish brown or black. **Female** has *black chin and throat*, and *white of breast extends to the under wing-coverts*. Feet pink or reddish pink. **Juvenile and immature** have similar white breast and wing pattern, but belly is dark; there are numerous transitional stages to full adult plumage. SIMILAR SPECIES: See Greater Frigatebird. STATUS AND DISTRIBUTION: Vagrant; one accepted sight record of an adult male at Watamu (Jan. 1980). See comments under preceding species. NOTE: Mann (1986) suggested that two subadult *Fregata* seen off the Kenyan coast in January 1970 were Christmas Island Frigatebirds, *F. andrewsi*, and this report has been cited by others. No formal record was submitted, however, and no convincing supporting evidence is available.

Lesser Frigatebirds. Male (left) and female.

SHOEBILL, FAMILY BALAENICIPITIDAE
(One species, endemic to Africa)

This unique bird of uncertain relationships shares several characteristics with storks, whereas the presence of powder-down patches and its habit of flying with neck retracted suggest affinities with herons. However, both skeletal evidence (Cottam 1957) and DNA–DNA-hybridization data (Sibley and Ahlquist 1985; Sibley, pers. comm.) indicate a closer relationship to pelecaniform birds.

SHOEBILL or WHALE-HEADED STORK *Balaeniceps rex*   **Figure below**

Length *c.* 120 cm (48"); stands *c.* 1 m tall. A huge, unmistakable, *all-grey* wetland bird with a distinctive *massive bill*. **Adult** pale bluish grey with slate-grey flight feathers; belly and under tail-coverts greyish white. A short pointed occipital crest is always erect or nearly so. Clog-shaped, hook-tipped bill variously described as mottled green and brown, yellowish horn or pinkish, with irregular blotches and streaks, but often appears grey. Eyes greyish to pale yellow; legs and feet dark slate-grey or blackish. **Juvenile/immature** darker grey, the upperparts tinged with brown. **VOICE:** Normally silent away from nest, except for frequent hollow-sounding bill-clattering. **HABITS:** Solitary, but several may gather at favoured feeding areas. Confined to papyrus swamps, marshy lake edges and flooded grasslands. Preys on fishes, particularly lungfish. Sluggish, standing stiff-legged and motionless for long periods. Walks with a slow, stately, deliberate pace, its huge toes enabling it to move easily over floating vegetation. Soars on thermals with head and neck retracted. **STATUS AND DISTRIBUTION:** Vagrant. Several early unsubstantiated reports from ne. Kavirondo Gulf, Lake Victoria, and the vicinity of Yala Swamp, notably in late autumn of 1899 (Johnston 1902) and in early 1960s prior to partial draining of the swamp (Britton 1985). Subadult photographed in the Musiara Swamp, nw. Mara GR (Sept.–Nov. 1994), and Amboseli NP (Dec. 1994; present at least to mid-1995).

Shoebill.

HERONS, EGRETS AND BITTERNS, FAMILY ARDEIDAE
(World, 65 species; Africa, 22; Kenya, 19; n. Tanzania, 18)

Long-necked, long-legged wading birds with spear-like bills for taking fish, frogs, insects or rodents. The toes are elongate, the middle and outer ones connected basally by a short web, and the middle toenail is pectinate. The wings are long and broad, flapped deeply and steadily in sustained flight, when the neck is prominently kinked and retracted (unlike storks, ibises, spoonbills and cranes). Posture varies from erect and elongated to short and crouched. When feeding or otherwise active, the neck may be stretched, but at rest it is fully retracted. The plumage is lax, with long, often lanceolate feathers on neck, breast and back, and there are well-developed hidden powder-down patches on the breast and sides of the rump. In some herons, long filamentous plumes adorn the head when breeding, at which time facial skin and sometimes other bare parts may become brightly coloured. The sexes are alike in most species.

Some, especially the stocky, relatively short-legged night-herons, are crepuscular or nocturnal. Bitterns are more solitary and secretive than most herons or egrets. Away from nesting colonies most species are not very vocal, and, except in bitterns, their calls consist mainly of loud croaks and squawks. Herons and egrets tend to feed in the open, typically in wet places, although some regularly hunt on dry ground. They generally nest in mixed colonies in trees or reeds, laying two to six pale bluish or greenish eggs that are incubated by both sexes. The nidicolous young are also fed by both parents.

LITTLE BITTERN *Ixobrychus minutus* | Plate 12

Length 27–38 cm (10.5–15″). A small heron with *pale forewing patches conspicuous in flight*. **Male** of nominate palearctic race has greenish-black cap, upperparts, tail and flight feathers contrasting with pale buff face, neck, underparts and wing patches. Eyes yellow; bill greenish yellow; legs and feet green. **Female** browner above, *streaked below*, and with smaller wing patches. **Juvenile** resembles female, but is more mottled above and more heavily streaked below. Breeding *I. m. payesii* is slightly smaller than nominate migrants, the adults with chestnut neck and sides of face. During courtship, bill flushes orange-red, eyes become red-brown; tarsi olive-green in front, yellow posteriorly (Hancock and Kushlan 1984). **Voice:** Flight note *kwer*, *quar* or *kerack*; also a squawking alarm cry. When breeding, gives a rapid *gak-gak-gak-gak* and a gurgling *ghrrrr* (Maclean 1984). **Habits:** Secretive. Freezes motionless with neck stretched and bill pointing upwards. Climbs about in thick vegetation. Fast-flying, the wingbeats interspersed with short glides, legs often dangling. **Similar Species:** Dwarf Bittern is wholly dark slaty grey above and wings lack light patches. **Status and Distribution:** Widespread in permanent and seasonal marshes where sedges and reeds provide cover. Resident *I. m. payesii* breeds at lakes Naivasha and Baringo, and at scattered localities north of Nairobi. Elsewhere, recorded during or immediately after periods of high rainfall. Local populations may be augmented by intra-African migrants from the south (May–Sept.). Nominate palearctic birds present in small numbers October to early May. **Note:** The Great, or Eurasian, Bittern, *Botaurus stellaris*, a large, stocky, thick-necked species, has been reported from Kenya on several occasions, but none has been confirmed.

DWARF BITTERN *Ixobrychus sturmii* | Plate 12

Length 25–30 cm (10–12″). Scarce and secretive. *Smaller than a Little Bittern.* **Adult** wholly *dark slate-grey above, buff below with heavy dark grey streaking* from throat to belly, and *black line down centre of foreneck*. Bill dark greenish with black tip; legs and feet yellowish green, becoming bright orange during courtship; eyes red-brown; bare lores and orbital skin bluish. **Juvenile** has pale buff feather edges above and is more rufous below. **Voice:** During breeding season a deep *hoo-hoo-hoo*. When flushed, utters a loud croak. **Habits:** Unobtrusive. Stands motionless and upright for long periods. Flies with slow steady wingbeats, the neck sometimes outstretched. **Similar Species:** Little Bittern has pale forewing patches. Young Green-backed (Striated) Heron is heavily streaked below, but is larger, paler, has whitish wing-covert tips and is less secretive. **Status and Distribution:** Widespread but uncommon in permanent and seasonal swamps with adjacent dense cover. All records are during or immediately after periods of high rainfall. At times reportedly fairly common in lower Tana River delta, where possibly resident. Has bred near Lamu, at Thika (June–July 1977), and displaying birds observed inland from Malindi (April 1985). Some May–September records may involve intra-African migrants from southern Africa.

WHITE-BACKED NIGHT-HERON *Gorsachius leuconotus* | Plate 12

Length 50–56 cm (20–22″). Retiring and seldom seen. Smaller than Black-crowned Night-Heron. **Adult** has largely black head with short dark plumes, *broad white eye-ring and yellowish loral skin*; throat white; neck and breast brownish rufous, contrasting with dark brown wings and back, the latter with a *long patch of silky white feathers, conspicuous in flight*. Eyes large, yellow (reportedly red, brown, chestnut or amber when breeding Maclean 1984); bill black with some yellow along base of mandible; legs and feet greenish or orange-yellow

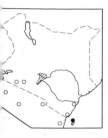

tarsi rather short. **Juvenile** lighter brown above than adult, spotted and streaked with white, the white back patch obscure, developing with age; underparts buff with pale tawny streaking. **Voice:** At night, a "clashing *taash-taash-taash*" (Maclean, *op. cit.*). In flight, a sharp *kraak*, more raspy than call of Black-crowned Night-Heron. Usually silent. **Habits:** Shy and secretive. Roosts by day in dense cover, not always by water. Strictly crepuscular and nocturnal. Stands quietly, waiting for prey. **Status and distribution:** Scarce along well-shaded, quiet streams and in mangroves. Scattered records suggest small numbers probably resident on parts of the Mara and Upper Tana Rivers in Kenya, and the Grumeti and Moshi Rivers in n. Tanzania. Recent sight records from mangroves at Mida Creek and near Shimoni (Ramisi River). Formerly reported breeding in mangroves on Pemba Island.

BLACK-CROWNED NIGHT-HERON *Nycticorax n. nycticorax* Plate 12
(Night Heron)

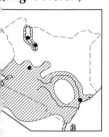

Length 56–61 cm (22–24"). Stocky and medium-sized, in flight rather owl-like with broad rounded wings. **Adult** has *black crown and back* with two long white occipital plumes; *wings, rump and tail grey*; face, neck and underparts white. Bill black; legs and feet pale yellow (briefly red during courtship); tarsi short; bare loral skin grey; eyes large and red. **Subadult** (third year) less clean-cut than adult, dark grey on crown and back, dirty white below; eyes brown. **Juvenile/immature** dark brown with white or buffy-white dorsal spots which disappear after a year or so, the greyish underparts streaked with dark brown. Bill largely yellow, becoming black; loral skin greenish, darkening to blue-black; eyes at first orange-yellow, turning brown; legs and feet yellow-green. **Voice:** Flight call a distinctive short *quok*, sometimes heard overhead at night. **Habits:** Solitary or in small numbers. Groups often roost in riverine trees. Mainly crepuscular and nocturnal, but abroad by day if no competition with other herons. Nests with other species in reeds or thickets near water. **Similar Species:** See White-backed Night-Heron. **Status and Distribution:** Locally common resident in vicinity of permanent water, breeding regularly at Garsen, sporadically elsewhere (Arusha NP, lakes Naivasha, Baringo and Turkana; formerly at Kisumu). Some East African birds may be palearctic migrants.

CATTLE EGRET *Bubulcus i. ibis* Plate 13

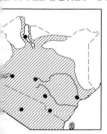

Length 50–56 cm (20–22"). A stocky, short-legged, 'heavy-jowled' white heron, hunched when resting, but neck extended when active. **Non-breeding adult** and **juvenile** plumage wholly white; legs and feet blackish at fledging, soon becoming greenish yellow or blue-grey; eyes and loral skin pale yellow; bill short and yellow. **Breeding adult** has deep buff crown, nape, back and breast plumes. Bill, eyes, lores, legs and feet bright red, all becoming orange-red during courtship, fading when egg-laying completed. **Voice:** Harsh croaks, e.g. *kark-kark, krok*, at breeding colonies; otherwise silent. **Habits:** Gregarious, often in dry grassland accompanying wild or domestic mammals. Flocks fly to and from large roosts in lines and V-shaped formations. Nests in large colonies in low trees, usually with other herons. **Similar Species:** Little Egret is more slender and graceful, with long, thin black bill, largely black tarsi and yellow toes. Yellow-billed Egret is larger, longer-necked, has black tarsi and toes at all ages. **Status and Distribution:** Common and widespread near wet places, in pastures, cultivation and dry grasslands. Breeds regularly at Kisumu and Garsen, sporadically at other localities, including North Kinangop and Emali.

LITTLE EGRET *Egretta g. garzetta* Plate 13

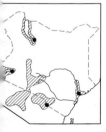

Length 55–65 cm (22–25.5"). A medium-sized slender white heron with long, largely *black bill*, black or mostly black tarsi, and *yellow toes* prominent in flight. Normal **white morph** in breeding plumage has two long (13–16 cm) and rather firm white occipital plumes, filmy and somewhat recurved 'aigrette' plumes arising from back and scapulars and reaching to tail tip, and elongate lanceolate feathers on upper breast. Longer plumes absent or reduced in non-breeding plumage. *Bill mainly black,* but typically *pale horn or dull flesh on basal half of mandible, particularly along gonys.* Eyes creamy yellow; normally *grey or bluish-grey bare lores and orbital skin* become (at least in extralimital populations) pale yellow, greenish yellow or dull peach colour at onset of breeding season, and lores turn bright orange at peak of courtship activity. Rare **dark morph** varies from *slate-grey or bluish grey to black* (depending on age), the chin and throat usually white. **Juvenile white morph** is white with no elongate plumes. **Immature** has somewhat longer pointed breast feathers and short dorsal plumes. Grey birds seen and photographed at Lake Magadi in 1960s and 1970s possibly represented juvenile or immature dark *garzetta* and not *E. (g.) dimorpha* (for which no positive inland record exists). *Combination of largely black bill and tarsi and yellow toes diagnostic,* except for coastal Dimorphic Egret. **Voice:** A soft or harsh *gwaa* and a short guttural *KOW* when flushed. **Habits:** Solitary or in

small groups, feeding in or near shallow water. Often dashes about in active pursuit of prey, but rests with slouched posture for extended periods. Foot-stirs to flush prey. Nests with other herons in low trees or shrubs near water, on the ground on rocky islets in Lake Turkana. **Similar Species:** Yellow-billed and Great Egrets are larger, with yellow bill (except briefly when breeding) and black toes. Cattle Egret has shorter yellow bill, greenish-yellow legs and feet. See also Western Reef Heron and Dimorphic Egret (main sources of confusion along the coast). **Status and Distribution:** Common and widespread on both fresh and alkaline waters, as well as along coastal creeks and estuaries. Infrequent on open shores at the coast. Breeds at Garsen, Kisumu, Lake Jipe, and on rocks of lava islands in Lake Turkana, where mixed pairs of dark and white morphs have been photographed. (These dark birds considered to be *schistacea* or *schistacea* x *garzetta* by some, but they are apparently identical in bill length/shape to white breeders on Lake Turkana and at Garsen.)

DIMORPHIC EGRET *Egretta (garzetta) dimorpha*   Plate 13

Length 55–65 cm (22–25.5"). Perhaps not specifically distinct from Little Egret, but an *entirely marine* bird in East Africa. **White morph** usually appears more slender and subtly longer-necked than Little Egret. A few individuals show small amounts of black streaking on body and wings. Legs and upper tarsi black, often with yellow or yellowish-olive 'anklets' extending upwards (and sometimes covering nearly entire front of tarsus) from the *yellow or yellowish-olive toes. These yellow areas become bright pink or orange-red at onset of breeding season. Lores and prominent narrow 'saddle' across base of maxilla grey in at least some non-breeding birds, but more often bright yellow, as is the bare orbital ring, these all turning bright deep pink during courtship;* eyes pale yellow. **Adult dark morph** (outnumbering white birds at least 2:1) blackish, except for white chin and upper throat, sometimes varying a narrow line down forecrown, and varying amounts of white (occasionally lacking) on the primary coverts as in *E. gularis,* this showing as a *small but conspicuous white patch in flight.* Many birds have white spots on head or are otherwise intermediate between dark and white morphs. Lores, orbital skin and 'saddle' at base of maxilla as in white morph; bill all black or the mandible with lateral yellow patch (but unlike Madagascan birds apparently never entirely or mostly yellow); tarsi greenish olive or black and olive; toes olive-yellow to orange. Some birds intermediate between dark and white morphs have mottled plumage. **Juvenile** and **immature** vary from slate-grey or pale grey to almost lavender-blue, becoming mottled when moulting into adult plumage. Bare parts as in non-breeding adults, but lores dark grey with narrow yellow line from mandible base to below eye. **Voice:** A low *gar* on take-off; similar or identical to call of Little Egret. **Habits:** Active, scurrying around in search of prey; stirs tidepools with feet; frequently wades belly-deep at low tide. Solitary or in small flocks. Breeds colonially on coral islets. **Similar Species:** Non-breeding Little Egret usually distinguishable by grey lores (breeding birds unlikely on marine shores or islands). Bill size not a reliable character; often appears longer in *dimorpha,* but available measurements (from Madagascar only) similar to those of *garzetta.* Rare dark Little Egret probably indistinguishable in the field. Western Reef Heron separated at all ages by bill colour. Black Heron is smaller, with shaggy crest. **Status and Distribution:** Locally common on open shores, coral reefs and tidal creeks south of Shimoni, including offshore Tanzanian islands. Breeds regularly on Kisite and Pemba Islands, where at northern extremity of its East African breeding range. Occasional north to Kilifi and Mida Creek. **Note:** *Egretta garzetta, dimorpha* and *gularis* are considered conspecific by some authorities.

WESTERN REEF HERON, *Egretta gularis schistacea*   Plate 13
(African Reef Heron)

Length 55–66 cm (22–26"). Resembles similarly sized Little Egret, but with a *longer, heavier and deeper bill* that is *yellowish, pinkish brown, horn-brown* or *brownish olive* and often appearing to *droop slightly at the tip.* **Adult white morph** has two long narrow plumes on occiput, elongate scapular 'aigrettes' extending beyond the tail, and lanceolate upper-breast feathers. Legs and feet olive-green or dark olive (apparently never black). **Adult dark morph** blackish, with well-defined white chin and throat, varying amounts of white on primary coverts (evident in flight), dark brown or brownish olive legs and feet, and *pinkish-brown, horn-brown* or *brownish-olive bill.* **Immature dark morph** light grey or slate-grey. Toes yellow or orange-yellow; eyes pale yellow, surrounded by greenish-yellow bare skin and yellow lores in both morphs. **Voice:** When disturbed, a guttural *kawww.* **Habits:** Generally solitary. Often stands with slouched posture and rests on tarsi in shallow water or on shore. Waits for prey or stealthily stalks prior to lightning-quick thrusts. Seldom dashes in active pursuit of prey, instead stalking in crouched position. **Similar Species:** Little Egret, with 20 per cent shorter wingspan than *gularis* (Cramp and Simmons 1977), distinguished with care by smaller, straighter, mostly *black* bill and tarsi. (Birds feeding in alkaline lakes may appear to have heavier and paler bills owing to encrusted soda deposits.) Cattle Egret is smaller, with shorter neck and bill. Yellow-billed and Great Egrets have black toes. See Dimorphic Egret. **Status and Distribution:** Uncommon non-breeding visitor from areas north of Kenya, especially in coastal mangroves south to Mida Creek and Kilifi. Frequently recorded at Lake Turkana, occasionally wandering south to lakes Nakuru and Magadi. Dark birds are mainly coastal but are not known to overlap with dark *E. (g). dimorpha* around Kisite Island near Shimoni.

BLACK HERON *Egretta ardesiaca*   Plate 13
(Black Egret)

Length 48–50 cm (19–20"). A *shaggy-crested, slaty-black* heron, *dark-eyed* and with conspicuous *orange or orange-yellow toes* (sometimes briefly red at onset of breeding); feet otherwise black, as are legs and bill. *Eyes dark brown* (*contra* current literature) and with narrow powder-blue orbital ring. **Adult** has *shaggy crest*. **Juvenile** duller, slightly paler and lacks head plumes. **VOICE:** An occasional low cluck, but generally silent. **HABITS:** Solitary or in small groups, feeding in shallows of marshy lake margins. Forms canopy over head by spreading wings up and forward down to water surface, possibly to reduce reflection, or to attract food to dark shelter. This pose maintained for several seconds while mud is stirred with foot to flush prey; flocks may canopy-feed in unison. Flies with steady quick wingbeats. Nests with other herons in trees or shrubs over water. **SIMILAR SPECIES:** Dark morphs of Western Reef Heron, Little Egret and Dimorphic Egret are larger, lack the shaggy crest and have white on throat. **STATUS AND DISTRIBUTION:** Local resident, mainly along coastal creeks, lakes and flood pools of the lower Tana River and Lake Jipe. Rare or absent at many apparently suitable inland sites. Currently breeds only near Garsen, formerly at Kisumu.

Feeding Black Herons.

SQUACCO HERON *Ardeola ralloides*   Plates 12 and 13

Length 46 cm (18"). Small and short-necked. Brownish and well camouflaged when standing, but in flight shows *conspicuous white wings, lower back, rump and tail*. **Non-breeding adult** buffy brown on upper back and scapulars, the head, neck and breast pale buff with dark brown streaks; belly white. Bill greenish yellow with dusky tip; lores yellow-green, eyes yellow; legs and feet dull yellowish green. **Breeding** plumage paler and buffier; streaking largely confined to head, which is adorned with black-edged white plumes; long cinnamon-buff plumes on upperparts, neck and breast; no streaks on underparts. Bill azure-blue with sharp black tip; lores blue or blue-green, legs and feet bright red at onset of nesting; eyes bright yellow. **Juvenile** as non-breeding adult, but breast more heavily streaked, wings (especially primary tips) brown-tinged, and tip of tail brown. **VOICE:** A harsh grating *krruk* when flushed, and repeatedly in breeding colonies. **HABITS:** Skulks in grass and reeds. Singles and loose groups stand camouflaged in waterside vegetation. Flies with quick shallow wingbeats. Nests in colonies in reeds or shrubs above water. **SIMILAR SPECIES:** See Madagascar Squacco Heron. **STATUS AND DISTRIBUTION:** Widespread and often common in swamps, along freshwater lakes with bordering or floating vegetation. Breeds regularly near Garsen, sporadically elsewhere (Lakes Jipe, Solai and Ol Bolossat); formerly at Kisumu. Many presumably are non-breeding visitors, some perhaps of palearctic origin.

MADAGASCAR SQUACCO or MALAGASY POND HERON *Ardeola idae*

Plates 12 and 13

Length 45–48 cm (17.5–18.75"). *Stockier and heavier-billed* than Squacco Heron. **Non-breeding adult** dark brown above, without buffy appearance of Squacco, and *head/neck streaking blacker and bolder, ending more abruptly against white lower breast and belly.* Bill olive-horn with blackish tip; lores, orbital skin and eyes yellow; legs and feet dull olive-yellow. **Breeding plumage** (rare in Africa) white, with pale buff wash on upperparts (becomes snow-white in Madagascar); long white plumes on nape, back, foreneck and breast. Bill cerulean blue with black tip; lores greenish; eyes yellow; tarsi and toes rose-pink. VOICE: A grating *krruk*, louder than call of Squacco Heron. HABITS: Solitary or in loose groups. Less secretive than Squacco. Stands on open grassy banks and frequents more open lake edges; perches in trees when disturbed. STATUS AND DISTRIBUTION: Regular non-breeding migrant from Madagascar, May–October, in coastal areas and inland to Mwea NR, Nairobi and Nakuru NPs and Ngorongoro Crater. Many go beyond Kenya and n. Tanzania, but small numbers remain near Mombasa, the Thika oxidation ponds and in the Mwea rice fields.

RUFOUS-BELLIED HERON *Ardeola rufiventris*

Plate 12

Length *c.* 39 cm (15.5"). Small, compact and dark. **Adult male** dark slate-grey with *chestnut 'shoulder' patches, belly, rump and tail.* **Female** sooty grey-brown, with conspicuous *buffy-white streak on chin and foreneck*; chestnut areas much as in male. Adults show chestnut wing-linings and much chestnut on inner upper wing surface in flight. Bill dark horn-brown with yellowish mandible, turning rufous brown when breeding; eyes, *lores and tarsi yellow*, all becoming bright pinkish red in breeding males. **Juvenile** resembles female, but neck and breast streaked with buffy brown. VOICE: A crow-like *kar*, and a croaking *kraak*. HABITS: Inconspicuous. Solitary or in small groups. Remains motionless for long periods in reeds and grass at water's edge. Usually flies only short distance before dropping back into cover. Breeds in colonies in reeds or partly submerged shrubby trees, generally alongside other herons. STATUS AND DISTRIBUTION: Local and uncommon, known only from a few widely scattered localities. Small numbers resident in permanent swamps in Tarangire NP and nw. Mara GR. Vagrants recorded from the Lake Victoria basin, Lake Baringo, Thika, Amboseli NP and Taita District.

GREEN-BACKED or STRIATED HERON *Butorides striatus atricapillus*

Plate 12

Length 40 cm (16"). A small, short-legged heron with characteristic hunched posture. **Adult** dark greyish green above with greenish-black erectile crown feathers; grey below with white throat and with a broad chestnut-buff line down foreneck. Legs and feet yellow (orange or red-orange when breeding); bill rather short, blackish with greenish-yellow base (wholly black at onset of breeding); eyes yellow (deep orange when breeding). **Juvenile** browner with buff or whitish streaks above, and whitish tips to wing feathers; buff, streaked dark brown, below. VOICE: A sharp *kyah* when flushed. Otherwise silent. HABITS: Shy and solitary. Creeps among low waterside roots and branches. Mainly diurnal, but also feeds at night. Known to use bait (e.g. paper, bread, twigs) in attempts to catch fish. SIMILAR SPECIES: Dwarf Bittern is smaller, wholly dark slate-grey above, heavily black-streaked on underparts, with dark line down centre of throat. STATUS AND DISTRIBUTION: Fairly common resident of coastal mangrove creeks, and lake and river edges with overhanging vegetation. Now scarce at Lake Turkana owing to falling water levels.

YELLOW-BILLED or INTERMEDIATE EGRET *Mesophoyx intermedia brachyrhyncha*

Plate 13

Length 61–69 cm. (24–27"). Suggests a small, short-necked Great Egret, but *bill smaller* and the *dark gape line extends back from bill only to below the eye*. Acquires long plumes on back and breast when breeding. Bill yellow, often blackish at tip, becoming orange-red (yellow at tip) at onset of breeding. Tarsi and toes blackish brown; legs (tibiae) paler brown, briefly pinkish red during courtship, but soon turning yellow for remainder of breeding season, when yellow line also extends down sides of tarsi. Lores yellow, turning bright green in breeding season; eyes yellow most of year, briefly bright red when courting. Colours of all bare parts revert to normal shortly after eggs are laid. **Juvenile** resembles non-breeding adult. VOICE: Usually silent away from nesting colony; may utter a low *kwark*. HABITS: Often solitary, but nests gregariously in low trees above water, often with other herons, storks and ibises. SIMILAR SPECIES: Great Egret compared above. Little Egret is smaller, with black bill and yellow toes. Cattle Egret, also smaller, is stockier, with (usually) yellowish legs and feet. STATUS AND DISTRIBUTION: Widespread, but seldom numerous away from breeding

colonies. Favours secluded swamp-edge habitats; scarce along coast. Breeds regularly at Kisumu and Garsen, sporadically at some Rift Valley localities.

GREAT EGRET *Casmerodius albus melanorhynchos*   Plate 13
(Great White Egret)

Length 85–92 cm (33–36"). A large white heron with long curved neck and a *black gape line extending from bill to behind the eye*. **Non-breeding adult** has *long yellow bill, black legs and feet, including toes*; lores dull yellowish green. **Breeding adult** develops long white back plumes; bill becomes wholly or partially black (much individual variation), the lores become bright green, and the normally yellow eyes briefly turn red. **Juvenile** and **immature** have black-tipped yellow bill. **VOICE**: A deep raucous croak, *krrrawk, krrrawk*; other sounds in nesting colonies include a guttural *rhaw* or *rhaa*. **HABITS**: Usually solitary, but scores may gather to feed. Often forages in deep water, with long neck held forward. Flies with slow, heavy wingbeats, the long neck bulging distinctively below. Roosts communally and nests among other herons in trees over water. Rather wary. **SIMILAR SPECIES**: See Yellow-billed Egret. **STATUS AND DISTRIBUTION**: Widespread and quite common in various wet inland habitats, along coastal creeks and on reefs. Breeds regularly near Kisumu and Garsen, sporadically elsewhere.

GREY HERON *Ardea c. cinerea*   Plate 11

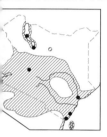

Length 90–100 cm (35–39"). A large grey-backed heron. **Adult** has *whitish head*, neck and underparts, and broad *black eye-line terminating in black nape plume*; also narrow black streaks down front of neck and *black carpal patches* on the wings. In flight, from above, *blackish flight feathers contrast with grey wing-coverts, back and tail; underside of wings uniformly grey*. Bill yellow, tinged brown below and on culmen; legs and feet yellowish brown (rear of tarsus and tibia more yellow). Eyes and lores usually yellow, but eyes, bill and tarsi become deep orange or vermilion during courtship. **Juvenile/immature** more uniformly grey (some individuals washed with brown), including crown and most of underparts, with white only on face and neck; no black epaulettes. Bill dark horn, becoming yellow in second year. **VOICE**: A harsh *hraaank* in flight. At nest, a deep grunting *ur-ur-ur-ur*. **HABITS**: Usually solitary except when breeding. Feeds by night and day in water or on dry land; also scavenges along coastline. **SIMILAR SPECIES**: Adult Black-headed Heron has black crown and nape (grey in immature), black legs, and white wing-linings. Purple Heron is slightly smaller and darker, the adult with black crown and belly, striped rufous neck and rufous wing-linings; immature much browner than Grey Heron. **STATUS AND DISTRIBUTION**: Widespread in small numbers in various wet habitats, favouring brackish or alkaline lakes and coastal flats. Breeds in a few widely scattered localities. Resident population possibly supplemented by palearctic birds, especially at Lake Turkana.

PURPLE HERON *Ardea p. purpurea*   Plate 11

Length 79–84 cm (31–33"). Richly coloured and *slender*, slightly smaller than a Grey Heron, with sinuous neck. **Adult** slate-grey above, with elongate chestnut scapular and back plumes when breeding, *black cap and occipital plumes, deep rufous face and neck with black stripe down either side*; whitish foreneck streaked with black; flanks chestnut; belly black. Bill dull yellowish, brown on culmen and tip; lores greenish yellow; eyes yellow, tinged orange at onset of breeding. Tarsi black in front, as are tops of toes; feet and legs otherwise yellowish. **Juvenile** and **immature** grey rather than black on head and hindneck, brownish on foreneck, and dirty white below; lacks chestnut flanks and black belly of adult. Much browner than young Grey Heron. **VOICE**: A harsh *kraak* or *kreek* when disturbed. **HABITS**: Solitary. Typically feeds in tall marsh vegetation, where difficult to see, but not shy. Nests colonially in low trees or shrubs over water, or in reedbeds. **SIMILAR SPECIES**: Goliath Heron is much larger, heavier, lacks black cap and neck stripes, has blackish bill. Purple Heron's flight like that of Grey Heron, with slow steady wingbeats, but kink of neck more exaggerated, wings less contrastingly patterned, feet project farther beyond tail. **STATUS AND DISTRIBUTION**: Widespread and locally common in extensive beds of reeds or papyrus. Breeds near Garsen, sporadically at Lake Jipe and at some Rift Valley sites. Wanders to seasonal wetlands.

GOLIATH HERON *Ardea goliath*   Plate 11

Length 120–152 cm (47–60"). *Huge size, grey-and-chestnut plumage*, and *large greyish-black bill* distinctive. **Adult** grey above with *rufous-chestnut head and neck, deeper chestnut carpal patches and belly*; white foreneck and breast streaked with black. Loral skin greenish grey; eyes yellow; legs and feet black. In flight, *wings appear uniformly grey above* with *chestnut wing-linings*. **Juvenile** browner with rufous-buff feather edges on upperparts; breast and belly buffy white, streaked with dark brown. **Immature** brownish grey above, the chestnut underparts

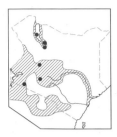

paler and more rufous than in adult; neck pattern obscure; lacks chestnut epaulettes; bill pale below. **Voice:** A deep raucous *koworrh-koworrh-worrh-worrh*. **Habits:** Solitary. Flies with slow ponderous wingbeats, legs and feet usually hanging below horizontal. Nests in isolated pairs or in small groups in reedbeds, on low tree boughs, or on waterside rocks. **Similar Species:** Purple Heron is smaller, more slender, with paler bill. **Status and Distribution:** Widespread but local and usually uncommon resident of larger lakes, rivers and permanent swamps. Breeds sporadically at lakes Baringo and Naivasha and along the Mara River, occasionally elsewhere, including Lake Turkana.

BLACK-HEADED HERON *Ardea melanocephala* — Plate 11

Length 84–92 cm (33–36"). A medium-sized grey-backed heron often seen on dry open grassland or cultivated ground. **Adult** has *most of head and hindneck black*, contrasting with *white throat and foreneck*. Upperparts darker than Grey Heron. In flight, shows strongly *two-toned underwing pattern, the whitish linings contrasting with black flight feathers*. Feet, legs and upper half of bill black; yellow eyes turn ruby-red at onset of breeding season. **Juvenile/immature** grey rather than black on head and hindneck, dusky grey on foreneck and generally greyish white below. **Voice:** A raucous croaking *kaaaak* in flight. At nest, a loud *kowk* and other calls. **Habits:** Solitary when feeding, but roosts and nests colonially, often in tall trees in towns and villages, sometimes in mixed colonies. Typically forages on dry ground, hunting insects and rodents, at times apparently scavenging. **Similar Species:** Grey Heron is larger and heavier, with uniformly grey undersides of wings, has yellow or horn-coloured bill, yellowish-brown legs and feet. **Status and Distribution:** Commonest and most widely distributed East African heron, although absent from much of arid n. and e. Kenya. Mainly resident. Not restricted to aquatic or littoral habitats. Long-established breeding colonies at Usa River, Njoro, and near Kisumu; several smaller colonies elsewhere.

HAMERKOP, FAMILY SCOPIDAE
(One species, endemic to Africa and Madagascar)

Of uncertain relationships, this unique bird shares with herons the pectinate middle toenail and rather long legs but does not resemble them in most other respects. Protein studies suggest that it is nearest to the storks. The sexes are alike.

HAMERKOP *Scopus u. umbretta* — Plate 11

Length 48–56 cm (19–22"). A heavy-billed brown waterbird with large 'hammer-shaped' crested head and short neck; bill, legs and feet black. **Juvenile** resembles adult. Flight buoyant, flapping and gliding on broad wings with neck extended. **Voice:** A loud strident yelping, *yik-purrrr, yik-yik-yik-purr-purr-yik-yik*. **Habits:** Usually solitary or in pairs. Highly vocal, with wing-raising display and, during courtship, frequent 'false mounting' that may involve several birds. Both sexes build massive nest of sticks and mud, with small side entrance hole, in crotch of tree. Lays three to six white eggs. Young are nidicolous and downy. Feeds largely on amphibians in and near shallow water. **Status and Distribution:** Widespread and fairly common resident of swamp edges, lakesides, sluggish rivers and streams. Wanders to flood waters and coastal lagoons.

STORKS, FAMILY CICONIIDAE
(World, 19 species; Africa, Kenya and n. Tanzania, 8)

Large, long-legged and long-necked birds with stout to very heavy elongate bills and basally webbed toes. The head may be largely bare or feathered, and plumage is usually black and/or white; there is little sexual dimorphism. Storks fly with neck and legs extended, and some soar on their long broad wings, often in flocks. Most are voiceless, but engage in bill-clattering when nesting. They feed in open grassland, cultivated fields and shallow water, mainly on aquatic and terrestrial animals, including insects, but diets vary. Some species are long-distance migrants. Our residents nest in trees, either colonially or as isolated pairs. They lay one to four plain whitish or greenish-white eggs that are incubated by both male and female. The nidicolous young are naked at hatching but acquire down later. They are fed by both parents.

WHITE STORK *Ciconia c. ciconia* Plate 9

Length 102–120 cm (40–48"). A large stork distinguished by *white body and tail* and contrasting black flight feathers. **Adult** has red bill, legs and feet (but legs and upper tarsi often white with the bird's excrement). **Immature** similarly patterned, but bare parts duller and flight feathers dark brown. **HABITS:** Usually gregarious, in loose flocks of a few birds to many hundreds or thousands, often soaring on thermals (especially when migrating) and assembling at large insect concentrations or grass fires. **SIMILAR SPECIES:** Yellow-billed Stork is distinguished in high flight by black tail. **STATUS AND DISTRIBUTION:** Palearctic migrant, mainly November–April, but a few remain all year, generally on grassland and grain fields above 1600 m; often numerous on the eastern Serengeti Plains and in Ngorongoro Crater. Regular passages November-December and March–April east of Lake Victoria; southbound flocks frequent east to Meru and Tsavo NPs. Young birds observed near Nakuru (Dittami and Haas 1982) may not have been raised in Kenya.

BLACK STORK *Ciconia nigra* Plate 9

Length 95–100 cm (37.5–39.5"). A large dark stork with white underparts and dull *red bill and legs.* **Adult** mainly black with purple and green gloss, white from lower breast to under tail-coverts; black wings show small white triangle next to body on underside. **Immature** brownish above, with dull olive-green bill, legs and feet. **HABITS:** Usually solitary. Feeds in shallow water or on short grass. Shier than White Stork. **SIMILAR SPECIES:** Abdim's Stork is smaller, with shorter greenish-grey bill, blue facial skin and white lower back. **STATUS AND DISTRIBUTION:** In Kenya, a regular palearctic migrant in small numbers, October–April, mainly near water, especially along the Athi–Galana Rivers. Regular in Nairobi NP, December–February; occasional in w. Kenya. Scarce throughout n. Tanzania.

ABDIM'S STORK, *Ciconia abdimii* Plate 9
(White-bellied Stork)

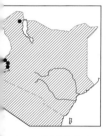

Length 76–81 cm (30–32"). A small black-and-white stork. **Adult** mainly black with purplish gloss, but *white from lower breast to under tail-coverts and on rump and lower back.* Bill dull grey-green with reddish tip; legs and feet greenish grey, tinged red on toes and tibiotarsal joints. Bare facial skin bluish, with red around eyes. **Juvenile** has adult pattern but is duller and browner; bare parts not described. **HABITS:** Gregarious, sometimes in flocks of hundreds or thousands. Forages in grassland and is attracted to insect concentrations, often associating with White Storks. Soars on thermals when migrating. Usually silent. **SIMILAR SPECIES:** See Black Stork. **STATUS AND DISTRIBUTION:** Mainly a non-breeding migrant from the northern tropics, late October to mid-April, frequenting open grasslands and cultivation below 2000 m. Large numbers associate with White Storks in the Mara GR and n. Tanzania. A few bred in n. and w. Kenya (near Lokitaung, Busia and Yala) during the 1960s, and in 1993–94 at Maseno.

WOOLLY-NECKED STORK *Ciconia episcopus microscelis* Plate 9

Length *c.* 86 cm (33–34"). **Adult** glossy *black with woolly white neck, white belly and long, stiff, white under tail-coverts projecting beyond the deeply forked black tail.* Forecrown blue-black, wings glossed with blue, the back and breast with purple; tibial feathers black. Blackish bill is red along culmen and at tip; dark red eyes are ringed with bare blackish skin; tarsi and toes dusky red. **Juvenile** and **immature** much duller and browner, with reduced gloss; crown dark at first, whitening with age. **HABITS:** Usually solitary or in pairs by water's edge; may stand motionless for long periods. Attends grass fires for burnt insects and reptiles. Nests in trees. Generally silent. **STATUS AND DISTRIBUTION:** Fairly common on coastal mudflats, lagoons and exposed coral reefs, and inland along streams and rivers in se. Kenya. Elsewhere, including much of n. Tanzania, an uncommon wanderer, although breeding recently confirmed in Mara GR.

SADDLE-BILLED STORK *Ephippiorhynchus senegalensis* Plate 9

Length *c.*145 cm (57"). An exceptionally tall, spectacular stork. **Adult** black and white with a *yellow saddle-shaped frontal shield* and pair of small, yellow (to partly red) wattles at base of the enormous *black-and-red bill. Pinkish-red tibiotarsal joints and toes* mark the otherwise dark legs and feet. Head and neck, upper and under wing-coverts, scapulars and tail black; rest of body and flight feathers white. Small bare pinkish-red patch on breast (not always evident). Eyes dark brown in male, bright yellow in female. **Juvenile** largely grey-brown, including bill (which lacks saddle). **Immature** duller than adult; flight feathers greyish; bill black and red but without saddle; legs and feet greenish. **HABITS:** Solitary or in pairs. Shy, but becomes approachable in protected

areas. Wades slowly in shallow water, striking at prey with bill; sometimes foot-stirs like Yellow-billed Stork. Pair roosts together and nests in tree. **STATUS AND DISTRIBUTION:** Local and uncommon resident of permanent swamps, freshwater lake margins and flooded grassland. Regular visitor to coastal lowlands north of Malindi, May–September. Breeding records from the lower Tana River, Meru and Nairobi NPs, Lake Naivasha, Laikipia, Lake Victoria, Mara GR, Shombole and Serengeti and Arusha NPs.

MARABOU STORK *Leptoptilus crumeniferus*   Plate 9

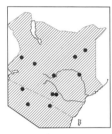

Length *c.* 152 cm (60″). Huge and unmistakable, with massive grey bill, naked pinkish head with white ruff at its base, and a bare pendent throat pouch (inflatable, thus varying in size). A second air sac lies beneath skin at base of hindneck; when inflated, this produces bright orange-red swelling just above the ruff. **Non-breeding adult** slate-grey above, with greenish gloss on wing-coverts; underparts white (often stained). Eyes brown, bill pale horn, sometimes tinged with pink; legs and feet black, but often 'whitewashed' with the bird's excrement. **Breeding plumage** paler blue-grey, with broadly white-edged secondary coverts and larger and fluffier white under tail-coverts. Bare skin brighter than in non-breeding bird, with throat pouch and most of head red, pale blue nape, black forehead and lores, and lines of black warts extending from ear region to occiput. **Juvenile** and **immature** resemble adults but are duller and with more hair-like feathers on head; wing feathers brownish with little gloss (becoming blackish with some gloss in second or third year); coverts pale-edged; bare skin often yellow-tinged. **VOICE:** Usually silent apart from bill-clattering and loud wheezy whine of air across flight feathers in low flight, but moans, moos and squeals at nest; courting bird gives a repeated hoarse whinnying, *wu-wuwuwuwuwuwuwuwa-ekk.* **HABITS:** Gregarious scavenger around offal and refuse dumps and at carcasses of large mammals, where often with vultures. Captures small reptiles and rodents with rapid jabs of bill, and can snatch low-flying swallows from the air. Soars and cruises at great height, with neck retracted. Inactive much of the day, standing motionless or squatting on tarsi. Roosts and nests colonially in trees. **STATUS AND DISTRIBUTION:** Widespread and locally common in open grassland and around towns and villages. Breeding colonies well established at Kitale, Wajir, Garissa, Kibwezi, Hunter's Lodge and Lake Manyara, smaller ones elsewhere, but total Kenyan breeding population only *c.* 300 pairs.

AFRICAN OPEN-BILLED STORK *Anastomus l. lamelligerus*   Plate 9

Length 81–94 cm (32–37″). A rather small blackish stork. **Adult** glossed purple and green. Unique feathers of underparts extended as stiff, lustrous, curly filaments (visible at close range). Large bill brownish, paler grey to greyish white basally, with a noticeable *tomial gap;* larger in male. Legs and feet black. **Juvenile/immature** duller and browner with whitish feather tips, the bill at first shorter and straighter with only a narrow gap, but soon developing adult size and shape. **VOICE:** Loud raucous croaking or honking, *horrrnkh-horrrnkh.* **HABITS:** Small groups feed on molluscs in or near shallow water. Perches and roosts in trees; nests colonially. Large flocks of presumed migrants circle high in the air. **STATUS AND DISTRIBUTION:** Widespread and locally common mainly below 1500 m on inland waters and brackish coastal lagoons. Nests regularly near Garsen and (a few) at Kisumu, but occasional large numbers in se. Kenya and ne. Tanzania are possibly migrants from farther south.

YELLOW-BILLED STORK *Mycteria ibis*   Plate 9
(Wood Ibis)

Length 95–105 cm (37.5–41.5″). A pinkish-white stork with *black tail* and flight feathers, *long yellow, slightly decurved bill,* and *bare red face.* **Adult** has bright pink or red legs and feet. **Juvenile** grey-brown with dull greyish-yellow bill, dusky orange face and brown legs. **Immature** resembles adult but lacks pinkish tinge to white body plumage and bare parts are much duller. **VOICE:** At breeding colonies adults utter a whining squeal; nestlings produce a braying sound. **HABITS:** Usually in small groups. Feeds in shallow water, mainly on fish; walks slowly with bill immersed, stirring with foot to disturb prey. Flocks spend much time resting on grassy banks or in trees. Roosts and nests communally. **SIMILAR SPECIES:** White Stork has all-white tail and much smaller red bill. **STATUS AND DISTRIBUTION:** Widespread and locally common on open lake edges, rivers, coastal estuaries, and other wet places. Breeds regularly near Kisumu, sporadically elsewhere.

IBISES AND SPOONBILLS, FAMILY THRESKIORNITHIDAE
(World, 34 species; Africa, 11; Kenya, 6; n. Tanzania, 5)

Large, long-necked wading birds which typically fly with flapping and intermittent gliding and with the neck extended. Most are gregarious, feeding in parties in shallow water, wet grassland, or forest clearings. Ibises have long decurved bills and relatively short tarsi; spoonbills have straight spatulate bills and long tarsi. The toes are webbed at the base. In all species the sexes appear alike, although females are slightly smaller than males. Some nest in isolated pairs; others breed colonially, at times with herons, constructing large nests of sticks in trees or shrubs. The two or three eggs are blotched and streaked with brown in most species, and are incubated by both sexes. The young are nidicolous and downy.

SACRED IBIS *Threskiornis a. aethiopicus*   Plate 10

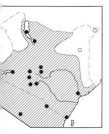

Length 64–82 cm (25–32"). **Adult** mainly white, with wrinkled *bare black head and neck* and *strongly decurved blackish bill.* Iridescent blue-black plume-like scapulars and long inner secondaries conceal the tail when wings are closed. Remiges tipped with glossy greenish black. Flanks tinged golden or brownish yellow when breeding. Eyes brown, with dark red orbital ring when breeding; legs and feet black (tarsi tinged red). *White wings with narrow black trailing edges* distinctive in flight. Adult shows bare red skin beneath wings near body, sometimes on adjacent breast and flanks. **Juvenile** has mottled black-and-white feathering on head and neck, lacks plumes, and has broader black wing edges; alula and primary coverts black. **Immature** may have partially feathered head, and some plume-like secondaries and scapulars which are iridescent green, not violet- or blue-black as in adult. **Voice:** Rarely, a harsh croak in flight; mostly silent away from nesting areas. **Habits:** Usually in groups. Probes for food in shallow water or soft mud, also forages on grassland, lawns and cultivated fields. Roosts communally in trees. Flies in V-formations between roosts and feeding sites. Nests mainly in large colonies, over water. **Status and Distribution:** Widespread and common in and near wet habitats, including coastal lagoons and estuaries. Breeds annually near Kisumu, Garsen and Lake Turkana, sporadically at several other localities. Some may be wholly resident; movements poorly known.

HADADA IBIS *Bostrychia hagedash brevirostris*   Plate 10
(Hadeda Ibis)

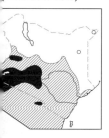

Length 76–89 cm (30–35"). *A stocky, dark, short-legged ibis* with highly iridescent green/purplish wing-coverts, whitish stripe below cheek, and generally dark brownish-grey plumage, the upperparts glossed with bronze. Mainly black bill shows prominent red culmen; legs and feet dark grey or black, toes sometimes crimson above; eyes appear silvery white, but iris is brown with white outer ring (said at times to be red). **Juvenile** duller and smaller than adult. **Voice:** A loud raucous *HAAA* or *HA-HAAA-DE-DAH* or *HAA-HAA-HAA,* usually in flight. **Habits:** Highly vocal, especially at dawn and dusk when flying to and from feeding grounds. Flight slow, rather jerky, bill angled downward. Roosts communally in trees, but pairs nest singly. Feeds in pairs or small groups. **Similar Species:** Young Glossy Ibis, also dark with some greenish gloss, is more slender, with longer bill, toes projecting beyond tail in more buoyant, graceful flight. African Green Ibis is crested, restricted to montane forests, and differs vocally. **Status and Distribution:** Widespread and locally common in higher-rainfall areas, on wooded streams, forest borders, grassy lakeshores, cultivation, lawns and suburban gardens.

AFRICAN GREEN IBIS or OLIVE IBIS *Bostrychia olivacea akeleyorum*   Plate 10

Length c. 74 cm (29"). A dark *forest* ibis resembling Hadada, but **adult** has a *loose mane-like crest* and more general greenish wash on head, neck and underparts; upperparts and wing-coverts iridescent green and bronzy. Bill dull dark red; bare skin on lores and above eyes dusky blue; eyes dark brown or (when breeding?) red; area below eyes to ear-coverts pale brown; legs and feet variously recorded as dull orange-brown with greenish tinge, pinkish brown or (breeding?) dull dark red. **Juvenile** and **immature** similar but duller and with shorter crest. **Voice:** A single alarm call, *GARR,* and a resonant *GARRA-GARRA* or *AKA-A* uttered by flying groups at dawn and dusk. **Habits:** Pairs or small parties feed in glades within dense forest. Runs along large branches of giant trees. Flight strong and direct. Rarely observed except when calling in crepuscular flight to and from roosts. A solitary breeder. **Similar Species:** Hadada Ibis lacks crest, has longer bill, white cheek stripe and different call. **Status and Distribution:** Scarce to uncommon local resident of highland forest. In Kenya, now confined to areas from 2000 to 3700 m on the Aberdares and Mt Kenya; in n. Tanzania known from southern slopes of Kilimanjaro and locally near 1000 m in parts of the East Usambaras. Formerly in the Nandi Forest. Unconfirmed reports from the Ngurumans.

GLOSSY IBIS *Plegadis f. falcinellus*   Plate 10

Length 55–65 cm (22–25.5"). A small, dark ibis with slender decurved bill and long legs. Appears black at a distance, but at close range **breeding adult** mainly chestnut with purple gloss, the back and wings iridescent green. Bill, legs and feet dull brown; bare pale blue or purplish lores are bordered above and below by narrow white lines. **Non-breeding adult** brownish black, flecked with white on head and neck. **Juvenile** and **immature** sooty brown with some greenish gloss above, head and neck brownish grey with some white spots. **VOICE:** A croaking *gra-gra-gra* in flight. **HABITS:** Gregarious; flocks may contain hundreds of birds, flying in compact lines, with buoyant wingbeats and long intermittent glides. Nests in trees over water, usually with other waterbirds. **SIMILAR SPECIES:** See Hadada Ibis. **STATUS AND DISTRIBUTION:** Widespread in permanent wetlands, on marshy lakeshores, rainpools and brackish coastal lagoons. Currently breeds only near Garsen. Many probably originate outside East Africa, some perhaps in the Palearctic.

*EURASIAN SPOONBILL *Platalea leucorodia*   Plate 10

Length 86–90 cm (34–35"). **Adult** differs from African Spoonbill (see below) in having *feathered area between eyes, black spatulate bill with yellow tip, and black legs.* May or may not show yellowish-buff area at base of neck. Bare orbital skin and that of gape, chin and throat yellow; some dark skin on lores; eyes red. In spring, develops partially yellow crest on nape and yellowish neck patch. **First-winter bird** has black primary tips, gradually assuming adult coloration during first year, the pinkish bill darkening from base, the pinkish legs turning olive-grey, then blackish; facial skin dark. **HABITS:** Like those of African Spoonbill with which it usually associates. **SIMILAR SPECIES:** Young African Spoonbill, also with blackish tarsi, has unfeathered face. **STATUS AND DISTRIBUTION:** Scarce migrant, recorded at Lake Turkana and less often at lakes Nakuru and Naivasha. Kenyan birds are generally thought to represent the nominate palearctic race, but *archeri* from Red Sea coast is also possible here.

AFRICAN SPOONBILL *Platalea alba*   Plate 10

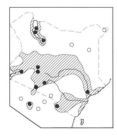

Length *c.* 91 cm (36"). A large white wading bird with a long spatulate bill. **Adult** has *bare red face,* grey bill with pink edges, and long pinkish-red legs; eyes pale blue-grey. **Juvenile** and **immature** have *dull yellow bill and facial skin, blackish legs and feet,* and *black primary tips.* **VOICE:** A double *ark-ark,* but usually silent. **HABITS:** Feeds by wading slowly in shallow water, bill immersed and sweeping from side to side. Flight graceful, with shallow wingbeats and long glides, often in lines and V-formations. Rests on one foot with bill tucked into scapulars. Nests communally in trees and shrubs over water or among rocks. **SIMILAR SPECIES:** See Eurasian Spoonbill. **STATUS AND DISTRIBUTION:** Widespread on inland waters. Breeds regularly near Kisumu and Garsen, and sporadically at several sites in or near the Rift Valley. Local on coastal saltpans, creeks and estuaries.

FLAMINGOS, FAMILY PHOENICOPTERIDAE
(World, 5 species; Africa, Kenya and n. Tanzania, 2)

Tall, slender wading birds of shallow saline or alkaline waters, characterized by a long sinuous neck, a lamellate bill bent sharply downwards at the midpoint, pink and white plumage, extremely long legs and short webbed toes. They fly in long skeins and V-formations with neck and legs fully extended, the pointed wings beating steadily. Both species feed with bill immersed, head upside-down, usually while wading, sometimes when swimming. Mud and water are taken in along the sides of the bill, then expelled past the filtering lamellae, the thick tongue acting like a piston. They are highly gregarious and nomadic. Breeding is often sporadic, always in large colonies, the nest a mound of mud with a shallow depression at the top to receive the one or two chalky, bluish-white eggs (which quickly stain brownish). Incubation is by both sexes, as is care of the downy nidifugous young.

GREATER FLAMINGO *Phoenicopterus (ruber) roseus*   Plate 10

Length 127–140 cm (50–55"). Very tall. White **adult** plumage washed with pink, the wing-coverts and axillaries bright coral-red; flight feathers black. *Bill pink with black tip;* legs and feet bright coral-pink. **Juvenile** brownish grey, with no red on wings; bill pale grey with black tip; eyes yellow; legs and feet grey. **Immature** white, tinged pink, with greyish head and neck, bill and legs gradually becoming pink. **VOICE:** A loud goose-like double honk *ka-hanh,* a conversational *kuk-kuk, kuk-kuk. . .,* a nasal *knyaaa,* plus other notes in display and at breeding colonies. Feeding flocks maintain a continuous 'kucking'. **HABITS:** Highly gregarious, flocks sometimes number

ing many thousands. Feeds primarily on invertebrates from bottom mud. Breeds in hundreds or thousands on open shores or small islands. **SIMILAR SPECIES**: See Lesser Flamingo. **STATUS AND DISTRIBUTION**: Largely confined to brackish and soda lakes of the Rift Valley, with major breeding sites at lakes Elmenteita and Natron. Ranges widely in small numbers, particularly to the coast, where regular at Mida Creek. Some coastal birds may be visitors from Arabia. **NOTE**: Some authorities consider the Old-World *roseus* specifically distinct from the New-World *P. ruber*.

LESSER FLAMINGO *Phoeniconaias minor* — Plate 10

Length 81–90 cm (32–35.5"). Considerably smaller than Greater Flamingo and more richly coloured. **Adult** mainly deep pink, with *dark red, black-tipped bill*, bright red legs and feet, and largely red wings with black flight feathers; eyes yellow. **Juvenile** greyish, with grey bill, legs and feet. **Immature** whitish, with no red in wings. **VOICE**: A low *murr-err, murr-err* at rest, and a high-pitched *kwirrik* in flight. Flocks produce a continuous humming or murmuring. **HABITS**: Gathers in immense numbers on Rift Valley soda lakes ,where often so closely packed that mass manoeuvring is necessary for sections of the flock to take off. Feeds by filtering microscopic blue-green algae (especially *Spirulina*) and diatoms. Nests in dense colonies on open mud. During wing moult, some birds in a colony remain flightless for three weeks (before, during or after nesting). **SIMILAR SPECIES**: Greater Flamingo compared above. **STATUS AND DISTRIBUTION**: Mainly confined to the Rift Valley soda lakes from Manyara north to Turkana. Hundreds of thousands breed regularly at Lake Natron, and occasionally at lakes Magadi and Logipi. Concentrations of feeding birds can exceed one million, especially at lakes Nakuru and Bogoria. Seldom recorded far from Rift Valley lakes.

DUCKS AND GEESE, FAMILY ANATIDAE
(World, 155 species; Africa, 55; Kenya, 24; n. Tanzania, 21)

Strong-winged, heavy-bodied and short-tailed waterbirds, the broad flattened bill with a nail-like tip and lateral lamellae for filter-feeding. The tarsi are short and thick, and the three front toes are webbed. Most species feed on small invertebrates, amphibians and plant material by diving, up-ending, or dabbling. Many also graze, and feed on grain. Nesting is solitary, usually in a lined hollow on the ground, sometimes in a hollow tree or old nest of some other bird. The three to 12 eggs are unmarked whitish buff or pale brown.

At hatching the nidifugous young are covered with down. They soon acquire a juvenile plumage, worn for only a few weeks, that resembles the adult female. The following first-winter (first basic) plumage displays the sexual dimorphism characteristic of many species; it develops through a head and body moult, but some or most juvenile wing feathers are retained. Adults usually undergo a complete post-breeding moult, shedding all remiges simultaneously and thus becoming flightless for a few weeks as they assume their non-breeding or 'eclipse' dress characteristic of males of palearctic species and a few southern-hemisphere breeders. This dull-coloured feather coat is retained for a month or two, then replaced by the bright breeding plumage in autumn or early winter. Northern ducks in partial eclipse plumage may be seen in East Africa, and some species (Northern Shoveler, Garganey) moult into a supplementary 'sub-eclipse' plumage, retained for several months before acquiring breeding dress. Females of palearctic species have moults corresponding to those of males, but the seasonal plumages of females differ little from one another.

Our classification of this diverse group follows Livezey (1986) and Madge and Burn (1988). Several subfamilies are represented in East Africa: Dendrocygninae (whistling ducks), Thalassorninae (White-backed Duck), Plectropterinae (Spur-winged Goose), Tadorninae (the duck-like geese *Sarkidiornis* and *Alopochen*) and Anatinae (typical ducks), the latter represented here by the well-marked tribes Anatini (dabbling ducks), Aythyini (diving ducks) and Oxyurini (stiff-tails). Whistling ducks are treated as a separate family by some authors.

FULVOUS WHISTLING DUCK *Dendrocygna bicolor* — Plate 15
(Fulvous Duck)

Length 45–53 cm (18–21"). Long-necked and long-legged. This and the following species stand more upright than typical ducks. **Adult** *rich rufous-brown* or fulvous below and on head, dark brown above with a broad *blackish line down back of neck*, and cream stripes forming a *broad pale line along the flanks*. In flight appears long-necked and broad-winged, and the feet project well beyond the tail; *buffy-white U-shaped patch on upper tail-coverts* separates brown back and wings from black tail. Eyes brown; bill, legs and feet greyish black. Little seasonal or sexual plumage difference. **Juvenile** duller than adult and the white upper tail-coverts less conspicuous. **VOICE**: A low whistle, *tsu-ee*, given in flight. Less vocal than White-faced Whistling Duck, although flocks produce a persistent whistling. **HABITS**: Shy. Gregarious, sometimes in flocks of hundreds. Feeds on plant mate-

rial by dabbling or diving. Often active at night. **SIMILAR SPECIES**: White-faced Whistling Duck has white face, shows no white on upper tail-coverts. **STATUS AND DISTRIBUTION**: Non-breeding visitor to freshwater and moderately alkaline lakes, flooded grassland, irrigated fields and rice paddies, mainly below 1500 m. Breeding suspected at Ahero (near Kisumu), but confirmed in our region only near Arusha (Feb. 1962) following exceptionally heavy short rains.

WHITE-FACED WHISTLING DUCK *Dendrocygna viduata* Plate 15
(White-faced Duck)

Length 43–48 cm (17–19"). Easily recognized by *white face contrasting with long blackish neck* and chestnut breast, lower neck and back; sides barred buffy white and dark brown; belly and tail blackish. Eyes brown; bill black with pale grey subterminal band; legs and feet greyish black. Flight outline similar to that of preceding species, but appears largely dark except for white face. **Juvenile** duller, with light brown face patch. **VOICE**: Usual call a sibilant three-note whistle, *swee-swee-sweeu*. **HABITS**: Similar to those of Fulvous Whistling Duck, the two species flocking together in favoured feeding areas, generally near open water. Nests on ground in tall grass or reeds. **SIMILAR SPECIES**: Fulvous Whistling Duck is much paler, shows white upper tail-coverts, no black belly in flight. **STATUS AND DISTRIBUTION**: Common and widespread below 1500 m on freshwater and slightly alkaline lakes and ponds, irrigated fields and rice paddies.

WHITE-BACKED DUCK *Thalassornis l. leuconotus* Plate 15

Length 38–40 cm (15–16"). A thickset dull brown diving duck with a short tail. Long nape feathers impart a *large-headed appearance*, and, except for the relatively large blackish bill with prominent strong nail, outline is more grebe-like than duck-like. Sides of head and neck tawny-buff, merging into the *dark crown and face*; shows *white patch at base of bill*; *body barred with tawny-buff*, more coarsely on flanks; white back/rump patch usually concealed on resting bird. In flight, looks tail-less and large-footed; the *white rump and lower back* contrast with generally dark plumage; wings plain. Eyes dark brown; legs and feet dark grey. Sexes alike. **Juvenile** similar but duller. **VOICE**: A clear two- or three-note whistle, *tu-wheet* or *si-weet-weet*. **HABITS**: Mainly in pairs or family groups, sometimes in flocks of 50 or more. Avoids open water, spending most of day resting among floating vegetation. Nests close to water, sometimes in old nest of grebe or coot. Reluctant to fly; prefers to escape danger by diving. If pressed, patters across water surface to take wing. **SIMILAR SPECIES**: See Maccoa Duck. **STATUS AND DISTRIBUTION**: Locally common resident on freshwater lakes and small ponds with abundant emergent vegetation. In Kenya, ranges from the coast up to 3000 m in central and western highlands, and large numbers are frequent on Lake Paradise, Mt Marsabit. Common in Arusha NP; smaller numbers on most other suitable lakes and ponds in n. Tanzania.

SPUR-WINGED GOOSE *Plectropterus g. gambensis* Plate 15

Length 75–100 cm (30–39"). The largest African waterfowl: an unmistakable *long necked and long-legged*, iridescent black-and-white goose. Sexes similar, but male substantially larger than female and with caruncles forming a low comb on base of bill; facial feathering somewhat more extensive in female. Glossy black with metallic green and bronze reflections; chin, throat and belly white. *Bill, bare loral and orbital skin, legs and feet dark pink*; eyes dark brown. In flight, shows white forewing patch above and below. **Juvenile** browner, with the lower face white-feathered. **VOICE**: In flight, a soft rolling or bubbling whistle, *cherrut* or *cherwit*; otherwise largely silent. **HABITS**: In pairs, small groups or flocks of 50 or more. Wary. Often flies to feeding areas at dawn, at dusk or at night. Usually nests on ground, at times in tree cavities or old Hamerkop nests. **STATUS AND DISTRIBUTION**: Locally common resident below 3000 m, especially on flooded grassland, swamps and freshwater lake edges. Wanders widely.

EGYPTIAN GOOSE *Alopochen aegyptiacus* Plate 15

Length 63–73 cm (25–29"). A large buffy-brown goose with *chestnut-brown eye patch* continuing around base of bill, similar small patch on lower breast, and narrow chestnut collar around lower neck. In flight, *white forewing* conspicuous against black primaries; secondaries edged with iridescent green. From below, white wing-linings contrast with dark flight feathers. Eyes orange; bill, legs and feet bright pink. Sexes similar, but con

siderable individual variation; some birds are noticeably greyer. **Juvenile** duller than adult, lacking face and breast patches, and with forewing panel grey, not white; bill, legs and feet yellowish grey. **VOICE:** In display, with neck stretched forwards, female utters a strident nasal *hur-hur-hur-hur-hur. . .* accelerating and becoming staccato; male has throaty wheezing or hissing, also with neck extended; both sexes give a honking *ha-ha-ha-ha-ha* before taking flight. **HABITS:** Swims with rear end held high. Usually in pairs, but may be gregarious when not breeding. Vegetarian, often grazing in fields. Nests on ground, on cliffs, in old raptor or Hamerkop nests. **SIMILAR SPECIES:** In flight at a distance, extralimital Ruddy Shelduck, *Tadorna ferruginea*, resembles this species in wing pattern, but has darker (rufous) body and shorter neck. **STATUS AND DISTRIBUTION:** Common inland breeding species as high as 3000 m on permanent lakes, ponds and sandy river banks. Wanders to some extent and occupies temporary pools. **NOTE:** The Ruddy Shelduck (see above) has twice been attributed to Kenya (Britton 1980; Short *et al.* 1990), but both reports were rejected by the East African Rarities Committee.

KNOB-BILLED DUCK, *Sarkidiornis m. melanotos*   **Plate 15**
(Comb Duck)

Length 56–76 cm (22–30"). A large black-and-white dabbling duck. *Head, neck and underparts white*, the head and upper neck finely speckled with black. Back and wings glossy black with green and bronze reflections. **Male** has large, fleshy, black comb at base of bill. In overhead flight, dark wings contrast with white body. **Female** smaller and with grey rump/lower back. Eyes dark brown; bill black, legs and feet dark grey. **Juvenile** considerably browner than adult on head and upperparts, mottled below and with trace of glossy green on wings. **VOICE:** A low croak when flushed; otherwise silent. **HABITS:** Typically in small flocks, at times in hundreds, loafing on pond margins. Feeds in shallow water and on land; often perches in trees. **SIMILAR SPECIES:** Distant Fulvous Whistling Duck might be mistaken for young Knob-billed, but is more richly coloured, has long-legged appearance and stands more upright. **STATUS AND DISTRIBUTION:** Widespread from coast to 3000 m, on freshwater lakes, ponds, swamps and flooded grasslands. Numbers fluctuate; most birds appear to be non-breeding visitors, but has bred in se. Kenya and in Serengeti NP.

AFRICAN PYGMY GOOSE *Nettapus auritus*   **Plate 15**

Length 30–33 cm (12–13"). A compact colourful duck about the size of a Hottentot Teal. Dark *green above with white face and neck; bright tawny-cinnamon on chest and flanks*. **Breeding male** has light green patches at sides of foreneck, and bright yellow bill with black nail; feet dark grey; eyes brown. In flight, looks small and dark with white belly, the dark wings with a large white patch on secondaries (above and below). **Eclipse male, female**, and **juvenile** lack neck patches and have dull greyish-olive bills. **VOICE:** Male gives a soft whistled *choo-choo-pee-pee*. **HABITS:** Usually in pairs or small groups among heavily vegetated secluded waters. Frequently dives. May perch in low trees over water. Flight fast and low. Not shy. **SIMILAR SPECIES:** Hottentot Teal is paler in flight and shows only narrow line of white on secondaries. **STATUS AND DISTRIBUTION:** Local and uncommon resident of coastal freshwater lakes and swamps with floating and emergent vegetation. Presumed wanderers recorded at Amboseli NP, Kiambu, lakes Turkana, Naivasha and Baringo, and at Port Victoria. No recent records from Lake Jipe or mainland n. Tanzania, but plentiful on Pemba Island.

MALLARD *Anas platyrhynchos*   **Plate 16**

Length 50–65 cm (20–25"). A rare bird in East Africa. **Male in breeding plumage** unmistakable, with *dark glossy green head and neck, narrow white collar* and *purplish-brown breast*. Belly white, sides of body pale grey, back darker, the scapulars black and buff; rump and upper tail-coverts black; two black tail feathers conspicuously curled up and forward; outer rectrices mainly white. Grey-brown wings have *white-bordered blue or purple speculum*; wing-linings white. Eyes dark brown; bill olive-green or yellowish with black nail; feet orange. **Eclipse male** resembles female, but bill yellowish, face and neck paler and contrasting more with much darker crown, large U-shaped markings on sides; breast less streaked. **Female** and **juvenile** variable, but generally buffy brown with dark brown streaking and mottling; crown, nape and eye-lines dark brown, contrasting with buffy-brown superciliary stripes, face and forecrown; wings as in male. *Bill usually dull orange with blackish markings*, but may be dull brownish, olive or yellowish brown. Eyes and feet as in male. **VOICE:** Female utters a repetitive *quack*; male has a soft *kreep*. **HABITS:** Gregarious and often with other duck species. Feeds chiefly by dabbling and up-ending. Flight strong but with shallow wingbeats. **SIMILAR SPECIES:** Female Gadwall is smaller, slimmer, has white patch on secondaries; smaller grey bill, yellow-orange at sides; feet yellower than in Mallard. Female Northern Pintail is slimmer, with long neck, plainer head and grey bill. Female Eurasian Wigeon is much plainer, with smaller grey bill. Feet of both pintail and wigeon also grey. **STATUS AND DISTRIBUTION:** Vagrant. Records of birds shot near Marsabit, 1928–29, undoubtedly of wild birds (presumably of nominate race but no specimens preserved). Reports from Lake Naivasha (Dec. 1938) perhaps based on feral birds. No satisfactory recent records.

AFRICAN BLACK DUCK *Anas sparsa leucostigma*   **Plate 16**

Length 48–57 cm (19–22"). A large sooty-black river duck with *bold white scalloping on upperparts* (forming bands on some individuals). Distinctive *blue or purplish-blue speculum bordered by white-and-black bands*, evident in flight and often on water. Bill pinkish or pinkish grey with black 'saddle' and nail; tarsi and toes yellowish, webs black; eyes dark brown. In overhead flight, white inner wing-linings contrast with generally dark wings. Sexes similar. **Juvenile** browner than adult, with sparse buff spotting above (sometimes nearly absent); dusky and white barring on belly; speculum dull; bill bluish grey. **Voice:** A Mallard-like *quack* (female) and a soft wheezy *peeshp* (male). **Habits:** Pairs haunt fast-flowing highland streams with wooded banks. Feeds by head-dipping or up-ending to take prey from beneath stones in strong current. Shy and readily takes to wing, flying low over water along river course. May roost on pools and in swamps at night. **Similar Species:** Yellow-billed Duck has bright yellow bill, blackish feet, is not boldly white-scalloped; in flight, shows less prominent speculum borders and more white on underside of wings. **Status and Distribution:** Uncommon and local on mountain streams above 1850 m in w. and cent. Kenyan highlands, most numerous on those flowing from Mt Elgon, Mt Kenya and the Aberdares; also on alpine ponds. Occasionally wanders lower during the rains. In n. Tanzania, similarly distributed on Mt Meru and Kilimanjaro; in the West Usambaras common above 1250 m, and in the East Usambaras recorded down to 450 m where suitable forest habitat remains.

CAPE TEAL *Anas capensis*   **Plate 16; Figure p. 331**
(Cape Wigeon)

Length 44–48 cm (17–19"). A *pale* dabbling duck with a distinctive *rose-pink bill*. Plumage mottled brownish grey, the head ash-grey with fine speckling. Eyes yellowish in males, orange-brown in females, varying individually; legs and feet dull yellowish brown. In flight, appears short-necked and big-headed, the wings dark brown above and showing a green speculum broadly bordered with white; underside of wings mostly dark grey. Sexes similar. **Juvenile** resembles adult, but underparts less spotted. **Voice:** Usually silent, but male occasionally utters a soft nasal whistle; female gives a low nasal quack. In display, male produces a "clear and fairly loud whistle, *oo-whee-oo*", the female a "decrescendo call of four to eight syllables, with the second the loudest" (Johnsgard 1978). **Habits:** Typically forms small flocks on soda lakes. Feeds by head-dipping and up-ending; occasionally dives. Rather tame. Bobs head when alarmed. Nests on ground under shrub. **Similar Species:** Red-billed Teal has red bill, but is darker above with dark brown crown and nape, and buff cheeks; shows large creamy-white patch on secondaries in flight. **Status and Distribution:** In Kenya, a common breeding bird, mainly resident on alkaline Rift Valley lakes, but wanders to fresh water. In n. Tanzania, common in Arusha NP and in smaller numbers at Lake Manyara, Ngorongoro Crater and Lake Lygarja (Serengeti NP).

EURASIAN WIGEON *Anas penelope*   **Plate 16**

Length 45–51 cm (18–20"). Medium-sized, with a *steep forehead, short blue-grey bill* (with black tip) and rather pointed tail. **Adult male in breeding plumage** has *chestnut head with yellowish-buff forehead and crown*, grey body, white line along wing, black under tail-coverts, and white patch at rear of flanks. Bill pale bluish grey with black tip, legs and feet dark grey. In flight, shows prominent white forewing, green-and-black speculum, and white belly. **Eclipse male** similar to female, but breast and sides rich chestnut with contrasting white belly and forewing, and white line along wing when at rest. **Female** either greyish or rufous-brown, finely mottled (appearing plain at distance), head paler in both morphs but blackish around eyes. In overhead flight, shows white belly and pale grey wing-linings with darker flight feathers and leading edge. Bill blue-grey with black tip and cutting edges. Female-like **juvenile** gradually moults into adult dress during autumn. **Voice:** Male gives characteristic loud whistled *wheeeoo*; female utters a low *grrr*. **Habits:** Gregarious, at times with other waterfowl. Dabbles, feeds on submerged plants by up-ending, and grazes waterside vegetation. Swims with pointed tail angled upwards. **Similar Species:** Female and young Northern Pintail distinguished by longer neck and bill, less contrasting white belly in flight; also by white bar along rear edge of speculum. **Status and Distribution:** In Kenya, a regular but generally uncommon palearctic migrant, late November–March, typically above 1800 m on freshwater lakes and ponds in the w. and cent. highlands and Rift Valley. Most numerous in Uasin Gishu, at lakes Turkana, Naivasha, Solai and Ol Bolossat. Scarce in n. Tanzania (no recent records).

Three East African teal species: Cape, (left), Red-billed, (upper), and Hottentot, showing wing patterns.

GADWALL *Anas s. strepera* Plate 16

Length 46–55 cm (18–22"). A medium-sized, rather dull-coloured dabbling duck (the male's handsome plumage appreciated only at close range). **Breeding-plumaged male** mainly *grey* with browner head and *black rear end*, some chestnut in upper wing-coverts; belly white. *Bill blackish; feet orange-yellow*; eyes brown. **Female and juvenile** mottled brown with rounded flank markings and dark eye-lines. *Bill greyish with orange sides* (yellower in juvenile). **Eclipse male** resembles female, but less coarsely marked and with less orange on bill. In flight (and sometimes on water), both sexes show *small square white patch on inner secondaries*, larger in male, small in juvenile. **VOICE**: Generally silent, but male gives a low whistle and a throaty *bek* or *nheck*; female utters a descending Mallard-like *kak-ak-ak-ak-ak*. **HABITS**: Associates with other dabbling ducks. Feeds by dabbling and up-ending. Usually shy. **SIMILAR SPECIES**: Female Eurasian Wigeon is plainer, has short grey bill and grey feet. Female Northern Pintail has grey feet and dull, white-bordered speculum. Female Mallard has less sloping forehead, its larger bill usually orange near tip and at base (rarely on sides like Gadwall); belly not sharply white, flank markings more pointed, crown and eye-lines darker. **STATUS AND DISTRIBUTION**: Rare palearctic migrant; ten Kenyan records (only two since 1944), mostly of single birds on freshwater lakes in the west, northwest and the Rift Valley.

COMMON TEAL *Anas c. crecca* Plate 16
(Green-winged Teal)

Length 34–38 cm (13–15"). A small dabbling duck little larger than a Hottentot Teal, with rather steep forehead and short bill. **Male in breeding plumage** has *chestnut head with buff-bordered iridescent green band from lores to nape*; body greyish with white horizontal line along side, and creamy under tail-coverts noticeable at a distance; breast buff, speckled with blackish. Bill, legs and feet slate-grey; eyes brown. **Eclipse male** resembles female but darker above and with less distinct line through eye. **Female** mottled brown, with dark greyish eye-lines. *Mostly grey bill is flesh-coloured at base of maxilla.* Shows pale line along under tail-coverts near each side of tail. In flight, both sexes appear small, short-tailed, short-necked, pale-bellied, and show a *bright green speculum* with white borders. **Juvenile** resembles female but has more heavily spotted belly and may show trace of dark cheek line from base of bill (less distinct than on Garganey). **VOICE**: Male has a high, soft, ringing *crreek-crreek*, female a short high-pitched *quack* when flushed.

Habits: Small groups or singles associate with other migrant waterfowl. Typically feeds near waterside vegetation. Rises abruptly and flies rapidly, usually low. **Similar Species**: Female Garganey is duller, greyer, shows no pink on bill base and lacks pale stripe along sides of under tail-coverts; also has flatter forehead, larger bill, more pronounced facial stripes. In flight appears longer-necked, with pale grey or grey-brown forewing, grey-brown speculum, relatively broad whitish trailing edge to secondaries and brighter, more extensive white on belly. **Status and Distribution**: Regular palearctic migrant in small numbers November–March, mainly above 1400 m, on small ponds, streams and lakeshores in and west of the Rift Valley, including Lake Turkana; occasional in Amboseli and Tsavo West NPs. Scarce in n. Tanzania (no recent records).

GARGANEY *Anas querquedula* Plate 16

Length 37–41 cm (15–16″). Teal-sized, with relatively long neck and large dark grey bill. **Male in breeding plumage** has bold *white stripe from eye to nape*, chestnut-brown head, neck and breast, and *pale grey sides*. In flight, shows *pale blue-grey forewing* and a *dark green speculum broadly bordered with white in front and behind*; overhead, the mainly white wing-lining contrasts with broad black leading edge. **Sub-eclipse male** plumage (replacing true eclipse plumage) resembles female, but with breeding-male wing coloration, brighter white throat, and broader streaking on head and neck. **Female** resembles female Common Teal, but is heavier, larger-billed and generally duller brown with *bolder head pattern*: dark crown and eye-lines contrast with pale buff stripes above and below eyes; also shows *short dark subloral lines* near base of bill. Speculum grey-brown; throat and belly brighter white than in Common Teal, and no pale stripe along under tail-coverts at edge of tail. Eyes dark brown or reddish brown; bill, legs and feet grey. **Juvenile** resembles female but has spotted belly and grey-brown eyes. **Voice**: Male gives a dry *krik-krik* and, in spring, a crackling *rrar-rrar-rrar*; flock continuously noisy; female has a harsh *gack*. **Habits**: Gathers in small groups or tightly packed flocks of hundreds or thousands. Prefers sheltered shallow pools and bays with emergent vegetation. Feeds like teal. Flight fast and agile. **Similar Species**: Female Common Teal compared above; juvenile shows suggestion of dark subloral lines, but these not well defined. Female and young Northern Pintail coloured much like Gargany but are larger and longer-necked, with plainer head and pointed tail. **Status and Distribution**: In Kenya, a common to abundant palearctic migrant, mainly late October to April. Widespread from near sea level to over 2500 m, on muddy or marshy lakeshores and sheltered ponds with emergent vegetation. Most numerous in w. and cent. Kenya, including the Rift Valley, at medium to higher elevations. Locally common on lower Tana River and in the southeast. Small numbers regular in Ngorongoro Crater, Lake Manyara and Arusha NPs in n. Tanzania.

YELLOW-BILLED DUCK *Anas undulata* Plate 16

Length 51–58 cm (20–23″). Mallard-sized, with a long, *largely bright yellow bill*. Plumage generally mottled dark brownish grey with broad pale feather edges, the head blackish. In flight, shows white wing-linings, green speculum (in nominate *undulata*, bordered with white lines at front and rear. Legs and feet vary from red-brown to dark grey; eyes red-brown; bill has some black on culmen, nail and commissure. Sexes similar (**female** duller, with paler bill). **Juvenile** resembles adult but has broader and buffier feather edges. The slightly darker northern race *rueppelli* has deeper yellow bill and a blue speculum. **Voice**: Female gives a hoarse descending Mallard-like *quack-quack-quack-quack*; male utters a soft low whistle. **Habits**: Pairs or small flocks forage in shallow water. Feeds by up-ending or dabbling; also grazes on land. Flight rapid but rather heavy. **Similar Species**: More slender female-plumaged Northern Pintail has longer neck and pale grey bill. African Black Duck is darker above with white scalloping, and pinkish or pinkish-grey bill. **Status and Distribution**: *A. u. undulata* is a widespread resident and wanderer, mainly above 1600 m in the cent. and w. Kenyan highlands, frequenting marshy freshwater lakes and ponds, marshy grassland and papyrus swamps; locally common at Lake Victoria, and small numbers are regular in Ngorongoro Crater; scarce elsewhere in n. Tanzania. Old records from Marsabit may refer to *A. u. rueppelli*, as may recent sightings of blue-speculumed birds at Ol Bolossat.

NORTHERN PINTAIL *Anas a. acuta* Plate 16

Length 51–65 cm (20–26″; including 4″ tail extension in male). Slender and long-necked. **Breeding-plumaged male** (Dec. onwards) has *dark brown head, white throat and neck stripe* and long *pointed central tail feathers*. Body grey, with buffy-white patch at rear of flanks and black under tail-coverts. Eyes yellow to brownish yellow; bill pale blue-grey with black culmen, tip and edges. Legs and feet dark grey. In flight, long neck, pointed tail and dark head obvious; speculum bronzy green. **Eclipse male** resembles female but has longer inner secondaries and green speculum. **Female** and **juvenile** mottled brown, sometimes with warm tawny tinge; face rather plain, slim-necked and with short pointed tail. Bill and feet grey; eyes brown. In flight, appears brownish with pale belly and *conspicuous white trailing edge on brown speculum*; underside of wings largely grey. Young male shows partly green speculum. **Voice**: Male gives a weak mellow *prrip-prrip*, female a series of quacks. Seldom

vocal. **HABITS:** Flocks in shallow water, often with Garganey or Northern Shoveler. Sometimes submerges when feeding. Swims buoyantly with tail elevated. Flight fast and graceful, often high with long neck outstretched. **SIMILAR SPECIES:** Female Eurasian Wigeon also has grey bill and feet, but is stockier and shorter-necked with clear-cut white belly. See females of Garganey and Gadwall. **STATUS AND DISTRIBUTION:** Locally common to abundant palearctic migrant, mainly November to early April, on ponds, freshwater and alkaline lakes, especially in the cent. and w. Kenyan highlands and the Rift Valley. Occasional in se. Kenya, including the Tsavo region and coastal estuaries. In n. Tanzania small numbers are regular on lakes in Ngorongoro Crater, Lake Manyara and Arusha NPs.

RED-BILLED TEAL *Anas erythrorhyncha*   Plate 16; Figure p. 331
(Red-billed Duck)

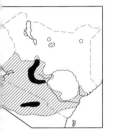

Length 43–48 cm (17–19"). A medium-sized duck with a *red bill, buffy-white cheeks* and *dark brown crown and nape.* Body plumage dark brown with broad pale feather edges, producing a scalloped or spotted appearance, especially below. Creamy-white and buff secondaries are crossed by a black band. Legs and feet dark grey; eyes brown. In flight, shows unique pattern of *whitish secondaries contrasting with otherwise dark wings.* Sexes alike. **Juvenile** duller than adult, streaked rather than spotted below; bill dull pink. **VOICE:** Male gives a soft whistling *whizzzt,* female a guttural *krraak.* **HABITS:** Not shy. Gregarious when not breeding. Feeds in shallow water by up-ending or dabbling; grazes on land. Nests on ground near water. **SIMILAR SPECIES:** Cape Teal has pink bill, finely speckled pale grey head, green speculum and dull yellowish legs and feet. Smaller Hottentot Teal shows similar head pattern, but has bluish-grey bill and green speculum. **STATUS AND DISTRIBUTION:** Common resident, subject to wandering and marked local seasonal fluctuations. Largely absent from coastal areas except the Tana and Sabaki estuaries, preferring freshwater and alkaline lake edges, ponds, marshes and temporary floodland.

HOTTENTOT TEAL *Anas hottentota*   Plate 16; Figure p. 331

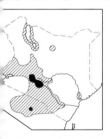

Length 30–35 cm (12–14"). The smallest resident duck. *Dark crown and patches on ear-coverts and hindneck contrast with pale buff face* and foreneck. Upperparts mottled dark brown; underparts buff with dark spotting and barring. *Greyish-blue* bill has black culmen, nail and edges; legs and feet dark blue-grey; eyes brown. In flight, shows dark brown wings and large green speculum with broad white trailing edge. Sexes similar, the female duller than male and with browner crown and less well-defined neck patch. **Juvenile** still duller, but pattern the same. **VOICE:** Take-off and alarm calls include a harsh *tsetzetze* and a higher *ke-ke-ke.* **HABITS:** Pairs and small groups associate with other dabbling ducks. Spends much time loafing on shores, often hidden in vegetation. Dabbles in shallows and forages in mud near water's edge. Flies low across water, with head and neck partially raised. Nests on ground near water. **SIMILAR SPECIES:** Red-billed Teal has red bill and buffy-white secondaries. **STATUS AND DISTRIBUTION:** Locally common to above 2500 m on well-vegetated freshwater and alkaline lakeshores, ponds, marshy pools and shallow reedy bays. Scarce in the coastal lowlands. Commonly makes movements of over 100 km.

NORTHERN SHOVELER *Anas clypeata*   Plate 16

Length 44–52 cm (17–20"). Readily identified in all plumages by the *oversized, semi-spatulate bill.* **Male in breeding plumage** (after late Dec.) has *dark glossy green head* and *large chestnut patch on sides and belly* contrasting with white breast and flank spot; under tail-coverts black. Bill black in breeding plumage, otherwise brown; *legs and feet bright orange;* eyes yellow to orange. Partial **eclipse male** somewhat resembles female, but has rufous on flanks and belly, darker brown head and darker feather edges on breast and sides. **Sub-eclipse male** intermediate between eclipse and breeding plumages, with a *whitish facial crescent* (often mottled) on dark head, and dark feather edges on underparts. Male in flight shows *pale blue forewing,* large green speculum with narrow white bar in front, and white wing-linings; appears 'front-heavy' owing to long bill, long neck and short tail. **Female** mottled light buffy brown, the head paler but hindneck and eye-stripe dark; tail pale-edged. Bill grey or brown with much orange along sides and at base; legs and feet orange; eyes brown. Flight pattern similar to that of male. **Juvenile** resembles female but duller, lacks green speculum and white wing-bar; eyes brown at first, becoming yellow; bill often mottled. **VOICE:** Male gives a gruff *took-took,* and in display a hollow liquid *g'dunk-g'dunk* (Madge and Burn 1988); female gives a double quack or short descending series of quacks. **HABITS:** Gregarious, sometimes in large flocks. Swims with rear end raised and head down, bill tip almost touching the water. Filter-feeds by swinging bill from side to side as well as dabbling. Pair formation begins in mid-winter. **SIMILAR SPECIES:** Other brown female ducks are readily sepa-

rated by their smaller, shorter bills. **STATUS AND DISTRIBUTION**: Locally common palearctic migrant, late October to early April, on alkaline and freshwater lakes and ponds in the Rift Valley and adjacent highlands; uncommon elsewhere.

Southern Pochards. Male (left) and female.

SOUTHERN POCHARD *Netta erythrophthalma brunnea*   Plate 16

Length 48–51 cm (19–20"). A large *dark* diving duck with a steep forehead. **Male** blackish below with chestnut flanks, dark maroon-brown on face and neck, blackish brown on upperparts. In flight, looks dark and long-necked, with *broad white band along entire length of the flight feathers*, also showing on the largely dark underside of the wing. Bill rather long, *bluish grey* with black nail; legs and feet dark grey; eyes bright red. **Female** dark brown, with unique head pattern: *whitish patch near base of bill and white crescent from behind eye to sides of neck*; under tail-coverts also white. Same flight pattern as male; bill and feet as in male; eyes red-brown. **Juvenile** light brown, darker on back, pale areas of face buff rather than whitish and restricted to area near bill base and throat; under tail-coverts whitish. Young male much darker than female on neck and underparts. **VOICE**: Male occasionally utters a low nasal *prerr-prerr* in flight, the female a descending nasal *krrrrow* (Maclean 1984). **HABITS**: Gregarious, often in compact flocks on open water. Dives frequently, but also feeds like dabbling duck. Patters across water when taking wing. Nests on ground, in tree cavities or in other birds' nests, not always near water. **SIMILAR SPECIES**: Female Maccoa Duck dark brown, but has pale line below eye. See Ferruginous Duck and Tufted Duck. **STATUS AND DISTRIBUTION**: Fairly common on both alkaline and freshwater lakes and ponds, especially in cent. Rift Valley and w. Kenyan highlands up to 3000 m. Generally scarce elsewhere and, although small numbers breed in cent. Kenya and n. Tanzania, it is mainly a non-breeding visitor with peak numbers between November and February.

COMMON POCHARD *Aythya ferina*   Plate 16
(Northern Pochard)

Length 42–49 cm (17–19"). A stocky diving duck with steep forehead and relatively long bill. **Male in breeding plumage** distinctive, with *very pale grey body* (almost white in bright sunlight), *rich chestnut head* and neck, and *black breast and rear end*. Bill broadly black at tip with wide pale grey subterminal band and darker grey base; eyes orange-yellow or red; legs and feet grey. In flight, shows broad *pale grey* stripe along the flight feathers, darker grey forewing and whitish wing-linings. **Eclipse male** resembles female but has greyer body, darker breast and more reddish eyes. **Female** brown on head, neck and breast, with diffuse pale greyish-buff or whitish areas at base of bill and on sides of head, and a pale postocular line; back dark grey-brown, sides and flanks paler and greyer. Bill has narrow pale grey subterminal band behind broad black tip; eyes brown. **Juvenile** more uniformly brown with some mottling below, reduced facial markings and no pale postocular line; bill entirely black or dark grey; eyes yellow-olive. Bare parts and plumage gradually assume adult features during winter. **VOICE**: Female sometimes utters a harsh growling *krrr* when flushed; male usually silent (Madge and Burn 1988). **HABITS**: Mingles with other diving ducks on open water. Shy. **STATUS AND DISTRIBUTION**: Rare palearctic migrant south of its normal African winter range. Five Kenyan records (Kisumu, Ol Bolossat and Lake Turkana), one from n. Tanzania (Arusha NP), all December–March.

FERRUGINOUS DUCK *Aythya nyroca*   Plate 16
(White-eyed Pochard)

Length 38–42 cm (15–16"). A *dark* diving duck, smaller than Southern Pochard. **Male in breeding plumage** ferruginous-brown or dark chestnut with blackish-brown back, at distance appearing blackish apart from *white under tail-coverts* prominent on resting birds. *Eyes white*; bill grey with black tip and narrow obscure pale grey subterminal band; legs and feet grey. Head more rounded than in Southern Pochard, with steeper forehead and shorter bill. In flight, both sexes appear dark with contrasting white belly, under tail-coverts and wing-linings. **Autumn male** similar to female but more chestnut on head and breast; eyes white. **Female** resembles male but duller and browner and with *brown eyes*. **Juvenile** resembles female, but with paler edges to back and flank feathers, paler and more buff on sides of head and foreneck, bill darker; eyes grey-brown. **Voice**: Female utters a harsh *gaaa*; male has whistling notes in display. **Habits**: Frequents open water, where small numbers occasionally join Southern Pochards. Rests higher in water than that species, tail angled upward. Shy and wary. Feeds by dabbling, as well as diving. **Similar Species**: Southern Pochard compared above. Dark female Tufted Duck also shows white under tail-coverts, but has shorter bill, different head shape with tuft or bulge at rear of crown, and usually yellow eyes (young birds and some females are dark-eyed). **Status and Distribution**: Scarce palearctic migrant (occasional small influxes), December–March, south of its main range. Recorded at lakes Naivasha and Nakuru, Ol Bolossat, Endebess, Marsabit, Thika and Nairobi.

TUFTED DUCK *Aythya fuligula*   Plate 16

Length 40–47 cm (16–18"). A diving duck with steep rounded forehead and tuft or bulge at rear of crown. **Male in breeding plumage** *black, with white sides, flanks and belly, and long drooping crest at back of head*. Bill blue-grey with narrow whitish subterminal band; eyes yellow; legs and feet grey. In flight, contrasting black-and-white pattern includes broad white stripe on secondaries shading to grey on primaries; much white on underside of wings. **Eclipse male** greyer or browner on sides and belly, with much shorter crest. **Female** dull dark brown, with *short crest or tuft on hindcrown*. Some birds show whitish areas on lores and/or white under tail-coverts (cf. Ferruginous Duck). Wing pattern like that of male. Eyes yellow, occasionally brown. **Juvenile** female-like, the typical buff feather edges largely gone by the time birds reach Kenya in autumn; full adult plumage usually not acquired prior to spring departure. Eyes brown at first, becoming yellowish. **Voice**: Female may utter low growling notes when flushed. Mostly silent, except when displaying. **Habits**: Solitary or in small groups on open water. Patters across surface when taking wing. Wary. **Similar Species**: See Ferruginous Duck. **Status and Distribution**: Scarce palearctic migrant, November–March, on Turkana and other lakes at medium to high elevations in cent. and w. Kenyan highlands. Rare elsewhere; wanderers recorded in Tsavo NP, Mombasa, Arusha NP and Ngorongoro Crater.

MACCOA DUCK *Oxyura maccoa*   Plate 16

Length 48–51 cm (19–20"). Squat and thick-necked. Swims low in water, often with the stiff tail angled upward. **Breeding male** rich chestnut with *black head* and bright *cobalt-blue bill*; centre of belly and under tail-coverts whitish. Eyes brown; legs and feet grey. Wings uniformly dark above; wing-linings somewhat paler. **Eclipse male**, **adult female** and **juvenile** dark brown with broad whitish line below eyes; lower face and throat also whitish; bill dull grey. Male's head more blackish. **Voice**: Generally silent, but male utters guttural croaks and whistles, as well as a vibrating *prrr* when displaying. Female gives a series of short grunts (Madge and Burn 1988). **Habits**: Usually in pairs or small groups. When alarmed, the body largely submerges. Dives frequently and feeds by filtering organisms from bottom mud. Reluctant to take wing, but flies rapidly and low after pattering across water for take-off. Nests near lake edge, often in old coot's nest. **Similar Species**: White-backed Duck is more mottled, lacks face pattern of female Maccoa and shows white rump and lower back in flight. Female Southern Pochard is also dark brown but has different face pattern. **Status and Distribution**: Rather uncommon and local resident on alkaline and freshwater lakes in the Kenyan Rift Valley and central highlands. Common at times in Arusha NP and on lakes in the Crater Highlands.

SECRETARY BIRD, FAMILY SAGITTARIIDAE

This unique species, confined to Africa, is distantly related to other Falconiformes. It is very long-legged with well-developed femoral muscles, reflecting adaptation to a pedestrian mode of life. It has a raptorial bill for dispatching living prey, but its toes are weak, with short and rather blunt claws unsuited to grasping.

SECRETARY BIRD *Sagittarius serpentarius*   **Plate 30**

Length *c.* 125–150 cm (49–59"). A large bird, usually seen walking with measured gait in open grassland, its *long-projecting central tail feathers and drooping head plumes* conspicuous, as are the long legs. Plumage mainly grey, with *crest, belly, leg and flight feathers* and *two broad tail bands black.* Bare orbital skin orange. **Juvenile** similar but duller. When soaring overhead, the black remiges and the projecting long legs and tail are diagnostic. **Voice:** A croaking *korr-orr-orr* in display, and mewing calls at roost; otherwise silent. **Habits:** Largely terrestrial, but soars high on thermals. Usually in pairs, hunting on foot for insects, rodents and reptiles, sometimes killing large venomous snakes. Attracted to grass fires, where it feeds on small dead animals. Nests and roosts in low trees, usually flat-topped acacias. **Status and Distribution:** Conspicuous, but nowhere common, on open plains, farmland, and grassland with scattered bushes and trees. Widespread in s. Kenya and n. Tanzania, mainly in areas of moderate rainfall, but scarce in w. Kenya and the arid north and east.

VULTURES, EAGLES, HAWKS, KITES AND ALLIES, FAMILY ACCIPITRIDAE
(World, *c.* 240 species; Africa, 77; Kenya, 57; n. Tanzania, 52)

Strong-flying birds of prey, typically with broad, rounded wings, short strong tarsi, and raptorial toes. They are usually solitary, although most vultures and some kites are gregarious. Females are larger than males, and may differ in appearance; in some species there are confusing immature plumages. Excepting the Osprey (in its own subfamily) and a few other unique forms, the majority comprise about eight natural groups. (The superficially similar but structurally different falcons are in a separate family.)

VULTURES: Seven very large species of open country, adapted to carrion-feeding and to extended periods of soaring on long, usually broad, wings. Except in the Lammergeier, feathering is reduced or absent on face and neck, the tarsi are unfeathered and the toes are better adapted to walking than to grasping. Most take to the air when late-morning thermals develop. They soar and glide at great heights, detecting carcasses (at which they assemble rapidly) by watching behaviour of other vultures, eagles and mammalian scavengers on or near the ground. Order and mode of feeding depend on bill size. They nest either singly or in loose groups in trees or on cliffs. Head, neck and bill colours are useful in identification; in flight, pattern of underside of wing and ventral body and overall shape are important.

AQUILA **EAGLES:** Three resident species, four palearctic migrants, mostly large brown or blackish birds of open country, with long broad wings and broad but rather short tails; bill long and powerful; tarsi feathered to the toes. Adults are quite uniform in colour; immatures paler, with more patterned rump and upper wing surfaces. They build nests of sticks in trees or on cliffs. Identification can be difficult, and depends mainly on flight silhouette, dorsal coloration, and wing pattern.

SNAKE EAGLES (*Circaetus*): Five species of medium-sized to large raptors, large-headed and thick-necked with long loose feathering on the occiput or nape, prominent yellow eyes and long bare tarsi. The wings are broad, the usually barred tail of medium length. Their main food is snakes, caught by swooping from a perch or after a period of soaring or hovering. Nests of sticks are placed in trees.

HAWK-EAGLES and ALLIES (*Hieraaetus, Lophaetus, Stephanoaetus, Polemaetus*): Powerful raptors of woodland and forest, ranging from medium-sized to very large. Tarsi are feathered. Adults are yellowish-eyed and dark above, with strongly patterned underparts and barred tail, but immatures may be markedly different. Their prey is mainly mammals and birds, captured after dropping from a perch, by a swift stoop from high soaring flight, or in a quick dash low among trees. The often bulky stick nests are constructed high in trees.

BUZZARDS: Medium-large, rather sluggish raptors of wooded or open, usually hilly country. True buzzards (*Buteo*) are thickset with broad wings and short square-cut or rounded tail, rather short bare yellow tarsi, and brown eyes. They soar with wings held in a shallow V and the tail widely fanned. Nests are in trees. Colour and pattern of tail, underparts and underside of wings are important in identification. The insectivorous Honey Buzzard (*Pernis*) is smaller-headed, yellow-eyed, and soars on long flat wings.

SPARROWHAWKS, GOSHAWKS and CHANTING GOSHAWKS: Small to fairly large birds of prey, slender-bodied with short, rounded wings and rather long tail. The bill is small and sharp, the tarsi bare, long and slender. The predominantly grey chanting goshawks (**Melierax**) are larger and longer-winged than accipiters. They fly with languid wingbeats and prominently perch upright on posts or trees. The Gabar Goshawk (**Micronisus**) resembles *Accipiter* in proportions, habits and hunting behaviour, but is like *Melierax* in coloration, voice and preference for dry habitats. True sparrowhawks (**Accipiter**) are fierce predators, specialized for agile pursuit of birds through branches in dense bush or forest; they often soar, especially on migration or over nesting areas. All are tree nesters. Species identification (especially of juveniles) can be difficult and relies heavily on pattern of head, underparts, upper tail-coverts and tail. Most adults are grey above and barred below. Males are noticeably smaller than females.

HARRIERS (**Circus**): Slim-bodied, long-winged hawks of open country where they hunt by quartering low over the ground, alternating periods of buoyant flight with short glides, checking to drop onto prey. They soar and glide with wings typically held in a shallow V. Tail and tarsi are long, the head small with a somewhat owl-like facial disc and small bill. Most are sexually dimorphic. Like its northern congeners which migrate to East Africa, our single breeding species is a ground nester, and feeds mainly on rodents and small birds. Identification is based mainly on body and head colour, and on rump, tail and dorsal wing patterns.

KITES: Graceful, buoyant fliers, and in the air **Elanus** and **Chelictinia** suggest a gull or tern; the Black Kite (**Milvus**) is more hawk-like. All are weak-footed, small-billed, with the tail slightly to strongly forked. They build nests of sticks in trees or appropriate those of other birds. Their food consists of small animals or (Black Kite) carrion.

OSPREY *Pandion h. haliaetus*   Plates 34, 39

Length 55–58 cm (22–23"). A large, long-winged raptor, dark brown above and white below with a narrow breast band of dusky streaks. *Head white with dark facial mask and yellow eyes; feet grey.* Flight outline distinctive, with frequently bowed and *well-angled wings*; appears *white below with conspicuous black carpal patches, black primary tips* and narrowly barred flight feathers and tail. At a distance may resemble a large gull. **VOICE:** An occasional melodious *chewk-chewk-chewk.* **HABITS:** Feeds on fish, caught by plunging feet-first; flies with slow loose wingbeats; hovers over water with dangling legs. Perches conspicuously on dead trees, posts, or on the ground. Sometimes dispatches prey on old nests of eagles or other birds (prompting erroneous nesting records). **SIMILAR SPECIES:** Juvenile African Fish Eagle, a possible source of confusion, has dark blotching on belly, shorter tail, brown eyes, and lacks facial mask. **STATUS AND DISTRIBUTION:** Uncommon palearctic migrant to lakes, rivers, coastal creeks and estuaries, mainly October–March; a few remain year-round, but not known to breed in East Africa.

AFRICAN CUCKOO-HAWK *Aviceda cuculoides verreauxii*   Plates 35, 43

Length *c.* 40 cm (16"). Slim and *crested.* Shape and colour pattern suggest a large cuckoo. Perched, the *long wings extend nearly to tip of the long tail.* **Adult male** brownish grey above; *greyer on throat and breast; rest of underparts white with rufous or chestnut barring;* tail blackish above with three broad grey bars. In flight, shows rufous and white wing-linings (appearing mainly rufous or chestnut at a distance) and dark barring on underside of flight feathers and tail. Upperparts appear quite uniform. Cere greenish yellow; eyes and tarsi yellow. **Female** browner, with broader, paler barring below. **Juvenile** dark brown above, with short whitish superciliary stripes, buff feather edging on back and wings; underparts and wing-linings white, heavily to very sparsely spotted; eyes grey; other bare parts as in adult. **VOICE:** A single explosive *tohew*; when breeding, a quick whistled *choo-titti-too* from perch. Soaring birds utter a mewing *peeoo.* **HABITS:** Solitary and retiring, frequenting dense cover. Low flight from tree to tree graceful, with buoyant wingbeats and glides followed by upward swoop to perch; soars in circles, mainly in display. Nest a collection of leafy twigs high in tree, too small to conceal sitting bird, but well hidden in foliage. Feeds on insects and lizards, largely caught on the ground. **SIMILAR SPECIES:** Juvenile African Goshawk lacks crest, has shorter and broader wings, and longer tarsi. Appears accipitrine in flight. **STATUS AND DISTRIBUTION:** Uncommon; scattered records from well-wooded habitats in the Kenyan highlands (two breeding records) and the southeast. Mainly a non-breeding visitor to cent. and s. Kenya including coastal lowlands north to the Boni Forest (May–Nov.; peak July–Sept.). Scarce in n. Tanzania, where known from Arusha NP and the Usambara Mts, and a single record from Serengeti NP (Feb. 1975).

EURASIAN HONEY BUZZARD, *Pernis apivorus*
(Western Honey Buzzard)

Plates 33, 39, 44

Length 52–60 cm (20–24"). Differs from true buzzards (*Buteo*) in slimmer body and *smaller head. When soaring, the long wings are held flat and straight,* and the small head noticeably protrudes. Glides with distal half of wing somewhat depressed. **Adult** *heavily barred below, with streaked throat.* Underside of wings whitish with *bold barring and prominent black carpal patches*; tail pattern diagnostic: *two dark bars near base, a broader one at tip.* Polymorphic: typically grey-brown above; some individuals uniform dark brown on body and under wing-coverts, others rufous, still others much paler and lightly marked below. All plumages, however, show characteristic flight feather and tail barring. Cere dark grey; *eyes bright yellow or orange* (unlike *Buteo* spp.); tarsi unfeathered and yellow. **Juvenile** *dark-eyed* and equally variable, but *small head* distinctive. Upperparts usually dark brown, but paler morph has light-mottled wing-coverts. Underparts blackish or dull rufous, or white with dark streaks and a *small black eye patch on all-white head.* Tail pattern less distinct than adult's, with four evenly spaced bars; underside of flight feathers darker than in adult, the barring less prominent; *pale primary patch* present in all juveniles. *Upper tail-coverts usually white.* **Voice**: A long, plaintive, whistling *ku-weeeeeeeeiuuu*, a shorter *pee-eeu* and various other notes on breeding grounds, but normally silent in Africa. **Habits**: Solitary, secretive and sluggish; perches on branches within or below tree canopy. May walk on ground to feed on insects. Flies with slow, deep wingbeats; soars and glides readily, but does not hover; expansive tail frequently tilted from side to side, widely fanned when soaring. **Similar Species**: Common (Steppe) Buzzard is larger-headed, with broader wings usually angled upwards when soaring, and with shallower, stiffer wingbeats; underparts and wings less boldly barred. It and other buteos are brown-eyed (as is young *Pernis*). Ayres's Hawk-Eagle heavily spotted beneath and barred on under wing surfaces, but has shorter wings and narrowly barred tail. Booted and Wahlberg's Eagles glide on long flat wings, but have dark unbarred flight feathers and plainer tails. **Status and Distribution**: Uncommon palearctic migrant in forest edge and rich woodland, October–April; mainly in the Kenyan highlands east of the Rift Valley and on the coast, but occasional west to the Ugandan border. Scarce in n. Tanzania.

BAT HAWK *Macheiramphus alcinus anderssoni*
(Bat-eating Buzzard)

Plates 37, 44

Length *c.* 45 cm (18"). A unique *crepuscular* hawk with *dark, long pointed wings, long tail* and *crested head.* Resembles a dark broad-winged falcon. Throat dark or whitish with black central streak; a white streak above and another below each eye. **Adult** otherwise blackish, with indistinctly barred tail. Eyes bright yellow; tarsi and toes whitish. **Juvenile** resembles adult but belly white or whitish. **Voice**: A high-pitched falcon-like *keerik-keerik-keerik.* **Habits**: Rests by day in tree canopy, sometimes in large isolated tree in town or village. Usually seen at dusk, when it emerges to hunt small bats and birds; cruises with glides and slow wingbeats, but swift and agile in pursuit of prey. Pairs display in full daylight; otherwise abroad only in low light or at night. Nest built of sticks in large leafy tree, often in towns supporting large bat populations. **Similar Species**: Falcons, which may hunt in the evening, are smaller and slimmer, their wings less broad basally. **Status and Distribution**: Uncommon and very local resident in higher-rainfall areas below 2000 m, frequenting forest edge and woodland. Few Kenyan breeding records, yet regular at Lake Baringo, Kakamega, Taveta and several coastal localities from Shimoni north to Malindi. Rare in n. Tanzania.

BLACK-SHOULDERED KITE *Elanus c. caeruleus*
(Black-winged Kite)

Plates 37, 43

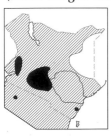

Length 31–35 cm (12–14"). A small, pale grey-and-white hawk with relatively large head and short tail; wings broad-based but long and pointed, with *large black 'shoulder' patch.* **Adult** grey above, with white face and underparts and small black eye patches; outer primaries contrastingly black beneath. Cere and feet yellow; eyes red or orange, rather large. **Juvenile** has *neck and breast tinged tawny,* the brown wing-coverts and scapulars edged with white and the black carpal patches white-spotted. **Voice**: Weak, rather shrill whistles, *eet-eet-eet-eet. . .,* and short chipping or chattering notes. **Habits**: Hunts in open grassy country, usually alone or in pairs, perching on wires or trees. At times crepuscular. Roosts in groups, but nests singly. Feeds largely on rodents, captured as bird drops to ground with wings extended above back. *Flight buoyant, slow wingbeats alternating with glides on raised angled wings; hovers persistently.* Nest of sticks, small and flat, usually low in small tree. **Similar Species**: Male Pallid and Montagu's Harriers are longer-tailed, with different wing patterns and flight habits. African Swallow-tailed Kite is more tern-like, with deeply forked tail, and lacks black shoulder patches. **Status and Distribution**: Widespread and fairly common in grassland, open savanna and cultivated country, especially in areas of moderate rainfall. Numbers may fluctuate seasonally. Breeds regularly in and around Nairobi NP.

AFRICAN SWALLOW-TAILED KITE *Chelictinia riocourii*   **Plates 37, 43**
(Scissor-tailed Kite)

Length 30 cm (12″). Elegant and *tern-like* with a *deeply forked tail; exceedingly graceful* in the air. **Adult** pure pale grey above and white below; underside of wing shows narrow black bar along edge of carpal area. Perched, the tail feathers project well beyond wing tips. Tarsi short and yellow; cere grey; eyes red. **Juvenile** much shorter-tailed; back and wing feathers edged with rufous. **VOICE:** A rasping chatter, various twittering sounds and a thin mewing call on breeding grounds. Silent away from nesting areas. **HABITS:** Gregarious, usually roosting and breeding colonially (up to 20 pairs), but sometimes flying alone or in pairs. Decidedly aerial, soaring, circling, hanging motionless against the wind with spread tail, or hovering. Builds nest of sticks with deep, grass-lined central cup, in shrub or low tree. **STATUS AND DISTRIBUTION:** Intra-African migrant; largely a non-breeding visitor from the northern tropics, but breeds locally at Lake Turkana, April–June, where at times fairly common. Regularly reaches dry grassland and open cultivation in cent. and (less often) se. Kenya, November–March, with occasional marked influxes. A disjunct resident population (22–24 birds from 1980 to 1990) accounts for frequent sightings in Longonot/Suswa area of the cent. Rift Valley.

Variation in Black Kites. Upper: M. m. migrans, *pale-eyed juvenile/immature; lower left:* M. m. migrans, *adult; lower right:* M. m. parasitus, *adult.*

BLACK KITE *Milvus migrans*   **Plates 34, 43, 44**
(Yellow-billed Kite)

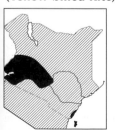

Length 51–60 cm (20–24″). A medium-sized brown raptor whose *shallowly forked tail is frequently spread and twisted in flight.* Wings long and narrow, noticeably bent at carpal joint. *Tarsi yellow.* **Adult** of Afrotropical race *parasitus* (Yellow-billed Kite) rather uniform warm brown (head and upperparts with some black streaking); *yellow bill* and *dark brown eyes;* underside of flight feathers and tail paler brown with indistinct barring. **Juvenile** buffier, paler below with distinct streaks; *bill black.* **Adult** of palearctic *M. m. migrans* has head and neck more greyish with black streaking and, in flight, a more prominent buffy bar across upper wing-coverts; black bill contrasts with yellow cere; eyes vary from bright brown to grey, pale yellow or ivory. **Juvenile/immature** paler than adult, with whitish streaks on head and underparts. In flight, shows pale area at base of primaries. Some presumed immature *migrans* are very pale-headed, creamy white on the face, with contrasting blackish eye-streak or eye patch; bill and eyes as in adult. Wintering Red Sea race *aegyptius* similar to *migrans,* but browner on head and neck, more rufous below and on the more distinctly barred tail; bill yellow in adult, blackish in immature. **VOICE:** In flight, a distinctive, quavering, two-parted whistle, loud and slowly uttered: *kiiiiiiiiiii-errrrrrrr,* the second part lower. Perched bird gives a long, plaintive, descending whistle, *wheeeeeeeeuu.* Aggression/excitement call *keeeeee-kik-kik-kik-kik.* **HABITS:** Associated

with man in villages, towns, at rubbish dumps, fishing sites and along highways. Opportunistic; feeds extensively on carrion but captures rodents, reptiles and young birds; steals prey from other raptors. Flight buoyant with slow wingbeats. **Similar Species:** *Aquila* eagles have more massive bills, feathered tarsi, lack the tail fork, and have different flight habits. Grasshopper Buzzard has pale yellow eyes and large rufous wing patches. **Status and Distribution:** Widespread and often abundant in open country with trees, especially near water, and around human habitation. *M. m. parasitus* is an intra-African migrant, breeding mainly September–March, but present all months at many sites. Nominate race a palearctic visitor and passage migrant, October–March, especially at medium elevations in cent. Kenya; the less common *aegyptius*, present at same time, said to be more coastal, but evidence lacking.

LAMMERGEIER *Gypaetus barbatus meridionalis* Plates 31, 32
(Bearded Vulture)

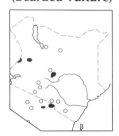

Length *c.* 110 cm (43″). A very large and distinctive vulture with *long, pointed, dark wings and long wedge-shaped tail.* **Adult** blackish above with conspicuous *white head and black facial mask with bristly 'beard'.* Underparts whitish or pale buff, with varying amounts of *rufous on neck and breast* (this adventitious colour from iron oxide, perhaps acquired during bathing in iron-bearing water or from dust-bathing). **Juvenile** generally dark brown, blackish on head and neck and paler brown below. Head of **immature** whitens with age as underparts become rufous brown, then gradually paler. **Voice:** At nest, a shrill *cheek-a-cheek-a-cheek.* In aerial display, a whistling *fweeee.* **Habits:** A solitary bird of cliffs and gorges. Soars over slopes with wings held slightly below horizontal, and glides, with occasional flaps, low over ground. Feeds on carrion, and has remarkable habit of dropping large bones on rocks to break them open. Probably kills some live prey. **Similar Species:** All-dark young Egyptian Vulture has wedge-shaped tail, but is much smaller, the tail relatively shorter, and it soars on flat, straight wings. **Status and Distribution:** Local and scarce resident on mountains and inselbergs, in Kenya on Mt Elgon, the Cheranganis, the Loldaiga Hills and Mt Kenya; formerly at Hell's Gate near Naivasha. In n. Tanzania on Kilimanjaro and Mt Meru; occasional near Gol Mts (Serengeti) and Ngorongoro Crater. Ranges far from breeding sites in search of food.

EGYPTIAN VULTURE *Neophron p. percnopterus* Plates 31, 32

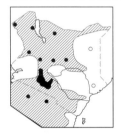

Length 58–71 cm (23–28″). Small and *slender-billed,* with comparatively narrow wings and a *wedge-shaped tail.* **Adult** *white or pale buff, with black flight feathers and bare orange-yellow face.* **Juvenile** entirely dark brown with grey facial skin. Body and wing-coverts of **immature** become paler with each moult; face orange-yellow by second year. Slim and graceful in flight, soaring with wings straight and flat. **Voice:** Occasionally hisses or grunts; rarely mewing or whistling sounds. **Habits:** Opportunistic, feeding mainly on meat scraps, birds' eggs and refuse. Uses stones to break open ostrich eggs; smashes smaller birds' eggs by dropping them on ground or rock. Cannot compete with larger vultures at carcasses. Perches in dead trees; usually nests on cliffs. **Similar Species:** See Palm-nut Vulture. **Status and Distribution:** Uncommon but widespread resident in open country with rocky crags, mainly in arid and semi-arid areas below 2000 m. Locally common in parts of the Rift Valley south of Lake Naivasha, and over much of n. Tanzania from Arusha District west to the Serengeti Plains.

HOODED VULTURE *Necrosyrtes monachus pileatus* Plates 31, 32

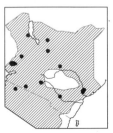

Length 65–75 cm (26–30″). A *small, dark brown* vulture with *slender bill* and a *short square tail.* **Adult** has *largely bare pink head and neck,* the *hindcrown covered with buffy-white down.* White down around tibial feather bases may be noticeable in flight, suggesting miniature Lappet-faced Vulture, but remex edges pale from beneath and body all dark. Eyes brown; feet pale blue. **Juvenile** has dark leg feathers and brownish tarsi; bare face and throat whitish (but can flush red with excitement, as in adult); down on hindcrown brownish. **Voice:** Essentially silent. Sometimes gives a high squeal at nest. **Habits:** Gregarious where common. A versatile scavenger, associating with human activities, but also accompanying larger vultures in game country. Feeds on scraps, offal, and carcass remnants; also at times on insects. Soars less than larger vultures. Roosts and nests in trees. **Similar Species:** Juvenile Egyptian Vulture, similarly slim-billed, has narrower wings, wedge-shaped tail, and feathered neck and hindcrown. Adult Lappet-faced Vulture is much larger, very heavy-billed, shows white stripe near leading edge of underside of wing, and has larger white tibial patches. **Status and Distribution:** Widespread but declining local resident below 3000 m. Present in most national parks and game reserves, but much less common than formerly; numbers around towns and villages now mainly in w. Kenya and lower Tana River area.

AFRICAN WHITE-BACKED VULTURE *Gyps africanus* Plates 31, 32

Length 89–98 cm (35–39"). A large vulture with broad wings and very short tail. **Adult** readily identified by *white lower back and rump*, conspicuous on take-off. Body brown, darker above but becoming paler and buffier with age, very old birds almost white. Underparts pale brown with faint paler shaft streaks; crop patch dark brown. Unfeathered head and neck blackish with sparse white down and whitish ruff at base of neck. *Bill heavy and blackish, cere grey; eyes dark brown;* feet dark grey. In flight, identified by *wholly pale wing-linings, contrasting with black flight feathers;* tail also black. **Juvenile** darker; body (including back), wing-coverts and ruff slaty grey, the pointed feathers streaked with white. Head and neck felted with cottony white down; head sometimes tinged brown. Skin of face and neck yellowish green with black spots; eyes blackish brown. Feathers of **immature** fade but remain streaked. Moult begins near end of first year, the new feathers rounded, not pointed. Birds become plainer and paler with age. Beginning about fourth year, back gradually whitens, becoming almost wholly white by sixth year. In flight, young birds appear largely dark brown beneath, the wing-linings with short white streaks and a long *narrow white line near leading edge.* **Voice:** Hisses, chatters and squeals at carcasses and roosts, but otherwise silent. **Habits:** Gregarious at carrion and at roosts in tall trees. Adapted to feeding on soft muscle tissue and intestines but unable to open up large carcasses. Nests in loose groups in trees. **Similar Species:** Rüppell's Griffon Vulture is slightly larger and longer-necked, lacks white lower back, and wings are dark beneath with narrow white bands near leading edge. Older birds have extensively scaled plumage, pale eyes and yellowish-horn bill. Immature high overhead difficult to distinguish with certainty. See young Lappet-faced Vulture. **Status and Distribution:** The common large vulture of most national parks and game reserves. Widespread and resident in all open or lightly wooded areas with large mammals, mainly below 2300 m. Absent from the Lake Victoria basin and coastal areas south of Malindi.

RÜPPELL'S GRIFFON VULTURE *Gyps r. rueppellii* Plates 31, 32

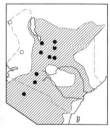

Length 95–107 cm (37.5–42"). Proportioned much like the preceding species, but **adult** and **subadult** easily identified by *long, heavy, yellowish-horn bill* and *'scaly' whitish edges on body feathers and upper wing-coverts.* Underparts whitish, somewhat mottled with brown feather bases. Head and long blackish neck mostly bare, with sparse dirty white down. Cere and facial skin grey, with sparse dirty white down on throat; *eyes yellow or amber;* crop patch dark brown; feet grey. In flight, *wing-linings show narrow white strip along leading edge* and *some more diffuse pale bands posteriorly.* **Juvenile** and **early immature** plumages tawny-fulvous, plain above and broadly pale-streaked below. Bill dark grey or blackish; eyes dark brown. Down on head and neck brown; neck skin reddish at first, soon darkening. In flight, older individuals with two or three pale bands on underside of wings distinguishable from young White-backed Vulture, but younger birds with only one white band may not be safely named. Full adult plumage reportedly takes six to seven years to acquire; bill becomes pale before iris colour changes. **Voice:** Hisses, grunts and querulous shrieks when feeding; otherwise silent. **Habits:** Competes with White-backed Vulture of similar habits and tends to dominate that species when both are present at carcasses. Nests and roosts on inaccessible cliffs, foraging over open plains. **Similar Species:** Adult White-backed Vulture has white or whitish back and pale under wing-coverts. Juvenile White-backed compared above. Young Lappet-faced easily confused unless head visible, but tail more wedge-shaped. **Status and Distribution:** Widespread and locally common in dry open country within range of cliffs. The most numerous large vulture in n. Kenya, and present in all national parks and game reserves. Breeding colonies at Mt Nyiru, Marsabit, Ololokwe, Hell's Gate NP, near Magadi, and the Gol Mts (e. Serengeti).

LAPPET-FACED VULTURE *Torgos t. tracheliotus* Plates 31, 32
(Nubian Vulture)

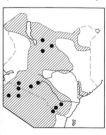

Length 98–115 cm (39–45"). Similar in size and soaring outline to Rüppell's Griffon, but with *more wedge-shaped tail.* **Adult** blackish brown with *white-streaked underparts.* Head and back of neck bare and pink (flushing red with excitement), and with *fleshy ear-like lappets on sides of face. Large bill ivory or pale yellowish horn,* brownish at base and with dark culmen spot; cere greyish; eyes dark brown; feet blue-grey. In flight, shows *dark under wing surface with narrow white stripe along leading edge and prominent white leg feathering.* **Juvenile** blackish, including underparts; bare head and neck skin pale dull pink but with lappets like adult; after first year acquires some white on back and upper wing-coverts, this gradually disappearing in older immatures. Tibial feathers take five to six years to become wholly white. Bill brownish horn. **Voice:** Occasional growling, yelping and grunting sounds, but usually silent. **Habits:** Dominant over other vultures; can open larger carcasses and eats skin, ligaments, and small bones not utilized by smaller species. Roosts and nests in trees on open plains. **Similar Species:** Hooded Vulture is much smaller, with dark lower wing surface, smaller white tibial patches and a much shorter and slimmer bill, these the only obvious differences from juvenile Lappet-faced when soaring at great height. Young Rüppell's and White-backed

confusable with young Lappet-faced in flight, but their tails more square-tipped. Young White-headed Vulture shows white line between secondaries and under wing-coverts in flight. **STATUS AND DISTRIBUTION**: Widespread and locally fairly common resident of open plains country with large herbivore populations. Present in all national parks and game reserves, but most numerous in Mara GR and Serengeti NP, where seasonally common (over 70 counted in one day) when wildebeeste herds and carcasses abound.

WHITE-HEADED VULTURE *Trigonoceps occipitalis* Plates 31, 32

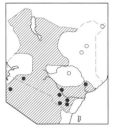

Length 78–84 cm (31–33"). A fairly large, short-tailed vulture with broad rectangular wings. **Adult** mainly blackish brown with *white crop patch, belly, leg feathers* and *largely white secondaries*, producing distinctive flight pattern. Inner secondaries of female white, those of male grey. Head and upper foreneck unfeathered and covered with white down; black ruff on hindneck. Bare facial skin pink, turning red in excitement; *bill bright pink with blackish tip* and pale blue mandible base, cere pale blue; eyes dark yellow or amber; feet pale pink. **Juvenile** has brown crown and lacks white on secondaries and belly, but is readily distinguished in flight by conspicuous white line between wing-linings and flight feathers. Bill pale pink, cere pale blue; eyes brown. **Immature** intermediate between juvenile and adult plumages, the latter probably taking several years to acquire. **VOICE**: Normally silent, but occasionally utters shrill chattering at carcasses. **HABITS**: Solitary or in pairs. Begins foraging early in day, and often arrives first at carcasses. Cannot compete directly with larger vultures, but powerful head and bill allow it, like Lappet-faced, to deal with tough sinews and skin. A 'clean' feeder, its plumage remains unbloodied at carcasses. Kills small mammals and young birds; also feeds on stranded fish and emerging termites. Roosts and nests in trees. **SIMILAR SPECIES**: See Lappet-faced Vulture. **STATUS AND DISTRIBUTION**: A rather scarce but widespread resident of open and lightly wooded country with large mammals. Present in most national parks and game reserves; most frequent in Mara GR and the Tsavo and Serengeti NPs.

SHORT-TOED SNAKE EAGLE *Circaetus gallicus* Plates 34, 40
(Short-toed Eagle; includes Beaudouin's Snake Eagle)

Length 61–68 cm (24–27"). A medium-sized, *pale*, 'bare-legged' eagle with *large rounded head and prominent yellow eyes*. **Adult** *C. g. gallicus* usually *grey-brown above, head and breast mottled with paler brown* and *rest of underparts white with sparse brown or chestnut spots and mottling*. Some birds are darker brown above and on the breast; others have whitish head and underparts with breast band of light brown markings, and with the ventral spotting and underwing barring nearly obsolete. In flight, wings appear mainly white below with narrow dark rear edges and tips, and usually barred remiges; wings brown above, the coverts somewhat paler. Tail grey with three dark bars. **Juvenile** closely resembles adult. **Adult** *C. g. beaudouini* is darker, with three or four indistinct tail bars, grey-brown upper breast, white *lower breast and belly narrowly barred with brown*. **Juvenile** streaked whitish on head but otherwise largely rufous-brown, the flanks, crissum and tail barred with brown, the wings and tail with darker brown. **Immature** (second year) has blotched underparts, later largely whitish, this plumage perhaps retained into early third year (Ferguson-Lees, in prep.). **VOICE**: *C. g. gallicus* silent in Africa; *beaudouini* vocalizations apparently unknown. **HABITS**: Solitary, perching on trees and poles. Soars with long broad wings held flat; frequently hovers. Feeds largely on reptiles. **SIMILAR SPECIES**: Immature Black-chested Snake Eagle may not be separable in the field. Osprey and Eurasian Honey Buzzard are narrower-winged, with prominent black carpal patches; Eurasian Honey Buzzard has differently spaced tail bands. **STATUS AND DISTRIBUTION**: Vagrant *C. g. gallicus* known here with certainty only from a specimen taken at Lake Turkana (27 Oct. 1988). Subsequent reports from Lake Nakuru NP, Kinangop, Mara GR and Tsavo East NP unconfirmed. Brown (1974) thought *C. g. beaudouini* "not uncommon" in Nyanza in the 1950s, but there are no specimens, photographs or documented sight records from Kenya. Report of an individual *beaudouini* attempting to breed with a Black-chested Snake Eagle on Raboor Island, Lake Victoria (Dec. 1953), and later sight records from w. Kenya are all unsubstantiated.

BLACK-CHESTED SNAKE EAGLE *Circaetus pectoralis* Plates 34, 40
(Black-chested Harrier-Eagle)

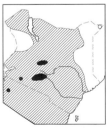

Length 63–68 cm (25–27"). A medium-sized eagle with long broad wings and a large rounded head. **Adult** *blackish brown on upperparts, head and breast;* otherwise white below. *Eyes large, bright yellow; bare tarsi whitish*. In flight from below, appears mainly white with black head and breast; underside of wings white, with barring on remiges; three broad black bars across tail. **Juvenile** paler, warmer brown above, and rufous on face and underparts. Underside of wing and tail plainer than in adult. *Eyes yellow*. Transitional **immature** may show whitish face and throat, dark breast band, and blotching on white underparts similar to Short-toed Snake Eagle. Blackish feathers first appear on throat and chest at age of six months. Probably acquires adult plumage in three years (Steyn 1982). **VOICE**: In display near nest, a musical *weeu-weeu* and a ringing *kwo-kwo-kwo* recalling African Fish Eagle. **HABITS**: Usually solitary. Perches prominently on

trees in open country. Soars, and frequently hovers with slowly beating wings. Preys largely on snakes. **SIMILAR SPECIES:** Adult Martial Eagle has same general pattern but is larger, broader-winged, with all-dark wing-linings, darker remiges, dark-spotted underparts, feathered tarsi, and short crest. Brown Snake Eagle is brownish below, not rufous-tinged like young Black-chested, and has a larger, more owlish head. See Short-toed Snake Eagle. **STATUS AND DISTRIBUTION:** Uncommon but widespread on lightly wooded plains and in more open country at all elevations. Recorded in all months, but apparently a non-breeding visitor in some areas. **NOTE:** Sometimes considered a race of *C. gallicus*.

BROWN SNAKE EAGLE *Circaetus cinereus* Plates 34, 40, 44
(Brown Harrier-Eagle)

Length 66–71 cm (26–28"). Plain brown, with a rounded, somewhat *owl-like head, yellow eyes and long bare whitish tarsi*. In flight, *silvery flight feathers contrast below with dark brown coverts*; wings nearly uniform dark brown above; three narrow pale bars on tail not always conspicuous. **Juvenile** resembles adult, but usually paler and sometimes with white mottling on nape and belly and/or white streaks on crown. **VOICE:** A loud *kok-kok-kok-kaaw* in soaring display. **HABITS:** Solitary and sluggish. Perches upright on treetops, from which it drops on prey, including large venomous snakes. At intervals flies with slow deep wingbeats to new perch; rarely hovers or hunts in flight; soars on long flat wings, mainly in display. **SIMILAR SPECIES:** Other all-brown eagles (Tawny, Steppe, Lesser Spotted, Wahlberg's and Booted) have feathered tarsi, darker flight feathers (from beneath) and unbarred tail; none has yellow eyes or an owl-like head. Juvenile Bateleur is large-headed but short-tailed and has dark brown eyes. Juvenile Black-chested Snake Eagle is rufous below. Juvenile Palm-nut Vulture has dull yellow face patch. **STATUS AND DISTRIBUTION:** A widespread, fairly common resident at low to medium elevations in bush, woodland, and cultivated country with scattered tall trees, favouring areas with baobabs. Few breeding records.

SOUTHERN BANDED SNAKE EAGLE *Circaetus fasciolatus* Plates 34, 40
(Southern Banded Harrier-Eagle; Fasciated Snake Eagle)

Length 55–60 cm (22–24"). A stocky, medium-sized eagle. **Adult** dark grey brown above, brown on head and breast; rest of underparts narrowly barred brown and white. *Tail moderately long, narrowly white-tipped*, the dorsal surface with *four broad black bands alternating with three grey or brownish-grey bands of equal width*; lower surface in flight shows two or three white bands and narrow white tip. Wings short and broad, mostly brown above and greyish white below, both wing-linings and flight feathers barred with dark brown. Eyes, cere, *tarsi and toes yellow*. **Juvenile** paler, buffy white below, the throat streaked with black; crown and nape brown, streaked with white; flanks and leg feathers barred with tawny or buff; dark tail bands (except subterminal one) narrower than in adult. Bare parts as in adult. Some **immatures** are pale, almost whitish, on the head and show suggestion of adult pattern below. **VOICE:** From perch, a high-pitched rapid *ko-ko-ko-ko-kaah* or *k-k-k-kaw-aw*, and a sonorous *kowaa*. **HABITS:** Retiring and secretive, typically perching in leafy cover, occasionally exposed on large branch. Hunts from perch, swooping to take its largely reptilian prey. Flies with quick, shallow wingbeats. Occasionally soars over forest. **SIMILAR SPECIES:** Adult Banded Snake Eagle has a single broad white tail band and less heavily barred underwing. Immature Banded and Black-chested Snake Eagles have whitish tarsi. **STATUS AND DISTRIBUTION:** In Kenya, an uncommon resident of coastal forest, ranging inland along the lower Tana River; one record from riverine forest near Voi (March 1971). In n. Tanzania, locally common in the East Usambara Mts.

BANDED SNAKE EAGLE *Circaetus cinerascens* Plates 34, 40
(Banded Harrier-Eagle; Smaller or Western Banded Snake Eagle)

Length 55–60 cm (22–24"). **Adult** differs from preceding species in having a *shorter tail with a single broad white band* and the *brown of the breast extends to flanks and belly*; white barring restricted to lower belly and underside of tail. Wings whitish below, with flight feathers prominently barred but coverts plain. Cere and bill base orange-yellow; eyes pale creamy yellow; tarsi and toes yellow. **Juvenile** *pale* brown above with light buff feather edges; crown whitish with dark streaks; *underparts greyish white or buffy white, darker buff on breast and with some brown on belly and leg feathers*. Tail paler brown than back, and with a dark terminal band. *Eyes and feet whitish*, cere yellow, bill brown. **Immature/subadult** birds variably streaked below, apparently later assuming a brown plumage with varying amounts of barring on flanks and belly. **VOICE:** In aerial display a loud staccato *kok-kok-kok-kok-ko-ko*, descending in pitch. From perch gives a repeated mournful *ko-aaagh*. **HABITS:** Rather sluggish. Solitary and inconspicuous. Often perches on bough of large tree near river or swamp. Flight direct, with quick wingbeats; circles during display. Feeds mainly on reptiles and amphibians captured on the ground or in trees. **SIMILAR SPECIES:** Southern Banded Snake Eagle com-

pared above. **STATUS AND DISTRIBUTION**: Scarce and very local in riverine woodland and forest patches at medium elevations. Scattered records from w. Kenya and locally along rivers on the eastern edge of the central highlands south to Kibwezi. Rare in n. Tanzania. No East African breeding record.

BATELEUR *Terathopius ecaudatus* Plates 32, 34, 40

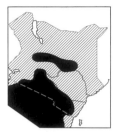

Length 55–70 cm (22–28"). Unique, with unmistakable flight silhouette: *long, broad-based wings have curved rear edge narrowing to pointed tip; chestnut tail extremely short; head large and owl-like*, cowled, with erectile feathers. Plumage *black, usually with chestnut back and grey upper wing-coverts* (*in **adult female** the secondaries also grey*). **Adult male** has snow-white wing-linings contrasting below with dark remiges; female's wings also white below, but black confined to tips and narrow trailing edges. *Cere, bare facial skin and feet bright red*. In pale morph, usually in more arid regions, back and tail vary from cream to pale brown. **Juvenile** largely brown, the underparts paler with darker brown streaks; *tail blackish brown, longer than adult's*. Cere and facial skin greenish blue-grey; eyes dark brown; feet grey. Transitional **immature** dark brown or blackish, with white mottling on underside of wings. Bare facial skin yellowish; feet pinkish. **VOICE**: Usually silent. When perched, sometimes produces a rather soft *ko-ko-ko-ko-koaaagh*, recalling Banded Snake Eagle. At nest, gives a barking *kow-er* and a chattering *ka-ka-ka-ka*. **HABITS**: Usually solitary. Glides continuously over open country with wings raised in marked V, canting frequently from side to side. Takes off with rapid shallow wingbeats but rarely flaps once airborne. Often rests on ground, regularly perches in trees, sometimes stands in water. Preys on birds, mammals (to dik-dik size) and snakes; at times eats termites and carrion. **SIMILAR SPECIES**: Brown Snake Eagle has similar cowled head and resembles immature Bateleur, but is more uniformly coloured, with longer tail, yellow eyes and bare whitish tarsi. **STATUS AND DISTRIBUTION**: Widespread; one of the commonest raptors of dry bush and grassland, ranging as high as 3000 m.

AFRICAN HARRIER-HAWK *Polyboroides t. typus* Plates 34, 35, 43
(Gymnogene)

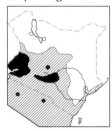

Length 60–66 cm (24–26"). An unusual, large grey hawk with a *small head* (but *long nape feathers*), *long black tail with a single broad white band*, and *long wide wings broadly tipped black; underparts finely barred black and white*. Bill black; eyes dark brown; *cere and bare face yellow*, the latter flushing pink or red-orange in excitement and when breeding. Tarsi exceptionally long and bright yellow. In flight from above and below, wings appear grey with broad black tips and trailing edges. **Juvenile** uniformly dark chocolate-brown above and below, including wing-linings; feathers of upperparts tipped paler brown; primaries tinged whitish at base and more or less barred; tail chocolate-brown with four narrow darker brown bands. Face dark grey; cere and bill greenish yellow, tipped black; eyes yellowish brown. Some juveniles show new *black* feathers on head and back. **Immatures** range from bright gingery or tawny-brown to blackish or dark chocolate-brown above, pale buff or whitish on forehead and forecrown, and streaked with pale buff on underparts. Pale tawny flank and leg feathers barred with brown; under tail-coverts broadly barred with rufous-brown. Tail much as in juvenile. **Subadult** paler below, with wide brownish-grey bars on tail; body plumage variable, lightly or heavily barred on belly, barred or unbarred on flanks. Some have virtually no dark markings, the entire underparts being pale tawny-buff. Young birds may be identified by overall proportions and small head. **VOICE**: Perched, a tremulous whistled *su-ee-oo* or *su-eeeeeeee*. In flight, a thin *peeeeeeeee*, and a plaintive *ur-eet ur-eet . . .* repeated indefinitely. Also *hweep-hweep-hweep. . .* (Steyn 1982). **HABITS**: Usually solitary; unobtrusive when perched. Flies with slow buoyant wingbeats and glides, and frequently soars. Searches trees systematically for insects and bird nests, clinging to trunk with wings flapping to maintain position while probing cavities with bill and feet. Similarly clings to weaver nests, from which it extracts eggs or nestlings. Also forages by walking on ground. Food includes small mammals, reptiles and invertebrates, as well as birds. Frequently mobbed by passerines, especially weavers. Nests in tall trees. **SIMILAR SPECIES**: The smaller chanting goshawks are differently proportioned, with feathered face, barred tail and no long nape feathering. **STATUS AND DISTRIBUTION**: Widespread but uncommon resident of woodland and forest up to 3000 m, typically in higher-rainfall areas. Often in modified, partly cleared habitats, suburban gardens and along wooded watercourses in drier country. Largely absent from arid n. and e. Kenya.

PALLID HARRIER *Circus macrourus* Plates 36, 43

Length 40–48 cm (16–19"). Slim and narrow-winged, with a rather long tail. Flight buoyant, tilting lightly from side to side; falcon-like when soaring. **Male** *lightly built, pale grey above* and white below with *small black wedge at wing tip*, the pattern quite gull-like. **Female** brown above, including upper wing-surface, with *white bar across upper tail-coverts* and *strongly barred tail*; underparts streaked buffy brown; flight feathers and tail pale grey below with dark barring. At close range, dark cheek crescent contrasts sharply with obvious pale collar, giving masked appearance. **Juvenile** and **immature** resemble female but are unstreaked pale rufous-buff below; underside of secondaries darker. **VOICE**: Generally silent on wintering grounds except for occasional chattering

near roost. **Habits**: Singles or small numbers hunt over open plains and perch on ground or low posts. Attracted to locust swarms and grass fires. Groups roost in tall grass, sometimes with other harrier species. **Similar Species**: Male Montagu's Harrier has entirely grey head, neck and upper breast, streaks on flanks, a black bar across the secondaries, and more black on wing tips. Female and young Montagu's are difficult to distinguish from Pallid, but have less conspicuous pale collar and more whitish face, are darker rufous and more streaked below. **Status and Distribution**: Palearctic migrant, locally fairly common on open grasslands and farmland, October to early April, ranging to above 2500 m. Much less numerous than formerly; usually outnumbered by Montagu's Harrier in the highlands, but often the more numerous species in se. Kenya and on the Masai Steppe in n. Tanzania.

MONTAGU'S HARRIER *Circus pygargus*   Plates 36, 43

Length 43–47 cm (17–18.5"). Similar to Pallid Harrier, but **male** has *narrow black bar across secondaries* and *much more black in wing tips* (outer eight primaries entirely black). Head, neck and upper breast dark grey; rest of underparts whitish, with some rufous streaking on flanks. Underside of wings pale, except for black primaries and two black bands across secondaries. **Female** brown above, with white rump band and strongly barred tail; underparts pale rufous-brown with darker streaking; flight feathers and tail pale grey below with dark barring. At close range, distinguished by lack of conspicuous pale collar and by whiter face contrasting with dark crescent on ear-coverts. Rare **dark morph** is charcoal-grey or sooty black in male, with or without silvery areas at base of primaries and tail, chocolate-brown in female with greyish-white primary bases which are plain, barred or mottled; tail boldly banded in female, essentially plain in male. **Juvenile** and **immature** resemble female above, *but underparts variably streaked and underside of secondaries darker.* **First-year male** has greyish head and upperparts and white belly combined with wing and tail pattern of adult female. **Voice**: Silent on wintering grounds. **Habits**: Solitary or in loose groups; roosts communally, sometimes with Pallid Harrier. Hunts over open grassy areas, quartering low; occasionally soars. Rests on posts and bare ground. **Similar Species**: Male Pallid Harrier is paler grey, lacks dark secondary bar, has much smaller amount of black on wing tips, and appears slimmer-winged. Female and immature difficult to separate from that species but facial mask is less distinct; young Pallid is pale rufous-buff below. **Status and Distribution**: Locally common palearctic migrant, mainly October to early April, in open grassland and farmland. Most frequent in higher plateau country between 1500 and 2500 m, in Uasin Gishu and Laikipia Districts, the Rift Valley highlands, Nairobi area, Mara GR, Serengeti NP and Ngorongoro Crater.

AFRICAN MARSH HARRIER *Circus ranivorus*   Plates 36, 43

Length 45–50 cm (18–20"). Smaller and more lightly built than Eurasian Marsh Harrier. Both sexes *brown above*, including crown and nape, with *whitish leading wing edges.* Underparts pale brown with dark streaking, more rufous on belly, legs and rump; tail narrowly barred above and below; primaries darker than coverts above, and flight feathers prominently barred below. **Juvenile** plainer and darker above than adult; dark brown below, with variable pale band across chest; nape and chin usually whitish, but crown dark. **Voice**: A high-pitched *fee-uu* during display flight. Alarm call a low ringing *kek-kek-kek-kek*. **Habits**: Usually solitary or in pairs. Flight and habits much as in Eurasian Marsh Harrier. Quarters grassy plains and valley bottoms as well as wetlands. Pair soars high over breeding marsh, calling repeatedly. Male also soars alone, descending in a series of steep dives. Builds nest of reeds and grass on marshy ground or in water. **Similar Species**: Female and young Montagu's and Pallid Harriers are easily separated from *ranivorus* by white upper tail-coverts, more strongly barred tail, and uniform brown upper wing-surface. Female and young Eurasian Marsh typically are pale cream on the head and lack rufous tinge on rump and underparts. **Status and Distribution**: Local and uncommon resident, mainly in vicinity of highland swamps and seasonal wetlands; scarce around Lake Victoria. No recent breeding records from Kenya, but has bred at Sanya Juu, West Kilimanjaro, in n. Tanzania.

EURASIAN MARSH HARRIER *Circus a. aeruginosus*   Plates 36, 43, 44
(Northern or Western Marsh Harrier)

Length 48–56 cm (19–22"). Rather heavily built (especially female); *broader-winged than other harriers.* **Male** of normal morph dark brown on back and wing-coverts; black outer primaries contrast sharply with *silvery-grey inner primaries, secondaries and tail; forepart of wing often cream;* head and underparts buff with darker streaks; underside of flight feathers pale grey except for black tips; wing-linings brown to whitish. **Female** generally dark rich brown, often with *forewing edge, and usually crown,* cream; dark brown face band separates cap from pale throat and variable *yellowish breast patch;* paler flight-feather bases tend to contrast below with dark wing-linings. **Juvenile** resembles female but darker, with more orange-yellow or brown cap, and may lack pale forewing.

Immature male gradually acquires dark wing tips, greyish tail and pale flight-feather bases; upper wing surface mainly brown. Rare **dark morph adult male** *all blackish above with silvery-grey tail; from below, shows a broad white wing band* formed by white flight-feather bases. **Dark morph adult female and juvenile** *brown with pale cream nape patch* and small white or tawny area at base of primaries below. **VOICE**: Generally silent in winter quarters. **HABITS**: Usually solitary, though several may quarter a single marsh or roost together. Hunting flight less buoyant, and often higher than that of other harriers. **SIMILAR SPECIES**: African Marsh Harrier has dark brown crown and nape at all ages, with heavily barred tail and flight feathers; adult rufous-tinged on rump and underparts. Dark-morph Montagu's Harrier separated from dark *aeruginosus* by much slighter build, more buoyant flight, narrower wings and banded tail. **STATUS AND DISTRIBUTION**: Widespread and fairly common palearctic migrant, October to early April, in w. and cent. Kenya and parts of n. Tanzania. Frequents lake edges, swamps, moist grassland and cultivation between 1000 and 2500 m.

GABAR GOSHAWK *Micronisus gabar aequatorius*   Plates 33, 36, 42, 44

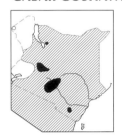

Length 28–36 cm (11–14″). A *small* accipiter-like hawk with short rounded wings and a rather long tail. **Grey adult** shows *broad white band on upper tail-coverts*; upperparts otherwise grey, as are head and breast; *belly, sides and flanks barred grey and white*; broad tail bands are blackish above, grey below. *Cere and tarsi red*; eyes dark red-brown. Plumage of **dark morph adult** black, except for grey barring on tail and flight feathers. **Juvenile** browner above than any *Accipiter*, with *white upper tail-coverts*; underparts white, with *brown-streaked throat and breast and brown barring on belly and flanks. Wings appear scaly*, with pale-edged upper coverts. **VOICE**: Distinct from any *Accipiter* of similar size: a reedy piping display note given from perch, *kwew-he, kwew-he, kwew-he . . .*, or *kik-kik-kik-kik-kik. . . .* **HABITS**: Solitary. Inhabits drier woodland and tends to perch in more exposed situations than accipiters, though often within canopy. Pursues birds swiftly through thick bush (accipiter-fashion; unlike chanting goshawks); also takes reptiles and insects on ground. Builds shallow stick nest, without added green leaves (unlike *Accipiter*). **SIMILAR SPECIES**: Juvenile Eastern Pale Chanting Goshawk is much larger, the breast less boldly streaked than young Gabar, and only the greater and median coverts are pale-edged; usually shows whitish superciliary stripes, lacking in Gabar. Ovambo and Little Sparrowhawks have white spots on upper tail-surface. Rare dark morph Ovambo has orange-yellow cere and tarsi. Shikra lacks white on upper tail-coverts. **STATUS AND DISTRIBUTION**: Widespread and locally common resident of woodland and thorn-scrub up to 2000 m, generally in low-rainfall areas.

DARK CHANTING GOSHAWK *Melierax m. metabates*   Plates 33, 36, 41

Length of male 43–51 cm (17–20″), of female 50–56 cm (20–22″). A large, grey, upright-perching hawk with long rounded wings, *pinkish-red or coral-pink cere and similar long slender tarsi*. **Adult** grey on upperparts, head and breast, the wing-coverts washed with brownish, as is back; posterior underparts barred grey and white; *white upper and under tail-coverts narrowly barred with grey*; primaries black, but rest of wings grey above and white below. Graduated tail has blackish central feathers, the others broadly grey-barred and white-tipped. **Juvenile** and **immature** dull brown above, with whitish superciliary stripes and *fully grey-barred upper tail-coverts*; brown, white-tipped tail broadly barred with darker brown. Underparts variable, sometimes much as in young Eastern Pale Chanting Goshawk, or the whitish throat streaked with dark brown and sharply defined from the plain or slightly mottled pale grey-brown breast band (in which narrow dark brown shaft streaks are visible at close range); rest of underparts and underside of flight feathers barred. Cere grey; eyes pale yellow; tarsi and toes yellowish olive. **VOICE**: During breeding season, a melodious piping *whee-pee-pee-pee* from perch or in flight; also a long-drawn high-pitched *kleee-yeu*. **HABITS**: Usually solitary. Typically quite fearless; perches prominently on small tree, shrub or post, from which it hunts lizards and snakes, less frequently birds (to size of spurfowl or guineafowl) and small mammals. Flies low, with slow shallow wingbeats alternating with glides; soars during breeding season. Occasionally walks on ground. Builds stick nest, usually without green leaves, sometimes cemented with mud, in acacia or other thorny tree. **SIMILAR SPECIES**: See Eastern Pale Chanting Goshawk. **STATUS AND DISTRIBUTION**: Two populations: one in nw. Kenya from Lokichokio south to Kongelai, the Kerio Valley, and lakes Baringo and Bogoria; the other mainly Tanzanian, in our area extending from Serengeti NP to southern and western Mara GR north to Aitong and Lemek, wandering to near Kisumu.

EASTERN PALE CHANTING GOSHAWK *Melierax poliopterus*   Plates 33, 36, 41
(Eastern Chanting Goshawk)

Length of male 46–54 cm (18–21″), of female 53–63 cm (21–25″). **Adult** distinguished from the preceding species by *yellow cere, longer orange-red tarsi, less fully barred or plain white upper tail-coverts* and generally

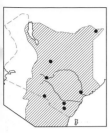

paler grey plumage, pure grey wing-coverts and less prominent tail barring; *under tail-coverts plain white with no trace of barring.* **Juvenile** and **immature** resemble Dark Chanting Goshawk except for the longer tarsi, and, in some individuals, a heavily dark-streaked breast. Upper tail-coverts show varying degrees of barring, this occasionally dark and heavy (unlike southern African *M. canorus,* in which the coverts are always plain white). These bars, however, are short and not reaching the feather edges, leaving much more white visible than in Dark Chanting, whose continuous barring extends completely across the covert patch. Under tail-coverts have finer, fainter, more widely spaced barring than in Dark Chanting. Fresh greater coverts (always?) white-tipped, as in adult. **Voice and Habits:** Similar to those of Dark Chanting Goshawk, the calls slightly lower-pitched. **Similar Species:** Dark Chanting Goshawk compared above. Gabar Goshawk is considerably smaller. Ovambo and Little Sparrowhawks show white spots on dorsal tail-surface and have orange-yellow cere and tarsi. **Status and Distribution:** Common in semi-arid bush country north, east and south of the Kenyan highlands, generally below 1600 m. Range is mainly east of the Rift Valley, but found in the Rift around lakes Turkana, Magadi and Natron; west of the Rift only in the drier eastern parts of the Loita plains. Nowhere resident alongside Dark Chanting Goshawk. **Note:** Considered conspecific with the red-cered Southern Pale Chanting Goshawk, *M. canorus,* of southern Africa by some authors.

AFRICAN GOSHAWK *Accipiter tachiro*   Plates 36, 42, 44

Length 38–46 cm (15–18"). A medium-sized, rather long-tailed hawk of wooded areas. **Male** *dark slate, almost black, above; whitish below with fine rufous or chestnut barring;* greyish sides of face contrast with white throat; tail with indistinct grey bars above, narrowly tipped white, sometimes with small white spots or bands on central feathers; underside of tail greyish, with brown bands across all rectrices or lacking on outer two pairs. Under wing-surface pale and narrowly barred. *Eyes and bare orbital skin yellow,* cere and feet yellow or greenish yellow. **Female** *much larger, browner above, more coarsely brown-barred below.* **Adult dark morph** *brownish black with grey tail bands.* **Juvenile** and **immature** dark brown above, the feathers at first rufous-edged; may show some white on nape; superciliary stripes white; *underparts white or buff with dark central throat stripe and large dark brown drop-shaped spots; flanks broadly barred; leg feathers more closely barred or with chestnut spots.* Eyes brown; cere greenish grey or olive; feet yellow. Spotted underparts gradually assume barred pattern as upperparts become slaty; eyes turn yellow by second year. **Voice:** A sharp, high-pitched *krit* or *quick* repeated at intervals of a few seconds, from perch or during circling flight. **Habits:** Unobtrusive except in soaring display (not confined to breeding season). Hunts mainly within forest, pursuing prey at speed through thick cover, occasionally in the open; may circle high over forest with loose flapping and gliding. Somewhat crepuscular. Feeds on birds, mammals and reptiles. Builds nest of sticks high or low in tree. **Similar Species:** Great Sparrowhawk is larger, blacker above and whiter below, with distinctive dark flank patches; young bird more chestnut or whitish below; dark morph wholly black except for white throat. Shikra is smaller and much paler. Ovambo Sparrowhawk has smaller head, grey chin and throat, grey barring below and large triangular white marks on central rectrices (these spots smaller, less conspicuous and differently shaped in African Goshawk if they show at all). Rare dark Ovambo is *red*-eyed, has cere and base of bill *bright orange or orange yellow,* and the middle toe is exceptionally long and slender. Juvenile African Cuckoo-Hawk resembles young African Goshawk, but has long wings (reaching almost to tail tip), shorter tarsi, and a short occipital crest. **Status and Distribution:** *A. t. sparsimfasciatus* is the most numerous *Accipiter* in more humid areas, widespread and fairly common in forest, rich woodland, dense secondary growth and wooded gardens from the coast up to 3000 m. The smaller *A. t. pembaensis* is endemic to Pemba Island.

SHIKRA *Accipiter badius sphenurus*   Plates 33, 36, 42
(Little Banded Goshawk)

Length 28–30 cm (11–12"). Small, pale, lightly built and compact, *blunt-winged* when soaring compared with Eurasian and Levant Sparrowhawks. **Adult** *wholly grey above* and on sides of face; *underparts finely barred with pale rufous or pinkish chestnut,* the throat white; compressed tail appears unbarred above, but shows five dark bars from below. (Female sometimes has dark terminal band on upper surface of tail.) Underside of wings whitish, with faint barring and darker tips. Cere, tarsi and toes yellow; eyes red in male, orange in female. **Juvenile** has *dark brown line down centre of throat, breast heavily blotched with russet-brown* and *rest of underparts barred with the same.* Upperparts brown, with buff-tipped wing-coverts. Five dark tail bars narrower than those of adult. Bill black; other bare parts yellow. **Immature** (after first moult) darker, with bolder, less blotchy ventral streaks and yellow eyes. May breed in this plumage. Assumes adult dress after second year. **Voice:** A rapid, high-pitched *kee-wick, kee-wick* (male), and a *kee-uh* or descending *keew-keew-keew* (female). Also an aggressive *kee-kee-kee-kee-kee.* Very vocal near nest. **Habits:** Solitary or in pairs. Perches within tree canopy or on exposed bough, from which it dashes to take prey on ground or, sometimes, in the air. Flight typically accipitrine; often soars. **Similar Species:** Little Sparrowhawk is

smaller and darker above, with white upper tail-coverts and large white spots on upper tail-surface; juvenile differently patterned on underparts. Gabar Goshawk has white upper tail-coverts, central rectrices barred on upper surface, grey throat and breast, and red tarsi. Juvenile Gabar is evenly streaked on breast, shows white upper tail-coverts in flight. See also Ovambo Sparrowhawk, Eurasian Sparrowhawk and Levant Sparrowhawk (all scarce). **STATUS AND DISTRIBUTION:** Widespread but rather uncommon resident of open woodland, savanna, bush and forest edge at low to medium elevations. Often along watercourses in dry country.

LEVANT SPARROWHAWK *Accipiter brevipes*   Plates 33, 42

Length 33–38 cm (13–15″). **Adult** suggests a large long-winged Shikra; medium-sized with relatively long, slender, falcon-like wings. Both sexes are plain above, with *darker cheeks than Shikra*. Unspread tail appears plain above, from below shows five or six narrow dark bars (a character valid for all age groups). Eyes *dark* red; cere greenish yellow; feet yellow. **Male** slaty blue-grey above with darker wing tips, white below with narrow chestnut barring concentrated on breast; *underside of wings white except for sharply defined black tips.* **Female** usually browner above than male, *heavily brown-barred below, and with prominent short streaks on throat;* wings lightly barred beneath. **Juvenile** browner than female, with whitish mark on hindneck, heavily spotted underparts, *black central throat stripe,* and undersides of wings are more strongly barred. In the hand, fifth primary (sixth from outermost) much shorter than ninth (only slightly so in Shikra). **VOICE:** Similar to that of Shikra. **HABITS:** Hunts low over ground with quick wingbeats and short glides, but is less dashing than most sparrowhawks. Tends to soar and glide more. **SIMILAR SPECIES:** Shikra is smaller, paler grey above, more pinkish (less chestnut) below, with wings more blunt and, from below, the tips lighter and less contrasting. Young Shikra is much less heavily marked. See also Eurasian Sparrowhawk. **STATUS AND DISTRIBUTION:** Rare palearctic migrant in bush or open country with scattered trees. Recorded once in Meru NP (Nov. 1983), three times in Tsavo West NP (Nov.–Dec. 1988, 1989).

LITTLE SPARROWHAWK *Accipiter minullus*   Plates 36, 42

Length 23–28 cm (9–11″). Very *small* and *rather short-tailed.* **Adult** dark slate-grey above, with *prominent white upper tail-coverts and two large round white spots* on compressed tail, appearing as broken white bars when feathers spread; underparts white, finely barred with brown, and washed with rufous on sides and flanks. In flight from below, remiges are narrowly barred, and pale tail is crossed by three broad dark bars. *Dark sides of head contrast with white throat.* Eyes yellow-orange; cere, rather short tarsi and toes yellow. **Juvenile** dark brown above with blackish crown, usually a *narrow band of white on upper tail-coverts* (lacking in some birds). Underparts with short, dark brown streaks composed of large circular or drop-shaped spots. *Tail dark brown with two or three white spots,* buff tip, three or four darker bars above and on inner feathers below (outer rectrices have twice as many bars underneath). Eyes pale grey or brown, becoming yellow; cere greenish, tarsi and toes yellow. Adult plumage probably acquired during second year. **VOICE:** A rapid, reedy, high-pitched *kek-kek-kek-kek-kek* (female) or a softer *kew-kew-kew-kew. . .* (male). Noisy when breeding. **HABITS:** Not shy, but usually perches in thick cover. Hunts small birds, sometimes in the open away from trees; flight fast, with much twisting and turning; glides briefly above trees but seldom soars. **SIMILAR SPECIES:** Gabar Goshawk is grey above, with pale grey sides of head, red cere and tarsi. Other small sparrowhawks lack white upper tail-coverts. **STATUS AND DISTRIBUTION:** Nominate *A. m. minullus* is a local and uncommon resident of forest, thick woodland (including riverine acacias), plantations and suburban gardens. It ranges widely in w. and cent. Kenya, although absent from the arid north and northeast and from much of n. Tanzania. The coastal lowlands are occupied by the paler race *tropicalis.*

OVAMBO SPARROWHAWK *Accipiter ovampensis*   Plates 36, 42, 44
(Ovampo Sparrowhawk)

Length 31–40 cm (12–16″). A rare, medium-sized hawk with a *rather small head.* **Adult** of usual **light morph** is plain slate-grey above and on face, chin and sides of throat, finely barred with grey or brownish grey below. Upper tail-coverts often barred with white; upper tail-surface grey, with four broad blackish bars, a white tip, and *triangular white marks along the rectrix shafts,* between the dark bars, showing as three or four white spots on the closed tail. At close range, the long, slim middle toe (35–45 mm) is a sure distinction from all other accipiters. **Dark morph** is almost wholly *dull black except for the white shaft spots on the dark grey tail,* and at times some white on upper tail-coverts; shows dark barring on the greyish underside of tail and remiges; wing-linings black. Eyes orange-yellow to dark red; *cere, base of bill, tarsi and toes bright orange-yellow or yellowish orange.* **Juvenile** dark brown above, sometimes with head largely buff, or streaked brown and black; *broad white superciliary stripes and dark patch behind each eye* create a masked effect. Underparts whitish or pale chestnut, with *narrow dark breast streaking* and *barred flanks.*

Eyes brown; cere and feet yellow. **VOICE**: A repeated high-pitched *wheet-wheet-wheet. . .*, a shorter, high-pitched whistle, *kee-kee, kee-kee, kee-kee*, and a slurred *QUEE-u*. **HABITS**: Solitary or in pairs, often in thick cover, but may perch in the open; swift, agile and graceful, readily capturing birds in flight. In s. Africa sticks used in nest construction may have green leaves, but nest is largely unlined. During breeding season soars overhead, calling loudly. **SIMILAR SPECIES**: Adult Shikra is smaller, more slender, finely barred with pinkish rufous below, has plain grey upper tail-coverts, no white shaft spots on tail. Adult Gabar Goshawk has grey head and breast and red (not orange or orange-yellow) tarsi and toes; melanistic Gabar is conspicuously barred on wings and tail above. Adult Little Sparrowhawk has yellow cere and tarsi, unbarred dorsal tail-surface with two oval white spots. African Goshawk is similar in size, but has larger head, dark brown or slaty upperparts, whitish throat, brown barring below, yellow eyes and a shorter middle toe; white marks on central rectrices are patches or bars, not triangular shaft spots. Melanistic Great Sparrowhawk is much larger than dark Ovambo, with yellow cere and tarsi, white throat and no tail bars. **STATUS AND DISTRIBUTION**: Local and rarely recorded resident of dry woodland or riparian groves, mainly at low to medium elevations. Twelve Kenyan specimens (1914–62) from Mt Elgon, Trans-Nzoia, Lumbwa, Nakuru, Makuyu, Nairobi and the Tsavo River. Recorded with certainty in recent decades only from nw. Mara GR and near Namanga. In n. Tanzania, known from one collected at Lembeni, North Pare Mts, in August 1959.

EURASIAN SPARROWHAWK *Accipiter n. nisus* Plates 33, 42
(Northern Sparrowhawk)

Length 28–38 cm (11–15″). A migrant *Accipiter*, both sexes uniformly coloured above, with no white on upper tail-coverts. Male much smaller than female. Underparts and underside of wings barred. Tail rather long, with four or five broad dark bars above and below. Eyes and tarsi yellowish orange, cere yellow. **Male** *slate-grey above*, with *sides of face chestnut and underparts barred chestnut-brown*. **Female** *dark grey-brown above, with whitish throat and conspicuous pale superciliary stripes* separating dark crown from dark ear-coverts; nape often whitish or cream; *underparts barred dark brown*. **Juvenile** resembles female but is browner above, with narrow, more ragged, 'saw-toothed' barring below, and streaking on throat and upper breast. **VOICE**: A chattering *kek-kek-kek-kek-kek-kek*. **HABITS**: Hunts alone in open country or woodland, preying on birds. In normal flight, quick wingbeats alternate with short glides on flat wings. Soars high when migrating. **SIMILAR SPECIES**: Rufous-breasted Sparrowhawk is plainer, brighter rufous below and darker above. Shikra is smaller and paler grey above, the ventral barring more pinkish; cheeks grey, central part of tail plain, and eyes red. African Goshawk is similar in size to female Eurasian Sparrowhawk, but more slaty above with dark cheeks, and juvenile has less prominent superciliary stripes. Levant Sparrowhawk has dark blue-grey cheeks, red eyes, the central rectrices plain above and more narrowly barred below; male's wings white below with distinct black tips. **STATUS AND DISTRIBUTION**: Scarce palearctic migrant, with fewer than 20 Kenyan records (Nov.–Feb.) from Lake Turkana, Tsavo West NP and wooded country in the cent. highlands. Two old specimens from near Moshi and Kidugallo in Tanzania, but no recent records.

RUFOUS-BREASTED SPARROWHAWK *Accipiter r. rufiventris* Plates 33, 42
(Rufous, Rufous-chested or Red-breasted Sparrowhawk)

Length 33–40 cm (13–16″). A medium-sized *montane* hawk with long tail and broad rounded wings. **Adult** slaty or blackish above, tail with a few broad bars; *cheeks, underparts and under wing-coverts largely rufous with little barring*; throat paler and under tail-coverts white. Underside of tail and flight feathers boldly barred. Eyes, cere and feet yellow. **Juvenile** dark brown above with rufous-edged feathers; *dark-streaked on centre of breast; barred with pale rufous on belly and flanks*; thighs plain dull rufous. Some brown-backed **immatures** are nearly plain rufous. Eyes, cere and feet yellow. **VOICE**: A staccato *kek-kek-kek-kek* like Eurasian Sparrowhawk. Also a long-drawn mewing *weeeeeeuu*. Alarm call a harsh *chek-chek-chek*. **HABITS**: Shy and unobtrusive, perching in forest trees and dashing to take birds in thick cover. Also hunts over farmland and montane grassland with alternating flapping and gliding. Occasionally soars over forest in breeding season. **SIMILAR SPECIES**: Male Eurasian Sparrowhawk (rare) is smaller, more barred below, female is browner and lacks rufous. Juvenile Gabar Goshawk resembles juvenile Rufous-breasted, but has broad white band on upper tail-coverts, is more boldly marked below, occupies different habitat. Juvenile rufous morph of Great Sparrowhawk distinguished by size. **STATUS AND DISTRIBUTION**: Local and uncommon resident of thick woods, highland plantations and montane forest at 1600–3000 m in the w. and cent. Kenyan highlands. Apparently not uncommon but infrequently seen. Rare in n. Tanzania, where recently recorded only from Arusha NP, Kilimanjaro, and at Shume, West Usambaras.

GREAT SPARROWHAWK *Accipiter m. melanoleucus*   **Plates 33, 36, 41, 42, 44**
(Black Sparrowhawk or Black Goshawk)

Length 46–58 cm (18–23"). Our largest *Accipiter*. **Normal adult** black above and white below, *with mottled black patches on sides and flanks; dark sides of head contrast sharply with white throat;* tail long, broadly barred above, whitish below with several narrow bars and broader dark terminal band; underside of wing white, with narrow dark barring on flight feathers. Except for black patches along sides, appears very white in overhead flight. Eyes dark red to amber; cere and feet yellow. Rare **dark morph** all black (including unbarred tail) except for white throat. **Juvenile** varies: one morph is dark brown above, *rufous or chestnut-buff below with short dark streaks on neck and breast,* pale morph is white below with dark streaks; eyes dark at first, later becoming greyish. **Voice**: A sharp *kyip*, and a loud ringing alarm call, *ku-ku-ku-ku-ku*. Usually silent away from nest. **Habits**: Solitary or in pairs, perches inconspicuously in shaded forest canopy and easily overlooked. Bold, usually wary. Food almost entirely birds, to size of guineafowl. Nests high in tree, sometimes in introduced *Eucalyptus*. **Similar Species**: African Goshawk is smaller, more slaty black above and barred below; juvenile is whiter below than young Great Sparrowhawk, and boldly marked with dark drop-shaped spots. **Status and Distribution**: Widespread and not uncommon in forest and rich woodland at the coast and in the w. and cent. Kenyan highlands, up to 3000 m, including many wooded suburban areas. Scarce in interior n. Tanzania, being absent from many seemingly suitable places.

GRASSHOPPER BUZZARD *Butastur rufipennis*   **Plates 33, 35, 43**

Length 41–44 cm (16–17"). A slim, medium-sized hawk, showing *large rufous wing patches* in flight. **Adult** brown above, darker on head; *throat white with dark central streak;* underparts largely pale tawny with black shaft streaks; tail barred above and below; underside of wings whitish. Base of bill, cere and feet yellow; eyes pale yellow. **Juvenile** rufous-tinged above, tawny-buff on head and underparts, with dark moustachial stripes; tail unbarred except for dark terminal band. Little yellow on bill; eyes brown. **Voice**: Generally silent on non-breeding grounds. **Habits**: Solitary or in small loose parties in open bush country, perching conspicuously on small bare trees. Not shy. Flies low, with slow buoyant flaps and glides; occasionally soars. Attracted to fires. Takes insect prey on the ground. **Similar Species**: Young chanting goshawks (with similar upright posture) lack rufous wing patches. Black Kite has shallowly forked tail. **Status and Distribution**: Non-breeding migrant from the northern tropics, mainly November–March, to bush, grassland and cultivated country. Regularly migrates through e. Kenya to and from Tsavo region and parts of the coastal lowlands, where some appear to winter. Scarce in n. Tanzania. Much less common than in former years, possibly owing to declines in breeding populations north of Kenya.

LIZARD BUZZARD *Kaupifalco m. monogrammicus*   **Plates 33, 35, 43**

Length 35–37 cm (14–15"). *A small, thickset grey hawk with reddish cere, short red tarsi* and a *dark central throat stripe.* Head, back and breast plain grey; upper tail-coverts white. Eyes dark red-brown with narrow red orbital ring. Posterior underparts *finely barred grey and white.* In flight, short tail is blackish with white tip and one or two broad white bands; underside of wings white with narrow grey barring. Browner **juvenile** has pale buff feather edges above, a less distinct throat stripe, brown eyes and more orange-yellow cere and tarsi. **Voice**: Generally silent, but during breeding season gives a clear melodious whistle, somewhat gull-like, *klioo-klu-klu-klu-klu*, repeated at intervals from perch; also produces a more prolonged, high-pitched mewing *peeeeeooooo*, and a lower *kraa-kraa*. **Habits**: Perches prominently on branch, utility pole or wire, scanning the ground below for prey (insects, reptiles, frogs, rodents). Flight low and undulating, with series of quick wingbeats alternating with descending glides on partly closed wings; rapidly swoops up to perch; soars above trees during display. **Similar Species**: Smaller Gabar Goshawk is longer-legged, has longer barred tail, prominent white upper tail-coverts, rounded wings and no throat stripe. It and all accipiters are more slender. **Status and Distribution**: Widespread in savanna, wooded grassland and cultivation; sometimes in suburban gardens. Common in coastal lowlands north to the Boni Forest. Elsewhere local and uncommon, occasional up to 2000 m near Kitale, though mainly in higher-rainfall areas below 1500 m. Scarce in n. Tanzania.

COMMON (STEPPE) BUZZARD *Buteo buteo vulpinus*   **Plates 33, 35, 39, 44**

Length 45–50 cm (18–20"). A small buzzard with relatively long wings and a moderately long tail; plumage variable, with pale brown, rufous and dark morphs. **Adult** usually warm brown above, *more mottled on head, throat and breast. Underparts barred brown* and white, usually with a *paler broad band across lower breast.* Eyes dark brown, cere and tarsi yellow. In flight from above, wings dark with *large pale patch in primaries;* on underside, this 'window' merges with large whitish panel on lightly barred secondaries, the entire area bordered by *black*

wing tips and trailing edges; mottled *black carpal patches* usually conspicuous. **Rufous morph** has rufous wing-linings, sometimes a paler bar on median coverts connecting to a broad pale band across the breast (or breast and wing-linings uniform fox-red); tail whitish or pinkish orange, plain, narrowly barred throughout, or with broad blackish subterminal band. **Brown morph** has tones more subdued; tail pale brown, but pattern as in rufous morph. **Dark morph** has blackish-brown body and wing-linings, pale grey tail finely black-barred throughout and with broad blackish subterminal band. **Juvenile** resembles adult of respective morph but is more streaked below, with less clear-cut dark trailing edge on wings, both above and below, and lacks dark subterminal tail band. Eyes pale yellowish or greyish brown; cere and tarsi as in adult. **Voice:** Silent in Africa. **Habits:** Flies with steady, rather shallow flaps and short glides, commonly soars with wings raised in a shallow V. Often solitary, but flocks of 50 or more are regular on migration. Perches on trees and posts, from which it drops to take insects or small vertebrates; attracted to termite hatches. **Similar Species:** Long-legged Buzzard easily confused with rufous morph but is longer-winged, usually with more whitish head and breast, much darker belly, and the tail often lacks any trace of barring (rarely true of Common Buzzard); also shows greater contrast between rump and tail. Dark morphs of the two species identical in plumage. Mountain Buzzard is darker brown above, less warmly coloured, whiter below with heavy streaking and blotching; generally at higher altitudes than Common Buzzard. **Status and Distribution:** Widespread and fairly common palearctic passage migrant, mainly October–November and in March, favouring woodland, forest edge, bush and cultivation with scattered trees. Winters in small numbers at medium to high elevations. A well-established migration route exists across Mt Elgon and immediately east of Lake Victoria.

MOUNTAIN BUZZARD *Buteo oreophilus* Plates 33, 39
(Forest Buzzard)

Length *c.* 45 cm (18″). A small *montane* buzzard, the **adult** brown above and whitish below, with *heavy brown splotching on breast, belly, flanks and wing-linings;* tibial feathers and under tail-coverts barred with rufous. Underside of flight feathers whitish, the secondaries barred and a distinct dark band on rear edge of wing. Tail brown above, pale greyish below with faint narrow barring, the subterminal bar broadest. Flight silhouette identical to that of Common Buzzard. Eyes greyish brown (not yellow), cere and tarsi yellow. **Juvenile** buffier below, more lightly marked than adult, and underside of flight feathers less sharply barred; tail bars all of equal width. Eyes pale yellowish brown; cere and tarsi yellow. **Voice:** A loud mewing *peeeoo-peeeoo;* calls frequently. **Habits:** Solitary or soars in pairs above montane forest and adjacent farm or moorland. Flight like that of Common Buzzard. Perches unobtrusively within forest or in the open, dropping to catch insects and small vertebrates. **Similar Species:** Common (Steppe) Buzzard usually warmer brown above and browner below, the markings much less bold, and typically showing a pale breast patch. Young of the two are easily confused, but Mountain Buzzard is generally much paler. **Status and Distribution:** Fairly common resident of montane forest between 2000 and 3500 m. In Kenya, on Mt Elgon, Mt Kulal, Mt Marsabit, the Ndotos, Maralal and in the w. and cent. highlands south to Ol Doinyo Orok (Namanga). In n. Tanzania, known from Mt Meru, Kilimanjaro, the North Pare Mts, West Usambaras, Arusha NP, the Crater Highlands and Mt Hanang.

LONG-LEGGED BUZZARD *Buteo r. rufinus* Plates 33, 35, 39

Length 55–65 cm (22–25.5″). Larger than other buzzards and with more *aquiline proportions.* Longer legs not a definitive character. Plumage variable. **Adult pale morph** typically warm brown above with *creamy-white head and neck,* rufous below with *darker chestnut-brown belly and leg feathers.* Some individuals creamy buff to nearly white below with no dark on belly. Eyes brown; cere, tarsi and toes yellow. In flight from above, flight feathers darker than wing-coverts, with *large white patch at base of primaries;* from below, white panels contrast strongly with *large dark carpal patches* (more pronounced than in Common Buzzard), wing tips and trailing edges; *tail very pale rufous to whitish orange, sometimes almost white,* and generally *with no visible barring* (unlike Common Buzzard); wing-linings rufous. **Rufous morph** has breast and under wing-coverts chestnut. **Dark morph** has body, head and under wing-coverts wholly blackish brown, the tail barred black and grey; contrasting flight-feather pattern as in light birds; plumage indistinguishable from dark Common (Steppe) Buzzard. **Juvenile** similar to light adults, with dark belly streaking and pale head, but tail usually barred; dark tips of secondaries and inner primaries more diffuse. Paler on head, body and wing-coverts than juvenile Common Buzzard, with oval or round (not crescent-shaped) carpal patch. Eyes yellowish-brown; cere and feet as in adult. **Voice:** Silent in Africa. **Habits:** Solitary or loosely associated with other migrating raptors. Wingbeats slower and deeper than those of Common Buzzard; wings held flatter when gliding, but slightly raised and held forward when soaring; *commonly hovers;* perches on poles, dead trees or on the ground. **Similar Species:** Common (Steppe) Buzzard compared above. Young birds of the two are much alike in plumage pattern and size, but dark carpal marks always smaller than those of Long-legged Buzzard. **Status**

AND DISTRIBUTION: Rare palearctic migrant, October–April; ten widely scattered Kenyan records from Lake Turkana, Marsabit, Nakuru, Kinangop Plateau, Nairobi, Narok and both Tsavo NPs.

AUGUR BUZZARD *Buteo a. augur*   Plates 33, 39, 44

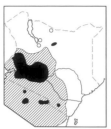

Length 55–60 cm (22–24″). A large buzzard with very broad wings and an *exceptionally short tail*, the latter *bright rufous* in **adult** (and frequently with a narrow black subterminal band). **Light morph** black above, including sides of head; underparts mainly white, with chin and throat black in **female**, white in **male**; tail and tail-coverts rufous; secondaries barred pale grey. Eyes dark brown; cere, tarsi and toes yellow. In flight from below, wings white with narrow black tips, trailing edges and crescent near base of primaries; short tail diagnostic. **Dark morph** (*c.* 10 per cent of individuals, more in some montane areas, e.g. Aberdares) characterized by wholly blackish underparts and under wing-coverts. **Light juvenile** longer-tailed than adult, brown above with buff wing-covert edges; pale buff underparts boldly streaked on throat, sides of breast and flanks; tail brown or reddish brown with narrow dark barring and a broader blackish subterminal band; secondaries barred above; lower wing pattern as in adult, but remiges faintly barred. Bare parts as in adult. **Dark juvenile** has uniformly brownish-black underparts and wing-linings, heavily barred flight feathers and tail. **Immature** plumage shows mixture of white and brown-streaked underparts. Adult plumage apparently acquired in second year. **VOICE**: A loud crowing *erawk-erahk-erahk*, and in display a longer, higher-pitched *ah-waaaa, ah-waaaa. . . .* **HABITS**: Solitary or in pairs. Perches on posts and dead trees. Soars on markedly raised wings. Frequently hovers or hangs motionless in strong wind or updraught. **STATUS AND DISTRIBUTION**: Common resident of hilly country above 1000 m. Characteristic of open or cultivated highlands between 1500 and 3000 m, particularly in w. and cent. Kenya and n. Tanzania. Also resident above 4000 m on moorlands of Mt Elgon, Mt Kenya and Kilimanjaro. Absent (except on isolated mountains) from n. and e. Kenya and the coastal lowlands.

AFRICAN FISH EAGLE *Haliaeetus vocifer*   Plates 34, 35, 40

Length 63–73 cm (25–29″). A large waterside eagle that soars on broad flat wings. **Adult** has entire *head, back, breast and tail white*, contrasting with black wings and *chestnut belly*, leg feathers and crissum. Bill black with yellow base; cere and bare facial skin bright yellow; eyes brown; feet yellowish. In flight, head projects well forward, and tail appears very short; wing-linings plain chestnut, underside of flight feathers black. **Juvenile** is streaky and unkempt-looking, mottled brown above, the *neck and breast whitish with heavy brown streaking and blotching; belly dark brown, streaked with white; tail dull whitish with broad dark tip; underside of wing shows pale panels on coverts and flight feathers*. Eyes brown; cere, tarsi and toes pale grey. **Immature** *largely white below and on tail*, contrasting with black wings and belly; *superciliary region blackish*. **Subadult** (third and fourth years) has head, neck and breast white, initially streaked black but gradually becoming immaculate; tail also largely white with some dusky at tip; belly black at first, later chestnut. Cere pinkish, gradually changing to yellow; feet dull yellowish. **VOICE**: A loud ringing or yelping *wee-ah, kyo-kyo-kyo-kyo*, somewhat gull-like, uttered with head thrown back, often in duet; male's call higher-pitched than that of female. **HABITS**: Usually in pairs near water. Feeds largely on fish; in some areas preys on waterbirds, especially flamingos; also eats carrion. Highly vocal. Young birds may stray to unusual habitats, sometimes far from water; breeds mainly near freshwater lakes and along coast. **SIMILAR SPECIES**: Most eagles are more uniformly brown, not streaked brown and white like young African Fish Eagle, which might also be confused with Osprey or Palm-nut Vulture. **STATUS AND DISTRIBUTION**: Common resident of coastal creeks and estuaries, inland lakes and rivers. Particularly common on some Kenyan Rift Valley lakes and parts of Lake Victoria.

PALM-NUT VULTURE *Gypohierax angolensis*   Plates 31, 34, 35
(Vulturine Fish Eagle)

Length *c.* 60 cm (24″). A large vulturine eagle with broad rounded wings and short rounded tail. **Adult** *white*, with *black lower back, scapulars, secondaries, greater coverts and tail base*. Overhead, black secondaries and primary tips contrast with otherwise white wings. Plumage often earth-stained. Bare orbital skin deep pink, red or orange; bill and eyes pale yellow; cere pale blue-grey; feet flesh-pink or yellowish. **Juvenile** *brown*, darker on secondaries and tail, with *dull yellow face patch* and black bill; eyes brown; legs and feet dull whitish. **Immature** mottled brown, black and white. **VOICE**: A low-pitched *pruk-kurr*, or *kwuk-kwuk-kwuk*, but largely silent. **HABITS**: Solitary. Perches in trees and walks on ground, scavenging along shorelines and floodplains. Soars well. Animal prey includes invertebrates (especially crabs), fish, amphibians, sometimes birds and mammals; feeds on fruits of palms where available (more so in other parts of Africa). Nests and roosts in tall trees. **SIMILAR SPECIES**: Adult African Fish Eagle has dark belly, dark wings, white tail; immature more streaked than young *Gypohierax* and lacks yellowish face patch. Egyptian Vulture has all-black primaries. It and young Hooded Vulture have narrow bills and fly with slow, heavy wingbeats. Juvenile African Harrier-Hawk and Brown Snake Eagle have longer tails and lack yellow facial skin. **STATUS AND DISTRIBUTION**: In Kenya, resident in areas with oil palms, mainly coastal lowlands south of Mombasa and in Shimba Hills NP. Also along Tana River to Meru NP. Smaller isolated populations at Lake Jipe, Taveta and along the Tsavo River. Wanders to Northern Uaso Nyiro and upper Tana Rivers and the Thika area. A common resident on Pemba Island, along parts of adjacent Tanzanian coast, inland to the East Usambaras. A few also resident around Moshi and at Lake Manyara NP.

Aquila eagles are exceedingly variable. Observers should not expect to identify every eagle that soars overhead or that appears over distant hills. Good views are necessary, and some birds cannot be positively named except by raptor specialists or after careful analysis of good photographs. As we have illustrated all major plumages and a few scarcer ones, our coverage should permit identification of 95 per cent of the brown eagles seen in our region. Nevertheless, rare plumages, together with moulting and bleached birds, produce variation beyond that which we can treat here. A few birds will not readily fall into any of the neatly described and illustrated categories. Serious students should consult Porter *et al.* (1981) and Hollom *et al.* (1988) for further information on these birds.

LESSER SPOTTED EAGLE *Aquila p. pomarina* Plates 32, 35, 38

Length 60–66 cm (24–26"). A large migrant eagle with long broad wings, rather buzzard-like in the air. Bill smaller than in Steppe Eagle, the yellow gape flange extending back only to below middle of eye; nostrils circular, not oval; *tarsal feathering less bulky* than in other species, making legs appear thin. In flight, *head projects less than in Tawny and Steppe Eagles*, and rear edge of wing is typically straighter. Soars with *wings held flat or slightly drooped, the short rounded tail fanned*. From above, often shows *whitish U on upper tail-coverts, a small pale area in primaries*, and *small white spot on centre of back*. From below, *remiges and tail usually appear darker than body and wing-linings*; latter typically brown but may be whitish or buff, or with paler areas in centre near the pale carpal crescent. **Adult** is dull brown, with head, neck and forewings somewhat buffier. **Juvenile** dark brown, typically with small yellowish or whitish patch on nape, similar streaks on underparts, and in fresh plumage variable whitish spots on greater (and sometimes median) coverts. Wing-linings may appear uniform with flight feathers; white upper tail-coverts and white patch in primaries more conspicuous than in adults; small whitish spots on tips of upper greater coverts and some median coverts quickly reduced through wear and seldom visible in the field. White rear flight-feather edges disappear by late autumn of first year. Adult plumage acquired in four to five years, after two moults. (Juvenile plumage lost in second year, after first moult.) **VOICE**: A barking *kow-kow-kow*. **HABITS**: Migrates alone or in groups. Frequently soars, glides or hangs motionless on updraughts. Perches in trees, but primarily a ground feeder, taking termites, grasshoppers and other insects. **SIMILAR SPECIES**: Tawny Eagle is usually paler above, warmer brown below, and has heavier bill; it lacks white upper tail-coverts and pale wing patches. Steppe Eagle has slightly longer tail, more curved rear wing edges, more protruding head with a longer bill; juvenile has broad white bar and white trailing edge on underside of wing. At close range, Tawny and Steppe show oval nostrils (not circular as in the two spotted eagles). Wahlberg's Eagle has a longer tail. Greater Spotted Eagle compared below. **STATUS AND DISTRIBUTION**: Palearctic migrant, late October to early April, mainly on southward passage (Nov. to early Dec.), favouring bush, open savanna and farmland, especially in cent. and se. Kenya. A few winter near Rift Valley lakes and in adjacent highlands.

GREATER SPOTTED EAGLE *Aquila clanga* Plates 32, 35, 38

Length 66–75 cm (26–30"). A scarce palearctic vagrant resembling Lesser Spotted Eagle, and some birds probably not distinguishable. In flight from above, both species show pale patch at base of primaries; in Greater Spotted this involves more feather shafts, but is less distinct at any distance. This species lacks the well-defined nape patch of young Lesser Spotted (but faded adult may show pale greyish-brown crown and nape). Soars and glides with flat or slightly drooping wings like that bird, but differs slightly in outline, with *broader wings and shorter tail*. **Adult** typically *darker* and duller than Lesser Spotted, rather uniform *sooty* brown above and below, with purplish gloss in fresh plumage; *wing-linings appear darker than flight feathers* (blackish brown, not warm dark brown as in Lesser Spotted); primaries show pale patch of shaft streaks above. **Juvenile** *generally blackish or sooty brown*. (Some freshly plumaged birds have rows of large white spots on wing-coverts almost obscuring the brown areas; others are nearly as unmarked as Lesser Spotted, but ground colour of upper wing-coverts contrasts little with flight feathers.) In flight from above, shows white U on upper tail-coverts, a white patch on the primaries, and lacks a well-defined pale nape patch; wing-linings dark, as in adult. **Pale morph** (juvenile only?) has blackish flight feathers in striking contrast with rufous-buff coverts and body. In flight, underside resembles those pale subadult Steppe and Lesser Spotted Eagles with pale coverts, but body and coverts are concolorous in Greater Spotted. Young Imperial Eagle also has buffy-brown wing-linings and body, but at close range appears well streaked, and inner primaries show a characteristic pale panel. Adult plumage acquired in four to five years.

SIMILAR SPECIES: Lesser Spotted Eagle and young Imperial Eagle compared above. Adult Steppe Eagle is all dark but has longer tail, more protruding head, and longer bill with gape extending farther back. **STATUS AND DISTRIBUTION**: Twelve accepted Kenyan records (Oct.–Feb., 1958–92), mainly from around Rift Valley lakes. One specimen (Lake Turkana, 19 Oct. 1958).

TAWNY EAGLE *Aquila rapax* Plates 32, 35, 38

Length 66–73 cm (26–29"). A resident brown eagle of non-forested areas. Often appears somewhat ragged, less elegant than other *Aquila* spp. At rest, close bird in profile distinguished from similar Steppe Eagle by the yellow *gape flange extending back only to below middle of usually pale brown eye*. **Adults** vary from dark tawny brown to pale buff and occasionally almost white; flight feathers and tail invariably dark brown; tarsi densely feathered; bill long and heavy, with oval nostrils. Northern *A. r. belisarius* is darker, less rufous, more streaky than widespread *A. r. rapax*. **Juvenile** *rapax* is usually pale, with dark brown eyes. In flight, the long rounded wings are held flat when gliding or soaring; tail broad and rounded, with buff upper coverts; also shows pale bars along upper wing-coverts and along rear wing edges; underside marked by a broken light line along edge of wing-lining and a pale panel in the inner primaries. **Immatures** vary: year-old birds (always?) pale cream or light buff, sometimes nearly white, with contrasting dark flight feathers; others dark (some almost blackish), often well streaked or blotched, and some show dark head and/or breast contrasting with pale body and wing-coverts. Adult plumage acquired in three to four years. **VOICE**: A barking *kiok* or *kowk*, plus other calls at nest. Not especially vocal, but more so than wintering palearctic eagles. **HABITS**: Solitary or in pairs. Perches infrequently on ground. Flapping flight appears rather heavy and clumsy. Kills mammals to size of dik-dik; also scavenges and feeds at carcasses with vultures, and eats termites; piratical, robbing other raptors of food. Nest large, shallow, often at very top of tree. **SIMILAR SPECIES**: Adult Steppe Eagle is darker brown; yellow of gape extends back to below rear margin of eye. Juvenile Steppe has distinctive white bar along middle of underside of wing, and broad white band on upper tail-coverts. Typical Lesser Spotted Eagle is darker below, with pale patch at base of primaries above, small white spot in centre of back and whitish U on upper tail-coverts. See juvenile Imperial Eagle. **STATUS AND DISTRIBUTION**: Widespread and fairly common resident of open country, bush and savanna at all elevations, mainly in dry areas. Most birds are *A. r. rapax*, but specimens (1958, 1959) from Lake Turkana have been identified as *belisarius*, also attributed to n. Kenya by Vaurie (1965). **NOTE**: Formerly considered conspecific with Steppe Eagle by some authors.

STEPPE EAGLE *Aquila nipalensis orientalis* Plates 32, 35, 38

Length *c*. 75 cm (30"). A large eagle, typically less scruffy-looking and more impressive than the resident Tawny Eagle. Flight outline like that of Tawny, with wings held flat and primary tips often slightly raised. The shorter *inner primaries create a slightly notched or pinched look* (especially in young birds, where the effect is greatly enhanced by the white tips of these feathers being viewed against a light sky). **Adult** dark brown with small buff patch on nape, and tail and flight feathers indistinctly barred; tarsi with bulky feathering; bill long and powerful. *Yellow gape extends back to a point below rear edge of dark brown eye*, and often appears wider, more prominent than gape of Tawny Eagle. **Juvenile** is paler, buffy or greyish brown, often with creamy nape and hindcrown. In flight from above, *blackish tail and flight feathers contrast with grey-brown wing-coverts*, shows *whitish patch at base of primaries, white stripe along coverts, white trailing wing edges* and a *broad white band on upper tail-coverts*. From below, the wing shows a broad white band parallel to the white rear border; belly whitish. **Immatures** variable; some birds show generally light wing-linings contrasting with blackish wing tips and dark brown body. During the six-year transition to adult plumage, the white underwing band is replaced by darker feathers, often producing a ragged effect, but the wing-linings become pale, always contrasting with the darker body. (At close range, the *strong flight-feather barring* bordered by a wider dark band provides a good mark.) Pale bands on the upper wing-coverts gradually disappear through wear and moult. **VOICE**: Generally silent in Africa. **HABITS**: Solitary or in small groups, sometimes scores together on migration. Feeds on the ground, attracted to termite emergences and to other insects; consorts with vultures at carrion. **SIMILAR SPECIES**: Adult Tawny Eagle is warmer brown; yellow gape flange extends only to below middle of eye. Juvenile Tawny lacks white line on underside of wing, has the bands on upper tail-coverts and wings buff rather than white, and remiges lack the heavy barring of Steppe Eagle. Somewhat smaller Lesser Spotted Eagle soars with straighter-edged and slightly drooping wings, has shorter tail and less protruding head, lacks broad stripe on underside of wing, has narrower, more U-shaped white band on upper tail-coverts. See Greater Spotted and Imperial Eagles. **STATUS AND DISTRIBUTION**: A common palearctic migrant in open country, late October to March, ranging up to 3000 m, mainly in semi-arid n. and e. Kenya, in and near the Rift Valley highlands, Mara GR and n. Tanzania. Most numerous during November–December passage. **NOTE**: Formerly treated as a race of Tawny Eagle by some authors.

*IMPERIAL EAGLE *Aquila heliaca*   Plates 32, 35, 38

Length 72–83 cm (28–33"). A large heavy eagle that soars with its long broad wings held flat, the square-tipped tail slightly spread, and the head markedly protruding. **Adult** blackish brown, with distinctive *pale crown and nape, pale greyish tail base and narrow white scapular stripes*. Eyes pale brown; cere and feet yellow. **Juvenile** *brownish buff with variable dark streaking, especially on breast*. In flight from above, pale wing-coverts contrast with blackish remiges and tail; also shows a narrow white bar along edge of coverts, a white patch in the primaries, and a broad white rump patch; below, a pale panel in inner primaries contrasts with otherwise dark remiges. **Early immature** still paler, with little streaking below. **Older immature** becomes mottled or blotchy as adult feathers appear; may show adult head pattern, reduced white markings above, and greyish dorsal tail base while still retaining pale feathers below and on wing-coverts. Full adult plumage apparently takes six or seven years to acquire. **Voice:** Generally silent in Africa. **Habits:** Single birds soar high over open country (usually with other *Aquila* eagles); rests on trees or dead snags. **Similar Species:** Steppe Eagle is smaller, stockier, with shorter and more wedge-shaped tail. Adult is darker below, lacks white on scapulars and grey tail base, and head is not so pale. Juvenile Steppe usually has conspicuous white line on underside of wing; otherwise resembles juvenile Imperial with buff body and pale undersides of inner primaries, but is smaller-billed, and both tail and flight feathers are browner. Greater Spotted Eagle is dark and much shorter-tailed. **Status and Distribution:** Scarce palearctic migrant, November–March, in grasslands at low or medium elevations. Nearly 20 Kenyan records (1962–92), mainly from the Rift Valley, Mara GR, Meru and Tsavo NPs. Recorded once in Tanzania (Olduvai, Jan. 1970).

WAHLBERG'S EAGLE *Aquila wahlbergi*   Plates 34, 38, 44

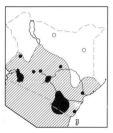

Length 55–61 cm (22–24"). A *medium-sized, slender* eagle, *little larger than a Black Kite*. A short occipital crest is not always conspicuous. Long-feathered tarsi give a rather 'baggy' appearance. Soars with its *long, parallel-edged wings held flat*, the *long, narrow, square-tipped tail* usually folded and the large head projecting far forward. Plumage of normal **dark morph** nearly *uniform dark brown*, but may show some golden-buff on crown and scapulars. In flight, *dark wing-linings and body contrast slightly with paler remiges, especially the primary bases*; dark tail shows indistinct barring below. Cere and feet bright yellow; eyes dark brown. In uncommon **pale morph**, buffy-white or cream body plumage contrasts with dark remiges and tail; underparts lightly marked with dark shaft streaks or spots. **Juvenile** resembles adult of dark morph, but underparts slightly paler. **Voice:** Seldom vocal, but clear shrill *kleeeee-ay* display call is distinctive; no other brown eagle has similar whistled call. Near nest, gives a yipping *kyip-kyip-kyip* or *kyop-kyop-kip-kip*. **Habits:** Often hangs against breeze with narrowed tail depressed; wingbeats quick, interspersed with glides. Sometimes migrates in small groups, but usually solitary or in pairs. Perches and nests in trees. Inconspicuous except when soaring. **Similar Species:** Other brown *Aquila* eagles are larger, bulkier, with broader wings and tail; none is crested. Dark Booted Eagle has narrower-tipped wings, a paler, frequently spread tail, light band across upper wing-coverts, and narrow whitish U-shaped band on upper tail-coverts. Brown Snake Eagle has bare tarsi, large head, bright yellow eyes, silvery under wing-surfaces, and barred tail. Black Kite is fork-tailed. **Status and Distribution:** Widespread; often the commonest eagle in woodland, bush and cultivation below 1800 m, typically in semi-arid country. Migratory; present mainly August–April, when it breeds; many presumably spend rest of the year to the north of Kenya.

VERREAUX'S EAGLE *Aquila verreauxii*   Plates 32, 34, 35, 38
(Black Eagle)

Length 82–96 cm (32–38"). A very large, powerful eagle distinctive in soaring flight, with its *long, distally broad wings narrowed at base*, raised in shallow V and the primary tips noticeably upturned. Tail quite long; large bill and head project well in front of wings. **Adult** *black*, except for *large white area on rump and back extending as lines along sides of upper back*, and *large white patches* on primaries (visible above and below). **Juvenile** rich tawny-brown, with *buff crown, nape* and *upper back*; upper wing-coverts scaled black and buff; *whitish back patch streaked with brown*. Face, neck and breast blackish, blending into buff on belly and legs. Cere and feet yellow. In flight, shaped as adult, but *wing-linings and primary patches pale buff*; remiges and tail barred below. **Immature** darkens as black gradually replaces the tawny-brown and buff areas. Adult plumage acquired after three or four years. **Voice:** A staccato *cluck*, a harsh alarm bark, *chyaw*, and a ringing *whaee-whaee-whaee*; gives a mewing *weeeeooo* in display. **Habits:** Soars along ridges and cliffs. Feeds primarily on hyraxes. Pairs perform spectacular swooping and somersaulting displays. Usually nests on cliff ledge, rarely in trees. **Status and Distribution:** Uncommon but widely ranging resident of open rocky hills, gorges and mountains above 1000 m. Prefers dry areas, including semi-desert; avoids heavily wooded slopes.

AFRICAN HAWK-EAGLE *Hieraaetus spilogaster*   **Plates 34, 41**

Length 60–65 cm (24–26"). A medium-sized *black-and-white* (adult) or *rufous* (young) eagle. Soars on long, flat, *very rounded wings distinctly narrowed* at the base; tail rather long. At a distance, flying **adult** appears black and white, with *whitish 'window' at base of primaries* conspicuous from above; *wings white below*, marked by *narrow black trailing edges* and a *broad mottled black band across the greater coverts*; remiges unbarred. *Tail with broad black tip* and several faint narrow bars. Short dark streaks on white throat and breast are visible at close range. Legs white. Cere and feet greenish yellow; eyes yellow. **Juvenile** dark brown above, *rufous with narrow black shaft streaks below* and on wing-linings; remiges white, faintly barred below; barred tail greyish. Eyes brown; cere and feet as in adult. **Immature** darker above than juvenile; underparts whitish, with broader dark streaks; eyes brownish yellow. Full adult plumage acquired in three or four years. **VOICE**: A musical *klu-klu-klu-klu-klu-klu*, or *kweee-u, kweee-u*; at nest, a harsher *ko-ko-ko-ko-kweeee-ko-ko*. **HABITS**: Soars frequently, alone or in pairs, and perches conspicuously in trees. Powerful and dashing, taking quite large birds (francolins, guineafowl) and hare-sized mammals. Nests on tree or cliff. **SIMILAR SPECIES**: Smaller Ayres's Hawk-Eagle lacks 'windows' in its more pointed wings, is heavily barred on remiges and tail, and has black primary shafts. Eurasian Honey Buzzard may show dark wing-linings but lacks broad black band formed by darker greater coverts below; has dark tail tip, but pattern otherwise differs. Much larger African Crowned Eagle has less contrasting wings, broader tail bands and narrower dark tail tip. Rufous juvenile Great Sparrowhawk is coloured like young African Hawk-Eagle, but has long bare yellow tarsi. **STATUS AND DISTRIBUTION**: Local and uncommon in open woodland or thorn-scrub with rocky hills and wooded watercourses; prefers drier country at low to medium elevations.

BOOTED EAGLE *Hieraaetus pennatus*   **Plates 34, 35, 41, 44**

Length 48–51 cm (19–20"). A *buzzard-sized* dimorphic eagle with rather narrow wings and long tail. Predominant **pale morph** warm brown above, head and neck more tawny or rufous-brown, streaked darker; underparts white, with thin brown streaking on breast. Easily recognized in flight from below by *dark flight feathers contrasting with white wing-linings and body*; tail greyish and *unbarred*, slightly rounded when soaring. Flying bird shows *broad buff band across upper wing-coverts*, and *narrow whitish U on upper tail-coverts* contrasting with dark remiges and tail. **Dark morph** is *uniform dark brown* on head, underparts and wing-linings, appears generally dark below except for *paler tail, small pale wedge in inner primaries* and *black patch at carpal joint*. Flying toward observer, *small white 'landing lights' at junction of wings and body* a diagnostic feature of both pale and dark morphs. Some birds intermediate between dark and light extremes. **Rufous morph** dull chestnut or tawny-brown on head and underparts; in flight, wing-lining shows distinctive contrast between dull chestnut forewing and broad black band on mid-wing. **Juvenile** resembles adult of same morph, but pale birds have chestnut wash below. **VOICE**: Generally silent in East Africa. (Highly vocal on palearctic and South African breeding grounds.) **HABITS**: Solitary. Soars and glides with wings flat, but relaxed-looking with primary tips slightly drooping, *tail usually slightly spread and flexed from side to side* as in Black Kite. Hunting flight fast and powerful; may stoop on prey from considerable height; feeds largely on birds but takes other vertebrates and winged termites. **SIMILAR SPECIES**: Wahlberg's Eagle can be confused with dark morph (as can rare pale Wahlberg's with pale Booted); Wahlberg's is larger, slightly crested, typically shows longer, narrower tail and broader-tipped wings; remiges paler than wing-linings below; no pale wing-bar or rump band from above. Ayres's Hawk-Eagle is heavily barred on tail, lacks dorsal flight marks of Booted. Distant Black Kite easily mistaken if slightly forked or square-cut tail not evident. **STATUS AND DISTRIBUTION**: Uncommon but regular and widespread palearctic migrant, mainly late October to early April, preferring dry woodland and bushy hillsides. Most frequent at low to medium elevations, including the coastal lowlands.

AYRES'S HAWK-EAGLE *Hieraaetus ayresii*   **Plates 34, 41, 44**

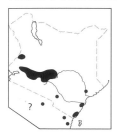

Length 46–56 cm (18–22"). A small stocky raptor, much smaller than African Hawk-Eagle. In flight, the broad rounded wings are held stiff and flat, the long tail slightly spread. Perched, **adult** appears blackish above with small *white forehead patch* (and sometimes superciliary stripes), white below with *heavy black spotting, black bars on leg feathers* and heavily barred tail; short occipital crest inconspicuous. Close view reveals *black primary shafts* (white in African Hawk-Eagle). Eyes yellow or orange, cere and feet greenish yellow. (Rare dark morph, unrecorded in East Africa, is black, with or without white on the breast and with barred tail.) Flying adult darker than African Hawk-Eagle below, with *barred remiges and no white 'windows' in the primaries*. May show *white 'landing-light' spots at junction of wings and body* as in Booted Eagle. **Juvenile** grey-brown above, with rufous from crown to upper back; *wing-coverts and scapulars scaly-looking, with white feather tips. Pale rufous superciliary stripes* usually present. *Underparts almost plain rich buff or pale rufous, very narrowly streaked with black on breast*. In flight, shows pale rufous wing-linings, barred remiges and tail. Cere and feet as in adult; eyes pale grey-brown. **VOICE**: Vocal only near

nest: a high whistling *wheep-hip-hip-hip-hip-wheeeep* in aerial display; a piping *kip-kip-kip* when perched. **HABITS**: Solitary. Perches in leafy tree cover. Flies briefly, sometimes soaring, above treetops. Takes medium-sized birds, stooping from a height with wing tips folded to tail, and pursues prey at speed through canopy. Nests in well-shaded part of tree, adding leafy twigs to nest at intervals. **SIMILAR SPECIES**: African Hawk-Eagle is larger, the flight feathers plain white below, and showing a whitish patch on primaries above; adult less heavily marked below. Pale Eurasian Honey Buzzard has longer wings, smaller head, different tail pattern and unfeathered tarsi. Adult Booted Eagle has unbarred tail; juvenile Booted is paler, less rufous than juvenile Ayres's and less heavily barred on wings and tail. Juvenile African Hawk-Eagle is similarly rufous or buff below, but lacks pale scaling on upperparts. **STATUS AND DISTRIBUTION**: Scarce and local resident of forest and rich woodland, preferring smaller patches and riverine strips where it can hunt over adjacent open country. Recorded up to 3000 m in the w. and cent. Kenyan highlands; also in the Shimba and Chyulu Hills, along the lower Tana River and in the Arabuko–Sokoke Forest. In n. Tanzania, known only from Arusha NP and the Usambara Mts. **NOTE**: Until recently, known as *Hieraaetus dubius*.

LONG-CRESTED EAGLE *Lophaetus occipitalis* Plates 32, 35, 44
(Long-crested Hawk-Eagle)

Length 53–58 cm (21–23"). Unique. Small and dark with a *long loose crest*. Perched **adult** appears entirely *blackish brown with broad grey tail bars and whitish tarsal feathering*. Bill black; cere, eyes and toes yellow. *Large white primary patches* are prominent (above and below) in flight. Flies with shallow flapping and gliding; soars with its short rounded wings held flat. **Juvenile** browner with some white mottling and a shorter crest. **VOICE**: When circling, a repeated screaming *keeeeeeah* or *keerr-wee*, sometimes with a sharp high-pitched *kek-kek-kek-kek* (which may be given separately). Also a repeated *kweew, kweew . . . .* **HABITS**: Solitary. Often perches on dead tree or roadside pole, intently peering downward for rodents and lizards, its floppy crest blowing in the breeze. Nests in tall trees, sometimes in introduced *Eucalyptus*; leafy green branches added at intervals during nesting. Known to eat figs. **STATUS AND DISTRIBUTION**: Widespread and locally fairly common in woodland, forest edge and partly cultivated country, typically at medium elevations but ranging up to 3000 m.

Note: Placed in the genus *Spizaetus* by some authors.

AFRICAN CROWNED EAGLE *Stephanoaetus coronatus* Plates 34, 39
(Crowned Hawk-Eagle)

Length 82–92 cm (32–36"). A *very large, crested* eagle with broad rounded wings and *long tail*; perches bolt-upright. **Adult** blackish brown above; head and *throat rich brown, rest of underparts tawny-buff, heavily barred and mottled with black; legs barred and spotted with black*. Eyes pale yellow; gape dull yellow; cere and *toes bright yellow*. In flight from below, wings show broad black trailing edges and diagnostic *rufous winglinings bordered by rows of large black spots*; remiges boldly barred. Tail whitish with three broad black bars. **Juvenile** *pale greyish*, the head and underparts white with some black spots on legs; buffy wash on breast; wings and tail barred as in adult, but winglinings pale rufous-buff. *Remiges and tail with four strong black bars*. Eyes and cere grey; bill black; gape flanges and toes light yellow. In about two years **immature** becomes more rufous on breast, shows black spotting on legs, later on head. Eyes gradually become paler. Adult plumage acquired after three or four years. **VOICE**: Male in high aerial display gives a melodious, far-carrying *kewee, kewee, kewee . . .* ; female calls a deeper *koowi, koowi, koowi. . .*, each note repeated 15–30 times. **HABITS**: Soars to considerable height over forest and often indulges in distinctive swooping display flight, flapping rapidly at top of each undulation; highly vocal. Singles or pairs usually perch inconspicuously in or under canopy. Flight remarkably silent and owl-like; some hunting crepuscular. Preys on mammals up to size of full-grown duiker or young impala, but particularly favours colobus monkeys; also kills guineafowl and monitor lizards; caches portions of large kills in trees. Builds huge nest of sticks, lined with leafy green twigs, high in forest tree. **SIMILAR SPECIES**: Juvenile Martial Eagle resembles juvenile Crowned, but Martial has longer wings with less distinctly barred flight feathers, shorter tail with several rather faint narrow dark bars, and all-white tarsi. **STATUS AND DISTRIBUTION**: Uncommon and local resident of large forest tracts, also relict patches and riverine strips in otherwise open country, from the coast up to 3000 m in the Kenyan highlands. In n. Tanzania, locally common in the Usambaras, on Kilimanjaro and in Arusha NP.

MARTIAL EAGLE *Polemaetus bellicosus* Plates 34, 39

Length 79–83 cm (31–33"). A *very large*, crested eagle with long, broad, wings and *short tail*. **Adult** *dark greybrown on head, upperparts and breast; rest of underparts white with small dark spots*; upper wing-surface rather uniform brown; *underside of wings dark*, the flight feathers indistinctly barred; tail lightly barred. Eyes yellow; cere and *toes blue-grey*. **Juvenile** and **immature** have face and *entire underparts (including tarsi and lightly mottled wing-linings)* white. Eyes brown; *cere and toes whitish or grey*. This plumage maintained through several

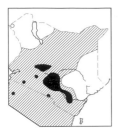

moults for four or five years. **Subadult** plumage, worn briefly, has throat and breast more spotted, under wing-coverts mottled with dark brown. **VOICE**: Although seldom vocal, utters a musical ringing *koweeo-koweeo-koweeo*. . . ; also a loud clear *klee-klee-klee, klooee, klooee, klooee* . . . in display; also a liquid *kluweeo* when perched. **HABITS**: Solitary or in pairs; usually shy. Soars at great height on steady flat wings with primary tips slightly upturned; rarely hovers. Perches prominently on bare branches, poles, dead trees. Feeds on large birds (including geese, storks) and medium-sized mammals, usually taken in long shallow dives from air or from high perch. Builds large nest of sticks with leafy lining, in tall isolated tree. **SIMILAR SPECIES**: Black-chested Snake Eagle is smaller, with white under wing-surface, more prominently barred flight feathers and tail and bare tarsi. African Crowned Eagle is a forest bird with longer barred tail, boldly barred wings, yellow (not whitish or grey) cere and toes, heavy ventral markings and chestnut under wing-coverts; juvenile and immature Crowned have black-spotted legs (like *adult* Martial). **STATUS AND DISTRIBUTION**: Widespread and reasonably common in open grassland and bush, mainly in drier areas at low to medium elevations, occasionally to 3000 m on high mountains.

FALCONS, FAMILY FALCONIDAE
(World, *c.* 63 species; Africa, 20; Kenya, 19; n. Tanzania, 16)

Although superficially hawk-like, falcons are anatomically distinct from other diurnal raptors, with fairly short tarsi, large and strong toes, and a short, well-hooked, powerful bill 'toothed' behind the tip. They are small to medium-sized birds with long pointed wings and moderate to rather long tails. Flight is typically swift and dashing, but they often soar on flat or slightly lowered wings. They hunt birds and small mammals by stooping or hovering, at times impressively diving on and striking avian prey in mid-air. Some also catch and consume aerial insects. Most species are solitary, but a few are gregarious on migration or at roosts. Usually they build no nest, but lay their eggs on cliff ledges, in tree cavities, or in old nests of other birds. Females are larger than males. Adults of many species support black 'moustache' marks. Young are duskier than adults and more streaked below. Species identification, often difficult, is based on a variety of structural characters and manner of flight.

PYGMY FALCON *Polihierax semitorquatus castanonotus*   **Plates 36, 46**

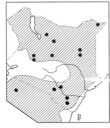

Length 19–20 cm (8"). Diminutive, thickset and somewhat shrike-like. **Male** mainly grey above, with white face, half-collar and underparts. **Female** similar but with *chestnut patch on back*. In flight, both sexes show prominent *white rump, white-spotted wings* and *black-and-white barred tail*. Cere, orbital ring and feet red, eyes pale brown. **Juvenile** washed rufous on back and buff on breast, with thin dark streaks from upper breast to belly. Young female shows more rufous, especially on back. **VOICE**: A high-pitched *kikiKIK* or *kiKIK-kiki*, commonly repeated. **HABITS**: Perches on exposed tree branches, from which it flies down to capture large insects and small reptiles. Usually uses unoccupied nest of White-headed Buffalo-Weaver for breeding. Bobs head up and down. Flight somewhat owl-like, low and undulating, with rapid wingbeats. **STATUS AND DISTRIBUTION**: Fairly common resident of bush and shrubby grassland in drier areas, below 1600 m, north, east and south of the Kenyan highlands. Range almost identical with that of White-headed Buffalo-Weaver. Absent from most parts of w. Kenya and the Lake Victoria basin.

LANNER FALCON *Falco biarmicus*   **Plates 37, 45**

Length 38–45 cm (15–18"). The commonest large falcon in East Africa. In flight, appears less compact and longer-tailed than Peregrine, with longer but *rather blunt-tipped wings*. **Adult** *F. b. biarmicus* is *slaty or grey-brown above, paler on rump, pale but below with sparse brown spotting*. Crown and nape rufous with blackish band from eye to nape, narrow blackish moustachial marks, and dark streaking on forecrown; pale buff cheeks extend almost to eye; tail with narrow pale barring. Wing-linings pale, but may have darker band across greater coverts. Cere, orbital ring and feet yellow. Adults of northern *F. b. abyssinicus* are more heavily streaked and barred below, and the crown is dark chestnut. **Juvenile** (both races) dark slaty brown above, often including crown; *heavily streaked underparts contrast with whitish throat, as do dark under wing-coverts with the pale flight feathers*. Cere and bare orbital ring blue-grey; feet pale yellow. **VOICE**: A harsh *kak-kak-kak* . . ., and a shrill *kiree-kiree*. **HABITS**: Pairs usually based on rock outcrop or cliff, also breeds in savannas or open woods where nests of other birds are available. Cruises with slow, shallow wing beats, but shows speed and agility in pursuit of birds in the air. Captures prey on ground following spectacular stoops. **SIMILAR SPECIES**: Peregrine is slightly smaller and darker, with shorter tail, more pointed wings, blackish crown and broader moustachial marks; adult is densely barred below. Flight silhouette compared above. See Saker and Barbary Falcons. **STATUS AND DISTRIBUTION**: Widespread resident in open dry country, especially near

cliffs and rocky gorges. The race *abyssinicus* ranges through n. Kenya south to Lake Baringo; more southern birds are nominate *biarmicus*.

SAKER FALCON *Falco c. cherrug*   Plate 45

Length 43–55 cm (17–21.5″). A rare northern migrant, slightly larger and more heavily built than Lanner, with broader-based wings; tail longer and wings a little narrower than in Peregrine, and wing tips less pointed in soaring flight. **Adult** differs from Lanner in *paler head*, this sometimes almost wholly white, and usually appearing so at a distance, but close view shows *narrow* dark moustachial streaks and dark postocular lines plus faint whitish superciliary stripes (lacking in Lanner). Back feathers and wing-coverts with rusty edges in fresh plumage. Brown wing bases and back contrast in flight with blackish primaries. *Brown tail shows pale yellowish spots at sides, the bars on the central rectrices incomplete.* (Adult Lanner has tail conspicuously and completely barred grey and rufous-grey across all feathers.) Underparts variable, often more heavily spotted than in adult Lanner. In flight, well-marked under wing-coverts may contrast with silvery remiges, although some birds are only sparsely streaked on greater coverts. Cere, bare orbital ring and feet pale yellowish. **Juvenile** more streaked on crown, darker above than adult; heavily streaked below. Difficult to separate from juvenile Lanner, but crown and nape usually paler (whitish). Juvenile Peregrine is darker above with heavier moustachial marks, and with underside of wings barred. Cere, bare orbital ring and feet grey or blue-grey. In flight, juvenile Saker's dark wing-linings contrast with almost translucent primaries (unlike Peregrine). **Habits:** Flies with slow wingbeats until prey is sighted, then quickly accelerates, making capture in air or less often on the ground after powerful stoop. Soars on flat or slightly lowered wings. **Similar Species:** Lanner and Peregrine Falcons compared above. **Status and Distribution:** Fewer than ten Kenyan records (several unsubstantiated), mainly in the Rift Valley between October and March. In Tanzania, recorded from West Kilimanjaro District (Feb. 1957) and Ngorongoro Crater (Jan. 1992).

PEREGRINE FALCON *Falco peregrinus*   Plates 37, 45

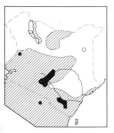

Length 33–48 cm (13–19″). Large, compact and fast-flying. **Adult** *blackish on crown. F. p. minor dark blue-grey above*, with *broad blackish moustachial marks* contrasting with white cheeks and chin; underparts creamy buff with heavy dark spotting and barring, most dense along sides and flanks. Eyes large, dark brown; cere, orbital ring, tarsi and exceptionally large toes bright yellow. Much larger migrant *F. p. calidus* is paler above, white below with reduced spotting and barring, and has narrower, more pointed moustachial marks. In flight, *wings relatively broad at base but pointed at tips, often appearing triangular in shape*; tail of medium length. Both races *generally dark, with white throat and breast*; lower back and rump *slightly* paler than back, and tail shows several narrow darker bars. Wing-linings narrowly barred, the remiges more coarsely, all appearing grey at a distance. **Juvenile** brown above, and heavily *streaked with dark brown below*; cheeks buff; may show crown streaking, paler brown nape and (often) superciliary stripes. Wing-linings more coarsely barred than in adult. Cere, orbital ring, tarsi and toes greenish yellow in *F. p. minor*. Juvenile *F. p. calidus* resembles juvenile Barbary Falcon, both quite different from resident *minor* in having buff crown and narrow streaking on underparts. **Immature** may show mixture of streaking and barring below. **Voice:** A shrill *kek-kek-kek-kek-kek-kek*. **Habits:** Usually solitary. Preys mainly on birds caught in the air, often stooping from a height at great speed, with wings nearly closed. Wingbeats stiff and shallow, interspersed with short glides when cruising, deeper and stronger when hunting. Breeds on cliffs, rarely on urban buildings. **Similar Species:** Adult Lanner is longer-tailed, has less pointed wings, is paler, has pale rufous crown and less pronounced moustachial stripes. Juvenile Lanner is considerably paler above than juvenile Peregrine, with narrower moustachial marks and blue-grey cere (yellowish in juvenile Peregrine). Taita Falcon is smaller, rufous below with white throat, shows prominent rufous nape patches and has distinctive flight. Eurasian Hobby is smaller, with narrower wings, shorter tail; streak-breasted adult has rufous leg feathers and crissum. See Barbary Falcon. **Status and Distribution:** *F. p. minor* is an uncommon but widespread breeding resident of cliffs in open country; sometimes seen around Nairobi city centre, where known to nest. Palearctic *calidus*, present October–March, probably accounts for most birds seen in atypical habitats.

BARBARY FALCON *Falco p. pelegrinoides*   Plate 45

Length 34–45 cm (13.5–17.5″). Resembles a small pale Peregrine in silhouette and flight habits. **Adult** *pale bluish grey above* with darker primaries; crown dark in centre, rufous at sides and on nape; forehead buffier; distinct dark line through eye to nape; usually *narrow dark moustachial streaks* and *large white cheek patch*. Underparts *pale pinkish buff*, with sparse brown barring on flanks and leg feathers. **Juvenile** warm *dark brown above*, with *narrow yellowish or buff collar on nape*; more sandy buff below with *narrow, light brown streaking*. (Juvenile Peregrine typically boldly streaked.) Cere, tarsi and toes blue-grey. **Similar Species:** Adult Lanner also has rufous on nape, but shows paler rump. Peregrine is much darker above, with little or no rufous on nape, has broader moustachial streaks and smaller cheek patches. More thickset Taita Falcon is extensively rufous-naped, but whiter on face, blacker on crown, plain rufous below and has parrot-like flight. African Hobby is darker, and entirely rich chestnut below. **Habits:** As for Peregrine Falcon. **Status and Distribution:** Apparently rare, in semi-arid regions. Status unclear and most records incompletely documented, some questionable. Collected once at Loyangalani, 4 November 1958 (Owre and Paulson 1968). An injured bird found at Timau, 21 February 1981, and various others reported seen in the Isiolo area 1981–83 (Thomsett 1989). Two reported in Tsavo West NP, Nov.–Dec. 1987 (Pearson *et al.* 1989), but details of the record not entirely convincing. **NOTE:** Sometimes considered conspecific with Peregrine Falcon.

TAITA FALCON *Falco fasciinucha*   Plates 37, 45

Length 28–30 cm (11–12″). A chunky falcon *shaped like a miniature short-tailed Peregrine, with long, broad-based wings. Wingbeats stiff, shallow, somewhat parrot-like.* **Adult** dark slate-grey above with a paler rump, distinctive *rufous nape patches, black crown and bold dark moustachial marks; chin and throat whitish or pale buff;* otherwise mainly rufous below, darker on flanks, with narrow dark shaft streaks. In flight, rufous wing-linings contrast with grey remiges; tail has indistinct dark bars and buff tip. Bill dark bluish slate with black tip; cere, eye-ring and feet yellow; eyes brown. **Juvenile** browner with buff feather edges above; more streaked below and with barred wing-linings. **VOICE:** Weaker than that of Peregrine. Apparent contact call a squealing *kree-kree;* alarm call a loud *kek-kek-kek-kek.* **HABITS:** Generally Peregrine-like. Perches at length on cliff faces; preys on birds and insects. **SIMILAR SPECIES:** Peregrine is larger, paler and strongly marked below, with little or no rufous on nape. Barbary Falcon is rufous-naped but paler above, has rufous on sides of crown, and underparts are pinkish buff with light barring. African Hobby has narrower wings and rich chestnut underparts. **STATUS AND DISTRIBUTION:** Rare near rocky crags, cliffs and gorges, usually in dry areas. Early Kenyan specimens from base of the Taita Hills and Voi, one from Nanyuki (March 1949). More recent sight records from Lewa Downs, Samburu GR, Ololokwe, Baringo, and near Lokitaung, and in Tanzania from the Gol Mts (Serengeti NP) and Olosirwa (Crater Highlands), but some of these inadequately documented. Reports from Amboseli and Magadi are erroneous.

EURASIAN HOBBY *Falco s. subbuteo*   Plates 37, 45
(Northern Hobby)

Length 30–36 cm (12–14″). A medium-sized, *slender falcon with long narrow wings reaching tip of the rather short square-tipped tail* on perched bird. **Adult** *dark slate-grey above,* including narrowly buff-barred tail; top of head and broad moustachial marks black, contrasting with white cheeks and throat; *underparts deep buff or creamy with broad blackish streaks; tibial feathers and under tail-coverts rich chestnut; wing-linings buff with dense dark spots.* Bill steel-blue; eyes dark brown; cere, orbital ring and feet yellow or yellow-orange. In flight, appears more slender than Peregrine, from below showing heavily streaked underparts and barred wings; *upper tail-surface unbarred.* **Juvenile** darker and browner above with pale buff feather edges; more heavily streaked below; leg feathers and crissum buff; cere, orbital ring and feet pale greenish yellow. **VOICE:** A repeated *kew-kew-kew-kew-kew.* . . . **HABITS:** Flies with stiff, regular wingbeats interspersed with short glides; rarely hovers. Agile, capturing insects, birds (including swifts) and bats. Often in loose groups, sometimes many together near rain storms. Attracted to grass and bush fires. Partly crepuscular. Roosts in trees. **SIMILAR SPECIES:** Peregrine is heavier and more compact, with broader wings, barred on underparts and upperside of tail. Female and juvenile Amur Falcon are more delicately built, longer-tailed, lighter below and on wing-linings; tail barred above, tarsi and toes orange or red; foraging flight more kestrel-like. Pale Eleonora's Falcon is longer-tailed, darker chestnut below, with contrast between dark wing-linings and paler remiges; foraging flight slow and relaxed. Juvenile Sooty Falcon is paler above than young Hobby, more diffusely streaked below, with slightly projecting central tail feathers. **STATUS AND DISTRIBUTION:** Widespread and fairly common palearctic passage migrant, mainly October to early December and late March to early May. Frequents open or wooded grassland, bush and farmland up to 2500 m, but scarce near the coast. Occasionally winters in the highlands.

AFRICAN HOBBY *Falco cuvieri*   Plates 37, 45

Length 28–30 cm (11–12″). A rather small, slim falcon with narrow pointed wings and short tail. **Adult** head pattern like that of Eurasian Hobby, but generally darker slate above and *underparts deep rufous,* with fine black streaks on breast and sides. Tail barred with blackish and pale rufous; wing-linings rufous with blackish streaks; flight feathers faintly barred with buff below. Bill steel-blue; cere, orbital ring and feet yellow; eyes dark brown. In flight, plain dark underparts and slender build identify it. **Juvenile** rufous below with *heavy streaking;* upperparts browner than in adult, the feathers rufous-tipped and tail more boldly barred. Greenish-white cere and orbital skin soon turn yellow; other bare parts as in adult. **VOICE:** A high *kiki-keeee,* and a harsher *kik-kik-kik-kik-kik-kik.* . . . **HABITS:** Solitary or in pairs; perches in tall trees; flight much like that of Eurasian Hobby. Partly crepuscular. Commonly feeds on emerging winged ter-

mites after rain. **SIMILAR SPECIES:** Eurasian Hobby is buff (not deep rufous) below, with more contrasting black streaking on body, and the wings are barred beneath. Taita Falcon is stockier, Peregrine-like, with rufous nape patches and white throat. **STATUS AND DISTRIBUTION:** Uncommon resident of forest edge and woodland patches, mainly in the Lake Victoria basin and w. Kenyan highlands up to 2200 m. Frequently seen along the lakeshore near Kisumu. Scarce in n. Tanzania.

RED-NECKED FALCON *Falco chiquera ruficollis*   Plates 37, 45
(Red-headed Merlin)

Length 30–36 cm (12–14"). A narrow-winged, kestrel-sized falcon typically *associated with Borassus palms.* When perched, wing tips do not reach tip of tail. **Adult** pale *blue-grey above* with fine black barring; *primaries and primary coverts darker; crown, nape and short moustachial stripes rufous;* malar stripes and postocular lines brown; *face and chin to upper breast white,* with a *broad pale rufous band across upper breast;* remaining underparts barred with black; narrowly barred tail has *broad black subterminal band,* conspicuous in flight. Wing-linings barred black and white, remiges barred black and grey; both appear evenly grey at a distance. **Juvenile** browner, darker, more streaked on head and neck, with broad blackish bars on upper wing-coverts. *Underparts dull rufous or creamy buff, with bold black bars on sides and flanks;* small elongate blackish spots on breast and belly. Cere, orbital ring and feet bright yellow; eyes dark brown in both adult and juvenile. **VOICE:** A shrill *keep-keep-keep.* . . . **HABITS:** Solitary or in pairs. Perches in trees, often hidden by foliage. Flight typically low and dashing, with quick wingbeats. Somewhat crepuscular. Feeds mainly on birds taken in flight, sometimes bats and terrestrial vertebrates. Uses old nests of other birds; usually in palms, but uses *Acacia tortilis* at Lake Turkana and perhaps elsewhere in n. Kenya. Favoured breeding sites occupied for years. **SIMILAR SPECIES:** Kestrels are less dashing, shorter-winged and differently patterned. **STATUS AND DISTRIBUTION:** Uncommon in low open country, especially with *Borassus* (sometimes *Hyphaene*) palms. In Kenya, widespread in coastal lowlands south of Mombasa and along the Tana and Galana Rivers upstream to Meru NP and Galana Ranch; also around Lokichokio, Lake Turkana and along the Northern Uaso Nyiro River. Rare in n. Tanzania away from the coast.

AMUR FALCON *Falco amurensis*   Plates 37, 46
(Eastern Red-footed Falcon)

Length *c.* 30 cm (12"). A *small, slim, usually gregarious* falcon, often seen gliding on scythe-like wings. **Adult male** slate-grey, with chestnut leg feathers, lower belly and crissum. In flight, the *white wing-linings* and *silvery-grey flight feathers* contrast with dark tail, body and wing bases. *Cere, narrow orbital ring and feet red.* **Female** has slate-grey upperparts and tail (with faint blackish barring), blackish crown and short moustachial marks on white cheeks. Underparts largely pale buff, blotched and barred with black; legs and crissum washed with pale rufous-buff. Tail and flight feathers boldly barred below. In flight, tail appears white below with broad black bars; wing-linings white with black mottling, remiges boldly barred with black. Cere and feet orange. **Juvenile** resembles female but is browner above, with paler crown, and more streaked below. **VOICE:** As for Red-footed Falcon. Usually silent, except at communal roosts. **HABITS:** Small parties, sometimes hundreds, often migrate with flocks of Lesser Kestrels or Eurasian Rollers. Roosts communally. Graceful and agile, flying with stiff regular wingbeats like Eurasian Hobby; soars and cruises with kestrel-like action, but wings held stiffly when gliding. Catches flying insects; occasionally hovers low above ground, but less persistently than kestrels. Attracted to grass fires and recently burnt areas. Perches on posts and dead trees. **SIMILAR SPECIES:** Eurasian Hobby is slightly larger, with narrower-based wings and shorter tail, unbarred above, its underparts deeper buff and more heavily streaked than those of female Amur. Male Red-footed Falcon has grey (not white) wing-linings; female Red-footed largely unstreaked rufous-buff below and on crown. **STATUS AND DISTRIBUTION:** Palearctic passage migrant, November–December and late March to early May, mainly in open country at low to medium elevations in cent. and se. Kenya. Large flocks pass through the Tsavo region on southward migration. Recorded in coastal lowlands in April. Few n. Tanzanian records, except near Lake Jipe and in Mkomazi GR.

*RED-FOOTED FALCON *Falco vespertinus*   Plates 37, 44, 46
(Western Red-footed Falcon)

Length 29–31 cm (12"). **Adult male** differs from more common Amur Falcon only in having *dark grey wing-linings.* Grey-tipped bill mostly bright orange-red, as are cere, orbital rings and feet. **Female** distinct, with *almost plain rufous-buff crown, nape and underparts;* black on head confined to moustachial marks and postocular streaks; sides of face and throat white; upperparts and tail barred with grey. In flight, rich buff wing-linings contrast with barred flight feathers. Bare parts as in male but duller. **Juvenile** browner above than adult female, and duller below, with streaked breast; pale streaked crown is separated from back by whitish collar. **First-year male** differs from juvenile in partial slate-grey plumage on body and wings. **VOICE:** A high-pitched *kew-kew-kew* . . .

at communal roosts. **HABITS:** As for Amur Falcon. **SIMILAR SPECIES:** Male Amur Falcon has white wing-linings; female Amur is blackish on crown and is heavily marked below, the wing-linings white with black mottling. See Eurasian Hobby. **STATUS AND DISTRIBUTION:** Rare palearctic passage migrant recorded four times in Kenya (Nyanza and Lake Elmenteita, Oct.; Nairobi NP, early May; Tsavo West NP, April).

DICKINSON'S KESTREL *Falco dickinsoni*   Plates 37, 46

Length 28–30 cm (11–12"). A small, robust kestrel with a relatively long tail. Dark eye surrounded by *broad, bright yellow orbital ring*. Adult *slate-grey above, with contrasting greyish-white head and rump*; underparts pale grey; *tail strongly barred* black and pale grey, as is under wing-surface. Tarsi and cere bright yellow. **Juvenile** browner, with *barred flanks; cere blue-green.* **VOICE:** Utters a high *keee-keee* alarm call on breeding grounds; otherwise mostly silent. **HABITS:** Solitary; perches upright on isolated dead trees, from which it flies to ground for prey; also takes insects and birds in the air; sometimes hovers. Not shy. **SIMILAR SPECIES:** Grey Kestrel is slightly larger, with less strongly barred tail and dark grey head and rump (not paler than back); bare orbital ring conspicuous but less pronounced than in Dickinson's. **STATUS AND DISTRIBUTION:** In Kenya, a vagrant recorded six times June–August, near Magadi, below Taita Hills, and in Amboseli, Nairobi and Meru NPs. Rare in mainland n. Tanzania, but a common resident on Pemba Island. Prefers open moist savannas, especially with *Borassus* palms.

ELEONORA'S FALCON *Falco eleonorae*   Plates 37, 44, 45

Length 36–40 cm (14–16"). A slender, streamlined falcon with *long narrow wings* and hobby-like head pattern; larger than Eurasian Hobby, with longer, slightly rounded tail. Adult of usual **pale morph** *slaty or sooty black above, with unbarred tail; underparts rich rufous-buff with black streaking; blackish wing-linings and dark trailing wing edges contrast below with pale unbarred flight-feather bases;* underside of tail faintly barred. **Adult dark morph** (rare on African mainland) largely blackish, the plumage appearing all dark at distance, but paler grey flight-feather bases and tail are evident at close range. Cere and orbital ring pale blue in males, pale yellow in females; feet yellow in both sexes. **Juvenile** browner above, with some buff feather edgings; underparts buff with heavy streaking; remiges and tail barred below, and wing-linings spotted, appearing brown in the field. **VOICE:** A high sharp *ki-ki-kik-ki-ki. . . .* **HABITS:** Swift and agile; pursues prey with deep, regular wingbeats, but forages with a slow, relaxed, almost kestrel-like action; glides and soars. Usually alone or in twos and threes. Partially crepuscular and often associated with rain storms. Feeds on birds and insects (especially winged termites) taken in the air. **SIMILAR SPECIES:** Eurasian Hobby is smaller, shorter-tailed, paler below, and with barred under wing-surface lacking contrasting pattern. Sooty Falcon is shorter-tailed and much greyer. **STATUS AND DISTRIBUTION:** Uncommon palearctic passage migrant, late October to November, occasional March to early May, in wooded country, bush and grassland, mainly in the cent. Kenyan highlands. Rarely recorded in n. Tanzania.

SOOTY FALCON *Falco concolor*   Plates 37, 46

Length 33–36 cm (13–14"). A fast-flying, medium-sized falcon with *long narrow wings;* moderately long tail has *two central feathers slightly protruding,* giving a slightly wedge-shaped appearance. **Adult** *nearly uniform slate-grey,* with slightly darker head and blackish wing tips; paler on back and rump; dark moustachial streaks are accentuated by pale chin. Cere and orbital ring lemon-yellow; feet orange-yellow to reddish in some males. **Juvenile** *buffy yellow below* with slate-grey streaking, often *solidly blotched on breast.* Hobby-like head pattern (slaty cap and moustachial marks, buff cheeks and chin). Cere bluish green; feet pale yellowish green. **VOICE:** A shrill *kikikik* or *ki-ki-lik.* **HABITS:** Usually in ones and twos. Cruises like Hobby, its stiff regular wingbeats interspersed with glides, but fast and agile when hunting. Preys on small bats, birds and insects. Mainly crepuscular. **SIMILAR SPECIES:** Eleonora's Falcon is larger, longer-tailed, with different foraging flight and contrasting underwing pattern; dark morph more blackish than typical Sooty Falcon. Grey Kestrel is much smaller and stockier, with shorter wings, tail bars, uniformly grey face, different habits and slower flight. Eurasian Hobby has black streaking and bolder face pattern than young Sooty Falcon. Juveniles of Eleonora's Falcon and Eurasian Hobby are less yellowish below, and with streaks, not heavy blotching, on breast. **STATUS AND DISTRIBUTION:** A North African/Arabian breeder, regular in small numbers as a passage migrant in cent., e.

and se. Kenya, late October to early December, and (sporadically) late February to early May; mainly in bush and grassland at low to medium elevations. Few n. Tanzanian records.

GREATER KESTREL *Falco rupicoloides arthuri* (White-eyed Kestrel)

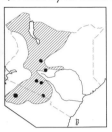

Length *c.* 36 cm (14″). *Stockier and larger-headed than Common Kestrel, with broader, less pointed wings.* **Adult** *pale-eyed*, largely rufous above, with *black streaks on head and bold black barring on back and wings*; underparts pale fawn or cinnamon, with dark streaks on breast and belly; rump and upper tail-coverts grey, barred darker; *tail dark grey, barred with black and tipped white. No moustachial marks.* Eyes creamy white to tan; cere and feet yellow. Dark rufous upper wing-coverts evident in flight; *from below, wings appear whitish with dark tips.* **Juvenile** resembles adult, but *flanks streaked* and flight feathers broadly tipped with buff; *rump and tail rufous with black barring.* Cere and orbital ring blue-green; *eyes brown.* **VOICE**: A double *kweek-kweek;* also sharp *chik* or *kwit* calls. Usually silent except near nest sites. **HABITS**: Perches conspicuously in open country, alone, in pairs, sometimes in loose parties. More sluggish than Common Kestrel; flight rather heavy; occasionally hovers but rarely soars. **SIMILAR SPECIES**: Female and juvenile Common and Lesser Kestrels are smaller, smaller-headed, less strongly barred and dark-eyed; both hover more regularly; they also differ vocally. **STATUS AND DISTRIBUTION**: Local resident of dry open plains with scattered trees and shrubs, at low to medium elevations. Fairly common on the Serengeti Plains, and in s. Kenya from Amboseli NP north to Nairobi; also around Naro Moru and Nanyuki. Population in n. and nw. Kenya, including both sides of Lake Turkana, presumably represents the paler Ethiopian race *fieldi*, but specimen evidence is lacking.

FOX KESTREL *Falco alopex*

Length 35–38 cm (14–15″). A large chestnut kestrel of dry rocky country. Larger than Common Kestrel, with narrow pointed wings and *long graduated tail.* **Adult** rich *chestnut with black streaking above and below; incomplete narrow bars on tail;* no moustachial marks. In flight, remiges dark brown above; tawny-buff wing-linings and whitish flight feathers below. Cere and rims of eyelids yellow; eyes pale brownish yellow; feet yellow-ochre. **Juvenile** more heavily marked than adult, tail more clearly barred. **VOICE**: A high-pitched *kee-kee-kee-kee. . .* ; usually silent except near nest sites. **HABITS**: Flies with quick, shallow wingbeats; frequently soars and glides along cliff faces. Mainly insectivorous. Usually in pairs, but semi-gregarious in n. Turkana. **SIMILAR SPECIES**: Female and juvenile of local dark race of Common Kestrel are duller, more spotted and barred above, with dark moustachial marks, barred under wing-surface, and much shorter, rounder tail with dark terminal band. **STATUS AND DISTRIBUTION**: Uncommon resident of arid and semi-arid areas with inselbergs and cliffs, locally common in n. Kenya near Lake Turkana and in the northwest around Lokichokio and Kamathia. Has wandered south to the Kongelai Escarpment, Lake Baringo and the Ngong Hills. A report from Lobo Lodge in northern Serengeti NP remains unsubstantiated.

GREY KESTREL *Falco ardosiaceus*

Length 30–33 cm (12–13″). *All grey, with a conspicuous broad yellow orbital ring;* cere, bill base and feet also yellow. *Wing tips do not reach tail tip in perched bird.* **Adult** shows dark shaft streaks at close range, and faint light barring on black tail and flight feathers, which appear plain at a distance. **Juvenile** more brownish grey than adult. **VOICE**: *keek-keek-keek* and a harsh twittering. **HABITS**: Flies low, with quick, shallow wingbeats; sometimes hovers. Sluggish; takes small mammals and insects, mainly on ground. Utilizes old nests of other birds (especially Hamerkop). **SIMILAR SPECIES**: Dickinson's Kestrel has paler greyish-white head and rump, strongly barred tail. Adult Sooty Falcon (unlikely in range of Grey Kestrel) is slimmer, with much longer and narrower wings, their tips extending beyond tail tip in perched bird. **STATUS AND DISTRIBUTION**: Uncommon resident of bushed and wooded grassland and savanna from the western Serengeti Plains, Mara GR and Nyanza north to Mt Elgon, occasionally east to Lake Baringo, Nakuru and the Kedong Valley.

LESSER KESTREL *Falco naumanni*

Length 29–33 cm (11–13″). A small falcon with long pointed wings and rather long, *slightly wedge-shaped tail* with broad black terminal band, and, at close range, diagnostic *white claws.* **Adult male** pale *chestnut on back, with crown to nape, rump and tail blue-grey,* the latter with *broad black terminal band;* underparts almost plain creamy buff or pinkish buff. Cere and orbital ring bright yellow, tarsi and toes orange-yellow. In flight, shows *blue-grey band across greater coverts,* largely chestnut forewing and blackish primaries; underside of wing whitish with dark tip. **Female** *rufous, spotted and barred with black above,* and with indistinct, dark moustachial streaks; underparts pale buff with fine brown streaking; wings buff below, with light spotting and barring. Bare

parts as in male. **Juvenile** much like female. **Voice:** A high-pitched *kikikikikikiki*. **Habits:** Gregarious, usually in loose flocks; roosts communally (sometimes thousands of birds) in trees. Attracted to grass fires. Flies with light shallow wingbeats and much gliding; hovers less persistently than Common Kestrel; spends much time catching insects. **Similar Species:** Slightly larger Common Kestrel is more heavily marked below and on underside of wings, has more rounded tail and black claws; male lacks grey band on wing-coverts. **Status and Distribution:** Locally common palearctic passage migrant and winter visitor in bushed, wooded and open grassland and cultivation, mid-October to early May. Most numerous February–April, in highland farming regions and on grassy plains in n. Tanzania and s. Kenya.

COMMON KESTREL *Falco tinnunculus* (Rock Kestrel)

Plates 37, 46

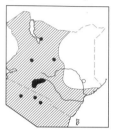

Length 30–33 cm (12–13″). A small falcon with long pointed wings, rather long tail and *black claws*. **Male** of migrant nominate race has *rufous back spotted with black*, blue-grey crown and nape; *grey tail* (sometimes with narrow black barring) has *broad black subterminal band and narrow white tip*; underparts pale buff, streaked with black. In flight, black tail band prominent; blackish primaries contrast above with rufous coverts; wings appear pale below, with faint spotting and barring. **Female** *rufous-brown, heavily spotted and barred with black above*, and with brownish moustachial streaks; tail chestnut, narrowly barred and with broad dark tip; more heavily streaked below than male, and more *heavily marked on underside of wings*. Both sexes have yellow cere, orbital rings and feet. **Juvenile** resembles adult female. Adults of local breeding race *rufescens* generally darker and more rufous below than nominate birds, the male more slaty on the head and on the noticeably barred tail. Coastal *archeri* is considerably smaller than similar *tinnunculus* and more heavily barred above. **Voice:** A shrill *kee-kee-kee-kee-kee-kee*, and *kik-kik-kik-kik.* . . . **Habits:** Solitary or in pairs. Perches on posts, wires or dead trees; preys mainly on small vertebrates and insects, taken on ground. Frequently hovers with tail fanned and depressed; often soars. Resident birds usually associated with rock outcrops and cliffs, but may nest in trees and buildings. **Similar Species:** Male Lesser Kestrel is plain-backed, paler overall, especially below, and has broad blue-grey bar on upperside of wing; female is less strongly marked on underside of wings and tail; white claws visible at close range. Greater Kestrel has more generally barred head and body, barred greyish rump and tail, whitish under wing-surface, lacks moustachial marks, and adults have pale eyes. Fox Kestrel has long, more graduated tail and is richer chestnut above and below. **Status and Distribution:** *F. t. tinnunculus* is a widespread palearctic migrant, mainly October–March, in bushed or open grassland and cultivation at medium to higher elevations. *F. t. rufescens* is an uncommon resident, mainly in the Rift Valley and adjacent highlands, usually near cliffs. The Somali race *archeri* was formerly reported from the Lamu area, but there are no recent records.

QUAIL AND FRANCOLINS, FAMILY PHASIANIDAE
(World, *c.* 177 species; Africa, 45; Kenya, 17; n. Tanzania, 11)

Compact terrestrial birds with sturdy legs, thickset rounded bodies and short wings and tail. Plumage is cryptically patterned above, sometimes boldly marked below. The birds occupy all habitats from semi-desert to forest, and from sea level to montane moorlands. They are sedentary residents, excepting the quail, and are generally found in pairs or small coveys. They prefer to avoid danger by running, taking wing as a last resort. Flight is fast and direct, with rapid wingbeats, although usually low and for only short distances. Most species are highly vocal at times, calls varying from the whistles of quail and Stone Partridge to the loud raucous cackling or grating calls of some francolins. All nest on the ground and lay large clutches. The young are precocial, and able to fly within a few weeks of hatching.

Quail are small birds, dumpy and rounded, seldom seen unless flushed. They might be confused with certain *Sarothrura* species (Rallidae) or button-quail (Turnicidae) which occupy similar habitats. Francolins and the bare-throated spurfowl are larger birds with heavier bills. Field identification relies on plumage pattern, and colours of bare parts and of flight feathers. Four species (Red-winged, Moorland, Orange River and Shelley's) show prominent rufous-chestnut remiges in flight. Adults of these have black bills and yellow feet, as do Ring-necked and Coqui (which lack large rufous wing patches). Except for Yellow-necked and Grey-breasted Spurfowl, the remaining species have red feet. Males of several species have prominently spurred tarsi. Apart from Coqui and Hildebrandt's Francolins, the sexes are alike or similar in plumage.

COMMON QUAIL *Coturnix coturnix*

Plate 27

Length 175–200 mm (7–8″). A small brown and buff bird, usually seen only when flushed from grass or cropland; appears *paler and more heavily streaked above* than female Harlequin Quail. **Adult male** *C. c. erlangeri* is chestnut-faced, with long whitish lateral crown stripes and a narrower central stripe; chestnut or buff throat encloses

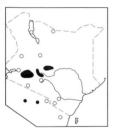

large dark central patch. Upperparts are largely sandy brown, mottled and barred with darker brown and rufous, and with prominent white shaft streaks on most feathers; underparts mostly pale buff, more rufous-buff on breast (marked by white shaft streaks); paler on belly; bold brown streaks on sides and flanks. **Female** paler than male, without dark face or throat patch, and with band of dark spots across upper breast; ear-coverts dark and head striped, as in male. *Buff bars on primaries* separate female from female Harlequin Quail in the hand, but this feature rarely of use in the field. Paler plumage, broad pale side stripes and breast spots are useful marks if underparts are visible. Eyes brown or red-brown; bill black; tarsi and toes yellowish, yellowish pink or pinkish brown. **Rufous morph** rufous-chestnut on throat, sides and flanks. **Juvenile** similar to adult female, but flanks heavily barred. Melanistic birds have been recorded. **Adult** of migrant *C. c. coturnix* is paler above and paler-faced than resident birds, especially on crown and back; both sexes have whitish cheeks, and spring male shows bolder throat mark, this bordered by white below. **VOICE:** Male's usual call a loud, rather metallic, trisyllabic *wheet, wit-it*, repeated several times, fairly high-pitched and quite ventriloquial. At times rhythm differs: *whik-wik, whik*. Several softer melodious and growling calls, and a low vibrant *wew-wew-wew* are audible at close range. In flight, gives a higher-pitched *tree-tree*. **HABITS:** Shy and retiring. Crouches and allows close approach, or runs with lowered head through the grass. Migrants are attracted to fallow fields. Active and most vocal at dawn and dusk. **SIMILAR SPECIES:** Female Harlequin is pale tawny below and spotted on sides of breast, less streaked on sides and flanks, and has unbarred primaries. Female Blue Quail is smaller, has barred sides and flanks. See Common Button-quail. **STATUS AND DISTRIBUTION:** *C. c. erlangeri* is a fairly common resident of grassland and farms between 1700 and 3000 m in the w. and cent. Kenyan highlands. Also known from the Crater Highlands, Arusha District and West Usambara Mts. Nocturnal migrants occasionally recorded in December at Ngulia in Tsavo West NP. Palearctic *C. c. coturnix*, possibly regular in n. Kenya, recorded at Lake Turkana, Huri Hills and Maralal; early specimens taken south to Kisumu, Nairobi, the Loita Hills and Tsavo.

BLUE QUAIL *Coturnix adansonii*   Plate 27

Length 125–135 mm (5–5.5"). *Small and dark.* **Adult male** *slaty blue*, appearing black at a distance, with *chestnut on innermost secondaries, wing-coverts and upper tail-coverts.* The *bold black-and-white face/throat pattern* includes *no white above eyes.* Bill black above, mandible largely blue-grey; eyes red; tarsi and toes dull yellow. **Female** dark brown above, streaked and vermiculated with buff, rufous and black. *Breast, sides and flanks heavily barred with black*; throat plain tawny-buff; belly and under tail-coverts white. Bill brownish horn; eyes red-brown; feet dull yellow. **Juvenile** resembles female but has pale shaft streaks on rump. **VOICE:** "A piping whistle of three notes going down the scale in semi-tones, the first loud and shrill, the others softer." Suggests call of Little Bee-eater (McLachlan and Liversidge 1978). **HABITS:** Shy; flushes reluctantly. Calls infrequently (unlike other quail). Prefers wet or inundated lush grassland. **SIMILAR SPECIES:** Male Harlequin Quail's bold face pattern includes white superciliary stripes. Female Common and Harlequin Quail are larger, with unbarred sides. Common Button-quail is buffier, with greater coverts usually pale-edged. **STATUS AND DISTRIBUTION:** Now a rare intra-African migrant in Kenya. Formerly bred near Kitale, Eldama Ravine and (1941) on the Ngong Escarpment. More recently known from a few scattered records during the rainy season, notably in the Mara GR. In n. Tanzania, recently recorded only from Mkomazi GR but may still breed on Pemba Island. **NOTE:** Often considered conspecific with the Asian *C. chinensis*.

HARLEQUIN QUAIL *Coturnix d. delegorguei*   Plate 27

Length 140–150 mm (5.5–6"). The most frequently seen quail. **Adult male** blackish brown above, streaked with buffy white. Black-and-white face/throat pattern includes *long white superciliary stripes continuing down sides of neck.* White of throat contrasts with *black central underparts* and *black-streaked rufous sides and flanks.* In flight, appears dark with small light streaks on back. Bill black; tarsi and toes dusky white or brownish pink. **Female** closely resembles adult Common Quail and difficult to distinguish in flight, but darker above, and pale tawny below, washed and mottled dusky brown, with variable amounts of *dark spotting* on sides of breast. In the hand, note *plain brown primaries without buff barring*, and *rich rufous-buff under tail-coverts.* Bill horn-brown. **VOICE:** Male's advertising call a fast two- to three-note *whit-whit* or *whit-whit-whit*, when close sounding more like *tswic-tswic-tswic. . .* (no pause after first note as in Common Quail, and the call more ringing and less mellow). Female may answer with soft *quick-ik*. When flushed, a squeaky rolled *skreeee*. **HABITS:** Highly gregarious, with locally large concentrations. Shy; flushes readily, but runs and hides after dropping again to ground. Quite vocal. Strongly nomadic, its movements coinciding with onset of the rains. Attracted to lights at night during migration, resulting in many fatalities. **SIMILAR SPECIES:** Female Common Quail compared above. See Common Button-quail. **STATUS AND DISTRIBUTION:** In Kenya, common and widespread in grasslands except in the north. Large numbers appear in November–December in Tsavo West NP; also annual concentrations on the Lake Victoria floodplain. In n. Tanzania, locally common November–December and from April to June, coinciding with heavy rains.

STONE PARTRIDGE *Ptilopachus p. petrosus* **Plate 27**

Length 240–290 mm (9.5–11.5"). A small, bantam-like bird of *rocky hillsides*, with a *rather long, broad cocked tail.* At a distance appears dark and almost uniform above. The fine barring, strongest on sides and flanks, is evident only at close range. Head 'scaly,' the small feathers paler-edged. Throat and neck are dark-speckled; breast buff in **male**, paler and more whitish in **female**. Bare facial skin dull red; eyes brown; bill dark reddish brown, red around nostrils and yellowish at tip; tarsi and toes dark red. **Juvenile** more distinctly barred above and below. Downy young has blackish-chestnut forehead, crown and centre of back; the dark brown face and underparts are speckled with black. **Voice**: A far-carrying whistled *oueek-oueek-oueek* or *weet-weet. . .*, sometimes more rolling, *rrr-weet, rrr-weet. . .*, often in duet or chorus. **Habits**: Sedentary, in pairs or small groups. Runs and hops rapidly over rocks and boulders, seldom flying; rarely, perches in trees when disturbed. Vocal at dusk and dawn. **Similar Species**: Crested Francolin often runs with cocked tail, but shows whitish superciliaries and pale streaks on back. Favours flat ground. **Status and Distribution**: Fairly common on rocky slopes and in gorges in nw. Kenya, from the Turkwell River gorge south to the Kongelai Escarpment; more local from Laikipia and Lewa Downs north to the Northern Uaso Nyiro River, Baragoi, the Ndotos and South Horr.

COQUI FRANCOLIN *Francolinus coqui* **Plate 27**

Length 215–265 mm (8.5–10.5"). Small, sexually dimorphic and subspecifically variable. **Adult male** *F. c. coqui* has *ochre face and neck*; *underparts barred with black and white* except for plain whitish-buff throat; crown and spot on ear-coverts rufous; upperparts generally grey-brown with buff streaks and black, rufous and buff cross-bars. Flight feathers brown, sometimes with traces of rufous on inner webs, but *no rufous wing patch*. Bill black, with yellow at base of mandible and gape; tarsi and toes yellow. **Female** has buffier face with *two black streaks on each side of head, the lower pair joining around the pale throat; upper breast vinaceous pink or pinkish brown, lower breast and belly buffy white and heavily barred with black, as are sides and flanks.* Western *F. c. hubbardi* has dark brown (not rufous) crown, grey breast and a plain, unbarred buff belly; some individuals may show traces of rufous (barred with black) on outer webs of primaries. Eastern and northern *maharao* equally variable, but more narrowly barred below, usually with some rufous on the primaries. **Juvenile** similar to female, but paler and more mottled rufous-buff above, buff below. **Voice**: Male has two common calls, a shrill, squeaky *KO-ki, KO-ki, KO-ki. . .* or *KWI-ki, KWI-ki. . .*, and *chur-INK-CHINK-CHERRA-cherra-cherra-cherra-cherra.* Alarm call a harsh *churr-churr.* Utters shrill squeaks when flushed. **Habits**: Noisy, especially near dusk. Usually in pairs or small groups. Shy and difficult to flush. Requires good grass cover, but may feed on open, nearly bare ground. Freezes if alarmed. Often walks slowly with neck outstretched almost horizontally. **Similar Species**: Shelley's Francolin somewhat resembles female but is considerably larger, with heavy chestnut markings on breast and sides. **Status and Distribution**: *F. c. coqui* is local and uncommon in coastal lowlands north to edges and openings in the Arabuko–Sokoke Forest, and inland to near Mt Kasigau. *F. c. hubbardi* is widespread and locally common in the central Rift Valley (especially near lakes Naivasha, Elmenteita and Nakuru), ranging to the western highlands and southwest to Mara GR and Serengeti NP. *F. c. maharao* is local and uncommon east of the Rift Valley from Tarangire NP and Arusha District north to Selengai and Machakos; disjunct population in the Huri Hills (and s. Ethiopia).

RING-NECKED FRANCOLIN *Francolinus streptophorus* **Plate 27**

Length 300–330 mm (12–13"). A rare western francolin with *rufous face and neck* contrasting with white throat and superciliaries; *hindneck and breast barred black and white*, forming a broad contrasting band. Upperparts mostly brown, with narrow buffy-white shaft streaks. Underparts rufous-buff, *blotched with dark brown*. Bill mostly black; tarsi and toes pale yellowish. **Female** resembles male, but has darker brown crown and cinnamon-barred underparts with broader buffy-whitish shaft streaks than those of male, and back, rump and upper tail-coverts are barred with buff. **Juvenile** undescribed. **Voice**: Ventriloquial; two dove-like coos, the first lower, followed by a drawn-out soft piping trill (Jackson 1938). Also a noisy flight call. **Habits**: Little known in East Africa. A shy and secretive bird of grass-covered rocky hillsides, solitary or in pairs or small coveys. In Uganda, males call from termitaria and other elevated perches at sunrise. Flight said to be especially rapid. Flushes silently. **Similar Species**: Coqui and Red-winged Francolins have black-and-white barring on hindneck and breast, but Coqui lacks heavy blotching below. Red-winged has rufous on breast below the black-and-white feathering. **Status and Distribution**: Early Kenyan records from the southern slopes of Mt Elgon, the Samia Hills near Busia, Maragoli Escarpment, and near Fort Ternan in the Nyando Valley. Bred on northeastern slopes of Mt Elgon in August 1993.

RED-WINGED FRANCOLIN *Francolinus levaillantii kikuyuensis*   **Plate 28**

Length 360–380 mm (14–15"). Large and warmly coloured; *much orange-buff on head*; breast mostly buff, with rufous streaks and some dark brown spots. *White malar streaks speckled with black and extending along sides of neck, forming a U-shaped band separated from white throat by an ochre or orange-buff band*; black-and-white feathering continues across lower throat/upper breast and around hindneck. Belly buff, vermiculated and broadly barred with black. *Mostly rufous flight feathers and primary coverts prominent in flight*. Bill blackish; tarsi yellow or yellowish brown. **Juvenile** duller; black-and-white pattern less distinct. **VOICE**: A shrill chattering squeal when flushed (as with other 'red-winged' species). Usual call a loud chanting *ki-al-de-werk* (van Someren 1925). The Kipsigis describe it as *tee-til-eet*. **HABITS**: In pairs or coveys of four to six birds. Shy and secretive. Flushes reluctantly, with startling whirr of wings and loud squeal. Calls from mounds or termitaria in early morning. **SIMILAR SPECIES**: Other 'red-winged' francolins lack the narrow rufous-ochre or orangey ring separating white throat from adjacent black-and-white feathering. Moorland Francolin is much larger and shows more rufous in the wings. **STATUS AND DISTRIBUTION**: Scarce resident of grasslands of the w. and sw. Kenyan highlands, where intensive agricultural development has severely restricted and fragmented its once extensive range. Recent records from Soy–Webuye–Kitale area (rapidly declining), and from Lumbwa, Koru, Lolgorien and nw. Mara GR. Two early specimens (July 1909) from n. Serengeti NP.

MOORLAND FRANCOLIN *Francolinus psilolaemus*   **Plate 28**

Length 400–460 mm (16–18"). A richly coloured francolin of *high elevations*. In flight, appears *dark and rusty-winged*. Sexes alike. **Adult** somewhat resembles Shelley's Francolin, but ground-colour of *underparts buff* or rufous-buff, not whitish, and *no heavy black bars on belly*. Sides of face orange-buff, extending as band from eyes down sides of neck, and bordered by lines of black-and-white speckling, the lower moustachial ones encircling the pale buff throat, separating it from the black-spotted rufous lower neck and upper breast; hindneck mottled black and rufous or deep buff. Otherwise buffy brown above, with cream shaft streaks and dark barring, the upper back washed with rufous-tawny. Breast buffy rufous with variable black spots; rest of underparts buff, heavily blotched with chestnut and finely barred with black. *Flight feathers extensively rufous*, as in preceding species. Bill dark brown, yellow at base of mandible; tarsi and toes pale brownish yellow. Birds on Mt Elgon, usually separated as *F. p. elgonensis*, are more rufous (especially on breast) than other Kenyan populations. **Juvenile** undescribed. **VOICE**: Not tape-recorded. Male's call said to be almost identical with that of Shelley's Francolin (Jackson 1938). Flushed birds squeal like Shelley's and Red-winged Francolins. **HABITS**: In pairs or family parties. Visits wheat fields for fallen grain. **SIMILAR SPECIES**: Shelley's Francolin (usually at lower elevations where the two sympatric) is compared above. Red-winged Francolin has ochre band between throat and black-and-white neck ring. **STATUS AND DISTRIBUTION**: Local and uncommon on higher parts of the Mau Escarpment, the Aberdares, and ranging down to 2300 m on the northern slopes of Mt Kenya where wheat fields now extend to the moorlands. Fairly common above 3000 m on moorlands of Mt Elgon.

SHELLEY'S FRANCOLIN *Francolinus shelleyi*   **Plate 28**

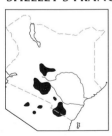

Length 280–310 mm (11–12"). A stocky, white-throated francolin. Sexes alike. Widespread *uluensis* has sides of head tawny-buff, with *black-flecked white postocular lines broadening on neck*; similar *wide black-and-white band extends down each side of neck to encircle the white throat*, and there may be a buff band around the throat, *outside* the black-and-white area. Upperparts light brown, blotched and barred with blackish brown, most feathers with buff shaft streaks. Ground-colour of underparts whitish, not buff or cream; breast and sides heavily streaked with chestnut; *lower breast and belly extensively black-barred*. Remiges show much rufous in flight. Bill black, yellow at base below; tarsi and toes dull yellow. **Juvenile** resembles adult. *F. s. macarthuri* of the Chyulu Hills is slightly darker than *uluensis*. **VOICE**: *F. s. uluensis* has a basically four-note *ski-UK skiki-eu* or *ker-kIRRr, ker-kek*, repeated several times. Utters a shrill squeal when flushed. **HABITS**: In pairs or small groups. Usually shy and secretive (but quite fearless in Nairobi NP). Crouches to avoid danger, readily hiding in tall grass. Reluctant to fly and usually goes only short distance. Most vocal at dusk. **SIMILAR SPECIES**: Red-winged Francolin has rufous-ochre or orange-buff ring between white throat and black-and-white 'necklace'; hindneck also black and white. Moorland Francolin of higher elevations has buffier throat, is rufous or rufous-buff on breast and without prominent black barring below. Both species show much more rufous in wings than does Shelley's. **STATUS AND DISTRIBUTION**: *F. s. uluensis* is locally common in grasslands with scattered acacias in the cent. and e. Kenyan highlands from Laikipia and Mt Kenya south to Naivasha, Ngong, Nairobi, Athi Plains, Machakos and Kajiado Districts, also disjunctly (subspecies?) in the Tsavo region from Bura and Taveta to Lake Jipe, with scattered Tanzanian records from Mkomazi GR, the North Pare Mts, Arusha NP and the Crater Highlands. The race *macarthuri* is endemic to the Chyulu Hills.

ORANGE RIVER FRANCOLIN *Francolinus levaillantoides archeri*   **Plate 28**
(Smith's Francolin; Archer's Grey-wing)

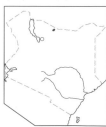

Length 290–305 mm (11.5–12"). A rare northern bird similar to Shelley's Francolin (the two possibly conspecific), but *creamy buff below with numerous short black streaks throughout,* sparse broad chestnut streaks on breast and flanks, *and inconspicuously barred with dusky on lower belly and crissum.* Juvenile undescribed. **Voice:** *Ki-KEET, ki-KIT,* the repeated phrase faster, more strident and higher-pitched than that of *F. shelleyi uluensis,* but otherwise similar. **Habits:** Little known. Shy, and apparently behaves much as Shelley's and Moorland Francolins. **Similar Species:** Shelley's Francolin has whitish underparts, the belly and crissum strongly barred with black. Moorland Francolin is more rufous or rufous-buff below, with black spots on rufous upper breast. **Status and Distribution:** Known in Kenya from a specimen collected at 1950 m on Mt Kulal in October 1973, and from sight records and tape recordings made in the Huri Hills (1100–1350 m) in November 1989. Also collected on Mt Moroto, ne. Uganda. **Note:** This form has been merged with Somali *lorti* by some authors.

CRESTED FRANCOLIN *Francolinus sephaena*   **Plate 27**

Length 240–300 mm (9.5–11.75"). Small and bantam-like, often seen *running with tail cocked* and *crown feathers raised. Largely black tail conspicuous in flight.* Plumage variable, especially below. **Adult male** *F. s. grantii* brown to rufous-brown above with *conspicuous white streaking.* Head well marked with *bold white superciliary and loral/subocular stripes* and *black moustachial stripes* that merge with rufous or brown spots around the plain white throat. Upper breast has band of triangular chestnut-brown spots; rest of underparts whitish or buff with coarse longitudinal vermiculations, these sometimes heavy on breast, sides and flanks, which may also be streaked with whitish. Flight feathers brown. Bill black, tarsi and toes dull red. **Female** and **juvenile** resemble male but are more vermiculated and barred; young birds are more broadly white-streaked above. Coastal *F. s. rovuma* lacks the dark moustachial stripes and has numerous short brown streaks on breast, belly, sides and flanks. Far-northern *spilogaster* is larger, with narrower ventral streaking. **Voice:** A high, strident, squealing cackle, given rapidly and often in duet or chorus, *kerra-kreek, kerra-kreek. . .*; and an antiphonal *kee, kek-kerra. . .*, repeated frequently, the first note uttered by one bird, second and third by another. **Habits:** In pairs or small noisy coveys, often on bare ground, dirt roads and tracks. Rests in shade of dense shrub during midday. Conspicuous and approachable where protected; secretive elsewhere. Roosts in trees. Vocal on moonlit nights and at intervals throughout the day. **Similar Species:** See Stone Partridge. **Status and Distribution:** Common and widespread in Kenya and n. Tanzania, typically in dry riverine scrub and dense thickets below 1500 m. Probably the most numerous Kenyan francolin, despite great declines in populated areas. Largely absent from the Lake Victoria basin (formerly common near Kisumu) and the w. and cent. highlands. Most Kenyan birds are *F. s. grantii.* The race *rovuma* ranges throughout the coastal lowlands, and *spilogaster* is known from the Moyale area.

SCALY FRANCOLIN *Francolinus squamatus*   **Plate 28**

Length 300–330 mm (12–13"). A stocky, dark 'red-legged' francolin of *forest or forest edge.* **Adult** dark brown on back and scapulars, with black-and-buff feather edgings; lower back, rump and upper tail-coverts vermiculated with dusky; markings less coarse and belly paler in birds west of the Rift Valley. Underparts paler than back, greyer brown and densely vermiculated with darker brown, especially on feather edges, producing *scaly effect;* chin whitish. *Bill entirely coral-red or vermilion,* said sometimes to be brown above and orange below (immatures?); bare postocular skin greyish yellow; tarsi and toes orange-red; one or two tarsal spurs in male. **Juvenile** resembles adult, but upperparts more rufous-brown with black arrowhead markings, and underparts barred with black and white. **Voice:** A loud grating *ke-RAAK, ke-RAAK,* or *kerrAK-KAK-KAK,* reiterated and increasing in volume; often given in chorus from roosting sites. **Habits:** Elusive. In pairs or small groups. Loudly vocal at dawn and dusk, sometimes at night. Forages in clearings and glades, but retreats to safety of forest when disturbed. Roosts in trees. **Similar Species:** Larger Jackson's Francolin has coarsely streaked chestnut-and-white underparts. **Status and Distribution:** In Kenya, widespread in highland evergreen forests and bamboo from Mt. Elgon, the Cheranganis and Mt Nyiru south to Mt Kenya, the Aberdares, Mau Forest, northern Nairobi suburbs (where now scarce), and disjunctly to the Chyulu Hills. In n. Tanzania, common in Arusha NP and on western slopes of Kilimanjaro. Has to some extent adapted to dense bush with disappearance of forest. Three rather poorly defined subspecies: *schuetti* mostly west of the Rift Valley and *maranensis* to the east; *usambarae* formerly in the Usambara Mts, but no recent records.

HILDEBRANDT'S FRANCOLIN *Francolinus hildebrandti* **Plate 27**

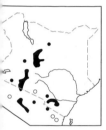

Length 320–410 mm (12.5–16"). A large, sturdy francolin with *pronounced sexual dimorphism*. **Adult male** *F. h. hildebrandti* is whitish below, *heavily spotted with black*, the marks large on breast, belly and flanks, smaller and more dense on throat and chin; neck with finer black-and-white streaks grading into whitish or creamy U-shaped markings on dark back. Upperparts mostly brown, finely and indistinctly vermiculated. Head largely grey with fine white speckling, the crown and ear-coverts brown, forehead and lores black. Bill brown above, orange-yellow at base, mandible and gape dark red, orange or orange-yellow; tarsi and toes usually coral-red, sometimes bright orange-yellow, the joints dusky; toes dusky black. In *F. h. altumi* upper breast is heavily spotted and mottled with blackish, but flanks only sparsely so. **Female** smaller, *rich tawny or rufous-buff below*, with some whitish feather edges; only a faint grey wash on the breast, the underparts appearing almost uniform buff in *F. h. hildebrandti*. Bill brown above, coral-red to reddish orange below and at gape; tarsi coral-red. **Juvenile** resembles female, but underparts more buffy brown, spotted and streaked (rather than blotched) with black; upperparts as in female, but more distinctly barred with black and rufous-buff. **Voice:** Advertising call a rapid, rather high-pitched and raucous *kek-kerek-kek-kek* and variations, often from several birds calling together. **Habits:** In pairs or small flocks, usually in dense scrub and thickets on rocky hillsides or flat ground. Dust-bathes in open places, including dirt roads. Roosts in trees. Highly vocal at dawn and dusk. **Similar Species:** Scaly Francolin is smaller, has brighter orange-red bill and scaly pattern below. **Status and Distribution:** Locally common in woodland, riparian forest, dense bush and forest edge in the central Rift Valley from Lake Manyara NP north to Nakuru, and in sw. Kenya from Narok to the Loita and Nguruman Hills, and eastern edge of the Mara GR. Also from Voi and Ngulia to Ololokwe, Maralal, Barsaloi, the Ndotos and Marsabit. Scattered n. Tanzanian populations in Tarangire and Arusha NPs (extending upward to the heath zone in the latter), the Crater Highlands and at Loliondo. Numerous and easily seen in Lake Nakuru, Hell's Gate and Arusha NPs. **Note:** Variation is clinal, and some authors recognize no subspecies. We treat as *F. h. altumi* birds of the Kenyan Rift Valley and western highlands from the Ngurumans to Elgeyu, Sotik and the Malawa River on the Kenyan/Ugandan border. Males of northern Kenyan birds, once separated as *helleri*, are more reddish-brown above and more extensively white below; females are more olive-brown, less greyish.

JACKSON'S FRANCOLIN *Francolinus jacksoni* **Plate 28**

Length 380–480 mm (15–19"). A *large, heavily streaked* francolin with *white chin/throat* and *red bill*. Narrow orbital ring, tarsi and toes also red. **Adult** boldly *streaked chestnut and white below*, generally rufous-brown above; lores chestnut. Female noticeably smaller than male. **Juvenile** duller than adult, with some barring on belly. **Voice:** High-pitched loud cackling reminiscent of Scaly Francolin. **Habits:** Forages in thick shrubby growth and adjacent openings. Uses dirt roads and tracks for dust-bathing (and drying plumage in wet weather). Typically shy, but confiding where protected. **Similar Species:** Scaly Francolin is smaller, with different ventral pattern. Moorland Francolin shows no red on bare parts. **Status and Distribution:** Endemic to East Africa. Common and widespread at edges of montane forest, in bamboo and giant heath between 2500 and 3500 m on Mt Kenya and the Aberdares. Smaller numbers in high parts of the Mau Forest and Cherangani Hills. Two sight records from Mt Elgon (one from the Ugandan side, where generally replaced by Moorland Francolin). Readily seen in the Aberdares.

CHESTNUT-NAPED FRANCOLIN *Francolinus castaneicollis atrifrons* **Plate 28**

Length 410–460 mm (16–18"). A large, *red-billed*, Ethiopian francolin with *black forehead and superciliary stripes*. This race quite plain, lacking the rich chestnut dorsal coloration and heavy ventral streaking of some other subspecies; only a faint rufous tinge to some feathers on sides of head. Crown dull brown; neck and back feathers widely bordered with dull white; black upper-back feathers with two buffy white U- or V-shaped markings; lower back, rump and upper tail-coverts olivaceous brown. *Underparts pale creamy buff*; foreneck feathers, below unmarked throat, have V-shaped brown centres, these fainter and diffuse on pale brown lower neck. Sides and flanks with dusky shaft streaks and faint sparse brown barring; leg feathers dull brown. Feet coral-red, the tarsi double-spurred in male; eyes dark brown. **Juvenile** undescribed. **Voice** (subspecies?): A loud raucous *kek-kek-kek-kerak* (Urban *et al.* 1986). **Habits:** In Ethiopia, inhabits broad-leaved forest edge and juniper woods, typically in small groups. Often feeds in the open during midday. Vocal throughout daylight hours. **Status and Distribution:** Known in Kenya from a single sight record south of Moyale (21 June 1975).

RED-NECKED SPURFOWL *Francolinus afer* **Plate 28**
(Red-necked Francolin)

Length 350–410 mm (14–16"). Plumage variable, but **adults** of all races have *bare red throat, orbital skin, bill, tarsi and toes* (bill blackish in juveniles). **Adult male** of coastal *F. a. leucoparaeus* has brown crown and black forehead; upperparts otherwise dark brown with blackish feather centres; sides of face grey-streaked. Upper breast greyish with black shaft streaks, *rest of underparts black with some white streaking*. In flight, pale brown

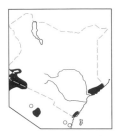

outer primary webs evident, but no prominent buff patch as in Yellow-necked Spurfowl. Tarsi spurred. **Female** smaller than male and with less prominent black belly patch; not spurred. **Juvenile** duller and browner, with blackish streaks on back and brown bars on underparts; feathered throat speckled with brown; feet greyish red and bill blackish. **Adult** of smaller *F. a. cranchii* is more uniform brownish grey, with sides of face mottled greyish black and dusky underparts with greyish-white vermiculations and sparse rufous streaking. **Voice:** A repeated squealing cackle, higher-pitched than similar call of Yellow-necked Spurfowl: *ku-WAAARK* or *ko-RAAAK*. **Habits:** Most active early and late in the day, in pairs or small groups. Spends little time in the open. Roosts in trees. Prefers moister habitats with denser cover than those occupied by Yellow-necked Spurfowl. **Similar Species:** Yellow-necked Spurfowl has yellow throat and shows conspicuous pale primary patches in flight. Grey-breasted Spurfowl (n. Tanzania only) has dark brown tarsi and orange or pinkish-red skin on face and throat. **Status and Distribution:** *F. a. leucoparaeus* inhabits coastal Kenyan lowlands north to the Shimba Hills, and from Lamu to the Boni Forest. *F. a. cranchii* is locally common in the Lake Victoria basin (especially Ruma NP), extending southeast to Mara GR and n. Serengeti NP. Also present (race?) in Tarangire NP. Birds in coastal Tanzanian lowlands south of Tanga and inland to Korogwe may represent the southern *melanogaster*.

YELLOW-NECKED SPURFOWL *Francolinus leucoscepus*   Plate 28
(Yellow-necked Francolin)

Length 345–430 mm (13.75–17"). A large, open-country francolin with *bare yellow throat* and orange or vermilion facial skin. **Adult** dark brown above with buffy white barring and shaft streaks. Underparts streaked dark brown and buffy white; bright yellow throat, deepening to orange on chin in some birds. Bill blackish, orange-red at base below; tarsi and toes dark brown or black. In flight, wings show *conspicuous pale buff patch in primaries.* Female smaller than male and lacks spurs. **Juvenile** resembles adult but is vermiculated with grey and blackish above, with paler yellow throat skin. **Voice:** Advertisement call a series of loud, raucous, grating notes, *ko-WAAARK, ko-WAAARK* lower-pitched than call of Red-necked Spurfowl. Also gives a longer *ka-WEEEERRRK ka-WEEEERRRK, KREEEK- kraak-kraak-kraak. . .,* fading at end of series. **Habits:** Pairs or small groups feed in the open, frequently on dirt roads and tracks, often digging in elephant dung. Males may call from termite mound or other eminence, or from cover. Confiding where protected. Runs from danger but also flies readily, sometimes far. Most active in early morning and evening. Roosts above ground. **Similar Species:** See Red-necked and Grey-breasted Spurfowls. **Status and Distribution:** In Kenya, fairly common and widespread in light bush and savanna, largely below 2300 m, although now numerous only in protected areas. Absent from the Lake Victoria basin and much of the highlands. West of Lake Turkana confined to the Ilemi Triangle and Ugandan border areas. Reaches the coast only between Sabaki and Tana Rivers. In n. Tanzania, widespread in thorn-scrub from Lake Jipe and Mkomazi GR west to the eastern Serengeti where it meets and hybridizes with Grey-breasted Spurfowl.

GREY-BREASTED SPURFOWL *Francolinus rufopictus*   Plate 122
(Grey-breasted Francolin)

Length 320–410 mm (12.5–16"). A n. *Tanzanian* endemic, similar in size to Yellow-necked Spurfowl, and with similar buff patch in primaries, but with *pinkish-red bill, white moustachial streaks, vermilion-orange facial skin* and orange or pinkish-red throat. *Tarsi and toes dark brown,* not red as in Red-necked Spurfowl; eyes dark brown; bill brownish orange, shading to greyish at tip, red at base. Upperparts grey-brown, with dark brown streaks throughout and broad chestnut streaks on upper back. *Sides of neck and breast grey* with sepia streaks, dull creamy-white belly streaked with chestnut and sepia. Female not spurred. **Juvenile** similar to adult, but with grey-and-black vermiculations on upperparts, black-and-white barring below. **Voice:** Similar to that of Yellow-necked Spurfowl. **Habits:** Generally in pairs or small groups in open acacia woodland and dense riparian thickets. Roosts in trees. **Similar Species:** Other spurfowl compared above. **Status and Distribution:** Locally common along the Seronera River valley in central Serengeti NP, ranging southeast to Lake Lygarja, where known to hybridize with Yellow-necked Spurfowl.

GUINEAFOWL, FAMILY NUMIDIDAE
(World and Africa, 6 species; Kenya and n. Tanzania, 3)

Sometimes treated as a subfamily of Phasianidae, these large terrestrial game birds have a sparsely feathered head and neck, characteristic pale-dotted and vermiculated dark plumage, and either a bony casque or feathered crest on a head small in proportion to body size. Sexes are alike. All are ground nesters, laying large clutch s of plain or speckled eggs. The nidifugous downy young are tended by both parents. Guineafowl are highly vocal, uttering distinctive strident rattling calls that often warn other animals of approaching danger.

CRESTED GUINEAFOWL *Guttera pucherani*   Plate 28
(includes Kenya Crested Guineafowl)

Length 46–51 cm (18–20"). A *forest* bird with *shaggy or mop-like crest* of curly feathers covering top of the head. Black **adult** plumage spotted with small round *bluish dots*, these extending up to the naked neck and throat in eastern *G. p. pucherani* (Kenya Crested Guineafowl). That form has *bright cobalt-blue neck, with red throat, foreneck and extensive orbital area*, red eyes, bluish-white bill and dark brown or blackish tarsi. In flight, shows pale brown wing patches. Western *G. p. verreauxi* has a somewhat shaggier crest, an *unspotted broad purplish-black collar* around lower neck, *dark brown eyes*, vermilion throat and foreneck but *no red on side of face*; dusky blue orbital skin and lores, rest of head and neck blue; bill dull light greenish above and pale blue below; feet dusky grey, darker on toes and bluish around the tibiotarsal joint. **Juvenile** *verreauxi* lacks blue spotting, is dusky below with buff and rufous feather edges, rusty brown on back and wing-coverts, where barred with black and rufous; buff feather tips and a blue wash on many feather bases; dark grey secondaries flecked with black and tipped with pale buff, the innermost with some blue barring; head ochre-buff, with black central line from bill widening to form black patch on hindcrown and neck; bill horn-brown; bare grey facial/throat skin grey; feet brownish. **Downy young** *dark brown* above, at first with broad buffy white stripes on scapular areas, later only sparse pale buff spots; crown blackish brown with rufous-buff central spot and stripe, tawny-buff lateral stripes bordered below by broad mottled brownish stripes extending to eyes and generally dark brown ear-coverts; wings mottled and barred with buff and cinnamon, buffier dorsally; underparts rufous-buff, pale buff on throat; feet yellow. **VOICE:** Commonly heard alarm call a fast rattling *chuk-chuk-chukkkkkrrrrr*, lower-pitched and less strident than calls of Helmeted Guineafowl. Flocks taking refuge in trees engage in loud cackling. Contact call a soft *chuk*. **HABITS:** Usual flocks of five to 20 birds break up into pairs for breeding. Shy and retiring, mostly in forest undergrowth, but in clearings and on paths or dirt roads at dawn or after heavy rains; regularly dust-bathes. Cocks tail when alarmed. Flies noisily into tree canopy if disturbed, and feeds on arboreal fruits as well as on terrestrial plant material and invertebrates. **SIMILAR SPECIES:** Helmeted Guineafowl, not in forest, has bony casque instead of crest; plumage spotted with white, not blue. **STATUS AND DISTRIBUTION:** *G. p. pucherani* is locally fairly common in wooded coastal areas north to the Boni Forest, ranging inland to Lake Manyara NP, and to the eastern edge of the cent. Kenyan highlands, meeting *verreauxi* (= *G. edouardi sethsmithi*) in the southern Aberdares. The latter race is uncommon in the western highlands from Mt Elgon and the Cheranganis south to the Nandi, Kakamega and Mau Forests, with smaller isolated populations south to Lolgorien, Mara GR and northern Serengeti NP. **NOTE:** With considerable reservation we follow Crowe (1978) in considering our two forms conspecific. These meet in the Kenyan highlands, but the situation there has not been carefully studied. We have seen no birds with intermediate characters. In southern Africa, *G. p. barbata* intergrades with *pucherani* and *edouardi*.

VULTURINE GUINEAFOWL *Acryllium vulturinum*   Plate 28

Length 61–71 cm (24–28"). A spectacular, tall, *long-tailed* guineafowl. **Adult** *black, white and brilliant cobalt-blue* with *striped lanceolate feathers* on neck, back and breast; lower breast and belly plumage bright blue on sides, black centrally. Rear half of body and wings black with white dots; secondaries edged with lilac. Bare head and neck grey, with band of short dense chestnut feathers on back and lower sides of head. Eyes red; bill dull pale yellowish green; tarsi and toes black. **Juvenile** grey-brown, mottled and barred with rufous-brown, buff and black; long neck and breast feathers much duller than in adults; blue underparts also dull; wings brown, barred with buff. **Downy young** yellowish buff with dark brown mottling, curved facial streaks and mid-dorsal stripe. **VOICE:** Usual call a strident metallic rattle or trill, *chink-chink-chink-cheenk-cheek-krrrrrrrrr*, when disturbed or threatened, higher-pitched than call of Helmeted Guineafowl. Lower-pitched *chink* contact notes are uttered by foraging birds. **HABITS:** Gregarious, in small or large flocks except when breeding. Feeds in open areas near cover. Tight groups rest in shade during hot hours. Roosts in tall trees at night, but rarely leaves ground in daytime. **STATUS AND DISTRIBUTION:** Locally common in dry bush (especially *Acacia* and *Commiphora*) and savanna in n. and e. Kenya, west to Lake Turkana, the Ndotos, Lumuruti and Isiolo. In the southeast, local in Tsavo East NP, at Maktau, Ngulia plains and Lake Jipe in Tsavo West NP, extending to Mkomazi GR and the Masai Steppe in n. Tanzania. Locally common on Kenyan coast from Larawa north to Kiunga.

HELMETED GUINEAFOWL *Numida meleagris*   Plate 28
(includes Tufted Guineafowl)

Length 58–64 cm (23–25"). A widespread guineafowl with a *bony casque on top of the head*. Bare skin of head and neck of **adult** largely blue; gape wattles racially variable in shape and colour. Plumage dark grey or black-

ish, densely fine-dotted and vermiculated with white. Eyes dark brown; bill pale grey ish or dull yellowish horn, with dense tuft of hard keratinous bristles (to 6 mm long) or cere; tarsi and toes blackish. Four races: northern *N. m. meleagris* has black lower hind neck merging into a dark grey collar finely barred with white; stumpy or elongated casque on crown mainly brownish horn in colour; bare facial skin and *flat rounded gape wattles pale blue*. Southern *N. m. reichenowi* has throat and entire hindneck from base of casque to collar black, facial skin blue with *somewhat pointed red gape wat tles*; long casque dark horn. *N. m. somaliensis* resembles *meleagris*, but has small stumpy casque, longer (to 24 mm) bristles at base of bill, a row of black filoplumes on midline of hindneck, and blue wattles that are somewhat pointed and red-tipped. *N. m mitrata* resembles *reichenowi*, but with smaller casque, wattles as in *somaliensis* and blue-grey facial skin. **Juvenile** grey-brown with small buff spots, rufous-brown barring (especially above) and fine black speckling; retains natal down on head. **Immature** has adult-like plumage, but neck well feathered and casque and wattles smaller. **Downy young** mottled rich brown and buff above, the broad dark brown median area enclosing two cream or pale tawny stripes. Dark brown crown bordered by long tawny lateral stripes, them selves bordered below by a solid dark line; another dark line from above eye to ear-coverts. Underparts tawny buff, more whitish on throat. Bill and feet rufous; eyes grey. **Voice:** Common alarm call a raucous staccato *kik kik-kik-kik-kaaaaaa*, the strident ending burring or trilling; also used for pre-roosting assembly. Contact call o soft metallic *chink* notes. **Habits:** Gregarious, in large flocks through much of year. Birds forage and dust-bathe in open areas, regularly walking, often in single file, to water. They roost in trees. Runs with wings partly raised the secondaries arched over the back. **Similar Species:** Vulturine Guineafowl stands taller, has conspicuous bright blue on breast, long lanceolate feathers on foreparts, chestnut on head. Crested Guineafowl is a forest bird with feathered crest. **Status and Distribution:** Widespread resident of bush, woodland, savanna and shrubby grassland, numerous in the south but uncommon in n. Kenya. *N. m. meleagris* ranges south to the edge of the cent. and w. Kenyan highlands; northeastern *somaliensis* is known south to Wajir. Populations south of the Equator are *reichenowi*, except for *mitrata* of coastal lowlands north to the Tana River.

BUTTON-QUAIL AND QUAIL-PLOVER, FAMILY TURNICIDAE
(World, 17 species; Africa, 3; Kenya, 3; n. Tanzania, 2)

Button-quail or hemipodes are small terrestrial grassland and bush birds resembling true quail of the genus *Coturnix* (Phasianidae), but differing behaviourally and anatomically. Both button-quail and Quail-plover run swiftly in cover, but in the open they may employ a peculiar chameleon-like forward-and-backward movement progressing extremely slowly. Like quail, they have plump rounded bodies, short broad wings (longer in *Ortyxelos*) and cryptic plumage, but the bill is more slender, the hind toe is absent and there is no crop. The sof short tail is barely visible in flight, which is only for short distances before the bird drops into cover and scurries away. The female is slightly larger and more brightly coloured than the male and she does the courting and vocal izing. Button-quail are thought to be polyandrous. The nesting season may be prolonged, with opportunistic breeding in any month if conditions are suitable. The female lays her blotched and spotted eggs (five to seven in *Turnix*, two in *Ortyxelos*) in a ground nest, where they are incubated mainly by the male. He also broods and feeds the young, which become independent before fully grown.

QUAIL-PLOVER *Ortyxelos meiffrenii*
(Lark Button-quail)

Plate 2?

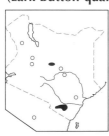

Length 112–130 mm (4.5–5"). A tiny grassland bird *suggesting a miniature courser o plover; in lark-like flight, the rounded wings are strikingly patterned rufous, black and white*. **Adult male** generally *rufous-brown above, with broad cream or pale buff super ciliary stripes and similar streaks on the back*. Some birds show a rufous-brown postoc ular line extending to side of neck, others are entirely pale around eyes except for rufous smudge on the ear-coverts. Underparts whitish, with the breast buff or with con spicuous rufous-bordered cream spots; sides may show rufous wash. Most wing-covert cream or white with some rufous markings. Dorsal pattern individually variable; in fresh plumage the dull rufous back feathers and scapulars have broad U-shaped whitish mar gins, smaller pale spots and a few black marks. Bill greenish brown to pale green, pale yellowish horn at base; culmen may be bluish brown; eyes light brown; tarsi and toe whitish flesh or creamy yellow, also said to be dark brownish pink in some birds. **Female** similar, but breast dark rufous-brown. **Juvenile** paler, less rufous than adult, and more vermiculated above. **Voice:** A soft low whistle likened to the sound of wind blowing through a pipe (Bannerman 1953). Not described in detail. **Habits** Solitary or in pairs. Runs rapidly and stands erect, but if intruder is close may crouch and freeze; chameleon-like locomotion used on bare ground or in sparse grass cover. Flushes silently, almost underfoot, and flies in some what undulating, erratic flight, quite like a *Mirafra* lark, slowing, further spreading wings and elevating tail before dropping into the grass. Somewhat nocturnal, at times active in rainy weather, and said to be vocal on moonli nights. **Similar Species:** All shorebirds have different plumage patterns. Button-quail and *Coturnix* quail have

more direct whirring flight and no pronounced wing pattern. **STATUS AND DISTRIBUTION**: Local and generally uncommon in semi-arid n. and e. Kenyan grasslands. Recorded from the Turkwell River, Lake Baringo, Samburu and Shaba GRs, Kora NR, Meru and the Tsavo NPs and Galana Ranch. In Tanzania, known only from Tarangire NP, but to be expected in the Mkomazi GR.

COMMON BUTTON-QUAIL *Turnix sylvatica lepurana*   Plate 27
(Little or Kurrichane Button-quail; Andalusian Hemipode)

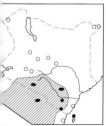

Length 140–150 mm (5.5–6"). A *tiny, very short-tailed, quail-like* bird, usually seen in flight, when *darker, grey-brown flight feathers contrast with pale buff and rufous wing-coverts.* Flight somewhat quail-like, but slower and more fluttery, less whirring; sometimes feet dangle at take-off; body appears more slender than that of true quail which have longer, narrower and more uniformly dark wings. Appearance more quail-like when squatting in grass or running. *Upperparts* of **Adult** *largely dull rufous-brown with indistinct scaly pattern and narrow black bars.* In fresh plumage, broad buffy-white edges of the longer wing-coverts (and of innermost secondaries, long posthumerals and a few scapulars) form a *long pale wing patch,* spotted with dull rufous and dark brown, and contrasting with the grey-brown primaries and outer secondaries. Forehead and sides of crown speckled buff and black, crown centre dull rufous with pale buff or cream median stripe; face pale buff, heavily speckled with black (may show small rufous ear patch); throat mottled pale buff, black-speckled at sides; *breast bright orange-rufous,* with *bold black U-shaped spots from sides to upper flanks.* Female more richly coloured than male. *Eyes cream or white;* bill pale grey; tarsi and toes pale flesh-pink. **Immature** duller, crown stripe less well defined, some dorsal feathers with white lateral spots, and underparts white or creamy buff with orange-buff wash and *band of dark brown spots across breast.* **Juvenile** has poorly defined central crown stripe, more white spots on dorsal feathers, sides of breast rufous-brown speckled with dark-bordered white spots, and a band of V-shaped dark spots across the breast. **Downy young** rufous-brown above, with pale buff central crown and superciliary stripes; underparts pale buff. **VOICE**: Courting female gives a deep resonant droning *hoom, hoom, hoom,* repeated frequently at short intervals. Sometimes develops into a kind of soft drumming (Sclater and Moreau 1932); slower and deeper than call of Red-chested Flufftail. Also has two long-drawn penetrating notes, the first high-pitched and longer, the second an octave lower and shorter (Chapin 1932). Male said to have a sharp *tuc-tuc,* or a high kestrel-like *kee-kee-kee-kee* (Urban *et al.* 1986). **HABITS**: Subject to local movements during rainy seasons, when often in loose or scattered groups, otherwise solitary or in pairs. When flushed, flies low for a short distance, raises wings for a split-second on alighting; runs rodent-like after landing and very difficult to flush a second time. Calls day and night, but most vocal at dawn and dusk. Female calls with bill closed and pointing downward, the extended neck much distended at sides. **SIMILAR SPECIES**: Black-rumped Button-quail has black rump, tail-coverts and tail, and an orange-rufous face (including superciliaries, which lack black speckling). *Coturnix* quail lack bright breast patch and show no contrasting wing pattern in flight. **STATUS AND DISTRIBUTION**: Locally common in dry and moist grassland, savanna and fallow cultivation. Recorded from all major grassland areas, particularly Serengeti NP, Mara GR, cent. Rift Valley, the Tsavo parks, and Arusha District. Sometimes attracted to lights at Ngulia (Tsavo West NP) during November–December rains.

BLACK-RUMPED BUTTON-QUAIL *Turnix hottentotta nana*   Plate 27
(Hottentot Button-quail)

Length 140 mm (5.5"). A scarce bird of moist or wet grasslands or marshy places. *Black rump, upper tail-coverts and tail* clearly visible in flight. Otherwise appears mottled brown and tawny above, with extensive fine black-and-white barring; scapulars broadly edged golden-buff or orange-rufous, forming a long streak on each side of back. Breast rich buff to orange-rufous, with short black-and-white bars on sides (sometimes across breast) and extending to flanks; belly white. Wing-coverts and associated inner wing feathers generally rufous and buff, but contrasting less with brown flight feathers than in the preceding species. **Male** has speckled malar area, black forehead and crown (sometimes pale rufous), and whitish or golden-buff throat; these orange-rufous in **female**. Bill dark brown, yellowish grey below; eyes usually pale creamy tan or whitish, but may be pale blue-grey; tarsi and toes pale pink or dusky white. **VOICE**: A *Sarothrura*-like *ooooop-ooooop* (Sinclair 1984); also a series of shorter resonant *hoo* notes. **HABITS**: Shy and secretive. Flies silently, fast and low for short distance before dropping into cover; runs after landing and seldom flushes a second time. **SIMILAR SPECIES**: Harlequin Quail, common in damp grassy places, has blackish-brown rump but with cream, not golden-buff or orange-rufous, streaks on back; distinguished by different flight, longer and more uniformly dark wings, more ample tail, rufous or rufous-brown posterior underparts (largely white in *Turnix*). In flight, body of Common Button-quail appears more uniformly rufous-brown above (although rump and upper tail-coverts are somewhat darker), and a contrasting pale patch formed by buff wing-covert margins is usually apparent. **STATUS AND DISTRIBUTION**: Now extremely scarce following extensive agricultural development in the Trans-Nzoia area of nw. Kenya, where once apparently regular; only two records from the Kitale area since 1950. To be sought in moist or partially flooded grasslands and at edges of marshes.

RAILS AND RELATIVES, FAMILY RALLIDAE
(World, 142 species; Africa, 26; Kenya, 17; n. Tanzania, 15)

This family displays considerable diversity of form, and includes the small, partly terrestrial flufftails (*Sarothrura*) as well as the large, heavy-set, aquatic coots and gallinules. Plumage patterns tend to be cryptic, and pronounced sexual dimorphism is exhibited only by the flufftails. All rallids have fairly short rounded wings and short tails, long tarsi and long slender toes. Flight appears weak and laboured, but several (*Crex, Porzana*) perform long-distance movements. Most species are associated with marshes and swamps, and a few inhabit forest or forest borders. With some exceptions, crakes and flufftails are skulking and secretive. The *Crex* species are typically grassland birds and, like the marsh-dwelling *Porzana*, have short bills. Our single *Rallus* is long-billed. Some species, notably the flufftails, are highly vocal. All nest on or near the ground, some on floating vegetation, laying two to several plain white or well-blotched and speckled eggs. The chicks are nidifugous, generally covered with black down.

WHITE-SPOTTED FLUFFTAIL *Sarothrura pulchra centralis*   Plate 26
(White-spotted Pygmy Crake)

Length 160–170 mm (6–7"). A bird of *streams in wooded areas*. **Adult male** has *chestnut head, neck, breast, upper back and tail*; rest of plumage *black with white spots*. **Female** rufous-chestnut as in male, but remainder of plumage *coarsely barred blackish brown and rufous*, the bars broadest on belly; tail rufous-brown, barred black. **Juvenile** browner than adult female, more extensively barred on breast. **Voice**: A short, whistled note repeated quite rapidly six to 14 times, *yew-yew-yew-yew-yew-yew. . .*, likened to tinkerbird's song, but louder, more mellow or bell-like. Also has a faster, higher-pitched *wuwuwuwuwuwu* when excited. **Habits**: Shy and skulking. Pairs or family groups may call throughout the day. **Similar Species**: Male Buff-spotted Flufftail (in places alongside White-spotted) has sandy-buff spots above; female Buff-spotted lacks rufous head, is less boldly barred above, and tail has broader buff bands bordered with black. **Status and Distribution**: Fairly common resident of forest and thick riverine bush from the Nandi and Kakamega Forests west to Busia District and the Ugandan border south of Mt Elgon.

BUFF-SPOTTED FLUFFTAIL *Sarothrura e. elegans*   Plate 26
(Buff-spotted Pygmy Crake)

Length 160–170 mm (6–7"). A *forest species*, usually not associated with water. **Adult male** bright rufous-chestnut on head, neck and upper breast; underparts otherwise *black, densely spotted with whitish and buff*; upperparts mainly dark brown with *extensive buff spotting*; tail barred rufous and black. **Female** brown above with paler buffy brown spots, each partly encircled with black; *underparts heavily barred* except for whitish throat, the breast and sides brownish with buff bars; belly paler, with broader dark brown bars; tail rufous-brown with several buff and black bands. **Juvenile** uniform sepia-brown, paler below, becoming white on mid-belly. **Voice**: A far-carrying, hollow-sounding, mournful wail, with the resonance of a tuning fork; starts low and rises in pitch near the end, and lasts up to four seconds. Calls repeated at intervals of several seconds in evening, at night or in early morning in wet misty conditions. **Habits**: Forages along narrow forest trails and near edges of clearings, usually concealed by dense rank vegetation. Crepuscular. **Similar Species**: See White-spotted Flufftail. **Status and Distribution**: Local and uncommon resident of Nandi and Kakamega Forests and the Kitale area in w. Kenya. Isolated records from Lake Turkana, Marsabit, Mt Kenya, Nairobi, Mara GR, the Mau, Chyulu Hills, Mt Kilimanjaro, East Usambaras and Pemba Island suggest a broader range. Believed subject to local movements during periods of heavy rain.

RED-CHESTED FLUFFTAIL *Sarothrura rufa*   Plate 26
(Red-chested Pygmy Crake)

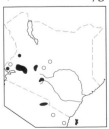

Length 150–170 mm (6–7"). A common flufftail of *swamps and marshes*. **Adult male** bright rufous on head, neck, breast and upper back; rest of *upperparts black with short white streaks*, changing into spots on the *largely black tail*. When flushed, front third of bird appears rufous, the rest black with fine white markings. Western *elizabethae* has longer white streaks and no spots. **Female** dark brown above with extensive buff speckling and feather edging, producing somewhat scaly or barred effect in *elizabethae*, more spotted with short broken bars in *S. r. rufa*. Tail dark brown or black, almost plain; throat white; rest of underparts buffy white with dark mottling and barring. **Juvenile** dusky black above, somewhat greyer below; chin, throat and mid-belly whitish. **Voice**: A series of upslurred whistles, about one per second and given in long series, *huer-huer-huer-huer huer* or *tui-tui-tui . . .*, often immediately followed by a high-pitched *ki-ki-ki-ki-ki-ki*. Speed and intensity vary. **Habits**: Elusive like other flufftails. Responds to imitations of call. **Similar Species**: Males of two preceding species show pale spots above. Male Streaky-breasted Flufftail has white breast streaked with

black. Female Striped Flufftail is most like female *rufa*, but has broadly barred tail and is confined to higher elevations. **STATUS AND DISTRIBUTION**: Common locally in marshy places up to 2700 m. *S. r. elizabethae*, in w. Kenya, extends east to Timboroa and Molo. Nominate *rufa* is known from Nyahururu, Rumuruti, Nanyuki, Nairobi and Thika in cent. Kenya, and the Arusha District, South Pare and East Usambara Mountains in n. Tanzania. Although formerly not uncommon on Pemba Island, reports from coastal areas of Kenya require confirmation.

STREAKY-BREASTED FLUFFTAIL *Sarothrura boehmi*   Plate 26
(Böhm's Flufftail, Streaky-breasted Pygmy Crake)

Length 160–170 mm (6–7"). A bird of *flooded grasslands*. **Adult male** has head and neck bright rufous-chestnut, with contrasting white throat. *Upperparts black with thin white streaks; breast and belly whitish with extensive dark streaking*. Wings longer than in most flufftails, but *black tail extremely short*. **Female** *blackish*, not brown, above, with fine white streaks and feather edges; much paler below than female Red-chested, *almost plain white on throat* and belly. **Juvenile** sooty black, with whitish throat and centre of belly. **VOICE**: A hollow hoot repeated about once every two seconds, *hooh. . . hooh. . . hooh . . .*, like a person blowing across an open bottle; also a higher-pitched, more rapidly repeated *gaWOO, gaWOO, gaWOO. . .* or *koo-AH, koo-AH. . .*, accelerating toward end of series, which may end with *blip-blip-blip-blip*. **HABITS**: Little known. Secretive, but responds to imitations of call. **SIMILAR SPECIES**: Male Red-chested Flufftail has similar upperparts, but is rufous on throat, breast and upper back; female brownish above. **STATUS AND DISTRIBUTION**: Scarce intra-African migrant, presumably from the southern tropics, following heavy rains in April and May. Early Kenyan records from Kitale, Kisumu and Machakos; several in Nairobi NP (May 1988), near Mumias (May 1990). Juvenile male captured at The Ark (Aberdare Mts), 14 July 1990.

STRIPED FLUFFTAIL *Sarothrura affinis antonii*   Plate 26
(Chestnut-tailed Crake)

Length 140–150 mm (5.5–6"). Restricted to *montane grasslands and moors*. **Adult male** chestnut-rufous on head, neck and upper breast, rest of underparts black with broad white streaks; black upperparts buff-streaked; *tail plain rufous*. **Female** dusky brown above, with extensive tawny or buff feather edges producing mottled and scaly effect; *tail broadly barred rufous and black* or (on birds from Mt Kenya and Aberdares) sooty with only slight traces of rufous. **VOICE**: A rather slow, repetitive hoot: *huuw-huuw-huuw-huuw. . .*, each note starting softly, increasing in volume and fading slowly away. Also produces a series of grunts, and a rapid *ti-ti-ti-tititi* that eventually fades to a lower *tee-tee-teee-teee*. **SIMILAR SPECIES**: Male White-spotted Flufftail also has rufous tail, but body and wings are spotted, not streaked. Female Buff-spotted Flufftail has barred tail and female Red-chested has similar back pattern, but both are unlikely in habitat of Striped. **STATUS AND DISTRIBUTION**: Seldom recorded. Early specimens collected above 3000 m in alpine grasslands on the Aberdares and Mt Kenya. Three recent records: 3200 m on Mt Elgon (Dec. 1969); near Satima Peak, Aberdare NP (Feb. 1974); one caught and ringed in high grassland of the Nguruman Range near Kenyan–Tanzanian border (June 1977), near site of collection in January 1909.

AFRICAN CRAKE *Crex egregia*   Plate 26

Length 190–230 mm (7.5–9"). *Short-billed*, with *barred sides* and *narrow white superciliary stripes*. **Adult** dark olive-brown above with dark feather centres, producing mottled appearance; white chin and throat; grey from sides of head to breast; *flanks and belly heavily barred black and white*. Bill grey, with pink or reddish base; eyes red or orange; bare orbital skin pink; *legs and feet pale olive*. Sexes alike. **Juvenile** has grey of face and breast replaced by dull brownish buff; flank barring more obscure and brown, not black; faint superciliary stripes. Bill dark brown, later becoming grey-brown like legs and feet; eyes grey-green, becoming hazel. **VOICE**: A short hard *kik* or *kak*, and a series of eight or nine rapid, high-pitched, whistling notes, somewhat trilled: *kik-kik-kik-kik-ik-ik-ikikiikikikik*; also has a harsh, Corncrake-like *churrr*. **HABITS**: Shy and skulking, usually solitary at grassy margins of swamps or in marshes. Runs through grass and sedges, crouched. Flushes reluctantly, flying a short distance with dangling feet and calling excitedly. **SIMILAR SPECIES**: Corncrake is slightly larger and buffier, shows prominent tawny wing-coverts in flight, and lacks heavy black-and-white barring below. Spotted Crake has white spots on neck, breast and wing-coverts, legs and feet olive-green, eyes red-brown. **STATUS AND DISTRIBUTION**: Local and uncommon intra-African migrant in wet grasslands and marshes, mainly April–September, during and immediately after the long rains. Has bred in w. and cent. Kenya and near Lake Manyara in n. Tanzania during May and June, but most records from the Lake Victoria basin, Lake Baringo and southern Kenyan coast, presumably non-breeding birds from the southern tropics.

CORNCRAKE *Crex crex*   Plate 26

Length *c.* 270 mm (10.5"). A buff-and-brown crake of *dry or recently inundated grasslands*, with *tawny-rufous wing-coverts diagnostic in flight*. Sexes similar. **Adult** olive-buff above with black streaks; head buff, with *broad*

grey superciliary stripes; neck and breast greyish tawny; throat and belly buffy white; *sides and flanks buffy white with broad brown barring*. Tail and under tail-coverts also barred. Spring bird acquiring breeding plumage has greyer neck and breast. Bill *pale* pinkish brown or flesh-brown; eyes light brown or hazel; legs and feet pale flesh-pink, not greenish or yellowish. **First-winter** bird is less heavily barred below. **VOICE**: Silent in Africa. **HABITS**: Shy and secretive; rarely observed unless flushed, when it flies short distance with dangling feet. Solitary or occasionally in groups on passage. **SIMILAR SPECIES**: African Crake lacks distinctive wing patches; breast is grey, and flanks are barred black and white. **STATUS AND DISTRIBUTION**: Local and uncommon passage migrant in grassland and savanna exceptionally up to 3000 m. Migration through the Kenyan highlands (Oct.–Dec. and March–April) is less marked than formerly, but regularly recorded in the Mara GR in April. Several recent records from Ngulia (Tsavo West NP), where attracted to lights at night in November and December. No recent records from n. Tanzania.

AFRICAN WATER RAIL *Rallus caerulescens* Plate 25
(African Rail)

Length 280–300 mm (11–12"). A large rail with *long red bill* and *red legs and feet*, *barred flanks* and red eyes. Sexes alike. **Adult** blackish on crown, but rest of upperparts dark brown; mostly dark slate-grey below, the chin and throat greyish white; *flanks barred black and white*; under tail-coverts white. **Juvenile** sooty brown above, and flanks heavily brown-barred; bill blackish or dull red; legs and feet dull red or red-brown. **VOICE**: A high-pitched *pree* followed by a rapid loud pumping *pi-pi-pi-pip-pip* . . ., also a loud *kew-kew-kew*. . ., the 10–20 notes gradually slowing and dropping in pitch. **HABITS**: Solitary or in pairs. Shy and secretive. When walking in the open at dawn or dusk, constantly flicks tail. Runs rapidly with long strides, and swims well. Flies low, with dangling feet. **STATUS AND DISTRIBUTION**: Uncommon but widespread resident of swamps, freshwater marshes and reedbeds from sea level to 3000 m. Most numerous from the cent. Kenyan highlands and Rift Valley south to the Mara GR, Amboseli NP, Lake Jipe and Arusha NP. Generally scarce in n. Tanzania.

BAILLON'S CRAKE *Porzana pusilla obscura* Plate 26
(Lesser Spotted Crake)

Length 160–180 mm (6–7"). *Flufftail-sized* and *short-billed*, mainly rich brown above and grey below. **Adult male** has warm brown upperparts *flecked with black and white on upper back and wing-coverts*. Face, neck and underparts largely slaty blue-grey, with flanks and crissum barred black and white, the lower belly grey and white. Bill dark green or greenish grey; eyes red; legs and feet greenish. Similar **female** whiter on chin, throat and upper breast. **Juvenile** has pale buff underparts mottled on breast and brown-barred on sides and flanks. **VOICE**: A dry rattling trill, *ti-ti-ti-ti-ti-ti-ti-tirrrrr*, lasting two or three seconds and frequently repeated, mainly at night. **HABITS**: Solitary, less often in small groups (migrants?). Forages on mud at edge of reedbeds or on floating vegetation. Flirts tail and continually moves head back and forth when walking. Shy. **SIMILAR SPECIES**: African Crake is larger, without white flecking on upperparts. Spotted Crake is also larger, its brown breast spotted with white. **STATUS AND DISTRIBUTION**: Uncommon in swamps, marshes, and lake edges with rank vegetation. Scattered records from Mara GR, Lake Kanyaboli, Eldoret, Baringo, Naivasha, the Aberdares, Thika, Mombasa and near Arusha. No East African breeding records. Population possibly augmented by palearctic *P. p. intermedia* between November and April. **NOTE**: The Little Crake, *Porzana parva*, has been reported near Thika in January, but presence in our area remains unsubstantiated. It resembles Baillon's Crake but is slightly larger, paler above, with *whitish scapular stripes*, a longer, thinner *olive bill* (*with red spot at base of maxilla in male*), and *unpatterned upper wing-coverts*.

SPOTTED CRAKE *Porzana porzana* Plate 26

Length 210–240 mm (8–9.5"). A *brownish, bar-flanked* marsh crake, *extensively white speckled* and with some narrow white streaking on upperparts. **Adult male** has face and throat slate-grey, profusely white-dotted; *neck and breast tinged brown* and dotted with white; lower breast and belly white, shading to sandy buff on under tail-coverts, sides and flanks. Eyes red-brown; *bill yellowish green or greenish yellow with red base; legs and feet olive-green to greenish yellow*. Sexes similar, but **female** has less grey on foreparts, and sides of head and neck are more heavily spotted. **Juvenile** generally browner than adult. **VOICE**: Alarm call a short *kreck* or *krrick*; generally silent in Africa. **HABITS**: Usually solitary, but in small groups when migrating. Less skulking than most crakes, feeding away from cover if not disturbed. Constantly flicks tail, showing buff under tail-coverts. **SIMILAR SPECIES**: African Crake lacks white spotting above; adult has

entirely grey neck, throat and breast and red eyes. Adult Striped Crake is rufous or cinnamon on under tail-coverts, has no red at base of bill. Juvenile Striped Crake lacks spotting and barring. **STATUS AND DISTRIBUTION**: Uncommon palearctic migrant, October–April, preferring dense vegetation in shallow standing water, marshes, and seasonally flooded grasslands. Kenyan records from Lake Turkana, Uasin Gishu, Kisumu, Londiani, Naivasha, Thika, Nairobi, Athi River, Tsavo and Mombasa, many during spring passage. No records from n. Tanzania, but several south of our region.

STRIPED CRAKE *Aenigmatolimnas marginalis* Plate 26

Length 200–225 mm (8–9"). A large-toed, heavy-billed crake. **Adult male** *rich tawny and buffy brown*, with crown and neck burnt orange; *upperparts streaked brown and white from base of neck to tail*, the upper tail-coverts brighter, more orange-brown. *Lower flanks and crissum tawny-rufous or cinnamon*, contrasting with greyish-white belly; *neck and face buffier; breast orange-buff*; sides and upper flanks olive-brown with white feather edges. Bill orange-brown; eyes golden brown with *orange or yellow orbital ring*; tarsi and very long toes jade-green. **Female** similar, but dark grey on head, paler *blue-grey on neck and breast*, the feathers white-edged; flanks and crissum as in male. Orbital skin, tarsi and toes yellowish green. **Juvenile** *unstreaked* plain brownish above with tawny-buff foreparts, and dull white belly and crissum. Bill yellowish brown; feet blue-grey. **VOICE**: A sharp repetitive *tak-tak-tak-tak* at night or on dark cloudy days. **HABITS**: Solitary; usually shy and secretive, but stands in the open on marsh vegetation to dry plumage after rain. Runs rapidly, and will freeze if pressed closely. Flicks tail when feeding. **SIMILAR SPECIES**: African Crake lacks white streaks, has boldly barred sides and flanks and red eyes. Spotted Crake has smaller dorsal streaks, brown-and-white-barred sides/flanks. Other *Porzana* species are spotted above, with smaller feet and bill, and show no bright colour on flanks and under tail-coverts. **STATUS AND DISTRIBUTION**: Scarce intra-African migrant, presumably from the southern tropics, mainly May–November. In Kenya, known from Kapsabet, lakes Baringo and Naivasha, Mt Kenya, Thika, Nairobi, Shombole, Amboseli, Mombasa and Karawa. Several Tanzanian records slightly beyond our limits.

BLACK CRAKE *Amaurornis flavirostris* Plate 25

Length 185–200 mm (7–8"). **Adult** unmistakable, with *plain dull black plumage, short greenish-yellow bill*, and *red legs, feet and eyes*. Sexes alike. **Subadult** resembles adult, but plumage duller black and the rump noticeably browner; eyes ruby-red, bill yellowish green, other bare parts bright orange-red. **Immature** *olive-brown above* and *grey below* (with variable amounts of white on cheeks and throat, absent in some Kenyan birds). Bill dull greenish yellow, becoming brighter with age; legs and feet pinkish-flesh colour, changing to bright orange; eyes pale brown, becoming dull red. **Juvenile** uniform *dark chocolate-brown*; bare parts blackish slate, later changing to dark flesh; bill slaty with pink base, becoming dusky greenish yellow. **Downy young** black, including eyes, unfeathered legs and feet; bill bright pink with dark median band, becoming darker until only basal third remains pink by onset of juvenile plumage (Parker and Parker, unpubl. ms). **VOICE**: A throaty *coo-crr-chrooo*, and a rippling, trilling *weet, eet, eet, eet*. Frequently utters a series of loud wheezing sounds from dense cover. **HABITS**: Usually in pairs, but a dozen or more may feed together in a small area. Neither shy nor particularly skulking; often forages in the open, and perches on partially submerged rocks, logs, occasionally on hippopotami. Flicks tail continuously when walking. Swims well, and escapes danger by diving. Active throughout the day. **STATUS AND DISTRIBUTION**: The most widespread rail; may appear on any swampy patch with open water and fringing vegetation. Common on all suitable Rift Valley lakes, throughout the Kenyan highlands, on the Kenyan coast and in much of n. Tanzania, including Pemba Island. Largely absent from arid n. and e. Kenya.

ALLEN'S GALLINULE *Porphyrio alleni* Plate 25
(Lesser Gallinule)

Length 260–300 mm (10–12"). A small, dark gallinule with *greenish-blue frontal shield* and *dark red bill*. **Adult** has *blackish head*, dark green upperparts and bright purplish-blue underparts except for white under tail-coverts. Eyes red or red-brown; legs and feet dark red. **Juvenile** dark brown above, with white chin and throat; pale buff below, with white belly; under tail-coverts rich buff. Bill brown with red base, frontal shield olive-brown; legs and feet pale pink. **Downy young** blackish (somewhat browner below), with silvery feather tips on face. **VOICE**: Calls include a sharp *KIK*, a metallic *kleerk* and a dry nasal *kekk*, either given singly or rapidly repeated; also produces a series of sharp, frog-like noises ending with a chur: *kik-kik-kik-kik-ki-kier-kier-kierr-kierr-kiurrrrrrrrr*; in flight, gives a sharp *kli-kli-kli*. **HABITS**: Shy and retiring. Partial to areas with water-lilies and other floating vegetation. Swims and dives well. Flicks tail when walking, and runs rapidly with lowered head. Frequently climbs in vegetation. **SIMILAR SPECIES**: Adult Purple Swamphen is larger,

with purplish-blue head, red frontal shield, massive bill. *Gallinula* species have olive or grey-green legs and feet. **STATUS AND DISTRIBUTION**: Local and usually uncommon in marshes, swamps and waterside vegetation up to 1900 m. Present all year at Lake Baringo, more numerous June–September. Scattered records from Busia District, Lake Naivasha, Thika, Nairobi and Amboseli NPs, Lake Jipe and Mombasa. Rare in n. Tanzania; may still breed on Pemba Island.

PURPLE SWAMPHEN *Porphyrio porphyrio madagascariensis*   **Plate 25**
(Purple Gallinule)

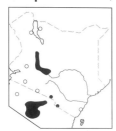

Length 380–460 mm (15–18"). *Large size* and *massive red bill* and frontal shield distinctive. **Adult** plumage mainly *blue and dull purple*, with bronzy-green back, scapulars and inner wing feathers, darker on rump and tail. Under tail-coverts white. Eyes red or red-brown; tarsi and toes dull coral-red or pinkish red. **Subadult** bluish and olive-brown above, generally pale grey on head, neck and underparts; bare parts duller than in adult. **Juvenile** dull brown below, but readily identified by heavy reddish bill. **Downy young** black, with sparse whitish filoplumes on head and back; sparsely bristled skin of forehead red; bill white, purplish red at base; legs and feet pink. **VOICE**: A wide variety of harsh shrieks, whistles, neighing, trumpeting, and especially grunting and cackling, sometimes in excited chorus. Contact call a clucking *aak aak aak . . .* or *cuk-cuk-cuk-cuk.* Alarm call a loud *kree-ik.* Male's voice lower than female's. **HABITS**: Solitary or in pairs. Feeds in the open away from cover in early morning and evening. Calls and probably feeds at night, as well as by day. Flight heavy and laboured. Runs rapidly through tangled vegetation. Favours areas with extensive growth of water-lilies. Mainly vegetarian, but also eats small aquatic animals. **SIMILAR SPECIES**: Much smaller Allen's Gallinule has smaller bill and greenish-blue frontal shield. **STATUS AND DISTRIBUTION**: In Kenya, a local and uncommon resident of dense swamps, papyrus and reedbeds in the Rift Valley. A few scattered population near Nairobi, Thika, Amboseli, Lake Jipe and Mombasa. Numbers greatly decreased in recent years from loss of habitat and introduction of Nutria (*Myocastor coypus*) to many lakes and swamps. Uncommon throughout n. Tanzania, but small populations in most freshwater swamps from Arusha NP west to Ngorongoro Crater and the Mbulu Highlands.

COMMON MOORHEN *Gallinula chloropus meridionalis*   **Plate 25**
(Common Gallinule)

Length 300–360 mm (12–14"). A perky dark swimmer, somewhat duck-like in shape. **Adult** has *yellow-tipped red bill* and *red frontal shield rounded posteriorly.* Plumage mainly slate-grey, blackish on head, slightly glossy olive-brown on the back. Conspicuous *line of broad white streaks along sides and flanks;* under tail-coverts white with black central patch. Eyes crimson to red-brown; legs and feet yellowish green with *orange-red 'garters' around tibiae.* **Immature** (first year) dark brown above, buffy slate below with some white on throat; flank stripes buff-tinged. Bill greenish brown, yellow toward tip, and gradually becoming red. **Juvenile** brown on head, neck, back and sides; *chin and throat buffy white; centre of breast and belly whitish;* bill and shield olive-brown; eyes grey-brown; legs and feet olive, with yellow tibial bands. **Downy young** black, with bare rose-red skin on head, bluish above the eyes, yellow on throat; bill pink with yellow tip; eyes dark brown; legs and feet black. **VOICE**: A single loud *quaarrk, krrik* or *kraak,* sometimes *kik-kik,* or *kek-kek-kek,* and a softer, less explosive *krrrruk.* **HABITS**: Swims in open water or among floating vegetation; dives readily; walks with high-stepping gait, flicking tail if apprehensive or alarmed. Frequently climbs into reeds or waterside branches. Solitary, in pairs or family groups. Not shy. **SIMILAR SPECIES**: Lesser Moorhen is smaller, the adult with largely yellow bill, red only on culmen; no red 'garters' on legs; juvenile paler and buffier; frontal shield pointed at base. **STATUS AND DISTRIBUTION**: Fairly common and widespread in w. and central Kenya, and in much of n. Tanzania, on fresh water with fringing vegetation and water-lilies. Local and uncommon in the coastal lowlands and at Lake Turkana.

LESSER MOORHEN *Gallinula angulata*   **Plate 25**

Length 230–270 mm (9–10.5"). A *small* moorhen with *largely yellow bill* with red culmen. *Red frontal shield pointed (not rounded) on forehead;* eyes red; legs and feet yellowish green, with no red tibial bands as in Common Moorhen. **Adult** dark grey, with line of white streaks on flanks; head blackish; back dark olive-brown. White under tail-coverts have black central line, noticeable when tail flicked upward as bird swims or walks. **Immature** paler and browner than adult, with *largely grey face and throat,* some black around base of bill; underparts generally pale brownish grey, more buffy brown on breast. Bill yellowish; frontal shield becoming orange with age. **Juvenile** olive-brown above, *whitish from chin to belly;* buff on sides of breast. Bill brownish yellow, dusky at base; eyes dark brown; legs and feet grey-green. **Downy young** black; bill black, white at tip, pink basally; frontal shield red-brown, purple at base; legs and feet blue.

rey. **VOICE**: A soft *pyup*, and a sharp high *kik* or *tik*. **HABITS**: Similar to those of Common Moorhen, but quite
₁y and tends to remain in or near cover; may forage on top of water-lily leaves. **SIMILAR SPECIES**: Adult Common
₄oorhen has red bill with yellow tip, and frontal shield rounded at base; also shows red 'garters' on legs; juve-
ile warmer brown above, paler below. **STATUS AND DISTRIBUTION**: Intra-African migrant on both permanent
₁nd temporary waters with ample fringing vegetation, local and uncommon April–August, during and after the
₁ng rains. Has bred in the Nairobi–Thika area and in Arusha District, but mainly a visitor to seasonal ponds in
₁e Lake Victoria basin, the central Kenyan highlands and coastal lowlands. Generally scarce in n. Tanzania.

RED-KNOBBED COOT *Fulica cristata*
(Crested Coot)
Plate 25

Length 410–460 mm (16–18"). A lobe-toed, *slate-grey* swimming bird with a *white bill
and frontal shield*. During breeding season, **adult** develops two dark red knobs at top of
frontal shield. These become dull and much reduced in size after nesting. Eyes red when
breeding, otherwise dull reddish brown; legs and feet olive or greenish when breeding,
slate-grey most of year. **Juvenile** dull brown above, flecked with white on head and
neck, whitish around base of bill and on throat; rest of underparts pale grey; bill, legs
and feet grey; eyes brown. **VOICE**: Common call, *hoo-hoo*. Also a harsh, somewhat
metallic *kik-kik* or *kriik*, sometimes *kekk* or *kerrk*; a bisyllabic *co-up*, a frog-like croak,
and various other calls. **HABITS**: Swims with pumping motion of head; patters across
water before taking wing. Dives frequently. Gregarious; may form post-breeding flocks
of 1,000+; numbers fluctuate on permanent waters, suggesting local movements, and
₁irds ringed in n. Tanzania have been recovered in cent. Kenya. **SIMILAR SPECIES**: Eurasian Coot, *F. atra*, not
₁nown in East Africa, would be difficult to distinguish as red knobs of *cristata* are evident only in breeding sea-
₁on and at close range. Loral feathering extends forward as a point at base of shield in Eurasian Coot, this exten-
₁ion rounded and blunt in Red-knobbed. Spread wing of Eurasian shows narrow strip of white on leading and
₁railing edges, lacking in Red-knobbed. **STATUS AND DISTRIBUTION**: Common to abundant resident of permanent
₁enyan waters up to 3000 m, most numerous in the highlands and on freshwater Rift Valley lakes. Absent from
₁he coastal lowlands and much of the north and east. Small numbers resident on most freshwater lakes in n.
₁anzania, particularly in the Crater and Mbulu Highlands.

CRANES, FAMILY GRUIDAE
(World, 15 species; Africa, 6; Kenya, 3; n. Tanzania, 1)

₁tately birds characteristic of marshes, wet grasslands, dry cultivated land and pastures. They are long-necked
₁nd long-legged, with the tibiae partly bare. Plumage, the same in both sexes, is generally grey, sometimes with
₁hite, chestnut and black. Some species have ornamental plumes or crests, and the large secondaries are
₁ecurved over the short tail. Many individuals pair for life, holding large territories when breeding, and per-
₁orming elaborate dancing displays. Outside the breeding season cranes tend to be gregarious, sometimes form-
₁ng large foraging flocks. Their flight is strong and often sustained, with head and neck always held below the
₁orizontal, imparting a distinctive hunchbacked appearance and readily separating them from flying herons and
₁torks. They often utter loud trumpeting calls in flight. The ground nest is a bulky mass of flattened marsh vege-
₁ation. The two or three greenish or bluish eggs are incubated by both sexes for about a month, and the nidi-
₁olous downy young are tended by both parents for two months or longer.

DEMOISELLE CRANE *Anthropoides virgo*
Plate 9

₁ength 97 cm (38"). A pale grey crane with black foreparts. **Adult** generally blue-grey, black from forehead to
₁he elongated breast feathers. White superciliary stripes extend to a tuft of long white feathers that droops along
₁indneck; flight feathers black; long inner secondaries extend and droop well beyond the dark grey tail. Eyes red;
₁ill olive-grey with reddish tip; legs and feet black. **Immature** duller and more ash-grey, the breast feathers and
₁ostocular tuft short and grey. Eyes brown. **VOICE**: A soft purring when feeding. In the air, a low raspy call.
HABITS: Where numerous, flies in V-formations; soars high on thermals. Feeds in open grassland, *Acacia* savan-
₁a; roosts in marshes. **STATUS AND DISTRIBUTION**: Palearctic vagrant, known from eight adults and one imma-
₁ture photographed at Ngomeni, near Malindi, Kenya, 15 January 1986, and reported again in March 1986, near
₁Mt Kenya.

GREY CROWNED CRANE *Balearica regulorum gibbericeps*
(Southern Crowned Crane)
Plate 9

Length 109–112 cm (43–44"). A colourful, tall *slate-grey* crane with *white, black and chestnut wings*; velvety
black forehead, crown and nape, with *crest of stiff, bristly straw-coloured feathers* on hindcrown (slightly smaller in female); *large bare white cheek patch bordered red above*; *long pendent red wattle* hangs from black throat.

Bill black; eyes pale blue; legs and feet black. **Juvenile** grey, with feathers of upperparts broadly edged rufous; head and neck rufous, with short tawny crest; cheeks creamy white; eyes brown. **Downy young** tawny, with brownish crown and nape. Bill black above, horn-brown below; eyes dark brown; legs and feet slaty grey or pink. **VOICE**: A loud honking from perch or in flight, members of a pair often calling in unison: *ku-waank, oo-waank. . .*, varied to *o-wahng, o-wahng. . .* or *ya-oo-ga-lunk. . . .* Gives low purring calls when feeding. A low booming sequence, often by several displaying birds in unison, may continue for several minutes. **HABITS**: Gregarious except in breeding season, sometimes in large flocks. Pairs perform elaborate display in all months of the year – mutual preening, head-bobbing, bowing and dancing, the latter involving high upward leaps with spread wings. **SIMILAR SPECIES**: Black Crowned Crane is darker, particularly on the neck; cheek patch largely pink, with smaller area of white. **STATUS AND DISTRIBUTION**: Fairly common and widespread in wetlands throughout w. and cent. Kenya, generally above 1300 m. Similarly distributed over much of n. Tanzania. Largely absent from extensive arid regions, but wanderers appear at Lake Turkana and in the coastal lowlands.

BLACK CROWNED CRANE *Balearica pavonina ceciliae*　　　　　Plate 9
(Northern Crowned Crane)

Length 92–97 cm (36–38"). A rare northern crane resembling the preceding species, but *generally black*, not slate-grey, in appearance, and with bare *face patch largely pink, only the upper quarter white*. Short throat wattle rose-pink. Eyes bluish white; bill, legs and feet black. **Juvenile** darker than young of Grey Crowned Crane, but with similar rufous feather edges. **VOICE**: Similar to that of preceding species, often a single *wonk* or *ka-wonk*. **STATUS AND DISTRIBUTION**: In our area, known from a few sight records along the northern shores of Lake Turkana.

FINFOOT, FAMILY HELIORNITHIDAE
(World, 3 species; Africa, Kenya and n. Tanzania, 1)

A shy, retiring, somewhat grebe-like waterbird with a long body, thin neck, and small head with a fairly long tapered bill. The short strong tarsi are set far back and the long toes are lobed, as in grebes, but the claws are well developed. As it swims, the bird pumps its head back and forth. It feeds on fish and large insects. When alarmed it submerges, often leaving only the head, or head and neck, above water, and it may patter across the water like a coot to seek safety along a shaded bank. On shore it waddles duck-like, but is said to run rapidly if necessary. It frequently rests on emergent rocks or logs. Our species is an able climber of riverine bushes and trees, the branches of which overhang the water, and it builds a substantial flat nest of grass and sedge culms among thick tangled vegetation in such places. The two or three eggs are apparently incubated only by the female.

AFRICAN FINFOOT *Podica senegalensis somereni*　　　　　Plate 25

Length of male 52–65 cm (21–26"), of female 45-50 cm (18-20"). An *elongate robust-bodied bird of shaded river banks. Swims with pumping neck motion*, the ample black tail spread out flat on the water surface. **Male** has crown and neck black, washed with iridescent green, a narrow *whitish line from the eye down each side of the neck*, and sides of face, throat and foreneck dark slaty blue; back dark brown with greenish gloss, rather heavily *white-spotted*, as are the brown sides and flanks. *Bill coral red*; eyes reddish brown; *feet bright orange-red*, the tarsi brownish behind; claws yellow. **Female** is duller, more brownish above, with white or buffy-white throat and foreneck, and a more *distinct white neck line*. Bill dusky above and at tip, most of mandible red; other bare parts as in male. **Juvenile** like female, but brown above with little or no white spotting; breast and flanks tawny-buff, faintly spotted; bare-part colours not recorded. **Downy young** chocolate-brown with rufous forehead, white supraloral spots, black eye-lines, whitish or pale brown cheeks, and white throat and belly; breast and flanks tawny-buff or dull rufous; bill blackish above, horn-brown below; eyes brown; feet orange-yellow to bright orange. **VOICE**: Generally silent, but sometimes utters a sharp *skwack* or a duck-like *kwack, kwak-wak-wak-wak*. Also said to give a repeated roaring or booming alarm note (Maclean 1984). **HABITS**: As for the family. **SIMILAR SPECIES**: Partly submerged darter might be confused, but bill is longer and more pointed, brownish, not red. **STATUS AND DISTRIBUTION**: A scarce resident of perennial rivers and streams with thick fringing vegetation. In e. Kenya, recorded on the Thika, Thura, Tana, Tsavo, Galana and

Mwachi Rivers; elsewhere on the Naro Moru, Mbagathi, Migori and Mara Rivers. In n. Tanzania, present in small numbers on rivers flowing off Mt Kilimanjaro in Moshi District, and in the East Usambaras.

BUSTARDS, FAMILY OTIDIDAE
(World, 25 species; Africa, 19; Kenya, 8; n. Tanzania, 6)

Large to very large terrestrial birds inhabiting grassland, bush and semi-desert scrub. All have rather short bills, long slender necks, stout bodies, short tails, and fairly long legs with only three toes on each foot. They walk in a steady and purposeful manner, head moving back and forth, pausing to pick up food items, which vary from insects and small lizards to flowers, fruits and seeds. Their flight is heavy, with slow deliberate wingbeats, the neck extended crane-like. Males are brighter and generally larger than females, especially in the larger *Neotis* and *Ardeotis* species. Plumage of most forms is cryptically vermiculated above, white, buff or black below. Bustards prefer to walk away from danger, but are nevertheless strong fliers. The smaller *Eupodotis* species can be quite vocal, whereas *Neotis* and *Ardeotis* are almost silent except during courtship, when males perform elaborate displays. All nest on the ground, with or without a scrape. (Nest and eggs of Hartlaub's Bustard remain unknown.) The downy young are nidicolous, cared for almost entirely by the female with bill-to-bill feeding for the first few weeks. Trapping of bustards for export to some Middle East countries has led to a significant decline of some species. Agricultural development seriously threatens the habitat and seasonal movements of several others.

DENHAM'S BUSTARD *Neotis denhami* Plates 29, 30
(Jackson's Bustard, Stanley's Bustard)

Length 84–116 cm (33–46"). A large bustard (males weighing 7–10 kg) with *bright orange-rufous hindneck*, less extensive in female. **Adult male** dark brown above, with much black-and-white mottling on wing-coverts, rufous on hindneck contrasting with light grey foreneck and breast; belly white. Head pattern includes black crown with white central stripe, prominent white superciliary stripes and black eye-lines. No crest. **Female** similar, but centre of crown brown, foreneck buffy with dark brown vermiculations. Both sexes have dull yellowish-white bill with dark culmen and tip, yellowish-white legs and feet, and dark brown to light hazel-brown eyes. **Juvenile** resembles adult, but shows considerable variation in neck and throat colour and extent of crown stripe. **Voice:** An infrequent barking *kaa-kaa*. Courting male gives a resonant booming call. **Habits:** Highly site-faithful, with individuals remaining in the same area for months at a time. Usually solitary, but several may gather at grass fires. Breeding males strut some hundreds of metres apart at a lek and employ a 'balloon' display with enormously inflated neck and breast and raised tail, this followed by a 'vertical' display with tail down, body nearly vertical, white ballooned breast and flared oblong of rufous nape raised so as nearly to conceal the head. **Similar Species:** Kori Bustard is crested, lacks rufous hindneck. Heuglin's Bustard is chestnut on breast, lacks black and white on wings. **Status and Distribution:** *N. d. jacksoni* is a local and uncommon grassland resident in cent. Serengeti NP, n. Masai Mara GR east to Narok and on the lower sw. slopes of the Mau Escarpment (1600–2000 m); main stronghold now the Laikipia Plateau and high grasslands northwest of Maralal. Presumed nominate *denhami* recently recorded in extreme nw. Kenya at Lokichokio, May–August. A threatened species in Kenya, its numbers now much reduced; probably fewer than 300 remain.

HEUGLIN'S BUSTARD *Neotis heuglinii* Plate 29

Length 66–88 cm (26–35"). A large northern bustard, variable in size; male larger than female and weighing up to 8 kg. Light brown above with darker brown and sandy-buff vermiculation and barring; *neck blue-grey; lower breast rich chestnut, bordered below by a narrow black band*; rest of underparts white. **Adult male** *black-faced* and with black crown that sometimes shows a narrow white central stripe; black extends to upper throat and to short occipital crest, which is raised in alarm; lower throat, ear-coverts and nape white. **Female** has black crown with white central stripe, but face and ear-coverts are mainly grey, chin white and throat buff; neck and breast as in male but generally paler. Adults *in flight show two or three white primaries contrasting with otherwise dark wings*. Bill of both sexes blackish above, yellowish below, dark horn at tip; legs and feet pale yellow; eyes dark brown in female, brown or dark red in male. **Immature male** resembles female, but has prominent white nape patch and blackish streak below and around eyes. **Voice:** Unrecorded. **Habits:** Little known. Shy, wary and nomadic; movements presumably governed by food availability. **Similar Species:** Arabian and Kori Bustards appear crested, with all-grey necks. Denham's Bustard is extensively rufous on hindneck and has black-and-white pattern on wing-coverts. **Status and Distribution:** Local and uncommon. Confined to the east side of Lake Turkana, mainly around the lava fields and thorn-bush north and northwest of Mt Marsabit. Also recorded from Ramu, El Wak, Garba Tula and Shaba GR, rarely wandering south to Bura, northern parts of Tsavo East NP, and the Galana Ranch.

KORI BUSTARD *Ardeotis kori struthiunculus* Plate 3

Length 105–128 cm (41–50"). A *very large, thick-necked, crested* bustard—the heavie
flying bird in tropical Africa (males weighing up to 18 kg or more). Sexes alike. **Adu**
dark to light greyish brown above, with neck and breast vermiculated grey, the feathe
filamentous and erectile. Black feathers of sides of crown and postocular stripes exten
back to straggling nape crest. *Chequered black-and-white pattern near bend of wir*,
and *black patches at sides of lower neck* diagnostic. Belly whitish. Tail broadly barre
black and white. In flight, shows pale diagonal band across upper wing-coverts, an
white-barred inner primaries. Bill mainly pale yellowish brown; legs and feet pale ye
lowish or creamy white; eyes yellowish. **Juvenile** and **immature** resemble adult but a
smaller. **Voice:** Normally silent, but displaying male gives a deep resonant *voomp*.
.voomp. . .voomp. **Habits:** Solitary or in pairs, although 15–20 birds may congregate
grass fires or on recently harvested wheat fields. Walks with long strides, often on open ground. Courting male
elaborate display may continue for several days, the lax neck feathers erected, the tail raised and spread
expose extensive, white, fluffy under tail-coverts (visible as a bright white spot from a distance of 2–3 km
Similar Species: See Arabian Bustard. **Status and Distribution:** Widespread in grassland between 700 an
2000 m, including dry areas of n. Kenya. Most numerous in Rift Valley highlands and south to Mara GR, Loi
Plains and Amboseli NP. Scarce and local in coastal lowlands from the Tana River south to the Tsavo NPs an
the Shimba Hills. Widespread in n. Tanzania, where most numerous on the Serengeti plains, January–March.

ARABIAN BUSTARD, *Ardeotis arabs* Plate 3

Length 84–91 cm (33–36"). A large crested bustard of far northern Kenya. Males weigh up to 10 kg. Resemble
Kori Bustard, but *without black on wing-coverts and on sides of lower neck.* **Adult** has several *rows of white*
cream spots across the wing-coverts. Forehead and crown centre greyish, sides of crown black, extending bac
to straggling crest; whitish superciliary stripes, blackish lines through eyes and along malar region; sides of hea
and neck finely vermiculated with grey; upperparts tawny-brown, the tail broadly barred; underparts cream
white. In flight, shows pale diagonal band across upper wing-coverts and white barring on inner primaries. Bi
pale yellowish horn, dusky at tip; legs and feet pale creamy yellow; eyes yellowish orange. Sexes similar. **Juveni**
duller than adult, with less distinct spots on wings. **Voice:** Usually silent, but gives a rasping or honking croa
pah pah, in display (Urban *et al.* 1986). **Habits:** Usually solitary or in pairs. Not especially shy. **Similar Specie**
Kori Bustard is larger, thicker-necked, darker above with black patches on sides of lower neck and a chequere
black-and-white pattern at bend of wing. **Status and Distribution:** Rare in extreme northern border areas. Pa
collected in Turkana, January 1932, and one photographed near Ileret, January 1989.

CRESTED BUSTARD *Eupodotis ruficrista gindiana* Plate 2
(Buff-crested Bustard, Red-crested Korhaan)

Length 46–53 cm (18–21"). A rather short-legged, black-bellied species of *thorn-scru*
and dry bush; the smallest East African bustard. **Adult male** tawny-brown above
marked with large, dark brown pointed spots and finer irregular brown-and-buff ba
ring. *Head almost plain sandy buff*, slightly greyer around eyes, light brown crown (wi
buff and dark brown speckling) and drooping *rufous-buff crest* (noticeable in display
Narrow black throat stripe extends down foreneck to black belly, contrasting with whi
on wing-coverts; most of neck buffy grey; breast grey, with white patches at side
Spread wing dark, with long white diagonal band near centre. Tail vermiculated blac
and white, appearing grey in flight except for broad black tips to all but central feath
ers. Bill dark grey; eyes pale cream; legs and feet darker cream. **Female** differs fro
male in more buff-flecked crown and nape, rufous-buff areas around eyes and ea
coverts, buff neck densely flecked and barred with brown, and lacks black foreneck streak. **Juvenile** resemble
female. **Voice:** Displaying male utters a variety of calls, including short series of melancholy whistles, *kwe*
kweu, kweu . . ., harsh strident calls and whistles continuing up the scale, finally ending on a sustained hig
note; also a descending high piping, *kee-keea, k'keea, k'keea . . .*, with something of the quality of Creste
Francolin's call. After aerial display, he gives a low *tuck-tuck-tuck, chuk chuk chuk chuk . . .* as he follows femal
Also a loud whistled *KWEEEE-kwer. . . KWEEEE-kwer-kwer . . .*, repeated continually on moonlit nights. **Habit**
Usually alone or in pairs. Secretive; tends to remain motionless behind shrub cover when under observatio
Vocalizations are followed by an impressive aerial display, ending with bird plummeting to the ground wi
closed wings which open only at the last instant. He then may walk behind the female, calling with neck ou
stretched horizontally and head feathers fluffed. **Similar Species:** Male Black-bellied and Hartlaub's Bustards a
slimmer, longer-necked and show largely white wings in flight; both are grassland species. **Status an**
Distribution: Fairly common and widespread in dry n. and e. Kenya, mainly below 1250 m. South of the hig
lands it ranges west into the Rift Valley only around Olorgesailie. In n. Tanzania, common on the Masai Stepp
west to Lake Natron and Tarangire NP. **Note:** Some authors consider *gindiana* specifically distinct from *ruficrist*

WHITE-BELLIED BUSTARD *Eupodotis senegalensis canicollis* Plate 29

Length 48–61 cm (19–24"). The only small East African bustard with a *white belly* in both sexes. **Adult male** largely vermiculated tawny-brown above and on breast; *neck bluish grey; side of head white, with black line along lower crown border* and *short black line below eye.* Rear of crown blue-grey, shading to blackish on forecrown and forehead. Black stripe down chin to throat, extending to lower malar region. Under tail-coverts sandy buff, barred with black. Bill deep bright pink, almost red when breeding, on basal half or more; tip and culmen dusky; eyes deep brown with narrow white peripheral ring; legs and feet pale creamy yellow. **Female** resembles male, but has blue-grey forehead and crown, tan cheeks with brown-and-buff-speckled subocular line; throat patch reduced to black-and-white speckling; lower throat and front of neck and breast sandy buff with fine dusky vermiculations. **Subadult male** has brownish face, white superciliary stripes, grey neck with white throat, and suggestion of blackish head pattern. Bill dull yellowish with dusky tip. **Juvenile** has greyish crown, largely whitish face with no black, tawny-buff neck whitish in front; blue-grey colour appears with age. **VOICE**: A very loud, harsh guttural *k'wuka WHUKa, k'wuka WHUKa . . ., or ka-warrak, ka-warrak . . .*, sometimes preceded by some low, frog-like *gaa* notes. **HABITS**: In pairs or family groups, and unlike other bustards young remain with adults for long periods. Noisy; individuals and groups frequently call to each other in morning and evenings. Courting male stretches neck up and forward, puffs out throat and raises crown feathers. **SIMILAR SPECIES**: Male Black-bellied and Hartlaub's Bustards show much white in the wings in flight. **STATUS AND DISTRIBUTION**: In Kenya, widespread in central, southern and southeastern grasslands and savannas, usually those with some shrub cover. Generally scarce in the far north, but there are scattered records from Lokichokio east to Moyale. Formerly common, but central highlands population greatly reduced in recent years. Widespread in suitable habitat in n. Tanzania, where most numerous in Serengeti NP.

BLACK-BELLIED BUSTARD *Eupodotis m. melanogaster* Plate 29

Length 58–63 cm (23–25"). A small bustard with thin neck and long legs. **Adult male** tawny-buff above, marked with brown and black, including on back and rump; *tail brown and buff with four or five narrow dark brown bars.* A thin black line down centre of foreneck, bordered narrowly with white, joins black underparts, which contrast with white edge of closed wing. *Neck almost uniformly buffy brown* with no obvious markings; top and sides of head buff with dark flecks; *lores and chin whitish*; throat dark with grey flecking. Whitish superciliary stripes border *thin black lines from eyes to black occipital feathers*, which form a short drooping crest. Spread wing mostly white above, with broad brown central wedge extending from base to median coverts. Outermost primary brownish black, most others with short black tips. Broad trailing edge of all but outermost secondaries black. Bill dull yellowish, dark brown on culmen; eyes light brown; legs and feet dull yellow. **Female** much plainer, similar to male above, largely buff below, fading to whitish on belly; *neck pale brownish with fine dark vermiculations* (appears plain at a distance). **Juvenile** duller, darker and with buff spots on wings; crown dark grey. **VOICE**: Although generally silent except for a rough *krak* of alarm, displaying male gives a short rising wheezy whistle, *zhweeeeee*, following which head is suddenly retracted onto the back. After a short pause, bird emits a popping *quock* or *plop* followed by a soft gurgling as head is slowly raised. **HABITS**: Calls with raised spread tail, often followed by short display flight with exaggerated wingbeats, after which bird dives to ground or glides down with wings raised in a V. Solitary except when breeding. **SIMILAR SPECIES**: Male Hartlaub's Bustard is somewhat stockier, with greyish neck, more contrasting head pattern, black lower back and rump and dark brown tail (usually concealed by wings, but evident in flight). Females difficult to separate; see Hartlaub's Bustard for distinctions. **STATUS AND DISTRIBUTION**: Local in open grasslands of the w. and cent. Kenyan highlands north to Mt Marsabit and the Huri Hills. In the south, present after heavy rains in Mara GR, Amboseli, Shimba Hills NP, and much of n. Tanzania from Mkomazi GR and Arusha NP west to the Lake Victoria basin.

HARTLAUB'S BUSTARD *Eupodotis hartlaubii* Plate 29

Length 61–71 cm (24–28"). Commonly mistaken for Black-bellied Bustard, but somewhat stockier and more contrastingly marked; bill thicker and appearing slightly heavier. **Adult male** has similar white-bordered black foreneck stripe connecting with black belly, but *hindneck greyish* rather than brown, and *side of face more sharply patterned*: large white spot on and below ear-coverts contrasting with *heavy black postocular line above* and with *another extending from eye to throat*, connecting to the black foreneck stripe. *Crown brownish black with whitish or buff speckling*; lores brownish or grey; suggestion of white superciliary stripes. Shows more white on the closed wing than does Black-bellied Bustard, has darker chin and throat (entirely black in presumed old birds, but in others a greyish 'pepper-and-salt' pattern darkening posteriorly). Black nape connects with black postocular lines. In flight, shows *black lower back and rump and dark brown tail* (faint narrow bars and ashy speckling evident only at close range); wings show more white than in Black-bellied Bustard owing to smaller and narrower dark wedge extending from body to coverts. Bill dull yel-

lowish horn with dark culmen; eyes brownish yellow; legs and feet yellowish. **Female** darker than female Blac■ bellied, with *cream line down foreneck; rest of neck streaked or somewhat spotted rather than finely vermic■ lated.* Upper breast with bold blackish markings, not fine vermiculations. *Lower back to tail generally grey, n■ brownish.* Bare parts as in male. **Immature male** shows dull adult pattern, no solid black on throat; eyes da■ yellow. Juvenile undescribed. **VOICE**: Silent most of year, but in breeding season male utters a three-part call: soft *click* followed by *pop!*, then (as head is lowered onto the breast) a deep prolonged *ooooooohm*. **HABIT** Solitary or in pairs. Generally prefers drier sites than Black-bellied Bustard, and is particularly attracted to bur■ ground. After heavy rains, both species may appear together in several localities. Displaying male struts wi■ raised tail, inflated throat and upper neck. **SIMILAR SPECIES**: Black-bellied Bustard compared above. **STATUS AN■ DISTRIBUTION**: In Kenya, rather local and uncommon in dry grasslands from the central highlands at Nairobi N■ southeast through Amboseli NP to the Tsavo NPs. Appears regularly after rains in Meru NP, and at Marsabit. Ra■ in n. Tanzania, with scattered records from Mkomazi GR, the Arusha District, and seasonally in e. Serengeti N■

JACANAS, FAMILY JACANIDAE
(World, 8 species; Africa, Kenya and n. Tanzania, 2)

Sometimes called lily-trotters, jacanas are long-legged, rail-like birds which inhabit swampy pools and marsh■ lake edges. Their exceedingly long toes and claws enable them to walk easily on floating vegetation, where the■ feed and nest, laying two to five tan eggs, heavily marked with black, on a sodden or floating wad of vegetatio■ sometimes on a bare water-lily leaf. Incubation and care of young is by male, who may brood and carry the■ under his wings.

AFRICAN JACANA *Actophilornis africanus* Plate 2■

Length 30–31 cm (12"). **Adult** unmistakable, with *chestnut wings and body, white fac■ and foreneck*, and *bright blue bill and frontal shield.* Lores, crown and hindneck black■ Legs and feet slate-grey or blue-grey, the long claws dark brown. *White underparts ■ **juvenile** glossy golden-yellow at sides of breast, rufous on flanks; also has *small grey ■ blue-grey frontal shield*, broad whitish-buff superciliary stripes and generally brow■ upperparts (darker on hindneck). Half-grown young distinguished from Lesser Jacana b■ small frontal shield, *uniform black cap and hindneck, chestnut secondaries and wing linings.* **Downy young** cinnamon-buff with black stripes above; crown rufous, wi■ black central and lateral stripes that converge on nape; face and underparts white■ **VOICE**: Various strident calls include a harsh rattle on take-off, a guttural *kyowrrr*, a gra■ ing *kreep-kreep-kreep*, and a loud, high-pitched, rapidly repeated trumpeting *weep■* *weep-weep-weeep*, not unlike call of some *Sarothrura* spp. **HABITS**: Forages for insects on water-lilies and othe■ floating vegetation or occasionally on muddy shores. Flies weakly on broad, rounded wings, feet dangling ■ trailing. Swims and dives readily, especially when annual flight-feather moult leaves the bird flightless. **SIMILA■ SPECIES**: Lesser Jacana compared above. **STATUS AND DISTRIBUTION**: In Kenya, a common and widespread res■ dent (though populations fluctuate greatly at some sites). Confined to fresh water with floating or emergent veg■ etation, from sea level to almost 3000 m, but largely absent from much of the arid north and east. Similarly wide■ spread in suitable habitat throughout n. Tanzania.

LESSER JACANA *Microparra capensis* Plate 2■

Length 15–16.5 cm (6–6.5"). Suggests juvenile African Jacana, but much smaller siz■ ordinarily diagnostic. Plumage *blackish brown above and white below, with golde■ rufous forehead, prominent white superciliary stripes*, and *cinnamon crown and nap■ Crown is shiny black in some*, presumably older, individuals. White face and side ■ head marked by *narrow rufous line from bill through eye to nape.* White underpart■ relieved by yellowish-buff patch on each side of neck and breast. Rump and tail cinna■ mon-rufous. In flight, shows *pale brown panel across wing* and *prominent white trai■ ing edge on black flight feathers*; underside of wing black. Bill pale brownish olive; eye■ hazel to dark brown, with narrow yellow orbital ring; tarsi and toes olive. **Juvenil■** resembles adult, but has buff feather edges above and *rump and upper tail-coverts ar■ black.* **Downy young** like that of African Jacana (Tarboton and Fry 1986). **VOICE**: A so■ *kruk* or *koop*, repeated several times; also a complaining higher *shrrree shree shree* or *see sree srrr*, and a so■ *tchrr-tchrr-tchrr.* **HABITS**: Forages on floating vegetation in ones and twos, but shy and easily overlooked. Flie■ readily and quite strongly; *raises wings on alighting, revealing black wing-linings.* **SIMILAR SPECIES**: See youn■ African Jacana. **STATUS AND DISTRIBUTION**: Very local and uncommon on ponds and lake edges with ampl■ floating vegetation. Small numbers present in parts of cent., w. and s. Kenya. In n. Tanzania, known only as a■ apparent vagrant in Arusha and Tarangire NPs. Formerly fairly common at Lake Jipe, but numbers greatly reduce■ in recent years.

PAINTED-SNIPES, FAMILY ROSTRATULIDAE
(World, 2 species; Africa, Kenya and n. Tanzania, 1)

Superficially like true snipes of the family Scolopacidae, these long-billed birds are in many respects more like rails or jacanas. Their eyes are large and set well forward, the elongate slender bill is hard-tipped and bent downward apically. In plumage and breeding behaviour there is notable reversal of the usual sex roles: the female is more brightly coloured than the male, and the male usually builds the nest (on the ground in marsh vegetation), incubates the four black-marked, buff eggs, and cares for the downy nidifugous young.

GREATER PAINTED-SNIPE *Rostratula b. benghalensis* Plate 24
(Painted Snipe)

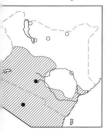

Length 23–26 cm (9–10"). A unique long-billed marsh-dweller, plump and short-tailed, with a striking head pattern. Both sexes show a *buff crown stripe, conspicuous white or yellowish eye-ring and postocular streak*, and a prominent *white stripe on side of breast*. Rows of *large black-bordered golden-buff spots on flight feathers give barred appearance to spread wings*; conspicuous golden V on back. **Female** is chestnut on neck and from face to upper breast, shading to black at sides of breast and on back, these areas separated from dark wings by the white stripe. Bill varies from pinkish orange or pale flesh-colour, greenish at base and paler at tip, to dull olive with reddish tip; eyes dark brown; tarsi and toes greyish green. **Male** paler and much less brightly coloured, the face and upper neck grey-brown and streaked; breast and back vermiculated and barred; wing-coverts buff-spotted. Bill brown with basal third greenish and tip blackish, or uniformly dull olive-brown. **Juvenile** resembles adult male but is paler on head, neck and back, and lacks distinct breast stripe. **Voice:** Usually silent when flushed. Breeding female gives a repeated hollow hooting, *koh-koh-koh. . .*, and a loud mellow *booo* like blowing across mouth of a bottle. Both sexes utter hisses, growls and clicking alarm calls. **Habits:** Skulking and secretive. Usually solitary or in pairs. Freezes when alarmed, flushing only on very close approach, then flying on rounded wings, feet dangling. Upon alighting, or when feeding, the rear end bobs up and down. Nocturnal and crepuscular, but also active on dull days, probing for invertebrates in soft mud; at night, may feed on grasslands or ploughed fields. **Similar Species:** True snipes are strongly streaked or barred on neck, breast and flanks; bills are generally longer and straighter. All lack bold golden-buff spots on flight feathers, and have different head patterns. Their flight is much stronger and they have narrower pointed wings. **Status and Distribution:** Widespread from sea level to over 2000 m, but uncommon, highly erratic and seasonal. Frequents marshy edges of lakes, ponds, swamps and irrigated areas. Largely absent from arid n. and e. Kenya.

CRAB-PLOVER, FAMILY DROMADIDAE

Warranting family status by virtue of its special features, this unique species differs from other shorebirds not only in structure, but also in its tunnel-nesting habits, single white egg and nidicolous young. It is endemic to the Red Sea region, breeding along the Gulf of Oman, Gulf of Aden and the southern Red Sea, wintering southward along the East African coast.

CRAB-PLOVER *Dromas ardeola* Plate 24

Length 38–41 cm (15–16"). A large coastal wader with *heavy, pointed, black bill* and generally *pied plumage*; body shape, stance and flight somewhat reminiscent of a thick-knee. **Adult** white, with black back, inner scapulars, wing tips and outer webs of primaries. Tail mainly white, central feathers grey. Crown and nape greyer in non-breeding plumage. **Juvenile** dark grey on back, streaked grey on crown and hindneck; inner wing feathers pale grey, not white. **Voice:** A low *kerrk*, and a sharper *chee-rruk* in flight. Flocks produce a continuous harsh chatter. **Habits:** Solitary or gregarious, often feeding in groups of 20–30 and gathering in hundreds at some tidal roosts. Forages plover-like, stalking crabs in intertidal areas, frequently picking and probing in the mud. Head often carried low, but long neck is stretched up and forwards when alarmed. Flight is usually low over the water, direct and unhurried, the neck extended and feet trailing, but at times flies higher in flocks, lines or Vs, the neck then retracted. **Similar Species:** Pied Avocet has thin upturned bill, longer and more slender tarsi and different plumage pattern. **Status and Distribution:** Migrant from breeding grounds on ne. African and Arabian coasts, present all months but largest numbers August–April. Normally confined to coastal mudflats, estuaries and coral reefs, especially around Lamu Archipelago, Mida Creek, and on s. Kenyan coast at Msambweni and Shimoni. Small groups frequently pass between the mainland and Pemba Island.

OYSTERCATCHERS, FAMILY HAEMATOPODIDAE
(World, 10 species; Africa, 2; Kenya and n. Tanzania, 1)

Large, heavily built waders with a distinctive, laterally compressed and colourful bill, sturdy pink legs, and each foot with three partially webbed toes. Oystercatchers inhabit coastlines around much of the globe, ours typically on rocky beaches and offshore islands. East African birds breed in the central Palearctic.

EURASIAN OYSTERCATCHER *Haematopus ostralegus longipes*   Plate 24
(Oystercatcher)

Length 40–43 cm (16–17"). A large pied coastal wader with a *bright orange-red bill.* **Adult** has *robust pinkish legs and feet,* red eyes and eyelids. Plumage brownish black above and from head to breast; white of underparts extends up beside bend of wing. In flight, shows *broad white stripe on rear of wing, and the white back, rump and tail base contrast with otherwise blackish upperparts and tail tip.* **Immature** and **non-breeding adults** have whitish collar across throat, lacking in breeding plumage. First-year bird is browner above than adult, with duskier and usually more pointed bill and *greyish legs and feet.* **Voice:** A plaintive, far-carrying *kleep* in flight, and a sharp repeated *kip!* or *pic!* **Habits:** Typically in ones and twos on rocky coasts, feeding on mussels; exceptionally in small groups. **Status and Distribution:** Uncommon palearctic migrant with a marked offshore passage along the East African coastline. Recorded annually, with sporadic records from lakes Turkana, Baringo and Nakuru.

AVOCETS AND STILTS, FAMILY RECURVIROSTRIDAE
(World, 10 species; Africa, Kenya and n. Tanzania, 2)

Slender graceful waders with thin bills and exceptionally long thin legs. The three toes are more or less webbed (the hallux vestigial or absent). Plumage is predominantly black and white. They are gregarious birds, breeding in small groups. The nest is a scrape in the ground, sometimes lined with pebbles, or a low mound of vegetation. The three or four spotted and blotched eggs are incubated by both sexes, and both care for the downy, nidifugous young.

PIED AVOCET *Recurvirostra avosetta*   Plate 24
(Avocet; Eurasian Avocet)

Length 43 cm (17"). Unmistakable, with *strongly recurved bill, long, slender blue-grey legs* and distinctive pied plumage. The black feathers become brownish with wear and fading. Eyes red (unlike in European birds). In flight, appears *largely white, with black on wing tips, wing-coverts, scapulars and crown;* feet project well beyond the tail. **Juvenile** has the dark plumage areas brown rather than black, and all white feathers are buff-tinged. **Voice:** A clear melodious *kluit* or *kleep.* **Habits:** Often in loose flocks numbering scores or hundreds. Feeds in shallows, sweeping bill from side to side; also swims, and up-ends to feed on the bottom of shallow ponds. Flight strong, on stiff wings. **Similar Species:** Crab-plover has heavy black bill and the wings show more black in flight. **Status and Distribution:** Widespread on inland waters, but with marked seasonal fluctuations. Numerous only on alkaline Rift Valley lakes. Small numbers breed at Lake Magadi in Kenya, and along most alkaline lakes in n. Tanzania. No evidence supports reports of palearctic birds in East Africa.

BLACK-WINGED STILT *Himantopus h. himantopus*   Plate 24

Length 38 cm (15"). A slender *black-and-white* wader with *thin, straight black bill* and *extremely long pinkish or red legs.* **Breeding male** glossy black above with mainly white head and neck, though hindcrown and nape occasionally dark grey. In flight, wings appear entirely black, both above and below; middle back also black, with pointed wedge of white extending from rump and upper tail-coverts; feet extend far beyond the whitish tail. **Breeding female** duller, less glossy, above than male, and head and neck white or merely with dark-tipped feathers. **Non-breeding adult** has white tips obscuring the greyish crown and nape, and appears mostly white-necked and white-headed. **Juvenile** sepia-brown from crown to back and wings, with extensive buff feather tipping; legs and feet duller, more greyish pink. In flight, shows pale trailing wing edges. **Voice:** A persistent piping *pip-pip-pip.* . . . **Habits:** Noisy and gregarious. Wades in deep water, picking insects from surface and at times immersing head and neck. Flight direct, with quick wingbeats. **Status and Distribution:** Widespread inland; common to abundant August–April on marshy pools and ponds, irrigated fields and edges of soda lakes. In coastal areas confined to muddy creeks and saltpans. More localized May–July, when small numbers breed, mainly in the Rift Valley from Magadi south to Lake Manyara NP. Some palearctic birds may reach n. Kenya.

THICK-KNEES, FAMILY BURHINIDAE
(World, 9 species; Africa, 4; Kenya, 4; n. Tanzania, 3)

These large and somewhat plover-like birds (known as dikkops in southern Africa, and one as Stone Curlew in Europe) inhabit stony or sandy semi-arid areas and shorelines. The group is characterized by the stout bill, large head, long yellowish legs with swollen tibiotarsal joints, large glaring yellow eyes, cryptically coloured body plumage and black-and-white flight feathers. Sexes are alike. The birds often stand with hunched posture, and they frequently squat on the tarsi to rest. They are largely crepuscular and nocturnal, feeding on insects and occasional small vertebrates, which they stalk plover-like, the walking or trotting gait interrupted by frequent stops. They also run rapidly, with head and neck extended. Flight is rapid, fluid and silent, the rather long tail obvious and white wing patches conspicuous. Their distinctive loud and semi-melodious calls, heard after sunset, are sometimes mistaken for those of nightjars. The two blotched eggs are laid in sand or on rocky ground, usually in a bare scrape devoid of nest material. Both sexes incubate and care for the precocial downy young.

EURASIAN THICK-KNEE or STONE CURLEW *Burhinus o. oedicnemus*   **Plate 17**

Length 40–44 cm (16–17"). Resembles resident Senegal and Water Thick-knees, with heavily streaked upperparts, neck and breast, but distinguished from them by a *narrow white bar on the lesser coverts bordered both above and below by black.* Legs and feet dull yellow. Bill smaller than in other species, black terminally with basal half or two-thirds yellow. In flight, shows black wing tips and trailing edge, with two white patches at base of primaries. Wings longer and more pointed than in other African thick-knees, and the wingbeats less fluttery. Feet do not project beyond tail. **Juvenile** paler, less heavily marked, wings at first lacking the well-defined contrasting black-and-white bands of adult. **VOICE:** A melodious *cur-LEEE.* Largely silent in East Africa. **HABITS:** Solitary or in small parties. Usually rests in shade by day. Squats or crouches flat on ground when approached. **SIMILAR SPECIES:** Water Thick-knee, a riparian bird, lacks lower black border to white wing-bar; shows broad grey panel on the closed wing. Senegal Thick-knee is more finely marked, has much less yellow on its larger bill (base of maxilla only); the closed wing shows no narrow white bar, but has a broad pale greyish panel with black along upper edge. **STATUS AND DISTRIBUTION:** A scarce palearctic migrant, October–March, in open sandy country or short grassland. Most records are from n. Kenya. Wanderers recorded south to Lake Nakuru, Nairobi and Amboseli NPs, Mara GR, and (once) Serengeti NP. Most birds presumably of the nominate race; there is no evidence to support reports of North African *saharae* from our region.

SENEGAL THICK-KNEE *Burhinus senegalensis inornatus*   **Plate 17**

Length 32–38 cm (12.5–15"). *Finely streaked* and with *no narrow white bar on the closed wing;* instead, a *wide, pale grey panel bordered above by black.* Bill proportionately large, *black* with yellow at base of maxilla; legs and feet yellowish. White primary patches prominent in flight. **VOICE:** A double whistled note, shriller than that of Eurasian and Water Thick-knees. Song *pi-pi-pi-pi-pi-PII-PII-PII-PII-PII-pii-pii-pii-pii-pii,* becoming louder in middle of series and then tapering off; resembles song of Spotted Thick-knee, but thinner and higher-pitched. **HABITS:** Prefers sandy country near water. Solitary or in pairs, sometimes in small flocks. Rests by day under dense bush or tree. Often forages along shorelines, at times near Water Thick-knees. Noisy at dusk. **SIMILAR SPECIES:** Water Thick-knee has narrow white bar on wing-coverts separated from pale grey panel by series of narrow black streaks; base of bill dull greenish, not yellow; legs more olive or greenish. Adult Eurasian Thick-knee is larger, more coarsely marked, has white band on wing-coverts bordered both above and below by black; immature has more uniformly brown wing. Spotted Thick-knee is spotted, not streaked, above. **STATUS AND DISTRIBUTION:** A local resident of sandy country near rivers, springs or lakeshores, confined to n. and nw. Kenya. Regular at Lake Turkana, occasional south to Lake Baringo.

WATER THICK-KNEE *Burhinus v. vermiculatus*   **Plate 17**
(Water Dikkop)

Length 38–41 cm (15–16"). More restricted to water's edge than other thick-knees. Closed wing shows a *broad grey panel narrowly streaked with black,* bordered above by narrow white and black bands, and by a black one below. Also differs from its relatives in having fine cross-bars and vermiculations on the body feathers, visible at close range, and a *dull greenish (not yellow) bill base.* Legs and feet olive or greenish. **Juvenile** somewhat more finely marked, with buff wing-covert edges. **VOICE:** At dusk and after dark, a rapid series of piping whistles, ris-

ing in pitch and volume, then subsiding with long melancholy notes, *wi-wi-wi-wi-wee-wee-WEE-WEE-WEE-WEE-WEE-WEEI-weeu-weeeu-weeeu-weeeu.* Alarm call a triple *kwa-lee-vee;* also a harsh *whee.* **HABITS:** Usually in pairs or small groups on open river banks or lake edges by day, especially when overcast. Somewhat more diurnal than other thick-knees, but most active and vocal at night (when ranging at least 1 km from water). Walks or runs with lowered head when disturbed, reluctant to fly. **SIMILAR SPECIES:** See Eurasian and Senegal Thick-knees. **STATUS AND DISTRIBUTION:** Locally common waterside resident throughout n. Tanzania and Kenya except at Lake Turkana, where replaced by Senegal Thick-knee. Most numerous at lakes Victoria and Jipe, along coastal creeks and on Pemba Island.

SPOTTED THICK-KNEE *Burhinus capensis*   Plate 17
(Spotted Dikkop)

Length *c.* 43 cm (17"). Boldly *spotted upperparts and lack of pronounced pattern or coverts of closed wing* distinguish this *dryland* species from other thick-knees. Face also browner and less patterned than in the others, and the tail strongly barred. Bill black, with basal third yellow; legs and feet yellow. In flight, shows double white primary patches, as do other thick-knees. Northern *B. c. maculosus* is brighter, more tawny, than the southern nominate race. **VOICE:** Mainly at night, a musical piping whinny, rising in pitch and volume and then subsiding: *pi-pi-pi-peo-PEO-PEO-PEO-PI-pi-pee-pee-pee.* Also has a rapid *qui-qui-qui-qui . . .,* or *pi-pi-pi,* and a descending *wuk-i-kik, wuk-i-kik, quee-quee-quee-quee-quee . . . .* **HABITS:** Solitary or in pairs in dry areas; rests in shade of shrub by day, crouching or walking away when approached. When flushed, flight low and silent, with rapid wingbeats; briefly holds wings spread upon alighting. Often encountered on roads and tracks at night. **SIMILAR SPECIES:** Other thick-knees are streaked, not spotted, above. **STATUS AND DISTRIBUTION:** Widespread and locally common resident of dry bush and savanna north, east and south of the Kenyan highlands, from the coastal lowlands up to 2000 m. Two races: *maculosus* in n. Kenya south to lakes Baringo and Bogoria, Samburu and Shaba GRs and Meru NP; *B. c. capensis* elsewhere.

COURSERS AND PRATINCOLES, FAMILY GLAREOLIDAE
(World, 18 species; Africa, 13; Kenya, 11; n. Tanzania, 6)

Somewhat plover-like birds of open habitats – deserts, grasslands and shorelines. Two subfamilies:

CURSORIINAE, including the rare (or vagrant) Egyptian-plover, *Pluvianus*, a unique waterside bird, and the commoner *Rhinoptilus* and *Cursorius*, long-legged ground birds that run rapidly and fly strongly. Some are crepuscular or nocturnal and difficult to observe. Sexes are alike. There is little or no nest, the one to three eggs laid on bare open ground. The downy young are nidifugous.

GLAREOLINAE, the pratincoles (*Glareola*), are medium-sized aerial feeders with very long pointed wings, short bill, legs shorter than in coursers, and usually a forked tail. Most are gregarious, nesting in colonies and forming large resting flocks. Sexes are alike. The nest is a scrape lined with a few pebbles or shells, and the two or three eggs are well marked. The young are as in Cursoriinae; they leave the nest in two or three days but are fed by both parents for a week or longer.

*EGYPTIAN-PLOVER *Pluvianus aegyptius*   Plate 17

Length 190–210 mm (7.5–8"). A rare northern waterside bird with strikingly patterned plumage: blue-grey above, *orange-buff below,* with black cap, sides of head, upper back and breast band contrasting with white superciliary stripes and throat. Short-legged and not very plover-like. In flight, the *broadly triangular wings are mainly white with broad black diagonal band,* black patch on forewing and narrow black trailing edge; short grey tail has white tip. Bill black and sharply pointed. Eyes dark brown, legs and feet blue-grey. **Juvenile** duller, with some rusty brown on head and wings. **VOICE:** A high-pitched *cherk-cherk-cherk,* usually in alarm. **HABITS:** Forages at water's edge, sometimes scratching (with both feet, following a forward jump), or running after prey, often with spread wings. Flight fast and flickering, low over water. Runs with spread wings upon landing. Unique nesting habits well known elsewhere: the eggs are covered with warm sand and cooled periodically by water carried on the adults' belly feathers; they hatch 'underground'. **STATUS AND DISTRIBUTION:** A resident of sandbars and sandy shores, common along the Omo River in s. Ethiopia, and the White Nile, but recorded only once from Kenya (near Todenyang, northwestern Lake Turkana, Aug. 1971).

TWO-BANDED COURSER *Rhinoptilus africanus gracilis*   **Plate 17**
(Double-banded Courser)

Length 200–240 mm (8–9.5"). A slender, thin-necked and large-eyed ground bird, scaly and buffy brown above, buff on face and neck, and with *two black bands across upper breast* (except in early juvenile plumage); underparts white. *Bold creamy-white superciliary stripes* separate dark (or mottled) cap from narrow dark eye-lines. Bill thin, dark, slightly decurved; eyes dark brown; legs and feet very pale yellowish. In flight, *dark brown outer primaries contrast with broad rufous band along rear of wing; white upper tail-coverts* form a narrow strip at base of the black tail; toes project well beyond tail tip. **Juvenile** sandier above and more finely marked; upper breast band faint in younger birds; outer primaries tipped with buffy white. **Voice:** A thin, plover-like *peeueee*, rising at end, and a sharper repeated *kik, kik, kik . . .* when flushed. Whistling alarm call *wheeu wheeu pip-pip-pip-pip-pip*. **Habits:** Usually in pairs. Nocturnal where daytime temperatures are high, but in many places active by day. Fairly confiding and approachable; seldom flies far when flushed. The single egg is laid among pebbles or mammal droppings. **Similar Species:** Heuglin's Courser is stockier, has chestnut stripe on neck and no rufous in wings. **Status and Distribution:** Rather uncommon and local resident of dry sandy or alkaline flats and short-grass plains, ranging through much of n. Tanzania north to the Loita Plains, Suswa, Olorgesailie, Kajiado, and Amboseli and Tsavo West NPs.

HEUGLIN'S COURSER *Rhinoptilus cinctus*   **Plate 17**
(Three-banded Courser)

Length 250–275 mm (10–11"). A fairly large, cryptically patterned courser with *broad mottled brown breast band bordered below by narrower black, white and chestnut bands; chestnut stripes, one from each side of the neck, converge in a point on the white breast*; rest of underparts white. Long pale superciliary stripes contrast with scaly brown crown and buffy-brown face patch. Bill black with yellow base; eyes brown; legs and feet yellowish. In flight, shows *white upper tail-coverts and outer rectrices* and rather uniformly dark wings. **Voice:** Alarm call a loud whistled *pieu*; after dark, a repetitive *whik-er, whik-er, whik-er.* **Habits:** Largely nocturnal, usually roosting in shade of bush by day. Appears on sandy roads and tracks at night, sometimes in small groups. **Similar Species:** Two-banded Courser has two narrow black breast bands. See also Violet-tipped Courser. **Status and Distribution:** *R. c. cinctus* is widespread but generally uncommon in semi-arid bush and scrub north, east and south of the Kenyan highlands, and into n. Tanzania east of the Rift Valley. The race *emini* ranges from Nyanza and the Mara GR south through Serengeti NP to Tabora District.

VIOLET-TIPPED COURSER *Rhinoptilus chalcopterus*   **Plate 17**
(Bronze-winged Courser)

Length 250–280 mm (10–11"). A fairly large courser with *long dark red legs*, plain brown neck and upperparts, a *single black band across lower border of brownish breast*; rest of underparts white. Bold head pattern, with *white forehead, superciliary stripes, postocular marks and sides of throat* contrasting with dark crown and face patch. Eyes large, *dark brown*, with narrow purplish-red orbital ring; bill black with dull red mandible base. Flight pattern suggests a *Vanellus* plover, with white rump, greyish diagonal wing-covert band, black flight feathers and white wing-linings. Diagnostic iridescent violet primary tips seldom obvious unless wings spread at close range. **Voice:** A penetrating trisyllabic *gee-leew-eee* resembling piping of Spotted Thick-knee, and a ringing *ki-kooi* (Sinclair 1984). Also a harsh flight call when flushed. **Habits:** Nocturnal; rests in shade of shrub by day. Sometimes seen on roads at night. **Similar Species:** Crowned Plover is stockier, has yellowish eyes, bright pinkish-red (not dull red) legs and black forehead. **Status and Distribution:** Local and uncommon in open bush and woodland. Mainly a non-breeding intra-African migrant from the southern tropics, May–November, recorded from ne. Tanzania and se. Kenya north to Malindi and Meru NP. Other scattered records include breeding in Tarangire NP (Dec. 1981).

SOMALI COURSER *Cursorius somalensis littoralis*   **Plate 17**

Length 200–220 mm (8–8.5"). A *pale,* long-legged ground bird of semi-arid plains in n. Kenya. **Adult** plumage generally creamy brown with *white belly and under tail-coverts,* and a distinctive head pattern: long white superciliary stripes bordered below by *black postocular lines which meet in a V on the nape,* as do the superciliaries; hindcrown grey. Largely black bill thin and decurved, brownish horn at base; *legs and feet pale yellowish cream.* Black primaries contrast in flight with pale brownish upper wing-coverts and grey secondaries as in Cream-coloured Courser, but, unlike that species, the wing-linings are mainly pale greyish and, *from below, inner portion of wing contrasts sharply with blackish distal half.* Tail mainly pale brown, with dusky subterminal spot on central feathers and broader blackish tips on the remaining ones, with white outer web of outer pair, and some white near tip of adjacent pair. **Juvenile** blotched and barred with dark brown above; bill yel-

389

lowish brown on basal half or more. **Voice:** A sharp *whit-whit* on ground and in flight. **Habits:** Diurnal; in pairs or small groups. Runs rapidly, stopping at brief intervals to feed or look around; bobs head. Prefers to run when approached, but may crouch and stretch neck forward. Flight noticeably jerky. **Similar Species:** Cream-coloured Courser is larger, sandier, has underside of wing entirely black, and relatively shorter bill and legs, the feet not projecting so far beyond the tail as in Somali Courser. Temminck's Courser is darker, with rufous crown, nape and upper belly. **Status and Distribution:** Locally common on short-grass plains throughout n. Kenya (west to Lokichokio, east to Mandera), extending south through Buffalo Springs and Shaba GRs and Meru NP to Tsavo East NP at Aruba and the adjacent Galana Ranch. **Note:** Although considered specifically distinct by van Someren (1922), generally treated as a race of Cream-coloured Courser until recently (cf. Pearson and Ash, in press).

*CREAM-COLOURED COURSER *Cursorius cursor* Plate 17

Length 210–240 mm (8.25–9.5"). A palearctic vagrant, sandier in tone than Somali Courser, with *underside of wing entirely dark*, and bill and tarsi relatively shorter. **Adult** has slightly different tail pattern (central feathers plain sandy buff, the others with narrow subterminal blackish bars). **Juvenile** tail pattern like that of adult, distinct from that of young Somali Courser, in which distal half of tail is barred. Dorsal body plumage more finely barred than in that species. **Voice:** Common call "a sharp piping whistle, rather harsh but liquid . . . ; often repeated" (Cramp and Simmons 1983). **Habits:** Those of Somali Courser. **Status and Distribution:** Rare or accidental visitor. Known only from sight records of several birds along the east shore of Lake Turkana, January–February 1987.

TEMMINCK'S COURSER *Cursorius temminckii* Plate 17

Length 190–210 mm (7.5–8"). Similar to Somali Courser in pattern, but *darker brown*, the *belly rufous with a blackish central patch* and crissum white; crown and nape rufous; black eye patches contrast with narrow pale superciliary stripes. In flight, black flight feathers contrast with generally pale brown upperparts; underside of wing entirely dark. Bill black or dusky; legs and feet whitish. **Juvenile** has duller head pattern and is somewhat barred above. **Voice:** A piercing metallic *enrr-enrr-enrr* or *keer-keer*, recalling a squeaking hinge. **Habits:** Diurnal; in pairs or small nomadic flocks, appearing (and often promptly breeding) on recently burnt grassland. Forages like preceding species. When alarmed, raises and lowers body by bending legs. **Similar Species:** See Somali Courser. **Status and Distribution:** The commonest and most widespread courser, largely allopatric with Somali Courser but the two sympatric in Tsavo East NP and perhaps elsewhere. Frequents areas of short grass (including airstrips) and open bush, being most numerous in parts of the Serengeti NP, Mara GR, Nairobi NP and around Naro Moru, breeding at up to 2000 m and wandering frequently to 2750 m. A seasonal visitor (occasionally breeding) to lower elevations at lakes Baringo and Magadi, Buffalo Springs and Shaba GRs, Tsavo East NP and the Tana River delta (plus an old record from Lamu), generally following periods of high rainfall.

COLLARED PRATINCOLE *Glareola pratincola fuelleborni* Plate 17
(Common Pratincole)

Length 240–250 mm (9.5–10"). On the ground, suggests a squatty, long-winged plover. In *graceful tern-like flight, a white patch on lower rump and upper tail-coverts* conspicuous; tail black, showing much white on outer feathers; *wing-linings chestnut*, sometimes mixed with brown; primaries and secondaries blackish with narrow white trailing edge. **Breeding plumage** plain brown, with *creamy-buff throat bordered by thin black line;* belly whitish. At rest, long pointed wings reach or exceed tip of *deeply forked tail.* Bill black, red basally; eyes brown; tarsi black. **Non-breeding adult** has less distinct throat border, and breast is more mottled. **Juvenile** has dark brown feathers of upperparts tipped with buff, and the pale throat lacks dark border; tail shorter than in adult. **Voice:** A chattering *kik, kik, kirrik.* **Habits:** Nests colonially, sometimes in isolated pairs. Noisy flocks assemble on lakeshores or riverine flats. Hawks insects in the air and runs after them on the ground. **Similar Species:** See Black-winged Pratincole. **Status and Distribution:** Locally common along lakes and rivers, mainly below 1800 m. Breeds April–September in low-rainfall areas below 1500 m, including lakes Turkana, Magadi and Manyara. Seasonal at most localities. Birds present alongside Madagascar Pratincoles at Sabaki on the north Kenyan coast regarded by some authors as *G. p. erlangeri*.

*BLACK-WINGED PRATINCOLE *Glareola nordmanni*   Plate 17

Length 230–255 mm (9–10"). At rest, appears darker brown, less sandy or buffy, above than Collared Pratincole. Distinguished in flight by entirely *black under wing-surface* (but Collared Pratincole can appear black-winged in poor light); also by *darker brown upperparts and forewing* showing *less contrast with flight feathers, lack of white on trailing edge of wing*, more extensive black loral area, and smaller amount of red on base of bill (not extending to nostril). **Juvenile** dark brown with buff-edged feathers above; wing-linings as in adult. **Voice:** Similar to that of Collared Pratincole, but lower-pitched and more strident. **Similar Species:** Collared Pratincole compared above. **Status and Distribution:** A palearctic migrant passing in large numbers west of Lake Victoria. The few Kenyan records are from Lake Naivasha (Oct. 1953), Lessos (Oct. 1969), north of Marsabit (March 1978), Lake Baringo (April 1981) and Mara GR (Nov. 1993).

MADAGASCAR PRATINCOLE *Glareola ocularis*   Plate 17

Length 230–250 mm (9–10"). Distinguished from Collared Pratincole by *shorter, shallowly forked tail*, generally *dark brown upperparts and breast*, a *rufous belly patch* contrasting with the white lower belly and crissum, and absence of white on trailing edge of wings. Dark cap and white subocular streak conspicuous, as are white upper tail-coverts; wing-linings chestnut. Bill black with red base; eyes brown; tarsi black. **Voice:** A repeated sharp *wick-wick-wick*. **Habits:** Highly gregarious. Rests on dunes and adjacent sand- or mudflats. Flocks hawk insects, especially in evening, often high in the air over open habitats and at times over coastal forest. **Similar Species:** Collared Pratincole compared above. **Status and Distribution:** A Malagasy migrant that spends its non-breeding season (April–Sept.) along the East African coast. Hundreds are regular at the Sabaki River estuary north of Malindi, the flocks augmented almost daily in August and early September; smaller numbers from Lamu south to the n. Tanzanian coast. Report of flocks at Kendu Bay, Lake Victoria (21–22 Aug. 1920) remains questionable.

ROCK PRATINCOLE *Glareola n. nuchalis*   Plate 17
(White-collared Pratincole)

Length 175–195 mm (7–7.5"). A *small, short-tailed pratincole* associated with *emergent rocks in rivers*. **Adult** mainly dark brownish grey, with white lower belly and crissum; narrow *white postocular stripes meet to form collar across hindneck* below the black cap. The only East African pratincole with dull *orange to coral-red tarsi*; bill also red, with black culmen and tip. In flight, white upper tail-coverts and tail base contrast with largely black, slightly forked tail; wings uniformly dark above, but with distinctive *short white stripe on centre of wing-linings*. **Juvenile** lacks collar and postocular stripes, has brownish-grey upperparts and breast finely spotted with buff; bill and tarsi dull orange-red. **Voice:** A faint *kip-kip*, and a harsh *kek-kek-kek*. In display, both sexes give a purring trill. **Habits:** In pairs or small groups perching on exposed riverine rocks, less often on tree limbs overhanging water. Hawks insects in the air, especially in early morning or late evening. **Similar Species:** Collared Pratincole is larger, with deeply forked tail, and has different head and throat patterns. **Status and Distribution:** Numerous resident pairs breed on rocks along the Nzoia River in w. Kenya, from Mumias south to Ukwala. Elsewhere, one was seen with Collared Pratincoles on the lower Tana near Garsen, February 1985.

PLOVERS, FAMILY CHARADRIIDAE
(World, 66 species; Africa, 30; Kenya, 21; n. Tanzania, 19)

A widespread family of 'shorebirds' characteristic of grasslands, fields, mudflats and beaches. All are compact and large-headed, with short straight bills and relatively long legs. The sexes are similar, usually plain above, although many species have white wing-stripes or wing-patches that are conspicuous in flight. The nest is a mere scrape in the ground where the two to four cryptically marked eggs are laid. The young are downy and nidifugous. Our species are distributed among three genera: *Vanellus*, large species (sometimes called lapwings), residents or short-distance migrants with broad, rounded wings, the head and breast often patterned, and most showing bold black-and-white wing markings and white-based black tail; *Pluvialis*, large, thickset palearctic migrants with long pointed wings, mottled upperparts, and distinctive black underparts in breeding plumage; *Charadrius*, the typical plovers, small, short-necked, and often with black-and-white head pattern and dark breast bands, represented by four resident species and six palearctic migrants in our region.

LONG-TOED PLOVER *Vanellus c. crassirostris*   **Plate 18**
(Long-toed Lapwing; White-winged Plover)

Length *c.* 31 cm (12"). A long-necked marsh plover with upright stance, *white face and foreneck*, black hindneck and breast; upperparts grey-brown; belly white. *Bill pink with dark tip*; legs and feet pinkish red; eyes and skin of eyelids darker red. In flight, *white forewing (including primary coverts)* and rump band contrast with black flight feathers and tail. **Juvenile** has feathers of upperparts edged with buff, black areas tinged brown, and buff mottling on the white wing-coverts. **VOICE**: A metallic *kik-k-k-k.* . . . **HABITS**: Forages jacana-fashion, in pairs or small groups, on floating vegetation or among sedges and grasses in shallow water. **SIMILAR SPECIES**: Blacksmith Plover has different head and wing patterns, black bill and tarsi. **STATUS AND DISTRIBUTION**: Fairly common local resident of marshes and permanent swamps in the Lake Victoria basin, occasionally up to 2200 m in Uasin Gishu and Trans-Nzoia Districts; also at lakes Baringo and Naivasha, Thika, Amboseli NP, Lake Jipe and along the lower Tana River. Kenyan range may be expanding eastward with drainage of many western swamps and marshes. In n. Tanzania, regular in the Lake Victoria area and Ngorongoro Crater, sporadic in Lake Manyara and Tarangire NPs.

BLACKSMITH PLOVER *Vanellus armatus*   **Plate 18**

Length 28–31 cm (11–12"). A distinctive black, grey and white plover of inland shores and wetlands. **Adult** has *black face, neck and breast, white cap,* broad white patch on hindneck and white belly; back and some scapulars black, and folded wings mainly grey. In flight, *black flight feathers contrast with grey upper wing-coverts*; wing-linings, rump and tail white, the latter with a broad terminal wedge of black. Bill, legs and feet black; eyes dark red. Sharp spine on carpal joint rarely visible in the field. **Juvenile** shows adult pattern, but white crown feathers tipped with brown, chin and throat whitish, and all black feathers buff-tipped. **VOICE**: A characteristic repeated *klink klink klink,* more rapid when alarmed (likened to a blacksmith hammering on an anvil). Alarm call near nest or young a screaming *kewah.* **HABITS**: Usually in pairs on dry ground near water, sometimes in loose flocks. Noisy and wary, flushing readily when alarmed. Feeds on crustaceans and other invertebrates. **SIMILAR SPECIES**: Spur-winged Plover has black cap, white cheeks and brownish back. See also Long-toed Plover. **STATUS AND DISTRIBUTION**: Common and widespread resident throughout n. Tanzania and into Kenya along the Rift Valley lakes and in wet areas with short grass and muddy shores in the adjacent central highlands. Ranges north to Lake Baringo and Maralal; also at Amboseli NP and Lake Jipe, wandering to the middle and lower Tana River and Tsavo East NP. Largely absent from the Lake Victoria basin and most of w. Kenya, although sporadic in Trans-Nzoia and Mara GR. Generally allopatric with Spur-winged Plover, except at Lake Baringo and in Amboseli NP.

SPUR-WINGED PLOVER *Vanellus spinosus*   **Plate 18**

Length 25–28 cm (10.5"). A medium-sized plover of inland waterways, plain brown above and with *black breast and upper belly joined to chin by a black mid-ventral line;* crown and hindneck also black, contrasting with *white cheeks and sides of neck.* In flight, a white diagonal bar separates brown forewing from black flight feathers; black distal half of tail contrasts with white base and upper tail-coverts; under tail-coverts and wing-linings also white. Bill, legs and feet black; eyes dark red. Sharp spur near bend of wing visible only at close range. **Juvenile** has black feathers tipped brown and speckled with white. **VOICE**: Alarm call a repeated metallic *pitt, pitt, pitt.* . .; territorial call a loud *ti-ti-terr-er.* **HABITS**: Often shy, but approachable where unmolested. In pairs or small noisy parties along water's edge. Feeds on insects, other invertebrates, also small lizards. Noisy both day and night. **SIMILAR SPECIES**: Crowned, Black-winged and Wattled Plovers show similar flight pattern from above, but they do not have extensive black underparts. Flying Blacksmith Plover appears similar from underneath but has black back and no white on upper wing-surface. **STATUS AND DISTRIBUTION**: Common and widespread resident of flats and areas of short grass along Kenyan rivers and lakeshores south to Kisumu, lakes Baringo and Bogoria, the Galana and Sabaki Rivers, Tsavo East and Amboseli NPs. A few inhabit the coast south to Garsen, although rarely on the open shore. Replaced by Blacksmith Plover on Rift Valley lakes from Bogoria south. Present most months at Lake Manyara NP, but only vagrants known elsewhere in n. Tanzania.

BLACK-HEADED PLOVER *Vanellus tectus*   **Plate 18**

Length *c.* 25 cm (10"). A distinctive dry-country plover with a *long, thin black crest. White chin and white nape patch are sandwiched between black of crown and neck;* back brown; underparts white. Eyes yellow; *base of bill, small loral wattles, legs and feet red.* White forehead patch is more extensive in the northeastern race *latifrons.* In flight, a long white diagonal wing-stripe contrasts with black tip and trailing edge; tail white with broad black terminal band. **Juvenile** has shorter crest and buff-tinged upperparts. **VOICE**: A short whistled *kir-kir-*

kir of alarm; mobbing call a loud, shrill *kwairrr*, less strident than that of most *Vanellus* plovers. **HABITS:** Pairs or small noisy parties inhabit open dry bush. Lays eggs on bare soil, sometimes at edge of sandy tracks. Feeds on insects and other invertebrates. **SIMILAR SPECIES:** Crowned Plover lacks crest and has different head pattern. **STATUS AND DISTRIBUTION:** In Kenya, a locally common resident of sparsely bushed dry areas at low elevations. *V. t. latifrons* ranges south to Meru NP, Kora NR, Tsavo East NP, and along the lower Tana River to Karawa; occasional in Tsavo West NP. One record from n. Tanzania (near Arusha, Aug. 1962). Nominate *tectus* is northwestern, extending south to the Kerio Valley and lakes Baringo and Bogoria.

SENEGAL PLOVER *Vanellus lugubris*   Plate 18
(Lesser Black-winged Plover)

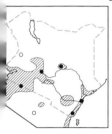

Length 22–26 cm (9–10"). A small lowland plover. **Adult** has dark grey upper breast separated from white belly by a *narrow black band.* Upperparts dark olive-brown, the head and neck dark grey with a *small white forehead patch* sharply defined from grey crown. Bill blackish, *legs and feet dark slate-grey or blackish;* inconspicuous *orbital ring dull yellowish; eyes yellow,* with narrow bright red outer ring at edge of iris. In flight, *white secondaries* contrast with otherwise dark wing feathers, and white upper tail-coverts and tail are conspicuous, the tail showing a broad subterminal black band. **Juvenile** has forehead patch and breast demarcation line partly obscured by pale feather tips, and wing-coverts are tipped with buff; legs and feet brown. **VOICE:** A melodious *kitti-kooee,* a shorter piping *klu-WIT,* oft-repeated, and a wailing alarm call. **HABITS:** In pairs or small groups. Wanders widely, often appearing shortly after grass fires, and nests on burnt or heavily grazed grassland. Active at night, and at least some migration is nocturnal. **SIMILAR SPECIES:** Larger Black-winged Plover, typically of higher elevations, has shorter dark red tarsi, dorsal plumage lacks olive tinge, head and neck are paler grey, and forehead patch is usually larger and more diffuse; wings show bold white diagonal stripe and black trailing edge in flight. **STATUS AND DISTRIBUTION:** Widespread but extremely local and nomadic in open or bushed grassland, especially in the Lake Victoria basin, along the south Kenyan coast and in ne. Tanzania; mainly below 1500 m, but wanders to higher areas and rarely north to Lake Baringo and Meru NP. Nowhere resident. Small numbers are regular April–August in coastal lowlands, June–August in the Tsavo NPs, November–May in the Lake Victoria basin, Mara GR and adjacent n. Tanzania, January–April in Arusha NP.

BLACK-WINGED PLOVER, *Vanellus melanopterus minor*   Plate 18

Length 26–27 cm (10.5"). A *highland* species resembling Senegal Plover, but slightly larger and heavier and with *much broader black band on lower breast;* white forehead patch also larger, not so sharply defined, and often with short pale superciliary extensions. Bill black; *legs and feet dull red; orbital ring purplish red; eyes orange-yellow.* More white on wings than in Senegal Plover; in flight, a *broad white diagonal band* separates brown forewing and black flight feathers. **Juvenile** pale brown on head, neck and breast; dorsal feathers broadly edged with buff. **VOICE:** *Che-che-chereek,* higher-pitched and more strident than call of Senegal Plover. When disturbed, gives a loud, rapid metallic *kay-kay-kay-kay. . .;* also has a softer, plaintive *titihoya.* **HABITS:** Usually in flocks on high grasslands or ploughed fields. Migrates altitudinally, breeding in the highlands March–July, then descending to lower elevations. Aggressive toward human intruders on breeding grounds. Nests in grass, often following burning, or on recently ploughed ground. Active at night. **SIMILAR SPECIES:** Senegal Plover compared above. **STATUS AND DISTRIBUTION:** Locally common resident of high grassland and cultivation between 1500 and 3000 m. In Kenya, widely distributed in the w. and cent. highlands and (outside the breeding season) in the Mara GR. In n. Tanzania, resident in the Crater Highlands and Arusha District, regularly moving lower after nesting.

CROWNED PLOVER *Vanellus c. coronatus*   Plate 18
(Crowned Lapwing)

Length 30–31 cm (12"). A conspicuous large plover of grassy plains, with brown back, brown chest and white belly. Easily identified by *white ring on black crown. Base of bill, long legs and feet red;* eyes yellow. In flight, shows *broad white diagonal wing-stripe,* white tail with broad subterminal black band, and white upper tail-coverts. **Juvenile** has more obscure head pattern and duller bare parts than adult, and numerous buff feather margins. **VOICE:** A strident *erEEK,* an excited *kree-kree-kreeip-kreeip,* or *WEEK-EEEK-EEEK;* a chattering *tri-tri-tri-tri* in display. **HABITS:** Pairs or small groups noisily protest any territorial intrusion. Feeds on insects, often extracted from dung of large mammals. Congregates into groups in late afternoon, these sometimes indulging in terrestrial and aerial displays. **SIMILAR SPECIES:** Black-headed Plover is crested, and in flight shows somewhat more white in wing (primary bases plus primary coverts). Black-winged, African Wattled and Spur-winged

Plovers have similar flight pattern, but primary coverts are black. **STATUS AND DISTRIBUTION**: Widespread and fairly common resident and wanderer on dry grassland and open savanna; often on cultivated ground; recorded as high as 3000 m. Absent from coastal lowlands south of Malindi and from much of the Lake Victoria basin.

AFRICAN WATTLED PLOVER *Vanellus senegallus lateralis*   Plate 18
(Senegal Wattled Plover)

Length 34 cm (13.5"). A large plover with *long yellow facial wattles* and smaller red ones on forehead. **Adult** generally greyish brown, with white forecrown, *black chin and throat, and streaked neck*. Legs, feet, eyes and bill yellow, the latter with black tip; sharp black spur near bend of wing. In flight, shows diagonal white wing-stripe, white upper tail-coverts and tail, the latter with a broad dusky subterminal band. **Juvenile** has small wattles, lacks black chin, and has the white forehead obscured. **VOICE**: A shrill high-pitched *kip, kip, kip*; alarm call *ke-WEEP, ke-WEEP*. **HABITS**: Usually solitary or in pairs near water. Nests on bare or sparsely vegetated ground, or among rocks. A slow, deliberate feeder. Raises wings vertically upon alighting. **SIMILAR SPECIES**: Black-winged and Crowned Plovers (with similar flight patterns) show much more white on underparts, and have dull red legs and feet. **STATUS AND DISTRIBUTION**: Local resident of damp short grass near lakes, swamps and streams. Fairly common in Mara GR and Serengeti NP, less so in the Lake Victoria basin and w. Kenyan highlands. Occasionally wanders east to Rift Valley lakes, including Turkana, and twice to Tsavo West NP.

BROWN-CHESTED PLOVER *Vanellus superciliosus*   Plate 18
(Brown-chested Wattled Plover)

Length *c.* 23 cm (9"). A small plover, accidental in our region. **Adult** shows *broad chestnut band on lower breast, black crown and nape, pale chestnut forehead and short yellow loral wattles*. Upperparts olive-brown, grey on face, neck and upper breast; belly white. Bill, legs and feet blackish; eyes yellow. In flight, shows short white diagonal wing-stripe, white upper tail-coverts and tail, with partial black subterminal band on the inner rectrices. **Juvenile** less brightly coloured, with brownish-grey face and neck shading to dull brown on breast. Hindcrown dark brown; forecrown and forehead dull rufous; wattles dull brownish yellow; orbital skin yellow; legs and feet olive. **VOICE**: A harsh, penetrating flight call, likened to squeak of a rusty hinge. **HABITS**: May associate with Senegal Plover on grasslands. Often on recently burnt ground. Active at night. **SIMILAR SPECIES**: Senegal Plover has no wattles, lacks chestnut on breast, and in flight shows broad white trailing wing edge. Flying juvenile Caspian Plover shows no white in wing. **STATUS AND DISTRIBUTION**: Non-breeding migrant from West Africa, visiting grasslands and lakeshores in central parts of the continent, July–October. Vagrant to Lake Victoria basin (specimens, Kisumu, 1916–17) and Ruiru, north of Nairobi (injured bird photographed, Jan. 1986). Northern Tanzanian records from Serengeti NP (Nov. 1962, Nov. 1985).

*PACIFIC GOLDEN PLOVER *Pluvialis fulva*   Plates 18, 21
(Lesser Golden Plover)

Length 23–26 cm (9–10"). *Smaller, slimmer and browner than Grey Plover, with entirely grey wing-linings and different call*. **Non-breeding adult** greyish brown above, spangled with pale golden-yellow, and *prominent buffy-yellow superciliary stripes extend well behind eyes*. Underparts lightly mottled greyish or brownish yellow, producing overall buff effect; belly and crissum white. In flight, shows only a faint wing-stripe, generally appearing uniformly brown above. Legs, feet and bill dark grey. In **breeding plumage**, yellow-spangled black upperparts are separated from black face and underparts by a broad white area at sides of breast continuing as a narrow white line along sides and flanks. **Juvenile** resembles non-breeding adult, but superciliary stripes more yellowish, breast mottled dull yellow and grey-brown; flanks and belly lightly barred with dark brown. **VOICE**: A clear whistled *tu-ee*, and a plaintive *klee*; also a dry *chuwit*. **HABITS**: Much like those of the common Grey Plover but more active, with comparatively rapid feeding gait. Favours grassy plains, as well as shorelines. **SIMILAR SPECIES**: Grey Plover is larger, heavier, greyer above, with white upper tail-coverts, prominent wing-stripe and black axillaries. Caspian Plover is

smaller, plainer above and with pale legs. The extralimital American Golden Plover, *P. dominica*, is known as a vagrant in southern Africa and might appear in our region. It is somewhat stockier, but with a longer primary extension than *fulva*, typically with four primary tips visible, whereas in *fulva* primaries almost entirely concealed by the posthumeral ('tertial') feathers; toes do not project beyond the tail in flight. Belly grey, not white, in non-breeding plumage. Breeding-plumaged birds show more white on sides of breast than *fulva*, but usually no continuous white flank line. **Status and Distribution**: Palearctic migrant recorded almost annually in East African coastal lowlands, particularly from the Tana River delta south to the Sabaki River and Malindi. Numbers usually small; flock of 57 in December 1985 exceptional. Scarce and irregular along Rift Valley lakes and at Aruba Dam in Tsavo East NP.

GREY PLOVER *Pluvialis squatarola* — Plates 18, 21
(Black-bellied Plover)

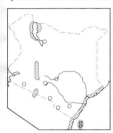

Length 28–31 cm (11–12"). A *large, stocky, shoreline plover with a stout black bill* and dark grey legs and feet. **Breeding plumage** (Aug.–Sept. and March–May) black from face to belly, and sides of neck and breast bordered by broad white line; under tail-coverts white. **Non-breeding plumage** mottled brownish grey above, white below with dusky mottling on breast; side of face marked by diffuse dark eye-line and smudge on ear-coverts, accentuating the pale superciliary stripe. In flight, shows *white upper tail-coverts and white streak on upperside of wings*, and from below diagnostic *black axillary feathers contrast with otherwise whitish wing-linings and belly*. **Juvenile** resembles non-breeding adult, but is browner and finely spotted with yellowish buff. **Voice**: A far-carrying trisyllabic whistle, *tlee-oo-ee*. **Habits**: Solitary or gregarious along the coast, where hundreds may gather at tidal roosts. Posture characteristically hunched; feeding behaviour lethargic. **Similar Species**: See Pacific Golden Plover. **Status and Distribution**: Palearctic migrant, August–April, common on coastal flats. Small numbers occasional on inland lakeshores, mainly in the Rift Valley. A few first-year birds remain all year.

RINGED PLOVER *Charadrius hiaticula tundrae* — Plates 19, 21

Length 18–20 cm (7–8"). Small and compact, with a single *dark breast band, narrow white collar* and a *stubby bill. Legs and feet orange*, the tarsi rather short. Crown and back dark brown, underparts white. In **breeding plumage** (September and April–May), bill orange with black tip, white forehead broadly bordered by black, and narrow white superciliary stripes contrasting with the black mask. In **non-breeding plumage**, black is replaced by dusky brown, the superciliary stripes are usually continuous with the pale forehead, and the bill may be all black. **Juvenile** resembles non-breeding adult, but breast band is paler, reduced in centre and sometimes broken; tarsi dull orange-yellow. In flight shows strong white wing-stripe; sides of rump, lateral tail-coverts and tip of tail also white. **Voice**: A distinctive melodious whistle with rising inflection, *too-li*; a sharper *too-i* or *wip* when alarmed. **Habits**: Usually in small loose groups with other shorebirds. Runs rapidly on beach or mudflats, stopping abruptly to peck at food items; also feeds in drier grassy habitats. **Similar Species**: See Little Ringed Plover. **Status and Distribution**: Palearctic migrant, common on coastal flats and beaches, and on inland lakeshores and river edges, September to early May. A few remain all year at the coast.

LITTLE RINGED PLOVER *Charadrius dubius curonicus* — Plates 19, 21

Length 15–17 cm (6–6.5"). Separated from the common Ringed Plover by *diagnostic call*, smaller and *less bulky build*, and *lack of obvious wing-stripes*. **Adult** also distinguished by *yellow orbital ring*, dull pinkish or yellowish legs and feet, and lack of orange on the bill (but there is a trace of yellow at base below). In **breeding plumage** shows a narrow white crown band behind the black frontal bar. **Non-breeding** bird has black replaced by brown, and the forehead and superciliary stripes are buff-tinged. **Juvenile** has smaller eye-ring and obscurely patterned brownish head; breast band usually broken. **Voice**: A far-carrying and descending *pee-o*. **Habits**: Solitary or in small groups, seldom mixing with other shorebirds. Wary. **Similar Species**: Ringed Plover discussed above. See Kentish Plover. **Status and Distribution**: Palearctic migrant, regular in small numbers October to early April, mainly on Kenyan Rift Valley lakes and along larger rivers. Local at the coast on dry flats and saltpans. Rare in n. Tanzania (few recent records).

KITTLITZ'S PLOVER *Charadrius pecuarius* — Plates 19, 21
(Kittlitz's Sandplover)

Length 14–15 cm (5.5–6"). A small buff-breasted plover. **Adult** *rich buff below*, and with *distinctive black-and-white head pattern*: white superciliary stripes and black eye-lines which meet around hindneck; forehead white,

bordered posteriorly by a black frontal bar. Toes and feet dark greenish grey. In flight, shows dark leading wing edge, white wing-stripe, white tail sides, and toes project beyond tip of tail; wing tips somewhat rounded. **Juvenile** lacks black frontal bar and bold face pattern, but buff forehead is continuous with pale superciliary stripes and band around nape; breast pale buff, with distinct brownish patches at sides. **Voice:** Flight note *trip* or *pip*; also a trilling *tri-rit-rit-rit*. Alarm call a rough *chrrrt*. **Habits:** Forages actively, in pairs or less often in small flocks. Feeds on dry flats as well as shore-lines. **Similar Species:** In juvenile and non-breeding White-fronted and Kentish Plovers, pale superciliaries do not join the nape band, and toes do not extend beyond the tail tip in flight. See juvenile Chestnut-banded Plover. **Status and Distribution:** Locally common on very short grass or bare ground near inland lakes and ponds below 2300 m, especially along Rift Valley lakeshores. Local at the coast, where confined to dry salt flats. Probably resident in most areas.

THREE-BANDED PLOVER   *Charadrius t. tricollaris*   Plates 19, 21

Length 18 cm (7"). A small plover with *two black breast bands, red orbital ring and paler red bill base*; greyish face marked by broad white superciliary stripes which meet around hindneck. Legs and feet red-orange; *eyes pale brown*. Back and wings dark grey-brown, tail rather long. In flight, shows narrow white wing-stripe and tail edges. **Juvenile** resembles adult, but head pattern is less distinct and feathers of upperparts have pale margins. **Voice:** A penetrating high-pitched *pi-peep* or *peeep* when alarmed or flushed. Display call described as a churring rattle uttered as white breast feathers are fluffed out (Beesley 1972). **Habits:** Usually solitary or in pairs, but may join other waders. Flight jerky, with seemingly erratic wingbeats. Largely sedentary, but wanders locally. **Similar Species:** Ringed and Little Ringed Plovers have only one black breast band, no red on the face. Extralimital Forbes's Plover, *C. forbesi*, prefers drier habitats and has more upright posture. **Status and Distribution:** Widespread resident along rivers, pools, lakes and dams, ranging up to 3000 m. In coastal lowlands, largely confined to lagoons and mangrove creeks, north to Malindi.

KENTISH PLOVER   *Charadrius a. alexandrinus*   Plates 19, 21
(Snowy Plover [American *C. a. nivosus*])

Length 15–17 cm (*c.* 6"). A small *pale* plover of sandy beaches and saltpans, grey-brown above and white below, with *fine dark bill, dark legs and feet, white hindneck collar*, and *dark patches at sides of breast* but no complete breast band. **Male in breeding plumage** has black frontal bar, black line through the eye, and white forehead continuous with short superciliary stripes; *cap usually tinged chestnut*, but individuals vary. In **female** and **non-breeding male**, black is replaced by brown. Tarsi usually dark grey, but sometimes tinged brown or yellowish. In flight, shows narrow white wing-stripe and white-sided upper tail-coverts and tail. **Voice:** A soft *kittip* or *teu-it*, some-times a simple *pit* or *pit-wit-wit*; alarm note a hard *prrrr*. **Habits:** Active; feeds more rapidly than Ringed Plover, but does not run with the speed of White-fronted Plover; flight especially rapid. Often mixes with other small waders. **Similar Species:** White-fronted Plover is usually washed tawny below, lacks dark breast patches and sharp white half-collar; it has a large white forehead patch, greenish-grey tarsi and shorter wings. Lesser Sandplover is larger, lacks hindneck collar and has more diffuse smudges at sides of breast. **Status and Distribution:** Palearctic migrant, regular in small numbers at Lake Turkana, October–April. Occasional on Rift Valley lakes south to Magadi and on Kenyan coast.

WHITE-FRONTED PLOVER   *Charadrius marginatus tenellus*   Plates 19, 21
(White-fronted Sandplover)

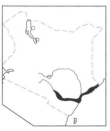

Length *c.* 16 cm (6"). A small plover, brown or rufous-brown above; white underparts often with *buffy or tawny wash and pale rufous patches at sides of breast. Broad white forehead band extends back to short superciliary stripes.* **Adult** shows black frontal bar and eye-lines, and often a *pale buff or rufous (not white) collar*. Bill black, *legs and feet greenish or yellowish grey*. Wing tips do not reach tail tip of standing bird. In flight, distinct white wing-stripe and white sides to rump and tail are conspicuous. **Juvenile** lacks black forecrown but has dark eye-lines; underparts whiter. **Voice:** A short low-pitched *wit*, and a dry trilling *trrrr* of alarm. **Habits:** *Runs very rapidly* on sandy beaches, *often at an angle* instead of straight ahead. Usually alone or in pairs, but occasionally in small groups. Nests in sand. Adults said to carry water to nestlings in belly feathers, like sandgrouse. **Similar Species:** Kentish Plover has white collar and distinct lateral breast patches, lacks rufous tinge above and below, and has blackish legs. Juvenile Kittlitz's Plover has pale superciliary stripes extending to hindneck, longer tarsi and toes which project beyond tail in flight. Adult

Chestnut-banded Plover shows a sharply defined, complete (though narrow) rufous breast band. **STATUS AND DISTRIBUTION**: Breeding resident of sandy n. Kenyan coastal beaches, in smaller numbers along the Galana and Athi Rivers on exposed sandbars. Non-breeding birds subject to some seasonal movements. Sporadic at Lake Turkana. Numerous only in coastal areas north of Malindi. **NOTE**: Breeding males in other parts of the species' range may show a complete breast band. Following Hayman *et al.* (1986), we consider East African birds *tenellus*; others would include them in *mechowi*.

CHESTNUT-BANDED PLOVER *Charadrius pallidus venustus* Plates 19, 21
(Chestnut-banded Sandplover)

Length 12–13 cm (c. 5"). A *small,* long-legged plover of *alkaline lakes;* wings short, the tips not reaching tip of the short tail in standing bird. **Adult** *the only small plover with a narrow chestnut breast band* on white underparts. Upperparts pale greyish brown. Both sexes show a broad white forehead patch and chestnut forecrown; **male** has black frontal band connecting to black eye-lines (lacking in female). *Bill slender* and black; legs and feet dark grey, the tarsi proportionately long. **Juvenile** has an *incomplete greyish breast band* and no black or chestnut. In flight, white wing-stripe and white sides of tail are obvious. **VOICE**: A soft *chup,* a dry *drreet* or *d'WEEu,* dropping in pitch at end; a plaintive *hweet* alarm call. **HABITS**: Gregarious, sometimes in hundreds. Typically tame. Often feeds in belly-deep water. **SIMILAR SPECIES**: No other small plover has a narrow chestnut breast band. Breeding-plumaged Lesser and Greater Sandplovers are much larger, with broad chestnut breast band. Non-breeding Lesser closely resembles juvenile Chestnut-banded, but is larger and relatively short-legged. Juvenile Kittlitz's Plover is browner above (less grey) than juvenile Chestnut-banded, with white nape and superciliary stripes. **STATUS AND DISTRIBUTION**: Common resident at lakes Magadi and Natron. Also known from the Suguta Valley south of Lake Turkana, and many smaller alkaline lakes in n. Tanzania from Serengeti NP east to Lake Manyara. Small numbers recorded in 1990s at Amboseli NP.

LESSER or MONGOLIAN SANDPLOVER *Charadrius mongolus pamirensis* Plates 19, 21

Length 19–21 cm (7.5–8"). Mainly coastal. Similar in size to Ringed Plover, with dark grey or blackish legs and feet (sometimes green-tinged); no pale band on hindneck. Compared with Greater Sandplover (with which it associates), Lesser has *more rounded head, shorter bill* and *shorter and darker tarsi; toes do not project beyond tail tip in flight.* **Non-breeding plumage** grey-brown above, with whitish forehead and superciliary stripes. Underparts white, with broad brownish-grey pectoral patches. Narrow white stripe on wings and white edges of tail and upper tail-coverts are evident in flight. **Breeding plumage** (April–May) distinctive, with *broad chestnut breast band and hindneck, black mask and forehead.* **Juvenile** buffier than non-breeding adult, with warm buff wash across breast, buff feather edges on upperparts and wing-coverts (wearing away by mid-winter). **VOICE**: A short hard *chitik* or *trrrrk,* distinct from usual soft call of Greater Sandplover. **SIMILAR SPECIES**: Greater Sandplover compared above. Kentish Plover is smaller, shorter-legged, with white collar and less conspicuous lateral breast patches. Juvenile Chestnut-banded Plover closely resembles non-breeding Lesser Sandplover, but is smaller and has numerous buff feather edges on upperparts. **STATUS AND DISTRIBUTION**: Palearctic migrant, common to abundant on coastal sandflats and mudflats from late August to early May. Some first-year birds present all summer. Regular in small numbers on Rift Valley lakes, especially Lake Turkana.

GREATER SANDPLOVER *Charadrius leschenaultii crassirostris* Plates 19, 21

Length 22–25 cm (8.5–10"). A medium-sized plover, larger than a Curlew Sandpiper, with a *large bill* and *greyish or greenish-grey legs and feet.* Compared to Lesser Sandplover, the *bill is longer and heavier, head more angular,* with forehead typically *more sloping, tarsi paler and longer,* and *toes project well beyond the tail in flight.* **Non-breeding plumage** as in Lesser Sandplover, but separated by above characters. In **breeding plumage** has chestnut band across upper breast, chestnut hindneck, and **male** shows *striking face pattern,* with black mask and frontal band enclosing a white forehead bisected by a black median line. **Female** may lack black mask. **Juvenile** resembles non-breeding adult but is generally buffier, with bright buff feather edges and breast patches. **VOICE**: A soft trilled *trrrrrri,* and a short dry *trrip.* **HABITS**: Gregarious, associating with other coastal waders, including Lesser Sandplover. Hundreds may gather at tidal roosts. **SIMILAR SPECIES**: Lesser Sandplover discussed above. Caspian Plover, typically in grassland, has broad dark breast band in female, more slender bill, bolder superciliary stripes, and its wing tips extend well beyond the tail at rest. Male Caspian in breeding plumage has dark brown hindneck uniform with rest of upperparts. **STATUS AND DISTRIBUTION**: Palearctic migrant, abundant on coastal beaches and sandflats, including offshore islands, mainly from August to early May, but many first-year birds remain all year. Small numbers recorded annually at Lake Turkana, but otherwise rare inland.

CASPIAN PLOVER *Charadrius asiaticus*   Plates 19, 21

Length 18–20 cm (7–8"). A *grassland* or lakeshore bird, suggesting a small Pacific Golden Plover. Shows *distinct pale superciliary stripes* and *white forehead,* a dark postocular area (and usually some dark on the lores), a *broad grey-brown breast band,* and yellowish (sometimes greenish or grey) legs and feet. Folded wings extend beyond tail tip, as do tips of toes in flying bird. In **non-breeding plumage**, upperparts, crown and postocular patches are brown, the breast band mottled. In **breeding plumage** (Jan.–April), **male** shows darker brown back, cap, hindneck and eye patches, contrasting with broad white superciliary stripes, face and throat; breast band chestnut, with blackish lower border. **Female** similar to non-breeding adult, but may show some chestnut on breast. **Juvenile** has bright buff feather edges above (including wing-coverts), and a mottled buff-and-grey breast band (not separate pectoral patches). **Voice:** A loud sharp high-pitched *tjeep* or *tchup;* also a soft *kik-kik-kik. . .,* and a shrill *quit* or *quick.* **Habits:** Gregarious, sometimes in large flocks. Often tame. Typically a grassland bird, but also feeds on muddy shores. **Similar Species:** Greater and Lesser Sandplovers have thicker bills, shorter wings (primary tips about level with end of tail), lateral breast patches and different head patterns; neither is likely on inland plains. See also Pacific Golden and Grey Plovers. **Status and Distribution:** Widespread and locally abundant palearctic migrant, typically on shortgrass plains, August–April. Large flocks winter in Serengeti NP and Mara GR, but February birds in Tsavo East NP are northbound migrants. Regular on muddy shores at Lake Turkana, where hundreds gather on northward passage, although generally scarce at other Rift Valley lakes and on the coast.

SANDPIPERS AND RELATIVES, FAMILY SCOLOPACIDAE
(World, *c.* 88 species; Africa, 44; Kenya, 32; n. Tanzania, 23)

A diverse, worldwide group. With the exception of one local nesting species, ours are migrants, arriving after having bred at high latitudes in the northern hemisphere (although several species remain here in small numbers throughout the year). Typically, these are long-necked, long-legged shorebirds or waders with slender bills, but there is much variation. Breeding plumage (seen here July–Sept. and Feb.–May) is usually brighter than the basic non-breeding dress. Juveniles (Aug.–Oct.) often have brightly patterned upperparts and may be sufficiently different from adults to be confusing. However, most have moulted into their first-winter body plumage by November, and then appear essentially like non-breeding adults (juvenile wing-coverts may be retained until spring). Flight patterns, involving wings, rump and tail, are important in identification; they are retained in all plumages. Calls also are diagnostic. Excluding a few unique species, our scolopacids can be conveniently grouped as follows: **(1) SNIPES (*Gallinago, Lymnocryptes*)**, superbly cryptic, long-billed marshbirds with large eyes placed well back, feeding by probing rapidly in 'sewing- machine' fashion. Pattern, wing shape and manner of flight are useful in field recognition. Shape, number and colour of tail feathers are important for naming birds in the hand. **(2) GREENSHANK and ALLIES (*Tringa*)**, slender, long-legged, medium-sized waders with white rump and barred tail, the wings almost unpatterned in most species. Loud ringing calls are useful in identification. **(3) CURLEWS (*Numenius*)**, large and brownish, with long decurved bills. **(4) GODWITS (*Limosa*)**, curlew-sized birds with long straight or slightly upturned bills. **(5) PHALAROPES (*Phalaropus*)**, formerly in a separate family, resembling dainty sandpipers but highly aquatic and typically pelagic, swimming in open water, where they often spin in circles, picking food from the surface. They are lobe-toed, and in breeding plumage females are considerably brighter than males. **(6) STINTS (*Calidris*,** in part), the smallest waders, and difficult to identify (hence treated in extra detail below). **(7) OTHER SMALL SANDPIPERS** include certain *Calidris* species, somewhat larger than stints, and the Broad-billed Sandpiper (*Limicola*). Most of these are distinctive and pose no special field-recognition problems.

LITTLE STINT *Calidris minuta*   Plates 20, 21

Length 130–150 mm (5–6"). The common East African stint; a tiny sandpiper with *short, fine, black bill and blackish legs and feet.* (Become familiar with the different plumages of this species before attempting to identify the others.) **Non-breeding adult** is grey-brown or grey above, and often shows a complete band of dusky speckling across the breast, this sometimes only suggested at the sides in **first-winter plumage,** which is much like that of non-breeding adult, but may show buff- or tawny-edged juvenile wing-coverts until midwinter or later. In flight, shows narrow whitish wing-stripe, white-sided dark rump and grey tail sides. **Breeding plumage** (Aug.–Sept. and April–May) can be *bright rufous-tinged, especially on crown, auriculars, scapulars and margins of most posthumerals ('tertials');* blackish or brown back feathers are edged with rufous, the colour at first obscured by whitish feather tips, which are gradually lost through wear; *whitish V on sides of back* and *another greyer V formed by pale scapular tips,* usually evident even in worn plumage. Wing-coverts light brown with broad rufous or deep buff edges. *Face and neck rufous with dusky streaks or speckling;* superciliary stripes and throat white. **Juvenile** (Sept.–Oct.) has *whitish forehead, face and underparts* (contrasting with dark cap and upperparts), a buff breast band (usually sharply streaked dusky brown at sides), and a *prominent buff or whitish V on the back.* Dusky lesser wing-coverts may be concealed by other feathers; if evident, the dark 'shoulders' suggest

Sanderling. **Voice**: A sharp high-pitched *chit* or *tit*, sometimes *chi-chi-chit* and *tilililili*. **Habits**: Gregarious, often in flocks of hundreds or thousands. Constantly active, picking insects and larvae from mud surface. Agile, with fluttery flight, frequently in tight flocks. **Similar Species**: Sanderling is much larger, with a stouter bill. Relatively plain-looking Temminck's Stint is more uniform above, greyer on breast, and has white tail edges, yellow-olive legs and a different call. See Red-necked and Long-toed Stints for distinction from those species. **Status and Distribution**: Widespread palearctic migrant, August–May, common to abundant on brackish and alkaline Rift Valley lakes. Along the coast, confined to lagoons, saltpans and mudflats.

*RED-NECKED STINT *Calidris ruficollis* Plate 20
(Rufous-necked Stint)

Length 130–160 mm (5–6.5"). A rare, dark-legged sandpiper, easily mistaken for Little Stint except in full **breeding plumage**, when *brick-red head, neck and breast* are obvious. **Non-breeding adult** differs subtly from Little. Look for the following: (1) *more elongate* but squatty appearance, owing to longer wings and shorter tarsi than Little Stint; (2) *paler grey upperparts* (less spotted or mottled, the dark feather centres reduced to fine shaft streaks, as they are in *adult* Little Stint); (3) *clear white wedge or line separating the more prominent greyish pectoral patch from front edge of wing*; (4) *darker lores*, contrasting more with whitish forehead. Said never to develop a complete breast band of dusky speckling as seen in some Little Stints (Veit and Jonsson 1984). Intermediate birds in **partial breeding plumage** usually show (1) slightly rufescent throat (always white in Little); (2) unmarked rufous areas of face and neck (these streaked or spotted with dusky brown in Little); (3) grey inner wing-coverts with dark shaft streaks (brown with broad buff or rufous edges in Little); (4) less prominent light V on back, evident only in fresh plumage (usually conspicuous in Little Stints, even in worn plumage). **Juvenile** is bright above, becoming greyer, more nondescript, with wear, and never shows pale V as does Little Stint. Wing-coverts and posthumerals ('tertials') pale grey, not dark-centred with bright buff or rufous margins as in Little Stint. Sides of breast are greyish with only a hint of buff in fresh plumage. **Voice**: A rolling *chirrk*, and a dry coarse *chit* or *chut* or *prip*, all too similar to calls of Little Stint to be useful. Also gives a sharp squeaky *week* and, when flushed, a short trilled *tirrwi-chit-chit*. **Habits**: Feeds energetically like Little Stint, picking food from mud surface, and is often with that species. Also probes deeply with bill. **Similar Species**: Little Stint compared above. Temminck's and Long-toed Stints have pale tarsi. **Status and Distribution**: An Asian species, recorded three times in Kenya: north of Malindi (May 1981), Lake Magadi (July 1987), and Mida Creek (Aug. 1989).

TEMMINCK'S STINT *Calidris temminckii* Plates 20, 21

Length 130–150 mm (5–6"). Comparatively *plain*, with rather short *yellowish or olive legs and feet, white tail sides*, and a short dark bill (often tinged olive at base). Usually in freshwater marshes, feeding inconspicuously among grasses and sedges. Relatively long tail imparts *elongate appearance*. Upperparts brown or greyish brown, with greyish and faintly streaked breast band. Superciliary stripes not pronounced, but the *narrow eye-ring* is evident in all plumages. In flight, shows broad dark rump centre and narrow white wing-stripe. *White outer tail feathers* (two pairs) evident when bird is flushed at close range. **Breeding plumage** dull, lacking pale dorsal V-marks or strong rufous tones, though back and scapulars show blackish feathers with pale rufous or buff margins, usually mixed with grey 'winter' feathers. Birds in full breeding plumage are unusual in East Africa. **Non-breeding plumage** uniformly dark grey above and across upper breast, appearing somewhat hooded; darker at sides of breast. **Juvenile** brownish or olive-brown above, scaly-looking with *buff feather tips*, and a *narrow blackish subterminal bar on some feathers (especially the anterior scapulars, which appear black-spotted)*; a brownish wash on the breast is especially pronounced at sides. Shows pale, somewhat diffuse superciliary stripes. **Voice**: A repeated trilling or ringing *tiririri* or *treee*, distinctive; also a longer *tititititititit* when flushed. **Habits**: Solitary or in small loose groups. Crouches horizontally when alarmed. Flight somewhat erratic. When flushed, often 'towers' with fluttery wingbeats. **Similar Species**: See Long-toed Stint. **Status and Distribution**: In Kenya, a local but regular palearctic migrant, October–April, near the southern limit of its wintering range. Typically on muddy edges of freshwater lakes and pools, with most records from the Rift Valley. Rare at the coast, and in n. Tanzania, where only two recent records (lakes Eyasi and Manyara).

LONG-TOED STINT *Calidris subminuta* Plates 20, 21

Length 130–150 mm (5–6"). Appears *smaller-headed and longer-necked* than the common Little Stint (with which it sometimes feeds). *Legs and feet pale yellowish or greenish, not black; toes (especially the middle) noticeably long and spindly, appearing oversized, and projecting beyond tail in flying bird* (unlike other African stints). **Non-breeding plumage** mottled dark brown above, with light streaking on neck and breast; *top of head and eye-lines dark, contrasting with prominent whitish superciliary stripes*. In flight, shows broad blackish rump centre, *greyish outer tail feathers*, and short white wing-stripe. Short, fine black bill is dull yellow at base of mandible. **Breeding plumage** rich tawny-brown above, with broad rufous and orange-chestnut and whitish feather edgings; may show indistinct whitish V on back. Dark crown, streaked with brown and rufous, contrasts with paler nape and the faint superciliary stripes. Neck and sides of breast heavily streaked, but the greyish-buff centre usually plain. **Juvenile** has *dark crown* finely streaked with rufous, distinct lateral crown stripes and white

superciliary stripes extending to back of head. Upperparts show two pale Vs formed by white feather tips on scapulars and back; dorsal feather edges vary from pale orange-buff to nearly chestnut. Breast finely streaked, often across the centre. Legs and feet dull yellow or olive. **Voice**: A soft rolling *cherrp* or *chulip,* at times reminiscent of Curlew Sandpiper; also a sharp *tik-tik-tik* (Hayman *et al.* 1986). **Habits**: Feeding behaviour like that of Little Stint. Crouches low when disturbed, but stands upright with stretched neck if alarmed. Often 'towers' when flushed; flight somewhat erratic. **Similar Species**: Temminck's Stint, also pale-legged, is plainer and longer-looking, with white outer rectrices, and shows a narrow pale eye-ring at close range. Little Stint has dark legs and feet (as does rare Red-necked). **Status and Distribution**: Rare palearctic migrant, recorded in Kenya nine times, November to early May, mainly on Rift Valley lakes, once from the coast at Malindi. Possibly overlooked. In usual Asian winter quarters favours marshes and mudflats.

PECTORAL SANDPIPER *Calidris melanotos*   Plates 20, 21

Length 200–230 mm (8–9"). A medium-sized brownish sandpiper with rather small head, short bill and *brown-streaked breast sharply demarcated* from white belly; male noticeably larger than female. In **non-breeding plumage** upperparts streaked black and rufous-brown, the back lined (somewhat snipe-like) with buff; pale superciliary streaks evident but not prominent; neck and breast buffy brown to whitish, finely and closely streaked with brown. *Bill, legs and feet dull yellowish olive.* In flight, appears dark-winged with suggestion of narrow pale wing-stripe; rump dark in centre, whitish on sides. **Juvenile** resembles adult but has stronger buff wash on breast. **Voice**: A distinctive reedy *krrik-krrik*; also a low *churk.* **Habits**: Walks slowly when probing in mud. Flight rapid and erratic. Stretches neck in alarm. **Similar Species**: Ruff does not have streaked 'bib' contrasting sharply with white belly, and back shows no snipe-like lines; in flight, reveals large white lateral patches along tail base. **Status and Distribution**: Northern vagrant, collected at Lake Naivasha (May 1952) and seen once at Mombasa (Sept. 1981). Prefers flooded fields, grassy marshes and muddy pond edges.

*DUNLIN *Calidris alpina*   Plates 20, 21

Length 150–220 mm (6–8.5"). A vagrant. In **non-breeding plumage** resembles the common Curlew Sandpiper but slightly smaller, typically more portly, with hunched posture, *shorter tarsi, much less conspicuous superciliary stripes and darker grey breast.* The long black *bill is decurved only near tip,* not evenly curved throughout its length as in Curlew Sandpiper. In flight, shows wing pattern of Curlew Sandpiper, but has no white on lower rump and upper tail-coverts. Dark rump centre and greyish tail sides suggest a Little Stint. Bright **breeding plumage** is mottled *rufous above,* with heavy streaking on neck and breast and a *black patch on belly.* **Juvenile** is buffy brown, with rufous scaling on crown and back; breast streaks expand into dark blotches on the flanks. **Voice**: A high nasal *treer* or *treerp* in flight. **Habits**: Flight strong and agile like Curlew Sandpiper's; gait more deliberate, less active when feeding. **Similar Species**: Curlew Sandpiper compared above. Smaller Broad-billed Sandpiper is squattier, with snipe-like head pattern, different bill shape and greyer non-breeding plumage. **Status and Distribution**: Rare palearctic migrant. In n. and w. Africa winters mainly on tidal estuaries and coastal mudflats, but the four Kenyan sight records are from Lake Nakuru (Oct. 1953), Lake Turkana (March 1970), near Nairobi (Oct. 1983) and Lake Baringo (Dec. 1991), all presumed to represent the nominate race.

CURLEW SANDPIPER *Calidris ferruginea*   Plates 20, 21

Length 180–230 mm (7–9"). A common wader, fairly long-legged and with a relatively long, *decurved black bill.* Our only small sandpiper with combination of all-white *upper tail-coverts and a long white wing-stripe.* **Non-breeding plumage** generally grey-brown above and white below, with prominent whitish superciliary stripes and faint streaking on neck and breast. Sides of rump white, central rump feathers dark-barred; upper tail-coverts pure white; legs and feet black. Partial chestnut **breeding plumage** commonly seen in August and April–May, most birds being mottled chestnut and white below, often with much white on belly and under tail-coverts; some blackish bars on flanks and belly. Back feathers and scapulars have chestnut and whitish edges. **Juvenile** (Sept.–Oct.) dark brown above with paler feather edging, and with pale cinnamon wash on breast. **Voice**: A soft *churrup,* usually when flushed; recalls Ruddy Turnstone, but softer, less sharp. **Habits**: Gregarious, in small groups or hundreds, foraging and roosting with other waders. Feeds with purposeful walking gait in shallow water, probing and occasionally picking at water surface for food. **Similar Species**: Much rarer Dunlin and Broad-billed Sandpiper also have long decurved bills, but are smaller (Broad-billed considerably so), shorter-legged and more heavily streaked. Broad-billed has bold superciliary stripes and is paler grey above in non-breeding plumage. Both have dark rump centre. Breeding-plumaged Red Knot is stockier, with much shorter bill. **Status and Distribution**: Palearctic migrant, abundant on coastal

mudflats, sandy beaches and coral shores, August to early May. More local inland, mainly on passage, but some remain on Rift Valley lakes until late May. A few first-year birds oversummer, seldom acquiring breeding plumage.

SANDERLING *Calidris alba*   Plates 20, 21

Length 200–210 mm (8"). A small *hyperactive* shorebird with *stout black bill*. Legs and feet also black, the tarsi rather short. *Whitish*-appearing **non-breeding adult** is pale grey above and white below, with grey smudge at each side of breast and *prominent black 'shoulder' mark*. Long white wing-stripe and white-sided dark rump conspicuous in flight; upper tail-coverts and centre of tail also dark. Traces of black-speckled rufous **breeding plumage** often present on head, breast and upperparts in August and late April; in spring acquires full plumage only after leaving East Africa. **Juvenile** (Sept.–Nov.) blackish above with pale buff spotting and feather edging, brown crown, dark loral spots and ear-coverts. Early in season, upper breast washed with buff and streaked with brown at sides. **VOICE:** A distinctive sharp *twick* or *kick-kick* in flight or when alarmed; sometimes gives a short trilling note. **HABITS:** Small groups or singles feed restlessly at water's edge, following waves and then retreating rapidly before the next breaker. Runs with body horizontal and head held low. Hundreds gather with other species at tidal roosts. **SIMILAR SPECIES:** Little Stint is similarly proportioned but much smaller, with thinner bill, browner upperparts and weaker call. **STATUS AND DISTRIBUTION:** Palearctic migrant, abundant on coastal beaches and coral flats from late August to April. Some remain all year. Occasional on inland lakes during southward passage, August–November. Some remain from November to April at Lake Turkana.

*RED KNOT *Calidris c. canutus*   Plate 22
(Knot; Lesser Knot)

Length 230–250 mm (9–10"). Distinctive. A *stocky*, medium-sized, coastal wader with *short neck and bill*. Legs and feet dull greenish, the tarsi short. **Adult non-breeding plumage** *pale grey and 'scaly' above,* with whitish superciliary stripes and fine black shaft streaks visible at close range. Underparts white, with faint streaks on neck and breast and fine barring or scalloping along sides and flanks. Some individuals have pale rufous wash on breast. In flight, shows narrow, short, white wing-stripe and whitish rump. **Breeding plumage** mottled chestnut and black above. Bright *rufous-chestnut below,* with variable black and brown speckling on white belly and crissum. **Juvenile** resembles non-breeding adult, but browner with buffy feather edgings and breast buff-tinged. **VOICE:** A whistling *twit-wit* in flight, and a low *utt* or *nutt.* **HABITS:** Feeds by probing, sometimes by pecking at surface organisms. Gregarious in usual wintering quarters, but only single birds are likely in East Africa. **STATUS AND DISTRIBUTION:** Palearctic vagrant, with five coastal records: Kiunga (Sept. 1961), Dar es Salaam (Nov. 1970), Mombasa (April 1973), Sabaki estuary (Sept. 1977) and Mida Creek (April 1993). Typically a bird of estuaries, coastal mudflats and sandy beaches.

BROAD-BILLED SANDPIPER *Limicola falcinellus*   Plates 20, 21

Length 165 mm (6.5"). Suggests a miniature snipe or a very long-billed stint. Intermediate in size between Curlew Sandpiper and Little Stint, with a *long dark bill kinked downward at tip.* **Non-breeding adult** pale grey above, including central rump and tail-coverts, the feathers white-edged. Head variable but always prominently streaked, the light *superciliary stripe forking in front of the eye* (upper branch, below crown, may be narrow and inconspicuous). Dark patagial/carpal patch often shows on the closed wing. Underparts white with indistinct grey spots or streaks on sides of breast and extending onto flanks. Blackish bill sometimes olive or yellowish at base, and the *short, dark brown tarsi* may be olive-tinged. In flight, appears *pale grey with broad black leading wing edges and dark flight feathers*, inconspicuous wing-stripe and white on sides of rump. **Juvenile** has bold *snipe-like pattern*, with broad white superciliaries and narrower buff stripes at sides and on centre of crown. Upperparts darker and brighter than in non-breeding adult; most blackish dorsal feathers edged with pale buff and white, those of back and rump margined with rufous-buff; shows pale double V on back. Blackish patagial/carpal area as in adult. A sharply defined band of dark breast streaks does not extend onto flanks. In flight shows *conspicuously black rump, central tail feathers and upper tail-coverts*; wing-stripe more conspicuous than in adult. **First-winter** bird resembles non-breeding adult. **VOICE:** A rough *chrreek* when flushed, and a quick *chitter-chitter* in flight. **HABITS:** Forages alone or in loose groups with other small waders. Relatively inactive; employs slow feeding action with persistent vertical probing. **SIMILAR SPECIES:** Non-breeding Dunlin is slightly larger, stands taller, has faint superciliary stripes, no black on leading wing edges and a differently shaped bill. Larger Curlew Sandpiper has different face pattern and white upper tail-coverts. **STATUS AND DISTRIBUTION:** Uncommon palearctic migrant from August to April, favouring open mudflats. Small numbers regular at the Sabaki estuary north of Malindi. Occasional at other coastal sites and on some Rift Valley lakes.

*BUFF-BREASTED SANDPIPER *Tryngites subruficollis* Plates 20, 21

Length 190 mm (7.5"). Small, plump and plover-like, typically with *entirely buff underparts* (brighter on throat and breast), but some autumn/winter birds are duller than usually illustrated and may be pale whitish buff with the usual dark flecking at sides of breast. Upperparts mottled buffy brown. *Pale buff face accentuates the dark eye,* and there is no obvious superciliary stripe. The bill is short and dark, the *legs and feet yellow.* Spread wing quite uniform above, with no white stripe; *underside white,* with dark carpal 'comma' and trailing edge; sides of rump buff. **VOICE**: Generally silent, but may give a low trilled *pr-r-r-reet* (Peterson 1980) and a low *churrp* or sharp *tik* when flushed. **HABITS**: Typically tame. Actions rather plover-like; stretches neck when alarmed. Prefers dry short-grass plains, dried mudflats; does not wade. **SIMILAR SPECIES**: Juvenile Ruff, also buff below and well marked above, is larger, has greenish or pale brownish-olive legs and feet; in flight, shows a narrow white wing-stripe and conspicuous white sides to rump and upper tail-coverts. **STATUS AND DISTRIBUTION**: Nearctic vagrant. One sight record from Lake Turkana (8 Dec. 1973).

RUFF *Philomachus pugnax* Plates 20, 23

Length of male 280–300 mm (11–12"), of female 230 mm (9"). A stocky, small-headed, long-necked wader with a rather short dark bill; *legs and feet of adults bright orange or pinkish.* **Non-breeding plumage** (Sept.–Feb.) mottled brown above and on sides of breast and flanks, with brownish-buff head and neck. In flight, a *distinctive light oval patch on each side of dark rump and upper tail-coverts,* with wings showing a long narrow white stripe. **Female breeding plumage** (March–May) and **male spring plumage** brighter, more distinctly patterned above and heavily mottled on neck, breast and flanks. **Male** usually has some pinkish or orange at base of bill; some have a striking white neck, others an entirely white head, upper back and scapulars. Breeding-plumaged male's elaborate ruff and head plumage acquired after departure from Africa, but early arrivals in August usually show black or rufous feathers on neck, breast and flanks. **Juvenile** scaled buff above and buffier below than adult; legs and feet greenish or brownish olive. **VOICE**: Infrequent flight note, *tooi;* usually silent. **HABITS**: Gregarious, in small groups or flocks of hundreds, typically feeding at water's edge, sometimes swimming in deep water. Rather sluggish, with deliberate gait. Not shy. **SIMILAR SPECIES**: See Pectoral and Buff-breasted Sandpipers. **STATUS AND DISTRIBUTION**: Palearctic migrant, mainly August–May, although a few first-year birds remain through summer. Common to locally abundant on muddy or marshy edges of freshwater and alkaline lakes, irrigated fields and flooded grassland. Most numerous in the Rift Valley and w. Kenyan highlands; scarce in coastal lowlands south of Mombasa.

JACK SNIPE *Lymnocryptes minimus* Plate 24

Length 190 mm (7.5"). A *small* snipe with *relatively short bill.* Pattern similar to that of Common Snipe, but has *double pale superciliary stripes bordering the dark crown,* and is more streaked on neck and breast. In flight, pronounced buff stripes evident on back, but *tail is dark and wedge-shaped, showing no white or chestnut.* **VOICE**: Usually silent, but may utter weak low-pitched calls when taking wing. **HABITS**: Flushes only at very close range; rises more slowly than Common Snipe and flies more directly, with only an occasional zigzag, usually alighting again within 50 m. Solitary or in small groups. **SIMILAR SPECIES**: Other snipes are larger, much longer-billed, and show a different head-stripe pattern. Common and African Snipes utter harsh notes when flushed. **STATUS AND DISTRIBUTION**: A scarce and somewhat sporadic palearctic migrant, here at the southern limit of its African range. In Kenya, recorded from the Rift Valley and cent. highlands in tall vegetation around lakes and swamps, mainly November–February. Two specimen records from n. Tanzania: Serengeti NP (Feb., early 1930s) and near Tabora (Dec. 1957).

COMMON SNIPE *Gallinago g. gallinago* Plate 24

Length 250–270 mm (10–10.5"). A cryptic, *long-billed* marshbird. Head shows pale central crown stripe and *pronounced black stripes above, through and below the eyes.* Back patterned rich brown and blackish, with *prominent golden-buff stripes along edges of scapulars.* Streaked and barred with brown from head to breast; rest of underparts white, the flanks with some dark barring. In flight, shows whitish trailing edge to secondaries and a *rufous-tipped tail with little white at the sides.* Tail of 12–18 feathers (usually 14), all fairly broad; wings narrow and pointed. **VOICE**: A loud rasping *scaaap* uttered on take-off. **HABITS**: Solitary, or more often in small groups. Sits tight. Rises explosively, giving harsh call and climbing quickly with rapid zigzagging and twisting; usually circles high for several hundred metres before dropping to ground. **SIMILAR SPECIES**: Somewhat darker African Snipe has slightly longer bill, but is best separated by its noticeable *breast/belly contrast, broader* and *more rounded wings, slower fluttery flight* and *prominent white tail sides.* For distinguishing Common Snipe from Great, Jack and Pintail Snipes, see those species. **STATUS AND DISTRIBUTION**: Palearctic migrant, common October–March, on lake edges, marshy ponds and flooded grassland. The most numerous snipe below 2000 m.

AFRICAN SNIPE *Gallinago nigripennis aequatorialis* Plate 24

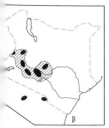

Length 300 mm (12″). On the ground, similar to Common Snipe, but *darker (more blackish) above*, and the *more boldly streaked neck and breast contrast strongly with white belly*. In flight, shows more white trailing edge to secondaries and conspicuous pale body stripes like Common Snipe, but has *broader, more rounded wings* with the white tipping on alula and primary and greater coverts more conspicuous against the generally dark upper wing-surface; *white sides of tail evident as bird alights*. **VOICE**: A harsh *scaap* or *scaip*, similar to that of Common Snipe. **HABITS**: Rises explosively and usually calls when flushed, but *flight slower and more fluttery than that of Common Snipe; flies lower, with less zigzagging*. Partly crepuscular and nocturnal. Circular breeding display flight (night or day) involves repeated stooping to near ground level with a low humming sound, *whur-whur-whur-whur. . .*, produced by the spread, vibrating outer tail feathers. **SIMILAR SPECIES**: Common Snipe compared above. Larger Great Snipe (also with white tail sides) has shorter bill, darker barred belly, and differs in wing pattern, shape, flight characters and voice. Jack Snipe is much smaller, with short bill. **STATUS AND DISTRIBUTION**: Local but fairly common resident of highland marshes and bogs between 1900 and 4000 m, but recorded as low as 1500 m. Widespread in the w. and cent. Kenyan highlands and Tanzania's Crater Highlands. Common on alpine moorlands of Mt Elgon, Mt Kenya and Kilimanjaro.

GREAT SNIPE *Gallinago media* Plate 24

Length 280 mm (11″). *Bulkier, darker and more barred (especially on flanks) than Common Snipe; bill somewhat shorter*. Further separated from that species by *broad white tail sides*, bold whitish wing-covert tips and spotted (not streaked) neck and breast. Tail feathers number 14–18 (usually 16). **VOICE**: Occasionally utters a monosyllabic croak when disturbed. **HABITS**: Rises rather slowly in usually silent, direct (not twisting) flight; bill is held more nearly horizontal than in Common Snipe. Sometimes feeds on dry ground. **SIMILAR SPECIES**: Common Snipe compared above. African Snipe also has white on sides of tail, but has much longer bill, unbarred flanks, and darker, more uniform and more rounded wings. **STATUS AND DISTRIBUTION**: In Kenya, an uncommon palearctic migrant, recorded mainly on passage October–December and in April and May. Frequents lake edges or flooded grassland, sometimes short grass or stubble. Few records from n. Tanzania.

PINTAIL SNIPE *Gallinago stenura* Plate 24

Length 250 mm (10″). A rare vagrant from Asia, similar in size, build and pattern to Common Snipe, the bill averaging only slightly shorter. With practice, distinguishable at close range by paler, less richly coloured upperparts, less prominent back stripes, and in flight by *paler, more fawn-coloured wings without noticeable white trailing edges* and *toes projecting well beyond the end of the short tail*. In the hand, readily identified by the *26–28 tail feathers, the outer eight pairs narrow and pin-like*. **VOICE**: Weaker and lower-pitched than that of Common Snipe, a reedy *krreek* or *squik*. **HABITS**: Rises more slowly and directly than Common Snipe; flight less powerful. **SIMILAR SPECIES**: Common Snipe compared above. May be impossible to separate in the field from Swinhoe's Snipe, *G. megala*, of Asia, not recorded in Africa but a potential vagrant. **STATUS AND DISTRIBUTION**: Three Kenyan records: two at Lake Naivasha (Jan. 1969, Jan. 1982), one near Mombasa (Oct.–Dec. 1981). In its usual s. Asian wintering areas, frequents ditches and floodland, also drier grassy areas.

BLACK-TAILED GODWIT *Limosa l. limosa* Plate 23

Length *c.* 400 mm (16″). A large, graceful, long-legged wader with a long straight bill. In flight, shows *broad white wing-stripe* and adjacent black trailing wing edge, plus *broad black tail band contrasting with white rump*. **Non-breeding plumage** dull brown above, light brownish on head, neck and breast; remaining underparts white. Narrow whitish superciliary stripes bordered below by dark eye-lines. Bill blackish with basal third pinkish; eyes brown; tarsi grey or blue-grey. In **breeding plumage** (March–April), head and breast are chestnut, the flanks, sides and belly white, barred with black. Base of bill orange-pink. **VOICE**: Usual note, *kik, keuk* or *quick*, and in flight a louder, excited *wicker-wicker-wicker* or *reeta-reeta-reeta*. **HABITS**: Feeds on muddy areas, often in deep water, usually in small flocks. **SIMILAR SPECIES**: Bar-tailed Godwit has shorter legs, slightly upturned bill, no bold wing-stripe and different rump/tail pattern. **STATUS AND DISTRIBUTION**: Palearctic migrant, October to early April, on marshy lake edges and irrigated areas. A few oversummer almost annually. More common than formerly, flocks of hundreds now recorded at lakes Turkana and Naivasha, and smaller numbers regular at Lake Nakuru, the lower Tana River and Ahero rice fields near Kisumu. Scarce elsewhere, including n. Tanzania, where sporadic in Serengeti, Manyara and Arusha NPs. Several thousand recently reported from Singida, just outside our area.

BAR-TAILED GODWIT *Limosa l. lapponica*   Plate 23

Length 380 mm (15"). A large, long-necked wader with a long *slightly upturned bill.* Tarsi shorter than those of Black-tailed Godwit, the toes barely projecting beyond the tail in flight. **Non-breeding plumage** *pale,* mottled brownish grey above, whitish below, lightly streaked on head, neck and breast; pale superciliary stripes prominent. In flight, shows *whitish rump patch narrowing to a point on the back,* a *finely barred tail* and *almost uniformly dark wings.* Bill blackish, with basal half pink or pinkish yellow; eyes dark brown; legs dark grey or blue-grey. **Breeding plumage** (sometimes seen Aug.–Sept.) mottled blackish and rich brown above, reddish chestnut on head and underparts. **VOICE:** A low *kirruk-kirrruk* in flight, but otherwise generally silent. **HABITS:** Singles or small numbers feed in shallow water along open shores. **SIMILAR SPECIES:** More gregarious Black-tailed Godwit has longer legs, straight bill, shows conspicuous white wing-stripe in flight, and prefers deeper water. **STATUS AND DISTRIBUTION:** Uncommon palearctic migrant to coastal areas, mainly August to October; some winter regularly in the Sabaki–Mida Creek area near Malindi. Scarce inland, with a few records from Rift Valley lakes. **NOTE:** Asiatic Dowitcher, *Limnodromus semipalmatus,* was earlier attributed to Kenya on the basis of a sight record from Lake Nakuru in November 1966. This, the sole African report of the species, was recently re-evaluated and rejected by the East African rarities committee. In all plumages this dowitcher resembles a small Bar-tailed Godwit, but has a heavier, straight, largely black bill.

WHIMBREL *Numenius p. phaeopus*   Plate 23

Length 400 mm (16"). A large dusky brown wader with *long bill decurved toward the tip* and *boldly striped head pattern.* Neck and breast heavily streaked, flanks and underside of wings barred. Bill blackish brown, paler brown or flesh-pink toward base; eyes dark brown; tarsi dull blue-grey. In flight, appears mainly brown above with narrowly barred tail and *white rump patch narrowing to a point on the lower back.* **VOICE:** A diagnostic rippling *pipipipipipipi* or *whiwhiwhiwhiwhi.* **HABITS:** Solitary or in small parties, locally in larger tidal gatherings, sometimes with other waders. Flight godwit-like, with rapid wingbeats. **SIMILAR SPECIES:** Eurasian Curlew is larger, with longer, heavier, more gradually decurved bill; it lacks head stripes, and has different call. **STATUS AND DISTRIBUTION:** Common palearctic migrant, present in all months on coastal beaches, mudflats, coral reefs and offshore islands, most numerous August–April. Occasional inland at lakes Victoria and Turkana; rare elsewhere.

EURASIAN CURLEW *Numenius arquata orientalis*   Plate 23
(Curlew)

Length 530–590 mm (21–23"). *Larger than a Whimbrel* and with a *proportionately longer and heavier bill continuously decurved throughout its length; lacks Whimbrel's pronounced head pattern* and is lighter, more buffy brown. Flight pattern similar to Whimbrel's, but *flight feathers paler* and the slower wingbeats somewhat gull-like. Bill dark brown, pinkish at base; eyes dark brown; legs and feet blue-grey. **VOICE:** Flight call, *quoi-quoi,* and a longer, more ringing *coor-lew* or *croo-li are characteristic.* Utters softer feeding calls and harsher notes when flushed. Loud song, sometimes heard in winter quarters, is a long melodious bubbling trill, accelerating and rising in pitch. Alarm call, a rapid *tuyuyuyuyu,* is reminiscent of Whimbrel's call. **HABITS:** Feeds more by deep probing than Whimbrel, but also picks at surface items. Wary. **STATUS AND DISTRIBUTION:** Uncommon palearctic migrant, regular in small numbers on coastal mudflats, mainly August–April. Flocks of up to 60 regular at Mida Creek near Malindi. A few present all year. Singles occasional on Rift Valley lakes, sporadically elsewhere in Kenya, also at Serengeti and Lake Manyara NPs and Ngorongoro Crater in n. Tanzania.

SPOTTED REDSHANK *Tringa erythropus*   Plate 22

Length c. 300 mm (12"). Large and slender, with a long neck, *long red legs* and *long, straight, red-based bill.* **Non-breeding plumage** grey above, with white spotting conspicuous on the wings; underparts white, the neck and breast faintly streaked; prominent whitish superciliary stripes contrast with conspicuous dark eye-lines. In flight, greyer above than Common Greenshank, white back and rump appearing as a more discrete patch, and white-spotted secondaries giving paler-looking rear wing edge; tail narrowly barred. Base of mandible, legs and feet orange or orange-red; eyes brown. **Breeding plumage** (April–May) *sooty black,* with whitish spots above and white barring on belly. White wedge on back and white wing-linings conspicuous in flight. Base of mandible dull dark red; legs and feet dark red or red-brown, at times orange-red on rear part of tarsi and tibiae. **VOICE:** In flight, a distinctive sharp rapid whistle, *chu-it,* the second note rising in pitch. Has a short *kip* of alarm, and a scolding *chick-chick-chick.* **HABITS:**

Solitary or in compact feeding groups; more active than Common Redshank, wading in deeper water, probing with head and neck submerged; swims readily, and up-ends to feed. Shy. **SIMILAR SPECIES**: Common Greenshank and smaller Marsh Sandpiper both have greenish legs, less obvious superciliary stripes, and more contrast between white rump and solidly dark wings. Common Redshank is browner, more heavily streaked, has more orange legs and pure white secondaries. **STATUS AND DISTRIBUTION**: Palearctic migrant, November to early May, regular in small numbers inland throughout Kenya and n. Tanzania on muddy or marshy lake edges, ponds and irrigated fields. Flocks of over 100 regular in rice fields at Ahero near Kisumu in w. Kenya.

COMMON REDSHANK *Tringa totanus ussuriensis*   Plate 22
(Redshank)

Length *c.* 280 mm (11″). Fairly large and long-necked; *base of bill, legs and feet orange-red.* **Non-breeding plumage** dull grey-brown above, white below, with light streaking on neck and breast; often shows white eye-ring; pale superciliary stripes indistinct. Flight pattern distinctive: *white inner primaries and secondaries contrast with dark outer primaries,* and *white rump patch extends in a wedge onto the back.* **Breeding plumage** more cinnamon-brown on upperparts, with underparts heavily and extensively streaked. **Juvenile** buffier below, with yellow-orange legs and feet. **VOICE**: When flushed, a ringing *tew-hew-hew,* initial note highest. Also a yelping *tuuu* or *tewk* of alarm. **HABITS**: Solitary or in small groups, wading in shallows or feeding on exposed mud. Bobs up and down when alarmed. Flight strong, the wingbeats quicker and jerkier than in Common Greenshank. **SIMILAR SPECIES**: Spotted Redshank, confusing in non-breeding plumage, is more slender, with longer darker red legs and longer bill, greyer above, and lacks white wing patches. **STATUS AND DISTRIBUTION**: In Kenya, a scarce palearctic migrant on inland lakes and ponds, coastal creeks and mudflats; small numbers winter regularly at Mida Creek and in the Tana River delta. Rare in n. Tanzania.

MARSH SANDPIPER *Tringa stagnatilis*   Plate 22

Length 230 mm (9″). *Slender* and thin-necked, with a *very fine, straight bill.* Suggests a diminutive, dainty Common Greenshank. *Long spindly tarsi and toes greenish yellow.* **Non-breeding plumage** pale brownish grey above, white below, with light streaking on sides of neck and breast. Pale superciliary stripes usually inconspicuous on the light face. In flight, *plain dark wings* contrast with *white rump extending to a point on the back;* tail narrowly barred. Bill brownish black, greenish grey toward base; eyes brown; legs vary from greyish green to yellow. **Breeding plumage** (Feb.–April) darker on upperparts, the head and neck more heavily streaked, and breast boldly black-spotted. Legs often yellow to orange-yellow. **Juvenile** (Aug.–Sept.) is much browner above, with cream feather edges. **VOICE**: A single rather dry *cheeo* when flushed; alarm call a sharp *chip,* often repeated. **HABITS**: Solitary or in small groups. Wades actively in shallow water, picking constantly at surface. Rather wary. **SIMILAR SPECIES**: Common Greenshank has similar pattern, but is larger and has a longer, stouter, slightly upturned bill, proportionately shorter legs, and different call. Non-breeding Spotted Redshank has red legs and feet, pronounced dark eye-stripe and distinct call. **STATUS AND DISTRIBUTION**: Palearctic migrant, mainly late August to April; some first-year birds oversummer. Common inland on muddy and marshy lake edges, irrigated fields, small pools and river banks. Particularly numerous on Rift Valley lakes. In coastal areas, confined to brackish pools and estuaries.

COMMON GREENSHANK *Tringa nebularia*   Plate 22
(Greenshank)

Length *c.* 300 mm (12″). Large and long-necked, with a long, *slightly upturned, thick-based bill* and *greenish legs and feet.* **Non-breeding plumage** brownish grey above, white below, with light streaking on sides of neck and breast. In flight from above, *plain dark wings separated by white rump and wedge of white on back;* white tail narrowly barred with black. Bill blackish, with basal half greenish grey or blue-grey; eyes dark brown; tarsi pale grey-green to greenish yellow. Browner **breeding plumage** (Feb.–April) is streaked and barred above, most heavily on face, neck and breast. **Juvenile** (Aug.–Sept.) is dark brown above with buffy feather edges, lightly speckled and barred on sides of breast. Yellowish-legged individuals recall American Greater Yellowlegs, *T. melanoleuca* (which has no white wedge on back). **VOICE**: A distinctive, far-carrying, fluty *tew-tew-tew,* usually given in flight; also a complaining *tyip.* **HABITS**: Solitary or in small groups, sometimes in larger gatherings on migration and at tidal roosts. Picks food from water surface and also scythes from side to side with bill held flat. Often wary. **SIMILAR SPECIES**: Marsh Sandpiper is smaller, more slender, with fine straight bill, proportionately longer legs. Non-breeding Spotted Redshank is paler and greyer above, has orange-red legs, straight bill, and prominent eye-line. **STATUS AND DISTRIBUTION**: Palearctic migrant, mainly late August to April, but many first-year birds oversummer. Common on coastal estuaries, mudflats and exposed coral; widespread on inland waters.

GREEN SANDPIPER *Tringa ochropus* Plate 22

Length *c.* 230 mm (9"). A *dark-backed* inland wader with *dark olive-green tarsi; underside of broad wings entirely dark,* contrasting in flight with white belly. Larger and stockier than Wood Sandpiper. **Non-breeding plumage** *deep olive-brown above* with fine whitish speckling; underparts white, with sides of breast olive. Faint streaking on face, neck and breast becomes much bolder in **breeding plumage**, February–April. White supraloral streak and narrow white eye-ring contrast with blackish eye-line. In flight, shows white rump, upper tail-coverts and tail, the latter with two or three black bars toward tip. Bill blackish brown, olive at base; eyes dark brown. **Juvenile** shows sparse dull buff spots above. **Voice:** A loud ringing *clewit-lewit* or *clewit-weet-weet,* mainly in flight. **Habits:** Solitary. Bobs up and down like Common Sandpiper. Takes off erratically, quite snipe-like, calling repeatedly. 'Towers' and descends in rapidly executed loops. **Similar Species:** Wood Sandpiper is smaller, less robust, has smaller white rump patch, browner upperparts, more prominent superciliary stripes, pale grey or whitish wing-linings and different call; tarsi rather longer and paler yellowish green or olive. Common Sandpiper teeters more than it bobs, has different flight pattern. **Status and Distribution**: Regular palearctic migrant, widespread in small numbers between August and early April, along inland lakes, rivers, streams and ditches, more often in riverine areas than other waders, and on mangrove-lined creeks and brackish lagoons at the coast.

WOOD SANDPIPER *Tringa glareola* Plate 22

Length *c.* 200 mm (8"). A *slender, delicately built* inland wader with *white superciliary stripes,* straight bill and *long yellowish-green or pale olive tarsi.* In flight, appears dark above with *white rump and upper tail-coverts;* white shaft of outer primary noticeable at close range; toes project well beyond tail. From below, *whitish wing-linings* merge with the white belly. In **non-breeding plumage,** *upperparts paler and browner than those of Green Sandpiper,* with faint buffy-white speckling. In **breeding plumage** (March–May), upperparts more boldly spotted, head, neck and breast pale brown with faint streaks, flanks boldly barred, and rest of underparts white. Bill blackish, olive- to yellow-green at base. **Juvenile** resembles non-breeding adult, but upperparts with more buff speckling. Bill brownish black. May remind Americans of Lesser Yellowlegs, *T. flavipes.* **Voice:** In flight, a loud *chiff-iff, chiff-iff-iff;* on the ground, a persistent sharp *chip-chip-chip. . .* of alarm. **Habits:** Typically in loose parties, but sometimes scores together. Feeds in shallow water or from floating vegetation, picking from surface. Rather wary. **Similar Species:** Green Sandpiper is slightly larger and heavier, also darker, with blackish wing-linings, more white on rump and tail, shorter and narrower superciliary stripes, a noticeable eye-ring, and different call; in flight, only tips of longest toes project beyond tail. Juvenile is less speckled above than young Wood Sandpiper. **Status and Distribution:** Palearctic migrant, widespread and common inland late July to early May, especially in marshy places, irrigated fields and lake edges. A few present all year on Rift Valley lakes.

COMMON SANDPIPER *Actitis hypoleucos* Plate 22

Length *c.* 190 mm (7.5"). A small, short-legged sandpiper with *teetering walk* and *stiff-winged quivering flight.* Shows dull white superciliary stripes, and *brownish patch on each side of breast encloses a white wedge* extending from belly along bend of wing. Fine barring visible on wing-coverts at close range, but wings appear plain olive-brown above at a distance. In flight, centre of rump and tail uniform with back, *white wing-stripe* and *barred white sides of the long rounded tail* conspicuous. Pied underwing pattern rarely noticed in the field. Bill grey, olive-grey or dark brown, ochre or sometimes pinkish at base. Legs and feet dull olive-grey, pale grey-green or rarely yellowish olive. **Breeding plumage** (March–April) noticeably streaked above and on neck and breast. **Voice:** Flight note, usually given when flushed, a high-pitched *twee-wee-wee.* Alarm call, usually from ground, a long-drawn *tweeee.* Display call, sometimes heard in East Africa, a repeated *twee-wit-it-it.* **Habits:** Forages alone along water's edge and perches on waterside rocks, tree roots and partly submerged hippopotami. Almost incessant teetering or bobbing motion is characteristic, as is the low direct flight, involving quick shallow strokes of bowed wings not rising above the horizontal, alternating with short glides. (In high flight or over some distance, wing action more like that of other small sandpipers.) **Similar Species:** Green and Wood Sandpipers are longer-necked, longer-legged, and show plain dark wings and white rump in flight. **Status and Distribution:** Palearctic migrant, common and widespread from mid-July to April, with pronounced passage August and September. Frequents lake and pool edges, river banks, ditches, water holes, forest streams, rocky and sandy seashores and estuaries.

TEREK SANDPIPER *Xenus cinereus* Plate 22

Length 220–250 mm (9–10"). An active coastal wader with a *long, upturned black bill,* orange to dull red at the base, and *short yellow-orange legs and feet* (sometimes brighter orange in April). **Non-breeding plumage** grey-

brown above, with blackish 'shoulders' sometimes conspicuous. Underparts white, the neck and sides of breast grey-tinged and faintly streaked. In flight, appears plain above except for *white trailing edge to secondaries*. **Breeding plumage** more streaked above and below, broadly so on scapulars, which may form a blackish V. **Voice**: A fluty *tuu-hu* or *tew-tew-tew* in flight; also a sharper *twit-wit-wit-wit*. **Habits**: Usually in loose groups with other waders at water's edge or in high-tide roosts. Makes short quick runs with body low and bill horizontal, suddenly changing direction; probes deeply with bill held nearly flat, and scythes like an avocet. Bobbing suggests Common Sandpiper. **Status and Distribution**: Palearctic migrant, late August to April, common on coastal creeks, saltpans, open mudflats and coral reefs. A few first-year birds regularly remain all year. Occasional along Rift Valley lakes in Kenya and n. Tanzania, August–November.

RUDDY TURNSTONE *Arenaria i. interpres*   Plate 23

Length 210–255 mm (8–10"). A plump coastal shorebird with *distinctively patterned plumage*, a *short, slightly uptilted, blackish bill* and *short orange legs*. **Non-breeding plumage** mottled dusky brown and black above; dark brown sides of face and bold blackish breast patch contrast with white chin and belly. Bold flight pattern involves broad white wing-stripe and white back and upper tail-coverts, with black bar across rump and broader black terminal tail band. **Breeding plumage** shows much rufous above and an *intricate black-and-white head/neck pattern*. **Juvenile** duller brown above (fresh feathers buff-edged) and on breast, with pale patches on head; legs and feet dull yellowish brown at first, rapidly turning orange. **Voice**: A hard *kitititit* or *tuk-a-tuk*, and a sharp *keeoo*. **Habits**: Small scattered parties actively forage among shoreline rocks and debris, turning over small stones and seaweed. **Status and Distribution**: Palearctic migrant, mainly late August to April, when common on rocky shores, weedy beaches and coral reefs. Small numbers occasional on Rift Valley lakes and at Lake Victoria, mainly September–November.

RED-NECKED PHALAROPE *Phalaropus lobatus*   Plate 22
(Northern Phalarope)

Length 180 mm (7"). Mainly pelagic. A dainty open-water bird with slender neck and *all-black, needle-like bill*. Usually seen in Africa in **non-breeding plumage,** grey above, with white sides of neck and underparts, and a *black eye patch*; white wing-stripe and dark centre of rump and tail prominent in flight. Tarsi short, dark grey or bluish grey; toes distinctly lobed. **Breeding female** acquires dark grey upperparts and breast with contrasting white chin, rufous patches on sides of neck, and buff lines on the back. **Breeding male** duller and more brownish above, with pale rufous-brown neck patches. **Voice**: A sharp *twick* or *kwick*. **Habits**: Solitary or in small groups on inland waters, but may be in large flocks at sea. Swims, often spinning in small circles and feeding on small surface organisms. **Similar Species**: In flight, Sanderling shows stronger wing-stripe, narrower tail with more contrasting pale sides, no black eye patch. See Grey Phalarope. **Status and Distribution**: Palearctic migrant, October April. Regular offshore, but scarce inland, where most records from Lake Turkana and other Rift Valley lakes. Rare in n. Tanzania, where singles or small numbers seen near Tabora (Oct. 1962), at Lake Lygarja, Serengeti NP (Jan.–Feb. 1975), and Arusha NP (April 1981).

GREY PHALAROPE *Phalaropus fulicarius*   Plate 22
(Red Phalarope)

Length c. 200 mm (8"). Slightly larger and more robust than Red-necked Phalarope, *paler and more uniformly grey* above in **non-breeding plumage.** Bill *shorter and thicker*, usually showing some yellowish at the base; tarsi brown or greyish. Toes brown with large yellow lobes. **Breeding plumage** bright rufous below, with *black cap and white face* patch; tarsi yellowish brown. **Voice**: A sharp, high-pitched, somewhat Sanderling-like *wit*, shriller than call of Red-necked Phalarope. **Habits**: Similar to those of preceding species. **Similar Species**: Red-necked Phalarope is slightly smaller, darker grey and more distinctly patterned above, with finer, needle-like bill. **Status and Distribution**: Rare palearctic migrant. Five sight records, most poorly documented. One photographed in Nairobi NP, September 1979.

SKUAS OR JAEGERS, FAMILY STERCORARIIDAE
(World, 7–8 species; Africa, 6; Kenya, 3; n. Tanzania, 1)

Gull-like seabirds sometimes considered a subfamily of the Laridae. They are hook-billed and piratical, pursuing other birds and forcing them to disgorge their food. Most are seen in flight, but occasionally one is observed standing beside the water or swimming with gull-like posture. Although typically marine, a few appear on Rift Valley lakes. Unidentified *Catharacta* skuas, rarely reported off the East African coast, are probably vagrants from southern oceans, whereas the three *Stercorarius* species are migrants from arctic breeding areas.

Adult *Stercorarius* in breeding plumage (possible here in August and again in spring) have a dark cap and distinctive projecting central tail feathers. All three species are polymorphic, with either predominantly white or dark brown underparts, but various intermediates exist between dark and light morphs. The sexes are alike. If seen well, adults can be identified by *shape of the central rectrices*. Barred winter adults (basic plumage) begin to moult back into breeding dress before they return north in spring. Most **juveniles** are brown (Long-tailed much greyer) and pale-barred above, dark-barred below, with pale wing-covert and scapular tips producing a scaly or neatly barred dorsal pattern. Some are darker, more sooty brown, with little pale tipping. Adult plumage apparently takes up to four years to acquire, so there are intermediate **immature** plumages, highly variable but distinct from the *juvenile* plumage of birds on their first southward migration. Their central rectrices are shaped like those of adults but are much shorter. Otherwise, young skuas show few plumage characters which permit species identification, and observers must rely on *shape*, *size* (especially *wingspread, compared with that of nearby species*) and *flight style*. For juveniles, one must also record (1) *general plumage colour*, (2) *shape of central rectrices* (short, and difficult to see, but diagnostic), (3) *bill shape and colour*, (4) *amount of white in primaries*, and (5) *tail-covert markings*. The ivory-white primary shafts show as a 'flash' of white on the upper wing-surface: five or six in Pomarine, three to five in Arctic, two in Long-tailed (sometimes a third pale brownish one can appear white); in any species the number visible depends on the extent to which the primaries are spread. It is risky to rely on this or any other single character for identification. Tail-feather shapes, though diagnostic, can be difficult to determine at certain angles or if the feathers are worn. Most skuas are not seen long enough or sufficiently near to permit careful study of subtle and variable field marks, precluding positive identifications in many cases. Good photographs are usually essential.

We are indebted to Kenn Kaufman for many of the fine points of skua distinctions included in the following species accounts.

POMARINE SKUA *Stercorarius pomarinus*
(Pomarine Jaeger)

Plate 8

Length 65–78 cm (25.5–31"), including 17–20 cm projection of central rectrices in adults. A *large* skua, *thick-necked, barrel-chested and broad-winged*, with steady, powerful, slow wingbeats, suggesting a large gull. *Bill long and deep, with strong hook and prominent gonydeal angle*; dark brown or grey, the *base often pale*. Eyes brown; feet black. **Spring adult** dark brown above, with blackish cap; predominant **pale morph** yellowish white below, darkly barred along sides and flanks, *usually* with a *mottled or barred dark breast band*; under tail-coverts dark brown. In flight, shows prominent white crescent at base of primaries above and below; *projecting central rectrices broad, twisted, and rounded at tips*. Uncommon **dark morph** wholly blackish brown below, mottled rather than evenly toned, with dull yellowish face. **Non-breeding adult** pale-barred on back, *dark-barred on upper tail-coverts*; cap margins blurred; chin and throat browner than in spring plumage, and barring stronger on flanks and under tail-coverts; projecting tail feathers shorter and more pointed. Some spring adults are intermediate between breeding and non-breeding plumages, often well barred below (especially on crissum). **Immature** similar to non-breeding adult, but wings more barred beneath and projecting rectrices short. Pale legs and feet gradually become black. **Juvenile** usually has *pale bill base* (grey, brownish or dull yellow) contrasting with black tip and with *dark malar area*. Head more uniformly dark than that of Arctic Skua, not paler on nape, faintly barred instead of streaked. More conspicuously barred on upper tail-coverts than Arctic Skua. Central rectrices broad, bluntly rounded to squarish, barely extending beyond the others (thus scarcely noticeable). Eyes brown; said to be dull white in some birds. Legs and feet pale blue; distal part of toes and webs black. **HABITS**: Deep, regular wingbeats of normal flight quickly change in swift and agile pursuit of gulls and terns. **SIMILAR SPECIES**: Slightly smaller Arctic Skua appears more falcon-like in flight, with narrower, more pointed wings and smaller tail; spring adult has longer and pointed central tail feathers. Juvenile has pale nape, paler face (less dark feathering on malar area adjacent to the all-dark bill), prominent pale tips on outer primaries (rare in Pomarine), and sharply pointed, more noticeably projecting central rectrices. **STATUS AND DISTRIBUTION**: Scarce palearctic migrant, October–March, with 13 Kenyan records (nine coastal, four from Rift Valley lakes). Tanzanian records from the Pemba Channel (Oct. 1989) and Zanzibar (Jan. 1993, Jan. 1994).

*ARCTIC SKUA *Stercorarius parasiticus* (Parasitic Jaeger)

Plate 8

Length 46–67 cm (18–26.5″), including 8–14 cm central rectrix projections. *Somewhat falcon-like* in flight. Wingspan about that of a Grey-headed Gull; slimmer than a Pomarine Skua, with narrower wings and, in **adult**, *narrow, pointed central tail-feather projections*. Bill variable in size, black, tinged olive or slate at base; eyes brown; feet black. **Dark morph** is *evenly dark smoky grey-brown*, not mottled-looking. **Light morph** sometimes lacks dark breast band; if present, this is evenly grey, neither mottled nor barred. White primary bases prominent on underside of wing. **Non-breeding adult** and **immature** resemble corresponding plumages of Pomarine; bill as in adult; blue-grey tarsal colour of juvenile gradually changes to black (often with much colour even in third-year birds). **Juvenile** brighter, warmer brown than young Pomarine or Long-tailed Skuas, with *rufous or tawny feather edgings producing scaly effect on back and wings*; underparts usually barred with uneven wavy lines except on flanks; *pale brown nape typically streaked like the face, malar area pale* (no dark feathers adjacent to bill as in Pomarine). *Upper tail-covert barring more brown and buff, less black and white, the bars wavy, not so straight and even as in Pomarine.* Bill uniformly dark blue-grey, more blackish at tip; eyes brown. **HABITS:** Flight rapid and dashing, often low, the powerful wingbeats alternating with long glides. Commonly pursues gulls and terns. **SIMILAR SPECIES:** Pomarine Skua, in addition to differences detailed above, is slightly larger and heavier, with broader wings and tail; projecting rectrices broad and rounded in adult; white wing flash generally more pronouced. Pale Pomarine usually shows a dark breast band. Long-tailed Skua is smaller and slimmer, with buoyant flight, little white in primaries. Juveniles compared above. **STATUS AND DISTRIBUTION:** Rare palearctic migrant. Three acceptable Kenyan records of adults near Malindi (April 1966 and 1980), one from Lake Turkana (Oct. 1983). Other skuas, thought to have been Arctics, seen at lakes Nakuru and Turkana (Sept.–Nov.) and the coast (Mar.–Apr.).

LONG-TAILED SKUA *Stercorarius longicaudus* (Long-tailed Jaeger)

Plate 8

Length 50–58 cm (19.5–23″), including 15–25 cm central rectrix projections. Quite graceful and *tern-like*; smaller, more delicate than the two previous species, the wings proportionately longer and narrower. **Spring adult (pale morph)** shows *neat, sharply defined black cap* separated by white collar from grey upperparts that are paler than in most Arctic Skuas. Primaries dark, *only two with white shafts; blackish secondaries contrast noticeably with greyish coverts* (an effect rarely created by Arctic's more uniformly dark wings). Underparts largely white, without breast band, but dark on belly and crissum; *tail streamers straight, pointed, about one-third of bird's total length.* Eyes brown; bill black (to horn-brown at base); tarsi grey-blue, or partly or wholly black. **Dark morph** very rare. **Non-breeding adult** generally buffy grey, dusky on face, collar and breast; tail projections shorter. **Immature** variable; usually much like non-breeding adult, but with mostly barred under wing-coverts and axillars. Tarsi blue-grey or partly black. **Juvenile** greyish above and *finely barred with white, less scaly or scalloped* in appearance than the two larger species; head often pale, at least on nape; face usually finely streaked. Breast typically uniform dark brownish grey; wing-linings, flanks, upper and under tail-coverts strongly barred *black and white*. Inch-long rectrix extensions blunt and rounded, at first with tiny sharp points (probably gone before birds reach African waters). Lacks buff primary tips of young Arctic Skua. Bill grey-blue with black tip; tarsi grey-blue; toes and webs blackish and pale pink. **HABITS:** Less piratical than the larger skuas. Flight more buoyant. Picks food items from water surface. **SIMILAR SPECIES:** Arctic Skua is larger, darker and browner, more like a medium-sized gull than a tern. See discussions above for details. **STATUS AND DISTRIBUTION:** Palearctic vagrant. Adult in breeding plumage photographed at Lake Turkana (25–26 Aug. 1961); immature, possibly of this species, seen at Lake Nakuru (21 Aug. 1989).

Antarctic Skua (left) and pale morph of South Polar Skua. Neither known with certainty from Kenya or n. Tanzania. Unidentified Catharacta *in our waters may include either or both species.*

Catharacta skuas

A skua seen at Kiunga on the north Kenyan coast, 6 August 1961, was reported as *C. antarctica madagascariensis* by Britton (1980), and other coastal *Catharacta* sightings have been reported (Aug. 1976, Jan. 1988, Dec. 1990, Dec. 1992). In view of possible confusion with South Polar Skua, *C. maccormicki*, as well as dark Pomarines, we cannot admit any *Catharacta* species to the Kenyan list without a specimen or satisfactory photographic evidence. The most likely large skua in southern Africa appears to be *C. a. madagascariensis* (= *lonnbergi*), but with reports of *C. maccormicki* and *C. antarctica* from Somalia, and records of the former from the Indian subcontinent, both would seem possible in Kenyan waters.

Antarctic Skua shows little or no contrast between underbody and underside of wing, the nuchal collar is faint or lacking, and the warm brown upperparts are more variegated, less uniform than those of South Polar Skua, which typically is colder brown above with a distinct pale nuchal collar; below, South Polar Skua shows marked contrast between the pale body and dark wings (**Fig. p. 409**). This latter species is polymorphic. In pale morph the head is light buff, similar to the underparts, and may have a contrasting dark cap. Dark morph is rather uniform slaty brown except (usually) for a faint nuchal collar. It typically shows a narrow pale band around base of bill. Intermediate morph shows less contrast between dark and light plumage areas.

GULLS, FAMILY LARIDAE, SUBFAMILY LARINAE
(World, *c.* 50 species; Africa, 23; Kenya, 8; n. Tanzania, 4)

Our species are mostly coastal scavengers and fishers, numerous at centres of human fishing activity. Some are regular and common on inland waters. Gulls are generally larger than terns, with broader and less pointed wings, shorter, heavier bills, and square-ended tails. They often settle on the water, but rarely dive. The sexes are alike, except for males being somewhat larger than females. Only two species breed in our region, nesting on the ground, among rushes or on floating platforms; eggs one to three, olive-brown or buff, heavily speckled or mottled.

Plumages are diverse. Typically, the smaller palearctic species appear adult in their second winter, medium-sized species in their third winter, and large gulls in their fourth winter. All undergo a post-juvenile moult when two to four months old, but retain their juvenile wing and tail feathers. In gulls, a partial prenuptial (prealternate) moult involves replacement of head and body feathers, some wing-coverts and inner wing feathers. The prolonged post-nuptial (prebasic) moult, resulting in winter (basic) plumage, replaces all feathers and may take up to five months to complete. Thus, there are numerous intermediate plumages to confound the observer. Important features to note are colour of bare parts, relative bill size, upper wing and tail patterns, and head markings.

SOOTY GULL *Larus hemprichii*   Plates 6, 7, 8
(Hemprich's Gull)

Length 44–47 cm (17–18.5"). A large, dark *coastal* gull, long-billed and with long, broad rounded wings. **Breeding adult** brownish grey above, with *sooty-brown head and greyish neck and breast; white collar on hindneck and small white marks above and below eyes* (most noticeable in breeding plumage); wings blackish above with white trailing edge; under wing-surface dark. *Bill yellowish, with black subterminal band and red tip;* legs and feet greenish yellow; eyes dark brown. **Non-breeding adult** similar, but hood paler and bare parts duller. **First-winter** paler and browner above, with pale-edged wing-coverts, brownish breast band, and pale head with some dark brown around eyes and on nape; primaries and bar along secondaries blackish, contrasting with paler forewing; *pale rump/upper tail-coverts contrast with black tail.* Bill blue-grey with black tip; feet dull grey or blue-grey; eyes brown. **Second-winter** bird similar but plainer, pale grey above (with contrasting dark remiges), and black confined to tip of tail. Full adult plumage attained in third year. **Juvenile** resembles first-winter bird, but body paler, the upperparts browner with scaly buff feather edges. **Voice:** Usual call a sustained screaming *keeow*, frequently repeated; also a more staccato *kek-kek-kek* and other calls at breeding colonies. **Habits:** Sociable, usually in groups and occasionally in many hundreds in mixed larid flocks. Nests on coral islands in a scrape or depression in the rock. Wingbeats slow and deliberate. **Similar Species:** White-eyed Gull (see note below) is similarly patterned and also has attenuated posterior owing to long wings, but is smaller, paler and greyer above, with slimmer black-tipped red bill and yellowish legs; first-year bird darker above than Sooty Gull, more uniformly brown. **Status and Distribution:** Present throughout coastal areas and offshore islands in most months, although scarce or absent from Malindi southward, June–September. Mainly a non-breeding visitor from ne. Africa and Arabia, although a few breed on islets off Kiunga on north Kenyan coast from July to October. **Note:** White-eyed Gull, *L. leucophthalmus* (Fig. p. 413), is a possible vagrant from the Red Sea, dispersing regularly to northern Somalia. It is paler and slimmer than Sooty Gull, with narrower, more pointed wings. Non-breeding adult has white-flecked black head (pure black and more sharply demarcated in breeding plumage) and prominent white crescents above and below eyes; slender dark red bill with black tip; feet yellowish. Juvenile is more uniform dark brown above than in Sooty Gull, lacking prominent pale edges on wing-coverts; blackish of head extends to nape; bill blackish; feet grey.

Jnconfirmed reports from the north Kenyan coast February–April, early 1950s to mid-1960s (Bednall and Williams 1989), and Lake Turkana, 4 April 1975.

HEUGLIN'S GULL *Larus heuglini*   Plates 6, 7

Length 60–66 cm (24–26"). A *bulky* gull, *patterned like Lesser Black-backed,* but slightly larger and heavier with somewhat larger bill. **Adult** medium grey to dark slate above, with white head and tail; outer primaries grade to blackish distally, and have small white tips with a small 'mirror' on outermost feather. Wings show white trailing edges. Bill heavy, yellow with a red or black-and-red gonydeal spot; some Kenyan birds (third year?) show a large black mandibular spot, others a nearly complete subterminal blackish ring around the bill, fainter on maxilla – a feature, in this group, supposedly unique to brown-eyed *armenicus* (Grant 1986). *Eyes pale yellow,* rim of the eyelids dark red; legs and feet yellowish. Birds assumed to represent nominate *heuglini* are dark above, some appearing almost as black as *L. f. fuscus* and in non-breeding plumage showing *greyish streaks on crown and neck.* Paler birds with medium grey to dark grey upperparts, little head streaking, and yellowish or flesh-pink feet appear to be *taimyrensis* – a variable population perhaps of hybrid origin – or at least assignable to the *taimyrensis–birulae* cline (P. Yésou, pers. comm.), but some dark grey birds may be *L. f. graellsii,* q.v. **First-winter** *heuglini* resembles comparable plumage of Lesser Black-backed Gull, but is generally paler than *L. f. fuscus,* with more barring and pale mottling above, more boldly marked on rump, and paler on underparts; head whitish. Said to lack black bar on greater coverts, and to show pale panel near base of primaries (unlike Lesser Black-backed Gull). Bill largely or entirely black, sometimes extensively pinkish with black tip; feet pinkish. **Second-winter** bird greyer (pale in some *taimyrensis,* more slaty in *L. h. heuglini*), with yellowish bill base; legs and feet described as either pink or yellow, but almost whitish in some birds. **VOICE**: Variable. Calls said to resemble those of Herring, *L. argentatus,* and Lesser Black-backed Gulls. **SIMILAR SPECIES**: Lesser Black-backed Gull compared above. See Kelp Gull. **STATUS AND DISTRIBUTION**: Regular or semi-regular palearctic visitors, sometimes in substantial numbers, from the Tana River delta to the Malindi/Sabaki area of the Kenyan coast, November–March; occasional elsewhere on the coast and reportedly at Lake Turkana (where possible confusion with *L. f. graellsii* must be considered). **NOTE**: Systematics of the entire *Larus fuscus/argentatus* complex are in dispute, and a definitive statement on allocation of forms is not yet possible. Some consider *heuglini* and *taimyrensis* to be races of Herring Gull, *L. argentatus;* others merge them with *L. fuscus.* A third school of thought, followed here, supports their separation as a third species owing to near-sympatry on the breeding grounds. *L. heuglini* may also include the forms *vegae, barabensis* and *armenicus.* Some of those, and perhaps *cachinnans* or *michahellis,* could reach East African waters. To date, the only large white-headed gulls collected in Kenya are *L. f. fuscus* and *L. f. graellsii,* although Cramp and Simmons. 1983) report a specimen of *heuglini* from Somalia; *heuglini* and presumed *taimyrensis* photographed numerous times near Malindi, 1980–94.

LESSER BLACK-BACKED GULL *Larus fuscus*   Plates 6, 7, 8

Length 51–61 cm (20–24"). Large, with *white head and tail* and (*L. f. fuscus*) *slaty-black upperparts* in **adult** plumage. Wings show white trailing edge above, with small white outer primary tips and white 'mirror' on outermost feather; *underside whitish, but dark near tip and dusky along trailing edge.* Bill typically yellow with red spot on gonys (variable dark markings in presumed third-year birds); eyes pale yellow, with narrow red eyelid rim; legs and feet usually yellow, but pinkish or greyish in some adult-plumaged birds. **First-winter plumage** mottled blackish brown above, paler on head, and neck strongly streaked; underparts greyish; flight feathers and their coverts blackish; tail white with broad blackish terminal band. Bill blackish; eyes, legs and feet dull pinkish flesh. **Second-winter** bird darker above, with tail band as in first-winter; bill blackish terminally, yellowish toward base. Full adult plumage attained in fourth year. Greyer *L. f. graellsii,* normally wintering in West Africa, has been collected once at Lake Turkana along with *L. f. fuscus.* First- and second-winter *graellsii* have especially dense head/neck streaking. (The Turkana specimen, a second-winter bird, had the bill mostly black terminally, extensively whitish on basal half, very pale tan eyes and whitish-flesh feet.) **SIMILAR SPECIES**: Upperparts of some Heuglin's Gulls are almost as dark as in *L. f. fuscus.* Heuglin's is slightly larger, heavier, with broader wings and stouter bill than Lesser Black-backed. See Kelp Gull. Grey-backed *L. heuglini taimyrensis* could be confused with *L. f. graellsii.* In the hand, it is seen to be long-winged (443–477 mm compared to 400–447 in *graellsii*). **STATUS AND DISTRIBUTION**: *L. f. fuscus* is a regular and at times common palearctic migrant, mainly October–April, along the Kenyan coast and larger inland lakes. Numbers recorded annually at Lake Turkana, particularly during the March–April northward passage. A few immatures present all year in Kenya, where Finnish- and Swedish-ringed birds have been recovered. *L. f. graellsii* is known in East Africa only from the Lake Turkana specimen (Allia Bay, 29 Nov. 1958) discussed above.

KELP GULL *Larus dominicanus* [*vetula*]
(Southern Black-backed Gull; Dominican Gull)

Plate

Length 58 cm (23"). A *large* vagrant black-backed gull with a *very heavy bill*. Generally *stockier and large headed than preceding two species*. In **adult**, upperparts black except for white trailing wing edges, whit primary tips and white 'mirror' on outermost primary. Wings of standing bird do not project so far beyond th tail as in Lesser Black-backed Gull. Bill yellow, with red or orange-red spot on gonys; orbital ring orange-rec eyes usually dark brown; in all plumages, legs and feet olive-grey or olive-yellow. In **non-breeding plumage**, fee may be blue-grey and crown may show some streaks. **Juvenile** (unlikely in East Africa) largely dark brown abov with buff feather edges and dark-barred whitish rump and upper tail-coverts; tail blackish, with white on edge and basal half of outer feathers. Head and underparts streaked with dusky; ear-coverts dusky, as are crescent above and below eyes; bill blackish. **First-winter plumage** mottled greyish brown above; whitish head an underparts dark-streaked, ear-coverts and area around eyes dusky; rump white with coarse dark barring; tai blackish. Eyes dark brown; bill and feet brownish. In **second-winter plumage**, head and underparts are cleare white with some brown streaking, more pronounced on breast, faint on head; back brown, primaries slate-grey and tail white at base. Bill and feet grey-brown becoming olive-yellow in spring. **Voice**: A plaintive *meew*, staccato *ko-ko-ko-ko* (Maclean 1984), and a loud *keeyok*. **Similar Species**: Adult Lesser Black-backed an Heuglin's Gulls have smaller bills and yellower legs and feet. Lesser Black-backed is smaller, appears slimme and longer owing in part to wings projecting farther beyond tail. **Status and Distribution**: Vagrant from s Africa. Adult photographed at Malindi, 2 January 1984.

GREY-HEADED GULL *Larus cirrocephalus poiocephalus*

Plates 5, 7,

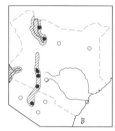

Length 41–43 cm (16–17"). A medium-sized *inland* gull with grey upperparts; wings o **adult** grey, with *white wedge* from carpal area to base of outer primaries; tip black wit white 'mirrors'; under surface quite dark. **Breeding adult** shows *pale grey hood*, darke along rear margin, and often a pink 'bloom' on the white underparts. Black primarie have white bases and white 'mirrors' on outer two pairs. Bill, legs and feet carmine eyelids coral-red; *eyes yellowish white*. **Non-breeding adult** has paler, less well-defined hood. **First-year plumage** differs in brownish diagonal bar across wing-coverts, dusk band along rear of secondaries, and a dark tail band; the white head shows blackish smudges on crown and behind eyes. Juvenile wings and tail retained, faded and worn Feet brownish red; bill pinkish with dark tip. **Juvenile** largely brown above, including crown and sides of head; tail white with dark brown terminal band; no mirrors or primaries. *Eyes dark*. **Voice**: A short harsh *garr* or a querulous *kwaar*. High-flying flocks are especially vocal **Habits**: Noisy and gregarious. At times feeds on the ground, and commonly on the wing, tern-like, hovering above water surface to seize emerging insects. Nests in clumps of water-lily leaves and floating islets of rottin vegetation. **Similar Species**: Non-breeding Black-headed Gull is slightly smaller, paler above, and dark-eyed Spread wing shows white wedge extending to the tip; wings paler below than in Grey-headed Gull. **Status and Distribution**: The most numerous gull on inland lakes, where locally abundant; breeds irregularly on severa Rift Valley lakes. Rare at the coast.

BLACK-HEADED GULL *Larus ridibundus*
(Common Black-headed Gull)

Plates 5, 7, 8

Length 34–37 cm (13.5–14.5"). A medium-sized, *dark-eyed* gull with pale grey upper-parts and a slender bill. Wings rather narrow and pointed, the upper surface with *long white leading edge from bend to tip; black confined to narrow line along primary tips* Diagnostic *dark brown hood* of **breeding adult** replaced by white in **non-breeding plumage**, the only dark feathers forming a *prominent blackish spot behind each eye* Bill, legs and feet red; eyes deep brown. **First-winter plumage** has leading edge o primaries white, rear edge of secondaries brown, and a brown diagonal bar across coverts; tail has blackish band. Legs and feet dull orange; bill orange-red with blackish tip. **Voice**: Similar to that of Grey-headed Gull. **Habits**: Typically sociable, usually with other larids although sometimes alone. Flight buoyant. **Similar Species**: Grey-headed Gull has black or blackish wing tips at all ages, and underside of wings is darker; adul has pale eyes. **Status and Distribution**: Since the early 1970s, a regular and locally common palearctic migrant to many Rift Valley waters, particularly Turkana and Nakuru. Small numbers elsewhere, including coastal sites. **Note**: Mediterranean Gull, *L. melanocephalus*, has been dubiously reported from Lake Turkana (April 1975) and Lamu (Aug. 1978). Adult differs from *ridibundus* in broader, more rounded wings that ar unmarked pale grey above (whitish near tip), a heavier dark red bill; black hood of breeding plumage extends to the nape. First-winter bird differs from young Black-headed Gull in having prominent black postocular patches, the outer part of wing largely blackish and trailing edge of the secondaries very dark. Resembles young Grey-headed Gull, but has more robust bill and lacks white wedge on upper wing-surface. Little Gull, *L. minutus*, has been dubiously reported once from Kenya (flock of 60, Lake Turkana, Jan. 1978). Adult of this small species has blackish under wing-surface; wings plain grey above. First-winter bird shows bold open blackish M-pattern across wings and back.

SLENDER-BILLED GULL *Larus genei* Plates 5, 7, 8

Length 38–46 cm (15–18"). A *pale-eyed* gull similar in colour and wing pattern to Black-headed Gull, but with *longer*, leaner appearance owing to *slender neck* and, in flight, a somewhat *longer tail*. **Spring adult** has a pink 'bloom' on underparts (not evident at distance in bright light) and a pure white head. In **non-breeding plumage** shows a faint grey mark behind the eye. Further distinguished from Black-headed Gull by *pale eyes, longer bill slightly drooping at tip and varying in colour from blackish red to bright orange*; legs and feet usually scarlet. In flight, shows *flatter forehead and distinctive long-necked, humpbacked profile*. When swimming, neck less upright than in Black-headed, with *head held forwards*. **First-winter** bird similar in plumage to first-winter Black-headed, but brown markings paler, the postocular ones less distinct, and bill and feet typically brighter orange-yellow. **STATUS AND DISTRIBUTION**: Scarce palearctic migrant, regular on lakes Turkana and Nakuru, where usually with Grey-headed and Black-headed Gulls. Rare elsewhere, including the coast. Has occasionally remained into July.

GREAT BLACK-HEADED GULL *Larus ichthyaetus* Plates 6, 7, 8

Length 57–61 cm (22.5–24"). A *large pale* gull with a *massive bill* and *long sloping forehead*. Standing bird *long-legged*, and has *attenuated rear end* owing to the long wing tips. *Wingbeats slow and heavy*. Huge bill and flat forehead give flying bird a characteristic *front-heavy appearance*. **Non-breeding adult** has pale grey upperparts, *largely white head with blackish shading around and behind eye*, and heavy streaking on hindneck. Upperside of wing shows white leading edge, outer primaries white with black markings near tip; underside whitish. Bill yellow with black subterminal band; legs and feet greenish yellow. **Breeding plumage** similar, but with *black hood* marked by conspicuous small white crescents around eyes. **First-winter** bird resembles non-breeding adult, but wing tips extensively blackish brown, forewing mottled brown, and blackish bar on secondaries contrasts with pale mid-wing; white tail has broad black terminal band. Bill greyish pink, tipped black; legs and feet grey. **Second-winter** bird has much greyer wings, and yellowish bill, legs and feet. **VOICE**: A raven-like croaking *kuraak*. **HABITS**: Often solitary. More shy than other large gulls, with which it associates. **STATUS AND DISTRIBUTION**: Uncommon palearctic migrant, December–March, fairly regular in small numbers at Malindi, the Sabaki River mouth and Lake Turkana. Rare elsewhere.

White-eyed Gull. No substantiated record from our region.

TERNS, FAMILY LARIDAE, SUBFAMILY STERNINAE
(World, 44 species; Africa, 23; Kenya, 17; n. Tanzania, 13)

Aquatic birds, mostly smaller and more slender than gulls, with forked tail and more pointed wings. Although sometimes placed in a family by themselves, their close affinities with gulls are unquestioned. They fly with grace and buoyancy, the bill often angled downward. Most dive to catch fish or other aquatic animals, sometimes plunging spectacularly after hovering kingfisher-like above the water. They rarely swim, and they come to land for roosting. Nesting is colonial, on the ground or in marsh vegetation.

Typical terns (*Sterna*) show a black cap in breeding plumage, this being partially lost after nesting. They mature during their second or third years, and many young oversummer in non-breeding areas. The freshwater marsh terns (*Chlidonias*) are dark bodied in breeding dress, but display marked seasonal plumage variation. The dark, white-capped noddies (*Anous*) are low-flying marine terns, usually seen far out at sea, where they hover and swoop to snatch food from the surface.

Tern identification requires attention to such subtle features as tail-tip/wing-tip relationship, relative bill and tarsus lengths (in perched birds), underwing patterns and flight styles.

GULL-BILLED TERN *Sterna n. nilotica*   Plates 3, 5

Length 35–38 cm (14–15"). Large and stocky; *pale grey above (including rump)* and *white below*. The gull-like impression produced by *heavy black bill, rather broad wings* and *shallowly forked tail* is enhanced by heavier flight than that of most *Sterna* species. Black cap of **breeding adult** is reduced to dark ear-coverts and streaks on nape in **non-breeding plumage**. In flight, darker trailing edge of outer primaries is visible from above and below. *Black tarsi* are longer and thicker than in most terns. **First-winter** bird is more white, less grey, than adult, but wing-coverts tipped with brown, and black on the head is confined to distinct facial patch; legs and feet brown. **VOICE**: A throaty *kirrr-uk, kay-ti-did* or *kay-rik*; also a repeated somewhat metallic *kaaak*. **HABITS**: Hunts with slow shallow wingbeats over exposed flats, lakes and marshes, picking prey from surface or hawking insects in the air; occasionally dives for fish. Congregates in hundreds at local roosts and feeding attractions. **SIMILAR SPECIES**: Other black-billed terns are more lightly built and have slender bills. **STATUS AND DISTRIBUTION**: Locally common palearctic migrant, mainly late August to early April, to the larger inland lakes, and in somewhat smaller numbers along the coast south to the Pemba Channel. Flocks regularly cross the eastern Serengeti Plains in n. Tanzania, January–March. A few are present much of the year on Rift Valley lakes.

CASPIAN TERN *Sterna caspia*   Plates 4, 5

Length 47–54 cm (18.5–21"). A *very large* tern with *heavy red bill* (tipped dusky), and shaggy crest on nape. Size, rather broad wings and only slightly forked tail may suggest a gull, but bill and habits are tern-like. **Adult** pale grey above, with slightly crested black cap, streaked with white in non-breeding plumage; underparts and rump white. Wings pale grey above, the primaries darker; whitish under wing has contrasting dark tip. Feet black. **First-winter** bird resembles non-breeding adult, but has brown-tipped wing-coverts, dusky secondaries and dark tail tip. Tail remains partly grey into first summer. **Juvenile** resembles immature, but brownish-black cap is streaked with greyish buff, sides of face blackish, white hindneck mottled with dark grey, the partly brown back feathers and scapulars are tipped with buff, and orange bill has dusky tip. Post-juvenile moult takes several months to complete. **VOICE**: A hoarse *kaaa*, a shorter *kark* and a heron-like *kraah-aah*. **HABITS**: Flies high and sometimes soars. Dives well, submerging completely. Small groups usually accompany other larids. **SIMILAR SPECIES**: Lesser Crested Tern can be confused at distance, when much smaller size is not apparent; the slimmer, straighter, orange or orange-yellow bill can appear reddish in low sunlight. **STATUS AND DISTRIBUTION**: Presumed palearctic migrant, regular in small numbers along the coast and at Lake Turkana; rare elsewhere, although recorded along the Tanzanian coast south of our region. Winters regularly in the Malindi/Sabaki area and at Lake Turkana.

GREATER CRESTED TERN *Sterna bergii*   Plates 4, 5
(Crested Tern; Swift Tern)

Length 46–49 cm (18–19"). A *prominently crested* coastal bird, slightly smaller than Caspian Tern. At rest, appears elongate, with long wings and *large pale yellow bill which droops at the tip*. Tail well forked. **Breeding adult** has *black cap separated from bill by narrow white band*. In **non-breeding plumage**, black is confined to hindcrown, occiput and nape. Upperparts rather dark grey in *S. b. velox*, paler in *S. b. thalassina*, but rump and tail pale grey in both races; blackish outer primaries form a dark wedge at wing tip, noticeable above and below. In *velox*, silvery-white inner primaries and secondaries contrast with dark grey forewing; underside of wing white except for dusky outer primary tips. Feet black. Greyer **first-year** bird similar to non-breeding adult, but with much grey-brown on wing-coverts plus darker carpal and secondary bars; grey tail feathers edged and tipped

with white. **Juvenile** darker grey above, barred and mottled with black and white, crown blackish brown with white-edged feathers, the crest browner; facial mottling dusky around eyes; *mid-wing paler* (lost by first winter), blackish-brown primaries, *dark brown carpal bar* and dark grey bar on secondaries; tail dark. **Voice**: A harsh *ki-ekk* or *kiii-rit*, a croaking *krrow*, and a high squealing *kreee-kreee*. **Habits**: Sociable; usually in small groups within mixed larid flocks. Flight powerful, with steady sweeping beats. **Similar Species**: Lesser Crested Tern is smaller, more lightly built, paler above (than *S. b. velox*), with smaller, brighter orange-yellow bill, all-black forehead in breeding plumage, but entire crown of non-breeding bird is white. **Status and Distribution**: *S. b. velox* is a non-breeding visitor from Somalia and the Gulf of Aden, common south to Malindi, especially November–June; occasional at Mombasa. *S. b. thalassina*, breeding in the western Indian Ocean, including Latham Island off Dar es Salaam, is sporadic along the coast south of Mombasa and around Pemba Island.

LESSER CRESTED TERN   *Sterna b. bengalensis*   **Plates 4, 5**

Length 35–37 cm (14–14.5"). A *crested* coastal tern with *long, straight orange or orange-yellow bill* and pale ash-grey upperparts. Tail deeply forked; wings proportionately shorter than in Greater Crested Tern, and flight more buoyant. Upperparts paler than in *S. bergii velox*. In **breeding plumage**, entire cap *black from bill to nape*. **Non-breeding adult** has white forehead, *crown and part of occiput white*, with *black largely confined to nape and postocular areas*; flight feathers silvery-edged; wing pale below with greyer primary tips. Feet black. **First-year** bird has dull yellow bill, blackish outer primaries and dusky secondaries. **Juvenile** (unlikely in our region) similar to first-year plumage, but back feathers and upper wing-coverts brown-tipped; head as in non-breeding adult, with dull greyish-yellow bill. **Voice**: Recalls Sandwich Tern; a rough *kik-kerruk* or *kirrik* or *kreek-kreek*; also a high-pitched *krrr-eeep* and some twittering notes. **Habits**: Gregarious, forming large flocks; associates with Greater Crested and Common Terns. **Similar Species**: See Greater Crested Tern. Caspian Tern is much larger, with a heavier red bill. **Status and Distribution**: Common non-breeding visitor from the Red Sea and Somalia, present along the coast in all months, especially November–April, when usually the most numerous and widespread tern. Extends up creeks and estuaries, and inland along the lower Tana River. Vagrants recorded on Rift Valley lakes, including Naivasha (photographed), Nakuru and Turkana. **Note**: Subspecific determination of East African birds varies. We follow Cramp (1985) in assigning these to the nominate race. Others refer to them as *par* or *arabica*.

SANDWICH TERN   *Sterna s. sandvicensis*   **Plates 4, 5**

Length 36–41 cm (14–16"). Another crested coastal tern, similar in size and build to Lesser Crested. Pale grey upperparts can appear white at a distance or in bright sunlight, when *slender, yellow-tipped black bill* may seem all black. *Short white tail is not deeply forked*. In **breeding plumage**, entire crown is black, the bill tip distinctly yellow. **Non-breeding adult** has white forehead and forecrown, less obvious yellow bill tip, and greyish-white wings with only a narrow dusky trailing edge below near tip. Feet black. **First-winter** bird has darker wing tips and brown flecking on wing-coverts. **Voice**: A grating *kirrick* or *keer-kwit*; also a lower *gwick* or *gwut*. **Habits**: Generally forages in ones and twos along sandy shorelines, often with other tern species. **Similar Species**: Lesser Crested Tern has orange-yellow bill, greyer upperparts and more deeply forked tail. Gull-billed Tern has heavier all-black bill. Common Tern is smaller, darker grey and with deeply forked tail. **Status and Distribution**: Uncommon palearctic migrant, mainly to the north Kenyan coast, where recorded almost annually from the Tana River delta south to Malindi. Vagrant seen at Lake Baringo, November 1991.

ROSEATE TERN   *Sterna dougallii bangsi*   **Plates 3, 5**

Length 33–38 cm (13–15"). A medium-sized coastal tern. *Slender build, generally white appearance, and long tail* of black-capped **breeding adult** distinctive. Upperparts very pale grey, the outer primaries forming a *darker grey wedge at wing tip*; *underside of wing entirely white*, as are rump and underparts, the latter with a rosy 'bloom' when fresh; *outer tail feathers exceptionally long, well exceeding wing tips in resting bird*. Long, thin bill, *usually black or black with red base* in non-breeding season, turns *largely or wholly bright scarlet* at breeding time, although many birds seen in and near nesting colonies have blackish bills; feet bright red. **Non-breeding adult** and **first-year** bird have white forehead and crown, shorter outer tail feathers, narrow black carpal bar on wing, and brownish-orange feet. **Juvenile** has whitish forehead, and scaly buffy-grey back contrasting with white rump and hindneck; feet black. **Voice**: A harsh *chirrik* or *chewik*, and a higher-pitched *aaar* or *aaak*; at nesting colonies utters an insistent chattering *kek-kek-kek-kek.*

HABITS: Flight exceptionally light, with quick shallow wingbeats. Away from colonies, usually scattered among other terns resting on the beach or in small feeding groups. **SIMILAR SPECIES**: Common Tern is darker grey above shows blackish trailing edge on outer wing from below, and has broader wings. White-cheeked Tern is mor compact, greyer above, with shorter bill and tarsi. Breeding birds of both species have grey underparts. **STATU AND DISTRIBUTION**: Small numbers present along coast throughout the year, especially between May and October, when most are in breeding plumage. Thousands breed in the Kiunga Archipelago, July–September, an less regularly on Whale, Kisite and Pemba islands.

COMMON TERN *Sterna hirundo* Plates 3, !

Length 31–35 cm (12–14"). A gregarious coastal tern. In **spring plumage**, pale gre above with white rump and tail; black cap separated from pale greyish underparts b white sides of face; *underside of wing whitish, with broad dusky trailing edge alon primary tips*. In resting bird, *wing tips reach the ends of the moderately long outer ta feathers. Bill usually all black* (turning scarlet with black tip in spring, after leaving Eas African waters); feet dull red or red-brown. **Winter adult** has shorter outer tail feathers white forehead and forecrown; lacks contrast between back and rump; blackish lesse coverts form a *broad carpal bar*, evident on closed wing. **First-year** bird resembles non breeding adult, but has dusky along trailing edge of secondaries; in August, may show remnant brown juvenile feathers above, sooty-brown ear-coverts, orange base of bil and orange feet. **VOICE**: A repeated *kik-kik-kik* and *KEE-agh* or *KEE-yarr*. **HABITS**: Flock of hundreds assemble on beaches and sandbanks, and thousands feed offshore beyond the reef. Flight rapid an graceful, with deep steady wingbeats. **SIMILAR SPECIES**: Breeding Roseate Tern is paler above, never show contrast between back and rump, has longer bill and longer outer tail feathers, underside of wing is pure white wingbeats are quicker and shallower. White-cheeked Tern is somewhat darker above, with whitish primaries, ir breeding plumage much darker below than Common Tern and with grey rump; non-breeding adult has narrowe carpal bar and less white on forehead than non-breeding Common; White-cheeked is more compact, with shorter tarsi, narrower wings, and has slightly faster wingbeats. **STATUS AND DISTRIBUTION**: Common to abun dant palearctic migrant along the coast, particularly late August–December and during April. Some spend the northern winter in East African waters, and many first-year birds are present April–August. Scattered records from some Rift Valley lakes. Although specimen evidence is lacking from our region, both the nominate race and *S h. tibetana* appear to be represented. There are ringing recoveries of nominate birds from both Kenyan and Tanzanian coasts, and measurements of some locally ringed birds fit those of *tibetana*.

WHITE-CHEEKED TERN *Sterna repressa* Plates 2, 5

Length 30–35 cm (12–14"). A dark grey marine tern, distinctive in **breeding plumage** with *broad white facial streak* below the dark cap. Upperparts, including rump and tail dark grey. Tail has long outer feathers equalling wing tips in resting bird. In flight, upper wing-surface appears dark grey except for *contrasting whitish primaries with long narrow blackish trailing edge* both above and below. (Primaries of worn birds in late summer may be uniformly dark and without obvious contrast.) Largely *grey wing-linings interrupted by whitish area on secondary coverts*. Bill coral-red with apical third or hal dusky; legs and feet dark red. **Non-breeding adult** and **first-year** bird have white under parts and forehead, medium grey upperparts, *broader black carpal bar* and *darker inner wing feathers than Common Tern*, and the *dark edge formed by black primary tips is longer than in that species; rump and tail also greyer,* outer rectrices little elongated. Bil and feet blackish. **Juvenile** paler grey above than first-year bird, the browner back showing much white feather edging; the largely grey wings have *conspicuously white primaries* and white-margined coverts; forehead, lores and much of forecrown white, with large blackish loral spot, tail tip brown. Basal half of mandible flesh-pink. **VOICE**: Usual call a loud *kee-ERR* or *kee-EEEK* (*second syllable accented*, unlike Common Tern's call). At nest ing colonies, more varied vocalizations said to resemble those of Common Tern. **HABITS**: Usually feeds beyond the reef (to 10 km from shore). Plunges or dips to surface, but seldom submerges. Small groups rest on beaches and exposed coral. Nests colonially on islets. **SIMILAR SPECIES**: Common Tern, in addition to wing-pattern differ ences discussed above, is paler, with broader wings, longer tarsi, slightly longer bill, and white rump and tail in breeding plumage. Inland Whiskered Tern has short tail and broad wings. **STATUS AND DISTRIBUTION**: Breeds off n. Kenya in the Kiunga Archipelago and on Tenewe Island south of Lamu, July–September, despite heavy preda tion by local fishermen. Present elsewhere along coast throughout the year, small numbers on shore, large flocks beyond the reef; hundreds regular north of Malindi, April–June. Uncommon south of Mombasa.

BRIDLED TERN *Sterna anaethetus antarctica* Plate 2

Length 30–32 cm (12–12.5"). A *pelagic* tern, dark above and white below, the *brownish-grey back usually sepa rated from black crown and nape by whitish hindneck; white forehead extends over and beyond eyes as narrow superciliary stripes*; sides of tail white. Bill and feet black. **First-year** bird has shorter tail than adult, the outer feathers with no white. **Juvenile** has pale-tipped dorsal feathers, mostly white underparts; less distinct head

pattern than adult, and wholly brownish tail. **Voice:** A growling *kararrr* and some softer notes from feeding birds. At breeding colonies, gives a barking *yup-yup* and various other calls. **Habits:** Solitary or gregarious, usually well offshore. Often feeds with other terns; snatches prey from water surface and dives. Perches on ships and floating debris, but rarely settles on water. **Similar Species:** Sooty Tern is larger, more blackish and uniform above, with broader and shorter superciliary stripes. **Status and Distribution:** Breeds in Lamu and Kiunga archipelagos (a few hundred pairs), and erratically on Whale Island off Watamu, July–September. Elsewhere, frequent well beyond the reef south to the Pemba Channel. Rare on mainland beaches and coral rag.

SOOTY TERN *Sterna fuscata nubilosa* Plate 2

Length 40.5–43 cm (16–17"). A large *pelagic* tern with *bounding* and *often soaring flight.* **Adult** *black above and white below, with broad white forehead and superciliary stripes*; tail black and deeply forked, with white outer edges. Bill and feet black. **First-year** bird as adult, but underparts variably dark, usually black from chin to breast. **Juvenile** mainly sooty brown, speckled with white; crissum and wing-linings pale grey or whitish. **Voice:** Usual call a loud, nasal *ker-wacky-wack*; also a prolonged *kreeeah.* **Habits:** Highly gregarious. Feeds mostly on squid by dipping to water surface, seldom dives. Reluctant to alight on water. **Similar Species:** Bridled Tern is smaller, shorter-winged, with browner mantle, whitish hindneck, and narrower white superciliary stripes which extend well behind eyes. **Status and Distribution:** Thousands nested on Tenewe Island near Lamu, July–September 1963, possibly in subsequent years, and c. 50 pairs on Kisite Island, August 1976. Egg-collecting by fishermen undoubtedly prevents regular breeding. Frequently observed at sea south to the Pemba Channel, but rare over or within the reef.

LITTLE TERN *Sterna a. albifrons* Plate 3

Length 22–24 cm (8.5–9.5"). Typical **breeding-plumaged adult** differs from that of the more numerous Saunders's Tern in *white of forehead extending to posterior margin of eyes or beyond,* and in paler wing tip (*blackish only on the outer two or three primaries, the outermost with a pale shaft*); differs further in white tail (ash-grey in *saundersi*), and typically bright yellow to reddish-orange feet (duller in *saundersi*). These supposedly distinguishing features are not always clear-cut, and some birds appear intermediate. **Non-breeding adult** and **first-winter** bird apparently indistinguishable in the field from corresponding plumages of Saunders's Tern. Both forms begin their southward migration after the crown moult (white feathers replacing the black), after Saunders's Tern has lost its contrasting wing pattern (see below), and when both forms have grey rump and tail except for white outer rectrices. **Voice:** Not certainly distinguishable from that of Saunders's Tern; described as a rasping *kyik* or *cherk* (Cramp 1985). **Habits:** As for Saunders's Tern. **Similar Species:** See Saunders's Tern. **Status and Distribution:** Apparently scarce, although status uncertain; four coastal Kenyan specimens (Malindi/Kilifi waters, April 1955 and 1959) and one from Lake Naivasha (April 1959). Several subsequent sight records from lakes Turkana, Baringo and Naivasha all unsubstantiated; also reported along the Tanzanian coast south of Dar es Salaam.

SAUNDERS'S TERN *Sterna (albifrons) saundersi* Plates 3, 5

Length 22–24 cm (8.5–9.5"). A *small*, predominantly coastal tern with narrow wings and rapid wingbeats. Closely similar to Little Tern, the two forms probably conspecific. **Breeding plumage** (seen here in spring) pale grey above with black cap, and *white forehead area extending back only to anterior margin of eyes,* the patch appearing more 'square' in side view than that of Little Tern, in front view triangular, not V-shaped as in Little Tern. *Outer three or four primaries black, forming a distinct dark wedge* contrasting with otherwise pale grey wings; thus shows more dark than Little Tern, which usually has only the outer two (but sometimes three) primaries black. Outer primary shafts are black in Saunders's, whereas outermost primary has a pale shaft in Little Tern. Rump, upper tail-coverts and central tail feathers ash-grey (paler, almost white, in breeding *albifrons*). Bill *yellow* with black tip; eyes brown; feet olive, dark reddish brown or pinkish brown, any yellow restricted to rear of tarsi and underside of toes (Chandler and Wilds, 1994). **Winter adult** has broad blackish band through eyes, connecting around occiput; crown and lores mostly white. Shows no distinctive wing pattern, owing to complex moult schedule that leaves inner primaries worn and dark by the end of breeding season, and not contrasting with the outer three. Bill brownish black by September, then all black until spring; feet usually yellowish brown. **Juvenile** has sandy-buff crown, nape, back and scapulars, the crown streaked with black; leading edge of wing blackish. Bill black with dull yellow base; feet greyish pink to yellowish brown. Post-juvenile moult begins in August, and by October most birds are in **first-winter plumage,**

similar to non-breeding adult but retaining dark-tipped rectrices and dark lesser coverts, the latter showing as a carpal bar (which, as in Little Tern, may be retained until the bird's second winter). Juvenile primaries are all replaced by April or May. VOICE: Less grating than most tern voices. Usual call *kidik*, or *kik-kik*; also *keeeee*, sometimes prolonged. HABITS: Gregarious, often forming large flocks. Flight hurried. Frequently hovers and feeds by diving. SIMILAR SPECIES: Little Tern compared above. Non-breeding Common and Roseate Terns are black-billed like non-breeding Saunders's, but are considerably larger and vocally distinct. STATUS AND DISTRIBUTION: Widespread and at times abundant migrant from exclusively marine breeding grounds in the southern Red Sea. Visits coastal areas, especially between Malindi and the Sabaki River mouth, in greatest numbers October–April; also recorded on the lower Tana River. Hundreds of *albifrons*-like terns sometimes present on Lake Turkana, although they are generally rare on inland lakes. Except for an adult *saundersi* collected at Ferguson's Gulf, 2 October 1953, identity of Turkana birds is uncertain; no evidence supports the suggestion by Clancey (1982) that they represent *S. a. guineae*.

WHISKERED TERN *Chlidonias hybridus delalandii*   Plate 3

Length 25–26 cm (*c.* 10"). Largest and most *Sterna*-like of the marsh terns. Black cap of **breeding adult** is separated from dark grey underparts by *white stripe on side of face*; under tail-coverts also white; upperparts uniformly grey. Bill and feet dark red. **Non-breeding plumage** recalls *Sterna* terns, with white underparts, black streak through eyes to nape, and black-flecked crown; bill and feet duller than in breeding bird. Silvery, black-tipped primaries show as narrow dark trailing wing edge. **First-year bird** resembles non-breeding adult, but shows darker bar across secondaries. **Juvenile** has dark brown hindcrown and nape streaked with grey, and the rich brown back (with buff feather edges) contrasts with pale grey wings, rump and tail. VOICE: A loud rasping *kerck*, *kerch*, or *kreek*. Near nest, calls include a longer grating *kirrrik*. HABITS: Often in company with other marsh terns, hawking insects over water. Nests in groups on floating vegetation in lakes and marshes. SIMILAR SPECIES: Other *Chlidonias* terns have shorter bills, shorter, blunter wings and less deeply forked tails. Non-breeding White-winged Tern has contrasting whitish rump and tail. STATUS AND DISTRIBUTION: Local resident, breeding opportunistically in small colonies in cent. Kenya and n. Tanzania (with some regularity at Lake Naivasha and Limuru). Otherwise, widespread but uncommon on most inland lakes and irrigation areas. Some n. Kenyan birds (especially those at Lake Turkana) may represent the nominate palearctic race.

WHITE-WINGED TERN *Chlidonias leucopterus*   Plate 3
(White-winged Black Tern)

Length 20–23 cm (8–9"). Commonest of the marsh terns. **Breeding adult** unmistakable, with *black body, head and wing-linings* contrasting with pale grey flight feathers and *white forewing, rump, tail and under tail-coverts*. Bill dark red; eyes brown; feet orange-red. In full or partial breeding plumage from March to May, and in August/September. Moulting adult has variably pied body plumage. **Non-breeding adult** mainly grey above, with blackish primaries and *whitish forehead/forecrown, collar, rump and tail*. White of underparts extends to wing-linings. Hindcrown and ear-coverts blackish, as is a small preocular spot. Bill and feet dark red to black. **First-year** bird resembles non-breeding adult, but wings have black carpal bar and dark grey secondary tips. In **juvenile**, *dark back* contrasts with *whitish collar, rump and wings* (latter with darker trailing edge and carpal bar). VOICE: A harsh *kreek-kreek*. HABITS: Gregarious, often in large flocks. Hovers above water, watching for prey. Sometimes hawks insects over land far from water, and is attracted to grass fires or ploughing operations; feeds on army worms and other insects. SIMILAR SPECIES: Non-breeding Whiskered Tern is slightly larger, longer-billed and more *Sterna*-like, its rump and more deeply forked tail uniform with rest of upperparts. STATUS AND DISTRIBUTION: Widespread, common to abundant palearctic migrant on larger freshwater and alkaline lakes. Scarce at the coast, except near lower Tana River. Many first-year birds oversummer at Lake Victoria and on Rift Valley lakes.

(*) BLACK TERN *Chlidonias n. niger*   Plate 3

Length 22–24 cm (8.5–9.5"). A marsh tern, although generally coastal or even pelagic in winter elsewhere in Africa. **Breeding-plumaged adult** *dark grey above, including wings*, and sooty black on head and underparts except for white under tail-coverts. Wing-linings whitish or pale grey; rump and tail dark grey. Bill blackish; feet dark red. **Non-breeding adult** and **first-winter** bird white below and on most of face and collar; slate of crown and nape extends to ear-coverts and cheeks; *grey rump and tail uniform with back*; *dark grey patches on sides of breast* diagnostic. VOICE: Generally silent in Africa. Spring migrants may give a double *kik-kik* or *keek-keek*. SIMILAR SPECIES: Non-breeding White-winged Tern shows contrast between grey back and white rump and tail, and lacks dark pectoral patches; bill is shorter and flight less buoyant, with quicker, shallower wingbeats. Non-breeding Whiskered Tern is also grey-rumped, but has different head pattern and paler grey wings with silvery primaries; juvenile Whiskered shows much dark brown on upperparts and brownish smudges on sides of breast.

STATUS AND DISTRIBUTION: Rare palearctic migrant. Sight records from Lake Nakuru (Sept. 1953), near Nairobi (Oct. 1980) and Thika (Feb. 1983). Some doubt surrounds a specimen (Natural History Museum, Tring) labelled as taken at Kisumu, 30 April 1916.

BROWN NODDY *Anous stolidus pileatus* (Common Noddy)

Plate 2

Length 36–45 cm (14–17.5"); wingspan 80+ cm (c. 32"). A dark brown seabird, larger than a Common Tern, with *wedge-shaped tail* and *greyish-white cap sharply demarcated from dark lores and ear-coverts*; forehead white, with narrow black band at base of bill connecting the black lores. Wings and tail almost black; underside of wings pale with dark margins. Bill and feet black. Plumage of **first-year** bird often much faded and worn, appearing paler than adult. It and **juvenile** have white restricted to forehead, plus white-tipped feathers on upperparts and wings. VOICE: A variety of calls, some low, harsh and croaking (rather raven-like); others shrill. Mostly silent at sea. Highly vocal day and night at breeding colonies and communal roosts. HABITS: Flight direct, with heavy wingbeats and short glides, usually close to sea surface; hovers and swoops to snatch food. Nests colonially on rocky islands. SIMILAR SPECIES: Lesser Noddy is smaller, more blackish, the wings more uniformly dark below; light cap extends to nape and merges evenly on lores and ear-coverts. STATUS AND DISTRIBUTION: Hundreds breed in the Lamu Archipelago, June–September, and on Latham Island off Dar es Salaam, November–February. Small numbers present offshore in all coastal areas throughout the year.

LESSER NODDY *Anous t. tenuirostris*

Plate 2

Length 30–34 cm (12–13.5"); wingspan c. 60 cm (23.5"). A marine tern, smaller than Brown Noddy, with proportionately *longer and thinner bill* and the *light cap extending from bill to nape, often to below the eyes, and not sharply demarcated* from dark lores and ear-coverts. Plumage appears less brown, more greyish black. In flight, *tail appears paler than the back* (the reverse in Brown Noddy), and the narrower wings are more uniformly dark below. Wingbeats more rapid and flight more erratic. VOICE: Usually silent away from breeding colonies. STATUS AND DISTRIBUTION: Rare, but probably overlooked. Perhaps regular in small numbers beyond the reef. Flock of 200 or more recorded near Mombasa, August–September 1976, and small numbers occasionally September–December off Kipini and Shimoni.

SKIMMERS, FAMILY RYNCHOPIDAE
(World, 3 species; Africa, 1)

Peculiar fish-eating birds allied to terns and gulls, and sometimes treated as a subfamily of Laridae. Their unique feeding behaviour is related to the odd, laterally compressed, knife-like bill; the longer mandible slices the water at a 45-degree angle as the bird flies rapidly back and forth, skimming the surface; the shorter maxilla snaps down, closing the bill on any food item encountered. The American Black Skimmer (*R. niger*), and perhaps ours as well, has remarkable cat-like eye pupils which contract to vertical slits. Skimmers breed along freshwater shores, laying their spotted eggs in a bare scrape in the sand. The young are precocial.

AFRICAN SKIMMER *Rynchops flavirostris*

Plates 4, 5

Length 38–40 cm (15–16"); wingspan *125–135* cm (50–53"). A long-winged blackish-and-white bird with tern-like flight. *Knife-thin scissor-like bill* (see above) *bright vermilion and yellow*, the longer mandible with a translucent tip in breeding season. **Breeding adult** almost black above (browner when worn), except for white on secondaries, upper tail-coverts and sides of forked tail; underparts white. Legs and feet red. **Non-breeding adult** has diffuse pale collar on hindneck and grey-brown crown feathers with white fringes. Bill paler, more yellow, and feet more orange than in breeding plumage. **Juvenile** much duller, with broadly buff-margined crown and back feathers; bill of newly flying young bird noticeably shorter than that of adult, brownish black, yellow basally and becoming more extensively yellow with age; legs and feet brownish yellow. VOICE: A sharp, loud *kip* or *kik*, repeated; also a harsh *kreeee*. HABITS: Gregarious. Generally shy and unapproachable. Spends much time resting on sandbanks and lakeshores. Flight slow, with quick upstroke. Foraging behaviour discussed above. Feeds by night as well as during the day. STATUS AND DISTRIBUTION: Uncommon and irregular at several widely scattered localities in Kenya. Most frequent and breeding in small numbers at Lake Turkana, with flocks present at Allia Bay throughout the year. Scattered records elsewhere on Rift Valley lakes and at the Sabaki estuary near Malindi. Rare in n. Tanzania.

SANDGROUSE, FAMILY PTEROCLIDAE
(World, 16 species; Africa,12; Kenya, 5; n. Tanzania, 3)

Not closely related to the Galliformes, these stocky terrestrial birds are more pigeon-like than grouse-like. Although traditionally treated as a family within the order Columbiformes, Sibley and Ahlquist (1985) consider them as Charadriiformes, nearer to Charadriidae than to Scolopacidae. Still others (Voous, 1973; Gill 1990) assign them to a separate order, Pteroclidiformes.

All species have long pointed wings for swift strong flight. However, the bill is short and the short tarsi are feathered to the toes. The birds are sexually dimorphic and rather cryptically patterned in brown, tan, buff and black. Males usually have one or more breast bands and bold head patterns, whereas females are duller and often extensively barred. Our species, all resident, mainly inhabit dry open country where they feed largely on seeds. Noted for their morning and evening flights to waterholes, they fly far from feeding and breeding areas, often congregating in great flocks. Sandgrouse build no nest, laying their two or three well-marked eggs on the ground. The downy young are provided with water carried from remote sources on specialized belly feathers of the male.

CHESTNUT-BELLIED SANDGROUSE *Pterocles exustus olivascens*   Plate 47

Length 265–280 mm (10.5–11"). The only East African sandgrouse with *yellowish-buff face* and *long, fine-pointed central tail feathers*. In flight, both sexes show *dark wing-linings continuous with the dark belly*. **Adult male** has sandy or greyish-buff neck and breast merging into the *dark chestnut belly*, and a narrow broken black breast band. Upperparts lightly scaled brownish buff or greyish buff, with large buff spots on the scapulars; similar broad area on wings partly spotted with black. Eyes brown; bill and feet bluish grey; orbital skin pale yellowish green. **Female** strongly barred buff and brown above, with streaked crown; neck and upper breast heavily streaked with brown spots, separated from broad creamy-buff breast band by narrow sepia line (sometimes double); belly dark brown, narrowly barred with buff toward sides. Large pale buff patch, and several rows of buff spots, on wings. **Immature** olive-grey above with faint dark bars and pale feather edges; breast greyish pink with fine black vermiculations; no breast band; belly dark, as in adult. **Juvenile** yellowish buff with rufous wash and extensive fine vermiculations. **Voice**: A repeated *gut-gurut, gut-gurut.* . . . Flock produces a low murmuring at water hole. **Habits**: Usually in pairs or small groups, but larger high-flying flocks fly to water after sunrise and before sunset, calling continuously. Crouches or creeps away if threatened. **Similar Species**: Yellow-throated Sandgrouse has dark belly and pointed tail, but central feathers not elongated; also larger, heavier, plainer above; male has broad black band bordering throat. Black-faced Sandgrouse has dark belly, but wing-linings are pale. **Status and Distribution**: Local in dry open country or light bush, mainly below 1500 m. Widespread in n. Kenya, west to Lokichokio and south to Lake Baringo, Isiolo, Meru NP, Garissa and Bura. A separate darker population in Kenyan–Tanzanian border areas ranges from Olorgesailie and the Loita Plains south across the Serengeti Plains and Lake Eyasi, east through Magadi, Lake Natron and Kajiado to Amboseli and the Tsavo West NPs, south through Mkomazi GR and the Masai Steppe to Dodoma District.

BLACK-FACED SANDGROUSE *Pterocles decoratus*   Plate 47

Length 210–230 mm (8–9"). A small, compact sandgrouse with pale wing-linings in both sexes. Dark-bellied **adults** have contrasting *broad whitish patch across lower breast*. **Male** barred buff and black above, with black from forehead to throat, and with white superciliary stripes meeting across the forecrown; white and buff areas of breast separated by a narrow black band. Bill pale orange or pinkish orange; eyes dark brown; bare orbital skin yellow; feet pale greenish yellow (tarsi white-feathered). **Female** barred on breast, more closely barred above; sides of neck black-spotted; no black on face and no white superciliary stripes. Bill brownish. Northern *P. d. ellenbecki* is paler, less heavily barred than nominate *decoratus*; southwestern *loveridgei* also paler, greyer, less buff than other races. **Immature** resembles adult, but has no black breast band and most feathers are edged with whitish; male shows hint of face pattern. **Juvenile** has rufous scapulars, wing-coverts are finely barred with black, and primaries have white-bordered rufous tips. **Voice**: *See-u* when taking wing, followed by a whistled *whit-wi-wheeer*. Also gives a *chucker-chucker-chucker* and a low *quick-quick-quick.* . . . **Habits**: Usually in pairs or solitary, often along dirt roads and tracks. Flocks fly to water after sunrise and before dusk, at times with Chestnut-bellied Sandgrouse. Flies high, calling frequently. **Similar Species**: Lichtenstein's and male Four-banded Sandgrouse have black and white on head but neither has a black throat. Four-banded shows a narrow white breast band; Lichtenstein's lacks white on breast and is strongly barred. Females of these lack pale breast patch of female Black-faced. **Status and Distribution**: Locally common in dry bush and shrubby grassland below 1600 m, east and south of the Kenyan highlands. Northeastern *P. d. ellenbecki* ranges south to the Northern Uaso Nyiro and Tana Rivers; *P. d. decoratus* extends south from Kajiado, Machakos and Tsavo East NP into n. Tanzania, mainly east of the Rift Valley. *P. d. loveridgei* ranges from the Loita Plains, Loliondo, w. Serengeti NP and the Maswa GR south to cent. Tanzania. Reported from the Karasuk Hills on Kenyan–Ugandan border (van Someren 1922), but

specimen evidence apparently lacking and the species otherwise not known in nw. Kenya. Birds from Olorgesailie and Mosiro not racially designated.

LICHTENSTEIN'S SANDGROUSE *Pterocles lichtensteinii sukensis*   Plate 47

Length 250–280 mm (10–11"). A stocky sandgrouse with short tail and closely barred plumage. Wing-linings pale in both sexes. **Male** has *black-and-white-banded forecrown and forehead*, and *yellow orbital skin* bordered behind by short white bar; neck, upperparts and belly barred black and buff; wings have additional white bars. *Large buff breast patch is crossed by narrow black band and bordered below by a second broader band.* Bill pinkish orange; eyes dark brown; feet pale to bright yellow with white tarsal feathering. **Female** narrowly barred black and buff almost throughout; *ill-defined forehead patch and superciliary stripes whitish, speckled with black;* some scapulars and wing-coverts have broad pale buff tips. Bill brownish; bare orbital skin pale yellowish green. **Juvenile** resembles female, but is duller and more closely barred. **VOICE**: A high whistled *chitoo* or *quitoo-quitoo*; also gives a low *quark-quark* and a soft *wheet. . . wheet. . .* in flight. **HABITS**: Solitary, in pairs or small groups. Flies low, just above the bushes or trees, coming to drink at water holes after sunset and before dawn. **SIMILAR SPECIES**: Black-faced Sandgrouse has broad white or cream breast patch; male has black throat and white superciliary stripes. Four-banded Sandgrouse has plain face and foreneck, the male with a white breast band and only one black forehead bar. **STATUS AND DISTRIBUTION**: Widespread in small numbers in dry, sparsely bushed country in n. Kenya, favouring broken stony areas with scattered acacias. Ranges south to Kapenguria, Lake Bogoria, and the Northern Uaso Nyiro River. Reported from the lower Tana River (Andrews *et al.* 1975), but no photographic or specimen evidence.

FOUR-BANDED SANDGROUSE *Pterocles quadricinctus*   Plate 47

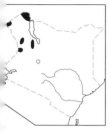

Length 250–280 mm (10–11"). Similar to Lichtenstein's Sandgrouse, but *plain buff from sides of face to upper breast* and with *three breast bands, the broad white central one bordered by chestnut above and black below.* Wing-linings pale in both sexes. **Adult male** has *black bar across the white forehead/forecrown,* and a black mark above each eye. Hindcrown rufous-buff with black streaks; upperparts otherwise largely sandy buff, barred and chequered with brown. Belly finely barred black and white. Bill dull orange-yellow; eyes brown; bare orbital skin and toes yellow; tarsal feathering white. **Female** *lacks breast bands and head markings; face, throat and upper breast rich buff;* lower breast barred buff and brown. Bill brownish. **Juvenile** more rufous than adults, with finer barring; primaries broadly tipped rufous and/or buff. **VOICE**: In flight, a whistled *pirrou-ee.* **HABITS**: In pairs or small groups during the day. Flocks form at dusk and fly to drinking areas: large numbers gather at springs in nw. border areas. Flies low. Apparently largely nocturnal, with flocks scattering to feed after drinking. **SIMILAR SPECIES**: Lichtenstein's Sandgrouse is finely barred neck and chest, and male lacks white breast band. See Black-faced Sandgrouse. **STATUS AND DISTRIBUTION**: Locally common in open or bushed grassland in nw. Kenya, generally in less arid country than Lichtenstein's. Recorded from Lokichokio, n. Turkana, the upper Turkwell River, Kodich, the n. Kerio Valley and locally on the Laikipia Plateau around Mugie.

YELLOW-THROATED SANDGROUSE *Pterocles gutturalis saturatior*   Plate 47

Length 270–300 mm (10.5–12"). A *large* stocky sandgrouse with *dark wing-linings* and a short graduated tail. **Male** has *pale yellowish-buff throat and sides of face bordered by black;* lores black, accentuating creamy-buff superciliary stripes; breast dark buffy grey, darker brown on remaining underparts (under tail-coverts more chestnut). Upperparts greyish to yellowish brown, with diffuse dark blotches on back and scapulars; dull rufous patch on wing-coverts with large, pale grey spots. Bill blue-grey; dark brown eyes surrounded by yellowish-grey skin; feet grey with brownish tarsal feathering. **Female** boldly mottled and barred black and buff above, contrasting with yellowish-buff superciliary stripes, face and throat; crown blackish brown and lores black, but no black line on throat and neck; lower neck and upper breast yellowish buff or ochre, with short black streaks and bars; lower breast and belly chestnut, barred with black. **VOICE**: A harsh *gluck-gluck-gluck* on take-off. In flight, *WHA-ha, WHA-ha. . .,* and *tweet-WEET, tweet-WEET. . . .* **HABITS**: Pairs and small groups feed on open short-grass plains, flocks gathering to fly to water holes in mid-morning. Wings produce much noise on take-off. **SIMILAR SPECIES**: Female Chestnut-bellied Sandgrouse has plain pale yellowish face, dark body and wing-linings, but is smaller, with broad pale area across lower breast, and very narrow elongated central tail feathers. **STATUS AND DISTRIBUTION**: Locally common on open grassland between 1500 and 1750 m in s. Kenya from the eastern Mara GR, Loita Plains, Kajiado, Nairobi NP, Selengai, Kimana and Oloitokitok, south through much of n. Tanzania west of the Masai Steppe.

PIGEONS AND DOVES, FAMILY COLUMBIDAE
(World, *c.* 310 species; Africa, 37; Kenya, 18; n. Tanzania, 16)

A distinctive group of plump, small-headed birds with soft dense plumage, pointed wings, short legs and a short bill with a soft bare cere. With strong swift flight, many perform extensive daily or seasonal movements, large numbers regularly gathering to feed on fallen grain in cropland. Most have characteristic cooing calls, important in identification. The green pigeons (*Treron*) are arboreal fruit-eaters with distinctive green and yellow plumage and loud sharp calls unlike the cooing of other columbids. Most *Columba* species are forest birds, feeding largely in fruiting trees, although a few are open-country ground feeders. The smaller turtle doves (*Streptopelia*) are mainly ground-feeding birds of dry country, with grey-brown plumage and pale-tipped tails. The small wood doves (*Turtur*) and the unique Namaqua Dove (*Oena*) also feed terrestrially, and usually perch low in vegetation. The sexes are alike or similar in most species. They build thin platform nests of twigs, usually in a tree or on a rock ledge, and lay one or two white or cream eggs. The nidicolous young are fed at first on a crop secretion known as 'pigeon's milk'.

AFRICAN GREEN PIGEON *Treron calva*
Plate 49

Length 250–280 mm (10–11"). A stocky, colourful arboreal pigeon. **Adult** *bright yellow-green on head and underparts*, greyish olive-green above, dull lilac at bend of wing; greater coverts and some secondaries edged with pale yellow, as are some primaries; crissum pale yellowish with dark grey feather centres, the longest coverts chestnut-tinged. Bill cream or yellowish with a reddish base and cere; eyes pale blue; orbital ring brown; feet scarlet. Races in Kenya and n. Tanzania are grey on the upper back. Tail green in coastal *wakefieldi*, greyish in inland races *brevicera* and *gibberifrons*. **Juvenile** duller, and without lilac on wings. **VOICE**: A long repeated song of numerous mellow trills followed by lower harsh creaking, barking, growling or whinnying, typically punctuated at the end with sharp *wick* or *tok* notes, often repeated. Also gives a separate *wik, ku-wik, k-ku-wik, ku-wik.* . . . Several birds may call in chorus. **HABITS**: Usually in flocks amid heavy tree foliage, perching quietly and well concealed during heat of day. Climbs easily and may hang upside-down to feed on fruit. Rarely comes to ground. **SIMILAR SPECIES**: Bruce's Green Pigeon, a northern species, has grey head and breast, and white bill with dull lavender cere. **STATUS AND DISTRIBUTION**: Locally common from sea level up to 2000 m in woodland, forest edge and open country with fruiting trees: *T. c. gibberifrons* west of the Rift Valley, north to Mt Elgon and Elgeyu, south to the Mara GR and Serengeti NP; *brevicera* mainly east of the Rift, north to the Northern Uaso Nyiro River and south to the Crater Highlands, and Arusha and Moshi Districts in n. Tanzania; *wakefieldi* coastal from the Somali border south to Tanga and inland to the Usambara Mts.

PEMBA GREEN PIGEON *Treron pembaensis*
Plate 124

Length *c.* 250 mm (10"). Endemic to Pemba Island, Tanzania. A grey-breasted pigeon with prominent purple 'shoulder' patch and chestnut, yellow and grey under tail-coverts. Head, neck and most of underparts dull, slightly olivaceous grey, with contrasting yellow lower belly and leg feathers; back and much of wings greyish olive-green, as are the yellow-tipped tail feathers. Bill greyish white or ivory with dull coral-red cere; eyes blue with purple outer ring; feet bright yellow or yellowish orange. **Juvenile** plumage unrecorded. **VOICE**: A soft *tiu. . .kiuriuu*, rather drawn out, but with little of the harsh grating quality typical of African Green Pigeon. Pakenham (1943) describes a longer call, a soft *kiu-tiu-kiutiu, kiwrikek-wrikek* followed by a soft purring *krrr, rrr, rrr*. **HABITS**: Small groups feed in the canopy, often in fruiting fig trees or palms. Largely silent. Tame around villages. Reportedly subject to local movements, probably governed by food supply. **STATUS AND DISTRIBUTION**: Fairly common in well-wooded parts of Pemba and adjacent coral islets.

*BRUCE'S GREEN PIGEON *Treron waalia*
Plate 49

Length *c.* 280–300 mm (11–12"). Differs from African Green Pigeon in *greyish head, neck and breast; belly bright yellow*; centre of under tail-coverts chestnut. *Bill whitish with dull lavender cere*; eyes blue, the iris red peripherally; narrow orbital ring yellow; *feet yellowish*. **VOICE**: Long 'creaking' song continuing with high sharp whistles, growls and yelping or yapping notes. **HABITS**: Usually in small groups feeding within tree canopy. Often around villages; commonly associated with fig trees, **SIMILAR SPECIES**: African Green Pigeon has yellow-green head and underparts and red feet. **STATUS AND DISTRIBUTION**: A savanna species, typical of watercourses in Kenya's northern border areas. Local and uncommon, with records from Lokichokio, Moyale and Ramu. Reports from the Suam River and Marsabit remain unsubstantiated.

TAMBOURINE DOVE *Turtur tympanistria* Plate 49

Length 200–220 mm (8–9"). A small forest dove with *rufous primaries* and grey-tipped outer feathers on the short dark tail. *Upperparts dark brown,* with contrasting *white fore-head and superciliary stripes* and blue-black spots on the wings. Bill dark purple, tipped black; eyes dark brown; feet maroon or purplish red. In flight, shows two dark bars across back. **Male** *entirely white below.* **Female** has less prominent face pattern and is grey from chin to flanks, white only on mid-belly. **Juvenile** has female head pattern, but is barred with tawny and dark brown on the back and has no wing spots. Underparts mainly brownish. **Voice:** A few slow, hesitant coos leading into 18 or 20 faster, evenly pitched notes, not decreasing in volume, and more prolonged than calls of Blue-spotted and Emerald-spotted Wood Doves, lower-pitched than Emerald-spotted. **Habits:** Singles or pairs forage on the ground, often in forest clearings or on paths. Flight fast, direct and low. Nests in foliage or creepers a few metres above ground. **Similar Species:** Blue-spotted and Emerald-spotted Wood Doves are grey on the head, pinkish below, with more prominent bars on back, and all-dark tail tip. **Status and Distribution:** Widespread and locally common in forest, woodland, moist bush and gardens in high-rainfall areas, from the coast up to 2500 m. Ranges north to Marsabit and Mt Nyiru, but absent from dry parts of n. and e. Kenya and from the Masai Steppe of n. Tanzania.

BLUE-SPOTTED WOOD DOVE *Turtur afer* Plate 49
(Red-billed Wood Dove)

Length 180–210 mm (7–8"). A small, compact ground dove. Replaces Emerald-spotted Wood Dove in *more humid habitats.* **Adult** resembles that species, especially in flight, but darker brown above, deeper buff on belly, with iridescent *blue spots on wings* and *yellow-tipped dark red bill.* Head grey; chin to breast pinkish. Eyes brown; feet purplish red. **Juvenile** browner than adult, barred buff above, with smaller, duller wing spots and dull brown bill. **Voice:** A few soft, well-spaced introductory coos leading into six to eight faster, even notes, *coo, cooo, cuwoo, coo, cuwoo, cu-cu-cu-cu-cu-cu-cu-cu,* slightly lower, less prolonged than call of Emerald-spotted Wood Dove. **Habits:** Forages alone or in pairs on the ground, usually within cover, sometimes on more open culti-vated fields. Calls from low concealed perch. **Similar Species:** Emerald-spotted Wood Dove compared above. Tambourine Dove is darker, white-faced, with fainter bands on back, grey-tipped outer tail feathers and dark bill. Extralimital Black-billed Wood Dove, *T. abyssinicus,* erro-neously attributed to Kenya, has dark blue metallic wing spots and a black bill with dull carmine base. **Status and Distribution:** In w. Kenya, common in forest edge, woodland, moist bush, and cultivation from Mt Elgon, Trans-Nzoia and Nyanza east to Nandi, the Mau and nw. Mara GR, occasionally wandering to the Rift Valley. North Tanzanian distribution fragmented: in Kenyan border areas west of the Mara GR, on Pemba Island and in the East Usambaras (where now rare).

EMERALD-SPOTTED WOOD DOVE *Turtur chalcospilos* Plate 49

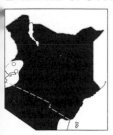

Length 165–200 mm (6.5–8"). A pinkish-brown, *dry-country* ground dove with bright *iridescent green wing spots.* In flight, shows *rufous primaries, two black bars across back* and a *broad dark tail tip.* Upperparts pale brown, greyer on head. Breast pinkish; otherwise buffy white below. *Bill all black in northern birds, dull red with black tip south of the Equator;* eyes dark brown; feet purplish red or maroon. **Juvenile** buff-barred above and with smaller and duller wing spots. **Voice:** A prolonged series of soft but penetrating notes, beginning slowly, with pauses, accelerating and descending in pitch: *cuwoo, cuwoo, co-oo-cuwoo coo cuwoo, cu-cu-cu-cu-cucucucucucucucucucucucu. . .,* more prolonged than Blue-spotted Wood Dove's call, somewhat higher in pitch than calls of either that species or Tambourine Dove. **Habits:** Solitary or in pairs. Forages in open when skies overcast, but otherwise keeps to shade. Calls from bush or low tree, from which flight is silent, but flushes from ground with loud wing-clatter. Flies low and erratically, usually not far. Pumps tail briefly upon alighting. **Similar Species:** Darker Blue-spotted Wood Dove has yellowish-tipped red bill and blue wing spots. **Status and Distribution:** Common and widespread in coastal forest, dry woodland, bush and cultivation, mainly below 1600 m. Scarce in the Lake Victoria basin, where largely replaced by Blue-spotted Wood Dove; absent from the Usambara Mts and Pemba Island.

NAMAQUA DOVE *Oena c. capensis* Plate 49
(Long-tailed Dove)

Length 200–225 mm (8–9"). A small, *long-tailed* dove with *rufous primaries* and *two black bands, separated by pale buff, across the lower back.* Upperparts largely grey-brown. Underparts and outer tail feathers mostly white, and several other rectrices white-tipped. **Male** is *black from forehead to upper breast,* head and neck otherwise grey; back greyish brown. *Bill yellow-orange,* dark carmine or purplish at base; eyes brown; feet maroon. **Female** has brown bill and whitish face with no black, generally grey-brown from chin to breast. **Juvenile** resembles

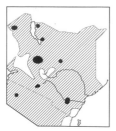

female, but has spotted throat and is barred with tawny and brown on back and wing-coverts. **VOICE:** A soft, plaintive two-note *hoo-ooooo*, rising slightly and repeated several times. Also has some rather sharp throaty notes. **HABITS:** Often solitary, but small groups gather at water holes. Perches on exposed branches and bushtops; feeds on open ground. Rises with wing-clatter, flying directly and swiftly. When alighting, raises tail and then lowers it slowly. Displaying male rises steeply, before descending with widely spread tail. Subject to pronounced local movements, and often concentrates at seed crops. **STATUS AND DISTRIBUTION:** Widespread and locally common in dry bush and edges of cultivation, mainly below 1600 m. Wanders up to 2000 m.

EASTERN BRONZE-NAPED PIGEON *Columba delegorguei sharpei*   Plate 49
(Delegorgue's Pigeon)

Length 240–300 mm (9.5–12"). A dark forest pigeon with grey or rufous-tinged underparts. **Male** has *broad white collar across lower nape*; head dark, with pinkish and green gloss on hindneck. Upperparts dark slate, with reddish reflections in strong light; tail black with a narrow dark grey tip. **Female** *rufous on crown and nape*, glossy coppery green on neck and upper back. Underparts dark buffy grey. Eyes dark red; bare eyelids pink to orange-red; bill blue-grey with contrasting pale tip; feet dull red. **Juvenile** dark grey-brown above and deep rufous below. **VOICE:** A distinctive *hu-hu-COO-COO-COO—hu-hu-hu-hu-hu*, the middle notes higher-pitched and emphatic, the beginning and ending soft and low. **HABITS:** Shy and usually in pairs or small groups in forest canopy, where it feeds extensively on fruit. Also walks on forest floor, and is attracted to salty earth in forest clearings (as at Mountain Lodge, sw. Mt Kenya). **SIMILAR SPECIES:** Olive Pigeon is larger, with yellow bill, feet and facial skin. Lemon Dove is brown above, with rufous nape, and cinnamon below. **STATUS AND DISTRIBUTION:** Locally common in Kenyan highland forest north to the Mathews Range and Mt Nyiru, south to Lolgorien, the Ngurumans and Ol Doinyo Orok (Namanga Hill). In n. Tanzania, at Mt Hanang, Arusha NP, on Kilimanjaro and the Usambara Mts. The few records from Kenyan coastal forests and Pemba Island probably involve wanderers from the Usambaras.

OLIVE PIGEON *Columba arquatrix*   Plate 49
(Rameron Pigeon)

Length 370–390 mm (*c*.15"). A *large*, heavy-looking, *dark* pigeon with *bright yellow bill, orbital patches and feet, white-speckled breast and wing-coverts*. **Adult** has pale grey hindcrown and nape, dusky pink upper back and *blackish rump and tail*. Upper breast dark purple, lower breast purplish slate, dotted with white; belly and under tail-coverts slate-grey. Eyes grey, greyish yellow or grey-brown. Sexes alike. **Juvenile** browner above than adult, with some blue-grey on wing-coverts and nape. Underparts rufous-brown, faintly white-spotted; breast feathers pale-edged. **VOICE:** A series of low notes, the first deep and rolling: *crrrooo, cw-w-w-oo, cw-w-oo, cw-w-oo.* **HABITS:** Small groups or good-sized flocks inhabit canopy of forest and woodland, also tall trees in cultivated areas. Undertakes extensive, high-flying, daily movements. Wings clatter loudly when taking flight. **SIMILAR SPECIES:** Speckled Pigeon is paler, with whitish rump and a grey tail with broad apical black band; its wing-coverts are more boldly spotted and the facial skin and feet are red. Female and young Eastern Bronze-naped Pigeon are smaller and browner, with dark bill and red feet. **STATUS AND DISTRIBUTION:** In Kenya, widespread and numerous above 1600 m in and near forest, north to the isolated mountains of Kulal, Nyiru and Marsabit, and south to the Ngurumans, Ol Doinyo Orok (Namanga) and the Chyulu Hills. In n. Tanzania, ranges from the Crater and Mbulu Highlands east to Arusha NP, Kilimanjaro, the Pare and Usambara Mountains (down to 915 m around Amani).

SPECKLED PIGEON *Columba g. guinea*   Plate 49
(Rock Pigeon)

Length 300–340 mm (12–13.5"). A large stocky pigeon, the adult with *red eye patches* and *vinous-chestnut or maroon back, scapulars and wing-coverts, the latter with bold triangular white spots*; head and underparts grey; neck and breast streaked with cinnamon; *pale grey rump appears white in flight; tail is grey with a broad black band at tip.* Yellowish eyes are surrounded by dull red bare skin; bill grey; feet red. **Juvenile** has brown head, rump and underparts, brownish orbital skin. **VOICE:** Common calls include a series of deep rough coos, uttered rapidly and increasing in volume: *whu-whu-whu-whu-whu-whu-whu-whu-WHU. . .*, and *ooWOO ooWOO wu-wu-wu-wu-wu.* Also has a rough 'bowing call', *hoo-uuu, hoo,* an owl-like *WHO-oo WHOO* or *whu-whooo* (the first note slurred upward), and a deep harsh *kworr.* **HABITS:** Usually in small groups. Flight fast, strong and direct. Feeds in open country, including culti-

vated areas. Roosts and nests on cliff ledges and buildings, occasionally in trees. **SIMILAR SPECIES**: Olive Pigeon has blackish rump and plain black tail, much smaller white wing spots; bare facial skin, bill and feet are yellow. Feral Pigeon lacks red face patches and white spotting. **STATUS AND DISTRIBUTION**: Widespread and locally common in n., w. and cent. Kenya, southeast to Tsavo. In n. Tanzania, from Kilimanjaro and Moshi Districts west to Serengeti NP and the Lake Victoria basin. Inhabits open country with rocks, cliffs and buildings, between 500 and 3000 m. Increasing urban populations established in Kisumu, Eldoret, Nakuru, Nairobi and Thika.

FERAL PIGEON *Columba livia*   Plate 49
(Rock Dove)

Length 320–330 mm (12.5–13"). The common city pigeon. Wild-type birds are blue-grey, darker on neck and upper breast, with green-and-purple iridescence. *Two black wing-bars* usually present. *Whitish or grey rump and black-tipped grey tail* recall Speckled Pigeon. Eyes orange; feet dark red. Urban birds are highly variable, the plumage predominantly pale cinnamon-brown, white, grey, black or some combination of these. Blackish birds are common in Nairobi and Mombasa. **VOICE**: A guttural *ooorrh*, and a cooing *cu-roo-oo-oo* or *oo-roo-coo*. **HABITS**: Gregarious. Roosts and nests on buildings. **SIMILAR SPECIES**: See Speckled Pigeon. **STATUS AND DISTRIBUTION**: Thriving urban populations of this European introduction have become established in our region during the last 30–50 years. Large numbers are now resident in most highland and coastal towns north to Kitale, Isiolo and Lamu.

LEMON DOVE *Aplopelia l. larvata*   Plate 49
(Cinnamon Dove)

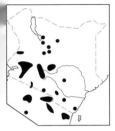

Length 240–250 mm (9.5–10"). A small, dark forest pigeon with a *whitish face*. Adult brown above, with bronzy green, violet and pinkish iridescence from mid-crown to back; tail brown, all but the central tail feathers obscurely grey-tipped; *underparts mostly rich cinnamon*; forehead, face and throat whitish. Eyes and orbital skin dark reddish; bill black; feet maroon. **Juvenile** dark brown on breast, the feathers rufous-edged like those of upperparts; belly rufous-buff; grey rectrix tips indistinct. **VOICE**: A deep, upslurred *whoo* or *cwoo*, repeated numerous times with short pause between notes. **HABITS**: Solitary or feeds in pairs on the forest floor, usually in shade. When disturbed, flies up with clatter of wings and drops back quickly into cover or alights on low branch. Usually wary, but becomes confiding in gardens where not molested. **SIMILAR SPECIES**: Female Eastern Bronze-naped Pigeon is larger and lacks white on face and throat. **STATUS AND DISTRIBUTION**: Widespread but rather uncommon. In Kenya, ranges from the isolated forests on the northern mountains of Kulal, Nyiru and Marsabit south through the w. and cent. highlands to Endau, Ol Doinyo Orok (Namanga) and the Chyulu, Taita and Shimba Hills. In n. Tanzania, on Mt Hanang, the Pare and Usambara Mountains, Kilimanjaro, Crater Highlands; also Lake Manyara and Arusha NPs.

RED-EYED DOVE *Streptopelia semitorquata*   Plate 48

Length 300–330 mm (12–13"). Largest of the black-collared doves. **Adult** has *dark red eyes* that appear black at a distance. Upperparts brown, with grey crown, whitish forehead and black nuchal collar; *wings entirely dark brown*. Face and underparts vinous pink, shading into grey on lower belly; *spread tail blackish at base with a broad grey terminal band*. Bill blackish; narrow maroon eye-ring discernible at close range; front of tarsi and tops of toes purplish red. **Juvenile** has pale rufous feather edging above and an obscure black nuchal band. Eyes brown; orbital skin grey. **VOICE**: Variable. (1) Syncopated call of six notes, the first two slower, last four faster, second or second and fourth notes accented: *coo COO, cu-cu-cu-cu* or *oo-woo, oo-WOO-oo-oo*, frequently repeated; (2) *wu-wu-wu-wu WOO-cu*, also repeated in series; (3) a deep rough or raspy *whu-whu-whu, whu*, last note low and guttural; (4) a soft double bowing call of raspy rolling quality, *WOOO-roo, WOOO-roo. . .* or *whrruu-whrruu. . .*; (5) somewhat nasal alighting call, *uh-RHAao* or *u-WHA*. **HABITS**: Usually solitary or in pairs, at times in small flocks. Sings, rests and feeds (on fruit) in trees; wary when foraging on the ground. Males sing in chorus early and late in day. Wings clap noisily on take-off. **SIMILAR SPECIES**: African Mourning and Ring-necked Doves are smaller, paler and greyer, with white (not grey) tail tips; eyes pale creamy yellow with prominent orange ring in African Mourning Dove, dark brown (appearing black) in Ring-necked. Dusky Turtle Dove has rufous-edged inner wing feathers and black smudge (not half-collar) on side of neck. **STATUS AND DISTRIBUTION**: Common and widespread in woodland, forest edge and gardens below 3000 m. Scarce or absent in drier parts of n. and e. Kenya and the Masai Steppe region of n. Tanzania.

AFRICAN MOURNING DOVE *Streptopelia decipiens*   Plate 48

Length 280–300 mm (11–12"). A *pale grey-brown 'collared' dove* of dry country, smaller and greyer than Red-eyed Dove. **Adult** has *pale yellow eyes ringed with orange-red*. Light grey-brown wings have *paler grey coverts*

along outer edges. Grey crown and sides of head contrast with pale pinkish neck and breast; throat, belly and under tail-coverts white; black half-collar across hindneck; *tail broadly white at corners* above, with four central feathers all dark; from beneath, tail appears black-barred with terminal half white. Bill black; eyes usually yellow, but varying to light creamy orange; feet pink. Eastern race *elegans* paler, with white extending from belly to lower breast. **Juvenile** is brown on top of head, lighter brown on breast; eyes pale brown. **Voice:** (1) *WHOO-woooo*, followed by a three-note rhythmical phrase accented on second syllable: *wu-WOO-oo, wu-WOO-oo, wu-WOO-oo . . .*, sometimes ending with *krrrrrrrrrow* or *uh-krrrrrrrrrrrow*; (2) *hoo-WOO, hoo-WOO, hoo-WOO*; (3) a descending throaty purring *aaaooow* on alighting. **Habits:** Usually in pairs or small groups, often along watercourses or near habitation. Feeds on the ground.

Not shy. Calls mainly in early morning and evening. **Similar Species:** Ring-necked Dove has dark eyes without red orbital ring. Red-eyed Dove (unlikely alongside African Mourning) is darker, with grey (not white) tail tip, pinkish face and dark red eyes. **Status and Distribution:** Locally common to abundant in bush and savanna, typically in sandy areas below 1400 m. *S. d. perspicillata* ranges through nw. Kenya, the Lake Victoria basin and low dry parts of s. Kenya and n. Tanzania. *S. d. elegans* of ne. Kenya extends south to Kilifi District, reaching the coast from the Tana River delta south to Karawa, north of Malindi.

RING-NECKED DOVE *Streptopelia capicola*   Plate 48
(Cape Turtle Dove)

Length 250–265 mm (10–10.5"). A *pale, dark-eyed* 'collared' dove. **Adults** grey-brown above, pale grey on outer wing-coverts; black half-collar across lower nape; top of head grey; sides of head and underparts pinker grey, lower belly and crissum white. Tail brownish grey, with narrow white edge and broad white corners; from beneath, similar to African Mourning Dove. Eyes almost black; bill black; feet dark purple. *S. c. somalica* paler and greyer than widespread race *tropica*. **Juvenile** similar, but many feathers edged with buff. **Voice:** (1) A rhythmic *cuc-CURRRoo, cuc-CURRRoo. . .*, or *wuh-ROOoo, wuh-ROOoo . . .*, repeated monotonously – a familiar sound of the East African bush; (2) *wuh-ka-RROOO, wuh-ka-RROOO. . .*, repeated; (3) bowing call a rolling *uk-carrrooooo, uk-carrrooooo*, etc.; (4) alighting call a high raspy, nasal *ka-waaaaaa.* **Habits:** Often in small groups, or larger flocks at drinking sites or food sources. Wings clatter loudly when taking flight. Calls throughout day, sometimes at night. Frequently bathes. **Similar Species:** Red-eyed Dove appears dark-eyed, but is larger and darker, with grey lower belly and grey (not white) tail tip. African Mourning Dove has pale eyes ringed with orange-red, and grey crown and sides of head. Laughing Dove lacks black on hindneck, is more rufous above and on breast, greyer on rump and wing-coverts. **Status and Distribution:** Widespread and often abundant in savanna, bush, cultivation and forest edge, mainly below 2000 m, but locally higher. *S. c. somalica* of e. and ne. Kenya ranges west to Lake Baringo, the Northern Uaso Nyiro River, Kibwezi, Namanga and Arusha; extends south in coastal areas to Mombasa. *S. c. tropica* elsewhere.

AFRICAN WHITE-WINGED DOVE *Streptopelia reichenowi*   Plate 48

Length 250 mm (10"). A pale 'collared' dove of far ne. Kenya, readily identified in flight by *prominent white crescent on forewing* (outer webs of greater and median coverts) and white-tipped tail. Perched at close range, the *white-feathered eye-ring* surrounding the *yellowish-orange eye* is distinctive. **Male** greyish on head and breast, with white chin, throat and belly; brownish-black half-collar across hindneck; back brown. Bill black; feet pink. **Female** browner on breast than male. **Juvenile** resembles female, but feathers edged with buff. **Voice:** In Ethiopia, a deep *kok-koorrr-kok-koorrr. . .*, repeated rapidly several times. Also a low repeated *crooo-crooo. . .* (Brown 1977). **Habits:** Usually in groups, often with other species, feeding mainly on ground. In Ethiopia, associates with Ring-necked and African Mourning Doves. **Similar Species:** Other *Streptopelia* species lack white on forewing. **Status and Distribution:** Confined to extreme ne. Kenya, where common along the Daua River between Malka Mari and Mandera on the Ethiopian border. Inhabits riparian woodland (especially sites dominated by palms), trees along irrigation ditches and in adjacent shrubby grassland.

EUROPEAN TURTLE DOVE *Streptopelia turtur*   Plate 48
(Turtle Dove)

Length 260–280 mm (10–11"). A small, slim dove with *black-and-white patch on sides of neck.* In flight, shows *grey band across the secondaries and larger wing-coverts*, and conspicuous *white outer tail edges.* **Adult** light brown above, more pinkish brown from head to breast; smaller *wing-coverts appear scaly, with conspicuous rufous margins.* Yellow eyes (the iris black peripherally) are ringed by pinkish skin; feet dark pink. **Juvenile** duller and without chequered neck patches; wing-coverts have white and tawny margins; brownish breast

appears scaly, with pale feather edges. **Voice**: A rolling purr, *rrrrrrr, roooooorrrr*. **Habits**: Gregarious in normal range, but only single birds recorded in Kenya. Feeds on the ground. Largely silent in non-breeding areas. **Similar Species**: Dusky Turtle Dove is slightly larger and much darker, with dark grey belly and grey tail tip. Laughing Dove is smaller, more rufous below, greyer wings lack scaly edging, and there are no neck markings. **Status and Distribution**: A palearctic species, casual in our region, where known from six sight records (some photographic documentation): Barsaloi (Oct. 1976); Samburu GR (Jan. 1981); Amboseli NP (Oct. 1983); Lake Baringo (Nov. 1989); Lake Turkana (Oct. 1990 and 1991). Subspecies uncertain.

DUSKY TURTLE DOVE *Streptopelia l. lugens*   Plate 48
(Pink-breasted Dove)

Length 280–300 mm (11–12"). A highland pigeon with greyish-white tail corners and a *bold black mark on sides of neck.* **Adult** dark grey-brown above, dark grey on head and underparts. *Prominent feather edging is greyish on lesser wing-coverts, more tawny on secondaries.* Eyes orange, surrounded by dark red skin; bill black; feet magenta. **Juvenile** paler and browner, with more extensive rufous feather edging. **Voice**: A deep, slow disyllabic *coo-or, coo-or, coo-or,* and a rough growling *oooh* repeated two to four times. **Habits**: Solitary or in pairs, with small groups or large flocks at food concentrations. Perches in tree canopy and on wires, often near cultivated fields. Small numbers attracted to suburban gardens in Nairobi, where quite confiding. **Similar Species**: Other doves lack solid black mark on sides of neck. Red-eyed Dove is much larger, with black half-collar on nape. **Status and Distribution**: Widespread and locally common in sparsely wooded country, forest edge, bamboo and cultivation between 1750 and 3200 m. Ranges from the Crater Highlands, Arusha NP and Kilimanjaro north through the Kenyan highlands to the Cherangani Mts, Maralal and Marsabit; also recorded at Moyale on the Ethiopian border.

LAUGHING DOVE *Streptopelia s. senegalensis*   Plate 48
(Palm Dove)

Length 220–230 mm (*c.* 9"). A small dry-country dove with *blue-grey wing-coverts* and white-cornered tail. Head pinkish grey, breast pinkish or vinous tawny, with *black-speckled rufous band* across front and sides of neck; belly and under tail-coverts whitish; back tawny-brown. Bill dark brown; eyes brown or brownish red; feet maroon. **Female** paler than male on head and breast, with less prominent rufous-and-black neck band. **Juvenile** similar, but lacks neck band, head is more rufous, the breast paler; some flight feathers rufous-tipped. **Voice**: A phrase of five or six rather high short notes delivered quickly and dropping slightly in pitch at the end: *oo, cu-cu-oo-oo* or *oo-oo-kuWOOoo*. **Habits**: Solitary or gregarious, flocking at drinking sites. Large concentrations assemble early in the dry season to feed on fallen seeds. Frequently bathes in water, and sun-bathes. Sings throughout the day, sometimes at night. Wings noisy when taking flight. **Similar Species**: Other dry-country *Streptopelia* doves are grey, with black half-collar. See European Turtle Dove. **Status and Distribution**: Widespread and common to abundant in open bush and dry cultivation, mainly below 1800 m.

PARROTS AND LOVEBIRDS, FAMILY PSITTACIDAE
(World, 358 species; Africa, 19; Kenya, 7; n. Tanzania, 6)

Compact, brightly coloured birds with large heads and powerful hooked bills, in which the movable maxilla is attached hinge-like to the skull. The nostrils open in a fleshy cere. The legs are short, the tarsi stout, and the first and fourth toes are directed backwards. Most African species are short-tailed, with narrow pointed wings. The distinctive flight is fast and direct, with rapid shallow wingbeats. With one exception, the sexes are alike in our species. Largely arboreal, they use the bill in climbing, and manipulate food items, usually fruits and seeds, with their toes. Typically noisy, all species produce loud squawking or screeching sounds, especially in flight. Parrots nest in tree cavities, where they lay two to four white eggs. Lovebirds also nest in tree cavities, as well as in old nests of swifts, holes in buildings or termitaria and among frond bases of palms; their eggs number up to seven or eight. In some species the young are naked at hatching, later becoming downy.

GREY PARROT *Psittacus e. erithacus*   Plate 47

Length 280–300 mm (11–12"). A rare parrot of west Kenyan forests, easily identified by its *grey body plumage* with *scarlet tail and tail-coverts.* Bare loral and orbital skin white; eyes yellow; bill black. **Voice**: A variety of

high-pitched screeches and whistles, in flight and when perched. **HABITS**: Small groups feed in the canopy of forest trees, and fly above treetop level to and from roosting areas in morning and evening. May perch in dead emergent trees. **STATUS AND DISTRIBUTION**: Owing to continuing forest destruction and resultant loss of nest sites, now endangered in Kenya, remaining only in the Kakamega Forest, where probably fewer than ten birds survive. Formerly fairly common and widespread throughout the Kakamega and Nandi Forests, ranging west to Mumias, east to Lessos and south to Nyarondo.

RED-FRONTED PARROT *Poicephalus gulielmi massaicus* Plate 47
(Red-headed Parrot)

Length 260–280 mm (10–11″). A robust, dark green highland parrot. **Adult** has *red forehead, crown, and leg feathers*. In flight, *red leading wing edges* and yellowish-green rump are noticeable. Bare orbital skin greyish yellow; eyes red-orange; maxilla ivory-horn, the tip and entire mandible blackish; feet dark brown. **Juvenile** has red body and wing patches replaced by brown, the crown buff. **VOICE**: Shrill, high-pitched screeching chatter in flight and when perched. **HABITS**: Pairs or small groups feed in treetops. May congregate in large flocks for roosting. Undertakes extensive daily flights to and from feeding areas. **STATUS AND DISTRIBUTION**: Widespread and locally common in *Podocarpus* and *Juniperus* forests between 2000 and 3200 m, in the w. and cent. Kenyan highlands on Mt Elgon and the Cheranganis, the Mau, Aberdares and Mt Kenya, with disjunct populations around Maralal and in the Ngurumans. Also on Kilimanjaro, in Arusha NP and parts of Tanzania's Crater Highlands.

BROWN PARROT *Poicephalus meyeri* Plate 47
(Meyer's Parrot)

Length 210–230 mm (8–9″). Distinctive, with *yellow crown band, 'shoulders,'* leading wing edges and wing-linings. Plumage otherwise rather dull: grey-brown on head, breast and upper back, green or blue-green from lower breast to under tail-coverts and on lower back and rump. Bare orbital skin dark grey; eyes dark red or red-brown; bill and feet blackish. **Juvenile** lacks yellow on crown and has less on wings; eyes dark brown. **VOICE**: A shrill, high *cheek-cheek-cheek*, and a screeching *chweeee*, mainly in flight. **HABITS**: Usually in pairs; shy and wary. Flight low and fast. Feeds on nuts, drupes, figs. **SIMILAR SPECIES**: Female African Orange-bellied Parrot shows no yellow in plumage and has dark brown wing-linings. Coastal Brown-headed Parrot lacks yellow on crown and upperside of wings, has olive-green upperparts and pale eyes. **STATUS AND DISTRIBUTION**: Locally common resident between 600 and 2000 m, in savanna, open woodland and riverine forest. Avoids montane forests occupied by Red-fronted Parrot. *P. m. saturatus* ranges north to Lokichokio and Lake Turkana, south to the Mara GR and Serengeti NP, east to Nanyuki and Naro Moru. *P. m. matschiei* of interior Tanzania extends north to Tarangire and Manyara NPs, but apparently does not reach s. Kenya.

BROWN-HEADED PARROT *Poicephalus cryptoxanthus* Plate 47

Length 240–250 mm (9.5–10″). Replaces Brown Parrot in the coastal lowlands. Largely olive-green above, brighter green on rump and underparts, with a *grey-brown head and neck* and *yellow wing-linings*. Bare orbital skin blackish; eyes pale creamy yellow; bill dark above, whitish below; feet black. **Juvenile** resembles adult but is duller throughout. **VOICE**: High screeching in flight: *chweer-eer chweer-eer chweek*. Also less piercing calls when perched. **HABITS**: Usually in small groups. Partial to baobab trees, but often roosts in coconut palms. **SIMILAR SPECIES**: Allopatric Brown Parrot has yellow on crown and wings, dark brown upperparts and dark red eyes. **STATUS AND DISTRIBUTION**: Local in coastal bush and woodland, including mangroves and coconut plantations, north to Lamu. Common near Kilifi, Shimoni and on Pemba Island, but scarce elsewhere. **NOTE**: We follow White (1965) in treating this species as monotypic.

AFRICAN ORANGE-BELLIED PARROT *Poicephalus r. rufiventris* Plate 47

Length 250 mm (10″). A dry-country bird, partial to *Commiphora* bush with baobab trees. Sexes differ. **Male** *bright orange on belly and wing-linings*, green on rump, tail-coverts and leg feathers; rest of plumage pale grey-brown. Eyes orange-red; bill, bare orbital skin and feet black. **Female** has *green belly* and *dark brown wing-linings*. **Juvenile** resembles female, but male shows some orange on belly and wing-linings. **VOICE**: A repeated

high screech, given in flight and when perched. **HABITS**: Usually in pairs, often perching in bare branches. Not shy. **SIMILAR SPECIES**: Brown Parrot is darker, with yellow on crown and wings. **STATUS AND DISTRIBUTION**: Fairly common and widespread in *Commiphora* bush and woodland in dry areas below 1200 m. Widespread in e. and ne. Kenya, ranging west to the Ndotos, Samburu GR, Lewa Downs, Embu and Selengai, extending into n. Tanzania in the Mkomazi GR and Masai Steppe west to Tarangire NP.

RED-HEADED LOVEBIRD *Agapornis pullarius ugandae*   Plate 47

Length 130 mm (5"). A tiny, bright green parrot with red *forehead, face and throat* (more orange in female) and pale blue rump. In flight, shows green and red tail with a black subterminal band, and black wing-linings. Bill red; eyes dark brown. **Juvenile** resembles adult, but has *yellowish face patch*. **VOICE**: A squeaky twittering *si-si-si-si* in flight. When perched, a sharp, thin *swee-seet* or *tswi-sitsit*, and a three- or four-note *skee-tee, tsyip-tsyip*. **HABITS**: Pairs or small groups feed unobtrusively on millet, sorghum and other grasses, perching at times in lower branches of trees and shrubs. **SIMILAR SPECIES**: Fischer's Lovebird, and Fischer's X Yellow-collared Lovebird hybrids are larger, with dusky or brownish head, yellow collar and white around eyes. **STATUS AND DISTRIBUTION**: Small numbers resident in bushed grassland and cultivation along the Kenya/Uganda border from Malaba and Malikisi south to Alupe and Busia, ranging east to the Sio River in Mumias District. Formerly more widespread, from Mt Elgon south to Kakamega and Nyarondo.

FISCHER'S LOVEBIRD *Agapornis fischeri*   Plate 47

Length 150 mm (6"). A Tanzanian lovebird with *orange-red forehead, cheeks and throat*; remainder of head dull olive-brown. Bright green above, with pale blue wash on upper tail-coverts; tail green with black subterminal band. Upper breast and collar yellow; belly, leg feathers and under tail-coverts green. Eyes brown; *orbital ring white*; bill red; feet pale grey. **Juvenile** duller than adults, particularly on head. **VOICE**: A shrill whistle and high-pitched twittering, both in flight and when perched. **HABITS**: Generally in small noisy flocks. Numbers congregate at water holes during dry seasons. **SIMILAR SPECIES**: See Yellow-collared and Red-headed Lovebirds. **STATUS AND DISTRIBUTION**: Endemic to n. Tanzania. Locally common on islands off the southern shore of Lake Victoria, ranging south to the Wembere River and east to Serengeti NP and the Lake Eyasi depression; wanderers recorded east to Babati and Arusha District. Formerly more numerous. A popular cagebird, with frequent escapes in Kenya (north to Isiolo), often hybridizing with the following species (see note below).

YELLOW-COLLARED LOVEBIRD *Agapornis personatus*   Plate 47

Length 130–150 mm (5-6"). Another small green-and-yellow lovebird with a red bill, white cere, and broad white ring of bare skin around eyes. Differs from Fischer's in its *dark brown head* and *broader yellow collar extending to the breast*. Back and rump green, upper tail-coverts pale blue; tail green with some dull orange markings and with black subterminal band on all but central feathers. Eyes brown; feet pale grey. **Juvenile** duller than adult, with some black on bill. **VOICE**: Shrill high-pitched screeching, from perch and in flight. **HABITS**: Usually in small groups. Often feeds low, sometimes on the ground. Nests in tree hollows or buildings. **SIMILAR SPECIES**: Fischer's Lovebird compared above. See note on hybrids, below. **STATUS AND DISTRIBUTION**: A Tanzanian endemic, locally common in the interior, ranging north to Babati and Tarangire NP. In Kenya, feral birds breed around Mombasa. Some near Lake Naivasha appear to be nearly pure *personatus*, but most are hybrids.

Feral and Hybrid Lovebirds: With the trapping and export of lovebirds from Tanzania dating back to the 1920s, and the subsequent release and escape of many birds in coastal cities, feral populations of both Fischer's and Yellow-collared Lovebirds have been present in Dar es Salaam, Tanga and Mombasa for over fifty years. In recent decades, East African aviculturists have released hundreds of captive-bred hybrids into the wild, where they readily become established. The hybrid lovebird population around Lake Naivasha comprised some 6,000 individuals in 1986, seriously competing with native cavity-nesting species. Smaller numbers also breed at Kisumu, Molo, Nakuru, Nairobi and Athi River, and wandering individuals can be expected anywhere.

TURACOS, FAMILY MUSOPHAGIDAE
(World and Africa, 23; Kenya, 11; n. Tanzania, 8)

Turacos (pronounced with accent on first syllable) are medium-sized to large arboreal birds with long broad tails and short rounded wings. They inhabit woodland and forest, as well as dry scrub and open bush country. All are more or less sedentary residents, undertaking only short-distance movements governed by food availability. Often gregarious, their presence is invariably revealed by a series of loud raucous calls, often given in chorus. Flight appears weak and laboured, but the birds rapidly run, climb and bound with great agility along branches or through thick vegetation. They have strong feet with semi-zygodactyl toes, the fourth one reversible. The sexes are alike in colour; plumage of most is dominated by green, purple or blue hues, and several have brilliant red primaries, prominent in flight. The go-away-birds and plantain-eaters lack bright colours. All species are crested and most have bare orbital or facial skin; their serrate bills are short and strong, sometimes brightly coloured, and expanded to form a frontal shield in *Musophaga*. They feed largely on fruits, flowers and buds, but also consume insects and snails. Nests are flat and rather flimsy, similar to those of pigeons and doves. The one to three eggs are whitish or pale blue. Incubation and care of the downy nidicolous young are undertaken by both sexes. Turacos are called louries in southern Africa. The family is endemic to this continent.

GREAT BLUE TURACO *Corythaeola cristata*   Plate 50

Length 70–75 cm (*c.* 30"). The largest turaco, readily identified by overall greenish-blue and yellow plumage, blue-black crest, red-tipped bright yellow bill, and *long wide tail with broad black subterminal band*. Belly, tibial feathers and under tail-coverts chestnut. No red in the wings. **VOICE:** A loud guttural *cow-cow-cow-cow*, and a deep, resonant, rolling *kurru-kurru-kurru*. **HABITS:** Pairs or small groups typically feed in forest canopy and often perch in tall emergent trees. Adaptable, persisting in cut-over areas with isolated large trees. Not shy; may feed and nest near dwellings and in wooded gardens. Glides from tree to tree on short broad wings. **STATUS AND DISTRIBUTION:** Small numbers are confined to the Kaimosi, Kakamega and South Nandi Forests in w. Kenya. Where not molested, survives quite well in small relict forest patches.

ROSS'S TURACO *Musophaga rossae*   Plate 50
(Ross's Lourie)

Length 51–54 cm (20–21"). A striking large turaco, dark *glossy violet-blue* with *bright crimson crest, yellow bill and frontal shield*. In flight, brilliant red primaries contrast sharply with dark body and tail. **VOICE:** A loud rolling *kkkow-kkow-kkow-kkow*, often repeated by others in the same or a nearby group; higher-pitched than calls of the green turacos. **HABITS:** Pairs or small flocks usually feed high in trees, but descend to fruiting shrubs at times. Highly vocal, members of a troop calling to one another from some distance. Not shy. **STATUS AND DISTRIBUTION:** Locally common in w. Kenya from Mt Elgon and Kapenguria south to the Nandi and Tugen Hills, West Mau, South Nyanza, Mara GR and northern Serengeti NP, typically in woodland, forest edge and riverine groves, wandering to open areas with scattered trees. Avoids deep forest.

PURPLE-CRESTED TURACO *Tauraco porphyreolophus chlorochlamys*   Plate 50
(Violet-crested Turaco)

Length 43–46 cm (17–18"). A dark turaco with *iridescent purple crown* and *shining green forehead, chin and lores. No white around eyes.* Hindneck, lower cheeks, neck and front of breast green; belly and leg feathers dull greenish grey. Back mostly greyish blue; wings, upper tail-coverts and tail violet-blue; primaries show much bright red in flight (outer webs brown). Eyes brown, bare orbital skin red; bill and feet black. **VOICE:** Call begins with a single, loud, high-pitched hoot, then continues as a raucous *'kaw-kaw-kaw. . .* typical of the genus. **HABITS:** Similar to those of other green turacos. Solitary or in pairs. **SIMILAR SPECIES:** Hartlaub's Turaco shows white markings on face. **STATUS AND DISTRIBUTION:** Rare and very local in open woodland and riverine forest, sometimes among scattered trees and tall euphorbias. Currently known only from Thika, Ol Doinyo Sapuk NP and the Mua and Ulu Hills in s-cent. Kenya; formerly near Embu, Machakos, Yatta Plateau, Kibwezi, lower Chyulu Hills and the Voi River, and near the coast in the Shimba Hills and near Shimoni. With continuing habitat destruction, now rapidly declining and endangered in our region. Known formerly in Lake Manyara NP, but no recent records from n. Tanzania.

SCHALOW'S TURACO *Tauraco schalowi*
(Livingstone's Turaco)

Plate 50

Length 40 cm (16"). The region's only turaco with a *long pointed crest* of white-tipped blue-green feathers, typically held erect. Green of head, neck and breast is set off by red orbital skin, and black-and-white feathers extending from lores to under and behind eyes; back and wings washed with blue; rump and tail violet-blue; belly and under tail-coverts dusky. Largely red primaries are showy in flight. *Bill dark red*; eyes brown; feet black. **VOICE:** A slowly uttered series of five or six rough, cawing barks, *haw, haw, haw. . .,* usually beginning with a shorter, much higher-pitched note. **HABITS:** Solitary or in pairs amid dense foliage. Shy. **SIMILAR SPECIES:** Black-billed and Hartlaub's Turacos have short crests. **STATUS AND DISTRIBUTION:** Confined to forests in the Mbulu and Crater Highlands, somewhat disjunctly in the Loita Hills and riparian woodlands along the Talek and Mara Rivers in the Mara GR, west and north to Lolgorien and Kilgoris. Occasional in northern and western parts of Serengeti NP. **NOTE:** Formerly considered conspecific with extralimital *T. livingstonii*. The subspecies *chalcolophus* is of doubtful validity.

BLACK-BILLED TURACO *Tauraco schuetti emini*

Plate 50

Length 40 cm (16"). A largely green *western* turaco with *short, rounded, white-tipped crest* and largely *black bill* (base of mandible dark red). Lower breast to under tail-coverts dusky; rump and tail violet-blue; primaries brilliant red; white line in front of and under the eye. Orbital skin red. **VOICE:** A repetitive raucous *khaw, khaw, khaw,* often continuing for 10–15 seconds. **HABITS:** Forages alone or in pairs in dense foliage of high forest trees. Shy and secretive. **SIMILAR SPECIES:** Hartlaub's Turaco has dark blue-black crest. Schalow's Turaco has long-pointed crest and dark red bill. **STATUS AND DISTRIBUTION:** Scarce; small numbers confined to the Kaimosi, Kakamega and South Nandi Forests in w. Kenya.

FISCHER'S TURACO *Tauraco f. fischeri*

Plate 50

Length 40 cm (16"). An *eastern* green-and-blue turaco with *white-tipped reddish crest*; posterior underparts blackish; primaries largely red. Bare red orbital skin is margined in front by a white line extending to the bill, and below by a small patch of black feathers; this in turn is bordered by white line extending below the ear-coverts. *Bill bright red.* **VOICE:** A repeated raucous call beginning slowly with two or three higher-pitched notes, quickly followed by guttural cawing. Less common is a softer *thukku, thukku* (Sclater and Moreau 1932). **HABITS:** Vocal but shy, remaining concealed in dense forest thickets. **SIMILAR SPECIES:** Other East African turacos lack red in the crest. **STATUS AND DISTRIBUTION:** Confined to coastal forests from Boni south to Tanga, inland along the Tana River to Garsen and Bura, also to the Shimba Hills, Mrima and the Usambara Mts.

HARTLAUB'S TURACO *Tauraco hartlaubi*

Plate 50

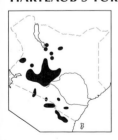

Length 43 cm (17"). The common *highland* turaco, *dark-headed* with *iridescent blue-black bushy crest*; side of face marked with *conspicuous white loral spot, white line from below eye to the neck* and *bright red orbital ring*. Throat, breast and upper back green; posterior parts glossy violet-blue. Bright red primaries conspicuous in flight. Bill dark red. **VOICE:** A series of rough, raucous *khaw* notes, harsher than those of the other green turacos. **HABITS:** Forages alone, in pairs or in family groups. Rather noisy. Less shy than most turacos. **SIMILAR SPECIES:** Schalow's and Black-billed Turacos are green-headed. Purple-crested Turaco has no white markings around eyes. **STATUS AND DISTRIBUTION:** An East African endemic, common and widespread in forests of the cent. and w. Kenyan highlands, between 1700 and 3000 m; also in isolated montane forests on Kulal, Nyiru and Marsabit, and from the Ndotos and Mathews Range south to the Ngurumans, Loliondo, Ol Doinyo Orok (Namanga) and Longido, the Chyulu and Taita Hills; also in montane areas of ne. Tanzania from Arusha NP, Mt Meru and Kilimanjaro to the Pare and West Usambara Mountains.

WHITE-CRESTED TURACO *Tauraco leucolophus*

Plate 50

Length 40 cm (16"). A green turaco with *largely white head*, the forehead and *crest blue-black*. Upper back and breast green; posterior parts deep violet-blue above, greyish and washed with violet below; much red in primaries. Bare orbital skin red; bill greenish yellow. **VOICE:** A high-pitched hoot followed by a succession of low raucous barks: *whoo, khow-khow-khow-khow khow. . . .* **HABITS:** Similar to those of other green turacos, but less secretive than some, often flying through open spaces between trees. Usually alone or in pairs in riverine

forest. **Similar Species:** No other turaco shows as much white on the head. Sympatric Ross's Turaco, also with yellow bill, is largely dark violet-blue. **Status and Distribution:** Locally common in nw. Kenya from the Suam River and Kongelai Escarpment to the Marich Pass, also in the Kerio Valley below Tambach, wandering east to the Tugen Hills, Baringo District and Marigat. A disjunct western population is resident around the Sio River in Mumias District. Favours riverine woodland and well-timbered hillsides; avoids heavy forest.

BARE-FACED GO-AWAY-BIRD *Corythaixoides personata*   Plate 50

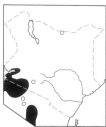

Length 48 cm (19"). A large dull-coloured bird with *bare black face, chin and upper throat*, bill also black. Forehead and crest ashy brown; sides of face, neck, and chest white; back, wings and tail grey-brown. A patch of light green on the breast merges into the pinkish-brown belly; posterior underparts white. *C. p. personata* has a more extensive green patch than southern *leopoldi*; underside of wings and tail also greenish; face appears less black than in *leopoldi* owing to numerous minute brown feathers. **Voice:** A loud, double *kow-kow*, frequently repeated by others in the group. **Habits:** Alone or in small groups; restless and noisy. Flight undulating. **Similar Species:** Eastern Grey Plantain-eater and White-bellied Go-away-bird have conspicuous white areas in wings and tail. **Status and Distribution:** *C. p. leopoldi* is a local and generally uncommon resident in sw. Kenya, ranging from Kisumu and Muhoroni south through Ruma NP (Lambwe Valley) and the Mara GR to Serengeti NP and southeast to the Crater Highlands, Lake Manyara and Tarangire NP. *C. p. personata* is known in Kenya from a sight record (May 1988) near the Ethiopian border west of Moyale.

WHITE-BELLIED GO-AWAY-BIRD *Corythaixoides leucogaster*   Plate 50

Length 50 cm (20"). A large grey-backed bird with *pointed grey crest* and *long black-and-white tail*. Grey breast contrasts with white belly and under tail-coverts; patch formed by white primary bases conspicuous in flight; *tail black with broad white median band*. Bill black in male, pea-green in female. **Voice:** Typical calls are a nasal *haa-haa-haa*, not unlike bleating of a sheep, and a single or repeated *gwa* (or *g'way*). Also has a somewhat cat-like whine. **Habits:** Often perches in treetops, frequently raising crest and elevating tail. Flies from tree to tree in loose straggling groups, calling loudly. **Similar Species:** Eastern Grey Plantain-eater, more western in our region, is browner, not pure grey, has bushy crest and different tail pattern. **Status and Distribution:** In Kenya, common and widespread in savanna and open woodland (particularly acacias), less so in bush country, mostly below 1500 m. Absent from coastal areas south of Malindi, the Lake Victoria basin, Mara GR and Serengeti NP. In ne. Tanzania, common throughout the Mkomazi GR, Masai Steppe, Tarangire NP and in low-lying areas east of the Rift Valley north to the Kenyan border.

EASTERN GREY PLANTAIN-EATER *Crinifer zonurus*   Plate 50

Length 50 cm (20"). A large grey-brown turaco, *dark-headed* with *shaggy white-tipped nape feathers* and a *long black-tipped tail*. Upperparts generally ash-grey with brown feather tips; throat to upper breast brownish; belly and under tail-coverts white with some brown streaks. White patch in wings and partly white outer tail feathers conspicuous in flight. Bill pea-green in male, yellow in female. **Voice:** Loud rapid yelping and cackling, including a *KWAH, kow-kow-kow-kow. . .* lasting 10–12 seconds. Also utters a high-pitched squeal. **Habits:** Solitary or in small noisy family parties. Flight undulating, suggesting a small hornbill. **Similar Species:** White-bellied Go-away-bird is greyer and long-crested, has white band across centre of tail. **Status and Distribution:** Locally common in open park-like country in w. Kenya, from Kapenguria and Mt Elgon south to Busia and the Lake Victoria basin, wandering to the Mara River and Tanzanian border areas, including Serengeti NP.

CUCKOOS AND COUCALS, FAMILY CUCULIDAE
(World, 138 species; Africa, 26; Kenya, 19; n. Tanzania, 17)

The typical cuckoos (Subfamily Cuculinae) are long-tailed, long-winged arboreal birds, some small and superficially passerine in general appearance, others larger and somewhat hawk-like or falcon-like in plumage and posture. The tail is graduated, the bill often stout and slightly decurved; the feet strong, with short tarsi and zygodactyl toes. Most are secretive, but breeding males have obtrusive and distinctive calls. Our species are brood parasites, each specializing on a different host species or group of species. Egg polymorphism corresponds to egg colours and markings of the particular species parasitized. Shortly after hatching, the nidicolous young cuckoo may evict eggs or young of the host species from the nest. The birds feed mainly on caterpillars. Several are migratory.

The non-parasitic coucals of the subfamily Centropodinae (sometimes elevated to family status) are bulky, clumsy-looking birds with long broad tails, short wings and coarse plumage, the feathers of head, neck and breast stiff and somewhat bristly, and the hind claw is relatively straight. Coucals tend to skulk in thickets and low rank cover, frequently coming to the ground where they feed on invertebrates and small vertebrate animals. The male constructs a loose globular grass and leaf nest with a side entrance. He alone incubates the two to six white eggs, and does most feeding of the young which at hatching are covered with bristly white down. The distinctive Yellowbill (Subfamily Phaenicophaeinae) is related to the Oriental malkohas. It builds an untidy cup-shaped nest of twigs in dense vegetation.

BLACK-AND-WHITE or JACOBIN CUCKOO *Oxylophus jacobinus* Plate 52
(Pied Cuckoo)

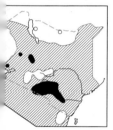

Length 330–340 mm (*c.* 13"). A medium-sized, *crested* cuckoo. **Adult** *O. j. pica* is glossy black above (with faint blue or green sheen) and white below. A small white patch at base of outer primaries is conspicuous in flight; tail long, graduated, prominently white-tipped. Bill black, feet slate-grey; eyes brown. *O. j. serratus* is greyish white below, with fine streaks on throat and breast. It also has a **dark morph**, *entirely black except for small white patch at base of primaries*. **Juvenile** brown above, buff-tinged below, with buff tail-feather tips. **VOICE**: Calls include a ringing *ker-wi-wi*, a sharp, excited *kikikikiki*, and a somewhat hornbill-like metallic yelping, *kyaOW-pi, kyaOW-pi, kyaOW-pi. . . .* **HABITS**: Usually solitary, sometimes in small groups, often in shrubs or low trees, where easily observed. Parasitizes babblers and bulbuls. **SIMILAR SPECIES**: Larger Levaillant's Cuckoo is more heavily built and still longer-tailed, with boldly streaked throat and upper breast; dark morph has white tail spots, unlike black *jacobinus*. Juvenile Levaillant's has rufous tips to the outer tail feathers. **STATUS AND DISTRIBUTION**: Rainy-season migrant throughout Kenya and n. Tanzania, seasonally common in bush, dry woodland and scrubby thickets, mainly below 1500 m. The race *pica* breeds in and west of the Rift Valley, March–August, also in se. Kenya, November and December. Common on southward passage in e. Kenyan plateau areas and in n. Tanzania November–January, yet scarce on return March–May. Large numbers move northwest across the Serengeti Plains in February and March. Coastal migrants in April and May are presumably *pica*, but may possibly include some migrants from India. *O. j. serratus* is an uncommon non-breeding visitor from southern Africa, April–September, ranging north to w. and cent. Kenya. **NOTE**: The two species of *Oxylophus* are often placed in the genus *Clamator*.

LEVAILLANT'S CUCKOO *Oxylophus levaillantii* Plate 52
(African Striped Cuckoo)

Length 380–400 mm (*c.* 15"). A *large* crested bird with *heavily streaked throat; tail proportionately longer than in Black-and-white Cuckoo*. **Adult** of **light morph** glossy black above (with faint bluish or greenish sheen) and white below, boldly streaked with black on throat and sides of neck, sometimes on breast; fainter streaks on sides. Shows conspicuous white patch at base of primaries and white tail-feather tips. Bill black; feet blue-grey; eyes brown. **Dark morph** black, apart from white primary patch and *white spots on outer tail feathers*. **Juvenile** brown above, wing-coverts strongly rufous; forehead, face and underparts buff; throat streaked; rectrix tips dull rufous; eyes reportedly yellow. **VOICE**: A low ringing *kuwu-weer, kuwu-weer. . .*, an excited *ku-wi-wi-wi*, and harsher, higher-pitched calls. Juvenile food-begging call a cat-like *nyaaa*. **HABITS**: Solitary. Skulks in thick leafy cover. Noisy. Parasitizes Arrow-marked and possibly Black-lored Babblers. **SIMILAR SPECIES**: Black-and-white Cuckoo compared above. Dark morph of that species has shorter tail with no white spots on outer feathers. **STATUS AND DISTRIBUTION**: Intra-African migrant along forest borders, in lush woodland and bush from sea level up to 2000 m. Most frequent west of the Rift Valley, May–September, with small numbers in se. Kenya and on north Kenyan coast, March–November. Few breeding records. Rare in n. Tanzania.

GREAT SPOTTED CUCKOO *Clamator glandarius*   Plate 52

Length 360–410 mm (14–16"). A *large, crested, buff-throated* cuckoo with a long narrow tail and *long pointed wings*. **Adult** grey-brown above, with white spots and three to four white wing-bars; broad blackish band through eyes, crest grey; white below, shading to cream or yellow-buff on breast and throat; tail feathers boldly white-tipped. Bill black, yellowish at base below; eyes brown or red, eyelids grey (reportedly sometimes red or orange); feet grey. **Juvenile** and **immature** resemble adults, but are more uniformly brown above, with *entire top of head black*, throat and upper breast deep buff, and *rufous primaries* conspicuous in flight; eyes red. First-year birds retain some chestnut in primaries and may show a few black crown feathers. **Voice:** Calls include a mellow whistling *kweeu, kweeu, kweeu. . .*, an excited, harsh *kiu-ku-ku-ker* or *kiu, kirru-kirru*, and a trilled *kirrrrrrrrrr* ending with several loud cackling notes. **Habits:** Shy and unobtrusive. In pairs in open areas, usually in tops of small trees. Parasitizes Pied Crow and starlings. **Status and Distribution:** Uncommon but widespread, except in arid n. and e. Kenya, in open woodland, savanna and cultivated country, from sea level to over 2000 m. Often in acacia groves. Mainly a migrant from the northern tropics, October–March, with marked passage across the Serengeti Plains, January–March. Present in parts of the Kenyan Rift Valley most of the year; several widely scattered breeding records.

THICK-BILLED CUCKOO *Pachycoccyx audeberti validus*   Plate 52

Length *c.* 360 mm (14"). A somewhat *hawk-like* cuckoo of coastal woods. Dark grey above and white below, with black-barred tail. Lacks crest; wings long and pointed. **Juvenile** *dark brown above with bold white spots*, white tips to wing-coverts and tail feathers, and sides of face white. **Voice:** Advertising call a repeated loud piping whistle, *REE-pipee, REE-pipee. . . .* Displaying bird gives a distinctive loud *weer-wik*; also a querulous *wheep-wheep-wheep* and a sharp vibrating *tititititititi.* **Habits:** Frequently perches on tops of tall trees. Restless and noisy. Cruising flight hawk-like and erratic, with deliberate wingbeats. Performs buoyant, floppy display flight above the forest canopy. Parasitizes Red-billed Helmet-shrike. **Similar Species:** Great Spotted Cuckoo, unlikely in coastal forest, is crested, slimmer and with longer, narrower unbarred tail. **Status and Distribution:** Uncommon local resident of Kenyan coastal forest and *Brachystegia* woodland from Sokoke north to Witu, and along the lower Tana River to Garsen.

BLACK CUCKOO *Cuculus clamosus*   Plate 51

Length 280–310 mm (11–12"). Resembles Red-chested Cuckoo in shape and size. **Adult** of nominate race is black, glossed with blue. It has small white spots on tips of tail feathers and may show *faint buff bars on under tail-coverts, sometimes on breast.* **Juvenile** and **immature** *dull sooty brown*. Both adult and immature of western race *gabonensis* (including '*jacksoni*') blackish above and strongly barred buff (or whitish) and black on belly, flanks and underside of wings; *throat, breast and sides of neck chestnut or rufous with variable black barring*; tail almost plain in adult, faintly barred in immature. **Voice:** Distinctive; an unhurried mournful whistle of three notes, the last rising: *wur, wur, wurEE* or *hoo, hoo-hurEEE*, repeated many times. Also a fast, harsh, excited-sounding *weurrri-weurrri-weurrri-WEURRRI*, or *cheudili-cheudili-CHEUDILI. . .*, rolling upwards and then fading away, often ending with a more subdued *chew-chew-tew-tew-tew*; imitated by robin-chats and other mimics. **Habits:** Solitary or in pairs. Approachable when calling, but usually well concealed in canopy. Flight fast and twisting. Nominate race parasitizes mainly bush-shrikes, but few actual breeding records. **Similar Species:** Male Red-chested Cuckoo can be easily confused with western *C. c. gabonensis*, but *throat grey*. Juvenile Red-chested has pale-edged crown and back feathers, is heavily barred below and on tail. **Status and Distribution:** *C. c. clamosus* is quite common (to judge from song frequency) and widespread in woodland, savanna and forest edge below 2000 m, north to the Turkwell River and the Ndotos, east to Kitui and Tsavo West NP, though largely absent from arid n. and e. Kenya, the coastal lowlands and parts of the Lake Victoria basin. Movements not clear, but some birds probably present in all months. Most, if not all, records of calling birds are during the rains: in w. Kenya and the Rift Valley, February–August; in se. Kenyan bush country during the short rains, November–February; and in Arusha District, January–March. Birds in the Kakamega and Nandi Forests ('*jacksoni*') are intermediate between *C. c. clamosus* and extralimital *C. c. gabonensis*.

RED-CHESTED CUCKOO *Cuculus s. solitarius*   Plate 51

Length 280–310 mm (11–12"). A slim, medium-sized cuckoo with a highly distinctive call. **Adult** dark slate-grey above, with *orange-rufous to chestnut-rufous upper breast*; throat pale buff in female, grey in male. Lower breast to under tail-coverts creamy white, the barring extending anteriorly into the rufous in some birds. Tail dark slaty grey, with outer feathers spotted and barred with white. Eyes brown; rim of eyelids yellow. **Juvenile** and **immature** *black above* and on throat and breast, with rest of underparts barred black and pale buff; white patch on

nape (sometimes obscure). Dark body feathers have narrow whitish tips, imparting scaly appearance. **VOICE:** Male has loud three-note call, descending in pitch: *wip-wip-weeu*, repeated many times. Female gives an excited *he-he-he-he-ha-he-ha-he* and an emphatic *quick-quick-quick.* . . . . **HABITS:** Shy and elusive, keeping to treetop foliage. Flight fast and direct. Almost exclusively parasitic on robin-chats, scrub robins and Spotted Morning Thrush. Vocal mainly just before and during rains. **SIMILAR SPECIES:** In w. Kenya, rufous-throated/breasted Black Cuckoos are black above, dark-barred below. Barred Long-tailed Cuckoo has similar call, but usually of four to five syllables; it is a smaller and longer-tailed bird, barred above and without rufous patch on breast. **STATUS AND DISTRIBUTION:** Common and widespread in w. and cent. Kenya and n. Tanzania. Breeds widely in forest edge and lightly wooded habitats (including suburban gardens) north to Mt Elgon and the Cheranganis and east to Meru, Kitui and Tsavo, but only a rare visitor to coastal lowlands. Movements little understood, but generally a wet-season visitor to arid northern border areas.

EURASIAN or COMMON CUCKOO *Cuculus c. canorus*   Plate 51

Length *c.* 310–330 mm (12.25–13"). A fairly large cuckoo with a long tail and long pointed wings. **Adult male** grey above, pale grey on throat and chest, otherwise barred black and white below; tail blackish, contrasting with back in flight, the outer feathers with large white terminal spots, smaller bar-like spots near shafts and on inner webs. *Bill blackish with yellow or greenish-yellow base*, more orange at gape; bare eyelids yellow; eyes orange-yellow. Dimorphic **female** either grey or bright rufous above, barred on breast, flight feathers and tail, with prominent whitish patch on nape, and rufous wash on sides of breast (absent in male); bare parts as in male. **Immature** variable, but always has strongly barred wings and tail: **rufous morph** less barred above than comparable adult; **brown morph** mainly brown above, most feathers pale tipped, wings and tail more blackish, underparts buff with brown barring; **grey morph** greyish or grey-brown, more or less barred above, and feathers whitish-tipped. **VOICE:** Well-known *cuc-koo* call not heard in East Africa. Female occasionally gives a chuckling *wuckel-wuckel-wuc-wuc-wuc-wuc.* . . . **HABITS:** Solitary. Shy, but often perches (somewhat horizontally) on open branch or bushtop. Flies low, fast and hawk-like, with shallow wingbeats and occasional glides. **SIMILAR SPECIES:** African Cuckoo has basal half of bill yellow, complete white bars across outer tail feathers and distinctive call. Both lesser cuckoos are much smaller and more compact, their underparts more heavily barred. **STATUS AND DISTRIBUTION:** Palearctic passage migrant, widespread in forest edge, woodland, savanna and bush, mainly below 2000 m, although rare in n. and e. Kenya. Small numbers present late October to December, mainly in se. Kenya and ne. Tanzania; more numerous and widespread in late March and April, when sometimes common in coastal areas.

AFRICAN CUCKOO *Cuculus gularis*   Plate 51

Length 305–330 mm (12–13"). Distinguished from very similar Eurasian Cuckoo by more *orange-yellow bill with distal half mainly black*, by *complete white bars (rather than spots or partial bars) on outer tail feathers*, and by *distinctive call.* **Male** grey above and from head to breast; otherwise white with narrow black barring below. Eyes orange; eyelids bright yellow. **Female** somewhat more brownish grey above than male, and barred breast often tinged with buff. Some closely resemble female Eurasian Cuckoo in the almost rufous tinge to sides of breast. *Eyes brown*; eyelids yellow. There is no rufous morph. **Juvenile** similar to young Eurasian, but rump, upper tail-coverts and crown entirely barred. **Immature** greyer above than Eurasian, with white spots and bars and white nape patch. **VOICE:** A soft but emphatic Hoopoe-like *oo-oo* or *hoo-hoop* (second syllable slightly higher), repeated several times. **HABITS:** Often perches upright, appearing quite hawk-like, especially when calling. Moves heavily when foraging in foliage. Flight like that of Eurasian Cuckoo. Sometimes calls at night. Parasitizes Common Drongo. **SIMILAR SPECIES:** Eurasian Cuckoo discussed above. Both of these larger species distinguished in flight from Asian and Madagascar Lesser Cuckoos by showing less contrast between back and tail. **STATUS AND DISTRIBUTION:** Intra-African migrant in dry acacia woodland, savanna and bush. Generally uncommon, but ranges widely from near sea level to over 2000 m. Movements not clear, but possibly moves in a clockwise direction following the rains, as calling birds are noted in Serengeti NP January–February, in cent. Kenya March–June, in Baringo District August–September, and in the Tsavo bush country November–December. Few records of breeding in our region.

ASIAN LESSER CUCKOO *Cuculus poliocephalus*   Plate 51

Length 260–280 mm (10–11"). Resembles a small Eurasian or African Cuckoo, but more compact and appearing *shorter-tailed*. Further differs from those species in dark tail and rump contrasting with pale back. **Male** grey above and from throat to breast, and boldly barred black and white on belly, sides and flanks. In many individuals, the buff crissum feathers also are heavily black-barred, but some others have the anterior and lateral under tail-coverts unbarred as in *C. rochii*, and a few have entirely plain coverts. Outer tail feathers marked with

large white spots. Bill blackish, with yellow at base of mandible. **Female** tinged tawny on breast and sides of neck, faintly barred on breast. **Immature** has tawny crown and nape, throat and breast, the latter barred; tawny bars on flight feathers and tail; some females barred with tawny-rufous above. **Voice**: Call of male, five or six staccato notes, middle ones higher pitched, *yok-yok chiki-chuchu*; rarely heard in Africa during northward passage. **Habits**: Unobtrusive, but not especially shy and often approachable. Tends to frequent thicker cover than Eurasian Cuckoo. Perches upright on low branches. Flight quick and darting. **Similar Species**: Eurasian and African Cuckoos compared above. Madagascar Lesser Cuckoo differs vocally; its under tail-coverts are more likely to appear plain, but this is not a reliable species distinction. **Status and Distribution**: Migrant from southern Asia, in forest edge, woodland and thick bush. At times quite common in coastal areas north to Malindi, March–April, often moving with Eurasian Cuckoos. Although little evidence of a major southward passage, there are several records from the Arabuko–Sokoke Forest and Ngulia (Tsavo West NP) in coastal and se. Kenya, late November–December. Recently recorded wintering in the West Usambara Mts.

MADAGASCAR LESSER CUCKOO *Cuculus rochii*　　　　　　　　**Plate 51**

Length 260–280 mm (10–11″). Unlikely at same time of year as the very similar Asian Lesser Cuckoo. Anterior and lateral under tail-coverts *usually* are pale cream or whitish buff, largely concealing the barred (or partly barred) inner coverts; longest central coverts often (always?) barred, but generally not visible in side view of bird. Appearance of coverts thus depends on angle of view and stage of moult. Furthermore, some female specimens from Zaïre, at least one of them immature, have *all* coverts heavily barred. Male is longer-winged than male Asian Lesser Cuckoo (162–174 mm, against 142–162 mm), but females of the two are the same size. Madagascar Lesser Cuckoo is present in Africa from *April to September*, the Asian species from November to April. Although some overlap occurs during April, newly arrived birds from Madagascar are then in *old worn plumage*, compared with freshly moulted Asian birds about to depart. **Voice**: Silent in Africa. Four evenly spaced mellow notes, *ko-ko-ko-ko*, the last lower in pitch than the others. **Habits**: Similar to those of Asian Lesser Cuckoo. **Similar Species**: Asian Lesser Cuckoo compared above. Eurasian and African Cuckoos are larger and stockier. **Status and Distribution**: Scarce and little-known migrant from Madagascar, mainly in forest edge, acacia woodland and thick bush. Most enter and leave Africa south of our area, but sight records from w. Kenya (Kapenguria, Saiwa NP, Kitale, Eldoret, Kapsabet, Mumias and Ng'iya districts) presumably represent this form, as do records from Lake Baringo (August), Nakuru (May) and Sokoke (August). Most Tanzanian records are from south of our area, but the species is known from the East Usambara Mts. **Note**: Considered conspecific with *C. poliocephalus* by some.

BARRED LONG-TAILED CUCKOO *Cercococcyx montanus patulus*　　**Plate 52**
(Barred Cuckoo)

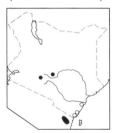

Length 320–330 mm (12.5–13″); tail 145–175 mm (6–7″). A medium-sized but small-bodied cuckoo with a *long, broad tail* and *relatively short wings*. Upperparts olive-brown with rufous and brown barring; underparts *boldly barred with black and buffy white*. Flight feathers and tail are rufous-barred, the outer rectrices also with white bars. Bill blackish above, yellowish below; eyes brown; orbital ring yellow; legs and feet dull yellowish. **Juvenile** streaked below, with some scaly mottling on throat. **Voice**: A repetitive whining whistle, *wee-weoo, wee-weoo, wee-weoo. . .*, the phrases rising in pitch and volume before stopping; these quickly followed by a ringing *wip-wip-weu-weu-wo*, suggesting Red-chested Cuckoo's call but usually of four or five notes. A variation begins with a raspy, nasal owlet-like *way-eu, way-eu, way-eu . . .*, changing to a loud *PEE-tu, PEE-tu . . .*, often repeated before the final series of repetitive *whee-wee-whew-yer* phrases. **Habits**: Shy and secretive. Calls repeatedly from forest cover, especially in evening and briefly at sunrise; also on moonlit nights. Flies low through forest. Parasitizes Sharpe's Akalat (Usambara Mts) and possibly African Broadbill. **Status and Distribution**: Locally common in forest between 1700 and 2100 m on the eastern slopes of Mt Kenya and southern slopes of the Aberdares; very common between 900 and 1600 m in the Usambara Mts. Probably resident, but vocal mainly October–March and doubtless overlooked at other times. Vagrants recorded at the coast September–November are believed to be wanderers from the Usambaras.

AFRICAN EMERALD CUCKOO *Chrysococcyx c. cupreus*　　　　　　**Plate 51**

Length 215–230 mm (8.5–9″). A brightly coloured forest cuckoo. **Adult male** *brilliant metallic green* with *golden yellow lower breast and belly*. Under tail-coverts barred black and white, sides of tail with white. Dark brown eyes ringed by bare blue-green skin; bill bright blue-green above, greyer below; feet bluish. **Female** shorter-tailed, iridescent green above with tawny or rufous barring; *wings rufous-barred; top and sides of head mainly rufous-brown, flecked with white behind eyes* and sometimes from forehead to nape; tail shining coppery green, the

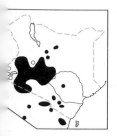

outer rectrices white with bronze-green spots or bars towards tip; *white underparts heavily or thinly barred with iridescent green* except sometimes on throat. Bill dull greenish horn; orbital skin blue; feet bluish. **Juvenile** resembles adult female, but crown and nape barred. Outer tail-coverts with, at most, a very narrow white edge, no broad white stripe as in young Klaas's Cuckoo. **Immature male** is barred green and white below, with much rufous on wings. **VOICE:** A repeated clear whistled call of four or five syllables, *teeoo*, *tchew-tui* or *diu, dew-dui*, rendered as 'Hello, Ju-dy'. **HABITS:** Highly vocal. Forages in canopy foliage, sometimes in lower branches, feeding extensively on caterpillars. Sun-bathes on branches at forest edge. Parasitizes various passerine birds. **SIMILAR SPECIES:** Adult Klaas's and Diederik Cuckoos are mainly white below and have different calls. Klaas's is smaller, adult has white postocular marks, dark breast patches and broad white tail edges. Juvenile Klaas's resembles female African Emerald, but lacks whitish flecking on head and nape, crown is barred with buff, and barring on underparts non-iridescent. Diederik has white spots on wings and red eyes. **STATUS AND DISTRIBUTION:** Local in highland forest, riverine woodland and well-timbered suburban gardens. Fairly common in the w. and cent. Kenyan highlands, the Mathews Range, Ndotos and Mt Marsabit. Also in the Chyulu and Taita Hills, the Usambara Mts, Kilimanjaro, Arusha and Lake Manyara NPs and Mt Hanang, occasionally wandering beyond these areas during the rains.

KLAAS'S CUCKOO *Chrysococcyx klaas* Plate 51

Length 160–180 mm (6–7"). An iridescent woodland cuckoo, the size of a small bulbul. *Broad white tail sides* are conspicuous in undulating flight. **Adult male** metallic green above with coppery reflections and *small white postocular marks*; underparts white, with *dark green patches on sides of breast*. Bill pale apple-green to olive-green (brighter when breeding); eyelids green, eyes dark brown; feet olive. **Female** may resemble male (although less shiny above and more heavily barred below), but usually has plain bronzy-brown head and nape; upperparts mostly barred iridescent green and coppery brown; central tail feathers coppery brown, the three outermost pairs white and each with a dark subterminal spot. Underparts whitish, narrowly barred along sides with olive or dusky brown. Bill dark green, blackish towards tip; *eyes grey-brown to pale brownish grey*; feet greenish dusky. **Juvenile/immature** shining green above, lightly barred with tawny-buff, including on crown (crown barring whitish in young African Emerald Cuckoo). Underparts, including throat and breast, heavily barred with brown, olive-brown or dark metallic green, the breast more or less washed with buff; *white outer webs of some lateral upper tail-coverts show as a short white stripe on each side of tail base*. **VOICE:** Three to five high plaintive whistles, *swhee-hee swhee-hee whee-hee-ki wee-ki*, or *weu-ki weu-ki weu-ki*, the series repeated three or four times per minute. **HABITS:** Frequents thick cover, but less secretive than African Emerald Cuckoo. Joins mixed-species parties. Usually sings from high perch, throwing head back with each call. Parasitizes warblers, sunbirds and other small passerines. **SIMILAR SPECIES:** Poorly seen flying bird may suggest a small honeyguide. Diederik Cuckoo is larger, with white spots on wings, heavily barred flanks and no white on sides of tail; adult has red eyes. Young Diederik shows white behind eye as does Klaas's, but has white wing spots and largely red bill. Female and young African Emerald Cuckoo resemble young Klaas's, but usually are flecked white on head and nape, and lack white on outer webs of lateral upper tail-coverts. **STATUS AND DISTRIBUTION:** Widespread and fairly common in woodland, forest edge, thickets and gardens between sea level and *c.* 3000 m. Absent from arid parts of n. and e. Kenya and the Masai Steppe of ne. Tanzania.

DIEDERIK CUCKOO *Chrysococcyx caprius* Plate 51
(Didric Cuckoo)

Length 178–190 mm (7–7.5"). Slightly larger than Klaas's Cuckoo, with conspicuous *white spots on the wings*. **Adult male** iridescent green above with coppery reflections; shows white superciliary stripe, often broken above the eye, and a row of *white spots along each side of tail*. Underparts white, with green barring on flanks. Bill black, grey at base; feet grey; *eyes red*. **Female** variable; browner above than male, often more barred below, with buff wash on throat and breast (but seldom, if ever, as prominently buff-throated as southern African birds). Some show iridescent green streaks on throat. Eyes rufous-brown, often yellow peripherally. **Juvenile** polymorphic; usually green with rufous barring above, broken white superciliary stripes, dark malar stripes, and much white spotting on wings and tail; flight feathers barred with rufous. Underparts heavily spotted, more streaked on throat, broadly barred on flanks and crissum. *Bill coral-red*, sometimes blackish above and at tip; eyes grey-brown; eyelids and feet grey. Some birds rufous above with green barring, and tinged rufous on throat and breast. **VOICE:** A persistent plaintive whistle, *kew-kew-kew-kewkiti* or *dee-dee-dee-DEEderik*. **HABITS:** Less shy and secretive than most cuckoos; calls from exposed treetop perches and in rapid quivering flight with spread, sometimes raised, tail. Ordinary flight direct and undulating. Parasitizes weavers, less often other small passerine birds. **SIMILAR SPECIES:** Vocally distinct Klaas's Cuckoo lacks wing spots and heavy flank barring, is smaller, with dark breast patches, and has white (not merely white-spotted) outer tail

feathers; also has brown eyes, never shows red on bill. **STATUS AND DISTRIBUTION**: Widespread and common in dry woodland, savanna, bush and cultivated country below 2000 m. Mainly a wet-season visitor in dry areas; and in n. and e. Kenya largely confined to vicinity of permanent water.

YELLOWBILL *Ceuthmochares aereus* Plate 52
(Green Coucal, Green Malkoha)

Length 330 mm (13″). A slender dark skulker with *conspicuous yellow bill* and with bright blue skin showing behind the red eyes; yellow lores grade into apple-green posteriorly. Western nominate race dark slaty blue above and grey below, with paler throat. Eastern *C. a. australis* glossy greenish grey above, olive-grey on head and underparts except for buff throat. **Juvenile/immature** more sooty above than adults, with paler brownish throat and breast, and buff wing-covert edges. **VOICE**: Arresting high-pitched staccato notes accelerating into a harsh trill, *kik kik, kik, kik-ki-ki-kikikikikikik*; and a wailing *kweeu-eeep, kweeu-eeep*; also gives various scolding sounds. **HABITS**: Forages unobtrusively, alone or in pairs, amid creeper tangles and dense foliage, but inquisitive and may remain in view for some minutes if lured into the open. Calls frequently. Builds an untidy cup-shaped nest of twigs in thick vegetation. At least some migration is nocturnal. **STATUS AND DISTRIBUTION**: Inhabits forest edge and tall dense thickets. *C. a. aereus* is uncommon in the Kakamega and Nandi Forests, ranging south to Kericho and Lolgorien. *C. a. australis* is present in coastal Tanzanian lowlands and on offshore islands, ranging north to the Usambara and North Pare Mountains, Arusha NP, Kilimanjaro and Taveta Districts, and along the Kenyan coast (mainly as a non-breeding migrant, May–Nov.) north to the Boni Forest. Occasional wanderers or migrants at Kiambu, Limuru, Kieni Forest, Samburu GR (June 1990), Ngulia (Nov. 1978, Dec. 1985) and Tsavo East NP (Nov. 1974, 1975).

WHITE-BROWED COUCAL *Centropus superciliosus* Plate 52

Length 400–410 mm (c. 16″). The common coucal. **Adult** distinguished by *dark crown separated from dark ear-coverts by yellowish-white superciliary stripes*. Back rufous-brown, wings rufous-chestnut, long heavy tail greenish black; underparts creamy white, with extensive cream streaking and dusky barring on sides. Shows conspicuous cream streaks on nape, sides of neck and back, and narrow buff bars on blackish rump and upper tail-coverts. Eyes red; bill black; feet black or bluish grey. Southern and western *C. s. loandae* is darker than nominate *superciliosus*, with black (not brown) crown in fresh plumage. **Juvenile** has less prominent *buff superciliary stripes* than adult, is streaked pale buff and brown from forehead to scapulars, barred with black on back and wing-coverts; tail bronzy greenish brown with faint buff bars (these whitish near rectrix tips); eyes red, at least by the time rectrices are fully grown. **VOICE**: A distinctive accelerating hollow cooing, *hoo-hoo-hoo-hoo-huhuhuhuhuhuhuhu. . .*, and a series of gurgling notes likened to water being poured from a bottle. Pairs duet, and several birds may call together. Alarm calls a loud hiss or a sharp *TCHUK*! **HABITS**: Skulks in shrubbery, tall grass and rank herbage. Makes short low flight when flushed, then quickly flops back into cover, landing awkwardly. Sometimes feeds on ground. Sun-bathes with drooped wings partly spread, the back and rump feathers erected. Calling bird perches upright, neck feathers erected, slowly lowering head until bill points downward. Eats a wide variety of animal food, mainly insects, but including young birds and eggs. Active and vocal at night in breeding season. **SIMILAR SPECIES**: Young Senegal Coucal and non-breeding and immature Black Coucal all lack pale superciliary stripes. **STATUS AND DISTRIBUTION**: Common and widespread in dense bush and moist vegetation below 2200 m, often near water. *C. s. loandae* is resident in much of n. Tanzania north to South Nyanza in sw. Kenya; supposedly nominate birds elsewhere, but precise limits of the two races unclear.

BLACK COUCAL *Centropus grillii* Plate 52

Length 380 mm (15″). Smaller and more compact than White-browed Coucal, with *shorter tail* and *shorter bill*. **Adult breeding plumage** *black, with orange-rufous wings.* **Non-breeding plumage** broadly barred rufous-buff and black on back and wings, *streaked tawny and black from forehead to scapulars*, these parts with bright cream shaft streaks, as are sides of breast, neck and wing-coverts; *no superciliary stripes; all rectrices narrowly barred with tawny*. Underparts buff, with semi-scaly dusky feather edges on lower throat and breast; some dusky barring on flanks. *Eyes dark brown*; bill brown above, pale blue-grey below; feet slate-grey. **Subadult breeding bird** has barred remiges and tail, and some barring is retained for first two years. **Juvenile** resembles non-breeding adult, but strong barring of upperparts continues to face and forehead; pale shaft streaks as in adult; *no defined superciliary stripes; rump and upper tail-coverts black with narrow dull buff or tawny bars*; flight feathers dull cinnamon with bold black bars; sides of breast mottled with brown and with cream shaft streaks; leg feathers and crissum barred black and buff. Eyes grey; bill dark brown above, paler below; feet dark blue-grey. **VOICE**: In breeding season, a double note, *kutuk. . .kutuk. .*

kutuk. . ., repeated over long periods; also a low hooting *hoo. . . hoo. . . hoo. . .*, and a 'water-bottle' call like that of White-browed Coucal but higher-pitched, faster and not rising at end. **Habits**: Much like those of other coucals. At times shy and secretive, creeping in tall moist grass and swamp vegetation; in savannas frequently perches on grass-tops and bushes, drying its plumage. Flushes reluctantly; flight heavy and clumsy. **Similar Species**: White-browed Coucal has pale superciliary stripes, and dark brown forehead/forecrown lacks streaks. Immature Senegal Coucal is longer-tailed. Adult and immature of both White-browed and Senegal Coucals have red eyes. **Status and Distribution**: Uncommon and local in swamps and seasonally wet grassland, often with little shrub cover. Small numbers breed in the Seronera Valley, Serengeti NP and Mkomazi GR (Dec.–Feb.) during seasonal rains; otherwise local in n. Tanzania. In Kenya, known from widely scattered localities, although only seasonal in some: Lake Victoria basin, Mara GR, Lake Baringo, Embu, Thika, Meru and Tsavo West NPs, Lake Jipe and on the coast from Watamu and Mida Creek north to the lower Tana River floodplain. Few breeding records.

SENEGAL COUCAL *Centropus s. senegalensis*   Plate 52

Length 380–410 mm (15–16"). A *small* coucal of relatively dry habitats in w. Kenya. **Adult** *plain black from forehead to nape*, rufous on back and wings, with black rump and tail and buffy-white underparts with shiny feather shafts. Eyes red. **Juvenile** is brown above, with creamy streaks and fine barring; wings barred brown, but primaries plain except at tips. Rump and upper tail-coverts barred blackish; underparts buff; tail blackish, with faint buff barring at tip. **Immature** similar, with long all-black tail. **Voice**: Dove-like call is similar to that of White-browed Coucal, but begins more slowly, descends and accelerates, *hoo-hoo-hoo-hu-hu-huhuhuhu. . .*, then slows and rises at the end, *. . . hoo hoo huhu.* 'Water-bottle' call much like that of White-browed. **Habits**: Skulks in dense growth, but is readily flushed. Flies weakly and heavily. Feeds on ground, but may ascend into trees. Like other coucals, may call at night. **Similar Species**: Blue-headed Coucal is larger, with top of head, nape and upper back shiny blue-black in adults. White-browed Coucal has pale superciliary stripes, lacking in juvenile Senegal. **Status and Distribution**: Locally common near the Ugandan border, mainly below 1300 m, in bush, thickets and sugarcane plantations in Bungoma, Busia and Mumias Districts.

BLUE-HEADED COUCAL *Centropus monachus*   Plate 52

Length 460 mm (18"). *Large* and heavy-looking. **Adult** *shiny blue-black from crown to upper back*; lower back and wings rufous, rump and tail black; underparts vary from creamy white to pale buff; eyes red. Western *C. m. fischeri* is darker, slightly more olive-brown on wings, than nominate *monachus*. **Juvenile** similar, but top of head dull black with fine dull buff shaft streaks; primaries barred throughout; underparts darker buff than in adult, dull rufous on breast and sides of neck; tail dark brown, with only very narrow buff barring toward tips of rectrices. Eyes red-brown; mandible pale. **Voice**: Slower and deeper than that of White-browed Coucal, *hoo, hoo, hoo, hoo-wu-wu-wu-wu-wu-wu hoo hoo, hu*, accelerating and dropping in pitch in the middle, then rising and slowing at end. Also has a raucous cackle. **Habits**: As for Senegal Coucal. **Similar Species**: Senegal Coucal is smaller, lacks blue tinge to black cap, is brighter rufous (less chestnut) on back and wings. Juvenile has blacker tail and largely plain primaries, with barring confined to tips. **Status and Distribution**: In Kenya, locally fairly common in papyrus swamps and marshy thickets; also in tea plantations in Nandi and Kericho Districts and the Nyambenis. The nominate race ranges sparingly in the w. and cent. highlands from Kericho east to Nyeri and Meru Districts, and south to the northern Nairobi suburbs. *C. m. fischeri* is widespread in the Lake Victoria basin north to Kakamega and Nandi Districts, south to Ruma NP (Lambwe Valley) and Kilgoris. One n. Tanzanian record: an early specimen from Kiniamongo (east of Musoma), January 1886.

OWLS are extraordinary birds, constituting the Order Strigiformes, which consists of two families with many features and habits in common. They are large-headed, with long rounded wings, a short, pointed, decurved bill, and long, strongly curved sharp claws. The outer toe is reversible. Most are nocturnal, some strictly so, but the forward-facing eyes see perfectly well in daylight. Their exceptional eyesight requires only a minute fraction of the light needed by humans, but most rely primarily on their exceptionally keen hearing for hunting. Barn owls, and perhaps others, can locate prey in total darkness. The soft plumage (which owls share with the equally nocturnal nightjars, Caprimulgidae), apparently aided by the serrated leading outer-primary edge, effectively muffles flight sounds and enables them to approach prey silently. (Pel's Fishing Owl, adapted to underwater prey, has not evolved mechanisms for silent flight.) Most owls eat rodents and large insects, seized with the powerful sharp claws and swallowed whole. Undigestible bones, fur and chitin are later regurgitated in pellet form. Numerous superstitions have developed from the traditional sense of mystery surrounding these secretive birds with their sometimes imposing nocturnal vocalizations. Ignorance often has led to their persecution—unfortunate, as owls are almost entirely beneficial to man's interests.

BARN OWLS, FAMILY TYTONIDAE
(World, 17 species; Africa, 3; Kenya and n. Tanzania, 2)

Barn owls differ from typical owls (Strigidae) in their heart-shaped facial disc surrounding small dark eyes. There are no 'ear-tufts'. The middle claw is pectinate (as in herons and some nightjars), the long slender tarsi are feathered and the toes are covered with bristles. Sexes are alike or similar, although females are larger than males. They nest in burrows, hollow trees, buildings, cliffs, old wells or simply on the ground, with little or no nest material. The four to seven white eggs are incubated by the female. Upon hatching, the downy young are tended by both sexes.

AFRICAN GRASS OWL *Tyto capensis* Plate 55
(Cape Grass Owl)

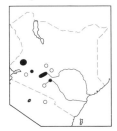

Length 360–400 mm (14–16"). A dark-backed, ground-nesting 'barn owl' with *whitish facial disc, dark brown lores* and *white-edged tail*. **Adult** *dark chocolate-brown above*, finely speckled with white. Underparts vary from tawny-buff to creamy white, with dark brown spotting dense on upper breast to rather sparse on belly and under tail-coverts. *Central tail feathers brown and unbarred*, the *others paler laterally* and *with a few dark bars*; *outer two pairs white*. Eyes yellowish brown to dark brown; bill pale pink; toes dull yellowish. Spread wing shows *tawny-buff area at base of outer primaries*, the patch much *less extensive than in Marsh Owl*; also shows a pale patagial area and *no white trailing edge*; wing-linings spotted and with a small dark carpal crescent. **Juvenile** has tawny-russet facial disc, white only toward throat, no white speckling on back, and golden-brown underparts with small black spots. **Voice:** A soft, Barn Owl-like screech, slightly lower-pitched and with a distinct ending, *schreeeeeeow*, given during the day in response to disturbance (from Marsh and Barn Owls or from humans). Common contact call a series of steady clicks, rising and falling in intensity, reminiscent of distant frogs except for a regular pause between the clicks, series interspersed with squeaks and snores, repeated frequently by adults bringing prey to nest; call changes to a more resonant *croick-croick* when feeding the young (Erasmus 1992). **Habits:** Nocturnal (in southern Africa somewhat crepuscular); shuns human habitation. When flushed, flies a short distance with long legs dangling, before dropping into cover. Hunts by quartering low over grass or marsh. Feeds primarily on rodents. **Similar Species:** Marsh Owl (in same habitat) is smaller, paler above with large buff primary patches, white trailing wing edges, and short legs (feet not extending beyond tail, but legs may also dangle in short flight); tail paler at sides but obviously barred. **Status and Distribution:** Scarce and local resident of moist highland marshes, grasslands and moors between 1600 and 3200 m, in the Crater Highlands of n. Tanzania, and in Kenya from the Mau, Aberdares and Mt Kenya to the Laikipia and Uasin Gishu Plateaux. Wanderers recorded from Kakamega Forest glades, Sotik, the Athi Plains and Arusha NP.

BARN OWL *Tyto alba affinis* Plate 55
(Common Barn Owl)

Length 330–360 mm (13–14"). A pale owl with *white heart-shaped face*. Appears large-headed and short-tailed in flight, ghostly white in headlight beams at night. **Adult** a delicate mixture of golden-buff and pale grey above, with considerable black and white flecking; tail yellowish buff, barred with grey-brown. Facial disc outlined by dark brown or black, and with a dark patch in front of each beady, deep brown eye; bill whitish. Underparts and entire underside of wings white, the former with small blackish dots. **Juvenile** resembles adult, but darker grey above, washed golden buff below. **Voice:** In flight, an eerie trilling screech, *schreeeeeeeeee or eeeSHEEEEeeee*. Hisses loudly at nest. **Habits:** Nocturnal and somewhat crepuscular. Nests in buildings, caves, wells and Hamerkop nests. Feeds on rodents, other small vertebrates and insects. Has head-swaying threat display. Frequently calls in flight. **Similar Species:** See African Grass Owl. **Status and Distribution:** Widely but spar-

ingly distributed at elevations from sea level to almost 3000 m. Often associated with man in urban and suburban areas; otherwise around cliffs and kopjes in many national parks and other largely uninhabited areas. Generally absent from arid n. and ne. Kenya, but several records from around Lake Turkana.

TYPICAL OWLS, FAMILY STRIGIDAE
(World, *c.* 160 species; Africa, 33; Kenya, 15; n. Tanzania, 13)

Varying greatly in size, these owls range from 15 to 66 cm (6 to 26 in.) in length. Their large eyes are usually surrounded by a broad facial disc, and their legs are shorter than in *Tyto*. Both tarsi and toes may be well feathered. Several species have well-developed erectile 'ear-tufts' arising from the forehead or occiput. (These have nothing to do with the internal ears or with hearing.) The dense, soft plumage makes the birds appear much larger than they really are, and provides effective insulation during long periods of inactivity. Cryptic feather patterns, plumage compression and ear-tuft erection of some species render them inconspicuous when resting during the day. The sexes are alike in colour, but females may be considerably larger than males. Some owls have different colour phases or morphs, some individuals being greyer, browner or more rufous than others, the differences independent of age or sex. *Glaucidium* species moult all of their rectrices at once, the renewed tail requiring several weeks to reach full length.

Owls occupy all land habitats from low deserts to alpine moorlands, although the majority inhabit woodland and forest edge. They are highly territorial and are generally sedentary, with long-distance migrations known in only a few species. All have distinctive calls, and are highly vocal during periods of full moon. A few species are moderately active by day.

With a few exceptions, they use old nests of diurnal raptors rather than building their own, or they lay their chalky-white rounded eggs in tree cavities, rock crevices or caves. Clutch size varies, and is dependent on the available food supply. Incubation is generally by the female, but the young are tended by both sexes.

SOKOKE SCOPS OWL *Otus ireneae*   Plate 56

Length 150 mm (6"). A small, polymorphic *coastal* species. *At night, the small ear-tufts are barely visible* in the field. **Grey morph** is brownish grey above with numerous small black and white dots, and larger buffy-white spots on scapulars that may be obscured by dark markings: facial disc rather dark buffy grey, outlined by black. Densely vermiculated underparts pale grey, more greyish brown on breast, with fine white-and-black speckling; prominent black-and-white markings on wing-coverts; primaries boldly barred black and buffy white; tail grey-brown with some incomplete dark brown bars. **Brown morph** differs in being rich vinous brown on head and breast, with white speckling and small black spots. **Rufous morph** *largely rufous, pale or bright,* and quite uniform except for short black crown streaks and white scapular spots (not always evident). Close view shows fine black speckling above, and some below, where there is also faint dark barring; *face dark rufous.* Eyes pale yellow; bill pale greenish yellow, pinkish grey on cere; feet dull greyish yellow. **Juvenile** undescribed. **VOICE:** A whistled *too-too-too. . .*, suggesting a tinkerbird, uttered as a series of eight to 10 notes repeated about ten times per minute. **HABITS:** Some crepuscular activity, but mostly nocturnal; highly vocal on nights of full moon. Roosts by day in dense thickets, ear-tufts erected and eyes reduced to slits. **SIMILAR SPECIES:** African Barred Owlet in the same habitat is larger and longer-tailed, barred on upper breast and back, boldly dark-spotted below, and with white on the wings. It is more likely to be seen during the day. **STATUS AND DISTRIBUTION:** Common resident of *Cynometra–Brachylaena* forest on red soil in the Arabuko–Sokoke Forest between Kilifi and Malindi on the Kenyan coast. Rare in *Brachystegia* woodland. Recently discovered from 200 to 400 m on lower slopes of the East Usambara Mts, ne. Tanzania.

PEMBA SCOPS OWL *Otus pembaensis*   Plate 124

Length *c.* 200 mm (8"). Confined to Pemba Island, where the only small owl. **Adults** vary from plain russet-brown above, with finely vermiculated pale rufous-buff underparts (often with some narrow streaking on head, breast and flanks), to entirely rich russet-brown or orange-rufous with little or no streaking. Pale buff spots on primaries and scapulars, the latter with small black tips. Eyebrows pale rufous; feathered tarsi rich buff, whitish posteriorly in some individuals. Bill dull greenish with black tip; eyes yellow. **Juvenile** resembles adult of respective colour morph. **VOICE:** A single monosyllabic *too* or *hoo*, repeated at irregular intervals. Male's call higher-pitched than female's. Courting pairs duet, calling in unison with one-second intervals between calls. At dusk, male gives four

or five hoots in quick succession, but reverts to single hoots for remainder of the night. **Habits:** Little known. Strictly nocturnal. **Status and Distribution:** Endemic to Pemba Island, where fairly common and widespread in clove plantations and forest. **Note:** Formerly considered conspecific with *O. rutilus* of Madagascar and the Comoro Islands.

EURASIAN SCOPS OWL *Otus scops* Plate 56

Length 175–185 mm (*c.* 7"). A small yellow-eyed 'eared' owl, difficult to distinguish from resident African Scops in the field. Brownish-grey or rufous-brown upperparts are finely vermiculated and speckled with dark grey, rufous and white; facial disc grey or grey-brown; sides of crown, inner part of ear-tufts and scapular edges pale buff or white, the large pale scapular spots vermiculated and black-tipped; primaries broadly banded buffy white and black. Underparts finely but densely vermiculated grey on a white or buffy-white background, with some heavy black streaks, numerous narrow dark shaft streaks and a few white bars; some birds show much cinnamon-rufous below. Eyes pale yellow; bill blue-black or brownish with black tip; cere brown or olive-grey. In the hand, note that 10th (outermost) primary is longer than 5th (the reverse in African Scops). The poorly differentiated *O. s. pulchellus* is more finely marked, and with more prominent pale spots on the back, than nominate *scops*. *O. s. turanicus* is paler than the other races. **Voice:** *Generally silent* in East Africa. On breeding grounds, a measured pure whistle, *peu . . . peu . . . .* **Habits:** Poorly known in winter quarters. Nocturnal. Apparently favours dense bush and thickets, avoiding heavy forest. **Similar Species:** Nominate race of African Scops Owl (a highly vocal resident) is slightly smaller and has broader black facial-disc borders. Said to be more boldly marked than Eurasian Scops, with heavier and more continuous black ventral streaking, but there is much variation. Some birds may not be separable except by primary measurements. **Status and Distribution:** Scarce palearctic migrant. Scattered Kenyan records November–March, from Nandi, Eldama Ravine and Mt Kenya south to Nairobi, Machakos and Kajiado Districts, the Tana River and Tsavo West NP. Known in Tanzania only from a specimen taken in the North Pare Mts, November 1958. Most records are of nominate *scops* or *pulchellus*, but pale birds ringed on December passage at Ngulia (Tsavo West NP), and a specimen from Bura on the Tana River, are referable to *turanicus*.

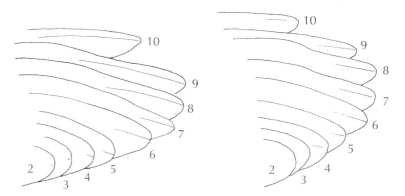

Wing-tip outlines of scops owls: Eurasian (left) and African (right). Note length of 10th primary.

AFRICAN SCOPS OWL *Otus senegalensis* Plate 56

Length 155–170 mm (6–6.5"). The common small 'eared' owl of savanna and bush country. Dimorphic, with some birds more rufous than others. Ear-tufts mainly dark, often with some white spots, but the inner edges not, or usually not, broadly pale as in preceding species. Most **adults** of the nominate race are dark grey above, streaked and mottled with black, often with buff or tawny on neck and wing-coverts, and the scapulars boldly white-spotted; primaries banded with dark brown and white or buffy white; facial disc grey (finely vermiculated), disc borders black, or brown and black, not meeting on chin. Underparts grey, finely vermiculated, with narrow dark shaft streaks, a few heavy, broad black marks, and some short white bars; centre of lower breast and belly paler, white centrally. Tail light grey-brown with several dark bars. At night, the ear-tufts may be inconspicuous. In the hand, 10th primary shorter than 5th or 4th. **Juvenile** similar to adult but washed with brown. *O. s. nivosus* is smaller and paler grey below, with a few light brown marks on the breast. **Voice:** A single short trill, *krru-*

uup or *k-k-krruup*, repeated many times at intervals of five to 10 seconds—a common night sound in suitable habitat; this varied to a soft purring *twrrr* or *terrrrup*. Less common calls include a louder *kukerow* and a shrill *weeeaow*. **HABITS:** Nocturnal, but may begin calling before dusk. Roosts in foliage among vines or against a tree trunk, its plumage compressed, ear-tufts vertically erect, and the eyes closed to mere slits. Mostly insectivorous. **SIMILAR SPECIES:** See Eurasian Scops Owl. **STATUS AND DISTRIBUTION:** *O. s. senegalensis* is a common and widespread resident of low-rainfall areas from 500 to 2000 m in Kenya and n. Tanzania. Prefers thorn-scrub, bush with scattered baobab trees, acacia woodland and savanna and grassland with large shrubs. *O. s. nivosus* is known from three specimens taken along the lower Tana River and in the Lali Hills of se. Kenya. **NOTE:** Formerly considered conspecific with *O. scops*.

WHITE-FACED SCOPS OWL *Otus leucotis*   Plate 56
(White-faced Owl)

Length 250 mm (10"). A pale grey owl of dry country, with *black-bordered white face*, golden-yellow eyes, and *narrow black streaks on the underparts*. Ear-tufts long, with much black, upperparts mostly vermiculated grey; white on scapulars and along edge of wing. Bill pale cream, more greyish at base and on cere. The race *granti* is darker and greyer, often with heavier dark ventral streaks, but some nominate birds are similarly dark. **Juvenile** resembles adult, but facial disc grey. **VOICE:** Usual call a mellow disyllabic *co-croor*, repeated at intervals of five to six seconds. In s. Africa also gives a rapid hooting, *ku-ku-ku-ku-ku-WHOO-OO*, the first notes staccato (Maclean 1984). **HABITS:** Pairs typically roost side by side in acacias, often quite exposed. When disturbed, becomes extremely cryptic by greatly compressing feathers, erecting ear-tufts, and closing eyes. Hunts from perch, dropping on prey (mostly scorpions). Nests in or on old bird nests. **SIMILAR SPECIES:** African Scops Owl is smaller, darker, grey-faced (as is young White-faced Scops), with much narrower black facial borders, smaller ear-tufts and different ventral pattern. **STATUS AND DISTRIBUTION:** Local and uncommon resident of dry bush and woodland between 300 and 1700 m. *O. l. leucotis* of nw. Kenya ranges south to the Turkwell and Kerio Rivers, Baringo, Samburu and Meru Districts; *O. l. granti* is scarce in South Nyanza, Amboseli and both Tsavo NPs, and rare in much of n. Tanzania. Sight records from the Tana River are not racially assigned.

CAPE EAGLE-OWL *Bubo capensis mackinderi*   Plate 55
(Mackinder's Eagle-Owl)

Length 510–610 mm (20–24"). A large highland owl with long brown ear-tufts and *orange or yellow-orange eyes*. Mottled tawny and dark brown above; *breast heavily blotched with dark brown, tawny-buff and white spots*; belly, feet and under tail-coverts whitish with brown and tawny barring. Bill black. **Juvenile** similar to adult but with shorter ear-tufts. **VOICE:** A deep *hoooo* or *ho-hooo* or *ho-hooo-ho*. Pairs apparently do not duet. **HABITS:** Roosts on rock ledges or in caves. Nests on ledges, or in stick nests of other raptors. **SIMILAR SPECIES:** Verreaux's Eagle-Owl is paler and more finely marked, and has dark eyes. Grey or grey-brown Spotted Eagle-Owl lacks bright tawny-buff coloration and is less heavily blotched on breast; ear-tufts are smaller, eyes yellow or brown. **STATUS AND DISTRIBUTION:** Local resident of alpine peaks and moorlands on Mt Kenya, Mt Elgon, the Aberdares and Mau Plateau; smaller isolated populations or pairs resident on cliffs and ravines in the Ngobit–Nakuru–Gilgil–Naivasha region, including Hell's Gate NP. Reports of large owls on the moorlands of Kilimanjaro (above 3000 m) may refer to this species (Grimshaw 1995), while a sight record at 2700 m on Mt Olosirwa, near Ngorongoro Crater, also requires confirmation.

SPOTTED EAGLE-OWL *Bubo africanus*   Plate 55

Length 430–480 mm (17–19"). A greyish or (more often) brownish 'eared' owl, finely barred below, with darker blotching on the upper breast; upperparts mottled dark brown, buffy and white, with some pale spots on back and wing-coverts. *Eye colour varies*. Northern *B. a. cinerascens* has pale brownish facial disc enclosing darker brown rings, grey-tipped bill and *dark brown eyes*. The paler *B. a. tanae* has a pale greyish facial disc with faint brown rings; top of head heavily spotted with white; eyes yellow, as are those of the larger *B. a. africanus*. Young birds resemble adults of their respective races, but tend to be browner and less spotted. **VOICE:** Male gives a mellow *ho-hoo* (second note lower); female utters a tremulous trisyllabic *hoo, whoo-hoo* in duet with the male or a few seconds later. Both sexes also give single *hoo* notes. **HABITS:** Nocturnal, calling at dusk. Usually hunts from low tree branch or roadside fencepost, but may run on ground after prey; feeds on large insects (at times around lights), other invertebrates, toads, small mammals and birds. Roosts by day in tree, cliff crevice or building, with compressed body plumage and erect

ear-tufts. **SIMILAR SPECIES**: Cape Eagle-Owl is much larger, with orange eyes and more boldly blotched ventral plumage. Paler milky-grey Verreaux's Eagle-Owl has whitish facial disc with broad black margins, dark brown eyes and bright pink upper eyelids. **STATUS AND DISTRIBUTION**: Fairly common and widespread between sea level and 2000 m, in varied habitats from rock outcrops, wooded ravines and gorges to forest edges, desert oases and suburban gardens. *B. a. cinerascens* ranges south to the Kerio Valley, Baringo, Isiolo, Meru and Wajir Districts; *B. a. tanae* is known along the Tana River from Garissa to Garsen and inland to the Lali Hills; nominate *africanus* in w., cent. and s. Kenya and throughout n. Tanzania. Rare in coastal lowlands, where known only from Mombasa and Lamu.

VERREAUX'S EAGLE-OWL *Bubo lacteus*   Plate 55
(Giant Eagle-Owl)

Length 580–660 mm (23–26"). The common large owl of acacia groves and riverine woodland. Pale milky grey or grey-brown below, with fine dark vermiculations visible at close range; upperparts pale grey-brown with whitish vermiculations. **Adult** has *whitish facial discs broadly bordered laterally with black. Eyes deep brown, with bright pink bare upper eyelids* conspicuous when bird blinks; ear-tufts broad, rather short, often inconspicuous. Bill pale creamy horn, dark grey at base, with blue-grey cere. **Juvenile** has narrower black facial borders, shorter ear-tufts. **VOICE**: A deep husky *hoo-hoo*, far-carrying, singly or in series of three to five calls. Female's voice deeper than that of male. Both sexes may give a more irregular grunting *wuh, wu-wuh-wuh*. **HABITS**: Nocturnal, but frequently hunts during early evening; often perches on exposed branches during daytime. Runs on the ground after prey, and wades into water after fish. Preys extensively on hedgehogs; also on birds and mammals to size of spring-hare and genets. **SIMILAR SPECIES**: See Spotted and Cape Eagle-Owls. **STATUS AND DISTRIBUTION**: Common and widespread from sea level to near 3000 m, in woodland, gallery forest and cultivation with surviving tall trees. Absent only from arid parts of n. and ne. Kenya.

USAMBARA EAGLE-OWL *Bubo vosseleri*   Plate 123
(Nduk Eagle-Owl)

Length *c.* 480 mm (19"). A large owl of Tanzania's Usambara Mountains. **Adult** tawny-brown above with darker brown barring; underparts creamy white, with heavy tawny-brown blotching on breast and widely spaced irregular darker bars on belly and under tail-coverts. Facial disc pale tawny, broadly black-bordered at sides; ear-tufts long and tawny-brown. Bill bluish white; *eyes dull yellowish orange or pale orange-brown* (not dark brown), with bluish-white eyelids; feet whitish. **Juvenile** resembles adult, but white-spotted scapulars form a distinct line, which disappears after first moult. Eyes probably brown. **VOICE**: A deep, far-carrying *ub-a-wb-a-wb-wb-a*, of several seconds' duration, ventriloquial and somewhat reminiscent of the 'winnowing' of Common Snipe (Evans *et al.* 1994). Captive birds have given a regular double note similar in quality to the call of West African *B. poensis* but distinct in pattern (White 1974). **HABITS**: Strictly nocturnal; vocal only after dark (20.00 to 04.30 hours), not at dusk or dawn. Presumably restricted to the forest canopy. **SIMILAR SPECIES**: No other eagle-owl inhabits the Usambaras. African Wood Owl is smaller and lacks ear-tufts. **STATUS AND DISTRIBUTION**: Rare endemic resident of evergreen forest and forested borders of tea plantations between 200 and 1500 m in the Usambara Mts. Possibly more numerous at lower elevations. **NOTE**: Formerly considered conspecific with West African *B. poensis*.

PEL'S FISHING OWL *Scotopelia peli*   Plate 55

Length *c.* 610 mm (24"). A large, round-headed, *rufous* owl of *riverine trees*. Upperparts finely barred with dusky; underparts paler rufous with dark brown streaks and spots; individually variable. Rufous-buff tail has narrow dark bars, most noticeable on underside. Eyes dark brown; bill black. **Female** paler than male. **Juvenile** still paler, at first *white with rufous wash* on head and underparts, the latter with faint dusky streaks; obscure dusky barring on back, heavier posteriorly. **VOICE**: An echoing hoot, often followed by a deeper and softer grunt: *hoooommmm-hut*, audible for a considerable distance; also a repeated horn-like *hoom, hoom*. Members of a pair may duet, the male starting with a grunting *uh-uh-uhu. . .* leading to higher *hoommm*, this answered by deeper hoot of female (Maclean 1984). Also gives a loud, descending wail, *weeeeaaow*. **HABITS**: Roosts by day in large shady trees whose branches overhang the water. Feeds on surface fish and other aquatic animals, hunted from low branch or river bank. Flushes noisily. **STATUS AND DISTRIBUTION**: Rare and local resident along major rivers from sea level to 1700 m. In Kenya, known from the Tana River upstream to Meru NP and Kiambere, and from secluded areas along the Mara River. Formerly recorded from Arusha Chini (south of Moshi), but no recent n. Tanzanian records.

PEARL-SPOTTED OWLET *Glaucidium perlatum licua* Plate 56

Length 180–190 mm (7–7.5"). A small, partly diurnal owl, *heavily rufous-streaked below*, and with prominent white eyebrows, generally whitish face and bright yellow eyes. *Long-tailed* (except in moult). Upperparts mainly warm brown, with two *large dark brown 'eye spots' on back of head*; crown and nape white-dotted. Rows of larger white spots form bands on flight feathers and tail. Bill greenish yellow. **Juvenile** resembles adult, but is less spotted on crown and back. **VOICE:** Variable. Most frequent is a prolonged series of loud penetrating whistles, *scheeu, scheeu, scheeu . . .*, rising in pitch and increasing in volume, at first accelerating, but notes gradually becoming more widely spaced and the pitch dropping slightly. Also gives a less harsh, higher-pitched *teeu*, repeated a few times or in a long accelerating series, the notes beginning softly and becoming progressively louder. Members of a pair often call to one another, sometimes duetting. Female's voice higher-pitched. **HABITS:** Perches conspicuously, and often mobbed by other birds when abroad by day. Flight strong and undulating. When disturbed, watches observer, not closing eyes like scops owls. When alarmed, pumps tail up and down, and wags it from side to side. Vocal day and night, especially at dusk. Feeds largely on arthropods. **SIMILAR SPECIES:** African Barred Owlet is spotted on lower breast and belly, barred above and on upper breast; lacks occipital 'eye spots' on nape. Scops owls are differently patterned, have small ear-tufts and shorter tails. **STATUS AND DISTRIBUTION:** Common and widespread in acacia woodland, savanna and riparian trees between 300 and 2000 m. Absent from the Lake Victoria basin, arid parts of n. and e. Kenya and coastal lowlands.

RED-CHESTED OWLET *Glaucidium tephronotum elgonense* Plate 56

Length 190–200 mm (7.5–8"). A small owl of west Kenyan *highland forests*. **Adult** distinctly *spotted below* with sepia or black (spots more dusky and diffuse on throat). *Rufous wash (sometimes faint) across breast and along sides* and flanks. Face largely light grey, with white eyebrows connecting along sides of bill and merging with white chin. Some birds have vertical band of black on each side of bill. Head and neck mainly dark grey; upperparts otherwise dark brown or rufous-brown. Wings vary from strongly rufous-washed, with tawny-banded flight feathers, to virtually plain dark brown above. Underside of wings white, with dark tips and black-banded flight feathers. Tail dark brown or black, with three or four large white spots on inner webs of central feathers; also on inner webs of outer feathers, where conspicuous from below. Eyes and feet bright yellow; bill greenish yellow. Sexes presumably alike, but individuals show considerable variation in colour intensity. **Juvenile** undescribed. **VOICE:** A series of four to 20 hollow whistled notes, mechanical-sounding and uttered at one-second intervals, *teu teu teu teu. . .*, or a more yelping *wook. . . wook. . . wook . . .* with intervals of several seconds between series. Sometimes a double note, *wu-wook, wu-wook . . . .* **HABITS:** Said to be partly diurnal, but usually roosts in tree cavities by day. Becomes active at dusk, hunting in forest openings and at edge. Pursues large insects in forest canopy at night. Also preys on birds and rodents. **SIMILAR SPECIES:** Pearl-spotted Owlet is heavily streaked below and occupies different habitat. **STATUS AND DISTRIBUTION:** Uncommon in Mt Elgon, North Nandi, Kakamega, Mau and Trans-Mara Forests. A report from the southern Aberdares remains unconfirmed.

AFRICAN BARRED OWLET *Glaucidium capense scheffleri* Plate 56
(Barred Owl)

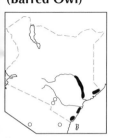

Length 200–215 mm (8–8.5"). An eastern owl, larger and with more rounded head than Pearl-spotted Owlet, but with equally prominent white eyebrows. Heavily *spotted on lower breast and belly, barred buff and brown across upper breast* and (narrowly and faintly) on upper back; tawny-brown collar on lower nape; many wing-coverts white-tipped. Facial disc grey-brown. Eyes yellow; bill greenish yellow. **Juvenile** resembles adult. **VOICE:** A series of six to 10 loud repeated notes, increasing and decreasing in volume: *kerr-kerr-kerr-kerr-KERR-KERR. . .* or *piu-piu-piu-piu-PIU-PIU-PIU-PIU-piu-piu-prr-prr-prrr. . .*, often followed immediately by a double trilled or purring whistle, the second note higher: *chrr-chrrrr, chrr-chrrrr*, repeated several times and increasing in volume. Also monotonously repeats a single note, *weu-weu-weu-weu-weu . . . .* **HABITS:** Nocturnal and partly diurnal, quite active at dusk and in early morning. Often perches in rather open sites during the day. Feeds on rodents, small birds, reptiles and amphibians, as well as arthropods. **SIMILAR SPECIES:** The smaller Pearl-spotted Owlet is heavily streaked below, has larger, more flat-crowned head, often flirts tail. **STATUS AND DISTRIBUTION:** Uncommon local resident of wooded coastal areas north to the Boni Forest and inland along the Tana River to Garissa. Scattered inland records from Kondoa, Mombo, Iltalal and Kibwezi.

AFRICAN WOOD OWL *Strix woodfordii nigricantior* Plate 55

Length 330–350 mm (13–14″). A medium-sized, *round-headed* owl with *dark brown eyes. Barred brown and whitish below*; facial disc pale buff, darkening to brown around eyes; broad eyebrows white in **adult**; crown and back dark brown with some white speckling, and with large whitish or buffy spots on scapulars; tail barred, rather long. Eyes dark brown, bare eyelids dark reddish; bill yellow. **Juvenile** resembles adult, but white facial areas duller, markings generally more diffuse, with less contrast. **VOICE**: Easily confused with that of Spotted Eagle-Owl. Individuals may give single hooting notes. Members of a pair often perform a duet, with a loud, tremulous, relatively high-pitched *WHOOOO* or *WHEEOW* or *oo-WOW-oo* from female answered by male's single low *hooo* or a longer *whu, hu-hu-hu, hu-hu*, or *ooo-wow-wow-wow-oo-waau*. **HABITS**: Nocturnal, but occasionally calls on overcast afternoons. Pairs roost in dense foliage or creeper tangles. Hunts from perch, dropping on small vertebrate prey, and catches moths and beetles in flight. **SIMILAR SPECIES**: Eagle-owls have ear-tufts (not always obvious); Verreaux's and northern race of Spotted have dark eyes, but their facial discs are black-bordered and plumage is not heavily barred below. **STATUS AND DISTRIBUTION**: Fairly common and widespread in coastal forest and woodland north to the Boni Forest, inland in n. Tanzania to the Usambara and Pare Mountains, Kilimanjaro, Arusha and Tarangire NPs, Mt Hanang and Ngorongoro; in Kenya to the Taita and Chyulu Hills, cent. and w. highlands, and north to the Cheranganis and Mt Ololokwe.

AFRICAN LONG-EARED OWL *Asio abyssinicus graueri* Plate 55

Length 420–440 mm (c. 17″). A rare *montane-forest* owl with *long, blackish-brown eartufts near centre of forehead, rich tawny-brown facial disc* and orange-yellow eyes. Upperparts dark brown with some paler tawny mottling. Underparts mottled tawny and dark brown on breast, with irregular tawny and whitish barring on belly. Tail heavily barred brown and pale tawny-brown. **Juvenile** undescribed. **VOICE**: Believed to be a disyllabic *OOOOO-oooomm*, drawn out and rising slightly in pitch. **HABITS**: Strictly nocturnal. May feed over moorlands adjacent to forest. Ethiopian birds roost in giant heath and prey largely on small mammals. **SIMILAR SPECIES**: Cape Eagle-Owl is much larger, with more laterally positioned ear-tufts and largely whitish belly and feet. **STATUS AND DISTRIBUTION**: Known from a single specimen taken in *Hagenia* forest at 3350 m on Mt Kenya, September 1961. Possible sight records from 2800 m on that mountain in August 1975, and at 3500 m in July 1992. **NOTE**: Often considered conspecific with the holarctic *A. otus*.

SHORT-EARED OWL *Asio f. flammeus* Plate 55

Length c. 380 mm (15″). A rare *yellow-eyed* ground owl of open areas. **Adult** *pale tawnybuff* with *broad dark streaks*, darker on breast; *facial disc pale buff, shading to dusky around eyes*; short ear-tufts in centre of forehead usually not noticeable. Bill blackish. Dark carpal patch on pale underside of wings conspicuous in flight. **VOICE**: Probably silent in Africa. **HABITS**: Partly diurnal. Favours open marshy areas, where it hunts in low flight, slowly flapping and gliding, then dropping on to prey. Roosts on or near ground in tall grass or bushes. **SIMILAR SPECIES**: Marsh Owl is much darker brown, has brown eyes. See African Grass Owl. **STATUS AND DISTRIBUTION**: Palearctic vagrant, known in our region from five Kenyan records, including an early specimen from Mt Elgon. Some perhaps ship-assisted, as recorded over the sea near Lamu (Nov. 1936) and off Mida Creek (Jan. 1971).

MARSH OWL *Asio c. capensis* Plate 55

Length 320–380 mm (12.5–15″). A *dark-eyed* brownish owl of *open grasslands*. Quite uniformly *dull brown* above, except for buff tail bars and *large pale buff patch in primaries conspicuous in flight*; secondaries darker with pale trailing edges. Wings appear long; underside shows large dark patch at carpal joint. Appears round-headed; short ear-tufts on forehead are seldom obvious in the field. Underparts brown, variably barred and vermiculated with buff. Female generally darker than male. *Eyes dark brown*; bill blackish. **Juvenile** has darker, blackish-rimmed facial disc. **VOICE**: A harsh croaking *zheeeow* or *creeow* when perched or when circling overhead. Also gives a shorter repeated croak, *crrk-crrk-crrk* or *quark*. Squeals near nest. Fledged young give hissing *shreeeeeeee* when soliciting food from adults. **HABITS**: Solitary, in pairs or small groups. Mainly crepuscular and nocturnal, but diurnal in cloudy weather. Watches for rodents from fenceposts, stumps or low trees, and also hunts by flying low over grass, abruptly twisting and dropping on to prey like a harrier. Roosts and nests on the ground. **SIMILAR SPECIES**: African Grass Owl is larger, with prominent white tail sides. Rare Short-eared Owl is paler above, not dark brown, and has yellow eyes. **STATUS AND DISTRIBUTION**: Locally common in areas of extensive grassland between 1300 and 2000 m, notably in n. Tanzania and Kenya north to the central Rift Valley, Nairobi NP and Mt Kenya; small numbers on the Laikipia Plateau and in Trans-Nzoia.

NIGHTJARS, FAMILY CAPRIMULGIDAE
(World, 75 species; Africa, 22; Kenya, 15; n. Tanzania, 10)

Crepuscular or nocturnal birds with marvellously soft owl-like plumage, intricately cryptic in pattern and coloration. They are big-headed, with large eyes, small weak bills, and well-developed rictal bristles for funnelling insect prey, caught on the wing, into the huge gape. Their feet are small and weak, the tarsi sometimes partly feathered, and the middle toenail pectinate. They spend their daylight hours well camouflaged on the ground or perched lengthwise on tree branches. Although solitary, numbers of nightjars may be attracted to insect concentrations. The eggs, incubated by both male and female, are laid on bare ground, rocks or leaf litter; there is no nest. The nidicolous downy young are cared for by both sexes. One of our species is a migrant from Eurasia; three others are mainly non-breeding intra-African migrants.

This group presents major problems in field recognition, though their nocturnal calls, once learned, are distinctive. Some species have long churring songs, others produce melodious whistles, and a few give series of yelping, chucking or chopping sounds. However, the four non-breeding visitors are largely or entirely silent in East Africa. Sight identifications made in the glare of vehicle headlights or spotlight beams often prove unreliable, and the birds are infrequently seen during daylight hours. Useful plumage features include general colour (several species exhibit grey, rufous, brown or buff morphs), extent of dorsal markings, and the amount and distribution of white (male) or buff (female) on wings and tail. The accompanying key (p. 453) will aid in identifying birds in the hand. Owing to their habit of alighting on roadways, many nightjars are killed by traffic; salvage of birds or wings in good condition for museum specimens (see p. 18) is worthwhile, as the status of several species remains poorly known. **NB:** In both key and text, wing measurements are from the bend or carpal joint to the tip of the longest primary. Wing moult can affect both wing formula and wing length.

FIERY-NECKED NIGHTJAR *Caprimulgus pectoralis*   Plate 53
(includes Black-shouldered Nightjar)

Length 225–240 mm (8.75–9.5"). A richly coloured nightjar, similar in size and pattern to Dusky Nightjar but *general colour warm brown* rather than grey-brown or dusky. (A rufous morph is known in s. Tanzania, but not from our area.) Eastern *C. p. fervidus* shows broad black streaks on the grey crown and black, cream and tawny scapulars, a broad rufous half-collar on hindneck and *rich rufous-brown ear-coverts*. There are small white moustachial lines and large white patches at sides of throat; upper breast dark rufous, finely barred with grey, black and buff. In flight, **male** shows *large white tail corners* (distal third of outer two feathers) and white spots near tips of outer five primaries; **female**'s pattern similar, but white areas buff-tinged. Wing structure similar to that of Dusky Nightjar but 10th (outermost) primary usually shorter than 7th; wing 150–176 mm. Western *C. p. nigriscapularis* has a generally brown crown with a rufous-margined black central streak, rufous half-collar marked with black, pale rufous sides of neck and inconspicuous buff moustachial lines. In the hand, note the deep rufous and buff underparts, often with sharp black barring on the under tail-coverts, black at bend of wing, and rufous speckling on the blackish tail; outer two rectrices white-tipped, central pair dark brown and rufous with five or six irregular narrow black bars; wing 147–159 mm. **VOICE**: *C. p. fervidus* has a quavering liquid whistle, trilled at the end, *keeyou-wurr, qu-weerrrrrr*; also *whi-whi-whippi-eeeu* and *tuwurrr, turrr-r-r-r*. *C. p. nigriscapularis* gives a similar *ki-yay-o, kee-yairrrrrr*, and *t'wip, tuwrr-r-r-r-r*. Both forms also have low chucking notes. **HABITS**: Behaviour of hawking from tree and returning to same perch distinctive. Vocal at dusk, before dawn, and throughout moonlit nights, singing from tree branches. **SIMILAR SPECIES**: Montane Nightjar of the highlands has similar but shriller voice. Dusky Nightjar, compared above, has churring call. **STATUS AND DISTRIBUTION**: *C. p. fervidus* is a fairly common resident of coastal forest, forest edge and rich woodland north to the Boni Forest, inland along the lower Tana River and in the Shimba Hills. Western Kenyan *nigriscapularis* is local and uncommon in Siaya, Mumias, Busia and Bungoma Districts, inhabiting riparian groves and moist thickets with low trees in grassland or cultivation. **NOTE**: These two forms are treated as separate species by some authors (Fry *et al.* 1988; Cleere 1995), but we now agree with others that there appear to be no significant differences between their calls, and that presumed morphological distinctions are not diagnostic (Louette 1990; Dowsett and Dowsett-Lemaire 1993).

MONTANE NIGHTJAR *Caprimulgus poliocephalus*   Plates 53, 123
(Abyssinian or Mountain Nightjar; includes Usambara Nightjar)

Length 210–230 mm (8.25–9"). A *dark* nightjar of the *highlands*. Widespread nominate race resembles Dusky Nightjar, with black-streaked crown, buff-spotted wing-coverts, and bold buff and black markings on the scapulars, but **male** has *outer two pairs of tail feathers almost entirely white*, as is a patch near tip of outer four primaries, conspicuous in flight. At rest, *head looks dark and rather plain, with contrasting buff or tawny-buff half-collar* on hindneck, and white throat patches; white tail areas usually concealed. **Female** has the spots near primary tips buff, not white, and a different tail pattern: outer web of outermost rectrices barred dusky and tawny, the *inner web buffy white almost to base*, and tip of next feather also buffy white. Wing 146–160 mm. Primary formula as in Dusky Nightjar. Male of smaller Tanzanian *C. p. guttifer* has dark rufous, not tawny-buff, half-collar, the white throat spots larger and bordered posteriorly with black, smaller white spots on the outer four primaries

and on tail (those on outermost rectrices 50–55 mm long). **Voice**: A shrill trilling whistle, *pee-yay-yo*, *pee-yairrrr* or *PEE-oo-Wlirrrrr*, higher-pitched than similar call of Fiery-necked Nightjar. *C. p. guttifer* gives a shorter but shriller *tureeeur-kurree*. Sclater and Moreau (1932) state that the call note of *guttifer* is a soft *kweep*, similar to that of nominate *poliocephalus*. **Habits**: Calls from tall trees and wires after dusk, before dawn and often through the night. **Similar Species**: Male African White-tailed Nightjar has similar tail pattern, but is much buffier and has dark-cheeked appearance; also has different call and prefers swampy grasslands. Dusky Nightjar shows much less white in tail. Gabon and Slender-tailed Nightjars have obvious whitish trailing secondary edges, only narrow pale tail sides, and churring calls. **Status and Distribution**: Resident. Nominate *poliocephalus* is common between 1500 and 3000 m in the w. and cent. Kenyan highlands north to Mt Elgon, the Cheranganis and Maralal, south to the Oloololo Escarpment (nw. Mara GR), the Nguruman Hills and Ol Doinyo Orok (Namanga), east to Mt Kenya and the Nyambeni and Chyulu Hills. In n. Tanzania, common in the Crater Highlands, Arusha NP and on Mt Kilimanjaro. Frequents forest edge and well-wooded areas, including suburban gardens. The race *guttifer* (sometimes considered specifically distinct) is local and uncommon between 1075 and 1700 m at forest edge and in grassland in the Usambara Mts, ne. Tanzania. **Note**: *Contra* Cleere (1995), Dowsett and Dowsett-Lemaire (1993) consider the vocal differences between races of *poliocephalus* to be merely dialectic. In addition, Louette (1990) considers there to be a cline of decreasing white in the outer rectrices from nominate *poliocephalus* through *ruwenzorii* to *guttifer*.

DONALDSON-SMITH'S NIGHTJAR *Caprimulgus donaldsoni*   Plate 53

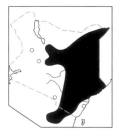

Length 180–190 mm (7–7.5"). The *smallest* African nightjar, usually richly coloured. *Scapulars always boldly edged with bright yellowish buff*, and *wing-coverts and breast marked with small buff or cream spots*; crown streaked with black. White throat patch conspicuous, as, often, are the pale moustachial lines. Common **rufous morph** *largely cinnamon-rufous to deep russet on head, upperparts and breast*, with black, grey and buff markings; back mostly grey, with scattered rufous feathers and fine dark vermiculations; central rectrices rufous or grey, finely speckled with dark brown. **Grey morph** generally brownish grey, browner on crown centre and scapulars, with tawny half-collar on hindneck; wings grey, brown and buff; central rectrices pale grey with seven to eight faint dark bars, these usually incomplete, sometimes obsolete. Less common **brown morph** similarly patterned, but colour generally grey-brown. Intermediate birds frequent. In flight, both sexes show white spots near tips of outer four primaries and white tail corners (tips of outer two pairs of feathers). Outermost webs buff in female. In the hand, small size diagnostic; wing 119–147 mm. **Voice**: A three-note whistled phrase, *pyew-yew-tew* or *tew-wi, piree*, repeated indefinitely. **Habits**: Hunts low over small area, with bouts of quick flapping followed by long glides. Vocal on moonlit nights, when it sings from the ground. Roosts under shrub during the day. **Similar Species**: Nubian Nightjar is larger and usually much paler, purer grey; scapulars have buffy-cinnamon or rufous tips instead of long yellow-buff edges. **Status and Distribution**: A locally common resident of dry eastern thorn-scrub and open bush from sea level to 1250 m, in Kenya ranging west to the Horr Valley, Lake Baringo and Loitokitok. In n. Tanzania, only in the Mkomazi GR and on the Masai Steppe west to Naberera. Often the commonest nightjar throughout the Tsavo region and e. Kenya, including ne. border areas.

NUBIAN NIGHTJAR *Caprimulgus nubicus torridus*   Plate 53

Length 210–230 mm (8.25–9"). A rather colourful nightjar of *dry country*. Typically *pale*, the *crown silvery grey with rufous-and-black markings in centre*; plumage otherwise sandy buff, brownish grey or light silvery grey, *with bright rufous-buff half-collar* on hindneck and numerous *large sandy or rufous-buff spots on wing-coverts*. Prominent white patch at each side of throat. Several tail feathers rufous with sepia bands, the central pair typically silvery grey with a few narrow blackish bands and fine vermiculations. *Large rufous wing patch* (greater coverts and bases of many remiges) conspicuous when bird is flushed during the day; in flight, appears generally pale or rufous with small white or buffy-white tail corners and, in **male**, a white bar formed by spots near tips of primaries 6–10. **Female** has male's tail pattern, but the white primary spots are smaller and tinged buff or rufous. **Rufous morph** tinged with cinnamon-rufous almost throughout, and most spots on wing-coverts deeper rufous. Uncommon **dark morph** generally browner, almost dusky, on throat and breast, but grey-crowned and with numerous large rufous-buff spots on upperparts. Some typically pale-bodied birds have dark tail with almost no rufous, the outer feathers mainly brown except for the white tips, the central pair deep sepia, obscuring the black bands; margins fringed with pale cinnamon. Wing 140–164 mm. **Voice**: A double, somewhat liquid *kwua-kwua*, steadily repeated at intervals of a few seconds; can recall distant barking poodle; sometimes becomes an excited triple note (Hollom *et al.* 1988). Also interpreted as *ow-wow* and said to be indistinguishable as a sonagram from call of Freckled Nightjar. Similar call heard at night in Dida Galgalu desert, n. Kenya (June 1975), but bird not seen, and no African recordings known. If *torridus* is mainly a non-breeding visitor to Kenya, it may be silent here. **Similar Species**: Smaller Donaldson-

Smith's Nightjar has prominent buff scapular edges. Dusky Nightjar is much darker above and on breast than the darkest *torridus*, and male shows larger white spots on tail corners. Plain and Star-spotted Nightjars are sparsely speckled above. **STATUS AND DISTRIBUTION**: Widespread in arid/semi-arid bush and bushed grassland between 600 and 1250 m, north and east of the Kenyan highlands. Ranges south through Meru and Tsavo NPs to border areas around Lake Jipe (but as yet unrecorded from Tanzania), mainly November–March. Largely and perhaps entirely a non-breeding visitor from Somalia, although June–August records from Samburu GR and Ijara suggest some birds present all year (collected adults have been in non-breeding condition, but a juvenile from Lodwar, 25 July 1956, may have been raised locally). **NOTE**: *Contra* recent treatment, we follow Mackworth-Praed and Grant (1952) in treating *taruensis* as a synonym of *torridus*, a variable bird ranging from greyish to bright rufous, with measurements encompassing those of *taruensis*.

FRECKLED NIGHTJAR *Caprimulgus t. tristigma*   Plate 54
(Rock Nightjar)

Length 230–255 mm (9–10"). A *dark, thickset* nightjar of *rocky places*, unique in its *almost uniform blackish-grey upperparts with fine pale speckling*; has few coarse markings and no contrasting colour on hindneck, appearing plain above except at close range. Head noticeably large; white throat patches more prominent in **male**, which in flight shows small white tail corners and white spots on inner webs of outer three or four primaries. **Female** has similar wing pattern but lacks white tail spots. In the hand, freckled pattern diagnostic; often a dusky streak on outer web of outermost rectrices of male; wing 184–205 mm. **VOICE**: A yelping two- or three-note *OW-wow* or *ow-WOW-WOW*, frequently repeated. Also an irregular *wuu-wu-wu-wuu*. Gives a triple *kluk-kluk-kluk* when disturbed. **HABITS**: By day, roosts on or among rocks, often exposed. Especially vocal just after sunset and before dawn, but also throughout moonlit nights. Locally, calls regularly from roofs of buildings. **SIMILAR SPECIES**: Plain Nightjar is smaller, paler, more uniformly coloured and with churring call. Star-spotted Nightjar is more uniform (small semi-stellate black spots on crown and scapulars visible only at close range) and with large white throat patches; also differs vocally. **STATUS AND DISTRIBUTION**: Local resident on rocky hills, escarpments and outcrops and in ravines between 600 and 2000 m along eastern edge of the cent. Kenyan highlands south to Tsavo and the Taita Hills; also common in the Tugen Hills and adjacent Kerio Valley, north to the Turkwell Gorge and Lokitaung. Scarce in n. Tanzania, although resident around kopjes in Serengeti NP.

STAR-SPOTTED NIGHTJAR *Caprimulgus stellatus simplex*   Plate 54

Length 220–230 mm (8.75–9"). A *stocky, plain-looking* nightjar of *arid northern Kenya*. Similar to Plain Nightjar but still plainer, and readily distinguished from it by *prominent white throat patch* (usually divided by dark midline) and smaller white tail corners; head appears larger and tail shorter than in Plain Nightjar. General plumage colour variable: rufous, grey, buff or sandy brown above, but always with *largely plain back* and *tiny, more or less stellate black spots on crown and scapulars*. Rufous birds have been mistaken for Nubian Nightjar in field and museum, but that species has larger spots on crown and conspicuous pale cinnamon spots on scapulars and wing-coverts. In flight, **male** shows small white tail corners (distal fifth of outer two feather pairs) and white spots on inner webs of outer three or four primaries. **Female** resembles male, but white wing spots smaller; differs from female Plain Nightjar in having white, not buff, patches on primaries and tail corners. In the hand, delicate dorsal markings unique; 7th primary about equal to outermost (10th), 6th to 9th emarginate (cf. Plain Nightjar); wing 151–162 mm. **VOICE**: A repeated yelping *pweu, pweu, pweu. . .* at c. 1.5 notes/sec., uttered from ground. Also a guttural *churr-krrk* (M. North). **SIMILAR SPECIES**: Plain Nightjar compared above. All other caprimulgids are more coarsely marked. Freckled Nightjar is darker, with extensive fine speckling and dorsal vermiculation. **STATUS AND DISTRIBUTION**: Locally common in n. Kenya on lava rock-strewn deserts with scattered areas of bare sandy soil. Ranges from northern border areas south to Lodwar, the southern end of Lake Turkana and Marsabit. Occasionally wanders south to the Kongelai Escarpment, Lake Baringo (specimen, Oct. 1986), northern Laikipia Plateau and Shaba GR. Some northern records possibly refer to nominate *C. s. stellatus*.

PLAIN NIGHTJAR *Caprimulgus inornatus*   Plate 54

Length 230 mm (9"). *Plain-looking, rather long-tailed* and with *no white throat patch*. Coloration variable (pale cinnamon, rufous, or grey-brown above), but delicate pattern constant: fine black speckling (less commonly narrow sparse black streaks) on crown and scapulars, and a few inconspicuous streaks on back and nape. Breast brownish, pale rufous or cinnamon, usually darker than throat and the finely barred belly. Shows pale bar across lesser coverts at rest. In flight, **male** shows *large white tail corners* (distal third of two outer feathers) and band of white spots across outer four primaries. **Female** similar, but white in wings replaced by buff, the outer rectrices not strongly barred at tips, but with no pale patches. In the hand, note long (148–166 mm) wing; outermost primary longer than 7th, and 7th much shorter than 8th; only 8th and 9th emarginate (cf. Star-spotted Nightjar).

VOICE: A prolonged, very rapid churring, almost buzzing, much like that of Eurasian Nightjar (not heard in East Africa). Apart from a low *chuck* when disturbed, mostly silent here, except perhaps in extreme nw. Kenya. HABITS: Spends the day among rocks or on ground, often under a bush. Crepuscular and nocturnal. Flies erratically, may clap wings when flushed. Sometimes alights in trees. SIMILAR SPECIES: Star-spotted Nightjar is also quite plain above, but shows much white on throat and less white in tail corners; wings are more rounded. Freckled Nightjar is larger and blackish grey, with distinctive voice. Perched Eurasian Nightjar also shows pale wing-bar, but is larger and boldly patterned. STATUS AND DISTRIBUTION: An intra-African migrant, regular in dry bush and bushed grassland between sea level and 1800 m. Mainly a non-breeding visitor, October–April. Breeds from Sudan east to nw. Somalia, possibly in nw. Kenya. Regular migrant through n. and e. Kenya, October–December. Spring records (March–April) indicate a northward movement through Olorgesailie, Tsavo, the Usambara Mts and the coastal lowlands.

AFRICAN WHITE-TAILED NIGHTJAR *Caprimulgus n. natalensis*   Plate 53
(Swamp or Natal Nightjar)

Length 210–225 mm (*c.* 8.5"). A buff-and-brown, dark-masked, west Kenyan species, boldly marked with *large black spots above (especially on scapulars)*; dark brown *breast heavily spotted with buff,* and *broad buff collar extends nearly from the whitish throat patch around hindneck*; mask, formed by prominent *dark lores and auriculars*, contrasts with pale *superciliary and moustachial stripes*. In flight, **male** shows *white tail sides* (outer two pairs of feathers white to near base) and white bar formed by spots on outer four or five primaries. Wing spots of **female** partly tinged buff or pale rufous; her outer rectrices buff-tipped, the outer web dirty white for most of its length. In the hand, note *large breast spots, unmarked pale buff belly and crissum*, and rather long tarsi; wing 145–167 mm. VOICE: A monotonous, long-continued *tsuk-tsuk-tsuk-tsuk. . .* or *chook-chook-chook. . .*; sometimes a harder, more emphatic *kew-kew-kew. . . .* In flight, utters a tremulous *wuwuwuwuwuwu.* HABITS: Crepuscular and nocturnal. Flies low. Often in tall grass along borders of woods and swamps, where it roosts on and calls from the ground, typically in small clearings. Occasionally perches on low tree branches. SIMILAR SPECIES: Male Montane Nightjar of the highlands, also with white-sided tail, is a dark *dusky* bird with plainer head and more contrasting tawny-buff half-collar restricted to hindneck; has whistling call. Gabon and Slender-tailed Nightjars have longer tails with narrower pale edges, and churring calls. STATUS AND DISTRIBUTION: Local and uncommon in wet grassland and grassy woodland edges and clearings, from Mt Elgon and Trans-Nzoia south through Kakamega, Mumias and Busia Districts to the Yala Swamp and Lake Kanyaboli. Has reportedly wandered to Lake Baringo. Numbers probably declining as western grasslands yield to sugarcane and maize.

DUSKY NIGHTJAR *Caprimulgus fraenatus*   Plate 53
(Sombre Nightjar)

Length 210–230 mm (8.25–9"). A thickset *dark* nightjar with a *rufous-tawny half-collar on hindneck, bold black and creamy-buff markings on scapulars, cream-spotted wing-coverts* and *dark ear-coverts*; otherwise dark grey-brown above with a few black streaks, heavily mottled with black on crown and upper back. Also shows narrow white moustachial lines and a large white patch at each side of throat; dusky brown breast finely barred with buff; belly buff with dark barring. Outermost primary about equal to 7th, and 7th to 9th emarginate; wing 152–174 mm. In flight, **male** shows white tail corners and white spots on outer three or four primaries. **Female** paler above than male, often much greyer; spots on primaries smaller and buff or pale tawny; tail corners dirty white. VOICE: A steady rapid churring, mechanical-sounding and may continue for 50 or 60 seconds, occasionally interrupted by a brief low *querk*. The churring may begin with a soft *wowka-wowka* or end with *kyow-kyow-kyow*. Flight note a liquid *quick*. HABITS: Roosts on ground; does not fly far when flushed. Flight consists of quick flapping and alternating glides. Active and vocal at dusk and dawn. Subject to local movements apparently related to vegetation cover. Favours areas with long grass and dense herbaceous growth. Sometimes calls from arborescent *Euphorbia* or tree branch well above ground. SIMILAR SPECIES: Equally dark Montane Nightjar has white or buff tail edges. Eurasian Nightjar is paler, greyer, longer-winged, longer-tailed and with streaked crown. Gabon Nightjar has narrow white (male) or buff (female) tail edges, pale trailing wing edges and, in male, a white wing-covert bar. Slender-tailed Nightjar has pattern of Gabon Nightjar and shows slightly projecting central rectrices. Fiery-necked Nightjar is more richly coloured, with rufous-brown cheeks, is more arboreal, and has whistling call. African White-tailed Nightjar is paler, buffier, and with more white in tail. STATUS AND DISTRIBUTION: In Kenya, wide-ranging in open bush, grassland and scrubby hillsides from below 650 m to 2000 m on slopes of Mt Elgon and Mt Kenya. Mainly in dry country from Maralal and the Laikipia Plateau, south through the central Rift Valley and adjacent highlands to Narok District and the Loita Plains, and Amboseli and Tsavo NPs. In n. Tanzania, a common resident throughout Arusha District west to Mbulumbulu and southeast to Same. Although formerly reported from Marsabit, Wajir and Kisumu, it remains largely absent from arid n. and e. Kenya, the Lake Victoria basin and the coastal lowlands.

EURASIAN NIGHTJAR *Caprimulgus europaeus* Plate 54

Length 240–265 mm (9.25–10.5"). A large nightjar, longer-winged and longer-tailed than most others. *Dark ear-coverts, blackish 'shoulder' feathers* and a *pale bar across lesser wing-coverts* often noticeable in resting birds. *Crown and upperparts streaked with black. Lacks contrasting half-collar on hindneck.* In flight, **male** shows white tail corners (tips of outer two rectrices) and white spots on outer three (sometimes four) primaries. These marks absent in **female** and **immature.** Nominate *europaeus* is brownish grey; shorter-winged *meridionalis* more silvery grey; *unwini* is paler grey, less extensively black-streaked and with unbarred under tail-coverts; *plumipes* is pale cinnamonbuff. In all races, 7th primary much shorter than outer three (nos. 8–10), and only 8th and 9th emarginate on outer web; wing 178–202 mm. VOICE: A sharp *quoik* or nasal *kweep* given on take-off and in flight; otherwise silent in Africa. HABITS: Perches on tree limbs more than most resident species. Agile and active, flying with deep wingbeats and short glides, ascending and then swooping low, but not skimming the ground. Although not vocal here, it responds to playback of recorded calls by flying nearby. SIMILAR SPECIES: Dusky Nightjar also has dark-cheeked look, but is shorter-tailed, generally darker, with mottled crown, contrasting hindneck and more white on primaries; female has buff primary spots and more rounded wing. STATUS AND DISTRIBUTION: Palearctic migrant, recorded mainly late October to November and late March to early April, when widespread and locally numerous in bushed, wooded and cultivated habitats from sea level to above 2000 m. Locally common in the Rift Valley and e. Kenya during southward migration, and northbound birds regular in the coastal lowlands. Distribution of subspecies unclear, but about 50 per cent of birds ringed in Tsavo West NP, October–November, are *unwini* and *plumipes*.

GABON NIGHTJAR *Caprimulgus fossii welwitschii* Plate 53
(Square-tailed or Mozambique Nightjar)

Length 210–230 mm (8.25–9"). Closely resembles Dusky Nightjar in body colour and pattern, but **male** distinguished from it by a *white bar across lesser coverts combined with white trailing edge of secondaries,* narrow white outer tail edges and corners. Shares these features with Slender-tailed Nightjar but *central tail feathers do not extend beyond the others.* Kenyan birds have white spots on outer five primaries, instead of on outer six or seven as in Slender-tailed. In **female,** pale areas of wings and tail largely cinnamon-buff. Presumed immature female shows less buff on outer rectrix, where replaced by dull brown near tip. Resting bird appears sooty brown, with tawny halfcollar on hindneck, densely mottled black crown, pale moustachial lines, prominent white throat patch (sometimes divided), broad black and golden-buff edging on scapulars, and dark ear-coverts. When flushed by day, male appears dark-winged except for the whitish bands; female shows more cinnamon-rufous in flight feathers, and the pale primary patch is half cinnamon (white reduced to inner webs of outer four feathers). Pale trailing wing edge obvious in flight. In the hand, distinguished from Slender-tailed Nightjar by *darker and shorter central rectrices,* which are brownish grey or grey-brown with *mostly complete broad black bands*; obsolete or no white or buff spot on 6th primary. Wing formula as in Dusky Nightjar; wing 149–170 mm. VOICE: A sustained low churring, easily confused with call of Dusky Nightjar, but *alternately accelerating and decelerating*; may end with a short *whoop.* Sometimes gives a hollow-sounding *a-whoop-whoop-whoop* in flight. Although locally vocal in Tanzania and possibly in Mara GR, no definite Kenyan records of singing birds. HABITS: Crepuscular and nocturnal; makes short hunting sallies low over ground or water. Occasionally perches on low bushes. Roosts by day in grass under shrub or tree. SIMILAR SPECIES: Slender-tailed and Dusky Nightjars compared above. STATUS AND DISTRIBUTION: Locally common in bushed grassland, woodland borders or clearings and river banks, mainly below 1500 m, usually in areas of moderate rainfall. Sometimes in places occupied by Slender-tailed Nightjar. Resident on Pemba Island and probably breeds locally in mainland cent. and n. Tanzania, ranging as a non-breeding visitor to Tsavo and coastal lowlands north at least to the Arabuko–Sokoke Forest and Mida Creek. Additional specimen records from Serengeti NP and Mara GR north to Kilgoris and Kericho, but reports from Olorgesailie, Kiambu and farther north require confirmation.

SLENDER-TAILED NIGHTJAR *Caprimulgus clarus* Plate 53

Length 215–245 mm (8.5–9.75"). A slim, long-tailed nightjar, *usually with central rectrices projecting 5–10 mm beyond the others* in females, up to 25 mm in males, these feathers typically pale grey or brownish grey and the transverse blackish bands narrow, incomplete, or obsolete on one web. Plumage otherwise as in Gabon Nightjar but somewhat paler and often greyer, top of head less black and more streaked than mottled. Wing 133–155 mm, the pattern as in Gabon and Long-tailed Nightjars, but well-developed white or buff spots on six or seven outer primaries (on only four or five in Gabon Nightjar). VOICE: A slow churring or chattering, continuing for several minutes, *chk-chk-chk-chk-chk-chk-chk.* . . or *tu-tu-tu-tu.* . . at six to eight notes/sec., with each note evident and steady except for slight acceleration toward end, and terminating with a soft *kyor-kyor.* Flight call *wik-wik-wicku-wik-wicku.* HABITS: Much like

those of Gabon Nightjar. Flies low and alights on bare ground, rock or stump, often flying only a short distance after being flushed. Commonly hawks insects around lights. Sings from ground or from low tree. Roosts on ground under shrub cover. **Similar Species**: Gabon Nightjar compared above. Female Long-tailed Nightjar often is more rufous, less dusky, usually with longer tail, the central rectrices less heavily marked and typically with at least nine bars (five to seven in Slender-tailed). **Status and Distribution**: Common and widespread resident of scrub and dry bush below 2000 m. Ranges throughout the coastal lowlands, the Rift Valley, and over much of dry n. and e. Kenya, south through Meru and Tsavo NPs to the Mkomazi GR, Masai Steppe and west to Serengeti NP. Largely absent from western border areas and the Lake Victoria basin, but several early specimen records from the shore of Lake Victoria at Kisumu. Northern Kenyan birds are the longer-tailed *apatelius*, intergrading north of the Equator with southern *C. c. clarus*. **Note**: Formerly considered conspecific with *C. fossii*, but vocally distinct. Has also been merged with Long-tailed Nightjar.

LONG-TAILED NIGHTJAR *Caprimulgus climacurus sclateri*　　　　　Plate 54

Length 265–395 mm (10.5–15.5"), including *200–265 mm (8–10.5") central tail feathers*. Generally resembles Slender-tailed Nightjar, except in tail length. Some birds washed with rufous, exceptional individuals almost chestnut. **Male** has narrow white tail edges plus white tips to outermost two pairs of rectrices. In flight, the long central feathers project straight out behind; *white spots on outer four primaries only*, plus *white trailing edges and wing-bars formed by tips of secondaries and lesser and median wing-coverts* respectively. **Female** has shorter tail; pale areas of wing partly buff. Wing 138–160 mm. Birds with tail in moult easily confused with Slender-tailed Nightjar. **Voice**: A steady, low-pitched, rapid churring, distinct from that of Slender-tailed and Gabon Nightjars; at distance has purring quality. Also a faint *tsip-tsip* and a twangy *chew-chew-chew*. **Habits**: Crepuscular and nocturnal. Forages low. Roosts on ground, but may perch on low tree branches at night. **Similar Species**: Slender-tailed Nightjar compared above. **Status and Distribution**: Scarce and local resident in savanna and bushed grassland in nw. Kenya. Probably resident around Lokichokio, but undertakes regular seasonal movements as shown by records south to the Lorugumu and Turkwell Rivers and east to Lake Turkana.

PENNANT-WINGED NIGHTJAR *Macrodipteryx vexillarius*　　　　　Plate 54

Length 230–254 mm (10–12"). **Adult male in breeding plumage** unmistakable, with remarkably *long inner primaries, the extremely elongated 2nd (9th from outside) forming pale 'pennants'* projecting over twice the bird's total length; these and broad white wing-bars contrast with largely black flight feathers. **Non-breeding male** (Jan.–Feb.) has short pennants. Plumage generally rich brown above, with black mottling on crown, a tawny half-collar, and bold black-and-buff marks on scapulars; also a large white throat patch and distinctive white belly. **Female** has *long tail* and noticeably *small head*; lacks pennants and wing-bars, and has the *flight feathers barred black and chestnut*; wings long and pointed. *Neither sex shows white in the tail. Outermost primary longer than adjacent one in male, usually so in female, unique among East African nightjars.* Wing of male 200–266 mm, female 177–195 mm. **Immature** plainer and more sand-coloured above, but with distinctive barred primaries as in adult female. **Voice**: A high-pitched bat-like or insect-like squeaking, *tseek-tseek-tseek . . .*, but generally silent away from breeding grounds. **Habits**: Migrates in flocks (often including males in breeding plumage) on southward passage. Begins foraging immediately after sunset, flying high above ground, swooping spectacularly. Rests on bare ground and on roads. **Similar Species**: Female Standard-winged Nightjar is smaller (wing <185 mm), with relatively shorter tail, and outermost primary always shorter than adjacent feather. Eurasian Nightjar resembles female Pennant-winged in size and shape. **Status and Distribution**: An intra-African passage migrant to and from breeding grounds in the southern tropics. Present in Kenya and n. Tanzania July to early September, returning January–February. Frequents bushed and open habitats in the Rift Valley, w. Kenya and the Lake Victoria basin. Casual at Nairobi and in the central highlands. Scarce in n. Tanzania.

*STANDARD-WINGED NIGHTJAR *Macrodipteryx longipennis*　　　　　Plate 54

Length 185–200 mm (7.25–8"). Smaller, darker and shorter-tailed than Pennant-winged Nightjar; pattern similar to female of that species, although general colour greyer. *Flight feathers barred blackish and rich tawny.* Shows tawny half-collar on hindneck, boldly patterned scapulars and black-mottled crown; *no white in wings or tail.* **Adult male in breeding plumage** has the shafts of 2nd *primary extraordinarily elongated, each terminating in a broad flag-like racquet*. In flight, these 'standards' appear as separate objects fluttering behind and above the bird. **Non-breeding male** and **adult female** similar, but without the standards. **Immature** more sandy above, with fewer markings. Wing 158–184 mm, more rounded than in Pennant-winged Nightjar, with outermost primary shorter than 9th, but 7th much shorter than 8th, and *lacking emargination* (as in Eurasian and Plain Nightjars). **Voice**: A high-pitched, strident, orthopteran-like trilling, *seeti-seeti-seeti-seeti. . .* or *tsi-tsi-tsi-tsi. . .*, but silent in non-breeding season. **Habits**: Migrates in loose groups; sometimes singly. Mainly nocturnal; does not fly so early

in evening as Pennant-winged Nightjar. Rests by day in shaded places. Standards are moulted after arrival in non-breeding quarters. **SIMILAR SPECIES**: Pennant-winged Nightjar compared above. Plain Nightjar somewhat resembles immature Standard-winged, but primaries are not boldly barred. **STATUS AND DISTRIBUTION**: An intra-African migrant, breeding from Gambia east to n. Uganda and s. Sudan between January and May, moving north in non-breeding season. Usually in bushed grassland or savanna. Rare in nw. Kenya, where displaying males observed at Lokichokio in late March 1988. Single stray males in full breeding plumage have been seen at Lake Baringo (Jan. 1979, 1984; Nov. 1990) and in Mumias District (Dec. 1989).

KEY TO KENYAN NIGHTJARS IN THE HAND

1.	Outer primaries boldly banded tawny and black to the tips	2
1.	Outer primaries not boldly banded to the tips (may have scattered spots)	3
2.	Wing over 185 mm; 7th primary emarginate	PENNANT-WINGED fem., juv.
2.	Wing under 181 mm; 7th primary much shorter than 8th, not emarginate	STANDARD-WINGED fem., juv.
3.	Wing more than 177 mm	4
3.	Wing less than 177 mm	7
4.	Innermost primaries greatly elongated	5
4.	Innermost primaries normal length, not elongated	6
5.	Primaries with black-and-white bases and tips; wing 200–230 mm	PENNANT-WINGED male
5.	Primaries not as above; wing under 185 mm	STANDARD-WINGED male
6.	Above, generally light greyish or pale brown with black streaks; dark patch at bend of wing; 7th primary shorter than outermost (10th) and not emarginate;wing 166–202 mm	EURASIAN
6.	Above, generally blackish grey with fine light speckling; 7th primary emarginate, longer than outermost; wing 184–205 mm	FRECKLED
7.	Wing under 133 mm	DONALDSON-SMITH'S
7.	Wing over 133 mm	8
8.	Wing with distinct white (male) or buff (fem.) rear edge to secondaries; usually a white or buff band across lesser coverts, another on median coverts	9
8.	Wing not so patterned (although some species may show pale tips to secondaries, especially Dusky, Nubian and Donaldson-Smith's Nightjars)	12
9.	Central rectrices greatly elongated; tail long and pointed; wing 129–161 mm	LONG-TAILED
9.	Central rectrices equal to the others or only slightly projecting	10
10.	Central rectrices projecting up to 25 mm beyond the others, quite pale, with narrow incomplete blackish bars, these often faint, sometimes obsolete on one web; crown clearly streaked; wing 133–155 mm	SLENDER-TAILED
10.	Central rectrices not projecting beyond rest of tail, usually darker grey-brown or brownish grey, and typically with broader, mostly complete black bands; crown often more mottled; wing 149–172 mm	11
11.	Light area at tip of outermost rectrix extending up entire outer web	GABON
11.	Light area at tip of outermost rectrix not extending up outer web, which is more or less barred with buff and black; pale bars on wing-coverts obsolete or lacking	DUSKY
12.	Size small; wing 147 mm or less; often pale or rufous; large rufous-cinnamon area in primaries and coverts sometimes conspicuous in spread wing; birds of dry country	13
12.	Size larger; wing 147 mm or more; often darker and duskier (if pale rufous, then with relatively plain upperparts)	14

13. Wing 119–147 mm, usually under 137 (av. 132);
scapulars broadly edged with yellowish buff; back and wings
rufous, brown or brownish grey, variously marked   DONALDSON-SMITH'S

13. Wing 141–153 mm, usually over 145 (av. 146);
each scapular tipped with a tawny-cinnamon spot, this larger on outer
web; back and wings often pale silvery grey or sandy grey with large
cinnamon-buff spots; extensive cinnamon-rufous patch conspicuous in spread wing   NUBIAN

14. Upperparts relatively plain and uniform, with only small fine markings;
no large bold spots or stripes   15

14. Upperparts boldly patterned with large markings   16

15. White throat patch absent; white tail corners of male large,
occupying a third to half the length of the outer rectrices;
7th primary much shorter than outermost (10th), not emarginate;
wing 148–166 mm   PLAIN

15. White throat patch(es) prominent; 7th primary emarginate,
about equal to outermost; wing 152–162 mm   STAR-SPOTTED

16. Outer rectrices buff or white nearly to base (males),
or (in female Montane Nightjar) only the inner web buffy white
to base (pale areas smaller in Usambara race of Montane Nightjar, not in this key)   17

16. Outer rectrices not as above, the white or buff (if any) confined to tips   18

17. Belly and crissum pale buff, unmarked; auriculars dark and contrasting
with pale buff superciliaries; entire breast boldly marked with large buff spots;
upperparts boldly marked. Wing 145–167 mm   AFRICAN WHITE-TAILED

17. Belly/crissum with dark brown bars; face largely dark,
ear-coverts not contrasting; buff breast spots mostly at sides;
wing 146–160 mm (in *C. p. poliocephalus*; shorter in race *guttifer* from
Usambara Mts, Tanzania, not included in this key)   MONTANE

18. Outermost primary longer than 7th   19

18. Outermost primary shorter than 7th; wing 147–174 mm   20

19. Wing 164 mm or less; tawny or buff half-collar on hindneck   NUBIAN

19. Wing 166–200 mm or longer; no half-collar on hindneck   EURASIAN

20. Auriculars dark brown; throat and breast (apart from white patch)
dusky or blackish brown, barred with buff; no rufous on face or breast   DUSKY

20. Auriculars rufous-brown; breast rufescent, vermiculated grey, black or buff   FIERY-NECKED

SWIFTS, FAMILY APODIDAE
(World, 93 species; Africa, 22; Kenya, 14; n. Tanzania, 12)

Seldom seen at rest, swifts are the most aerial of birds, highly specialized, masterful fliers with long, slender wings and short square-tipped or forked tails. The head is flattened, with large eyes, the bill tiny but the gape wide. All four toes are directed forward, their claws curved and sharp for clinging to vertical surfaces; the tarsi are very short. On the wing, swifts superficially resemble swallows, but their distinctive flight is direct and fast with stiff-winged flapping and much gliding, sometimes very high. The plumage is mainly black, grey or brown, frequently offset by a white rump, tail-coverts, throat or belly; the sexes are alike. Juveniles tend to be browner and duller than adults. Most species are gregarious, and flocks may produce screaming, rasping or trilling calls. Swifts spend long periods aloft catching insects, their sole food. Some are colonial, others solitary breeders; most nest in crevices under overhangs on cliffs and buildings, in caves or trees, one species on the undersides of palm leaves. The nest of twigs, plant fibre and feathers is glued together and to the substrate with the birds' saliva.

One of our species is a palearctic migrant, another an apparent non-breeding visitor from Somalia. The others are resident and presumably breed in our region, although evidence is lacking for several. Field identification is difficult, and sight records must be treated with caution. Many dark-rumped *Apus* swifts, especially in coastal areas, cannot be positively identified on the wing given the present state of our knowledge.

SABINE'S SPINETAIL *Rhaphidura sabini*   **Plate 57**

Length 90–100 mm (3.5–4"). A rare *white-bellied* swift associated with western Kenyan forests. *Long white upper tail-coverts cover centre of tail*; rest of upperparts, throat and breast glossy blue-black. White plumage areas of

some individuals have long black shaft streaks. **VOICE**: A weak, high-pitched twittering *tsu-sit-sit-sit sireeeeeeeeee sit-sit-sit*. **HABITS**: Forages in pairs or small groups, usually high above forest, but attracted earthward by low-flying insects, and may feed just above ground over clearings ahead of advancing thunderstorms. Flight fluttery, but less bat-like than that of Böhm's Spinetail. **SIMILAR SPECIES**: Allopatric Böhm's Spinetail is smaller and much shorter-tailed. **STATUS AND DISTRIBUTION**: Formerly uncommon, now rare, in Kakamega Forest and on Mt Elgon. Few recent records.

MOTTLED SPINETAIL *Telacanthura ussheri stictilaema*   **Plate 57**
(Mottled-throated Spinetail)

Length 125 mm (5"). Sooty black with a broad white rump. Resembles Little Swift, but *throat and breast mottled* dark brown and whitish, and a *narrow white band extends down from sides of the white rump and across the lower belly* near the vent. Tail square-tipped or slightly rounded, with the feather shafts extending as spines (not visible in the field). Flight more fluttery, and appearing more laboured than that of Little Swift; wings longer, but secondaries shorter and narrower near body than in Little Swift (although wing shape of that species can appear similar under some flight conditions). **VOICE**: A soft *tt-rrit, tt-rrit*, and a longer *shree-shree-skiii-skirrrrrrrrrreeeee* or *chiti-chiti-chiti skir-rrrreeeeee*. Chapin (1939) refers to a rasping *kak-k-k-k-k*. **HABITS**: In pairs or small groups, foraging around or over trees, sometimes with Little Swifts, and typically in deciduous woodlands dominated by baobab trees; nests in hollow tree or well shaft. **SIMILAR SPECIES**: Little Swift compared above. **STATUS AND DISTRIBUTION**: Uncommon in dry woodland and open forest at low elevations, occasionally up to 2200 m. Ranges in coastal lowlands from Tanga north to the Tana River, inland in Kenya along the upper Tana and Galana/Athi river systems to Kibwezi, Kitui, Meru NP and the Nyambenis; in n. Tanzania to the Usambaras and Tarangire NP. Although usually associated with baobab trees, it is regular around the southwest corner of Mt Kenya, at Kiganjo and Mountain Lodge, September–January, with wanderers reported from the s. Aberdares (Kieni Forest).

BÖHM'S SPINETAIL *Neafrapus boehmi sheppardi*   **Plate 57**
(Bat-like Spinetail)

Length 78–85 mm (3–3.25"). A *tiny swift, appearing tailless* in the air; *broad wings with pointed tips and pinched-in look near body*; belly white, upperparts black with broad white rump patch; throat, breast and sides brownish grey. Wings have faint bluish gloss. **VOICE**: A distinctive *sitsitsit-see-tsew* or *sitisitCHE-chew*. Also a high-pitched *srree-srree-seeep*. **HABITS**: Solitary or in pairs, foraging above or around tree canopy. Flight bat-like, slow, fluttery and erratic. Nests in hollow tree or well shaft. **SIMILAR SPECIES**: See Sabine's Spinetail. **STATUS AND DISTRIBUTION**: Local and uncommon resident of woodland and forest edge, especially near baobab trees. Most frequent in coastal lowlands north to the Tana River delta, inland to the Shimba Hills and Usambara Mts. Disjunct population resident in Kitui and Kibwezi Districts of s. Kenya, where sympatric with the more numerous Mottled Spinetail. Wanderers reported north to Meru Forest.

SCARCE SWIFT *Schoutedenapus m. myoptilus*   **Plate 57**

Length 160–170 mm (*c.* 6.5"). A small *slim* swift, appearing uniformly grey or brown-ish except for *slightly paler greyish throat*. Wing length similar to that of Little Swift, but *tail long and deeply forked, pointed when closed*, recalling African Palm Swift. **VOICE**: Distinctive metallic clicking, *tik, tik . . .*, preceding or following a short rapid trill or a nasal chittering. **HABITS**: Feeds alone or with other swifts. Flight rapid and darting, with quick wingbeats. **SIMILAR SPECIES**: African Palm Swift is paler and greyer, with longer and narrower outer tail feathers. Other dark-rumped swifts are heavier-bodied, with more shallow tail fork and whiter throat. **STATUS AND DISTRIBUTION**: Typically a species of highland forest, but also over open grassland and bush, descending at times as low as 1000 m. Common on and around Mt Kenya and often elsewhere in the cent. and w. Kenyan highlands; also Arusha NP, Kilimanjaro and the West Usambaras in n. Tanzania. Recorded in the Ngurumans, Mara GR, Kakamega, Kapenguria, the Laikipia Plateau, Mathews Range, and from lower elevations near Isiolo, Thika, Nairobi, Ngulia (Tsavo West NP) and Mt Kasigau. No confirmed record of breeding in our region.

AFRICAN PALM SWIFT *Cypsiurus parvus*   Plate 57

Length 140–155 mm (5.5–6"). A small, *slender, plain brownish-grey* swift with a very *long pointed tail* (*deeply forked when spread*) and *narrow pointed wings*; throat not distinctly paler than body. Plumage has faint greenish gloss, slightly stronger in western *C. p. myochrous*. **Voice:** A thin, high-pitched twittering scream, *skiiirrrrrrrrrrr*. **Habits:** Pairs or small groups typically forage low, often around palm trees. Using saliva, bird glues its tiny nest to underside of palm or *Dracaena* leaf; eggs also glued to the nest lining. Flight graceful and darting, with quick wingbeats and less gliding than most swifts. **Similar Species:** Scarce Swift is heavier, darker and browner, shows slightly paler throat and has a shorter tail; is more likely over highland forest. **Status and Distribution:** Widespread resident and wanderer, mainly below 1400 m, but breeds locally up to 1800 m. Especially common in coastal districts. *C. p. laemostigma* ranges throughout the coastal lowlands and inland to *c.* 36°E. *C. p. myochrous* is restricted to western areas, including the Lake Victoria basin.

EURASIAN or COMMON SWIFT *Apus apus*   Plate 57
(Swift; European Swift)

Length 160–178 mm (6.25–7"). A medium-sized swift, largely sooty black (*A. a. apus*) or paler sooty brown (*A. a. pekinensis*) with a noticeable whitish throat, more prominent in *pekinensis*. *Upper surface of wings almost uniform in colour with upper back*, the inner feathers *not* forming a contrasting paler patch. **Immature** resembles adult, but forehead pale, loral areas anterior to the black spot whitish and contrasting, joining with the white throat to give a white-faced appearance. Body feathers more distinctly pale-margined than in adult. In the hand, this species distinguished from the following three swifts by 10th (outermost) primary being distinctly shorter than 9th, instead of nearly equal length. *A. a. apus* also shows the least distinct ventral barring of any. **Voice:** Believed usually silent in East Africa. The loud *screeee* or *scirrrr*, commonly heard on breeding grounds, may not be given in Africa. **Habits:** Usually gregarious in parties or flocks over open country, often with other swift species. Flight fast and powerful, with deep wingbeats. **Similar Species:** African Black Swift has darker (more blackish) body which contrasts above with pale secondaries and greater coverts. Nyanza Swift also with pale inner-wing area, is smaller and browner and has weaker flight. Mottled Swift is larger, browner, mottled below, and has less distinct pale throat. See Forbes-Watson's Swift. **Status and Distribution:** Palearctic migrant in open areas at low to medium elevations, sometimes over forest. Common on passage in w. Kenya, September–November; in Tsavo area and (mostly *pekinensis*) coastal lowlands, November–December. Flocks of silent drifting swifts seen at dusk off Watamu may represent *pekinensis*. Moves northwards in March and early April. Often present December–February over the Mara/Serengeti grasslands, and in wetter years in the Tsavo–Kibwezi–Taveta–Moshi region.

AFRICAN BLACK SWIFT *Apus barbatus roehli*   Plate 57

Length 160–175 mm (6.25–7"). *Blackish-bodied* with a white or whitish throat, like Eurasian Swift. Similar to that species in size and build, but *dark body contrasts above with paler secondaries and greater coverts*, which show as a light patch when bird banks or is viewed against dark background. Forehead always dark, without pallid appearance of many Forbes-Watson's or immature Eurasian Swifts. Underparts obscurely 'barred' (basal part of each feather paler brown than dark subterminal portion, which contrasts with white or whitish tip), more so than in Eurasian Swift, from which distinguished in the hand by outer two primaries being of equal length. Tail fork pronounced, but more shallow than in Eurasian Swift. **Voice:** A shrill twittering scream from displaying flocks. **Habits:** Gregarious, often in flocks of 100 or more around rock outcrops and over open farmland or highland forest. Often flies with other swift species. Nests and roosts in cliff crevices, in holes in forest trees (especially those with large strangler figs), and in isolated giant trees in largely cleared land. **Similar Species:** Partly sympatric Nyanza Swift shows similar dark-body/pale-secondaries contrast, but is somewhat smaller and sooty brown, not blackish; whitish throat less prominent. Eurasian Swift discussed above. Forbes-Watson's Swift is coastal. **Status and Distribution:** Locally common in parts of the w. Kenyan highlands, breeding mainly between 1600 and 2400 m. Ranges from Mt Elgon and the Cheranganis south to the Mau, Trans-Mara region and Mara GR, with smaller numbers in the Taita Hills, Arusha NP, North Pare and Usambara Mts. May wander far from forest, as shown by specimens taken at Isiolo. Few confirmed breeding records.

NYANZA SWIFT *Apus niansae*   Plate 57

Length 140–150 mm (5.5–6"). A distinctly *brown* swift with less contrasting *dull whitish chin and throat* than in the slightly larger African Black Swift. Like that species, *shows contrast between body and paler secondaries from above*. These remarks apply to the common *A. n. niansae*. Small *A. n. somalicus* (see below) is paler and greyer

brown, quite like extralimital *Apus pallidus*, which it further resembles in its large whitish throat patch. **Voice**: A descending twittering scream, reedy and strident, *zhiiii-iiiuuuuuu* or *riiiieeeeeee*, often by many birds in chorus. **Habits**: Gregarious. Often around or near rocky outcrops. Breeds colonially in cliff crevices, rarely in buildings. Noisy at breeding sites. Sometimes flocks with African Black and Mottled Swifts. **Similar Species**: African Black and nominate Eurasian Swifts are more blackish or darker brown and have more prominent whitish throat patches. (*A. apus pekinensis* is paler brown but seen mainly in and near the coastal lowlands, as is Forbes-Watson's Swift.) Mottled Swift is considerably larger, longer-tailed, and lacks dorsal-body/inner-wing contrast of Nyanza. **Status and Distribution**: *A. n. niansae* present in dry rocky country at medium and higher elevations in much of w. and cent. Kenya; common to abundant in the Rift Valley highlands and in Arusha NP. Breeds in large numbers (alongside Mottled Swift) in Hell's Gate NP near Naivasha. A specimen of the northeast African *A. n. somalicus* was collected near Mt Kenya on 2 March 1936. This form was originally considered conspecific with the Pallid Swift, *A. pallidus*. Periodic sight records of pale swifts with prominent white throats, from Samburu GR, Mt Kenya, Meru, Embu, the Nyambenis and Taita Hills, may refer to *somalicus* and/or *pallidus*, but in the absence of specimens their identity remains questionable. (*A. pallidus brehmorum* has been collected at Moroto, Uganda, near the Kenyan border.)

FORBES-WATSON'S SWIFT *Apus berliozi bensoni* Plate 57

Length 160–170 mm (6.25–6.75"). A sooty-brown *coastal* swift with well-forked tail. *Large white throat patch* prominent, as is *whitish forehead* of some individuals. (Others lack pale forehead feather tips and are grey-brown to the bill, although black pre-orbital spot always contrasts with pale sides of face and white throat; note, however, that immature Eurasian Swift can appear equally pale-faced.) Distinguished from Eurasian Swift in the hand by essentially equal length of outer two primaries, and by much *more prominent white tipping to feathers of underparts*, a feature *very rarely* visible in the field in low-flying birds. Bill lengths also differ; tomium of *bensoni* 18–20 mm, compared with 16–18 mm in *pekinensis*. Plumage generally paler than adult nominate Eurasian, but virtually identical to that of *A. a. pekinensis* (seasonally common in coastal regions) except for longer outermost primary and white ventral feather tipping. **Voice**: Probable Forbes-Watson's Swifts, tape-recorded by R. Behrstock, gave repeated nasal metallic, burry notes, *dzhhh, dzhhh. . .*, when flying towards presumed roosts on offshore islands, these calls distinct from known vocalizations of similar East African swifts. Said also to have a strident chittering scream, shorter and less shrill than that of Eurasian Swift (Fry *et al.* 1988). **Habits**: Gregarious, often in silent flocks over or adjacent to forest. **Similar Species**: Eurasian Swift, discussed above, may at times be numerous at and near the coast. African Black and Nyanza Swifts, neither of which is likely in the coastal lowlands, distinguished by dorsal-body/inner-wing contrast. **Status and Distribution**: Scarce and poorly known non-breeding migrant to coastal Kenyan lowlands, recorded October–February (specimens 6 Dec.–26 Jan.) over the Arabuko–Sokoke and Gedi Forests, Kilifi, and south to Diani, Gazi and Shimba Hills. Flocks of highly vocal swifts at dusk over Mida Creek (Nov.–Dec.), and flying towards Whale Island, probably this species. Breeds in sea caves in se. Somalia.

MOTTLED SWIFT *Apus a. aequatorialis* Plate 57

Length *c.* 200 mm (8"). An impressively *large* grey-brown swift with *mottled underparts* (visible at close range) and an indistinct whitish throat patch. Somewhat paler than the smaller Nyanza and African Black Swifts with which it often associates. Upper wing-surface uniform in colour with back. Long-winged and long-tailed. Size obvious when with other swifts, but can appear deceptively small when alone. **Voice**: Individuals and flocks vocal around nesting/roosting sites. Calls comparatively low-pitched, rapid and shrill: (1) *tsirrrrrrrrrrrrrrr, tsit-tsit-tsit;* (2) *skwi-skwi-skwi-skwi skwirrrrrrrrrrrrrrrr;* (3) *skiree-skiree chk-skiree-tsit;* (4) *zh-zh-zhrrrrrrirrrr.* **Habits**: Flies with deep powerful wingbeats and very fast glides; gregarious, and often accompanies smaller swifts. Breeds colonially in crevices on cliff faces. **Similar Species**: Slightly smaller African Black and Eurasian Swifts are darker, the whitish throat more prominent; African Black and Nyanza Swifts show contrasting pale secondaries and greater coverts from above. **Status and Distribution**: Fairly common and widespread up to 3000 m or higher, typically around cliff faces and rocky crags, but wanders widely across open country, frequently following rain storms. Ranges widely in n. Kenya from the Turkwell River gorge and the Cheranganis east to Mt Nyiru, Mt Kulal and Mt Marsabit, and south through w. and cent. Kenya to n. Tanzania's Crater Highlands, Arusha District, Mt Meru, Kilimanjaro, and the Pare and Usambara Mountains. Large numbers breed in Hell's Gate NP, near Naivasha, alongside Nyanza Swift.

WHITE-RUMPED SWIFT *Apus caffer*   Plate 57

Length 140–150 mm (5.5–6"). A *slim* black swift with contrasting *white throat* and *narrow U-shaped whitish rump* patch; *slender tail deeply forked* when feathers spread, but usually closed and *appearing pointed*; wings narrow and pointed, the secondaries with narrow whitish tips and edges. **VOICE:** A short chatter, each note distinct, *chree-chree-chree-chree-chree*; and near nesting colony a longer trill, beginning with several separated *tsip* notes. **HABITS:** Usually in pairs or small parties, often with other swifts. Nests on rocks, beneath bridges or under eaves of houses; typically utilizes old nests of Red-rumped and Striped Swallows, but may build its own nest in crevice among rocks or in tree. **SIMILAR SPECIES:** Horus and Little Swifts are stockier and have broader white band across rump. Tail of Horus Swift is more shallowly forked, that of Little Swift short and square-tipped. **STATUS AND DISTRIBUTION:** Seldom numerous, but widespread in rocky areas, open country and around towns, from the coast to over 2500 m. Scarce or absent from arid areas of n. and ne. Kenya. Range within our region closely parallels that of Red-rumped Swallow.

HORUS SWIFT *Apus h. horus*   Plate 57

Length 130–150 mm (5–6"). A rather stocky black swift with broad *greyish-white band across rump* and *whitish throat patch* extending onto breast. Tail moderately forked but outer feathers somewhat bowed and not attenuated, providing distinctive shape when spread. **VOICE:** A buzzy or reeling *rrrrreeeeeeeeeee-ew*, lower-pitched than that of White-rumped Swift, given near nesting colony. **HABITS:** Gregarious near colonial nest sites, but often feeds alone or in small groups over lakeshores and open country. Nests and roosts in earth banks, utilizing tunnels vacated by bee-eaters, kingfishers or martins. **SIMILAR SPECIES:** White-rumped Swift is slimmer, with more deeply forked tail and narrower white rump band. Little Swift is smaller, with square-tipped tail. **STATUS AND DISTRIBUTION:** Locally common breeding visitor between 1600 and 2000 m in cent. Kenya (especially cent. Rift Valley) and Tanzanian border areas from Lake Natron east to Kilimanjaro. Large numbers arrive for breeding in March, and disappear by September. Only occasional in other months. Wanderers recorded north to the Horr Valley (specimen) and east to Tsavo and the Taita Hills (sight records, Oct.–Dec.). Range within our region closely parallels that of White-fronted Bee-eater, with which it shares breeding sites.

LITTLE SWIFT *Apus a. affinis*   Plate 57

Length 120–140 mm (5–5.5"). A small *stocky* swift with a *short, square-tipped tail*. Head sooty brown, paler on forehead and with narrow dull whitish line above black lores. Otherwise black, except for *white throat and square white rump patch which extends onto flanks*; outer tail feathers pale greyish brown. **VOICE:** A shrill chittering trill, *tsitsitsitsitsitsitsi. . .*, or *si-si-tsiti-tsireeeeeeeeeeeeeee*. **HABITS:** Highly gregarious, often in flocks of hundreds; flies with other swift species. Vocal near nesting or roosting sites at dawn and dusk, wheeling in tightly packed flocks. Nests colonially under eaves of buildings or bridges, and in less populated areas on cliff faces and in gorges. **SIMILAR SPECIES:** White-rumped and Horus Swifts have forked tails. Mottled Spinetail has darker-mottled throat, white band across lower belly, is somewhat longer-winged but with shorter secondaries. **STATUS AND DISTRIBUTION:** Widespread resident, common to locally abundant from sea level up to 3000 m, foraging over all types of country and now occupying towns and villages where nesting sites were formerly lacking. Largely absent from arid parts of n. and e. Kenya.

ALPINE SWIFT *Apus melba africanus*   Plate 57

Length 210–220 mm (8.5"). A uniquely patterned *large* swift, dark brown with white underparts, latter crossed by a *broad brown breast band*; tail well forked. **VOICE:** At nest sites, a high-pitched, rising and falling scream. **HABITS:** Usually flies high, sometimes with other swifts. Nests in colonies on high rock faces. **STATUS AND DISTRIBUTION:** Presumably breeds on rocky crags above 4000 m on the higher mountains (Elgon, Kenya, Meru and Kilimanjaro). Most frequent near these massifs, but wanders widely with other swifts, recorded as far afield as Mt Marsabit, Mara GR, Serengeti, Tarangire, Amboseli and the Tsavo NPs, less often over the Arabuko–Sokoke Forest and other coastal areas near Malindi. No evidence supports the supposition that nominate *A. m. melba* reaches Kenya.

MOUSEBIRDS, FAMILY COLIIDAE
(6 species, all endemic to Africa; 3 in Kenya and n. Tanzania)

Mousebirds, or colies, are conspicuous elements of the East African avifauna, inhabiting gardens and cultivation as well as bush, savanna and forest edge. Consumers of fruit, flowers, buds and foliage, they rouse the ire of gardeners, but they consume vast quantities of insects. The common name stems from their habit of scampering mouse-like along branches; they climb well, using bill and feet, and frequently hang upside-down or assume other odd positions. They are short-billed, crested birds with a long, stiff graduated tail. The tarsi are short and thick, the sharp-clawed toes strong and the outer ones reversible. When clinging to a branch, the second and third toes (and sometimes the first and fourth) are directed forward. The birds roost communally, tightly bunched together. Flight is straight, with whirring beats of the short wings alternating with long glides. Although gregarious, they are solitary breeders, building cup-shaped nests in shrubs or trees and laying two to four whitish eggs, sometimes with a few brown markings.

SPECKLED MOUSEBIRD *Colius striatus*   Plate 58

Length 300–360 mm (12–14"). A *brown* mousebird with *brown crest*, greyish-white or silvery-grey cheeks, duskier around eyes and on throat, and the buff-tinged breast finely speckled with dusky. Fine barring on neck, throat and breast visible at close range (more conspicuous in the paler coastal race). Bill black above, with small blue spot on culmen, pinkish below, sometimes black-tipped; feet deep rose-pink with blackish claws; orbital skin dusky; iris colour varies from brown in coastal *mombassicus*, to greenish yellow and white, as well as brown, in the interior races. **Juvenile** has short crest, bare blackish nape and a narrow pale stripe down centre of back; maxilla pale greenish or black, mandible black or grey. **VOICE:** Usual contact call a soft *siu-siu;* in flight, *chew* or *chew-chew;* a *zik-zik* of alarm; a harsh *cheek-tseek-chiack* (and variations); sometimes a longer thin *seeeeeeeet, tseet chireeeeeet,* plus other soft weak notes.
HABITS: Bold yet suspicious around humans. Highly social, feeding together, 'loafing' and allopreening. Birds frequently hop along on the ground, where they dust-bathe and sometimes eat soil. They roost in tight groups of 12–20 or more, clinging to one another and becoming torpid on cold nights. **SIMILAR SPECIES:** White-headed Mousebird is greyish, white crested and has a whitish bill. **STATUS AND DISTRIBUTION:** Widespread and common resident from sea level to above 2500 m, in a variety of wooded, bushed and cultivated habitats but avoiding forest and arid country. Several intergrading races: interior *kikuyuensis* in the Kenyan highlands and other high-rainfall areas from Marsabit south to the Chyulu Hills and adjacent areas of n. Tanzania; *mombassicus* in coastal Kenya, interior ne. Tanzania and the Usambaras; *affinis* in coastal Tanzanian lowlands; and *cinerascens* in n. Tanzanian areas not occupied by other subspecies.

WHITE-HEADED MOUSEBIRD *Colius leucocephalus*   Plate 58

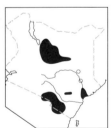

Length 300–310 mm (12"). A *greyish,* rather broad-tailed mousebird with *creamy-white crown, crest and cheeks* and bare, dark grey orbital skin. *Neck, back and breast narrowly barred black and white;* otherwise greyish to ashy white above, with a white streak on the back conspicuous when not concealed by the wings. Underparts tawny-buff, more vinaceous buff on breast and flanks. Eyes brown; bill pale bluish grey or bluish white above, pale buff below, darker toward tip of maxilla but pale at extreme tip; feet bright coral-pink to pinkish red. Northern *C. l. turneri* is darker than the southern nominate race, and more heavily barred on hindneck. **Juvenile** has buff throat and breast. **VOICE:** A squeaky chattering of dry thin notes, *tsik chiki-chiki;* a simpler *tsip-sip-sip. . .* or *tsik-tsik-tsik;* also a descending *tsip-tsip tseeeeeeeer.* **HABITS:** Parties haunt thick shrubbery and creeper tangles in dry country. More secretive than Speckled Mousebird. **SIMILAR SPECIES:** Speckled Mousebird is browner and darker-billed; lacks white on crown. **STATUS AND DISTRIBUTION:** Local resident in dry bush below 1400 m. The uncommon *C. l. leucocephalus* has a fragmented distribution from ne. Tanzania at Mkomazi GR and Tsavo West NP at Maktau, east to Voi and Maungu, northwest to Kimana, Selengai and western boundary of Amboseli NP; also disjunct populations along the Tiva and lower Tana Rivers north to Bura and possibly Garissa. Northern *turneri* ranges from the Horr Valley and Marsabit south to Samburu and Shaba GRs, the Northern Uaso Nyiro River and Isiolo District.

BLUE-NAPED MOUSEBIRD *Urocolius macrourus*   Plate 58

Length 330–355 mm (13–14"). A *slender-tailed,* ash-grey mousebird with *crested head and bright turquoise-blue nape patch.* Northern *U. m. abyssinicus* has more white on throat and a darker breast. Bill red above with broad black tip, mandible black; bare orbital and loral skin crimson; feet purplish red, the tarsi grey-brown behind. **Juvenile** lacks blue on nape, has pink facial skin and greenish bill. **VOICE:** A plaintive far-carrying whistle, *peeee, peeeeeeeeeee;* also shorter calls of same quality, *pyee, pyee, pyee. . .* or *pew t'lew,* repeated. **HABITS:** Usually in small groups, but flocks of 30–50 gather in fruiting trees. Far-flying (unlike Speckled Mousebird), moving rapidly from tree to tree over considerable distances. **SIMILAR SPECIES:** Speckled Mousebird is brown, not grey;

has different flight habits. **STATUS AND DISTRIBUTION**: Typically a dry-country species, usually avoiding the moister habitats frequented by Speckled Mousebird. *U. m. pulcher* is widespread and common in Kenya and n. Tanzania in bush, savanna and open acacia woodland up to 1900 m; also in coastal shrub savanna north of Malindi. *U. m. massaicus* is limited to ne. Tanzania, from the lowlands around Arusha and Kilimanjaro and the Masai Steppe region east to coastal lowlands near Tanga. *U. m. abyssinicus* ranges along the Kenyan/Ethiopian border east to Moyale.

TROGONS, FAMILY TROGONIDAE
(World, 39 species; Africa, 3; Kenya and n. Tanzania, 2)

Constituting a separate order, trogons are distinctive, colourful forest dwellers with large heads, short necks, and long broad tails. The feet are weak with very short tarsi, two toes (the third and fourth) directed forward, two (first and second) backward. At the base of the short curved bill are well-developed bristles. The wings are short and rounded, with strongly curved primaries. The plumage is dense, lax and loosely attached to the thin skin. Males of our species are bright red below and iridescent green above; females are duller. Trogons are stolid birds, typically perching upright with hunched posture. As they remain still for extended periods they are easily overlooked, despite their bright colours. Taking wing suddenly, they snatch insects, especially caterpillars, from twigs or foliage, and they hawk insects in flight. Our species are not frugivorous. They nest in natural tree cavities, laying two or three plain white eggs. The young are naked at hatching.

NARINA TROGON *Apaloderma narina*   Plate 58

Length 300 mm (12″). **Adult male** brilliant metallic green, with lower breast to under tail-coverts bright geranium-red; inner secondaries and median coverts finely barred black and grey; tail dark blue-green, with *three outer pairs of feathers white*. Bill deep yellow, merging into greenish white at tip; gape flanges apple-green; exposed postocular, rictal and gular skin yellowish green and bright blue, that above eyes pale blue; eyes chestnut-brown; narrow orbital ring blue, greenish on coastal *A. n. littoralis*, which has somewhat bronzier green feathering above and is paler, more pinkish red below. A long streak formed by white remex bases is conspicuous on underside of wing in flight. **Female** brown on face and throat, greyish pink on breast, red on belly and crissum. Bare facial skin blue or bronzy blue-green. **Juvenile** duller bronzy green above, with broad white tips to wing-coverts and inner secondaries; underparts grey with fine buff barring, the breast more mottled with brown. Bill dull yellow, orange at the gape; orbital ring white, the iris dark brown. **Immature** resembles adult female, but inner secondaries are white-tipped and there is less pink on the belly. **VOICE**: Somewhat ventriloquial. A soft double hoot, *hroo-HOO* or *oh-COO*, repeated several times, the second note of each pair usually slightly higher and accented, the series beginning softly and becoming louder. Bare gular skin inflates with each note. **SIMILAR SPECIES**: Bar-tailed Trogon is slightly smaller, with darker head and throat, violet on breast and with barred outer tail feathers. **STATUS AND DISTRIBUTION**: Mainly resident. *A. n. narina* is widespread but uncommon in forest and rich woodland, mainly at low to medium elevations, but also in highland forests of n. and w. Kenya, from Mts Elgon, Kulal, Marsabit and the Mathews Range south to the Kakamega, Nandi and Mau Forests, Nakuru NP, Nairobi suburbs, Mara GR, Lolgorien, the Ngurumans, and Kibwezi and Taveta Districts. In n. Tanzania, fairly common in Arusha and Lake Manyara NPs, but scarce elsewhere, ranging west to Serengeti NP. The race *littoralis* (= '*littorale*') occupies coastal woods north to the Boni Forest, inland to the East Usambaras, Shimba Hills and the lower Tana River.

BAR-TAILED TROGON *Apaloderma vittatum*   Plate 58

Length 280 mm (11″). **Adult male** bright green above, the head and throat blue-black with bronzy-green gloss; *sides of breast iridescent violet, blue and blue-green*; underparts otherwise bright red; inner secondaries and median coverts barred black and grey; tail mainly bluish or purplish black (central six rectrices), with *outer three pairs of feathers barred black and white*. White streak on underside of flight-feather bases conspicuous in flight. Eyes reddish brown or dull orange; bill yellow or greenish yellow; patches of bare skin below eyes *yellow or orange*, one above eyes yellow or grey. **Female** has brown head and light cinnamon breast. **Juvenile** white-bellied, with wing-coverts and inner secondaries tipped buffy-white. **VOICE**: Higher-pitched and more yelping than that of Narina Trogon. Male's song a fairly high-pitched *yaow, yow, yow, yow. . .* or *wuk-wuk-wuk-wuk. . .*, beginning softly and increasing in volume. Female utters a whining *chee-uu*. **SIMILAR SPECIES**: Narina Trogon has no tail barring. **STATUS AND DISTRIBUTION**: Uncommon resident above 1600 m in forests of the w. and cent. Kenyan highlands, and in parts of Tanzania's Crater Highlands, Arusha NP, Mt Kilimanjaro, the North Pare Mts and West Usambaras. Typically at higher elevations than Narina Trogon, but the two overlap in Kakamega Forest and Arusha NP. Has disappeared from the Nairobi area in recent years.

KINGFISHERS, FAMILY ALCEDINIDAE
(World, 94 species; Africa, 18; Kenya, 11; n. Tanzania, 10)

Small to medium-sized birds with large heads, long and often heavy pointed bills, short legs and small feet with strongly syndactyl toes. The largely piscivorous *Alcedo*, *Megaceryle* and *Ceryle* inhabit aquatic environments, but *Ispidina* and *Halcyon* may prey on insects, lizards and other terrestrial forms far from water. Most kingfishers are solitary, typically perching quietly and scanning the ground or water for long periods, darting down or plunging for prey. Their flight is direct and rapid. Most nest in long tunnels which they excavate in earth banks, but some breed in tree cavities; they lay three to eight white eggs. Except for one casual visitor from central Africa, our species are residents, although certain subspecies are migratory. We prefer to maintain the traditional family with its three subfamilies, each of which Sibley *et al.* (1988) and Fry *et al.* (1992) elevate to family status.

GREY-HEADED KINGFISHER *Halcyon leucocephala*   **Plate 59**
(Chestnut-bellied Kingfisher; Greyhooded Kingfisher)

Length 200–210 mm (*c.* 8"). A medium-sized, dry-country kingfisher with *bright cobalt-blue rump and tail*, *all-red bill* and red feet. **Adult** *H. l. leucocephala* is *chestnut-bellied* and *black-backed*, the scapulars with much concealed white; wings blue and black. Head and breast pale grey-brown; throat white, lores black. Wing-linings chestnut, with black spot near wrist, undersides of secondaries and tips of primaries black, the latter mostly white. Blue of wings has strong violet cast in coastal *H. l. hyacinthina*. Migrant *pallidiventris* is greyer on head, pale grey on upper back, and the chestnut is replaced by pale tawny. **Juvenile** duller than adult, the underparts buff, with grey barring on neck and breast; bill and feet dusky red. **VOICE**: Various calls include a piping *tieu*, *WEEU-WEEU chrrtili weeu-ti-weeu*, a sharp chattering *chirrrr-r-r-r-r*, falling in pitch, a loud sharp *TSI-TSI-TSI-TSI*. . . (the notes irregularly grouped and uttered in long series, sometimes alternating with a high wavering twitter), a clear *tew-uuuuuuuuuu*, and a clear descending *piuu piuu piuu*. . . **HABITS**: Perches on low branches, bushes or wires and drops to ground to take insects and small vertebrates. Conspicuous in vocal display, pivoting on perch with vibrating wings spread to show their boldly patterned undersides. **SIMILAR SPECIES**: Brown-hooded Kingfisher has buffy-white belly with pale cinnamon on flanks only, some streaking on sides; head is darker, with brownish-grey ear-coverts. Mangrove Kingfisher has paler blue back and wholly white belly. **STATUS AND DISTRIBUTION**: Common in bushed and wooded habitats up to 2200 m, often near watercourses, but absent from arid parts of n. and ne. Kenya. *H. l. leucocephala* present almost throughout, the breeding population augmented by migrants from the northern tropics November–April. *H. l. hyacinthina* is an uncommon resident of coastal lowlands and offshore islands from Tanga north to the Boni Forest, inland to Tsavo East NP and along the Tana River to Bura. *H. l. pallidiventris* is a migrant from the southern tropics between April and September, ranging north to Kendu Bay, Bungoma and Nandi Districts of w. Kenya.

BROWN-HOODED KINGFISHER *Halcyon albiventris*   **Plate 59**

Length 190–200 mm (7.5–8"). Another dryland kingfisher with an *all-red bill*. Usually in larger trees and inhabits thicker woodland than Grey-headed Kingfisher, from which it differs in *pale buff or buffy-white belly* and half-collar on hindneck. Head light brownish grey or grey-brown, with black around eyes and on lores, brownish ear-coverts, and slightly streaked pale brown crown bordered below by faint whitish superciliary stripes. Flanks deep buff or cinnamon, lightly and narrowly streaked in *H. a. prentissgrayi*. Wings black and azure-blue (*paler than in Grey-headed Kingfisher*), the linings pale cinnamon-rufous; tail dull azure, the rump much brighter. **Male** has black back, that of **female** sooty brown. Feet mostly orange, the tarsi brownish in front. Coastal *H. a. orientalis* has paler and essentially unstreaked crown; underparts plain, except for a few blackish shaft streaks on the buffy flanks. **Juvenile** has nuchal collar less well defined than in adult, crown and back browner, underparts more streaked, and sides of breast lightly but darkly scalloped; bill dusky red. **VOICE**: Usual calls a loud, repeated strident phrase of four or five notes, falling in pitch, *KIEU*, *KI-ki-ki-ki*; and a rapid descending trill, *PI-iiiiiiiirrrrr*. Also has a more even, drawn-out *pi-ee-ee*, *pi-ee-ee*. . . **HABITS**: Usually perches on exposed branch or wire. Pairs display with spread wings, pivoting and calling. Feeds mostly on insects, but also takes small vertebrates, including birds. **SIMILAR SPECIES**: Adult Grey-headed Kingfisher compared above. Mangrove and Woodland Kingfishers are blue on back, and Woodland has black-and-red bill. **STATUS AND DISTRIBUTION**: Common resident and partial migrant in woodland, savanna and forest at low to medium elevations: *H. a. orientalis* in coastal lowlands north to Lamu and the Boni Forest, inland along

the Tana River to Garissa, in the Shimba Hills and the East Usambaras; *prentissgrayi* in interior e. Kenya and Tanzania from Meru NP, Masinga Reservoir, Thika, Kitui and the Chyulu Hills south to Arusha, Tarangire and Lake Manyara NPs. Wanderers reported from Lake Baringo, Laikipia Plateau and Samburu GR.

WOODLAND KINGFISHER *Halcyon senegalensis* Plate 59

Length 200–220 mm (8–8.75"). A medium-sized kingfisher whose *bicoloured bill, red above and black below*, separates **adult** from all other East African species. Back azure-blue, underparts pale grey and white; wing-coverts and primary tips black but wings otherwise bright azure, as are upper tail-coverts and tail. Southern *H. s. cyanoleuca* has top and sides of head pale blue, contrasting less with back than in grey-headed *H. s. senegalensis*; lores and narrow eye-ring black in both races, the black extending as a point behind eye in some *cyanoleuca*. Maxilla bright red with some black at tip; mandible usually black, but partly red in some presumed immatures; eyes brown; feet blackish. **Juvenile** has dusky bill, sometimes partly red; buffy-grey sides of neck and breast marked with blackish vermiculations. **VOICE**: Loud and strident; a staccato note followed by a slightly rising, then descending, 'laughing' trill: *KEWK, kirrrr-r-r-r-r*; at times omits the initial note, especially when two birds duet. Also gives a short series of rapid notes on one pitch, *ski-ski-ski-ski*, sometimes doubled or tripled, *kiKEE-kiKEE-kikiKEE*, often extending into an excited twitter. **HABITS**: Usually in pairs in leafy trees. Noisy, especially in breeding season. Typically nests in tree cavity. Aggressive. Feeds on insects, small reptiles, some fish and occasionally small birds. **STATUS AND DISTRIBUTION**: Locally common resident and inter-tropical migrant in wooded and cultivated areas west of the Rift Valley, particularly the Lake Victoria basin, Mara GR and Serengeti NP. Presumably sedentary *H. s. senegalensis* is sometimes seen alongside *H. s. cyanoleuca*, a migrant from the southern tropics, April–September, when present mainly in the Rift Valley from Lake Manyara and Tarangire NPs north to lakes Naivasha and Baringo, Trans-Nzoia, the Turkwell River and Lokichokio.

MANGROVE KINGFISHER *Halcyon senegaloides* Plate 59

Length 215–230 mm (8.5–9"). A *coastal* species. Red-billed **adult** resembles sympatric Brown-hooded Kingfisher, but *bill stouter, head grey* and *back pale greyish blue*. Rump bright azure (as in Brown-hooded); wing-coverts black; flight feathers appear mainly azure on closed wing. Underparts generally whitish, minutely vermiculated with grey on breast, sides and flanks. Sexes alike. **Juvenile** resembles adult but is much duller, with head, breast and sides washed with yellowish buff, finely vermiculated and speckled with dusky. Bill brownish, gradually becoming red. **VOICE**: In breeding season, a series of sharp separated notes accelerating into a descending chatter, *KYI, KYI, KYI, ki-kik-ki-kikikikikiki*. **HABITS**: Perches conspicuously on wires, low boughs or projecting branches. Feeds on crabs, insects and lizards, occasionally fish. Nests in tree cavities or in earth banks. **SIMILAR SPECIES**: Brown-hooded Kingfisher is black-backed, with brownish-grey head and ear-coverts. Allopatric Woodland Kingfisher has black-and-red bill. See juvenile Grey-headed Kingfisher. **STATUS AND DISTRIBUTION**: Locally common resident throughout the coastal strip, including offshore islands, from Tanga and Pemba Island north to Kiunga, inhabiting mangroves, dense bush, woodland, forest and gardens. Extends inland along the lower Tana River to Garsen and the Tana River Primate Reserve.

STRIPED KINGFISHER *Halcyon c. chelicuti* Plate 59

Length 160–175 mm (c. 6.5"). A small *drab-coloured, streaky* kingfisher of *dry bush and open wooded country*. Mostly grey-brown and dull blue above, but *in flight shows bright azure lower back, rump and upper tail-coverts*. Forehead to nape pale buffy grey in **male**, browner in **female**, heavily streaked dark brown; narrow black lines from eyes connect around lower nape, bordering whitish (and faintly streaked) sides of head and nuchal collar. Underparts white, with pale *buff breast, sides and flanks streaked with brown*. Upper back and scapulars brown; tail dull greyish blue. Closed wings show much pale blue on remiges. In **male**, wing-linings and basal half of primaries and secondaries white, with large dark brown patch near wrist; white on remiges bordered by broad black band, the tips silvery grey. **Female**'s underwing pattern paler, without black band. Bill dark brown or blackish above, orange-red below, darker near tip; eyes dark brown; feet dull red. **Juvenile** generally paler, with little or no blue in wings, but crown darker brown and less boldly streaked than in adult; breast feathers with narrow dusky crescentic tips; mandible dusky red. **VOICE**: Distinctive and far-carrying: *KEW, kerrrrrrrrrr*, the lower-pitched trill descending and repeated. **HABITS**: Solitary or in pairs. Vocal, particularly in early morning and evening. Bobs head frequently. Members of displaying pair face each other, calling with tails cocked, repeatedly spreading and closing wings. Feeds on insects and some small vertebrates. Nests in tree cavities, and frequently parasitized by honeyguides. **SIMILAR SPECIES**: Brown-hooded Kingfisher has dark back and wing-coverts, brighter all-red bill and brighter blue wing feathers. **STATUS AND DISTRIBUTION**: Common and widespread from sea level to above 2000 m, in open woodland, savanna, tall bush and cultivation with scattered trees, although largely absent from dry n. and e. Kenya.

HALF-COLLARED KINGFISHER *Alcedo semitorquata tephria*   **Plate 59**

Length 180–190 mm (7–7.5"). Scarce and local. **Adult** bright *cobalt-blue above and rich tawny below*, with a *long black bill*; throat whitish; white patch on side of neck and diagnostic *blue patch on each side of breast*. Eyes brown, feet red. **Juvenile** duller below, scaled greyish on breast. **VOICE**: A high-pitched sibilant *tseeep* or *tsip-ip-ip-eep*. Song a very thin *tsip-tsip-tsiueep-tseep, tsiu-tseep-tseeueep-seep. . ..* Otherwise mainly silent. **HABITS**: Perches inconspicuously on low branch or stump by water. Dives steeply to catch fish and small crabs. Flight low, fast and direct. **SIMILAR SPECIES**: Shining-blue Kingfisher, a western vagrant, is darker ultramarine-blue on head and wings, has chestnut underparts with no blue on breast. Young Malachite Kingfisher with black bill is commonly mistaken for Half-collared, but is smaller, with brownish, not blue, cheeks and no blue breast patches. **STATUS AND DISTRIBUTION**: Known with certainty only from a few well-wooded streams flowing off Mt Kilimanjaro and in the East Usambaras. Formerly bred in Kitovu Forest, Taveta District. Few recent records.

SHINING-BLUE KINGFISHER *Alcedo quadribrachys guentheri*   **Plate 59**

Length 160–175 mm (*c.* 6.5"). Casual along wooded streams in w. Kenya. Mainly deep ultramarine-blue above, with *centre of back and rump glossy cobalt-blue*. Underparts bright chestnut, except for whitish throat; patch on side of neck buffy white or pale tawny-buff. Eyes dark brown, *bill black*, feet red. **VOICE**: A sharp high *cheet*, given mainly in flight, and a high-pitched *seet-seet-seet-seet*. **HABITS**: Shy and unobtrusive. Perches on shaded roots or branches over water. **SIMILAR SPECIES**: Half-collared Kingfisher in se. Kenya and ne. Tanzania has paler, more cobalt-blue upperparts, is paler below, with blue breast patches. Juvenile Malachite and African Pygmy Kingfishers also have blackish bills, but are much smaller. **STATUS AND DISTRIBUTION**: A forest species of w. and cent. Africa. Six Kenyan records of single birds: Nandi District (specimen, Nov. 1905); Kakamega Forest (Nov. 1974–Jan. 1975); near Alupe, Busia District (Aug. 1990, Oct. 1993); near Kapenguria (June 1992); near Mungatsi, Mumias District (Oct. 1992).

MALACHITE KINGFISHER *Alcedo cristata galerita*   **Plate 59**

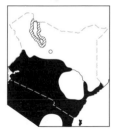

Length 115–120 mm (*c.* 4.5"). A small waterside kingfisher with a *shaggy crest*. **Adult** has *bright red bill and feet*. Upperparts deep blue, *top of head (down to eyes) turquoise, barred with black*; underparts and sides of head orange-rufous; throat and patch on side of neck white. **Juvenile** has *blackish bill*, is more greenish blue above and paler below than adult. **VOICE**: A sharp, high-pitched *seek*, usually in flight, and a squeaky chattering song, *tsiii-tsi-tswitswitswi tsewi-chui-chichi-chui. . ..* **HABITS**: Perches low over water and dives for small aquatic prey. Flight fast, straight, very low over water. Nests in holes in banks. **SIMILAR SPECIES**: African Pygmy Kingfisher, usually not a waterside bird, lacks crest and has chestnut between eye and the blue cap, and on the hindneck. See Half-collared Kingfisher. **STATUS AND DISTRIBUTION**: Common and widespread, frequenting fringing vegetation along open water, from coastal creeks up to 3000 m. Regular at Lake Turkana, but otherwise virtually absent from arid n. and e. Kenya and from the Masai Steppe of n. Tanzania.

AFRICAN PYGMY KINGFISHER *Ispidina picta*   **Plate 59**

Length 105–114 mm (4–4.5"). A diminutive forest or woodland kingfisher similar to Malachite Kingfisher but *lacks crest* and *blue cap does not extend down to eyes*. **Adult** has *red bill*, dark blue upperparts, and the cap is dark blue (not turquoise), barred with black. Orange-rufous face is washed with rich *lilac on ear-coverts* in nominate birds. Throat white, rest of underparts light orange-rufous, darker on sides of breast. Pale, almost white, on belly in southern race *natalensis*, which also shows small blue patch on posterior ear-coverts, adjacent to the white spot. Feet orange-red. **Juvenile** more greenish above, with *black bill*. **VOICE**: A thin, high-pitched *seet*, usually given in flight. Song a variable, prolonged, sharp, high twittering, *chewtiCHIchew chewtiCHEEtew skitise-see tseu-tsieeu-chewtitseu tsip tseu tseu tseu. . ..* **HABITS**: Unobtrusive. Usually perches in shaded shrub or on low tree branch and darts into grass for insects. Nests in earth banks. **SIMILAR SPECIES**: Malachite Kingfisher is crested and has long turquoise or greenish-blue crown feathers, these much paler than the hindneck and back; lacks lilac on ear-coverts and shows no rufous above the eyes. **STATUS AND DISTRIBUTION**: *I. p. picta* is a fairly common resident of wooded and riparian areas of w. Kenya, ranging north to Pokot District and Lokichokio; less numerous in coastal forest and upper Tana riverine woodland, Mwea NR, Machakos and Taveta Districts and the Tsavo NPs. In n. Tanzania, a scarce resident in Arusha, Lake Manyara and Serengeti NPs, and replaced by resident *I. p. natalensis* on Pemba Island and parts of the coastal mainland. That race also present April–September as a non-breeding migrant from s. Africa in coastal forests north to Malindi, inland to the East Usambaras and possibly other eastern areas.

463

GIANT KINGFISHER *Megaceryle m. maxima*   Plate 59

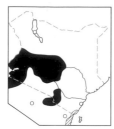

Length 380–430 mm (15–17"). A *crow-sized* kingfisher, dark-crested, with white throat and a *large black bill*. Upperparts dark slate, finely spotted and barred with white. **Male** has *chestnut breast, white belly* and black-and-white-barred flanks. **Female** is *chestnut-bellied*, with *densely black-and-white-speckled breast*. Eyes brown, feet black. **Juvenile** male resembles adult male, but has some chestnut on sides and flanks, and chestnut mixed with black on the breast; juvenile female has whitish band between breast and belly. **Voice**: A sharp raucous *kyaahk* or *kahk*, often repeated many times from perch; also *skyak-skyak-skyak-skirrrrrrrrr* and a chattering *keririririririri*. . .. **Habits**: Usually shy. Perches motionless, often well concealed, on bough by wooded stream or shady pool. Feeds on fish, freshwater crabs and frogs. Rarely hovers. Flight heavy, low and direct, with somewhat irregular wingbeats. Nests in burrow in river bank. **Similar Species**: Much smaller Pied Kingfisher is white below with one or two narrow black bands; habitually hovers. **Status and Distribution**: Uncommon resident along wooded banks of perennial rivers, streams and lakes. In Kenya, largely confined to the w. and cent. highlands above 1500 m, but present at lower elevations (Kiboko, Kitovu Forest, also on the upper Tana and Athi Rivers). In n. Tanzania, present on most well-wooded streams flowing off Mt Meru and Kilimanjaro, and sparingly in the Usambaras. Wanders to coastal lowlands as far north as Kilifi, and recorded once at Lake Turkana.

PIED KINGFISHER *Ceryle r. rudis*   Plate 59

Length 230–250 mm (9–10"). A *black-and-white* kingfisher associated with *open water*. Flat-crested crown bordered below by broad white superciliary stripes; ear-coverts black, cheeks and underparts white, except for two black breast bands in **male**, and one (broken centrally) in **female**. Eyes dark brown; bill and feet black; gape flanges bluish grey. **Juvenile** resembles female, but face, throat and breast are tinged brown, breast band greyish and gape pink. **Voice**: Various high calls: *tsiree-eee, tsiktsiktsik*. . ., a repeated *tsee-ee TSEU*, and *kwik. . . kwik*. . ., repeated frequently, from perch. On take-off, a sharp, reiterated *kikety-kick* or *tsikititsik*. **Habits**: Usually in pairs or small family groups. Nests co-operatively in burrows, sometimes in small colonies. Not shy. Feeds mainly on fish, caught by plunging from perch or after hovering. Flicks tail in excitement. **Similar Species**: Much larger Giant Kingfisher has partly chestnut underparts in both sexes. **Status and Distribution**: Common on lakes, ponds, rivers and coastal creeks, ranging up to 2300 m. Frequents open as well as wooded shores. Widespread except in n. Kenya, where suitable habitat is confined to Lake Turkana and the Daua River.

BEE-EATERS, FAMILY MEROPIDAE
(World, 25 species; Africa, 18; Kenya, 11; n. Tanzania, 9)

Sleek, attractive aerial feeders with long pointed wings, slightly decurved bills and small weak feet with syndactyl toes. Their tails are rather long, and in some species the two central rectrices extend well beyond the others. The body plumage is compact, often slightly lustrous, and shades of green predominate in a majority of species. Bee-eaters typically perch with upright posture, frequently moving the tail forward and back. Some are gregarious and highly social. In chilly weather, and when roosting, several birds may huddle closely together, side by side. Most larger species are colonial breeders, typically forming flocks, making long foraging flights and hawking insects high in the air. The smaller ones tend to be less gregarious, nesting in scattered pairs, making short foraging sallies and returning with prey to a perch. The birds devenom bees and wasps by rubbing them against a branch. Most are quite vocal, with simple but often pleasing liquid calls. Nesting is in burrows excavated in earth banks or sometimes in almost flat ground. The two to four white eggs are incubated by both sexes. The nidicolous young are naked at hatching.

EURASIAN BEE-EATER *Merops apiaster*   Plate 60

Length 260–280 mm (10.5–11"). A large greenish-blue and rufous-brown bee-eater with a *yellow throat* narrowly black-bordered below. **Adult male in spring** (after Jan.) has *golden-yellow scapulars that form a bold V* along the rufous-brown back; rump yellowish. Forehead white, crown rufous-brown; mask black; upperparts otherwise greenish blue, the greener wings with a large rufous patch; tail green, the *central feathers pointed and projecting an inch* beyond the others. Bill black; eyes red; feet purplish brown. In **non-breeding plumage** (Aug.–Oct.), back is green, crown green-tinged (sometimes rufous only at sides), scapulars greenish blue, and the yellow throat shows only a faint dark border; central rectrices not greatly elongated. Many early-winter males are intermediate between the two above plumages. **Female** differs from spring male in her paler underparts, greener scapulars, and green feathers mixed in the rufous wing areas.

First-winter bird generally greenish with rufous-brown crown, the pale yellow throat with only a suggestion of the dark border; scapulars pale green or buff; back and wings dull olive, with little rufous; central rectrices not projecting. Flying overhead, birds in all plumages show translucent pale rufous wings with broad black rear edges. **Voice:** A rolling liquid *klroop-klroop*, or *chrreep-eep*, far-carrying. **Habits:** Gregarious, commonly feeding in small migratory flocks high overhead, calling constantly. Also hawks insects from high perches. **Similar Species:** Blue-cheeked and Madagascar Bee-eaters have much longer tails, green upperparts, and lack the large yellow throat patch; calls are less fluty. Immature Madagascar without long central rectrices is most similar, but has cinnamon-buff throat and no rufous on crown. **Status and Distribution:** Widespread palearctic passage migrant in grassland, savanna, open woodland and cultivation from sea level to over 2000 m. Common on southward passage, September–November, more sporadic on return in March and April. Some winter at medium elevations in w. and cent. Kenya and in n. Tanzania.

MADAGASCAR BEE-EATER *Merops s. superciliosus*   Plate 60
(Olive Bee-eater)

Length 230–240 mm (9–9.5″), plus up to 70 mm (2.75″) extension of central rectrices. Elegant, slim and long-tailed. Distinguished from Blue-cheeked Bee-eater by duller *olive-green (not bright grass-green) upperparts* and *dark olive-brown crown, white (not pale blue) forehead and cheek stripes. Superciliary stripes usually white* but may be pale yellow or blue; chin whitish, throat dull rufous. *Underside of wings ochreous, not cinnamon or rufous.* Bill and feet black; eyes wine-red. **Juvenile** lacks tail streamers and has greenish crown, scattered pale blue feathers on green back, cinnamon-buff throat and pale blue breast merging with pale green belly. Eyes brown. **Voice:** A persistent rolling *t'rreeo, t'rreeo* or *krreep, krreep*, sharper than call of Eurasian Bee-eater, but almost identical to that of Blue-cheeked. **Habits:** Similar to those of Blue-cheeked Bee-eater. **Similar Species:** Blue-cheeked Bee-eater compared above. See Eurasian Bee-eater. **Status and Distribution:** Fairly common non-breeding migrant May–September (from the Zambezi Valley and perhaps Madagascar and the Comores). Also a local, generally uncommon and erratic breeding resident in some coastal areas, notably Lamu and Pemba islands. Has bred (Sept. 1975) along the Tana River in Meru NP. Seasonally common in low bush and lightly wooded habitats, often beside water. Birds in e. Kenya November-March may be enroute to or from breeding grounds in Somalia.

BLUE-CHEEKED BEE-EATER *Merops p. persicus*   Plate 60

Length 230–245 mm (9–9.5″), plus up to 70 mm (2.75″) central tail-feather projections. A slender, long-tailed, *bright green* bee-eater with black mask, mostly white forehead, green crown, pale blue cheeks and *pale blue or whitish superciliary and cheek stripes. Turquoise or blue-green cheek patch* is *always conspicuously brighter than the surrounding green plumage; yellow chin* merges with russet throat. Bill and feet black; eyes wine-red in male, orange-red in female. Underside of wings *coppery rufous*. **First-winter bird** duller, more olive than adult, sometimes retaining pale-edged juvenile feathers; forehead green, narrowly yellowish at bill; chin pale yellowish buff grading into rufous-buff throat patch, paler (yellowish or whitish) at sides. Moult apparently completed in wintering areas; young indistinguishable from adults by mid-winter. **Voice:** Flight call a rolling *prruuik* or *krreep-krreep* similar to that of Eurasian Bee-eater, but softer, less melodious, more distinctly disyllabic. **Habits:** Hawks insects in long pursuit flights, frequently over water. Flocks often migrate high overhead, and also gather on wires and dead trees. **Similar Species:** Madagascar Bee-eater has brown crown, white facial stripes rarely bluish (superciliaries may be pale yellow), and a larger dull rufous throat patch. Extralimital Little Green Bee-eater (see note below) is bright green with long tail feathers, but is much smaller than Blue-cheeked and has a narrow black band across the lower throat. **Status and Distribution:** A regular palearctic migrant, late October to early April, in open bush, wooded lake edges and swamps below 1500 m. Locally common at lakes Victoria, Baringo, Jipe and Manyara, in mangroves along the lower Tana River and coastal creeks south to Tanga. **Note:** Little Green Bee-eater, *M. orientalis*, has been mentioned as a scarce visitor to n. Kenya (Fry *et al.* 1988) on the basis of an erroneous record.

CARMINE BEE-EATER *Merops nubicus*   Plate 60

Length 240–260 mm (9.5–10″), plus up to 100 mm (4″) central rectrix extension. A large *red and blue* bee-eater with long central tail feathers. **Adult** of northern *M. n. nubicus* has *turquoise-blue head and throat*, the bright forehead and chin separated by black mask; most of underparts and the back pinkish red; wings and tail carmine (streamers largely blackish); rump, upper and under tail-coverts bright pale blue. Bill black; eyes crimson; feet grey. Vagrant *nubicoides* differs in having chin, *throat and cheeks bright pink*; eyes dark brown. **Juvenile** *nubicus* brown on nape, more rufous on upper back; scapulars and inner secondaries olive-brown with pale blue edgings; tail dull carmine, tipped with brown. Chin and throat blue; breast brown with pinkish feather edges; belly pale buff; upper and under tail-coverts pale blue. Most body feathers pale-tipped. **Voice:** A loud *gra-gra-grra* from perch. In flight, a repeated *cheo-cheeo-cheeo, chrrip, chrrip*, or *kyee kyeeo*. Also a shorter *chrk* or

tewp, and according to Fry (1984) a commonly double, deep throaty *krunk* or *trunk*. *M. n. nubicoides* gives a rolling *rrik-rak* (Maclean 1984). Feeding flocks produce a continuous chatter. **HABITS:** Highly gregarious. Forages in low flight or by hawking from tree branch, wire or (*M. n. nubicus*) from the back of some mammal or large ground bird. Attracted to grass fires and to insects disturbed by domestic stock. Forms large roosts, particularly in coastal mangroves. Nests in large colonies, sometimes on almost flat ground. **STATUS AND DISTRIBUTION:** *M. n. nubicus* breeds erratically in northern border areas, March–June; with us mainly as a non-breeding migrant from the northern tropics, September–March, especially to the coast, where common locally south to Tanga; occasional in bushed grassland and cultivation in se. Kenya and some Rift Valley localities. Vagrant *M. n. nubicoides* recorded at Lake Kanyaboli (June 1972) and in the Kedong Valley, near Kijabe (July 1977). **NOTE:** The two forms are treated as separate species by some authors.

WHITE-THROATED BEE-EATER *Merops albicollis*   Plate 60

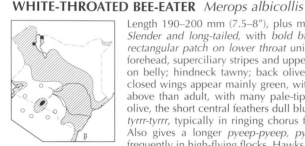

Length 190–200 mm (7.5–8"), plus median rectrix extension of nearly 125 mm (5"). *Slender and long-tailed*, with *bold black-and-white head pattern. Black crown and rectangular patch on lower throat* unique; these and black mask contrast with white forehead, superciliary stripes and upper throat. Much of body pale green, almost white on belly; hindneck tawny; back olive-green, becoming pale blue on rump and tail; closed wings appear mainly green, with ochre-buff flight feathers. **Juvenile** more olive above than adult, with many pale-tipped feathers; chin and throat light yellow; tail olive, the short central feathers dull blue-green with darker tips. **VOICE:** A high strident *tyrrr-tyrrr*, typically in ringing chorus from a flock, reminiscent of Eurasian Bee-eater. Also gives a longer *pyeep-pyeep*, *pyueep-pyrrrrrrr*. **HABITS:** Gregarious and vocal, frequently in high-flying flocks. Hawks insects from tree branches or wires. Often raises black crown feathers in excitement. **SIMILAR SPECIES:** Madagascar Bee-eater lacks black crown and throat patch. **STATUS AND DISTRIBUTION:** Widespread non-breeding migrant from the northern tropics, September–April, locally common in dry bush, woodland and forest edge below 1400 m, including coastal lowlands south to Tanga. Small numbers breed in northernmost Kenya, April–May, and erratically around Lake Magadi and Olorgesailie in the south.

WHITE-FRONTED BEE-EATER *Merops b. bullockoides*   Plate 60

Length 225–235 mm (8.5–9.5"). A colourful bee-eater with a square-tipped tail. Upperparts mainly green; black mask offset by *whitish forehead, white chin and cheeks, and bright red* (very rarely yellow) *throat; crissum and upper tail-coverts deep blue;* hindcrown, nape, breast and belly pale cinnamon-buff. **Juvenile** much paler than adult; bluer above, with little or no red on throat. **VOICE:** A deep, somewhat nasal *gaaaa* or *gharrra*, and a sharp *kwaank* of alarm. **HABITS:** Gregarious and noisy. Hawks insects from small trees, but rarely flies high. Nests in small socially organized colonies in cliff burrows. **STATUS AND DISTRIBUTION:** Locally common resident of bush and woodland, especially brushy eroded gullies and watercourses in the cent. Kenyan Rift Valley from Mt Suswa north to Menengai, also on the lower slopes of Kilimanjaro and Mt Meru in n. Tanzania; smaller populations in the Kerio Valley and nw. Mara GR. Occasionally wanders.

BLUE-HEADED BEE-EATER *Merops m. muelleri*   Plate 60

Length 190 mm (7.5"). A dark-plumaged bird of *western Kenyan forests.* **Adult** mainly *deep blue* with *russet back* and *scarlet chin,* latter surrounded by black malar areas, sides of neck and lower throat; *forehead pale frosty blue,* darker on crown. Bill and feet black; eyes red. **Juvenile** more ochre-brown on back, dusky turquoise below; cheeks, throat and upper breast dusky; chin bluish, with little or no red. **VOICE:** Song a medley of well-spaced notes, some strident or piercing, others soft and nasal: *cherik, nyaa, sherik SKIEEK-skirk, chrrrr SKERIK . . ..* Calls include a weak *tssip-tssip-tseeseeseesee* and a single thin *tseep* or *tseeup.* **HABITS:** Usually solitary. Perches unobtrusively, usually on high twigs along forest tracks or at clearing edges, but sometimes nearer ground. Hawks small butterflies and hymenopterans, swooping fast and low for some distance, then returning to the same perch. Nests in earth banks and road cuttings in forest. **STATUS AND DISTRIBUTION:** Uncommon local resident of the Kakamega and South Nandi Forests. Formerly at Nyarondo, Lerundo and on Mt Elgon, where no suitable habitat remains.

LITTLE BEE-EATER *Merops pusillus*   Plate 60

Length 145–160 mm (*c.* 6"). The smallest bee-eater; bright green above, with long *black mask bordering the yellow throat.* **Adult** has triangular *black patch on lower throat,* narrowly margined above with bright blue, and

below by chestnut or cinnamon-brown on breast and belly. Flight feathers rufous with greenish edges; secondaries broadly tipped with black, producing striking flight pattern. Slightly notched *tail cinnamon-rufous, with green central feathers* and *broad black terminal band*; narrow white rectrix tips disappear with wear. Bill black; eyes red or pale orange; feet dark brownish grey. Blue superciliary stripes are evident in M. p. *cyanostictus*, though barely discernible in the race *meridionalis*. **Juvenile** *pale greenish below*, yellow on throat with no black patch; belly buff-tinged, breast indistinctly streaked; eyes brown. **VOICE**: Usual call a soft, sibilant *tseep* and a slightly disyllabic *teesip* or *tseup*, repeated numerous times. Also gives a rather sharp *tsip, tsip, tsip. . .*, alone or with additional notes to form a song: *tsip-tsip-tstip-teesip-siddip-seedle-tsip-tsip-tsee*. **HABITS**: Not colonial; usually in pairs or family groups. Commonly nests in river banks. Makes quick feeding sallies from bush or grass stem, with low gliding return to the same or nearby perch. **SIMILAR SPECIES**: Slightly larger Blue-breasted Bee-eater has *purplish-blue throat patch* and shows narrow white stripe between black mask and yellow throat. Cinnamon-chested Bee-eater occupies different habitat, is larger, darker below, has white cheeks, and a green tail with black-and-white tip. **STATUS AND DISTRIBUTION:** Common from sea level to over 2000 m in open country with shrubs and small trees. M. p. *cyanostictus* ranges through much of Kenya, intergrading with mainly n. Tanzanian *meridionalis* in the w. Kenyan highlands.

BLUE-BREASTED BEE-EATER *Merops variegatus loringi*   Plate 60

Length 165–175 mm (c. 6.5"). A small *west Kenyan* bee-eater of *humid areas*. Closely resembles the slightly smaller Little Bee-eater, but both adult and juvenile have narrow *whitish cheeks* below the black mask. Adult's *throat patch is dark purplish blue*, not black, and is bordered above with bright blue. Bill and feet black; eyes orange-red. **VOICE**: Lower-pitched, less sibilant than that of Little Bee-eater: *tseuk, tseuk, tseuk. . .* or a more song-like *tseuk-tseuk-tseuk-cherrik-chewk*, with or without a terminal trilled *trrrip*. **HABITS**: Similar to those of Little Bee-eater. **SIMILAR SPECIES**: Little Bee-eater compared above. Larger Cinnamon-chested Bee-eater has rich chestnut breast, more green in the tail, and occupies wooded habitats at higher elevations. **STATUS AND DISTRIBUTION**: A locally common resident of moist grassland and edges of papyrus swamps at Usengi and around the Yala Swamp (Lake Victoria basin). Formerly ranged east to Kisumu.

CINNAMON-CHESTED BEE-EATER *Merops oreobates*   Plate 60

Length 200–215 mm (8–8.5"). A highland species of more wooded habitats than the smaller and paler Little Bee-eater. **Adult** has *chestnut breast* and *largely green tail with broad black subterminal band and white tip*; inner webs of most tail feathers faintly edged with dull cinnamon. *Lacks blue superciliary stripes* present in Kenyan races of Little and Blue-breasted Bee-eaters. Back bright green; *cheeks white* posteriorly below black mask. Bill black; eyes red; feet brownish grey. **Juvenile** bluish green on upperparts; throat entirely yellow, *breast greenish* with infusion of pale cinnamon; belly and flanks buff, under tail-coverts pale green or greenish buff. **VOICE**: A high *tsip* or *tseeip*, stronger and more persistently uttered than calls of Little Bee-eater. Song *siddip-siddip*, *tsip-tse-tsee*. **HABITS**: Perches and feeds around canopy of tall trees, occasionally near ground, in pairs or small groups. Small colonies breed in earth banks, road-cuttings or quarries. **SIMILAR SPECIES**: Adult Little and Blue-breasted Bee-eaters compared above. Juveniles of these have more rufous in tail than Cinnamon-chested, but are best distinguished by size and habitat. **STATUS AND DISTRIBUTION**: Locally common resident of open forest, forest edge, woodland and suburban gardens between 1600 and 2300 m, occasionally up to 3000 m. Widespread in the w. and cent. Kenyan highlands, north to the Ndotos, Mt Nyiru and Mt Marsabit, east to Mt Kenya, south to Machakos and Nairobi Districts, Mara GR and the Nguruman Hills. In n. Tanzania, in the Crater Highlands, Lake Manyara and Arusha NPs, Mt Meru, Kilimanjaro, North Pare Mts and the West Usambaras.

SWALLOW-TAILED BEE-EATER *Merops h. hirundineus*   Plate 122

Length 195–215 mm (c. 8"). A green bee-eater with a long, *deeply forked, bluish tail* in all plumages. Resembles the preceding three species in its bright green upperparts, black mask and yellow throat, but always has *green underparts* and **adult** has narrow blue band on lower throat. Blackish trailing edge of rufous flight feathers conspicuous in flying bird. Bill black; eyes reddish; feet dark. **Juvenile** duller than adult, with chin and throat greenish white and no band on lower throat; eyes dark brown. **VOICE**: Resembles that of Little Bee-eater, but calls drier and less sibilant. **HABITS**: Forages in pairs or small groups. Somewhat nomadic, and attracted to recently burnt areas. **SIMILAR SPECIES**: Little, Blue-breasted and Cinnamon-chested Bee-eaters have nearly square-tipped tails, and adults are cinnamon or chestnut below. Juveniles of those species have green on breast and some pale yellow on throat, but all lack forked tail. **STATUS AND DISTRIBUTION**: The northern race *heuglini* (recorded several times near Kenyan territory in the Sudan and Uganda) can be expected as a vagrant in the extreme northwest of our region. The nominate southern race ranges north to Tanga in Tanzania. Old reports of specimens attributed to Vanga and the Shimba Hills in se. Kenya cannot be verified.

SOMALI BEE-EATER *Merops revoilii*   Plate 60

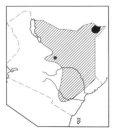

Length 155–165 mm (6–6.5"). A small *pale* bee-eater of *dry bush and desert*. Often looks scruffy and dishevelled. *Lower back, rump and upper tail-coverts lustrous cobalt-blue*, contrasting in flight with greener back; some buff on neck. Black mask bordered above by narrow blue superciliary stripes. *Throat white; breast and belly pale cinnamon-buff*; under tail-coverts light cobalt-blue. Wings and tail dull greenish blue. Flight feathers pale cinnamon on bases of inner webs, and the wings appear pale rufous in flight. Bill black; eyes dark red; feet grey to dusky pink. **Juvenile** duller than adult, but otherwise similar. **Voice:** An infrequent, soft warbling whistle, slightly descending and becoming fainter in mid-series, *turee-turee-turee-turee-turee*. **Habits:** Solitary or in pairs. Perches low and behaves much like Little Bee-eater. During hot weather stands high on perch, legs stretched. Nests in road cuttings and in the sides of deep wells. Confiding in the north, but normally wary along southern edge of range. Largely silent except for bill-snapping. **Similar Species:** Little Bee-eater has large black patch on lower part of yellow throat, and its black-tipped tail is largely cinnamon-rufous. **Status and Distribution:** Locally common in n. and e. Kenya from Lake Turkana and Mandera south to Isiolo District, also Meru, Tsavo East and (recently) Tsavo West NPs. Few breeding records.

ROLLERS, FAMILY CORACIIDAE
(World, 12 species; Africa, 8; Kenya, 5; n. Tanzania, 4)

Robust, upright-perching coraciiform birds with large heads, strong and rather corvine bills (the nostrils more or less concealed by the frontal feathers) and short tarsi. The outer toe is basally united to the middle one and is reversible. The sexes are similar, with much blue or purplish, and sometimes rufous or cinnamon, in the plumage. They are somewhat aggressive birds, perching prominently on vantage points in open country, from which they either drop on their arthropod and vertebrate prey (*Coracias*) or pursue aerial insects (*Eurystomus*). They regurgitate pellets of undigested chitin and bones. In flight, rollers are exceptionally agile, and the name derives from their exuberant diving and rolling aerial displays, which are accompanied by harsh croaking calls. They nest in cavities in trees or termitaria, laying two to four white eggs. The nidicolous young are naked at hatching; they are cared for by both sexes. One of our species is a palearctic migrant.

EURASIAN ROLLER *Coracias g. garrulus*   Plate 61

Length 300–310 mm (12"). A stocky *greenish-blue* bird *without long tail feathers*. **Spring adult** has *cinnamon-brown back*, with forehead and supraloral areas whitish; bend of wing, lower back and rump bluish purple. Wings flash bright blue and black in flight, the black-tipped dark blue flight feathers contrasting with turquoise wing-linings from below. Tail greenish blue, the central feathers dull olive, the outer ones black-tipped and very slightly attenuated. Eyes pale to medium brown, bare orbital skin greyish black; bill brownish black; feet yellowish to olive-brown. **Autumn adult** duller, with many feathers brown-tipped, the back more rufous. **First-winter bird** browner, pale greenish blue on head and wing-coverts, little or no purplish on rump or wings, and no black spot on outer tail feathers; bill slightly pinkish at base. **Voice:** A croaking *ugrr-ugrr-ugrr . . .* or *yaaak, aggh,* etc. Also a harsh noisy *kaarr*. Not very vocal in East Africa. **Habits:** Often solitary, but in loose flocks on migration. Flight rather crow-like, with deep wingbeats and glides, the wings appearing longer than in African-breeding rollers. **Similar Species:** Abyssinian Roller has long outer tail feathers, shorter wings with quicker beats. Lilac-breasted Roller, also long-tailed, has lilac throat and (usually) breast. **Status and Distribution:** Palearctic passage migrant, late October to April, common in dry open woodland and shrubby habitats (mainly below 1500 m) in e. Kenya and ne. Tanzania, where migrating flocks are frequent. Small numbers also regular on autumn passage in and west of the Rift Valley and in spring along the coast. At least the majority of East African birds are referable to the nominate race. The paler *C. g. semenowi* winters commonly in southern Africa, and there are specimens from our region.

ABYSSINIAN ROLLER *Coracias abyssinica*   Plate 61

Length 390–430 mm (15.5–17"), including *long (120–250 mm) outer tail feathers*. A streamlined roller of dry northern regions; resembles Eurasian Roller in coloration. **Adult** *bright azure-blue* with rufous-brown back, purplish-blue rump; whitish forehead, superciliary stripes, chin and throat streaks, and dusky lores. *Vivid purplish-blue flight feathers have basal third or half (and coverts) azure, conspicuous in flight.* Dark purplish-blue 'shoulders' may be concealed in perched bird. Eyes brown, and bare postocular skin black; bill black and promi-

nently hooked; feet ochre-yellow or yellowish brown. Duller **juvenile** has crown, hind-neck and breast tinged olive-brown, and no elongated outer rectrices. **Voice**: A repeated raucous *aaaaarr, aaaaarr. . .* or *sckaaaa, sckaaaa . . .* from perch. In aerial display, a harsh *ga-ga-ga-ga-ga-ga-gaarrrr-gaarrrrrr*, building in volume and intensity. **Habits**: Usually solitary, but sometimes forms groups near fires or termite swarms. Aggressive, noisy and conspicuous. Performs spectacular rolling display flights. **Similar Species**: Eurasian Roller lacks elongated outer rectrices and can be mistaken for young Abyssinian Roller (or an adult missing its long feathers), but is stockier, less brilliantly plumaged, and has black flight feathers. Lilac-breasted Roller has lilac on lower throat and (usually) breast. **Status and Distribution**: Locally common resident west of Lake Turkana in dry bushed grassland and riverine *Acacia* woodland. Wanders October–March south to Pokot District, Kerio Valley and Baringo and Nakuru Districts, occasionally to Nyanza, Laikipia, and Samburu and Mara GRs. Also a sporadic visitor from se. Ethiopia to the Moyale–Ramu–Mandera area of extreme ne. Kenya.

LILAC-BREASTED ROLLER *Coracias caudata*   **Plate 61**

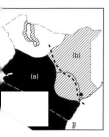

Length 320–350 mm (12.5–14"), including outer rectrices which extend 80-90 mm beyond rest of tail. A gaudily coloured bird with *bold white superciliary stripes, fore-head and chin.* **Adult** glossy blue-green on crown and nape, and with *largely lilac throat and breast* in *C. c. caudata.* Lilac confined to throat, chin and lower face in *C. c. lorti,* which has greenish-blue breast, sometimes with a central patch of vinaceous lilac; remaining underparts of both races azure-blue; bend of wing bright dark blue; rump and outer webs of black flight feathers purplish blue. *Flight feathers brilliant turquoise-azure basally, in flight forming (with coverts) large patch contrasting with dark wing tip.* Back greenish brown; tail vivid greenish cobalt-blue, the central feathers olive. **Juvenile** much duller, without elongated outer rectrices; crown and nape brownish, forehead buffy, superciliary stripes indistinct; throat and breast rufous-tawny with broad, diffuse buffy-white streaks. **Voice**: Loud and raucous: *keer, ka, kek-ke-ke-kek-keer-keer,* or a repeated guttural *errrack yecck yecck* and variations, sometimes terminating in a very loud *KRAAA-KRAAAACK.* Aerial displays usually end with a harsh chuckling. **Habits**: Solitary or in pairs, often perched prominently on bush, tree or wire. Flight rapid; dives and loops in noisy display. Aggressive toward other species. Preys on invertebrates, lizards and some-times small birds. **Similar Species**: Eurasian and Abyssinian Rollers lack lilac throat/breast. **Status and Distribution**: Fairly common and widespread resident and wanderer (less numerous than formerly) in dry open bushed and wooded habitats and cultivation up to 2000 m. *C. c. caudata* ranges throughout n. Tanzania, and Kenya north and east to Pokot, Maralal, and the Northern Uaso Nyiro and Tana Rivers, wandering to Lake Turkana. *C. c. lorti,* mainly a non-breeding visitor from Somalia, ranges west to Marsabit, south to Meru NP, Garissa and Garsen, some reaching the Tsavo NPs (Jan.–March).

RUFOUS-CROWNED or PURPLE ROLLER *Coracias n. naevia*   **Plate 61**

Length 330 mm (13"). Robust and strong-billed, with a square-tipped tail; lacks the extensively blue body plumage of the previous three species. **Adult** has *face and under-parts purplish brown, streaked with white,* a *rufous crown bordered by conspicuous white superciliary stripes and white nape patch.* Upper back olive-green, lower back lilac, rump purple, and tail dark purplish blue with brownish-green central feathers; upperside of wing mostly dark blue and purplish brown, the primaries basally white on inner webs, blue-green near tips of outer webs. Eyes dark brown; bill black; feet olive-brown. **Juvenile** olive-green below with broad white streaks, these narrowing and more pinkish on throat. **Voice**: A harsh, guttural, repeated *gah* in flight, accompanying upward flight and twisting descent. Other calls are a deep nasal *wukhaa,* or *ka-karaa* repeated several times, a repeated throaty, somewhat bustard-like *guggiow* or *keeoh,* and a rough chuckling *chk-chk-chk-chk-chk. . .* **Habits**: Solitary. Perches conspicuously. Rather sluggish, but performs rapid rolling, twisting and tumbling display flight. Pugnacious, pursuing other species, including raptors. Drops or flies to ground for prey. Flight direct, with quicker wingbeats than those of Eurasian Roller. Subject to local movements or partial migrations. **Similar Species**: Smaller Broad-billed Roller is darker, with short yellow bill. Young Lilac-breasted Roller has rufous-tawny breast, often with some lilac feathers, broader pale streaks on underparts, differently coloured wings, no white nape patch. **Status and Distribution**: Uncommon but wide-spread in dry woodland and bush with scattered large trees. Ranges up to 2000 m, occasionally higher, but largely avoids the coastal lowlands. Becomes seasonally numerous in some areas of Kenya (Baringo District, both Tsavo NPs), yet inexplicably scarce in much of Tanzania. Numbers fluctuate as a result of poorly understood movements; birds from the northern tropics believed responsible for some influxes.

BROAD-BILLED ROLLER *Eurystomus glaucurus* Plate 61

Length 240–270 mm. (9.5–10.5"). Small, dark and compact, with a *short, broad yellow bill*. **Adult** rich cinnamon-brown above, with blue rump and tail; underparts deep lilac; flight feathers and outer wing-coverts mainly deep blue. Crissum dark greyish blue in nominate birds from Madagascar (pure blue in other races). *E. g. suahelicus* has all upper tail-coverts deep blue; in *afer*, the central coverts are brown, and the rest greenish blue. Eyes brown; feet olive or olive-brown. **Juvenile** dull rufous-brown above, lores blackish; head to upper breast duller brown; otherwise greenish blue or dull azure below. Bill yellowish with brown culmen and tip. **VOICE**: A deep harsh *kaaar, kyaaar, kyaaaar*, and a chattering *kakakakaka-kaa-kaa-kakaka*. **HABITS**: Prefers more thickly wooded areas than other rollers. Perches prominently on high trees. Normally solitary or in pairs, but migratory flocks visit w. Kenya and Pemba Island. Crepuscular, pairs wheeling around treetops in erratic noisy evening flights. **SIMILAR SPECIES**: All *Coracias* rollers have longer, dark bills. **STATUS AND DISTRIBUTION**: Uncommon to locally common in woodland, forest edge and open country with tall trees, mainly below 2000 m, but absent from arid n. and ne. Kenya. *E. g. suahelicus* is a widespread resident from Mt Elgon, the Cheranganis, Samburu, and the Tana River southward, but in interior n. Tanzania mainly a breeding migrant, August–March. West African *E. g. afer* has been recorded in the Lake Victoria basin of w. Kenya. The nominate Madagascan race is known from Pemba Island, and flocks in w. Kenya in July–September may represent this form.

HOOPOE, FAMILY UPUPIDAE

The single species of this coraciiform family is widespread in the Old World. It is a smartly patterned, crested bird with a very slender long bill with which it probes for insects, mostly as it walks somewhat jerkily on the ground. Its tarsi are short but the toes are relatively long, the third and fourth fused basally. The cavity nest may be in a tree, earth bank or wall. Only the female incubates, but both sexes care for the nidicolous young. The four to six eggs are pale blue, greenish or dark olive-brown. Eurasian birds are migratory, whereas some African populations are resident. Southern forms are more richly coloured than those in the north, and females may differ from males in wing pattern. Some authors have considered the African-breeding races as a species separate from *U. epops*, but there are no obvious differences in habits or vocalizations (unlike in *marginata* of Madagascar), and some populations are intermediate in plumage. It seems preferable to consider them conspecific.

HOOPOE *Upupa epops* Plate 61

Length 255–280 mm (10–11"). Unmistakable, with pinkish-rufous, tawny or cinnamon head, neck and underparts, and the *pointed black-tipped crest frequently raised in fan-like fashion. Bold black-and-white wings and tail* are especially striking in *wavering, erratic, butterfly-like flight*. **Adult male** *U. e. africana* is more richly coloured above and below than northern nominate birds, and lacks the whitish subterminal band on the crest feathers. **Female** is smaller, duller below, with whitish abdomen and dusky-streaked flanks. **Juvenile** is darker, more earth-brown. At all ages *africana* has *largely white secondaries in the male*, but resembles *nominate birds in the female. In both sexes, the primaries are entirely black*. All nominate *epops* show a conspicuous white band across the primaries, as do northern tropical *waibeli* and *senegalensis*. The latter has a *pale* tawny body, whereas that of *waibeli* is *rich* tawny, almost as dark below as *africana* and (in the male) with largely white secondaries, obvious in flight. In many respects, *waibeli* is intermediate in plumage between nominate *africana* and *epops*. Both sexes of the latter are pale pinkish cinnamon, somewhat sandy above, whitish on lower belly, sometimes with dusky streaks on flanks. **VOICE**: A low, penetrating *hoop-hoop* or *oo-poo-poo*, repeated after short interval, from tree or ground. (Cf. African Cuckoo.) **HABITS**: See family account. Usually solitary or in pairs. Often shy (especially northern birds). Usually flies to tree if disturbed. **STATUS AND DISTRIBUTION**: Widespread in open woodland, bush, savanna and cultivation, mainly below 2000 m. *U. e. africana*, a breeding resident north to about 2° N, is fairly common throughout (though numbers fluctuate seasonally). *U. e. waibeli* is mainly a non-breeding migrant from the northern tropics, recorded south to Nakuru (regularly) and Nairobi Districts; also resident in extreme nw. Kenya around Lokichokio. *U. e. senegalensis* is known in extreme ne. Kenya from sight records near Moyale and Mandera, and it may be present along the border with Somalia; also specimen records from near Lake Turkana at Lodwar and the Horr Valley. *U. e. epops* is a regular palearctic migrant from October to March, mainly in dry areas of n. Kenya, but reaching Lake Elmenteita, Athi River and Tsavo West NP; in Tanzania, recorded from Dar es Salaam (Oct. 1972) and Lake Manyara NP (Feb. 1990).

WOOD-HOOPOES AND SCIMITARBILLS, FAMILY PHOENICULIDAE
(World and Africa, 8 species; Kenya, 7; n. Tanzania, 4)

These African endemics are slim, small-bodied birds with long, slender, graduated tails, broad rounded wings, narrow decurved bills and short, thick (sometimes partly feathered) tarsi. The plumage is largely iridescent black with green, violet or blue sheens. The sexes are alike or similar. Wood-hoopoes are agile arboreal birds, climbing and clinging to boughs and trunks, often hanging upside-down. The tail may be used as a brace, as in woodpeckers, but the unspecialized rectrices become badly worn as a consequence. All species feed mainly by extracting arthropods from bark crevices or decaying wood. At times, foraging birds also hammer like woodpeckers. Prey is swallowed whole, sometimes after being beaten vigorously on a branch or in a crevice. Woodhoopoes nest in tree cavities, and some breed co-operatively. The three to five eggs vary from plain pale turquoise or dark grey to blue with brown spots and blotches.

The larger *Phoeniculus* species usually travel in small noisy, chattering parties, moving from one tree to the next with floppy, jerky flight. Individual, racial and age variation, combined with effects of different light conditions on the iridescent plumage, renders field identification unreliable in many cases. The smaller scimitarbills (*Rhinopomastus*) are quieter and less gregarious. DNA studies suggest separation of these genera at the family level, but there do not appear to be significant morphological differences. We therefore maintain the traditional family treatment here.

WHITE-HEADED WOOD-HOOPOE *Phoeniculus bollei jacksoni*   Plate 62

Length 300–355 mm (12–14″). The only *highland-forest* wood-hoopoe. **Adult** iridescent green with an individually variable *whitish head* (buff on crown), blue-glossed wings, and long blue-and-purple tail. No white in either wings or tail. Bill and feet red. **Juvenile** duller and blacker, with *black bill*. Some immatures are highly glossed, with dull red bill, and many have black head feathers intermixed with white. **Voice**: A rippling chuckling chatter, higher-pitched than similarly patterned call of Green Wood-hoopoe; often prolonged: *shk-chk chickchickichichichichichi-ch-ch-ch-ch-ch*, often by several birds together. Also a descending trilled *chirrrrrrrrrrrrrrrr*. Contact call a soft mellow *krrr*. **Habits**: Those of the genus. Travels in pairs or noisy parties. Feeds on fruits, as well as on insects and other arthropods. **Similar Species**: Juveniles of related species are also dark-billed but do not inhabit highland forest. Pale-headed morph of Forest Wood-hoopoe, probably extirpated from Kenya, has shorter, straighter bill and a different call. **Status and Distribution**: Fairly common and widespread resident in w. and cent. Kenyan highland forest, mainly from 2000 to 3000 m. Ranges north to Mt Elgon, the Cheranganis, Maralal, the Aberdares, Mt Kenya and the Nyambeni Hills, and south to the Kakamega and Mau Forests, Ngong Hills (formerly), nw. Mara GR and the Nguruman Hills. In n. Tanzania, only at Loliondo near the Kenyan border.

FOREST WOOD-HOOPOE *Phoeniculus castaneiceps brunneiceps*   Plate 62

Length *c.* 260 mm (10″). A small polymorphic central African species of uncertain status in w. Kenya (see below). Head of **male** variable: *light chestnut-brown, buffy white, pale brown or black with green gloss*; **female** always brown-headed. No white in either wings or tail. Back iridescent blue-green; lower breast and belly dull black; tail violet; wings dark blue with greenish gloss. *Bill grey, shading to black at base, yellow from gape along cutting edges to tip*; eyes brown; feet black. **Juvenile** similar to adult, but shorter-billed and duller, with head darker brown. **Voice**: A plaintive yelping *ueek ueek ueek. . .*, the quality slightly suggesting gull or African Fish Eagle, typically given from high conspicuous perch. A rapid, high-pitched twittering chatter, given by one or more birds, recalls that of White-headed Wood-hoopoe. **Similar Species**: Adult White-headed Wood-hoopoe (in different habitat) has decurved red bill and distinctive call; dark-billed juveniles are longer-tailed than young *castaneiceps*. **Status and Distribution**: Doubtless extirpated (and unlikely to reappear owing to extensive deforestation along the Kenyan/Ugandan border). Probably always rare in w. Kenya, although van Someren (1916) described birds collected along the Sio River in Mumias District and later secured others on the Ugandan side of Mt Elgon. Chapin (1939) referred to birds from North Kavirondo and possibly had examined van Someren's specimens, which cannot now be traced. Ligon and Davidson (in Fry *et al.* 1988) erroneously included Kitale within the species' range.

GREEN WOOD-HOOPOE *Phoeniculus purpureus*   Plate 62
(Red-billed Wood-hoopoe)

Length 325–370 mm (13–14.5″). The commonest wood-hoopoe. Does not always appear green (usually blue and purple in the shade); tail mostly violet, with large white spot near tip on outermost two or three pairs of feathers. **Adult** of *P. p. marwitzi* green-glossed on neck, back, throat and breast (throat tinged with blue or violet in some birds). Wings largely blue and violet-blue, with some white on primary coverts and *broad white bar across primaries conspicuous in flight*; rump purplish black; belly dull greenish black; *bill and feet typically bright red*, but mandible and culmen black in some breeding females. Bill of female shorter and less curved. The northwestern race *niloticus*, ranging south to lakes Baringo and Bogoria, is larger-billed and darker than *marwitzi*, with

crown and nape green or blue-green, wings and central tail feathers violet or violet-blue; inner secondaries purple, not blue; upper back and breast somewhat bluer green than in *marwitzi*, and white bar on primaries broader. **Juveniles** of both races dull black, with entirely brownish chin and throat, faint iridescence; *short black bill and black feet* gradually becoming red during first year. **Immature** has black maxilla, metallic green throat feathers margined with pale tawny. **Subadult** has more bronzy wash, is less pure green than full adult plumage. A specimen from South Horr, possibly a hybrid with *P. somaliensis*, has a long, mainly black bill, red at the base and along nearly the entire culmen. **VOICE:** A repeated chuckling, usually with one bird beginning slowly, *wuk. . .wuk . . .*, then several call together, the loud chattering chorus accelerating, and the pitch rising and falling: *whuh, wuk, wuk-ukuk, ukchuk-chuck-chukchukchukch-ch-ch-ch.* Also a single loud *kuk* when alarmed, and a braying *waaa.* Foraging note an abbreviated *uk.* **HABITS:** Those of the genus. Flocks defend large territories with noisy group displays, featuring bowing and swaying with wings and tail spread. Co-operative breeders; nest-helpers continue to feed young long after fledging. Several birds may roost together in tree cavity. Flight undulating; birds follow one another flying from tree to tree; on landing, may 'see-saw' back and forth, calling excitedly. **SIMILAR SPECIES:** Violet Wood-hoopoe, not known west of the Rift Valley, is distinguished *with care* by mostly violet-blue iridescence on head, back and breast, with *only the chin and throat green* (and not always conspicuous). Black-billed Wood-hoopoe has largely black bill (often red toward base below). All young wood-hoopoes have blackish bills (shorter and straighter than in adults), and plumage is much less iridescent than that of adults; some juveniles probably not separable in the field, but usually accompany adults. Common Scimitarbill is smaller, with black bill and feet, rounded tail tip. **STATUS AND DISTRIBUTION:** *P. p. marwitzi* is a fairly common and widespread resident in acacia woodland and other open wooded habitats, mainly below 2800 m, in n. Tanzania and in Kenya north to Mt Elgon, the Laikipia Plateau, Northern Uaso Nyiro River, Mathews Range and the Tana River. Replaced by *P. p. niloticus* in the northwest, south to Lake Bogoria, and by *P. somaliensis* in much of ne. Kenya. Possibly hybridizes with the latter.

BLACK-BILLED WOOD-HOOPOE *Phoeniculus somaliensis*   Plate 62

Length 330–350 mm (13–14"). Known with certainty only in *ne. Kenya.* **Adult** resembles Green Wood-hoopoe, but *bill black, sometimes red at base, more slender and more strongly decurved; iridescence more blue, less violet.* In *P. s. somaliensis*, crown and nape are glossed with blue; back and breast dark violet-blue; wings green or bluegreen; chin blue with some turquoise gloss, and belly dull black; tail violet with white subterminal spots on outer three rectrices. Feet bright red. Ethiopian *P. s. neglectus* is slightly greener on head and upper back, with lower back brighter violet; also heavierbilled than nominate race. **Juvenile** *neglectus* dull black, with blue or greenish-blue wash above, tawny-buff feather edges on chin and throat, blue or violet wash on black lower throat and breast; wings and tail as in adult, except for faint white primary tips; bill and feet blackish. **Immature** resembles adult, but throat with deep purple and blue sheen, no green or copper in crown. **VOICE and HABITS:** Similar to those of Green Wood-hoopoe. **SIMILAR SPECIES:** Adults of Green and of Violet Wood-hoopoes usually have red or largely red bills, but bill may be black with red base in young Green. Race *marwitzi* of that species mainly glossed green on body, violet on tail; race *niloticus* is violet on inner wing feathers and tail. Violet Wood-hoopoe is more uniformly violet-blue. **STATUS AND DISTRIBUTION:** *P. s. somaliensis* is a fairly common resident of open bush and riparian woodland in much of ne. Kenya. It ranges west at least to Lodwar, but western and southern limits are not clearly defined. The suggestion (Fry *et al.* 1988) that *P. p. niloticus* and *P. s. neglectus* are sympatric around Lake Turkana requires substantiation. **NOTE:** Formerly considered a race of Green Wood-hoopoe.

VIOLET WOOD-HOOPOE *Phoeniculus damarensis granti*   Plate 62

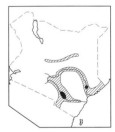

Length 345–375 mm (14–15"). In and near dry *riverine woodlands east of the Rift Valley.* Similar to Green Wood-hoopoe in size, appearance and habits, but **adult** *violet-blue on crown, nape, back and wings, as well as on breast and tail; lower throat green.* Bill red, sometimes black at base; feet red. **Juvenile** duller, sooty black, with buff-streaked chin and throat; bill blackish, almost straight, shorter than in adult, gradually becoming red and curved. **VOICE:** Resembles that of Green Wood-hoopoe, but somewhat louder and harsher. **HABITS:** Similar to those of Green Wood-hoopoe. Often in association with doum palms. Known to raid weaver nests to feed on eggs. **SIMILAR SPECIES:** Green Wood-hoopoe also shows violet gloss on tail; race *marwitzi* of that species has green neck, back and breast; northwestern *P. p. niloticus* has violet inner secondaries and tail; often misidentified as *granti.* Black-billed Wood-hoopoe has largely black bill, sometimes red at base and on mandible; iridescence more blue and violet-blue on head and body. **STATUS AND DISTRIBUTION:** Local and uncommon resident (?) in eastern dry bush and riverine woods, mainly below 1000 m. Specimen evidence from Taveta, both Tsavo parks, Kibwezi, Kitui, Meru NP, and the Tana, Athi–Galana–Tiva and Northern Uaso Nyiro Rivers. Irregular in many localities. Northern limits unclear, owing to frequent confusion with other species. *Not known in or west of the Rift Valley.*

COMMON SCIMITARBILL *Rhinopomastus cyanomelas schalowi*   **Plate 62**
(Greater Scimitarbill)

Length 280–300 mm (11–12"). A small wood-hoopoe with a *strongly decurved black bill* and *black feet*. **Adult** plumage blackish with violet-blue gloss; **female** duller below than male. In flight, shows *white bar across primaries* (and at times some white on primary coverts), white subterminal spots on outer two pairs of tail feathers. **Juvenile** resembles adult, but bill is shorter and straighter. **VOICE**: Usual advertising song a mournful *woui* or *poui* given in groups of two to seven notes for an extended period, the groups separated by intervals of a few seconds. Also gives a faster *woueek-week-week-weeek* and a descending *kui-kui-ker-ker-ker-ker-ker*. **HABITS**: Solitary, in pairs, less often in small groups, but individuals regularly join mixed-species flocks. Often works on tree trunks and forages much like *Phoeniculus* spp. Sings while foraging or from treetop perch. **SIMILAR SPECIES**: Abyssinian Scimitarbill is smaller, orange-billed, and has no white in wings or tail. Juvenile Green Wood-hoopoe is larger, with more pointed tail, straighter bill and some buff on throat; bill and feet show some red, except in very young birds. **STATUS AND DISTRIBUTION**: A fairly common and widespread resident of open woodland, savanna and bush across much of n. Tanzania and Kenya north to the Cheranganis, Laikipia Plateau, the Ndotos and the Tana River; also in coastal woodlands from Tanga north to the Boni Forest. Avoids arid areas. **NOTE**: The Black Scimitarbill, *R. aterrimus*, is mapped (as *R. cyanomelas*) as occuring in extreme n. Kenya by Lewis and Pomeroy (1989), but, although it is attributed to Kenya by Short *et al.* (1990), we know of no evidence to support addition of this species to the Kenyan list. However, *R. a. notatus* ranges south nearly (or actually) to the Kenyan/Ethiopian border and may extend into our region. It has a *shorter, less strongly curved dark bill*, a *short and only slightly graduated tail* with variable white spot on the outer rectrices, and a broad white bar across the primaries. Unlike more western races, *notatus* has *little or no white on the primary coverts*. Its calls include a plaintive mournful *wuoi wuoi wuoi wuoi*, strongly suggestive of *R. cyanomelas*, and *week-week-week . . .*, recalling Forest Wood-hoopoe. See Fig. below.

Black Scimitarbill.

ABYSSINIAN SCIMITARBILL *Rhinopomastus minor cabanisi*   **Plate 62**

Length 230–240 mm (9–9.5"). A small dry-country scimitarbill with *no white in wings or tail*. **Adult** has long, *strongly decurved, bright orange bill* and black feet; black plumage glossed dull violet above; tail bluer, somewhat rounded, shorter than in Common Scimitarbill. **Juvenile** duller than adult, with dusky bill. **VOICE**: A chattering *keree-keree-keree-keree-keree. . .*, each note rising and then falling in pitch; also a loud yelping *kwee-u* or *peu*, repeated up to 15 times, the notes varying slightly in pitch. **HABITS**: Solitary or in pairs; sometimes in small groups, often with mixed bird parties. Flight undulating. Forages in wood-hoopoe fashion; acrobatic. **SIMILAR SPECIES**: Common Scimitarbill has black bill, shows white in wings and tail. **STATUS AND DISTRIBUTION**: Rather uncommon resident of bush and open woodland in dry regions, mainly below 1400 m. Widespread in interior n. Tanzania. In Kenya, absent from high-rainfall areas of the w. and cent. highlands, Lake Victoria basin and coastal lowlands.

HORNBILLS, FAMILY BUCEROTIDAE
(World, 56 species; Africa, 24; Kenya, 12; n. Tanzania, 9)

Medium-sized to large birds noted for their long, ridged or casqued bills, these sometimes of remarkable shape. Excepting *Bucorvus*, most are short-legged birds with stout tarsi, and have the second, third and fourth toes fused at the base. Plumage is basically black and white, occasionally brown, and there is some bare skin on the face and throat. Eyes, bill and casque may be brightly coloured, and several species exhibit well-developed facial and gular wattles. All have long eyelashes. Their wings are rather short, the tail long. Flight is buoyant, with repeated flapping and gliding, undulating in the smaller *Tockus* species, and distinctly audible, especially in the large *Bycanistes*, in part because of air rushing between the bases of the remiges, which lack under wing-coverts.

Some hornbills are sedentary and territorial throughout the year, whereas others congregate into post-breeding flocks and undertake local movements in search of food. They are omnivorous, favouring fruit and insects. In most species, after mating, the female seals herself into the nest cavity (in tree or cliff face) with mud. As incubation begins, the entrance hole is reduced to a small slit through which the male feeds his mate and their young. Incubation lasts from 25 to 40 days, and young are fed for 45 to 85 days. The female undergoes a complete moult during this period. She is the first to emerge, leaving the young to reseal themselves in with excrement until they are ready to leave. Hornbills are quite vocal. Most *Tockus* species have simple monotonous clucking or piping calls, and the large *Bycanistes* are extremely noisy, with loud braying, bleating or quacking.

The huge terrestrial ground hornbills (*Bucorvus*) differ in several respects from other hornbills, and some authors treat them as a separate family. The bare throat is inflatable, owing to its underlying air sac. Both species are largely carnivorous, and *B. leadbeateri* is a co-operative breeder. They nest in cavities, but do not seal the entrance as do other hornbills.

SOUTHERN GROUND HORNBILL *Bucorvus leadbeateri*   Plate 30

Length *c.* 1 m (38–40″). A large-billed, *turkey-sized* terrestrial bird, *black-plumaged* except for *white primaries*, conspicuous in flight. **Adult** has *bright red bare skin* around eyes and on neck, where usually somewhat inflated; eyes pale yellow; bill black, with small casque at base above. **Sexes** similar, but female smaller and with small violet-blue patch on chin and upper throat. **Juvenile** sooty brown, with smaller and greyer bill; eyes greyish, facial skin brownish yellow. **Voice**: A deep resonant *ooom, ooom, ooo-ooom*, or *oomp-oomp-oomp*. Sometimes more grunting, *uh-uh-uh*, or a single *ugh*, quite lion-like. Often calls just before dawn, the sound far-carrying. **Habits**: Pairs or small groups walk about (on distal part of toes) in search of insects and small vertebrates (to size of squirrel or young hare). Normally takes flight only when disturbed or alarmed. Regurgitates undigested food remains in pellet form. Each pair has several 'helpers.' Courtship may involve all adult males in the group, but only the dominant male copulates. Nest cavity is in tree, cliff or earth bank. **Similar Species**: See Abyssinian Ground Hornbill. **Status and Distribution**: Widespread but patchily distributed in open grassland and savanna from interior n. Tanzania north to Nairobi NP, the cent. Rift Valley, Kakamega, Mt Elgon, Kapenguria and Ortum, but increasing agricultural development in the Kenyan highlands has severely reduced numbers in recent years. **Note**: The species is often called *B. cafer*, but see Browning (1992).

ABYSSINIAN GROUND HORNBILL *Bucorvus abyssinicus*   Plate 30

Length *c.* 1 m+ (40–43″). **Adult male** differs from the preceding species in having a yellow patch at the base of the maxilla, an *open-ended cylindrical casque*, and *bare blue skin* around eyes and on the throat; skin on lower neck red; eyes brown. **Female** smaller, the *bare skin entirely dark blue*. **Juvenile** dark sooty brown with undeveloped casque; bluish-grey skin around eyes and on throat. **Voice**: A series of deep booming grunts, *uuh, uh-uh-uh* and *who-OOru OO-ru*, slightly higher-pitched than call of Southern Ground Hornbill; not unlike the grunt of a leopard. **Habits**: Similar to those of preceding species. Eats reptiles and other small vertebrates, also fruits and large seeds. **Similar Species**: See Southern Ground Hornbill. **Status and Distribution**: Scarce local resident, mainly below 1000 m, in nw. Kenya south to the Kerio Valley and Baringo District and east to Lake Turkana. Generally in more arid areas, with poorer grass cover, than those favoured by Southern Ground Hornbill.

RED-BILLED HORNBILL *Tockus e. erythrorhynchus*   Plate 63

Length 40–51 cm (16–20″). A small black-and-white hornbill with a *slender orange-red bill*. **Adult male** blackish brown above, with *white streak down centre of back*; crown dark grey; superciliary stripes, neck and underparts white; primaries black; *wing-coverts spotted with white*; central tail feathers black, outermost pair white, others black and white. Bill orange-red, black at base below; eyes brown; feet black. **Female** similar but smaller, and does not always have black mandible base. **Juvenile** has smaller, duller bill and buffy-white spots on the wing-coverts. **Voice**: A long series of similar notes, beginning faintly, becoming louder and more run together:

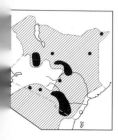

uk. . .uk. . .uk, wuck, wuck, wuck-wuck-wuck-WUCK-WUCK-WUCK-WUCK-WUCK, uhWUK, WUK-WUK-uhWUK-uhWUK. . ., or wuk-wuk-wuk-kaWUKwa-kaWUKa-wuka-wuka. . ., higher-pitched than similar calls of related *Tockus* species. **HABITS:** Feeds largely on the ground; forms foraging flocks after breeding. Flight slow, deeply undulating. Pair often duets, wings raised above back; heads are bowed and bodies moved up and down as calls accelerate. **SIMILAR SPECIES:** Other similarly patterned *Tockus* species have differently coloured bills. **STATUS AND DISTRIBUTION:** Common and widespread in dry thorn-bush below 1400 m. Absent only from the coastal lowlands, the Lake Victoria basin and heavily forested areas.

EASTERN YELLOW-BILLED HORNBILL *Tockus flavirostris*   Plate 63

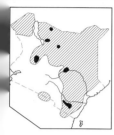

Length 50 cm (20"). Black and white, with a *heavy yellow bill.* **Adult** blackish above, with broad white streak down back; crown and nape black; broad superciliary stripes, neck and underparts white; *wings heavily spotted with white;* central tail feathers black, others mainly white with black subterminal band. Yellow eyes ringed with dusky bare skin; bare throat patches pink in **male**, black in **female**. **Juvenile** has a smaller, dull yellowish bill mottled with dusky; upper breast streaked with dark grey; eyes dull grey. **VOICE:** A series of clucking notes, often very prolonged, increasing in intensity at end, *wuk-wuk-wuk-wuk-wuk-wuk-wuk-wuk-wuk-wuk-wuk-wuk-WUK-WUK-WUK-WUK-WUK. . .*; deeper than call of Red-billed Hornbill. **HABITS:** Much like those of Red-billed Hornbill. Often symbiotically associated with Dwarf Mongoose (*Helogale*), feeding on insects disturbed by the troop, and warning them of possible predators. Perched display-ing birds raise and fan wings, bow heads and rock bodies forward and back. **SIMILAR SPECIES:** Red-billed Hornbill is similarly patterned, but bill red and more slender. **STATUS AND DISTRIBUTION:** Uncommon but widespread resident between 500 and 1200 m in much of n. and e. Kenya. Most numerous in areas with *Commiphora* and baobab trees, ranging south to the Kerio Valley and Baringo District, and in the east extending south along the Somali border throughout Tana River District and from the Tsavo NPs into ne. Tanzania's Mkomazi GR and adja-cent edge of the Masai Steppe; also around Longido and along Tanzanian/Kenyan border north of Arusha. **NOTE:** East African *flavirostris* is now considered specifically distinct from the southern African *T. leucomelas,* differing vocally and in colour and extent of the bare facial skin.

VON DER DECKEN'S HORNBILL *Tockus deckeni*   Plate 63

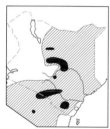

Length *c.* 47 cm (18.5"). A small black-and-white hornbill with a *heavy bill (two-toned red and ivory with black tip in* **male**, *entirely black in* **female***)* and *no white spots on wing-coverts.* **Adult** plumage black above, including crown, white on centre of back and sides of head, but with some dark grey streaks on ear-coverts; throat, neck and underparts white; wings black, with some white on central secondaries showing in flight; back, rump and central tail feathers black; outer rectrices white with black tips. Bare orbital skin black; eyes brown; throat patches flesh-pink; feet black. **Juvenile** resembles female, with blackish-horn bill, but has small white spots on wing-coverts. **VOICE:** A continuous low and even chucking, *cukcukcukcukcukcukcukcuk. . .*, or *whuh-whuh-whuh. . .*, with little variation. **HABITS:** Similar to those of preceding species, including symbiotic relationship with Dwarf Mongoose. **SIMILAR SPECIES:** Adult Jackson's Hornbill has white spots on wing-coverts. **STATUS AND DISTRIBUTION:** Fairly common and widespread in thorn-scrub, bush and savanna throughout dry interior e. Kenya and n. Tanzania. Absent from nw. Kenya (where replaced by Jackson's Hornbill), the coastal lowlands south of Malindi, the Lake Victoria basin and high-lands above 1600 m.

JACKSON'S HORNBILL *Tockus jacksoni*   Plate 63

Length *c.* 50 cm (20"). Resembles Von der Decken's Hornbill, the two considered conspecific by many. **Adult** Jackson's differs in its *white-spotted wing-coverts.* **Male** also has mainly *orange-red bill with creamy-yellow tip.* **Female** has all-black bill. **Juvenile** resembles adult, but bill blackish or mixed with dull orange-red. **VOICE:** A monotonous series of notes on one pitch, like that of Von der Decken's but higher, louder, more hollow and often slower, each note more distinct: *wek-wek-wek-wek-wek. . ., wukk-wukk-wukk . . .*, or *wok-wok-wok. . .* **SIMILAR SPECIES:** Von der Decken's Hornbill compared above. **STATUS AND DISTRIBUTION:** Common in nw. Kenya west of Lake Turkana, south to Nasolot NR, the Kerio Valley and Baringo District. Status on eastern side of Lake Turkana uncertain. No known overlap with the preceding species in the Turkana area, but specimens of both collected at the base of Mt Nyiru.

HEMPRICH'S HORNBILL *Tockus hemprichii* **Plate 63**

Length 56–58 cm (22–23"). A rather large, dark hornbill with a *dull reddish bill* and *white-striped tail* (two feathers down each side adjacent to the black outer feather); lacks white streaks on head. **Adult male** dark brown above, the top and sides of head washed with grey; throat, neck and chest dark brown; lower breast and belly white; wings dark sooty brown, the coverts and secondaries narrowly white-edged. Bare skin around eyes and on throat black; eyes dark brown; bill dull maroon-red with dark tip, brighter red below; feet black. **Female** is smaller, with duller red, dusky-based mandible, and pale dull greenish gular skin. **Voice:** A series of high-pitched yelping whistled notes: *queeo, pipipipipipipipipi*, or *pwik, kwiwiwiwiwiwiwi*; also *pi-pi-pi-pi-pi-piew*. Call note a sharp *QUEEo or PEEo*; sometimes *KWI-KWI*. **Habits:** Typically inhabits rocky hills and gorges; breeds in cliff crevices. Feeds in the air (catching bees, termites, etc.) and in trees and shrubs; robs buffalo-weaver nests. Non-breeders wander in small groups some distance from nesting areas. Flight slow and buoyant. **Similar Species:** Crowned Hornbill has brighter red bill, white streaks behind eyes and different tail pattern. **Status and Distribution:** Uncommon and local in semi-arid rocky parts of n. and nw. Kenya between 900 and 1200 m. Most numerous on the Kongelai, Tambach and Kabarnet Escarpments, and near Lake Baringo. Wanders regularly to the Laikipia Plateau, Mogotio and Menengai Crater; also recorded from northern border areas at Lokichokio, Kamathia, Huri Hills and Moyale.

CROWNED HORNBILL *Tockus alboterminatus* **Plate 63**

Length 55 cm (21.5"). Blackish or brownish black with a *white belly, white tail corners* and a *red bill*. **Adult** has *white streaks from above eyes to nape*; head *slightly crested*. Bright red bill, orange-tinged at base, and with a low ridge-like casque; bare orbital and gular skin black; eyes dull yellow; feet black. **Female** resembles male but is duller, with smaller bill and greenish-yellow skin on throat. The eastern race *T. a. suahelicus* is much paler above than the almost black-backed *geloensis*. **Juvenile** lacks ridge on bill, has greyish eyes and brownish wing-covert edges. **Voice:** A shrill, piercing piping or whistling: *squeek, pyi-pyi-pyi-pyi-pyi. . .* or *pew-pew-pew-pew-pew*; in display, the repeated notes grouped together, rising and falling in pitch. Contact note a single loud *KWEE* or *QUEW*. **Habits:** Pairs or small family groups feed mainly in tree foliage, but may hawk termites, moths and other insects from perch. Courting pairs call with bill pointing upward, the birds rocking rhythmically back and forth with each phrase. Flight appears laboured and weak. **Similar Species:** See Hemprich's Hornbill. **Status and Distribution:** *T. a. geloensis* is fairly common in woodland and forest edge up to 3000 m in the w. and cent. Kenyan highlands, and in n. Tanzania at Loliondo, the Crater and Mbulu Highlands, Lake Manyara, Tarangire and Arusha NPs and on Kilimanjaro. *T. a. suahelicus* occupies similar habitat in coastal lowlands from Tanga north to the Boni Forest, including Pemba Island, ranging inland along the lower and upper Tana River gallery forests, to the Shimba Hills, both Tsavo NPs, Taveta, Kibwezi and Kitui Districts, the Usambara Mts and Mkomazi GR. Birds on Mt Kulal and the Ndotos not racially assigned.

AFRICAN GREY HORNBILL *Tockus nasutus* **Plate 63**

Length 51 cm (20"). A dull grey-brown hornbill with a *long white stripe from eye to nape and another down centre of back*; wings sooty brown, all feathers edged white; bare skin on throat dark grey; eyes red-brown; throat and breast pale greyish brown; belly white. Bill of **male** *black, with creamy-white patch at base of maxilla*, narrow cream or pale yellowish lines/ridges across base of mandible; low ridge-like casque along culmen in nominate race, this narrowly tubular and extended forwards in *T. n. epirhinus*. **Female** similar but *bill tip is dark red* and *basal half of maxilla cream*. **Juvenile** dull brown, with buffy-white wing edgings and smaller bill; female shows more yellowish cream on the maxilla than male. **Voice:** A penetrating rhythmic piping, *ki-ki-ki-ki-ki-ki, pi-KEW pi-KEW pi-KEW curee-curee-curee-curee*; a simpler *PEW-ku, PEW-ku, PEW-ku. . .*; and a more strident descending *PEW, PEW, pew, pew. . ..* **Habits:** Usually in pairs. Flight buoyant and deeply undulating. Displaying birds point bills skyward, rock back and forth and flick wings. **Similar Species:** Crowned Hornbill is larger and darker, with red bill and yellow eyes. **Status and Distribution:** *T. n. epirhinus* is widespread in n. Tanzania, rather local and uncommon in Kenyan coastal lowlands. The nominate race is widespread in savanna and open acacia woodland over much of interior Kenya, absent only from the arid north and east and the western highlands. Subject to local movements, with numbers fluctuating seasonally. **Note:** The Pale-billed Hornbill, *T. pallidirostris*, endemic to *Brachystegia* woodland south of our area, has been attributed to Kenya on the basis of a specimen allegedly from near Taveta, collected by V. G. L. van Someren, but the single Pale-billed Hornbill taken by him is from Mgeta near Morogoro.

TRUMPETER HORNBILL *Bycanistes bucinator* **Plate 63**

Length *c.* 60 cm (23.5"). A large hornbill, typical of coastal and riverine forests. Largely black above, but white on upper tail-coverts and *rear half of wings* (tips of secondaries and inner two pairs of primaries) conspicuous in flight; some scapulars may also show white tips; a few grey streaks on sides of head. Throat and upper breast black, otherwise white below. Bill blackish in **adult,** casque large in male, smaller and terminating halfway along bill in female; eyes red-brown; *bare skin around eyes and on throat dark purple to purplish pink, sometimes bright pink*; feet black. **Juvenile** has rudimentary casque and greyish eyes. **Voice:** Loud, high nasal braying, *NHAAA NHAAA NHA-HA-HA-HA-HA-HA . . .*, often prolonged; also a low guttural croak when feeding. **Habits:** Often in large noisy flocks. Roosts communally. Flies far in search of fruiting trees, sometimes over open country. **Similar Species:** Silvery-cheeked Hornbill has no white in wings, more on lower back. Black-and-white-casqued Hornbill has much white in wings, but is a western bird, not in range of Trumpeter. **Status and Distribution:** Locally common in Kenyan coastal forests from the lower Tana River south to Tanga. Inland populations in Taveta, Kibwezi, Thika and Maua Districts and along the upper Tana River. No actual breeding records from ne. Tanzania, where local in the East Usambaras (fairly common in adjacent lowlands) and North Pare Mts; rare elsewhere. **Note:** Some authors place this and the following three species in the genus *Ceratogymna.*

SILVERY-CHEEKED HORNBILL *Bycanistes brevis* **Plate 63**

Length *c.* 70 cm (27–28"). A very large pied hornbill with *all-black wings,* breast and upper back contrasting with *white lower back, rump and upper tail-coverts.* Belly and under tail-coverts also white. Black tail shows conspicuous white corners in flight. **Adult male** has silvery-grey feather tips on cheeks and ear-coverts, and a *very large, mostly cream-coloured casque* projecting to or beyond the bill tip; bill otherwise dark brown, with yellowish band at base. Eyes brown; *bare orbital skin dull grey or blue-grey* (brighter in breeding season?); feet black. **Female** slightly smaller than male and casque lower, restricted to basal half of maxilla and tapered or abruptly truncated in front, coloured like rest of bill; *orbital and loral skin pale pink.* **Juvenile** has brown-tipped feathers on sides of head, throat and breast, and a much smaller bill, the casque as in male. **Voice:** Loud raucous braying, *RAAAH RAAAH RAAAH RAAAH. . .*; also softer grunting and quacking calls when feeding. **Habits:** Forages in pairs or large noisy flocks, and roosts communally in tall trees. Feeds almost entirely in canopy foliage. Mainly frugivorous, but hunts small animals and tears open birds' nests for eggs and young. Wanders far, daily and seasonally, from usual highland-forest habitat in search of fruiting trees (regularly visiting those in Nairobi gardens). Often associates with Trumpeter Hornbill. **Similar Species:** Trumpeter Hornbill has smaller, darker bill and more white on underparts; in flight, shows much white in wings, has white on upper tail-coverts but none on rump or back. Allopatric Black-and-white-casqued Hornbill shows much white in wings (both perched and in flight), more white in tail, has differently shaped bicoloured casque. **Status and Distribution:** Locally common in highland Kenyan forests east of the Rift Valley, from the Ndotos south to Nairobi and Thika; also in Kibwezi and Taveta Districts, the Chyulu and Taita Hills, and coastal lowlands north to the Arabuko-Sokoke Forest. In ne. Tanzania, common and widespread in the Usambara and Pare Mountains, on Kilimanjaro and in Arusha and Lake Manyara NPs. Disjunct (seasonal?) population in the Nguruman and Loliondo forests astride the Kenyan/Tanzanian border, west of lakes Magadi and Natron. Few breeding records.

BLACK-AND-WHITE-CASQUED HORNBILL *Bycanistes subcylindricus subquadratus* **Plate 63**

Length *c.* 70 cm (27–28"). A large *western* hornbill, distinguished from Silvery-cheeked by *extensive white wing area* (secondaries and broad tips to greater coverts) and more white in the tail. **Adult male** has high, laterally flattened, wedge-shaped casque (much shorter than that of Silvery-cheeked), cream at base but apical half black like rest of bill. Bare skin around eyes dull greyish pink; eyes reddish brown; feet blackish. Casque of **female** reduced to low projection at base of bill, bare loral and circumorbital skin pale pink, becoming red in breeding season; otherwise similar to male. Silvery-grey facial feather tips are less conspicuous than in Silvery-cheeked Hornbill. **Juvenile** has no casque, has brown facial feathering and grey eyes. **Voice:** Very loud bleating or braying *AAAR HAAARH, AAARH. . .*, or *AAAK AAAK AAAK AAAK-AAAK-AAK-AK,* producing a remarkable din when many birds call together. Contact note a single querulous *AARK.* Utters softer guttural notes when feeding. **Habits:** Similar to those of preceding species. Large numbers roost together, usually in pairs, making long flights to and from tall trees in morning and early evening, often using the same site for years. Pairs engage in allopreening. Frugivorous, but takes many insects and small vertebrates. **Similar Species:** Silvery-cheeked Hornbill compared above. Eastern Trumpeter Hornbill is allopatric. **Status and Distribution:** Locally common west of the Rift Valley in forest between 1600 and 2400 m, from Mt Elgon and the Cheranganis, Kakamega and Nandi Districts, Kabarnet, Eldama Ravine, Molo and Kericho Districts, south to the Mau and Trans-Mara Forests, Lolgorien and western parts of the Mara GR and Serengeti NP.

BARBETS AND TINKERBIRDS, FAMILY CAPITONIDAE
(World, *c.* 80 species; Africa, 41; Kenya, 22; n. Tanzania, 17)

Like their relatives on other continents, African barbets are stocky, large-headed birds with stout pointed bills. Many of ours are brightly coloured and strongly patterned, but others are clad in uniformly dull hues. The sexes are alike or similar. In the larger species, the bill is proportionately longer and heavier, with the maxillary tomia coarsely notched or 'toothed'. All have well-developed rictal and chin bristles, and *Gymnobucco* has bristly nasal tufts. Their wings are short and rounded, providing direct, strong but rather laboured (and typically audible) flight. With four exceptions, the tail is quite short. The tarsi are short and strong, the zygodactyl toes well adapted to clinging to trees; the terrestrial forms hop rather awkwardly on the ground.

The majority are highly frugivorous, but all include insects in their diet, and the ground nesters are largely insectivorous. They regurgitate pellets of undigested fruit stones and chitin. Tinkerbirds and some other arboreal barbets regularly join foraging mixed bird parties. Our species are all resident. Most are associated with trees, nesting and roosting in cavities excavated in soft wood, but *Trachyphonus* species breed in holes dug in termitaria or in the ground. Two to five white eggs are laid at the bottom of the cavity, usually without nesting material. Incubation and care of the nidicolous young are shared by both parents. Some barbets live in pairs and are strongly territorial, but others are social. Co-operative breeding is known in a few and suspected in others. The nest and eggs of Eastern Green Tinkerbird and Black-throated Barbet remain undescribed. Some authors place our barbets in a separate family (Lybiidae), but, although the semi-terrestrial *Trachyphonus* species have no counterparts among Asian or Tropical American forms, the family generally seems quite homogeneous.

GREY-THROATED BARBET *Gymnobucco bonapartei cinereiceps*   Plate 64

Length 165–175 mm (6.5–7"). A dark barbet with *pale eyes* and two prominent *erect tufts of brownish or straw-coloured bristly feathers at base of bill*. **Adult** dark brown (with indistinct paler shaft streaks), the head greyer to almost black on face and forehead; elongate buff spots behind the nasal tufts. Eyes cream or pale yellow; bill black, sometimes slightly bluish at base; feet black. **Juvenile** more uniform, nearly chocolate-brown, with less distinct shaft streaks, shorter and darker nasal tufts, dark grey eyes, and brownish-black bill yellowish at the base. **VOICE:** *Chew* or *whew* notes, repeated several times, and a sharper *yeek*, also in series. A nasal *nyaaa* and a buzzy *spzzz* when several birds are together. **HABITS:** Social, often in small vocal groups in dead treetops, from which they sometimes hawk aerial insects. Flies long distances to fruiting trees. **STATUS AND DISTRIBUTION:** Fairly common in highland wooded areas of w. Kenya, from Mt Elgon and Kapenguria south to the Nandi, Kakamega and Mau Forests, reaching the nw. Mara GR at Lolgorien and the forested slopes of the Olololoo Escarpment.

WHITE-EARED BARBET *Stactolaema leucotis kilimensis*   Plate 64

Length 170–180 mm (6.5–7"). A pied barbet with a *broad white streak extending from near eye and flaring on side of neck*; belly white, *rump and upper tail-coverts white or whitish* mixed with dark brown; plumage otherwise black (faintly glossy on head and breast) or blackish brown. Eyes dark brown; orbital skin, bill and feet black. **Juvenile** resembles adult, but is more blackish, the bill pale (dull yellowish or pinkish) at base; orbital skin probably dull pink, as in extralimital *S. l. leucotis*. **VOICE:** A harsh rolling *chreeer* or *kyeeeee*, often in groups of three or four; and a loud piercing *tseu tseu tseu tseu*. Several birds together produce various chattering and trilling notes. **HABITS:** Solitary or in small groups. Perches for long periods on dead branches of tall trees. Joins mixed-species flocks in fruiting trees (sometimes away from forest). **SIMILAR SPECIES:** Spot-flanked Barbet, in different habitat, has different distribution of black on underparts, large white moustachial streaks extending to the breast, and yellow wing edging. **STATUS AND DISTRIBUTION:** In Kenya, local and uncommon in forest edge and riparian woods on the Nyambeni Hills and lower slopes of Mt Kenya at Meru and Sagana; formerly near Nairobi; also in the Chyulu, Taita and Shimba Hills, and the coastal Diani and Ganda Forests. In ne. Tanzania, common in the Usambara and Pare Mountains, around Kilimanjaro, on Mt Meru and in Arusha NP.

GREEN BARBET *Stactolaema o. olivacea*   Plate 64

Length 150–155 mm (6"). A stolid, *dull olive* bird of *coastal forests*. **Adult** dark greenish olive above, more yellow-green on wings, paler on underparts; head and chin dark brown. Eyes dull red or orange (iris brownish around the pupil); bill black; feet blackish, the toes yellowish beneath. **Juvenile** duller than adult; eyes brown. **VOICE:** A loud, repetitive *tyok tyok tyok. . .*, or *chock chock. . ..* Sometimes duets, and one calling individual often stimulates another. **HABITS:** Frequently vocal, but difficult to locate high in forest trees. Attracted to fruiting branches in subcanopy. Solitary or social; several birds forage (and sometimes roost) together. **SIMILAR SPECIES:** Eastern Green Tinkerbird is much smaller, smaller-billed and much more active; also differs vocally. **STATUS AND DISTRIBUTION:** Common in Kenyan coastal forests from the Tana River delta south to Mrima and Shimoni. In ne.

Tanzania, largely absent from the coast but common in the East Usambaras (much less so in the West).

SPECKLED TINKERBIRD *Pogoniulus scolopaceus flavisquamatus*   Plate 65

Length 115–130 mm (4.5–5"). A central African bird, probably no longer present in w. Kenya. *Dull, scaly-looking* and larger than other tinkerbirds. **Adult** olive-brown above, the feathers edged and tipped yellowish; flight feathers irregularly yellow-edged and appearing spotted; crown blackish with some yellow spotting; underparts mottled, the chin and throat whitish (often with faint dark barring), shading into olive-yellow on breast (sometimes orange-tinted) and belly; sides of breast and flanks streaked and spotted with dusky brown. Iris colour varies from yellow in females to greyer or pale brown with whitish or yellowish outer ring in males; orbital skin blackish; bill black. **Juvenile** resembles adult, but throat often distinctly barred and bill yellowish at base, especially below. **VOICE:** Typical call differs from that of other tinkerbirds in that the syllables increase in number as the series continues; starts with a single *pok* or *cok*, repeated slowly, doubled to *cokok. . .*, tripled, *cokok-kok*, and finally becoming four or five rapidly uttered syllables, *cokok-kok-kok-kok*, etc., continuing for many seconds; middle portion of series closely resembles call of Common Quail, (Chapin 1939). Less frequent is a more typical tinkerbird-type *tok, tok, tok . . .*, and a faster trill recalling that of Moustached Green Tinkerbird. **HABITS:** In Uganda, favours clearings or forest edges with numerous large trees. Sometimes forages on large branches. Joins mixed-species flocks. **STATUS AND DISTRIBUTION:** Known in Kenya from an old and unsubstantiated sight record from the Kakamega Forest, and a specimen collected near Kitale (apparently examined by Chapin, but now untraceable).

EASTERN GREEN TINKERBIRD *Pogoniulus simplex*   Plate 65
(Green Tinker Barbet)

Length 90 mm (3.5"). A tiny olive bird of *coastal forest*. Upperparts yellowish olive-green with *lemon-yellow rump patch*; wings blackish, with *yellow wing-bars and flight-feather edging*; indistinct dull whitish line from bill to below eye; tail black, the outer feathers with very pale olive edging. Underparts dull olive-yellow to greyish yellow-olive. Eyes grey-brown or brown; orbital skin grey; bill black, with basal third yellow or orange-yellow below; feet blackish. **Juvenile** duller than adult, with entire basal half of bill yellow. **VOICE:** A rapid high-pitched trill, sometimes preceded by a single *pop* or *tok*; differs from similar call of sympatric Yellow-rumped Tinkerbird in being higher-pitched, somewhat faster, and often shorter; however, *simplex* may give slower trills at times. Utters a series of harsh grating notes when interacting with another individual. **HABITS:** Solitary or in mixed-species flocks, especially at fruiting trees. Typically forages in tangled undergrowth; sometimes flycatches. Puffs up yellow rump feathers when singing. **SIMILAR SPECIES:** Moustached Green Tinkerbird is a highland species with white moustachial stripes. Larger Green Barbet is much heavier, bigger-billed and lacks yellow rump. Yellow-rumped Tinkerbird is mostly black and white, with a striped face. **STATUS AND DISTRIBUTION:** Local and uncommon resident of undisturbed coastal forest from Arabuko–Sokoke, Shimba Hills NP, Shimoni and Mrima south to Tanga, and inland to the foothills of the East Usambaras, meeting *P. leucomystax* around Amani.

MOUSTACHED GREEN TINKERBIRD *Pogoniulus leucomystax*   Plate 65

Length 90–100 mm (3.5–4"). A *highland-forest* bird, olive-green with two *yellow wing-bars* (lower one often faint), *yellow rump* and *distinct white moustachial stripes* widening towards the neck. **Adult** mostly dark olive-green above, more yellowish green on head, and with a bright golden-yellow rump patch; wings blackish, with narrow yellowish wing-bars, and some flight feathers edged with yellowish white. Underparts greyish yellow-olive, darker on breast; belly pale yellowish. Eyes brown; bill blackish, with basal third (or more) of mandible dull yellow or whitish; feet black. **Juvenile** resembles adult, but has brighter yellow underparts. **VOICE:** A dry rapid *chk-chk-chk-chk-chk* in groups of several syllables, then a pause before next series as in Yellow-rumped Tinkerbird's call, but whole series faster and of different quality. Also has variable trills, fast or slow, sometimes changing tempo within a series, often beginning slowly and gradually accelerating (from six to *c.* 20 notes per second). Occasionally, a sharp, somewhat woodpecker-like *pi-pik!*, repeated a few times. **HABITS:** Solitary or in pairs. A canopy bird, but comes lower to feed in fruiting

creepers and shrubs; favours mistletoe (*Loranthus*) berries. Quite vocal. **SIMILAR SPECIES**: Eastern Green Tinkerbird, generally at lower elevations, lacks prominent white moustachial streaks and differs vocally. **STATUS AND DISTRIBUTION**: Fairly common between 1400 and 2500 m in forests from Mt Elgon and Mt Nyiru south to Mt Kenya, the Aberdares, Mau and northern Nairobi suburbs. Smaller populations in the Nguruman, Chyulu and Taita Hills, Arusha NP, Kilimanjaro, and the Pare and Usambara Mountains (where as low as 900 m at Amani).

YELLOW-RUMPED TINKERBIRD *Pogoniulus bilineatus*   Plate 65
(Golden-rumped Tinkerbird or Tinker Barbet)

Length 95–110 mm (3.75–4.25"). A *stripe-faced, black-backed* tinkerbird with a bright *golden-yellow rump*. **Adult** mostly glossy black above, with two yellow wing-bars and yellow-edged flight feathers; black head marked by long white superciliary stripes extending to neck from above eyes, and broader lines meeting over base of bill, extending back beneath eyes and across cheeks, separating the broad black moustachial stripes from the whitish throat; breast greyish, sides greyish olive, belly pale yellow. Eyes grey-brown, dark brown or red; orbital skin dark grey; bill black; feet greenish grey or blue-grey. Coastal *P. b. fischeri* is whiter on the throat, has less grey on the breast, more yellow on sides, and differs vocally from the widespread highland race *jacksoni*. **Juvenile** has yellowish-green or olive-green feather tips (sometimes extensive) on crown and upper back; bill yellowish horn-brown. **VOICE**: Commonly calls throughout the day, the notes not loud but far-carrying. Normal call of highland birds is a fairly slow series: *tonk-tonk-tonk-tonk. . .* or *tok, tok, tok. . .*, typically delivered in groups of three to seven notes, with a brief pause between groups, but the calling continuing for several to many minutes. A vocal session usually begins with groups of three or four notes, increasing in number as singing progresses or if another individual calls or appears nearby; groups rarely exceed eight or nine notes. Also produces a slower, more deliberate *whonk, whonk, whonk. . .* and a harsh *krreek, krreek, krreek. . .*, both in series. Usual song of coastal race is a single *pup*, quickly followed by a rapid dull trill (see Eastern Green Tinkerbird). **HABITS**: Solitary, but joins mixed-species flocks and mingles with other barbets in fruiting trees; takes many insects, some caught on the wing. Forages at various heights. **SIMILAR SPECIES**: Adult Yellow-fronted and Red-fronted Tinkerbirds have coloured forehead patches and white-striped backs, but are similar vocally and easily misidentified by voice alone. **STATUS AND DISTRIBUTION**: Common in forest (including clearings and edges), dense thickets, riverine woods and suburban gardens up to 3000 m. *P. b. jacksoni* (including '*alius*') ranges from Mt Elgon, the Cheranganis and Maralal, south across the Laikipia Plateau to Mt Kenya, the Aberdares and Nairobi; in the west, extends south to the Nandi, Kakamega and Mau Forests, Kilgoris, Lolgorien and the nw. Mara GR. *P. b. fischeri* (including '*pallidus*') ranges throughout the coastal lowlands from Tanga north to the Shimba Hills and Arabuko–Sokoke Forest.

RED-FRONTED TINKERBIRD *Pogoniulus pusillus affinis*   Plate 65

Length 90–106 mm (3.5–4.25"). A *dry-country* tinkerbird with a black-and-white-*striped face* and, in **adult**, a *scarlet forehead*. Upperparts black, heavily streaked with yellowish white from crown to upper back; rump and upper tail-coverts yellow; tail and wings blackish, the flight feathers and coverts broadly edged with golden yellow. Underparts pale yellowish, buffier on breast and flanks. Eyes dark brown; bill and feet black. **Juvenile** resembles adult, but lacks scarlet forehead patch. **VOICE**: Calls include a repeated metallic *tonk, tonk, tonk, tonk. . .*, a hollow, sometimes rather nasal *tok-tok-tok-tok. . .*, each note distinct and given in long series (often 20 or more) without pause, and a faster, more trilled series of piping notes which may alternate with popping sounds. Also has some harsh croaking notes. **HABITS**: Usually solitary. Forages low and high in foliage, on twigs and on larger branches, where it taps like a woodpecker; also flycatches. Joins mixed-species flocks. **SIMILAR SPECIES**: Red-fronted Barbet is much larger with a heavier bill and broad yellowish superciliary stripes. In areas of overlap, Yellow-rumped Tinkerbird could be confused with juvenile Red-fronted (which lacks red) but face patterns differ and Yellow-rumped is not streaked on the back. **STATUS AND DISTRIBUTION**: Fairly common in acacia woodland and taller thorn-scrub from the coastal lowlands up to 2000 m. Ranges north to the Kerio and Turkwell rivers, Mt. Kulal, Loyangalani, Marsabit and northeastern border areas. Absent from northern parts of the Lake Victoria basin and in western border areas where replaced by *P. chrysoconus*. After breeding may move from usual dry habitat to higher wetter sites.

YELLOW-FRONTED TINKERBIRD *Pogoniulus c. chrysoconus*   Plate 65

Length 100–115 mm (4–4.5"). Similar to the preceding species, but larger, heavier-billed, and, in most **adults**, the *forehead bright golden yellow*; no long white superciliary stripes; also *more lemon-yellow below*, and white cheeks separated from throat by thin black moustachial streaks. Eyes dark brown; bill black; feet greenish black. Forehead patch rarely orange-red, but face pattern readily separates such birds from Red-fronted Tinkerbird. **Juvenile** resembles adult, but lacks yellow on forehead. **VOICE**: Recalls that of Yellow-rumped Tinkerbird, but more uniform, with no periodic pauses within a series: a simple repetitive *tok tok tok toktok. . .*, almost identical to some calls of Red-fronted Tinkerbird. Often changes to *tu tu tu tu. . .*, the note repeated at rate of one or

two per second. Also has a disyllabic *cok-ok, cok-ok, cok-ok. . .*, and a rolling, almost trilled *cok-k-k-k, cok-k-k-k . . .*. **HABITS**: As for Red-fronted Tinkerbird; responds to playback of taped calls of that species. **SIMILAR SPECIES**: Red-fronted Tinkerbird compared above. Yellow-rumped Tinkerbird is evenly black from forehead to lower back. Both species unlikely within range of Yellow-fronted. **STATUS AND DISTRIBUTION**: Locally common in w. Kenya from Malaba and Busia border areas east to Bungoma, Mumias, Kisumu and Chemelil. Inhabits wooded riparian strips, forest edge, savanna, thickets, suburban shade trees and gardens at up to 1500 m. Rare south of Ahero, where replaced by Red-fronted Tinkerbird.

YELLOW-SPOTTED BARBET *Buccanodon d. duchaillui*   Plate 64

Length 150–165 mm (6–6.5"). A black-and-yellow barbet of *western Kenyan forests*. **Adult** crimson on forehead and crown, velvety blue-black from hindcrown to back, the last *spotted with bright yellow,* as are some wing-coverts; *broad yellow stripe from eyes to sides of neck;* greater coverts and flight feathers edged with yellow. Sides of face blue-black, as are chin, throat and breast; heavily barred with yellow on belly (sides and flanks become largely black as the yellow feather tips wear away); rump and upper tail-coverts also yellow-barred. Eyes brown; bill black; feet dark slate-grey. **Juvenile** duller than adult, with *black crown and forehead. Bill orange or yellow with black tip*; eyes grey; orbital skin pinkish; underparts more extensively (but duller) yellow than adult. **VOICE**: A two-second purring or snoring call, *zhr-r-r-r-rrrrrrrrrr.* Several birds may engage in a group chattering. **HABITS**: Solitary or in groups; joins mixed-species parties. Arboreal and usually high in canopy, but fruiting creepers lure it into the undergrowth. **SIMILAR SPECIES**: Rare Hairy-breasted Barbet lacks red, side of face shows a *white* stripe above ear-coverts and a white moustachial stripe; chin to breast streaked black and white. **STATUS AND DISTRIBUTION**: Local and uncommon resident of the Nandi, Kakamega and West Mau Forests of w. Kenya. Reported from Mt Elgon (Short *et al.* 1990).

HAIRY-BREASTED BARBET *Tricholaema hirsuta ansorgii*   Plate 64

Length 165–180 mm (6.5–7"). A canopy-feeding barbet of the Kakamega Forest. **Adult** glossy black on forehead and face, with white superciliary and moustachial stripes, the former not extending above the lores; crown and rest of upperparts brownish black, finely spotted with yellow; most wing feathers yellow-edged; *throat streaked black and white*; breast yellow, with fine black hair-like tips to some feathers (as on lower throat); *lower breast, sides, flanks and under tail-coverts paler yellow or greenish yellow, spotted with black*; flanks also barred. Eyes reddish brown or red; orbital skin dark grey; bill black; feet bluish or greenish grey. Yellow plumage of **female** more gold or orange-gold. **Juvenile** is less spotted, more barred, below; bill horn-coloured, with black base; feet pale grey. **VOICE**: A deep short *hoop* or *oork,* slowly repeated for up to 30 seconds; usually given in short series, faster than similar call of Yellow-billed Barbet. **HABITS**: Solitary, in pairs or in mixed-species flocks. Arboreal and inconspicuous, usually remaining within cover, but occasionally visits fruiting trees at forest edge. **SIMILAR SPECIES**: Smaller Yellow-spotted Barbet has red forehead and is black-throated, with a single yellow line on each side of neck. **STATUS AND DISTRIBUTION**: Rare resident, confined to taller trees of the Kakamega Forest, w. Kenya.

RED-FRONTED BARBET *Tricholaema diademata*   Plate 64

Length 145–165 mm (5.75–6.5"). A thickset dry-country barbet. **Adult** has *red forehead patch, yellow-streaked black upperparts,* and *yellow rump; broad yellowish superciliary stripes* border the black cheeks and ear-coverts; wings and tail spotted and edged with yellow. Underparts creamy white in *T. d. diademata*, with a few large blackish spots on lower flanks; *T. d. massaica* spotted or streaked on flanks and belly. Eyes brown or red-brown; bill blackish or dark grey, paler at base; feet dark grey. **Female** has less red on head. **Juvenile** duller, with browner bill, and little or no red. **VOICE**: A series of up to 15 loud hollow notes, *hoop-hoop-hoop. . .*, often in duet; faster than call of Spot-flanked Barbet. Hoopoe-like in quality. **HABITS**: Solitary or in pairs. Rather sluggish, foraging slowly in low trees and shrubs; sometimes comes to the ground for insects. **SIMILAR SPECIES**: Red-fronted Tinkerbird is much smaller and smaller-billed, and has conspicuous black moustachial stripes. **STATUS AND DISTRIBUTION**: Uncommon in dry woodland (especially *Acacia* and *Combretum*): *T. d. diademata* in n. Kenya, from the Kongelai Escarpment, Kerio Valley and Mt Nyiru south to Baringo, Maralal, Laikipia, Isiolo and Meru Districts; *T. d. massaica* from Siaya, Kisumu, Nakuru, Naivasha, Nairobi, Machakos and Kitui Districts, south through much of dry interior n. Tanzania.

SPOT-FLANKED BARBET   *Tricholaema lacrymosa*
(Spotted-flanked Barbet)

PLATE 64

Length 125–140 mm (5–5.5"). A small, *black-bibbed* barbet, *heavily spotted on sides, flanks and under tail-coverts*. Black above, with bold white superciliary and submoustachial stripes, the latter joining white of foreneck at sides of bib; browner rump and upper tail-coverts heavily streaked with pale yellow; long broad whitish stripes on scapulars. Wing shows yellow bar on greater coverts, and all but outer few flight feathers are edged with pale yellow. Underparts creamy white below the bib; black side/flank spots drop-shaped in *T. l. lacrymosa*, smaller and more rounded in western *radcliffei*. **Adults** of both races have yellow or yellow-orange eyes in male, brown or red in female. **Juvenile** has the black plumage areas greyer and is brown-eyed. **VOICE**: A loud *hook. . . hook. . . hook. . .*, slower and higher-pitched than comparable call of Red-fronted Barbet, the notes given at rate of about one per second. Also a croaking *grrrk, grrrk. . .*, a low *yek, yek, yek. . .* given in series, and a harsh nasal *nyaaa*. **HABITS**: Solitary or in pairs. Usually feeds in low trees; partial to figs. **SIMILAR SPECIES**: Black-throated Barbet, typically in drier regions, has yellow spots above, lacks black spots below. **STATUS AND DISTRIBUTION**: Locally common between 600 and 2100 m in moist to moderately dry woodland and tall riverine vegetation, generally occupying areas of higher rainfall than does Black-throated. *T. l. lacrymosa* ranges from the Kongelai Escarpment, Mt Nyiru and Meru, south through the Tsavo NPs to Mkomazi GR and Moshi and Arusha Districts in ne. Tanzania. *T. l. radcliffei* (includes 'ruahae') occupies Kenyan/Ugandan border areas south of Mt Elgon, the Lake Victoria basin, and Mara GR south to Serengeti NP, the Crater and Mbulu Highlands, Lake Manyara and Tarangire NPs and western edges of the Masai Steppe. Sympatric with *T. melanocephala* in several eastern areas, especially after periods of high rainfall.

BLACK-THROATED BARBET   *Tricholaema melanocephala stigmatothorax*

Plate 64

Length 125–140 mm (5–5.5"). A dark brown-and-white barbet of *dry* bush country. Head pattern like that of Spot-flanked Barbet, but occasional birds show yellow, orange or red speckling on forehead. Upperparts blackish brown, with *elongated bright yellow spots on back* and yellow streaks on rump; upper tail-coverts tipped with yellowish white. *Brown of throat and breast narrows to point* on the white belly (where sometimes ending in a red or orange spot). In worn birds, the dark plumage areas are browner, the yellowish marks narrower and whiter. Eyes brown; bill black, paler below at base; feet dark grey. **Juvenile** darker, with duller yellow spots and feather edging; bill greyer. **VOICE**: A series of four to six harsh grating notes, rapidly uttered and slightly descending: *skwi, tchee-tchew-tchew* or *ka-kaar-kaar-kaar-kaar*. Also produces a harsh nasal *nyaaa*. **HABITS**: Solitary, in pairs or in small groups. Forages low in trees, frequently in shrubbery. Frugivorous, but captures flying insects and eats numerous insect larvae. **SIMILAR SPECIES**: Spot-flanked Barbet differs vocally, has spotted sides, no yellow spots on back. **STATUS AND DISTRIBUTION**: Fairly common and widespread in dry bush and thorn-scrub below 1500 m. Ranges over much of n. and e. Kenya (though absent from the coast), south through the Tsavo region to the Mkomazi GR and west across the Masai Steppe to Tarangire NP; also near the Kenyan border north of Arusha and west to lakes Natron and Magadi.

WHITE-HEADED BARBET   *Lybius leucocephalus*

Plate 64

Length 180–190 mm (7–7.5"). A *white-headed, white-rumped* barbet of the highlands. Racially variable: *L. l. senex* is *white, except for the wings and middle of back*; *L. l. albicauda* is *white-tailed* like *senex*, but flanks, belly and wings are dusky brown, spotted with white. These two races interbreed. *L. l. leucocephalus* differs in having a *black tail*, dusky *brown lower breast and belly with white streaks*, white-spotted scapulars and wing-coverts and white-tipped inner secondaries. In all races, eyes dark brown; bill black, the maxillary tomium with one large 'tooth'; feet slate-grey to greenish grey. **Juveniles** blotched dull brown on head and underparts, tail partly or wholly brown, bill horn-brown with indistinct 'tooth' or none; eyes grey. **VOICE**: Differs racially; typical guttural churring or growling group vocalizations rather babbler-like. Those of two or more *L. l. albicauda* include a 10- to 15-second series of notes building in intensity from a soft beginning, then fading at the end: *chrrchrr-grr, grraak gwak, grrh, grrh, chrr-OW-chrrOW-chrrCHOW-chrrCHOW-chrr-tchao chrrak-akk-akk-akk-akk*. Comparable call of *senex* a still harsher, loud wheezy chattering, *ch-ch-ch-ch-zhizh, zhizh-zhizh-zhizh-zhizh-tchee-tchee-tchee . . ..* Also gives separate *skyrrrr* or *chwrrr* notes. Pairs of *L. l. leucocephalus* duet with unsynchronized clear *pewp* notes, the series ending with *yit* or *it-it-it* (Short and Horne, in Fry *et al.* 1988). **HABITS**: Social, often in small groups. Several adults incubate and also tend nestlings. Closely associated with fruiting fig trees, but also feeds on insects, some taken on the ground; occasionally flycatches. Noisy displays include exaggerated bowing, head-swaying, tail-spreading and wing-flicking. Sometimes taps, woodpecker-like, near nest cavity. **SIMILAR SPECIES**: White-headed Buffalo-Weaver has different habits, orange-red rump, white wing patches and dark line on face. **STATUS AND DISTRIBUTION**: Locally fairly common in riverine woodland, cleared forest with scattered trees, tall moist bush and wooded suburban gardens. *L. l. leucocephalus* ranges in w. Kenya from Ruma NP (Lambwe Valley) and Kisumu north to Mt Elgon and the

Kongelai Escarpment; *senex* in the central Kenyan highlands, mainly east of the Rift Valley, at Meru, Embu, Nairobi, Thika, Kitui and the Chyulu Hills, meeting and apparently interbreeding freely with southwestern *albi-cauda*. The latter ranges from Lolgorien, Mara GR and the Loita Hills through interior n. Tanzania to Serengeti, Lake Manyara, Tarangire and Arusha NPs and the North Pare Mts; also to Taveta and Bura (Taita Hills District) in se. Kenya. Formerly along the Voi River and occasional at Mombasa.

BLACK-BILLED BARBET *Lybius guifsobalito* Plate 64

Length 150–165 mm (6–6.5"). A black-bodied, red-faced barbet of western border areas. **Adult** blue-black, with *red face, throat and upper breast*; flight feathers brownish and *broadly edged pale yellow* (and with white on inner webs); *coverts black with white streaks*. Eyes reddish brown; orbital skin grey; bill black, maxillary tomium usually with one 'tooth'; feet dark grey or blackish. **Juvenile** resembles adult, but red areas more orange and forehead and crown mainly dull black; chin brown with whitish shaft streaks; throat brown with some red feather tips. **VOICE**: Main call an antiphonal duet, preceded by chattering or grating notes, with one bird giving a repeated higher double *kik-ka*, the other a lower *apoot*, the performance consisting of 10–20 *kik-ka-apoot* phrases (Short and Horne, in Fry *et al.* 1988). Recalls similar call of Black-collared Barbet. Also gives a single *wupp*. **HABITS**: Solitary, in pairs or in small groups. Often perches on tops of tall euphorbias, utility poles and other exposed places. **SIMILAR SPECIES**: Extralimital Red-faced Barbet, *L. rubrifacies*, west of Lake Victoria, has blackish-brown throat and breast, red restricted to face and ear-coverts; juvenile lacks red on head. **STATUS AND DISTRIBUTION**: Locally common along the Kenyan/Ugandan border, from Mt Elgon, Malaba and Busia east to Mumias, Kisumu, Muhoroni, Songhor, Koru and Kapsarok, south to Ruma NP, Lolgorien, Tanzanian border areas and Musoma.

BLACK-COLLARED BARBET *Lybius torquatus irroratus* Plate 64

Length 180–190 mm (7–7.5"). Restricted to *coastal woods*. A colourful bird, with *red forehead, face and throat* and *broad black 'collar' across upper breast*; underparts below the black band pale yellow (rarely orange-yellow). Crown and upper back black; lower back and rump brown, with fine brown, black and yellowish vermiculations; wings dark brown with pale yellow feather edges. Eyes chestnut, purplish red or brown; orbital skin dark grey; bill large and black, with one or two large maxillary 'teeth'; feet blue-grey. **Juvenile** blackish brown on forehead and face; throat and breast brown, with scattered red feathers appearing with maturity; bill brown, yellow at base of mandible; eyes grey. **VOICE**: A sprightly antiphonal duet, *KEE, pup-up KEE, pup-up. . ., KEE* from one bird, *pup-up* from the second, repeated numerous times and often preceded or followed by a babbler-like guttural chatter, *cheew-chewchewchew. . .*. A repeated *pup, pup, pup. . .* is given by single bird. **HABITS**: Usually in pairs. Often perches high in dead trees; noisy and aggressive at fruiting trees or shrubs; forages among large branches and in foliage of smaller twigs. **SIMILAR SPECIES**: Brown-breasted Barbet has white belly and black leg feathers, no black collar. **STATUS AND DISTRIBUTION**: Locally fairly common in moist open woodland, scrub and gardens with fruiting trees in coastal lowlands north to the Boni Forest, inland to Shimba Hills NP and in riparian forest along the lower Tana River.

BROWN-BREASTED BARBET *Lybius melanopterus* Plate 64

Length 180–190 mm (7–7.5"). A *white-bellied, red-faced* eastern barbet with a *brown breast*; *leg feathers and small patch on flanks black*. **Adult** has red forehead, face and throat, the latter with whitish shaft streaks (and brown feather bases evident in worn birds); crown to upper back grey-brown to blackish brown, with bright red feather tips in fresh plumage; brown rump, blackish upper tail-coverts, brown breast feathers and wing-coverts all have white shaft-streaks. Tail blackish. Eyes brown or reddish brown. Bill pale, brownish or greyish horn, yellowish or whitish at tip and along cutting edges; one or two maxillary 'teeth,' lacking in **juvenile,** which has much less red, largely brown throat and grey-brown breast. **VOICE**: Usual call a loud *whaak whaak whaak. . .*, three or more notes per series. Does not duet. **HABITS**: Social; several often perch together in dead trees. Forages in trees and low shrubbery, congregating in fruiting fig trees. Rather sluggish, but frequently flycatches from dead treetops. **SIMILAR SPECIES**: See Black-collared Barbet. **STATUS AND DISTRIBUTION**: Local and uncommon in coastal woodland, forest edge and cultivation from Tanga north to Lamu, ranging inland along the Tana River to Garissa, and from Shimba Hills west to ne. Tanzania in the Mkomazi GR, North Pare Mts, lower slopes of Kilimanjaro and Mt Meru, and throughout Arusha and Moshi Districts, extending into Kenya from Taveta and Rombo to Bura and Wundanyi in Taita Hills District, and along the Voi River in Tsavo East NP.

DOUBLE-TOOTHED BARBET *Lybius bidentatus aequatorialis* Plate 64

Length 205–215 mm (8–8.5"). A black-and-red barbet with a *large ivory-coloured bill* and *yellow eye patch*. **Adult male** mostly black above, with a small white patch on lower back and a narrow rosy wing-bar; crown with some red streaking; *ear-coverts, cheeks and most of underparts bright red*, the flanks, leg feathers and under tail-coverts black; *white fan-shaped patch* usually conspicuous on sides. Maxillary tomium has two large 'teeth.' Eyes whitish or yellow; orbital skin bright yellow or greenish yellow; feet pinkish brown to dark brown. **Female** has blackish streaks on the red sides immediately above the white patches. **Juvenile** shows much less red below, has more greyish brown on throat and sides, and grey orbital skin; feet whitish; tomial 'teeth' reduced or lacking. **VOICE:** A harsh *kekk* or *krrek*, singly or repeated; also a three- to five-second purring *krrrrrrrrrrrrrrr-ik*. **HABITS:** Solitary or in pairs, but several may roost together. Travels far to fruiting fig trees; flycatches (especially for emerging termites), and may cling to tree trunks when foraging; actively flicks tail when excited. **STATUS AND DISTRIBUTION:** Fairly common in open moist woodland, forest edge and patches, and in cultivation with trees, between 1300 and 2300 m in w. Kenya, from Mt Elgon, Kapenguria and Nandi Districts south through the Lake Victoria basin, western Mau Forest, Kilgoris and Lolgorien to the Mara GR and western Serengeti NP.

YELLOW-BILLED BARBET *Trachylaemus purpuratus elgonensis* Plate 64

Length 230–255 mm (9–10"). A striking long-tailed barbet with *vivid yellow bill and facial skin*. Upperparts black with blue gloss. A narrow white patch from bend of wing along forepart of wing usually concealed in perched bird. *Forehead, crown and postocular area deep maroon, more reddish on neck and bright crimson along lower edge of a dark chest band*, the latter blackish but 'frosted' with short silvery-pink streaks; *lower breast and belly yellow*, grading into large yellow spots on otherwise black sides and flanks. Eyes red or orange-red; feet olive-slate. **Juvenile** similar but duller, with less red, no frosty pink on throat and breast, and more extensively yellow below; eyes brown. **VOICE:** Usual call (a common forest sound) is a low *whook* or *hoop*, uttered once or twice per second for an extended period; may be varied to a disyllabic *wha-ook*. Displaying birds give a soft *wunk-wunk, oonk-oonk-oonk*; in duet, both give rapid *chaaa* calls leading to a rapid *wuk-wuk, wuk-wuk-wup . . ..* **HABITS:** Solitary or in pairs. Sluggish; perches quietly in lower canopy or dense vines (where difficult to see, despite frequent calling). Displays marked by bowing of duetting birds. Largely frugivorous, but also eats insects and snails, some taken from the ground. **SIMILAR SPECIES:** Sympatric Yellow-spotted and Hairy-breasted Barbets are black-billed, shorter-tailed, and have no yellow facial skin. **STATUS AND DISTRIBUTION:** Locally fairly common in w. Kenyan highland forests between 1500 and 2800 m. Ranges from Mt Elgon, Saiwa NP, the Nandi and Kakamega Forests south to the Mau and Trans-Mara Forests, Molo and Lolgorien. **NOTE:** Now often placed in the genus *Trachyphonus*, but differs greatly from those open-country social species in plumage, behaviour and vocalizations.

CRESTED BARBET *Trachyphonus vaillantii suahelicus* Plate 122
(Levaillant's Barbet)

Length 230–240 mm (9–9.5"). A handsome orange, yellow and black Tanzanian barbet with *prominent black crest* and nape outlining a *red-speckled yellow face*. **Adult** glossy blue-black above with variable white feather tipping; remiges browner and white-barred; lower-back feather margins and rump yellow; upper tail-coverts crimson. Long black tail barred with white except on central feathers, and in fresh plumage shows a *broad white tip or subterminal band*. Face, lower crown, throat and sides of neck yellow, with variable red feather tipping; chin pale yellow to orange; small black-and-white patch on ear-coverts. White-spotted black breast band subtended by red streaks on otherwise mainly pale yellowish lower breast and belly. Under tail-coverts yellow with red tips. Bill heavy, *pale yellow or greenish yellow*, and dusky-tipped; orbital skin black; eyes mainly red-brown; feet brownish grey to blackish. **Juvenile** browner, less glossy blue-black, paler yellow on face. Bill darker than adult's; orbital skin grey; eyes brown. **VOICE:** A sustained unmusical purring, somewhat like the ringing of a muffled alarm clock, lasting up to 20 seconds. Pairs often duet, and nearby birds may join in. Alarm call a loud sharp rattle, *kek-kek-kek-kek-kek*, similar to that of Red-and-yellow Barbet. **HABITS:** Singles or pairs forage near or on ground, but never far from cover. Prefers areas with an abundance of termitaria. Roosts and nests in tree cavities, unlike others of the genus. **SIMILAR SPECIES:** Red-and-yellow Barbet has red bill, heavily spotted upperparts, and lacks crest. The smaller d'Arnaud's Barbet shows little or no orange-red on face. **STATUS AND DISTRIBUTION:** Local and uncommon, in our area only at Lake Manyara and Tarangire NPs (where sympatric with Red-and-yellow Barbet), and around edges of cultivation in the West Usambaras.

RED-AND-YELLOW BARBET *Trachyphonus erythrocephalus*   Plate 64

Length 200–225 mm (8–9"). A *gaudily spotted, reddish-billed, red-faced* barbet with bright *white ear patches*. **Adult male** of nominate race *boldly white-spotted* above, with a black-and-white-speckled band across the yellow breast, yellowish-white tail spots, and boldly barred outer tail feathers; rump yellow, upper tail-coverts red and yellow; under tail-coverts red with yellow tips. *Crown slightly crested and glossy black*. Throat and upper breast orange, yellower at sides, with a long median black patch. Bill buffy red, orbital skin dark grey, eyes yellow-brown or red-brown; feet blue-grey. **Female** similar but browner (as are worn males), and *crown red with black spots*; throat more evenly orange, with no black patch; breast band narrower and incomplete. **Adult** *T. e. versicolor* is paler, more yellow, with less red on head (superciliary areas largely yellow). Extreme northeastern *T. e. shelleyi* is smaller, much paler below, with little orange on throat and breast. **Juveniles** (all races) are yellower than adults and with little orange; dorsal spots cream or yellowish, not white; throat greyish; eyes grey. **Voice:** Loud rollicking duets characteristic of open bush country, *ko-quedeely-kwo, ko-tweedely-kwo,* repeated over and over. Alarm call a woodpecker-like *ki-ki-ki-ki.* **Habits:** Social. Pairs duet from top of termitarium, rock or bush, sometimes joined by other individuals. Forages mostly on ground; omnivorous. Excavates nest holes in termitaria, earth banks or road cuttings. Confiding where not persecuted. **Similar Species:** The smaller d'Arnaud's Barbet shows little or no orange-red coloration, has different face pattern, horn-coloured or blackish bill. In n. Tanzania see Crested Barbet. **Status and Distribution:** Locally fairly common and widespread in dry bush, woodland, savanna and scrub with suitable terrain and termitaria for nesting. *T. e. versicolor* ranges across much of n. and nw. Kenya south to the Kerio Valley, lakes Baringo and Bogoria and Meru NP; intergrades with Ethiopian *T. e. shelleyi* in the extreme northeast. Nominate *erythrocephalus* is widespread in s. Kenya, from the Kedong Valley, Olorgesailie and Magadi east to Amboseli, the Tsavo NPs, and the lower Tana River; in n. Tanzania, from Mkomazi GR and the Masai Steppe west to Tarangire and Lake Manyara NPs, the Crater Highlands, Olduvai Gorge and Lake Natron.

D'ARNAUD'S BARBET *Trachyphonus darnaudii*   Plate 64
(including Usambiro Barbet)

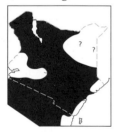

Length of *T. d. boehmi* and *darnaudii* 165–180 mm (6.5–7"), of *usambiro* 180–190 mm (7–7.5"). A *boldly spotted* barbet of grassland and bush. Reminiscent of the preceding species, but smaller, with *no red on face*, and the entire *underparts black-speckled* excepting the *bright red under tail-coverts*. Pronounced racial differences. **Adult** mainly dark brown above with bold white spots. *Forehead and crown yellow or orange and yellow, speckled with black* (*usambiro* and nominate *darnaudii*), or *entirely black* (*boehmi*); rump dull yellow, indistinctly barred with brown. Face yellow or orange-yellow, heavily black-spotted, as are yellow or orange-tinged throat and upper breast; *large black patch on lower throat* and an irregular black-and-white-spotted band across breast; otherwise pale yellow below with blackish speckling, fainter on sides but broadening to faint bars on lower flanks; tail barred with black and yellowish white, the central feathers mostly dark brown. Southwestern *T. d. usambiro* is larger and stockier, with a more distinct breast band and *heavy barring on lower breast and belly*; head appears larger and more rounded than in other races, and plumage lacks orange tones. Eyes brown or reddish brown in all races. Bill of *darnaudii* brownish grey or light greyish horn, paler below and at tip, darker on culmen; that of *boehmi* blackish at tip and often on much of maxilla, the pale areas brownish to pinkish horn; bill of *usambiro* typically *black or blackish*. Feet grey or brownish grey. Birds along Kenyan/Tanzanian boundary near Lake Victoria, with general appearance of *boehmi*, have vocalizations of *usambiro*. **Juvenile** resembles adult, but crown of nominate *darnaudii* is dark brown with few or no light spots, and underparts are paler yellow, brownish on throat; eyes grey. **Voice:** A characteristic sound of open bush and dry scrub. Rising-and-falling duet of *boehmi* and *darnaudii* resembes that of Red-and-yellow Barbet: *tu-wa-tee-tootle, tu-wa-tee-tootle. . .* or *qu-wa-tew-chupup . . .,* repeated numerous times. Distinct duet of *usambiro* typically harsh, grating, almost squealing: *cherk-a-SKRRRRRK* or *Uk-ki-YERRRK,* monotonously repeated, quite unmusical and not rising and falling in pitch; a rather squeaky reedy *kuWEEER* also repeated by duetting birds. **Habits:** In pairs or small groups (usually three or four birds). Typically, excavates roosting and nesting holes in flat ground. Forages in low bushes and on the ground. Omnivorous. Often confiding. **Similar Species:** See Crested and Red-and-yellow Barbets. **Status and Distribution:** Common in bushed grassland and dry scrub. *T. d. darnaudii* in nw. Kenya south to Kongelai, the Kerio Valley and Baringo District; *boehmi* east of the Rift Valley, south through Tana River District and the Tsavo NPs to ne.Tanzania, where ranges west to Tarangire and Lake Manyara NPs and Lake Natron; *usambiro* in heavily overgrazed parts of Masailand in Narok District, throughout the Mara GR and Serengeti NP to western edge of Ngorongoro Conservation area near Olduvai. **Note:** *T. d. usambiro* ('Usambiro Barbet') is considered specifically distinct by some authors (but see Short and Horne 1985a, b). Unstudied population along Kenyan/Tanzanian border around Muhoro Bay on Lake Victoria may prove intermediate between *boehmi* and *usambiro*.

HONEYGUIDES, FAMILY INDICATORIDAE
(World, 17 species; Africa, 15; Kenya, 9; n. Tanzania, 6)

Drab-coloured, superficially passerine-like, arboreal birds with much white in the tail. The well-known guiding behaviour, whereby a bird leads humans or ratels to bees' nests (and from which the English and scientific family names are derived), seems to be restricted to the Greater Honeyguide. All studied species are brood parasites, with barbets and woodpeckers serving as principal hosts of the *Indicator* species, which frequently harass these cavity nesters. The small, sharp-billed honeybirds (*Prodotiscus*) lay their eggs in open nests of passerines.

Honeyguides are stolid and rather inactive, often remaining still for long periods before abruptly flying with rapid and sometimes undulating flight, flashing their white outer tail feathers. Some are quite vocal, and certain species have favourite calling sites used for years. The dainty honeybirds are reminiscent of warblers in their movements. They and the smaller honeyguides sometimes feed by fluttering about amid foliage, and they may hawk insects in the air. If seen well, most species may be identified in the field, but some are difficult to name with certainty. Except in the Greater Honeyguide, sexes are alike and young birds are similar to adults, but less sharply marked.

Honeyguides feed on wax as well as insects, thus explaining their predilection for bees' nests. Some species are scarce and poorly known. The more common ones are widespread but easily overlooked. They may be seen near arboreal bee hives and around tree cavities where bees are in evidence, and can at times be baited with honeycomb. The species are all resident.

GREATER or BLACK-THROATED HONEYGUIDE *Indicator indicator* Plate 67

Length 180–190 mm (7–7.5"). Most often seen in *undulating flight*, the *white outer tail feathers* conspicuous. When perched, appears as an upright compact bird, the tail from below appearing white, with dusky markings at edges and tip. **Adult male** greyish brown above, with brown-and-white-streaked upper tail-coverts. *Black throat patch*; greyish breast may be washed with yellow; belly and under tail-coverts white. Golden 'shoulder' patch, often partly concealed; wings otherwise dark brown. Bill usually pink, but may be dull white or pale horn-brown; eyes dark brown; feet grey. **Female** plain brownish above, with pale-edged wing feathers; below, light grey (rarely a few black throat feathers), becoming white posteriorly; bill dull brown with some pink or entirely dark grey; eyes grey-brown. **Juvenile** *yellow-throated*; upperparts olive-brown, with unstreaked white patch on central upper tail-coverts; belly and crissum creamy white.
Immature often retains many yellow chin and throat feathers following the incomplete post-juvenile (first prebasic) moult. **VOICE**: Usual call of male a loud, monotonous, rolling *WHEET-cher, WHEET-cher. . .* or *WHIT-purr, WHIT-purr. . .*, repeated over and over; this varied to *WHEP-eew-irr. . .*, the trilled second and third notes suggesting a Striped Kingfisher's call. Guiding call of both sexes is a dry chattering rattle, likened to shaking a box of matches back and forth. Female gives loud *wit* or *weet* notes when interacting with barbets. **HABITS**: Males 'sing' for extended periods from favoured trees. Near such call sites, courting (?) birds produce a whirring, rustling or clapping sound with wings or tail. Also gives a deep, vibrating *bvoOOOmmm*. **SIMILAR SPECIES**: Lesser Honeyguide is smaller, bright yellow-olive above, with dusky malar stripes and whitish loral spots. Scaly-throated Honeyguide is heavily marked on throat and breast. **STATUS AND DISTRIBUTION**: Rather local yet widely distributed in Kenya and n. Tanzania, from sea level to over 2500 m in open forest, savanna, acacia woodland, thornscrub, tall bush, and cultivation with scattered trees. Absent only from arid parts of n. and ne. Kenya.

SCALY-THROATED HONEYGUIDE *Indicator variegatus* Plate 67

Length 180–190 mm (7–7.5"). An inconspicuous arboreal bird of dense foliage, compact and *heavy-billed*, with *spotted or scaly lower throat, breast and sides*; chin streaked. **Adult** has upperparts dull greenish olive or yellowish olive, brightest on wings. Belly and under tail-coverts dull whitish. Head olive-brown, streaked whitish on forehead and crown. From below, the dark-marked white tail and black-tipped pinkish mandible are noticeable. Bill yellow along tomia; orbital skin olive-green or blackish; eyes brown; feet olive or greenish grey. **Juvenile** more greenish than adult, with more prominent spots or bars, more white in tail, and a narrow yellowish eye-ring. **VOICE**: An ascending purring trill, varying in quality and reminiscent of an insect or frog, and lasting two to four seconds or more. Begins slowly, then accelerates as pitch slightly rises. Other notes include a prolonged *chee-tii, chee-tii* (van Someren, in Mackworth-Praed and Grant 1952), and a loud, vibrant, rolling trill, *trrrreeeeee* or *treeee-phew*, likened to a policeman's whistle. Also gives a short soft chatter and various buzzing notes. **HABITS**: Unobtrusive. Joins mixed-species flocks. Calls from favoured tree, as do Greater and Lesser Honeyguides. Feeds extensively on beeswax and insects; also eats figs. Reported 'guiding' of humans and ratels to bee hives remains undocumented. **SIMILAR SPECIES**: Female Greater Honeyguide may also show pink on bill but is plain-breasted. Honeyguide Greenbul (w. Kenyan forests) has thinner bill and male has whitish eyes. **STATUS AND DISTRIBUTION**: Uncommon in woodland, savanna, riparian groves and forest edge from sea level to over 2500 m. Widespread in coastal forest north to the Boni, and inland along the Tana River, in the Shimba Hills and Usambara Mts. Largely absent from arid n. and ne. Kenya and much of dry interior n. Tanzania.

LESSER HONEYGUIDE *Indicator minor teitensis*   Plate 67

Length 130–140 mm (5–5.5"). A small and unobtrusive stub-billed bird, olive-grey to (usually) yellow-olive above, greyer on the crown and cheeks. **Adult** has *whitish loral spots and dusky sub-moustachial or malar stripes*. Underparts pale grey to dark ashy grey with olive tinge; chin and belly whitish; some dark streaks on flanks; underside of tail white, with dark tips and corners. Bill black, with extreme base of mandible pinkish white; eyes brown; feet greyish. **Juvenile** lacks loral spots and malar stripes; head and upperparts greener than adult, underparts greyer, with streaked throat; bill greyish. **Voice**: A far-carrying *klee-eu* or *pew*, repeated many times, the series followed by a brief pause before resumption. Less frequent is a repeated clear song-like *twee-wiweet*. . . with variations. Also gives a trill or rattle, sometimes in flight. **Habits**: More active than the preceding two species. Gleans in foliage and flycatches. Often displays aggressively toward other honeyguides and nearby smaller birds when around bees' nests. Flight rapid, level or undulating. Feeds on bees, other insects and beeswax. Produces rustling, whirring or clapping sounds with wings or tail, sometimes as a single *whurrr* or *wh-whrrrr*. Responds to imitations of barbet calls. **Similar Species**: Thick-billed Honeyguide has darker underparts and is restricted to heavy forest. Female Greater Honeyguide is larger, brownish above and lighter below than Lesser, lacks white loral spots and dusky malar stripes. Pallid Honeyguide is brighter, more golden olive above, with no hint of dark malar stripes. **Status and distribution**: Locally common and widespread from sea level to 2000 m or higher in acacia and riparian woodland, forest clearings, bushed grassland, savanna and cultivation with scattered trees. Largely absent from arid n. and ne. Kenya, although resident on Mt Nyiru and Mt Marsabit.

THICK-BILLED HONEYGUIDE *Indicator c. conirostris*   Plate 67

Length 150 mm (6"). A dark *forest* honeyguide with *deep grey or olive-grey breast*, sometimes obscurely streaked, and a stout blackish bill (grey or pinkish at base of mandible). **Adult** generally yellowish olive above, yellower on rump; wings may appear more golden yellow owing to bright flight-feather edgings; head and upper back dusky. A whitish loral spot or streak (sometimes quite narrow) extends to bill base; dim dusky malar stripes (faint in female) not sharply set off from grey face; posterior underparts and sometimes chin whitish; flanks faintly streaked. Tail white beneath, with dark corners and tip. Eyes dark brown, bare orbital skin greenish grey or blackish; feet greenish, grey or blackish. **Juvenile** greener and darker than adult, with chin and throat streaked dusky. **Voice**: Only a husky *kiss-kiss-kiss-kiss* or *tssp-tsssp* noted in our area. Songs recorded in West Africa said to be indistinguishable from those of Lesser Honeyguide. **Habits**: Similar to those of Lesser Honeyguide. **Similar Species**: Lesser Honeyguide is slightly smaller, paler grey below and less contrastingly streaked above. Where sympatric with Thick-billed in w. Kenya, Lesser is confined to forest edges, clearings and more open acacia and riverine woodland. Farther east, where Thick-billed is absent, Lesser inhabits forest. Sympatric Least Honeyguide is smaller, noticeably streaked above and dark greyish olive below; adult shows distinct facial pattern of *black* malar stripes, *conspicuous* white loral spots and usually a *prominent* pale mandible base, but these marks less well defined in young birds. Honeyguide Greenbul is larger, longer-billed, greener above, and lacks the yellowish streaks on the wings. **Status and distribution**: A local and uncommon resident in interior of several w. Kenyan highland forests from Mt Elgon, the Cheranganis and Saiwa NP south to the Kakamega and Nandi Forests. In some areas (Saiwa and Nandi) being replaced by Lesser Honeyguide as extensive forest tracts disappear. Reports from nw. Mara GR require confirmation.

LEAST HONEYGUIDE *Indicator exilis pachyrhynchus*   Plate 67

Length 110–130 mm (4.25–5"). A *small* dark honeyguide of w. Kenyan forests. **Adult** has *black sub-moustachial or malar stripes, white loral spots*, and usually a *conspicuous pale mandible base* (bill rarely all black). *Facial marks and dorsal streaking more distinct than in sympatric Thick-billed Honeyguide*. Underparts greyish olive or olive-grey, heavily streaked on flanks, faintly on sides, sometimes on throat. Tail white below, with dark tip and corners. Eyes brown, orbital skin blackish or greenish grey, feet olive or blackish. **Juvenile** less distinctly streaked above and darker below than adult; may lack loral spots, and malar stripes indistinct or lacking. **Voice**: Usually a short dry trill; less often a song-like *pew-pew-wheet-wheet* or *tew-tew-wheer wheer wheer*. . .. **Habits**: More active than larger honeyguides. Gleans from large branches and amid canopy foliage; occasionally flycatches. Flight rapid and strongly undulating. **Similar Species**: Thick-billed Honeyguide compared above. Lesser Honeyguide is paler and occupies more open habitats. Allopatric Pallid Honeyguide, also paler, lacks dark malar and dorsal stripes. **Status and Distribution**: Local and uncommon in forest and along forest edge in the Kakamega, Nandi, Sotik, Kericho and Mau forests of w. Kenya. Also known from Kapenguria (specimen, April 1962). **Note**: The Dwarf Honeyguide, *Indicator pumilio*, is a central African species formerly attributed to the Kakamega Forest (Zimmerman 1972). Re-examination of the single specimen by ourselves and others suggests that it is merely an aberrant Least Honeyguide. *Indicator pumilio* is a *tiny* bird (length under 4"; weight 13–14 g), dark grey and

usually faintly but obviously streaked below and on crown. From beneath, its *bill is noticeably narrow*, not as broad as in *exilis*.

PALLID HONEYGUIDE *Indicator meliphilus*   Plate 67
(Eastern Honeyguide)

Length 110–130 mm (4.25–5"). A paler eastern counterpart of the Least Honeyguide. **Adult** light grey below, the chin and upper throat whitish with fine dusky streaks; *golden olive and appearing nearly plain above* (feather centres darker but contrasting little with paler edges); often greyer about the face; has *white loral spots* (not always distinct) but *lacks dark malar stripes*. Bill small, conical, dark grey with pinkish mandible base; bare orbital skin grey; eyes dark brown; feet blue-grey. **Juvenile** darker grey below, more yellowish green above; lacks white loral spots. **VOICE**: Song *pwee, pa-wee, pa-wee-wit* . . ., the latter phrase repeated about once per second 20 or more times. Also a song-like *pwee-wee-wee-wee-wee* (Short and Horne, in Fry *et al.* 1988). **HABITS**: Inconspicuous, usually in foliage. Feeds on insects and beeswax; sometimes flycatches and forages on tree trunks. At times sways body and/or head sideways as if to obtain a better view. Frequently fans tail like *Prodotiscus* spp. Produces 'winnowing' sound, probably by wings, in circular flight near song perches (Short and Horne, *op. cit.*). Side-to-side body movements, when peering for insects, said to be distinctive (Carter 1978). **SIMILAR SPECIES**: Least Honeyguide of w. Kenyan forests is much darker below, more streaked above, the adult with black malar stripes. Lesser Honeyguide only slightly larger, and malar stripes often sufficiently indistinct as to be confusing; bill size and shape, however, diagnostic. **STATUS AND DISTRIBUTION**: In Kenya, local and uncommon in wooded areas from Sigor and n. Kerio Valley southeast to Maralal, Laikipia Plateau, eastern slopes of Mt Kenya, Thika, Nairobi, Hell's Gate NP, Southern Uaso Nyiro River, Ol Doinyo Orok, Kibwezi, Taveta, Arabuko–Sokoke Forest and Shimba Hills NP. Old Tanzanian records from Lake Manyara, Usa River, North Pare and Usambara Mountains, and coastal lowlands north of Tanga. **NOTE**: Includes birds formerly considered under the name *I. narokensis* ('Kilimanjaro Honeyguide').

WAHLBERG'S HONEYBIRD *Prodotiscus r. regulus*   Plate 67
(Brown-backed Honeybird; Sharp-billed Honeyguide)

Length 120 mm (4.75"). Warbler-like in appearance and behaviour. Dull *brown above*, with *much white in the tail*. Chin and throat greyish white; breast pale grey, fading to creamy white on belly and under tail-coverts. Plumage lax and fluffy; silky-white feathers flanking lower sides of rump normally concealed, but erected in display. *Tail of adult shows an inverted-T pattern*, the central feathers and tip dark. Eyes brown; bill and feet dark grey or blackish. **Juvenile** paler above than adult and yellowish below, with outer three pairs of rectrices entirely white; gape flanges orange. **VOICE**: Song a short buzzy trill. Calls include a high *tseeu-tseeu*, a loud rasping *zeet-zeet* in flight, a single *zeep* or *tseeet*, and a soft chatter. **HABITS**: An active foliage-gleaner, often foraging with other small birds; usually in trees, but descends to feed near ground. At times moves the head in a peculiar circular motion (more lateral than vertical). Spreads tail widely in undulating flight, or when flycatching or displaying. Parasitizes cavity-nesting birds and those which build globular or bag-like nests with side entrance holes. **SIMILAR SPECIES**: Other honeybirds are greenish above, more typical of true forest (but all visit wooded gardens and forest edge). The smaller honeyguides are thick-billed and less active. Brown Parisoma shows only narrow white tail edges. **STATUS AND DISTRIBUTION**: Local and uncommon in bush, acacia savanna, forest edge and riparian woodland, mainly near and in the highlands, ranging up to nearly 2000 m. Recorded in Kenya from the Kongelai Escarpment and Sigor, the Laikipia Plateau, Nandi Hills, Lake Nakuru NP, Nairobi, Southern Uaso Nyiro River, the Chyulu and Taita Hills, Tsavo West NP, Shimba Hills and Kilifi District. In n. Tanzania, known from Serengeti NP (old records), Arusha and Moshi Districts and the North Pare Mts.

CASSIN'S HONEYBIRD *Prodotiscus i. insignis*   Plate 67
(Western Green-backed Honeybird)

Length 115 mm (4.5"). An *olive-backed* species of w. Kenyan forests. Resembles Eastern Honeybird but darker below and brighter above, more golden olive-green. Sides of face greyish olive; underparts rather dark olive-grey, paler in centre of belly; under tail-coverts paler, more brownish or yellowish grey or yellowish white. Bill small and blackish, pale greenish yellow at the gape; eyes dark brown; feet greyish. **Juvenile** greyer, less olive-green than adult; gape flanges creamy white. **VOICE**: Little known apart from infrequent soft chattering. A weak *whi-hihi* reported in West Africa. **HABITS**: Restless, much like the preceding species. Habitually spreads the conspicuously patterned tail; also flicks tail and wings as it actively forages in foliage. Joins mixed-species flocks. **SIMILAR SPECIES**: See Eastern Honeybird. **STATUS AND DISTRIBUTION**: A scarce resident of forest edge and clearings around Kakamega and Kaimosi. Formerly in the Yala River Forest Reserve.

EASTERN HONEYBIRD *Prodotiscus zambesiae ellenbecki* Plate 67
(Green-backed Honeybird; Slender-billed Honeyguide)

Length 110 mm (4.25"). The only *olive-backed* honeybird *east of the Rift Valley*. **Adult** greyish below (buff-tinged on breast), with whitish lower breast, belly and under tail-coverts; tail white with four dark central feathers. Has patch of normally concealed white feathers on each side of rump. Upperparts and wings olive, washed with yellowish green. Bill blackish; eyes brown; feet slate-grey. **Juvenile** paler and greyer below than adult and less greenish, more yellowish olive, above. Washed with buff below. **Voice:** Inadequately described. Sometimes gives a squeaky chatter, but usually silent. A harsh *skeee-aaa* heard from an apparently courting bird (Malawi; Benson 1952). **Habits:** An active restless foliage-gleaner. Joins mixed-species flocks. Flight undulating. In display, bobs head and fluffs plumage to reveal white rump patches. White-eyes are apparently the main hosts, but also known to parasitize sunbirds and small flycatchers. **Similar Species:** See Cassin's Honeybird. Small honeyguides (*Indicator*) are thicker-billed and show different tail patterns. **Status and Distribution:** Fairly common in woodland, including riparian strips, dry forest and suburban gardens in highlands east of the Rift Valley. In n. Tanzania, known from the Pare and Usambara Mountains, Arusha and Moshi Districts, Lake Manyara NP and Oldeani. In Kenya, from Nairobi, Limuru, Kiambu, Thika, Naro Moru and Meru Districts. Occasional in coastal *Brachystegia* woodland in the Arabuko–Sokoke Forest.

WRYNECKS AND WOODPECKERS, FAMILY PICIDAE
(World, 215 species; Africa, 31; Kenya, 16; n. Tanzania, 12)

The woodpeckers (Subfamily Picinae) are the most specialized of bark-foraging birds, differing from the related barbets (Capitonidae) in their straight, chisel-tipped bills, long barbed tongues (with which they extract ants and insect larvae from bark crevices or holes in wood), and stiff pointed tail feathers, which provide support on tree trunks. Their strong zygodactyl toes with sharp nails enable them to cling to smooth boles and branches. Our species forage little on the ground. They are associated with more or less arborescent woody vegetation and are present in all forested and bushed habitats (where they are generally much less numerous than are woodpeckers in tropical American or Asian forests). All are sexually dimorphic in head colour or pattern. They are resident birds, generally in pairs that maintain frequent vocal contact. They are aggressive in defence of their territory, which is proclaimed by vigorous 'drumming,' a loud rapid tapping on some resonant object such as a hollow dead branch. Flight is direct and undulating, usually not sustained. All species roost and nest in cavities which they excavate in trees, laying two to five white eggs directly on wood chips with no nest material added. Incubation is by both sexes, and the young are tended by both parents.

The two wrynecks, distinct enough to occupy a separate subfamily (Jynginae), are superficially unlike woodpeckers, having soft rounded tails and cryptic nightjar-like plumage and lacking sexual dimorphism. Only occasionally do they cling to tree trunks, and they feed almost exclusively on ants and termites. One species is resident, the other a palearctic migrant.

EURASIAN WRYNECK *Jynx t. torquilla* Plate 65
(Northern Wryneck)

Length 175–180 mm (7"). An unusual bird, at a distance appearing mottled brownish grey with a *broad dark streak down nape and back*, and narrower streaks on the scapulars. Typically perches vertically, with the *pointed bill angled upward*. At close range the intricately patterned dorsal plumage is evident, mainly vermiculated brownish grey with darker brown barring on sides of the crown, brown ear-coverts, a dark grey band down each side of the neck from the eye, brownish-black mid-back and finely vermiculated rump and tail, the latter with irregular blackish bars. **Adult** pale buff below, with *dark brown* wavy bars on flanks and belly, finer barring on throat and breast. Eyes brown; bill and feet pale brown. **First-winter** bird paler grey above, less barred on throat and breast. **Voice:** A harsh *kwee-kwee-kwee-kwee. . .*, but apparently silent in East Africa. **Habits:** Retiring and inconspicuous. Forages on the ground, where it hops with raised tail, and in trees. Flight undulating. **Similar Species:** Red-throated Wryneck has rufous throat, upper breast and crissum, and is streaked, not barred, on lower breast and belly. **Status and distribution:** A scarce palearctic migrant, with 14 scattered Kenyan records (1969–92) from Lokichokio, Lake Turkana, Huri Hills, Mt Marsabit, Saiwa, Nakuru and Meru NPs, Busia, Siaya, Mumias, Nairobi and Machakos Districts and the Chyulu Hills. Unrecorded in Tanzania.

RED-THROATED WRYNECK *Jynx r. ruficollis* Plate 65
(Rufous-breasted Wryneck)

Length 180–190 mm (7–7.5"). **Adult** resembles Eurasian Wryneck, but has *bright rufous chin, throat and upper breast*. Upperparts mainly grey-brown, finely vermiculated and spotted, with a *broad dark streak from hindcrown to back*, barred face and forecrown, and black-spotted scapulars. Lower breast and belly creamy white with vari-

able black streaking; flanks and under tail-coverts dull rufous, the latter barred with black; tail with several blackish bars. **Juvenile** darker and more heavily barred than adult, with duller, lightly barred rufous throat and breast. **Voice:** A short series of loud squealing notes, *yeea, yeea, yeea. . .* or *pyee, pyee, pyee, pyee*, repeated after an interval of several seconds. **Habits:** Solitary or in pairs. Perches on fenceposts and dead trees; forages on or near the ground. Nests either in natural cavities or in old woodpecker or barbet holes. **Similar Species:** See Eurasian Wryneck. **Status and Distribution:** Uncommon. Resident, but presence erratic in many areas. Inhabits acacia woodland, forest edge, gardens and cultivation with scattered trees. In Kenya mainly between 1400 and 2500 m, from Mt Elgon, the Wei-Wei River, Maralal, Laikipia Plateau, the Aberdares and Mt Kenya south to Rapogi, Lolgorien, Mara GR, Nguruman Hills and the Nairobi area; most numerous and regular in Lake Nakuru NP. In n. Tanzania, known from a few sight records along the Mara GR/Serengeti NP border at Sand River and near Loliondo.

NUBIAN WOODPECKER *Campethera nubica* Plate 66

Length 200 mm (8"). The combination of *dark malar stripes* (mainly *red in male, black with white speckles in female*) and *spotted underparts* distinguishes this widespread species from other similarly sized Kenyan woodpeckers. **Adult male** crimson-red from forehead to nape and with whitish superciliary stripes; olive-brown upperparts are heavily spotted with creamy white, more barred on the wings; *dull yellow tail barred with olive-brown*, the feather *shafts bright yellow*. Sides of face narrowly streaked black and white; red malar stripes contain some black feathers; throat creamy white, breast and sides heavily black-spotted, the flanks black-barred. Eyes red; bill dark grey; feet grey or greyish green. **Female** resembles male, but red confined to the nape; crown and malar stripes black with small white spots. *C. n. pallida* is paler than nominate *nubica*, with smaller spots. **Juvenile** darker and browner above and more heavily spotted below; chin, throat and breast often appear streaked; moustachial stripes black; eyes greyish. **Voice:** A duet of loud strident notes, *tyee, tyee, tyee, tyee-tyee-tyee-tyee-tyee, tee, tee*, accelerating, sometimes slowing again at end; one bird begins, the second soon joins in, more or less synchronizing its notes with those of the first. Series repeated several times. **Habits:** Forages alone but maintains vocal contact with mate. Feeds in trees and on the ground; consumes large numbers of ants. Drums on poles and dead trees. **Similar Species:** Green-backed Woodpecker lacks malar stripes, has speckled throat. Adult Mombasa and Golden-tailed Woodpeckers are *streaked* on the breast, olive-green on back; Golden-tailed is blackish on throat. Much smaller Cardinal Woodpecker is also streaked below. In n. Tanzania, see also Bennett's Woodpecker. **Status and Distribution:** *C. n. pallida* is uncommon in coastal Kenyan lowlands from Kilifi north to Lamu (formerly south of Mombasa). Intergrades inland with nominate *nubica* in the Tsavo region and along base of the eastern plateau. Elsewhere in Kenya, *C. n. nubica* is fairly common and widespread in acacia woodland, bush and savanna up to 2300 m, absent only from forested areas and the arid northeast. In n. Tanzania, it ranges east to Arusha NP and lowlands around Kilimanjaro, and south through the dry interior to Tabora, Kilosa and Iringa Districts. Birds in Mkomazi GR not racially assigned.

BENNETT'S WOODPECKER *Campethera bennettii scriptoricauda* Plate 122

Length *c.* 180–190 mm (7–7.5"). A largely *Tanzanian* bird resembling Nubian Woodpecker, but *throat centrally speckled, not plain white.* **Female** *lacks dark malar stripes*, is slightly *more yellowish above* and with the back more narrowly barred; also lacks conspicuous brown ear-coverts of other races (may show trace). Bill slate-grey above, *mandible extensively to largely pale yellow*; culmen more curved than in Nubian, and bill narrower between the nostrils. **Voice:** Territorial calls of southern African birds described as a neighing *ddrahh, ddrahh, ddray-ay, ddray-ay, dray-ay*, and *wi-wi-wi-wi* (Short and Horne, in Fry *et al.* 1988); said to be like calls of *scriptoricauda*. Call note a short *churr*. **Habits:** As for Nubian Woodpecker. Sometimes feeds on ground. Said to drum more softly than Golden-tailed Woodpecker. **Similar Species:** Nubian Woodpecker compared above. Female Green-backed Woodpecker is smaller and with spotted green upperparts. Mombasa and Golden-tailed Woodpeckers are streaked on breast. **Status and Distribution:** Known from around Kilimanjaro, the North Pare Mts and from Handeni southward. V. G. L. van Someren (1922) considered the species as ranging north along the coast to Lamu, and specifically mentioned at least one specimen from Mombasa. We have examined an adult male (Field Museum 195254), labelled by van Someren as collected on the Kenyan mainland near Mombasa, 20 July 1918. **Note:** This form treated as a full species by van Someren (*op. cit.*), as a race of *C. nubica* by Peters (1948) and Mackworth-Praed and Grant (1952), merged with *C. bennettii* by White (1965), and reported to intergrade freely with the nominate race of that species in Malawi (Benson and Benson 1977). Collection of *nubica* and *scriptoricauda* at base of Mt Kilimanjaro (15 Aug. 1967) provides the only evidence of sympatry, unless *scriptoricauda* still ranges northward along the Kenyan coast. Distribution of the two forms in our region requires further study.

MOMBASA WOODPECKER *Campethera mombassica* **Plate 66**

Length 200 mm (8"). An *eastern* woodpecker, golden green with *fine white spotting above, streaked below.* **Adult male** has olive forehead, red-edged grey crown and largely red nape; greyish ear-coverts and sides of face with darker streaks; malar stripes mixed red and black; yellowish-white underparts have blackish-brown streaks (heavier on breast). Tail barred brown and yellowish, with bright yellow shafts. Eyes reddish; bill slate-grey, tinged greenish below; feet greyish olive. **Female** has olive-green forehead and crown speckled with buffy yellow. **Juvenile** resembles adult female, but is more heavily streaked and has brown or grey eyes. **Voice:** An accelerating nasal *keeoank-yaaaank-yaaaank-yaaank-yaank-yank-yank, yuk*; also a rough *ghrrrrrrk.* **Habits:** Forages in large or small trees, usually in leafy cover where inconspicuous. Associates with mixed-species flocks. Feeds largely on ants. Not known to drum. **Similar Species:** Bennett's and Nubian Woodpeckers are spotted, not streaked on breast. Smaller Green-backed Woodpecker is spotted below and lacks malar stripes. Western Golden-tailed Woodpecker is blackish on throat and upper breast and barred with yellowish white above. **Status and Distribution:** Locally fairly common in forest and coastal woodland from Tanga north to the Boni Forest, inland along the Tana River to Garissa, Shimba Hills NP and the Usambara Mts. **Note:** Formerly considered a race of *C. abingoni.* Reports of a specimen from Kilimanjaro, and of hybrids with *C. a. suahelica* from Moshi, indicate the need for further field studies in n. Tanzania.

GOLDEN-TAILED WOODPECKER *Campethera abingoni* **Plate 66**

Length 200 mm (8"). A western counterpart of the preceding species, less yellowish below and with *dense black streaking from chin to upper breast, sides and flanks; spotted only on belly.* Upperparts olive-green in *C. a. kavirondensis*, more yellowish green in *suahelica*, with pale cream spots merging into bars on rump and upper tail-coverts; white ear-coverts are streaked with black. Eyes dark red; bill slate-grey. **Adult male** mostly red from crown to nape. **Female** has blackish forehead and crown densely spotted with white. **Juvenile** more heavily streaked below, more barred on belly and sides than adult; malar stripes black with white spots. **Voice:** A single, drawn-out, penetrating *skweeeeeeea.* **Habits:** Tends to forage low and in mid-level of trees, often working a small area for long periods. Drums softly. Feeds largely on ants. **Similar Species:** Mombasa Woodpecker is allopatric. Smaller Green-backed Woodpecker has black-speckled throat and no malar stripes. Allopatric Speckle-breasted (Uganda Spotted) Woodpecker is small, speckled below, with brown forehead and forecrown. **Status and Distribution:** Uncommon *C. a. kavirondensis* is local in forest and riverine woodland in sw. Kenya, from Lolgorien and the Mara River south to w. Serengeti NP. *C. a. suahelica* is uncommon in Arusha NP, Moshi District and North Pare Mts of n. Tanzania, but range limits are poorly known. Species attributed without details to the Chyulu Hills (Short *et al.* 1990), where not recorded by the 1938 van Someren Chyulu expedition.

GREEN-BACKED or LITTLE SPOTTED WOODPECKER *Campethera cailliautii* **Plate 66**

Length 150–160 mm (6–6.5"). A small *green-backed* woodpecker with *no malar stripes. Sides of face, neck and throat yellowish white with black speckling.* **Adult** of nominate race greenish and profusely spotted with yellowish white above; tail dull greenish yellow with olive-brown shafts. Yellowish breast spotted with round black dots, these smaller on lower belly and crissum. **Male** has dull red forehead and crown with some dark streaking, and a bright red nape patch. Black forehead and crown of **female** are dotted with white. Eyes reddish brown; bill dark grey; feet olive-green or greenish grey. **Juvenile** resembles adult female but has grey eyes. *C. c. nyansae* is slightly larger and brighter green above than eastern birds, has fine short streaks above, and the ventral spotting merges into barring on belly and sides. **Voice:** A fairly rapid *uweek uweek uweek uweek. . .*, the note repeated 20 times or more. Also a shorter *kwee-kwee-kwee* or *kerree.* **Habits:** Unobtrusive. Feeds alone or in pairs, mainly on ants and termites. **Similar Species:** Cardinal and Golden-tailed Woodpeckers have streaked underparts. Nubian and Mombasa Woodpeckers have prominent malar stripes. **Status and Distribution:** Local and uncommon. Nominate *cailliautii* occupies coastal lowlands north to the Boni Forest and inland along the Tana River to Bura, the Shimba Hills and East Usambaras. *C. c. nyansae* ranges from Mwanza and w. Serengeti NP north to the Mara GR, Lolgorien and South Nyanza. Reports from the Tugen Hills require confirmation.

FINE-BANDED or TULLBERG'S WOODPECKER *Campethera tullbergi taeniolaema*
Plate 66

Length 175–190 mm (7–7.5"). A *greenish* woodpecker of *montane forests; finely barred body* appears plain at a distance. Upperparts olive-green, browner on wings and tail and bright red on nape. Blackish vermiculations on face, ear-coverts, neck and throat merge into narrow bars on breast and belly, broader bars on flanks. Bill dark

slate-grey above, paler blue-grey below; eyes wine-red or red-brown; feet olive. **Male** has dull red forehead and crown (the feathers basally black); in **female** these areas black with small white dots. **Juvenile** more greyish green, with darker barring on underparts; forehead and crown olive-black with fine white spots, though red of adult male develops early; eyes brown. **Voice**: A loud *kweek-kweek-kweek. . .*, the series often prolonged. **Habits**: Solitary or in pairs. Forages mainly in forest canopy, where often a member of mixed-species flocks. Feeds extensively on ants. **Status and Distribution**: Locally fairly common between 1750 and 3000 m in Kenyan forests from Mt Elgon and the Cheranganis south to the Mau, Lolgorien and nw. Mara GR, the Aberdares, Mt Kenya, Nyambeni Hills and northern Nairobi suburbs. Small disjunct population in the Nguruman Hills and nearby Loliondo District of n. Tanzania.

BUFF-SPOTTED WOODPECKER *Campethera nivosa herberti* Plate 66

Length 140–150 mm (5.5–6"). A small olive woodpecker of *forest undergrowth* in *western Kenya*. **Adult** plain yellowish olive-green above, with brown tail and white-spotted brown primaries; pale yellowish-olive throat and sides of face are streaked with brown. *Underparts largely olive (darker on breast) and profusely spotted with dull yellow*; barred pale dull yellowish white and olive on flanks. Bill blackish, bluer at base below; orbital skin dull olive; eyes dark red; feet olive. **Male** has olive-brown forehead and crown and bright orange-red nape. **Female** lacks red, is brownish olive from forehead to nape. **Juvenile** resembles female, but crown greyish and eyes brown. **Voice**: A slightly descending rattling trill, *kee-kee-kee-kee-kee-kee-kee*, and a soft dry *chk chk chk-chk chk*. **Habits**: Usually feeds in undergrowth and low trees, often on fine twigs and stems. Excavates nest cavity in termitarium or dead branch. Feeds extensively on ants. **Similar Species**: Larger Brown-eared Woodpecker has chestnut-brown patch on side of head. **Status and Distribution**: Uncommon in forest, forest edge and dense second-growth in the Kakamega and South Nandi Forests. Formerly on Mt Elgon.

BROWN-EARED WOODPECKER *Campethera c. caroli* Plate 66

Length 180–190 mm (7–7.5"). Now restricted to the *Kakamega Forest*, w. Kenya. *Large chestnut-brown patch on ear-coverts* unique. Top of head dark brown, back and wings golden olive; tail blackish; lores, superciliary region and throat spotted with buff; mainly olive underparts densely spotted with dull yellowish white. Bill grey or bluish grey, tinged olive; orbital skin greyish olive; eyes red or brown; feet olive. **Male** has red on hindcrown and nape; **female** dark brown from forehead to nape. **Juvenile** more olive-green above, with cinnamon-rufous ear patch and streaked chin, more barred on belly. **Voice**: A short *kwaa-kwaa-kwaa* (Short and Horne, in Fry *et al.* 1988), a single drawn-out *uwheeeeeeu*, and a low trilled *trrrrrrrr*. **Habits**: Solitary and shy. Seldom vocal and not known to drum. Forages unobtrusively on large trees, vines and saplings, sometimes low. Feeds on ants and other insects. **Similar Species**: Often sympatric Buff-spotted Woodpecker lacks brown on ear-coverts. **Status and Distribution**: Uncommon resident of primary and dense secondary forest remnants in Kakamega District. Formerly on Mt Elgon.

SPECKLE-BREASTED or UGANDA SPOTTED WOODPECKER *Dendropicos poecilolaemus* Plate 65

Length 140 mm (5.5"). A *small west Kenyan* woodpecker of forest edge and semi-open areas, *finely speckled (or weakly barred) on the breast*. **Adults** yellow-olive above, with traces of barring from lower back to upper tail-coverts, the coverts and rump feathers faintly red-tipped. Tail brownish with yellow feather shafts. Wings brown, the flight feathers barred and spotted with yellow; coverts yellow-edged. Cheeks and ear-coverts whitish, faintly streaked or spotted, and with indistinct dark moustachial stripes. Chin and throat white with fine dark flecking; rest of underparts pale yellow-olive, spotted on upper breast, faintly barred on sides and flanks; a few indistinct short streaks on belly. Eyes red-brown; bill blackish; feet olive. **Male** has *brown forehead and forecrown*, red hindcrown and nape. **Female** *brown on forehead, black from crown to nape*. **Juvenile** grey above and below, with little yellow; faintly black-barred on upperparts; little or no red on rump and upper tail-coverts, but both sexes *red-crowned* (brighter and more extensive in male), with *black nape and postocular areas*; eyes brown. **Voice**: A dry rattling *che-che-chi-chi-chichi*. **Habits**: Often forages low, especially in isolated trees or riverine shrubs. **Similar Species**: Cardinal Woodpecker has streaked breast. **Status and Distribution**: Local and uncommon in riverine woodland, forest edge and partly cleared ground from Mt Elgon and Kapenguria south to Nandi (early specimens), Busia, Mumias, Yala, Ng'iya and Ukwala Districts.

CARDINAL WOODPECKER *Dendropicos fuscescens* Plate 65

Length 130–140 mm (5–5.5"). The most numerous *small* woodpecker. A variable *streak-breasted* species represented in East Africa by four distinct races, three of which (*massaicus, hemprichii* and *hartlaubii*) are savanna and forest-edge forms, contrastingly '*ladder-backed*', thus differing from other small woodpeckers. *D. f. lepidus*, of forest and heavy woodland, is relatively plain olive above, with faint dark barring usually visible only at close range. In more detail: (1) *D. f. massaicus* is narrowly barred dark brown and whitish above, washed with yellowish orange on rump and upper tail-coverts; wings and tail dark brown, with pale yellowish barring on flight feathers and coverts; rectrices with yellow shafts; whitish face and sides of head marked with fine dark streaks and long white superciliary stripes; malar stripes dark brown; underparts pale yellow, with heavy dark brown breast streaking merging into barring on sides, flanks and crissum. **Male** plain brown on forehead and forecrown; hindcrown and nape red. **Female** has brown forehead, black crown and nape. Eyes red or red-brown; bill blackish, sometimes dull light blue-grey below; feet greenish grey or greyish olive. **Juvenile** duller than adult, both sexes with red crown patch. (2) *D. f. hemprichii* resembles *massaicus*, but is more sharply barred above, has white (not yellowish) barring on wings, and orange-red rump and upper tail-coverts. (3) *D. f. hartlaubii* is more olive-brown above, more yellow-olive below with paler olive-brown streaking. (4) *D. f. lepidus* has golden-olive upperparts with darker olive barring, white-spotted wings, and pale yellowish underparts with brown streaking, this less distinct on the belly. **VOICE:** A soft, rather slow rattle, *kwee, kwee, kee-kee-kee-kikik*, descending and fainter at end; repeated several times. Also a more chattering *chwi-chi-chi-chi-chi* and a trilled *tri-tri-tri-tri-trrrrrrr*. **HABITS:** Forages on large branches as well as among small twigs; agile, often working undersides of limbs. Singles or pairs may join mixed-species flocks. Quite vocal, but drums softly. **SIMILAR SPECIES:** Other small woodpeckers have *spotted* underparts. **STATUS AND DISTRIBUTION:** *D. f. hemprichii* ranges widely in e. and ne. Kenya from Mandera, Moyale and Marsabit south to the Northern Uaso Nyiro and Tana Rivers, and in coastal lowlands from the Boni Forest south to Kilifi; *massaicus* elsewhere in the northern and eastern lowlands south of *hemprichii*, including the Mombasa area, interbreeds with that race and with *hartlaubii* of se. Kenyan/Tanzanian border areas from the Chyulu Hills south into n. Tanzania; *lepidus* ranges throughout the w. and cent. Kenyan highlands, up to 2600 m, interbreeding with *massaicus* in all contact zones. Specimens from the East Usambaras (500–1150 m) have been assigned to *lepidus* by Ripley and Heinrich (1969).

BEARDED WOODPECKER *Dendropicos namaquus* Plate 66

Length 230 mm (9"). *Large* and dark, with *broad black malar and postocular stripes* on a *whitish face*. Upperparts olive-brown with narrow whitish barring, yellow-tinged on rump and upper tail-coverts, some of the latter faintly orange-tipped; rectrix shafts yellow. Chin and throat white; underparts of *D. n. namaquus* otherwise olive-brown, closely barred with dull white or olive-yellow. **Male** has *white-speckled black forehead and forecrown*, red hindcrown/occiput and black nape. In browner *D. n. schoensis,* the black facial stripes are longer and join at sides of lower neck; greyish underparts are more spotted than barred. **Females** of both races lack red, have entire top of head black, with white spots on the forehead. Eyes maroon-red; bill grey; feet olive-grey. **Juvenile** resembles adult, but upperparts more olive with less distinct barring. **VOICE:** A shrill *kwik-kwik-kwik. . .*, repeated several times; suggests call of Grey-headed Kingfisher. **HABITS:** Not very vocal, but loud tapping reveals presence, often high in trees. Drumming rather slow with last three or four taps separated. Shy; flies far when disturbed. **SIMILAR SPECIES:** Yellow-crested Woodpecker (w. Kenyan forests) has unbarred back. **STATUS AND DISTRIBUTION:** Widespread *D. n. namaquus* is uncommon to fairly common in acacia and riverine woodland, forest edge and savanna between sea level and 2600 m throughout interior n. Tanzania and north to the w. and cent. Kenyan highlands, Meru and Tsavo NPs, and in coastal lowlands from Kilifi north to the Tana River gallery forests. *D. n. schoensis* is local and uncommon on northern Kenyan mountains (Loima, Nyiru, Marsabit, Ndotos, Mathews Range) and from Maralal, the Karissia Hills and Laikipia Plateau south to the Kerio Valley and Baringo District. Generally absent from the Lake Victoria basin, extreme se. Kenya, the Masai Steppe and Usambara Mts.

YELLOW-CRESTED WOODPECKER *Dendropicos xantholophus* Plate 66

Length 200–230 mm (8–9"). A *large, dark* woodpecker of *western Kenyan forests*. Head pattern resembles that of Bearded Woodpecker, with two broad dark facial stripes and black forecrown sparsely spotted with white, but *forehead is brown*. Inconspicuous *golden-yellow hindcrown* of **male** may appear mottled owing to black feather bases showing through; nape black. Dull olive-brown upperparts washed with yellow on rump and upper tail-coverts; may show a few whitish bars on back. Tail black. Except for whitish throat, underparts are dark brown to olive-brown, spotted and barred with white on flanks, sometimes on belly. Bill blackish above, greenish grey below; eyes red or reddish brown; feet olive-brown or greenish. **Female** resembles male but lacks yellow on head. **Juvenile** (both sexes) has yellow-tipped hindcrown feathers, more olive upperparts, and greyer underparts with more barring and less spotting than adults. **VOICE:** A trilled, somewhat honeyguide-like *kerrreee, kerreee, kerrreee* followed by a descending *kwi-kwi-kwi-kwi*. **HABITS:** Solitary. Noisy, with loud tapping and frequent

rapid drumming on dead trees and large branches, the sound accelerating at end (reverse of Bearded Woodpecker's). **SIMILAR SPECIES:** Bearded Woodpecker (unlikely in Yellow-crested's habitat) compared above. **STATUS AND DISTRIBUTION:** Uncommon in interior of heavy forest on Mt Elgon and in the North Nandi and Kakamega Forests.

GREY WOODPECKER *Dendropicos goertae* Plate 66

Length 180–190 mm (7–7.5"). A *grey and golden-olive* woodpecker showing *bright red rump and upper tail-coverts* in flight. Crown and nape of **male** also bright red, as, usually, is a patch on mid-belly and crissum (extensive in *D. g. rhodeogaster*, small to obsolete and orange or yellow in western *centralis*). Back and wings generally golden olive, the flight feathers and tail mainly brown with some barring. Most underparts almost plain grey with some indistinct barring. Grey face more patterned, with suggestion of superciliary and malar stripes in *centralis*. Bill slate-grey or black, the mandible paler; eyes red or brown; feet greenish grey. **Female** similar but lacks red on the head. **Juvenile** more greenish olive above, more barred below, with little red on belly; eyes grey. **VOICE:** A weak *ch-ch-reeek-reeek-reeek*, a fast rattling *wik-wik-wik-wik-wik-wik. . .*, a louder *chwi-chwi-skew-skew-CHREE-CHREE-CHREE-chree-chree-chree*, softer at end, and a still more emphatic *SKWI-SKWI-SKWI-skwi-skwi-skwi-skwi*. **HABITS:** Solitary, in pairs or in family groups. Forages on stumps, exposed roots and fallen branches, as well as in trees. Catches winged termites in the air. Vocal, but drums infrequently. Where sympatric with Olive Woodpecker (Arusha NP and Kilimanjaro), *goertae* generally avoids heavy forest. **STATUS AND DISTRIBUTION:** *D. g. centralis*, merged with the nominate race by Short (1982), is fairly common in savanna, open woodland and cultivation in w. and cent. Kenya north of the Equator, although absent from the arid north. *D. g. rhodeogaster* ranges widely from Mt Kenya, Nyeri and Kisumu south into the Lake Victoria basin and Serengeti NP, and to the Crater Highlands, Lake Manyara, Tarangire and Arusha NPs and on lower western slopes of Kilimanjaro. **NOTE:** Some authors treat *rhodeogaster* (including Ethiopian *spodocephalus*) as a separate species.

OLIVE WOODPECKER *Dendropicos griseocephalus kilimensis* Plate 124

Length 160–170 mm (c. 6.5"). A red-rumped *Tanzanian* forest woodpecker, suggesting the preceding species, but *dark olive, not grey, on breast* and with an *unbarred blackish tail*. **Adult male** has a dull golden olive-green back, and is red from crown to nape, on rump and on upper tail-coverts (but no red on belly as in extralimital races); forehead, sides of head and throat grey. Underparts yellowish olive, more greyish on belly and crissum. Wings brown, with remiges spotted or barred with white on inner webs and edged greenish yellow. Bill dark grey, paler and more bluish on mandible; eyes red-brown; feet greyish olive. **Female** has entirely grey head. **Juvenile** greyer and less yellowish below, darker olive-green above and paler red on rump. **VOICE:** A laughing *yeh-yeh-yeh-yeh-yeh*, and various other calls including *week-week-week* and a loud *QUEEK!* of alarm. Does not give long rattle like Grey Woodpecker. **HABITS:** Single birds or pairs feed by probing on mossy or lichen-covered branches, often delivering lateral blows with head angled to one side. Frequently moves sideways and backwards. Forages mainly in small trees and on thinner branches. Often a member of mixed-species flocks. **SIMILAR SPECIES:** See Grey Woodpecker. **STATUS AND DISTRIBUTION:** Local in heavy forest on Mt Meru (scarce), Kilimanjaro, and the Pare (scarce) and Usambara Mountains. Most numerous in the West Usambaras between 1500 and 1850 m.

BROWN-BACKED WOODPECKER *Picoides obsoletus* Plate 66

Length 120–135 mm (c. 5"). A *small brown-and-white* woodpecker with *boldly white-spotted wings*. Back dull brown (blackish brown in *P. o. crateri*); rump to tail brown, broadly barred with white; side of face white, with large brown ear patch and malar stripe. Whitish underparts have fine faint brown streaks (darker and heavier in *crateri*). Top of head entirely brown in **female**, with red occipital patch in **male**. Bill black above, grey below; eyes red-brown; feet greenish grey. **Juvenile** darker than adult, somewhat barred on underparts and with red on crown in both sexes (more extensive in male). **VOICE:** A loud, slightly descending *SQUEE squee squee squee. . .* and a more chattering or twittering *chew-chew-CHEW-CHEW-chew-chew-chew-chew*. **HABITS:** Unobtrusive. Forages on slender branches, eating fruits and insects. Solitary or in pairs. **SIMILAR SPECIES:** Some Cardinal Woodpeckers (*D. f. lepidus*) are nearly plain on the

back, but olive, not dull brown, with plainer face, less heavily spotted wings, and yellow on the tail. **STATUS AND DISTRIBUTION**: Local and uncommon in woodland, forest edge and wooded suburban gardens. *P. o. ingens* ranges widely in the cent. Kenyan highlands and Rift Valley from Maralal and the Laikipia Plateau south to Thika, Kiambu and Nairobi Districts. In w. and sw. Kenya, known from the Kongelai Escarpment, Kapenguria and Saiwa NP, south to Kisumu and Kericho Districts, Lolgorien, nw. Mara GR, Nguruman Hills, and at Loliondo in n. Tanzania. *P. o. crateri* ranges from the Crater Highlands south to Mbulu and Nou. Recent records from the Shimba Hills (Oct. 1987) and near Arusha (Sept. 1985) not racially assigned.

BROADBILLS, FAMILY EURYLAIMIDAE
(World, 14 species; Africa, 4; Kenya and n. Tanzania, 1)

Our single representative of this largely Asiatic family is a small, thickset arboreal forest bird with large head and broad flat bill, short tarsi and strong syndactylous toes. The tail is short, the wings rounded. The nest is a bulky mass of plant material, usually with a long straggling 'tail' and side entrance hole, suspended from a low horizontal branch.

AFRICAN BROADBILL *Smithornis capensis*   **Plate 68**

Length 130 mm (5"). A *boldly streaked*, flycatcher-like bird; crown black in male, grey in female of eastern races, blackish in western *S. c. meinertzhageni*. Upperparts largely olive-brown with black streaks; white bases of lower-back and rump feathers usually concealed at rest. Underparts creamy white or buff, with heavy black streaks on breast and flanks. *S. c. meinertzhageni* and *suahelicus* are both less buff below than the more narrowly streaked *medianus*. **VOICE**: A loud, strident vibrating sound like that of an old-fashioned automobile horn: *PR-R-R-R-R-R-RRRRRRUP* or *KRRRRRRRROOOOO*, produced during display flight or at rest. A soft plaintive *tui-tui-tui* or *twee-o, twee-o . . .* may alternate with the louder sound or be given separately. **HABITS**: Perches upright on low horizontal branches. Shy, inconspicuous and often silent. Both sexes perform remarkable display flight, describing a circle of c. one metre diameter around perch on rapidly vibrating wings, puffing out white on back and rump, and giving the 'klaxon-horn' call (see above). **SIMILAR SPECIES**: Female African Shrike-flycatcher, in w. Kenyan forests, is heavily streaked below, but bill is much longer and flight feathers, rump and crissum are tawny-rufous. **STATUS AND DISTRIBUTION**: Scarce and seldom recorded resident of heavy forest, including dense riparian strips. Three races: *S. c. meinertzhageni* restricted to Kakamega and North Nandi Forests, w. Kenya; *medianus* formerly in montane areas east of the Rift Valley from Mt Kenya and the Ngaia Forest south to Nairobi suburbs and the Chyulu Hills, but now rare in Kenya (recorded on southern slopes of Mt Kenya, Jan. 1983), and in n. Tanzania known from the Usambara Mts, lower slopes of Mt Meru and Kilimanjaro, Arusha NP, Mbulumbulu in the Crater Highlands, and Marang Forest; *suahelicus* occupies coastal lowlands in the Shimba Hills and the Arabuko–Sokoke Forest. Everywhere declining with forest clearance.

PITTAS, Family PITTIDAE
(World, 31 species; Africa, 2; Kenya and n. Tanzania, 1)

Secretive, brightly coloured terrestrial forest birds, long-legged and short-tailed, with rounded wings. Sexes alike. Our species is an intra-African migrant from the southern tropics.

AFRICAN PITTA *Pitta angolensis longipennis*   **Plate 68**
(Angola Pitta)

Length 180 mm (7"). A plump, somewhat thrush-like bird of the forest floor. Black crown and sides of face contrast with broad creamy-white superciliary stripes and white throat. Upperparts mainly dark green, but *'shoulders' and rump brilliant cobalt-blue; white patch at base of primaries conspicuous in flight*. Breast buff; belly and under tail-coverts bright red. **VOICE**: Has a querulous scolding *skeeow* (Moreau) and a deep short trill followed by a sharp wing-clap. Usually silent during the non-breeding season. **HABITS**: Solitary and elusive. Noisily scratches for insects and molluscs in leaf litter. Flirts tail as it walks. Runs rapidly when alarmed, occasionally flying or jumping to low tree branch. Flight fast and direct. **STATUS AND DISTRIBUTION**: Rare non-breeding migrant from the southern tropics, mainly April–October. Formerly more or less regular in many coastal forests north to Watamu and Gedi, but few records after 1983. Widely scattered reports elsewhere in our area are largely of exhausted or dead vagrants in highland areas (Usambara Mts, Arusha District, Ngorongoro Crater, Nairobi, Timau and Kongelai).

LARKS, FAMILY ALAUDIDAE
(World, 83 species; Africa, 67; Kenya, 21; n. Tanzania, 15)

Cryptically patterned, terrestrial birds of open areas, most larks are stouter-billed and generally bulkier than the superficially similar pipits (Motacillidae) of the same habitats. Like pipits, many larks have the hind claw elongate and sometimes straight. They walk, at times with a shuffling gait, and can run rapidly. Some are migratory or nomadic, subject to poorly known movements. They may be abundant one year, rare or absent the next, the movements doubtless related in part to rainfall and resultant vegetation changes affecting the seeds and insects on which they feed. All species nest on the ground, typically in grass tufts, laying two to six speckled whitish, greyish or buffy eggs.

Identification is complicated by subspecific variation, different colour morphs and by wear and fading, which markedly affect appearance. Larks have but one annual (post-nuptial) moult, so worn birds are frequently encountered, even during the breeding season. Differences between these and freshly feathered individuals of the same species can be striking. Abraded birds appear more uniform in tone as light feather tips and edges wear away, leaving only the dark central portions, which become browner. General plumage coloration is often correlated with soil colour. The sexes are alike or (in sparrow-larks) different. Juveniles tend to have speckled or scaly upperparts. Some species are poorly known, represented by only a few museum specimens, and rarely identified in the field.

SINGING BUSH LARK *Mirafra cantillans* Plate 71

Length 130 mm (5″). An often nondescript lark with prominent *white tail edges*. In fresh plumage, **adult** of *M. c. marginata* is *streaked grey-brown and buff*, with *conspicuous pale buff superciliary stripes*, *dark cheeks* and a necklace of *spotted streaks across the breast*. *Rufous or rufous-buff flight-feather edges* (disappearing with wear) can make wings appear largely rufous in flight. A *dark postocular line* accentuates the *brown or rufous-brown ear-coverts*, which are separated from *dark lateral patches* by partial whitish collar, these marks much reduced and *pectoral patches absent in very worn birds* (including some breeding adults). Rare individuals almost as dark as White-tailed Larks, but differ in brighter feather edges, fainter breast spots, and less white in the tail. Bill dark brown above, largely dull pink below. Some northwestern birds light rufous-buff, with fine black submarginal line on each inner-wing feather. In the hand, exposed nostrils and short outer primary distinguish this and other *Mirafra* species from *Calandrella* larks. **Juvenile** buffier than adult, *scalloped with pale buff* feather edges on crown and back; wing edgings more rufous; brighter inner secondaries show dark submarginal lines near the buff edges; ear patch less rufous; bill mainly pale pinkish, with some greyish blue on maxilla. **Voice:** Song a prolonged medley of 'tsips', trills, warbling and scratchy notes, fluctuating in pitch and intensity, some notes distinct, others run together, and often ending in a buzzy trill, e.g. *tsip-tsip-tsip chirrrrip tchew tchew TCHEW TCHEW TCHEW tchweep tchweep tchweep tsi-tsi-tsi-tsi tew tew-tew-tew-twi chewi chewi . . ..* Shorter songs include *chk chk tsitsitsiki-zreeeeeeeeeeeee* (from perch) and *tsit tsit tsit chreet chreet chreet tsikitswik-sik srisrisrisrisrisrisrisri* (in flight). **Habits:** Typically in pairs or small loose groups. Flushes silently, flying swiftly and low, suddenly flopping into grass. Displaying male sings in low hovering flight, in high circling or from bushtop. **Similar Species:** Somali Short-toed Lark is more coarsely streaked above, with pale sandy-buff (not rufous) primary edges, broad pale eye-ring, heavier bill and concealed nostrils. White-tailed Lark is blackish above, with dark breast spots. Rare blackish morph of Flappet Lark shows buff or tawny tail edges. See Friedmann's Lark. **Status and Distribution:** *M. c. marginata* is locally common below 1500 m in bushed or open grassland. Subject to local movements during or after periods of high rainfall. Ranges from Turkana and Marsabit south to lakes Magadi and Natron, Tsavo West NP and, in Tanzania, lowlands around Arusha, Moshi, Mt Meru and Kilimanjaro. Widespread in drier areas of the Rift Valley. Presumed northern breeders appear to move south with November–December rains through Tsavo West NP, where migrants ringed at night. Replaced by White-tailed Lark in sw. Kenya. Birds near Sudanese border (specimens, Nadapal) may represent an eastern population of *M. c. chadensis*.

WHITE-TAILED LARK *Mirafra albicauda* Plate 72
(Northern White-tailed Bush Lark)

Length 130 mm (5″). Appears *blackish* compared with other grassland larks, and shows *much white in the spread tail* when flushed. Typical **adult** mottled black and stone-grey above, with some buff feather edgings on back (occasionally faded browner, enhancing resemblance to Singing Bush Lark). Wings dark brown with broad pale buff edgings, some rufous on primary coverts; bases of secondaries and inner primaries with much cinnamon-rufous (evident in flight), but *only outer two primaries edged rufous*. Tail blackish, with entire outer pair of feathers and outer web of next pair white; some white on third pair. Superciliary stripes and area behind ear-coverts whitish. Upper breast buff with fine blackish spots and with dark patch at each side. Eyes hazel-brown; bill dusky above, pinkish white below; feet pinkish horn. Appears short tailed in the air. **Juvenile** coloured like adult, but scaly above with buff feather tips. **Voice:** Distinctive song of separated sharp or throaty notes with an occasional whistle; lacks Singing Bush Lark's trills: *tsik trrr chi-chi tsik chrr tsik-tsik tsyuk. . .*, or *skyrr skwee kyrr skwik skeree chik-chik trrit-trit trew*. **HABITS**: Solitary or in pairs. *Prefers dense grass on black 'cotton' soils; usually avoids overgrazed areas*, but may nest in bare places. When flushed, flies a short distance and drops. Displaying male's circular song-flight takes place far above ground. **SIMILAR SPECIES**: Singing Bush Lark is browner, often has paler (brown) breast spots; frequently sings from bushes or while hovering. Blackish morph of Flappet Lark shows deep buff or tawny tail edges and slimmer bill. Dark morph of Williams's Lark, only in lava desert, is heavily spotted on chest, thicker-billed, and almost patternless on back. See Friedmann's Lark. **STATUS AND DISTRIBUTION**: Uncommon resident of grassy plains and bushed grassland, mainly in the highlands from 1350 to 1850 m. Locally common on the Athi–Kapiti plains south of Nairobi, in West Pokot, Siaya and Kitui Districts, and a disjunct population on Lewa Downs near Timau. Also in Mara GR, Serengeti NP and the Ardai Plains west of Arusha.

WILLIAMS'S LARK *Mirafra williamsi* Plate 72

Length 140 mm (5.5"). A *heavy-billed, almost plain-backed* lark of *northern lava deserts*. Outer tail feathers white. Upperparts quite uniform compared with the boldly streaked preceding species, the back feathers much less prominently buff-edged. Worn *williamsi* show no pale dorsal streaks, and *dark streaking is more prominent on crown and nape than on back*. Overall dorsal colour varies from rufous to nearly black, matching the red soil and lava rocks of the habitat. **Adult rufous morph** uniformly bright above, but back duller and browner than wings; limited buff feather margins form a few narrow pale streaks in centre of back. Fresh rufous or rufous-brown inner wing feathers and central rectrices have pale reddish-buff margins separated from feather centre by a narrow black submarginal line; rufous scapulars, lower-back and rump feathers of some adults marked with a similar black subterminal bar. *Primaries strongly rufous-edged, sometimes forming a long panel on the closed wing*; wing-coverts rich brown with contrasting pale rufous-buff margins. Sides of head well patterned: rufous-brown ear-coverts spotted with dark brown and bordered above by whitish-buff or rufous-buff superciliary stripes joining a whitish post-auricular area (not always conspicuous). Lower *throat and chest sparsely spotted with dark brown* sometimes mixed with rufous; below this is a streaky band of rufous flanked by *rufous-brown pectoral patches*. Eyes bright brown; *bill pale* flesh-pink to brownish-grey above, or grey only on culmen, otherwise *flesh-white or ivory*; feet heavy, dull white (appearing pink in the field). **Adult dark morph** has *deep vinous-brown or blackish upperparts*; sides of face blackish with some chestnut; superciliary stripes buff. Margins of flight feathers rufous. *Breast mottled chestnut and dusky*, with *bold blackish pectoral patches*; *flanks heavily streaked*; small spots along sides of throat (and sometimes in centre). Bare parts as in rufous morph. **Juvenile** unknown. **VOICE**: Take-off note a short metallic *tseu*. Song a thin rather scratchy effort punctuated by louder, sharper notes towards the end: *tsit-tsitsit-sit-sureet-eet, tse-tseetsuleu-eet-sueet . . . chuck tseet tserk tsuk tsuk tser-SREET tsur-SREET tsri-tsri tsur-SREET tsri-tsri-tsri tsur-SREET . . .*. **HABITS**: Secretive (unlike Masked Lark in same habitat). Feeds alone at edges of small sandy patches amid lava rocks. Scuttles rodent-like among rocks and low shrubs; may walk ahead of slowly moving observer, but when flushed or pressed closely becomes wary and disappears. Rarely perches above ground except on low rocks, where it stands high on the hot substrate. Male displays briefly at sunrise, within three metres of ground, progressing forward with slow, jerky, laboured flight. Toward end of performance, body and tail hang almost vertically, each forward flap of the broad wings accompanied by the sharp *tsur-SREET* phrase. For several seconds while singing he remains stationary, flaps hard to maintain position, then drops to the ground. **SIMILAR SPECIES**: White-tailed Lark lacks vinous or reddish tone, and inhabits luxuriant grassland. Singing Bush Lark and Friedmann's Lark (in adjacent grassier habitat) are boldly streaked above, more lightly marked below, have more prominent superciliary stripes and lack chestnut on breast. **STATUS AND DISTRIBUTION**: A Kenyan endemic known from rocky desert plains with sparse short grass and low shrubs on red lava soils north of Marsabit (locally common in Dida Galgalu Desert). Also locally east and northeast of Isiolo in uniform stands of low *Barleria* shrubs on rocky lava desert.

FRIEDMANN'S LARK *Mirafra pulpa* Plate 71

Length 130 mm (5"). A rare bird resembling Singing Bush Lark but more richly coloured and more heavily streaked above, especially on nape and upper back, the streaking enhanced in fresh plumage by broad pale feather edges; superciliary stripes somewhat less prominent. Singing birds readily distinguished vocally and by *prominent white throat*. Further differs from Singing Bush Lark (race *marginata*) in its *reddish-brown* (not grey-brown or sepia) central rectrices, inner wing feathers and coverts each showing a *fine dark submarginal line separating feather centre from the pale edge*. (Dark line also present on feathers of juvenile *M. cantillans* and in some adults in nw. Kenya.) Dark, usually streaked ear-coverts accentuated by a white postauricular half-collar continuing partly around hindneck, where obscured by dark streaking. Breast streaks aggregated into prominent patch at each side of upper breast; sides and flanks with diffuse brown streaks. In fresh plumage, *head appears streaked* (more scalloped in *cantillans*); *scapulars and wings rufous-brown, more reddish than the back*. Wing-coverts rufous-brown, edged with pale rufous or tawny. Bill slightly heavier than in *M. c. marginata*, dark horn-brown above, paler horn or pinkish below; feet pinkish. **Rufous morph** more reddish overall, less contrastingly patterned, the white areas washed with warm buff and pale collar much less distinct; may show some rufous at sides of breast with the brown streaks. **Juvenile** resembles young *cantillans,* but much more rufous on the wings, back and nape. **VOICE**: A distinctive whistled *uREEu* or *ooEEoo,* accented in middle and nearly trisyllabic, repeated at one- or two-second intervals from top of bush or tree, as well as during laboured circular song-flight. **HABITS**: Gregarious territorial birds share habitat with Singing Bush Lark, Red-winged and Flappet Larks. Elevates crown feathers when singing, leaning forwards and fluffing out the white throat. Vocal at night and throughout the day. In Ethiopia, Mearns recorded it rattling its wings like a Flappet Lark. **SIMILAR SPECIES**: Singing Bush Lark compared above. White-tailed Lark has blackish upperparts. Somali Short-toed Lark shows marked facial pattern, lacks rufous in primaries. Fawn-coloured Lark has thinner bill, little white in tail, much rufous in primaries but almost none elsewhere in wings. Flappet Lark lacks white in tail. Williams's Lark lacks contrasting dorsal streaks, is more densely spotted or blotched below, and has heavier bill. **STATUS AND DISTRIBUTION**: Known from six specimens and a few sight records (those in Tsavo West NP, Dec. 1992, involving at least 150 individuals). Recorded in dense or very short grassland with sparse shrub cover. Irregular in both Tsavo parks (where it may breed), November-January, April-May and August; two have been caught at night with other migrants at Ngulia. A single bird photographed in Mkomazi GR (Sept. 1994) is the sole Tanzanian record. Otherwise known from near Kibwezi and Archer's Post, Kenya, and s. Shoa, Ethiopia.

RUFOUS-NAPED LARK *Mirafra africana* Plate 72

Length 150–180 mm (6–7″). A *large, stocky, short-tailed* lark with conspicuous *rufous wings in flight.* **Adults** variable. Highland race *athi* streaked buff, brownish grey and blackish above, scapulars more spotted; *no distinct rufous nape*; broad superciliary stripes and sides of head buff, with dark postocular line and fine spotting on ear-coverts. Most wing feathers broadly buff- or tawny-margined in fresh plumage; coverts pale rufous with dark central spot; long rufous panel on closed wing formed by bright primary edges. Throat unmarked whitish or pale buff; upper breast streaked with triangular dusky spots, grading into rufous mottling on lower breast. Tail feathers greyish with tawny edges and narrow dark submarginal lines. Eyes light brown; bill blackish above, pinkish below; feet pale pinkish. Western *tropicalis more reddish brown above with contrasting blackish streaks, rufous on hindcrown and nape,* and with outer webs of outermost tail feathers entirely rufous. *M. a. harterti* of se. Kenya still brighter rufous. **Juveniles** of all races darkcrowned, with bold dark spotting on breast and at sides of foreneck. **VOICE**: Usual whistled song is a repetition of a single phrase such as *weet-ureet, ti-e-EW, chi-witu-EEE* or *tew-tew-tewi-li.* A more complex song *twee-tew-pewi-CHEE pewiCHEE,* likewise repeated, and a prolonged complex series of sputtering, chirping and short whistled notes. **HABITS**: Perches conspicuously on fences and other low perches. Rises from ground with jerky fluttering wing action, but sustained flight direct and somewhat undulating. Walks and stands with upright stance. **SIMILAR SPECIES**: Flappet Lark is smaller, slimmer, more scalloped or spotted above, and relatively longer-tailed; rufous morph resembles *M. a. harterti* but is less heavily streaked above, with broader rufous tail edges and shorter bill. Red-winged Lark is larger and longer-tailed, with prominent dark pectoral patches (less distinct in juvenile). Fawn-coloured Lark is slimmer, has smaller bill, bright white superciliary stripes, black loral lines and thin white tail edges. **STATUS AND DISTRIBUTION**: Widespread and often common resident of open plains and bushed grassland from 1200 to 3000 m in the highlands. Three widely intergrading races: western *tropicalis* from Mt Elgon, Trans-Nzoia and Uasin Gishu Districts south to the Lake Victoria basin, South Nyanza, Mara GR, Serengeti NP, the Crater and Mbulu Highlands and Mt Hanang; *athi* from Maralal, the Laikipia Plateau and the cent. Rift Valley, south through the Mau and cent. Kenyan highlands to the Loita Plains and Loliondo, also to Nairobi, Kajiado and Machakos Districts, around Mt Meru and Kilimanjaro and throughout Arusha District; *harterti* on the Simba and Emali Plains of s. Kenya.

RED-WINGED LARK *Mirafra h. hypermetra* Plate 72

Length 215–230 mm (8.5–9″). *Suggests Rufous-naped Lark,* and like that species shows *much rufous in the primaries* (especially in flight), but larger, longer-tailed, and with *dark patches on sides of chest* (inconspicuous in worn birds). **Adults** dimorphic, some generally rufous, others greyish. Most individuals buff below and patterned grey-brown and black above; rump and upper tail-coverts barred with black; inner wing feathers like back, but narrow submarginal black line separates feather centre from pale margin. Tail plain brown, with narrow buff feather edges in fresh plumage. Superciliary stripes and sides of head buff, mottled or speckled with brown and black; whitish lower throat and upper breast with triangular black spots. Eyes light brown; bill dark horn-brown above, pinkish below, varying markedly in length; feet pale flesh-pink. **Juveniles** also dimorphic, barred and scalloped above with pale feather tips, and lightly spotted on breast; sometimes only a hint of adult's black pectoral patches; *face pale (especially around eyes).* Bill brownish, pink at base; may appear confusingly short. **VOICE**: Clear whistles, loud, melodious and variable, typically variations on a single phrase: *tew-EE-tew, tew TEW-e-tew, WEE-tew, WEE-tew. . . , pee-tu-wee, teree-teree, cheet-twertiLEE . . ..* Also has a clear bubbling *tree, turquireedo-qureee-qureee* (last two notes higher), and complex

songs uttered continuously for several minutes, with imitations of Singing Bush Lark, Pink-breasted Lark, Ashy Cisticola and other species. **HABITS**: Much like those of Rufous-naped Lark, but regularly perches in shrubs and low trees, from which it sings and makes short vertical song-flights. Also sings while hovering. On ground, often assumes very upright stance with stretched neck. **SIMILAR SPECIES**: Allopatric Rufous-naped Lark has shorter tail, and adult lacks prominent pectoral patches; juvenile may show such patches, but is more boldly spotted below, darker-crowned and shorter-tailed than Red-winged Lark. *M. africana harterti* can be confused with rufous morph of Red-winged, but is stockier and lacks the pectoral patches. Flappet Lark is much smaller, more barred or scal-loped above, lacks pectoral patches and shows broad tawny or rufous tail sides. **STATUS AND DISTRIBUTION**: Locally common resident of bushed grassland below 1300 m in northern and eastern lowlands from the Huri Hills and Marsabit District south to Samburu and Shaba GRs, Meru and the Tsavo NPs, Taveta, Lake Jipe and into ne. Tanzanian lowlands in the Mkomazi GR and Masai Steppe, west to Tarangire NP and Lake Burungi. Prefers lower, drier country than Rufous-naped Lark, with no known range overlap. **NOTE**: Birds along Sudanese border north of Lokichokio appear to represent the small race *kidepoensis*, not yet collected in Kenya.

FLAPPET LARK *Mirafra rufocinnamomea* Plate 72

Length 130–138 mm (5–5.5"). Suggests a small, slender Rufous-naped Lark with *tawny or pale rufous outer tail feathers* and *more spotted or barred upperparts*; crown streaked. Pale superciliary stripes contrast with dark ear-coverts. Underparts tawny or rufous, with band of brown or dark rufous spots across upper breast. Typical **adult** russet-brown above; the more rufous-backed individuals may show only faint barring with some thin black shaft streaks. Coastal birds are the dull earth-brown race *fischeri* (of which a more heavily barred, cinnamon-brown morph is known). The bright rufous or chestnut *torrida* is widespread inland. Western *kawirondensis* is darker (with a rare blackish morph), less obviously barred than eastern birds, the markings more streaky. Colour of underparts varies in all races. Bill dark brown above, pale pinkish horn below; feet pinkish or pale brown. **Juvenile** more barred above than most adults. **VOICE**: A slow melodious song, the phrases well separated: *te-ew. . . eee eetieu. . . eet pee-ee. . . eet pee-ee. . . wee-it whur. . .weet we-EW. . . wee eetiEW. . .*; also a shorter *tuwee tuwee*. **HABITS**: Solitary and in pairs, inconspicuous except for breeding male's loud rattle-like 'flappeting' from high above ground: *prrt. . . prrt. . . prrrrrrrt. . .*, presumably produced by the wings, employed in undulating, circling courtship flight and when disturbed. Sings from fencepost, termite mound or shrub. Rises from grass with jerky flight, flies on rapidly quivering wings, then often drops straight down. **SIMILAR SPECIES**: More common Rufous-naped Lark is larger, heavier, proportionately shorter-tailed, much larger-billed, streaked rather than barred above. Fawn-coloured Lark is slimmer-billed, with whitish (not buffy) eyebrows, blackish loral lines and thin white tail edges (sometimes earth-stained). Neither of these species 'flap-pets'. **STATUS AND DISTRIBUTION**: Fairly common but local in short grass, shrubby savanna and edges of dense bush below 1500 m. Three races: *fischeri* throughout coastal lowlands north to Kiunga and inland to the lower Tana River, Rabai, Shimba Hills and Korogwe; *torrida* in n. and e. Kenya at the Huri Hills, Marsabit District, Laikipia Plateau, Meru NP, Thika, Simba and Kibwezi Districts, Tsavo East and West NPs, and in ne. Tanzania from Mkomazi GR, Arusha and Moshi Districts and Mbulumbulu south through the interior to Dodoma; *kawirondensis* in the Lake Victoria basin and Mara GR south to Serengeti NP and Maswa GR.

COLLARED LARK *Mirafra collaris* Plate 72

Length 130–150 mm (5–6"). A bright rufous-backed *northern* lark, the **adult** with a *black-and-white collar across the nape and sides of neck*, distinct white superciliary stripes and throat, and a *narrow black band across lower throat*; rest of underparts pale buff, with some cinnamon mottling on breast and sides. Tail and wings largely black, the primaries tipped and edged white; feathers of upperparts, including inner wing feathers and coverts, pale-margined in fresh plumage. **Juvenile** has black spots on back and dusky spots on lower throat. **VOICE**: A plaintive ascending whistling song delivered from tree or during descent in flight (Mackworth-Praed and Grant 1955). **HABITS**: Usually solitary. Wary, elusive, and runs rapidly. Reportedly 'flappets' like a Flappet Lark. **SIMILAR SPECIES**: Several other larks are rufous above, but all lack the distinctive neck markings. **STATUS AND DISTRIBUTION**: Scarce and local in thorn-bush on red sandy soils in n. Kenya, from Mandera, Moyale and Marsabit Districts south to Habaswein, Garissa and Hola. Reportedly common in areas supporting *Acacia turnbulliana*. In Somalia, inhabits tussock grass with low shrubs (Ash and Miskell 1983).

FAWN-COLOURED LARK *Mirafra africanoides intercedens* Plate 72

Length 140–165 mm (5.5–6.5"). A *trim, slender-billed,* often sharply patterned lark, the *dark cheeks contrasting with bold white superciliary stripes and black lores.* **Adult brown morph** rich brown with broad black streaks, paler (and somewhat greyer) on hindneck; primaries edged rufous or cinnamon. Tail dusky, the central feathers rufous-edged, and outer webs and tips of the outermost feathers whitish or buffy. Throat white; underparts other-wise pale buff, the breast slightly darker and with lines of angular dark spots. **Rufous morph**, bright dark rufous

above and buffier below, is more frequent at lower elevations; rare dark **grey morph** (almost blackish above when worn) known from the Loita Plains to Naivasha and Nakuru; birds in northern deserts are noticeably pale. Eyes brown; bill dark grey or horn-brown above, basal half or more of mandible pale pinkish flesh; feet greyish flesh. **Juvenile** streaked brown and buff on back, with rufous flight feathers and dusky lores. **Voice**: A short high, thin song: *seet suweet sweet-sweet*, variable but often with the terminal double *sweet*. Also a colourless *tsee-tsee*, *tsi-tsi-tsi-tsitsi*. **Habits**: Solitary or in pairs. Sings from shrub, rock or fence wire, sometimes in flight. **Similar Species**: Pink-breasted Lark is paler, its breast mottled with pinkish or pale rufous; it lacks white superciliary stripes. Flappet Lark has broad tawny or pale rufous tail edges and buff superciliary stripes. Grassland Pipit is more sand-coloured and shows much more white in tail. In far ne. Kenya, see Gillett's Lark. Juvenile Pink-breasted Lark lacks rufous in the wings and has pale lores. **Status and Distribution**: Locally common, especially in the Rift Valley, from 500 to 1800 m in open thorn-bush and shrubby grassland on semi-arid sandy soils. Ranges widely in Lodwar, Marsabit, Maralal, Isiolo and Pokot Districts, through much of s. Kenya and across n. Tanzania from Serengeti and Tarangire NPs, Lake Natron, Longido and Ngare Nairobi to foothills of the North Pare Mts, Mkomazi GR and the Masai Steppe.

GILLETT'S LARK *Mirafra gilletti*   Plate 72

Length 155–170 mm (6–6.75"). A rarely recorded bird of *extreme northeastern Kenya*. Resembles a rufous Fawn-coloured Lark, but is slightly larger and less distinctly streaked above (especially on crown), with *grey rump and upper tail-coverts*, and light brownish-rufous (instead of sepia) streaks on the breast. **Juvenile** unknown. **Voice**: Undescribed. **Habits**: Solitary or in pairs. In Somalia, displays marked predilection for hard stony ground among sparse thorn bushes; not a grassland bird (Archer and Godman 1961). **Status and Distribution**: Known in Kenya only from specimens, apparently of the race *arorihensis*, taken near Mandera and El Wak along the Somali border in May 1901 (Miskell and Ash 1985).

PINK-BREASTED LARK *Mirafra poecilosterna*   Plate 72

Length 150–165 mm (6–6.5"). A slender *pipit-like* lark that commonly *perches in trees*. *Face pale rufous to pinkish cinnamon, with variable mottling of the same colour on breast and sides*. Crown dark grey with fine dusky streaks; back and wings brownish grey, mottled with dusky. Brown wings and tail have narrow pale feather edges, but show *no rufous. No white in tail*. Bill and eyes brown; feet pale pinkish flesh. **Juvenile** paler than young Rufous-naped and Flappet Larks; lacks dark lores of Fawn-coloured Lark. **Voice**: Usual note a simple *tseet-tseet* or *pwee*. Song a series of up to seven rather squeaky high, thin notes, often running into a short, descending, squeaky chatter (K. Kaufman, pers. comm.), or a shorter *tseet-tseetsew-seet* or *tsit-tsit-tseu-tseet*, the last note higher. **Habits**: Feeds on ground, alone or in pairs, but often flies to elevated perch when disturbed. Sings from exposed branch on top of shrub or tree. **Similar Species**: Fawn-coloured Lark, of similar proportions, is darker and browner, with dark cheek patches, bold white eyebrows and thin white tail edges; lacks grey crown. See Red-throated Pipit. **Status and Distribution**: Locally common in bushed and wooded grassland on sandy soils at 150–1500 m, typically in dry *Acacia* and *Commiphora* scrub, often with little or no grass cover. Ranges widely north, east and south of the Kenyan highlands (though absent from coastal lowlands, the Lake Victoria basin and the southwest); in ne. Tanzania, at Longido, Kahe, Mkomazi GR and eastern parts of the Masai Steppe.

DUSKY LARK *Pinarocorys n. nigricans*   Plate 122

Length 190–200 mm (7.5–8"). A large, *dark thrush-like* lark. **Adult male** dark sooty brown above, the feathers buff-edged in fresh plumage; *buffy-white superciliary stripes and areas around eyes contrast with dark ear-coverts, and malar and moustachial stripes*. Underparts buffy white, with bold streaks of blackish-brown spots on breast and flanks; belly and under tail-coverts white. Bill horn-brown, fading to yellow at base of mandible; eyes brown; feet whitish. **Female** paler, with less prominent facial pattern; breast pale buff, streaked with brown. **Immature** similar but duller, and with much buffy-brown feather edging on upperparts. **Voice**: A soft *wek-wek-wek* repeated three to six times in flight (Maclean 1984). **Habits**: Forages restlessly, stopping and flicking wings after each stop. Favours recently burnt ground. **Status and Distribution**: Breeds in the miombo zone of w. Tanzania. Known in our region only from a single specimen taken in Arusha NP, October 1962.

SPIKE-HEELED LARK *Chersomanes albofasciata beesleyi*   Plate 122

Length 115 mm (4.5"). A northern Tanzanian lark with *upright carriage* and fairly *long decurved bill*. *Very short white-tipped tail* conspicuous in flight. **Adult** streaked and mottled blackish brown above, the head and back feathers margined (in fresh plumage) with whitish or pale cinnamon; hindneck and some upper back feathers broadly cinnamon-edged. Face, superciliary stripes and throat white; auriculars cinnamon. Breast rufous-cinnamon with necklace of dark brown streaks, these extending sparsely onto the flanks; remaining underparts paler

rufous. Tail brown, all except central feathers white-tipped. Bill blackish grey above, pale whitish horn below; eyes bright red-brown; feet pinkish flesh. **Juvenile** lacks rufous on the nape and shows less white feather tipping on upperside than in adult; breast diffusely speckled with brown, the feathers white-tipped; rest of underparts paler than in adult; remiges broadly margined with buff or whitish; wing-coverts white-tipped. **Voice**: In flight, a trilled *piree* or *tirrr*, repeated several times. Alarm note a harsh *skeee*. Southern African races sing *chip-kwip-kwip-kwip*, *ti-ti-ti-ti-ti*, *chirri-chirri-chirri* (Maclean 1984). **Habits**: Solitary or in small groups. Flight undulating, with spread tail. Digs with powerful swipes of the bill. Rarely perches above ground. **Status and Distribution**: This race known only from overgrazed, treeless, short-grass plains near Kingerete, 30–50 km north of Arusha.

GREATER SHORT-TOED LARK *Calandrella brachydactyla longipennis* Plate 71

Length 130–140 mm (5–5.5"). A palearctic vagrant, *pale*, with a *short dull yellowish bill*, broad buffy-white superciliary stripes bordered below by dark postocular lines, and wide white tail edges. Ear-coverts and lores dusky. Brownish crown (rufous-tinged in male) marked with fine dark lines. Upperparts streaked pale buffy brown and blackish; upper tail-coverts more tawny and unstreaked. Tips of some greater coverts, margins of primary coverts and outer web of outermost primary white or pale buff. Tail blackish, the outer pair of feathers half black, half white; next pair with narrow white edge. Area on sides of neck and underparts buffy white, the flanks faintly brown-tinged; small dusky pectoral patches not prominent in autumn birds; lower throat faintly spotted. Bill pale yellowish horn with dusky culmen; eyes brown; feet brownish pink. **Voice**: A chittering call when flushed. **Similar Species**: Somali Short-toed Lark is darker, with streaked breast, and larger bill. **Status and Distribution**: Accidental; normally winters from the Sahel to ne. Ethiopia. Known in Kenya from two specimen records (Athi River, 14 Nov. 1899, and near Mombasa, 19 Dec. 1964). **Note**: Included in *C. cinerea* by Vaurie (1959).

RED-CAPPED LARK *Calandrella cinerea* Plate 71

Length 140–150 mm (5.5–6"). A gregarious highland lark with *dark rufous crown, nape, sides of breast and upper tail-coverts*. May appear crested. **Adult** rather pale grey-brown above and whitish below; most primaries edged with rufous, the outermost with white. Throat, superciliary stripes and area around eyes also white. Tail dark brown, the outer two pairs of rectrices edged white (noticeable in flight). The race *saturatior* is brighter, more rufous above than the somewhat greyer *williamsi*. **Juvenile** lacks rufous; upperparts appear scaly, with light feather edges; breast dark-spotted, with dusky patch at each side. **Voice**: A hard *chip* or *chirrip* (sometimes double) when flushed. Flocks in flight produce a soft twittering. A brief aerial song, infrequently heard, consists of a few thin, harsh notes. **Habits**: Typically in flocks on bare ground. Stands upright to look about. Courting bird struts with erect crest, drooped wings, spread and cocked tail. Flight low and undulating. **Status and Distribution**: *C. c. williamsi* is widespread and common, mainly above 1200 m, on short grass in the cent. Kenyan highlands, ranging from the Uasin Gishu and Laikipia Plateaux south to the Kedong Valley, Nairobi NP, Athi and Kapiti Plains and Amboseli NP. *C. c. saturatior* ranges over the Mara GR, Loita Plains and in n. Tanzania from Serengeti NP east to the Crater Highlands and Arusha District.

SOMALI SHORT-TOED LARK *Calandrella somalica* Plate 71
(Rufous Short-toed Lark; Athi Short-toed Lark)

Length 130–140 mm (5–5.5"). A 'spectacled' lark of dry grassy plains. **Adult** *C. s. athensis* is dark brown and sandy buff, heavily streaked above, with a *large pale eye-ring or subocular semicircle joining the creamy-buff superciliary stripe and postauricular area*; ear-coverts dark. In fresh plumage, buff edges of wing feathers are prominent, but vanish through wear prior to the annual moult. Outer pair of tail feathers mostly white, but often inconspicuous in the field; central rectrices almost black. Underparts buffy white, with dark spots on upper breast and pectoral patches at the sides. Eyes dark brown; *bill light brownish pink*, dusky on culmen; feet brownish pink. In the hand, readily separated from *Mirafra* species by concealed nostrils and by outermost primary being elongated like the others, not half the length of the next feather. **Juvenile** apparently undescribed. Northern race *megaensis* is paler, more sandy buff, especially on wing-coverts; head and neck may show rich buff wash; bill pinkish. **Voice**: A short low trill, *trrrit*, when flushed; flock produces a chittering sound. Prolonged trilling flight song of *athensis* recalls European Skylark (*Alauda arvensis*): *trr-trr-treer, treer-treet-treer-trtrtrtr-tlee-tlee-treer*. . . . Song of presumed *megaensis* consists partly of distinct notes interspersed with rapidly delivered medleys of scratchy and clear notes plus an occasional canary-like trill; suggests songs of both Greater and Lesser Short-toed Larks (*C. brachydactyla* and *C. rufescens*) but with more distinct notes, e.g. *chlip-chlip-slureet, chree-chree-chree-chree, quree quree, tyee-tyee-tyee, squiree*. . ., and *tsk-tsk-chukwee-chreeee, swee-sweet-swereet, screet-weet, squirrrrrr*. **Habits**: Gregarious, in small to rather large flocks

flying rapidly and low over the plains. Tends to avoid shortest grass, preferring areas with denser tufts which provide better cover. Has high-soaring song-flight on fluttering wings; also sings from ground. Erects crest in display. **Similar Species**: White-tailed Lark is more blackish above, has fainter breast spotting, and typically inhabits taller grass. Singing Bush Lark lacks the distinctive facial pattern and usually shows prominent rufous primary edges. See also Williams's and Friedmann's Larks. **Status and Distribution**: Locally common resident and wanderer on open short-grass plains from 1200 to 1850 m. Movements probably determined by heavy seasonal rains, after which many birds may suddenly appear. *C. s. athensis* is southern, from Nairobi NP, the Athi, Kapiti and Emali Plains south to Arusha District in n. Tanzania. Formerly ranged north to Naivasha and the plains below Mt Kenya. Sight records from Buffalo Springs GR (March 1978) and the Huri Hills (Nov. 1989) probably of *megaensis*, and hundreds south of Maralal (displaying, Nov. 1991) almost certainly of that race. Photographic or specimen documentation of northern birds desirable. **Note**: Often considered conspecific with palearctic *C. rufescens*.

MASKED LARK *Spizocorys personata*   Plate 71

Length 140–150 mm (5.5–6"). A distinctive northern desert lark with white throat, *black face* and *heavy pink or yellowish-horn bill*. Head and neck grey-brown with black shaft streaks; back similar, but broadly streaked with black; wings blackish brown with rufous feather edges. Underparts mainly greyish or cinnamon-brown. Northern *S. p. yavelloensis* noticeably greyer above, with grey breast; southern races browner. Eyes light hazel-brown; feet flesh-pink. **Voice**: Call, in flight or on ground, a rolling *chew-chichew, chew* or *tew-tew-tutew-tew*, and a thin metallic *tsik-tsik tseedleee*. Calls include a high-pitched *treeeeeee*, a single *chew* and a double *djew-djew*. On the ground utters a repeated high *tee tee tee tee*. **Habits**: Feeds in small groups on bare ground. Not shy; easily approached on foot. Seems to avoid roadsides. Perches prominently on rocks, often standing erect with neck stretched. **Status and Distribution**: Locally common at 600–1400 m in n. Kenyan deserts with or without sparse low shrubs (e.g. *Barleria*) and with little or no grass cover. Three races: *yavelloensis* from Ethiopian border and the Huri Hills south to the Dida Galgalu Desert; *mcchesneyi* on the Marsabit Plateau; and *intensa* in eastern Shaba GR and adjacent country between Isiolo and Garba Tula. Partial to areas of lava rock on red soils, a habitat shared with Williams's Lark. Birds south of Loyangalani (Aug. 1983) not racially assigned.

SHORT-TAILED LARK *Pseudalaemon fremantlii*   Plate 71

Length 140 mm (5.5"). A unique *long-billed and short-tailed* lark with a conspicuous *vertical black mark below the eye* and extending partly around ear-coverts. White superciliary stripes and dark patches on each side of foreneck add to the distinctive face pattern. Usual **adult grey morph** generally streaked greyish and black above; wings blackish brown, with broad sandy-buff edges in fresh plumage. Tail short, square-tipped, dark brown, with outer web of outer feathers largely white (disappearing with wear). May appear slightly crested. Lower throat/upper breast sparsely spotted with brown; rest of underparts white, buff-tinged on breast and along sides and flanks, the latter lightly streaked black and rufous. **Rufous morph** has rufous upperparts. Northern birds (*megaensis*) noticeably paler than southern *delamerei*. Eyes hazel-brown; bill stout, lead-grey above, creamy below; feet pinkish. **Juvenile** has feathers of upperparts and wings tipped whitish, and small brown spots on the breast. **Voice**: Take-off note a distinctive sharp *tewi*. Song a slow deliberate whistle delivered from the ground: *seeu seeu. . . seeu seeu seeu. . . seeu seeu TEWleu*, slightly slurred. **Habits**: Wanders in pairs or small groups, sometimes with *Calandrella* larks. Digs by using its bill 'shovel-fashion'. Shelters under low shrubs in midday. **Similar Species**: Masked Lark has black facial mark but otherwise lacks contrasting head pattern. **Status and Distribution**: Locally common on dry, often over-grazed, short-grass plains from 1000 to 1700 m. Subject to irregular local movements. Southern *P. f. delamerei* ranges from Nairobi NP and the Athi–Kapiti Plains south to Amboseli NP and the Arusha area, west to the Crater Highlands and Serengeti Plains. *P. f. megaensis* is known from the Ethiopian border south to Marsabit District; sight records from the Leroghi Plateau near Maralal probably represent this race.

CRESTED LARK *Galerida cristata somaliensis*   Plate 71

Length 165–170 mm (6.5–6.75"). A *conspicuously crested, pale buff or sand-coloured lark* of *sandy deserts* in northern Kenya. **Adult** mottled with dusky above; no contrast between upper tail-coverts and rump. Underparts mostly white, the breast pale tan and dusky-spotted. Primaries pale brown with tawny edges; tail mostly dusky, the outer feathers with entire outer web and tip buff. Eyes brown, bill dusky, feet pale brown. **Juvenile** scaly above, with buffy-white feather tips and speckled crown; back and wings brighter buff; breast streaks more diffuse, and bill shorter and darker than in adult. **Voice**: Calls include a thin *tee-tewit* and a slurred *seeureet* (higher at end), given in flight or from the ground. Take-off note *cherrreet*. Songs loud, clear and sweet: (1) a slurred liquid *ti-TSI-oo, EEE-tsew-seeet*; (2) a musical *tee-tee-tew TEW-e-tew*; (3) *sree-sree-reeu*; (4) *tew p'tew p'tew*; (5) a longer *weee-twee, tewee-tew, twee-too-ee-tooee. . .* given from the ground. Complex warbling song

of these phrases and a few scratchy notes, plus mimicry of other species, may last for 30 seconds or longer. **Habits:** Usually in pairs; apparently does not flock. Digs vigorously with bill when foraging. **Similar Species:** Thekla Lark is darker above and shows contrast between paler upper tail-coverts and darker rump; breast markings darker, usually much more prominent; prefers rocky desert. **Status and Distribution:** Fairly common in sparsely vegetated sandy desert, and in sand patches amid lava-rock desert from 400 to 900 m. Ranges throughout the Lake Turkana basin, and south in the Rift Valley to Lokori and Kapedo, east to Turbi and Marsabit Districts and the Kaisut Desert.

THEKLA LARK *Galerida theklae huriensis*   **Plate 71**
(Short-crested Lark)

Length 160–165 mm (6.25–6.5"). A *conspicuously crested* lark of *rocky places* in arid northern Kenya. *Overall tone much darker and less sandy than Crested Lark,* the dorsal streaks and *breast spots heavier and blacker.* (Heavily marked extremes of Crested Lark seldom, if ever, as boldly spotted on the breast as G. t. huriensis.) Crest and *bill slightly shorter* than in Crested Lark. *Light grey upper tail-coverts contrast with darker grey-brown rump;* pale parts of tail slightly more rufescent than in Crested Lark. In the hand, note that short outer primary is slightly longer than the primary coverts (shorter than coverts in Crested Lark). Eyes hazel-brown, bill dusky, feet pale pinkish brown. **Juvenile** buffier than adult, with pale feather edges above; breast streaks faint. **Voice:** Common call a short buzzy *chureeeeet,* unlike thin clear whistles of Crested Lark. Short songs from perched bird: *sweet seet sureet-tsew* and *tseet-tseet-chreet, chureet, tsurreeeeeee.* In flight display, groups of scratchy notes and short trills precede a faster, longer and complex twittering. Mimics other species. **Habits:** Similar to those of Crested Lark, but typically inhabits rocky or stony ground. In pairs or small groups; often approachable. Unlike Crested Lark, seldom digs forcefully with bill. Has extended circling display flight with fluttery wingbeats, to height of 30 m or higher. **Similar Species:** Crested Lark, compared above, has different calls and is almost always on sandy substrate. **Status and Distribution:** Locally common in rocky lava desert, at 400–1300 m, from the Huri Hills, Allia Bay, North Horr and Turbi south to Loyangalani and Marsabit Districts. Particularly numerous in the Dida Galgalu Desert. **Note:** Considered a race of the Asian *G. malabarica* by some authors.

FISCHER'S SPARROW-LARK *Eremopterix leucopareia*   **Plate 71**

Length 115–120 mm (4.5–4.75"). A gregarious sparrow-like or finch-like lark, quite compact and short-tailed. **Adult male** has *large white cheek patch contrasting with dark throat and mid-ventral line;* greyish brown above, with darker rufous-tinged crown. Underparts whitish. **Female** dull grey-brown with dark mottling, and with buff nape band, faint pale superciliary stripes and *broad black line from belly to under tail-coverts* (not easily seen); throat buff, usually somewhat mottled. Some apparent females have throat and breast dark brown or blackish. **Juvenile** mottled above with pale feather edges, and with a pale buff nape patch, long tawny wing panel formed by flight-feather edges, and a small blackish belly patch. **Voice:** Call note a low *chirrup* or *seet-eet.* Flocks utter a soft twitter. When breeding, a simple short song recalling a repeated *Passer* chirp, given incessantly in rather high flight. **Habits:** Large flocks break up in breeding season, but numerous pairs nest in a loose 'colony'. Sings from the ground and in flight. Displaying male erects crest, showing chestnut-brown nape and ear-coverts. **Similar Species:** Other sparrow-larks are thicker-billed, with whitish outer tail feathers. Dark male Chestnut-headed shows prominent circular white crown patch; female is paler and buffier than female Fischer's, with no dark mid-ventral line. Male Chestnut-backed is strikingly patterned black, chestnut and white; female shows rufous or chestnut wing-coverts. **Status and Distribution:** Common resident and wanderer on short-grass plains in drier areas between 600 and 1800 m, ranging from Kongelai, Maralal, Buffalo Springs GR, Isiolo and Meru NP south to Nyanza, the Loita Plains, Magadi, Amboseli area and Tsavo West NP, and throughout n. Tanzania from Serengeti NP, Lake Natron, the Crater Highlands, Arusha and Moshi Districts and the Mkomazi GR southwards.

CHESTNUT-BACKED SPARROW-LARK *Eremopterix leucotis madaraszi*   **Plate 71**

Length 130 mm (5"). A dark nomadic sparrow-lark with a predilection for black 'cotton' soils. **Male** *chestnut on back and wing-coverts;* black on head, neck and underparts, except for *large white patch on side of head and at sides of breast,* plus a *narrow whitish band on nape.* **Females** vary from rather like male to darkly mottled or pale, but always show *rufous or chestnut wing-coverts and black face, foreneck and centre of belly;* some are blackish-crowned and densely streaked on throat and breast. Both sexes have *whitish or pale grey upper tail-coverts and outer rectrices,* conspicuous in flight. **Juvenile** similar to juvenile Fischer's Sparrow-Lark, but with *heavier bill.* **Voice:** Call a sharp rattling *chirip-cheew.* Song varied, rather soft, e.g. *chitichu ch-ch-ch CHIwieu, ch-ch-*

ch CHIwieu. **HABITS:** Highly gregarious, sometimes in mixed flocks with *E. signata.* Not shy. Usually flies low. Several pairs may nest near one another. Sings from the ground and in flight. **SIMILAR SPECIES:** Other sparrow-larks are paler. Female Chestnut-headed has rufous superciliary stripes. Female Fischer's has dark mid-ventral line (often difficult to see). **STATUS AND DISTRIBUTION:** A scarce and erratic wanderer in semi-arid areas north, south and southeast of the Kenyan highlands, somewhat regular only in parts of Meru and Tsavo East NPs. Ranges through interior n. Tanzania, appearing sporadically in Arusha, Tarangire and Serengeti NPs and on the Ardai Plains. Everywhere subject to extensive local movements. Formerly recorded in the coastal lowlands from Manda Island, the lower Tana River and Malindi.

CHESTNUT-HEADED SPARROW-LARK *Eremopterix signata* Plate 71

Length 115–120 mm (4.5–4.75"). A pale sparrow-lark of *northern Kenya.* **Male's** *crown and nape auburn, chestnut or blackish,* with a *large circular white area on centre of crown;* white patches on sides of head bordered by dark throat and band on neck; back pale brown. Underparts white with broad black central stripe. Outer tail feathers whitish. **Female** sandy buff, with *whitish patch on each side of head* and *pale rufous superciliary stripes.* **Immature male** resembles female, but has *dull chestnut throat and upper breast* and *blackish mid-ventral patch* on lower breast and belly; suggests a lighter-coloured, larger-billed female Fischer's Sparrow-Lark. **Juvenile** pale brown and scalloped, with sandy-buff face and nape; buff breast band mottled or streaked dusky. Freshly plumaged birds show pale buff wing-feather edgings; some individuals more uniformly tawny-brown above and heavily streaked below. **VOICE:** A sharp *chip-up* (Tomlinson 1950). Song described as a short twittering. **HABITS:** In pairs or in flocks of 30–40 birds. Flies low, suddenly dropping to ground. Regularly visits water holes. Sings from the ground and in flight. **SIMILAR SPECIES:** See Fischer's and Chestnut-backed Sparrow-Larks. **STATUS AND DISTRIBUTION:** Locally common on dry short-grass plains and in nearly bare lava desert. Widespread in n. Kenya, particularly in the Dida Galgalu and Kaisut Deserts near Marsabit. Range has recently extended south into Tsavo East NP, where now resident near Aruba. Wanders east to the lower Tana River and to coastal dunes between the Tana and Sabaki Rivers, rarely farther south along the coast. Nominate *signata* and the more western *harrisoni* reportedly meet near Lake Turkana, but limits of the two races uncertain. Generally little or no overlap with Fischer's Sparrow-Lark, although both are known from Buffalo Springs GR and Meru NP.

WAGTAILS, PIPITS AND LONGCLAWS, FAMILY MOTACILLIDAE
(World, *c.* 63 species; Africa, 35; Kenya, 21; n. Tanzania, 17)

Small to medium-sized ground birds, mostly slim with fairly long legs and slender pointed bills. The moderate to long tail, with white or buff outer feathers, is habitually pumped up and down in wagtails and pipits. Forward-and-backward head motion is often exaggerated, especially in wagtails, and all species walk rather than hop. Motacillids are insectivorous birds, some of them gregarious, feeding along shorelines and streamsides, in grassland or other open habitats, less often in forest openings. Our species include palearctic migrants and breeding residents. The nest is an open cup, usually well concealed on the ground or set into a bank. Wagtails are slender and long-tailed, with unstreaked plumage, mostly black and white, yellow and grey. Pipits are somewhat lark-like, cryptically streaked brownish and buff above, and with similar elongated inner secondaries ('tertials'). They can be difficult to identify; the most useful field characters are colour of outer tail feathers, extent of streaking both above and below, and vocalizations. In the hand, wing formula and length of hind claw may be diagnostic. The aberrant Golden Pipit shows much yellow and appears especially long-legged, with lower part of the tibiotarsus unfeathered (an approach to this is seen in Malindi Pipit). Longclaws are more robust, shorter-tailed, and with more rounded wings than pipits. Their plumage is cryptically patterned above, yellow or pink below, often with a black collar. The tarsi and toes are long and stout, the hind claw extremely long.

AFRICAN PIED WAGTAIL *Motacilla aguimp vidua* Plate 69

Length 200 mm (8"). The common *black-and-white* wagtail of towns and countryside. **Adult** mostly black above, including top of head, with black mask and broad breast band, and with large white wing patch and broad superciliary stripes; tail black, with white outer feathers. Bill, tarsi and toes black; eyes dark brown. **Juvenile** brownish grey where adult is black, washed brownish on flanks; breast band may be brown. **VOICE:** Call a whistled *tuwhee* or *tseet-tseet-tseet. . .,* thin but loud. Song a sustained sequence of melodious whistling and piping notes, *weet-weet, wip-wip-wip, weet-wee-wee. . . .* **HABITS:** During the day, usually solitary or in pairs, walking with pumping tail on bare ground, muddy shores, grassland and lawns. Very confiding, often on and about houses. Each evening gathers in hundreds at communal tree roosts. **SIMILAR SPECIES:** See White Wagtail, Cape Wagtail. **STATUS AND DISTRIBUTION:** Widespread and common resident n city suburbs, villages, farms, forest clearings, lake and river edges, and around water holes or habitation in more arid areas. Absent from much of n. and ne. Kenya.

WHITE WAGTAIL *Motacilla a. alba*   Plate 69

Length 190 mm (7.5"). A *long-tailed* grey-and-white bird characteristic of muddy shores. White sides of head contrast with black or dark grey crown and nape and a *black crescent across upper breast*. Spring birds (Feb.–March) may also have black chin and throat. Upperparts mainly grey; underparts white; tail black with white outer feathers; wings black with white feather edgings and two white bars across coverts. **Adult male** has broadly white forehead and is black from crown to nape. Bill, tarsi and toes black; eyes dark brown. **Female** and **first-winter** birds may show little white on forehead and have entirely grey nape and crown. **Juvenile** has olive-tinged grey crown and narrow breast band, sometimes retained into December. **Voice:** A high-pitched double *tschizzic*, given mainly in flight. **Habits:** Territorial, often in pairs. Roosts colonially in trees. **Similar Species:** Mountain Wagtail of highland streams is more bluish grey above, has dark facial markings, a narrower breast band, more white in tail, and differs vocally. Cape Wagtail resembles juvenile White, but is much darker above and buff-tinged below. African Pied Wagtail more robust and differently patterned. **Status and Distribution:** Palearctic migrant, November to early March, along lakes, rivers and at sewage works. Common at Lake Turkana; uncommon elsewhere, but regular in the cent. Kenyan highlands at Mogotio and Nairobi area oxidation ponds. Rare in Tanzania, where known only from Lake Manyara (Jan. 1969) and Dar es Salaam (Jan. 1975).

GREY WAGTAIL *Motacilla c. cinerea*   Plate 69

Length 190–205 mm (7.5–8"). An especially *long-tailed, pale-legged* wagtail, *grey above, with yellowish-green rump*. Underparts yellow, with pale buff flanks, throat either white or (in spring male) black; superciliary stripes whitish. In flight, shows white outer tail feathers and *long white band across base of secondaries and inner primaries*. Bill black; eyes dark brown; *tarsi and toes pinkish brown or brownish flesh* (not black). **Voice:** Call note like that of White Wagtail, but more metallic and staccato: a sharp *chitik!*; alarm call a shrill *si-heet*. **Habits:** Usually solitary, foraging along streams. Pumps tail vigorously during feeding pauses; flies with long undulations. **Similar Species:** White and Mountain Wagtails lack yellowish rump and are white below. Yellow Wagtail is olive-green or olive-brown above, without contrasting rump, and has shorter tail. **Status and Distribution:** Uncommon but widespread palearctic migrant, late September to March, mainly along fast-flowing highland-forest streams below 3000 m in the w. and cent. Kenyan highlands and the Crater Highlands of n. Tanzania. Occasional on passage at lower elevations, including some coastal sites.

MOUNTAIN WAGTAIL *Motacilla clara torrentium*   Plate 69
(Long-tailed Wagtail)

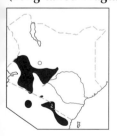

Length 172–192 mm (6.75–7.5"). Slender, *long-tailed* and characteristic of *highland streams*. **Adult** *light blue-grey on back* and with a *narrow black breast band*; wings black with pale feather edgings and two white bars on the coverts. Outer three pairs of tail feathers white; central ones black. Blackish face has contrasting narrow white superciliary stripes and white eyelids. Bill black, mandible sometimes grey at base; eyes dark brown; legs pinkish or grey-brown. **Juvenile** similar, but browner above, somewhat buffier below, with breast band reduced or absent. **Voice:** On take-off a loud *chizzik*. Song a sustained series of trilled musical phrases and short sibilant notes: *tsrrrrup, tsrrrrup . . . tsu-tse-seu, tsweu-tswii, trrrip . . ..* **Habits:** Solitary or in pairs, running actively on streamside rocks and banks, the tail in constant motion. Sometimes forages along forest tracks. **Similar Species:** Grey Wagtail, another streamside bird, has yellowish rump and underparts. Cape Wagtail has shorter tail with less white (on only two outer pairs of feathers), and back is olive-brown, not blue-grey. **Status and Distribution:** Local resident and wanderer, characteristic of highland streams under 3000 m, but recorded as low as 700 m at Taveta and even lower in the East Usambara Mts. Often alongside the migratory Grey Wagtail.

CAPE WAGTAIL *Motacilla capensis wellsi*   Plate 69
(Wells's Wagtail)

Length 192–205 mm (7.5–8"). Dull-plumaged and relatively *short-tailed*. **Adult** *dark olive-grey* or *olive-brown* above and on face, with *narrow buffy-white superciliary stripes* and dusky lores. Underparts creamy white, sometimes with faint salmon-pink wash, especially on centre of lower breast and belly, with dusky breast band and olive-grey sides of breast and flanks. Blackish-brown wings show much pale feather edging. Tail blackish, with

outer two feathers largely white. **Juvenile** resembles adult, but brownish above with buff wing edgings and more yellowish below. **VOICE:** Call note a piping *tweep*. Song a jumble of twittering notes, *tweep-tweep-tweep, witititi, cheep-tweep,* etc. **HABITS:** Usually solitary or in pairs, foraging purposefully on muddy or marshy shores or floating vegetation. Rather shy. **SIMILAR SPECIES:** Brown-tinged juvenile African Pied Wagtail has large white wing patch and broader superciliary stripes. Mountain Wagtail is slimmer, longer-tailed, paler blue-grey above. Female and immature Yellow Wagtail lack black breast band. Some immature White Wagtails with grey crown and narrow breast band resemble Cape Wagtail but are paler above and nearly pure white below. **STATUS AND DISTRIBUTION:** Uncommon resident and wanderer, on shallow lake and swamp edges, moist grassland, forest clearings and cultivation, generally above 2000 m in the w. and cent. Kenyan highlands from the Mau and Trans-Mara east to Mau Narok, Naivasha, the Aberdares, and Nyeri and Nairobi Districts.

YELLOW WAGTAIL *Motacilla flava* Plate 69

Length 175–185 mm (7"). Slightly smaller than most wagtails, and somewhat shorter-tailed. Upperparts olive-green or brownish; underparts yellow or yellowish white; pale superciliary stripes usually prominent. Wing edgings creamy buff; tail black, with white outer feathers. **Adult male** has *yellow throat;* **female** *whitish or buff from chin to upper breast.* Head pattern of male varies according to race: *M. f. flava* has blue-grey crown separated from darker grey face by broad white superciliary stripes; *M. f. thunbergi* has dark grey crown but blackish face, with no white superciliary stripes or these short and narrow; *M. f. lutea* has greenish crown and face with broad yellow superciliary stripes, the forehead, face or (in some spring birds) most of head yellow; *M. f. feldegg* is black-headed with no superciliary stripes; *M. f. beema* resembles *flava,* but top of head and face pale grey; *M. f. leucocephala* is still paler, with largely whitish head. **Females** not racially distinguishable; top of head and face olive-brown or grey-brown and superciliary stripes buff or whitish; body coloration brighter and head pattern sharper in spring. **First-winter** birds resemble females, but show more distinct white wing-bar and usually are more whitish below; some show faint necklace of spots on breast. Young males usually acquire some of adult head pattern in December. **VOICE:** A characteristic *tseeip* or *tseer* in flight. **HABITS:** Gregarious; flocks or small groups feed actively on shorelines and short grass, especially around domestic animals. Individuals also forage on lawns and roadsides. Forms large night roosts in swamps, tall grass or trees. **SIMILAR SPECIES:** Cape Wagtail is similar in build but larger, darker above and less yellow below, with a black chest band. Grey Wagtail has greenish-yellow rump and longer tail. **STATUS AND DISTRIBUTION:** Widespread, common to abundant palearctic migrant, September to mid-April, mostly below 2500 m and mainly in more humid areas. Frequents marshes, lake and swamp edges, cultivation and short grassland; thousands assemble at sewage works. *M. f. flava* present throughout, predominating in the Rift Valley; *lutea* largely in drier eastern areas; *beema* in small numbers, mainly alongside *flava* in the east; *thunbergi* primarily western, especially near Lake Victoria, but common throughout during April passage; *feldegg* in small numbers with marked preference for wetlands in the Lake Victoria basin; *leucocephala* occasional at Nairobi, recorded once near Arusha in n. Tanzania.

TAWNY PIPIT *Anthus c. campestris* Plate 70

Length 165–170 mm (6.5"). A slender *pale* pipit with a rather long white-edged tail. **Adult** almost uniform sandy brown above and *with only a few short dark brown streaks on buff breast.* Face shows prominent creamy-white superciliary stripes, largely brownish lores and ear-coverts, and narrow dark brown malar streaks. Much pale wing edging; buffy-white edges of median coverts contrast strongly with almost blackish centres. Bill dark brown, base of lower mandible flesh-pink; eyes dark brown; tarsi and toes pale yellowish flesh-colour; hind claw short. **First-winter** bird more heavily streaked across upper breast, scalloped or strongly streaked above. **VOICE:** A loud *tseep* or *tseuc* on take-off and landing; recalls Yellow Wagtail. **HABITS:** Wagtail-like, with rather horizontal carriage; walks or runs rapidly, frequently pumping tail up and down. **SIMILAR SPECIES:** Grassland Pipit resembles immature Tawny, with similar tail pattern and wing formula, but differs vocally and is less wagtail-like, with heavier bill, longer legs and long hind claw, and with more upright carriage. Long-billed Pipit is much darker and duller above, deeper buff below, with buffy-white outer tail feathers and more rounded wing. **STATUS AND DISTRIBUTION:** Rare palearctic migrant to Kenya, where recorded fewer than ten times on short dry grassland south to Lake Nakuru, Nairobi, Meru and Tsavo West NPs and Lamu District.

GRASSLAND PIPIT *Anthus cinnamomeus*   **Plate 70**
Richard's Pipit; Grassveld Pipit)

Length 158–170 mm (6–6.5"). The common East African pipit, rather long-legged and long-tailed, buffy brown above with distinct dark streaking. *Face pattern bold, with pronounced pale superciliaries and dark malar stripes; pale buff below, with short dark streaks across upper breast;* tail broadly edged white. Bill blackish brown, base of mandible yellowish; eyes brown; tarsi and toes pale flesh-brown. In the hand, note long hind claw, extensive white toward tip of the second tail feather from the outside, and wing formula (5th primary much shorter than outer four and not emarginate toward tip). Freshly plumaged **adult** and **immature** have broad pale buff feather edges above; in worn adults these largely disappear. The bird known as 'Jackson's Pipit', *A. (c.) latistriatus,* is a very dark bird, possibly not conspecific (see discussion below). **Juvenile** darker, more dusky above, with heavy dark brown breast streaks extending to flanks; back blotched or spotted with black, the feathers narrowly tipped with pale buff. Coastal *A. c. annae* is paler, duller, greyer and slightly smaller than widespread inland *lacuum* described above. **VOICE**: When flushed, a sharp *chip* or *trip*. Song *tree-tree-tree* or *sreet-sreet-sreet-sreet,* sometimes continuing as *chew chew chee chew chew-chew-chew,* from low perch or in cruising display flight. **HABITS**: Sometimes gregarious, commonly forming small groups, but singles and pairs frequent. Walks with strutting gait; carriage erect when alert. Perches on posts and bushes. Flight undulating. **SIMILAR SPECIES**: Long-billed Pipit is larger and darker, with longer bill and tail, less distinctly streaked above; has buffy-white tail sides, slightly shorter hind claw (7–12 mm as opposed to 11–15 mm), and the emarginate 5th primary is a little shorter than the outer four. Tree and Red-throated Pipits are smaller, more extensively streaked below, with smaller bills and shorter legs. Plain-backed Pipit is larger, almost unstreaked above, with buff tail edges. See Tawny Pipit. **STATUS AND DISTRIBUTION**: *A. c. lacuum* is widespread and often common in open habitats to above 3000 m in open or bushed grassland, cleared or burnt ground and cultivation. Absent only from arid country north of about 2° N in w. Kenya and 2° S in the east. *A. c. annae* is coastal. **NOTE**: Our bird is often considered conspecific with either palearctic *richardi* or the widespread *novaeseelandiae*. With some misgivings, we follow Clancey (1990) and others in treating the African birds as a separate species. The enigmatic Jackson's Pipit, *A (c.) latistriatus,* described from Mumias in 1899, has not been positively recorded again in Kenya. At times it has been considered a race of Long-billed Pipit (from which it differs in wing formula), a full species (most recently by Clancey 1984, 1990), or as a dark morph or race of Grassland Pipit. In its *dark blackish-brown dorsal plumage* and *deep buff underparts with broad blackish streaks which extend to the flanks,* it resembles the dark *A. c. itombwensis,* but differs from it and most other races of *cinnamomeus* in its shorter hind claw (7–10 mm) and pinkish-grey, not yellowish, mandible. It may well represent a distinct species, but its biology remains unknown and few specimens have been collected. This form, whatever its taxonomic status, appears to be a vagrant in w. Kenya from as yet unknown breeding grounds. Two dark birds, possibly *latistriatus,* were seen alongside Grassland Pipits at Muhoro Bay, Lake Victoria, in early August 1993.

LONG-BILLED PIPIT *Anthus similis hararensis*   **Plate 70**

Length 170–180 mm (6.75–7"). A *large, stocky* pipit with *relatively long bill, legs and tail.* **Adult** dusky brown above with diffuse streaking, becoming more uniform and almost blackish brown above as plumage becomes abraded, losing the paler dorsal feather edges. Buff superciliary and dark brown malar stripes prominent. *Underparts warm buff,* with whiter chin and throat and *inconspicuous dark breast streaking;* wing feathers edged with warm buff; *sides of tail buffy white.* Bill pinkish at base below; tarsi pinkish flesh. In the hand, shows short curved hind claw, the pale area on penultimate outer rectrix confined to tip, and the emarginate 5th primary only slightly shorter than the outer four. **Juvenile** dark, with pale dorsal feather margins and deep tawny or rufous edges to the wing feathers and outer tail feathers. Spotting on breast extends as streaks onto the flanks. **VOICE**: A metallic two-syllabled *che-vlee.* Song a repeated series of disjointed notes, *chreep. . . shreep. . . chew-ee . . .,* from the ground or in fluttering display flight. **HABITS**: Usually solitary or in pairs, at times in small groups. Perches on rocks, mounds and shrubs. Stands erect when alert. *Lacks tail-pumping motion of other pipits.* **SIMILAR SPECIES**: Grassland Pipit is slightly smaller and shorter-billed, buffier and more distinctly streaked. Plain-backed Pipit is plainer, smaller-billed, has deeper buff edges to relatively shorter tail, which is frequently in motion during foraging. **STATUS AND DISTRIBUTION**: Local and uncommon resident of thinly grassed stony or rocky hillsides and dry gullies, from sea level to above 2500 m. Absent from the Lake Victoria basin and most of e. and ne. Kenya, although recorded along the coast around Lamu (possibly *A. s. nivescens*). Locally common around cent. Rift Valley scarps, Mt Kulal, Arusha NP and Mt Hanang.

PLAIN-BACKED PIPIT *Anthus leucophrys*   **Plate 70**

Length 165 mm (6.5"). *Plain-looking,* **adults** essentially unstreaked above and with only *short faint breast streaks.* Broad-looking tail *buff, not white, at sides.* Pale superciliary stripes evident, but distinct malar stripes often lacking. Bill blackish brown above and at tip, mandible largely yellowish pink. *A. l. zenkeri* west of the Rift Valley shows *narrow dark malar streaks* and is rather *dark brown above with contrasting rufous-buff wing edgings* and

with *deep buff underparts*. Central Kenyan *goodsoni* is paler and sandier above and below, the breast streaks pale and diffuse. **Juvenile** browner, with pale buff wing edgings, and more distinctly streaked on breast than adult; lighter areas in tail deeper buff or tawnier than in adult. **Voice:** Alarm/flight call a thin soft *chissik*; on take-off, a sparrow-like *t-t-tit*. Song (*goodsoni*) a monotonous sparrow-like *chwee, chweep, cheew* or *tchwip-shee-cheree*, from ground or low perch. **Habits:** Solitary or in pairs in open short-grass areas with patches of bare ground. Pumps tail; perches on rocks and mounds. **Similar Species:** Long-billed Pipit is darker, has longer bill and longer tail with whitish outer feathers, prominent malar streaks and heavier body streaking. **Status and Distribution:** Locally common resident of short-grass plains and cultivation at medium elevations, often overgrazed areas with patches of bare ground, scattered bushes and termitaria. The western race *zenkeri* ranges from Mt Elgon south to Nyanza, Mara GR, northern and western Serengeti NP; *goodsoni* (see Note below) is common in the Rift Valley from Nakuru south to Suswa, the Loita Plains, e. Mara GR and into n. Tanzania from Loliondo and the western side of Lake Natron to the dry eastern Serengeti Plains and Lake Eyasi, also in high grasslands east of the Rift Valley at Laikipia, Ngobit, Naro Moru and Machakos. Both forms have been collected at Nakuru and in eastern Mara GR; they are said to intergrade at Maralal and Kakamega (Britton 1980), but we have seen no specimens that support this. Birds from Moyale, Mt Nyiru and at 3400 m on Mt Hanang (Feb. 1946) are not assigned racially. **Note:** *A. l. goodsoni* closely resembles the southern Buffy Pipit, *A. vaalensis*, and is considered a race of that species by some authors, but we are not aware that it differs in either voice or behaviour from other races of *A. leucophrys*.

MALINDI PIPIT *Anthus melindae*   Plate 70

Length 145–158 mm (5.75–6.25″). A heavily streaked *coastal* bird similar in size and structure to Grassland Pipit, but *bill bright yellow or orange-pink at base of mandible*. Appears long-legged, the *tibiae partly bare; tarsi yellow to orange-flesh colour*. Streaking on *dark grey-brown upperparts* indistinct, but *underparts heavily and extensively streaked*; sides of tail white; pale superciliary stripes and dark malar stripes prominent. In the hand, white in penultimate outer tail feather restricted to tip. **Juvenile** resembles adult, but bill and tarsus colour much duller. **Voice:** Flight call *tsweep*; also *tirrip-tirrip-tirrip*. Song a repeated *creer* or *kwee* from low perch. **Habits:** Forages alone or in pairs, or in small loose groups. Stands upright during feeding pauses and moves tail infrequently; perches on low shrubs. **Similar Species:** Grassland Pipit is paler, more sandy buff, more distinctly streaked above but with only narrow band of streaks on breast, duller feet and (especially) bill, outer tail feathers more extensively white, and 5th primary shorter. **Status and Distribution:** Confined to short-grass areas subject to seasonal flooding. Locally common along the n. Kenyan coast from Ngomeni north to Karawa; widespread, though less numerous, in the Tana River delta north to Baomo.

TREE PIPIT *Anthus trivialis*   Plate 70

Length 152 mm (6″). A slim, sedate pipit typical of *forest edges or other open areas with trees*. Light *warm olive-brown* above, heavily streaked on back, but rump and *upper tail-coverts almost plain*. Underparts buffy white, with *sharp blackish streaks across breast* but becoming more obscure on flanks. Malar stripes are prominent, and a narrow pale eye-ring is evident at close range. Outer tail feathers largely white. Bill dark brown, pale flesh-pink at base of mandible; tarsi and toes pale flesh-brown. In the hand, shows short curved hind claw, very fine streaks on rump/upper tail-coverts, and bluntly pointed wing tip with 6th primary usually much shorter than outer three. **Voice:** A single *tseep* in flight, usually given as bird rises; also a high pitched *seet-seet-seet* of alarm. **Habits:** Usually in small groups, foraging unobtrusively on ground. Perches commonly on low tree branches, to which it usually flies if disturbed. Flight strong and undulating. Pumps tail during feeding pauses. **Similar Species:** Red-throated Pipit in non-breeding plumage has whiter underparts and more extensive side/flank streaking, less olive upperparts and well-streaked rump; bill also finer. Grassland Pipit is larger, with longer bill and legs, more distinct superciliary stripes, and different call. In the hand, both Red-throated and Grassland Pipits show long hind claw, and in Grassland 6th primary is little shorter than outer three. **Status and Distribution:** Palearctic migrant, October to mid-April, frequenting forest clearings, open woodland, cultivation and gardens, mainly at medium to higher elevations. Widespread and common to abundant in the highlands between 1500 and 2500 m; more local in lower, drier bush habitats in se. Kenya. Few records from the arid north and northeast, the coastal lowlands and ne. Tanzania.

RED-THROATED PIPIT *Anthus cervinus*   Plate 70

Length 140–150 mm (5.5–6″). A small, heavily marked pipit of open wet places. Upperparts brown or grey-brown, *well streaked from back to upper tail-coverts*, and with *bold streaking on the whitish breast and flanks*; outer tail feathers edged white. Many individuals show *pink on face* from January onward; in full **breeding**

plumage (March–April), whole face, throat and upper breast may be bright tawny-pink. Tarsi and toes pale brown. In **non-breeding plumage,** distinguished from Tree Pipit by *heavily streaked rump/upper tail-coverts* and *bolder streaking on sides and flanks*, less olive appearance, finer bill, and somewhat shorter tail; also by call, and in the hand by long, slightly curved hind claw and outer four primaries almost equal in length. **VOICE:** Usual call a high-pitched thin *teeze* or *seeu*, at times a double, slightly accented *see-seeu*, longer and more piercing than call of Tree Pipit; another call is a short *tew*. **HABITS:** Usually in small groups on wet ground. Forages with low horizontal carriage, pumping the tail. Perches on fence wires and posts. Flight more jerky, less undulating, than Tree Pipit's. **SIMILAR SPECIES:** Tree Pipit compared above. Grassland Pipit is larger, slimmer, with longer legs and bill, ventral streaks confined to breast. **STATUS AND DISTRIBUTION:** Palearctic migrant, in our region between late October and mid-April, along muddy or marshy lake edges, irrigated fields and in wet grassland from the coast to above 2500 m. In Kenya, most numerous in the Rift Valley (especially at lakes Turkana and Baringo) and adjacent highlands. Uncommon in n. Tanzania, although regular in the Crater Highlands, Arusha NP and around Kilimanjaro.

STRIPED PIPIT *Anthus lineiventris*   Plate 70

Length 170–180 mm (7"). A *large, strong-billed* pipit of rocky hillsides in ne. Tanzania and se. Kenya. Olive-brown above, with heavy streaking; pale buff below, with *long streaks extending to belly and under tail-coverts.* No other large pipit is so extensively streaked below. Shows prominent buff or white superciliary stripes, white outer tail feathers (plus much white on inner web of adjacent pair as well), and diagnostic *greenish-yellow edges to wing and tail feathers.* Bill dark brown above, buffy horn below; eyes brown; tarsi stout, light pinkish brown. **VOICE:** Song a melodious whistling *whip-chew-chew whitty-pee-tee-tee, whip chew-chew . . .* **HABITS:** Solitary or in pairs, foraging among stones and grass tufts. Wary and unobtrusive. Runs up and over rocks in crouched attitude. May fly to tree when disturbed, and sings from low trees. **SIMILAR SPECIES:** Long-billed and Grassland Pipits are much less heavily streaked below and lack the distinctive greenish-yellow wing edgings. **STATUS AND DISTRIBUTION:** Local resident of thinly grassed rocky slopes with scattered trees and shrubs. In Kenya, known only from between 1500 and 2000 m in the Taita Hills, where scarce. (Reports from the Chyulu Hills require confirmation.) In ne. Tanzania, uncommon in the Pare and Usambara Mountains and on the Mbulu Escarpment above Lake Manyara NP.

BUSH PIPIT *Anthus caffer blayneyi*   Plate 70
(Little Tawny Pipit; Bushveld Pipit)

Length 126–135 mm (5–5.25"). A *miniature* pipit, sandy buff, with bold dark brown streaks on back; rump and upper tail-coverts nearly plain. Underparts buffy white, the breast and flanks streaked with dark brown. *Face rather plain, the buff superciliary stripes narrow.* Tail dark brown with white outer feathers. Bill dark brown above, pinkish brown below; eyes brown; tarsi and toes pale flesh-pink. **VOICE:** Call a sibilant *tzee-eep;* song a repeated *zweep-tseer.* **HABITS:** Usually solitary or in pairs. Wary. Forages among leaf litter and grass tufts. May fly to tree or fence wire when flushed; flight jerky and erratic. **SIMILAR SPECIES:** Sokoke Pipit is more boldly streaked below and is restricted to coastal forest. **STATUS AND DISTRIBUTION:** Local and uncommon in savanna, bushed and wooded grassland and open acacia thickets, favouring areas where heavy grazing by large mammals has reduced the amount of grass between bushes (Stronach 1990). Partially nomadic, its movements coinciding with onset of rains. Common in cent. and n. Serengeti NP, ranging north to Mara GR and the Loita Hills. Recorded sporadically from Tarangire NP and Monduli north to Kajiado, Konza, Simba and Ngong Districts.

SOKOKE PIPIT *Anthus sokokensis*   Plate 70

Length 120 mm (4.75"). A small *coastal-forest* pipit with *heavy black streaking both above and below*, that on the underparts broader on breast, sharper and narrower on sides and flanks. Rump and upper tail-coverts rufous-tinged. Tail short, with pointed feathers, the outermost white-edged. Pale buff superciliary stripes narrow and indistinct; lores buff; ear-coverts streaked buff and brown. Wings with much pale feather edging and *two prominent wing-bars.* Tarsi and toes pale flesh-pink. **VOICE:** Contact call a high-pitched descending *sweer* or *tseeer* from ground or tree perch. A very high-pitched flight song is delivered above forest openings and over the canopy; it consists of a repeated phrase, *eee-see* or *su-eeee-see* (middle note highest), each phrase separated from the next by a brief but distinct pause. **HABITS:** Solitary, shy and easily overlooked; calls as it forages among leaf litter on forest floor. Often flies to high perch when flushed. **SIMILAR SPECIES:** Other coastal pipits inhabit grasslands, (Grassland Pipit occasionally visits grassy tracks along woodland edges). **STATUS AND DISTRIBUTION**: Endemic to coastal East Africa. In Kenya, confined to the Arabuko–Sokoke Forest, particularly dense *Afzelia*-dominated stands on white soil, but also, at least formerly, in more open *Brachystegia*-dominated woodland; also in the Mkongani Forest, Shimba Hills (Oct. 1992). Although collected near Moa (north of Tanga), November 1931, all recent Tanzanian records are well south of our area.

GOLDEN PIPIT *Tmetothylacus tenellus* Plate 68

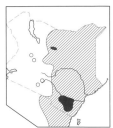

Length 128–160 mm (5–6.25"). A distinctive long-legged pipit of dry country. **Male** unique, with *bright yellow underparts, bold black breast band, yellow superciliary stripes* and *largely yellow wings*; rump and sides of tail also yellow; back and scapulars streaked dark brown and yellow-olive. *In flight, appears mostly yellow with black wing tips and a dark inverted T on the yellow tail.* Bill brown, darker on culmen and gonys; eyes brown; bare tibiotarsi, tarsi and toes pale pinkish brown. **Female** brown above with dark streaking, faintly yellowish below, wing and tail feathers edged with brighter yellow. Both sexes have yellow underwing surfaces. **Juvenile** *closely resembles Grassland Pipit*, streaked pale buff and brown above, with broad whitish superciliary stripes and brown streaks across breast; *centre of belly faintly yellow-tinged*, and *suggestion of streaks on sides and flanks*; bill dark above, dull pinkish-flesh colour below; tarsi and toes brownish pink, and the *long bare tibiotarsi* darker and browner. **VOICE**: Song a series of sibilant whistles from perch or in display flight, *tsi-tsi-tsi-tsi, tsur-tsur, tsi-tsi-tsi-tsi* . . . **HABITS**: In pairs when breeding, but most of year in small loose flocks. Frequently perches on trees and bushes, tail moving up and down. Male has distinctive fluttering song-flight and planes to ground from treetop with wings raised in V over back. **SIMILAR SPECIES**: Grassland Pipit resembles juvenile Golden (see above). **STATUS AND DISTRIBUTION**: In Kenya, ranges widely in dry bushed grassland and open savanna, mainly below 1000 m, from Marsabit, Samburu and Shaba GRs, Meru, Amboseli and the Tsavo NPs eastward, including coastal lowlands. Occasional west to Lake Baringo, Nairobi NP and Olorgesailie. Numbers fluctuate erratically; may be locally common after rains. In n. Tanzania, known from Longido, Arusha District and Mkomazi GR (during Dec.–Feb. rains) and from parts of the Masai Steppe and Usambara foothills.

YELLOW-THROATED LONGCLAW *Macronyx croceus* Plate 68

Length 200–222 mm (8–8.75"). A stocky, yellow-breasted, open-country bird, larger than any pipit, its *white tail sides and corners conspicuous in flight.* **Adult** warm brown above with darker streaking; *superciliary stripes and underparts bright yellow, with broad black band across breast* (sometimes less extensive in female) curving upward to base of bill; short dark streaks on lower breast. Coastal *M. c. tertius* is smaller and brighter than nominate *croceus*. **Juvenile** buffy yellow with indistinct band of short streaks on breast, and scalloping above; some individuals rufous-tinged, especially in fresh plumage. **VOICE**: A reiterated whistling *teuwhee* or *twee-eu* from bushtop or in flight. Longer song a far-carrying whistled *tirrEEoo, trip-tritri* or *twitilew-tree-eurr,* usually from perch. Alarm call a loud piping *whip-pipipipi, tuwhip-pipipipi.* **HABITS**: Solitary or in pairs foraging in grass, but regularly perches on trees, bushes, or posts. Flight low, bursts of stiff wingbeats alternating with glides. **SIMILAR SPECIES**: Pangani Longclaw has streaked, pale buff flanks and under tail-coverts, and more orange throat. Sharpe's Longclaw is smaller and lacks breast band. **STATUS AND DISTRIBUTION**: Widespread and locally common resident of open and bushed grassland and cultivation between sea level and 2200 m. *M. c. croceus* occupies mesic areas with rank grass in w. and cent. Kenya south to Mara GR and Serengeti NP. *M. c. tertius* ranges throughout coastal lowlands north to the lower Tana River and Boni Forest.

PANGANI LONGCLAW *Macronyx aurantiigula* Plate 68

Length 190–203 mm (7.5–8"). **Adult** resembles Yellow-throated Longclaw, but *flanks buffy white with dark streaks, throat orange-yellow* (more contrasting in male) and *breast with narrower black band and more heavily streaked at sides* than in Yellow-throated. Streaking of upperparts paler; yellow on underparts confined to centre of breast and belly. Bill brown or black above, pale horn below with blackish tip; eyes brown; upper eyelid orange-yellow, lower more yellowish; tarsi pale pinkish brown, toes darker. **Juvenile** buff below, with yellowish wash on breast, incomplete band of breast streaks; tarsi and toes pinkish grey. **VOICE**: Song *syeet syeet syeet, churrie churrie, which which which-which, tee-er tee-er tee-er* . . . , each note repeated two or more times. At times gives a single, very high-pitched *teeeeeeee.* **SIMILAR SPECIES**: Yellow-throated Longclaw compared above. **STATUS AND DISTRIBUTION**: Common resident of dry grassland below 1500 m in e. and se. Kenya, from Meru NP and Kora NR south to Amboseli and Tsavo NPs, west to the Athi Plains; reaches the coast north of Malindi and in the Tana delta area (where sympatric with Yellow-throated Longclaw). In n. Tanzania, ranges from Mkomazi GR west to Arusha, Tarangire and Lake Manyara NPs. Sympatric with Rosy-breasted Longclaw on the Ardai Plains west of Arusha.

SHARPE'S LONGCLAW *Macronyx sharpei*   **Plate 68**

Length 160–170 mm (6–6.75"). A *highland* bird, smaller than Yellow-throated Longclaw and lacking black collar; upperparts more boldly marked with rufous- or buff-edged black streaks. Underparts bright chrome-yellow, with streaks across breast and along flanks. White prominent at sides of tail, but less extensive at corners than in Yellow-throated Longclaw. **VOICE**: A series of thin whistles rising in pitch: *tew tyo tew tee* or *tyo tyo tew-tee*. Calls include a sharp *tsit*, a long plaintive *tweeeee* and a thin rising *seeeu*. **HABITS**: Forages alone or in pairs in grass or other low herbaceous vegetation. Difficult to see until flushed, after which bird quickly drops again into cover. Rarely perches on bushes. Flight stiff-winged like that of Yellow-throated Longclaw. **SIMILAR SPECIES**: Yellow-throated Longclaw compared above. Lowland Pangani Longclaw has solid breast band, more orange throat, and paler flanks. **STATUS AND DISTRIBUTION**: Endemic to Kenya. A local and generally uncommon resident of short grassland between 2400 and 3400 m on Mt Elgon, the Uasin Gishu, Mau and Kinangop Plateaux, southern slopes of the Aberdares and northern slopes of Mt Kenya. Always at higher elevations than Yellow-throated Longclaw, with few areas of overlap.

ROSY-BREASTED LONGCLAW *Macronyx ameliae wintoni*   **Plate 68**
(Pink-throated Longclaw)

Length 190–200 mm (7.5–8"). A slender, *red-throated* longclaw. Warm brown with dark streaking above. **Adult breeding male** has bright rosy-red *chin and throat bordered by broad black band* across breast and curving narrowly upwards to bill base; centre of breast and belly pale to bright salmon-pink, flanks buffy white and streaked; superciliaries pale buff. **Female** much paler below, with *salmon-pink wash on throat and belly*. Flying adult shows pale patch formed by buffy-white edges of lesser coverts (unless plumage much worn). Tail appears longer than in other longclaws, the white conspicuous only at sides, not corners. **Juvenile** scalloped above, *buff below without breast band, pinkish on belly (sometimes in centre only)*. **VOICE**: Song a squeaky whistled series of notes, *pink-pink-pink-zheeenk* with a wheezing final syllable, often given in hovering display flight. Call a plaintive *chuit-chuit*, and in alarm or excitement a sharper *chwit* or a metallic *tyang*. **HABITS**: Shy. Solitary or in pairs. When flushed, returns to ground promptly; runs rapidly; infrequently perches in bushes. Flight less stiff-winged, more pipit-like, than that of other longclaws. **SIMILAR SPECIES**: Juvenile Pangani Longclaw might be mistaken for this species, but has no pink on belly. **STATUS AND DISTRIBUTION**: Local and uncommon in the cent. Kenyan highlands, mainly in open wet grassland at medium elevations. Ranges from Maralal, Laikipia Plateau, Mt Kenya, Naro Moru and Ngobit south to Nakuru and Nairobi NPs and the Athi Plains; also locally in the Lake Victoria basin and from the Mara GR south to the Serengeti Plains and Ngorongoro Crater, east to Lake Manyara NP and the Ardai and Sanya Plains in Arusha District. Partially nomadic, with rainfall-related movements.

SWALLOWS AND MARTINS, FAMILY HIRUNDINIDAE
(World, 82 species; Africa, 42; Kenya, 18; n. Tanzania, 19)

Among the most graceful of birds, hirundines are slim, long-winged fliers whose insect food is taken entirely on the wing. In most species the tail is long and forked, with the outer feathers sometimes much elongated. The bill is short, flattened and with a wide gape; the feet are comparatively small. Although swallows superficially resemble swifts (Apodidae), their wings are broader and less scythe-like, their flight slower, more fluttery and graceful. Plumage is often brown or glossy blue above (sometimes with a rufous, white or grey rump) and buff or rufous below, while some species are black. The sexes are similar. Swallows tend to be gregarious when feeding, and some breed colonially. Most build a nest of mud pellets—either a half-cup plastered to a wall, or retort-shaped with an entrance tube and affixed below an overhang. Some species, however, are cavity nesters, using holes in trees, in earth banks or in flat ground. The white or pale pinkish eggs may be plain or speckled. Field identification is based mainly on plumage, tail shape, and flight characteristics. Bare-part colours are quite uniform and unnecessary for identification; they are omitted from most of the following species accounts. Length measurements are inclusive of the long outer tail feathers.

BANDED MARTIN *Riparia cincta*   **Plates 73, 74**

Length 140–150 mm (5.5–6"). A *large brown-backed* swallow with a broad brown breast band across largely white underparts; sometimes a mid-ventral line of brown feathers extends from breast to belly, especially in the race *erlangeri*. Lores black, with contrasting *white supraloral lines*; *wing-linings white*. Tail almost *square-tipped*. **Adult** plain dark greyish brown above. **Juvenile** similar, but wing-coverts and secondaries broadly edged with tawny-buff. **VOICE**: Song a short *chirip-cherip-chee-chirup-tsri-ereee*, sometimes ending in a trill. Calls include a rapid *chrink-cherrunk, tsri-tserrunk*, a low *chee cho* on taking wing (van Someren 1956) and a long nasal *schwaanh*. In flight, several birds utter an irregular metallic churring. **HABITS**: Forages low over grassland in small

loose parties, or alone. Flight slower, more leisurely and less fluttering than that of most swallows. Perches on wires and grass stems. Nests in sand banks. **SIMILAR SPECIES**: Sand Martin also has white throat and brown breast band, but is smaller, with clearly forked tail, brown wing-linings and no white supraloral lines. **STATUS AND DISTRIBUTION**: *R. c. suahelica* is locally common in open or lightly bushed grassland up to 3000 m over much of the Kenyan highlands, extending south to the Mara GR, Emali Plains, Amboseli NP and Lake Jipe; also across n. Tanzania from the Mkomazi GR and Arusha District to the Crater Highlands, Tarangire and Serengeti NPs. Ethiopian *R. c. erlangeri* has been collected at Naivasha, and occasional sight records from around Lake Turkana (Nov.–Feb.) and Bura, Tana River District (March), probably represent this race.

PLAIN MARTIN or AFRICAN SAND MARTIN *Riparia paludicola ducis* Plates 73, 74
(Brown-throated Sand Martin)

Length 110–120 mm (4.5"). *Brown-backed*, with *grey-brown throat, breast, sides and wing-linings*, becoming whitish on belly and under tail-coverts; tail slightly forked. **Juvenile** resembles adult, but has buff feather edges on somewhat greyer upperparts. **VOICE**: Song *chee, wer-chi-cho wer-chi-cho* (van Someren 1956), sometimes given in flight. Also a short descending trill, a low *chi-choo*, and a rough *chrrk* or *chickereek*. **HABITS**: Gregarious. Flight fluttery and rather slow, with few long glides. Perches, sometimes in tight flocks, on wires, grass stems and dead trees. Nests colonially or in scattered pairs, excavating tunnels in earth banks. **SIMILAR SPECIES**: Sand Martin has a white throat and underparts with brown breast band. Rock Martin shows white tail spots, is pale cinnamon on throat and upper breast. **STATUS AND DISTRIBUTION**: Widespread and often common in open country near water: typically from 1300 to 2500 m in the Kenyan highlands, and in n. Tanzania in Arusha NP and the Crater Highlands. Recorded north to Lake Turkana (where possibly *R. p. schoensis*), east to Lake Jipe and Mombasa, and south to Serengeti, Lake Manyara and Tarangire NPs.

SAND MARTIN or BANK SWALLOW *Riparia r. riparia* Plates 73, 74

Length 110–120 mm (4.5"). *Brown-backed*, with a *dark brown breast band* across otherwise white underparts. **Adult** brown or grey-brown above; wing-linings dark brown; tail well forked. **Juvenile** shows buff or cream feather edges on upperparts, and a rufous-buff wash on the head. **VOICE**: A rough twittering, *ch-ch-ch-ch-chi-chi-chi-chi*, but usually silent when alone. A continuous deep churring at concentrations. **HABITS**: Gregarious, at times in large flocks, often with other swallows. Feeds over water or open country. Flight rather fluttery, close to trees and low vegetation or at times much higher. Numbers gather on wires and at roosts in swamps and reedbeds. Comes to ground for dusting and sun-bathing. **SIMILAR SPECIES**: Banded Martin is similarly patterned but larger, with white wing-linings and supraloral lines. Plain Martin has brown throat and breast with no distinct band. **STATUS AND DISTRIBUTION**: Widespread and locally abundant palearctic migrant, September–May, mostly near lakes below 1800 m. Winters commonly in the Lake Victoria basin, and, although small numbers reach the Kenyan coast, it is generally scarce in e. Kenya and ne. Tanzania (main passage periods Sept.–Oct. and March to early May).

GREY-RUMPED SWALLOW *Pseudhirundo g. griseopyga* Plates 73, 74

Length 130–140 mm (5–5.5"). A small, slender swallow of open grassland. **Adult** has *grey-brown crown sharply demarcated from glossy blue-black back*, and contrasting *pale brownish-grey or ash-grey rump* and slightly darker upper tail-coverts. Variable (usually short and narrow) whitish superciliary stripes. Underparts dull white (or creamy white on breast and belly) with grey or light brown wash, and small brown smudge on each side of breast; for brief time early in breeding season, chin, throat and breast are tinged with salmon-pink. Tail dull bluish brown with no white spots; well forked, with narrowly elongated outer feathers. Feet pinkish brown. **Juvenile** duller above, with little or no gloss, often with more prominent white superciliary stripes and larger pectoral patches; inner secondaries tipped buff, rump browner and outer tail feathers shorter. **VOICE**: Calls include a weak nasal *waanh* or *phew*, a harsh *chrree-chrr-chrr*, and a rough *chirrk, tsr-chrrrr*, the latter calls recalling some notes of Plain Martin. Infrequent song a weak sibilant twitter, *tsitsertsi-tsi-sisi*. **HABITS**: Forages low over open ground, usually in small loose flocks. Flight fluttering and rather slow. Perches on grass stems, low twigs and clods of earth. Nests in small rodent holes in flat open ground, occasionally in banks and abandoned termitaria. Scarcely checks flight speed before diving into nest holes. **SIMILAR SPECIES**: Common House Martin has snow-white or greyish-white rump, is more thickset, with broader-based wings, dark blue-black crown, and less deeply forked tail; flight more lively, usually higher and with more gliding. **STATUS AND DISTRIBUTION**: Local and usually uncommon on grassy flats or open cultivation, often with

a preference for recently burnt grassland, from Mt Elgon, Kapenguria and the Laikipia Plateau south to the Lake Victoria basin, cent. Rift Valley, Narok District, Loita Plains and to Tanzania's Crater Highlands. Occasional (post-breeding birds?) on the Serengeti and Ardai Plains, and vagrants reported north to Marsabit and Lake Turkana. Population in Kenyan Rift Valley possibly augmented by austral winter migrants. Numbers fluctuate seasonally, but the species breeds regularly in the Kedong Valley, June–August. **NOTE 1**: Maintained as generically distinct by recent authors because of its breeding habits and white eggs, characters shared with Australian *Cheramoeca* (cf. Sheldon and Winkler 1993), but morphologically differs little from most *Hirundo* species. **NOTE 2**: A single specimen described as *H. andrewi*, taken from a flock of swallows at Lake Naivasha in April 1965, has been treated as subspecifically distinct (Dowsett 1972; Keith *et al.* 1992), but it may be only an aberrant individual, darker grey-brown below and with more dark on sides of chest than in typical birds.

BLUE SWALLOW *Hirundo atrocaerulea* Plates 73, 74

Length 165–230 mm (6.5–9"). A slender, dark swallow of open or bushed grasslands in w. Kenya; appears all black at a distance. **Adult** *dark shining blue* with velvety-black lores; *tail deeply forked, with long, very narrow, streamer-like extensions to blackish outer feathers*, in male these 10 cm (4") or more in length; no white tail spots. Normally concealed long white and black-and-white feathers on sides and flanks sometimes show as conspicuous white patch on resting birds. **Juvenile** sooty black, with brownish throat; tail lacks long outer feathers. **VOICE**: Contact calls a harsh *tchur* and a soft *tchup-tchup*. A unique twittering *wi-wi-wi-wi-wi-wi* given by courting male prior to departure to breeding grounds. **HABITS**: Solitary or in small groups; flight low, graceful and swift. Courting male glides and hovers above female with wings raised. Perches on wires, reeds, grass stems and low shrubs. Roosts communally in areas of tall grass. **SIMILAR SPECIES**: Black Saw-wing might be mistaken for Blue Swallow with moulting tail, but is differently shaped and lacks blue gloss. **STATUS AND DISTRIBUTION**: Generally scarce intra-African migrant, April–September, from breeding areas in southern Africa. Ranges north to shrubby grasslands in w. Kenya (Ruma NP, Mumias, Busia and Bungoma Districts). Occasional concentrations of over 100 birds. Presumably passes through n. Tanzania on migration, but only two records: Korogwe (April) and Serengeti NP (Aug. 1994).

WIRE-TAILED SWALLOW *Hirundo s. smithii* Plates 73, 74

Length 120–175 mm (4.5–7"). A dainty swallow with *entirely white underparts* except for narrow blue-black patch on each side of upper breast. No other white-breasted swallow has *wholly chestnut cap* and *long wire-like outer tail feathers* (sometimes missing or broken). **Adult** dark metallic blue above, with chestnut forehead and crown bordered below by black and blue-black band from bill to nape. Wing-linings white. Spread tail shows *prominent white spots*. **Juvenile** duller blue than adult, dull brownish on top of head, and white underparts buff-tinged; lacks long outer tail feathers. **VOICE**: Song a Barn Swallow-like twittering *chirrrik-erreeek*. Contact call a short *chwit* or *twit*. **HABITS**: Confiding. Usually in pairs, often near water. Flight fast and darting. Plasters cup-shaped mud nest to wall, bridge or rock face. **SIMILAR SPECIES**: Extralimital White-throated Swallow (see below) has dark breast band. Ethiopian Swallow has incomplete breast band, is chestnut only on forehead. **STATUS AND DISTRIBUTION**: Widespread and locally fairly common resident below 2100 m in moist grassland, cultivation, and woodland edges, especially near streams and lakeshores. Ranges through much of our region, including offshore islands, but largely absent from waterless areas of n. and ne. Kenya.

BARN SWALLOW *Hirundo r. rustica* Plates 73, 74
(Swallow; Eurasian Swallow)

Length 150–190 mm (6–7.5"). A medium-sized swallow with *shiny dark blue upperparts and breast band*, and underparts varying from white to deep buff. **Adult** has *rufous-chestnut forehead and throat* (more buff when worn and faded); *deeply forked tail* (especially in male) shows *prominent white spots*. **Juvenile** (Sept.–Dec.) duller, faintly bluish-glossed above; *forehead and throat pale buff*; chest band dusky brown. Wing-linings buffy white (as in adult); outer tail feathers slightly elongated. **VOICE**: Song a rapid, squeaky twittering with dry trills, e.g. *tsik-churreek-tsreek-tsrrreeek tsirk-tsirk tsureeeek tsrrrrrrrrr skirrrri-skirrreeek tuk-strrrreeeeeeee*. Contact call *wit-wit*. **HABITS**: Usually in scattered flocks; large numbers assemble on wires or in trees; gathers in large numbers to roost in swamps or reedbeds. **SIMILAR SPECIES**: Angola Swallow is greyer below, with broken breast band, and lacks long outer tail feathers. Ethiopian Swallow has white or buff throat and incomplete breast band. **STATUS AND DISTRIBUTION**: Palearctic migrant, widespread and generally abundant from late August to early May. Favours grassland, marshes and lakeshores from sea level to almost 3000 m. Arrives in w. Kenya in late July or early August; marked passage September–November and March–April. Occasional from late May to August at higher elevations.

WHITE-THROATED SWALLOW *Hirundo albigularis*   Plate 122

Length 140–170 mm (5.5–6.75"). **Adult** suggests a Barn Swallow, but has *snow-white throat bordered by a blue-black breast band* (narrower in centre than at sides, not of even width as in the preceding species). Wings broader than Barn Swallow's, with white linings. **Juvenile** is duller, lacks chestnut on forehead and has a brownish breast band. **Voice:** Sharp twittering alarm calls and high-pitched thin notes which may be extended in a song-like series, *tsrik-tsreek-tsreek-tsirit-seet-seet* or *sureet-sreet-sreet-sreet*. **Similar Species:** Barn Swallow compared above. Wire-tailed Swallow lacks breast band and has rufous-chestnut crown as well as forehead. **Status and Distribution:** Accidental from southern Africa. A bird collected over open water at Lake Jipe, ne. Tanzania, 25 July 1957, is the only East African record.

ETHIOPIAN SWALLOW *Hirundo aethiopica*   Plates 73, 74

Length 125 mm (5"). Smaller than Barn Swallow; **adult** more steel-blue above, with *chestnut restricted to forehead*. Tail forked and white-spotted, but narrow outer feathers shorter than in adult Barn Swallow. Throat and upper breast buff or very pale rufous in nominate birds, white in the northeastern race *amadoni*, and partly margined below by a *broken blue-black breast band*. Remaining underparts white or whitish. **Juvenile** less glossy, more dusky above and with buff forehead; outer tail feathers not elongated. **Voice:** Contact call a soft *cht*. Song a prolonged squeaky twittering. **Habits:** Usually in pairs or family parties along exposed rocky coastlines, or around human settlements in open areas. Builds open half-cup mud nest on wall of building or coral cave. **Similar Species:** Barn Swallow compared above. Angola Swallow is larger, and grey-brown below. Wire-tailed Swallow has entire top of head rufous, and much longer, narrower outer tail feathers. **Status and Distribution:** The common resident swallow of the coastal strip from Tanga northward. Also widespread in n. Kenya, including the Lake Turkana basin, ranging south to the Kerio Valley, Marsabit, Laikipia Plateau, Lake Baringo, and Nanyuki and Nakuru Districts. Most Kenyan populations represent the nominate race. *H. a. amadoni* of Somalia ranges south in coastal areas to Kiunga, Lamu and possibly Malindi. Records from El Wak and Mandera not racially assigned. Few breeding records away from the coast.

ANGOLA SWALLOW *Hirundo angolensis*   Plates 73, 74

Length 140–150 mm (5.5–6"). Suggests a *short-tailed* stocky Barn Swallow with *dingy grey-brown underparts* and *dusky wing-linings*. **Adult** bright glossy blue above; *rufous of throat extends to breast, the dark pectoral band narrow and incomplete*; under tail-coverts conspicuously dark-centred; tail well forked, with *large white spots*. **Juvenile** duller than adult, with buff throat and small tail spots. **Voice:** Song a weak twittering, sometimes given in flight. **Habits:** Forages low, in pairs or small groups. More sluggish, less graceful than Barn Swallow. Frequently settles on wires or shrubs. Attaches half-cup mud nest beneath bridge or under eaves of buildings, sometimes on cliffs. **Similar Species:** Barn Swallow has a complete broad breast band, whitish or pale buff underparts and wing-linings, rufous is confined to throat, and adult has longer outer tail feathers. Ethiopian Swallow is white below, with unmarked under tail-coverts and pale wing-linings. **Status and Distribution:** Widespread in w. Kenya, locally fairly common in northern parts of the Lake Victoria basin, ranging to Mt Elgon, Nakuru, Nyahururu and Nanyuki Districts, sparingly to the nw. Mara GR (apparently only Nov.–April: B. W. Finch) and the Mara Region of n. Tanzania, including parts of Serengeti NP.

RED-RUMPED SWALLOW *Hirundo daurica emini*   Plates 73, 74

Length 180 mm (7"). Rufous-bellied, with *blue-black under tail-coverts*. **Adult** shiny blue-black above with contrasting *rufous rump*; ear-coverts dull brown; postocular area and sides of head rufous, the colour extending narrowly onto sides of the largely blue nape. Most of underparts and *wing-linings rufous-chestnut*; throat paler. Tail dark and plain, well forked, with long outer feathers. **Juvenile** paler, with shorter tail and tawny tips to inner wing feathers. **Voice:** Flight notes include a soft *chmp*, a drawn-out *queesch* and *skeek-eek*. Alarm note a short *keer*. Song a few widely spaced metallic notes of 'squeaking-hinge' quality: *yaannh . . . . . quer-yaannh . . . . . skiaaaannh . . . . . cher-yaanng*. **Habits:** Forages in pairs or small groups over open grassland, often near rock outcrops or human dwellings. Flight slower and heavier than Barn Swallow's. Perches freely on wires and dead trees. Builds retort-shaped mud nest in cave, building, road culvert or under bridge, where plastered to overhanging projection. **Similar Species:** Mosque Swallow is larger, with white wing-linings. Rufous-chested Swallow has no rufous on face or nape and the dark blue extends down to below eyes. Both species have rufous under tail-coverts. **Status and Distribution:** Widespread and fairly common from 1200 to over 2500 m in the Kenyan highlands, ranging north to the Ndotos, Mt Nyiru, Mt Marsabit and south to Tanzania's Crater Highlands, Serengeti, Lake Manyara, Tarangire and Arusha NPs. Scarce over much of lowland n. and e. Kenya and ne. Tanzania, and absent from coastal areas. Mainly resident, but seasonal in some localities.

MOSQUE SWALLOW *Hirundo senegalensis*   **Plates 73, 74**

Length 200–210 mm (8"). Distinguished from Red-rumped Swallow by *large size, snow-white wing-linings, rufous auriculars and under tail-coverts*, and *pale buffy cheeks and throat*. **Adult** glossy blue-black above, except for rufous rump. Tail entirely dark in *H. s. saturatior*, with white spots on inner webs of most rectrices in the eastern race *monteiri*. **Juvenile** paler on neck, rump and underparts; secondaries and wing-coverts edged with tawny. **Voice:** Slowly uttered, semi-musical song of creaking, whining and metallic notes, e.g. *muree rrrang crrik-crrik meeeu mreeeeeu rrrrreeeerang-rrrang*. Varied calls include a short nasal *haaarrnk*, a descending *tseeeu*, a cat-like *meeu* and various guttural notes. **Habits:** Pairs forage high and regularly perch on dead treetops or wires. Flight rather slow and leisurely, brief periods of quick fluttering followed by a glide. Builds gourd-shaped mud nest in hollow tree (especially baobab), occasionally below overhang on building. **Similar Species:** Red-rumped Swallow has blue-black under tail-coverts. Rufous-chested Swallow is blue-black on head and nape. Both have rufous wing-linings. **Status and Distribution:** Widespread but uncommon resident of forest edges and clearings, light woodland and cultivation below 2600 m. Most numerous in Nyanza, parts of the Kenyan highlands and coastal localities; absent from arid n. and ne. Kenya. *H. s. monteiri* ranges throughout n. Tanzania and in coastal lowlands north to the Boni Forest, inland to Voi and Kibwezi and along southern Kenyan border areas; intergrades with the northern and western *saturatior* near Nairobi.

RUFOUS-CHESTED SWALLOW *Hirundo semirufa gordoni*   **Plates 73, 74**
(Red-breasted Swallow)

Length 180–190 mm (7–7.5"). Medium-sized and glossy blue-black above, with *rufous rump, underparts, and wing-linings. Dark blue top of head extends below eyes and across ear-coverts,* giving a hooded appearance. Spread tail shows white spots; outer tail feathers much elongated in adult. **Juvenile** browner above, paler below than adult, with buff-tipped secondaries and relatively short outer rectrices. **Voice:** Unique song of growling and prolonged descending squeals, *chureek-cherrrrow-chiteeeerpereee squeeeeeeeee chrrierrow*. Also utters a plaintive *seeurr-seeurr* (Maclean 1984). Alarm call *weet-weet*. **Habits:** Usually solitary or in pairs; at times in small flocks, especially when roosting. Flight swift. Perches on wires, dead tree branches and rocks. Nests in road culverts, holes in termitaria, under bridges or in hollow trees, constructing flask-shaped nest of mud pellets. **Similar Species:** See Mosque and Red-rumped Swallows.

Status and Distribution: Uncommon in bushed grassland and moist open country below 1700 m in the Lake Victoria basin and east to Mumias, Kakamega, Nandi and Muhoroni Districts, south to Lolgorien, Mara GR and Mara Region of n. Tanzania. Mainly a wet-season visitor in many areas.

LESSER STRIPED SWALLOW *Hirundo abyssinica unitatis*   **Plates 73, 74**
(Striped Swallow)

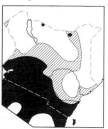

Length 150–175 mm (6–7"). Unique in our region: *rump and most of head rufous,* entire *underparts boldly streaked* black on white. **Adult** metallic blue-black on back, sometimes showing white feather bases; tail blue-black with elongated outer feathers, these and next two pairs with *large white spots* on the inner webs; wing-linings mostly white. **Juvenile** duller, with some blackish on head; tail shorter than in adult. **Voice:** Song a nasal or tinny *rronh rrenh reenh rroonh reenh*, ascending or descending, usually introduced by some thin squeaky or buzzy notes; distinctive and pleasing. Flight note *seent*. **Habits:** Breeds in scattered pairs, otherwise gregarious and often in flocks of hundreds. Forages over grassland, along forest edges and around houses. Flight fast and darting, but with less speed and more gliding than Barn Swallow. Builds retort-shaped mud nest under overhanging projection, usually on buildings. **Similar Species:** Other rufous-rumped, blue-backed swallows are unstreaked below and dark blue on top of head. **Status and Distribution:** Widespread and locally common in varied habitats from sea level to over 2000 m in w., cent. and s. Kenya, and throughout n. Tanzania, including Pemba Island. Doubtless resident in some lowland areas, but largely absent from the highlands during the cold dry season (June–Aug.), returning as a breeding visitor with the rains.

ROCK MARTIN *Hirundo fuligula fusciventris*   **Plates 73, 74**

Length 110–120 mm (4.5"). A small, dark swallow with pale *cinnamon throat and upper breast*, and showing *white spots in the spread tail*. **Adult** sooty brown above, paler grey-brown below; wings quite broad at base, tail slightly forked. **Juvenile** similar, but feathers of upperparts tipped with buff. **Voice:** Notes include a low *wick* or *wik-wik*, a high-pitched *sree*, and some soft mellow twittering. Seldom vocal. **Habits:** Usually in pairs or small loose groups, often with other swallows and swifts; rarely far from breeding sites. Flight appears leisurely, with much gliding. Builds cup-shaped mud nest on cliff, rock outcrop or building. **Similar Species:** Plain Martin has

dull brown throat and breast, no tail spots. Mascarene Martin is streaked below. Young Common House Martin shows pale grey rump. **STATUS AND DISTRIBUTION**: Widespread and often common resident in much of Kenya and n. Tanzania around kopjes, cliffs, gorges, quarries and tall buildings, typically between 1500 and 3000 m, but as low as 400 m in rocky gorges near Lake Turkana. Absent from coastal lowlands (in our region), and rare throughout the Lake Victoria basin.

COMMON HOUSE MARTIN *Delichon u. urbica*   Plates 73, 74

Length 140 mm (5.5"). Small and rather thickset; glossy blue-black above with *white rump* and with *white underparts*, these sometimes tinged buffy brown in winter. Tail plain black and well forked. *Tarsi and toes uniquely white-feathered.* **Juvenile** browner above, tinged dusky below, and with greyish markings on rump. **VOICE**: When perched, *bzreet, dzreet-dzreet cherrrang*; in flight, *dzurreet-dzeet chri-eet chree-eeet* and various higher notes. Contact call a harsh grating *chirrt* or *chirrup*; alarm note a shrill *tseep*. **HABITS**: Gregarious; often with other swallows or swifts. Typically forages high either over forest or in open country, often near cliffs and rocky hills; feeds low during early morning or in cloudy weather. Flight fluttery but strong, with much flapping and short glides but no long swoops. Said to sleep on the wing. **SIMILAR SPECIES**: See Grey-rumped Swallow. **STATUS AND DISTRIBUTION**: Fairly common palearctic migrant, typically in flat or hilly country between 1600 and 3000 m, but also lower (900–1000 m) on passage (Sept.–Nov. and late March to April). Numbers winter locally in the Kenyan highlands east to Meru and the Nyambenis, south to Mt Meru, Kilimanjaro and the Crater and Mbulu Highlands. Recorded once in June, at Samburu GR.

MASCARENE MARTIN *Phedina borbonica madagascariensis*   Plates 73, 74,

Length 125–140 mm (5–5.5"). A small, stocky swallow, *sooty brown* above, the generally whitish underparts *heavily streaked with dark brown from throat to belly*; sides and flanks heavily washed with grey-brown. Almost square-tipped blackish tail shows no fork when spread; wing-linings dark. **VOICE**: A wheezy *phree-zz* (Clancey *et al.* 1969). **HABITS**: Usually gregarious; mixes with other swallows. Flight sluggish, with alternate fluttering and gliding, usually high. Perches in trees, on wires and on buildings. **SIMILAR SPECIES**: Plain Martin is paler above, plain brown on throat and breast; tail more clearly forked. Lesser Striped Swallow is blue-black and rufous above and has white tail spots. **STATUS AND DISTRIBUTION**: Casual visitor from Madagascar. Formerly (1925–28) recorded from Pemba Island. Four recent records: 16 at Lake Jipe, June 1978; one at Watamu, June 1980; two north of Malindi, August 1989; and 100+ with Plain Martins at Lake Jipe, June 1993.

BLACK SAW-WING or ROUGH-WING *Psalidoprocne holomelas*   Plates 73, 74

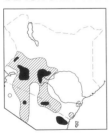

Length 135–155 mm (5.25–6"). An all-black swallow with a distinctively shaped tail. **Adult** male *P. h. massaicus* has faint greenish gloss (duller in female) and grey-brown wing-linings; *tail longer than body, rather broad but very deeply forked* (less so in female). **Juvenile** similar but duller, with no gloss and shorter tail. Coastal *P. h. holomelas* is shorter-tailed and noticeably smaller (wing 95–106 mm, against 110–119 mm in *massaicus*). **VOICE**: Flight calls include *dzrrt-tsireeee* and a squealing *sqweeu*, a sharper *tseeeu-tseeu*, and a soft *chirp*. Perched birds may give a nasal *chirranu-chirranu*, slightly drongo-like in quality; also *chirr-chirr-cheeru*. **HABITS**: Flight graceful; hawks around treetops or along forest edges and tracks, often just above ground. Frequently perches on leafless twigs. Excavates nest burrow in bank or road cuttings. **SIMILAR SPECIES**: Almost uniformly dark juvenile White-headed Saw-wing usually shows slightly paler throat, is duller, more sooty or brownish black, tail is less forked and body appears stockier. **STATUS AND DISTRIBUTION**: *P. h. massaicus* is a common resident of forests, wooded hillsides and high grasslands at 1600–3200 m in the w. and cent. Kenyan highlands south to the Ngurumans, Chyulu and Taita Hills, Tanzania's Crater and Mbulu Highlands, Arusha NP, Mt Meru, Kilimanjaro, and the North Pare and Usambara Mountains. The smaller nominate race is an uncommon resident of the Shimba Hills and Arabuko–Sokoke and Marafu Forests. **NOTE**: The Eastern Saw-wing, *P. orientalis*, a species with white wing-linings, was described in 1899 from near Pangani, at the northern edge of its range and near the southern boundary of our area (5° 30' S). Unknown north of there, it was mistakenly attributed to Kenya by Short *et al.* (1990).

WHITE-HEADED SAW-WING or ROUGH-WING *Psalidoprocne a. albiceps*

Plates 73, 74

Length 125–150 mm (5–6"). A *black* swallow with *white on the head*, stockier and with shallower tail fork than the preceding species. **Adult male** *white-headed* with black eye-lines. **Female** has *whitish throat*, and sooty feathering often intermixed with some white on the crown. **Juvenile** *almost uniformly sooty brown*, somewhat paler on throat. **VOICE:** Generally silent, except for an infrequent soft *brzt*. **HABITS:** Much like those of Black Saw-wing, with which it often associates. Flight fast and low along forest edges and clearings; often perches on low twigs. Nests in holes in banks. **SIMILAR SPECIES:** Black Saw-wing resembles juvenile White-headed, but is more slender; a deeper black, and has a much more deeply forked tail. **STATUS AND DISTRIBUTION:** Locally common resident of shrubby grassland, light woodland, cultivation, forest edges and glades in w. Kenya. Ranges from Mt Elgon and the Cheranganis south to the Nandi and Kakamega Forests, Lake Victoria basin, Mara GR and the Nguruman Hills; sporadic in cent. Kenyan highlands east to Embu and Machakos and in the Taita Hills. In n. Tanzania, uncommon in the Mara Region, Serengeti NP, and the Crater and Mbulu Highlands (locally common around Mt Hanang).

BULBULS, FAMILY PYCNONOTIDAE
(World, *c*. 130 species; Africa, 58; Kenya, 25; n. Tanzania, 17).

Except for the ubiquitous Common Bulbul, these are largely retiring, secretive birds, somewhat thrush-like but with shorter, weaker tarsi and toes and usually a shorter bill. The plumage is lax and soft, with hair-like filoplumes on the nape. (The aberrant genus *Nicator*, once considered a shrike, has long and strongly scutellate tarsi, as well as a heavy hooked bill; it may well belong elsewhere.) DNA research suggests that bulbuls are not related to the cuckoo-shrikes as proposed in the past. Their closest living relatives may be warblers and white-eyes (Sibley and Ahlquist 1990).

Some species are decidedly arboreal, but the majority inhabit dense undergrowth and creeper tangles, and several spend much time on the ground. Certain greenbuls and the brownbuls habitually travel in small, often quite vocal groups. Songs, while variable, tend to be lively and cheerful, typically penetrating, and with repeated notes or phrases. Many species indulge in spirited chattering, chuckling or churring, and some have nasal alarm or distress calls. A few are remarkably quiet, their vocalizations poorly known. Within some species, notable vocal differences exist between eastern and western African populations.

Most bulbuls erect their crown feathers when excited; several puff out the throat plumage as well. Dominant plumage colours are shades of olive, yellow and brown; the sexes are generally alike, but males are noticeably larger and often longer-billed. A few species exhibit notable subspecific differences in size. Young birds resemble adults, though often darker and darker-eyed than adults, and with somewhat pointed rectrices—useful for ageing birds in the hand. Juveniles are revealed as such by plumulaceous body feathers, more prominent rictal areas, and sometimes different bare-part colours. Forest greenbuls can be extremely difficult to distinguish, and positive identifications require care. *Andropadus* is the most troublesome genus in this respect, most species being olive-green, fairly uniform in tone or with greyer head or underparts; the tail may be chestnut-tinged. *Phyllastrephus* species are longer-billed than *Andropadus*, often with more olive-brown or rufous plumage tones. They are more insectivorous than *Andropadus*, hence less likely to be attracted to fruiting trees and creepers. Important considerations in greenbul identification are: (1) foraging level and behaviour; (2) tail colour (olive or rufous-tinged); (3) throat/breast colour; (4) colour of bare part; (5) bill size and shape (short and rather broad-based in certain *Andropadus*, long and slender in most *Phyllastrephus* species); (6) vocalizations; and (7) range (some are strictly confined to either eastern or western forests; others are highly localized).

All of our pycnonotids are residents, wandering only locally, and forest species exhibit great site tenacity. The typical nest is a thin cup of plant materials, usually low in a shrub or tree. Most species lay only two spotted, whitish or pinkish eggs. Some employ elaborate ruses to lure observers away from nest or young, with fluttering, death-feigning or 'broken-wing' displays.

CAMEROON SOMBRE GREENBUL *Andropadus c. curvirostris*
(Plain Greenbul)

Plate 76

Length 160–170 mm (6.5"). A dark brownish-olive greenbul of *tall understorey shrubs and creeper tangles* in west Kenyan forests. Does not extend into the canopy; *usually forages between 3 and 10 m* above ground. **Adult** has *noticeable greyish-white eyelids*, short slender black bill, olive-grey throat and yellow-olive belly contrasting with *darker olive breast*; dark olive tail is washed with rufous. Some (young?) individuals are very dark-chested. Feet dark olive or greenish grey. **Juvenile** much brighter yellow on belly, greyer (less olive) on throat, breast and flanks; bill tipped yellowish olive. **VOICE:** Seldom heard but distinctive song of repeated slow, rather mournful, clear whistles, *wheetu-WEEu, wheetu WEEu . . .* (West African birds have at least two song types: a trilling *quureee-turr-chweeeeeee*, and a low, slowly whistled *turwee-twur-twur* or *weeee tur-tureeee*.) Common call a short mellow trill: *chreeeeeee* or *pureeeeeee*, dropping slightly at the end. **HABITS:** Singles and pairs often accompany mixed-species feeding parties. Forages in tops of tall shrubs and among tangles of vines. Less skulk-

ing than some greenbuls. **SIMILAR SPECIES:** Sympatric Ansorge's and Little Grey Greenbuls are much smaller, with brighter eye-rings, and have different habits. Little Greenbul, less often seen, is more secretive, more uniformly olive, has an olive throat, broader-based bill, often shows light yellowish-brown feet. **STATUS AND DISTRIBUTION:** Fairly common in the Nandi and Kakamega Forests of w. Kenya, and recently reported from the Migori River near Lolgorien. Formerly at Mumias and Mt Elgon.

LITTLE GREY GREENBUL *Andropadus gracilis ugandae*   Plate 76

Length 150 mm (6"). A *small* western greenbul, remarkably like the commoner sympatric Ansorge's Greenbul, but *belly brighter, distinctly olive-yellow, almost pure yellow centrally.* **Adult** has olive upperparts, with *more greyish-olive head* and a *narrow white eye-ring.* Chin, throat and upper breast pale olive-grey, shading to yellowish on belly; flanks bright tawny, under tail-coverts pale brown. Tail and upper tail-coverts brown, washed with rufous. Eyes brown or brownish grey; bill black; feet dull greyish olive to blue-grey. **Juvenile** of *ugandae* undescribed; that of nominate West African *gracilis* is brighter olive-green above and brighter yellow below than adult, and has *yellowish eye-ring* and base of bill; eyes brown; feet olive. **VOICE:** Not positively recorded in our region, and song descriptions from West Africa are unsatisfactorily differentiated from those of Ansorge's Greenbul. In West Africa, its call is said to consist of five rapid, jaunty notes, *wheet-wu-wheet-wu-wheet,* rising at the end (Fishpool *et al.* 1994). In Uganda said to have a three-syllabled *HWEET-hwet-hwut,* the second and third notes shorter and descending in tone (L. Fishpool, pers. comm.). The latter song, however, is confusingly like that of (collected) w. Kenyan *A. ansorgei.* In Gabon and Cameroon, phrases of *gracilis* recorded by C. Chappuis (1975) are terminally accented: *twick tu-wee-tu-WEE, chuwi-weeu-WEE, wick-weu-WI,* or *tweee-u-WEE.* Call note a single *twit, tchick* or *tchuk.* **HABITS:** Solitary or in pairs, foraging among smaller tree branches and limbs at middle and lower levels, often conspicuously on outermost twigs, and often low. Seldom in high canopy or undergrowth. Occasionally joins mixed-species flocks. **SIMILAR SPECIES:** See Ansorge's Greenbul. Cameroon Sombre Greenbul is larger, darker (particularly on breast), its eye-ring more greyish; it is an undergrowth bird, less likely than *gracilis* to forage on slender tree branches. **STATUS AND DISTRIBUTION:** In our region, confined to the Kakamega Forest in w. Kenya, where scarce.

ANSORGE'S GREENBUL *Andropadus ansorgei kavirondensis*   Plate 76

Length 145 mm (5.75"). The *olive-grey belly* and *narrow white eye-ring* mark this *small,* rather short-tailed greenbul of the Kakamega Forest. **Adult** has olive-brown head and upperparts, *grey throat, olive-grey breast and belly,* and *warm rufous-olive or ginger-brown flanks;* tail brown with faint rufous wash. Eyes brown or red-brown; bill dark brown; feet greyish olive. **Juvenile** resembles adult, but head and breast greyer. **VOICE:** In Kenya, an infrequent, thin three-note whistle: *weet-wurt-eet,* the last note highest; also a descending chatter or rattle reminding Americans of a Brown-headed Cowbird, *Molothrus ater.* Typical songs recorded by Chappuis (1975) in Cameroon and Gabon vary from *wiku-WEE-wee* to *tur-WEE-wee* or *tswee-cheu-TWEE,* some terminally accented like songs of *A. gracilis.* **HABITS:** As for Little Grey Greenbul, but tends to forage somewhat higher. **SIMILAR SPECIES:** Much rarer Little Grey Greenbul has yellowish belly; both it and Ansorge's Greenbul are smaller, paler, and with more conspicuous white eye-rings than Cameroon Sombre Greenbul. Shelley's Greenbul (race *kakamegae*) has entire head grey (darker on crown and nape), is more uniformly yellowish olive beneath. Little Greenbul is more uniformly olive (including throat), has short, broad bill, no eye-ring, stays hidden in undergrowth. **STATUS AND DISTRIBUTION:** Fairly common and easily seen in the Kakamega Forest, w. Kenya. Formerly recorded from the Nyarondo Valley and southern slopes of Mt Elgon.

LITTLE GREENBUL *Andropadus virens*   Plate 76

Length 150–160 mm (*c.* 6"). A small olive greenbul, *short-tailed* and with a *short, broad bill.* **Adult** generally *darker olive below than most other small greenbuls,* the *olive throat is more or less uniform with breast,* middle and lower belly yellow; some birds (immature?) are dark-breasted. Tail and upper tail-coverts brown with rusty wash. Eyes dull grey-brown; bill blackish brown, with corners of mouth more or less yellow; feet yellowish orange or yellowish brown. Coastal birds (*zombensis*) are brighter and lighter olive above than those in w. Kenya, the belly paler yellow. **Juvenile** *A. v. virens* is darker on crown and with browner wings than adult and yellowish throat; yellow of belly dull, more restricted; under tail-coverts pale olive; *feet dull brown or yellowish brown.* **VOICE:** Song of *A. v. zombensis* a protracted hurried chattering, a jumble of notes usually beginning with some

fairly low-pitched guttural sounds like *kwirk-kwirk-kwirk* or *chuk-chuk-chuk*, accelerating into *chwukawuk-cherchickalee-chuck-chuck-chuck-tuwerrtlii-tuk-tuk* rapidly run together and sometimes ending with a short high note. Western birds have shorter (2–3 seconds) song, recalling that of Yellow-whiskered Greenbul but much faster and more even in pitch, not becoming progressively louder from a faint beginning; ending may be either lower- or higher-pitched: *chippity choppity chipity chop*, or *chippity chop chippity cherp p'CHEEEEee* with the last note a thin upslurred whistle. Alarm call a rapid chatter. **Habits:** Shy and skulking; remains in dense undergrowth, avoiding exposed perches. **Similar species:** Cameroon Sombre Greenbul, sympatric with Little in w. Kenya, has noticeable eye-ring, forages higher and utilizes exposed perches. Juvenile Yellow-whiskered Greenbul has similar broad bill, but has bright orange feet, dusky malar streaks, dark dusky olive throat and breast, tawny crissum and a longer bill. Toro Olive Greenbul is slimmer, paler and more greyish below, lacks pure yellow belly, has much longer bill and dark rufous tail. **Status and Distribution:** *A. v. zombensis* is locally common in coastal forest and thickets north to the Mombasa area and inland to the East Usambaras and Shimba Hills; ranges (at least formerly) north to Kilifi, where scarce. Slightly paler population in Arusha and Moshi Districts of n. Tanzania sometimes separated as the race *marwitzi*. In w. Kenya, *A. v. virens* (including '*holochlorus*') known from the Kakamega and Nandi Forests, riverine strips in Busia, Mumias and Rapogi Districts, and along the Migori River near Lolgorien south to Tanzanian border areas.

YELLOW-WHISKERED GREENBUL *Andropadus l. latirostris* Plate 76

Length 165–180 mm (6.5–7"). A common forest greenbul. **Adult** readily identified by the prominent *yellow streak on each side of the throat*. With these 'whiskers' compressed, the bird may appear yellow-throated. Upperparts dark brownish olive, including top and sides of head; tail dark reddish brown. Underparts dull olive, lighter and browner on flanks, and pale yellow in centre of lower breast and belly. Eyes dark brown; bill blackish; feet dark brownish orange to yellowish brown, sometimes bright orange-yellow. **Juvenile** *lacks yellow whiskers*, is browner above, less yellowish in centre of belly, has *pale tawny under tail-coverts*, *bright orange or orange-yellow feet*, and *mottled yellow-orange and black bill*. Yellow whisker marks of moulting **immature** are narrow and less prominent than adjacent dark malar areas. **Voice:** The protracted chattering is a dominant feature of many forests. The four- to six-second song is delivered in short choppy bursts, typically beginning very faintly, becoming progressively louder, then stopping abruptly: *chuk, chik, chuk, chip, tsup chik-chik-chik tsuk chik-chik-tsuck*, repeated after 20–30 seconds. Quality reminiscent of Little Greenbul's song, but much slower, the individual notes more distinct. **Habits:** Often solitary; joins other greenbuls at fruiting trees, but seldom seen in mixed-species flocks. Forages at all levels, and frequently attends ant swarms. Some individuals sedentary, others nomadic, appearing in marginal habitats. Where common (as in Kakamega Forest), inquisitive and not shy. **Similar species:** Juvenile Little Greenbul is much like young Yellow-whiskered, but its throat is yellowish olive, under tail-coverts pale olive, and feet dull brown or yellowish brown. **Status and Distribution:** The most numerous greenbul from 1500 to 3000 m. Abundant in w. Kenyan forests and well-developed riparian undergrowth from Mt Elgon and the Cheranganis south to Eldama Ravine, Molo, Mau Narok, Njoro, the Trans-Mara and Lolgorien Forests, the Nguruman Hills and, in n. Tanzania, at Loliondo. East of the Rift Valley, ranges from Mt Nyiru, the Ndotos, Mathews Range and the Karissia Hills south to the Nyambenis, Mt Kenya, the Aberdares, Nairobi and Ol Doinyo Orok (Namanga Hill). **Note:** We follow Keith *et al.* (1992) in considering w. Kenyan *eugenius* and eastern *saturatus* synonymous with nominate *latirostris*.

SLENDER-BILLED GREENBUL *Andropadus gracilirostris* Plate 76

Length 170–180 mm (7"). A *slim, slender-billed* species of the *forest canopy*. Longer-tailed than other *Andropadus*, but with no obvious field marks; *from below, appears plain grey against the sky*. **Adult** bright olive above, duller on crown; underparts pale grey, more whitish on throat, belly and under tail-coverts; tail brownish olive above, much paler below. Bill and feet black; eyes brick-red or reddish brown. **Juvenile** browner on upperparts, duller grey below than adult. **Voice:** A distinctive short *cu-WEE-a* or *chew-WAYa*, repeated. The short song, *twick-CHEWsee-tseu* or *chik-WEEo-chew*, is much less frequent. **Habits:** Arboreal, typically foraging quietly among topmost canopy leaves, but ripening subcanopy berries lure it into lower branches. Solitary or in pairs, but joins other greenbuls at fruiting trees. **Similar species:** Cameroon Sombre Greenbul is darker, especially on head and breast, with shorter bill; forages among tall shrubs. Ansorge's and Little Grey Greenbuls are smaller, with darker underparts and rufous tinge to the short tail. **Status and Distribution:** Fairly common below 2400 m in w. and cent. Kenyan forests, from Mt Elgon, Kapenguria, the Ndotos, Mathews Range and Mt Kenya south to the Kakamega, Nandi, Lolgorien, Trans-Mara and Mau Forests, the Aberdares and northern Nairobi suburbs. Two similar subspecies, *percivali* and *gracilirostris* (including '*congensis*'), intergrade in w. Kenya.

SHELLEY'S GREENBUL *Andropadus masukuensis*   Plates 75, 123

Length 165–170 mm (6.5″). A forest species, frequently seen *clinging to tree trunks*. *Grey head* of **adult** *A. m. kakamegae* (perhaps specifically distinct) contrasts with bright greenish-olive upperparts (including tail) and yellowish-olive underparts. Narrow, *dull white eye-ring* is noticeable; crown and nape darker grey than face, almost dusky in some worn birds. Eyes red-brown or bright brown; bill dusky or black above, blue-grey below; feet slaty blue or blue-grey. **Juvenile** paler-headed but otherwise like adults. **Adult** of Tanzanian *A. m. roehli* has mainly *olive-green head* with *only the face and throat greyish*; underparts dull greyish olive. **HABITS:** *A. m kakamegae* rather shy and silent; forages at all levels, in leafy vine tangles and on large tree trunks, systematically probing bark crevices and epiphytic bryophyte clumps. Trunk-foraging not reported for *roehli*. **VOICE:** Voice of *kakamegae* unrecorded, despite extensive observation; apparently a nearly silent bird. *A. m. roehli* utters a fairly loud and simple *ke-kew-ke-kew-ke* (Dowsett-Lemaire, pers. comm.), a soft nasal *kwew, kwa, kwew* (Sclater and Moreau 1932). In Tanzanian mountains south of our limits, a soft *chewki-chewki-chewki-chewki* tape-recorded (Svendsen and Hansen 1992). **SIMILAR SPECIES:** Mountain Greenbul of race *usambarae*, also grey-headed, has crown narrowly black-bordered; race *kikuyuensis* more closely resembles Kenyan *A. m. kakamegae*, but has much brighter underparts, more conspicuous eye-ring, is stockier, and tends to be at higher elevations. Little Grey and Ansorge's Greenbuls both smaller, lack all-grey head, and appear shorter-tailed. Cameroon Sombre Greenbul is darker, especially on head and breast. **STATUS AND DISTRIBUTION:** In w. Kenya, *A. m. kakamegae* is locally common in the Nandi and Kakamega Forests; also recorded from the Mau and Trans-Mara Forests; formerly on Mt Elgon. One sight record from montane forest above Kericho (June 1979). Tanzanian *A. m. roehli* is fairly common in the Usambara and South Pare Mts, ranging as low as 500 m in the East Usambara foothills.

MOUNTAIN GREENBUL *Andropadus nigriceps*   Plates 75 and 123
(Olive-breasted Mountain Greenbul)

Length 180 mm (7″). An often conspicuous *montane-forest* greenbul restricted to higher elevations. Three distinct races in our area: **Adult** *A. n. kikuyuensis* of western and central Kenya has *entire head slate-grey*, contrasting with bright yellowish-olive underparts (olive-yellow on belly) and greenish-olive back, wings and tail; *broken greyish-white eye-ring* readily visible at close range. Eyes brown or red-brown; bill black; feet greenish grey to blue-grey. Of the two southern races, *A. n. nigriceps* has *blackish forehead and crown* and dark grey hindneck; face and most of underparts grey, the belly washed with pale yellow; flanks, sides and crissum yellowish olive; upperparts, including tail, darker olive than in *kikuyuensis,* and eye-ring greyer. *A. n. usambarae* is grey-headed like *kikuyuensis*, but with *black superciliary stripes extending from the lores*; plumage otherwise as in nominate *nigriceps*. **Juveniles** of all races darker than adults, and with dull olive underparts; eyes brown or grey-brown. **VOICE:** Inadequately studied; song of Kenyan *kikuyuensis* apparently unrecorded, but alarm note a short grating *churr*. Song said by Dowsett-Lemaire (1990) to be a low, nasal, husky phrase of 1.5–2 seconds, rich in harmonics, and lacking the boisterous cheerful quality of extralimital *chlorigula*, now generally considered to be specifically distinct (Green-throated Greenbul). Rwandan *kikuyuensis* said to have "a bustling continuum of low nasal, husky notes all on one pitch—notes run into one another", and "a more defined phrase of 6–8 distinct notes, repeated with minor variations: *jur-jitjur-dejur-jur-jerry*, last note upslurred." Voice of *A. n. usambarae* in the Usambaras described as *hee-her-hee* (Sclater and Moreau 1932). Northern Tanzanian races said to have "a conversational *kwew-ki-kwew-ki-kwew*, like Shelley's Greenbul" (Keith *et al.* 1992), but some published voice descriptions may be based on misidentifications. **HABITS:** Solitary or in pairs, often with mixed-species flocks at forest edge as well as in interior. Forages from undergrowth into the subcanopy, and gathers with other greenbuls at fruiting trees. **SIMILAR SPECIES:** Shelley's Greenbul is slightly smaller, slimmer and with less conspicuous eye-ring. Stripe-cheeked Greenbul has olive-green head, with dark grey cheeks and ear-coverts. **STATUS AND DISTRIBUTION:** *A. n. kikuyuensis* is locally common at up to 3300 m in the w. and cent. Kenyan highlands on Mt Elgon, the Cheranganis, Nyambenis, Mt Kenya, the Aberdares, and in Mau and Trans-Mara Forests. Nominate *nigriceps* is known in n. Tanzania from Mt Hanang, the Crater and Mbulu Highlands east to Mt Kilimanjaro and Arusha NP, and north to Loliondo and the Nguruman Hills. *A. n. usambarae* ranges commonly in the West Usambara and South Pare Mts occasionally north to the Taita Hills in se. Kenya. **NOTE:** Formerly considered conspecific with West African *A. tephrolaemus*.

STRIPE-CHEEKED GREENBUL *Andropadus milanjensis striifacies*   Plate 75

Length *c.*190 mm (7.5″). A *bright yellowish-olive* greenbul, almost *golden yellow on the belly*, with *dark face and contrasting pale eyes*. **Adult** uniformly olive above from forehead to tail, with blackish lores, grey cheeks and ear-coverts, the latter with whitish streaking visible only at close range. Chin greyish, breast bright yellowish olive, sides and flanks darker and contrasting with yellow belly. Eyes pale bluish grey, or rarely yellow (specimen label datum from North Pare Mts: Dowsett 1974). Bill black; feet brown or olive-brown. **Juvenile** resembles adult but is duller and greyer below, with faintly streaked ear-coverts and brown eyes. **VOICE:** Contact call *ookeri* or *u-ki-rii*. Taita Hills birds have two 'songs': (1) a prolonged monotonous loud *piku-piku-piku-piku* . . .

or *tchiku-tchiku-tchiku*. . .; (2) a more slowly uttered *qua quee-qua qua-quee-qua*. . ., varied to *cha-CHWEE-kwa*, *cha-CHWEE-kwa-kwa* and *chuck CHWEE chuck chuck*. .., such phrases altered in excitement to *kwi-kwa-kwa-KWEEri* and *chwi-chwa-choo-kwa-CHWEERi*. In the Chyulus, *churru-hichu-hichu-hichu-hick*, terminal note higher (van Someren 1939). Usambara birds give a throaty *ukkeri-ukkeri-ukkeri*, sometimes followed by a rising trill (Sclater and Moreau 1932). **HABITS:** Less shy than many greenbuls, often easily viewed at forest edge, where several may gather to feed on small fruits. Forages from mid-level into the canopy, where it hops or creeps along branches. Usually solitary or in pairs. **SIMILAR SPECIES:** Mountain Greenbul is smaller, duller, with all-grey head and whitish eyelid feathering. Shelley's Greenbul is also smaller, with duller, more greyish-olive underparts in race *roehli*. Yellow-bellied Greenbul has darker olive-brown head and upperparts. All three are dark-eyed. **STATUS AND DISTRIBUTION:** In n. Tanzania, locally common in forest and forest edge in Arusha NP, the North and South Pares, Usambaras and on lower slopes of Kilimanjaro and Mt Meru. Ranges north to the Taita and Chyulu Hills in se. Kenya; also known on Mt Monduli and Ol Doinyo Orok (Namanga Hill).

ZANZIBAR SOMBRE GREENBUL *Andropadus importunus*   Plate 75
(Sombre Bulbul)

Length 150–175 mm (6–7"). A *plain-looking, pale-eyed greenbul* of *thickets and scrub*, common in coastal lowlands, where readily visible on roadside wires and bushtops. **Adult** *A. i. insularis* has uniform brownish olive upperparts, including sides of head; underparts pale yellowish olive, slightly browner on flanks. Eyes cream; bill black; feet dark olive-brown. Central Kenyan birds were described as *A. i. fricki* on basis of prominent yellow eye-ring in adult birds. This feature is also present in **juveniles** of the race *insularis*. **VOICE:** Songs (*insularis*) include a short, rapid, slurred *chweleee-tuweeueet-tuweeuleet*, higher and thinner at end; also *we-up-tchup-cheu-tew-WEEa* and *chuk, chreep churrreeep chweeeo* or variations. Usual call note a terminally accented *cheerurIP* or *wheerUP*. Also utters an emphatic, police-whistle-like *prrrreeep*, repeated indefinitely. **HABITS:** Highly vocal; frequently in full song in the midday heat. Often conspicuous when singing; otherwise shy, skulking in thick vegetation. Frugivorous. **SIMILAR SPECIES:** Widely sympatric Yellow-bellied Greenbul is larger, darker olive-brown on upperparts, and with dark reddish eyes. **STATUS AND DISTRIBUTION:** The race *insularis* is common and widespread in coastal lowlands north to Kiunga and the Somali border; inland in ne. Tanzania to the East Usambara foothills, Mkomazi GR, North Pare Mts and the slopes of Kilimanjaro; also in e. and se. Kenya along the Tana River to Garissa, Kora NR and Meru NP, and through Tsavo East NP to Kasigau, Taveta, Rombo, Chyulu Hills, Mtito Andei, Kibwezi and Emali. Highland *A. i. fricki* (including '*kitungensis*') is known from Thika, Embu and Meru Districts; type specimen (but no subsequent records) from the Ndoto Mts.

GREY-OLIVE GREENBUL *Phyllastrephus cerviniventris*   Plate 76

Length *c*. 155 mm (6"). 'Pale-footed Greenbul' would be a better name, as the *straw-coloured, greyish-white or light flesh-pink tarsi and toes* are this drab bird's best field mark. **Adult** pale dull brown above, faintly tinged olive; tail and upper tail-coverts brownish rufous. *Narrow whitish eye-ring* obvious at close range. Throat pale buff; breast pale greyish olive-brown, shading to buff on belly, with tawny wash on sides, flanks and crissum. *Eyes orange-yellow or golden brown*; bill brownish horn or blackish above, but mandible *largely pale horn or whitish*. **VOICE:** Varied but distinctive. Calls include a somewhat raspy *yeckk yeckk yeckk* . . ., a repeated *cherkiyeck*, a rapid *chirrrridichirr* or *chewki-chiki-chew-chew-chew*. . ., all with quality reminiscent of Yellow-bellied Greenbul's voice. Also gives a *weh-weh-weh-weh* and a mournful whistling *hee-heu, hee-heu, hee-heu*. **HABITS:** Forages in pairs or small, highly vocal groups, with marked preference for dense streamside vegetation and ground-water forest. Typically shy and skulking, foraging low in undergrowth and leafy tangles not far above ground, constantly flicking wings and tail. Partly terrestrial. **SIMILAR SPECIES:** The two brownbuls are brighter brown. Fischer's and Cabanis's Greenbuls are larger, with prominent white or cream-coloured throats. **STATUS AND DISTRIBUTION:** In Kenya, local and uncommon in forest undergrowth and riparian thickets below 1500 m; one population in Kiambu and Thika Districts of cent. Kenya, another in Kenyan/Tanzanian border areas near Loitokitok, Taveta, Moshi and Arusha Districts. Also known from Bura (Taita District), Lake Manyara NP and East Usambara foothills at Mombo. Formerly in the Meru–Tharaka District, from where described as *P. c. lonnbergi*, a slightly darker form.

TORO OLIVE GREENBUL *Phyllastrephus hypochloris*   Plate 76

Length 155–170 mm (6–6.75"). An elusive west Kenyan forest bird, dark and with no distinctive markings, but *fairly long blackish bill* separates it from confusing *Andropadus* species. **Adult** *uniform dull olive above, except for dark rufous tail; underparts pale olive, obscurely streaked yellow and grey*. Feet dull greenish or bluish-grey;

eyes brownish orange to russet-brown. In the hand, bill is seen to be shorter and much broader at base than in Cabanis's Greenbul. **Juvenile** paler below, with light rufous under tail-coverts, brown eyes, and dark brown bill with yellow commissure and tip. Resembles adult of sympatric Cabanis's, but is dark-eyed, duller above and below, more uniformly greyish olive on upper breast and belly, and the pale throat is duller and less contrasting. **Voice:** Not known with certainty. A bird believed to be of this species uttered a loud song of three or four notes with quality of Little Greenbul's song, and consisting of a short phrase, *titiwah*, lower-pitched at the end, or *titutawah* rapidly repeated two to four times. Call reportedly a shrill harsh chatter, *chrrrrrrrrrrtitiwah*, often preceding the song (Keith *et al.*1992). **Habits:** Solitary and shy. Forages in dense under-growth, usually low, in Kakamega Forest. In w. Uganda, ascends into middle strata and inhabits tangled vegetation along forest and stream edges. **Similar species:** Canopy-inhabiting Slender-billed Greenbul is paler and greyer. Little and Cameroon Sombre Greenbuls have short bills; the latter has whitish eye-ring, as do the smaller Little Grey and Ansorge's Greenbuls. Cabanis's Greenbul has pale tan or grey eyes, a light yellowish throat, is generally yellower below and browner on the back. **Status and Distribution:** Local and uncommon in Kakamega Forest, w. Kenya. Formerly on Mt Elgon and at Lerundo. Sometimes considered a race of West African *P. baumanni.*

CABANIS'S GREENBUL *Phyllastrephus cabanisi*   Plate 76
(includes Olive Mountain or Placid Greenbul)

Length 165–190 mm (6.5–7.5"). A long-tailed, slender-billed, *highland-forest* greenbul with olive or olive-brown upperparts, *bright rufous-brown tail* and *pale throat.* **Adult** *P. c. placidus* east of the Rift Valley, is olive-brown above, darker and browner on crown; brownish side of face and ear-coverts contrast with narrow whitish eye-ring and *creamy-white chin and throat;* variable greyish-olive wash on breast, sides and flanks; tibial feathers and crissum brownish. Bill brownish horn to grey, lighter below and at base; eyes usually pale brown or grey, but said to be dark ochre and reddish in some birds; *feet blue-grey or slaty blue.* **Juvenile** *placidus* reportedly dark rufous-brown above, and underparts described as blotchy brown and creamy with brown flanks, more cinnamon on leg feathers and crissum. **Immature** more olive above than adult and darker on breast, sometimes with a distinct olive-grey chest band. **Adult** of western *P. c. sucosus* much brighter olive, less brown-tinged above, than *placidus,* the back contrasting more with the *strongly rufous-tinged upper tail-coverts and tail;* eyelid feathers creamy grey. *Underparts pale yellow,* with greyish-olive shading across breast, sides and flanks; dark sides of breast accentuate the *pale yellow throat;* leg feathers and crissum brownish olive. Bill dusky horn, more bluish at base of mandible. *Eyes pale greyish tan or pale grey; feet bright blue-grey or greyish blue.* **Juvenile** and **immature** *sucosus* bright olive above and with pale *yellow underparts* (brighter than adult), more olive on sides and breast; eyelids dull yellowish. Bill of immature black, with yellowish tip, tomia and gape; eyes pale olive-brown; feet greenish grey. **Voice:** A common forest sound; an abrupt harsh *chrrrk, chrrrrrk, chrrrrk-chrrrk, chwerrt-chwerrt,* or a more rolling, somewhat less grating *prrip-prip-perrup-perrup. . .,* or *pru-ip, pru-ip, peerrip peerrip prrup prrup. . .,* prolonged, the notes loud and explosive or softly uttered in fussy scolding fashion. Also various nasal complaining notes. **Habits:** Pairs or family parties work through undergrowth, repeatedly flicking wings and dipping tail. Bird raises feathers of crown and throat when excited or inquisitive. More responsive than most greenbuls to 'pishing' and playback of recorded calls. **Similar species:** Several sympatric greenbuls show rufous tails; Yellow-whiskered and other *Andropadus* species are shorter-billed and dark-eyed. Slender-billed Greenbul is a canopy bird and pale greyish below. Scarce Grey-olive Greenbul has obvious pale feet. Northern Brownbul is more uniformly brown above, without a contrasting rufous tail, and has reddish eyes. See Fischer's Greenbul. **Status and Distribution:** Common and widespread in forest, forest edge and riverine thickets from 900 to 2700 m. *P. c. placidus* ranges east of the Rift Valley from mts Kulal, Nyiru and Marsabit, the Mathews Range and Ndotos, south through the cent. Kenyan highlands to Mt Kasigau and the Taita and Chyulu Hills; also in Arusha NP, on Mt Meru, Kilimanjaro, and the Pare and Usambara Mountains in ne. Tanzania. *P. c. sucosus* (including *nandensis* and *ngurumanensis*) ranges from the Crater and Mbulu Highlands (where some specimens appear intermediate with *placidus*), Loliondo, the Ngurumans, Lolgorien and Olololoo Escarpment north to the Trans-Mara, Mau, Kakamega and Nandi Forests, Mt Elgon, Saiwa NP and the Cheranganis. Birds from Ol Doinyo Orok (Namanga Hill) and Maralal not racially assigned. **Note:** Some authors maintain *sucosus* and *placidus* as separate species.

FISCHER'S GREENBUL *Phyllastrephus fischeri*   Plate 76

Length 170–180 mm (7"). A *white-throated, pale-eyed* bulbul of *coastal forest,* usually in small groups on or near the ground. **Adult** pale brownish olive above, top of head no darker than back, becoming *dull rufous on upper tail-coverts and tail.* White chin and throat contrast with brownish-olive breast and flanks; belly also white. Inconspicuous narrow whitish eye-ring around white, cream, yellowish or pale tan eyes. Male's bill much longer and more slender than that of female. **Juvenile** resembles adult, but *belly pale yellow* and *eyes grey;* upperparts, breast and flanks somewhat darker. **Voice:** Foraging call *prurrit prurrit,* varied with a protracted dry chattering, *cherrrrh-cherrrrh-cherrrrh . . .,* a sharper *chiccck-chicccck-chiccck. . .,* and a repeated rapid *chweeeeeeeeeooh,*

chreeeeeeeeeoh . . ., slightly falling in pitch. Chattering may be interspersed with occasional shorter and louder notes. It may also "accelerate into a distinctive four to five-note form, in which first note is longest, loudest and highest, the following notes on a descending scale: 'WREEE-ga-ga-ga-ga' " (Keith *et al.*, 1992). **HABITS**: Forages in low vegetation and on forest floor. Shy and secretive, but frequent chattering (often involving more than one bird) reveals its presence, calling accompanied by tail-flirting and wing-flapping. **SIMILAR SPECIES**: Both brownbuls are dark-eyed. Sympatric Terrestrial Brownbul lacks marked olive tone to upperparts and flanks. Northern Brownbul is purer brown, brighter rufous on the tail. Cabanis's Greenbul is allopatric. **STATUS AND DISTRIBUTION**: Common in forest and woodland undergrowth from the Boni Forest southwards along the coast, inland along the lower Tana River, in the Shimba Hills and up to 600 m in the East Usambaras.

NORTHERN BROWNBUL *Phyllastrephus strepitans* Plate 76

Length 155–180 mm (6–7"). *Bright brown on back and tail, with strongly rufous-tinged wings, upper tail-coverts and rump* (unlike Terrestrial Brownbul). **Adult** has whitish-buff chin and throat less sharply defined than in Terrestrial Brownbul; grey-brown breast and flanks, pale buff belly and crissum. Narrow whitish eye-ring inconspicuous, but at close range contrasts with the russet or reddish-brown eyes; bill black with pale tomial streak; feet bluish grey, darker (particularly the toes) than in Terrestrial Brownbul. **Juvenile** resembles adult, but top of head and upperparts duller; eyes dull brown. **VOICE**: A rapid chattering reminiscent of *Turdoides* babblers, continues for five to ten seconds and is frequently repeated; higher-pitched than call of Terrestrial Brownbul, typically faster: *skrrrk-skrrrrk-kk-kk-kk-kk-kk. . .* or *chichichichichichichichichi-chk, chik-chik-chik . . ..*
Often slower and softer at beginning and end: *chiak-chiak- chiak chchchch SKEYOW skeyow chyow chyow chyow chyow.* Frequently given in partially synchronized duet with mate or in chorus with several birds. **HABITS**: Often inhabits dry scrub; usually low or in tangles of creepers. Travels babbler-like through undergrowth in noisy family parties. Restless, repeatedly flicking wings. **SIMILAR SPECIES**: Terrestrial Brownbul compared above. Adult Fischer's Greenbul has pale eyes. Cabanis's Greenbul has contrasting rufous tail, but back is dark brownish olive, the eyes usually tan or grey. **STATUS AND DISTRIBUTION**: Fairly common and widespread in dry thickets, woodland and forest edge throughout the coastal lowlands (where sympatric with Terrestrial Brownbul), inland along the Tana River to the edge of the Kenyan highlands, and through the Tsavo NPs to Mkomazi GR and southern slopes of Kilimanjaro. In n. Kenya, from Shaba and Samburu GRs, Lake Baringo and the Kerio Valley north to Lokichokio, Lake Turkana, Marsabit, Moyale and Mandera Districts.

TERRESTRIAL BROWNBUL *Phyllastrephus terrestris* Plate 76
(Terrestrial Bulbul)

Length 170–190 mm (6.75–7.5"). Closely resembles the more common (and partially sympatric) Northern Brownbul, but often in moister habitat and *mainly coastal* in distribution. **Adult** *less rufous above* than Northern Brownbul, particularly on wings and tail, and bill slightly larger. *Throat whitish, contrasting with darker breast*; whitish belly has faint yellow streaks, visible only with bird in hand; under tail-coverts pale dull rufous. Eyes red or red-brown; feet pale greyish lavender or light purplish grey. Interior race *bensoni* somewhat more olive-brown above than coastal *suahelicus*, more olive (less brown) on breast and flanks, and with more yellow streaking on underparts; whitish eyelids less prominent. **Juvenile** (*suahelicus*) paler and brighter than adult, more rufescent on wings (thus more like Northern Brownbul). Bare parts not described, but eyes of young *P. t. intermedius* (southern Africa) dark grey, bill pinkish brown, and feet pale brownish pink. **VOICE**: A rough chattering, somewhat lower in pitch than that of Northern Brownbul: *chrrrrrk, chrrk-chrrk, chrrrrrk*, etc. Several birds calling together produce a churring sound. **HABITS**: Much like those of preceding species. Noisily scratches for snails and insects on forest floor. Shy but inquisitive. **SIMILAR SPECIES**: Northern Brownbul is brighter, more reddish brown, than adult Terrestrial and lacks olive tint. Adult Fischer's Greenbul has pale eyes. (*P. t. suahelicus* is intermediate between *strepitans* and *fischeri* in the degree of olive on upperparts.) Cabanis's Greenbul is somewhat less brown above, has more contrasting reddish tail, and (in adult) pale grey or greyish-brown eyes. **STATUS AND DISTRIBUTION**: *P. t. suahelicus* is local and uncommon in moist wooded coastal lowlands north to the Boni Forest, ranging inland to the Shimba Hills and forest patches on the lower Tana River floodplain. In the interior, the scarce race *bensoni* is known only from early records in the Meru and Chuka Forests, between 1200 and 1400 m. A specimen from Mt Endau, attributed to this species by Tennant (1964,) is actually *P. strepitans*, casting doubt on a subsequent sight record from near Murang'a (Lewis and Pomeroy1989).

YELLOW-STREAKED GREENBUL *Phyllastrephus flavostriatus tenuirostris* **Plate 76**
(Yellow-streaked Bulbul)

Length 180–200 mm (7–8″). A pale, long-billed forest greenbul with a habit of *constantly raising or flicking one wing at a time*, revealing the yellow wing-linings. **Adult** olive above, with *grey head*, whitish lores and eyelids, somewhat browner on wings and tail; chin and throat white; pale greyish breast and belly marked with *faint light yellow streaks* rarely visible in the field; flanks pale olive; under tail-coverts brownish yellow. Eyes dull olive-grey; bill blackish brown; feet pale grey or blue-grey. **Juvenile** apparently not described; that of cent. African *P. f. olivaceogriseus* yellow-bellied, with dusky olive-green breast. **Voice:** A series of distinct loud notes: *chwick chwerk chk chk chee qu-qu-qu chew chikichick, yerk quip chikichick . . .*; or more distinctly two-parted, with three or four nasal whistled notes followed by clear faster whistling, *yerk, chwip chweep cheweep whew-whew-whew-whew*, accelerating and slightly descending. Alarm note a metallic chatter (Sclater and Moreau 1932). Contact call a repeated *quee-chew*. **Habits:** Solitary, in pairs or noisy groups, or accompanying mixed-species flocks. Not shy. Forages in middle and upper levels, gleaning from foliage, working over large branches and clinging to tree trunks. Peculiar wing-flicking distinctive. **Similar species:** Tiny Greenbul is much smaller, warbler-like, and forages mainly in undergrowth. Terrestrial Brownbul also has faint yellow ventral streaks, especially in the interior race *bensoni*. **Status and Distribution:** Fairly common in forest on the Usambara and South Pare Mountains in ne. Tanzania. Status uncertain in Kenya, where known only from two specimens (near Murang'a, April 1917, and Mt Kasigau southeast of Voi, Nov. 1938).

TINY GREENBUL *Phyllastrephus debilis* **Plate 76**
(Slender Bulbul)

Length 128–138 mm (5–5.5″). A small *warbler-like* bird of eastern forest undergrowth. **Adult** of coastal *P. d. rabai* has mainly olive-green upperparts, with *sharply defined grey head*, and greyish-white *underparts streaked with yellow*. Eyes usually white, creamy or yellowish, but sometimes brown, red-brown or grey (variation perhaps age-related); bill blue-grey or brownish, paler below and on sides; feet black, grey or brown. *P. d. albigula* has a more olive (less grey) crown, is greyer below with fewer yellow streaks than in *rabai*; eyes yellow or yellowish orange. **Juvenile** not well described, but in *rabai* lores and top of head are greenish instead of grey; eyes probably brown. **Voice:** Song a series of short *chit* or *tut* notes variously combined with lower, more nasal *nya* or *dya* sounds, e.g. *chitchitchit, chit-nya-nya-nya*. Alarm or contact call of *albigula* a gurgling *chrrrrrr*, of *rabai* a rasping *chicididididi*, rising in pitch; sometimes with a low *churr* or a nasal *nnyeh nnyeh*. **Habits:** Active, in pairs or small groups in forest undergrowth, less often in low trees; sometimes solitary; may join mixed-species flocks. Sings from canopy in very early morning only (Keith *et al.* 1992). **Similar species:** Yellow-streaked Greenbul is much larger and with different habits. **Status and Distribution:** Generally uncommon. *P. d. rabai* now scarce in the Arabuko–Sokoke Forest and apparently absent from Rabai and most other s. Kenyan coastal sites, but extends up to 450 m in Shimba Hills NP. In ne. Tanzania it reaches the East Usambara foothills, there replaced above 300 m by *P. d. albigula*, which also ranges throughout the West Usambaras.

HONEYGUIDE GREENBUL *Baeopogon i. indicator* **Plate 75**

Length 190–195 mm (7.5″). A forest-canopy species of western Kenya; dark, with a *largely white tail* patterned somewhat like a honeyguide's, the resemblance heightened in flight. **Adult** has dark olive-green upperparts, grey chin and throat, greyish-olive breast and flanks, shading to buffy on belly and crissum. Tail olive-green centrally; rectrices otherwise white, with yellow outer webs and black tips. *Eyes white, cream or pale grey in male, grey or brown in female*, often with olive tinge; bill black; feet dark grey. **Juvenile** (male) similar to adult, but browner on crown and greyish white on belly; outer three pairs of rectrices entirely white; eyes dull greyish buff. **Voice:** Loud and distinctive. Several slurred, slightly squealing whistles with a prolonged, descending final note, the latter somewhat buzzy in quality and often fading away, *keerriup keeup kuileep turee TZEEeeeeewwww*. Frequent variations include *weeti-p'tew, p'teew* and *weetilee-whew, wheeti-'p'weet, p'wheeeeeeeu*. Also a squealing cat-like *teeueeep*, or *squeeeueee*, the pitch dropping in the middle; sometimes interspersed with the song. **Habits:** Usually calls from concealed perch high in canopy, often at forest edge. Forages at all levels, depending on location of fruiting trees and vines. Vocal throughout the day. **Similar species:** All honeyguides (Indicatoridae) show different patterns of dark and light in the tail, have stubbier bills, differ vocally and have dark eyes. **Status and Distribution:** Local and uncommon in the Kakamega and Nandi Forests of w. Kenya. Formerly at Mt Elgon and the Yala River Forest Reserve.

YELLOW-BELLIED GREENBUL *Chlorocichla flaviventris centralis*   **Plate 75**
(Yellow-bellied Bulbul)

Length 200–215 mm (8–8.5"). A large, dark-headed greenbul, olive-brown above, *yellow below* and with prominent *white upper eyelid* (lower-lid feathering less conspicuously whitish). Dark *crown feathers frequently erected into a low bushy crest.* Chin and throat pale yellow; rest of underparts rich yellow, with olive wash on breast and flanks. Eyes dark red or brown; bill blackish; feet slate-grey. **Juvenile** duller; head no darker than back; underparts paler than in adult; eyes grey-brown. **Voice:** A distinctive, querulous, somewhat nasal *qui quaaaa quer qua queree qwa*; or *quar-tooa, quar-tooa,* slowly delivered, the notes well spaced. Also *rreeek, rrreeek, rrreeek, yerrr,* alternating with continued chattering. A reiterated *kerr quar, kerr quar. . .* serves as a contact note. Two birds may call together asynchronously. **Habits:** Solitary or in small groups, sometimes with mixed-species flocks. Quite vocal, but shy and skulking. Usually in forest undergrowth. **Similar species:** Adult Zanzibar Sombre Greenbul, sympatric with Yellow-bellied in many areas, is pale-eyed, typically in more open scrubby habitats and differs vocally. **Status and Distribution:** Fairly common in coastal forest, thickets and dense bush north to the Boni Forest and Somali border, inland along the Tana River to Bura, and in Shimba Hills NP. In n. Tanzania, small numbers present in the East Usambaras, around base of the North and South Pare Mountains, at Lake Manyara NP and on Mt Hanang. Also known from the Sagala, Ngulia and Chyulu Hills, Kibwezi, Mt Endau, western Nairobi suburbs and near Meru, but now scarce in cent. Kenya, where most suitable habitat has been cleared for agriculture. Formerly along the Voi River in Tsavo East NP and in Taveta District.

JOYFUL GREENBUL *Chlorocichla laetissima*   **Plate 75**

Length 200–210 mm (8–8.25"). A large golden-yellow greenbul of w. Kenyan forests, unique in our area. **Adult** *bright yellowish olive above,* with dark-centred crown feathers appearing scaly in close view; short yellowish superciliary stripes and yellow eyelid feathers. Tail dark olive with yellowish feather edges. *Chin, throat and belly bright yellow,* tinged greenish on breast, sides and flanks. Bill black; eyes bright chestnut; feet blue-grey. **Juvenile** browner above, washed with greenish below. **Voice:** A cheerful rollicking or bubbling chatter usually announces the presence of a group. A typical series (4–5 seconds): *chuck-chuck-chweek-kweek-kuardl-chuker-erk-querk.* Courting bird calls *chukliSKEEskeu, chwukiliSKEEskew* over and over. **Habits:** Small noisy parties move through canopy or middle levels of forest, often near clearings. Displaying bird raises and pumps tail, droops wings and puffs throat feathers while singing. **Similar species:** Yellow-bellied and Zanzibar Sombre Greenbuls are more eastern. Female Petit's Cuckoo-shrike tends to be solitary and lethargic, is usually silent and has black-and-yellow wings. **Status and Distribution:** An uncommon but conspicuous resident of forests from Mt Elgon and Saiwa NP south to Kericho, West Mau and Lolgorien Districts, and nw. Mara GR (Olololoo Escarpment). Most numerous in the Kakamega Forest.

YELLOW-THROATED LEAF-LOVE *Chlorocichla flavicollis pallidigula*   **Plate 75**

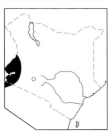

Length 210–220 mm (8.5"). A *large, noisy, pale-throated* greenbul of riverine thickets and tangles in *western Kenya.* Often appears large-headed, with raised crown and throat feathers. **Adult** dusky olive above, *crown greyer and somewhat dappled or scaly; olive-brown tail* feathers edged with greenish olive. *Chin and throat yellowish or cream;* rest of underparts greyish olive-brown, faintly grey-streaked, the breast feathers with white shaft streaks. Eyes dull yellow to light brown in male, greyish white in female; bill black; feet brownish grey to dark grey. Tarsi long for a bulbul. **Juvenile** resembles adult, but browner, less olive, above and with a whitish throat. **Voice:** Loud rattling, chattering and squeaky notes conveying an impression of anger or irritation, e.g. *skyow-skyow-chyowk-chyowk, ch-ch-ch-ch-chchchchch. . .*, with variations. Several birds may call together. **Habits:** Small, highly vocal family groups forage low in dense foliage, less often up to middle levels in taller trees, scolding all intruders. Individuals follow each other closely, one landing on a perch just vacated by another. Flicks wings and puffs out throat feathers when disturbed. **Similar species:** Cabanis's Greenbul, also with prominent pale throat, is smaller, with rufous-brown tail. **Status and Distribution:** Locally common in riverine thickets, gallery forest and suburban gardens in the Lake Victoria basin. Ranges from Saiwa NP and Kitale south through Bungoma, Busia, Mumias and Kakamega Districts, throughout South Nyanza to Tanzanian border areas. Generally scarce east of 35° E.

COMMON BULBUL *Pycnonotus barbatus*   **Plate 75**
(Yellow-vented, Dark-capped, or Black-eyed Bulbul; includes White-eared Bulbul)

Length 150–190 mm (6–7.5"). One of East Africa's best-known birds. **Adult** of widespread *P. b. tricolor* dusky brown above, almost black on head and throat; underparts otherwise white, with *prominent yellow under tail-coverts.* Male considerably larger than female. The small eastern and northern race *dodsoni* ('White-eared

Bulbul') has whitish ear-coverts, mottled breast markings and often more conspicuous whitish rectrix tips. Tanzanian *layardi* has black crown and face. Bill, orbital skin and feet black and eyes dark brown in all races. Eyes of some birds in the southern Kerio Valley (Fig. below) prominently ringed by bare white orbital skin (like *P. xanthopygos*, White-eyed Bulbul, of Arabia and the Middle East). **Juvenile** rufous-tinged above, generally duller and paler than adult. **Voice:** Common calls of *P. b. tricolor* include: (1) *kwick, kwerk kwee*; (2) *kwee kwit kwert keert*; (3) *kwee kerr-oh*; (4) *chuip churtle-eu*, often dropping in pitch. Songs involve repetition of one note: *churtle-churtle-churtle-churtle*, or *wurtilee-wurtilee-wurtilee*. All may be given separately or intermingled. In excitement, variations on these and others explode in a jumble of frantic-sounding notes. Continues to sing after sunset. Greeting vocalization *cheedle cheedle cheedlelit*, given with partly raised wings (van Someren 1956). Calls of *dodsoni* are higher and more shrill than those of *tricolor*, e.g. (1) *pwhic-pwer*, (2) *chwiki-chwiki-chwiki*, (3) a sharp *tchreek, turtur-eeek*, (4) *treek tur, chireeek*. **Habits:** Usually in pairs, but several call in chorus, especially at dawn, and numbers gather at fruiting trees with other birds, and presumed family groups remain together after breeding. Bold and fearless of man. Omnivorous, feeding on vegetable material and insects; sometimes flycatches. A nuisance at open safari-lodge dining areas, varying its diet with sugar, butter and table scraps. **Status and Distribution:** Common in most wooded and shrubby natural habitats, and readily adapts to artificial ones (especially suburban gardens). Virtually ubiquitous, except above 3000m and in dense forest. *P. b. tricolor* ranges throughout w. and cent. Kenya and n. Tanzania west of the Rift Valley; *layardi* in Tanzania east of the Rift and in s. Kenya around Taveta, Rombo and Loitokitok; *dodsoni* over much of n. and e. Kenya south to Mkomazi GR in ne. Tanzania. Races freely interbreed in contact zones.

Common Bulbul. Variant with white orbital ring (southern Kerio Valley).

RED-TAILED BRISTLEBILL *Bleda syndactyla woosnami* Plate 75

Length 205–230 mm (8–9"). A large, stocky bulbul of the forest floor and low undergrowth in western Kenya. Conspicuous *pale blue or bluish-white orbital skin, bright yellow underparts, plain rufous tail* and dark brownish-olive back identify **adults**. Eyes of male blood-red, those of female brown; bill black above, the mandible pale blue-grey; feet pale grey or pinkish grey. **Juvenile** more or less *rufous above* and *on sides and flanks*, and with *yellowish orbital skin*. **Voice:** A series of four or five quavering, minor-key, descending notes: *QUEEE, queee, queee, queee*. Much less frequent is a short monotonous *tung-tung-tung-tung-tung*. . . lasting for several seconds. West African birds give a distinctive, evenly pitched *querr-querr-querr-kiqurr, qurrrrrr-qurrrrrr*. . . *qurrrrrrrr*. . ., with quality of Yellow-bellied Greenbul's notes. **Habits:** Solitary or in pairs. Shy and skulking, usually on or near ground and frequently with ant columns. Regularly joins mixed-species foraging flocks. **Similar species:** Several other greenbuls have rufous tails, but none combines that feature with bright yellow underparts and pale orbital skin. **Status and Distribution:** In our region only in w. Kenya, where fairly common in North Nandi, Kakamega, and Iruru Forests; also on Mt Elgon, and recorded in Saiwa NP (Nov. 1989).

EASTERN NICATOR *Nicator gularis*   **Plate 75**
(Yellow-spotted Nicator)

Length 200–230 mm (8–9"). Unique in our region. A long-tailed, pale-spotted bird of eastern forests and dense thickets. **Adult** olive-green above, with a grey crown, dusky wings with olive feather edgings and *large yellow spots on wing-coverts and secondaries*; the grey chin, throat and breast pale to white on belly; *under tail-coverts and tips of tail feathers yellow*. Lores yellow in male, white in female. *Bill heavy, hooked*, somewhat shrike-like, brownish horn or grey-brown; eyes light brown; feet blue-grey. **Juvenile** at first has unfeathered face. **Immature** has yellow-tipped remiges and wing-coverts. **Voice:** Alarm call a powerful *TSUCK*; also a softer *tsuk-tsuk* and a whistled *WEE-oo*. Song a loud, liquid whistling, *WEEo WEE, WEE-EE-OO-choWEE*, and a pleasing *chwik, cheerrk, chwick, wherrreek, cho-CHIDilee*, the softer notes mainly audible at close range. Commonly mimics other species. **Habits:** Shy and skulking, but highly vocal. Flicks wings nervously when disturbed. Solitary or in pairs. Forages in dense tangles, sometimes on ground, but sings from high, well-concealed perches. **Status and Distribution:** Fairly common in coastal woods and thickets north to the Boni Forest, inland in n. Tanzania to the East Usambaras, Ambangulu, Mkomazi GR, the North Pare Mountains and s. Moshi District. In Kenya to Mt Kasigau, Sagala and Ngulia Hills, Taveta, Kibwezi and Endau; also along the Tana River to Bura. In the north, known from Mt Uraguess (near Wamba) and the Karissia Hills (near Maralal), but current status in both localities uncertain. **Note:** Considered an aberrant bush-shrike (Malaconotidae) by some authors. The very similar (and possibly conspecific) *N. chloris* has been recorded on the Ugandan side of Mt Elgon.

BABBLERS, CHATTERERS AND ILLADOPSES, FAMILY TIMALIIDAE
(World, *c.* 265 species; Africa, 42; Kenya, 14; n. Tanzania, 9)

Most of our species are either sturdy, often conspicuous and obtrusive birds (*Turdoides*) or small, secretive forest dwellers (*Illadopsis*). All are brownish and somewhat thrush-like, but stronger-footed, with shorter rounded wings. The longer-tailed babblers and chatterers, named for their boisterous vocalizations, frequently 'sing' in duet or chorus as the birds skulk in thick shrubbery or assemble after flying weakly, one by one, across openings. Decidedly social, several birds roost together and rest side by side during the day, often preening one another. They are mostly ground foragers, but freely perch in shrubs and low trees. Although normally retiring, they become bold and confiding around safari lodges and in gardens. Their nests are rough structures of roots, twigs and stems, hidden in dense shrubbery or creepers. Iris colour is important in identification of *adult* babblers: red in Hinde's, orange or yellow in Arrow-marked, Scaly, and Brown, white in Northern Pied and Black-lored. Rather plain juvenile plumage is replaced soon after fledging.

Very different from *Turdoides* are the five illadopses (*Illadopsis* and *Kakamega*), shy, skulking, terrestrial forest birds. Solitary or in family groups, they feed on invertebrates in the leaf litter and lowest shrub stratum of deep forest, seldom venturing into the open. The *Illadopsis* (formerly *Trichastoma*) species are master skulkers, difficult to identify in the field. All are similar in appearance, and their habits and habitat almost preclude good views. Vocal distinctions exist, but there may be no certainty that a calling bird is the one eventually seen, as three species inhabit certain Kenyan forests, and four are possible in some. Most respond poorly, if at all, to playback of recorded songs or to vocal lures. Of our four species, Brown Illadopsis is the most easily identified, especially when its evenly tawny-buff underparts (except for pale throat) are visible; however, Pale-breasted appears almost identical in a side view. Scaly-breasted is relatively distinctive if its scaly underparts can be seen; it is also larger-footed than Pale-breasted, but songs of the two can be similar. Mountain Illadopsis is the only species in montane forest above 2200 m (but it ranges down to *c.* 1500 m, overlapping with the other three). Only Pale-breasted need be considered in n. Tanzania, where the local race is greyer and less buff than that in w. Kenya. Male illadopses are noticeably larger than females; plumage is the same in both sexes, as in *Turdoides*.

The African Hill Babbler (*Pseudoalcippe*) is a small arboreal bird of highland forest, distinct from other East African timaliids and from its Asian relatives (*Alcippe*). Restricted, in our region, to northeastern Tanzania are the two controversial *Modulatrix* species. Both are shy, secretive forest-floor dwellers. Although frequently included in Turdidae, these birds have reported syringeal differences, their juveniles are unspotted, and to some workers their behaviour is more suggestive of timaliids, especially *Kakamega*. We place them here following Jensen and Brogger-Jensen (1992). As with other members of the family, they are resident species.

BLACK-LORED BABBLER *Turdoides sharpei*   **Plate 89**

Length 220–230 mm (9"). Grey-brown, with *black lores* and *white eyes* (**adult**); plumage variable. Nominate *T. s. sharpei* has pale brownish-grey ear-coverts and somewhat mottled underparts, with lighter feather edges and dark shaft streaks on chin and throat feathers (but without white-pointed tips or spots). Birds around Naivasha are more pale-throated and have darker wings and tail; they may appear quite frosty-headed. The race *vepres*, near Nanyuki, looks like a different species, with *chin and often the entire throat snow-white*; *rest of underparts dark brown* with narrow pale scaly feather edges, and more streaked on belly; back, wings and tail also dark brown. This form is highly variable within its small range, possibly reflecting past hybridization with Northern

Pied Babblers, a species apparently not now present in Nanyuki District. Birds on Lewa Downs are very different from more typical *vepres* nearer Nanyuki, sometimes suggesting a streaky-breasted Northern Pied. **Immature** of *T. s. sharpei* resembles adult but has dark eyes. **Voice**: Single birds utter a rough single or double note, *waaach* or *sqwaa-a*, repeated several to many times; also a muffled *wher-ha* or *kurr-ack*. In duet or chorus various harsh phrases, sometimes in long series, *ch-WAACKa WAACKa wAACKa. . .* or *wuk-wuk-wuk ye-ack, wee-ack wee-ak cherakkk-akk-akk. . .*, or *CHURRRi CHURRi CHURRi chchchchchch chichiwaka-chichiwaka . . .*, often slower than many babbler vocalizations. **Alarm** note a cat-like *nyaaa*. **Habits**: Small flocks or family groups forage for insects in shrubbery and tall grass; generally restless, noisy and suspicious. Especially vocal in early morning and late afternoon. **Similar Species**: Arrow-marked and Brown Babblers have yellow or orange eyes and pointed white tips to throat and breast feathers. See also Northern Pied Babbler. **Status and Distribution**: *T. s. sharpei* is locally common in w. Kenya at elevations between 1000 and 1900 m in forest edge, acacia thicket and dense bush, from the Kongelai Escarpment, Mt Elgon, and Busia, Kisumu and Kendu Bay Districts southeast to Lolgorien, Narok and Mosiro, and in the cent. Rift Valley north to Rongai and Solai. In n. Tanzania known only from early specimens taken in Serengeti NP and on Mt. Hanang. East of the Rift Valley only on the Laikipia Plateau south to Nanyuki District where the local *T. s. vepres* displays variation suggesting past hybridization with Northern Pied Babbler around Timau and Lewa Downs. **Note**: Formerly considered conspecific with the southern African *T. melanops*.

ARROW-MARKED BABBLER *Turdoides jardineii* Plate 89

Length 215–230 mm (8.5–9″). A *yellow- or orange-eyed* grey-brown babbler with conspicuous *lustrous sharp white tips to feathers of throat and upper breast*; crown and nape feathers have less prominent white tips and dark centres; lores, chin and auriculars brown, the latter indistinctly streaked. Flanks dark grey-brown with pale shaft streaks; belly mottled pale buff and grey-brown. Bill and feet black. **Immature** resembles adult except for dark brown eyes. **Voice**: Boisterous chuckling and chattering much like that of other babblers: *waaCHA, waaCHA*, repeated, or *chyaa-chyaa-chyaa. . . chchchchchchchch. . . chyah-chay-chyah. . .*, sometimes slowing and then accelerating again. The somewhat buzzy chatter, often involving two or more birds, may be continuous or given in short bursts. **Habits**: Similar to those of Black-lored Babbler. **Similar Species**: Brown Babbler has whitish lores and chin, more scaly white feather edges on throat and breast, with the sharp white tips much less pronounced. **Status and Distribution**: Locally common in acacia and riverine woodland, forest edge and bush. Two intergrading races: *T. j. emini* west of the Rift Valley from Endulen and locally in Serengeti NP north through Mara GR and Narok District to the central Rift Valley at Naivasha (where sympatric with Black-lored Babbler) and Nakuru NP (where common). East of the Rift in Tanzania, *T. j. kirki* ranges north to Lake Manyara and Tarangire NPs with old records from near Kilimanjaro, Taveta and Amani. Replaced by Brown Babbler north of the Equator.

BROWN BABBLER *Turdoides plebejus cinereus* Plate 89

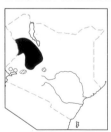

Length 215–220 mm (8.5″). **Adult** generally dull brown, *yellow-eyed*, and *grey-faced* with *whitish lores and chin*; upperparts brown, the crown and nape slightly mottled in fresh plumage (less so as pale margins disappear through wear, leaving dark feather centres); ear-coverts light grey. Underparts grey-brown; *throat and breast feathers with small white tips* and darker centres; belly and flanks uniformly pale dull greyish brown. Bill and feet black. **Immature** similar but brown-eyed. **Voice**: Recalls Arrow-marked Babbler. Variable chattering and chuckling calls include a slow *tsuk-tsuk-tsuk. . .*, a rapid *chkchkchkchk. . .*, a harsh *skyrr, skyrr, skyrr, skyrr, chwrrr-chwrrr-chrrr-chrrchrrchr*, and a buzzier communal *chwerryer chwerryer chwerryer. . ..* Scold note a repeated buzzy *CHAY-o*, given with partly spread and raised wings and fanned tail. **Habits**: As for the preceding two species. **Similar Species**: Arrow-marked Babbler has dark lores and ear-coverts; chin not noticeably pale; white feather tips on breast larger and more sharply defined; belly and flanks more mottled or streaked. **Status and Distribution**: Uncommon and local between 600 and 1500 m in n. Kenya, occupying thick bush, acacia and riverine woodland in Pokot and Maralal Districts, the Turkwell and Kerio Valleys, south to Mogotio, Rumuruti and Nanyuki Districts, extending south of the Equator only near Kisumu, Muhoroni and Fort Ternan. No overlap with Arrow-marked Babbler.

SCALY BABBLER *Turdoides s. squamulatus* Plate 89

Length 220–230 mm (9″). A *scaly-looking coastal* babbler with largely *whitish chin*. **Adult** with orange-yellow eyes. Upperparts dark olive-brown, the crown, throat and neck feathers scaled with whitish edges; *auriculars and lores dark blackish brown*. Bill and feet black. **Immature** brown-eyed. **Voice**: A distinctive throaty *wuk-a-ha, wuk-a-ha . . .* and *ch'wuk ch'wuk . . .*, most reminiscent of Black-lored Babbler. Less vocal than other *Turdoides*. **Habits**: Furtive. Small groups skulk in very dense cover. Shier than most *Turdoides* species. **Similar Species**:

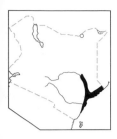

Brown Babbler (unlikely alongside Scaly) also light-chinned, but has paler lores and ear-coverts. Arrow-marked Babbler (present in coastal thickets south of our area) has prominent white feather tips on underparts. **STATUS AND DISTRIBUTION**: Local and uncommon in lowland thickets and dense forest-edge undergrowth from Mombasa north to the Boni Forest, and inland along the Tana River to Bura and Garissa. Reports south of Mombasa require confirmation. Birds near Ramu Dimtu and Ramu on the south bank of the Daua River (Kenyan/Ethiopian border) show much white on the head, more than in white-throated *jubaensis* from the nearby Juba River in s. Somalia; they reportedly resemble the more distant *T. s. carolinae*. See Ash (1981) for details of northeastern birds.

HINDE'S BABBLER *Turdoides hindei*   Plate 89
(Hinde's Pied Babbler)

Length 200–230 mm (8–9″). **Adult** a motley *red-eyed* babbler with varying amounts of *broad white feather edging on dark head and back,* plus white wing-covert and secondary tips. Upperparts generally blackish, wings and tail browner, *rump chestnut-brown; flanks and crissum tawny-cinnamon.* Some birds are much darker than others, and certain individuals suggest partial albinos. **Immature** duller and browner than adult, with dark brown eyes. **VOICE**: Harsh chuckling and chattering, *cherak-chwak-chakchakchakchak . . .* or *kwerak-chk-chk-chk.* **HABITS**: Noisy groups forage in dense shrub growth, including dry *Lantana* thickets. **SIMILAR SPECIES**: Allopatric Brown and Arrow-marked Babblers have yellow or orange eyes and prominent *pointed* white markings on underparts; both are plainer brown above, without the white scaling of Hinde's. Adult Black-lored and Northern Pied Babblers have white eyes. **STATUS AND DISTRIBUTION**: Scarce and very local Kenyan endemic, restricted to eastern and southern edges of the central highlands from 1300 to 1500 m; known from several localities in Meru, Embu, Karatina, Murang'a, Thika and Machakos Districts on fringes of cultivation and in river valleys, also in Mwea NR. Formerly at Athi River and in Kitui, Mwingi and Chuka Districts. Reduction in range coincides with increased agricultural development. Sympatric with Northern Pied Babbler, but not known to associate with it.

NORTHERN PIED BABBLER *Turdoides hypoleucus*   Plate 89

Length 200–230 mm (8–9″). A *white-eyed,* brown-backed babbler with *white underparts* bordered by a *dark brown patch on each side of the breast* and *dark brown sides.* Upperparts dark brown, the forehead and crown feathers paler-edged. Lores black to dark brown; ear-coverts blackish brown. *T. h. rufuensis* is greyer above than nominate *hypoleucus,* with distinct light scaly crown-feather margins. Eyes clear bluish white; bill mostly black; feet greenish grey. **Immature** resembles adult but is dark-eyed. **VOICE**: A variety of loud raucous chattering, churring and chuckling calls. **HABITS**: As for other babblers. Wanders in small family parties or flocks of 10–12 birds, always near thick cover. Restless and noisy. Tame and confiding in suburban Nairobi gardens. **SIMILAR SPECIES**: Black-lored Babbler, our only other white-eyed *Turdoides,* generally has dark underparts, but in parts of Nanyuki District the local *T. sharpei vepres* shows marked plumage variation including complete brown breast band or heavily streaked underparts. **STATUS AND DISTRIBUTION**: An East African endemic. *T. h. hypoleucus* is local in bush, savanna, forest edge and gardens east of the Rift Valley, from Meru and Nyeri Districts south through the cent. Kenyan highlands to the Tanzanian border; occasional in Arusha NP and northern Kilimanjaro District. Present also on the Yatta Plateau south of Kitui. *T. h. rufuensis* is fairly common in parts of e. Tanzania south of our region, ranging north to Tarangire and Lake Manyara NPs and northeast to the East Usambaras at Amani. A record from Mbulumbulu (May 1945) probably represents *rufuensis.*

RUFOUS CHATTERER *Turdoides rubiginosus*   Plate 89

Length 190–200 mm (7.5–8″). A fairly long-tailed bird, brown above, mostly *cinnamon-rufous below.* **Adult** has *white or pale yellow eyes.* Underparts almost solidly rufous in some birds, the throat and mid-belly paler in others. At close range, forehead shows short silvery streaks; these also present to some degree on breast. Bill pale yellowish horn or dull brown; feet pinkish-flesh colour. Eastern *T. r. heuglini* is darker overall, rufous-tinged above (especially on head), with indistinct black shaft streaks on head and back. Western *emini* has greyer crown with extensions of the forehead streaks. **Immature** more rufous above than adult, the light forehead streaking reduced. **VOICE**: Common call a shrill descending *tschyeerss,* repeated many times at intervals of two to three seconds. Also various chattering, growling and squealing calls; a soft *queer,* and a longer quavering whistle. **HABITS**: Less vocal than other *Turdoides*; small groups quietly forage on ground or in low shrubbery. Flight slow and laboured. **SIMILAR SPECIES**: Scaly Chatterer lacks rufous tones, has scaly-edged throat and breast feathers, and has conspicuous patch of bare skin around eyes.

STATUS AND DISTRIBUTION: Common and widespread in dense bush and thicket below 1500 m. To some extent replaced in dry *Commiphora* scrub by Scaly Chatterer. *T. r. rubiginosus* occupies much of n. and e. Kenya, south to Mtito Andei, Amboseli NP, the Athi and Kapiti Plains, and the Southern Uaso Nyiro River. The race *heuglini* occupies coastal lowlands north to Kiunga, inland to Voi, Taveta, Mkomazi GR and southern Kilimanjaro lowlands. Tanzanian *emini* is west of the Rift Valley, from Lake Eyasi and drier areas of Serengeti NP and Maswa GR southwards. Sight records from Ramu and Mandera Districts in extreme ne. Kenyan border areas probably refer to *T. r. sharpei*. Birds in the Lake Victoria basin and Lake Manyara NP not racially assigned.

SCALY CHATTERER *Turdoides aylmeri* Plate 89

Length 210–230 mm (8.25–9"). A duller version of Rufous Chatterer, rich brown above and pale cinnamon-brown below, the *broad buff feather edges of throat and breast feathers producing a scaly effect*; lores ashy. **Adult** shows prominent *bare blue-grey patch around pale yellow eyes*; bill pale horn-yellow; feet pale brown. Northern *boranensis* has darker centres to throat feathers, and Tanzanian *mentalis* is generally more greyish brown than eastern *kenianus*. **Immature** browner than adult, with duller bare parts, the eyes and bill brown. **VOICE**: An odd, rather feeble "squeaking wood-screw" sound, varied by a thin high-pitched chatter and broken whistling (Fuggles-Couchman and Elliott 1946). **HABITS**: Similar to those of Rufous Chatterer. **SIMILAR SPECIES**: Rufous Chatterer has more rufous underparts, lacks large bare patch around eyes. **STATUS AND DISTRIBUTION**: Local and generally uncommon in dry *Commiphora* scrub north, east and south of the Kenyan highlands, typically in drier areas than Rufous Chatterer but the two often sympatric. Three races: *boranensis* in n. Kenya from around South Horr south to Barsaloi; *kenianus* from Meru NP and Garissa south through Galana Ranch and the Tsavo parks to Mkomazi GR and North Pare foothills; *mentalis* in dry interior e. Tanzania from Lake Natron and the Masai Steppe south to the Dodoma Region. Sight records near Olorgesailie, Magadi and elsewhere in s. Kenya may also represent *mentalis*.

AFRICAN HILL BABBLER *Pseudoalcippe a. abyssinica* Plate 90
(Abyssinian Hill Babbler)

Length 150 mm (6"). Somewhat robin-like. An arboreal forest bird with a *small, slim bill*, *bright rufous-brown back* and *contrasting grey head and nape*. Grey underparts are faintly mottled or streaked with white, paler on belly; *flanks and leg feathers washed with yellowish brown*. Eyes brown to bright red (when breeding?); bill black above, paler below; tarsi and toes greyish blue. **VOICE**: Variable. Usually a clear melodious song, suggesting a thrush or oriole, composed of separated whistled phrases with frequent changes in pitch, e.g. *weu-tu-whu-yo-WUtu-CHeu*; *CHEWi-WEUto-wuchiWItew*. Sometimes a pure slurred whistling, *weu-TEEU-tu-WEU-weu-weu* or *pee tew, turWEEoo-heu, whurr quip-WEEo*, surprisingly low-pitched. Other songs higher, with more scratchy notes, *tchh, churwee-churwee, skeek skweee skwee-tsur, chreer seet-see twer seet-seet. . ..* **HABITS**: Pairs or singles forage for fruits and insects in low tree branches and tall undergrowth. Often vocal after sunset. **SIMILAR SPECIES**: Adult Mountain Illadopsis, a darker, stockier terrestrial skulker, has grey of head more restricted, merging with olive-brown back and nape (sharply demarcated in hill babbler); underparts dark slaty grey, with no white on belly. **STATUS AND DISTRIBUTION**: Widespread in highland forest, including riparian strips, between 1500 and 3000 m. Ranges throughout the w. and cent. Kenyan highlands north to the Ndotos, mts Kulal, Nyiru and Loima, south to the Mau and Trans-Mara Forests, the Chyulu and Nguruman Hills. In n. Tanzania at Loliondo, the Crater and Mbulu Highlands, Arusha NP, Mt Meru, Kilimanjaro, the Pare Mts and the West Usambaras.

SPOT-THROAT *Modulatrix s. stictigula* Plate 123

Length 170 mm (6.75"). A dark, chestnut-tailed forest bird of the ground stratum in Tanzania's Usambara Mts. **Adult** has a noticeable *whitish or greyish eye-ring* around the large dark eye, largely *rufous breast and sides,* and dull buffy-white throat marked with small dark spots visible only at close range. Upperparts brownish olive; flanks and crissum tawny-rufous; belly whitish. Bill black, partly grey below; eyes brown; feet dark brown, the toes paler. **Juvenile** resembles adult, but throat is less speckled and chin/throat patch less distinct. **VOICE**: Songs recorded by Svendsen and Hansen (1992) in the Udzungwa Mts consist of loud, shrill slurred whistles with some long-drawn higher notes, *skureet chierreet siureeee sreet seeu sheeu-tsi-chiu, seeeeeet, swee-ir-si-REEO*, the final note often loudest. Also gives a shorter *chiu chi-chi-CHEEO* and a shrill, descending *siuuuuu*, repeated several times. **HABITS**: Rather noisy, but shy, running or fluttering along forest floor when approached. Stays low. Hops with tail slightly elevated, probing in leaf litter and flicking leaves with bill. Restless, seldom still. **SIMILAR SPECIES**: Dappled Mountain Robin and Pale-breasted Illadopsis have no chestnut on underparts. **STATUS AND DISTRIBUTION**: In our region, only in the Usambaras, both East (rare) and West, where common between 900 and 2200 m; more numerous above 1500 m.

DAPPLED MOUNTAIN-ROBIN *Modulatrix orostruthus amani*   **Plate 123**

Length 170 mm (6.75″). A rare, streak-breasted forest bird of the East Usambara Mts in ne. Tanzania. **Adult** generally brownish olive-green above, with the lores and sides of face dark olive; upper tail-coverts and tail russet-brown, the rectrices mainly olive-brown with reddish-tinged outer webs. Underparts pale yellow, more whitish on throat, with broad olive streaks on breast, upper belly and (more densely) flanks; lower belly and crissum washed with ochre, sometimes heavily. Bill brown or black, mandible whitish at base; eyes brown; feet pinkish grey. Very rounded wings said to be obvious in flight. Sexes alike. Juvenile olive below, darker and greener on breast. **Voice:** Several song types (of *M. o. sanje* in the Udzungwa Mts), all rapidly delivered and of short, clear melodious stanzas, at times quite oriole-like, e.g. *qu qu-we wurdilee WEE-yew* or (*twee*) *turLEEa*; a different, repetitious yet melodious chattering is more bulbul-like: *chiquea chiquea chiquea*. Main call is a rising fluty whistle, *hoooo-reee*, the ending much higher-pitched (Svendsen and Hansen 1992). **Habits:** Elusive, and presumably forages on ground, preferring dense undergrowth along streams. **Similar Species:** Spot-throat has tawny-rufous underparts with spotted throat and immaculate breast. Cabanis's Greenbul and Pale-breasted Illadopsis, somewhat similar above, have plain underparts. **Status and Distribution:** In our region, a rare inhabitant of undisturbed montane forest, this race restricted to the East Usambaras. Other races farther south in e. Tanzania are much more common. **Note:** Placed by some authors in a separate genus, *Arcanator*.

GREY-CHESTED ILLADOPSIS *Kakamega poliothorax*   **Plate 90**

Length 165 mm (6.5″). A thrush-like bird of the forest floor and undergrowth; relatively small-billed and long-legged; *bright mahogany-rufous above*, more dusky on crown, wings and tail. Throat and centre of belly whitish, shading to pure *grey on breast and sides*. Eyes red-brown; bill black; tarsi and toes slate-blue. **Juvenile** apparently undescribed. **Voice:** Variable song short, clear and loud, the rapidly uttered phrase somewhat oriole-like: (1) *tew-tu-TEW-wieu*, (2) *kew-ki-KEWI-eu*, (3) *wi chi-yow kiWEEo*; sometimes more bulbul-like: *werk-kiyer-l'week* or *choik-kiyer-WEEK*. Calls include *tseetseetseetsee* and a slightly churring *kwerriyer, kwerriyer* or *churriyer, churriyer*. **Habits:** Solitary, shy and skulking. Little known. See Mann *et al.* (1978). **Similar Species:** Adult Mountain Illadopsis, also grey-breasted, is much smaller, darker brown above, and has olive-brown flanks. See juveniles of that species and Brown Illadopsis. Brown-chested Alethe appears bright brown above in dappled forest light, but has light superciliary stripes and brownish breast band. **Status and Distribution:** Scarce resident of forest undergrowth at 1550–2000 m in the Kakamega and Nandi Forests of w. Kenya. Formerly recorded at Lerundo and Mt Elgon.

BROWN ILLADOPSIS *Illadopsis fulvescens ugandae*   **Plate 90**

Length 140–150 mm (5.5–6″). *Longer-tailed and larger-billed* than its relatives. *Whitish throat* of **adult** contrasts with *otherwise tawny-buff underparts*. Upperparts brown, the head darker; *lower edge of grey cheeks and ear-coverts dusky, forming weak malar stripes*. No hint of scaly pattern on breast; flanks only slightly darker than belly. In the hand, throat feathers are seen to be entirely whitish, not basally dark as in Pale-breasted Illadopis. Eyes bright brown or orange-brown; bill black above, pale blue-grey below; feet purplish grey or blue-grey. **Juvenile** almost rufous on back and wings; eyes dull brown; bill brown, with base of mandible paler; feet dull maroon. **Voice:** Variable, but usually a combination of a few short notes preceding longer minor-key whistles, the latter often with a pronounced twang: (1) *yik, youuuuuuuuuu*, (2) *yik chickik p'chyowww*, (3) *whik peeeeee, pyerrrrrr*, (4) *whik whik chik-ti-fownnnnn*, (5) *tsik, tsik, CHICK-ti-fownnnn* or '*dictaphone*'. The twangy '*-taphone*' given by one bird, the varied *chik* or *tsik* notes by its presumed mate perched close by (positive identifications based on tape-recorded, collected birds). Dawn song (which may end with the twang of regular diurnal songs) is described by Chapin (1953) in Zaïre as "a long-drawn husky whistle. . . often introduced by a couple of shorter, less musical attempts, and as the whistles are slowly repeated they vary characteristically about half a tone, always low in the scale". Alarm note a nasal *tchaa* or *chwaa*. **Habits:** Forages in pairs or small family groups; spends more time above ground in low shrubbery than other illadopses, investigating vine tangles and clusters of dead leaves. Sometimes responds to 'pishing' and squeaking, unlike its relatives. Joins mixed bird parties, and appears to be entirely insectivorous. Builds nest in low shrub. **Similar Species:** See Pale-breasted and Scaly-breasted Illadopses. **Status and Distribution:** Fairly common in the Kakamega Forest in w. Kenya and nearby Kabras (Malaba Forest), although populations appear to fluctuate from year to year. Upper altitudinal limit probably *c.* 1600 m.

MOUNTAIN ILLADOPSIS *Illadopsis p. pyrrhoptera*   **Plate 90**

Length 120–134 mm (4.75–5.25″). A small, dark skulker of *montane forest*. **Adult** *dark* rufescent olive-brown above, greyer and somewhat scaly on the crown; upper tail-coverts dull rufous-brown, contrasting, as bird darts

into cover, with the dark brown tail. *Dark grey face, breast and sides contrast with pale grey throat and brownish flanks and crissum*; belly grey, somewhat lighter than breast. Eyes light brown; bill grey, darker above and dull yellowish at base; feet purplish grey. **Juvenile** brighter russet-brown above than adult. **Voice**: Song of penetrating descending semitones, *TWEEK twe tyew tu-wer tu-wer*, mingled with much low chucking and chattering. Very different is the quality of Ugandan birds' songs (Keith and Gunn 1971), confusingly like Brown Illadopsis, with short semi-staccato notes and longer descending minor-key semitones: *chick-waaaa-fiyownn* or *chikchi-fiyaaaa chiyaaaaa chiown*; sometimes more varied notes, e.g. *quili-waaa yew-yew-yeaow*. Two or more birds call together, producing a duet as in Brown Illadopsis. **Habits**: Solitary or in groups of four or five individuals, creeping on or near the ground, generally in thick forest undergrowth; forages wren-like through tangled fallen branches, recalling Evergreen Forest Warbler in the same habitat. **Similar Species**: Grey-chested Illadopsis is larger, longer-tailed, longer-legged, with bright mahogany-rufous back. Other illadopses are at lower elevations and have paler underparts. African Hill Babbler is longer-tailed, grey-throated and arboreal. **Status and Distribution**: Locally common in montane-forest undergrowth (1500–2800 m) west of the Kenyan Rift Valley, from Mt Elgon, Kapenguria and the Cheranganis south to North Nandi, Mau and Trans-Mara Forests. Rare (at least formerly) in Kakamega Forest, perhaps wandering from the Nandi.

PALE-BREASTED ILLADOPSIS *Illadopsis rufipennis*   Plates 90, 124

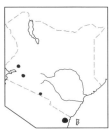

Length 125–140 mm (5–5.5"). Dull and olive-brown, paler below than Scaly-breasted Illadopsis; *I. r. rufipennis* is smaller and has a smaller bill than that species, but sexual size differences blur this distinction. *Whitish throat and belly* accentuated by a faint *dull olive-buff or pale brownish breast band, sides, flanks and crissum*. **Adult** *I. r. rufipennis* is *greyish about the face*, with *essentially no dark feather edging on breast*. Eyes rufous (to buff around pupil); bill dusky above, blue-grey below; *feet grey with blue, purplish or brownish tinge, usually darker than in Scaly-breasted*, but sometimes pale yellowish white. Nominate *rufipennis* has breast, sides, flanks and crissum concolorous. In the hand, note that the pale throat feathers are dark basally (these feathers entirely pale in Brown Illadopsis); rictal bristles shorter and weaker than in Scaly-breasted; tarsus length 23–27 mm. Rictal skin and *mandible base bright yellow to orange*, bill tip black; eyes dull tan. Tanzanian *I. r. distans* has large bill, the breast band is pale cold grey, not warm buff or pale brown; flanks and crissum olive-brown. Maxilla mostly black, mandible pale grey with basal third horn; tarsi fleshy brown, toes olive-grey. **Juvenile** *I. r. rufipennis* has tawny lesser-wing-covert tips, is somewhat brighter brown above than adult and *grey-faced* (no rufous or cinnamon as in Scaly-breasted Illadopsis). Some of the brighter dorsal feathers with light shaft streaks persist into first adult plumage. **Voice**: Virtually no information on Kenyan birds (which seem almost non-vocal, or their songs not distinguished from those of *I. albipectus*). In West Africa the nominate race supposedly sings *tuik yeeee PEEE* or *twik eeee WEEEE*, distinctly reminiscent of Scaly-breasted (but birds not collected following recording). In Zaïre, Chapin (1953) attributed to *rufipennis* "an ascending series of three or four short whistles, introduced by one or two low chirps or clucks", but following these songs he collected both this species and *I. albipectus*, and "for 30 years . . . wondered how two distinct species [of Illadopsis] could utter notes so closely similar". Call note is a harsh *chack*. *I. r. distans* (Usambara Mts) commonly utters a slow human-like whistle, often preceded by a softer short note: (*twik*) *wureet weeee* or *tuit wureet uweeee*, this frequently answered by another bird. Alarm note a grating *ka-a-a-a* followed by a throaty *kwo-kwo* (Sclater and Moreau 1932). Much 'conversational' churring between members of a group. **Habits**: Furtive and shy, living entirely on or near the ground in dense forest undergrowth. Usually in pairs or small groups. **Similar Species**: Scaly-breasted Illadopsis typically shows dark feather edges below; plainer individuals closely resemble *rufipennis*, but usually have paler tarsi. Young Scaly-breasted has rufous feathers around and behind eyes; mandible base and gape dull pink or yellowish. Brown Illadopsis is more uniformly tawny-buff below, including the belly, is larger and longer-looking, and less restricted to ground foraging. Mountain Illadopsis resembles *I. r. distans*, but is *dark* grey below. **Status and Distribution**: *I. r. rufipennis* is locally fairly common in the Kakamega and South Nandi Forests, populations possibly fluctuating annually or seasonally; fewer records in recent years. In ne. Tanzania, *I. r. distans* is a common resident of the East Usambara Mts, less numerous at Ambangulu (1220 m) in the West Usambaras. Two adults recorded in Kenya on Ol Doinyo Orok near Namanga (Bennun *et al.* 1986) and one in the Trans-Mara Forest (Bennun 1991) showed plumage characteristics of *distans*. A unique report of the species at 2300 m in the Cheranganis (Britton 1980) probably refers to Mountain Illadopsis. **Note**: Apparently distinctive voice, larger bill and plumage differences suggest that the race *distans* may not be conspecific with *rufipennis*.

SCALY-BREASTED ILLADOPSIS *Illadopsis albipectus barakae*   Plate 90

Length 130–155 mm (5–6"). Another drab skulker of the forest floor. **Adult** olive-brown above, grey on forehead and above and behind eyes. Throat pale grey; dark-margined grey or pale olive-grey breast feathers have *scaly appearance* in most, but not all, birds (non-squamate ones more common in Uganda). Well-marked individuals are not only scaly-breasted, but also scaly on the olive-brown sides and white belly, less so on the back. Eyes

brown; bill blackish above, pale grey below; *long tarsi whitish grey to greyish pink* with faint purple tinge (usually paler than in Pale-breasted Illadopsis). In the hand, note strong rictal bristles, dark bases of pale throat feathers, and tarsus length of 26–30 mm. **Juvenile** brighter than adult, faintly yellowish on breast; head browner, less grey, with conspicuous *rufous supraorbital and eyelid feathers*, this colour extending to the fore-head and above the ear-coverts in some. (Some of these brighter feathers remain on immatures in first adult plumage.) Eyes brown; bill black above, dusky brown below, dull pink or yellowish basally, with yellow gape; tarsi and toes whitish or pinkish grey. **Voice:** Usual song, heard repeatedly in some w. Kenyan forests, is composed of two or three ascending, semitone, minor-key notes, often preceded by a softer introductory note inaudible at a distance: (1) *t'eee eee EEE*, (2) *t'wick yee EEEE*, (3) *wik, weu UR WEE*, or (4) *chip yew WEE*, the louder notes penetrating and far-carrying. These songs commonly heard in the Kakamega Forest (where this species is common) in seasons when few or no Pale-breasted Illadopses (*q.v.*) are netted or observed. Seldom heard is a high-pitched warbler-like *see-u, see-u, see-u* preceded by a soft twittering *titititititititi.* **Habits:** Almost entirely terrestrial, walking about in leaf litter under heavy forest. Usually solitary or in pairs. Sometimes near, but perhaps not part of, mixed-species flocks. More vocal (or with longer song season) than other illadopses. **Similar Species:** Pale-breasted Illadopsis shows only a hint of scaly breast feathers, the breast band is buffier, more sharply defined; rictal bristles are weaker, and the shorter (23–27 mm) tarsi are bluish or brownish grey. Juvenile Pale-breasted has bright yellow or orange mandible base. Brown Illadopsis is uniformly buff below except for white throat, shows no trace of dark feather edges, and has darker (purplish or blue-grey) tarsi. **Status and Distribution:** Common in low undergrowth in the Kakamega (where usually the most numerous illadopsis) and Nandi Forests from 1600 to 2100 m.

THRUSHES, CHATS AND RELATIVES, FAMILY TURDIDAE
(World, *c.* 300 species; Africa, 126; Kenya, 49; n. Tanzania, 40)

Small to medium-sized birds which occupy a broad range of habitats, from heavy forest to open plains. They are longer-legged than the related warblers and flycatchers (which some ornithologists unite with thrushes in the family Muscicapidae). The bill is moderate in length and rather slender; the eyes tend to be large. Some species are undistinguished in appearance, but others have bold facial patterns, brightly coloured underparts, or distinctly patterned tails. The sexes usually are similar, although conspicuously different in some wheatears, chats and *Irania.* Juveniles are more or less spotted. Our breeding thrushes are mainly solitary in habits, but migrants of some species gather in small groups. Most forest thrushes are shy and elusive birds of shaded undergrowth or forest floor, often feeding with other birds on invertebrates flushed by columns of army ants. Many stand quite upright when alert; some habitually raise and lower the tail, or cock it up and over the back; others flirt and spread the tail, or flick the wings. Songs of resident species vary from unimpressive to powerful and melodious, and some species are among Africa's finest songsters. Twelve of our species are long-distance migrants from the Palearctic; the remainder are African residents. The typical nest is an open cup of plant material, sometimes rein-forced with mud and placed in a shrub or tree, but several species build in tree cavities, rock crevices or holes in earth banks and termitaria. The eggs vary from immaculate to well spotted.

WHITE-STARRED ROBIN *Pogonocichla stellata*   Plates 93, 124
(Starred Robin; White-starred Forest Robin or Bush Robin)

Length 150 mm (6"). A small forest thrush with a distinctive bright tail pattern in all plumages. **Adult** has *bright yellow underparts*, blue-grey head, olive back, grey wings (in some races with greenish feather edgings), and a *yellow tail with black central feathers and tip* (yellow confined to extreme tail base in Mt Elgon race). Shows a small white spot in front of each eye; another, on the lower throat, is narrowly bordered by black and concealed when bird is at rest, but conspicuous when throat extended in song. Races differ in intensity of yellow and in colour of wing edgings. **Juvenile** olive-green above, with pale spots; underparts dull yellow with heavy black chevron-shaped mark-ings; tail as in adult. This remarkably persistent plumage (worn for up to three months in southern African races) moults into an **immature** or **subadult** dress that is retained for up to two years in s. Africa (few data from our area). In the better-known forms, this plumage is uniformly olive from forehead to upper tail-coverts, but underparts vary racially: mottled yellow and olive in *intensa*; dull pale yellow with grey mottling in *helleri* and *orientalis*; olive with narrow yellow streaks in *macarthuri.* **Voice:** Alarm notes a soft *krrrrrrr* or harsh *pirrut-pirrut.* Song (of both sexes) a repeated series of squeaky phrases interspersed with low chattering: *ski-skurEE-skurEW, chrrg-chrr-chrr, ski-skurEE. . .* or *wi-wur-wihi, wi-wur-wihi, chrr-ch-chrr-chrr, wi-wur-wihi . . .*; a softer version, with more creaking quality, alternates two notes, *treee-tur, treee-tur, treee-tur. . .* At least some Tanzanian birds have a distinctive clear song, *tuEET tuEET tuEET, eet eet tuEET. ..* , interspersed with a somewhat clicking or ticking chatter. **Habits:** Shy and secretive. Singles or family groups forage in forest-floor leaf litter, perching near ground and frequently following ant columns; may feed on fruits in the canopy. Flirts and spreads the tail. **Status and Distribution:** Locally common in lower stratum of forest, forest edge and bamboo in highlands between 1600 and 3000 m. In non-breeding season, descends to 500 m or lower in ne. Tanzania and se. Kenya. Six races in our area: *P. s. intensa* is widespread in the Mbulu and Crater Highlands, Longido, Monduli and Loliondo areas of n. Tanzania, ranging north through Kenya from Ol Doinyo Orok (Namanga Hill) and the Ngurumans north to the Cherangani and Karissia Hills, Mathews Range, the Ndotos, Mt Nyiru and Mt Kulal; *orientalis* occupies the Usambaras; *guttifer* on Mt Meru and Kilimanjaro; *helleri* on Mt Lossogonoi, the Pare Mts, Mt Kasigau and the Taita Hills; *macarthuri* is restricted to the Chyulu Hills, and *elgonensis* to Mt Elgon.

SWYNNERTON'S ROBIN *Swynnertonia swynnertoni* subsp.   **Plate 123**

Length 118–125 mm (4.5–5″). A small Tanzanian thrush suggesting a White-starred Robin, but with *rich yellow flanks and breast*, and a white crescent across the lower throat bordered below by black or dark grey. White belly and crissum conspicuous, as tail is often carried at 45° angle. Flanks washed with olive. Bill black; eyes brown; feet pale greyish pink. **Adult male** dark grey on head, wings and tail, bright olive-green on upper back; lower rump, upper tail-coverts and tail grey. **Female** duller than male; head more olive, and throat pale buffy grey. **Juvenile** brown above, with buffy-yellow spots; breast pale yellow with brown feather tips; belly and crissum mottled grey and white. Bill horn-brown with greyish tip. **Immature** browner above than adult female, paler on underparts. **Voice**: Song a sweet, high, leisurely whistled series of four (occasionally three or five) notes, slightly slurred, the first one or two higher, *didi durdur* (T. Evans, *pers. comm.*). Birds in the Udzungwa Mts (south of our region) usually sing three notes, *teeee ter tew*, penetrating and semi-mechanical, the quality reminiscent of Black-faced Rufous Warbler or some *Batis* species. **Habits**: Forages alone or in pairs in forest undergrowth and on ground, flicking leaf litter about with the bill. Prefers more open areas of forest floor than White-starred Robin, and less shy than that species. Perches low, dropping on prey flushed by ant columns. Appears to be restricted to the least disturbed areas of forest. **Similar Species**: White-starred Robin is bright yellow below, with smaller (often concealed) white throat spot, and has yellow on rump and tail. East Coast Akalat is yellow on the throat. Both species have whitish supraloral marks, lacking in Swynnerton's. **Status and Distribution**: Rare. Known in our region only between 200 and 550 m in East Usambara lowland forests, well north of other known localities, and possibly representing an undescribed race.

FOREST ROBIN *Stiphrornis erythrothorax xanthogaster*   **Plate 93**

Length 110–115 mm (4.5″). A small bird of forest undergrowth, probably accidental east of Uganda. **Adult** olive-brown above, including tail; *throat and upper breast yellow-orange*; sides of breast and flanks grey, rest of underparts white. Shows *blackish cheeks* and *white spot in front of each eye*; bill black. **Juvenile** paler and tawny-spotted above; cheeks grey; throat creamy white; lower neck and breast tawny and grey; bill pale horn-brown. **Voice**: In Uganda, a high-pitched squeaky and repetitive *ter-ter twee ter ter churrri* (Keith *et al.* 1992). Common call a low hoarse *ch-chic* (Chapin 1953). **Habits**: Skulking and shy. Largely terrestrial, foraging among leaf litter in mature forest. Sings from low in undergrowth, tail cocked and wings quivering. Regularly gathers at ant swarms. **Similar Species**: Equatorial Akalat is more uniform apricot below, this colour extending to sides of breast and belly; lacks supraloral spots, dark cheeks. **Status and Distribution**: Typically a bird of lowland rainforest. Known in our area from one specimen collected near Kipkabus, w. Kenya (2500 m), 16 April 1966.

USAMBARA GROUND ROBIN *Sheppardia montana*   **Plate 123**
(Usambara Akalat)

Length 135–145 mm (c. 5.5″). A small, drab, long-legged robin of the *West Usambara forests* in ne. Tanzania. **Adult** *dull brownish olive* with *dark reddish-brown upper tail-coverts* (rectrices brighter on outer webs). Whitish preorbital area, and a *usually concealed supraloral streak of orange-rufous* (the feathers olive-tipped) becomes visible during courtship excitement, in territorial defence or at ant swarms. Throat and belly dull white; breast, sides and flanks olive-grey; under tail-coverts buffy white. Bill black; eyes brown; feet lead-grey to purplish grey. **Juvenile** blackish brown above, densely mottled with pale yellowish buff on back and wing-coverts; underparts (especially breast) heavily mottled greyish white and dark brown. Eyes dull brown; bill blackish; feet silvery blue-grey or dark purplish grey. **Voice**: Song short and clear, *twi-tew LEEtiew* or *wi-TEW-TWI-i-chew*. Also said to give a series of extended high notes on the same pitch, *ee, seebee ee hee-hee ee seebee hee lichee seabee* (Keith *et al.* 1992). Call note a short guttural *querr* or *wurr*. Alarm call a repeated nasal *jaanh*. **Habits**: Unobtrusive. Inhabits montane-forest undergrowth, often perching for long periods less than a metre above ground. Frequently attends ant swarms in company with other forest thrushes. **Similar Species**: Sharpe's Akalat is smaller, much brighter, with orange-buff underparts and greyish superciliary stripes. Juvenile White-starred Robin has black-and-yellow tail. **Status and Distribution**: Fairly common endemic resident of the West Usambara Mts in Tanzania, where restricted to montane forests between 1650 and 2300 m at Mazumbai, Shagayu and Shume. Locally common above 2000 m. **Note**: Formerly placed in *Alethe* (Mackworth-Praed and Grant 1955) and *Dryocichloides* (Britton 1980).

SHARPE'S AKALAT *Sheppardia sharpei usambarae* Plate 123

Length 120 mm (*c.* 5"). A robin-like bird of Tanzania's Usambara Mts. Duller and paler than Equatorial Akalat of w. Kenya, with *short pale grey superciliary stripes.* **Adult** plain brownish olive above, browner on upper tail-coverts and tail; *ear-coverts, sides of neck and underparts dull orange-buff;* belly white. Bill black; eyes dark brown; feet pale purplish grey or pinkish brown. **Juvenile** blackish above, with short buffy-orange streaks or spots; underparts buff, more orange on breast, scalloped with black or dark brown. **VOICE:** Song a tinkling warbler-like series, accelerating at end: *tee tu-wi tu-teetu-ti* or *tee, see see tuweee tuweeti.* Alarm call a more raspy chatter mixed with clear staccato notes. **HABITS:** Shy and skulking in open forest understorey. Forages on or near the ground, and occasionally follows ant columns. Emerges onto trails at dusk and dawn. **SIMILAR SPECIES:** Usambara Ground Robin behaves similarly, but is much duller, with longer tarsi and without orange-buff coloration. **STATUS AND DISTRIBUTION:** Fairly common forest resident from 900 to 1600 m in the East and West Usambara Mts. Descends as low as 600 m during cold periods in July and August.

EQUATORIAL AKALAT *Sheppardia a. aequatorialis* Plate 93

Length 120–130 mm (4.75–5"). A small robin-like bird of *west Kenyan highland forests.* **Adult** *grey on lores and around eyes,* olive-brown above, more *russet on rump, upper tail-coverts* and on edges of the brown tail feathers. *Underparts dull apricot-orange, white in centre of breast and belly;* sides of breast olive-brown or grey-brown. Concealed white supraocular feathers presumably used in display, as in *S. gunningi.* Eyes brown; bill black; feet purplish blue-grey. **Juvenile** dark brown and mottled with tawny above and below, white on centre of belly. **VOICE:** Usual note a soft *whit.* Alarm call a low rattling *grrrrrrr* or *prrer.* Easily overlooked song is a low quavering *erriyerrk* or *yeeerrrr,* repeated every one or two seconds, mournful, and slightly reminiscent of African Scops Owl's call. **HABITS:** Generally solitary, although several may gather at ant swarms. Shy and retiring; perches low and unobtrusively in shady undergrowth for long periods, but feeds on forest paths at dawn and dusk. **SIMILAR SPECIES:** Vagrant Forest Robin has prominent white loral spots, and bright orange-yellow confined to throat and breast. Juvenile Grey-winged Robin has tawny superciliary stripes (later becoming white), blue-grey 'shoulders' and plain tawny-orange tail. Sharpe's and East Coast Akalats are allopatric. **STATUS AND DISTRIBUTION:** Locally common resident between 1600 and 2200 m in wooded areas from Kakamega and Nandi Districts south to the Sotik, Kericho, Mau and Trans-Mara Forests. Formerly on Mt Elgon.

EAST COAST AKALAT *Sheppardia gunningi sokokensis* Plate 93
(Gunning's Robin)

Length 110–122 mm (4.5"). A *coastal-forest* bird. **Adult** olive-brown above, with *blue-grey lores, superciliary stripes and wing-coverts;* mostly *orange-yellow underparts* with white on belly, the orange flanks faintly washed with olive. Erectile white feathers above and in front of each eye usually concealed, but prominently exposed in displaying bird. Eyes brown; bill black; feet pinkish brown. **Juvenile** dark brown above and below, with tawny spotting; flanks pale yellowish. **VOICE:** Song of displaying male a clear rapid warbling, *uweela-uweela. . .* or *tureea-tureea-tureea,* with little change in pitch and lasting two or three seconds; repeated many times, the phrases sometimes run together as monotonous uniform warbling for a minute or more. A low, possibly vocal, *prrrt* accompanies flirting of wings and spreading of tail. **HABITS:** Shy and retiring. Conspicuous only in display, when male is vocal. Perches low in dense understorey of evergreen coastal forest. Feeds on or near ground, often with other species attending ant swarms. **SIMILAR SPECIES:** See allopatric Sharpe's and Equatorial Akalats. **STATUS AND DISTRIBUTION:** Fairly common in undergrowth of the Arabuko–Sokoke and East Usambara lowland forests. Also known from Shimoni, Shimba Hills, Rabai, and from gallery forest along the lower Tana River (from Garsen to Wenje). To date, no records from coastal Tanzania north of Dar es Salaam.

GREY-WINGED ROBIN *Sheppardia p. polioptera* Plate 93
(Grey-winged Ground Robin; Grey-winged Akalat)

Length 140–150 mm (5.5–6"). A western forest bird, with characters of both an akalat and a robin-chat. **Adult** resembles a small robin-chat, with *dark slate-grey crown* and *broken white superciliary stripes* underlined by blackish lores and narrow postocular patch; variable white supraloral spot near nostrils. Underparts orange-rufous, centre of belly white with heavy rufous wash. Upperparts largely olive-brown, contrasting noticeably with blue-grey wing-coverts; tail and upper tail-coverts *dark rufous.* **Juvenile** recalls adult Equatorial Akalat, with nearly plain *rufous-orange or orange-buff underparts, tawny or rufous superciliary stripes,* dark brown crown with fine rufous streaks, and largely *blue-grey wing-coverts,* some at first tipped with rufous, as are many head

feathers. Upperparts otherwise olive-brown with a few tawny or rufous spots, which soon disappear; rump and tail rufous. Long tarsi and toes pale pinkish purple. **Immature** resembles juvenile but has few or no light feather tips above, narrow (and often obscure) whitish superciliary stripes and black lores. **VOICE:** Usual calls a soft *chut*, and *kwik-kwik-kwik*. Songs include a rather soft, high-pitched *sureee-ta-twee-tuweee*, and a prolonged call in which each note is repeated: *tweet-tweet-tweet, turr-turr-turr, siweet-siyerrr, seet-seeet, titiur-titiur, turee-turee-turee. . ..* **HABITS:** A ground dweller. Adults shy and skulking, but young not timid and may feed in the open. Often forages along forest streams, probing in leaf litter, flicking leaves. Perches quietly on low branches, with semi-hunched posture, for extended periods. **SIMILAR SPECIES:** White-browed and Blue-shouldered Robin-Chats are larger, black-crowned, extensively black on sides of head, with longer superciliary stripes and brighter orange tail feathers. Equatorial Akalat readily confused with late juvenile/early immature, but lacks blue-grey on wing-coverts. **STATUS AND DISTRIBUTION:** Local and uncommon resident of forest undergrowth from 1250 to 2000 m in w. Kenya, from Mt Elgon, Kapenguria and Saiwa NP south to Kakamega (rare), Kaimosi, Nandi, Sotik and West Mau Forests; also in gallery forest at Rapogi, Lolgorien and along the Migori River. **NOTE:** Opinions continue to differ on the generic placement of this species. Plumage of juvenile, erectile supraocular tufts and unpatterned tail suggest that it is closer to *Sheppardia* than to *Cossypha*.

OLIVE-FLANKED ROBIN-CHAT *Cossypha anomala mbuluensis*   Plate 122
(Olive-flanked Ground Robin)

Length 140–145 mm (*c*. 5.5"). An atypical robin-chat of n. Tanzania's Mbulu Highlands. **Adult** blackish above, with *narrow white forehead band extending into long white superciliary stripes*; rump dull rufous-brown; upper tail-coverts and tail sides brighter orange-rufous, contrasting with blackish central rectrices and tail tip. *Throat white, breast and sides dark grey, flanks washed with olive-rufous* and *crissum orange-rufous.* Bill black; eyes dark brown; feet dark brown. **Juvenile** apparently undescribed. (That of *C. a. grotei* in the Ukaguru and Uluguru Mts is mottled and speckled dark brown and buff above and on breast; centre of belly and crissum nearly immaculate pale buff; upper tail-coverts buff or rufous. Tail pattern presumably like that of adult.) **VOICE:** Song described as a whistled *fe-FUUUUUR* (Keith *et al.* 1992) or a rich but mournful pair of notes, descending in pitch. Responds strongly to playback of its own voice, but not to those of related forms in the Uluguru and Mbeya mountains (R. Stjernstedt, pers. comm.). Alarm call a short, loud harsh note. **HABITS:** Solitary or in pairs. Forages on ground or low in vegetation. Flicks wings as it slowly raises and lowers the tail. Often attends ant swarms. **SIMILAR SPECIES:** Other robin-chats are rufous on the breast. **STATUS AND DISTRIBUTION:** Restricted in our region to the Nou Forest (4° 05′ S, 35° 30′ E) in the Mbulu Highlands of n. Tanzania.

RED-CAPPED ROBIN-CHAT *Cossypha natalensis*   Plate 92
(Natal Robin)

Length 155–175 mm (6–7"). A robin-chat with a *mainly rufous-orange head;* dark eyes conspicuous on the bright face. **Adult** *mostly bright orange-rufous,* with *slaty blue on back, scapulars and wings;* crown rufous (brighter in coastal birds) or indistinctly streaked with black; central tail feathers blackish. Bill black; eyes brown; feet pinkish brown. **Juvenile** mottled blackish and rufous above; underparts tawny, with dusky mottling. **VOICE:** Common call a slightly trilled, two-syllabled *prreep-prrup*, monotonously repeated. Alarm note a guttural *gurr*. Song a rich melodious whistling, often including much mimicry of other bird species: *twee tew, twee tew, chwe-witi-tew, tutu-tutu, tee-tew. . .* or a longer *tew-tew t'weetew, tsiwe-titi-tew, tutututu siweu, chidledew, ti-wew-weu-wew. . ..* **HABITS:** Highly vocal, but shy and skulking. When disturbed, often darts into low cover, flashing its orange-and-black tail. Forages on or near the ground, often joining mixed-species parties at ant columns. Jerks tail and flicks wings. Occasionally follows small mammals (e.g. elephant-shrews) for invertebrates that may be flushed. Bathes regularly in pools or water-filled hollows. **SIMILAR SPECIES:** Most other robin-chats have black and white on head; Grey-winged Robin has no black in tail. **STATUS AND DISTRIBUTION:** *C. n. intensa* is a common intra-African migrant from the southern tropics, late April to November, to wooded habitats in the coastal lowlands, and scattered inland localities in ne. Tanzania, w. Kenya, and gallery forest along the Tana River upstream to Garissa. *C. n. hylophona* breeds uncommonly in riverine forest and thickets in s. Kenya at Taveta, the Ngurumans, Mara GR, and Lolgorien and Rapogi Districts, with smaller isolated populations at Endau (Kitui District), Ngaia Forest (near Meru) and Uraguess (near Wamba). Movements of inland birds little known, particularly in n. Tanzania. Virtually absent from coastal areas between December and March.

RÜPPELL'S ROBIN-CHAT *Cossypha semirufa*   **Plate 92**

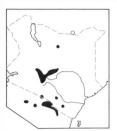

Length 180–185 mm (7"). A *highland-forest* species closely resembling the more wide-spread White-browed Robin-Chat, with black top and sides of head, prominent long white superciliary stripes, and orange-rufous underparts, rump and outer tail feathers. *Central tail feathers blackish, not light brown*; back, scapulars and wings dark slate-grey; superciliary stripes slightly narrower than in White-browed Robin-Chat. Bill black; eyes brown; feet dark brown. Northern nominate race is smaller, and more olive and less slaty above, than the widespread *C. s. intercedens.* **Juvenile** similar in pattern, but superciliary stripes absent or faint, and with black scalloping (often dense) on under-parts, back and scapulars; crown marked with pale olive speckling and rufous streaks; wing-coverts rufous-spotted. **Voice:** Variable but distinctive song consists of repeated loud whistles; mimics a remarkable range of bird species and other sounds, also persis-tently repeats a three-note phrase with a somewhat rolling accented initial sound: *rrrri-pru-ru, rrrri-pru-ru, rrri-pru-ru. . ..* Alarm a guttural *rack-k-k-k.* **Habits:** Rather shy and skulking, foraging among ground vegetation and leaf litter. Highly vocal in late evening, when it often feeds on open paths and clearings. Pugnacious, chasing other birds from feeders and bathing spots. **Similar Species:** White-browed Robin-Chat, compared above. Cape Robin-Chat is duller, grey from breast to belly. **Status and Distribution:** Common resident of highland forest, forest edge, riverine thickets and wooded suburban gardens from 1400 to 2300 m. *C. s. semirufa* is known from high forest on Mt Marsabit and near Moyale. Southern *C. s. intercedens* ranges widely in the cent. Kenyan high-lands east of the Rift Valley south to Ol Doinyo Orok (Namanga Hill), the Chyulu and Taita Hills, and in n. Tanzania at Longido, the Crater Highlands, Arusha NP, Mt Meru, Kilimanjaro and the Pare Mountains.

WHITE-BROWED ROBIN-CHAT *Cossypha heuglini*   **Plate 92**
(Heuglin's Robin)

Length 190–200 mm (7.5–8"). The most widespread East African robin-chat. **Adults** strikingly coloured, with black top and sides of head separated by *long white supercil-iary stripes.* Back brownish olive, scapulars dark olive-grey; wing-coverts dark blue-grey; rump and upper tail-coverts rufous. Underparts and tail orange-rufous, except for *light brown central rectrices.* Bill black; eyes dark brown; feet pinkish brown. **Juvenile** mottled and scalloped tawny and black above, with rufous spots on crown and large tawny spots on wing-coverts; superciliary stripes indistinct. Underparts rufous, scal-loped with black. **Voice:** A harsh *tserk-tserk* of alarm. Song an extended variable series of repeated rich, melodious, whistled phrases, starting softly but markedly increasing in volume, each repetition louder and more rapidly uttered than the previous one *pwirri-pi-pirrr, Pwirri-Pi-Pirrr, PWIRRI-PI-PIRRR. . .,* or *oodle-teedle-teedle, OODLE-TEEDLE-TEEDLE, OODLE-TEEDLE-TEEDLE. . .,* or *we-KEEa, WEKEEa, WEKEEA . . .,* mostly at dawn and dusk. Members of a pair duet or sing antiphonally, the female giving a high-pitched *seeeeet*; sometimes the pair together chat-ters *tickety-tickety-tickety* or *CHUCKitee CHUCKitee CHUCKitee.* Less of a mimic than Rüppell's Robin-Chat. **Habits:** Highly vocal and retiring, sometimes shy, but tame and confiding in gardens with dense shrubbery. Feeds on ground, often in exposed areas, and sings from both low and high perches. **Similar Species:** Rüppell's Robin-Chat, more of a forest species, has darker, slatier back, darker slaty-black wings and blackish central tail feathers. Cape Robin-Chat is smaller, and largely grey below. **Status and Distribution:** Common in acacia and riverine woodland, moist thickets, secondary growth, gardens, and forest edge. Avoids arid country and many highland areas occupied by Rüppell's Robin-Chat. Nominate *heuglini* ranges from the Mbulu Highlands and the Oldeani District of n. Tanzania west to Serengeti NP and Lake Victoria, and east to Lake Manyara and Tarangire NPs; also over much of western and central Kenya north to Mts Loima, Marsabit and Nyiru and the Mathews Range. The smaller *C. h.intermedia* inhabits coastal lowlands north to the Boni Forest, inland along the Tana River to Garissa; also to Rombo and the Usambara foothills. Formerly along the Voi and Galana Rivers.

BLUE-SHOULDERED ROBIN-CHAT *Cossypha cyanocampter bartteloti*   **Plate 92**

Length 150–160 mm (*c.* 6"). A small, extraordinarily skulking robin-chat of *west Kenyan forests.* **Adult** head pattern recalls White-browed Robin-Chat, with long white supercil-iary stripes extending to nape. Back and wings dark, slate-grey with *bright blue 'shoul-der' patches* (sometimes largely concealed); *rump buffy olive*; upper tail-coverts orange-rufous, as are the sides of the tail; central rectrices and outer edge of outermost pair black. *Underparts rich tawny-buff*, darker on flanks; white in centre of belly. Bill black; eyes dark brown; feet brownish grey. **Juvenile** mottled tawny and blackish above, the crown and wings rufous-spotted; underparts pale tawny, with black markings on breast. **Voice:** Common call a guttural dry croaking. Sustained song of low chuckling and clear whistles, each note or phrase tending to be repeated several times; may begin with slow rising whistles, followed by louder and softer phrases, *chreek chreek WUKERI-TEW-TEW-TEW, chick-chick-chuck-chuck chi-chew WHI-WHEW WEE-WHEW, WIKIYEW WIKIYEW tootoo-wee-wee, weetu weetu-weetu. . ..* Other songs entirely of melodious clear whistles, *wee-tee-tee-tee, tu-tee-tu, tooi-tooi-tooi. . ..* A remarkable mimic of other birds and human whistling. **Habits:** Very shy. Forages near and on the

ground in forest undergrowth; seldom leaves dense cover. Most vocal at dawn and dusk. **SIMILAR SPECIES**: White-browed Robin-Chat avoids deep forest, lacks blue 'shoulder' patches, and orange-rufous outer tail feathers lack black edges. **STATUS AND DISTRIBUTION**: Local and rather uncommon resident between 1500 and 2000 m in the Kakamega, Kaimosi and Nandi Forests of w. Kenya. Formerly on Mt Elgon.

SNOWY-HEADED ROBIN-CHAT *Cossypha niveicapilla melanota*   Plate 92
(Snowy-crowned Robin-Chat)

Length 205–220 mm (8–8.75″). A *large, black-backed, white-capped* robin-chat of *western Kenya*. **Adult** has forehead and sides of head black, a broad white patch from crown to upper nape, separated from the back by an *orange-rufous collar* (more distinct than in other robin-chats). Entire underparts, rump, and most of tail orange-rufous; back, scapulars, wings, *central rectrices (and outer webs of outer pair) jet-black*. Bill black; eyes dark brown; feet dark brown. **Juvenile** lacks white on head, has the crown brownish and densely speckled with rufous; back mottled dark brown and rufous; rump and tail as in adult, but central rectrices dark brown; underparts rufous (paler on throat), scalloped with dark brown. **VOICE**: Contact call a whistled *wheeeeo-wheeeeo-wheeeeo*. Song a loud, sustained, rapidly delivered mimicking of numerous bird species (and other sounds) interspersed with powerful whistles. Alarm note a low *churrr*.

HABITS: Those of other robin-chats. Skulks in undergrowth; feeds mainly on or near ground, but may sing from treetops. Active and highly vocal at dusk. **SIMILAR SPECIES**: White-browed Robin-Chat has different head pattern, and back and central tail feathers are dark olive-grey or olive-brown. **STATUS AND DISTRIBUTION**: Fairly common local resident of remnant forest patches and moist streamside thickets, mainly between 1500 and 2000 m. Ranges from Mt Elgon, Kapenguria and Saiwa NP south along the Kenyan/Ugandan border to the Lake Victoria basin, South Nyanza and Lolgorien; east to Kakamega, Nandi Hills, Kericho and Sotik Districts, and the Mau and Trans-Mara Forests.

CAPE ROBIN-CHAT *Cossypha caffra iolaema*   Plate 92
(Robin Chat; Cape Robin)

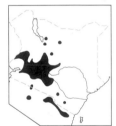

Length 160–170 mm (*c.* 6.5″). A small, *grey-bellied* robin-chat of highland gardens and forest edge. *Tawny-orange throat and breast* of adult contrast with *pale grey flanks and belly*; short white superciliary stripes separate dark grey crown from black sides of face. Back, scapulars and wings olive-grey; rump and tail rufous, the latter with brown central feathers. **Juvenile** brown above, with tawny-buff spots and streaks; underparts buff, scalloped with black. **VOICE**: Alarm call a low *turr-da-da*. Anxiety note a plaintive descending *peeeeuu*. Song a series of whistled phrases, repetitive and halting: *teeu-cheeo. . . cheeo-tu-teeo. . . teeo-teeo-tu-weeoo. . ..* Mimics other species. **HABITS**: Forages in the open, on the ground; in many places tame and confiding. Also gleans bark and foliage in tall trees. Commonly parasitized by Red-chested Cuckoo. **SIMILAR SPECIES**: Other sympatric robin-chats have entirely orange-rufous underparts. **STATUS AND DISTRIBUTION**: Common resident between 1500 and 3000 m or higher in towns, villages, suburban gardens, tea and coffee plantations and wooded habitats. Ranges from Mt Nyiru, Mt Kulal, and the Mathews Range, Karissia Hills, Cheranganis and Mt Elgon, south through the w. and cent. Kenyan highlands to the Chyulu and Taita Hills, Morijo, Loliondo, the Crater Highlands, Arusha and Moshi Districts, Kilimanjaro, the Pare Mts and West Usambaras. Particularly common in Nairobi suburbs. Does not extend east of longitude 38° except in the Taita Hills and West Usambaras.

BROWN-CHESTED ALETHE *Alethe poliocephala*   Plate 90

Length 145–155 mm (*c.* 6″). A long-legged, short-tailed forest thrush. **Adult** mainly dark chestnut-brown above, the dusky head marked by *whitish superciliary stripes*. Underparts dingy white, with *grey-brown breast band and flanks and a white throat*. Head dusky, with blackish area around eyes. Tail dark brown. Eyes red-brown; bill black; long tarsi and toes pale whitish pink. The central highland race *akeleyae* is larger, duller and greyer about the face than western *carruthersi*. **Juvenile** blackish brown above, heavily spotted with dull orange; breast buff and white with black scalloped markings, otherwise greyish white below. Eyes brown; bill dusky brown, yellowish at base of mandible; feet pinkish white. **Immature** closely resembles adult, but is duller and often retains some orange spots on upperparts. **VOICE**: Note a hollow *keu*, repeated at intervals; also a repeated double call, *tseeeep tyerrrr*, the first note higher and thinner, the second descending. Song of soft, widely separated minor-key single notes alternating with a double one: *pew. . . . .pew-pee. . . . . pee. . . . . tew-tee. . . . . pee. . . . . pew-pee. . .* Less often gives four to eight mournful minor-key whistles, descending and accelerating, *pee pee pee pee pee-pee. . ..* Utters a rough *chaggh* around ant swarms, and an ascending *schleeee*. **HABITS**: A shy skulking bird of forest floor and undergrowth; regularly attends ant columns; frequently appears on forest paths at dawn, dusk and after rains. **SIMILAR SPECIES**: In some

areas, sympatric *Illadopsis* species have similar habits, but are slightly smaller, less sharply patterned, lack white superciliary stripes and tend to be more secretive. **STATUS AND DISTRIBUTION**: Widely distributed resident of Kenyan forest undergrowth at medium to high elevations. *A. p. carruthersi* (includes '*nandensis*') is fairly common west of the Rift Valley, from Mt Elgon and Saiwa NP south to Kakamega, Nandi, West Mau and Trans-Mara Forests; *akeleyae* is scarce in the central highlands from the Ngaia Forest, Nyambenis, and the Meru and Embu Forests south to Kieni, Gatamayu and Kiambu District. Formerly in Nairobi suburbs (last record a nesting pair in 1976).

WHITE-CHESTED ALETHE *Alethe fuelleborni* Plate 123

Length 170 mm (6.75″). A dark-backed, *white-bellied,* terrestrial thrush of *Tanzanian mountain forests. Face dark brown, tinged grey above the eyes.* **Adult** mostly dark olive-brown to chestnut-brown above, becoming dark rufous on rump and upper tail-coverts; tail chestnut. Central underparts white, bordered with *dark grey from neck to flanks.* Variable grey feather tips (usually faint) make breast appear somewhat scaly. Bill black; eyes red-brown; feet pale greyish pink. **Juvenile** marked above with tawny-orange spots, these more streaky on head, and black feather tips; entire *underparts appear scaly, with blackish feather margins* and orange mottling; flanks greyish orange; under tail-coverts pale orange. **VOICE**: Common call a loud, somewhat buzzy, ascending *zhurreeee* or more whistled, upslurred *querrrrr-quiiiiiii*; sometimes a shorter, faster *yerr-terwii.* Such phrases may also initiate the song, a variety of whistled notes. Also gives a penetrating whistled note, *wheeu*; alarm call a rattling *skreeee.* **HABITS**: Shy and elusive, remaining near ground in thick forest understorey. Attends ant swarms and joins mixed-species flocks, often displaying aggression towards smaller forest thrushes in the same aggregations. Flicks wings and tail when alarmed. **SIMILAR SPECIES**: Pale-breasted Illadopsis is much smaller and has grey underparts. **STATUS AND DISTRIBUTION**: Common resident of forest undergrowth between 500 and 2200 m in the Usambara Mts. Some birds may disperse lower during the July–August cold season. One record from the South Pare Mts (Feb. 1960). **NOTE**: We follow Keith *et al.* (1992) in considering this species as monotypic.

RED-TAILED ANT THRUSH *Neocossyphus r. rufus* Plate 91

Length 220–225 mm (8.5″). A plain, uniformly coloured thrush of coastal forests. **Adult** warm brown on head and back, otherwise rufous; central rectrices darker. Eyes brown; bill blackish; feet pale purplish. **Juvenile** resembles adult, but duller and more olive-brown above, more tawny-olive below. **VOICE:** Common call a descending sibilant, mournful *peeeyew* or *twit-teeeyew*, sometimes more elaborate: *tsip-wi-wheeeer* or *seeyew-peeeyew*, repeated frequently. Song consists of these notes followed by a long descending trill, accelerating and dropping in pitch. Gives a trilling *chrrrr-chrrrr* call around ant swarms. **HABITS**: Shy and skulking; more often heard than seen. Forages on ground among leaf litter, sometimes in small groups. Before dawn and at dusk, leaves forest cover to feed along sandy roads and paths. Regularly follows ant columns, perching on stumps and low branches above the insect swarm and uttering its dry trills; dominates other attendant species. **SIMILAR SPECIES**: Brownbuls and Fischer's Greenbul are brown above and show a reddish tail, but are smaller, slimmer, and lack rufous underparts. **STATUS AND DISTRIBUTION**: Fairly common resident of lower and middle levels of coastal forest and woodland north to the Boni Forest, inland along the lower Tana River to Bura, the Shimba Hills and up to 950 m in the East Usambara Mts.

WHITE-TAILED ANT THRUSH *Neocossyphus poensis praepectoralis* Plate 91

Length 200 mm (8″). A dark, west Kenyan forest thrush with *large white tail corners* and a *broad rufous stripe across the primaries noticeable as the bird flies away.* Upperparts generally sooty brown, paler on throat and upper breast; rest of underparts dull rufous. Eyes brown; bill black; feet pinkish-flesh colour. **Juvenile** undescribed. **VOICE**: Usual call a one-second-long, shrill, ascending whistle, *weeeeeeeeeeet* or *wurrreeeeeeet*, repeated frequently. Alarm note, a sharp *sip-sip*, and also a low sharp *prrt-prrt* when flushed or in excitement. Seldom-heard song rich and *Turdus*-like, *wurreeet t'ree ueeeeeet. . ..* **HABITS**: Secretive, but feeds on forest paths and bathes in roadside rain-pools at dusk and dawn. Sometimes sings from 10–15 m high in tree. Flicks tail when alarmed. Regularly attends ant swarms. **SIMILAR SPECIES**: Sympatric Brown-chested Alethe has shorter tail lacking white corners. **STATUS AND DISTRIBUTION**: Local and uncommon resident between 1700 and 1900 m in the Kakamega and Nandi Forests of w. Kenya. **NOTE**: Kenyan (and Ugandan) birds are decidedly variable; we do not recognize the races *kakamegoes* and *nigridorsalis.*

SPOTTED MORNING THRUSH *Cichladusa guttata*   Plate 92
(Spotted Morning Warbler; Spotted Palm Thrush)

Length 160–170 mm (6.5"). A slim spotted thrush of scrub and thicket, *rufous-brown* above with a *bright rufous tail*, conspicuous as the bird dashes into cover. **Adult** buffy white to pale buff below, with *large black spots* surrounding throat and extending down flanks; shows small white superciliary stripes. Eyes brown; bill and feet black. Nominate *guttata*, in nw. Kenya, is paler and duller, more whitish below, than the darker, more richly coloured and heavily spotted *intercalans*. Coastal *rufipennis* is smaller, paler buff below, and with smaller spots. **Juvenile** resembles adult, but has smaller, browner spots and is more streaked on throat and chin. **Voice:** Usual varied song consists of powerful clear whistled phrases, often introduced with a chuckling sound, and including mimicry of other species. Less complex song may begin with a penetratingly loud, descending whistle, *EEEEEEEEU. . .* or shorter *ee-eu*, repeated several times and leading into groups of simple notes, e.g. *ee-eu ee-eu ee-eu kewi-kewi-kewi, EEEEEEEU. . . tweedle-tweedle-tweedle. . ..* A characteristic low call, *PEE-u-priri-PEEEu*, is given at all times of day, as is the harsh scolding *chaaaaa* or *skurrrr* of alarm. Prolonged, near-perfect imitations of Greater Honeyguide and other species are frequent. **Habits:** Retiring. Skulks in shrubbery and dense thickets, but becomes confiding around game-park lodges and in gardens, where it forages in the open. Feeds entirely on the ground, singly or in pairs, with much flicking of wings and raising of tail. **Similar Species:** Scrub robins have more prominent superciliary stripes, wing-bars and black-and-white tail tips. See Collared Palm Thrush. **Status and Distribution:** Common resident of thickets and dense bush below 1600 m, especially along dry watercourses. Widespread north, east and south of the Kenyan highlands, but absent from the southwest and Lake Victoria basin. Three races: northwestern *C. g. guttata* from Lokichokio and Turkana District (west of the lake) south to Kongelai, Kerio Valley and Baringo District; *intercalans* southeast of Lake Turkana, from the Horr Valley, the Ndotos, Samburu and Shaba GRs, Meru NP and Kora NR south to Athi River, Olorgesailie, Kajiado, Amboseli and the Tsavo NPs and, in n. Tanzania, at Longido and Lake Natron, the Masai Steppe region, Pare foothills, Lake Manyara and Tarangire NPs and Mkomazi GR. Coastal *C.g. rufipennis* is rare or absent south of Malindi (where more or less replaced by *C. arquata*).

COLLARED PALM THRUSH *Cichladusa arquata*   Plate 92
(Morning Warbler)

Length 175–180 mm (7"). A *pale-eyed coastal* thrush typically asociated with *palm groves*. **Adult** has a diagnostic *narrow black band outlining the pale buff throat and upper breast*. Upperparts warm rusty brown, more rufous on *rump, tail and wings*. Face, neck and sides of breast grey, underparts otherwise tawny, shading to rufous-buff on under tail-coverts. Eyes whitish or pale yellow; bill black; feet brown or grey. **Juvenile** *lacks black throat border*, is mottled with blackish above and with brown below, streaked on crown and nape; eyes brown. **Voice:** Call a piping *weet-weet*; alarm note a shrill *preee*; also a chatter. Song a medley of melodious whistled phrases and harsh scratchy notes, including mimicry of other birds. **Habits:** Forages in pairs or small groups on and near the ground, in and around riparian thickets; typically associated with *Borassus* palm savannas, where it often sings from high perches. Hops about with the long tail elevated, and slowly pumps it up and down while flicking the wings. Nests in palm or dense shrub, sometimes under eaves of buildings. **Similar Species:** Spotted Morning Thrush is spotted below, lacks black throat border, has dark eyes. **Status and Distribution:** Local resident in coastal lowlands north to Lamu, inland to the Shimba Hills, Mariakani and along the lower Tana River to Wenje. Fairly common on Kenyan coast south of Gazi.

NIGHTINGALE *Luscinia megarhynchos*   Plate 93

Length 160–170 mm (c. 6.5"). A skulking brown thrush with a *rufous tail, rufous-tinged rump* and rather plain head. Breast and flanks pale greyish brown; rest of underparts whitish. **Adult** *L. m. africana* is rich brown above, with slight rufous tinge on head; the larger *hafizi* is paler, with greyer-brown back contrasting with bright rufous rump and tail; darker eye-lines more distinct. **First-winter** bird resembles adult, but usually shows buff wing-covert tips. **Voice:** A plaintive *whet*, a hard *tucc*, and a grating *krrr*. Loud rich song (commonly heard Dec.–March) consists of repeated phrases such as *cheoo-cheoo-cheoo. . ., jugg-jugg-jugg. . .* and *pichu-pichu-chipuchi;* may be preceded by an introductory whistled crescendo, *whee-WHEE-WHEE.* **Habits:** Mainly solitary. Shy and secretive. Feeds on the ground in dense cover, hopping with drooped wings; cocks tail and flicks wings when excited. Active and vocal at dusk and dawn, and may sing from low perch throughout morning hours. **Similar Species:** Sprosser is darker and shorter-tailed, safely distinguished only by darker, faintly mottled breast and noticeable malar stripes, or by song (in the hand, by more pointed wing and smaller outer primary; see Fig. p. 541). **Status and Distribution:** Palearctic migrant, November–March, typical of leafy scrub, green bush and woodland thickets below 1800 m, mainly in cent. and se. Kenya, including the coastal lowlands; also in ne. Tanzania from Lake Manyara NP, Babati, Arusha, Moshi and Tanga Districts.

Locally common to abundant, especially along watercourses. Marked passage in November. Uncommon west of the Rift Valley. Most inland birds are *africana*, but *hafizi* predominates in coastal lowlands. Small numbers in the Lake Victoria basin and Nyanza are probably nominate *megarhynchos* (known from Uganda, but not yet collected in Kenya).

SPROSSER or THRUSH-NIGHTINGALE *Luscinia luscinia*   Plate 93

Length 160–165 mm (6.5"). Slightly darker above than Nightingale, and the *greyish-brown breast has variable amounts of dark mottling*; whitish chin and throat bordered by dark malar stripes; centre of belly whitish. Dark rufous-brown tail contrasts less with back than in Nightingale. Tarsus colour varies from pinkish to dark grey-brown. **First-winter** bird resembles adult, but usually has small buff tips to greater coverts. **VOICE:** A high-pitched whistling *wheet*, especially at dawn; a dry, harsh croaking *kh-krrrrrk*, and a quieter *tuc*. Rich and powerful song (regularly heard in Kenya) includes whistles, harsh grating sounds, and a loud *chook-chook-chook;* is less liquid, with more guttural notes than Nightingale's song, the phrases more poorly defined and without the introductory crescendo. **HABITS:** A skulker, much like Nightingale but generally more approachable. Feeds mainly on the ground, often raising, spreading or flicking tail from side to side. Birds on autumn passage commonly occupy territories for two weeks or more. **SIMILAR SPECIES:** Nightingale compared above. Female Common Redstart is slimmer, paler brown above, has dark central tail feathers and is more arboreal. Red-tailed Chat has blackish tail centre and tip, shows narrow pale eye-ring. **STATUS AND DISTRIBUTION:** Palearctic migrant, widespread and common to abundant east of the Rift Valley on southward passage (over 31,000 ringed Nov.–Dec. in Tsavo West NP, 1969–95). Less numerous from late March to mid-April, when sometimes along the coast. Winters locally inland in se. Kenya and Mkomazi GR in moist bush and woodland undergrowth. Scarce in and west of the Rift Valley, where recorded sporadically in autumn.

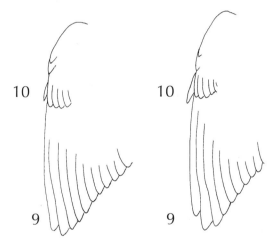

Wing outlines of Sprosser or Thrush-Nightingale, (left) and Nightingale, (right). Note size of 10th primary and position of 9th primary tip.

WHITE-BROWED SCRUB ROBIN *Cercotrichas leucophrys*   Plate 92

Length 140–165 mm (5.5–6.5"). A common, brightly patterned chat of bush and scrub. **Adult** shows pronounced *white superciliary stripes* and a *rufous tail with black subterminal band and white corners.* Underparts are whitish, with streaks on throat and breast. Two groups of subspecies. 'Red-backed' *zambesiana*, *brunneiceps* and *sclateri* are warm brown to brownish olive above, more rufous on rump and darker on head, the breast streaks blackish and distinct: *zambesiana* shows two white wing-bars, whereas *brunneiceps* has both wing-bars and white-edged inner secondaries; *sclateri* is similar to *brunneiceps* but smaller, with more tawny-brown back and paler streaks. 'White-winged' *vulpina*, *leucoptera* and the paler *eluta*, birds of more arid country, are rufous above, with pale grey-brown head, and have greyish, less distinct breast streaking; broad wing-covert and secondary edges form a large white wing patch. Sexes alike. **Juvenile** mottled black and tawny; tail pattern as in adult. **VOICE:** Alarm note, a sharp *skirr* or *skee-ip*, sometimes extended. Songs loud, variable and highly repetitive, generally shriller in white-winged races, which sing one phrase indefinitely with no variation, e.g. the *sweet-sweet-sweet-siaweet-sweet* or *wureet see-titi-yew* of *C. l. leucoptera*. *C. l. vulpina* has similar short songs such as *suree-sweet chew chew. ..* , but also more varied, often

longer medleys of slurred whistles and shrill piping notes: (1) *sieu pee-pee-pee-pee*, (2) *sieut-swit-chruree peee-pee-pee-pee*, (3) *tee-twee-tweeo, teet-wet-weo-twer, see-see-seeutwer, tchwee-tchweeo* . . .. Also characteristic of *vulpina* are somewhat chattering or rattlings songs, e.g. *churee chi-chi-chichcichichichi* and *tsuree tsi-tsi-tsi-tsi-tsi-tsi*. Red-backed *C. l. zambesiana* repeats clear slurred whistles interspersed with other notes: *siureeet-sreet-swureet-cheet*; sometimes a more rhythmic but equally repetitive *see-surEET, see-surEET* . . . or *t'weeoTWEET, t'weeoTWEET*. . .. *C. l. brunneiceps* gives loud monotonous whistled songs such as (1) *tee-tew t'pee* or *ch'wee tew tuwee*. .. , (2) *werra-weeo, werra-weeo*. . . *werr-wi-weeo, werr-wi-weeo*. . .., *ureet-reet-reet*, changing after countless repetitions to *ureet-tulee*. . .; it also sings a slurred, almost *Turdus*-like *slureet sreet turr chichichi*. **HABITS**: Shy and restless. Spends much time on ground, where it normally hops when foraging, but may run rapidly if disturbed. Raises and fans tail over back and droops wings. Sings from near tops of shrubs or well concealed within. **SIMILAR SPECIES**: Brown-backed Scrub Robin has similar pattern, but is dark brown above, rufous only on rump and tail, and with broader black tail band. Rufous Bush Chat lacks white in wings. **STATUS AND DISTRIBUTION**: Common and widespread resident of bush and scrub, mainly below 1500 m. Despite some intergradation (apparently known only between *brunneiceps* and *vulpina* around Simba), the three 'red-backed' and three 'white-winged' races are largely separated ecologically, the latter in drier country. Red-backed *zambesiana* ranges west and south of the Kenyan highlands and through Tanzania's Lake Victoria and Mara regions to Serengeti NP, also in coastal lowlands from Mombasa north to the Tana delta; *brunneiceps* in s. Kenya at Naivasha, from west of Nairobi southeast to Emali, Sultan Hamud and Machakos, and along the Rift Valley into n. Tanzania at Lake Natron, plus the Crater Highlands and areas west of Kilimanjaro and Mt Meru; *sclateri* in Tanzania, from the Mbulu Highlands east to Tarangire NP and Lolkissale. White-winged *leucoptera* ranges across much of n. Kenya south to the Kerio Valley, Samburu GR, Lake Baringo, Meru NP, Embu and Magadi; *eluta* in extreme ne. Kenya and Somali border areas south to the Tana River; *vulpina* in dry interior se. Kenya, including the Tsavo NPs and Taita District south to lowlands east and south of Kilimanjaro. **NOTE**: This and the following three species are frequently placed in the genus *Erythropygia*.

BROWN-BACKED SCRUB ROBIN *Cercotrichas hartlaubi*   Plate 92

Length 150 mm (6"). A *highland* scrub robin, similar in size and habits to the preceding species, but *dark brown above*, with *rufous rump and tail base, broad blackish terminal tail band* and white tips to all but central tail feathers; bold white superciliary stripes and wing-bars. **Adult** greyish buff below, with faint breast streaks. **Juvenile** similar, but mottled on crown and breast and with buff superciliaries. **VOICE**: Song loud, cheerful and protracted, including clear whistled notes, e.g. (1) *pripri-weeoo-wee-oo-wi-wee-oo*. . ., (2) *weet wurdleyu EE-tsee*, (3) *s'weet s'weet suree-EU*, or shortened to (4) *trrreee-EU*. Any of these phrases may be repeated many times with little variation. Some songs are of simpler phrases, in which members of a pair may duet. **HABITS**: As for preceding species. **SIMILAR SPECIES**: 'Red-backed' races of White-browed Scrub Robin have more distinct breast streaking, mainly rufous tail, and paler, brighter brown back. **STATUS AND DISTRIBUTION**: Uncommon local resident of shrubby thickets, riverine woods, gardens and forest edges in the Kenyan highlands, between 1500 and 2200 m, from Mt Elgon, Kakamega, Nandi and West Mau east to Naro Moru, Meru, Embu, Thika, Kiambu and Nairobi Districts.

EASTERN BEARDED SCRUB ROBIN *Cercotrichas q. quadrivirgata*   Plate 92
(Bearded Robin)

Length 140–165 mm (5.5–6.5"). An *eastern* scrub robin with *striking black-and-white face pattern*: broad white superciliary stripes bordered by black above and below, brown crown and ear-coverts, black moustachial and malar stripes. Breast band and flanks tawny; belly and under tail-coverts white; *tail black, white-tipped except for central feathers*; wings grey and black, with small white patch on primary coverts and another at base of primaries. **Juvenile** mottled black and tawny above and on breast. **VOICE**: Call note a loud *chuk*; alarm call *chuk-churrr* or *chak-chak-chizzzzz*. Song sustained and varied, of whistled notes repeated to form musical phrases sometimes lasting many minutes and often preceded by three slow whistles, *whee, yeeu, weee*. Songs may be delivered slowly with significant pauses between phrases, *wurk-wurk*. . . *oodle-ee-EE-oo*. . . *churrchurr*. . . *wurkilee-ee-ee*. . .*wurkelee-eeo-eeo*. . .. Others are faster, the phrases run together and less melodious: *tsee-chiu wit-wi, twe-twe-twe, witu-witu, chiu-chiu, t-t-t-teeu, weet chrrrr weet chickitseet* . . .. **HABITS**: Shy and secretive. Feeds on the ground, usually within dense cover. Sings from concealed perch in undergrowth, less often from high in tree. Somewhat crepuscular. **STATUS AND DISTRIBUTION**: Common resident of dense moist thickets, shrubby woodland, forest undergrowth and gardens in the coastal lowlands north to the Boni Forest; inland along the lower and middle Tana River to Garissa, at Ngaia Forest (near Meru), Mt Endau, Kibwezi and Kitovu Forests, and the North Pare Mts. Two specimens collected west of Lake Manyara were described as *C. q. brunnea* (Ripley and Heinrich 1966). Reported presence in Tarangire NP requires confirmation. Formerly along the Voi and Galana Rivers.

RUFOUS BUSH CHAT *Cercotrichas galactotes*   **Plate 92**
(Rufous Scrub Robin)

Length 150 mm (6"). A migrant species, differing from resident scrub robins in having *no white in the wings*. Mostly plain grey-brown or buffy brown above, rufous on rump and upper tail-coverts, with pale buff superciliary stripes and dark eye-lines. Underparts light buff, whitish on belly in *C. g. familiaris*. Long graduated *rufous tail boldly tipped black and white*, frequently fanned and cocked over the back. *C. g. syriacus* is slightly darker, less grey-toned above than *familiaris*. **Voice**: A sibilant *sseeeep* and a squeaky double *si-sip*. The sweet warbling song apparently is not sung in East Africa. **Habits**: Feeds on the ground, frequently perching on fallen dead branches in or near shrub cover. Habitually moves tail up and down, and cocks it far forward, often spread, while drooping the wings. **Similar Species**: White-browed Scrub Robin, with similar tail pattern and in the same habitat, has white on wings and streaks on breast. **Status and Distribution**: Palearctic migrant, November to early April, widespread and common in coastal scrub and dry bush below 1000 m in the east; more local in n. Kenya, south to Baringo and Samburu GR. A regular passage migrant (Nov.) in Tsavo West NP and the Chyulu Hills, but fewer than five records from ne. Tanzania. Most birds apparently *C. g. familiaris*.

IRANIA or WHITE-THROATED ROBIN *Irania gutturalis*   **Plate 93**
(Persian Robin)

Length 150–170 mm (6–6.75"). A handsome migratory thrush of dry bushland thickets. **Male** readily identified by *white throat and superciliary stripes* contrasting with *black cheeks*, dark grey upperparts and *black tail*. Breast, flanks and wing-linings rufous-orange to pale cinnamon; belly and under tail-coverts white. Eyes brown; bill and feet blackish. **Female** has black tail but is brownish grey above, with plain greyish head, mottled grey-brown breast and *orange-buff flanks and wing-linings*. **First-winter** bird resembles adult female, but has whitish spots on greater coverts; adult body plumage acquired in December. **Voice**: A grating *krrrk* call. Sings a warbling subsong, and occasionally, from January onward, a distinctive long song of fluty whistles and scratchy, chattering or slurred notes, portions almost parrot-like in quality: *skwee-churrilee-cheek-cheek-cheek-chur-skweeilew-chur-chur-chur, skwer skweeereri-tsik-tsik tsi-tsi-tsi. . ..* **Habits**: Solitary or in loose groups. Shy; skulks in dense cover; spends much time on and near ground. Often cocks tail above back, droops wings; in alarm, stretches upward, slowly raising and lowering tail. **Similar Species**: Other small thrushes with white superciliary stripes and/or rufous-orange on underparts have brown or rufous tails. **Status and Distribution**: Locally common palearctic migrant, November to early April, in dry thickets and scrub, often along gullies and watercourses. Winters mainly in areas dominated by *Acacia* and *Commiphora* north and east of the Kenyan highlands, from Isiolo and Meru Districts south through Kitui, Tsavo NPs and Taita District. Few records west of the Rift Valley, but in n. Tanzania small numbers winter in Serengeti, Lake Manyara and Tarangire NPs, Olduvai Gorge and the Masai Steppe region. Marked southward passage (Nov./Dec.) through Tsavo West NP.

COMMON REDSTART *Phoenicurus p. phoenicurus*   **Plates 90, 93**
(Eurasian Redstart)

Length 140 mm (5.5"). A slim, robin-like bird, both sexes with *bright chestnut tail* with darker central feathers. **Adult male** grey above, with striking *black face and throat*, the feathers white-tipped when fresh; broad white stripe from forehead to above eye obscured by grey feather tips in fresh autumn plumage. Breast bright chestnut, belly whitish. **Female** much duller, with pale eye-ring and brownish ear-coverts; otherwise uniform brown on head and upperparts, and buffy brown below. **First-winter male** has adult pattern largely obscured by buffy-white feather tips. **Voice**: A high liquid *tic* or *quick* and a thin plaintive *hweet*, the two sometimes run together, *whit-tic-tic*. Song a short squeaky warbling ending in a mechanical trill, rarely heard in East Africa. **Habits**: Solitary; rather shy; perches low in trees or in bushes. Active, with characteristic tail-shivering. Feeds partly on the ground, but also makes flycatching sorties. **Similar Species**: Red-tailed Chat resembles female Redstart, but is stockier, darker and greyer, with blackish band across tail tip; flicks wings frequently. **Status and Distribution**: Palearctic migrant, October–March, mainly in dry woodland, thicket and riparian shrubbery. Regular in small numbers in w. and nw. Kenya, to a lesser extent at Maralal and in the cent. Rift Valley. Scattered records elsewhere south and east to Buffalo Springs GR, Kajiado, Ngulia and Voi.

COMMON STONECHAT *Saxicola torquata axillaris*   **Plate 93**

Length 125 mm (5"). A small, plump, upright-perching chat of open country. *Pale rump* conspicuous in low flight. **Adult male** has *black head, throat and upperparts* marked with *white collar and rump* and *long white wing patch*;

underparts white, with centre of breast chestnut; tail black. **Female** mottled brown and buff on head and upperparts, white wing panel smaller than in male, and more *tawny on breast and flanks.* Bill and feet black; eyes dark brown. **Juvenile** mottled blackish brown above and on head, mottled buffy brown below. **VOICE**: A grating *hwee-trr-trr* or *terk-terk*; also a plaintive *weet*. Male has cheerful interrupted warbling song of short notes and repeated phrases, these typically separated by two-second intervals. **HABITS**: Solitary or in pairs. Perches on wires, fenceposts and bushtops, watching the ground for insects. Jerks wings and tail repeatedly. **SIMILAR SPECIES**: Whinchat resembles female, but is slimmer, has less upright stance, shows pale superciliary stripes, dark cheeks and white patches at base of tail. **STATUS AND DISTRIBUTION**: Common resident of rank herbage, cultivation, tea plantations, grassy hillsides and moorland, usually above 1800 m. Widespread in the w. and cent. Kenyan highlands, the Chyulu and Taita Hills, and Tanzania's Crater and Mbulu Highlands, Arusha NP, Mt Meru, Kilimanjaro, North and South Pares and the Usambara Mts.

WHINCHAT *Saxicola rubetra*   Plate 93

Length 125 mm (5"). A small migratory chat of open areas, perching prominently like a Stonechat, but posture less upright and outline of head less rounded. Well-patterned **spring male** is *mottled brown above, including rump,* the *black cheeks and ear-coverts bordered by broad white stripes* above and below; underparts orange-buff. *White patches across major wing-coverts, at base of primary coverts, and at sides of tail base,* all conspicuous in flight. **Female** and **winter male** have brown or mottled cheeks, buff superciliary stripes, smaller wing patches than in spring male; underparts creamy buff. **VOICE**: A persistent *hu-tuc* or *hu-tuc-tuc*. Infrequent song is a brief, clear warbling mixed with rattling notes, the short phrases often given in long series. **HABITS**: Generally solitary. Watches for prey from grass stems, low bushes and fenceposts. **SIMILAR SPECIES**: See Common Stonechat. **STATUS AND DISTRIBUTION**: Palearctic migrant, late September to early April, in moist grassland and savanna, bushland clearings and cultivation. Mainly western, but regular in small numbers at several central Rift Valley localities. A few winter in w. Kenya and the cent. Rift Valley. Rare in se. Kenya and in n. Tanzania, where fewer than five records from Serengeti and Arusha NPs.

NORTHERN WHEATEAR *Oenanthe oenanthe*   Plate 94

Length 140–152 mm (5.5–6"). A terrestrial bird of open country, grey or brown above and pale buff below, with white rump/upper tail-coverts and white tail with black T-pattern on tip and central feathers. **Adult male** unmistakable in **breeding plumage** (Jan.–April), when *black wings and facial mask* contrast with white superciliary stripes. Pale-brown-backed **female** has darker brown ear-coverts and buff superciliaries; *dark brown wings contrast with paler upperparts at rest and in flight.* Both sexes have dusky wing-linings. **Autumn/winter male** shows much brown above, the mask often brownish. **First-winter** bird resembles adult female, but wing feathers more broadly edged with pale buff. Typical **male** of *O. o. libanotica* has paler grey upperparts than nominate *oenanthe,* and the buff wash on underparts confined to throat and upper breast; black tail band narrower. **Female** *libanotica* is browner above than that of nominate race. **VOICE**: A grating *chack-chack* or *eek-chack-chack*. Song, occasionally heard in East Africa, consists of variable short phrases including whistles, trills, harsh *chack* notes and frequent mimicry. **HABITS**: Perches upright on ground, rocks or low bushes, alone or in scattered groups. Moves tail up and down. Flies low, showing prominent white rump, tail-coverts and tail base. Defends winter territories. **SIMILAR SPECIES**: Female and first-winter birds are easily confused with other wheatears. The plainer, more uniform Isabelline Wheatear is slightly larger, more robust, and paler, especially on wings; it also has a heavier bill, thicker and longer tarsi, broader black tail band, and white (not grey) wing-linings. Female Pied Wheatear is darker brown, especially on throat and breast, with black wing-linings. **STATUS AND DISTRIBUTION**: Common palearctic migrant, late September to March, in short-grass savanna, cultivation and on open plains, mainly above 600 m, but small numbers regular on passage in coastal areas. Most numerous and widespread on southward passage, October/early November, when ranging exceptionally up to 3800 m. Winters mainly in greener areas between 1300 and 2000 m.

PIED WHEATEAR *Oenanthe p. pleschanka*   Plate 94

Length 145–152 mm (5.75–6"). A small wheatear of dry bush country, with a *large white rump/tail area* and *black wing-linings.* **Spring male** is black above, on throat and on upper breast, with top of head, hindneck and underparts whitish; flight feathers blackish brown. Occasional males are white-throated, becoming buff on breast, with black restricted to a facial mask. **Autumn/winter male** (Oct.–Dec.) mottled, with feathers of upperparts tipped brown, those of the crown grey-tipped. **Female** somewhat darker, ashier brown above than Northern Wheatear, and dusky brown on throat and breast; pale dorsal feather edging in fresh plumage produces mottled effect. Browner **first-winter male** has blackish throat with many feathers light-tipped; wing feathers buff-edged. In all plumages, rump/tail pattern as in Northern Wheatear, but *white extends farther up rump, and black band across*

tail tip is narrower (occasionally broken). **Voice:** A soft *perrt*, and a harsh *chack* or *zack*. Song or subsong (occasional Feb./March) a repeated short *tri-tri-trreeee-tri*, the last note trilled (Keith *et al.* 1992). **Habits:** Like those of Northern Wheatear, but habitually perches on shrubs and low tree branches, and feeds mainly by ground sallies. **Similar Species:** Male Abyssinian Black Wheatear, also black above with pale crown, has orange-buff rump and tail base. Isabelline and Northern Wheatears are larger-billed, longer-legged, paler sandy brown above and on breast than female Pied; they have more pronounced superciliary stripes and pale (not black) wing-linings. See Black-eared Wheatear. **Status and Distribution:** Palearctic migrant, October–March, often common in open and bushed grassland, scrub and acacia woodland, preferring hilly or stony country between 400 and 1500 m. Less numerous than Isabelline and Northern Wheatears. Largely absent from the coastal strip and Lake Victoria basin, and relatively uncommon in n. Tanzania.

BLACK-EARED WHEATEAR *Oenanthe hispanica melanoleuca*   Plate 94

Length 145 mm (5.75"). Accidental in our area. Resembles Pied Wheatear in plumage, form and habits. **Adult male** differs in *cream or whitish back continuous with pale cap and contrasting* with *black outer scapulars, wings* and *ear-coverts.* Black throat continuous with black cheeks and ear-coverts in some birds; others are white-throated. **Female** of this race difficult or impossible to separate in the field from female Pied Wheatear which has similar rump/tail pattern and black wing-linings. Typically slightly paler, less mottled above, and paler on breast, the ear patch usually darker, more distinct and without distinct superciliary stripes. **First-winter male** has much brownish feather tipping on crown and back, but generally is much paler above than Pied Wheatear. **Voice:** Call a rough *grrt*, similar to call of Pied Wheatear. **Status and Distribution:** Palearctic vagrant, in our region south of its usual African wintering range. One caught and photographed at Athi River near Nairobi, 23 March to 5 April 1984; another seen at Lake Baringo, 2 December 1994.

*DESERT WHEATEAR *Oenanthe deserti* (*deserti?*)   Plate 94

Length 145 mm (5.75"). A wheatear with an *almost wholly black tail;* accidental in East Africa. **Male** with black throat and face, dark wings contrasting with buffy-brown upperparts, and sandy-buff underparts. Often shows a paler line on scapulars; rump buffy white. *Black of wings continuous with throat patch* (unlike Northern and Black-eared Wheatears). **Female** variable, light sandy buff to greyish buff on head and breast. **Voice:** A plaintive whistled *heeu;* also a short soft chatter. **Similar Species:** Other wheatears show considerable white or buff in the tail. **Status and Distribution:** Palearctic vagrant, recorded once at Kiunga, on the Kenyan/Somali border (17 Feb. 1984, two adult males observed at very close range). All specimens from Somalia are of the nominate race (Ash and Miskell 1983).

ISABELLINE WHEATEAR *Oenanthe isabellina*   Plate 94

Length 152–172 mm (6–6.75"). A pale wheatear of *open dry country.* Both sexes resemble a female Northern Wheatear, but are somewhat *larger, more uniformly coloured* and with white wing-linings. In flight, shows *lack of contrast between pale brown wings and sandy-brown back* (but confusing first-winter Northern Wheatear has fresh broad buffy wing edgings which reduce contrast). Isabelline has a more robust bill, somewhat longer and heavier tarsi, and the slightly broader superciliary stripes are more diffuse in front of the eyes; tail has broad dark brown or black terminal band. Lores blackish in spring, greyer in autumn. **Voice:** Usual call *chack* or *chack-chack*, like Northern Wheatear's; also a high-pitched *wheet-whit* and a loud whistled *wheew.* Sometimes utters subdued song on wintering grounds. **Habits:** Tends to stand more upright than Northern Wheatear. **Similar Species:** Northern Wheatear compared above. Pied Wheatear is smaller, has more white in tail and black wing-linings. **Status and Distribution:** Widespread palearctic migrant, common to abundant October–March in open or bushed dry grasslands or barren plains, usually below 2000 m. Subject to local movements in response to heavy rains or grass fires.

ABYSSINIAN BLACK or SCHALOW'S WHEATEAR *Oenanthe lugubris schalowi*
(Mourning Wheatear [in part])   Plate 94

Length 152–160 mm (6–6.75"). A resident wheatear with *orange-buff or rufous in rump and tail.* **Male** *largely black, with white belly,* pale brown crown more or less streaked with black, *orange-buff rump and under tail-coverts* and *tawny-rufous on outer rectrices;* tail with black T-pattern. **Female** sooty brown above, including cap; pale brown from chin to breast, with darker streaking; belly and tail-covert/tail pattern as in male. **Juvenile** dusky brown, faintly speckled with pale buff; rump and tail as in adult. **Voice:** Song short and rapidly delivered, mainly of grating, somewhat buzzing notes, *skeerrreeet-siweek-chiureek,* repeated with short pauses; variable. **Habits:** Solitary or in pairs. Often tame and confiding. Perches freely on rocks or boulders and in associated vegetation.

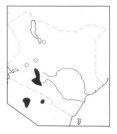

Nests in rock crevices or earth banks. **SIMILAR SPECIES:** Male Pied Wheatear has nearly pure white cap and white rump, and less black on the breast; its tail band is narrow, and pale parts of rectrices white, not buff. Juvenile Capped Wheatear is paler than young *schalowi* and has conspicuous superciliary stripes. **STATUS AND DISTRIBUTION:** Fairly common resident of boulder-strewn slopes, hillsides and eroded gullies in the central and southern Rift Valley and associated highlands. Ranges from Nakuru and Ol Kalou south to Narok and Olorgesailie, with two disjunct n. Tanzanian populations in the Crater and Mbulu Highlands, and around Mt Meru in Arusha District. Two birds seen on Mt Kulal (Aug. 1985) were possibly of the nominate Ethiopian race. **NOTE:** Merged with Mourning Wheatear, *Oenanthe lugens*, by some authors, but differs in behaviour, voice and plumage of both sexes.

HEUGLIN'S WHEATEAR *Oenanthe (bottae) heuglini* Plate 94
(Red-breasted Wheatear [in part])

Length 130–140 mm (5.5"). A slim, dark wheatear with a *dull brick-red breast* veiled with whitish or buff in fresh plumage. Sexes similar. **Adult** *dark* brown, almost blackish, above except for *buff rump*, the feathers tipped with rufous-buff when fresh; upper tail-coverts and basal half of all except central tail feathers white; rest of tail black. Blackish mask bordered above by white superciliary stripes; cheeks to throat whitish or rufous-buff, shading into the darker breast; belly much paler, whitish in some birds. Wing-linings spotted with reddish buff. **Juvenile** dark brown above, spotted with deep reddish buff; chin, throat and breast russet with dark brown feather tips. **VOICE:** Call a harsh *chack*. Song, not recorded in our area, said to be extended and complex. **HABITS:** Rather shy. Perches on rocks and low shrubs. Droops wings and flicks tail; often perches with horizontal stance. Prefers black 'cotton' soil and short-grass areas; attracted to burnt ground. **SIMILAR SPECIES:** Extralimital Red-breasted Wheatear, *O. bottae*, of highland savanna, tussock grass and moorland in Ethiopia, is a larger, chunkier, more upright-perching bird. Its brighter rufous breast is clearly separated from the white throat; narrow superciliary stripes and wing-linings are cream-coloured. Juvenile Capped Wheatear shows mottled buffy-brown underparts with trace of a breast band. **STATUS AND DISTRIBUTION:** A poorly known species in extreme nw. Kenya, where (seasonally?) fairly common around Lokichokio. Recorded east to Lake Turkana following heavy rains in June–July 1974 and 1975, and at Lodwar in March 1986 and at Todenyang in February 1988. One collected at Kisumu, 24 July 1917. **NOTE:** Usually considered a race of the montane *O. bottae*, but differs morphologically, ecologically and behaviourally.

CAPPED WHEATEAR *Oenanthe pileata livingstonii* Plate 94

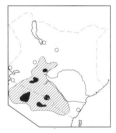

Length 165–170 mm (c. 6.5"). An upright-perching grassland wheatear. Sexes alike. **Adult** has *broad black breast band, black forecrown and sides of head* contrasting with white forehead, superciliary stripes and throat. Upperparts mainly brown above, shading to black on crown, cinnamon-brown on rump. Upper tail-coverts and sides of tail base white, rest of tail black. **Juvenile** brown, spotted with buff above; underparts pale buff, with dark mottling on throat and breast. **VOICE:** Song a short medley of trills, melodious whistles and some harsh notes; includes imitations of other bird species. Alarm calls include a thin *sueet* and varied ticking notes. **HABITS:** Solitary or in pairs. Forages on the ground; stands upright on rocks, termitaria or fenceposts, bobbing head when alarmed; also flicks wings and pumps tail up and down. Nests in hole in open ground, often in rodent burrow. Engages in short fluttery song-flight and frequently sings on moonlit nights. Attracted to recently burnt areas. **SIMILAR SPECIES:** See Heuglin's Wheatear. **STATUS AND DISTRIBUTION:** Fairly common and widespread on open and lightly bushed grassland from cent. Kenya and Mara GR south through much of upland n. Tanzania. Largely resident above 1400 m; at lower elevations mainly a non-breeding visitor, April–September.

RED-TAILED or FAMILIAR CHAT *Cercomela familiaris* Plate 90

Length 150 mm (6"). Quiet and unobtrusive, grey-brown above and paler greyish below, with *rufous rump and tail, the latter with blackish central feathers and tip*; *narrow pale eye-ring* and brownish ear-coverts. Centre of belly whitish. **Juvenile** mottled dusky and buff, with adult tail pattern. **VOICE:** Song a soft mixture of whistles, chattering and churring, *chur-chur-chur, sureet-sweet-sweet, her-chack-chack-chack. . .*, etc. Call note a shrill but not very loud whistle; alarm call *chak-chak* or *whee-chak-chak*. **HABITS:** *Flicks wings frequently* and slowly raises and lowers tail. Solitary or in pairs; perches on rocks, stumps or low tree branches; feeds on ground. Nests in crevices, holes in earth banks and among tree roots. **SIMILAR SPECIES:** Female Common Redstart is less greyish, and chestnut tail lacks dark tip. Brown-tailed Rock Chat is more uniform brown. **STATUS AND DISTRIBUTION:** Local and uncommon resident on rocky hillsides and escarpments with shrubs and small trees. Small numbers present in nw. and sw. Kenya around the Suam and Kongelai Escarpments, Kerio Valley, Kito Pass, Olololoo Escarpment (nw. Mara GR), Lolgorien, and around kopjes and rocky hills in Serengeti and Lake Manyara NPs. Reports from the Lake Turkana basin and Huri Hills require confirmation. Northwest Kenyan birds may be *C. f. omoensis,* but no specimens are available; southern birds are *C. f. falkensteini.*

BROWN-TAILED ROCK CHAT *Cercomela scotocerca turkana*   **Plate 90**

Length 140 mm (5.5"). A *plain drab chat of rocky country in n. Kenya.* Tail dark brown (very narrowly and inconspicuously edged with rufous-brown, as are upper tail-coverts). Upperparts otherwise dull brown, relieved by more rufous-brown ear-coverts and rump; wings faintly buff-edged in fresh plumage. Underparts uniform grey-brown, slightly paler than back. Bill and feet black; eyes large, dark brown, surrounded by *narrow pale tan eye-ring.* Sexes and age classes similar. **VOICE**: Call note *chuke-chuke.* Song a thin but loud rapid phrase, *seeseesuweet* or *tcheesueet,* repeated frequently at several-second intervals. **HABITS**: Solitary or in pairs. Unobtrusive, but rather tame. Spends long periods perched quietly upright on shrubs or small trees around rocky cliffs and lava fields. Persistently flicks wings and tail when on ground or upon returning to perch. **SIMILAR SPECIES**: See Red-tailed Chat. The sympatric and superficially similar African Grey Flycatcher is much greyer, with shorter tarsi and bill, streaks on crown, and spends less time on the ground. **STATUS AND DISTRIBUTION**: Local and uncommon resident of open rocky bush country at 400 to 1500 m in dry parts of n. Kenya, from Lokichokio east to Lake Turkana and Mt Marsabit, south to Baringo District and the Shaba and Samburu GRs.

ALPINE CHAT *Cercomela sordida*   **Plate 90**
(Hill Chat; Moorland Chat)

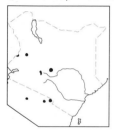

Length 135–150 mm (5.5–6"). A *tame, stocky brown chat of alpine habitats,* with conspicuous *white patches on sides of rather short tail.* Darkest on head and upperparts. Bill and long legs black; eyes dark brown. The two Tanzanian races are darker above and greyer below than Kenyan birds. **Juvenile** faintly barred above and mottled with darker brown on breast. **VOICE**: Call a soft chirping *werp-werp.* Song a loud metallic piping (Elliott and Fuggles-Couchman 1948). **HABITS**: An active bird, in pairs or small groups. Stands bolt-upright on rocks and boulders. Flicks tail and wings; often spreads tail feathers, displaying the white patches. Nests in grass tufts or in tops of giant ground-sels (*Senecio*), but feeds on or near ground. **SIMILAR SPECIES**: Female Northern Wheatear (possibly on moorlands, Oct.–March) is paler brown above, with contrasting rump and tail pattern. **STATUS AND DISTRIBUTION**: Common resident of alpine moorlands. Three races in our area: *C. s. ernesti* on Mt Elgon, the Cheranganis, Aberdares and Mt Kenya, from tree line to over 4000 m; *hypospodia,* on Mt Kilimanjaro, is the commonest bird above 3400 m and ranges to nearly 5200 m; *olimotiensis* inhabits the Crater Highlands of n. Tanzania at Engamat, Embulbul, Olosirwa and Ol Olmoti, from 2400 to 3500 m. Small population on Mt Meru not racially determined.

NORTHERN ANTEATER CHAT *Myrmecocichla aethiops cryptoleuca*   **Plate 90**

Length 175 mm (7"). A *stocky, dark sooty-brown chat of open country.* **Adult** shows *large white wing patches in flight.* Eyes brown; bill and feet black. Female slightly browner than male, with faint buff feather edging on throat in fresh plumage. **Juvenile** sooty brown throughout. **VOICE**: Varied piping and whistling calls. Song an attractive prolonged mixture of high thin whistles, rattling trills, and tsicking notes: *chwerchiwee tserk, chiwerchiwee, tsick-tuweee tuwee, teeruweeeer tsick, tchu chiwer. . ..* **HABITS**: Usually in pairs or small groups; several birds may display and sing together. Nests and roosts in tunnels excavated in earth banks and termite mounds, or in aardvark dens and other ground openings. **SIMILAR SPECIES**: Sooty Chat is slightly smaller, with no white in primaries; male deep black with white shoulder patch, female entirely dark sooty brown. **STATUS AND DISTRIBUTION**: Fairly common resident of dry, often eroded grassland in the w. and cent. Kenyan highlands. Largely absent from the Mara GR, where replaced by Sooty Chat. In n. Tanzania, locally common at Loliondo, the Crater Highlands and on the eastern Serengeti Plains.

SOOTY CHAT *Myrmecocichla nigra*   **Plate 90**

Length 155–160 mm (6–6.25"). Another stocky, rather short-tailed dark chat of open country. **Male** *glossy black,* with *white patch at bend of wing* (sometimes largely concealed in perched bird). Eyes brown; bill and feet black. **Female** and **juvenile** *plain sooty brown.* **VOICE**: A prolonged, sweet but thin musical song, sometimes given in flight: *wee tewee tuweer, skwik-skueeeer, cueee-eeeee-cuweeeer, eee-euwee-tee, tseuwee-tew-skeweeer-tsi-tsueet. . ..* Mimics other species. **HABITS**: Rather tame. Raises and lowers tail, sometimes teetering slightly. In

pairs or small groups, frequently associated with termitaria, on which it perches and in which it often nests and roosts; also digs nesting tunnels in roofs of aardvark or porcupine burrows and in road cuttings. **SIMILAR SPECIES**: Both sexes of Northern Anteater Chat show large white patch in primaries. **STATUS AND DISTRIBUTION**: Locally common resident of open grassland with scattered shrubs in sw. Kenya from Lolgorien and Mara GR south to northern Serengeti NP. Largely allopatric with Northern Anteater Chat, preferring moister areas.

CLIFF CHAT _Thamnolaea cinnamomeiventris subrufipennis_   Plate 92
(Mocking Chat; White-shouldered Cliff Chat)

Length 200 mm (8"). A large, colourful, long-tailed chat of _rocky cliffs and ravines_. **Male** glossy black, with _large white 'shoulder' patch, rufous rump_ and _upper tail-coverts_ and _bright orange-rufous underparts_. Narrow white band separates rufous belly from black breast. Eyes dark brown, bill and feet black. **Female** similar in pattern, but dull _slate-grey on head, breast and back_, and no white in the wings. **Juvenile male** duller than adult, with less white on wings. **VOICE**: Song a loud continuous fluty warbling, replete with rapid-fire mimicry of other species; also a long series of well-spaced and varied phrases, some sweet, others harsh: _tseeu tseeu, week-week-week, chir-chir-chir, tseuk tseuk tsuCHEEO, tsur WEEo tsik. . .._ Echoes in gorges, enhancing its effect. **HABITS**: Perches on boulders or low tree branches. Slowly raises and lowers tail, bringing it far above back, often fanned wide. Usually in pairs. **SIMILAR SPECIES**: Little Rock Thrush shows much rufous in tail. **STATUS AND DISTRIBUTION**: Local and rather uncommon in rocky gorges, on slopes and sheer rock faces, up to 2200 m, from Lokichokio, mts Kulal, Marsabit and Nyiru, the Ndotos and Kongelai Escarpment south through cent. and s. Kenya (most numerous on Rift Valley scarps) to Serengeti, Lake Manyara and Tarangire NPs, Mkomazi GR and the West Usambara Mts.

COMMON ROCK THRUSH _Monticola saxatilis_   Plate 91
(Rock Thrush; Mountain Rock Thrush)

Length 170–190 mm (6.5–7.5"). A _stocky_ thrush with _rather short rufous tail_. **Spring male** (March–April) _blue-grey on head, throat and back, dark rufous on underparts and wing-linings; whitish patch on lower back_. **Female** _mottled brown above_, buff with _dark crescentic markings below_; no white on back. Eyes brown; bill mostly black; feet dark brown. **Autumn male** resembles female, but shows some white on lower back, grey on crown and throat and (largely hidden) rufous bases to feathers of underparts. Transition to spring plumage occurs slowly during late winter. **VOICE**: A soft _chack-chack_ and a low throaty _kschirrrr_, but generally silent. **HABITS**: Usually solitary. Perches upright on ground, rock or stump. Forages on the ground, becoming quite tame in many areas. **SIMILAR SPECIES**: Little Rock Thrush is much smaller, with a relatively longer tail; in male, blue-grey of throat extends to breast, and rump is dark rufous like the tail; female lacks strong mottling and barring. **STATUS AND DISTRIBUTION**: Fairly common palearctic migrant, late October to early April, favouring dry open grassland and cultivation, especially where trees and rocks provide suitable perches. Widespread from sea level to over 2000 m, except in heavy forest and the more arid areas of n. Kenya.

LITTLE ROCK THRUSH _Monticola r. rufocinereus_   Plate 91

Length 155 mm (6"). A small resident thrush with grey and rufous underparts. **Male** smoky or brownish grey above, pure grey or bluish _grey from chin to breast; rest of underparts and rump rufous; tail darker rufous, with black central feathers and tip_. **Female** duller above, _ash-grey on throat and breast_. **Juvenile** spotted with buff above and mottled buff and blackish below; rump and tail as in adult. **VOICE**: Song a short _tsurr-sureet, skeee, tsee-ee-tsurrrr_ or _steeee skurrree skirrrrrr_, the phrases fading terminally. **HABITS**: Solitary, in pairs or in family parties. Unobtrusive and decidedly crepuscular; perches upright on rocks and low branches. Nests in rock crevices or walls, occasionally in cleft of tree. **SIMILAR SPECIES**: Female Cliff Chat is larger, with a blackish tail. Red-tailed Chat and female Common Redstart are pale brown or buff below. **STATUS AND DISTRIBUTION**: Local and uncommon between 1400 and 2000 m in the w. and cent. Kenyan highlands, frequenting rocky slopes, gorges, forested ravines and old quarries. Most frequent on the Rift and Kerio Valley scarps; also resident on Kongelai, Elgeyu, Tambach, Laikipia and Olololoo Escarpments, as well as in the Ndotos, Tugen Hills, Ololokwe, Mweiga, Loldaiga, Hell's Gate and Nakuru NPs, Elmenteita, Naivasha and the Ngong Hills. Rare in n. Tanzania, where currently known from Longido, the western scarp above Lake Natron, and at Lobo Lodge, n. Serengeti NP.

SPOTTED GROUND THRUSH *Zoothera guttata fischeri*   Plate 91
(Spotted Thrush)

Length 190–200 mm (7–8"). A large, terrestrial, migratory thrush of coastal forests. *White below, with bold black spots.* Olive-brown above, with two rows of *large white spots across the wing-coverts. Pale buff face has two heavy black vertical bars on cheeks and ear-coverts.* Small white tail corners are noticeable in flight. Eyes dark brown; bill large, dusky, pinkish at base below; feet pale flesh-pink. Sexes and age classes alike. **Voice:** A sibilant *tsee-tseee*; otherwise silent in non-breeding quarters. **Habits:** Solitary, shy and unobtrusive. Feeds in leaf litter on the forest floor, digging in the soil with its heavy bill; often flies to low tree branch when disturbed. **Status and Distribution:** Confined to humid coastal forest. Scarce and local non-breeding migrant from the southern tropics, April–October. Recorded north to Lamu, but most records from the Gedi and Arabuko–Sokoke Forests.

ORANGE GROUND THRUSH *Zoothera gurneyi*   Plate 91
(Orange Thrush)

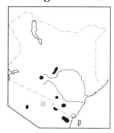

Length 180–205 mm (7–8"). A shy ground bird of eastern forests. **Adult** brownish above, *orange-rufous below,* whitish on belly; *incomplete narrow white eye-ring* and *greyish ear-coverts crossed by an oblique whitish or buffy band;* two conspicuous *white wing-bars.* Eyes brown; bill dark brown, variable in size, especially long (to 20 mm) in *Z. g. chuka; tarsi* yellowish. Upperparts racially variable: olive-brown in *chuka,* grey in *otomitra,* grey-brown with contrasting greyish crown in *chyulu.* **Juvenile** shows prominent wing-bars and is mottled brown below. **Voice:** Loud clear songs vary from (1) short and simple without repetition of notes in the phrase, e.g. *tew turee keeu -turlP* or *wuree tew-tew,* to (2) a series of melodious, sometimes slurred whistles repeated several times before the same is done with a different phrase, e.g. *reee-eee tureee-tew, reee-eee tureee-tew. . . erreee tew-tew rriiiii, erreee-tew-tew-rriiiii. . .*. Very high, barely audible, 'whisper' notes are frequent between the whistled phrases. Longer warbling phrases may be given rapidly and continuously with others to form a more complex extended performance. Some songs less clear, more quavering, e.g. *quee qui-urrrrr tur-turileee weet-weet.* Call notes include *querk* and *cureek.* **Habits:** Usually solitary. Shy and skulking. Feeds on the forest floor, but sings from high in the canopy as well as from low dense cover. Often vocal until early afternoon, resuming again in evening. **Similar Species:** Abyssinian Ground Thrush (mostly above 2000 m, and allopatric except on Mt Kenya and s. Aberdares) is richer brown above, the head mostly orange-brown and with a broader, complete eye-ring and no grey on ear-coverts; bill also smaller; underparts darker orange-rufous or orange-brown. **Status and Distribution:** Uncommon forest resident from near sea level to over 2000 m: *Z. g. chuka* in the s. Aberdares and on the eastern slopes of Mt Kenya (Meru, Irangi, Chuka); *Z. g. chyulu* in the Chyulu Hills; *Z. g. otomitra* on the Taita Hills, and in n. Tanzania at Mbulu, Oldeani, Mt Meru (reportedly to 2400 m, in bamboo), Arusha NP, North Pare Mts and the Usambaras (900–1200 m, sparingly to 1830 m). Some movement in cold seasons to lower elevations (e.g. 260–280 m on Mrima Hill, se. Kenya; 450 m in the East Usambaras).

ABYSSINIAN GROUND THRUSH *Zoothera piaggiae*   Plate 91

Length 190 mm (7.5"). Generally replaces the similar Orange Ground Thrush at higher elevations in western and most of central Kenya, and on higher Tanzanian mountains. Best distinguished by *complete broad white eye-ring* and *no pale band on ear-coverts.* **Adult** olive-brown above, with *two bold white wing-bars;* ear-coverts rufous-olive. *Forehead and underparts deep orange-rufous;* centre of belly and crissum white. Eyes brown; bill blackish; *tarsi* whitish-flesh colour. The two Kenyan races are browner-backed, western *piaggiae* more olive above and paler below, *kilimensis* more orange-brown on the breast; Tanzanian *rowei* paler below, more olive above than either northern race. Sexes alike. **Juvenile** tawny above and on head; underparts mottled brown; wing-bars prominent. **Voice:** Song of classic thrush quality, composed of clear whistles with a few softer, harsher notes, some phrases almost trilled. Certain songs recall those of Orange Ground Thrush in that a phrase is repeated several times before switching to another. Other songs involve less repetition: *wurr teeu weeu. . . wur-weeu-tiWEE, (wichu-tsik) trrrrweeeu, seesurrWEE, tiuwee (chikuchik) wurweeotuweee. . ..* **Habits:** Solitary, shy and skulking. Feeds on ground, usually in dense forest undergrowth. Sings from concealed low perches just before dawn and after dark. **Similar Species:** Orange Ground Thrush compared above. **Status and Distribution:** Uncommon resident of forests between 2000 and 3300 m in the w. and cent. Kenyan highlands, particularly favouring the bamboo zone on Mt Kenya. *Z. p. piaggiae* ranges west of the Rift Valley from Mt Elgon and the Cheranganis to North Nandi, Eldama Ravine, Sotik, Mau and Trans-Mara Forests. *Z. p. kilimensis* on mountains east of the Rift (Nyiru, Kulal, Marsabit, Karissia Hills, Uraguess, Aberdares and Mt Kenya); also on Kilimanjaro. *Z. p. rowei* is confined to the Loliondo and Magaidu Forests in n. Tanzania and the Nguruman Hills in s. Kenya.

OLIVE THRUSH *Turdus olivaceus*   **Plates 91, 124**
(Northern Olive Thrush)

Length 205–215 mm (8–8.5″). The common large thrush of the highlands. **Adult** *T. o. abyssinicus* is dark olive-brown above, with *bright orange bill and bare orbital ring*; lores black; chin and throat buffy white with dusky streaks, becoming *greyish olive-brown on breast*; *dull tawny-orange on flanks and most of belly*; white under tail-coverts streaked dusky; feet brownish orange. **Juvenile** darker: blackish brown above with small orange-tawny tips on wing-coverts; an almost solid band of brownish-black spots extends across the breast and onto the dull orange flanks; throat dull greyish buff, streaked with dusky; belly pale dingy orange, fading to whitish on crissum. The three Tanzanian races are all darker above: *deckeni* duller than *abyssinicus*, darker on upperparts and breast, more brownish tawny on sides and flanks; *oldeani* still darker and more sooty grey, the flanks grey-brown without tawny hue; *roehli* nearer *abyssinicus*, but darker on chest and white from centre of breast to belly, with bill more reddish. **Voice**: Full song consists of clear short phrases of rising and falling notes, often with a higher, softer terminal trill, *wheeu - wheee - wheeu - wheee-wheeu-trrrrrrri*. Some songs have a distinct reeling quality: *reeee-rreeeeetew-eeeeeee. . .*; short dawn song a rolling, reedy *trrrip-trreeEET*; other song phrases include *weeu-HEE* and *tuwee-teelieu*; midday song a sweet, high-pitched *swee-turr-TEE-turr*, or *tsurr-TCHEE-tsurr-tsee-tsur*, the phrase repeated at intervals. Calls include a soft *chk-chk-chk*, a harder, guttural *gew* or *gew-gew*, and a scolding *tsrk, tsrk*. **Habits**: Forages on open ground or in forest-floor leaf litter, but flies to trees when disturbed. Often confiding, feeds on lawns in the manner of an American Robin, *T. migratorius*, or European Blackbird, *T. merula*. **Similar Species**: African Thrush is paler, less rufous on flanks, with a yellow bill. See Taita Thrush. **Status and Distribution**: A common resident of forest edge, woodland and gardens. *T. o. abyssinicus* ranges throughout the Kenyan highlands, including northern montane 'islands' of the Ndotos, Nyiru, Kulal and Marsabit, and between 1500 and 3400 m on Mt Kenya, and south to the Nguruman and Chyulu Hills and into n. Tanzania at Loliondo (an old record from Moyale is not entirely satisfactory); replaced by Taita Thrush in Taita Hills forest. Three other races restricted to n. Tanzania: *T. o. oldeani* in the Mbulu and Crater Highlands, on mts Lolkissale, Hanang and Meru; *roehli* in the North Pare Mts and Usambaras; *deckeni* on Kilimanjaro, at Monduli, Kitumbeine, Longido and Ol Doinyo Orok (Namanga Hill).

TAITA THRUSH *Turdus (olivaceus) helleri*   **Plate 91**

Length 215 mm (8.5″). A very rare thrush of the *Taita Hills forest*. **Adult** differs from Kenyan race of Olive Thrush (absent from the Taitas) in being *much darker above*, and *blackish from head to breast*; *orange-rufous restricted to flanks*; *belly and under tail-coverts white*. Bill and feet bright orange; bare *orbital ring and postocular patches orange-yellow*; eyes blackish brown. **Juvenile** duller and browner on upperparts; scapulars and wing-coverts with orange tips and shaft streaks; breast heavily mottled, becoming paler on belly. **Voice**: Not known with certainty. A short *wee sewee slewp* and *wee tewer tuwee* (rising at end) may be attributable to Taita Thrush, but singing birds not observed. Archived tape recordings purportedly of this species are of Orange Ground Thrush and Rüppell's Robin-Chat, highly vocal species of the Taita forests (and difficult to observe when singing.) **Habits**: Shy and skulking; keeps well hidden in dense thickets and undergrowth; spends most of its time digging with its strong bill in forest-floor leaf litter. Occasionally perches on stumps or fallen logs, but rarely ascends above eye-level. Does not venture into secondary growth, scrub or cultivation. **Similar Species**: *T. olivaceus abyssinicus* compared above. Darker-backed *T. o. deckeni* and *T. o. oldeani* of n. Tanzania all have some tawny-orange on the belly; *T. o. roehli* is dark brownish olive from chin to breast. Bills of these forms are considerably smaller than that of *helleri*. **Status and Distribution**: Endemic to the Taita Hills, se. Kenya, where now confined to the remnant Ngangao and Mbololo forest patches (endangered; few pairs remain). Reports from Mt Kasigau require confirmation. **Note**: Considered a race of Olive Thrush by many authors.

AFRICAN THRUSH *Turdus pelios centralis*   **Plate 91**

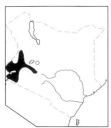

Length 205–215 mm (8–8.5″). A largely *western* thrush with a *yellow bill*. Resembles a faded Olive Thrush. **Adult** grey-brown above, paler and greyer below, with light tawny flanks and dusky throat streaking. Eyes bright brown; bare skin behind eye dusky brown; feet light grey, pale buff, or pale brownish green. Sexes alike. **Juvenile** greyish below, mottled on breast and flanks. **Voice**: An extended caroling dawn song of clear and slurred whistles, a few notes slightly quavering and throaty; most notes/phrases repeated two or more times: *tureep tureep tureep weeu-weeu-weeu-cureep-churEEP. . .* or *trierieu trierieu ureetew-ureetew. . . slurreeep slurreeep swrp-swrp-swrp, weet-tweeyu tweeyu. . ..* **Habits**: Solitary and rather unobtrusive; more timid than Olive Thrush. Feeds in the open but flies to cover if alarmed. Sings extensively in early morning and evening. **Similar Species**: Olive Thrush is darker, with more rufous underparts and an orange bill. **Status and Distribution**: A fairly common resident of forest edge, woodland, cultivation and gardens below 2000 m from Mt Elgon and Kapenguria south to the Lake Victoria basin, South Nyanza and

Lolgorien Districts, east to the Kerio Valley, Kabarnet, lakes Baringo and Elmenteita, Lake Nakuru NP and locally on the w. Laikipia Plateau (*fide* Short *et al.* 1990). Sympatric with Olive Thrush in many areas around 2000 m elevation. To be expected in the Mara Region of n. Tanzania.

BARE-EYED THRUSH *Turdus tephronotus*   Plate 91

Length 200 mm (8"). An *eastern* thrush with a conspicuous *broad area of bare orange-yellow skin around the eyes*. **Adult** grey above and on breast, *tawny-orange on flanks and belly; throat white, with pronounced black streaking*. Bill and feet orange-yellow. **Juvenile** pale greyish below, with mottled breast. **Voice**: Calls include a rattling *chrrrrrr*, a soft mellow *tew-tew-tew* or *qu-qu-qu-qu*, and *tsyik-tsyik-tsyik*. Song, repeated at intervals, is basically a short quavering trill followed by or interspersed with one or more higher-pitched notes: (1) *quirrrrrrrrr turr chik*, (2) *squirrrrr-qyrrr tyip-tyip tew-tew-tew*, (3) *kewerr-kewrrr s'leep-yee-eee*, (4) *huu-huu-tsri-tsritsritsritsri*. **Habits**: Shy and skulking, but may be confiding near dwellings. Forages on ground inside thickets and in dense *Commiphora* scrub, digging with its powerful bill. **Similar Species**: Olive Thrush, of higher and moister habitats, is dark olive-brown above, with a bright orange bill, lacks white throat, and the orbital ring is narrow. **Status and Distribution**: Uncommon but widely distributed in eastern bush and dry woodland below 1600 m from northeastern border areas, Wajir, the Ndotos and Horr Valley south to Kajiado, Namanga, Tsavo and Taita Districts; also in coastal scrub south to the Mombasa area. In n. Tanzania, ranges from the Mkomazi GR and Masai Steppe west to about 37° E. Rare in coastal Tanzanian lowlands, where replaced by Kurrichane Thrush.

KURRICHANE THRUSH *Turdus libonyanus tropicalis*   Plate 124

Length 220 mm (*c.* 8.5"). Southern counterpart of the Bare-eyed Thrush. Broken *dark malar streaks border the whitish throat* of **adult**. Breast buffy grey; flanks bright buffy orange; upperparts plain brownish grey. Eyes brown; narrow orbital ring yellow; bill orange; feet pale pinkish flesh. **Juvenile** has buff spots on the wing-coverts, blackish spots on breast, sides and flanks; bill brownish. **Voice**: Common call a whistling *tsi-tseeoo*. Alarm note a thin whistle, often given when flushed. Pleasing short song *rrreeeee treeeeee qurileeeee*, and a higher sweet *tsurrreeeeee*. **Habits**: Feeds on the ground, quickly taking cover when alarmed. Confiding near dwellings, but shy elsewhere. Although typically a miombo-woodland species, in our area frequents gardens and light woods. Sings in early morning and evening. **Similar Species**: Bare-eyed Thrush is more rufous on belly and shows prominent orange-yellow orbital skin. **Status and Distribution**: Barely reaches our area in coastal Tanzanian lowlands and the East Usambara foothills. Several old records from around Tanga and Amani, and a sight record in 1994 from Tanga.

FLYCATCHERS, FAMILY MUSCICAPIDAE
(World, *c.* 100 species; Africa, 34; Kenya, 15; n. Tanzania, 12)

Small, arboreal insectivorous birds with somewhat flattened, broad-based triangular bills. Except in the migratory *Ficedula*, the sexes are alike, mostly grey or brown above and pale below. The juvenile plumage is spotted. Agile birds, most species feed by hawking insects in the air; many also take prey from the ground, and some glean from canopy foliage. Typically solitary or in pairs, they perch unobtrusively and most have unimpressive voices. The nest is cup-shaped, usually high in a tree fork or hole. Some species formerly included in this family are now treated under Platysteiridae and Monarchidae. Our flycatchers are ecological equivalents of the quite distantly related New World tyrant flycatchers, Tyrannidae.

SPOTTED FLYCATCHER *Muscicapa striata*   Plate 87

Length 135–145 mm (*c.* 5.5"). A *long-winged, streak-crowned* flycatcher; generally grey-brown above and whitish below, with diffuse *dusky streaks on breast*. Crown slightly peaked, with blackish streaks conspicuous on the pale brownish-grey background. *Wings extend to mid-tail when perched*; most feathers margined with white or grey. Eyes dark brown; tarsi short; bill and feet black. **Voice**: An insistent thin *tseet* or *see-tseet*, repeated several times; sometimes a longer *tsee, tsi-tsik*. **Habits**: Usually solitary. Perches upright on low branch, post or fence. Hawks for insects, returning to same perch. Flicks wings when calling and on alighting. **Similar Species**: African Grey and Pale Flycatchers are more robust, with heavier tarsi; both lack breast streaks, have more rounded crowns and shorter wings. See Gambaga Flycatcher. **Status and Distribution**: Palearctic migrant, October–April, in light woodland, riverine acacias, bush with scattered trees, gardens and forest edge, from sea level to over 2200 m. Widespread and often

common on passage. Winters more locally, mainly south of 1° N, notably in the Rift Valley highlands, dry south-eastern plateau country and in coastal lowlands, including Pemba Island. Our birds are mostly of the greyer eastern *M. s. neumanni*, but nominate *striata* is also represented.

GAMBAGA FLYCATCHER *Muscicapa gambagae*   Plate 87

Length 120–130 mm (4.5–5″). Resembles Spotted Flycatcher but slightly smaller, with *shorter wings* (primaries do not extend beyond upper tail-coverts) and more rounded head; tends to perch more horizontally than that species. **Adult** appears *essentially unstreaked on crown* (although darker feather centres produce slight streaked or mottled effect at close range); crown slightly darker brown than back. Whitish eyelids form narrow eye-ring, broken in front by dark loral spot; another narrow line of whitish feathers from nostrils along upper rictal area. Diffuse, *grey-brown or pale brown breast streaks (varying individually) less sharply defined than in Spotted Flycatcher*, brownish from sides of breast to flanks. Secondaries and wing-coverts pale-margined in fresh plumage. Dusky brown tail feathers have very narrow whitish edges and tips, often reduced by wear and not noticeable in the field. Bill dusky brown above, buff or yellowish below; eyes dark brown; feet dusky brown. **Juvenile** spotted with buff above and on head; breast brown-streaked. Buff spots subject to early wear, often disappearing before the streaked breast feathers are moulted. **VOICE:** Call a distinctive *chick*, or *zick-zick-zick*, or *zickzick-tzicktzick*, much sharper than any note of Spotted Flycatcher. **HABITS:** Much like those of Spotted Flycatcher; seldom perches more than five metres above ground. Flicks wings when calling. **SIMILAR SPECIES:** Spotted Flycatcher compared above. African Grey and Pale Flycatchers are larger, with longer tarsi, and both differ vocally. African Dusky Flycatcher is smaller, darker brown, shorter-tailed, and in different habitat. **STATUS AND DISTRIBUTION:** Local and uncommon in dry bush, acacia woodland along streambeds, and in low, broad-leaf tree savanna, generally below 1600 m. Most records between November and April, but has bred in the Kerio Valley. Otherwise recorded at scattered localities in n. Kenya, from Mt Elgon and Baragoi east to Wamba, Shaba GR, Isiolo, Garissa and Bura, south to Galana Ranch and the Tsavo parks. Night passage of juveniles noted at Ngulia, Tsavo West NP, during November (once with heavy passage of Spotted Flycatchers), indicative of at least local movements.

AFRICAN DUSKY FLYCATCHER *Muscicapa adusta*   Plate 87

Length 100–111 mm (*c.* 4″). A small, somewhat dumpy brown flycatcher with a short tail. **Adult** plain brown above, variably grey-brown below, with whitish throat and belly (with suggestion of faint streaks in some birds). At close range, *narrow pale tan eye-ring* marks an otherwise plain face. Three similar subspecies: southeastern *murina* has breast and sides dark olive-grey, throat and belly washed with buff; the widespread *interposita* is warmer brown above, and tinged warmer buff on throat and breast; northern *marsabit* is richer rusty olive-brown above and more rufous-buff below. **Juvenile** has large pale buff spots on upperparts and breast; base of mandible yellowish. **Immature** loses spots, except for buff tips to greater coverts, pale secondary edges; richer brown on breast and buffier on belly than adult. Mandible base pale. **VOICE:** Call note a thin, sibilant repetitive *ss-s-s-st* or *tseee*, also a sharp *trrt-trreet*. **HABITS:** Unobtrusive and mainly silent. Confiding. Perches upright on prominent low twig or fence wire, and makes frequent flycatching sallies, returning to same perch. Flicks wings, but less frequently than Spotted Flycatcher. **SIMILAR SPECIES:** Spotted Flycatcher is larger, longer-winged, whiter below, with prominent crown and breast streaks. Chapin's Flycatcher is larger, greyer, has short pale supraloral streaks, is more arboreal. See Gambaga Flycatcher. **STATUS AND DISTRIBUTION:** Common resident of highland forest edge and other well-wooded situations, including suburban gardens, between 1200 and 3000 m or higher. *M. a. marsabit* is known from Marsabit and Moyale. *M. a. interposita* ranges throughout the w. and cent. Kenyan highlands, north to the Ndotos, Mt Nyiru and Mt Loima, south to Mara GR and the Nguruman Hills; in Tanzania at Loliondo, Mt Kitumbeine and Serengeti NP. *M. a. murina*, mainly Tanzanian, ranges from the Crater and Mbulu Highlands east to Arusha NP, Mt Meru, Kilimanjaro, the Pare and Usambara Mountains and the Taita and Chyulu Hills in se. Kenya. Birds on Ol Doinyo Orok (Namanga Hill) and nearby Longido are not racially assigned.

CHAPIN'S FLYCATCHER *Muscicapa lendu*   Plate 87

Length 125–130 mm (5″). A rare arboreal forest flycatcher of w. Kenya. **Adult** dark brown above, dingy greyish below, darker on the breast, with *short pale grey supraloral stripes*. Bill short, mostly black, grey at base of mandible; corners of mouth yellow; eyes brown; feet dull blue-grey. **Juvenile** resembles adult, but wing-coverts and secondaries tipped with buff; base of mandible yellowish. **VOICE:** A repeated short dry trill, *bzzzt-bzzzt-bzzzt-bzzzt*, each note one second or less in duration. **HABITS:** Quiet, unobtrusive and sluggish; perches upright on tree branch, often in foliage, typically 10–20 m above ground. Makes long sallies for insects, sometimes dropping nearly to ground, but returning to high perch. **SIMILAR SPECIES:** Dusky Flycatcher is smaller and darker, and shows no supraloral stripes. **STATUS AND DISTRIBUTION:** Scarce resident of the Kakamega and North Nandi Forests.

SWAMP FLYCATCHER *Muscicapa aquatica infulata* Plate 87

Length 130–140 mm (5–5.5"). A western *lakeside species*. **Adult** dark brown above, with *broad brown breast band*, white throat and white belly; brownish along sides and flanks. Bill and feet dark brown; corners of mouth yellow; eyes dark brown. **Juvenile** *heavily* spotted above; breast mottled brownish white and streaked with dusky. **Voice**: Song a soft squeaky *weesaseet-tsit-seetaseet*. Alarm note a sharp *pzitt*. **Habits**: Quiet and unobtrusive. Perches beside water on grass stems and reeds, from which it hawks aerial prey or drops to pick insects from low aquatic vegetation. **Status and Distribution**: A fairly common resident of lakeshore vegetation, in our region largely confined to the Lake Victoria basin, including Yala Swamp and Lake Kanyaboli; also at Saiwa NP. Wanderers recorded east to the Mara GR and south to the Grumeti River in w. Serengeti NP.

ASHY FLYCATCHER *Muscicapa caerulescens* Plate 87
(Blue-grey Flycatcher)

Length 130 mm (5"). A pale *grey or blue-grey* flycatcher of forest edge. **Adult** *M. c. brevicaudata* blue-grey above, darker on wings and tail; underparts washed with blue-grey on breast and sides, whiter on throat and belly; side of face shows *blackish loral line* and a *short white supraloral streak connecting with narrow white eye-ring*. Bill black above, blue-grey below; eyes dark brown; feet slate-grey. Eastern *M. c. cinereola* is paler, more ashy grey, lacking bluish tone of *brevicaudata*. **Juvenile** heavily spotted dark brown and buff above, speckled blackish on underparts. **Voice**: Song a rapid sibilant, slightly descending *tsip-tsip-tsetse-tseu*. **Habits**: Perches inconspicuously on mid-level twigs; stance less upright than that of Spotted and African Dusky Flycatchers. Darts to catch aerial insects; flicks wings on return to perch. **Similar Species**: See Lead-coloured Flycatcher. **Status and Distribution**: Uncommon and local resident of forest edges and riverine and acacia woodland from sea level to 1800 m. Western *M. c. brevicaudata* is known from the Kakamega Forest and Kerio Valley (scarce), and birds of riverine areas at Lolgorien, Mara GR, Loita Hills and Serengeti NP may represent this race. *M. c. cinereola* ranges through the coastal lowlands north to the Boni Forest, inland along the Tana River to Bura, Shimba Hills and in n Tanzania to the Usambara and Pare foothills, with small populations in the Kitovu, Rombo and Kibwezi Forests; sporadic records from Tsavo East NP north to Machakos District. Birds in Lake Manyara NP not racially assigned. Formerly known from Nairobi, Kiambu and Embu Districts.

WHITE-EYED SLATY FLYCATCHER *Melaenornis fischeri* Plates 87, 124
(Slaty Flycatcher)

Length 150–170 mm (6–6.5"). A grey or blue-grey highland flycatcher. Side of face with conspicuous *broad white eye-ring* in the widespread, more blue-grey nominate *fischeri*, the ring narrow in slate-grey *nyikensis* of Tanzania. **Adult** *slaty blue-grey* above, greyish white below; underparts paler in *nyikensis*. Bill blue-grey with black tip; eyes dark brown; feet black. **Juvenile** grey, with whitish spots above and mottled black streaking on underparts. **Voice**: A short, barely audible, high-pitched *seee* or *eeeea*, sometimes extended to a chattering descending trill. Alarm note a loud *zit*. **Habits**: Usually quiet and solitary. Perches upright on low branch of tree or shrub; frequently clings to rough tree trunks. Quite active; hawks insects, but also flies to ground to feed. Confiding and decidedly crepuscular. **Similar Species**: Largely allopatric Ashy Flycatcher is smaller, paler and daintier, its eye-ring narrow and connected to short white supraloral streak. **Status and Distribution**: *M. f. fischeri*, common between 1350 and 3000 m at forest edge and in various wooded habitats, is widespread in the w. and cent. Kenyan highlands north to the Mathews Range, the Ndotos, mts Nyiru, Kulal and Loima (but oddly absent from Mt Marsabit); ranging south to Lolgorien, nw. Mara GR, the Nguruman and Chyulu Hills, Ol Doinyo Orok, and in n. Tanzania to Loliondo, Monduli, Arusha NP, Mt Meru, Kilimanjaro and the North Pare Mts. Southern *M. f. nyikensis* ranges north to the Crater Highlands. Birds from the Mbulu Highlands are considered intergrades with *fischeri*. **Note**: Formerly considered conspecific with *M. chocolatina*.

NORTHERN BLACK FLYCATCHER *Melaenornis edolioides* Plate 88
(Black Flycatcher; Western Black Flycatcher)

Length 180–190 mm (7–7.5"). A *dull blackish* flycatcher of *n. and w. Kenya*. **Adult** *dull blackish slate*, with *browner wings*. Tail long, almost *square-tipped*. *Eyes dark brown*; bill and feet black. The northeastern race *schistacea* is slightly paler and greyer than widespread *M. e. lugubris*. **Juvenile** blackish, liberally spotted with tawny. **Voice**: Song a soft sibilant *sweetchy*, repeated at short intervals (Chapin 1953). Also various harsh scolding calls. Juveniles give a single repetitive *seep*. **Habits**: Typically perches quietly on bushtop or low twig. Flies to ground for most prey, returning to same perch. Somewhat crepuscular. **Similar Species**: Allopatric Southern Black Flycatcher has glossy blue-back plumage. Common Drongo has forked tail, red eyes and larger bill. **Status and**

DISTRIBUTION: *M. e. lugubris* is a locally common resident west of the Rift Valley, between 1100 and 1800 m, in bushed and wooded habitats, favouring clearings and edges of cultivation; ranges from Mt Elgon and Saiwa NP south to Mara GR and Serengeti NP, east to Kakamega, Nandi and Kericho Districts. Reports from Lake Turkana require confirmation. *M. e. schistacea* ranges south from the Ethiopian highlands to Moyale.

SOUTHERN BLACK FLYCATCHER *Melaenornis pammelaina*   Plate 88

Length 180–185 mm (7"). A somewhat drongo-like flycatcher of *dry country east and south* of the preceding species' range. **Adult** *glossy blue-black*, with a long, square-ended tail. Bill and feet black; eyes dark brown. **Juvenile** dull sooty black, with tawny-buff spotting above, tawny scaling below. **VOICE**: Usual song a thin, high-pitched *tsee-tsee-sweeu, tsee-swooi, tsee-tsee. . ..* Dawn song also high-pitched and squeaky, but longer: *seet-skeet-sisi, skreee-tsew-tsreet seeet seeet.* Call note *tzeer.* **HABITS**: Perches quietly, usually on low leafless branch. Hawks insects, feeds on the ground, and gleans from foliage. **SIMILAR SPECIES**: Northern Black Flycatcher has dull plumage. Common Drongo is slightly larger, has splayed forked tail, larger bill and red eyes, is more noisy and aggressive. Male Black Cuckoo-shrike has yellow skin at gape and more rounded tail. **STATUS AND DISTRIBUTION**. Locally common resident of dry woodland (especially acacia), bush and margins of cultivation, mainly east of the Rift Valley and below 1800 m. In Kenya, ranges from Rombo, Loitokitok, Amboseli and the Tsavo NPs north through the eastern plateau to Kibwezi, Simba, Sultan Hamud, Nairobi, Lake Nakuru, Nairobi and Meru NPs, Naro Moru, Ngobit, Laikipia, the Samburu and Shaba GRs, Mathews Range and the Ndotos; also along the lower Tana River and in the Boni Forest. Although mainly a southern African species, in our region suprisingly scarce in ne. Tanzania, recorded only from Lake Manyara and Tarangire NPs, Arusha District and the East Usambara Mountains.

AFRICAN GREY FLYCATCHER *Bradornis microrhynchus*   Plate 87

Length 140 mm (5.5"). The common round-headed *greyish* flycatcher of *dry country*. **Adult** grey above, paler grey below, with whitish throat and belly; under tail-coverts white or pale tawny-buff. At close range shows *dusky streaks on crown*, but lacks streaking on breast. Inner secondaries and wing-coverts edged with white. Northern *B. m. neumanni* is browner grey above, pale buff below with suggestion of a dark breast band, shows whitish forehead and noticeable superciliary stripes; eastern *burae* is rather pale grey; southeastern *taruensis* is smaller and markedly darker than *burae* adjoining it to the north; southern/southwestern nominate *microrhynchus* is larger and darker grey. *Bill entirely black*; eyes brown; feet black. **Juvenile** has pale streaks on head, buff spots elsewhere above, dark scaling and mottling on breast; paler than young Pale Flycatcher, and throat unstreaked. **VOICE**: Song a soft squeaky *wit-wer-tsip, twititi . . ..* Call note a thin squeaky *see.* **HABITS**: Usually in pairs or family groups. Perches on shrub or low tree branch; feeds mainly by dropping to ground. Largely silent. **SIMILAR SPECIES**: Pale Flycatcher lacks crown streaks; all races slightly browner, usually somewhat larger, with slightly longer tail and with longer bill which is pale at the base. Spotted Flycatcher is slimmer, with more pointed wings, streaked breast, more peaked head shape. **STATUS AND DISTRIBUTION**: Common and widespread resident of dry woodland and bush, especially among acacias, up to 2000 m. Absent from the coastal strip, and less numerous in the more humid highlands and the west. Four races: *B. m. neumanni* (= *erlangeri*) in n. Kenya south to Kapenguria, Maralal and Wajir; *burae* in dry thorn-bush of eastern Kenya west to Garba Tula and Shaba GR, south to the Lali Hills, Ijara and the lower Tana River valley; *taruensis* around Tsavo East NP and south to the Tanzanian border; nominate *microrhynchus* in s. and sw. Kenya from Thika and Narok Districts, south through all of n. Tanzania except the coastal lowlands. The latter race intergrades with *neumanni* between Meru and the Athi River; *taruensis* and *burae* closely approach one another, apparently without intergrading; *taruensis* intergrades with *microrhynchus* around Simba (Traylor 1970). **Note**: *B. m. neumanni* was considered the species *pumilus* ('Little Grey Flycatcher') of Mackworth-Praed and Grant (1955). The genus *Bradornis* is merged with *Melaenornis* by some authors.

PALE FLYCATCHER *Bradornis pallidus*   Plate 87
(Pallid Flycatcher)

Length 150–170 mm (6–6.75"). A common light *brownish* flycatcher, generally in moister habitats than the preceding species. **Adult** slimmer than African Grey Flycatcher, with longer tail, *longer bill* and *no streaks on crown*; usually shows *pale tawny* (*not white*) wing edgings. *B. p. subalaris* is rather pale sandy brown above, with almost no trace of the dark breast band evident in the darker brown southern races *griseus* and *murinus*. Bill

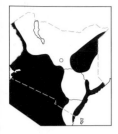

black, with pale mandible base; feet black; eyes dark brown. **Juvenile** spotted with buff or tawny above and with dark streaks on throat, breast and flanks. Northeastern *bafirawari* ('Wajir Grey Flycatcher') is pale grey-brown above, white below, with pale grey-brown breast band and flanks; it is the only subspecies adapted to dry thorn-bush country, normally a habitat of African Grey Flycatcher. **VOICE**: Song a high twittering, *tree-tricky-trit-tricky-chee-witty. . .*, less squeaky than song of African Grey Flycatcher. Calls include a soft *churr* and a thin *see-see*. **HABITS**: Often in pairs. Perches upright on low branches. Drops to ground to feed. **SIMILAR SPECIES**: African Grey Flycatcher compared above. Spotted Flycatcher has streaks on crown and breast, longer wings and peaked crown. Gambaga Flycatcher is smaller, with indistinct breast streaking. **STATUS AND DISTRIBUTION**: A locally common resident below 2000 m in lightly wooded or bushed country and along borders of riverine woods. Typically inhabits areas with stands of *Croton* trees and *Combretum/Terminalia* thickets. Four subspecies in our region: *murinus* from nw. border areas at Lokichokio and Mt Elgon south through the Kenyan highlands to Mara GR, the Chyulu and Taita Hills, and in n. Tanzania from Serengeti NP east through the Crater Highlands to the Mt Meru and Kilimanjaro foothills; *bafirawari* in dry thorn-bush of ne. Kenya from El Wak and Wajir south to Garissa, west to Garba Tula District; *griseus* from Voi and Taveta Districts south to Mkomazi GR and Tarangire NP in ne. Tanzania; *subalaris* in coastal lowlands from Tanga north to the Boni Forest, inland to the East Usambaras, Shimba Hills NP, Maji ya Chumvi, Taru and the Lali Hills, and along the lower Tana River to Bura. **Note**: The eastern *subalaris* appears not to intergrade with neighbouring *griseus*. It has been suggested that the two may not be conspecific (Traylor 1970), the apparent gap between their ranges as narrow as 80 km (50 miles). The two forms differ in measurements, as well as colour.

SILVERBIRD *Empidornis semipartitus*   Plate 87

Length 175–180 mm (7"). A uniquely coloured western flycatcher of open areas. **Adult** bright *silvery grey above* and *rich tawny-orange below*; tail rather long. Bill and feet black; eyes brown. **Juvenile** well marked above with black-bordered tawny spots; mottled buff and black on throat and breast. **VOICE**: Songs typically short, repeated many times, phrases varying from a slightly thrush-like *sur-eet-itisew* to those with the terminal note higher: *eee-cheri-chee* or *ee-sleeur-eeee* or *sweet siursur-eet-seet*. Also a longer *eep-eep churEEerip, eeep-eep cherip chchch, eee*, embellished with additional short chattering notes and an occasional *seep*. **HABITS**: Often in pairs perched prominently on low branches, dead trees or wires. Takes prey from the ground. **STATUS AND DISTRIBUTION**: Locally common resident in bush and savanna (especially with acacias), mainly below 1600 m. One population in northwest Kenya around Lokichokio and Kongelai, and from the Kerio Valley and Baringo District south to Mogotio and Rongai; another in the Lake Victoria basin (South Nyanza, Mara Region of n. Tanzania) and from Keekorok (s. Mara GR) south to Serengeti NP and Maswa GR. Local movements or post-breeding wandering reflected by records from Lake Turkana, Laikipia, Nakuru, Nairobi, Tarangire NP and Same.

LEAD-COLOURED FLYCATCHER *Myioparus plumbeus*   Plate 87
(Grey Tit-Flycatcher; Fan-tailed Flycatcher)

Length 140 mm (5.5"). A restless, *warbler-like* bird, frequently *raising, fanning and wagging its tail*. **Adult** blue-grey above and whitish below, with pale grey wash on throat and breast; under tail-coverts faintly tinged tawny. Shows whitish lores, short, narrow whitish superciliary stripes and white eyelids; *long blackish tail conspicuously white-sided*. Bill black above, blue-grey below; eyes brown; feet blue-grey. Similar to an American gnatcatcher (*Polioptila*) in appearance and behaviour. **Juvenile** browner above than adult, with buff spots on wing-coverts; underparts pale brown. Best identified by size, behaviour, and white outer tail feathers. **VOICE**: A plaintive repeated *peerri-peeeerr*. **HABITS**: Usually solitary. Actively forages in shrubs and low trees, moving constantly with much tail motion as it gleans insects from leaves and twigs. **SIMILAR SPECIES**: Ashy Flycatcher, in same habitat, lacks white in tail, has bolder face pattern and is much less active. **STATUS AND DISTRIBUTION**: Local and uncommon resident of bush, riverine forest and acacia woodland, mainly below 2000 m. Nominate *plumbeus* is western, from the Suam River, Kongelai Escarpment and the Marich Pass to the Kerio Valley and Baringo District. *M. p. orientalis* occupies coastal lowlands north to the Arabuko–Sokoke and Boni Forests, inland to the East Usambara foothills, and riverine woodlands in the Moshi and Arusha Districts and around Taveta and Kibwezi. One collected on the upper Tana River in Embu District, July 1963. Formerly common along the Voi River in Tsavo East NP.

SEMI-COLLARED FLYCATCHER *Ficedula semitorquata*   Plate 87

Length 130 mm (5"). A compact flycatcher with long wings, short tail, rounded head and small bill. **Spring male** (Feb.–March) black above and white below. Shows large white panel on inner part of closed wing, a smaller patch at base of primaries and often a short, *narrow bar across median coverts*. Has white forehead, white

extending from throat to below ear-coverts, white sides to tail and grey rump patch. **Female** and **first-winter male** grey-brown above and white below, with ashy wash on breast. Pale wing areas buff-tinged and less extensive, confined to edges of inner secondaries ('tertials') and to bar on tips of greater coverts, a small mark at base of primaries, and often a faint narrow bar across median coverts. Flight feathers and tail dark brown; rump may show pale grey patch. **Adult male in autumn/winter** retains striking black-and-white wing and tail patterns, but body and head as in female. **VOICE:** A repeated sharp *dzit*. **HABITS:** Forages in tree canopy, often quite high; stance often more horizontal than Spotted Flycatcher. Hawks insects in flight, changing perches frequently. **SIMILAR SPECIES:** See Collared Flycatcher. **STATUS AND DISTRIBUTION:** Uncommon palearctic migrant in the west, September–April, mainly on passage but also overwintering in forest edge, woodland and open country with scattered trees. Recorded from Mt Elgon, Kakamega Forest and Mara GR; rare east to Nakuru and Nairobi. All Tanzanian records are from south of our region.

COLLARED FLYCATCHER *Ficedula albicollis*   Plate 87

Length 120–130 mm (5"). **Spring male** differs from Semi-collared Flycatcher in having a *complete broad white collar around hindneck* and a *white rump patch*; lacks white bar on median coverts. **Female and autumn/winter male** usually indistinguishable in the field from Semi-collared, although some may show complete greyish collar. In the hand, *feathers of lower hindneck show diagnostic whitish subterminal crescents*, lacking in Semi-collared. Pale buff median-covert bar not reliable (usually evident in *semitorquata*, sometimes faintly present in *albicollis*). **VOICE AND HABITS:** Similar to those of Semi-collared Flycatcher. **SIMILAR SPECIES:** Semi-collared Flycatcher compared above. **STATUS AND DISTRIBUTION:** A palearctic migrant whose route to southern African winter quarters lies to the west of our region. Known here from a single record (Ng'iya, Nyanza, 2 Oct. 1972).

WARBLERS, FAMILY SYLVIIDAE
(World, *c.* 350 species; Africa, *c.* 200; Kenya, 101; n. Tanzania, 68)

A diverse group of small, slender-billed insectivorous birds (only distantly related to the nine-primaried New-World wood-warblers, Parulidae). Although sometimes merged with thrushes, babblers, and flycatchers, we treat them as a separate family as they represent a cohesive group conveniently considered apart from the rest of the muscicapid assemblage. The genera *Cisticola, Prinia, Spiloptila, Apalis, Heliolais, Camaroptera, Calamonastes* and *Eminia* are sometimes separated as the family Cisticolidae, a treatment which is at best tentative and neglects consideration of other distinctive 'African warblers' such as *Bathmocercus* and *Phyllolais*. We follow a more traditional course here and retain all in Sylviidae. Differences between genera in this family are readily apparent to the practised observer. The following brief summaries (excluding monotypic genera) cover general aspects of plumage, structural characters and habits not necessarily repeated in the species accounts.

Locustella. Shy, *skulking*, dull-plumaged warblers with *broad rounded tails*, noticeably *long under tail-coverts*, fine pointed bills and long toes. They characteristically inhabit dense scrub and herbaceous tangles or edges of marshy vegetation, where they remain near the ground, often bobbing their tails. They are seldom seen to fly. Our three species are palearctic migrants, only one of them regular in East Africa.

Acrocephalus. Brownish, long-billed warblers with large strong feet and slightly rounded, graduated tails; under tail-coverts long and prominent, but not so exaggerated as in *Locustella*. All except Sedge Warbler are quite plain and difficult to identify by plumage characters alone. Subtle colour differences between species must be considered with care, and with due regard for plumage wear and age. Freshly plumaged birds are richer in colour (more rufescent) and show greater contrast in wing edgings, rectrix tips and orbital markings than faded worn birds. Wing formula may be useful in distinguishing birds in the hand (Fig. p. 560). All are shy (but often inquisitive) skulkers, typically inhabiting reedbeds, swamps, moist thickets or herbaceous undergrowth. They frequently climb about in reeds or papyrus, but in winter quarters may be far from water. Five of the eight East African species are palearctic migrants.

Hippolais. Our four species, all palearctic migrants, resemble *Acrocephalus* in being plain above, with long (but fairly broad-based) bills and rather flat heads (crown feathers may be raised in excitement). Their tails are more square-ended, tipped white at the corners (except in Icterine Warbler), and the under tail-coverts are shorter than in *Acrocephalus*. Pale lores give a more 'bare-faced' appearance, and the three commonest species are grey or grey-brown above, not rich brown or olive-brown. They inhabit shrubbery and trees in dry woodland, bush and scrub. See Fig p. 562.

Sylvia. Relatively stout warblers characterized by short bill, rounded head and square-tipped tail. Plumage is predominantly grey-brown. Four migrant species visit our region from Eurasia.

Phylloscopus. Small, typically arboreal birds, mostly olive- or yellowish-tinged, with pointed wings, and slender booted tarsi. In addition to the well-known palearctic species with fine bills and pointed wings we include here the resident East African woodland warblers formerly (and perhaps better) placed in *Seicercus*. These have somewhat broader, flatter and more flycatcher-like bills (nostrils almost hidden by the frontal feathers) and more rounded wings; the long tarsus is partly scutellate, not booted. Two species build domed nests of plant material on or near the ground.

Bradypterus. Elusive warblers of dense damp forest undergrowth, rank herbage, and swamp vegetation. They have moderate straight bills, strong feet, short rounded wings, and the tail feathers may be soft and broad or stiff and narrow, often frayed and ragged. The typical nest is a deep cup of leaves, grass, plant fibre or hair, well hidden in dense low cover. Four resident species in our region.

Chloropeta. Flycatcher-like, brush- or papyrus-inhabiting warblers with wide flat bills, forwardly directed frontal feathers, well-developed rictal bristles, and large tarsi and toes; plumage of the two commoner species yellow below.

Hyliota. Two resident arboreal species with slender bills and long, pointed wings; plumage black above, yellowish or pale tawny below, and with some white on the wings. The nest is cup-like, built in high tree branches. This genus may be misplaced in Sylviidae.

Apalis (accent on the initial 'A'). Moderate- to long-tailed resident warblers of wooded areas, either in trees or in undergrowth. They are attractive, often confiding and of appealing habits; certain species habitually engage in exaggerated wing and tail movements. Most are quite vocal, and several give loud monotonous chipping notes for extended periods. They forage in pairs or small family groups, and regularly join mixed-species flocks. The usual nest is a purse-like bag of moss, lichen and spider web, with a top opening at one side, placed in a tree or shrub, but *A. pulchra* often reconditions an old nest of a camaroptera or sunbird. The eggs are highly variable. Prinias, Long-tailed Cisticola and Buff-bellied Warbler might be mistaken for birds of this genus. *Spiloptila* has been included in *Apalis* and may not warrant generic separation.

Cisticola. A large genus of mainly African warblers, treated in detail on pages 570–571.

Prinia. These and the possibly congeneric *Heliolais* (Red-winged Warbler) are long-tailed, typically low-foraging residents reminiscent of certain cisticolas. *Prinia* is believed by some to be polyphyletic and is divided into several monotypic genera, a course not followed here. They perch with the long tail raised at a jaunty angle, and often utter insistent chipping or peeping notes. Some are shy, others easily observed. Their nests are of the tailorbird type, beautifully woven and typically sewn between leaves or within a single large leaf, often in a tall herbaceous plant.

Sylvietta. The crombecs are stump-tailed little warblers of bush, woodland and forest, searching foliage and twigs or creeping around large branches in short jerks quite like nuthatches (Sittidae). They travel in pairs or with mixed-species flocks, and are often tame and confiding. The nest, a pendent pouch or bag of spider web, moss and plant material, is typically attached to a drooping branch.

Eremomela. Tiny, short-tailed and short-billed resident warblers of bush, woodland and forest. All are restless, flitting from bush to bush or through the tree tops, usually providing only brief observation. They travel in pairs or small parties, and sometimes join mixed species flocks. The nest is a small cup, either in a vertical fork or suspended from the rim between horizontal twigs.

Calamonastes and **Camaroptera.** Slender, short-winged residents of bush and forest. Although sometimes considered congeneric, and with similar nesting habits, the two groups appear quite distinct. Wren-warblers are rather long-billed brownish birds whose long tails are frequently in motion; they inhabit dry scrub and woodland, particularly *Acacia* and *Commiphora*. Camaropteras are shorter-billed, stub-tailed, olive or grey-and-olive birds, skulking in moist forest and forest-edge undergrowth.

RIVER WARBLER *Locustella fluviatilis* Plate 96

Length 130–140 mm (*c.* 5.5"). A secretive bird of rank undergrowth, usually located by its call. **Adult** dark olive-brown above, except for faint pale superciliary stripes. Sides of breast and flanks olive-brown, *chin and throat whitish, upper breast with soft dark streaks*; centre of belly whitish; buffy-brown under tail-coverts conspicuously pale-tipped. Bill horn-brown above, pale pinkish below; eyes dark or light brown; tarsi flesh-pink. **First-winter** bird similar to adult, sometimes yellowish on face and throat. **VOICE:** Call a repeated high-pitched *chik, chik* or *p'chick*. Song (occasionally heard late Dec. to April) a metallic *zizizizizizizizizi* in bursts lasting from a few seconds to over half a minute. **HABITS:** Those of the genus. Always shy and secretive. **SIMILAR SPECIES:** See Savi's Warbler. *Acrocephalus* warblers of similar size lack breast streaks, have more prominent superciliary stripes, shorter unmarked under tail-coverts, and less rounded tail. **STATUS AND DISTRIBUTION:** Palearctic passage migrant, November to early January and late March to April, in moist green thickets and rank herbage, often

along dry watercourses. Recorded from the eastern edge of the Kenyan highlands from Samburu GR and Meru District south to Kitui and Tsavo. Most numerous during southward passage. Small numbers winter around Mtito Andei. One Tanzanian record (Arusha NP, April 1968).

GRASSHOPPER WARBLER *Locustella naevia*   **Plate 96**

Length 120–135 mm (4.5–5.5"). Accidental in our region. Appears slender and tapered as it creeps or runs away; at rest may look more compact. Upperparts *warm olive-brown, with broad black streaks* on the back, rufous-tinged rump faintly streaked; tail rather long and often faintly barred. Faint, short, pale superciliary stripes. Underparts dull whitish to pale yellow or pale rufous, with variable spotting across the lower throat; breast and flanks brownish; *long, finely streaked, buff under tail-coverts*. Variation apparently independent of geography, age or sex. Bill dark brown above, pale yellowish brown below; tarsi pinkish. **Voice**: Call note a sharp *tuck, tchik* or *pitt* or *pitch*, repeated more rapidly in alarm. Song a high-pitched continuous insect-like reeling or buzzing. **Similar Species**: Sedge Warbler is more boldly marked above, with conspicuous broad white or buff superciliary stripes and unstreaked rufous rump. **Status and Distribution**: Known in East Africa only from one caught and photographed in the Nguruman Hills, 17 June 1977. The West Asian race *straminea* has wintered in Ethiopia (Ash 1978).

SAVI'S WARBLER *Locustella luscinioides fusca*   **Plate 96**

Length 130–145 mm (5–5.5"). Another vagrant, much like River Warbler but warmer brown above, the throat plain or bordered below with a necklace of *faint* diffuse spots; pale tips to under tail-coverts less pronounced. Shows short indistinct buffy-white superciliary stripes, and rufous-brown wash on flanks. **Voice:** A sharp *chik* or *pitch*. Alarm call a dry chatter. Song a far-carrying reel similar to that of Grasshopper Warbler, but lower-pitched and more mechanical-sounding. **Similar Species**: River Warbler compared above. Eurasian Reed Warbler has more pronounced superciliary stripes, paler underparts, shorter under tail-coverts and less rounded tail. **Status and Distribution**: Palearctic vagrant, here south of its normal African wintering range. Recorded twice at Ngulia, Tsavo West NP (6 Dec. 1975 and 21 Dec. 1987).

SEDGE WARBLER *Acrocephalus schoenobaenus*   **Plate 96**

Length 125–130 mm (5"). Distinguished from other small *Acrocephalus* by *bold cream superciliary stripes, heavily streaked back*, and *plain rufous-tinged rump* which contrasts with the *dark blunt tail*. Underparts of **adult** buffy white, more yellowish buff on flanks. Bill blackish brown, yellow at base of mandible; eyes brown; tarsi greyish. **First-winter** bird yellower or buffier than adult, with a necklace of faint spots across upper breast. **Voice**: A harsh *churr* and a sharp repeated *tuck*. Song, a prolonged medley of harsh and sweet notes, faster, less rhythmic and more 'buzzing' than that of Eurasian Reed Warbler, and less intense than on breeding grounds. **Habits**: Usually in small loose groups, foraging low in aquatic or waterside vegetation. Flies low, with tail spread and drooped. Somewhat less skulking than its relatives. **Similar Species**: Rare Grasshopper Warbler is much less boldly marked, lacks prominent superciliary stripes and has very long, streaked under tail-coverts. **Status and Distribution**: Palearctic migrant, November to early May. Winters commonly in waterside scrub and emergent vegetation on lake edges, mainly in w. and cent. Kenya above 1800 m, more locally in se. Kenya (e.g. Lake Jipe) and n. Tanzania. More widespread and locally abundant on April–early May passage, when sometimes in dry habitats. Migrants reported at up to 3000 m (Lewis and Pomeroy 1989).

GREAT REED WARBLER *Acrocephalus arundinaceus*   **Plate 95**

Length 180–190 mm (7–7.5"). Our largest migratory warbler, appearing heavy, with a long, fairly thick bill, *narrow but well-defined creamy-buff superciliary stripes*, and an ample tail. Upperparts olive-brown, often with rufous-tinged rump; sides of breast and flanks creamy buff to pale tawny-buff; whitish *throat faintly streaked in adults*. Bill horn-brown, the mandible pink at base; *tarsi usually pale brown in adults, typically darker or greyer in first-year birds*. *A. a. zarudnyi* more greyish above, less warmly tinged than nominate *arundinaceus*, and with paler underparts. **First-winter** birds appear paler, more yellowish tawny above, especially on rump; throat unstreaked. Underparts mostly cinnamon-buff. **Voice**: A loud harsh *chack*. Song loud, rhythmic and far-carrying, of harsh grating and croaking notes each repeated two or three times: *chirrk-chirrk kreek-kreek skyuk-skyuk syrrik-syrrik-syrrkk krruk-krruk . . ..* Sings regularly in winter quarters. **Habits**: Those of the genus. Usually soli-

tary. Flies low, with tail slightly fanned. Wintering birds often sedentary on territories for weeks. **SIMILAR SPECIES**: Basra Reed Warbler is much smaller, with a more slender bill, colder olive-brown upperparts and whiter underparts with no throat streaks. The smaller, less robust swamp warblers are more closely associated with water and very different in voice; they have shorter and more rounded wings and dark greyish tarsi. Greater Swamp Warbler is much greyer below. **STATUS AND DISTRIBUTION**: Palearctic migrant, November–April, typically in tall rank grass, reedbeds and green thickets, often near lakes and rivers. In Kenya, small numbers winter around Lake Victoria, in the central highlands and along the lower Tana River. Locally common on April passage in and east of the Rift Valley. Both *A. a. arundinaceus* and *A. a. zarudnyi* are reported from Kenya. Few records from n. Tanzania, although wintering birds reported near Lake Eyasi (Jan. 1960) and northbound migrants recorded near Arusha and on Pemba Island in April.

BASRA REED WARBLER *Acrocephalus griseldis*   Plate 95

Length 145–160 mm (5.5–6.25"). Duller and much smaller than Great Reed Warbler, with distinctive *long slender bill and dark greyish tarsi*. All plumages *uniformly cold grey-brown or olive-brown above*; underparts white, with buff tinge confined to sides of breast and flanks; throat never streaked. Whitish superciliary stripes prominent and pale eyelids noticeable with close view. Rather long tail, slightly fanned in flight, appears darker than rest of upperparts. **VOICE**: Call note a harsh nasal *chaarr*. Song structurally similar to those of Eurasian Reed and Great Reed Warblers, but low and subdued, less strident and less rhythmic: *chwik-chwak-chook-charra, tchuk-tchuk-whee-er skweek skwak skuiir, swerwee cherak cherak. . .*, lacking power and grating quality of Great Reed Warbler's song, not all notes repeated in pairs, and some elements of the song run together; recalls song of Yellow-whiskered Greenbul. Sings from December to March. **SIMILAR SPECIES**: Great Reed Warbler is larger, thicker-billed, warmer brown above, with (usually) rufous-tinged rump, and faintly streaked throat. Vocally distinct Lesser Swamp Warbler is warmer brown above, with brighter upper tail-coverts and rump, buffier underparts and short rounded wings. Eurasian Reed Warbler is slightly smaller, shorter-billed and shorter-tailed, paler above, with warm brown or rufous rump, less prominent superciliary stripes and browner tarsi. See also Marsh Warbler. **STATUS AND DISTRIBUTION**: Palearctic migrant, November to mid-April, in dense moist thickets and rank vegetation along ditches, often on seasonally inundated ground. Regular southward passage (Nov. to mid-Dec.) through Tsavo West NP (where over 1,000 ringed at Ngulia, 1972–93). Winters commonly in the lower Tana River valley from Baomo to Karawa; scattered records inland to Naivasha and in coastal lowlands south to Tanga and beyond. Relatively scarce on northward passage, along coast and inland to Tsavo region, in early April.

EURASIAN REED WARBLER *Acrocephalus scirpaceus fuscus*   Plate 95

Length 125–135 mm (5–5.5"). An olive-brown warbler, *often rufous-tinged above, especially on rump*. Underparts whitish, with buff wash across breast and on sides. *Narrow white eye-ring* (broken in front and behind); pale, moderately pronounced superciliary stripes. Bill thin and rather long; tarsi vary from pale brown to dark greenish brown (generally darker in young birds); toes often darker. Most Kenyan birds are of the pale eastern race *fuscus*, but warmer-coloured individuals may represent the nominate race. **VOICE**: Call notes include a soft *tchurr* and a louder harsh *skurr*. Song a rhythmic series of strident grating or squeaky notes, each repeated two or three times: *chup-chup-chic-chic-weet-weet-chip-churric-whit-whit-tsurric-tsurric. . ..* Commonly sings from December to March. **HABITS**: Those of the genus. Wintering birds often sedentary on territory for many weeks. **SIMILAR SPECIES**: For distinction from very similar African Reed Warbler and Marsh Warbler, see those species, also Fig. p. 560. Basra Reed Warbler is larger, with longer bill, more prominent superciliary stripes and greyish tarsi. **STATUS AND DISTRIBUTION**: Palearctic migrant, late October to early May, in green thickets, rank grass, reedbeds, hedges and scrub near cultivation. Winters commonly in the Lake Victoria basin, with smaller numbers between 1200 and 1800 m on eastern edge of the cent. Kenyan highlands from Meru south to Nairobi. Scarce and local farther east, with occasional records from Ngulia in Tsavo West NP. April passage at times marked through the Rift Valley and adjacent highlands. Few records from n. Tanzania, but northbound migrants noted in the North Pare and East Usambara Mountains, mid-March to late April.

AFRICAN REED WARBLER *Acrocephalus baeticatus*   Plate 95

Length 115–130 mm (4.5–5"). A small warbler similar to the preceding species. Widespread *A. b. cinnamomeus* plain, *rather pale, reddish brown above* (brightest on rump) and *warm buff below,* with throat and centre of belly whitish. Lores and superciliary stripes pale buff, as is the narrow eye-ring. Tarsi pale brown to grey or greenish grey. In the hand, distinguished from Eurasian Reed Warbler by shorter wing (under 58 mm) with more rounded tip (9th primary shorter than 5th; 9th usually longer than 6th in Eurasian Reed). Juvenile closely resembles adult.

A. b. suahelicus of Pemba Island is larger. **Voice:** Common note a repeated short churr. Song as in Eurasian Reed Warbler, a prolonged rhythmic tshic-chic-churric-churric . . ., thin, scratchy or squeaky. Mimics other species. **Habits:** Those of the genus. **Similar Species:** Eurasian Reed and Marsh Warblers are larger, more olivaceous above, more whitish below, with longer, more pointed wings. Marsh Warbler has whiter throat, typically pink tarsi and more rounded head, and differs vocally. Fulvous young Lesser Swamp Warbler is larger, heavier, darker, with strong blackish tarsi and toes. **Status and Distribution:** Resident. A. b. cinnamomeus is wide-ranging but local in rank grass, dense moist thickets, swamps and waterside shrubbery in the Lake Victoria basin and cent. Kenyan highlands. Also known from Tarangire NP north and east to the Crater Highlands, Amboseli NP, Lake Jipe and Mkomazi GR. Singles ringed in December in Tsavo West NP suggest some local movement. A. b. suahelicus is fairly common on Pemba Island in gardens, bush, thickets and forest on coral rag and small islets.

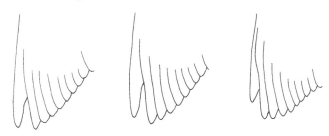

Wing-tip outlines (left to right) of Acrocephalus species: Marsh Warbler, adult Eurasian Reed Warbler and African Reed Warbler. The rudimentary 10th (outermost) primary is not shown. Note position of notch on 9th primary and position of the tip of that feather relative to tips of others.

MARSH WARBLER Acrocephalus palustris   Plate 95

Length 125–130 mm (c. 5"). Similar in size, build and coloration to race fuscus of Eurasian Reed Warbler, from which distinguished only with difficulty as follows: (1) slightly shorter and broader bill and more rounded crown, thus a less attenuated, more Sylvia-like head shape; (2) upperparts more uniform olive-brown, lacking rufescent tinge to rump (except in some first-autumn birds); (3) pale cream throat at times contrasts with more yellowish-buff breast; (4) tarsi typically pinkish brown (but often dark greenish brown in young birds); (5) in the hand, best criterion is position of notch on inner web of 9th primary (Fig. above) though this character does not separate first-autumn birds, and additional measurements of toe span (smaller in Marsh) and bill (shorter/wider in Marsh) may be needed (Pearson 1989). **Voice:** A harsh dry tchahh, kaahh or t-cherr similar to Eurasian Reed Warbler's note; also cha-cha-cha, a soft tuc, and a hard Hippolais-like chek. Full song (Feb.–April) a prolonged rich, varied warbling including mimicry of numerous palearctic and African birds; many notes distinct and well separated, others slurred and run together; liquid trills are characteristic. **Habits:** Those of the genus. **Similar Species:** Eurasian Reed Warbler discussed above. African Reed Warbler is smaller, brighter, much more rufescent above and buffier below. Basra Reed Warbler is larger, with longer bill and dark grey tarsi. **Status and Distribution:** Palearctic migrant, common to locally abundant on southward passage (Nov. to early Jan.) in broad range of scrub and bush habitats in cent. and se. Kenya. Much less numerous April to early May, when also present in coastal lowlands. Small numbers winter locally inland in se. Kenya, depending on length and success of the short rains. Ecologically widespread, mainly below 1600 m on migration, but rare in and west of the Rift Valley. Few records from n. Tanzania, where recorded November–February and April to early May in the Mkomazi GR and the East Usambara Mts.

GREATER SWAMP WARBLER Acrocephalus rufescens ansorgei   Plate 95

Length 165–180 mm (6.5–7"). A large, dull-coloured, strong-footed denizen of papyrus swamps in w. Kenya, with actions reminiscent of a Great Reed Warbler. Long slender bill obvious, and long dark tarsi and large toes often noticeable. **Adult** dingy grey-brown above, except for rufescent rump; underparts dull greyish, strongly tinged with brown or dull tawny on sides and flanks; throat and belly almost white, but throat/breast contrast less than in Lesser Swamp Warbler. Short, ill-defined superciliary stripes do not extend far behind eyes. Bill dusky brown above, buff below; corners and interior of mouth dull yellow (evident in singing bird). Tarsi dark bluish or greenish grey; toes similar, but yellowish beneath. **Juvenile** tawny or yellowish brown above and washed with pale tawny on underparts, quite different from adult. **Voice:** Alarm note a single or double chock. Other calls low and throaty, kweeok or kierok. Song a mixture of

gurgling and harsh churring phrases separated by short pauses, *churr, churr, chirrup, chuckle, cwiurok . . .*, or *krip-krr-krr-krr, kikweu-kikwer-kikweu, kieru-kwee-kwee-kwee*. **HABITS**: Creeps and hops among reed stems and drops onto water-lily leaves in pursuit of insects. Inquisitive, and responsive to vocal lures. **SIMILAR SPECIES**: See Lesser Swamp Warbler. Vocally distinct Great Reed Warbler is heavier, with stouter bill, longer wings, whitish and buff underparts and (usually) faint streaks on throat. Basra Reed Warbler, unlikely on geographic grounds, is more whitish below, more olive-brown above. **STATUS AND DISTRIBUTION**: Common resident of papyrus swamps around the Winam (Kavirondo) Gulf of Lake Victoria, from the Yala Swamp and Lake Kanyaboli east to Kisumu and Homa Bay. Reports from 2000 m in Nandi District probably refer to Lesser Swamp Warbler.

LESSER SWAMP WARBLER *Acrocephalus gracilirostris* Plate 95

Length 140–158 mm (5.5–6"). A common warbler of wet places. **Adult** brown above, brighter on rump; dull greyish-white superciliary or supraloral stripes rather indistinct; eyelids greyish white. *Throat white, contrasting with darker breast*; underparts otherwise whitish or greyish, darker on sides of breast and on flanks. Bill dusky brown, with mandible base salmon-pink, dull yellow, or grey; *inside of mouth bright orange or scarlet*; *corners of mouth bright yellow or orange*; tarsi dark olive-grey, blue-grey or black. **Juvenile** brighter, with tawny or fulvous upperparts. Age and abrasion affect appearance, as do subspecific differences. Highland *A. g. parvus* dark tawny-brown throughout above, the rump only slightly more rufescent; grey-brown to brownish tawny on flanks, sides, under tail-coverts and across breast. Western *jacksoni* is duller and paler brown, more greyish and less warm-toned both above and below, the belly and under tail-coverts almost white. The smaller *leptorhynchus* of eastern lowlands is tawny or olive-brown above, the rump and upper tail-coverts brighter (almost rufous) and more contrasting; flanks and under tail-coverts tinged with tawny-buff. **Juveniles** of all races more rufescent above than adults. **VOICE**: Prolonged song a pleasing series of musical and harsh notes, clearer and higher-pitched than the more guttural voice of Greater Swamp Warbler, e.g. *shkioo, cherk, tweeeoweeowew squeeo-squeeo squeeo squeeo, quewk weeoweeoweeo, chee-chee-chee-chee. . .* Some songs more rolling, *chrree-churree-churree, chrrrrr chak-chak, chirrweeoweeo-weeo-weeo, tsrrrk tsirrrr seeo-chick*. Calls include a harsh *chaa*, a hard *tchuck* and a low *chierok*. **HABITS**: Those of the genus. Usually in pairs in waterside vegetation. Quite vocal. **SIMILAR SPECIES**: Greater Swamp Warbler differs vocally, usually has pale buff mandible, and gape and mouth-lining are dull yellow, not bright orange; male appears much larger and coarser (but large male *gracilirostris* approaches small female *rufescens* in size). Basra Reed Warbler is longer-billed and more olive-toned above, with more prominent superciliary stripes, has whiter underparts and longer and more pointed wings. African Reed Warbler is warm brown above, but is smaller, has paler tarsi and smaller bill than bright juvenile Lesser Swamp Warbler. **STATUS AND DISTRIBUTION**: Locally common resident of cattails, bulrushes, reedbeds, papyrus, marsh grasses and lakeshore shrubbery. Three races: *A. g. jacksoni* on the islands and shoreline of Lake Victoria; *parvus* in the w. and cent. Kenyan highlands from Eldoret, Kapsabet and Nandi Districts east to Lake Baringo, Naivasha and Nairobi, and in n. Tanzania at Arusha NP, Monduli, the Mbulu Highlands and Lake Manyara and Serengeti NPs; *leptorhynchus* in coastal lowlands north to the lower Tana River, inland to the Usambara Mts, Lake Jipe, Taveta, Amboseli NP and Kibwezi District.

OLIVACEOUS WARBLER *Hippolais pallida elaeica* Plate 96

Length 120–130 mm (4.75–5"). Our smallest and commonest *Hippolais*, plain grey-brown above and whitish below. The distinct whitish superciliary stripe does not extend behind the eye, and a narrow white eye-ring is noticeable at close range. Bill pale orange or pinkish white below; tarsi pinkish grey to brownish grey. **First-winter** bird greyer above. Autumn adults grey and usually in very worn plumage. **VOICE**: Usual call a persistent hard, repeated *tac. . .tac* or *trrt. . .trrt*. Commonly sings a prolonged scratchy warble, with suggestion of an underlying Eurasian Reed Warbler-like rhythm: *shweek-chirri chirri seek-sik, siriskeei-chur-chweek chirr, seek-seek . . . .*. **HABITS**: Forages *Phylloscopus*-like in shrubs or in the canopy of larger trees. Habitually calls and flicks tail downward when foraging. Often sings during hot hours of the day. **SIMILAR SPECIES**: Upcher's Warbler is larger and paler grey, with longer bill, bulkier tail, and different song. Marsh and Eurasian Reed Warblers have similar head shape, but are richer brown above, less white below, and show darker lores. Marsh Warbler has similar hard call note. See Olive-tree Warbler. **STATUS AND DISTRIBUTION**: A palearctic migrant, late October to early April. Widespread and common in bush and dry woodland from sea level up to 1800 m; typically in large acacias, especially along dry river-beds, but also inhabits *Commiphora* woodland; shows preference for *Balanites* shrubs.

UPCHER'S WARBLER *Hippolais languida* Plate 96

Length 135–145 mm (*c.* 5.5"). An active grey-backed bird, distinctly larger than Olivaceous Warbler, with relatively *longer, slimmer bill, paler and greyer upperparts*, and *longer, bulkier white-edged blackish tail constantly in motion*. Narrow whitish superciliary stripe readily discernible, as is white on upper (and usually lower) eyelid. Recently moulted birds show *pale panel on closed wings formed by edges of secondaries*. Base of mandible

pinkish; tarsi pinkish grey. **Voice**: A *tuc, tuc* call, somewhat softer than that of Olivaceous Warbler and less persistently uttered. During February and March sings a prolonged song with sweet, somewhat warbling musical quality, suggestive of a *Sylvia* (especially Barred Warbler): *chuk-chuk-chuk swee-wee, skwiawer skiuirrri-ceek, chr-chr, tsi-tsi-tswee-swer.* **Habits**: Forages within low shrubs and tree canopy. Pumps tail or slowly wags it sideways; also engages in fanning and circular waving of tail, reminiscent of a shrike. **Similar Species**: Olivaceous Warbler is smaller, browner, shorter-billed, shorter- tailed, with less obvious pale wing panel, and different tail action; voice also different. Olive-tree Warbler is larger, with heavier bill, longer tarsi, more prominent wing panel, darker cheeks and less distinct superciliary stripes. **Status and Distribution**: Uncommon palearctic migrant, November to early April (main arrival Dec. to early Jan.). Winters in hot, dry bush country, mainly below 1200 m. Locally common east of the highlands, and widespread in small numbers throughout the arid north. Regular southward migration through Tsavo NPs, but in n. Tanzania known only from near Moshi and the East Usambaras.

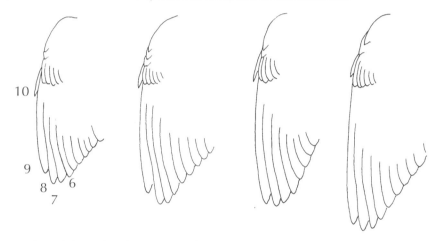

Wing outlines (left to right) of migrant Hippolais warblers: Olivaceous, Upcher's, Icterine and Olive-tree. Note length of 10th primary, and position of 9th primary tip relative to tips of primaries 8, 7 and 6.

OLIVE-TREE WARBLER *Hippolais olivetorum* Plate 96

Length 152–160 mm (6–6.25"). A large, slim-looking, *greyish* warbler with *long and rather stout bill* and *long grey or blue-grey tarsi.* *Flat-headed,* but erects crown feathers when excited. **Adult** brownish grey above and whitish below, the breast creamier. Wings often appear browner than back. Superciliary stripes shorter and narrower, and cheeks darker, than in Upcher's and Olivaceous Warblers. Eyelids white, as in those species. In fresh plumage, shows promient *pale panel on closed wing,* more conspicuous than in Upcher's. Tail grey, with narrow (and usually indistinct) white outer edge and tips. *Bill flesh-pink below, bright yellow or orange at base;* culmen dark. **First-winter** bird resembles adult. **Voice**: Usual note a loud harsh *chack* or *tcheck.* Alarm call a harsh nasal *chaaarr.* Song, occasionally heard in East Africa, is harsh and grating, somewhat reminiscent of Great Reed Warbler: *tchek-chek-kak-kak-kok, kek kek, chuk-chuck-chuk . .,* often prolonged. **Habits**: Less skulking than Upcher's Warbler, feeding more in outer canopy of low trees or in shrubs. Commonly flicks tail, but without the exaggerated movements of that species. **Similar Species**: Upcher's Warbler is smaller and paler, with finer bill which lacks yellow or orange tinge to mandible base, less noticeable wing panel and very different song. Olivaceous Warbler is still smaller, with thinner bill, and shows either a faint pale wing panel or none. Adult Barred Warbler also large and grey, but has stubby bill, longer tail and is pale-eyed. (Some young Barred Warblers have dark eyes.) **Status and Distribution**: Uncommon palearctic migrant, mainly east of the Rift Valley, usually recorded on passage October to early December (when regular in Tsavo West NP and near Isiolo), and less frequently March–April. Small numbers winter around Archer's Post/Isiolo, Lake Baringo, in Tsavo East NP and near Mombasa in dry open woodland and bush, but main wintering areas are from cent. Tanzania southwards. Scattered Kenyan records from the coastal lowlands, the lower Tana River and Ukwala in Nyanza. Few n. Tanzanian records away from Arusha and Lake Manyara NPs.

ICTERINE WARBLER *Hippolais icterina*   Plate 96

Length 135 mm (5″). A long-winged *Hippolais* with relatively short, broad bill. Adult's olive and yellow plumage may suggest a *Phylloscopus*, but lores are pale and there are no dark eye-lines. Crown feathers erected in excitement. **Adult** greenish-tinged above and with *pale yellow superciliary stripes and underparts*, narrow yellowish eye-ring, and in fresh plumage a *prominent wing panel* formed by yellowish edges of secondaries. Mandible and edges of maxilla dull white or pinkish; tarsi blue-grey. **First winter** bird usually greyer, sometimes with little yellow and inconspicuous wing panel. **VOICE:** A hard *tac*, a distinctive slurred *wipperueet*, and a less common *uwee*. Song a loud sustained mixture of musical and discordant notes, slightly reminiscent of Marsh Warbler, including mimicry. **HABITS:** Active, but with more deliberate movements than any *Phylloscopus*. Tends to forage within foliage, and usually sings from high in tree. **SIMILAR SPECIES:** Melodious Warbler, *H. polyglotta*, with shorter, more rounded wings and browner tarsi winters entirely in West Africa. **STATUS AND DISTRIBUTION:** Uncommon palearctic migrant, October–April, usually in open woodland or among scattered trees, but also in green bush and gardens. Small numbers winter regularly in open acacia woodland in Mara GR and Serengeti NP. Although most records are from in or west of the Rift Valley, it is also known from Nairobi, Ngulia (Tsavo West NP) and the Mombasa area.

BARRED WARBLER *Sylvia nisoria*   Plate 96

Length 155–165 mm (6–6.5″). A *large*, robust, usually *pale-eyed* warbler with a relatively long tail. General appearance can suggest a small shrike. Some first-winter birds resemble a large Garden Warbler. **Adult male** varies from brownish grey to pale grey above with pale scaling and wing-bars, whitish below with *extensive dusky barring*. *Long tail* shows white corners and narrow white edges. Bill horn-brown, yellowish or pink at base of mandible; eyes pale to bright yellow; heavy tarsi and toes brownish grey or pinkish. **Female** slightly browner grey with reduced barring, especially above (the brownest individuals less distinctly barred); less white on tail tip than in male. *Eyes pale yellow*; tarsi grey. **First-winter** plumage plain grey-brown above, with wing-coverts and flight feathers edged or tipped whitish; underparts buffy white, with *barring confined to flanks and under tail-coverts*, at times faint. Some show short buff superciliary stripes and whitish eyelids; *iris colour varies from dark brown to pale grey-brown* or ochre, sometimes with a yellowish outer ring. **VOICE:** A harsh *chack-chack* or *ch-ch-check*, and a chattering *chi-chi-ti-titititititit*. Contralto song (frequent Feb.–March) is varied, short or prolonged, includes rich musical notes and harsher sounds: *chweek tsuricheek chwerk tsweck, swee-swer-iliusweek-sweeik, chwa-chwa-sweek. . ..* Similar to song of Garden Warbler, but softer and less 'throaty'. **HABITS:** Shy and skulking; less lively than many warblers. Feeds in shrubbery and low trees. Erects crown and forehead feathers and pumps tail when excited. Flight heavy, low and direct, with tail slightly spread. **SIMILAR SPECIES:** Common Whitethroat is smaller, browner, with pale rufous wing edging and more white on sides of tail. Garden Warbler resembles some first-winter Barred Warblers, but lacks white on outer rectrices. Olive-tree Warbler is also large and grey, but slimmer, with (usually) a flat forehead, noticeable short superciliary stripes, dark eyes, and long pointed bill with orange-yellow at base below. **STATUS AND DISTRIBUTION:** Common palearctic migrant, late October to early April, in dry scrub, thickets and woodland, especially in *Commiphora* and succulent *Salvadora* bushes; mainly below 1200 m. Winters in Kenya in dry riverbeds in the Turkwell and Kerio Valleys, near Lake Turkana and South Horr south to Lake Baringo, Isiolo, Meru NP, Kitui, Mtito Andei, the Tsavo NPs and Mkomazi GR. More widespread on passage, but seldom recorded west of the Rift Valley.

COMMON WHITETHROAT *Sylvia communis*   Plate 96

Length 135–140 mm (c. 5.5″). A rather long-tailed warbler, brown or grey-brown above, with *pale rufous wing-feather edgings*, and a *white throat contrasting with pale buff underparts*. Tail prominently white-edged. **Adult male** usually has grey crown and ear-coverts, and pinkish wash on breast. Eyes pale yellowish to reddish brown; tarsi pale brown. **Female** has browner crown, little or no pink on breast and pale brown eyes. **First-winter** bird resembles female, but browner above and eyes usually darker grey-brown. **VOICE:** A harsh *chaar* or low *chur* and a hard *tek*. Subdued song a rather scratchy prolonged warbling, higher-pitched than that of Garden Warbler, most notes thinner and less distinct; commonly heard December–March. **HABITS:** Solitary or in loose groups, sometimes with Barred Warbler. Active, foraging among foliage of bushes and small trees. Often raises crown feathers and slightly elevates tail. **SIMILAR SPECIES:** See Garden Warbler and immature Barred Warbler. **STATUS AND DISTRIBUTION:** Locally common palearctic migrant, late October to April, preferring leafy scrub, scattered bushes, and small trees in dry country (especially *Acacia* and *Commiphora* woodland), typically between 800 and 1200 m. Winters commonly north and east of the Kenyan highlands, from Isiolo and Meru NP south to Nairobi, Machakos, Kitui, Kibwezi, Taita and into ne. Tanzania. More widespread on passage (Nov.–Dec. and April), when at times numerous in Mara GR, Arusha and Tarangire NPs and Mkomazi GR. Our birds represent the eastern races *icterops* and *volgensis*.

GARDEN WARBLER *Sylvia borin* Plate 96

Length 135–145 mm (5.5–5.75"). A *compact, stubby-billed, plain-looking* warbler with a noticeably *rounded head*, and *bland or 'gentle' facial expression,* with subdued pattern of *short greyish or pale buff superciliary stripes, narrow pale eye-ring accentuating the dark eye,* a dusky loral spot and short postocular line. *Upperparts uniformly dull grey-brown,* relieved only by narrow whitish primary tips in fresh plumage; may show a touch of white above primary coverts at very edge of wing. Underparts pale buff, darker across breast and along sides and flanks. The European nominate race is browner than the widespread *S. b. woodwardi.* Bill brown, paler (pinkish, yellowish or horn) at base; eyes dark brown to grey brown; tarsi grey or dark horn-brown. **Voice:** A sharp *teck-teck.* Song (subdued Sept.–Nov., more frequent and powerful in March and April) rich and low-pitched, not rapid, but most notes connected and given in long series with few pauses, *sweet-swer-wuriwur, swer-sweet-sweet, tsukiseet-seet, chwer-seet-wurasweet-chweri-cheek* . . . . **Habits:** Unobtrusive. Singles or small loose groups forage deliberately in leafy bush or tree canopy; lacks 'nervous' wing and tail movements of some warblers. **Similar Species:** Olivaceous Warbler is grey-brown but smaller than Garden, with flat forehead and longer pointed bill. Young Barred Warbler is larger, longer-billed and longer-tailed, and has pale wing-bars. Female Blackcap has contrasting reddish-brown crown. **Status and Distribution:** Palearctic migrant, mainly between 1000 and 1600 m in moist bush, leafy woodland and forest edge, late Setember to April. Common on southward passage in the Lake Victoria basin, Kakamega, Mara GR and Serengeti NP, and in e. Kenya from the edge of the highlands to Kibwezi and the Tsavo parks. Marked northward migration through cent. Kenya and the Rift Valley during April. Small numbers winter in n. Tanzania from Serengeti NP east to the Usambaras, and from the edge of the Kenyan highlands to Kibwezi and Tsavo West NP. Most birds represent the eastern race *woodwardi,* but nominate European birds are also known in Kenya.

BLACKCAP *Sylvia atricapilla* Plate 96

Length 140–148 mm (5.5–5.75"). A compact, robust warbler with distinctive contrasting crown colour. **Adult male** grey below, brownish olive-grey above, with *black crown;* tail dusky black, with outer feathers brown-edged. Bill black, more blue-grey at base; eyes hazel-brown; tarsi dull greyish blue or dark slate. **Female** and **first-winter** birds olive-brown above, with contrasting *reddish-brown cap,* duller in young birds; underparts dull creamy or buffy tan, paler on throat; eyelids (especially lower) narrowly whitish. Eyes of immature dark brown; tarsi grey-brown. *S a. dammholzi* generally paler and greyer above and whiter below than nominate *atricapilla.* **Voice:** A hard *tac tac.* Song a subdued varied warbling which may lead into a series of pure fluty notes; mimetic. Sings increasingly from January to March. **Habits:** Forages low in scrub and undergrowth, often in small parties. Feeds extensively on fruit. Some individuals territorial in winter, with regular song posts. **Similar Species:** Garden Warbler lacks crown patch. **Status and Distribution:** Common palearctic migrant, late October to early April, in woodland, forest edge and gardens, generally between 1600 and 2600 m, but as low as 1000 m in the East Usambaras. Winters commonly in the w. and cent. Kenyan highlands south to Serengeti and Arusha NPs, and all ne. Tanzanian mountains, including the Crater and Mbulu Highlands. Most birds represent *S. a. dammholzi,* the nominate race being relatively scarce in our region.

WOOD WARBLER *Phylloscopus sibilatrix* Plate 96

Length 110–125 mm (4.75–5"). An active arboreal warbler. **Adult** distinguished by its bright greenish upperparts, *bright yellow superciliary stripes* and *yellow throat and breast sharply demarcated from the white belly.* Wings are longer (extending beyond tail base) and the tail shorter than in Willow Warbler. Bill brown above, yellowish below; tarsi yellowish brown. **First-winter** bird has somewhat greyer upperparts than adult, and is paler yellow on throat and breast. **Voice:** A plaintive *puuu.* Song a high-pitched *vit-vit-vit-vit-vit* or *sit-sit-sit* . . ., accelerating into a trill. **Habits:** Typically forages high in trees. Often holds wings low, the tips drooping below tail base. Frequently flycatches. Does not customarily flick wings or tail. **Similar Species:** Willow Warbler and Chiffchaff are less green above and lack contrast between breast and belly. Yellow-throated Woodland Warbler has brown crown, grey underparts and shorter wings. **Status and Distribution:** Scarce palearctic migrant (fewer than 25 Kenyan records, mainly of southbound birds), November to early April, in broad-leaved trees and woodland at medium elevations, and recorded once in coastal mangroves. The few Tanzanian sight records are unsubstantiated.

CHIFFCHAFF *Phylloscopus collybita abietinus* Plate 96

Length 110–115 mm (c. 4.5"). Closely resembles Willow Warbler, but browner or buffier on breast and flanks, yellow-olive on wing edgings; tarsi typically *blackish or dark brown* (rarely light brown); superciliary stripes

somewhat less pronounced; has slightly more rounded head shape and smaller bill, which, combined with shorter wings, produces a subtly more compact impression. In the hand, distinguished by different wing formula (Fig. below). **VOICE:** The *hweet* call tends to be more monosyllabic than that of Willow Warbler, but varies. Distinctive song (usually from tall forest trees) is an irregular repetition of two notes, one slightly higher-pitched than the other: *chif chaff chif chif chaff. . .*, given from January onward. **HABITS:** Solitary. Feeds in tree canopy or lower branches. Restless, with much rapid wing-flicking plus vertical pumping and lateral twitching of tail. **SIMILAR SPECIES:** Willow Warbler compared above. See Wood Warbler. **STATUS AND DISTRIBUTION:** Uncommon palearctic migrant, November to early March, in montane forest between 2000 and 3500 m. Winters regularly on Mt Elgon, Mt Kenya and the Aberdares. Occasional at lower elevations on passage. Records of singing birds from Marsabit, the Cheranganis, Mau Narok, Kakamega and the Trans-Mara Forests. Single trapped migrants examined at Lake Kanyaboli (March) and Ngulia (Dec.). In n. Tanzania, known only from three early specimens (Jan.–March) from Mt Kilimanjaro.

Wing outlines of Willow Warbler (left) and Chiffchaff. Note position of 9th primary tip and emargination details.

WILLOW WARBLER *Phylloscopus trochilus*   Plate 96

Length 110–120 mm (*c.* 4.5″). A small warbler, olivaceous above and whitish below, with pale yellow superciliary stripes, dusky and yellowish streaking on throat and breast, and yellow at bend of wing. Tarsi typically pale yellowish brown, sometimes dark blackish brown; rarely, toes and lower tarsi yellow, upper tarsi dark. **Adult** plumage variable. Some adults of *P. t. acredula* are well streaked with greenish and with yellow below, others much browner above and whiter below. The race *yakutensis* lacks olive and yellow tones, is grey-brown above, dull white below, greyish across the breast, and has whitish superciliary stripes. Most **first-winter** *acredula* have more extensive yellow below. **VOICE:** Call note, *hooweet*, very similar to that of Chiffchaff but more disyllabic. Song a melancholy liquid cadence of similar notes on a descending scale, typically starting faintly, becoming louder, then fading away, but with more distinctly phrased ending: *sweet sweet suEEtu.* **HABITS:** Sometimes flicks wings and regularly pumps tail up and down (but apparently lacks the lateral twitch of Chiffchaff). Partial to acacia trees, but feeds in vegetation at all levels, from weedy herbs to tree canopy. **SIMILAR SPECIES:** Wood Warbler is brighter, with sharply defined yellow throat and breast. Chiffchaff not easily distinguished, but slightly browner, with less distinct superciliary stripes, tarsi usually black, wing more rounded (Fig. above). **STATUS AND DISTRIBUTION:** Palearctic migrant, mid-September to early May. Winters commonly in woodland, forest edge and in bush with scattered small trees, mainly in w. and cent. Kenya at medium elevations. More widespread on passage, especially during northward movement, late March to April. Eastern Siberian *P. t. yakutensis* present in small numbers, but most Kenyan birds represent the e. European–cent. Siberian race *acredula.*

UGANDA WOODLAND WARBLER *Phylloscopus budongoensis*   Plate 96

Length 95–105 mm (*c.* 4″). A tiny arboreal warbler of w. Kenyan forests, easily overlooked except for its distinctive song. **Adult** olive-green above and on the sides; underparts whitish. Creamy-white superciliary stripes bordered below by black eye-lines. Tarsi dark brown, bill largely black. **Juvenile** dark on crown, slightly more olive on breast and flanks than adult. **VOICE:** A sweet song of four or five high notes, thin yet fairly loud: *see-su-su-eet* or *see-see-su-weet.* **HABITS:** Solitary or in pairs, sometimes in mixed-species flocks. Usually forages in

middle or lower tree branches in forest interior, descending to ground level only when breeding. **SIMILAR SPECIES**: Green Hylia, in the same forests, is larger and much stockier, has heavier bill and different song. Palearctic *Phylloscopi* are paler below, and face patterns are less bold. **STATUS AND DISTRIBUTION**: Fairly common resident in Kakamega Forest; much less numerous in the nearby North and South Nandi Forests. Formerly at Nyarondo.

BROWN WOODLAND WARBLER *Phylloscopus umbrovirens mackenzianus*   Plate 96

Length 105–120 mm (4–4.5"). A highland warbler, mostly *warm brown above, with bright olive-green wing edgings; pale tawny superciliary stripes bordered below by dark eye-lines. Underparts greyish white, the flanks tawny or rusty;* under tail-coverts yellowish; bend of wing pale yellow. Bill horn-brown above, yellowish below; eyes brown; tarsi greyish pink. **VOICE**: Usual song a clear descending series of musical notes, *tu-ti-teeo-teeo-teeo-teew*, or *titiri-titiri-cheeo-tu-tu*. Another is a long series of repeated phrases, *tseu-tsi-tsee-tsee chew, weechu weechu weechu, tsuchee tsuchee tsuchee, sweet sweet sweet sweet. . .*, typically with a brief pause after each group of similar notes. The song interspersed with occasional rapid trills. Alarm note *tu-wiu*. **HABITS**: In pairs, small family parties, or mixed-species flocks in trees or shrubbery. **SIMILAR SPECIES**: Allopatric Uganda Woodland Warbler is olive-green above and on sides, lacking tawny or rufous wash on flanks. **STATUS AND DISTRIBUTION**: Fairly common resident of montane forest and woodland, bamboo and giant heath between 1500 to 3300 m or higher, from northern mountains (Kulal, Nyiru, Marsabit, Loima and Elgon), the Ndotos, Karissia Hills and the Cheranganis south through the w. and cent. Kenyan highlands, Mau and Trans-Mara Forests, the Nguruman and Chyulu Hills, all n. Tanzanian mountains (except the South Pares and Usambaras), the Crater and Mbulu Highlands and Mt Hanang.

YELLOW-THROATED WOODLAND WARBLER *Phylloscopus ruficapillus minullus*
Plate 102

Length 100–110 mm (4–4.5"). A colourful warbler of montane forest in se. Kenya and ne. Tanzania. Olive-green above, with *lemon-yellow face, throat and under tail-coverts; crown and nape tawny-brown;* dark line through eye; grey wash on breast; flanks oliveyellow and grey. **Juvenile** duller, with yellowish-olive wash across breast. **VOICE**: Call a high-pitched *seeu*. Songs sweet and variable, e.g. (1) *tee-tuitee-tuitee,* (2) *see-see seesee seet,* (3) *tee, tew tew tew tew,* (4) *twee, tewi tewi tewi tewi,* the first note highest, (5) *tee-pe-tee-pe-tee, pe-pe-tee,* and (6) *uree-tsee-tsuiEEsee.* May suggest call of European Coal Tit, *Parus ater.* **HABITS**: Pairs or family groups forage actively among trees and (less often) in undergrowth, at times with mixed-species flocks. **SIMILAR SPECIES**: Wood Warbler has white under tail-coverts and no brown on head. **STATUS AND DISTRIBUTION**: Common in forest and forest edge below 2300 m in the South Pare and West Usambara Mts; also in the East Usambaras, descending as low as 500 m. In Kenya, confined to forest in the Taita Hills, where fairly common in the limited remaining habitat.

GREEN HYLIA *Hylia p. prasina*   Plate 96

Length 120 mm (4.75"). A *stocky, dark* warbler of w. Kenyan forests. **Adult** plain dark olive above, darker on head, with *long pale yellowish superciliary stripes* and dark lores and ear-coverts. Cheeks paler, brighter olive. Chin whitish; underparts otherwise olive-grey, darker along sides and obscurely streaked on throat. *Fairly strong black bill* and stout body separate it from most sources of confusion. **VOICE**: A loud, penetrating double whistle, *tyee-tyee* or *tee-yeu,* the first note higher. Also a rapid harsh chatter, *chreeeeee-che.* **HABITS**: Usually solitary. Forages in low trees and undergrowth; does not regularly join mixed-species flocks. Nest globular, in shrub or low tree, loosely built of dead leaves and plant down. **SIMILAR SPECIES**: Uganda Woodland Warbler is smaller, more slender and much paler on belly. **STATUS AND DISTRIBUTION**: Rather uncommon resident in the Kakamega and Nandi Forests; formerly on Mt Elgon.

LITTLE RUSH WARBLER *Bradypterus baboecala*   Plate 95

Length 128–145 mm (5–5.75"). A skulking, dark brown warbler of swamps and marshes, conspicuous only in display, when it flies low over the water or reeds with audible wing-rattling, its ample tail well spread and held downward. *Short black streaks on lower throat* are usually diagnostic, but not always easy to see and racially

variable, finer and sometimes almost lacking in *B. b. moreaui.* Colour of upperparts varies racially in **adults**: rich rufous-brown in *elgonensis,* dark olive-brown in *centralis,* pure dark brown in *moreaui,* which otherwise resembles nominate southern African birds. Shows narrow whitish superciliary stripes; rich buffy brown extends from cheeks across breast, separating whitish throat and belly; flanks and under tail-coverts olive- or tawny-brown. Dark brown tail narrowly barred with black and tipped with pale brown. Bill black, base of mandible blue-grey; eyes brown; *tarsi brownish pink,* toes darker. **Juvenile** richer brown above, buffy to yellowish below, throat streaks narrower and sometimes extending along sides of lower neck. **VOICE:** Call note a single *chup.* Song of *B. b. elgonensis* (and *centralis*) a thin *seet* or sharper *zrip* or *zri* repeated 10–18 times, slowly at first, then becoming faster and still faster as the notes gradually fade away: *zri - zri - zri - zri-zri-zri-zizizizizizizizi;* quality reedy and somewhat insect-like. Southeastern *B. b. moreaui* has similar 'bouncing-ball' pattern, but a much deeper, louder *turr - turr -turr-turr turr-turrturrturrturr* or *chwerk, chwerk . . . cherk-cherk-cherkcherkcherkcherk . . .,* the eight to 18 notes all on same pitch, less measured, and acceleration less pronounced than in *elgonensis;* virtually identical to song of nominate southern African birds, to tape recordings of which *moreaui* responds, though it ignores those of *elgonensis.* The latter, together with *centralis* and perhaps other forms, may constitute a species distinct from the southern populations. **HABITS:** Skulks in low swamp or marsh vegetation. Gives characteristic song when flying a metre or so above wet substrate or across water in narrow hippo trails amid tall sedges or reeds. A few wing sounds, *prrt-prrt-prrt,* regularly terminate each vocal display flight. **SIMILAR SPECIES:** Broad-tailed Warbler (which in flight may produce audible wing whirring) lacks throat streaks, has much larger tail and very long, pale-tipped under tail-coverts. Evergreen Forest Warbler has dark streaks on lower throat, but inhabits forest undergrowth. **STATUS AND DISTRIBUTION:** Locally fairly common in large perennial swamps, as well as stream edges. The race *elgonensis* ranges from the Kenyan highlands to Laikipia and Trans-Nzoia Districts; also in the Mara GR and the Lake Victoria basin. *B. b. moreaui* inhabits coastal lowlands north to the lower Tana delta, and inland to the East Usambaras, Arusha and Moshi Districts, Lake Jipe, Taveta and Amboseli NP. *B. b. centralis* just reaches our area in n. Tanzanian swamps south of Lake Manyara and Tarangire NPs and the Mbulu Highlands.

WHITE-WINGED WARBLER *Bradypterus carpalis*   **Plate 95**

Length 165–170 mm (6.5"). A distinctive warbler of extensive papyrus swamps, in our region confined to the Lake Victoria basin. **Adult** unique, with *heavily streaked throat and breast,* white belly, *white or creamy patch on carpal area of wings,* and *white-tipped wing-coverts.* Upperparts dark brown. Bill mostly black; eyes dark brown; feet brownish. **Juvenile** less clearly streaked below, dusky brown on sides, flanks and centre of belly; some creamy white on bend of wing, but wing-coverts not white-tipped. **VOICE:** A succession of short loud notes, audible for several hundred metres, with almost metallic resonance, starting slowly, accelerating, then fading away: *tsyik, tsyik, tsyik, tsyik-tsyik tyur-tyur-tyur-turturturtur,* often followed by four or five loud explosive whirring wingbeats. Little Rush Warbler has similarly patterned song, but where sympatric with *carpalis* its songs are weaker and much higher-pitched. **HABITS:** Highly vocal, but keeps to dense papyrus stands, where it forages low down among the stem bases. Shy but inquisitive. **SIMILAR SPECIES:** Swamp warblers and other *Acrocephalus* species may be seen in papyrus stands, but none has the unique pattern of White-winged Warbler. **STATUS AND DISTRIBUTION:** Locally common resident in the interior of papyrus swamps. In Kenya, known from the Yala Swamp, Lake Kanyaboli and Usengi east to Kisumu and Kendu Bay.

EVERGREEN FOREST WARBLER *Bradypterus lopezi*   **Plate 95**

Length 128–145 mm (5–5.75"). A dark, dull bird of dense undergrowth and ground cover in highland forest. Deep olive-brown above, with light superciliary stripes; dark greyish olive below, paler on chin and centre of belly; *short diffuse blackish streaks on lower throat and upper breast* diagnostic, but inconspicuous. *Tail feathers usually much frayed and pointed. B. l. usambarae* is warmer brown above and less grey below than *mariae.* **VOICE:** Songs vary in pitch and accenting, but most consist of one note or short phrase repeated eight to 20 times with little variation. Some begin softly and become louder: (1) *p'chew-p'chew-p'chew-p'chew-p'chew . . .;* (2) a crescendo *cher-TEE cher-TEE cher-TEE. . .* or *tur-CHEE tur-CHEE,* somewhat apalis-like. Other songs more even-pitched: (3) *chewi-chewi-chewi-chewi. . .,* (4) *wuchi-wuchi-wuchi. . .,* varied to (5) a slower, softer *tewsi, tewsi, tewsi . . .;* and (6) *chu-CHUi, chu-CHUi, chu-CHUi . . ..* Call note a hard sharp *TCHEW!* or *chi-CHEW;* this varied to *CHIR-U, CHIR-U* in *usambarae,* and sometimes preceded by a high-pitched *see-see* (Sclater and Moreau 1933). Also has thin chattering annoyance notes. Two birds may call in duet. **HABITS:** A master skulker. Hops and creeps in low vegetation and debris, with tail slightly elevated; flits quickly between adjacent perches, but usually flies only a metre or two. **SIMILAR SPECIES:** Juvenile Cinnamon Bracken Warbler, also dark brown above, is longer-tailed (unless quite young), more yellowish below. Little Rush Warbler has blackish throat streaks, but is warmly coloured

on sides and flanks and inhabits swamps and marshes. Mountain Illadopsis is more robust, its tail rarely appearing threadbare. **Status and Distribution:** Local and generally uncommon resident of highland forest. *B. l. mariae* ranges between 1700 and 3000 m in the w. and cent. Kenyan highlands from Limuru north and west to the Aberdares, Mt Kenya, North Nandi, Elgon, and Mau and Trans-Mara Forests; also in the Chyulu Hills. In n. Tanzania in the Crater Highlands around Oldeani and Karatu, also Arusha NP, Mt Meru and Kilimanjaro. Tanzanian *usambarae* ranges north to the East and West Usambaras (between 900 and 2200 m) and the Pare Mts, extending to the Taita Hills in se. Kenya.

CINNAMON BRACKEN WARBLER *Bradypterus cinnamomeus* Plate 95

Length 142–150 mm (5.5–6"). A richly coloured warbler of bracken and briars. **Adult** *rufous-brown* (to dark brown in Chyulu Hills birds), with prominent *pale superciliary stripes* and *whitish throat and belly*. The tail feathers, broad when fresh, soon become worn and narrowed. Throat and belly whitish, underparts otherwise strongly rufous-tinged. **Juvenile** darker dusky brown above, olive-brown and yellowish below. **Voice:** Call note a soft *tseep*; also a scolding *chrrrr*. Song of *B. c. cinnamomeus* a loud *slow* trill, *cheee, chur-wr-wr-wr-wr-wr-wr-rrr-rrr-rrrr*, or *twee, twee, tu-ur-ur-ur-ur-ur-rrrrrrrr. B. c. rufoflavidus* gives a less rolling or trilling *chew, tswee-tswee-tswee-tswee* or *t'see, chee-chee-chee-chee* (Sclater and Moreau 1933). **Habits:** Shy and skulking, typically in clearings or forest edge, rarely in forest interior, where usually replaced by Evergreen Forest Warbler. **Similar Species:** Adult Evergreen Forest Warbler is dark brown, not rufous, with blackish streaks on throat; juvenile much less yellow than young Cinnamon Bracken Warbler. **Status and Distribution:** Locally common resident of highland-forest edges and clearings, overgrown roadsides and brushy bamboo, mainly above 2000 m. Nominate race widespread in the w. and cent. Kenyan highlands north to Mt Nyiru; *rufoflavidus* in n. Tanzania's Crater and Mbulu Highlands, Mt Hanang, Arusha NP, Mt Meru, Kilimanjaro and the West Usambaras. Darker birds in the Chyulu Hills, s. Kenya, originally named *B. c. chyuluensis*, now generally included within *rufoflavidus*. Other border populations in the Nguruman Hills and nearby Loliondo are not racially assigned.

BLACK-FACED RUFOUS WARBLER *Bathmocercus rufus vulpinus* Plate 101

Length 120–130 mm (c. 5"). A unique, *black-faced* bird of w. Kenyan forest undergrowth. **Adult male** *bright rufous,* with black extending from forehead and face to centre of breast and upper belly. Bill black; eyes dark red or red-brown; feet dark blue. Concealed bright blue skin of neck may be visible in singing males (but no observation as yet supports this). **Female** has male's pattern, but olive-grey replaces the rufous. **Juvenile** dark olive or olive-grey, with central underparts much lighter; no black; male shows some rufous on wings and tail; female uniformly drab, best identified by shape and size if not seen with adult. Young male later shows rufous patches on sides and splotches of black on underparts. **Voice:** Loud, extremely penetrating, slowly uttered and prolonged notes easily mistaken for an insect sound; often given antiphonally by a pair, but male also sings alone: *EEEENH. . . EEEENH. . . EEEENH. . .*, or *FEEE, FEEE, FEEE . . .*, a characteristic sound of some western forests, ventriloquial and hard to pinpoint. Quality similar to that of illadopsis voices. Call note a loud *chip*. **Habits:** Secretive, but highly vocal. Skulks in bracken and other low vegetation along forest trails and near edges of clearings. **Status and Distribution:** Common in forest undergrowth from Sotik and Kericho north to the Kakamega and Nandi Forests and southern slopes of Mt Elgon.

AFRICAN MOUSTACHED WARBLER *Melocichla mentalis* Plate 95
(Moustached Grass Warbler)

Length 185–190 mm (c. 7.5"). A *large*, skulking, brown-backed warbler with a *long, broad, blackish-brown tail* showing buff feather tips. **Adult** rich brown above, rufous-tinged on forehead, rump and upper tail-coverts. *Black malar streaks* contrast with white cheeks and throat; *lores and area around eyes white;* dark ear-coverts show white shaft streaks at close range. Underparts tawny, except for white chin, throat and lower belly. *Eyes yellow or cream;* bill black above, mostly pale bluish grey below. *M. m. orientalis* barely distinguishable from nominate birds, but slightly paler and more rufous-brown on back. **Juvenile** dark-eyed, lacks rufous on head, and has buff-tipped wing-coverts. **Voice:** Utters a wheatear-like *tuckk* (Sclater and Moreau 1933) and a loud chattering annoyance call, *chi-chi-chi-chi. . . ..* Songs loud, sprightly and hurriedly delivered, of loud sharp notes and short warbling or bubbling phrases, with numerous changes in pitch: (1) *twip-twip-twip-twip chiWEE chipity-chip teu teu teu,* (2) *tsyk, tchuk TSYUK TSYUK TSYUK TSYUK chordilee-ideleee churdle-tweeee,* or (3) *chip chip churdelee churdelee chew* and variations (the almost bulbul-like quality well conveyed by Chapin's memory aid: "chirp-chirp-chirp-chirp, doesn't it tickle you?"). Some songs have higher wispy notes added: (4) *tsi-chireeee WIDDLEY WIDDLEY WEE, tsip-tsyip tsyip tsee, cheree cheree CHEW-CHEW-CHEW tyee.* **Habits:** Shy and skulking. Haunts low brushy vegetation, especially where grass is

tall and undisturbed along streamsides. Sidles up grass stems to sing. When alarmed, flicks tail and drops into cover. **SIMILAR SPECIES**: Broad-tailed Warbler is a plain pale bird, smaller and daintier except for its exaggerated tail. **STATUS AND DISTRIBUTION**: Local and uncommon in rank herbage and dense grass along streams. The nominate race ranges in w. Kenya from Mt Elgon and Saiwa NPs to South Nyanza, Ruma NP (Lambwe Valley), Mara GR and Serengeti NP (one record, Aug. 1985); also disjunctly from Meru NP, Embu and Nairobi, south to Selengai, Simba, Kibwezi, the Taita and Chyulu Hills, and to Kilimanjaro and Arusha Districts in Tanzania. *M. m. orientalis*, also Tanzanian, extends from the East Usambaras (old records around Amani and the Sigi Valley) south to the Pangani River and Dar es Salaam; formerly in Tsavo East NP.

BROAD-TAILED WARBLER *Schoenicola brevirostris alexinae*   Plate 95
(Fan-tailed Warbler)

Length 154–160 mm (6"). A skulking, brown-backed, dark-tailed warbler of wet grasslands, small-bodied but with a *remarkably broad graduated tail; wide black rectrices pale-tipped, as are the very long grey-brown under tail-coverts.* **Adult** tawny-brown above, darker on crown, greyer on sides of neck; wings more dusky, the feathers edged with rufous. Faint pale superciliary stripes visible at close range. Underparts white, tinged with tawny on breast, sides and flanks. Bill black above, bluish horn below; eyes brown; feet pale brownish pink. Birds in the Chyulu Hills are darker. **Juvenile** similar to adult, but underparts yellowish-tinged. **VOICE**: Song a weak metallic *cheep. . . cheep. . . cheep. . . cheep. . .*, or *simp . . . simp . . .*, from perch or in aerial display flight. Call notes a harsh *chick* and a sharp *prit-prit.* **HABITS**: Creeps about in coarse grass. Usually seen when flushed from underfoot, going only a short distance with laboured flight, tail fanned and bobbing, before dropping out of sight; flushed again only with difficulty. Displaying male circles in a wide spiral, the wings producing a soft whirring sound, then sails down on set wings to perch on tall grass stem. **SIMILAR SPECIES**: Little Rush Warbler lives in dense reedbeds, differs vocally from Broad-tailed and makes louder, more rattling, wing noises; its brown tail is much smaller and lacks pale feather tips. African Moustached Warbler is larger and bulkier, with distinctive head pattern and less exaggerated tail. **STATUS AND DISTRIBUTION**: Local and uncommon resident of wet grassland or low sedge meadows between 1150 and 2150 m from Mt Elgon south to Nyanza, Ruma NP and the Mara GR, east to Nakuru and Nairobi NPs, Thika and disjunctly to the Chyulu Hills. In n. Tanzania, not uncommon in Serengeti NP, along the northern base of Mt Meru and in Arusha NP. Less common than formerly as tall grass gives way to overgrazing and cultivation. **NOTE**: Sometimes considered conspecific with the Indian *S. platyura*.

PAPYRUS YELLOW WARBLER *Chloropeta gracilirostris*   Plate 102

Length 135 mm (5.25"). A scarce inhabitant of dense *papyrus swamps* fringing Lake Victoria. Resembles Mountain Yellow Warbler, but with slimmer bill, larger tarsi, *much longer toes and claws*, and *no yellow on lores*. **Adult** olive-brown, strongly rufous-washed on wings, lower back, rump and tail. Underparts yellow, rufous-tinged on flanks and under tail-coverts. Bill brown; eyes orange-rufous; mouth-lining red-orange; tarsi and toes black. **VOICE**: Song sibilant or semi-whistling: a short series of notes described as *to-tslo-wee*, or *trslo-tschlee-wo*, or *tschlee-ow* (S. Keith). Chapin referred to it as *chwee-chwee-chwee*. An erratic singer. **HABITS**: Much like those of swamp warblers or reed warblers, hopping between papyrus stems in low foraging. **SIMILAR SPECIES**: Mountain Yellow Warbler compared above. **STATUS AND DISTRIBUTION**: Local resident of extensive papyrus stands, in our area known only from the Yala Swamp, Lake Kanyaboli, Kisumu and Kendu Bay.

DARK-CAPPED YELLOW WARBLER *Chloropeta natalensis massaica*   Plate 102
(African Yellow Warbler; Yellow Flycatcher)

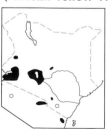

Length 135–140 mm (5.5"). A yellow-breasted, *flycatcher-like* warbler of low rank vegetation, with broad bill, well-developed rictal bristles, and often upright posture, but has long tarsi and strong toes. **Adult** bright *yellow below*, more olive on flanks; olive-brown above, with *contrasting sooty-brown crown* (olive-black in Chyulu Hills birds); supraloral lines yellow. Bill dark brown above, pale pinkish buff or dull ochre below; eyes brown; tarsi and toes grey or blackish. **Juvenile** tan or dull ochreous tawny, with brown crown. **VOICE**: Song a short but musical warbling, *twiya twiya, wichuwichu wichu*, and a brief *chui chui, chuweya.* Alarm note a harsh *check.* **HABITS**: Forages in low shrubs and herbage; sidles up and down grass stems. Sings from exposed perch, but when alarmed drops into vegetation and sneaks away. Often raises crown feathers. **SIMILAR SPECIES**: See Mountain Yellow Warbler. **STATUS AND DISTRIBUTION**: Uncommon resident of rank herbage, grass and brush, especially along streamsides or other moist sites between 1100 and 2300 m. Ranges from Mt Elgon and Saiwa NPs south to Kakamega, Nandi, Kericho, Sotik and Nyanza, east to the Aberdares and Nairobi and Meru Districts; also in the Chyulu and Taita Hills, Arusha and Moshi Districts, lower slopes of Kilimanjaro and the Usambaras (occasional).

MOUNTAIN YELLOW WARBLER *Chloropeta similis*   **Plate 102**

Length 120–140 mm (4.75–5.5"). More warbler-like in habits and appearance than Dark-capped Yellow Warbler, which it largely replaces at higher elevations, usually along forest edges, although the two overlap around 1900 m on Kilimanjaro. **Adult** uniformly olive-green above, the crown coloured like the back. Wings and tail more dusky, but with bright olive edgings. Loral line (or spot) and underparts bright yellow. Bill dark brown, paler at base below. **Juvenile** generally greenish olive, darker above. **VOICE:** A slow melodious song with slurred whistles, canary-like warbling and trills, *turee tsk-tsk, sureeeee tur-tur-treeeeee chur, seewuree tchip-tchip-tchip-tchip*, or *reee-tew, purrreeee, skeeaskew, purreet-reeet*; variable, usually short, but with a wide range of pitch. **HABITS:** Actively gleans insects from foliage in typical warbler fashion. Forages low. **SIMILAR SPECIES:** Adult Dark-capped Yellow Warbler has flycatcher-like posture and dark brown crown; juvenile buffy tan or ochre-buff below. **STATUS AND DISTRIBUTION:** Locally fairly common resident in dense forest-edge vegetation, bracken and bamboo from 1850 to over 3000 m in the w. and cent. Kenyan highlands, from Mt Nyiru, Mt Elgon and the Cheranganis to the Nandi, Mau and Trans-Mara Forests, the Aberdares, Mt Kenya and the Nguruman Hills. In n. Tanzania, known from Loliondo, the Crater and Mbulu Highlands, Mt Hanang, Arusha NP, Mt Meru and Kilimanjaro.

CISTICOLAS (accent on second syllable) are small grass- or bush-dwelling warblers with a reputation for defying field determination. Species distinctions can be subtle, and complicated by racial, seasonal and individual variation, prompting coverage of this group in exceptional detail here. Our treatment applies only to populations within Kenya and northern Tanzania, as appreciable differences may exist between local subspecies and those in other parts of a species' range. (For example, the nominate race of Singing Cisticola in Ethiopia has a stripe-backed non-breeding plumage, whereas Kenyan birds are always plain-backed.) Cisticola identification involves consideration of the following: **(1) Distribution.** Some species (e.g. Rattling, Winding, Siffling, Stout, Pectoral-patch) are geographically widespread, although each has its preferred habitat. Certain others are decidedly localized, e.g. Carruthers's in Lake Victoria's papyrus swamps, Red-pate along the Sudan border and Rock Cisticola on barren outcrops in the south. Some are altitudinally limited: Hunter's, Wing-snapping and Aberdare, for example, are rare below 2500 m. Several, e.g. Long-tailed, Whistling, Chubb's, Foxy and Black-backed, are restricted to the west. All species are resident. **(2) Voice and behaviour** are important (although non-breeding cisticolas tend to be retiring and silent). Most species have several vocalizations, and, whereas basic song patterns are quite constant, considerable variation exists between (and within) populations. Certain species duet or sing in chorus, some, such as Hunter's and Chubb's, habitually and vigorously. Courtship behaviour may be conspicuous and diagnostic. Pectoral-patch, Wing-snapping and Black-backed are among the so-called 'cloud-scrapers' noted for their high aerial display flights accompanied by loud wing-snapping. Tape recordings are useful for study, but some cisticolas respond to playback of similar species' voices, prompting caution in using this approach in establishing identifications. **(3) Size and proportions.** Several small species (Pectoral-patch, Wing-snapping, Desert, Black-backed and Zitting) are very short-tailed. Levaillant's tail is noticeably long and slim, that of Long-tailed exceptionally so. Tail length varies between breeding and non-breeding birds in most species which have seasonal plumage changes. Sexual size differences may be negligible, or (in the robust Stout, Aberdare and Croaking) great enough to be confusing at times. **(4) Plumage colour and pattern** are not especially varied and there is little sexual dimorphism. The **distinction between streaked and unstreaked species,** however, is important. Essentially plain-backed cisticolas are Singing, Red-faced, Rock, Trilling, Whistling, Chubb's, Foxy, Long-tailed, the coastal race of Rattling, and breeding-plumaged Siffling and Red-pate. Hunter's and Tiny are obscurely streaked. All others have well-streaked upperparts. Obvious **contrast between head and back** characterizes Levaillant's, Winding, Stout, Red-pate and a few others. **Presence or absence of crown or nape streaking** can be diagnostic (but these streaks, like those on the back, may be difficult to see at a distance, in harsh light or on worn birds). **Colour of face and underparts** (particularly if reddish, as in Lynes's and Red-faced) is noteworthy, as is the **colour of the tail-feather tips,** but the possibility of earth-staining by red soil should be borne in mind. It is important to appreciate **differences between abraded and fresh, unworn plumage,** as effects of feather wear combined with sun-bleaching can be considerable. Thus, the rufous-tipped feathers that produce the red-capped appearance of a Winding Cisticola can bleach and wear off, leaving the bird brownish- or grey-crowned. Similarly, the wearing-away of the olivaceous tips from a Red-faced Cisticola's back feathers produces a slaty effect later in the season, and both light rectrix tips and rufous primary edges are much reduced or worn individuals. Some silent birds in poor plumage cannot be safely named.

Although cisticolas elsewhere in Africa typically have distinct breeding and non-breeding plumages, this is true of few East African populations. Ours generally moult only once per year and wear a 'perennial' dress (resembling either the breeding or the non-breeding plumage of extralimital races of the species). Within Kenya and northern Tanzania, seasonal differences are exhibited by Black-backed, Long-tailed and certain populations of Siffling and Croaking, and in inland populations of Winding Cisticola *some* individuals acquire a noticeably different non-breeding plumage. A few Zitting Cisticolas also moult twice per year. **(5) Bill size** varies from small and thin to noticeably stout. **(6) Colour of bare parts** is of limited value. Bill colour varies somewhat with breeding condition, age and sex, and is not useful in distinguishing species. Most male cisticolas have the inside of the bill and mouth jet-black, conspicuous when they sing. The mouth-lining is pale pinkish (rarely black) in most adult females, yellow-ochre in juveniles. The feet (tarsi and toes) are typically pale flesh-pink in adults, more yellowish in juveniles. The eyes usually are light (hazel) brown in adults, grey or brownish grey in young birds. **(7) Juvenile plumage** tends to be tinged with rusty above, and often with yellow below (sometimes quite bright). Variation in ventral colour exists even within some local populations. No adult cisticola has yellowish underparts. **TAXONOMY and NOMENCLATURE**: Our treatment of this genus involves a few changes from earlier East African bird books. We consider *C. angusticaudus* specifically distinct from southern African *fulvicapillus*. We also separate *distinctus* from *C. lais,* following Lynes (1930) and Sibley and Monroe (1990). However, *contra* some authors we continue to maintain *mongalla* as a race of *C. ruficeps,* for the reasons given in the species account. The coastal race of *C. galactotes* may prove to be specifically separable from inland birds, but its poorly studied vocalizations appear to resemble rather closely those of southern African *galactotes* populations. Affecting several *Cisticola* names is an International Code of Zoological Nomenclature ruling (1985) to the effect that all compound Latin nouns which end in *-cola* are to be treated as masculine; this results in changed gender for some well-known specific and subspecific epithets which formerly ended with the feminine 'a'.

SINGING CISTICOLA *Cisticola cantans* Plate 97

Length 130–145 mm (5–5.75"). A plain-looking highland bird. **Adult** has *dull rufous crown and wing edgings contrasting with unstreaked grey-brown back;* face buffy or whitish with a black subloral spot (more noticeable in males). Underparts whitish, tinged with buff, greyer on sides. Inside of bill and mouth-lining black in *both* sexes. **Juvenile** rustier above than adults, with less contrast between rufous and brown areas; underparts white; bill yellowish with brown culmen; eyes greyish. **VOICE**: Loud, emphatic two- or three-syllabled phrases such as *wee-chew, tchew-whip, tchee-tchew-WHIP, ju-whee, o-ki-WEE,* etc., variously combined or a single phrase repeated. Members of a pair may duet, one giving a repeated low *trr, trr,* the other singing short song phrases. Alarm call *srrt-srrt-srrt.* **HABITS**: Active pairs or family groups rapidly work through undergrowth, with cocked tails in motion, wings frequently drooped. Wary, but not unduly shy. Quite vocal. Sews nest between leaves in manner of prinias or Asian tailorbirds (*Orthotomus*). **SIMILAR SPECIES**: Red-faced Cisticola is russet about the face, shows faint rufous superciliary stripes, lacks contrast between rufous wing edgings and the duller brown back, has no dark subloral spot, is more richly coloured below, and occupies lower, wetter sites. **STATUS AND DISTRIBUTION**: Common and widespread in edge situations and gardens. Prefers dense herbaceous and shrub growth of a 'soft' and luxuriant nature; largely avoids wetter sites occupied by Red-faced Cisticola, but shuns dry, harsh, thorny cover. Common between 1300 and 2500 m. Two races: *belli* in w. Kenya around Mt Elgon and Siaya NP; *pictipennis* in the Kenyan highlands from Kakamega, Kaimosi and Nandi Districts, east to the Aberdares, Mt Kenya and the Nyambenis, south to the Mau, Nairobi, Machakos and Kitui and (disjunctly) Taita Hills Districts, and in n. Tanzania, at Arusha NP and lower slopes of Mt Meru and Mt Kilimanjaro. Reports from the West Usambaras require confirmation. A specimen record attributed to the Shimba Hills by Lewis and Pomeroy (1989) is erroneous.

RED-FACED CISTICOLA *Cisticola erythrops sylvia* Plate 97

Length 130–140 mm (5–5.5"). A skulking warbler of low wet places. **Adult** plain and *russet-faced.* Forehead and dim superciliary stripes more reddish than the crown, which, like the wings, does not contrast with the back. Upperparts generally olive-grey, becoming more slaty with wear; *underparts tinged with rufous-buff or tawny,* sometimes strongly. Bill blackish above, grey below with dusky tip (male), or greyish pink with brown culmen (female). **Juvenile** paler, buff-faced, rusty-tinged above, white below. **VOICE**: Sometimes confusingly like that of Singing Cisticola, but songs more emphatic, with many staccato notes, e.g.: (1) a group of repeated phrases, *pickup pickup pickup pickup TWEE TWEE TWEE pickup pickup. . . CHWEE CHWEE CHWEE pick pick pick tsee tsee tsee. . .;* (2) *wuCHEE, wuCHEE, wuCHEE. . .;* (3) an ascending series of excited *cheer* or *chwee* notes; (4) *chic-chic-chic-chic. . . CHEEP CHEEP CHEEP. . . CHEER CHEER CHEER!* (Chapin 1953: Zaïre); (5) a rising series of shrill, harsh reedy or wiry notes, ending emphatically with strongly accented *chew-WHEER!* or *chew-WHIP!;* (6) *weet, cheeraweet cheeraweet. . ..* **HABITS**: Elusive and hard to watch, but highly vocal. Forages low in dense vegetation. Male conspicuous when singing from low perch, but drops into cover if alarmed. Performs slow butterfly-like flight in breeding season. Nest sewn between leaves (e.g. *Solanum*), like that of Singing Cisticola. **SIMILAR SPECIES**: Singing Cisticola lacks reddish facial tone and is whiter below; its reddish wing edgings contrast noticeably with the grey-brown back; it occupies drier ground, but may be alongside Red-faced. Although skulking, Singing Cisticola is much easier to observe. **STATUS AND DISTRIBUTION**: Local in rank herbage and shrubbery of riverbeds, ravines and other damp habitats, between 500 and 2400 m. Sometimes common, especially in and near the Lake Victoria basin; also in the Kenyan highlands from Mt Elgon and Saiwa NP south to Mara GR, Serengeti NP, and from se. Mt Kenya to Thika and Nairobi NP, and (disjunctly) to the Taita Hills at Wundanyi. In ne. Tanzania, locally common in the Usambaras, less so in Arusha NP; old specimen records from the coastal lowlands near Tanga and Baricho (Malindi area).

ROCK CISTICOLA *Cisticola aberrans* **Plate 97**
(Rock-loving or Lazy Cisticola)

Length 130 mm (5"). A *plain-backed, rufous-crowned* cisticola of *barren rock outcrops and sparsely vegetated boulder-strewn slopes.* (Few East African specimens exist, and seasonal plumage differences within each race are poorly known.) In **breeding plumage**, *C. a. emini* of sw. Kenya and adjacent Tanzania has *greyish-brown back and wings contrasting with rufous crown and nape*, median and greater coverts narrowly edged and tipped with tawny-rufous, buff or cream lores and *long superciliary stripes*, and greyish ear-coverts. Underparts variably buff, sides and flanks tawnier and with a greyish wash; under tail-coverts rich rusty buff or yellowish buff; leg feathering rufous-brown; tail brown above, rather indistinctly pale-tipped with poorly defined subterminal dark band. At close range, a narrow buff eye-ring is evident. Bill blackish, paler below at base; feet pinkish. **Non-breeding plumage** undescribed; may resemble that of eastern *C. a. teitensis,* for which only a presumed non-breeding plumage is known. This is brighter brown above than breeding *emini*, the rufous extending from the nape onto the back; rusty buff of face and underparts less bright than in (at least some) *emini*, the throat and lower belly whitish; terminal tail spots larger and brighter, pale grey with no rufous tinge. **Juvenile** undescribed. **Voice**: Contact call of *C. a. emini* is a somewhat mournful, disyllabic piping *pee-u*, repeated, and a squeaky *squee-a or squee-e-a.* Alarm call an insistent nasal *tchaa* or *zheea*, often repeated, and sometimes followed by a rapid *tsip-tsip-tsip-tsip* or a louder and more churring *tsir-rrrrrrrrr* to form a song: *squee, chchchchchchch* or *skiew, skieee, chrrrrrrrrrrr.* In Zaïre, *C. a. petrophila* gives a simple dry trilling or buzzing resembling that of the American Chipping Sparrow, *Spizella passerina*, but louder (Chapin 1953). A "complex jumble of sweet and harsh notes interspersed with churring" also reported from a sw. Kenyan bird (Finch 1987). Voice of *C. a. teitensis* unrecorded. **Habits**: Unobtrusive. Scampers mouse-like among boulders and over bare rock faces; forages between rocks and within crevices; scolds from low shrubs and rocks, tail often cocked over the back and flicked frequently in alarm, as are the wings. **Similar Species**: Rattling Cisticola, whose back streaks can be inconspicuous in harsh light, inhabits rocky hills but prefers well-vegetated sites. Allopatric Lynes's Cisticola, often among rocks, is heavily streaked above. Trilling Cisticola is partially sympatric with *emini* in nw. Mara GR, is ecologically distinct, and has dull chestnut crown, indistinct superciliary stripes, larger bill and shorter tail. **Status and Distribution**: *C. a. teitensis* is known from four old specimens and a few sight records in se. Kenya and ne. Tanzania (Taita and Sagala Hills near Voi, Tsavo West NP, Mkomazi GR and the West Usambaras), *C. a. emini* from three specimens collected years ago near Mwanza and s. Lake Victoria; recent sight records and photographs from nw. Mara GR and Serengeti NP probably are of this latter form. A published record of the species from Limuru is doubtless in error. **Note**: The southern African Lazy Cisticola is considered conspecific with our birds by most authors, but is perhaps correctly treated as a separate species by Sibley and Monroe (1990).

TRILLING CISTICOLA *Cisticola w. woosnami* **Plate 97**

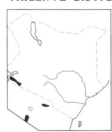

Length 120–145 mm (4.75–5.75"). A *bulky, large-billed, western* cisticola, its dull chestnut crown and wing edging contrasting only slightly with the plain brown back. Tail spots noticeable only in flight when feathers are spread. Underparts white, washed with yellowish buff on breast, sooty grey on flanks; leg feathers rufous-brown; lores dull white. *Bill prominently curved,* black above, grey below (male) or whitish pink with dark culmen (female). **Female** much smaller, paler, redder on head than male. **Juvenile** more rufous above, yellow below, with grey eyes, yellow-ochre bill. **Voice**: Song a rather ventriloquial, soft, far-carrying trill, *trrrrrrrrrrrrrrRRRRRRRRRRRRRRRRRR* lasting several seconds and increasing in volume; often preceded by a loud metallic *quink . . . quink. . .* or *quip. . . quip.* Alarm or scolding calls include a single *tchaaa* and an emphatic nasal *cha-cha-cha.* **Habits**: Sings from perch with quivering tail, turning head and thus changing apparent volume and direction of song. Usually shy. Builds spherical nest with side entrance hole in grass, low shrubs. **Similar Species**: Allopatric Whistling Cisticola has dusky crown, larger and heavier bill, whistling songs, and lives in less open country. Partially sympatric Rock Cisticola has more contrasting rufous crown, prominent superciliary stripes, smaller bill, and occupies rocky sites. **Status and Distribution**: Inhabits open woods and grassy hillsides with scattered shrubs and abandoned cultivation between 1000 and 2000 m in sw. Kenya, where locally fairly common in nw. Mara GR, Lolgorien and Rapogi Districts and Ruma NP. In n. Tanzania, known from Arusha and Lake Manyara NPs, Moshi District and Mt Hanang, though few recent records.

WHISTLING CISTICOLA *Cisticola lateralis antinorii* **Plate 97**

Length 125–140 mm (5–5.5"). A *plain, heavy-billed, west Kenyan* cisticola; a darker, duller, *dusky-crowned* edition of Trilling Cisticola. Black tail spots well defined even on central feathers (most obvious in flight). Male much larger than female. **Adult** uniformly sooty brown, darker on crown, somewhat paler on rump and upper tail-coverts, with dull rufous wing edgings; whitish underparts faintly buff-tinged on breast, grey on flanks; leg feathers rufous-brown. Rare rufous-backed adults are known elsewhere, but unreported from our region. Bill blackish with some grey on gonys in male, whitish pink with brown culmen in female; feet brownish flesh. **Juvenile** similar to that of Trilling Cisticola and best distinguished by accompanying adults. **Voice**: Unique loud

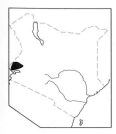

rich whistling songs of several patterns: (1) *keuw, keuw, keuw, keuw. . .,* (2) *whoi, chu-chu-chu-chu-chu-chu-chu* (reminding Americans of *Cardinalis cardinalis*), (3) *tew-tew tutu WICHew* (recalling Northern Waterthrush, *Seiurus noveboracensis*), (4) *witilew t'wee tew,* (5) a somewhat nuthatch-like *kree, kew-kew-kew-kew-kew,* (6) a repetitious *tweety tweety tweety. . .* Other calls include a scolding chatter and well-spaced *tew* or *chew* notes, and a short *chea* of alarm. **HABITS:** Often sings from treetop (up to 15–20 m). Wary; skulks in undergrowth, alone or in family groups. Builds ball-shaped nest like Trilling Cisticolas. **SIMILAR SPECIES:** Adult Trilling Cisticola, in more open-country, has reddish crown, shorter and more curved bill, trilling song. Juveniles of the two nearly identical except for bill. **STATUS AND DISTRIBUTION:** Scarce and local in riverine under-growth, forest edge and clearings, moist woodland, damp bush and thickets between 1200 and 1850 m. Ranges north of Trilling Cisticola, from northern shore of Lake Victoria at Bar Olengo, Bondo and Ng'iya north to Mumias and Kakamega Districts; an old record from foothills of Mt Elgon.

HUNTER'S CISTICOLA *Cisticola hunteri*   Plate 97

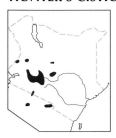

Length 140–145 mm (5.5–5.75"). A *slim, black-lored, fairly long-tailed* cisticola of high elevations, dark and sombre in plumage but *animated and vocal.* At a distance or in dim light, **adult** appears plain dark brown above, except for chestnut or chestnut-brown crown, but broad diffuse streaks or mottling on back and crown evident at close range. (Birds on Kilimanjaro are more heavily streaked than most; those on Elgon less so and nearly plain-backed.) Underparts vary from light to dark grey or (Mt Elgon) dusky. All birds on higher mountains (except Mt Meru) duller and darker than lower populations. **Juvenile** somewhat rustier above, whiter below than adult; bill yellow-ochre with dark culmen. **VOICE and HABITS:** Display involves exuberant duetting or chorus-singing in which two or more birds enthusiastically bob, flutter and pump their spread tails near one another, often on a bushtop. One of a pair sings *weet-cheeeeer* or *see-wit-cheeeeer,* the other simultaneously or alternately gives a long reeling trill, *tweeeeeeeeeeeeerrrrrrrrrr,* the perfor-mance repeated several to many times in quick succession, and with increasing excitement and activity. Shy except when courting, calling from cover with short trilling *trrrr* notes. Builds ball-shaped nest with side entrance, low in herbage. **SIMILAR SPECIES:** Chubb's Cisticola looks and behaves much like Hunter's; crown of *chubbi* is lighter and brighter, contrasting with the back. Still plainer and bulkier Trilling and Whistling Cisticolas differ in behaviour and habitat. Whistling is dusky on crown; Trilling dull chestnut-crowned, its bill heavy and curved. Singing Cisticola shows reddish wing edging and is much paler below. Each species is vocally distinct. **STATUS AND DISTRIBUTION:** Common in highland shrubbery, tangles, bracken and rank herbage in forest openings, edges and overgrown gardens, also in bamboo, giant heath and moorland shrubbery, between 1550 and 4400 (typically above 2400) m. Ranges from Mt Elgon (above 2500 m; Chubb's largely below that level) and the Cheranganis east to Nyahururu, Mt Uraguess, Mt Ololokwe, the Aberdares, Mt Kenya and the Nyambenis, south to the Mau, Ngurumans, Loliondo, the Crater Highlands, Mt Meru and Kilimanjaro.

CHUBB'S CISTICOLA *Cisticola c. chubbi*   Plate 97

Length 135–140 mm (5.25–5.5"). A *plain, black-lored* western species. **Adult** much like Hunter's Cisticola, but shorter-tailed, brighter rufous on crown and nape, and with *no streaks* on the back. Creamy-white breast is washed with grey at the sides, buff on flanks and crissum; leg feathers and tail tip pale rufous. **Juvenile** similar but duller; bill yellow-ochre with dark culmen. **VOICE and HABITS:** Song an antiphonal duet; also much ener-getic piping, chattering or babbling as the birds (a pair or group) bob and bow excit-edly, with tails spread and erect; the phrases *chwee-wheeo, whi-cheery* and *see-whi-cheery* are distinctive, more shrill than Hunter's but with the same reeling quality. Alarm a short chatter. Snaps wings in display. Like Hunter's, conspicuous when singing (duets all year); otherwise retiring. Builds spherical ball-type nest in low shrub. **SIMILAR SPECIES:** Hunter's Cisticola (alongside Chubb's on Mt Elgon) compared above. Singing Cisticola has contrasting reddish wing panel. See Trilling and Whistling Cisticolas. **STATUS AND DISTRIBUTION:** Locally common in w. Kenya between 1600 and 2500 m (usually below 2000 m) in dense shrubbery and tangles of stream valleys, forest clearings and borders, along brushy roadsides and in thick bush, from Mt Elgon and Saiwa NP south to Kakamega, Nandi, Eldama Ravine, Kericho, Sotik and Lolgorien Districts.

FOXY CISTICOLA *Cisticola t. troglodytes*   Plate 97

Length 95 mm (3.75"). A *small, richly coloured* northwestern species. **Adult** bright rufous above, warm buff below, *with no obvious tail spots,* but central rectrices blackish toward tip, others black with broad rufous edges. *Eyes grey;* bill brownish pink. **Juvenile** duller above than adult, yellow below. **VOICE:** Common call a soft *tsit, tsit-tsit,* and a rapid series of similar wispy notes may serve as a song, *tsiptsiptsiptsip. . ..* **HABITS:** Forages in tall grass, but flies into trees when alarmed. Sings from low treetops. **SIMILAR SPECIES:** Rare reddish juvenile Whistling Cisticola is grey-eyed like adult Foxy, but larger and with yellow-ochre bill. **STATUS AND DISTRIBUTION:**

Uncommon and local in open woodland and *Erythrina–Combretum* savanna with tall grass. Old specimens from lower Mt Elgon and the Cheranganis, Suk and w.Turkana Districts. Recent records (1993–94) from ne. Mt Elgon, where suitable habitat is rapidly disappearing.

TINY CISTICOLA *Cisticola nanus*   Plate 97

Length 85–90 mm (3.5"). Distinctive. A *very small, short-tailed* cisticola of dry country east of the Rift Valley. **Adult** clean-cut, with *bright rufous crown, light loral lines* and clear white or buffy-white underparts. The *faintly streaked pale grey back* may appear plain. **Juvenile** rufous-tinged above, the crown duller and not contrasting; underparts yellowish, tinged buff on breast, sides and flanks. **VOICE:** Call note *churr-it-it* (Benson 1946). Song a loud, rapid clear whistling: *TEW-teu-eet, t'TCHEW-tchew-eet, t'TCHEW-tchew-eet. . .*, or *tidiTUwe, tidiTUwi, tidiTUwe. . .*, the phrase repeated and with numerous high-pitched *tsick* or *tseep* notes interspersed; some songs consist largely of these thinner notes. Also a simpler, monotonous *tseetsiup-tseetsiup-tseetsiup . . .*. **HABITS:** Forages from ground level into tall shrubs and low trees; usually sings from high perch. Courtship flight involves short spurts of flight on whirring wings with occasional quick swerves or sideslips (Lynes 1930). Builds ball-type nest in grass tuft among low shrubs. **SIMILAR SPECIES:** Long-tailed Cisticola has long tail. Red-pate Cisticola is confined to nw. border areas. **STATUS AND DISTRIBUTION:** Widespread but uncommon in acacia woodland, savanna, thorn-bush and shrubby thickets between 500 and 1300 m. Ranges from Ethiopian border areas south through Samburu and Shaba GRs, Meru and Tsavo NPs to ne. Tanzania at Mkomazi GR, South Pare foothills and Naberera. Rare west of the Rift Valley, but has reached Baringo District, the Loita Hills and Lake Natron.

*RED-PATE CISTICOLA *Cisticola ruficeps mongalla*   Plates 97, 98

Length 105 mm (4"). A small, seasonally varying cisticola of *northwestern border* areas. Bill rather large for size of bird. **Breeding adult** plain or faintly mottled dull grey-brown above, with noticeable *white supraloral stripes* and *dull rufous forehead, crown and nape*. **Non-breeding adult** has *short white superciliary stripes, bright rufous crown and nape*, and broad dark brown back streaks (when unworn, with contrasting pale buff feather edges). A blackish subloral spot is most evident in males. In both plumages, chin and throat creamy white, shading to buffy white on breast, with some grey at the sides; tail brown, the outer feathers pale-edged and most white-tipped. Bill blackish above, greyer below; feet pinkish. **Juvenile** resembles non-breeding adult, but is duller, with yellowish underparts. **VOICE:** Songs include (1) a rapid insect-like trill on one pitch, of one to two seconds' duration: *tsee-seeseeseeseeseesee*; (2) a trill followed by three or four forceful, terminally accented double notes: *teeeeeeeeeeeeeee tseWE tseWE tseWE tseWE*; (3) a repeated *weuTSE weuTSE weuTSE. . .*. **HABITS:** Pairs forage in shrubs, largely avoiding both grass and trees. Builds spherical nest low in grass or broad-leaved plant. Courtship display undescribed. **SIMILAR SPECIES:** Allopatric Long-tailed Cisticola is much longer-tailed. Tiny Cisticola is smaller, brighter and very short-tailed. **STATUS AND DISTRIBUTION:** Sight records from thorn-bush near Lokichokio, nw. Kenya (Aug. 1990). **NOTE:** Sometimes considered specifically distinct from other Red-pate Cisticolas, but both *mongalla* and *scotoptera* are versatile vocalists sharing the same basic trilling song and perhaps other sounds. These two birds and nominate *ruficeps* are morphologically similar to one another, and all three forms intergrade in the basin of the upper White Nile (Lynes 1930).

LONG-TAILED or TABORA CISTICOLA *Cisticola angusticaudus*   Plate 97

Length 98–105 mm (4"). *Slender* and *prinia-like*, with a long, thin dark tail (shorter in non-breeding plumage), often cocked; *crown and nape bright rufous*; back plain grey-brown. **Juvenile** has duller rufous-brown crown, darker brown back; underparts tinged yellow. **VOICE:** Song three-parted: *see-chew-chew* or *chew-see-see*. Reportedly sings a rapid series of 15–50 ringing notes on one pitch, but this not recorded in our region. **HABITS:** Pert and active; usually in pairs or small groups foraging in low trees or shrubs and down into the grass. Favours grassy stands of *Acacia gerrardii*. Sings from perches 5–10 m high. Builds ball-type spherical nest low in grass. **SIMILAR SPECIES:** Tiny Cisticola has short tail. Red-fronted Warbler is more uniform above, shows conspicuous white in tail. Tawny-flanked Prinia is paler, tawny-buff below, and lacks rufous on crown. **STATUS AND DISTRIBUTION:** Local and generally uncommon in open acacia woodland and thorn-bush in sw. Kenya, from Kendu Bay, Ruma NP, Rapogi and Lolgorien Districts to the Mara GR and n. Serengeti NP. **NOTE:** Sometimes considered conspecific with s. African *C. fulvicapillus*, which not only

differs vocally in areas of sympatry but has the reduced outer primary broad and blade-like, not narrow, acute and short as in *angusticaudus,* whose adjacent primaries are distally emarginated on the outer web (Irwin 1993).

LEVAILLANT'S CISTICOLA *Cisticola tinniens oreophilus*   Plate 98
(Tinkling Cisticola)

Length 125 mm (5"). A slender, *wetland* cisticola with *bright rufous tail, wing edgings, crown and nape; back and nape heavily streaked* (sometimes so densely as to appear black-backed), in conspicuous contrast with rufous areas. Upper tail-coverts mottled black and rufous; tail rufous, with rusty-white tips and outer edges. Underparts white with rusty-buff wash, the sides and flanks with varying blackish streaking; leg feathers pale rufous-brown. **Adult** has forehead and most of the crown plain rusty red, but streaked in the paler-backed **juvenile,** which may have yellowish underparts. **VOICE:** Brief song, sometimes described as tinkling, but more often a rapid warbling or partly trilled *tee-tiurrrrip* or *che-cheeureeeueep,* with slight terminal accent and frequently repeated with little variation. Alarm calls *trrt-trrt* and a high *tee-tee-tee.* **HABITS:** Sings from low perches in or near wet places. Flies low, with weak jerky motion, flirting the long, slim tail. Builds ball-like nest, typically taller than it is broad. **SIMILAR SPECIES:** Winding Cisticola is boldly streaked above, but in breeding plumage the stripes are black on *grey;* shorter tail lacks reddish tint, and rump and upper tail-coverts grey, not rufous. Non-breeding Winding is less distinct, but head is streaked from forehead to nape, and general plumage tone is sandy buff, not rufous. **STATUS AND DISTRIBUTION:** Local in permanently wet sites from 2000 to 3000 m in the w. and cent. Kenyan highlands. Inhabits sedges, reedbeds, tall waterside grass and marshy meadows with tussock grass. Ranges from Eldoret, Uasin Gishu and Elgeyu to Mau Summit, Molo, Nyahururu, Ol Bolossat, the Aberdares, Kinangop Plateau and Mt Kenya (rare).
NOTE: In southern Africa, the name Tinkling Cisticola is applied to *Cisticola rufilatus.*

WINDING CISTICOLA *Cisticola galactotes*   Plate 98
(Black-backed Cisticola)

Length 110–130 mm (4.25–5"). A slender, *boldly streaked* bird typical of wet places. Most **adults** of *Cisticola g. amphilectus* have bright rufous crown and wings. In **normal perennial plumage,** this inland race has rufous forehead and face, *pale grey back heavily streaked with black,* and *grey tail with an extensive black subterminal area;* dark pectoral patches often present. *Some* individuals assume a **non-breeding plumage,** with buff-edged back feathers, tawnier underparts, streaked crown, and the central rectrices brown and grey, or brown with black subterminal patch and shaft streak. Small coastal race *haematocephalus* has perennial dress only, is paler, less heavily streaked and much less reddish, also noticeably whitish-faced, less rufous on crown (none in worn plumage), and lacks marked pectoral patches. It resembles inland Tanzanian *suahelicus,* whose general dorsal colour is intermediate between those of the two Kenyan forms.
Juveniles of all races pale yellowish below; these and **first-year** birds have crown and back streaked buff and black, as in non-breeding adults. **VOICE and HABITS:** Usual song of *amphilectus* is a repeated dry winding or creaking trill, likened to winding a clock; somewhat insect-like, *krrrrrrRRRRRRRRRRRRRRRrrrrrrrrrr.* Other vocalizations include (1) a weak rasping *zhreeeeeeeeee;* (2) a ringing *chwee-chwee-chwee-chwee,* each note sometimes nearly disyllabic: *tchwee-tchwee. . .;* (3) a short loud *chew-chew-chew-chewip;* and (4) a series of *trit-trit* notes given by displaying male as he flies back and forth low over grass. Sings from grass stems, branches or wires, often away from water. Builds ball-type nest *c.* 1 m above ground, often well decorated with spiders' egg cases. Retiring and secretive except during courtship. *C. g. haematocephalus* bleats rather than trills, giving an upslurred *brrrrRRIP;* also has an excited twittering *tic-titic-tic-tic-titic* call, sometimes given in dancing flight around bushes. **SIMILAR SPECIES:** Carruthers's Cisticola of western papyrus swamps has dull brown (not reddish) wing edgings, darker chestnut crown, largely blackish tail, thinner and straighter bill. Levaillant's Cisticola resembles non-breeding Winding, but is slimmer, bright rufous and black above, with unstreaked crown in adults. Stout Cisticola is heavier, broader-tailed, with dull tawny wing edging; often on drier ground. **STATUS AND DISTRIBUTION:** In Kenya, *Cisticola g. amphilectus* is common and widespread below 2000 m except in the dry north and northeast, preferring low damp areas, swamps and lake edges, less often occupying nearby dry grass and thickets. Where sympatric with Carruthers's, confined to *edges* of papyrus stands. *Cisticola g. suahelicus,* common in interior Tanzania, intergrades with *amphilectus* in s. Kenya and the Lake Victoria basin. *Cisticola g. haematocephalus* is the most conspicuous coastal cisticola, occupying varied wet and dry habitats, including low dune vegetation, from the Somali border south to Tanga and Dar es Salaam.

CARRUTHERS'S CISTICOLA *Cisticola carruthersi*   Plate 98

Length 125–130 mm (5"). A streak-backed cisticola resembling preceding species, but strictly confined to the *interior of western papyrus swamps.* **Adult** differs from Winding Cisticola in its *brown wing edgings,* plain *dusky or blackish tail, chestnut-brown crown,* and slimmer, straighter bill. **Juvenile** has lighter brown crown and back, the latter lightly streaked with dark brown, quite unlike bold pattern of adult; underparts faintly tinged yellow-

ish; eyes grey; feet yellowish flesh; bill dusky pink below. **VOICE**: Two-part song, a chatter followed by a rapid series of high scratchy or squeaky notes, these run together and higher-pitched at the end: *chchchchchchchch tsik-tseeosisitseek*, or *tswi-squee-squee-squee tsik-cheeoreeoo-tseek*. Annoyance notes include a loud, nasal, scolding *cheeya!* or *nyaaa!*, and a protracted scolding *wick-tsyik-tsyik-tsyik. . ..* **HABITS**: Forages among bases of papyrus plants, and sings from low or mid-level or in flight between stems. Not shy. **SIMILAR SPECIES**: Sympatric Kenyan race of Winding Cisticola, compared above, has unique reeling or 'winding' song. Other possibly confusing species are in different habitats. **STATUS AND DISTRIBUTION**: Endemic to papyrus stands around Lake Victoria, from northern shore of Winam (Kavirondo) Gulf south through Kisumu to Homa Bay.

STOUT CISTICOLA *Cisticola robustus nuchalis* Plate 98

Length 110–140 mm (4.25–5.5″). A *stocky* grassland cisticola. **Adult** has *unstreaked bright rufous nape* contrasting with buffy-grey, black-streaked back, and reddish-brown crown also streaked with black. **Male** large and robust; **female** much smaller. Wing edging pale dull buff or buffy brown. *Short blackish* tail has buff feather edges and dull whitish tips, conspicuous in flight. Underparts creamy or buffy white. **Juvenile** bright yellow below in fresh plumage, with both crown and nape black-streaked. **VOICE**: Song types include (1) two or three introductory notes followed by a short musical trill, *twi-twi-TWRRRRRRRRRRRR*; (2) a thinner lisping *tsee tsee tsiptsiptsiptsiptsip*; (3) a long, descending, almost tremolo series of identical notes, *tew-tew-tew-tew-tew-tew. . .,* rapidly run together. Calls include a loud *chip-chip-chip* and a softer *tsi-tsi-tsi-tsi*. **HABITS**: Less vocal than many cisticolas. Avoids short-grass plains. Male sings from low shrub or tall grass stem, sometimes in the air as he makes a low jerky flight with spread tail. Builds flimsy ball-type nest on or just above ground, weaving living grass stems over and around the structure. **SIMILAR SPECIES**: Aberdare Cisticola (only above 2300 m) is somewhat darker throughout, its rufous nape patch black-streaked and duller than in Stout, its outer tail feathers grey-tipped and its wings slightly brighter. Winding and Levaillant's Cisticolas are slimmer, long-tailed, and have contrasting reddish wing edgings. Other species with combination of bright rufous nape and boldly streaked grey-and-black mantle are differently proportioned. **STATUS AND DISTRIBUTION**: Widespread and locally common between 1200 and 2500 m in rolling tall grassland with moist hollows and scattered small shrubs, around Mt Elgon, in Trans-Nzoia and Uasin Gishu Districts, from Rongai and Nanyuki south to the Ngong Hills, Nairobi NP, Athi and Kapiti Plains, Loita Hills, Mara GR and Serengeti NP. Also from lower slopes of Mt Meru and Kilimanjaro east to Taveta, Maktau and Lake Jipe grasslands. Formerly at Laikipia.

ABERDARE CISTICOLA *Cisticola aberdare* Plate 98

Length, 120–150 mm (4.75–6″). A *dark, montane* version of Stout Cisticola, the two forms once considered conspecific. *Rufous nape streaked with black*, hence *not conspicuous and contrasting*, the back streaks heavier, wing panels more rufous, and tail somewhat longer than in Stout Cisticola. **VOICE**: Typical songs include (1) *pieu pieu pieu pieu twirrrrrrr chip-chip-chip*, (2) *pieu pieu pieu pieu tew-tew-tew-tew tschweep tchweep tchweep chew-chew-chew-chew-chew*, (3) a series of short trills, *tchweeeeeeee, tchweeeeeee. . ..* Scold note *piew* or *pew-pew*. **HABITS**: As for Stout Cisticola. Nest undescribed. **SIMILAR SPECIES**: See Stout and Croaking Cisticolas. **STATUS AND DISTRIBUTION**: A Kenyan endemic, locally common in moist grasslands *between 2300 and 3700 m* around Molo, Mau Narok and on the Aberdares.

CROAKING CISTICOLA *Cisticola natalensis* Plate 98

Length 130–140 mm (5–5.5″). A *streaky, stout-bodied* cisticola with a *heavy decurved bill*; often associated with *tall grass* on slopes and hillsides. Usual **perennial plumage** streaked or mottled dark sepia and pale brown above, but some birds (particularly in w. and se. Kenya, including the Chyulu Hills) assume a **non-breeding dress** (Aug.–Oct.) that is boldly striped black and tawny above, rich buff below (especially on flanks), and with a considerably longer tail. Pale superciliary stripes more evident in female. **Adults** in perennial plumage show *some rufous on the nape*, usually faint, but quite pronounced in the race *kapitensis*; crown rusty buff, well mottled with dark brown. *C. n. matengorum* less prominently streaked than *kapitensis*. *C. n. argenteus* is paler and greyer. **Juveniles** similar to non-breeding adults, but with yellowish underparts. **VOICE**: Variable but distinctive. One type involves unique 'klunking' notes, e.g. *k'lonk-i, chee-u-onk, chee-wunk, keeong-wip, tweeonk* or *tsiunk*, one or more repeated several times and often changing into a rasping or croaking *kwerrrrrrrrrrrrr*. Less metallic notes, e.g. *whut-CHI* or *chiop-chiop* or *wreeenh-YUK!* (an aspiratory wheeze followed by a sharp explosive note), may be given in series with no embellishments. Other songs include *klee clock, tu-tu-weh,* and a single rolling *rrreek* or other note repeated indefinitely. Aerial vocal-

izations are composed either of klunking notes or of guttural, croaking or wheezing sounds: *kur-r-ruk, krrk, krrk . . .*, or *prrt-prrt-prrt . . .*, some probably made by the wings, given as male circles high above ground. Alarm note an emphatic *chee-YRRR* or *chi-WUNK*, sometimes rather frog-like. **Habits**: Similar to those of Stout Cisticola, but song perch more often 8–10 m above ground in low tree. Circular display flight a jerky butterfly-like cruise, 10–15m high, with short harsh guttural vocalizations. Builds nest like that of Stout Cisticola, with green grass forming dome, in thick grass tuft. **Similar Species**: Stout Cisticola has brighter nape and a smaller bill, but some *C. n. kapitensis* approach that species in bill size. Aberdare Cisticola (only above 2300 m) has a shorter bill and black-streaked rufous nape. All confusing species have noticeably smaller bills. **Status and Distribution**: Generally uncommon in tall grassland with scattered shrubs, grassy bush, woodland and acacia groves below 2200 m. Four races: *kapitensis* from Mathews Range and the Nyambeni Hills south to Thika, Nairobi, Machakos and Sultan Hamud; *strangei* from Mt Elgon south to the Lake Victoria basin and Kericho District; *matengorum* in n. Tanzania, and north in Kenya to the Mara GR, Chyulu and Shimba Hills and Mombasa; *argenteus* on Mt Marsabit and the Huri Hills.

RATTLING CISTICOLA *Cisticola chiniana* — Plates 97, 98

Length 115–145 mm (4.5–5.75"). The common streak-backed brush-inhabiting cisticola in many areas, usually seen chattering from bushtop or low tree. A medium-sized species with white or whitish lores and *no well-defined superciliary stripes*. Back usually brown, variably streaked; greyish pectoral patch on each side of breast, largely grey-brown flanks, and brown tail with dull white tipping except on central feathers; blackish subterminal tail spots most distinct on underside. Much subspecific variation. **Adult** has *low-contrast, dull rufous wing edgings and crown* (brightest in *C. c. ukamba*). Western *C. c. victoria* and the duller (less reddish) *fischeri* are heavily streaked on the back; most races also have top of head streaked, but the large highland *humilis* is plain-crowned, as is eastern *heterophrys*, which is so faintly streaked on the *greyish* back as to appear plain, and its *crown, wing edgings and tail more rufous* than on inland birds. Northern *fricki* (like *keithi* just south of our limits) has distinct seasonal plumages, unlike most Kenyan *chiniana* populations. In breeding *fricki*, the pileum is heavily streaked with dark red-brown, the remaining upperparts have bright tawny feather edgings, and breast and flanks are rich buff. Birds in this plumage differ from sympatric *C. bodessa* only in their (often) deeper buff underparts, (often) buffier-tipped rectrices, and more uniform wing-feather edgings (less contrast between those of flight feathers and those of coverts and inner secondaries). Non-breeding *fricki* resembles perennial dress of *C. c. humilis*. **Juveniles** of most or all races rustier above than adults, usually pale yellowish on underparts and about the face. **Voice**: Loud and usually distinctive, despite much variation. Typical songs consist of two to four rasping or grating introductory notes followed by a harsh trill or rattle, e.g. (1) *chr chr chititititititititititi*, (2) *chi chi chi chrrrrrrrrrr*, (3) *tsee, chuchuchu*, (4) *sk-sk-skiirrrrrrrrrrr*. The rattle may be brief or prolonged, less often followed by additional short notes or lacking. Less common songs: (5) *chuk-chuk-chuk tswi-tswi-tswi-tswi*, (6) *tseutseu seetsitisew* or (7) *tsi-snaa, tsitsiTSEEsee*. **Habits**: Usually in thorny vegetation (except near the coast). Individuals and family groups feed conspicuously on ground in grass or shrubbery. Male sings from bush- or treetop, sometimes high. Wary but not shy. Builds spherical nest just above ground in green vegetation or dead branches. **Similar Species**: Lynes's Cisticola is reddish-faced, prefers rocky hillsides or gorges. The much brighter Winding Cisticola has more contrasting rufous crown and wing panels, bolder streaking on a grey back, and (usually) a blackish or greyish tail; coastal Windings are duller. Carruthers's Cisticola inhabits papyrus swamps. Croaking Cisticola is larger, heavier, with a stout, more curved bill. Levaillant's Cisticola is brighter, slimmer, rufous-tailed and marsh-dwelling. All have distinctive songs. In n. and e. Kenya, see Boran and Tana River Cisticolas, respectively. **Status and Distribution**: Widespread and common, mainly in dry shrubby habitats below 2000 m. *C. c. heterophrys* inhabits rank vegetation as well as coarse thorn-scrub in coastal lowlands from Lamu south to Tanga and Dar es Salaam, inland to the East Usambaras and lower Tana River. Ethiopian *fricki* extends south to Mt Marsabit, intergrading with *humilis* north of Mt Elgon and the northern Uaso Nyiro River. The highland race *humilis* ranges from Mt Elgon, Maralal and Mt Kenya south to the cent. Rift Valley and Nairobi, intergrading with *C. c. ukamba*, which extends from Embu and Kitui south to Machakos, Simba, the Tsavo parks, Taita Hills, Magadi, and the South Pare and West Usambara Mts in n. Tanzania. *C. c. victoria* ranges from Kakamega and Nandi Districts south through the Lake Victoria basin to the Mara GR and Serengeti NP. *C. c. fischeri* occupies interior north-central Tanzania from the Crater and Mbulu Highlands east to Arusha and Moshi, possibly intergrading with extralimital *keithi* near Lake Manyara and Tarangire NPs, and with *victoria* in the Ngurumans, sw. Kenya. Reports from Moyale unconfirmed, *C. c. fricki* apparently sympatric with *C. b. bodessa* on Mt Marsabit.

LYNES'S or WAILING CISTICOLA *Cisticola (lais) distinctus* — Plate 98

Length 140–146 mm (c. 5.5"). Suggests Rattling Cisticola, but *russet-tinged on face and underparts*. Wing edgings pale reddish brown; *back grey, dappled or streaked with black* and contrasting with the streaked reddish crown. Tail long, tipped with dull reddish buff. **Juvenile** slightly yellowish below; otherwise resembles adult. **Voice**: Varied song-calls include (1) a reiterated loud thin whistle, *peee* or *peeet*, at times preceding a dry trill: *peeeee peee peee peee squirrrrrrrrrr*; (2) a similar trill given alone, without introductory notes; (3) *t'pee t'pee t'pee t'pee*

chwer-chwer-chwer-chwer-chwer; (4) a variable series of harsh notes, e.g. *squee squee squee*, *wich-wich-wich*, *squi WEE-WEE-WEE*, *skerk-cher wee-wee-wee chrk*, *tsur-wee-we-wee*; (5) a rough wiry *spiiiiiii* or *swirrrrr*, embellished with other notes in a rather discordant medley: *tsk-tsk squeeeee tsk-tsk spiiiiiii tswi-tswi-chwink-chwink-chwink*. . . .. Call note a simple loud *SPEEEEE*. Alarm calls include a loud shrill *SPEEK SPEEK SPEEK* . . . and a squeaky *tspTSEEa* or *tskSWEEA*. **HABITS**: Restless, secretive and shy; flits and scurries among shrubs and boulders, calling frequently; runs mouse-like on rocks and ground, recalling Rock Cisticola. Calls from rock or low shrub, with tail elevated and partly spread. Unlike Rattling and some other similar cisticolas, appears not to have favoured perches for persistent singing. **SIMILAR SPECIES**: Sympatric race of Rattling Cisticola and Boran Cisticola are both browner, much less grey on back, less reddish on face. Rock Cisticola is unstreaked above. Ashy Cisticola is much greyer, more uniformly streaked on upperparts. **STATUS AND DISTRIBUTION**: A locally common East African endemic, inhabiting grass and bushes in rocky ravines, on hillsides or in gorges (often alongside Rattling Cisticola, which occupies the flatter terrain). Ranges in the cent. Rift Valley from Lake Nakuru and Hell's Gate NPs, south through the Kedong Valley to the Ngong and Loita Hills, Lukenya Hill (30 km southeast of Nairobi) and the Gol Mts in e. Serengeti NP in Tanzania. Early specimen records from Laikipia Plateau and Mt Uraguess; also from Mt Kulal (1958–59). **NOTE**: Considered conspecific with s. African *C. lais* by several recent authors, but plumage and habitat differences are pronounced, and vocalizations require further study. Kenyan *distinctus* exhibit little or no response to taped songs of s. African *C. l. lais* in preliminary playback experiments. The geographically intermediate form *semifasciatus* may prove to be more closely allied to *distinctus* than to *lais*.

BORAN CISTICOLA *Cisticola b. bodessa*   Plate 98

Length 130–140 mm (5–5.5"). A *northern* species closely resembling Rattling Cisticola, and formerly considered conspecific, but *crown browner (less rufous)* than in Rattling, and usually so *faintly streaked* as to appear plain; back more mottled, less boldly streaked; wing-coverts appear light-margined when fresh, contrasting more with the reddish-buff flight-feather edges than in sympatric race of Rattling; underparts whiter, less buff. Plumage differences subtle and affected by abrasion and earth staining. Rely on voice. **Juvenile** faintly yellow on face and underparts, probably indistinguishable from young Rattling Cisticola. **VOICE**: Song short (1.5–2 sec.) loud, emphatic and *hurriedly uttered*, usually with some less rapid initial notes: (1) *tchip-tchip-tchip-chipi CHU-uuuuuuuu*, (2) *ti-ti-ti TliiiiiiiiiiiiiiiiiiiiiiEW*, (3) *ch-ch-ch-ch-CHUchichichi*, or with initial part also rapid, (4) *chuchuchu CHIchichichichichichi-chichichiCHEW*. Quality may recall Whistling Cisticola. A loud *chip* or *tsip* may be repeated indefinitely as an agitation note, often accelerating quickly and leading into the song. **HABITS**: As for Rattling Cisticola, but Boran usually sings 3–10 m above ground, higher than is usual for Rattling in known areas of sympatry. Prefers uneven, often steeper terrain than Rattling Cisticola. **SIMILAR SPECIES**: Rattling Cisticola compared above. Ashy Cisticola is greyer-looking, with no rufous on wings, no contrast between crown and back, and more melodious song. **STATUS AND DISTRIBUTION**: Uncommon and local in n. Kenya, typically on rocky, grassy hillsides with thickets, dense scrub and low trees. Known from Moyale, Marsabit, Mt Kulal and Maralal, the Kongelai, Iten and Tambach Escarpments, ne. Elgon, Kito Pass, Laikipia Plateau and northern slopes of Mt Kenya around Lewa Downs.

TANA RIVER CISTICOLA *Cisticola restrictus*   Plate 99

Length 130 mm (5"). An enigmatic streak-backed cisticola known only from the lower Tana River. Resembles a pale Lynes's Cisticola. Also suggests both Ashy and Rattling Cisticolas, reported to sing like the latter, and perhaps a mere variant of that species or of hybrid origin. Underparts almost white, *pale grey on sides of breast and flanks*; crown *finely streaked and faintly to rather strongly rufous-tinted* (thus distinct from the duller back); back and rump narrowly streaked with dark brown, the pale feather edges varying from warm buffy brown or pale rufous-brown (March–June) to dull pale grey-brown (the single September specimen); *wing edgings only faintly rufous*. Buff-tipped greybrown tail somewhat longer than that of Ashy Cisticola. In the hand, no white bases to nape feathers, thus differing from Ashy Cisticola. Differences between specimens may reflect existence of distinct breeding and non-breeding plumages. **Juvenile** unknown. A specimen in apparent immature dress is particularly rufous on the crown. **VOICE and HABITS**: Poorly documented. Song of one collected bird reportedly like that of Rattling Cisticola (A. Forbes-Watson, label datum on topotype). **SIMILAR SPECIES**: Most closely resembles Lynes's Cisticola in plumage, tail length, and (apparently) little sexual size dimorphism, but occupies distinct range and markedly different habitat. Duller-crowned *restrictus* specimens resemble Ashy Cisticola, which has uniform, more broadly streaked upperparts with white bases to the nape feathers, and (in Kenya) a proportionately shorter, white-tipped tail; Ashy also lacks grey wash on sides. Some *restrictus* show rufous tinge to crown, and resemble Rattling Cisticola, a browner bird with contrasting rufous wing edgings. (*C. restrictus* more closely resembles upland *C. chiniana ukamba* than the virtually plain-backed sympatric *C. c. heterophrys*.) Coastal Winding Cisticola is more streaked above, and has wing edgings noticeably more rufous than the back. **STATUS AND DISTRIBUTION**: Known from seven specimens collected in semi-arid bush on flat sandy or black 'cotton' soils at Mnazini, Garsen and Karawa in the lower Tana River basin, and at Ijara and Sangole, 50 km east of the river. Holotype from Karawa in 1932; all others 1962–72. No subsequent records.

ASHY CISTICOLA *Cisticola cinereolus*   **Plate 99**

Length 130 mm (5"). A *greyish or brownish-grey, dry-country* cisticola with a *pleasing song. Adult pale and uniformly streaked above*, the dark brown feather centres bordered with grey; crown slightly browner than the back. Side of face plain, with whitish loral spot and very narrow white eye-ring. No rufous wing edgings. Tail feathers white-tipped. Underparts mostly white, with buff or pale tawny wash. Bill flesh-pink with brown culmen. In the hand, note white nape-feather bases. **Juvenile** browner and buffier above, light buff below, sometimes with yellowish wash. Eyes grey; bill yellow-ochre with brown culmen; feet yellowish pink. **VOICE**: The most musical cisticola song, somewhat lark-like; warbling, loud, rapid and accelerating. Variations include (1) *chiew-chiew, tawa-tiwi-twiwi* (rising), (2) *tee-tee-tee-titititititew* (falling), (3) *chew chi-weeto* (last three syllables also used as an alarm call), (4) *twi-twi-twi-tweeo*, or (5) *sri, sree-turee turEEileu*. Distress/annoyance calls a sharp *tsee tseet tseet tseet* and a monotonous *pee-pee-pee . . .* Songs regularly imitated by Red-winged Lark. **HABITS**: Usually solitary. Male sings conspicuously from shrubs or to three metres high on low treetop. Not shy. Builds ball-shaped nest with side entrance hole near top. **SIMILAR SPECIES**: Siffling Cisticola is smaller, browner, less strongly marked, with unstreaked nape, grey (not white) rectrix tips and weak lisping song. Often sympatric Rattling Cisticola is much browner, has harsh chattering calls. Boran Cisticola also browner and has more contrasting plain crown. Lynes's Cisticola is brighter, with obvious reddish face, inhabits rocky gorges and ravines. Croaking Cisticola is larger, browner, bigger-billed, and usually in tall grass. Rare Tana River Cisticola is typically browner, usually more reddish-crowned, grey-sided, with buff-tipped rectrices. **STATUS AND DISTRIBUTION**: Locally fairly common in dry bush and scrub, mainly below 1300 m and east of the Rift Valley, from the Huri Hills and Mt. Marsabit south through Samburu and Shaba GRs to the lower Tana River, Tsavo and Amboseli NPs, Mosiro and Magadi; less commonly in ne. Tanzania, at Lake Natron, Engaruka, Longido, Sanya Plains and Mkomazi GR. Specimen and sight records from the Kenyan/Sudanese border area near Lokichokio (Dec. 1978, Aug. 1990) may represent an undescribed race.

SIFFLING CISTICOLA *Cisticola brachypterus*   **Plates 97, 99**
(Short-winged Cisticola)

Length 110–120 mm (4.25–4.75"). A small, nondescript cisticola with an undistinguished song; essentially lacks useful field marks. Upperparts either plain or well streaked; whitish lores mark an otherwise featureless face; underparts buff, darker on flanks. Western *C. b. brachypterus* differs seasonally. **Breeding adult** plain and nearly uniform rich brown above, sometimes slightly dappled; wings somewhat rufous; light tail tip well defined and *grey* above. Mouth-lining black in male, pinkish in female. **Non-breeding adult** has mottled crown, bold back streaking; tail longer than in breeding plumage, the central feathers rufous-edged. Other races have a streaky perennial plumage, that of highland *katonae* with both crown and back boldly streaked, but nape only faintly marked (creating a plain-collared effect); west Kenyan *kericho* somewhat less patterned, and redder in tone; coastal *reichenowi* a dull-coloured edition of *katonae*, with redder, plainer crown and fainter back streaks. **Juvenile** somewhat streaked above, tinged yellow and rusty buff below; tail longer and broader than in adult. **VOICE**: A feeble, high-pitched monotonous 'siffling' or lisping sound, like whistling softly through the teeth, delivered from low bush or tree: *ssiwi-ssiwi-ssiwi* or *ssuswi-ssuswi-susswi* or *tsip, tseeek, tsup,* last note slightly lower, the typically three-parted phrases often separated from one another by other softer notes. Another song, *ssee-ssee-ssee-ssee,* drops slightly in pitch. More structured is a scratchy *su-SEET su-SEET su-SEET* repeated over and over (second syllable accented). Alarm note a squeaky *tsick.* **HABITS**: Often flies into shrub or tree when disturbed. Singing male may permit close approach. Courting *reichenowi,* and *isabellina* of e. and s. Tanzania, indulge in apparently silent, slow, upward-spiralling flight to as high as 60 m, followed by circling with pumping tail slightly spread, then a spectacular steep dive with audible swish of wings. Displaying *katonae* (usually) has much less impressive antics, only limited circling some 10 m above ground, followed by return to the song perch. (These behavioural differences suggest that two species may be involved.) Usually builds ball-type nest near ground in grass, but in the Usambara Mts Moreau found nests 3 m above ground in stunted trees. **SIMILAR SPECIES**: Pectoral-patch, Wing-snapping, Zitting, Black-backed and Desert Cisticolas are more boldly patterned, and usually deliver aerial songs. Some Pectoral-patch males have largely plain crowns, but are stub-tailed birds of open plains. Ashy Cisticola is larger, greyer, more obviously streaked, and with a loud musical song. Boran and Rattling Cisticolas are larger and longer-tailed. **STATUS AND DISTRIBUTION**: Fairly common and widespread from sea level to over 2000 m in open bush, savanna, shrubby grassland, grassy woodland openings and forest edge. Most numerous race is interior *katonae,* from the cent. Rift Valley and Laikipia Plateau south to Nairobi, Kajiado, Machakos and Simba Districts, the Chyulu and Taita Hills, and in n. Tanzania from the Crater Highlands east to Arusha and Moshi Districts. It inter-

grades with nominate *brachypterus* in w. Kenya from Mt Elgon and Kapenguria south to the Lake Victoria basin, and presumably also with *kericho* in the West Mau–Kilgoris region. Coastal *Cisticola b. reichenowi* occupies coastal lowlands from Kiunga south to Tanga and inland to the lower Tana River basin, Shimba Hills and the East Usambaras.

ZITTING CISTICOLA *Cisticola juncidis uropygialis*   Plate 99
(Fan-tailed Cisticola; Fan-tailed Warbler)

Length 105 mm (4"). A *short-tailed, heavily striped* little bird of grassy terrain. **Male** has *rusty-buff rump and pale collar contrasting with black-striped crown and back*; underparts buffy white; tail brown, the central feathers darker but pale-edged. **Female** less contrasting above, whiter below. Kenyan birds normally have only one annual moult and wear a perennial plumage, but there is some irregularity, and adults from Tanzania north to Kitui, Embu and Thika may moult into a **non-breeding plumage** in the dry season: brighter with longer tail, paler sandy back-feather edges and buffier rump. Rare erythristic birds, with overall rufous wash on underparts, are known from Pemba Island. **Juvenile** rustier above than adult, yellowish below. **Voice and Habits:** Aerial song consists solely of sharp scratchy notes, *tseek . . . tseek . . . tseek . . .*, or *zit . . . zit . . . zit. . .* at one- or two-second intervals, each note synchronized with the low point of a dip in the courtship flight. Alarm call a rapid *zitzitzit.* Male conspicuously displays within 30–40 m of the ground, cruising back and forth with strongly undulating flight; never snaps wings. Skulking non-breeding birds are practically silent. Builds bottle-shaped nest of soft grasses with top entrance. **Similar Species:** Rare western Black-backed Cisticola, is darker with darker tail. Desert Cisticola of dry short-grass plains has nearly black upper tail-surface (with pale tip); juvenile seldom, if ever, yellow below. Pectoral-patch and Wing-snapping Cisticolas are much shorter-tailed, have different displays. **Status and Distribution:** Local on moist lacustrine flats or in abandoned cultivation, rarely above 2000 m. Common in the Lake Victoria basin, around most Rift Valley lakes, and from Mara GR, Magadi, Nairobi, Amboseli and Tsavo West NPs south into n. Tanzania, where widespread from Serengeti NP east to Lake Manyara, Tarangire and Arusha NPs. In n. Kenya, recorded at Lokichokio, Marsabit, Ramu and the Northern Uaso Nyiro River; also in coastal lowlands from the Tana River delta south to the Sabaki River near Malindi, Mombasa and locally on Pemba Island.

DESERT CISTICOLA *Cisticola aridulus tanganyika*   Plate 99

Length 105 mm (4"). A small striped cisticola of *dry short-grass plains; resembles Pectoral-patch Cisticola, but has longer tail and unstreaked light rufous-buff rump.* **Adult** buffy white below, more tawny on breast and flanks; tail blackish with a pale tip. **Juvenile** more rufous above than adult; underparts white, not yellow. **Voice and Habits:** Aerial song a single, repetitive tinking *pinc . . . pinc . . . pinc . . .*, or *twing . . . twing . . .*, the note repeated several times at half-second intervals; sometimes more disyllabic: *tuink, tuink . . . .* Audible wing-snaps with or between groups of notes. Apparent distress call, delivered in erratic low cruising flight, is a dry, sharp *tuk . . . tuk . . .*, accompanied by wing-snaps, about one per second. Singing male conspicuous on low perches and in flight. Non-breeding birds retiring and unobtrusive. Wing-snapping softer than in other species and never given in high display flight; possibly restricted to alarm situations. Display itself merely a low circular cruising without embellishment. Builds ball-shaped or elliptical nest with side entrance, in grass tuft. **Similar Species:** See Pectoral-patch and Wing-snapping Cisticolas (both shorter-tailed and usually in more luxuriant grass). Rare western Black-backed Cisticola in non-breeding plumage has reddish rump and nape contrasting with largely black crown and back; crown chestnut in breeding plumage. Zitting Cisticola has subterminal black spots on paler brown tail, occupies taller grass cover, often near lakes, never open dry plains (but the two may be closely adjacent). Juveniles of these species yellow below. **Status and Distribution:** In n. Kenya, locally common on dry grasslands between 600 and 1700 m, from n. Turkana, Koobi Fora, the Huri Hills and northern edge of the Dida Galgalu Desert south to Marsabit, the Kaisut Desert, and Buffalo Springs and Shaba GRs. Farther south, ranges from Elmenteita, Hell's Gate and Nairobi NPs, the Athi and Kapiti Plains, and Kajiado to Amboseli and the Tsavo NPs. In n. Tanzania around base of Mt Meru, becoming locally abundant on the Sanya and Ardai Plains; the commonest cisticola throughout Masailand and west to Serengeti NP.

BLACK-BACKED CISTICOLA *Cisticola e. eximius*   Plate 99

Length 105 mm (4"). A small species of *western grasslands*, rare and possibly extirpated from Kenya. Stub-tailed **breeding male** *brightly coloured, with reddish rump and upper tail-coverts, dark chestnut crown, black-streaked back* and *rusty-buff flanks.* Much longer-tailed **non-breeding male**'s *black crown* is narrowly streaked white and separated from black back by plain or faintly streaked *red-brown semi-collar;* rump and upper tail-coverts as in breeding plumage. Pectoral patches fainter than in *C. brunnescens;* tail black except for white tip (as in Wing-snapping and Pectoral-patch Cisticolas, but their tails very short). **Female** resembles non-breeding male, but is shorter-tailed. **Juvenile** rusty above, brightly tinged yellow on throat and breast. **Voice and Habits:** Flight song

varies, but most notes repeated several times: (1) *tsi tsi tsi tsi, tsew tsew tsew, tsi tsi tsi*; (2) *chew chew chew, tsweet tsweet tsweet chuchuchuchuchuchu wiwi-TWI* (accented terminal note higher); (3) a high *tsureet-eet-eet-eet*; and (4) a longer *stur seet-seet-seet tsur-tsur-tsur tee-tee-tee-tee-turrr teeeeeeeeee*. Calls while ascending (to 50–60 m) and throughout the circular cruising (with wing-snapping) and during the final, nearly vertical plunge (with audible whir of wings). Builds spherical nest near ground in grass tuft, weaving green grass blades over the roof. **SIMILAR SPECIES**: Wing-snapping Cisticola, of higher elevations, has dark chestnut or almost black crown, and is shorter-tailed than breeding Black-backed, but the black-crowned *non*-breeding Black-backed is longer-tailed than *ayresii*. Desert Cisticola of dry short-grass plains has lighter, more buff-and-black back pattern. Pectoral-patch Cisticola is uniformly buff-and-black-striped above or with buffy-brown crown; it shows little or no collar or rump contrast. Zitting Cisticola has more patterned brown tail, black-streaked brown crown and back, duller rump, and is longer-tailed than breeding Black-backed. Each is vocally distinct. **STATUS AND DISTRIBUTION**: Formerly in open short-grass meadows (dry or seasonally flooded) at *c.* 1200 m near Mumias and Yala in w. Kenya. Not recorded in recent decades.

PECTORAL-PATCH CISTICOLA *Cisticola brunnescens*   Plate 99
(Pale-crowned Cisticola)

Length 90–100 mm (3.5–3.75"). A *diminutive, stub-tailed, grassland* species, prominently *streaked buff and black above*, often showing a faint collar across nape, but the streaked *rump no brighter than the back*; black tail tipped with white. **Breeding male** has *unstreaked chestnut* (fading to reddish buff) *crown centre contrasting with dark-streaked nape and back*; sides of crown typically mottled with dusky, forming dark lines above the superciliary stripes. Reddish-buff underparts have blackish or dusky patch on each side of breast. These and dark subloral spots faint or obsolete in **non-breeding plumage** (both sexes), which is brighter, *uniformly streaked above* from forehead to upper tail-coverts; black inner secondaries ('tertials') have sharp cream-coloured edges in fresh plumage. **Breeding female** resembles non-breeding male, but forehead and forecrown are rufous. Eastern *C. b. hindii* is slightly paler than western *nakuruensis*.

Juvenile resembles non-breeding adult, but is rufous-tinted above and bright yellowish below. **VOICE AND HABITS**: Variable flight-song a monotonous repetition of sharp *tsik* or *tsip* notes, sometimes accelerating, and often accompanied by loud wing-snaps: *tsik tsik tsik* (SNAP) *tseet tseet tseet* (SNAP) *sheek cheek cheek* (SNAP) *tsip, tsip tsk tsk-tsiktsiktsiktsik . . .*; the terminal accelerated chatter uttered as the bird descends. A separate wing-snap may be given along with each vocal *tsip*, and at times a short volley of snaps. Snapping (always?) ceases prior to the descent. The display flight itself typically a steady circling with few or no pronounced undulations. Series of *tsip* calls and occasional wing-snaps also given from grass-stem perch. Builds compact ball-shaped nest just above ground in grass tuft, with living grass blades bent down to form a woven canopy over the top. **SIMILAR SPECIES**: Male Wing-snapping Cisticola, of higher elevations, is brighter and darker above, with reddish rump and sometimes black crown; female is more like *brunnescens*, but usually brighter on rump. Voice and display distinct. Wing-snapping, Pectoral-patch and breeding Black-backed Cisticolas are very short-tailed; tails of Desert, Zitting and non-breeding and juvenile Black-backed are appreciably longer. Juvenile Wing-snapping is brighter yellow below than Pectoral-patch; juvenile Desert has whitish underparts. **STATUS AND DISTRIBUTION**: Locally common in Kenyan grasslands between 1400 and 2000 m (formerly overlapping with Wing-snapping Cisticola above 1700 m in the Ngong Hills); ranges up to 2500 m in n. Tanzania with no competition from Wing-snapping. *C. b. nakuruensis* occupies the cent. Kenyan highlands from the Laikipia Plateau south through the Rift Valley and adjacent grasslands to the Loita Plains, Mara GR, Serengeti NP and the Crater Highlands. *C. b. hindii* ranges east of the Rift Valley from Thika and Nairobi NP south across the Athi and Kapiti Plains to the Meru and Kilimanjaro foothills and the Ardai Plains west of Arusha. Huri Hills population in n. Kenya possibly represents nominate *brunnescens* from s. Ethiopia. The race on Mt Hanang in the Mbulu Highlands of n. Tanzania is *C. b. cinnamomeus*.

WING-SNAPPING CISTICOLA *Cisticola ayresii mauensis*   Plate 99
(Ayres's Cisticola)

Length 85–90 mm (3.25–3.5"). A tiny grassland bird of *high elevations*. Resembles Pectoral-patch Cisticola, but brighter and darker above, and still shorter-tailed in breeding plumage. *Rusty-tinged rump contrasts with boldly streaked buff-and-black back*; pale collar and faint pectoral patches evident. The black tail has whitish feather tips and edgings. **Breeding male** *becomes black- or chestnut-crowned* as wear reduces the narrow pale feather edges of non-breeding plumage; *forehead dark rusty red*, usually mottled with black; lores grey or dusky; underparts strongly tinged with rusty-buff. Bill dark grey. **Non-breeding male** has longer tail (like that of *Cisticola brunnescens*), brighter upperparts with broad rusty buff feather edges, rump bright rust-red; head like the back, with no rufous on forehead. **Female** resembles non-breeding male, but lores entirely whitish, and pectoral patches absent or reduced to a few short streaks. Bill paler

than in male; mandible flesh-pink. **Juvenile** resembles non-breeding adult, but paler and rustier above, yellowish below. **Voice and Habits**: Breeding male performs high circling display flight after ascending steeply and silently to 50–75 m. Once aloft, he circles and swoops, uttering a high-pitched, wispy, squeaky, yet fairly musical song: *tsi-tsi-tsu TUwi-TUwi wi-wi* (last two notes higher) or *tsee, seese, seese-see*, or *seet sweeet twee turee seet twiulee . . .*, or *tsu-TSEW-wi chew werk* (dropping at end). With each dip in his circular cruising, he rapidly and loudly snaps his wings, rattle-like, suggesting Flappet Lark's display sound. After four or five minutes he stops singing and dives steeply earthwards, uttering a rapid *tsiktsiktsik . . .*, often giving a final upward spurt and more wing-snapping before his final descent into the grass. Also snaps wings in erratic low flight when alarmed. Builds nest like that of preceding species. **Similar Species**: Pectoral-patch Cisticola is more uniformly streaked above or with plain rufous (never black) crown centre; its wing-snaps are given singly and usually are well spaced; plumage most like female *ayresii*, but rump and nape lack distinct rufous tinge. Longer-tailed Desert Cisticola ranges entirely below Wing-snapping. Non-breeding male Black-backed Cisticola (rare, mostly lower elevations) is longer-tailed, with largely black crown and back separated by rufous collar. Zitting Cisticola, also ranging lower, has longer brown tail, does not snap wings in display. **Status and Distribution**: Locally common in Kenya between 2150 and 2800 m in dry to rather wet grasslands, including dense tussock grass in marshy meadows, rarely down to 1700 m, where (formerly, at least) alongside Pectoral-patch Cisticola. Ranges from Kaptagat, Elgeyu, Molo and the Mau, east to the Aberdares, Ol Bolossat, Ol Kalou, the South Kinangop Plateau and Mt Kenya (scarce). Formerly on the Ngong Hills near Nairobi. Lynes (1930) reported specimens of *C. a. entebbe* from 1150 and 1350 m in the Nyando Valley and near Kisumu, but there are no other Kenyan records of this race.

TAWNY-FLANKED PRINIA *Prinia subflava melanorhyncha* Plate 101

Length 110–128 mm (4.25–5″). A sprightly tawny-brown warbler with *creamy-white superciliary stripes, blackish lores*, and a long narrow tail showing a dark subterminal band and pale feather tips. **Adult** has creamy-white underparts, with the *flanks, tibial feathers and under tail-coverts pale tawny*. Bill blackish; eyes hazel-brown; tarsi and toes flesh-pink. **Juvenile** similar, but yellow or yellowish below and bill paler. **Voice**: A monotonous, measured *cheeup cheeup cheeup . . .* or *chrt chrt chrt . . .* or *chip chip chip . . .*, repeated 15–20 times; also a dry *brzzt*, a harsh scolding *sbeee*, and a long-drawn *cheeeee*. **Habits**: Forages in vocal pairs or small groups, mostly in shrubbery. Tail frequently held high and wagged back and forth. Inquisitive and often tame. **Similar Species**: Pale Prinia of drier country has pale brownish-grey upperparts and lacks tawny on flanks. **Status and Distribution**: Common in scrub, grassy and brushy borders, cultivation and forest edge throughout w., cent. and s. Kenya, n. Tanzania, and in coastal lowlands north to Lamu. Where sympatric with Pale Prinia (Baringo District and the Tsavo NPs), Tawny-flanked occupies more verdant sites. The nominate race may reach nw. Kenya at Lokichokio.

PALE PRINIA *Prinia somalica erlangeri* Plate 101

Length 115–120 mm (4.5″). Inhabits drier country than the similar Tawny-flanked Prinia, from which **adult** differs in its *plain creamy-white underparts* with no tawny on flanks, and *pale brownish-grey or ash-grey back*. **Juvenile** tawny or sandy above, with *buff breast and flanks*. **Voice**: A buzzy note repeated without variation six to many times, *dzik, dzik, dzik, dzik . . .* (Benson 1946) or *zhree zhree zhree . . .*, the notes distinct or (less often) connected. **Habits**: Usually forages in more open vegetation than preceding species, often on the ground. Sews nest to grass stems. **Similar Species**: Tawny-flanked Prinia is more richly coloured, both above and below. **Status and Distribution**: Widespread and fairly common in dry n. and ne. Kenya south to Pokot, Baringo, Isiolo and Garissa Districts; also Galana Ranch and Tsavo East NP, and (wanderers?) south to Tsavo West NP.

BANDED PRINIA *Prinia bairdii melanops* Plate 101

Length 115 mm (4.5″). A distinctive warbler of western forests. **Adult** *heavily barred black and white below*, with centre of belly white. Upperparts dark brown, black on head, with *white tips to wing-coverts, secondaries and tail*. Eyes yellowish. **Juvenile** brown-eyed; grey or brownish grey on throat and breast, with faint barring. **Voice**: An emphatic ringing *plee plee plee . . .* or *pink pink pink . . .* given in prolonged series; also a metallic *tu-tu-tu-tu-tu-tu* and *pipik-pipik-pipik. . ..* Call note a hard *chip*. **Habits**: Forages in pairs or restless family groups, low in undergrowth. Skulking, but at intervals hops with flicking wings and elevated tail to tops of bracken or low shrubbery. Only partially roofs over its nest, which is not sewn to supports. **Similar Species**: White-chinned Prinia somewhat resembles juvenile Banded, but lacks spots on wing-coverts and tail. **Status and Distribution**: Locally common between 1600 and 3000 m in rank herbage along forest paths and edges in w. Kenya, from Kakamega and Nandi Districts south to Sotik, Kericho, Mau and Trans-Mara Forests, east to Mau Narok and (rarely) Molo. Formerly on Mt Elgon.

WHITE-CHINNED PRINIA *Prinia leucopogon reichenowi*   Plate 101

Length 120–138 mm (4.75–5.5"). A long-tailed *western* warbler. *Upperparts bluish grey; throat creamy white;* belly and under tail-coverts buff or pale tawny. Scaly-looking forehead and black lores are noticeable at close range. Eyes dark red; feet pink. **Juvenile** resembles adult but is paler below. **VOICE:** Typically a loud excited chattering, produced by two or more individuals calling together. Song of individual bird *tsu-tsu chipichew,* or *tswipi-chew chew-pi-chew tswe tsipi-tsew.* **HABITS:** Forages in low undergrowth, usually in noisy groups. Not shy. **SIMILAR SPECIES:** Chubb's Cisticola behaves similarly, but is brown-backed. See juvenile Banded Prinia. **STATUS AND DISTRIBUTION:** Common in w. Kenyan woodland, regenerating forest, damp bush and dense rank herbage between 1100 and 2400 m, from Mt Elgon and Saiwa NP south through Busia, Mumias, Kakamega, Nandi, Kericho and Sotik Districts to the Lake Victoria basin, South Nyanza, Lolgorien, Kilgoris and extreme nw. Mara GR at Kichwa Tembo. Also locally in the Kabarnet Forest.

RED-WINGED WARBLER *Heliolais erythroptera rhodoptera*   Plate 101

Length 120–140 mm (4.75–5.5"). *Prinia-like,* with *rich maroon-rufous wings.* Upperparts brownish grey in **breeding plumage**, otherwise dull rufous-brown with dark sides of face; whitish underparts washed with tawny or rich buff, brighter posteriorly. The *long, strongly graduated tail is white-tipped* and with *black subterminal spots.* Bill quite long, thin, slightly decurved, brown above, pale pink or whitish below, becoming black when breeding; eyes light yellowish brown; feet dull yellowish. **Juvenile** resembles non-breeding adult, but has faint or obsolete tail markings. **VOICE:** Song a loud monotonous *tseep tseep tseep tseep tseep.* Other calls include a thin *sit-sit-sit. . . .,* and a high-pitched churring. **HABITS:** Restless. More arboreal than most prinias; forages in shrubbery, but flies to trees when disturbed, and sings from topmost branches of tall tree or shrub. **SIMILAR SPECIES:** Long-tailed Cisticola is rufous on crown but not on wings. Tawny-flanked Prinia lacks rufous in wings, has creamy superciliary stripes. Both are smaller, with smaller bills than *Heliolais.* **STATUS AND DISTRIBUTION:** In w. Kenya, recorded in shrubby grassland, open grassy woods and abandoned cultivation near Fort Ternan (Aug. 1918), Ng'iya (May 1969) and near Muhoroni (1989–92). Fairly common in parts of e. Tanzania, ranging north to foothills of the East Usambaras and Tarangire NP. **NOTE:** Placed in the genus *Prinia* by some authorities.

GREY WREN-WARBLER *Calamonastes simplex*   Plate 100

Length 130 mm (5"). A *dark brownish-grey* bird of undergrowth in dry bush country, attracting attention by *slowly moving its black tail up and down.* At close range, **adult** shows *faint whitish barring on dark grey sides and flanks* and pale rufous or tawny leg feathering. Bill black; eyes red; *tarsi and toes blue-grey.* **Juvenile** paler below, with still fainter barring; bill horn-brown. **VOICE:** A distinctive sharp call, rather like rapidly striking two stones together: *chuk chuk chuk . . .* or *tsuk, tsuk, tsuk, tsuk . . .,* repeated steadily. **HABITS:** Rather shy, foraging low, alone or in pairs, in dense bush. Tail almost continuously in motion. Builds a spherical nest with side entrance, low in herbage, stitched with plant fibre or spiders' silk to living leaves. **SIMILAR SPECIES:** See Pale Wren-Warbler. **STATUS AND DISTRIBUTION:** Fairly common and widespread below 1300 m in bush, woodland and thickets north, east and south of the Kenyan highlands, and in ne. Tanzania from Lake Natron east to Longido, the lowlands south of Kilimanjaro, Mkomazi GR and the Masai Steppe.

PALE WREN-WARBLER *Calamonastes undosus*   Plate 100

Length 130 mm (5"). Paler and browner than Grey Wren-Warbler, *tail uniform with rump and back,* not darker as in that species, and *tarsi and toes pinkish orange. Underparts greyish white, with conspicuous barring* on throat, lower breast and upper belly. Eyes dull red; bill black. **VOICE:** A rather sharp, measured *wheet* or *weeu,* repeated several times, with an occasional more plaintive trisyllabic note: *weeu, weeu, weeu, weeu, weeu, teeueet.* **HABITS:** Shy and retiring. Forages around trunks and bases of small acacias, but sings from upper canopy of tall shrubs. Tail motion less persistent than that of Grey Wren-Warbler. **SIMILAR SPECIES:** Grey Wren-Warbler compared above. **STATUS AND DISTRIBUTION:** Widespread but generally uncommon between 1500 and 1700 m in s. and north-cent. Tanzania, reaching our area from Serengeti NP and Loliondo north to the Mara GR and Loita Hills of sw. Kenya. **NOTE:** Formerly considered a race of *C. simplex,* but differs both vocally and morphologically.

583

GREY-BACKED CAMAROPTERA *Camaroptera brachyura*   **Plate 103**
(including Grey-backed and Green-backed Bleating Warblers)

Length 95–105 mm (*c. 4"*). A small, noisy warbler of tangled vegetation and forest undergrowth. Most **adults** grey-backed, with *bright olive-green wings* and a *short grey tail with indistinct dark subterminal band*. Northern races *abessinica* and *tincta* are dark slaty to grey-brown above, dull white or grey below and on face. Coastal *erlangeri* is grey-crowned, grey-backed (but with extensive olive-green on scapulars and wings), silky white below, sometimes with a faint grey tinge on throat and sides. Southeastern *C. b. pileata* has dark grey forehead and crown, olive-green back, wings and tail, and pale grey face and underparts. In **non-breeding plumage**, certain races are browner above, and the bill paler, but seasonal differences less pronounced here than elsewhere in Africa. Eastern **juveniles** (*erlangeri* and *pileata*) uniformly brownish olive above, including tail, yellowish or yellow-olive below; bill pale horn-brown. Young of inland races resemble adults, but are paler, with or without yellow wash on underparts. **VOICE**: Usual calls of inland birds a repeated hard *CHITIP CHITIP CHITIP . . .*, and a loud, continuous, petulant *pyaa pyaa pyaa . . .* or *tee-tee-tee-tee. . .* ; also a querulous bleating *squeeee*; alarm calls include *chiwerk* or *cheeack* and a short, loud *spee*. Less common vocalizations include a very rapid, machine-gun-like *brrrrrrrt* and a hard *ch-ch-ch-ch-ch-ch*. Coastal birds give an insistent *pyeek pyeek pyeek . . .*, repeated indefinitely. **HABITS**: Forages in shrubbery, creeper tangles and on the ground; usually in pairs. Shy, but inquisitive. Wings are held low, tail elevated. Makes loud *trrip trrip* sound with wings. Sews nest inside two large shrub or sapling leaves punctured near their edges and stitched together with spiders' silk and bark fibre, forming a pocket with opening near top and to one side; another leaf may be stitched over top to form a roof. **SIMILAR SPECIES**: Western Olive-green Camaroptera is brighter and more uniformly olive above, without back/wing contrast of present species. **STATUS AND DISTRIBUTION**: Common except in the arid n. and e. Kenya, typically in deciduous and evergreen forest, dense bush and gardens. Olive-backed *pileata* ranges throughout coastal Tanzanian lowlands, to extreme se. Kenya at Vanga and Shimoni, and inland to the East Usambaras. Other races are grey-backed (sometimes treated as a separate species, *C. brevicaudata*): *erlangeri* in interior ne. Tanzania (including the Usambaras, where intergrading with *pileata*) and coastal Kenya, from Gazi and Shimba Hills NP north to the Boni Forest, inland to the edge of the cent. Kenyan plateau; *griseigula* in north-cent. Tanzania, Mara GR, Amboseli and Tsavo NPs north to Narok, Nairobi, Eldoret, Kapenguria and Maralal; *abessinica* in northern border areas from Mandera, Moyale, Lake Turkana and Lokichokio south to Marsabit, Nasolot NR and Baringo District; *tincta* in w. Kenyan border areas south of Mt Elgon and east to Mumias and Kakamega Districts.

OLIVE-GREEN CAMAROPTERA *Camaroptera chloronota toroensis*   **Plate 103**

Length 96–102 mm (4"). A small, *short-tailed* warbler of *western forests*. **Adult** dull brownish olive above, the wings brighter olive-green. *Sides of face, including lores and short superciliary stripes, tawny*. A broad diffuse tawny brown band across the lower throat and breast extends down sides and becomes duskier on the flanks; belly and chin whitish; thighs dull rufous. **Juvenile** *olive-green above, pale yellow to yellowish white below, with lower throat, breast and flanks olive*. Some individuals have dark greenish throat and breast contrasting with pale yellowish chin and belly. **VOICE**: Usual call a plaintive *wheet-wheet*. Song a loud and remarkably prolonged ventriloquial effort, consisting of a single short penetrating note repeated for several minutes without pause: *pee-ee-ee-ee-ee-ee-ee-ee-ee-ee-ee-ee-ee-ee-ee-ee-ee-ee-ee . . ..* An infrequent song is a prolonged *tewi-tewi-tewi-tewi . . ..* Annoyance call a clear *pwee, pwee, pwee . . ..* **HABITS**: Skulks in undergrowth, but forages and sings in creeper tangles and dense foliage in lower tree canopy. **SIMILAR SPECIES**: Young Grey-backed Camaroptera is yellowish below but greyer above than *chloronota*, with contrasting olive-green wings; it is less likely inside forest (though the two may overlap at forest edge). Green Crombec is much shorter-tailed, longer-billed, dingier, lacks tawny face, is not a forest species. **STATUS AND DISTRIBUTION**: Common in forest undergrowth in the Kakamega and Nandi Forests of w. Kenya. Formerly on Mt Elgon.

YELLOW-BREASTED APALIS *Apalis flavida*   **Plate 100**
(formerly Black-breasted Apalis)

Length 105–130 mm (4–5"). A common arboreal warbler with a broad *yellow breast band*, yellow-olive upperparts, grey on the head, and *tail feathers (except central pair) with conspicuous yellowish tips*. **Adult's** yellow breast band often has a *central black spot*, reduced or lacking in females and some males. Racially variable: western *caniceps* has entire top of head grey, little or no black on the breast in any plumage, short tail (31–44 mm), and small, pale yellowish or whitish rectrix tips; *golzi* is also grey from forehead to occiput, but long-tailed (45–55 mm) and with a large black breast spot; *A. f. pugnax* (formerly *flavocincta*) has only forehead, forecrown and sides of face grey, broad yellow breast band with central black spot in male, and is longer-tailed than *golzi*, with broad yellow rectrix tips. These races are green-tailed. Northern *A. f. flavocincta* (formerly *malensis*) has *brown uppertail surface, grey is confined to the forehead*, and has yellow and olive-green breast band with *no black spot in any plumage*, and *pale yellow to whitish tail-feather tips*; tail 46–62 mm in length. Eyes (all races)

red-brown; bill black; feet pale pinkish flesh. **Juveniles** dull yellowish olive or brownish olive above, paler than adult, with yellow breast band or patch, noticeable whitish eye-ring, and horn-coloured bill. Juvenile *caniceps* has yellow chin, throat and breast. **VOICE** (*A. f. pugnax* and *caniceps*): *chidiup chidiup chidiup . . ..* Male also gives a hard, almost metallic, camaroptera-like *chidip chidip . . .* or *chip-ip chip-ip chip-ip*, to which female answers *cheeea-cheea-cheea-cheea*. Other songs include *cheedo cheedo cheedle cheedle cheedle*, or *chier chier chier*, and a distinctive *sqieeu-kik-kik-kik-kik-kik*. Call note a single *cheerr*. Voice of *flavocincta* similar to that of other races, but faster and higher-pitched. **HABITS**: Forages mainly in trees, favouring acacias. In pairs or with mixed-species flocks. In excitement, elevates and spasmodically spreads tail. Usually nests within two metres of the ground. **SIMILAR SPECIES**: Bar-throated Apalis (*A. thoracica griseiceps*) has black band across white breast, yellow on belly and grey-brown head. **STATUS AND DISTRIBUTION**: Ranges widely in savanna, woodland, forest edge and wooded gardens. Our races are: *caniceps*, uncommon in the Lake Victoria basin (Siaya and Kisumu Districts); *pugnax*, common and widespread in the Kenyan highlands from the Karissia Hills south to Mt Meru and Kilimanjaro in Tanzania, and said by Britton (1980) to reach the coast at Lamu and Manda islands; *flavocincta* across n. Kenya, from Lokichokio to Moyale and Mandera, south to Wajir, Marsabit, Maralal and Baringo Districts, the Kerio and Turkwell Valleys, and including '*neglecta*' in coastal lowlands north to Bura on the lower Tana River and inland to Lali (Tsavo region) and the Usambara Mts, where intergrading with *golzi*, the latter known in Kenya only from the Taita Hills. **NOTE**: We follow Traylor (1986a) in treating northern birds as *flavocincta*, those in central Kenya as *pugnax*. The race *flavocincta*, clearly related to *viridiceps* of Somalia, is considered an incipient species by Hall and Moreau (1970) and is given full specific status ('Brown-tailed Apalis') by Sibley and Monroe (1990). It and *pugnax* were collected near Lotonok in the Kerio Valley in July 1926 (Granvik 1934), but both forms may not be resident there.

CHESTNUT-THROATED APALIS *Apalis p. porphyrolaema* Plate 100

Length 114–125 mm (4.5"). An arboreal warbler of highland forest. **Adult** *grey*, with *rufous chin and throat*; outer tail feathers with inconspicuous pale tips and edges. Eyes red-brown; bill black; feet brownish-flesh colour. **Juvenile** somewhat paler and more olive-grey above, with *yellowish chin, throat and cheeks*; rest of underparts yellowish white. **VOICE**: Distinctive; a thin high-pitched trill preceded by one or two chipping notes: *chi-chi trrrrrrrrrrrr*, or a simpler *chirrrreeeeeeeeeeee*, repeated several times. **HABITS**: Usually in pairs. Feeds mainly in the canopy, but occasionally visits lower trees and undergrowth. Active, with much body movement, drooping and partly spreading wings, raising and fanning tail. **SIMILAR SPECIES**: Female Buff-throated Apalis has pale tawny-buff throat and upper breast, blackish-brown back and white belly. **STATUS AND DISTRIBUTION**: Fairly common from 1700 to over 3000 m in forest, riparian groves and forest edge from Mt Elgon and the Cherangani Hills east to Maralal and the Karissia Hills, the Aberdares and Mt Kenya, south to the Mau Forest and the Nguruman Hills; also at Loliondo and the Crater Highlands, n. Tanzania.

BUFF-THROATED APALIS *Apalis rufogularis nigrescens* Plate 100

Length 107 mm (4"). An arboreal bird of *western forests*. Dimorphic, the two sexes formerly treated as separate species. *Lower tail-surface appears white* (as in Grey Apalis), and upperparts blackish brown in both sexes. Underparts of **male** creamy white, faintly buff on throat. Bill black; eyes hazel; tarsi dark brownish purple, toes light brown. **Female** *tawny-buff from chin to upper breast*; belly whitish. Bill black; eyes orange; tarsi grey-brown, toes contrastingly pink. **Juvenile** *greyish olive* above, the *female faintly washed with buff on chin and throat; male evenly yellow below*. **VOICE**: Two songs: *sureet sreet sreet sreet sreet sreet*, and a loud emphatic *chirrip* or *chidip* (recalling *Yellow-breasted Apalis*), often with a slightly trilled quality, accent varying, repeated four to 12 times. **HABITS**: Solitary, in pairs, or roving as part of a mixed-species flock in the canopy. **SIMILAR SPECIES**: Chestnut-throated Apalis resembles female, but is grey below, with a rufous throat. Black-headed Apalis suggests male, but longer tail is dark beneath, with white feather tips. Tail of Grey Apalis appears all white below, but crown is brownish and underparts wholly white. **STATUS AND DISTRIBUTION**: Locally common in w. Kenya between 1700 and 2400 m on Mt Elgon and in the Kakamega and Nandi Forests; formerly at Mumias.

GREY APALIS *Apalis c. cinerea* Plate 100

Length 120–125 mm (4.75"). An active warbler of highland-forest canopy. *Tail appears wholly white from beneath*. **Adult** grey above, with the *crown brown* in **male**, grey-brown and contrasting little with the back in **female**. Underparts and outer three pairs of tail feathers white. Bill black; eyes rufous-brown; tarsi pinkish brown. **Juvenile** *dull olive-brown above*, more olive on back; *tinged yellow below*, especially on throat. Eyes and bill brown; tarsi grey. **VOICE**: A somewhat metallic *chip chip chip chip . . .* or *chip-it chip-it . . .*, the note repeated up to 30 times, by both sexes; also an infrequent high trill ending with a few chipping notes. **HABITS**: Forages

actively in treetops and undergrowth, frequently spreading the tail; sometimes hovers at foliage. Often accompanies mixed-species flocks. Not shy. **SIMILAR SPECIES:** Male Buff-throated Apalis (western only) is blackish brown above with faintly buff throat. Black-headed Apalis is darker above, the tail blackish with white feather tips. In Nguruman Hills and Tanzania, see Brown-headed Apalis. **STATUS AND DISTRIBUTION:** Common in forest between 1700 and 3000 m from Marsabit, the Ndotos, Mathews Range, Karissia Hills, Maralal, Cheranganis and Mt Elgon south to Kakamega, Nandi, Kabarnet, Eldama Ravine, Mau and Trans-Mara Forests; also the Aberdares, Mt Kenya and Nyambenis, Kiambu and Nairobi Districts, and from the Nguruman Hills to Loliondo in n. Tanzania.

*BROWN-HEADED APALIS *Apalis alticola*   Plate 100

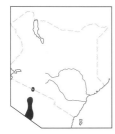

Length 120–126 mm (c. 4.75"). A southern species closely resembling Grey Apalis. **Adult** has *crown and face dark chocolate-brown or rufous-brown; outer tail feathers grey with white outer webs and tips*, not entirely white, and next three pairs of feathers have small white tips. Sexes alike. *Eyes pale orange or orange-brown;* bill blackish; feet flesh-pink or brownish pink. **Juvenile** slightly more olive-grey above, faintly tinged with yellow below; base of mandible horn-brown. **VOICE:** A loud *chip-it, chip it . . .* recalling Grey Apalis, but sometimes accelerated as a rattle. **HABITS:** Similar to those of Grey Apalis, but where sympatric with that species in the Nguruman Hills apparently restricted to forest edge, not ranging through forest interior. **STATUS AND DISTRIBUTION:** Fairly common in the Mbulu and Crater Highlands of n. Tanzania, ranging north to Loliondo, and to the Nguruman Hills in sw. Kenya.

BLACK-HEADED APALIS *Apalis melanocephala*   Plate 100

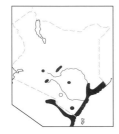

Length 120–150 mm (4.75–6"). A *dark-backed* arboreal species *with black face* and *creamy-white underparts*. **Male** *A. m. melanocephala* is dusky or brownish black above, darker on head, black on sides of face; breast sometimes buff-tinged; tail dark grey or brownish grey with white feather tips. Eyes red-brown; bill black; feet pinkish brown. **Female** paler above with faint olive tinge, the face contrastingly blackish. The darker, very long-tailed race *nigrodorsalis* is velvety brownish black above, the female tinged olive on the back. *A. m. moschi*, also long-tailed, is paler dusky grey above. **Juvenile** greyish olive above, black on lores and under eyes, pale yellow from chin to breast and along mid-ventral line to belly. **VOICE:** Loud and monotonous, but less chipping than that of Grey Apalis: *wheet wheet wheet wheet wee wee wee . . .* or *uwee uwee uwee . . .* Two birds may call together. **HABITS:** Arboreal; sings and forages in leafy canopy or subcanopy. Often accompanies mixed-species flocks. **SIMILAR SPECIES:** See Grey Apalis and male Buff-throated Apalis, both of which have the tail largely white below. **STATUS AND DISTRIBUTION:** *A. m. melanocephala* is common in coastal forest from Tanga north to the Boni Forest, inland to the East Usambaras (up to 900 m), Shimba Hills and lower Tana River gallery forests. *A. m. moschi* common between 1000 and 2130 m in interior e. Tanzanian forests north to the West Usambara and Pare Mountains, Kilimanjaro, Mt Meru, and to Mt Kasigau in se. Kenya. *A. m. nigrodorsalis* is uncommon in the cent. Kenyan highlands from Nairobi north to the Aberdares, Mt Kenya and Meru Forests. Specimens from Mt Endau and the Chyulu Hills appear intermediate between *nigrodorsalis* and nominate coastal birds.

BLACK-THROATED APALIS *Apalis j. jacksoni*   Plate 100

Length 116 mm (4.5"). A handsome warbler of Kenyan highland forests. **Male** has *black face and throat*, and *long white malar stripes;* crown and nape dark slate, back and rump bright olive-green; underparts greenish yellow, brightening to lemon-yellow on belly. Bill black; eyes dark brown; tarsi brownish pink. **Female** duller, with paler grey crown, face and throat. **Juvenile** still duller, greenish yellow on crown and throat in female, greyer in male. **VOICE:** Loud and rather varied, a monotonously repeated *chu chu chu . . .* or *chip chip chip . . .*, sometimes sounding like *kreek-kreek-reek-reek-reek . . .*, or disyllabic *che-chip, che-chip . . .* or *tuTEE-ku, TEE-ku, TEE-ku . . ..* Typically, these are duet performances by members of a pair, but notes are neither perfectly synchronized nor regularly antiphonal. More than two birds may call together at times. **HABITS:** Forages in pairs or small groups. Prefers tall trees at forest edge, where often in lower branches; occasionally descends into undergrowth. **SIMILAR SPECIES:** See White-winged Apalis (lower Tana River only). **STATUS AND DISTRIBUTION:** Fairly common between 1700 and 2400 m from Mt Elgon and the Cheranganis south through the Kabarnet, Kakamega (scarce), Nandi, Mau and Trans-Mara Forests to Lolgorien and the Ngurumans; east of the Rift Valley from Meru, Mt Kenya and the Aberdares south to Limuru and northern Nairobi suburbs.

WHITE-WINGED APALIS *Apalis c. chariessa*   **Plate 100**

Length *c.* 125 mm (5"). A rare bird of the lower Tana River gallery forests. **Male** glossy greenish black above, with *white stripe on wing* formed by edges of outer secondaries and inner primaries. *Throat and cheeks white*, with lower throat and foreneck black. Underparts otherwise bright yellow, deepening to orange on the breast; tail (except central feathers) tipped white. **Female** has head, sides of face, wings, tail and part of lower neck grey, the back and rump olive-green. **Juvenile** resembles adult female, but centre of lower neck yellow. **Voice** (of *A. c. macphersoni* in Malawi): A rather slow, repeated *tweety tweety* . . . and a more rapid *teety-teetup* or *tweety-chy* (Benson and Benson 1947). **Habits:** Arboreal, frequenting tall riverine trees, where reportedly forages with mixed-species flocks. **Similar Species:** Black-throated Apalis of highland forest has entire throat black, lacks white wing-stripe. **Status and Distribution:** Known from three specimens collected at Mitole (1878) and near Baomo in 1961, both localities less than 40 km north of Garsen. (Although the Mitole forest was cleared by the mid-1960s, patches of apparently suitable habitat remain in the Tana River Primate Reserve near Baomo.)

BLACK-COLLARED APALIS *Apalis p. pulchra*   **Plate 100**

Length 115–125 mm (4.5–5"). An attractive, *tail-wagging* warbler of forest undergrowth and creepers. *Broad black breast band* and *rufous flanks and belly* distinctive. Upperparts dark grey; tail with mainly white outer feathers and white tips on all but central pair. Eyes light reddish brown or hazel; bill black; feet dusky grey, more pinkish on the toes. **Juvenile** has dark grey breast band. **Voice:** A series of loud complaining notes, variously interpreted as (1) *pweu PYEE PYEE PYEE PYEE* . . . , (2) *cher, CHEWI CHEWI CHEWI.* . ., (3) *T'WEE T'WEE T'WEE* . . ., (4) *PEET-PEET-PEET, PEET*, and (5) *kwi-kwi, kwer kwer*. **Habits:** Confiding, but keeps to dense cover. The long, expressive tail, held high and often well forward, is in constant side-to-side motion. **Similar Species:** Allopatric Bar-throated Apalis lacks rufous flanks and belly. **Status and Distribution:** Fairly common between 1600 and 2400 m in Kenyan highland forest, especially along overgrown edges and clearings. Ranges from Mt Elgon, Saiwa NP and the Cheranganis south through Kakamega and Nandi Districts to the Mau and Trans-Mara Forests, east to Nairobi, the Aberdares, Mt Kenya and Meru District.

BAR-THROATED APALIS *Apalis thoracica*   **Plate 100**

Length 114–116 mm (4.5"). A rather stocky apalis, represented in our region by four distinct races. **Adult** *A. t. griseiceps* is brown-capped (or cap ash-grey in Chyulu birds), bright yellowish olive on the back, with a *narrow black band across the white breast* and lemon-yellow lower belly. **Juvenile** more greenish on head, with less distinct breast band. **Adult** *A. t. murina* differs in having *grey upperparts and little yellow* on the belly. The similar *A. t. pareensis* has white underparts, with a trace of yellow on the lower belly and flanks. *A. t. fuscigularis* (Taita Hills) is very different, with brownish chin and *entire throat and breast black*; rest of underparts yellowish; upperparts mostly dark grey, brownish on the crown. Eyes creamy white or pale yellow in all forms. **Voice:** Song of *murina* involves repetition of the same syllable in moderately fast sequence, with short pause between sequences: *tjil tjil-tjil tjil tjil-tjil tjil* . . ; alarm call loud, sharp, almost metallic, one note uttered in rapid sequence without pause, *tik-tik-tik-tik* (Ripley and Heinrich 1966). Usual call of *griseiceps* is a frequently repeated *pii*, slightly disyllabic and resembling notes of Black-headed Apalis or Grey-backed Camaroptera; also a harsh *tsewi* (Sclater and Moreau 1933), and a trilling *pirri-pirri* (Mackworth-Praed and Grant 1955). *A. t. fuscigularis* has a loud penetrating *chwee-chwee-chwee* . . . or *chewik chewik chewik*, reminiscent of songs of more southern races; also some high thin notes. **Habits:** Usually in pairs, typically in forest undergrowth or lower parts of canopy. *A. t. fuscigularis* is shy and unresponsive to 'pishing' or to playback of vocalizations (unlike some southern races). **Similar Species:** Black-collared Apalis has rufous on flanks and belly. See Yellow-breasted Apalis. **Status and Distribution:** *A. t. murina* is fairly common and widespread in Tanzania, reaching our area in the West Usambaras. The race *pareensis* is confined to the South Pare Mts; *griseiceps* is scattered from the Mbulu Highlands, Oldeani, Kitumbeine, Longido, Monduli, Arusha NP and Mt Kilimanjaro (fairly common), reaching Kenya in the Chyulu Hills, where local and uncommon in forest and forest-edge scrub; *fuscigularis* is restricted to the Taita Hills. **Note:** *A. thoracica* as traditionally recognized is made up of at least 16 forms, some of which may prove to be specifically distinct. *A. t. fuscigularis* differs strikingly in plumage from the band-breasted races and is reminiscent of the black-chested *lynesi* on Mt Namuli in n. Mozambique, with which it may have close affinities. The group has received little field study.

LONG-BILLED APALIS *Apalis m. moreaui*   **Plate 123**

Length 110 mm (4.25"). A *long-billed* grey warbler of Tanzania's East Usambara Mts. Upperparts plain olive-grey, with forehead and lores tinged with tawny; underparts pale grey; tail grey and quite short. Sexes alike. **Juvenile**

undescribed. **VOICE**: A whistled *tcheu-tcheu-tcheu-tcheu-tcheu*, sharp and mechanical. At times almost disyllabic: *tchwee-tchwee . . .* or *t'wee-t'wee . . .*. **HABITS**: Shy and elusive. Forages in dense tangles of vines, often at forest edge. Sings, apparently infrequently, from vines just above ground (Stuart and Hutton 1977). **STATUS AND DISTRIBUTION**: A rare and extremely local endemic of the East Usambaras, where known only between 900 and 1000 m around Amani. Formerly recorded only from dense forest undergrowth, but the few recent records are from small valleys amid cultivation or around tea plantations, suggesting major habitat change likely (relating to forest destruction in the area). **NOTE**: Taxonomic position in doubt; placed in *Orthotomus* by Hall and Moreau (1970), Fry (1976) and Sibley and Monroe (1990), although the nest remains undescribed and the bird itself poorly known.

RED-CAPPED FOREST WARBLER *Orthotomus m. metopias*   Plate 123

Length 100 mm (4"). A long-billed, chestnut-headed warbler of the Usambara Mts. **Adult** brownish above, tinged greyish on wings and tail; most of head and neck chestnut; underparts white, with sides of breast and flanks greyish. Eyes brown; bill and feet black. **Juvenile** duller and greyer than adult, with olive-yellow wash on underparts. **VOICE**: Song two short loud notes followed by a trill. Call a soft *swee-swee-swee* or more wiry *siree-siree-siree . . .* Sometimes utters a low humming *mmi, mmi.* **HABITS**: Shy and secretive. Inhabits dense forest undergrowth, foraging in small groups and easily overlooked. Builds a typical tailorbird type of nest, sewn into large leaves. **STATUS AND DISTRIBUTION**: Common in the West Usambaras between 1200 and 2150 m; rare in the eastern range, where formerly known from Amani at 900 m.

RED-FRONTED WARBLER *Spiloptila rufifrons*   Plate 100
(Red-faced Apalis)

Length 110 mm (4.25"). A *rufous-capped* apalis-like warbler of *dry bush; tail long and black, white-tipped* except for central feathers, often *held erect and wagged from side to side*; underparts creamy white. Wing-coverts and inner secondaries variably edged white. Some birds have only the forehead rufous; in others, this colour extends to the nape or beyond. The race *rufifrons* (includes 'smithii') is grey-brown above; *rufidorsalis* is brighter, with entire back washed rufous and more tawny underparts. What appear to be fully adult males with black band across upper breast (*rufidorsalis* only) are now seldom reported. **VOICE**: Songs (*S. r. rufifrons*) include a simple *tick tick tick tick tick . .* (Benson 1946: Ethiopia), a high *tsee-it tsee-it tsee-it. . .*, suggesting a thin apalis song, and a louder *chee-ip chee-ip chee-ip. . ..* Alarm call *seep-seep* or *speek, speek. S. r. rufidorsalis* gives a *spi-spi-hee-hee-hee* (Moreau). **HABITS**: Pairs actively forage near ground in sparse, often leafless scrub, the tail erect or bent forward over the back and wagged almost incessantly. **SIMILAR SPECIES**: Long-tailed Cisticola of southwestern grassy savannas has shorter tail little darker than back and with less well-marked white feather tips. **STATUS AND DISTRIBUTION**: Uncommon in arid bush and thorn-scrub between 400 and 1200 m. *S. r. rufifrons* ranges throughout n. Kenya south to the Kerio Valley, Baringo, Isiolo, Wajir and Garissa Districts, and along the Tana River to Bura and Ijara, with a disjunct population in the south from Mosiro, Olorgesailie and Lake Magadi south into Tanzania at Lake Natron and across the Masai Steppe to the Pare foothills, Mombo, Mkomazi GR and around Lake Jipe. *S. r. rufidorsalis* appears to be confined to Tsavo East NP, near Voi, Maungu, Aruba and the Lali Hills. **NOTE**: Placed in the genus *Apalis* by some authors, in *Urorhipis* by others.

GREY-CAPPED WARBLER *Eminia lepida*   Plate 101

Length 150 mm (6"). An unusual, rather thickset warbler. **Adult** bright yellowish green above, with a *grey crown bordered by a broad black line* through the eyes and around occiput; *throat patch and bend of wing chestnut*; underparts greyish white. **Juvenile** similar but duller, with little chestnut on throat. **VOICE**: Male's song loud and variable, with reeling, trilling and/or explosive notes, e.g. (1) *churrrrrrrr, WEE-WEE-WEE-WEE*, (2) *WHER-CHEEW-CHEEW-CHEEW-CHEEW*, (3) *tu-tu-tu WHEE WHEE*, (4) *twee twee chu-chu-chu-chu*; to these, female often adds a loud *WIRRRRRRR*. Call a short trilled *treeee.* **HABITS**: Secretive and stays well hidden, but highly vocal, especially during rainy season. Pairs duet from low rank cover. Builds conspicuous large nest (resembling mass of flood debris) on branch above streambed or other opening; domed, with side entrance near top, and with long loose ends of bark strips and rootlets hanging free; sometimes modifies an old weaver's nest. **STATUS AND DISTRIBUTION**: Fairly common between 1100 and 2500 m in the Lake Victoria basin, the w. and cent. Kenyan highlands, and south to Tanzania's Crater Highlands. Usually in dense vines and other thick cover on overgrown river banks, in dark damp ravines, brushy forest edges and old gardens.

KRETSCHMER'S LONGBILL *Macrosphenus k. kretschmeri* **Plate 101**

Length 140–145 mm (5.75"). A *greenbul-like* forest bird with *white eyes* and *long straight bill*. Adult generally dull olive above, more yellowish olive below, with greyish throat and olive-brown tail. Bill blackish above, paler below; eyes whitish; feet whitish flesh or lilac-pink. **VOICE**: A distinctive, somewhat bulbul-like, four-note song, uttered about once every five seconds for long periods: *week, tyeuk-er-eek* or *tweet, euker-rik*. Contact note a clear *ker-ip*; alarm call a low *charr* (Sclater and Moreau 1932). **HABITS**: Highly vocal at times, but exceedingly shy and skulking, favouring dense vine tangles and deep thickets, where it sings from concealed perches. **SIMILAR SPECIES**: Sympatric Little Greenbul is stockier and has a much shorter bill. Tiny Greenbul is more olive on head, greyer below, and has yellow eyes. Grey-olive Greenbul is browner above, with a more rufous tail. **STATUS AND DISTRIBUTION**: Uncommon to scarce resident at forest edge and in forest undergrowth from 900 to 1550 m, in our region now apparently restricted to the Usambara Mts in ne. Tanzania, where not uncommon at Ambangulu. Formerly in forests extending down from Mt. Kilimanjaro to Moshi, and (until the 1920s) to Kitovu Forest in Kenya's Taveta District, where now extirpated owing to severe habitat destruction.

NORTHERN CROMBEC *Sylvietta brachyura* **Plate 103**

Length 80 mm (3"). A 'nuthatch-warbler' with a *distinct facial pattern*. **Adult** *S. b. leucopsis* uniformly pale grey above; underparts rufous, fading to *whitish on throat and belly*. Side of face marked by whitish superciliary stripe (pale tawny in western *S. b. carnapi*) and *grey or dusky eye-line*. Bill mostly grey, darker above; eyes light brown or reddish brown; feet brownish pink. **Juvenile** resembles adult, but has tawny-tipped wing-coverts. **VOICE**: Song a short *chiorchi-chiririchi chiorchi-chiririchi*. Calls include a dry *trrr*, a sharp double *tick-tick* and an excited *chichichichi*. **SIMILAR SPECIES**: Larger Red-faced Crombec is plain-faced and uniformly rufous-buff below. **STATUS AND DISTRIBUTION**: Fairly common in open woodland and bush; widespread but scarce in the highlands. *S. b. carnapi* ranges along the north shore of Lake Victoria at Ukwala, Ng'iya and Lake Kanyaboli; also in drier northern parts of Trans-Nzoia District. *S. b. leucopsis* is widespread north, east and south of the Kenyan highlands from Lokichokio, Turkana, Marsabit and Mandera Districts south to Baringo and Isiolo Districts, Meru, Amboseli and Tsavo NPs, the lower Tana River and coastal areas north of Lamu; it reaches Tanzania around Lake Natron and Longido, and in the northeast at Lembeni, Same and the Mkomazi GR (where common).

RED-FACED CROMBEC *Sylvietta whytii* **Plate 103**

Length 90 mm (3.5"). A plain-looking crombec with *uniformly rufous or rufous-buff face and underparts*, grey upperparts; *no dusky eye-lines or light superciliary stripes*. **Adult** of northwestern *S. w. abayensis* is more olive-brown above, and coastal *minima* is paler, than the richly coloured, more widespread *jacksoni*. Bill blackish; eyes hazel-brown, reportedly pale yellow in *minima* (Jackson 1938); feet flesh-pink. **Juvenile** tawny-grey above, with tawny-edged wing-coverts. **VOICE**: Contact note between members of a pair is a dry *chick*. Song a thin, decidedly patterned *WEE-see-see, WEE-wee-see* or *see-si-si SEEEEE*, repeated several times; varied to a rhythmic *chichirri-chichirri-chichirri*. Less common is a louder *chit-wit-weer-CHWEER-CHWEER-CHWEER*, repeated at short intervals. **SIMILAR SPECIES**: Northern Crombec is paler, with well-marked face; favours drier habitats. **STATUS AND DISTRIBUTION**: Fairly common in bush, open woodland and forest edge, mainly below 2000 m and typically in areas of higher rainfall than those occupied by Northern Crombec. *S. w. abayensis* ranges from Lokichokio to s. Turkana and Pokot Districts; *jacksoni* in w., cent. and s. Kenya from Mt Elgon, Trans-Nzoia, Baringo and Meru Districts, south through interior n. Tanzania from Serengeti NP east to Lake Manyara, Tarangire and Arusha NPs, the Masai Steppe and Mkomazi GR, in Kenya intergrading from Kibwezi to Murang'a with southeastern *minima*, which is uncommon in coastal lowlands north to Lamu and the Boni Forest.

SOMALI LONG-BILLED CROMBEC *Sylvietta isabellina* **Plate 103**

Length 95 mm (3.75"). A *pale* crombec of arid *northern and eastern Kenya. Bill nearly as long as the head.* Upperparts pale ash-grey, with whitish superciliary stripes; underparts buffy white or cream, occasionally with some pale tawny on the flanks. Bill blackish; eyes brown; feet pinkish brown. **Juvenile** duller than adult, with slightly mottled throat. **VOICE**: Song a repeated *tichit-tichit-tiri-chirichirichirichiri*. **SIMILAR SPECIES**: Yellow-vented Eremomela, often in same habitat, has shorter bill and some pale yellow on lower belly and vent region. Mouse-coloured Penduline Tit has longer tail and shorter bill. Red-faced Crombec is much more brightly coloured throughout. **STATUS AND DISTRIBUTION**: Local and uncommon resident of dry *Acacia* and *Commiphora* scrub and open bush from northern and northeastern border areas south through Samburu and Shaba GRs, Meru and Tsavo East NPs and Galana Ranch, wandering to the Tsavo River and Maktau areas of Tsavo West NP.

WHITE-BROWED CROMBEC *Sylvietta l. leucophrys*   Plate 103

Length 90–95 mm (3.5–3.75"). An 'eye-browed' crombec of highland forest, usually seen creeping about in tangled undergrowth and among vines. **Adult** dark olive above, with *chestnut-brown crown, conspicuous white superciliary stripes* and *yellow-green wing edgings*. Dark chestnut streak through eye adds to the striking head pattern. Bill pinkish brown above, paler greyish pink below; eyes dark reddish brown; feet bright flesh-pink. **Juvenile** upon leaving nest has chocolate-brown crown *with no trace of superciliary stripes*, pale yellow lower breast and belly, *brown from chin to chest and along sides*, where paler. **Immature** has pale greenish-yellow superciliary stripes, and dark olive-brown of breast extends in a point onto centre of the throat. **VOICE**: Song short, clear and ending in a trill: *tee-tee-tee-trrrrrrrrrrrrrrrrr*. **STATUS AND DISTRIBUTION**: Local and uncommon resident above 1500 m in forest and bamboo from Mt Elgon and Saiwa NPs south through Kakamega (scarce), Nandi, Mau and Trans-Mara Forests, east to the Aberdares, Limuru, Tigoni, Naro Moru and Mt Kenya. Formerly in Nairobi area forests and suburbs.

GREEN CROMBEC *Sylvietta virens [baraka]*   Plate 103

Length 85–90 mm (3.5"). A *dull-coloured, slender-billed western* crombec. **Adult** dark olive or olive-brown above, with traces of brighter olive-green on primaries, visible on unworn birds in good light. *Crown and nape sepia-brown; sides of face, throat and chest warmer tawny- or cinnamon-brown*; chin whitish; rest of underparts greyish, almost white in centre of belly. Indistinct, short, pale buff superciliary stripes noticeable at close range. Bill mostly blackish brown, long and thin; eyes light brown; feet pinkish brown. **Juvenile** paler than adult, with distinctive greenish-yellow wash on underparts. **VOICE**: Songs variable, typically loud and rapidly delivered: (1) *stereeetisu, seet-seet-seet*, (2) *skireet-sew eet-se-sew*, (3) *sit-sit-stueetsisew CHEEsu CHEEsu*, (4) *sitsuweet sitsueeet tsu-seeteeu-sitsueet-sweeet*, (5) *chit-chitisee chitisee*. Call *chi-chi-chit*. **HABITS**: Forages in low trees and shrubbery, in pairs or with mixed-species flocks. Highly vocal. **SIMILAR SPECIES**: Short-tailed juvenile Olive-green Camaroptera, easily mistaken for this species, is a forest bird, yellowish or yellowish white below and olive, not brown, on breast and flanks, sometimes on throat. Adult camaroptera with its tail feathers missing is even more similar, but wings brighter olive and face tawny. Female sunbirds have decurved bills. **STATUS AND DISTRIBUTION**: In our region confined to Busia and Mumias Districts in w. Kenya, where locally common in dense high bush and thick secondary woods along streams. Not in primary forest. Possibly restricted to areas below 1200 m. Reports from Kakamega Forest not substantiated. Our race presumably *S. v. baraka*, the species being known in Kenya only from sight records and tape recordings.

YELLOW-BELLIED EREMOMELA *Eremomela icteropygialis*   Plate 102

Length 90–95 mm (3.75"). A small, short-billed and short-tailed warbler of moist bush. **Adult** greyish above, faintly olive on the lower back, and usually with *some bright yellow on underparts*. Dusky streak through eyes and faint whitish superciliary stripes in some populations. Chin, throat and breast white; belly to under tail-coverts bright lemon-yellow in *E. i. abdominalis*. Yellow paler and restricted to lower belly in western *griseoflava*, the colour only marginally more extensive than in Yellow-vented Eremomela. Bill dark brown above, paler below; eyes hazel; feet grey or blackish. **Juvenile** paler yellow below than adult, and often extensively washed with olive on back. **VOICE**: Song a repeated, short, cheerful *cheri-chee-chit-chit CHWEER* or a shorter *chee-churi CHEEa*. Call note a high *chit*. **HABITS**: Tit-like, but actions more deliberate; progresses in short hops among branches and quick flights between adjacent trees. Forages on twigs and in foliage; also extracts insects from flowers. Usually solitary or in pairs. Rather shy. **SIMILAR SPECIES**: Yellow-vented Eremomela occupies drier areas, is paler, with yellow restricted to the lower belly and around vent, and shows no trace of olive on the lower back. Yellowish-bellied penduline tits have heavier, more conical bills. **STATUS AND DISTRIBUTION**: Widespread but uncommon resident of open woodland and bush (especially moister *Acacia* and *Combretum*) below 1900 m. Absent from arid e. Kenya, where replaced by Yellow-vented Eremomela. *E. i. abdominalis* occurs in n. Kenya at Moyale and Mandera and ranges from Isiolo District and Meru NP south to Nairobi and Magadi Districts, Amboseli and Tsavo West NPs and the Tana River delta; in n. Tanzania, from Namanga and Longido to the base of Mt Meru, west to Lake Natron, south to Tarangire NP, the Masai Steppe and Mkomazi GR. *E. i. griseoflava* is western, from Lokichokio and nw. Turkana, south to Kongelai, Pokot and Maralal Districts, lakes Baringo and Bogoria, Nakuru, Narok and Kisii Districts, the Mara GR, Loita Hills, Serengeti NP and Maswa GR.

YELLOW-VENTED EREMOMELA *Eremomela flavicrissalis*   Plate 102

Length 85 mm (3.5"). A tiny warbler of *arid n. and e. Kenya*; suggests a small, pale Yellow-bellied Eremomela with the *yellow paler and restricted to the lower belly/vent region*, often difficult to see in the field. Under tail-coverts largely white. **VOICE**: A high *sureet-seet-seet-seet* or *seet-seet-seet-seet*. **HABITS**: Similar to those of

preceding species. Becomes vocal as country greens following good rains. **SIMILAR SPECIES:** Most Yellow-bellied Eremomelas are much brighter and more extensively yellow below; the race *griseoflava* is more confusing, but its yellow extends slightly higher on the belly, and the lower back has an olive tinge. Mouse-coloured Penduline Tit has heavier, more conical bill. **STATUS AND DISTRIBUTION:** Local and uncommon in arid scrub, low bush and semi-desert below 1200 m. Ranges from e. Turkana District to Marsabit, Moyale and Mandera, south to Samburu, Shaba and Kora reserves, the lower Tana River (Meru NP to Bura), Galana Ranch and Tsavo East NP. A sight record from Mkomazi GR (Nov. 1994) is the first from Tanzania. In some northeastern border areas sympatric with Yellow-bellied Eremomela, but ecologically separated.

GREEN-CAPPED EREMOMELA *Eremomela scotops*   Plate 102

Length 100–110 mm (4"). An active arboreal warbler of open wooded areas. **Adult** *pale ash-grey above, with greenish-yellow or olive-green crown, sides of head and part of nape,* and *bright lemon-yellow superciliary stripes.* Lores dusky. Colour of underparts varies: coastal *E. s. occipitalis* has the entire underside pale yellow; *kikuyuensis* in cent. Kenya is bright yellow on throat and breast, otherwise yellowish white below; south-western *citriniceps* has greyish-white belly. Bill black; *eyes pale* yellow to whitish; feet flesh-pink. **Juvenile** paler than adult, more olive above. **VOICE:** When feeding, a short, low musical trill, *turrrrrrrr*, and a churring alarm call. Songs (*E. s. citriniceps*) a loud repeated chatter, *tsip-tsip, chip-chip-chip-chip*, and a uniform *tew-tew-tew-tew-tew-tew*. **HABITS:** Moves through canopy or shrubbery alone, more often in small groups or with bird parties. Loudly snaps bill when flycatching. Reportedly makes snapping sound with wings. Several birds may roost together, huddled side by side on branch; nest may be built co-operatively by several individuals (Maclean 1984). **SIMILAR SPECIES:** West Kenyan Green-backed Eremomela has prominent white throat, rest of underparts yellow. Allopatric Yellow-throated Woodland Warbler has tawny-brown crown. **STATUS AND DISTRIBUTION:** Local resident of open woodland, bush, forest edges and clearings, riparian trees, and sometimes gardens. Range disjunct: *E. s. citriniceps* is uncommon to scarce from Kendu Bay, Lolgorien, Mara GR and Loita Hills to n. Serengeti NP; *kikuyuensis* is scarce in Thika and Embu Districts; *occipitalis* scarce in open *Brachystegia* woodland in the Arabuko–Sokoke Forest. Old records from the East Usambara foothills.

GREEN-BACKED EREMOMELA *Eremomela pusilla canescens*   Plate 102

Length 112 mm (4.5"). A white-throated, green-and-yellow warbler with grey head and a *broad blackish streak through the eye.* **Adult** olive-green above, grey on crown and nape; white on throat and foreneck, otherwise yellow below. Bill black; eyes buffy yellow to pale hazel-brown; feet brownish pink. **Juvenile** adult-patterned, but more olive above and paler yellow below. **VOICE:** Songs rapid, somewhat guttural, the phrases rising and falling: (1) *erreee-turtreeeureeee-tureeeutree*, (2) a more rolling *urrreet-urreet-rreet-rreet*, or (3) *reelu reelu reelu*, commonly given by several birds together. Call a thin *see-see*. **HABITS:** Typically in small vocal groups or with mixed-species flocks. Forages in foliage of low trees and shrubs. Not shy. **SIMILAR SPECIES:** See Green-capped Eremomela. **STATUS AND DISTRIBUTION:** Local resident, formerly fairly common, in savanna, open woodland (especially *Combretum/Terminalia*), shrub-covered hillsides and riparian trees in w. Kenya, from the northeastern slopes of Mt Elgon to the nearby Kongelai Escarpment, and on shrubby hillsides in the Kerio Valley. Old records from Muhoroni, Kericho and Sotik Districts, where little suitable habitat remains.

TURNER'S EREMOMELA *Eremomela turneri*   Plate 102

Length 84–88 mm (3.25"). A *tiny,* grey-backed warbler of western Kenyan forest tree-tops. **Adult** has *black band across the lower throat,* broad black eye-lines, and *chestnut forehead patch* extending back over the eyes; chin and throat creamy white, breast to belly greyish. Bill black; eyes brown; feet pale pinkish. **Juvenile** olive-brown above, with no chestnut on head or merely a faint rufous wash; pale yellow below, with only a suggestion of breast band or unmarked; difficult to identify high in canopy. **VOICE:** A high-pitched rapid series of eight to 10 notes, only slightly fluctuating in pitch, *titititi-titititi*, followed by a slightly louder *si-si-chick* or *weet-su-sweet*. Begging young give a chattering *it-it-eet-chit-chit*. **HABITS:** Confined to forest trees, foraging high in the canopy or subcanopy, often with mixed-species flocks. **SIMILAR SPECIES:** Juvenile resembles other young eremomelas, but these unlikely in forest canopy. Female sunbirds have longer bills. **STATUS AND DISTRIBUTION:** In our region known only from Kakamega Forest, where uncommon in and along edges of primary and second-growth forest. Formerly along the Yala River.

BUFF-BELLIED WARBLER *Phyllolais pulchella*   Plate 100

Length 95–100 mm (3.75–4"). A small *plain* warbler of acacia woodland and savanna. **Adult** dull grey-brown (with slight olive wash) above and pale *creamy yellow below*, with a *featureless face*. Narrow blackish tail has white sides and tip. Tarsi and toes pale pinkish brown; bill grey, with base of mandible pinkish; eyes pale brown. **Juvenile** darker above and more yellowish below than adults. **VOICE**: Contact call *cht-cht-cht-cht* or *cher cher chit*. Song a dry ascending trill, uneven, with a terminal buzzy chip or two: *chirrrrrreerrrr-chk* or *zhrrrrrreeeeeerreet-chewk-chk*. **HABITS**: Pairs or family groups forage inconspicuously in tops of acacia trees, especially the yellow-barked *Acacia xanthophloea* and *A. abyssinica*. Joins mixed-species flocks. Builds felted purse-shaped nest. **SIMILAR SPECIES**: Poorly seen Willow Warbler might be mistaken for this species, but resemblance superficial; its superciliary stripes are more pronounced, wings are longer and the tail has no white. **STATUS AND DISTRIBUTION**: Fairly common resident between 600 and 2000 m in acacia-dominated habitats from Lokichokio, Lodwar, the Turkwell and Kerio Valleys, Mt Elgon and Trans-Nzoia east to Maralal, Laikipia, Samburu and Shaba GRs and Meru NP; south through w., cent. and s. Kenya to n. Tanzania, where equally widespread from Serengeti NP east to the Crater and Mbulu Highlands, Mt Hanang, Lake Manyara, Tarangire and Arusha NPs. Absent from much of eastern Kenya, but may just reach Tsavo West NP. Formerly in Tsavo East NP.

BROWN PARISOMA *Parisoma lugens jacksoni*   Plate 101
(Brown Tit-Flycatcher)

Length 130–135 mm (5.75"). A *plain dull brown* warbler partial to acacia trees. Upperparts dark brown; underparts paler dusky brown, almost whitish on belly, with lower flanks and under tail-coverts faintly buff; dull whitish chin and sides of throat indistinctly mottled with dusky brown; *tail narrowly edged and tipped with white at corners*; small amount of white on edge of wing alongside dark alula. Bill black; eyes red-brown; feet dark grey. **VOICE**: Short song begins with a husky slurred whistle, *zuree serichew wurEET* or *wureet TWEEotew*; sometimes ends in a trill: *dzree suicherrrrrrr*. Alarm call a loud, tit-like scolding *chee-chee-chee-chee* or *skwee-skwee-skwee*. **HABITS**: Unobtrusive. Usually in pairs. Actively gleans for insects in tit-like manner. **SIMILAR SPECIES**: Smaller Buff-bellied Warbler is pale creamy yellow below, with conspicuous pink on mandible. Migratory *Hippolais* warblers are paler and show superciliary stripes. **STATUS AND DISTRIBUTION**: Local and uncommon resident of acacia woodland and savanna between 1600 and 2400 m in the Kenyan highlands, from Mt Elgon, Trans-Nzoia and Laikipia south to Kakamega, Rongai, Nanyuki, Naivasha and Nairobi Districts; also from the Nguruman Hills to Loliondo and the Crater Highlands. Most numerous in and near the Rift Valley where *Acacia abyssinica* and *A. xanthophloea* are common.

BANDED PARISOMA *Parisoma boehmi*   Plate 101
(Banded Tit-flycatcher)

Length 120 mm (4.75"). A distinctly patterned arboreal warbler, and, like the preceding two species, partial to groves of acacia trees. **Adult** greyish brown above and white below, with a *black band across upper breast, black spots on throat, tawny under tail-coverts* (bright in southern birds, dull in northern *P. b. marsabit), much white wing edging* and a *white-edged black tail*. Bill dark above, light below; eyes pale yellow; feet dark grey. **Juvenile** has buffy wing-covert edges; lacks breast band and throat spots. **VOICE**: Song of 'bouncing-ball' pattern, sometimes ending in a rapid trill: *chip. . . chip, chip, chip-chip-chip-ipipipipipip*, or *prit-prit-prit-pruprupririririririri*. **HABITS**: Usually in pairs, actively feeding in acacias (especially *A. tortilis*), often on low exposed branches. Accompanies mixed-species flocks. Quite vocal. **SIMILAR SPECIES**: Some adult Red-fronted Warblers have a diffuse blackish breast band, but are otherwise dissimilar and usually feed near the ground. **STATUS AND DISTRIBUTION**: A fairly common resident of acacia savanna, bush and woodland below 1700 m. *P. b. marsabit* ranges from Marsabit and South Horr Districts south to Isiolo and Nanyuki Districts, Samburu and Shaba GRs and Meru NP. *P. b. boehmi* is southern, from the Mara GR and Serengeti NP east to Amboseli and the Tsavo NPs, Mkomazi GR and the Masai Steppe.

SOUTHERN HYLIOTA *Hyliota australis*   Plate 101
(Mashona Hyliota)

Length 114 mm (4.5"). A dark-backed arboreal warbler with a *broad white band across the wing-coverts* in both sexes. **Male** *velvety brownish black* above, including ear-coverts; **female** *grey-brown* above. Both sexes have tawny-yellow underparts and a slightly forked tail with white-edged outer feathers. Bill black above, the mandible blue-grey with black tip; eyes dark brown; feet dark lead-grey. *H. a. usambarae* is slightly smaller, the underparts deeper in colour, more buff-tinged, and the outer rectrices have a little white at their bases. **VOICE**:

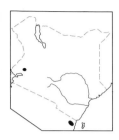

Song of squeaky whistles leading into a warbling trill (Maclean 1984). Call note a sharp *tsik*. **HABITS**: Solitary, in pairs or with mixed-species flocks. Active and warbler-like in habits. Flycatches and gleans in tree canopy at forest edge, where often hidden in foliage. Sometimes forages in plantations of exotic trees. **SIMILAR SPECIES**: Yellow-bellied Hyliota has metallic blue gloss on upperparts, and is usually in open savannas or on shrubby hillsides. **STATUS AND DISTRIBUTION**: *H. a. slatini* is an uncommon resident of the Kakamega and Nandi Forests in w. Kenya. *H. a. usambarae* is restricted to elevations between 350 and 1000 m in the Usambara Mts, ne. Tanzania.

YELLOW-BELLIED HYLIOTA *Hyliota flavigaster*   Plate 101
(Yellow-breasted Hyliota)

Length 115–120 mm (*c.* 4.5″). Patterned like the preceding species, with tawny-yellow underparts and dark upperparts and with an elongated white patch across wing-coverts, sometimes onto bases of innermost secondaries ('tertials'). **Male** *iridescent blue-black above* and tawny-yellow below. **Female** *dark grey above, appearing almost blackish, and with faint blue-green lustre.* **Juvenile** buff-barred above, paler below than adult. **VOICE**: A disyllabic *seek-seek* or *pit-seet* that may lead into a short sputtering song. **HABITS**: Somewhat tit-like. Travels in pairs, in small groups or with mixed-species flocks. Gleans in canopy or in low shrubs; also flycatches. Builds small lichen-covered cup-like nest in tree fork. **SIMILAR SPECIES**: See Southern Hyliota. **STATUS AND DISTRIBUTION**: Local and uncommon resident of savanna, open woodland (especially *Combretum*/*Terminalia*) and tall bush. Two disjunct populations in w. Kenya at 1700 m elevation: one on northeast slopes of Mt Elgon, the nearby Kongelai Escarpment, and the Nambale District; the other from Fort Ternan/Kapsoit, Kericho and Sotik Districts south to Lolgorien and the Olololoo Escarpment (nw. Mara GR), occasionally wandering to the Sand River area on the Kenyan/Tanzanian border.

WHITE-EYES, FAMILY ZOSTEROPIDAE
(World, *c.* 82 species; Africa, 10; Kenya, 3; n. Tanzania, 4)

Small, brush-tongued tropical birds, warbler-like in actions and appearance, but of uncertain taxonomic affinities. Coloration is typically yellow or olive, sometimes greyish below, but all have conspicuous white or silvery-white eye-rings for which the group is named. The iris colour is brown; bills are mostly black, and feet bluish grey in all of our species. The sexes are alike, and young birds differ little from adults. Habits vary little among species (and are not discussed separately below). White-eyes are common in wooded habitats, moving among trees and shrubs in restless twittering flocks or in pairs, feeding on insects and small fruits, as well as on nectar and juices from soft fruits obtained by using the brush-tipped tongue. Most species are gregarious except in the breeding season, indulging in various group activities. They frequently perform mutual preening and roost in clusters, often huddled against each other on a perch. The nest is a pendent cup of plant material and spider web suspended from a horizontal fork, the nest rim level with the twigs (like nests of New World vireos). At least two species are parasitized by the honeybird *Prodotiscus insignis* in East Africa.

Species limits vary, often confusingly, with different authors. The distinctive, non-intergrading montane forms, here considered races of *Z. poliogaster*, are variously merged with *Z. senegalensis* or maintained as several separate species by others. Mt Kulal birds, originally described as a race of *Z. pallidus*, may well belong with that species. The pale *flavilateralis*, now considered a race of Abyssinian White-eye, is placed in *senegalensis* and called Yellow White-eye by some authors. Here, *senegalensis* comprises *Z. virens*, the Green White-eye of some earlier East African works.

ABYSSINIAN WHITE-EYE *Zosterops abyssinicus*   Plate 102

Length 102 mm (4″). A small, relatively *pale yellow* white-eye, greenish yellow above (with greyish tinge in northern *jubaensis*). Underparts of our subspecies pale powdery canary-yellow with no trace of greenish, somewhat duller in *jubaensis*. *No contrasting yellow forehead patch*. Black on face confined to feathers at base of mandible and below the *narrow white eye-ring*; no black on lores. **VOICE**: Buzzing and twittering call notes given repeatedly by foraging groups. Song unrecorded. **SIMILAR SPECIES**: Largely allopatric Yellow White-eye has greenish sides and flanks, is brighter yellow below, greener above, and the eye-ring is broader. Yellow-bellied Montane White-eye is larger, with much broader eye-ring and usually broad contrasting yellow forehead patch. **STATUS AND DISTRIBUTION**: Locally common resident between sea level and 1800 m in bush, savanna, forest edge and gardens. Ranges from northern border areas south along lower slopes of the cent. Kenyan highlands and adjacent areas, mainly in and east of the Rift Valley, to n.

Tanzania at Mbulumbulu, Tarangire NP, lowlands near Arusha, Same and Mkomazi GR; also in coastal lowlands from Ngomeni north to the Somali border at Kiunga, and inland along the lower Tana River to Baomo. Specimens from Lotonok, north of the Cherangani Hills (July 1926) provide the only definite record west of the Rift, although there are sight records from the Kongelai Escarpment (Sept. 1988, July 1994). A familiar bird in northern Nairobi suburbs, where sympatric with *Z. p. kikuyuensis*, and present alongside *Z. p. silvanus* in the Taita Hills. Far-northern birds, south to lowlands around Mt Kulal, are considered *jubaensis*, all others *flavilateralis*.

MONTANE WHITE-EYE *Zosterops poliogaster*   Plates 102, 124
(includes Kikuyu, Taita, Kulal, South Pare and Broad-ringed White-eyes)

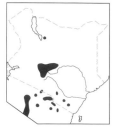

Length 110–120 mm (4.5–4.75″). A polytypic group of *highland* forest forms, perhaps embracing more than one species. The widespread central Kenyan *kikuyuensis* is large (115–120 mm) and bright (greenish above, yellow below), with *very broad eye-ring*, a *broad, well-defined golden-yellow forehead band* and black lores. On Kilimanjaro and Mt Meru, *eurycricotus* also has the *broad eye-ring but no yellow on forehead*, and *underparts are mostly dark greenish*, with some yellow on throat. Equally large *mbuluensis*, of other Tanzanian mountains (except South Pares) and the Chyulu Hills, is golden yellow below, but *yellow forehead is not sharply defined*, merging with the yellow-green crown, and the eye-ring is somewhat narrower. Small (110–113 mm) *grey-bellied* form *silvanus* of the Taita Hills has a *broad eye-ring but no yellow on the forehead*; *winifredae*, in the South Pare Mts, is also *grey-bellied, but has yellow forehead and throat*, and the eye-ring is relatively narrow. The form *kulalensis* of Mt Kulal has a relatively narrow eye-ring margined by black below and on lores, and a distinct yellow forehead; dark grey sides and flanks contrast with the limited greenish yellow of throat and upper breast, and with the pale yellowish-white mid-ventral streak from breast to the yellow crissum. Female *kulalensis* only faintly yellowish white on the belly and paler grey on sides and flanks than male. **VOICE:** Typical white-eye buzzing or twittering from a moving flock. Distinctive foraging calls of *silvanus* include a clear, slightly querulous but not buzzing *kweer-a-ree-ree* or *rree-tree*, *ter-ree-tee* or *kwerakwee-kwee-kwee*. Comparable call of *Z. p. kikuyuensis* is *whii-tu-tu-her-tu* or *whii-tew*. Song of *silvanus* a slow, slightly rising-and-falling warbling, *see tee tew chew, tew see te tew see-chew. . .*; that of *kikuyuensis* a similar *zhree zhree zhri zhree zhri zhree zhri zhew*. Songs of *kulalensis* and *winifredae* unrecorded. **SIMILAR SPECIES:** Abyssinian White-eye is smaller, paler, has narrow eye-ring, and narrower yellow forehead patch not contrasting with crown. Yellow White-eye (mainly western) is more greenish, with contrasting but much narrower forehead band; eye-ring width varies, but never as broad as in *kikuyuensis*. **STATUS AND DISTRIBUTION:** Locally common resident of highland forest, forest edge and wooded gardens between 1500 and 3400 m. Grey-bellied forms isolated on Mt Kulal, n. Kenya (*kulalensis*), Mt Kasigau and the Taita Hills (*silvanus*), and the South Pare Mts (*winifredae*). *Z. p. kikuyuensis* occupies the cent. Kenyan Highlands from Meru District, Mt Kenya and the Aberdares south to Nairobi. Mostly Tanzanian *mbuluensis* ranges from Mt Hanang, the Mbulu and Crater Highlands, Mt Ketumbeine and Longido to the North Pare Mts, and in Kenya to Ol Doinyo Orok (Namanga Hill) and the Chyulu Hills. *Z. p. eurycricotus* is present in Arusha NP, on Kilimanjaro and Mt Meru, at Essimingor, Lossogonoi and Lolkissale.

YELLOW WHITE-EYE *Zosterops senegalensis*   Plate 102
(includes the former Green White-eye)

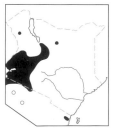

Length 115 mm (4.5″). The common northern and western *forest* white-eye, darker, greener above and brighter yellow below than Abyssinian White-eye, and distinguished from yellow-bellied forms of Montane by the *much narrower eye-ring* and *limited forehead band*. Black of loral area extends back under the eye-ring. *Sides, flanks and often a diffuse band across the breast are greenish*, at times contrasting noticeably with yellow throat and belly. The widespread race *jacksoni* shows signs of intergradation with Ugandan *stuhlmanni* at Kakamega, with the yellow forehead band often obscure and the back sometimes lightly washed with cinnamon. *Z. s. stierlingi* of Tanzania's Usambara Mts is darker green above and on the flanks, and deeper yellow below, than *jacksoni*. **VOICE:** Contact and other calls include a repeated rolling, raspy *sreeeep* and a faster *sreep-sreep-sreep*. At and shortly after dawn, sings a rising-and-falling series of 12–30 burred notes of typical white-eye quality, often introduced by four or five clear slurred notes: *tree-turri weeeu-teu, dzree-dzriri-dzree chrirri-tseeu-tseu zhree-zhree chew-chew-chew dzi-chew dzi-chew dzi-chew tzee-zizi-chew*. Song repeated frequently, sometimes by two or more birds, but seldom continues long after sunrise. **SIMILAR SPECIES:** Abyssinian and Montane White-eyes described above. Yellow warblers and Little Yellow Flycatcher lack the prominent eye-rings. **STATUS AND DISTRIBUTION:** Common resident of most western wooded and forested habitats above 1100 m. In the absence of Montane White-eye on Mt Elgon, *senegalensis* extends to 3400 m in giant-heath and moorland zones. *Z. s. jacksoni* ranges from mts Marsabit, Nyiru, Loima and Elgon, the Ndotos, Mathews Range and the Karissia Hills south through the w. Kenyan Highlands to Lolgorien, Mara GR, the Loita and Nguruman Hills and into n. Tanzania at Loliondo. Ugandan *stuhlmanni* is said to intergrade with *jacksoni* in w. Kenya from Busia and Ng'iya to Kakamega, and there are specimens of *stuhlmanni* from Kapenguria. *Z. s. stierlingi*, common in e. Tanzania, reaches our area in the Usambaras. Records from Serengeti NP and Mangola (near Lake Eyasi) not racially assigned.

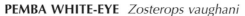

PEMBA WHITE-EYE *Zosterops vaughani*   **Plate 124**

Length 100–105 mm (*c.* 4"). The only white-eye on Pemba Island. Yellow, brighter on forehead, crown and underparts, with prominent black loral spot and very narrow white eye-ring; faint olive wash on flanks. **VOICE**: A high sweet song, shorter than that of Yellow White-eye: *sreet, seweet-sureeteet-twerila-eeta-eet*, or *weet, su-weeet-see-sur-seeiwee-see*, the first note distinct, the others often run together in a brief warbling. **STATUS AND DISTRIBUTION**: Endemic to Pemba Island and adjacent coral islets, where abundant. **Note**: Treated by some authors as a race of *Z. senegalensis*, a species absent from the adjacent mainland coastal region.

TITS, FAMILY PARIDAE
(World, *c.* 50 species; Africa, 15; Kenya, 5; n. Tanzania, 3)

The true tits are small, rather plump arboreal birds, their tails longer and their short bills less conical than those of penduline tits (now treated as a separate family, Remizidae). The sexes are alike or nearly so, and black-and-white patterns predominate. Except when breeding, tits tend to be sociable, moving in noisy restless groups of their own kind or with mixed-species parties. Busy, active and acrobatic birds, they often hang upside-down as they forage for insects and larvae on twigs and branches. They occupy various wooded habitats, and all nest in tree cavities, laying three to five white eggs with reddish speckling.

NORTHERN GREY TIT *Parus thruppi barakae*   **Plate 103**
(Somali Tit)

Length *c.* 115 mm (4.5"). A small, dry-country tit, black on head, throat and breast, with a *large white patch from bill to sides of neck*, and a broad black mid-ventral streak extending downward from the breast. **Adult** is mainly grey above with whitish wing edgings, and usually shows a white spot on the nape. Sides greyish white, sometimes with a faint tawny wash. Eyes brown; bill black; feet slate-grey. **Juvenile** has adult pattern, but black parts duller, and wing and tail edgings buff. **VOICE**: Clear whistled songs, *twee-tew-tew-tew* or *tui-tui-tui-tui*, usually of four to six notes, frequently repeated. Contact note a buzzy *chya chya*. Annoyance call a harsh raspy nasal *chewy chewy chewy chewy*, or *tchwaa, tchwaa. . ..* **HABITS**: Singles, pairs or family groups forage in low trees and shrubs, attracting attention with frequent scolding calls. Territorial male sings from treetop. **SIMILAR SPECIES**: White-bellied Tit lacks white cheek patches and black ventral streak. **STATUS AND DISTRIBUTION**: Fairly common resident of *Acacia* and *Commiphora* scrub north and east of the Kenyan highlands, mainly below 1000 m. Ranges from Lokitaung and northern border areas (east of Turkana) south through Marsabit District and the Horr Valley to Baringo and Isiolo Districts, Meru and Tsavo NPs and the Mkomazi GR in ne. Tanzania.

NORTHERN BLACK TIT *Parus leucomelas guineensis*   **Plate 103**

Length *c.* 145 mm (5.5"). A *black* tit with a *large white patch on wing-coverts*; flight-feather edges and wing-linings also white. **Adult's** black plumage glossed with violet; *eyes pale yellow*; bill and feet black. **Juvenile** duller, with no gloss, the white wing patch tinged yellowish; eyes greyish. **VOICE**: Calls weak and rasping. Song a clear reiterated *chu-wee* (Chapin 1953). **HABITS**: Typical of the genus. Usually in pairs or family groups. Takes insects on the wing. **SIMILAR SPECIES**: Dusky Tit is a forest species with no white in plumage and with red eyes. **STATUS AND DISTRIBUTION**: Sporadic wanderer from Uganda to w. Kenya, in moist bush, woodland and forest edge. Early records from Mt Elgon, Saiwa Swamp, Bungoma and in the Nyando Valley. More recent sight records of single birds at Kapenguria (April 1972), w. Pokot (Nov. 1985) and near Mumias (Dec. 1989).

DUSKY TIT *Parus funereus*   **Plate 103**

Length 130–140 mm (5–5.5"). An all-dark west Kenyan forest species. **Adult male** blackish slate with very slight green gloss. **Female** slightly duller and greyer. Eyes red; bill black; feet blue-grey in both sexes. **Juvenile** similar to female, but with faint brownish wash on throat, breast and sides of face, and narrow whitish wing-covert tips; eyes brown. **VOICE**: A loud persistent *see-er, see-er, see-er*. **HABITS**: Pairs or small vocal groups often join mixed-species flocks in canopy or lower tree branches. **SIMILAR SPECIES**: Northern Black Tit has yellow eyes, white wing patches, in different habitat. Vieillot's Black Weaver in same forests is larger, deeper black, and has yellow eyes. **STATUS AND DISTRIBUTION**: Fairly common in the Kakamega and Nandi Forests. Formerly on Mt Elgon.

WHITE-BELLIED TIT *Parus albiventris*   **Plate 103**
(White-breasted Tit)

Length 140–145 mm (c. 5.5"). A largely black tit with contrasting *white belly* and *large white patch on wing-coverts*. Remiges and outer tail feathers conspicuously white-edged in fresh plumage. Under tail-coverts and wing-linings also white. Eyes brown; bill black; feet slate-grey. Female slightly duller than male. **Juvenile** much duller than adult, with yellowish-tinged wing edgings. **VOICE**: A harsh *tss-tss-tcher-tcher-tcher*. Infrequent song *chee-er-weeoo, chee-er-wheeoo*. **HABITS**: Restless and vocal. Forages in shrubs or tree canopy; often with mixed-species flocks in acacia woodland. **STATUS AND DISTRIBUTION**: Fairly common and widespread resident of savanna, dry woodland, forest edge and suburban gardens, generally above 1200 m. Ranges throughout the Kenyan highlands, from Mt Kulal and Mt Nyiru, the Ndotos and Mathews Range south to the Lake Victoria basin, Mara GR, Nairobi, Machakos and Kibwezi Districts, Amboseli and Tsavo NPs. In n. Tanzania from Serengeti and Lake Manyara NPs and the Mkomazi GR, but largely replaced in Masailand by Red-throated Tit.

RED-THROATED TIT *Parus fringillinus*   **Plate 103**

Length 115–120 mm (c. 4.5"). A small rufous-headed tit of n. Tanzania and s. Kenya. *Blackish crown* contrasts with pale dull *rufous-buff face, throat and breast*. Adult has grey back; black wings and tail with white feather edges. Eyes brown; bill bluish horn, paler below; feet dark grey. **Juvenile** browner on crown and back. **VOICE**: A repeated rattling *tsi-chur-ur-ur-ur*, or a persistent *see-er, see-er, see-er*. Annoyance calls short bursts of a chattering *ch-ch-ch-ch*, often with some squeaky notes. **HABITS**: Pairs forage alone or with other species. Favours acacias. **STATUS AND DISTRIBUTION**: An East African endemic, fairly common and widespread between 1000 and 1600 m in Masailand in s. Kenya/n. Tanzania, from Serengeti, Tarangire and Arusha NPs across much of the Masai Steppe, and north (less commonly) through the Mara GR and Loita Plains, Namanga, Kajiado and Oloitokitok Districts to Lukenya and the southern boundary of Nairobi NP at Athi River. In places, sympatric with White-bellied Tit.

PENDULINE TITS, FAMILY REMIZIDAE
(World, 10 species; Africa, 7; Kenya and n. Tanzania, 2)

Tiny short-billed birds formerly treated as a subfamily of the Paridae, which they resemble in general habits. They differ in their short tails and their sharp conical bills. Plumage is quite uniform and dull-coloured, and the sexes are alike. Pairs or small groups forage in trees and shrubs like warblers or parids, but they are even more agile and acrobatic in their search for insects. They are frequent visitors to parasitic mistletoe flowers and blossoming acacia trees. Our two species differ little in habits. The unique nest is a remarkable, tightly woven, felt-like bag of plant down with a tubular side entrance near the top, and suspended from a thin branch of a tree or shrub. That of *A. caroli* (and presumably also that of *A. musculus*) has a false opening below the real entrance hole, which reportedly is closed by the bird on leaving and sometimes after entering. The nest is used for roosting during the non-breeding season. Both species lay several pure white eggs. See Fig. p. 597.

MOUSE-COLOURED PENDULINE TIT *Anthoscopus musculus*   **Plate 103**

Length 65–85 mm (2.5–3.25"). A tiny tit-like bird of dry country, plain, short-tailed and with a short sharp, bill. Upperparts grey to brownish grey; *forehead same colour as crown*; underparts pale creamy or whitish, often with a faint buffy tinge on flanks and belly; also a trace of buff on lores and ear-coverts. Side of face marked only by a short dark eye-line. Eyes brown; bill black; feet slate-grey. **Juvenile** resembles adult. **VOICE**: High-pitched and sibilant: a rattling *di-di-di-di-di-di* and a thin *tsee-tsi tsee-tsi tsee-tsi. . .*; also shorter squeaky *tsi* and *tsrr* calls.

Similar Species: African Penduline Tit, typically in higher-rainfall areas, has forehead paler than the crown, although faded and pale individuals of *A. c. sylviella* can be mistaken for Mouse-coloured; they are buff, not whitish, below and on the forehead, with noticeably buff ear-coverts. Buff-bellied Warbler is long-tailed. Eremomelas and crombecs are larger and longer-billed. **Status and Distribution**: Widespread but rather local and uncommon resident of bush, savanna and open acacia woodland in semi-arid areas north and east of the Kenyan highlands, ranging from n. Kenya south to Baringo and Isiolo Districts, Meru and the Tsavo NPs, Lake Jipe, the North Pare foothills and Mkomazi GR.

AFRICAN PENDULINE TIT *Anthoscopus caroli*   **Plate 103**

Length 80–85 mm (3–3.5"). Another very small, short-tailed bird with a short, sharp bill, usually in moister regions than *A. musculus* and differing from it in *brighter plumage and pale forehead*. Seen much less frequently than that species. Plumage variable: *A. c. sylviella* grey above with no olive tinge, deep buff or pale rusty buff below, *forehead usually rusty buff*, sometimes paler; *A. c. sharpei* of the Lake Victoria basin is darker below, with whitish forehead; southeastern *robertsi* is greyish or greyish olive above, buffy to yellowish or pale tawny below; western *roccattii* is *bright greenish olive* above, with *yellowish forehead and underparts*, the lower abdomen slightly buffy. **Voice**: *A. c. sylviella* gives a high, thin simple trill, somewhat metallic and of two or three seconds' duration: *sreeeeeeeee-ee-ee-ee*. Other calls (subspecies?) include a rasping *chiZEE*, *chiZEEE*, *chiZEE* and a squeaky *skee-chi-skee-chi-zee*. **Similar Species**: Mouse-coloured Penduline Tit is paler, lacks pale forehead, and inhabits drier country. Eremomelas and crombecs have longer, differently shaped bills. **Status and Distribution**: Widespread but uncommon and local in open woodland, savanna, and along forest edge in areas of moderate to high rainfall, mainly below 2000 m on the periphery of the w. and cent. Kenyan highlands. Four subspecies (two east of the Rift Valley, two west). *A. c. sylviella* in interior eastern Kenya from Murang'a and Kitui south to Voi, Taita Hills, Simba, Athi River and Kajiado, and to Longido and Kibaya in n. Tanzania. Precise limits of *sylviella* and *robertsi* unclear, the latter formerly known in coastal Kenyan lowlands from the Tana River south to Mombasa, inland to Taru, Samburu and the Usambara Mts, but no recent records; also collected at Naberera in the Masai Steppe of ne. Tanzania. *A. c. roccattii* ranges from Mt Elgon to the Kongelai Escarpment, Kapenguria, Saiwa NP and Bungoma District; *A. c. sharpei* from Kakamega south to the Lake Victoria basin, Lolgorien, Mara GR, the Nguruman Hills and Serengeti NP. Birds from Lake Baringo, Kerio Valley and Nakuru District not racially assigned.

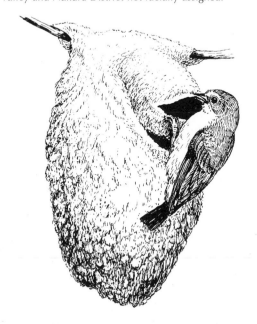

African Penduline Tit at nest, opening 'lips' of the entrance tube (usually closed to an inconspicuous horizontal slit when bird is away from nest). Before entering, upper edge of lip is pushed up with bill, the lower one pulled down or held with the feet. Dark area behind bird's tarsus represents the normally more conspicuous false entrance leading to a blind pocket in front of the real nest chamber concealed behind the thick padded wall.

CREEPERS, FAMILY CERTHIIDAE
(World, 7 species; Africa, 2; Kenya, 1)

Our single species (formerly placed in the monotypic family Salpornithidae) differs from holarctic treecreepers in that the tail is not specialized for support, being soft and rounded, and held away from the bark during climbing. Like other creepers, it has a slender curved bill, strong feet, and sharply curved claws adapted to bark-clinging. The sexes are alike, and plumage is cryptically patterned. The nest is a compact lichen-covered cup in or near a horizontal tree fork, the three eggs pale turquoise with dark spots and blotches.

SPOTTED CREEPER *Salpornis spilonotus salvadori*   Plate 103

Length 140 mm (5.5"). A small *tree-climbing* bird with a thin, decurved bill. Entire upperparts dark brown with extensive *bold white spotting*; strong white superciliary stripes. Underparts lighter, with brown and white spotting and mottling; tail boldly barred black and white. **Juvenile** resembles adult. **Voice**: A shrill, thin, high-pitched *sweepy-swip-swip-swip*; sometimes a single *sweee*. Southern African birds utter a sharp *kek-kek-kek-kek* (Maclean 1984). **Habits**: Forages on trunks and large branches, fluttering and climbing from the bottom upwards, then flying to next tree. Favours large, flat-topped acacias. Flight undulating and woodpecker-like. Joins foraging mixed-species flocks. **Status and Distribution**: One of Kenya's most endangered species, now extirpated from many areas owing to continuing loss of habitat. It remains (1994) a scarce and very local inhabitant of acacia savanna and open woodland around Kapenguria in nw. Kenya. Early in the 20th century, recorded from Kitale and Kaimosi to Elgeyu and Londiani.

MONARCH FLYCATCHERS, FAMILY MONARCHIDAE
(World, 98 species; Africa, 15; Kenya, 7; n. Tanzania, 5)

Small active birds of tree canopy in forest, woodland and gardens. Excepting *Erythrocercus*, they are slender, crested, with long to very long graduated tails, rather broad flat bills and slender tarsi. The sexes are alike or similar; juveniles differ from those of true flycatchers (Muscicapidae) in their unspotted plumage. Most are foliage-gleaners, but they also snatch aerial prey. They build neat cup-shaped nests, typically using mosses and lichens, in a tree fork a few metres above ground. The usual two eggs are whitish, with various dark or reddish markings concentrated in a zone around the larger end.

LITTLE YELLOW FLYCATCHER *Erythrocercus holochlorus*   Plate 102

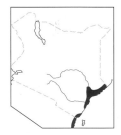

Length 95 mm (3.75"). A *warbler-like* bird of coastal forest, yellow-olive above and *bright yellow below*; wing feathers edged somewhat brighter yellow. Face rather plain, but shows narrow yellowish eye-ring at close range. Eyes dark brown; bill pale brown above, flesh-pink below; feet pale yellowish brown. **Voice**: Songs sweet, snappy and warbler-like: (1) *wee-see-SEEu si-SEEu-WEET*, (2) *sweeti-seeu-see-SEEu*, (3) *sweechee-seeu*, (4) *trrrrrrrrr-wichi-see-see*. Any of the songs may be modified by addition of a chattering trill, as at start of example 4. Call note an emphatic loud *cheu*; also said to give a plaintive *zee-zee* similar to call of Collared Sunbird (Williams and Arlott 1980). **Habits**: Pairs forage actively in forest canopy and mid-level vegetation. Joins mixed-species flocks. **Similar Species**: The much larger, thicket-dwelling yellow warblers of the genus *Chloropeta* are absent from the coast. **Status and Distribution**: Common in primary and secondary forest and moist thickets in coastal lowlands north to the Boni Forest, inland along the lower Tana River, in the Shimba Hills, and to 1000 m in the East Usambara Mts.

AFRICAN BLUE FLYCATCHER *Elminia longicauda teresita*   Plate 88

Length 140 mm (5.5"). A dainty little crested monarch, *cerulean blue* above with noticeable black lores; breast pale blue-grey, otherwise white below. *Long graduated tail is repeatedly fanned*. Eyes brown; bill and feet black. **Juvenile** paler, with buff-edged feathers above. **Voice**: Song a rapid, thin, featureless sputtering, *chiti-chi-chee-chee spitisti chitisi chi-chi-chi chitisee chit . . .*, and a sharper *dzreet tsit stereeeu tsit-tsit-tsit tsereee tsit . . ..* Call notes include a sharp high *chink* and thin *chee*. **Habits**: Lively and conspicuous, fanning tail, drooping wings, twisting about and darting between perches. Usually in pairs or small groups in lower or outer part of tree canopy or among shrubs, actively searching foliage and flycatching. **Similar Species**: Allopatric White-tailed Blue Flycatcher has conspicuous white outer tail feathers. Dusky Crested Flycatcher is much darker and duller, and has different habits. **Status and Distribution**: Locally common in forest edge, woodland and gardens below 2400 m in w. Kenya, from Mt Elgon, Kapenguria and

Saiwa NP, south through Busia, Mumias, Kakamega and Nandi Districts to the Kericho and Kilgoris Forests, Lolgorien and w. Mara GR.

WHITE-TAILED BLUE FLYCATCHER *Elminia albicauda*   Plate 124

Length 140 mm (5.5"). A crested Tanzanian monarch, less blue than the preceding species, especially on the breast, and with *much white in the tail*. Outer rectrices entirely white. Head streaked with whitish and pale greyish blue. **Voice:** Call note a sharp *tip-tip*, alternating with whistled *teereet* notes (Vincent 1935). Also an occasional short burst of pretty warbling (Chapin 1953). **Habits:** As for the preceding species. **Similar Species:** African Blue Flycatcher compared above. **Status and Distribution:** Locally common in forest edge and gallery forest, reaching our area from the Mbulu Highlands north to the Karatu and Marang Forests of the Crater Highlands.

WHITE-TAILED CRESTED FLYCATCHER *Trochocercus albonotatus*   Plate 88

Length 130 mm (5"). A lively crested monarch of montane forest, the *frequently spread graduated tail broadly edged and tipped with white*. **Adult** has black head and throat, dark grey upperparts, grey breast and flanks and whitish belly; wings uniformly blackish. *T. a. subcaeruleus* slightly paler above than nominate *albonotatus*. **Juvenile** has dark grey face and throat. **Voice:** Common call a high-pitched metallic *pink-pink*. Song of four or five thin sharp notes, *tseu, tseu-tseu-tseu*, sometimes faster and more twittering. **Habits:** Conspicuous. Pairs forage restlessly among lower-and mid-strata foliage, twisting, turning and fanning the tail and pursuing flying insects. Not shy. **Similar Species:** Blue-mantled Crested Flycatcher is more bluish grey above, with white wing markings and whiter underparts; lacks white in tail; female has mottled throat. Dusky Crested Flycatcher is more uniform slaty blue on body, with plain dark tail. **Status and Distribution:** *T. a. albonotatus* is fairly common between 1850 and 2500 m in the w. and cent. Kenyan highlands, from Mt Elgon and Saiwa NPs south to the North Nandi, Kericho, Mau and Trans-Mara Forests, and east to Ndaragwa, s. Aberdares, eastern slopes of Mt Kenya and the Nyambenis. *T. a. subcaeruleus* is common in ne. Tanzania from 900 to over 2000 m in the Usambara Mts, with some cold-season movement to lower elevations.

BLUE-MANTLED CRESTED FLYCATCHER *Trochocercus cyanomelas bivittatus*   Plate 88
(Crested Flycatcher)

Length 130–135 mm (c. 5"). A small eastern-forest bird with *prominent long floppy crest* erected in display or excitement. **Adult male** *glossy blue-black on head, throat and breast*; upperparts mostly slaty blue, with *conspicuous white wing patch*; belly white; tail plain and dark. **Female** paler, with grey head and upperparts, conspicuous white eye-ring and two *narrow white wing-bars*; underparts white, except for *grey-mottled breast*. **Juvenile** resembles female, but has buff-tipped wing-coverts. **Voice:** Calls include a rasping *zhi* or *zhi-wa* and a harsh *zwer-zwer-zwer-zwer*; also a high penetrating twitter, *tit-titititititi*, and a repeated *skwi-yaa-yaa* followed by some high, soft whistled notes. Songs a loud mellow *kew-wu-wu-wu-wu* and *tew-witi-tew-ti-tee-tew*, at times ending with several chips. **Habits:** In pairs or solitary, often with mixed bird parties. Retiring and shy. Flits and searches restlessly in forest undergrowth, sometimes in dense lower-canopy foliage. Fans tail. Rather acrobatic, clinging to one side of a branch, then the other. **Similar Species:** The more blackish White-tailed Crested Flycatcher has white in tail, plain wings and greyer underparts; is generally at higher elevations. **Status and Distribution:** Inhabits forest below 1800 m. Most numerous in the coastal lowlands north to the Boni Forest (but now decidedly uncommon in many areas). In Kenya, ranges inland to Mt Kasigau and Kitovu Forest (Taveta District), the Chyulu Hills and Mt Endau. Records from the Meru Forest (June–Nov. 1993) and w. Nairobi suburbs (Aug.–Sept. 1994) were the first in cent. Kenya in recent decades. In n. Tanzania, scarce and local below 900 m in the East Usambara Mts. More widespread in Arusha and Moshi Forests, including Arusha NP, and between 1500 and 1750 m in the North Pare Mts.

DUSKY CRESTED FLYCATCHER *Trochocercus nigromitratus*   Plate 88

Length 130 mm (5"). A small, dark crested monarch of *west Kenyan forest undergrowth*. **Adult male** *dark bluish slate*, with *top of head, wings and tail black*. Eyes dark brown; bill black; feet dark bluish. **Female** and **juvenile** duller and less bluish than male. **Voice:** Contact note a rather harsh *tick*. Annoyance call a harsh chattering. Song of clear, shrill, short notes, *sreet tseeu seet* (last note higher) or *sreet, tseu* (the second lower). Any of these notes may be given singly. **Habits:** Unobtrusive. Solitary or in pairs in dense undergrowth. Forages actively, but may perch quietly for some time. **Similar Species:** White-tailed Crested Flycatcher, at higher elevations, has white in

tail and on belly. **STATUS AND DISTRIBUTION**: Uncommon in the Kakamega Forest. Also recorded from the Chemoni Forest, Nandi Hills, and formerly from Mt Elgon.

AFRICAN PARADISE FLYCATCHER *Terpsiphone viridis*   Plate 88

Length 175–190 mm (7–7.5″) excluding *long central tail feathers, which may extend 6–7″ beyond other rectrices.* A medium-sized dimorphic monarch with dark crested head and *grey belly*. **Rufous morph** bright orange-rufous on back and tail. **White morph** has white back and tail and much white in wings. Bill and narrow bare eye-ring cobalt-blue to purplish blue. *T. v. ferreti* is glossy greenish black from head to breast, the male with a large white wing patch. Eastern *ungujaensis* may lack white in the wings, shows whitish on belly and at times on under tail-coverts; coastal birds, considered *plumbei-ceps,* have dark head, dull bluish black from forehead to nape, and generally lack white in wings. **Female** and **young male** have only slightly elongated central rectrices. **VOICE**: Various rasping calls such as *chwee-chwee-chwee; zwa-i-zer; zhweet-zhwait; wiZHEER;* and *skwee-chi-chi-chwee.* Variable brief song of rapidly delivered mellow ringing notes, *whee-wheeo-whit-whit* (Sclater and Moreau, 1933), *tu-whiddle tuWEE,* or *zwitty-weep-weepa-weep.* **HABITS**: Solitary or in pairs. Rather bold and conspicuous. Perches on low or mid-level branches and flies out to capture aerial insects. **SIMILAR SPECIES**: Red-bellied Paradise Flycatcher is orange-rufous from breast to under tail-coverts. **STATUS AND DISTRIBUTION**: *T. v. ferreti* is widespread and common in woodland, bush, forest and gardens from the coast up to 2500 m, but absent from arid parts of n. and ne. Kenya. Most records of breeding are from the highlands and adjacent areas; white morph is common in eastern bush country but generally scarce at higher elevations. *T. v. ungujaensis* is common in ne. Tanzania from the Usambara Mts southward, intergrading with *ferreti* in the North Pare Mts and Moshi District; *plumbeiceps* ranges along the coast north at least to the Arabuko–Sokoke Forest, mainly as a non-breeding visitor from the southern tropics, but some individuals may breed on Pemba Island.

RED-BELLIED PARADISE FLYCATCHER *Terpsiphone rufiventer emini*   Plate 88

Length 160–200 mm (6.25–8″). A *west Kenyan forest-interior* bird with an entirely *orange-rufous* body. **Adult male** has *black head and throat* sharply separated from colour of back and breast; black flight feathers are edged with orange-rufous; crest short or lacking. Central tail feathers of most birds only slightly elongated, but sometimes extending well beyond rest of tail. **Female** similar, but may be somewhat greyer on throat. Hybridizes with preceding species, producing intermediates with well-developed crests, elongated central tail feathers, grey or whitish breast feathers, a little white on the wing, or some combination of these characters. **VOICE**: Call note a harsh *zhre-zhre* or *zree-zree,* much like that of African Paradise Flycatcher. **HABITS**: Solitary or in pairs, often moving through the lower and middle forest strata with mixed-species flocks. **SIMILAR SPECIES**: African Paradise Flycatcher often shows white in wings, black of throat extends onto breast and merges with grey of belly, crest is longer, and central rectrices of male typically extend far beyond rest of tail. **STATUS AND DISTRIBUTION**: Confined to the Kakamega Forest, where increasingly scarce, possibly being genetically 'swamped' through interbreeding with African Paradise Flycatcher as forest decreases and the remnant stands increasingly opened. Most birds observed in recent years appear to be hybrids.

BATISES, WATTLE-EYES AND RELATIVES, FAMILY PLATYSTEIRIDAE
(World, 28 species; Africa, 27; Kenya, 13; n. Tanzania, 8)

Small birds with somewhat flattened bills and pronounced rictal bristles, formerly considered muscicapids but now believed to be near relatives of helmet-shrikes and vangas (Sibley and Monroe 1990), as suggested by DNA similarities as well as morphology and nest construction. We treat them as a separate family, following Traylor (1986c). The two *Bias* species are unique, sexually dimorphic, flycatcher-like birds. The main groups, batises and wattle-eyes are treated separately below.

BATISES (pronounced with a long 'a') are small insectivores found in pairs or small family groups. They are primarily foliage-gleaners, but also indulge in flycatching. Some species are quite vocal. True songs are supplemented by quaint piping contact notes and are often accompanied by audible wing sounds—*prrrt, prrrt, brrrt* or *firrrrup*—as the bird flies from branch to branch. Bill-snapping is frequent. General behaviour, not discussed in the following species accounts, is quite uniform throughout the genus. Most batises are confusingly similar in plumage. Males are grey, black and white, with a black breast band; females have some chestnut or tawny below, often including a breast band. Both sexes show a white spot on the nape. The partly white, silky rump feathers are puffed out in display, as in puffback shrikes.

Species recognition requires knowledge of crown colour, relative tail length, throat pattern, eye colour and extent of the superciliary stripes, although the latter is affected by plumage wear and also by the degree of feather erection; a batis can show conspicuous superciliaries one minute and none the next. Crown colour may require close scrutiny: grey feathers become more blackish with wear, and a glossy black cap can appear deceptively lighter in strong light. Width of the breast band varies, and is not always reliable for species distinction; it varies individually and possibly geographically. Our six *Batis* species, all resident, tend to segregate geographically and/or ecologically, although two, and sometimes three, may be sympatric in some areas. The common Chin-spot is widespread inland, typically at higher elevations; it does not reach the coastal lowlands occupied by Forest Batis (in dense evergreen thickets and forest) and Pale Batis (more open or drier woodland). Black-headed overlaps with these two at the coast but is usually in semi-open or edge habitats—scrub, savanna, mangrove-swamp borders and (formerly) Mombasa-area gardens. The western race of Black-headed is more restricted to savanna or bushed grassland than the partly sympatric Chin-spot of woodland patches and riparian strips with a more continuous canopy. Pygmy and the little-known Grey-headed Batises are dry-country birds whose ecological distinctions are not entirely clear, although Pygmy inhabits open tall bush or thin scrub-savanna with uniformly low, sparse tree cover. Grey-headed, barely known in Kenya, may prefer slightly less xeric sites with more or higher trees.

WATTLE-EYES are forest birds sporting brightly coloured orbital wattles. The *Platysteira* species are relatively slender, with ample tails, *Dyaphorophyia* plump and stub-tailed. Most are glossy black and white, often with some chestnut; one species is bright yellow and olive. As in *Batis*, the long fluffy rump feathers can be raised in a puff above the back. These birds also share with *Batis* various wing-flicking sounds and they have intriguing semi-musical songs. The nest, like that of *Batis*, is a neat compact cup covered with lichens and cobwebs and placed in a small fork or horizontal tree branch.

CHIN-SPOT BATIS *Batis molitor* Plate 86

Length 105–110 mm (4–4.25"). The most widespread batis. **Adult female** readily identified by sharply defined *dark chestnut throat spot.* **Adult male** has a broad black breast band. The *slate-grey crown* can appear blackish when worn, but still appears lighter than the jet-black ear-coverts, which usually contrast with narrow white superciliary stripes extending back to the white nape spot (not always conspicuous). Long wing-stripe, sides of neck, most of underparts and edges of tail white. Eyes chrome-yellow or (in immatures?) greenish. **Juvenile** resembles female, but has buff feather tips on black upperparts and on the dark breast band. **Immature male** like adult female; **immature female** brown above, with tawny median wing-coverts. VOICE: A penetrating song of several clear piping whistles in descending semitones, reminiscent of a Common Wattle-eye: *hee-her, hee-her. . .* or *hee-her-her. . .*, the higher initial note sometimes repeated indefinitely. Also gives a metallic descending *weenh whenh wherr* or *tee quee queu*, oft-repeated. A soft *querk querk querk* is uttered by courting birds, and there is a harsh scolding *chh-chh-chh-chh* or *ch-chk* of annoyance. **SIMILAR SPECIES**: Male Black-headed Batis has jet-black or blackish crown of same shade as ear-coverts. Allopatric Pale Batis is shorter-tailed and paler grey above; female has paler, more diffuse patch on throat and paler breast band. Forest Batis is smaller, still shorter-tailed, orange- or red-eyed, the female extensively tawny or cinnamon below, with no throat spot; also shows conspicuous tawny wing band. Smaller Pygmy Batis inhabits drier country, has short white line leading from bill to eye only; female lacks throat spot. Rare Grey-headed Batis of northern border regions has shorter tail, larger nape spot. Male Common Wattle-eye is uniformly glossy black above, with much narrower breast band, red eye-wattles and no white superciliary stripes. **STATUS AND DISTRIBUTION**: Fairly common and widespread between 600 and 2600 m in woodland, riverine forest and wooded suburban gardens. Absent from the Lake Victoria basin, coastal lowlands, much of arid e. and ne. Kenya, and ne. Tanzania.

BLACK-HEADED BATIS *Batis minor* Plate 86

Length 105 mm (4"). **Adult male** much like Chin-spot Batis, but *crown jet-black* in western *erlangeri* (same hue as ear-coverts), *medium grey, dark charcoal-grey or blackish* in nominate eastern race. *Long white superciliary stripes extend to or almost to nape* (but can appear shorter, depending on wear and feather arrangement). **Female** has a *dark chestnut breast band* and no throat spot. Eyes yellow in both sexes. **Juvenile** blackish above with buff speckling, like young Chin-spot. VOICE (*B. m. erlangeri*): Notes tend to be more drawn out, less sharp, than those of Chin-spot Batis. Common call a penetrating, monotonously repeated *eent eent eent . . .* or *reehn reehn. . .*, given by both sexes. Members of a pair may call antiphonally, the notes well separated and unhurried. Male also has a clearer whistled song, a repeated *ureet-eet, ureet-eet. . .*, and another beginning with a high introductory *seent*, followed by *wree wree wree wree*. Female has a rough *skaow* of alarm or annoyance.(Eastern *B. m. minor* gives a thin, slightly ascending *ureet-weet-weet* or *yeeo-eet-eet* of similar penetrating quality to voice of western

birds.) **Similar Species**: Male Chin-spot Batis has grey crown (can look dark when worn, but never as black as the ear-coverts). Rare Grey-headed Batis also has long superciliary stripes, but is grey or bluish grey on crown. **Status and Distribution**: *B. m. minor* is uncommon to locally fairly common in savanna and open woodland in coastal lowlands, including edges of mangrove stands, inland along the lower Tana River, to Mt Endau, the Tsavo NPs, Kibwezi and Mkomazi GR. *B. m. erlangeri* occurs in w. Kenya at Lokichokio and from Mt Elgon and the Kongelai Escarpment south through Busia, Mumias and Kisumu Districts to South Nyanza, east to slopes above the Kerio Valley near Kabarnet. Sympatric with *B. molitor* in Kapenguria and Kabarnet Districts, but typically in more open woodland, wooded grassland or tall-grass savanna with small thickets, scattered broad-leaved trees (e.g. *Erythrina, Terminalia, Ficus*) and tall euphorbias.

FOREST BATIS *Batis mixta*   Plates 86, 124

Length 95 mm (3.75"). A small, *short-tailed* batis of coastal forest and some ne. Tanzanian mountains. *Eyes orange or red*, not yellow. **Adult male** has broad breast band. Coastal adult **female** (*B. m. ultima*) distinctive, with *frosty cinnamon throat and upper breast, long black mask bordered above with white*, and *tawny wing-stripe* formed by the larger coverts and edges of inner secondaries ('tertials'). Female *B. m. mixta* (Tanzanian highlands) is darker, more chestnut below, with reduced superciliary stripes and brown eyes. **Juvenile** resembles adult female, but speckled with buff above. **Immature** similar to female, but crown olive-brown. **Voice** (*B. m. ultima*, Sokoke): A hollow, minor-key *yeu* or *ooo* repeated at three- to four-second intervals, and often alternating with mate's identical call; also a rough nasal *rrrannh*, repeated in series. Song a monotonous hollow piping (much like that of Chestnut Wattle-eye), long-continued and at times ventriloquial. A soft *nyemp* may be given at intervals with the piping. Annoyance call a mechanical *ch-ch-ch-ch* in repeated series. Piping of nominate *mixta, eee . . . eee . . . eeeuk . . . eee . . . eeeuk . . .*, the notes given at intervals of two to four seconds; annoyance call *ch-ch-ch-chchchch cheenh*. **Habits**: Kenyan *ultima* customarily inhabits lower forest strata, often foraging within a metre of the ground, whereas *mixta* is at least partially a bird of high forest canopy, from which it calls persistently. When vocalizing, head is raised and neck puffs out like bellows (Sclater and Moreau 1933). **Similar Species**: Male Pale Batis (in coastal Kenya, virtually restricted to *Brachystegia* stands) has yellow eyes and narrow breast band. Black-headed Batis is larger, longer-tailed and yellow-eyed. **Status and Distribution**: *B. m. ultima* is fairly common in Kenyan coastal forest and tall evergreen thickets from the Arabuko–Sokoke Forest south to the Shimba Hills, Shimoni and Mrima Hill. *B. m. mixta* is locally common between 1500 and 2300 m in submontane forests in Arusha NP and on Mt Meru, Kilimanjaro and the Pare Mts. Fairly common from 300 to over 2000 m in the Usambara Mts, where Lawson (1964) reported intergrades between the two races; birds in the East Usambara lowland forests, however, appear closer to *ultima* (T. Evans, *pers. comm.*).

PALE BATIS *Batis soror*   Plate 86
(East Coast or Mozambique Batis)

Length 90–95 mm (c. 3.5"). An *eastern woodland* species, replacing Chin-spot Batis in coastal areas. **Male** slightly paler grey above and *shorter tailed* than Chin-spot (but not stub-tailed like Forest Batis); best separated by range and accompanying **female,** in which the *throat patch is pale tawny and diffuse*, and the *breast band pale tawny or cinnamon*, not dark chestnut. Eyes yellow in both sexes. **Voice**: Male's song a soft metallic piping, *yeenk-yeenk-yeenk-yeenk . . .*, or an almost creaking *trree trree trree . . .*, the series often coinciding or alternating with female's louder and harder *pik-pik-pik-pik. . .* Notes may alternate with soft *whit* notes and *prrrt* of wings. Harsh alarm calls like those of Chin-spot Batis. **Similar Species**: Chin-spot Batis (female) has sharply defined chestnut throat patch and breast band. Sympatric Forest Batis has shorter tail, orange or red eyes, occupies evergreen woods. See Black-headed Batis. **Status and Distribution**:
Fairly common in coastal woodland in the Arabuko–Sokoke Forest (mainly in *Brachystegia*) and in the same habitat north of the Sabaki River. Reported occurrence along the lower Tana River requires confirmation. In ne. Tanzania, ranges up to 1000 m in the East Usambara Mts. Nowhere overlaps in range with Chin-spot Batis, but status unclear in several areas.

PYGMY BATIS *Batis perkeo*   Plate 86

Length 87–96 mm (3.5–3.75"). A *short-tailed*, grey-crowned batis of *arid and semi-arid country*. Patterned like Chin-spot Batis, but *white on face reduced to supraloral stripes only, or lacking*; breast band (narrow in centre to 15–18 mm broad at sides) black in **male**, *orange-tawny* in **female**, which usually shows a faint *buff wash on the white throat* (may be pale cinnamon at sides of throat). Eyes golden yellow in female, almost orange-yellow in male. **Voice**: Penetrating piping notes suggesting those of Black-headed Batis, but typically sharper, more ringing, less drawn out, *ting, ting, ting*, sometimes in long measured series of 20 or more identical notes. Sometimes

the note slightly more extended, *pee, pee, pee* . . . or *een, een, een*. . . **SIMILAR SPECIES**: Male Grey-headed Batis has broader breast band and longer superciliary stripes; female's breast band is chestnut. See Chin-spot Batis. **STATUS AND DISTRIBUTION**: Fairly common in dry regions at low and intermediate elevations. In n. and e. Kenya, ranges from the Ethiopian border south to West Pokot, Baringo and Bogoria Districts, Samburu and Shaba GRs, Meru and Tsavo NPs and to the Mkomazi GR in ne. Tanzania. Prefers uniformly low acacia scrub-savanna.

GREY-HEADED BATIS *Batis o. orientalis*   **Plate 86**

Length 96–105 mm (*c.* 4"). A northern species, known with certainty in our region only from Moyale. Alleged specimens from north of Garsen and Lamu District have proved to be Black-headed Batises of nominate race, some individuals of which are more grey- than black-crowned. Much like the slightly smaller sympatric Pygmy Batis, but *long superciliary stripes extend back nearly to, or actually merge with, the broad white nape spot*; tail also is somewhat longer. *Breast band typically broad*, not narrow as in eastern Black-headed Batis. *Crown blue-grey* to medium grey, similar to Pygmy Batis, but always noticeably contrasting with the jet-black ear-coverts (unlike Black-headed Batis). **Female** has *chestnut* (not tawny) *breast band* and pure white throat. Eyes yellow in both sexes. **Immature male** may have black-and-chestnut breast band. **VOICE**: Song of Ethiopian birds, described by Benson (1946) as *WEET, weet, weet, seerr* (final note softer,) would appear distinctive, but recent Ethiopian recordings are of clear piping whistles almost indistinguishable from those of Kenyan Chin-spot Batis, and which stimulate immediate vocal response from that species. **SIMILAR SPECIES**: Shorter-tailed Pygmy Batis differs vocally and has white supraloral stripes not extending behind eyes (sometimes scarcely visible); female's breast band orange-tawny instead of chestnut, and her throat tinged with buff or pale cinnamon. Black-headed Batis in eastern Kenya and Somalia often mistaken for Grey-headed, even in the hand, as crown colour ranges from black to medium grey. Relationship between these two species is as perplexing here as near Lake Chad, where Vielliard (1972) reports an apparent cline between *B. o. chadensis* and *B. m. erlangeri*. The latter form in w. Kenya has black or blackish crown, the lower edge of which (above eyes) can appear greyish. Wings of male *B. minor erlangeri* measure 58.5–67 mm, those of *B. orientalis* 52–59 mm; tails 43–51 mm and 39–41.5 mm, respectively. **STATUS AND DISTRIBUTION**: Status uncertain, but only two definite Kenyan specimens (Moyale, Oct. 1910). Misidentifications cloud interpretation of data based on sight reports, none of which is documented or convincing. Published statements of abundance around Lake Turkana are entirely unsupported, and reports (1970s and early 1990s) from Samburu GR and elsewhere likewise without substantiation. As yet, no evidence of this species west of Moyale, despite much collecting at intervals since 1912 from Isiolo north through Turkana to sw. Ethiopia. Possibly ranges rarely in n. Kenya, as specimens are known from se. Sudan and (one) from Mt Moroto, Uganda. A bird of dense thorn-scrub in s. Ethiopia, where sympatric with Pygmy Batis.

COMMON WATTLE-EYE *Platysteira cyanea nyansae*   **Plate 86**
(Wattle-eyed Flycatcher; Brown-throated or Scarlet-spectacled Wattle-eye)

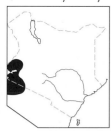

Length 120–130 mm (4.75–5"). **Adult male** glossy black above, white below, with a black breast band, *long white wing-stripe*, white outer tail feathers and prominent *scarlet wattle* above each eye. **Female** greyer above, and entire *throat and breast dark maroon-chestnut*. Eyes of both sexes blue-grey, with narrow white inner ring around pupil. Buff-speckled **juvenile** has tawny wing-stripe and pale buff throat and breast. **Immature female** grey above, with tawny-rufous wing-stripe, and scattered chestnut feathers on throat, cheeks and forehead; underparts white, with clouded chestnut band across breast; eye-wattles dull orange-red. **VOICE**: A distinctive and appealing song of somewhat mechanical-sounding notes, in variable groups of three to five, often given by both members of a pair: *eee-tee-EENH-eu, ee-EENH-eu, sherrink rawnk rink, ee-ee-ree-eu* and variations. Gives a buzzy alarm note and various churring calls. **HABITS**: Solitary or in pairs, foraging restlessly in trees and shrubs; seldom pursues flying insects. Flight jerky, with audible *frrip-frrip* sounds from wings. Often snaps bill. **SIMILAR SPECIES**: Black-throated Wattle-eye lacks white wing-stripe, female has black throat. Black-headed and Chin-spot Batises are smaller, without eye-wattles, and show conspicuous white superciliary stripes. **STATUS AND DISTRIBUTION**: Western. Locally common in woodland, forest edge, moist riverine bush and gardens at up to 1850 m, from Ugandan border areas, Bungoma and Webuye Districts, and the Kakamega and South Nandi Forests south to the Lake Victoria basin, Lolgorien, Mara GR, Loita Hills and into northern and western parts of Serengeti NP. At lower elevations than western race of Black-throated Wattle-eye.

BLACK-THROATED WATTLE-EYE *Platysteira peltata*   Plate 86

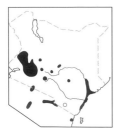

Length 130 mm (5"). Resembles previous species in appearance and habits, but **male** has *entirely dark wings*; underparts white, with *narrow black breast band*; tail narrowly edged with white. Bill black; eye-wattles scarlet, eyes dark grey with narrow white ring around the pupil. **Female** similar, but entire throat and upper breast black. **Juvenile** has narrow tawny edges to wing-coverts and inner secondaries; lacks broad tawny stripe of Common Wattle-eye; breast buffy white. **VOICE**: Song a *Batis*-like *er-er-fee-eu*. Also gives a loud, reiterated metallic *jing* (Chapin 1953). Calls include a harsh *zik-keek* and a sharp staccato *chit-chit-chit* or *keek keek keek* of alarm. **HABITS**: Similar to those of preceding species. **SIMILAR SPECIES**: Common Wattle-eye has long white wing-stripe. *Batis* species lack eye-wattles. **STATUS AND DISTRIBUTION**: Local and rather uncommon in highland-forest patches and other wooded habitats, including moist bush and gardens. *P. p. mentalis* ranges between 1950 and 3000 m in and west of the Rift Valley, from Mt Elgon and the Cheranganis south to the North Nandi, Kericho, Mau, Trans-Mara and Nguruman/Loliondo Forests, and east to Kabarnet, Nakuru and Elmenteita. Nominate *peltata* is uncommon in coastal lowlands north to Witu and Lamu, inland along the Tana River to Bura, in the Shimba Hills and to 1000 m in the East Usambara Mts, also locally at Mt Endau, in Meru, and Nyeri Districts, n. Nairobi suburbs, and the Kitovu Forest, Taveta District; in n. Tanzania, locally common in gallery forests around Arusha, Moshi, in the North Pare Mts, and in the Crater High-lands from Karatu and Marang Forests south to Mbulu. Birds from Laikipia and Ndaragwa not racially assigned.

CHESTNUT WATTLE-EYE *Dyaphorophyia c. castanea*   Plate 86

Length 95–100 mm (*c.* 4"). A small, plump species of western Kenyan forests. Appears almost tailless. Sexes very different. **Adult male** has black crown, upper back and wings, and a *broad black breast band* contrasts with *white throat, collar, lower back and posterior underparts*; feathers of hind-crown rather long and erectile, forming a low crest in display or alarm. **Female** *chestnut above and on breast*; rest of underparts white; top of head dull purplish grey. Both sexes have *purple wattles surrounding eyes*. **Juvenile** resembles adult female, but is white below with band of pale grey and chestnut across breast. **VOICE**: A rather loud, extended, tinkerbird-like *tonk-tonk-tonk-tonk*. . . may continue for nearly two minutes without a break (in contrast to sympatric Yellow-rumped Tinkerbird, which pauses periodically in its singing); this advertising call is seldom heard. Displaying male gives a penetrating hollow *p'qwonk* or *twonk*, repeated six to 10 times, and mingled with nasal *chwaa* notes, a hiccough-like *p'kwup*, and sharper *pwick* and metallic *kwink* notes, plus various popping and snapping sounds produced by wings and bill—all delivered in an unobtrusive, apparently patternless medley, often inaudible at a distance. **HABITS**: Forages actively in tall shrubs and low trees, 3–7 m above ground, seldom lower; less often in canopy, 30 m high (typically delivers the 'tinkerbird' song from high perches). Frequently in groups, or with mixed-species flocks, but shy and difficult to see except in extended vocal courtship displays, which may involve several birds. **SIMILAR SPECIES**: Adult Jameson's Wattle-eye has turquoise wattles, lacks white on throat, is black above. Young Jameson's has pale chestnut throat bordered below by dusky, and dark grey upperparts. **STATUS AND DISTRIBUTION**: Confined to the Kakamega and South Nandi Forests, where fairly common.

JAMESON'S WATTLE-EYE *Dyaphorophyia jamesoni*   Plate 86

Length 80–90 mm (3–3.5"). A tiny, stub-tailed bird of west Kenyan forest undergrowth. **Adult** has *large turquoise-blue eye-wattles* and a bright chestnut patch on each side of neck; upperparts otherwise glossy greenish black, as are throat and breast; posterior underparts silky white. Eyes dark red-brown; feet light purple. Female greyer above than male. **Juvenile** dark grey above, white below, with pale chestnut throat and upper breast. **VOICE**: Apparently much less vocal than other wattle-eyes. A subdued *chawuk-chawuk-chawuk*. . . and a very soft *wuk, wuk, wuk*. . . are the usual calls heard; both audible only at close range. **HABITS**: Forages at lower levels, often near the ground, and in denser forest undergrowth than Chestnut Wattle-eye. Shy. Flying bird can produce loud wing-snapping noises (likened by Chapin to diminutive firecrackers), probably in display. **SIMILAR SPECIES**: Male Chestnut Wattle-eye has white throat and collar, white back and purple wattles. **STATUS AND DISTRIBUTION**: Confined to Kakamega and South Nandi Forests, where fairly common.

YELLOW-BELLIED WATTLE-EYE *Dyaphorophyia concreta graueri*   Plate 86

Length 90 mm (3.5"). Another small wattle-eye of west Kenyan forests. **Male** dark olive-green above, *bright golden yellow* below. Eyes dark maroon, with narrow lavender ring around pupil; feet purple; *eye-wattles bright apple-green*. **Female** similar but duller above, chestnut from throat to upper breast. Bare parts as in male, except for blue-grey feet. **Juvenile** greyish above, pale yellow below. **VOICE**: A distinctive emphatic *tchwik! tchwik!* or *whick! whick! whick!*, variously repeated and sometimes leading into a full song: *whick! whick! tch'wee*

WHERNK!, the last note strongly accented and frequently repeated by itself. All notes have a whistled nasal quality and possess considerable carrying power. **HABITS**: Solitary or in pairs. Shy. Inhabits undergrowth and lower mid-level of forest, particularly well-shaded sites with clumps of *Dracaena*. **STATUS AND DISTRIBUTION**: Scarce in the Kakamega and South Nandi Forests, slightly more common in North Nandi.

AFRICAN SHRIKE-FLYCATCHER *Bias flammulatus aequatorialis*   Plate 87

Length 150–160 mm (*c.* 6"). A compact flycatcher-like bird of the forest canopy in w. Kenya. Sexes markedly different. **Male** glossy black above, with white rump and underparts. **Female** brown above, with rufous rump and edges to wing and tail feathers; chin to belly white with *long brown streaks; lower belly and crissum rufous*. Black bill rather long, the maxilla with prominent terminal hook; eyes of both sexes bright red to dark orange. **VOICE**: A musical *chuik*, and a whistling call. Female has a churring note (Mackworth-Praed and Grant 1955). **HABITS**: Perches quietly, alone or in pairs, typically high and often on large limbs near edge of forest opening. Slowly wags tail from side to side. Sallies to catch flying insects. **SIMILAR SPECIES**: Female can be mistaken for African Broadbill, which is smaller, shorter-billed and with black streaks on underparts. Male somewhat resembles a puffback shrike (*Dryoscopus*). **STATUS AND DISTRIBUTION**: An uncommon resident of the Kakamega and North and South Nandi Forests.

BLACK-AND-WHITE FLYCATCHER *Bias musicus changamwensis*   Plate 88
(Vanga Flycatcher)

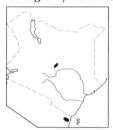

Length 130 mm (5"). A compact flycatching bird with a *pointed crest* and rather short tail. **Adult male** has upperparts, entire head and breast glossy greenish black, rest of underparts white; shows a small white patch near edge of wing. **Adult female** black on top and sides of head, otherwise tawny-brown above, white below with chestnut tinge. *Eyes yellow* in both sexes. **Juvenile** resembles adult female, but top of head streaked brown. **VOICE**: A harsh *chuur* uttered on the wing. Loud song, also given in flight, a sharp series of varied whistled notes, *wit-tu-wit-tu-tui-tu-tu. . .* or *twi-twi-trwirri-tuwoo . .*, with pronounced changes in pitch. **HABITS**: Usually vocal and conspicuous, in pairs or small groups in forest canopy, along or near forest borders. Hawks aerial insects. Displaying male performs slow circular flight, with hesitant wingbeats, around nest tree. Normal flight slow and flapping. **STATUS AND DISTRIBUTION**: Rare local resident. Formerly present in coastal Kenya (Rabai, Takaungu, Changamwe, Mombasa), where now apparently extirpated. In the 1990s, recorded in cent. Kenya from Meru and Ngaia Forests and along northern boundary of Meru NP (Campi ya Nyati). In ne. Tanzania, scarce and local between 300 and 1500 m in the Usambara Mts.

HELMET-SHRIKES, FAMILY PRIONOPIDAE
(World and Africa, 9 species; Kenya and n. Tanzania, 5)

The typical helmet-shrikes are noisy sociable birds, restlessly travelling through bush or woodland in parties of a few to 15 or 20 individuals. They feed mainly among branches and foliage. *Eurocephalus* is more sedentary and shrike-like than *Prionops* and takes most of its food from the ground. It is sometimes placed in the Laniidae, but it builds a neat, compact, well-camouflaged nest like *Prionops*, and it has scutellation extending down the sides as well as the front of the tarsus, unlike true shrikes. Several helmet-shrikes possess circular, more or less pectinate eye-wattles. The firm plumage is black and white or of other contrasting pattern. The sexes are alike. At least some *Prionops* species breed co-operatively and roost communally, with several birds serving as helpers from nest-building to feeding of the young. Eggs are white or coloured, with markings concentrated around the larger end.

WHITE-CRESTED HELMET-SHRIKE *Prionops plumatus*   Plate 85
(Helmet Shrike, White Helmet Shrike; includes Curly-crested Helmet-shrike)

Length 170–250 mm (6–10"). The commonest and most widespread helmet-shrike, usually encountered in small wandering flocks. A *black-and-white* bird with *bushy frontal crest*; **adult** has bare yellow wattles around bright *yellow eyes*. Displays a prominent *white band across the primaries* in flight, which is rapid and undulating. Racially variable in plumage and size: formerly regarded as a separate species, the curly-crested *cristatus* is large

605

(210–250 mm, 8–10"), with little or no white on the closed wing, much like smaller and more moderately crested *vinaceigularis* (190–195 mm, 7.5"); still smaller *poliocephalus* (170–180 mm, 6–7") has a long white wing-stripe and a very short crest. **Juvenile** tinged brown above, with white-tipped wing-coverts; eyes brown, with no wattles. **Voice:** *P. p. poliocephalus* gives a buzzing, growling *cheeeeeeayh, zheeeeeayh, chickichichichi, zheeeeeeayh. . . zheeeeeeeayh. . . chikichik . . .*; also a faster, noisy, rough *cherrow cherrow cherrow cree cree cerwow cerwow*. Song of *P. p. cristatus* a squeaky *tsirreek tsrick srech, chreek-chreek*, and a rapidly repeated nasal *KWEE-we-wiro* or *CHIri-ri-ro*. All races have various harsh scratchy calls and strident chattering by the flock. **Habits:** Noisy and gregarious, always on the move; flocks cover a large area, foraging like starlings or tits among branches or hopping about on the ground, calling constantly. Frequently snaps bill. **Similar Species:** Grey-crested Helmet-shrike lacks eye-wattles, has part of crest dark grey and more or less erect; much larger than mostly allopatric *P. p. poliocephalus*, with similar wing pattern. **Status and Distribution:** Local and generally uncommon in open woodland, riverine acacias and dry bush. *P. p. cristatus* is northwestern, ranging east to the Turkwell River delta, Lake Turkana, south to Mt Elgon, Trans-Nzoia, the Kerio Valley and Baringo District; *vinaceigularis* in e. Kenya, from Mandera, Wajir, Moyale and the Horr Valley south to Laikipia, Meru and Tsavo NPs, Taveta and Taita Districts, Mkomazi GR and along the lower Tana River to Galana Ranch and lowlands in Garsen, Malindi and Kilifi Districts; *poliocephalus* is mainly a non-breeding visitor, May–September from south of our region to Serengeti, Lake Manyara and Tarangire NPs (breeding reported), Loliondo and Arusha Districts and the Mkomazi GR, north in Kenya to the Loita and Chyulu Hills, Kibwezi, Machakos and Kitui Districts and formerly or rarely to Nairobi, overlapping with the preceding race in several southeastern areas.

GREY-CRESTED HELMET-SHRIKE *Prionops poliolophus*   **Plate 85**

Length 240–260 mm (9.5–10"). A large and conspicuously crested helmet-shrike, similar in plumage to the preceding species. Eyes yellow, but *no eye-wattles; hind part of crest dark grey*, quite erect. Wings show a long white stripe and, in flight, a white band across the primaries. **Juvenile** undescribed; young in nest appear largely brownish white. **Voice:** Single *chwerr* notes and rolling, descending, churring phrases, such as *chichi cherrrrro*. These elaborated upon with additional harsh, scratchy, chattering and bill-snapping by several birds in group vocalizations, e.g. *chikiki-chi-chirrrrow chi-chirrro che-chiwow-cherrow chk chk skrrk cherrk. . . .* **Habits:** Gregarious and restless; feeds quietly, but flock noisily scolds any intruder. **Similar Species:** The race *poliocephalus* of White-crested Helmet-shrike has similar wing pattern, but is much smaller and with a very short crest. **Status and Distribution:** Local and uncommon from Serengeti NP, Mara GR, Loliondo, the Loita and Nguruman Hills north to Narok District, and in the Rift from the Kedong Valley north to Lake Elmenteita and Lake Nakuru NP. Typically in *Acacia drepanolobium* (whistling-thorn) or *Tarchonanthus* (leleshwa) woodland.

RETZ'S HELMET-SHRIKE *Prionops retzii graculina*   **Plate 85**
(Retz's Red-billed Shrike; Red-billed Helmet-shrike)

Length 190–205 mm (7.5–8 "). A handsome bird showing conspicuous white in the tail as a flock takes flight. **Adult** *black, with tan back, white belly and tail corners, short shaggy frontal crest, serrated red wattles surrounding the yellow eyes,* and white spots on inner webs of primaries (absent in some individuals). *Bill red,* orange in younger birds, with *extreme tip yellow.* **Juvenile** has black replaced by dull brown; bill dull horn-brown; eyes brownish(?); eye-wattles present in immature bird. **Voice:** Varied chattering, churring or grating sounds, often by several birds together. Individuals give a harsh rolling *tchurEEo* or *tsurrrEEoo-errrEEo,* or a descending creaky trill, *crrrrrreeeeeo,* these given alone or quickly repeated several times and often followed by a clearer *RRRREEO cho-wo cho-wo cho-wo,* or *choCHo, cho-CHO, cho-CHO.* **Habits:** Restless and highly gregarious, sometimes in mixed flocks with Chestnut-fronted Helmet-shrike. Feeds in foliage and hawks flying insects. Somewhat starling-like, but flight weak and fluttery, interspersed with gliding. Parasitized by Thick-billed Cuckoo. **Similar Species:** Chestnut-fronted Helmet-shrike is smaller, slate-grey above, with bluish eye-wattles and chestnut forehead patch. **Status and Distribution:** A fairly common resident of coastal woods north to the Boni Forest, more local inland in riverine forest, acacia savanna and wooded groves along the Tana River to Meru NP, Kamburu and Mwea NR, and south to Kiboko, Kibwezi Forest, Chyulu Hills and the Tsavo NPs; formerly in Kiambu and Nairobi Districts. Also inland in n. Tanzania in Arusha NP, Mkomazi GR and the Usambara Mts.

CHESTNUT-FRONTED HELMET-SHRIKE *Prionops scopifrons*   **Plate 85**

Length 165–178 mm (6.5–7"). A small, slate-grey helmet-shrike with white belly and under tail-coverts, large white tail corners, a *chestnut frontal patch* of short bristly feathers, and pectinate *bluish wattles* surrounding

golden-yellow eyes. Inland race *keniensis* shows more white in the tail, and chestnut forehead patch is darker, with a narrow dark grey (not white) band between it and the dark crown. **Juvenile** described as having blackish forehead and white-tipped alular feathers; it probably lacks wattles and is brown-eyed. **VOICE**: A unique loud churring or chattering with a strange nasal whirring or humming quality, often accompanied by softer whistled notes, e.g. *char-rer wit-wit-chirro, trree trree trree trree*. Call note a sharp *shuk*! **HABITS**: Often flocks with Retz's Helmet-shrikes and other birds. Somewhat tit-like; forages in foliage and on branches; may cling to tree trunks. Snaps bill. **SIMILAR SPECIES**: See Retz's Helmet-shrike. **STATUS AND DISTRIBUTION**: *P. s. kirki* a locally common resident of Kenyan coastal woods north to the Boni Forest and in Shimba Hills NP. In ne. Tanzania, nominate *scopifrons* occupies the East Usambara foothills. (A flock at 1230 m in the North Pare Mts, 20 Aug. 1984, was north of its normal range.) The rare *P. s. keniensis*, formerly known from near Marsabit and in Meru and Embu Districts, is now reduced to small numbers in the remnant Meru and Ngaia Forests.

NORTHERN WHITE-CROWNED SHRIKE *Eurocephalus rueppelli* Plate 85

Length 190–210 mm (7.5–8″). A stocky, dark brown-and-white bird, often perching conspicuously or gliding from tree to tree on stiff wings, the prominent *white crown, nape and upper tail-coverts* contrasting with otherwise dark upperparts in **adult**; tail blackish, with extreme bases of rectrices white. *Large dark brown patch on side of head and neck extends forward under the eye.* Rest of face and underparts white, except for *dull brown patch on sides.* Bill and feet black; eyes dark brown. **Juvenile** has *pale bill, greyish-brown forehead and crown*, with *black around and below eyes*; brownish *patches at sides connected by narrow band across breast.* **VOICE**: Call a harsh *kaak-kaak* or *weeyer WOK, weeyer WOK* (the *o* long); also gives similar notes in series: *chrrk, wirk-wirk, yerk-yerk, wuk-wuk, yerk. . .*, or *yerk yeck-yeck-yeck.* Juvenile gives a sharp, piercing *skeet.* **HABITS**: Somewhat sociable, usually in pairs or groups of three or four. Restless, but not so flighty as other helmet-shrikes; perches in one place for extended periods, watching the ground for arthropod prey. Sustained flight distinctively quivering or fluttery. **STATUS AND DISTRIBUTION**: A common and widespread resident below 1600 m in dry bush and open woodland (especially *Acacia* and *Commiphora*). Numerous in Samburu, Shaba and Mkomazi GRs, Meru, Amboseli, Tsavo East, Tsavo West, Tarangire, Lake Manyara and Serengeti NPs. Absent from moist w. Kenyan border areas, the Lake Victoria basin and coastal lowlands south of Malindi.

SHRIKES, FAMILY LANIIDAE
(World, 26 species; Africa, 17; Kenya, 14; n. Tanzania, 8)

Most true shrikes are bold and aggressive birds of relatively open country. The head is large, with a short hooked bill, and the narrow tail may be quite long. The sexes are alike or similar, although most female fiscals differ from males in their small chestnut flank patches. Adult plumage commonly includes black, grey, white and chestnut coloration, but most juveniles are brownish with fine barring. Some shrikes are solitary, spending much time on exposed perches, from which they drop on to small vertebrate and invertebrate prey. Others are gregarious, associating in noisy social groups. Harsh scolding vocalizations are the rule, but some produce musical notes. The nest is a bulky cup of grasses and other plant material in bush or tree; the eggs of most species are spotted. Five of the East African shrikes are regular palearctic migrants.

YELLOW-BILLED SHRIKE *Corvinella corvina affinis* Plate 84

Length 300–310 mm (*c.* 12″). A very *long-tailed* grey-brown shrike with pale buff underparts. **Adult** profusely *streaked with black above and below*; ear-coverts dark brown. *Rufous primary bases are conspicuous in flight*, and most individuals show a small rufous patch on the flanks. *Bill and eyelids yellow*; eyes dark brown; feet dark grey-brown. **Juvenile** barred and mottled rather than streaked. **VOICE**: A variety of harsh, rasping, buzzing calls is given by a flock. Individuals also utter a repeated *scis-scis.* **HABITS**: Highly sociable; usually in small noisy parties actively foraging in low trees and undergrowth. **STATUS AND DISTRIBUTION**: Uncommon local resident of open woodland, savanna and bushed grassland at medium to high elevations in w. and nw. Kenya. Now essentially localized on the northeastern slopes of Mt Elgon around the Suam River from Kanyakwat to Kongelai and Kacheliba, with small numbers occasionally reported around Soy and Awasi. Formerly more widespread (including Kitale, Nandi, Lumbwa, Muhoroni, Kibigori and Sotik, where its habitat now replaced by cultivation).

MAGPIE SHRIKE *Urolestes melanoleucus aequatorialis* (Long-tailed Shrike)

Plate 84

Length 345–435 mm (14.5–17"). A large black shrike with a *very long pointed tail*, long white patch on scapulars and secondaries, a smaller spot formed by white primary bases, and a greyish-white rump; tail feathers white-tipped in fresh plumage. **Female** resembles male, but has white patches on flanks. **Juvenile** browner than adult. **VOICE:** Various loud squeaky or squealing whistles, often from small groups in chorus, *KWEEKio KWEEKio . . ., kee-ur keeureek . . ., TWEO WHEEO WEEO. . .* and *tlee-teeooo . . .*, the phrases repeated and variously combined. Also harsh sparrow-weaver-like *squee-er* notes and a grating, scolding *skaaa*. **HABITS:** Usually in pairs or small groups perched conspicuously on bushtops or small trees. Flirts tail as it calls. Flight rapid and undulating. **STATUS AND DISTRIBUTION:** Locally common in acacia bush and savanna over much of interior Tanzania, reaching our area in Serengeti, Lake Manyara and Tarangire NPs, and a few pairs resident in e. Mara GR near Siana Springs. Formerly (or sporadically) elsewhere in and near the Mara GR. **NOTE:** Sometimes placed in the genus *Corvinella*.

RED-BACKED SHRIKE *Lanius collurio*

Plate 85

Length 165–180 mm (6.5–7"). Small, compact and rather short-billed. **Adult male** *chestnut or red-brown on back,* emphasizing the *grey crown and rump.* Black facial mask, white chin and throat; rest of underparts pinkish; flight feathers blackish, rarely showing a small white patch at base of primaries; tail black with white edges (more extensive at base). *L. c. collurio* and the paler *pallidifrons* have bright rufous-chestnut back; *L. c. kobylini* is duller (rufous and brown tones at times obsolete), and the grey extends from nape onto the back. **Female** brown above and on face, greyer on head and rump, creamy white below, with barring on breast and flanks; tail brown or chestnut-brown above, greyish below. **First-winter** bird resembles adult female, but top of head and rump are same tone as the back, varying from grey-brown to russet-brown, and barred with black. **VOICE:** Alarm call a harsh repeated *chack.* A soft scratchy warbling song is heard after January. **HABITS:** Generally solitary, but sometimes in loose groups. Usually perches low on bush, fence or tree branch. Flight low, rapid, not undulating. **SIMILAR SPECIES:** First-winter Red-tailed Shrike is slightly paler and greyer, and less heavily barred above, than corresponding plumage of Red-backed; slightly more rufous upper tail-surface difficult to assess without direct comparison, but usually provides some contrast with sandy-brown back; chestnut underside of tail diagnostic in the hand, sometimes obvious in the field. Wing formula also differs (see below). **STATUS AND DISTRIBUTION:** Common passage migrant (Nov.–Dec. and April) in open habitats with shrubs and small trees from sea level to over 2200 m. Some winter regularly in greener parts of se. Kenya and ne. Tanzania, including coastal areas, where *L. c. kobylini* is the most numerous subspecies. Northward passage generally occurs farther east than the southward movement, heaviest in and east of the Rift Valley.

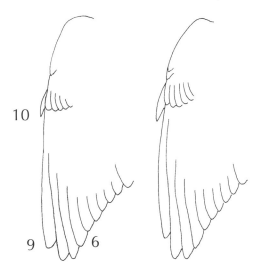

Wing outlines of Red-backed Shrike, (left), and Red-tailed Shrike, (right). Note position of 9th primary tip and, in Red-tailed, emargination on 6th primary.

RED-TAILED or ISABELLINE SHRIKE *Lanius isabellinus*   **Plate 85**

Length 165–180 mm (6.5–7"). Similar to Red-backed Shrike in size, build and habits, but usually *paler*, and the slightly longer tail is more often cocked at an angle from body. **Adult male** *L. i. phoenicuroides* pale brown above, more rufous on crown, chestnut on rump and tail; underparts whitish; black mask bordered above by narrow whitish superciliary stripes; blackish flight feathers show white patch at base of primaries. *L. i. speculigerus* is paler, more sandy brown above and creamier below. **Female** and **first-winter** birds resemble corresponding plumages of Red-backed Shrike, but show reduced barring, and the tail appears slightly more chestnut (both above and below), contrasting more with the pale brown upperparts. Female often shows cream patch at base of primaries. In the hand, separated from Red-backed by having 9th primary much shorter than 6th (see Fig p. 608). **VOICE**: 'Chacking' alarm and contact calls, and soft warbling song similar to that of Red-backed Shrike. **HABITS**: Much like those of Red-backed Shrike, with which it shares habitat during migration. **SIMILAR SPECIES**: Red-backed Shrike compared above. **STATUS AND DISTRIBUTION**: Common palearctic migrant, November to early April, in dry bush, scrub and cultivation below 1700 m, generally east of the Rift Valley, south into ne. Tanzania; especially numerous in the Tsavo NPs and Mkomazi GR. Most of our birds are *L. i. phoenicuroides*. **NOTE 1**: Formerly considered conspecific with Red-backed Shrike, with which it is known to hybridize. **NOTE 2**: The type of *L. i. isabellinus* is from Arabia, and apparently is an example of the Mongolian form that migrates to Africa (G. Nikolaus, pers. comm.). This race is referred to by most authors to date as *L. i. speculigerus*. Both forms may now have to be re-named (cf. Cramp and Perrins 1993: 455).

LESSER GREY SHRIKE *Lanius minor*   **Plate 84**

Length 200–220 mm (8–8.5"). A medium-sized shrike with pointed wings and fairly long tail. **Spring adult** (March–May) pale grey above and white below, with *black mask extending to forehead*. White outer tail edges and white patch at primary bases conspicuous in flight; *underparts tinged pink*. **Autumn adult** has forehead mixed grey and black. **First-winter** brown-tinged above, with no black on forehead. **VOICE**: Call note a harsh *chek*. Song a sustained twittering, including some harsh notes. **HABITS**: Solitary. Perches prominently on bush, tree or wire. Rather wary. Flight strong and undulating. **SIMILAR SPECIES**: Grey-backed Fiscal is larger, with longer, white-based tail and black scapulars; it has rounded wings and much weaker flight. Taita and Somali Fiscals have entire top of head black. In w. Kenya, see Mackinnon's Fiscal. **STATUS AND DISTRIBUTION**: Common and widespread palearctic passage migrant, late March to early May, in grassland, open bush and cultivated country from the coastal lowlands to above 2200 m. Occasional in autumn, but southward migration occurs largely to the west of our region.

Great Grey Shrike.

*GREAT GREY SHRIKE *Lanius excubitor pallidirostris*
Figure p. 609

Length *c.* 230 mm (9"). An open-country shrike, accidental in our region. Longer-tailed and with more rounded wings than Lesser Grey Shrike. Has *no black on forehead* (or a very narrow strip at base of bill), and white superciliary stripes separate black mask from grey crown. Graduated tail black centrally, broadly white at sides. Shade of grey on upperparts, presence or absence of pink tinge to white underparts, and amount of white in wing all vary subspecifically. Some individuals show faint barring on breast. *L. e. pallidirostris* is generally pale, with a horn-coloured bill, and no black frontal band at base of maxilla. **Voice:** Varied notes include a harsh *sheck-sheck* and a more nasal *sheenk-sheenk*. **Habits:** Perches high on exposed pole, wire or bushtop. Flight undulating. **Similar Species:** Lesser Grey Shrike and Grey-backed Fiscal both have black forehead. **Status and Distribution:** One sight record, 17 February 1988 (Pearson *et al.* 1989), from near Kibish in the Ilemi Triangle, an area administered by Kenya, but usually mapped as part of the Sudan. The site is some 400 km south of the species' normal African range.

MACKINNON'S FISCAL *Lanius mackinnoni*
(Mackinnon's Shrike)
Plate 84

Length 200 mm (8"). A slender western shrike of forest edges. **Adult** dull grey above, with *wholly black wings* and white scapulars; tail narrow and graduated, black with white corners. *Black facial mask* is bordered by *white superciliary stripes.* Underparts white. **Female** shows patch of chestnut on flanks. **Juvenile** grey above with narrow dark bars, white below, with fine barring on chest and flanks. **Voice:** Call a musical *chick-erea.* Rich, varied and warbling song includes mimicry of other species. **Habits:** Solitary or in pairs. Perches unobtrusively on bush or low branch at edge of forest or in clearings, seldom far above ground. **Similar Species:** Grey-backed Fiscal is larger, with black forehead and white in wings. First-winter Lesser Grey Shrike, unlikely in same habitat, shows prominent white patch in primaries and lacks white superciliary stripes. **Status and Distribution:** Uncommon local resident between 1500 and 2000 m in shrubby grassland, along borders of cultivation and forest edges in the w. Kenyan highlands from Nandi and Kakamega Districts south to Kericho, Sotik and Kilgoris. Recent records from Saiwa NP and nw. Mara GR. Formerly on Mt Elgon and at Elgeyu.

GREY-BACKED FISCAL *Lanius excubitoroides*
Plate 84

Length 250 mm (10"). A large western shrike with pale grey back and *broad white side panels at base of the long, broad black tail;* a wide black mask extends from forehead to sides of neck. **Adult** has black wings and scapulars and white underparts, the **female** with small chestnut patch on flanks. Western *L. e. intercedens* is larger than nominate *excubitoroides; boehmi* is also large, but more dusky grey above. **Juvenile** pale brownish above with narrow barring, and with buffy-white underparts. **Voice:** A chattering *teudleeoo-teudleeoo* and similar sounds, often developing into an excited chorus. **Habits:** Sociable; pairs or noisy groups gather on wires or branches, chattering, waving their tails and fluttering their wings. When dispersing, they follow one another in slow flight. **Similar Species:** Lesser Grey Shrike has grey scapulars, long pointed wings, and a shorter tail without broad white panels at base. See Mackinnon's Fiscal. **Status and Distribution:** Locally common resident at low to medium elevations in wooded grassland, *moist* acacia bush, gardens and cultivation. Occupies areas of higher rainfall than Long-tailed Fiscal. *L. e. intercedens* ranges from Mt Elgon and Kapenguria south to the Lake Victoria basin at Kisumu, Ahero, Kendu Bay and Ruma NP; nominate *excubitoroides* in the Kerio and Rift Valleys from Baringo District south to Naivasha and Longonot, occasionally east to the Laikipia Plateau; Tanzanian *boehmi* reaches our area in Serengeti NP, the Mara GR and Loita Hills.

LONG-TAILED FISCAL *Lanius cabanisi*
Plate 84

Length 300–310 mm (12–12.5"). A large eastern shrike with dark back and a *long, rounded black tail* (small white basal area of rectrices is usually concealed by coverts, and inconspicuous narrow white tips are evident only in fresh plumage). **Adult** black from forehead to wings, dark grey on back, white on rump and upper tail-coverts; underparts and patch at base of primaries also white. Female shows some chestnut on flanks. **Juvenile** grey-brown above, with narrow black barring; rump buff and underparts buffier than in adult. **Voice:** A variety of chattering scolding calls, including a harsh *chit-er-row;* also a mellow whistle. **Habits:** Conspicuous; often in small noisy groups on bushtop, wire or low tree, excitedly waving tails from side to side. **Similar Species:** Common Fiscal is smaller, with narrower, white-sided tail, white scapulars and *black* back. Taita Fiscal has much shorter, white-sided tail and pale grey back. **Status and Distribution:** Common resident from sea level to 1600 m in bushed grassland, dry savanna and edges of cultivation, mainly east of the Rift Valley. Ranges from Isiolo District, Meru NP and lowlands southeast of Mt Kenya

to Thika, Nairobi, Namanga, Amboseli and the Tsavo NPs. In Tanzania, south to Lake Manyara and Tarangire NPs east across the Masai Steppe to Lake Jipe and Mkomazi GR. Also in coastal lowlands north to the lower Tana River delta and Lamu District.

TAITA FISCAL *Lanius dorsalis*   Plate 84

Length 200–205 mm (*c.* 8"). A short-tailed, *dry-country* shrike. **Adult** *pale grey on back,* black on hindneck, top and sides of head; wings black, except for white patch in primaries; graduated black tail has white sides and corners; underparts white, with some chestnut on flanks in female. **Juvenile** dark grey above, finely barred with dusky, wing-coverts and inner secondaries edged with buff; white with sparse dark barring below. **Voice**: Song a quaint mixture of churrs, hollow sounds and ticking notes, *chwaaa pikereek chrrrrrrr yook pikerchik . . . skyaaa, week kiook-tiureek tik . . ..* **Habits**: Solitary. Usually perches on shrubs and low trees. Flight direct, seldom high. **Similar Species**: Somali Fiscal has white tips to secondaries and slightly longer tail. Lesser Grey Shrike has grey top of head, longer wings and undulating flight. Long-tailed Fiscal is larger, with much longer, all-black tail and dusky back. **Status and Distribution**: Common resident of open bush and savanna in dry country below 1500 m. Widespread north and east of the Kenyan highlands, and locally south to n. Tanzania from Olorgesailie to lakes Magadi and Natron, Olduvai, se. Serengeti NP and Lake Eyasi, Lake Manyara and Tarangire NPs, in lowlands around Arusha, the Masai Steppe and Mkomazi GR. Absent from coastal lowlands south of Malindi.

SOMALI FISCAL *Lanius somalicus*   Plate 84

Length 200–205 mm (*c.* 8"). A medium-sized shrike of barren *northern Kenya*. Suggests Taita Fiscal, with glossy black top and sides of head, pale grey back and white underparts, but *broad white tips to secondaries* show as bird swoops up to perch; wings otherwise black, with small white patch in primaries. Black tail has prominent white sides. **Female**, unlike those of other fiscals, lacks chestnut on flanks. **Juvenile** brownish above, with buffy edges to wing-coverts and secondaries; some faint barring on scapulars. Underparts buffy white. **Voice**: Common note a low churring alarm call. Song composed of short variable phrases, *bur-ur-ur bit-it-it . . .* **Habits**: Similar to those of Taita Fiscal. **Similar Species**: Taita Fiscal has shorter tail with less white, and lacks white tips to secondaries. **Status and Distribution**: Uncommon local resident of low semi-deserts with scant vegetation. Ranges throughout the Lake Turkana area east to Turbi and Marsabit, south to Kapedo and Laisamis, occasionally wandering to Baringo, Wamba and Merti Districts.

COMMON FISCAL *Lanius collaris humeralis*   Plate 84

Length 210–230 mm (8–9"). A slender shrike with a *long, narrow tail*. **Adult** *dull black above* from forehead, becoming dark grey on lower back, rump and upper tail-coverts (latter often paler); *white scapulars form a prominent V*. Black wings show small white area at base of primaries; tail black with white sides, and most feathers white-tipped. Underparts white, with dull chestnut flanks in female. **Juvenile** brown above, finely barred with buff and black; pale scapular areas whitish or buff, well defined. Underparts brownish white with dusky barring and vermiculation. **Voice**: Usual call a harsh grating *ghreeee* or *ghree ghree ghree*, sometimes accompanied by two soft piping notes from bird's mate. Also gives an extended plaintive *tweeeeeer*, soft and reedy. Song consists of varied phrases, including piping and rasping notes. **Habits**: Perches conspicuously on bushes, posts or wires, usually alone or in pairs. Bold and aggressive. Impales orthopterans and other prey on acacia thorns or sisal leaf-tips. Flight low and direct. **Similar Species**: Larger Long-tailed Fiscal has longer, broader and more rounded tail, lacks white scapulars, has greyish-black back. **Status and Distribution**: Common resident between 1400 and 3000 m in all types of open country including cultivation and suburban gardens. Widespread throughout the w. and cent. Kenyan highlands south to Serengeti NP and the Crater and Mbulu Highlands. Absent from coastal lowlands and much of n. and e. Kenya, but resident on isolated northern mountains (Marsabit, Nyiru and Kulal), in the Ndotos and in Mathews Range. Regular in the Chyulu Hills and occasional in the nearby Taita Hills. In ne. Tanzania, common in Arusha District and in all highland areas from Mt Meru and Kilimanjaro to the Pare and Usambara Mountains.

WOODCHAT SHRIKE *Lanius senator niloticus*   Plate 84

Length 180–190 mm (7–7.5"). Slightly larger and more thickset than Red-backed Shrike, with a short, square-tipped tail. **Male** white below, black above, with *rufous or chestnut crown and nape* and *white on rump, upper tail-coverts and tail base*; scapular and primary patches also white. **Female** similar, but duller and browner above. **First-autumn** bird barred brown above, with pale scapulars and rump, faintly barred breast and flanks; some adult feathering, including rufous on nape, present by November. **Voice**: Common call a dry chattering *schrrrrret*

or *kschaaa*; warning call similar to that of Red-backed Shrike. Song variable, with whistles, trills and mimicry. **HABITS**: Conspicuous; perches on bushtops, posts and wires. **SIMILAR SPECIES**: Masked Shrike has different head pattern, and in flight appears dark above except for white scapulars and wing patch. **STATUS AND DISTRIBUTION**: Uncommon palearctic migrant, November–March, in w. and nw. Kenya, regularly south to Busia and Baringo Districts and northern Mara GR. One record from Nairobi NP (29 Sept. 1989). Favours grassland with small scattered acacias.

MASKED SHRIKE *Lanius nubicus*   Plate 84
(Nubian Shrike)

Length 170 mm (6.75"). A slim, narrow-tailed shrike with *orange-buff sides and flanks*; shows *white on scapulars, forehead, superciliaries*, at base of primaries and narrowly along sides of tail. **Adult male** otherwise *black above, including rump and upper tail-coverts*. **Female** similarly patterned, but brownish instead of black; flank patches duller. **First-autumn** bird barred brownish grey, with paler forehead and superciliaries; scapular patches prominent, but no orange-buff on flanks; adult feathering appears by late November or December. **VOICE**: Occasionally a hard chattering *chek-chek*; also a *krrrr* much like that of Woodchat Shrike. Generally silent. **HABITS**: Less conspicuous than most shrikes, often perching in thick shrubbery or within canopy of small trees. **SIMILAR SPECIES**: Woodchat Shrike has white rump and upper tail-coverts, rufous or chestnut crown and nape. **STATUS AND DISTRIBUTION**: Scarce palearctic migrant, annual at Lake Baringo, 1982–91. Individuals also recorded at Lake Kanyaboli (Nov. 1969) and Lake Naivasha (March 1994). Typically winters in acacia groves near water.

BUSH-SHRIKES, FAMILY MALACONOTIDAE
(World and Africa, 45 species; Kenya, 23; n. Tanzania,16)

Endemic to Africa, bush-shrikes are retiring birds, many of them foliage-gleaners, generally difficult to study as they seek concealment amid dense vegetation, although their vocalizations are sufficiently loud and unusual to attract attention. Most are striking birds, the plumage of many contrastingly patterned, either brightly coloured or black and white; the sexes may be alike or different. The often barred juvenile plumage is soon replaced by an immature dress similar to, but not necessarily identical with, adult plumage. Several species are aptly named 'bush-shrikes,' but others inhabit understorey or canopy in dense forest, woodland and garden shrubbery. Some feed on and near the ground, and all prey on insects and other invertebrates; larger species capture small vertebrate animals as well. The nest is a neat compact cup or frail platform of twigs recalling a dove's nest, in a tree or shrub, and the two or three speckled eggs are whitish or pale greenish. Although often treated as a subfamily of the true shrikes (Laniidae), the two groups do not appear to be closely related. All species are resident in our region.

BRUBRU *Nilaus afer*   Plate 82

Length 125–130 mm (*c.* 5"). A small, chestnut-sided bird of low savanna trees; not suggestive of other bush-shrikes. **Adult male** black above, with white superciliary stripes, *broad white streak down middle of back and a narrower one on each wing*; *sides and flanks chestnut*. Eyes brown; bill and feet grey. **Female** has black replaced by brown or blackish brown, and shows some dark streaks on the throat. Eastern/northeastern *N. a. minor* has paler chestnut or rufous sides than western *N. a. massaicus*. **Juvenile** heavily barred white, buff and blackish brown above; white below with irregular brown bars. Flight feathers edged and tipped buff or tawny; tail buff-tipped. **VOICE**: Male gives distinctive, prolonged, trilling or purring sound, droning and slightly metallic in quality, *kuuuurrrrrrrrrrr*, not loud but far-carrying; female frequently answers in a lower tone. Also gives a penetrating high whistled *wutitititititi*. **HABITS**: Actively gleans in treetops; occasionally forages like a nuthatch. Partial to groves of acacias, and often joins mixed-species flocks. **SIMILAR SPECIES**: Chin-spot Batis bears a slight resemblance but has no rufous side stripes. **STATUS AND DISTRIBUTION**: Widespread and often common in savanna, open woodland and bush with tall trees. Two subspecies: *massaicus* in w. and cent. Kenya south to Lake Natron, Loliondo, Serengeti NP and Maswa GR; *minor* in n. and e. Kenya, extending south to n. Tanzania east of the Rift Valley. Absent from coastal lowlands and from highlands above 2500 m.

BLACK-CROWNED TCHAGRA *Tchagra s. senegala* Plate 82
(Black-headed Bush-shrike)

Length 195–210 mm (*c.* 8"). A brown-backed bush-shrike with *bright rufous wings and white-tipped black tail* prominent in flight. **Adult** has *solid black crown margined by bold whitish or buff superciliary stripes.* Underparts white. Eyes dark *blue* (**female**) or *purplish blue* (**male**); bill black; feet greenish grey. **Juvenile** duller, with brownish crown, less bold head stripes, brownish-grey eyes, underparts dull ochre or buff. **VOICE:** Distinctive *slow whistling song* consists of clear lilting phrases run together in a pleasing sequence, often descending in pitch, *chwee, chew, chewee, chee, chewi* . . , or *teyo, weeo, queeo, tew,* or *queeo tew EEo-tew, tew, tew, tew.* Calls include a harsh *churr,* a low *tchuk,* and a descending soft rattle, *chrrrrrrrr.* Alarm call a clear liquid *chu-tu-woi.* **HABITS:** Inhabits dense shrubbery, usually near the ground. Skulking. Sings from concealed perch or on the wing. Aerial courtship flight begins with loud wingbeats, continues with extended whistling song. **SIMILAR SPECIES:** Smaller Brown-crowned Tchagra is brown on top of head and has brown eyes. Black cap of male Marsh Tchagra extends down below eyes; female has white superciliary stripes but is smaller than Black-crowned Tchagra and shows broken blackish V on back. **STATUS AND DISTRIBUTION:** Locally common between sea level and 1850 m. Widely sympatric with Brown-crowned Tchagra, and in similar shrubby and wooded habitats. Although absent from much of n. and e. Kenya, present in the extreme northwest near Lokichokio (and old records from Moyale and Karo Lola); also in coastal lowlands (where more numerous than Brown-crowned) north to the Boni Forest.

BROWN-CROWNED TCHAGRA *Tchagra australis* Plate 82
(Brown-headed Bush-shrike)

Length 175–185 mm (*c.* 7"). Resembles the larger Black-crowned Tchagra but *brown crown centre* bordered by a *narrow black line above the buffy white superciliary stripes.* Eyes brown, not dark blue; bill black; feet blue-grey. Coastal *littoralis* is smaller and paler than the two inland races. **Juvenile** buff or ochreous tawny below, head stripes much less pronounced; bill horn-brown, not black. **VOICE:** Song rapid and explosive, unlike that of preceding species, usually with some oriole-like whistles: *WEEo, WEwo-wo, WEEwo kew kew kew tu-tut-tu-tu,* or *queeri, TWEEo, weeo weeo weeo-kew-kew-kew-kew.* . . A more varied effort begins with some soft notes and a short descending whinny, *tok-tok-tok queero SKWIAAaaaa tyu-u-u-u-u-u-u.* Flight song a long, rapid series of *weeo* or *weewo* notes beginning loudly and gradually diminishing, with increasingly prolonged syllables. Usual call note a low *cheerk,* but also gives a single oriole-like whistled *quweeo.* **HABITS:** Feeds methodically on or near ground in dense shrubbery. Sings from bush-top, accompanied by much posturing and extreme tail movement. Fluttering vocal courtship flight given with loudly beating wings, erected rump feathers and broadly fanned tail. **SIMILAR SPECIES:** Adult of larger Black-crowned Tchagra has jet-black crown; brownish-crowned juvenile is duller, lacks narrow black lines above the superciliary stripes, has brownish feet and bill and greyer eyes. Three-streaked Tchagra is smaller and paler, with black central crown stripe. **STATUS AND DISTRIBUTION:** Common in bush, woodland, shrubby grassland and overgrown cultivation between sea-level and 2000 m. Western *T. a. emini* ranges from Mt Elgon and Saiwa NP east to the Laikipia Plateau and Nairobi, south to the Mara GR and Serengeti NP; *T. a. minor* occupies much of e. and se. Kenya, along the Tana River to Bura, at Lamu and throughout n. Tanzania east of *emini; T. a. littoralis* is in the coastal lowlands north to Malindi, inland to the Shimba Hills and East Usambara foothills. Largely allopatric with Three-streaked Tchagra, but the two coexist in parts of Tsavo East NP and Lamu District.

THREE-STREAKED TCHAGRA *Tchagra jamesi* Plate 82

Length 165 mm (6.5"). A small tchagra with white-tipped tail and rufous in the wings like others of the genus, but paler greyish brown above, with a *black streak of variable width down centre of crown and nape, and one on each side of the head through the eye.* The peculiar iris pattern, a ring of silvery dots surrounding the pupil, is rarely discernible in the field. The eastern race *mandana* is sandier and less grey above than nominate *jamesi,* has a broader central crown stripe, and sides of crown are paler. **VOICE:** A melodious flight song similar to that of Brown-crowned Tchagra, an emphatic series of downslurred whistles, *wi-weo-weo-weo-weo* or *chweeo-chweeo-chweeo.* Protests with a nasal scold, *chuwaa* or *chwaa-chwaa,* and *cherraa-cherraa.* **HABITS:** Skulking like other tchagras. Usually solitary or in pairs near the ground in low thorny thickets. Performs fluttering song-flight followed by quick dive into shrubbery. **SIMILAR SPECIES:** See Brown-crowned Tchagra. **STATUS AND DISTRIBUTION:** *T. j. jamesi* is local and uncommon below 1000 m in dry thorn-bush in n. and ne. Kenya, south to the Nasolot NR and Kerio Valley, lakes Baringo and Bogoria, Samburu and Shaba GRs, Meru and Tsavo NPs, and into n. Tanzania in the Mkomazi GR. *T. j. mandana* is confined to the vicinity of Manda and Lamu islands, ranging west to Witu and the Tana delta.

MARSH TCHAGRA *Tchagra minuta* Plate 82
(Blackcap Bush-shrike)

Length 150–190 mm (6–7.5"). A small tchagra of *swampy grasslands; solid black cap* identifies the **adult male**. Ear-coverts, chin and throat white, shading to rich buff on remainder of underparts. *A black V on the back* is prominent except in the smaller and paler coastal *reichenowi. Bill black; eyes rose-pink or red;* feet dark grey. **Female** has *white superciliary stripes* and a black streak through the eye. **Juvenile** resembles female, but has a distinctive *whitish crown* and horn-coloured bill. **VOICE**: Alarm note a hoarse *charr;* also a scolding *kiop, klock,* or *tchup.* A short warbling song, *tewayo tuwaro,* given in low flight, suggested to Chapin the words 'today or tomorrow.' **HABITS**: Favours grassy areas more than other tchagras. Behaviour relatively sluggish; often perches for long periods on tall grass stems. **SIMILAR SPECIES**: See Black-crowned Tchagra. **STATUS AND DISTRIBUTION**: Local and uncommon in tall grass and rank herbaceous growth in damp hollows and along edges of swamps or streams; sometimes on drier grassy hillsides or in sugarcane. Western *T. m. minuta* ranges from Kapenguria and Saiwa NP south through Kakamega, Nandi and Mumias districts to the Lake Victoria basin and South Nyanza, wandering to Mara GR and w. Serengeti NP (Grumeti River); formerly in the cent. Kenyan highlands from Murang'a and Thika to Nairobi, but no records in recent decades. Coastal *reichenowi* formerly known from Dar es Salaam, the East Usambara Mts, Mombasa and Lamu, but few recent records (Pugu Hills near Dar es Salaam, and near Amani, East Usambaras).

BOCAGE'S or GREY-GREEN BUSH-SHRIKE *Malaconotus bocagei jacksoni* Plate 82

Length 158–165 mm (6–6.5"). A *forest-canopy* species in *western Kenya.* In the tree-tops, **adult** appears black above and white below, with prominent *white lores, forehead and superciliary stripes.* Viewed closer, back appears dark grey and a faint buff wash is noticeable on breast and sides; crown, nape, cheeks, sides of neck, flight feathers and tail black; *no white in wings.* Bill black; eyes dark red-brown; feet grey. **Juvenile** tinged yellow and faintly barred with grey below, barred yellowish and black on grey above; wings and tail with light greenish feather edgings and buff tips. **VOICE**: A monotonous, loud, clear whistle, usually a double *peeeu-peeeeu* or *pureet-ureet,* sometimes *tweee-teeeeu,* the second note lower. Also a rapid, clear whistled *uwee-wee-wee-wee-wee,* all on same pitch. Also harsh scolding notes. **HABITS**: A methodical foliage-gleaner, moving slowly and deliberately; easily overlooked when silent; occasionally feeds in the subcanopy or forest-edge saplings. **SIMILAR SPECIES**: Males of Northern and Pink-footed Puffbacks lack white forehead, lores and superciliary stripes. Black-backed and Pringle's Puffbacks are more eastern and southern. **STATUS AND DISTRIBUTION**: Uncommon in the Nandi and Kakamega Forests. Formerly at Nyarondo and Kericho.

SULPHUR-BREASTED BUSH-SHRIKE *Malaconotus sulfureopectus similis* Plate 83
(Orange-breasted Bush-Shrike)

Length 165–175 mm (6.5–7"). A colourful bird of acacia woodland and savanna. **Adult** olive-green above and yellow below, with grey crown, *orange breast, narrow black mask and yellow superciliary stripes.* Eyes dark brown. **Immature** yellow below, greenish above with grey head and upper back, but no striking facial pattern. **Juvenile** similar, but finely barred with dusky on head, breast, flanks and upperparts. **VOICE**: Song (sometimes recalling opening notes of Beethoven's 5th symphony) a short ringing whistle of four to eight notes, *twi-twu-twu-twurrr* or *whi-whi-whi-whi-her,* the last note lower and more emphatic; or first note slightly lower-pitched, *kew-tee-tee-tee-tee-tee-tee.* A characteristic sound of acacia woodland, as is the clear whistled *hooi hooi hooi* plus various rasping and clicking calls. **HABITS**: Shy and skulking, but highly vocal. Often joins mixed-species flocks. **SIMILAR SPECIES**: Grey-headed Bush-shrike is much larger, with massive bill and yellow eyes; lacks black mask and yellow superciliary stripes. **STATUS AND DISTRIBUTION**: Widespread and fairly common in acacia woodland, *Erythrina* bush and savanna, also thickets, riparian groves and forest edge, mainly below 2000 m. Absent from arid n. and e. Kenya.

BLACK-FRONTED BUSH-SHRIKE *Malaconotus nigrifrons* Plate 83
(Many-coloured Bush-Shrike)

Length 180 mm (7"). A handsome arboreal bird of *montane forest.* **Adult** *olive-green above ,with grey head and upper back,* and a *black forehead band extending back as a mask* through the ear-coverts. Of the four colour morphs in East Africa, golden-breasted birds are most numerous. The red-breasted form (either scarlet or dull orange-red) is known from the Cherangani Hills, Elgeyu-Maraquet, Meru, Nairobi and Mt. Kilimanjaro. Some Kenyan birds are red only from chin to breast, with yellow abdomen; others are orange below. Buff-breasted individuals recorded from Mt Kenya, the Taita Hills and the Usambara Mts; rare black-breasted males known only in the East Usambaras. **Immature** yellowish olive-green above, with the crown, ear-coverts, nape and upper back grey in at least some individuals (reportedly olive in others); narrow eye-ring greyish white; wing-coverts and tail

feathers tipped with yellow; underparts generally olive-yellow, more olive at sides, bright yellow on belly and lower breast. **Juvenile** resembles immature, but diffusely barred with dusky olive. **Voice:** Various hollow bell-like phrases, e.g. *whoop-whoop*, frequently repeated; or *kwo-kwo kwo, whoop-WEEup . . .*, or *WHEEo worik, WEEo worik. .*, or a simple *oook*, any of these commonly answered by mate's nasal rasping *CHAAAAAAA , NYAAAA* or *SHNARR* which may also be given alone as an alarm. A soft mellow *woo woo woo woo . . .* or *uwoo-uwoo* is performed as a duet. In the Usambaras, a soft *oo-poo* sometimes combined with a mechanical *click-clack* (Sclater and Moreau 1933). **Habits:** Usually shy. Pairs forage for insects in canopy foliage, often with mixed species flocks. Responsive to playback of voice. **Similar Species:** Immature and juvenile Sulphur-breasted Bush-shrike suggest comparable plumages of this species, but habitat differences separate them. **Status and Distribution:** Locally fairly common in highland forest on Mt Elgon, in Saiwa NP, the Cheranganis, Elgeyu-Maraquet and the Tugen Hills; also in the Kericho, Mau, Trans-Mara, Lolgorien, Nguruman, Meru, Embu and s. Aberdare forests and the Taita Hills. Formerly in n. Nairobi suburbs (most recent record Nov. 1980). In n. Tanzania, resident in submontane forest in Arusha NP and on Kilimanjaro, also common and widespread from 900 to 2200 m in the Pare and Usambara Mts (down to 300 m in the East Usambaras during cold seasons). Also known from the Marang Forest above Lake Manyara.

DOHERTY'S BUSH-SHRIKE *Malaconotus dohertyi* Plate 83

Length 180 mm (7"). A colourful bush-shrike of *highland-forest undergrowth*. **Adult male** *bright red on forehead and throat, the latter separated from yellow belly by a broad black band* which extends up around throat and through the eyes. Under tail-coverts also red. Back and wings green, tail black. **Female** differs in having narrow and faint olive-green edges and tips to the tail feathers. Rare yellow morph lacks red. **Juvenile** olive-yellow above (more buff on head and back), heavily and closely barred with black; wings greenish olive, many feathers edged with buff; narrow yellow eye-ring; underparts yellow, tinged olive on breast and sides, finely (and sometimes densely) barred with dusky except on belly; under tail-coverts dull pink with faint dark bars; tail dusky olive. **Voice:** Song a whistled phrase of short notes, *we-week u-week-u-week*, and an almost liquid *wurk wurk wurwurwurwurk*, varied to *weeo-weeo weeo weeo-werk*, slightly accented terminally. Call note *quip*, followed by a rising whistled *whee-u* (Chapin 1954). **Habits:** Normally secretive and shy, remaining in dense forest undergrowth and tangles, but confiding and sometimes easily seen at The Ark (Aberdare NP), where it feeds on ground in and near shrubbery. **Similar Species:** Four-coloured Bush-shrike of eastern lowlands has yellow, orange or red-orange forehead and superciliary stripes. **Status and Distribution:** Uncommon and local in thick scrub and undergrowth, dense secondary growth, and edge thickets, especially where mixed with bracken and bamboo, generally above 2200 m on Mt Elgon, the Cheranganis, Mt Kenya, Aberdares and the Mau. Old records from Limuru, Kiambu, Kericho and Sotik.

FOUR-COLOURED BUSH-SHRIKE *Malaconotus quadricolor nigricauda* Plate 83
(Gorgeous Bush-Shrike)

Length 180 mm (*c.* 7"). A bird of *eastern lowland* forest and thickets. Much like montane Doherty's Bush-shrike but *forehead and superciliary stripes orange or yellow*, sometimes red-tinged; *breast below the black band is red* in **adults**. Tail of male black, that of female olive-green. Female's red throat shows some yellow feathers, and the belly and crissum have little red. **Immature** plain olive above and on flanks; throat orange-yellow tinged red posteriorly; lower breast and belly more lemon-yellow; lores and eye-ring yellow. **Juvenile** similar with some barring below. **Voice:** A loud clear whistled song: *hooi-hooi-hooi-hooi. .*, and various harsh scolds. **Habits:** Shy and retiring, yet inquisitive; skulks in the densest of undergrowth where hard to see, but responds to imitation or playback of song. **Similar Species:** See Doherty's Bush-shrike. Young Sulphur-breasted Bush-shrike has grey on head. **Status and Distribution:** Local and uncommon in coastal forest and thickets north to Lamu, inland along the lower Tana River, on Mt Endau (at 1600 m) and Mt Kasigau, Shimba Hills NP and the North Pare Mts (1100–1800 m). Formerly known from the Chyulu and Sagala Hills, Tsavo East NP (Voi River) and East Usambara foothills; no records from these localities in recent decades, but an immature caught at Ngulia, Tsavo West NP, December 1973, may have wandered from the nearby Chyulu Hills.

GREY-HEADED BUSH-SHRIKE *Malaconotus blanchoti* Plate 83

Length 226–252 mm (9–10"). A *large, yellow-bellied, grey-headed* bush-shrike. *Massive black bill and bright yellow eyes* impart distinctive facial expression to **adult**. Variable rich chestnut patch on breast (and sometimes flanks) in *M. b. approximans,* lacking in northwestern birds. **Immature** paler. **Juvenile** pale yellow below, mottled brown on head; bill brownish horn; eyes brown. **Voice:** A far-carrying (yet often soft) hollow, whistled *whoonh,* this mechanical-sounding note repeated monotonously for an hour or more. Other repetitive notes may be thinner or squeakier, e. g. *wheeu. . ., wheeu. . .,* and may be preceded by soft notes audible only at close range; they

may also be accompanied by a variety of clicks, ticks or clinks. Also gives a single metallic bell-like note, and a harsh rasping alarm. One song, *wik-uraaanh-uraaanh-uraaanh . . .*, the main note repeated five to 12 times, may be given by one bird or in duet by members of a pair. **HABITS:** Usually in pairs; skulking and elusive. Often forages in tree canopy. Highly vocal. **SIMILAR SPECIES:** Sulphur-breasted Bush-shrike has much smaller bill, dark eyes, yellow superciliary stripes and narrow black mask. **STATUS AND DISTRIBUTION:** *M. b. approximans* is widespread but uncommon in bush and woodland, especially riparian strips, north and east of the Kenyan highlands, usually below 1500 m, including the coastal lowlands north of Mombasa, and south into n. Tanzania east of the Rift Valley. A disjunct population ranges from Lolgorien and nw. Mara GR south to the Nguruman Hills, Loliondo and cent. Serengeti NP. The northwestern *catharoxanthus* ranges from the Karasuk Hills to near Mt Elgon, locally as high as 3000 m. **NOTE:** Van Someren (1932) described a specimen (subsequently lost) said to have been obtained in the Kakamega Forest and which resembled both West African *M. monteiri* and *M. b. catharoxanthus*. It had much white on the head and entirely yellow underparts. Kakamega is close to the southern limits of *catharoxanthus*, and the moot specimen was possibly an aberrant (perhaps partially albinistic) example of that form. Hall and Moreau (1970) considered it *M. monteiri*, and it has been included under *M. cruentus* (Fiery-breasted Bush-shrike) by others, including Lewis and Pomeroy (1989); both species are extralimital.

ROSY-PATCHED BUSH-SHRIKE *Rhodophoneus cruentus*   Plate 83

Length 220–234 mm (8.75–9.25"). A unique dry-country species, *slim, pinkish tan above, with large white tail corners* and a conspicuous *rosy-red rump patch.* **Male** of the southern *R. c. cathemagmena* has the rose-coloured throat and breast patch bordered by black. Largely north of the Equator is *R. c. hilgerti*, less rosy tan above, the male with no black. **Females** of both races have a black-bordered white throat. **Juvenile** shows numerous buffy feather edges on back and wings. **VOICE:** Duet or antiphonal singing by members of a pair is a loud, piercing, somewhat slurred *TWEE-u, TWEE-u . . .* or *TSWEE-UR, TSWEE-UR. .*, repeated indefinitely. **HABITS:** In pairs. Decidedly terrestrial; runs rapidly across ground between bushes; flies low, just above ground. Pairs display and call for long periods from bushtop, facing one another, stretching high and extending bills skyward, wings drooped at sides, calling monotonously over and over as above. **SIMILAR SPECIES:** Tchagras show white tail corners but otherwise bear little resemblance. **STATUS AND DISTRIBUTION:** Locally fairly common in arid bush and semi-desert with scattered shrubs, usually below 1300 m: *R. c. hilgerti* in n. and e. Kenya from Lokichokio, n. and e. Lake Turkana, Marsabit, Moyale, Mandera and Wajir Districts south to Samburu and Shaba GRs, Meru NP, Kora NR, Garissa and Bura; *cathemagmena* from the Tsavo parks west to Amboseli, Kiboko, Olorgesailie and Mosiro, south to Lake Natron, lowlands north of Arusha, the Ardai Plains, Tarangire NP, the Masai Steppe and Mkomazi GR. The two races are not known to intergrade.

BLACK-HEADED GONOLEK *Laniarius erythrogaster*   Plate 83

Length 205–215 mm (8–8.5"). An impressive *black-and-red western* bush-shrike. **Adult** scarlet below except for black tibial feathers and *yellowish-buff lower belly and crissum;* upperparts glossy black, sometimes with a few white spots on wing-coverts, and some usually concealed white on the lower back. Eyes white or yellow. **Juvenile** blackish brown with faint buff barring above; underparts closely barred yellowish buff and black; eyes brown. Birds in post-juvenile moult boldly mottled with red and black. **VOICE:** Male gives a loud, resonant somewhat bell-like whistle, *Oiyo* or *WEEyo*, to which female immediately responds with a harsh grating *TURRRR* or *KSSRRRRR*, sounding like violent tearing of cloth. Another song is a hollow whistle, *chuyo-chuyo, chyochochocho*, involving both members of a pair. Alarm calls include a loud rapid *chk-chk-chk. .*, the notes run together in a continuous rail-like chatter. **HABITS:** Usually in pairs. Hides in undergrowth, but attracts attention with loud calls. Inquisitive and responsive. **SIMILAR SPECIES:** Papyrus Gonolek has yellowish crown. **STATUS AND DISTRIBUTION:** Common in dense bush, wooded patches, thickets, gardens and shrubby cultivation in the Lake Victoria bBasin, east to Muhoroni and Migori, and in n. Tanzania in the Mara Region and w. Serengeti NP. Locally fairly common along the Suam River at Kongelai, in Nasolot NR and parts of the southern Kerio Valley, occasionally wandering to Marigat and Lake Baringo. Birds in northern border areas at Lokichokio and northern Lake Turkana (Omo River delta) represent southern limits of Sudanese and Ethiopian populations. **NOTE:** Sometimes considered a race of *L. barbarus*.

PAPYRUS GONOLEK *Laniarius mufumbiri*   Plate 83

Length 190 mm (7.5"). A black-and-red gonolek restricted to *western papyrus swamps*. Resembles preceding species, but **adult** has *dull golden-yellow crown;* shows variable white spotting on wing-coverts; posterior underparts dingy white, and throat somewhat orange-tinged, not pure red. **Immature** dull (not glossy) black above,

with some pale feather tips; crown dull greyish olive; underparts brick-red to yellowish pink with yellowish buff throat. **Juvenile** undescribed. **Voice:** Double mellow whistles: *yong-yong* or *chyo-chyo*; may be varied to *yoo yong-yong*. **Habits:** Skulks in papyrus. Occasionally overlaps territory of Black-headed Gonolek at swamp edges, particularly in disturbed areas, but *mufumbiri* rarely leaves the papyrus except for short flights over open water. **Similar Species:** Black-headed Gonolek compared above. **Status and Distribution:** Locally common. Restricted to papyrus stands along Lake Victoria, east to Kisumu and Kendu Bay. An old report from Mt Elgon, repeated by some recent authors, is doubtless in error.

LÜHDER'S BUSH-SHRIKE *Laniarius l. luehderi*   Plate 83

Length 175 mm (7"). Restricted to forests in western Kenya. *Adult orange-tawny on crown and from throat to breast*, with a *broad black mask. Upperparts mainly black, with long white wing-stripe*; belly white. **Juvenile** largely olive above with rufous upper tail-coverts, and buffy yellow below, finely barred with blackish except on pale yellow belly and dark rufous tail. Wing-coverts and secondaries edged with yellowish or buff. **Voice:** Common call a throaty, somewhat rolling, amphibian-like *whook* or *wurrk*, sometimes followed by a low *chk-chk-chk* from second bird. Song a liquid whistling *weeo-k'wee* apparently given by males and females together. **Habits:** Generally in pairs, foraging in undergrowth and creeper tangles. Shy and retiring, but at times inquisitive. Quite vocal. **Similar Species:** Black-fronted Bush-shrike is grey and olive above, lacks white wing-stripe. Red-naped Bush-shrike is allopatric and in different habitat. **Status and Distribution:** Locally fairly common in forest undergrowth, creeper tangles and thick riparian growth from Mt Elgon, Kapenguria and Saiwa NP, the Nandi, Kakamega, Kericho, Mau and Trans-Mara Forests south to Lolgorien, the Migori River and Olololoo Escarpment, nw. Mara GR.

RED-NAPED BUSH-SHRIKE *Laniarius ruficeps*   Plate 83

Length 180 mm (7"). An eastern bush-shrike with *orange-red crown and nape* separated from *prominent black mask* by narrow white superciliary stripes; forecrown black in *L. r. rufinuchalis*, orange-red in *kismayensis*. Male has grey or grey-and-black back, olive-grey in female; wings black with *long white stripe*; tail also black, with white-edged outer feathers; underparts pinkish or cream, becoming white on belly and throat. **Juvenile** largely olive-grey with dull white underparts. **Voice:** A continuously repeated *kwoi kwoi kwoi . . .*, and a low whistling *whooi-whooi. . .* Harsh notes include a loud *K-K-K-K-K-K-K* and a repeated scolding *KWERR, KWERR . . .* Reportedly duets like other bush-shrikes. **Habits:** Shy and secretive; skulks in dense shrubbery and thickets, often near the ground. Sings from bushtops just after dawn. **Similar Species:** Lühder's Bush-shrike of western forests is tawny on crown and throat, lacks white on outer tail feathers. **Status and Distribution:** Locally common in dry bush country below 1000 m in e. and ne. Kenya. *L. r. rufinuchalis* ranges from Garissa, Mwingi, Kitui and Mutomo Districts south to Mtito Andei, Ngulia, Maungu, Taru and Galana Ranch. Numbers may vary seasonally. Also known from Mandera and Wajir Districts, but status unclear in the northeast. *L. r. kismayensis* is common around Kiunga and adjacent border areas.

TROPICAL BOUBOU *Laniarius aethiopicus*   Plate 82

Length 195–210 mm (*c.* 8"). A *robust* pied bush-shrike. **Adult** *white below*, mainly *black above*. The four subspecies in our region differ in the amount of white in the wing: only on middle coverts in *L. a. ambiguus*, longer and forming a longitudinal stripe along the major edges in *major*, on the middle coverts and edges of some secondaries in *L. a. aethiopicus*, and lacking in *L. a. sublacteus*, which also has an all-black coastal morph. **Juvenile** resembles adult, but feathers of upperparts variously tipped with tawny or ochre and underparts dull white with limited dusky barring (young *sublacteus* lacks these dark bars); nominate *aethiopicus* has breast and flanks pale brown, some dusky barring beneath and tawny feather tips above. **Voice:** Variable but distinctive. Common song of highland *ambiguus* is a short bell-like or metallic duet, *hooo-i-hoo* or *onk-hi-wong* or *ki-wahng*, sounding as if a single bird were calling (which sometimes is the case), the phrases oft-repeated. Calls include a quavering prolonged *hooooooooooo*, a *quu-wi* or *qui-u* and *kwi-u-eee* from male, accompanied by *heur* or *hoooo* from female. Another duet a repeated *hoo-anh* or *hoo-wanh*, the second note apparently that of the female. Courting male gives a harsh jarring *SCHRANG! SCHRANG!* to which female responds *oo-yuu*. Adults near nest or young give a low *chewk*, often double. Common duet of *L. a. sublacteus* in the East Usambaras, *hoongg-a-hoongg* (Sclater and Moreau 1933). **Habits:** Typically secretive and shy, skulking in dense cover, but confiding around many national park lodges and in gardens where it may forage on the ground away from cover. Usually in pairs. **Similar Species:** More arboreal Black-backed Puffback

is smaller, with white rump in male, grey in female; white of face extends above eyes in female; both sexes show white wing-feather edgings. Fiscals differ in posture, proportions and habits. In coastal thickets, Slate-coloured Boubou can be mistaken for sympatric all-black morph of *L. a. sublacteus*, but is dull bluish-slate, not glossy black. **STATUS AND DISTRIBUTION**: Widespread and common in woods, tangled shrubbery, forest edges and gardens. *L. a. ambiguus* occupies highlands east of the Rift Valley, from Mt Kulal and Marsabit south to the Chyulu Hills, Mt. Meru, Kilimanjaro, the Arusha and Moshi districts; western *L. a. major* ranges from Mt Elgon and the Kitale area east into the Rift Valley at Nakuru, Elmenteita and Naivasha, and south to the Lake Victoria basin, South Nyanza, Mara GR, n. Tanzania's Mara Region, Serengeti NP, Loliondo, and the Crater and Mbulu Highlands; *L. a. aethiopicus* just reaches our area at Moyale in ne. Kenya; *L. a. sublacteus* ranges through the coastal lowlands north to Lamu, inland along the lower Tana River to Bura and Garissa, also to Shimba Hills NP, Mt Kasigau, the Sagala and Taita Hills, and in ne. Tanzania to non-forested areas of the East Usambara and North Pare Mts and Lake Jipe.

SLATE-COLOURED BOUBOU *Laniarius funebris* Plate 82

Length 185–200 mm (7.25–8"). **Adult** *entirely dark slate-grey, with a blackish head* and heavy shrike-like bill. **Male** dark bluish slate, **female** a little paler. Inconspicuous white spots near tips of some rump feathers evident in the hand. Eyes brown; bill and feet black. **Juvenile** dull blackish brown-barred with black below. **VOICE**: Loud and variable; one common phrase a flute-like *cho-ko-WI*, given by male and often followed by female's harsh snarling *CHUERR* similar to the *CHERRK* alarm note. **HABITS**: Noisy, but shy and skulking, although more confiding in some national parks and game reserves. In pairs, on or near ground in thick vegetation. Displaying male erects long, white-based rump feathers like a puffback shrike, producing a piebald puff over the back, against the raised and widely fanned tail. **SIMILAR SPECIES**: Black flycatchers, drongos and male cuckoo-shrikes differ in bill shape and behaviour. Coastal all-black morph of Tropical Boubou is glossy black. Fülleborn's Black Boubou differs vocally, and in our region is restricted to the West Usambara Mts. **STATUS AND DISTRIBUTION**: Widespread and often common in scrub, bush and thickets below 2000 m, except in extreme e. and ne. Kenya, coastal lowlands south of Malindi, Ugandan border areas south of Mt Elgon, the Lake Victoria basin and South Nyanza. Characteristic of dry bush, but also inhabits acacia woodland and overgrown cultivation.

SOOTY BOUBOU *Laniarius leucorhynchus* Plate 82

Length *c.* 210 mm (8.25"). A vagrant in our region. **Adult** plumage sooty black or brownish black throughout, female slightly less glossy than male. Eyes reddish brown or brown; bill and feet black. Bill of **juvenile/immature** ivory white. **VOICE**: Male has a fluty whistle, *oo-oo-oo*, preceded or followed by female's grating *skaaaa*. **HABITS**: A shy and skulking bird of dense forest undergrowth and overgrown thickets. **SIMILAR SPECIES**: Other all-dark boubous are in non-forest habitats or are allopatric. **STATUS AND DISTRIBUTION**: Accidental. Known from a single specimen collected in the Kaimosi Forest, w. Kenya, in April 1931.

FÜLLEBORN'S BLACK BOUBOU *Laniarius fuelleborni* Plate 123

Length 185–195 mm (*c.* 7.5"). A *slaty-black* bush-shrike of *Tanzanian mountain forests.* **Adult** uniformly dark, the female somewhat less black about the head and with a faint olivaceous wash on the breast; has no white in rump feathers. Eyes brown; bill and feet black. **Juvenile** said to be dark olive-grey above, olive-green or olive-grey below. **VOICE**: Male has short, pleasing, liquid song, *wick-wick WEE* or *wit-WEET* or *hooi-hooi*, varied to *wu-wu-WEET* or *o-EKK, o-EEK*; may be preceded or followed by a melodious descending *turrrrrrrr* or rapid *u-u-u-u-u* from the female. Duets include *weeuweetu-WEE, oogle-WEEK, ooi-ooi-ooWEE* and *wuk-WEEK k'WEEEE* and a harsh *nyaaa-skereeeee.* Alarm call a repeated hard click (Sclater and Moreau, 1933). **HABITS**: Pairs inhabit undergrowth, creeper tangles and low trees. Quite vocal. **SIMILAR SPECIES**: Allopatric Slate-coloured Boubou, not a forest species, is more bluish slate in colour. **STATUS AND DISTRIBUTION**: In our area confined to the West Usambara Mts where a common resident between 1500 and 2200 m.

NORTHERN PUFFBACK *Dryoscopus gambensis* Plate 82

Length 180–190 mm (7–7.5"). A large-billed arboreal bush-shrike. **Adult male** *dull* white below and mostly black above. Distinguished from Black-backed Puffback (which nowhere overlaps with range of this species) by *larger size, stouter bill, less pure white underparts* and *grey scapulars. Rump is grey* (as in female Black-backed). Bill and feet black. *Eyes bright orange-red.* Far-northern *D. g. erythreae* is darker-backed than the widespread race *malzacii*. Distinctive **female** *tawny-buff below,* dusky brown above, the wing-coverts and secondaries edged with buff (not white). **Juvenile** resembles adult female, but has buff wing-feather edges and grey feather tips on head and back. **Immature** buffy white below (male) or with deeper tawny underparts (female). **VOICE**: A whistled note, *keow* or

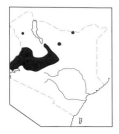

keewu, repeated several times after a short pause. Varied call notes include a sharp *kek*, a *chuck-chack* of alarm, a harsh, slow *wrrich, wrrich, wrrich*, and a rasping *zhiuu* or *zhrraanh*. **HABITS:** Arboreal, descending to tops of tall undergrowth; stealthy and secretive, but presence revealed by frequent calls. **SIMILAR SPECIES:** Black-backed Puffback compared above. Pringle's Puffback of dry bush country is much smaller, has conspicuously pale mandible base, white tail tip and edges; female much paler below and with distinctive facial pattern. **STATUS AND DISTRIBUTION:** Generally *north* of the Equator. *D. g. malzacii* is fairly common in lightly wooded areas from Bondo, Ng'iya and Nandi Districts east to Elmenteita, Lake Nakuru NP and the Laikipia Plateau, ranging north to Mt Elgon, Kapenguria, the Cheranganis, Horr Valley, Mts Loima, Nyiru and Marsabit. *D. g. erythreae* is known from northern border areas near Moyale.

BLACK-BACKED PUFFBACK *Dryoscopus cubla* Plate 82
(Puffback)

Length 148–175 mm (6–7"). A clean-cut, *red-eyed* arboreal bush-shrike. **Adult** males have *bright* white underparts and *black-and-white upperparts. Black cap of **male** extends to below eyes. **Female** has white supraloral stripes* and sides of face; rump grey. Bill and feet black. Inland birds (*hamatus*) have white-edged wing feathers. Distinctive coastal race *affinis* has all-black wing feathers, and female has prominent black loral streaks. (Intergrades common where ranges overlap.) **Immature** tinged buff below and on wings. **Juvenile** resembles female, but buff below and greyer on flanks; underparts dull black with grey feather tips; bill brownish. **VOICE:** Notes include a repeated TSUIK; a prolonged harsh *ki-eeh*; a loud repetitive hollow whistle, *WEEO* or *tu-WEEEO*; an emphatic grating *TCHEW . . . TCHEW . . ;* and a clearer *TYEW . . . TYEW.* Courting male calls *chak-chak-chak* on the wing. Coastal *affinis* incorporates a version of *TYEW* note into a varied series of other calls, each repeated several times: *tsik-tsik-tsik-tsik skweea, chyaa chyaa chyaa kyah kyah kyah, TYEW TYEW TYEW TYEW.* **HABITS:** Often in mixed-species flocks, usually in trees, not undergrowth. Displaying male puffs out long soft rump feathers to form a remarkable white ball, then bows, droops vibrating wings and spreads tail. He makes short 'butterfly' flights with the puff expanded, and may drop vertically through the air with raised wings. Courting birds audibly click their wings. **SIMILAR SPECIES:** Male Northern Puffback is more robust, with larger bill, dull white underparts, grey rump (like female Black-backed), buff-edged scapulars and orange-red (not blood-red) eyes. In dry e. and ne. Kenya, see Pringle's Puffback. Tropical Boubou is larger, black above except (usually) for white wing-stripe. Fiscal shrikes are longer-tailed and have different habits. **STATUS AND DISTRIBUTION:** Mainly *south* of the equator. Fairly common in forest, woodland, riparian strips and wooded gardens from sea level to 2000 m. *D. c. hamatus* (includes *nairobiensis*) is widespread east and west of the Rift Valley from South Nyanza and the Lake Victoria basin east to Nairobi, Mt Kenya and Meru NP, ranging south throughout all inland areas of s. Kenya and n. Tanzania. *D. c. affinis* occupies the coastal lowlands north to the Boni Forest, inland along the lower Tana River to Bura, and the Shimba Hills.

PRINGLE'S PUFFBACK *Dryoscopus pringlii* Plate 82

Length 135–140 mm (c. 5.5"). A *small, dry-country puffback with bicoloured bill* and *grey scapulars.* **Male** resembles a diminutive Northern Puffback, but *basal half of mandible pale* and *tail edged and tipped with dull white* (obvious only in fresh plumage); a brownish-grey wash across breast and along flanks. *Eyes crimson.* **Female** *entirely light grey-brown above* with *whitish wing edgings;* side of face marked by *inconspicuous white eye-ring;* lores and underparts dull white tinged with pale buff on breast and flanks. Narrow white rectrix tips soon wear away. Bare parts as in male. **Juvenile** resembles female, but duller. **VOICE:** A sharp repeated *keu*, which may be given by several birds. **HABITS:** An active foliage-gleaner, typically with mixed-species flocks moving through undergrowth or low trees. **SIMILAR SPECIES:** Northern Puffback is much larger, the female richly coloured below and with orange eyes; male's bill entirely black, tail lacks white edges and tip. Black-backed Puffback is also larger, has black scapulars and all-black bill. **STATUS AND DISTRIBUTION:** Local and uncommon in dry *Acacia* and *Commiphora* bush and low woodland below 1000 m in e. and ne. Kenya from Mandera, Moyale and Marsabit, south to Meru NP, Kora NR, Kitui District, Mtito Andei, and the Tsavo NPs; a small disjunct population (limits unclear) in nw. Kenya's Turkwell Valley. In ne. Tanzania, recorded at Lake Jipe, Mkomazi GR and Lembeni.

PINK-FOOTED PUFFBACK *Dryoscopus angolensis nandensis* Plate 82

Length 152–155 mm (6"). A canopy species, in our region confined to forests in w. Kenya. **Male** has *black crown, nape* and *upper back,* with lower back and rump *pale grey,* underparts white. Eyes dark brown (narrowly edged with bright cobalt-blue); eyelids reddish grey; bill black, feet lavender-pink. **Female** grey-headed, *rich tawny-buff below except for white belly and under tail-coverts;* back, wings and tail olive-brown. Bare parts as in male. **Juvenile** similar to female, but duller. **VOICE:** An emphatic *TCHEW, TCHEW, TCHEW. . .*, the note repeated up

to 30 times. Also a harsh churring sound. **HABITS**: Arboreal; forages in high foliage and on large subcanopy branches. Usually in pairs. Not especially vocal. **SIMILAR SPECIES**: Bocage's Bush-shrike, also in forest canopy, suggests male Pink-footed Puffback, but has white forehead, lores and superciliary stripes, dark rump and dark feet. Female Northern Puffback resembles female Pink-footed, but is larger, browner above, with buff or tawny wing edgings and bright orange eyes. **STATUS AND DISTRIBUTION**: Uncommon in Kakamega and Nandi Forests. An early specimen reported from Mt Elgon at 2400 m (8000 ft). A report from the Tugen Hills requires confirmation.

CUCKOO-SHRIKES, FAMILY CAMPEPHAGIDAE
(World, 82 species; Africa, 10; Kenya, 6; n. Tanzania, 4)

Despite the name, these birds have no affinities with either shrikes or cuckoos. Our species are starling-sized, with rather long, pointed wings and ample, slightly rounded tails. The tarsi are short and the bill is quite small, with very slight terminal hook, in most species. The dense matted feathers of the lower back and rump may be partly erected, giving the bird a humpbacked, somewhat trogon-like outline. In the hand, the stiff pointed shafts of these feathers are readily detectable. Of our two genera, the *Campephaga* species are smaller and exhibit pronounced sexual dimorphism. Males are mainly glossy blue-black, with the rictal skin often swollen into short, brightly coloured gape flanges; female plumage is yellow, olive and whitish, extensively barred in some. In the larger *Coracina* species, the sexes are similar (males slightly larger). All cuckoo-shrikes are quiet, unobtrusive arboreal birds, solitary or in pairs, often accompanying mixed-species flocks. They feed on insects (particularly larvae) gleaned from foliage, and to some extent on fruit. The nest is a shallow pad of plant material, usually bound with spider web to a high tree branch. Eggs (undescribed for some species) are one or two in number, greenish or bluish and heavily speckled with brown, olive or grey.

BLACK CUCKOO-SHRIKE *Campephaga flava*   Plate 81

Length 175–200 mm (*c.* 7–8"). A sluggish arboreal bird of bush and woodland. The black **male** has a blue or slightly greenish-blue sheen, and at first suggests a drongo or glossy starling, but the fleshy *gape is dull yellow or orange-yellow*, and tail tip is rounded or square. Some birds show a black-edged yellow 'shoulder' patch, variable in size. In others, median coverts are black with broad yellow edges. Many have no yellow. Eyes dark brown; bill and feet black; mouth-lining yellow or orange (said to be red in southern African birds). In the hand, note that inner webs of primaries are strongly washed with yellow. **Female** greyish olive above and mostly whitish below, *heavily black-barred* and suggesting a small cuckoo; shows noticeable dark eye-streak and *bright yellow wing and tail edgings. Underside of tail appears mostly yellow*; may show some dusky near base (and elsewhere if rectrices spread or moulting). Some yellow on sides of breast, leg feathers and rump. **Juvenile** resembles adult female, but is spotted with blackish above, and spotted rather than barred below; tail feathers pointed rather than rounded. Moulting **immature** mottled glossy black and white below, often with some barred white juvenile feathers remaining. **VOICE**: Call notes high and sibilant. Advertising songs include a rather shrill, loud *tutututu chee-chee-chee-chee wureet-reet-seetiti* and *tu, chri-chri-chri-chri-chri-chri*. Also gives a high-pitched insect-like trill, *tririririririririrri*, and a sharper *trreeu*. **HABITS**: An 'edge' or second-growth species, rarely entering true forest. Shy and lethargic, sometimes perching quietly, except for occasional wing-flicking, for long periods. Feeds amid foliage and briefly hovers to remove prey from leaves. Normal flight floppy and undulating. In quivering display flight, erects lower-back and rump feathers. Territorial male sings from low treetops. **SIMILAR SPECIES**: Square-tailed Drongo has large bill and red eyes. Male Red-shouldered Cuckoo-shrike has large scarlet epaulettes; female slightly greyer than female Black, with less yellow on outer tail feathers. Male Petit's Cuckoo-shrike has more obvious, bright orange-yellow gape. Male Purple-throated Cuckoo-shrike has purple gloss on throat. **STATUS AND DISTRIBUTION**: Although some populations probably are resident (breeding recorded at several localities in s. Kenya and n. Tanzania), the species is mainly a non-breeding migrant from the southern tropics, May–October, when widespread and fairly common in bushed, wooded and forest-edge habitats, including those in coastal lowlands north to the Boni Forest. Inland, it ranges north to the w. and cent. Kenyan highlands, occasionally to Lake Turkana and northern border areas.

RED-SHOULDERED CUCKOO-SHRIKE *Campephaga phoenicea*   Plate 81

Length 180–200 mm (7–8"). A *west Kenyan* bird suggesting a Black Cuckoo-shrike, but glossy blue-black **adult male** has *large scarlet epaulettes*. (These are modified lesser and median coverts, some of the latter basally yellow; bases of greater coverts also yellow, in worn birds showing as a yellow edge to the epaulette, or making this appear orange or deep orange-yellow.) Swollen *gape flanges pale pink*. Eyes brown; bill and feet black.

Female closely resembles that of Black Cuckoo-shrike, but *underside of tail feathers black with broad yellow tips*, instead of largely yellow with limited dark basal area; *crown and back grey-brown with olive tinge*; rump and upper tail-coverts black-barred (as, sometimes, are back and scapulars). Narrow dark eye-line accentuated by whitish eyelids. *Underparts whitish with numerous dusky bars.* Wing feathers have bright yellow margins. Tail dark olive-brown above, and *yellow on outer three pairs of feathers confined mainly to tips.* **Juvenile** resembles female, but *spotted (not barred)* above and below, and tail feathers pointed. **VOICE:** Rarely heard. Male has "soft double whistle or a bell-like note" (Chapin 1953). **HABITS:** Where sympatric with other *Campephaga* spp. (e.g. near Kakamega), mainly a savanna or open-woodland bird, with *flava* in second-growth woods or forest edge, slightly overlapping *petiti* and *quiscalina* of the forest. Often remains hidden in heavy foliage, seldom perching on exposed branches. Typically in trees, but sometimes in undergrowth. **SIMILAR SPECIES:** See Black Cuckoo-shrike. **STATUS AND DISTRIBUTION:** Scarce and local presumed resident in dense moist bushed grassland, riverine woods and savanna from Uganda into w. Kenya in the Malaba, Alupe, Mumias, Kakamega and Nandi Districts. **NOTE:** Formerly considered conspecific with Black Cuckoo-shrike.

PETIT'S CUCKOO-SHRIKE *Campephaga petiti* Plate 81

Length 185–190 mm (*c.* 7.5"). A *west Kenyan forest* species. **Adult male** glossy blue-black and closely resembling Black Cuckoo-shrike, but *bright orange or orange-yellow gape much more conspicuous*; narrow bare orbital ring dull apple-green; mouth-lining orange-yellow. Eyes dark brown. In the hand, note the entirely dark primaries. **Female** *largely yellow* (duller on back), *almost unmarked below* (a few bars on sides of chest), but *heavily barred with black from back to upper tail-coverts*; rump brighter yellow. Crown and nape plain olive. Side of head shows short yellowish superciliary stripe, broader black eye-line and whitish eyelids. Wings blackish, with bright yellow wing-bars and secondary edges; remiges edged bright yellow on inner webs. Tail olive and black, edged and extensively tipped yellow. **Immature male** resembles female, but at least some birds *essentially unmarked above* except on wings. Dark yellowish olive from nasal feathering to middle of nape, paler on upper back and scapulars, with obscure barring; lower back, rump and upper tail-coverts plain rich yellow, duller, more ochre, in centre, brighter at sides. Tail as in female, largely yellow below; rectrices not pointed. *Underparts plain bright yellow*, duller and paler on chin, *with band of faint blackish bars across upper breast.* Side of head marked by broad blackish eye-line and black-streaked, yellowish-grey ear-coverts; pale yellowish eyelid feathering and dull yellow superciliary stripe more obscure than in adult female. Inner edges of primaries edged bright yellow. Bill and feet black; gape and inside of mouth bright yellow-orange; eyes dark brown. **Juvenile** resembles adult female or immature, but *head and underparts spotted with black* and tail feathers pointed. **VOICE:** Song a high-pitched, scratchy warbling: *sueet-sueet, siueet-seet-seet-sireet.* Infrequent call note a short whistled *seep.* **HABITS:** Perches quietly on exposed twigs in middle or high canopy; forages in foliage, on large tree branches and trunks. May join mixed-species flocks, but usually solitary. **SIMILAR SPECIES:** Male Black and Purple-throated Cuckoo-shrikes have less conspicuous gape flanges; female Purple-throated has grey head and plain olive wings. **STATUS AND DISTRIBUTION:** Fairly common resident of the Kakamega and Nandi Forests.

PURPLE-THROATED CUCKOO-SHRIKE *Campephaga quiscalina martini* Plate 81

Length 178–192 mm (7–7.5"). A *highland* bird of *forest and forest edge*. Slightly heavier-looking and broader-tailed than Black Cuckoo-shrike. Blue-black **male** has dull *purple gloss on throat and neck*, this less prominent on rest of underparts (which nevertheless lack the blue-green or greenish-blue sheen of Black Cuckoo-shrike. Wings, rump and rectrix edges shiny greenish blue. Inner webs of primaries entirely black. Velvety-black feathers at base of culmen and on lores somewhat better developed than in Black Cuckoo-shrike. Rictal skin yellow or orange, but *often inconspicuous and not swollen; mouth-lining red or orange-red* (obvious when the bird 'gapes'); eyes brown; bill black; feet greyish. **Female** *plain olive above, with contrasting grey head, whitish or greyish throat*, streaked cheeks, dark eye-lines and narrow white superciliary stripes. Underparts yellow, variably barred with black, especially on breast, sides and flanks. Underside of tail feathers olive-grey with yellowish tips. Mouth-lining orange. Occasional birds lack barring on underparts. **Juvenile** resembles female, but darkly barred above, lightly barred below, head browner and wing-coverts tipped white. Tail mostly yellowish olive-brown, with ill-defined dull yellowish feather tips and outer edges. Moulting **immature male** mottled olive and black above, yellow and black below. **VOICE:** Song a monotonously repeated slurred whistled note, *sweep* or *tseeu*, loud and shrill. **HABITS:** Similar to those of Petit's Cuckoo-shrike, but often forages higher and in dense foliage. **SIMILAR SPECIES:** Males of preceding three species lack purple gloss on throat, and differ vocally. Petit's Cuckoo-shrike, the only other species likely in forest, shows bright orange-yellow gape flanges and the mouth-lining is yellow or yellow-orange; females have blackish wings and tail with yellow feather edging, and no contrasting grey head. Black forest starlings show chestnut in wings.

STATUS AND DISTRIBUTION: Uncommon local resident of wooded areas between 1700 and 2500 m in the Kenyan highlands, from Mt Elgon, Cherangani Hills, Maralal and Mt Kenya south to the Kakamega, Nandi, Kabarnet, Mau and Trans-Mara Forests, Lolgorien and the Ngurumans. In n. Tanzania, known from an early specimen from n. Serengeti NP, and sight records from Loliondo, Arusha NP, Mbulumbulu and Mt Hanang.

GREY CUCKOO-SHRIKE *Coracina caesia pura*   Plate 81

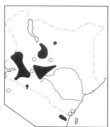

Length 210–220 mm (*c.* 8.5"). A rather *uniformly grey* cuckoo-shrike of *highland forest.* Forehead paler grey; large whitish eye-ring conspicuous. Sexes similar, but **male** has blackish lores and dusky chin; **female** paler below, especially on chin. **Juvenile** finely barred above and below, with whitish flight-feather edging and white tail-feather tips. **Immature** resembles adult, but may retain some spotted or barred juvenile feathers, especially on posterior underparts. VOICE: A descending nasal *meeeaa*, somewhat cat-like, and a feeble, rather sharp and high-pitched *tseeu* or *tsiu-tsiu*. In southern Africa, said to have a "weaver-like chattering," a "sneeze-like *chi-oo*", and a "high-pitched drawn-out *peeeeoooo*, similar to quiet whistle of Red-winged Starling" (Maclean 1984). HABITS: Usually forages in high foliage or on trunks and large branches. Quiet, and often perches motionless for long periods. STATUS AND DISTRIBUTION: Fairly common but local resident between 1600 and 3000 m in the Kenyan highlands, ranging from Mt Elgon, the Cheranganis, Mt Nyiru and Mt Marsabit south through the Ndotos, Mathews Range and Maralal to the Nyambenis, Mt Kenya, the Aberdares, Mau and Trans-Mara Forests, Lolgorien, nw. Mara GR and the Nguruman Hills. In n. Tanzania, at Loliondo and in the Usambara Mts. Isolated birds reported from w. Serengeti NP (Aug. 1970), Mrima Hill (Nov. 1983) and Shimba Hills NP (May 1990) may represent wanderers.

WHITE-BREASTED CUCKOO-SHRIKE *Coracina pectoralis*   Plate 81

Length *c.* 250 mm (10"). A large, sturdy-billed, *grey-and-white* cuckoo-shrike of savanna and woodland. Upperparts mainly light grey (paler on head); primaries and outer rectrices black; *lower breast and belly white.* Eyes brown; bill and feet black. **Male** has *dark grey throat and upper breast.* **Female** has *whitish forehead, incomplete eye-ring and chin; throat and upper breast are pale grey.* **Juvenile** barred black, grey and white above; black-spotted below. VOICE: Male gives a soft whistled *duid-duid,* female a drawn-out trilled *chrreeeeee;* also a weak squeak (Maclean 1984). HABITS: Solitary or in pairs. Gleans foliage, large tree branches and trunks; may hawk insects; flight flapping and gliding. Frequently joins mixed-species flocks. SIMILAR SPECIES: Grey Cuckoo-shrike, a highland-forest bird, has grey belly. STATUS AND DISTRIBUTION: Scarce. Recorded in extreme w. Kenya at Mt Elgon, in Busia and Kakamega Districts (few records in last 50 years) and Tsavo River (July 1914); in n. Tanzania, at Arusha NP (Nov. 1969) and Kondoa District (Jan. 1982).

DRONGOS, FAMILY DICRURIDAE
(World, 24 species; Africa, 4; Kenya, 3; n. Tanzania, 2)

Drongos are distinctive, black-plumaged birds of uncertain relationships. They are small to medium-sized, with rather long, more or less forked tails, the outer feathers of which are splayed out terminally in some species. The head is large and quite flat, and the bill stout, somewhat hooked, and basally subtended by strong rictal bristles. The tarsi are short. Sexes are alike. Decidedly aggressive toward hawks, eagles and large corvids, habitually pursuing them in the air, drongos nevertheless seem tolerant of other small birds in their territories. They are mainly insectivorous and feed by flycatching or pouncing on their prey, which is held down with the toes and dispatched in raptorial fashion. The nest is a shallow flattish cup placed in a horizontal fork of a tree branch. The usually three eggs are whitish, typically spotted and blotched with chestnut, brown and purple; sometimes unmarked.

COMMON DRONGO *Dicrurus adsimilis*   Plate 81
(Fork-tailed Drongo)

Length 230–260 mm (9–10"). A conspicuous black bird with a *long, prominently forked 'fish-tail'* (less deeply forked in n. Kenya). Inner webs of flight feathers greyish tan, producing a pale silvery flash in flight. **Adult** plumage mainly glossy blue-black, except for velvety-black forehead. *Eyes red;* bill and feet black. **Juvenile** blackish brown on head and crissum; dull dark grey-brown on rest of underparts, with extensive buff tips to body feathers (later much reduced by wear). Less deeply forked tail than adult, and with amber, grey-brown or light yellowish-grey eyes. **Immature** is uniformly blue-black but less glossy than adult, *brown-eyed,* with shallow tail fork and a conspicuous yellowish-white gape. Whitish-edged lesser under wing-coverts often conspicuous at edges of wings. VOICE: Diurnal song of varied short phrases or single notes, often rasping, twanging or banjo-like in quality, the

performance unhurried and with frequent (sometimes long) pauses: one example *tsrinki-tsrinki-styaow, chwinki, tsr-skwinki-skwink . . .*; another *skerrik . . . tchwang, skiiing, seeeeek, tsurik-tssrng-cherrinka. . . .* Certain notes may be delivered in synchronous duet with mate. Song may also include parrot-like squeals, other discordant sounds and mimicry. A simpler song consists of a repeated *wurchee-wurchee* with occasional other notes. Prolonged pre-dawn song of well-separated phrases contains fewer metallic notes: *swittsit squierk, squier-cherk, chak-chak, sqwaang, whuk-skwerk, stweeek, chuk-cherk . . . wee-eet, chrr . . . yerk-yerk, SKLEEH, cherrer-weeeet . . . cherang-skeeeeee, twer, chup . . .*. Call note a nasal *chwang*. **HABITS**: Perches conspicuously on exposed branches, from which it hawks insects. Solitary or in pairs, and may join mixed bird parties. Noisy and pugnacious. Sings through heat of the day and sometimes at night. Flight undulating and easy, often tumbling and twisting; agile in pursuit of large birds. **SIMILAR SPECIES**: Male Black Cuckoo-shrike has brown eyes and unforked tail, different habits. Southern Black Flycatcher is brown-eyed, has smaller bill, smaller tarsi and shallow tail fork. **STATUS AND DISTRIBUTION**: A widespread and common resident in dry woodland, savanna, cultivation and forest edge, from the coast up to 2200 m. Most birds are of the nominate race, said to intergrade with *divaricatus* in n. Kenya.

VELVET-MANTLED DRONGO *Dicrurus modestus coracinus* **Plate 81**

Length 240–280 mm (9.5–11"). A *deeply 'fish-tailed' forest* bird. Differs from Common Drongo in being much *less glossy below* and with a *velvety-black back and rump. Inner webs of flight feathers blackish*, imparting no silvery wing flash in flight. Eyes orange-red to deep scarlet; bill and feet black. **Juvenile** brown-eyed, presumably barred beneath as in Common Drongo. Dull **immature** has pale rictal skin and less deeply forked tail. **VOICE**: Song prolonged, halting, semi-musical, and many notes with a pronounced twang; much repetition of notes or phrases: *tsik, chk cher we wee-wee-weu, stik tser-eu, stick ter-eu, tsik-ter wee-tsiktwer-wee-wee, tser tsuk, chk ker-wee squanh, chick cher wi squanh. . .* Has various harsh scolding calls. **HABITS**: Unobtrusive and rather shy. Does not venture into open habitats, but forages near small openings or tracks within forest. **SIMILAR SPECIES**: Common Drongo compared above. Smaller Square-tailed Drongo has almost no tail fork. Male forest cuckoo-shrikes have smaller bills, rounded or square tail tips. **STATUS AND DISTRIBUTION**: Scarce resident of the Kakamega Forest, w. Kenya. Formerly on Mt Elgon.

SQUARE-TAILED DRONGO *Dicrurus ludwigii* **Plate 81**

Length 180 mm (7"). A small forest drongo with a *slightly notched tail* and bright *orange-red to deep red eyes*. **Male** glossy black (duller, more bluish or purplish, less green in the western race *sharpei*). **Female** all black in *sharpei*, but with dark slate-grey underparts and (rarely?) whitish-tipped under tail-coverts in eastern birds. Lacks pale-winged appearance in flight. Bill and feet black. **Juvenile** resembles female, but is speckled pale grey on mantle and breast. Eyes brown. **VOICE**: Less jangling and more structured than song of Velvet-mantled Drongo, variable but often with repeated phrases, typically loud, strident or ringing: (1) *SKI-tsi-chee si-chee-chee see-see*, (2) *chi-see SEEEET si-chee-chee*, (3) *cherk, chichi chwerk-chwerk*, (4) *cherk whuit whuit whuit*, (5) *wheu-tuit, wheu-tuit . . .* In s. Africa, varied song includes loud twanging *tswing-tswing-tswing* phrases (Maclean 1984). Calls a harsh rasping *chyaa*, a ringing *WEEK-yer* and *yerk-yerk*. **HABITS**: Solitary or accompanying foraging bird parties. Hunts from a perch like other drongos, but more secretive, usually in leafy cover, low or high. Often twitches tail sideways. Calls persistently. **SIMILAR SPECIES**: See Common and Velvet-mantled Drongos. Southern Black Flycatcher has dark brown eyes, finer bill and longer tarsi. Black male cuckoo-shrikes (*Campephaga* spp.) are smaller-billed, often show colourful gape flanges, have more rounded head, shorter and more rounded tail. **STATUS AND DISTRIBUTION**: *D. l. ludwigii* (includes *munzneri*) is a locally common resident of forest and moist thickets in coastal Tanzanian lowlands and up to 2000 m in the Usambara Mts. In Kenya, it ranges in gallery forest along the lower Tana River from the delta north to Bura and Garissa, east to the Witu and Boni Forests. *D. l. sharpei* is uncommon in the Kakamega and South Nandi Forests of w. Kenya; formerly on Mt Elgon.

ORIOLES, FAMILY ORIOLIDAE
(World, 29 species; Africa, 9; Kenya, 6; n. Tanzania, 4)

Arboreal, starling-sized birds, *Oriolus* species are not to be confused with New World orioles (Emberizidae: Icterinae). Our species are stout-billed and long-winged, with rather short tails and tarsi. The sexes are alike or, as in the two migratory species, quite different. Plumage is largely yellow and olive, often with black on head or wings. Most species are shy and remain hidden in high foliage, their presence revealed only by loud fluty whistles. They are typically solitary, although numbers congregate in fruiting trees, and they frequently join mixed-species flocks. The diet consists mainly of insects, but some species are known to eat fruits and flowers. Foraging movements are rather slow and deliberate, but flight tends to be swift and undulating. The typical nest is a well-woven cup or flimsy basket of grasses, moss and lichens, suspended from a slender horizontal tree fork. The two handsome eggs are pinkish or white with brown and lavender markings. Two of our species are long-distance migrants. All are behaviourally similar, and habits are not discussed separately below.

BLACK-HEADED ORIOLE *Oriolus larvatus rolleti* Plate 80

Length 200–215 mm (8–8.5"). The most commonly seen dark-headed oriole, distinguished from its close relatives by *greenish-olive central tail feathers, yellowish-edged inner secondaries* and *largely grey greater coverts.* Note habitat and range. **Adult** (sexes alike) yellowish olive above and bright yellow below, with black head and throat; black primaries narrowly edged greyish white, and primary coverts with conspicuous white spot; *outer secondaries broadly edged whitish grey,* the inner black and olive with low-contrast pale dull yellowish edges. *Closed tail olive above* (the central feathers darker near tips) and yellow below; when spread, shows large yellow corners. Bill deep pink, pale pinkish horn or maroon; eyes red. **Juvenile** resembles adult, but head duller, the feathers edged with yellowish green; yellow half-collar on sides of neck; back obscurely marked with short dark streaks. Throat dull yellow, with *dense black streaks* which extend to breast and sides, where *narrow and distinct.* Eyes grey-brown; bill dull black; feet pale grey. **VOICE**: A short liquid whistle, *ku-WEEo* or *weelka-WEEo* or *QU-o-wo,* and a shorter *keeWO* or *CLUeo,* repeated at regular intervals; alarm call a harsh *kwarr.* **SIMILAR SPECIES**: Montane Oriole of mountain forests has a more contrasting pattern, with black central tail feathers and more black in the wings. Western Black-headed Oriole (only in Kakamega Forest) also has olive central rectrices, but has largely yellow-olive inner wing feathers and greyer, less whitish, wing edgings. **STATUS AND DISTRIBUTION**: A widespread and common resident from sea level to 2300 m, mainly in acacia woodland and well-timbered savanna, but also locally in mangroves. Where sympatric with other black-headed orioles, restricted to non-forest habitats or forest edge. Absent from arid n. and e. Kenya.

MONTANE ORIOLE *Oriolus percivali* Plate 80

Length 195–215 mm (7.75–8.5"). A *highland-forest* bird, similar in voice, habits and coloration to Black-headed Oriole but plumage pattern of **adult** more sharply contrasting, with deeper black and brighter, more extensive yellow. *Central tail feathers black,* not olive as in Black-headed Oriole, and *wings with more black.* White spot on primary coverts, and whitish stripe formed by edges of outer secondaries; *inner wing feathers mainly black but both inner and outer webs contrastingly margined with yellow-olive.* Details of wing pattern often hard to see, and subject to wear and to the effects of hybridization (see below), but the *greater coverts mainly dull yellowish,* with less grey than in Black-headed; that portion of secondaries above the white primary-covert spot is *black,* not grey, hence contrasting more with the greater coverts. Entire back brighter yellow, less olive, than in related species. **Juvenile** resembles juvenile Black-headed Oriole, but much less heavily marked on breast, with faint narrow grey streaks below the dark throat/breast patch. **NOTE**: Occasionally hybridizes with *O. larvatus* in remnant forest patches north of Nairobi, where birds in intermediate plumages may be expected. **VOICE**: Similar to that of Black-headed Oriole and not always distinguishable. Typical are a short *e'YO* or *EE-yo,* and a squealing *chaeWEE* or *CHWEE,* which may flow into a liquid *qua-WEEo.* Common is a loud *weeka-ku-WEEU,* to which female may reply with a higher *weekla-wee-er.* **SIMILAR SPECIES**: Black-headed Oriole has olive central tail feathers, largely grey secondary coverts; broad yellowish-buff edges to inner wing feathers. **STATUS AND DISTRIBUTION**: A locally common resident from 1850 to 3000 m in forested Kenyan highlands from Mt Elgon and the Cheranganis south to the Mau, Trans-Mara, Aberdares and Mt Kenya. **NOTE**: Formerly considered a race of *O. nigripennis* (Mackworth-Praed and Grant 1955) or of *O. larvatus* (White 1962). Hybrids with the latter (see note above) reflect incomplete reproductive isolation from that species, the two increasingly in contact as forest habitat of *percivali* shrinks.

WESTERN BLACK-HEADED ORIOLE *Oriolus brachyrhynchus laetior* Plate 80

Length 205–215 mm (8–8.5"). Restricted to the *Kakamega Forest,* where the only oriole. **Adult** resembles Black-headed Oriole, but *outer secondaries edged with slate-grey, not whitish. Exposed webs of inner wing feathers mainly yellowish olive, with no pale yellow edges;* largely black inner webs also lack contrasting pale edges. (These wing features difficult to see under normal field conditions.) *Central tail feathers yellowish olive,* not darkening terminally. Eyes red; bill dull pink; feet grey. **Juvenile** has dark olive head indistinctly streaked with black. Eyes brownish red; bill dark horn; feet grey. **VOICE**: A rapid *tututuWEEah* or *cucuWEEa,* more shrill than calls of Black-headed and Montane Orioles, at times with a squealing quality. Some shorter, more fluty calls resemble those of related species. **SIMILAR SPECIES**: See Black-headed and Montane Orioles. **STATUS AND DISTRIBUTION**: In our area, known only from the Kakamega Forest, w. Kenya, where a fairly common resident.

GREEN-HEADED ORIOLE *Oriolus chlorocephalus amani* Plate 80

Length 215 mm (8.5"). A distinctive *coastal* forest species. **Adult** with back, *head, throat and chest rich olive-green*. Underparts and *collar on hindneck bright yellow*; wings pale blue-grey, with no white spot on primary coverts; tail dark green with yellow corners and sides. Bill pink, eyes red. Sexes alike. **Juvenile** streaked with olive-green below; yellowish on chin and throat; wing-coverts tipped yellow; bill dark. **VOICE**: Similar to that of Black-headed Oriole, slightly more liquid, the phrases often less abrupt: *ku-WEE-oo* or *kwee-WO* (each utterance accompanied by a quick fanning of the tail). A longer *onk-onk-co-WOyo* or simpler *coWOyo* are characteristic, as is a distinctive nasal mewing *kweee-aaah* or *nyrr-thrrr*. **SIMILAR SPECIES**: Juvenile Black-headed Oriole shows some dark greenish olive on head, but has blackish streaking on underparts, dark eyes and dark bill. **STATUS AND DISTRIBUTION**: Local and uncommon resident of some coastal Kenyan forests from Diani and Shimba Hills NP north to Arabuko–Sokoke (where appearing in the 1980s; not yet known to breed locally). Also common from 200 to 1200 m in the Usambara Mts of ne. Tanzania.

AFRICAN GOLDEN ORIOLE *Oriolus auratus* Plate 80

Length 200 mm (8"). In all plumages (unless badly worn), distinguished from Eurasian Golden Oriole by *broadly yellow-edged greater coverts and secondaries*. **Adult male** bright golden yellow, with conspicuous *black streak around and behind eye*. Wings black, with *broad yellow feather edges*; tail mostly yellow, with black central feathers (yellow extends to base of outer rectrices in southern race *notatus*, but not in nominate *auratus*). Bill dull brownish red; eyes bright red; feet blue-grey. **Female** yellowish olive above, with yellow upper tail-coverts; eye-stripe olive-grey; underparts yellow, with olive wash on sides of breast and some short olive streaks; sides of tail narrowly black. Bare parts as in male, but duller. **Juvenile** and **immature** similar to adult female above, but underparts with heavy blackish streaks. Easily confused with streaked female or first-winter Eurasian Golden Oriole, but *bend of wing mainly yellow-olive*, not noticeably darker than sides of neck and scapulars as in that species, *greater coverts and secondaries yellow-edged*, and *grey postocular streak* suggests adult head pattern. Bill black; eyes dull brown; feet slate-grey. **VOICE**: A liquid *cuWEERo* and *turereeo-ki*, and a longer *weeka-la-weeoo*, the phrases typically more fluty and prolonged than those of Black-headed Oriole. Alarm note a harsh mewing *mwaaa* or *mwaaarr*. **SIMILAR SPECIES**: Eurasian Golden Oriole compared above. **STATUS AND DISTRIBUTION**: *O. a. notatus* is a non-breeding migrant from the southern tropics, present mainly April–August in woodland, forest edge and well-timbered savanna, locally common in coastal lowlands, including Pemba Island, north to the Tana River and Lamu District; inland, far more common in Tanzania than Kenya, ranging north and west to the Lake Victoria basin and the w. and cent. Kenyan highlands. Nominate *auratus* from the northern tropics is known from the southern slopes of Mt Elgon and the northeastern base of the Cheranganis; sight records from Baringo and Kapedo Districts may be of this form.

EURASIAN GOLDEN ORIOLE *Oriolus o. oriolus* Plate 80

Length 210–230 mm (8.25–9"). **Adult male** bright yellow, with *black wings* (except for yellow spot on primary coverts), *black lores*, and black tail with yellow corners. Bill dark pink; eyes crimson or brick-red; feet dark slate-grey. **Female** yellow-olive above with brighter yellow upper tail-coverts, usually *whitish below with dark brownish streaks*; *wings dark olive-brown, with little or no pale feather edging*; dark 'shoulder' area contrasts with scapulars and sides of neck. Tail blackish with yellow corners. **Older female** has yellow underparts, washed olive on throat and breast, with narrow olive streaks; rather like dull male, but *loral spot olive-grey*. Bill pinkish red; eyes reddish brown; feet grey. **First-winter** bird (both sexes) has brown bill and (usually) yellow-tipped median coverts; fresh primaries with whitish edges and tips. Female resembles whitish-breasted adult, but underparts more heavily streaked with dark brown. Male more yellow on chest and belly, with little streaking; sometimes yellow only on sides, flanks and crissum, otherwise greyish white and streaked like adult female; tail more blackish. **VOICE**: A liquid fluty whistle, *weeka-laweela-weeoo*, or a shorter *weelawoo*; also a harsh *kraa* or *kree-er*, and a *churr* of annoyance or alarm. **SIMILAR SPECIES**: African Golden Oriole has dark eye-streak (black in adult male, olive-grey in other plumages) extending well behind eye, extensive yellow wing edging, and some yellow on sides of tail. **STATUS AND DISTRIBUTION**: A palearctic passage migrant, October–December and again late March to April, in woodland, savanna, riparian forest and wooded gardens. Recorded annually on southward passage in cent. and se. Kenya, much less regularly in n. Tanzania. On return, common to abundant in coastal lowlands from Tanga north, coinciding with April fruiting of introduced neem trees (*Azadirachta*) in Kilifi and Malindi Districts. A few occasionally overwinter in the Tsavo region.

CROWS AND ALLIES, FAMILY CORVIDAE
(World, 118 species; Africa, 15; Kenya, 7; n. Tanzania, 4 [1 introduced])

This family contains the largest of the passerines, mostly conspicuous and highly adaptable birds, often numerous around human habitation, where their raucous nasal calls are a common sound. Our species are all residents, one of them introduced. They are entirely or mainly black-plumaged; some show white, grey or brown. The bill is strong, often heavy, and the nostrils are concealed by forward-directed bristles. The feet are large and strong. The tail varies greatly in length and shape; wings are broad and, in *Corvus*, often used for soaring. Corvids are omnivorous, predatory, scavenging birds, gregarious for much of the year. They build bulky bowl-shaped nests of sticks in trees or on cliff ledges. Eggs typically are blue-green or bluish, splotched and streaked with dark colours, although those of the Cape Rook are buff or salmon-pink with purplish spots. *Corvus* species typically have brown irides and blackish bills and feet; unless distinct, bare-part colours are excluded from the species accounts.

PIAPIAC *Ptilostomus afer* — Plate 80

Length 35 cm (14"). A distinctive, small, blackish corvid with a *long, graduated tail* that soon fades to dull light brown. Wings generally dusky brown, the *primaries lighter brown, almost silvery grey beneath, appearing noticeably paler in flight.* **Adult** body plumage mainly black with faint purplish or bluish gloss; rump and upper tail-coverts dark brown. Eyes *purple or violet,* with an inner ring of reddish brown around the pupil; bill and feet black. **Juvenile** has brown eyes and pink or pinkish-red bill with brown or black tip, this colour persisting for some months in immature birds. **Voice:** Call a shrill piping *pee-ip* repeated in series; also a short rasping *kweer* (Chapin 1954). Alarm note a harsh scolding chatter. **Habits:** Sociable. Where numerous, often in small flocks in the vicinity of *Borassus* palms, in the tops of which it nests in scattered pairs. Feeds on the ground, often with domestic (or wild) mammals, sometimes perching on their backs. Walks and runs as well as hops. Flies with rapid wingbeats. **Similar Species:** Long-tailed *Onychognathus* starlings show much chestnut in primaries, have narrower bills with less strongly curved culmen. **Status and Distribution:** Scarce and local resident (or visitor from Uganda) in w. Kenya; records from Busia, Alupe, Mumias, Maseno and Kisumu, in bushed grassland below 1300 m.

HOUSE CROW *Corvus s. splendens* — Plate 80

Length 33 cm (13"). A slender *black-and-grey* crow with relatively large bill and with fairly long tail extending well beyond wing tips in perched bird. **Adult** with *black forecrown, face and throat* (to central breast). Nape, neck and lower breast dull buffy grey, shading to sooty grey on the belly. Crown glossed with purplish; back greenish black; wings and tail black, well glossed with green, blue and purple. **Juvenile** duller, more brownish black and paler grey, than adult. **Voice:** *kwaa, kwaa,* more nasal and higher-pitched than call of Pied Crow. **Habits:** A scavenger near towns and villages, bold but wary. Gregarious. Forages on the ground, and forms large roosts in trees. Harasses and kills small birds; very destructive to eggs and nestlings. **Status and Distribution:** An introduced and increasing coastal resident which in places has displaced the Pied Crow. Introduced to Zanzibar last century, soon spreading to Dar es Salaam, Tanga, Pemba Island and Mombasa, where first noted in 1947. Now abundant and ubiquitous on Mombasa Island, and spreading on adjacent mainland south to Diani, north to Malindi (where common by late 1980s), and inland to Mackinnon Road. Control measures initiated in early 1990s.

BROWN-NECKED or DWARF RAVEN *Corvus (ruficollis) edithae* — Plate 80

Length 46 cm (18"). An all-dark corvid of *arid northern Kenya.* 'Desert Crow' would be a better name. Size, proportions and voice like those of Pied Crow (with which it has interbred). *At rest, wing tips extend to tip of moderately long wedge-shaped tail.* Bill rather long and slim, but less extreme than in Cape Rook. **Adult** *sometimes dark brown on head;* upper back bronze-glossed; rest of upperparts, wings and tail black, with faint bluish or purplish-blue sheen. *Concealed bases of lanceolate throat feathers and those of nape and breast snow-white, evident in display or when feathers disarranged by wind.* **Juvenile** light brown (sometimes almost rufous) on head, underparts and upper back; basal portions of neck and breast feathers whitish, not pure white. **Voice:** A nasal croaking, *kwaar-kwaar-kwaar,* recalling Pied Crow; this varied to *waaa* or *yaaa.* Other calls include a short metallic *onk, wonk* or *kwonk,* a double *rrawnk-rrawnk,* a guttural rattle or purr, and a flat *yack, yack,* like similar call of Pied Crow. **Habits:** Usually in pairs or small groups; at times with Cape Rooks. Feeds on the ground. A fearless scavenger, attracted to villages and camps. Nests in acacia trees, sometimes in small loose colonies. **Similar Species:** Fan-tailed Raven has broader wings, very short tail, and thicker bill. Cape Rook is slender-billed with lax neck feathers and more rounded tail. **Status and**

DISTRIBUTION: Locally common on arid plains and in semi-deserts throughout n. Kenya, ranging south to Kapedo, Laisamis, Mado Gashi and Wajir. **NOTE**: Our bird possibly not conspecific with extralimital *C. ruficollis*, compared with which *edithae* is somewhat smaller, and differs in more consistently white (instead of sometimes dusky) neck-feather bases, shorter primary extension, shorter and more slender bill, tree-nesting (instead of generally cliff-nesting) habits, and in at least some vocalizations.

PIED CROW *Corvus albus* Plate 80

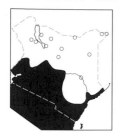

Length 46 cm (18″). Easily identified by *white breast and belly continuous with broad white collar across hindneck*; **adult** plumage otherwise glossy black. **Juvenile** similar but duller, the white feathers dusky-tipped. **VOICE**: Commonly a harsh, rather nasal *kwah* or *kwar, kwar*, more rasping in alarm. Various other sounds include a snoring *khrrrr*, a hard hollow *clock, clock . . .*, a nasal *whawnk* or *aahnk*, a flat *ack-ack* and a throaty *glupp*, some of these given with raised head and exaggerated movements of wings and tail. Displaying bird gives a low creaky growl, *urrrrrkkk*, answered quickly by mate's higher clicking *tkkk*; these sounds accompany deep bowing, with fluffed head feathers, partially spread wings and the bill pointing straight down. **HABITS**: Usually in pairs or small flocks, although large numbers roost together or soar on rising thermals. Flicks wings on alighting. Nests in trees. Allopreening regular between mated birds. **SIMILAR SPECIES**: White-naped Raven is larger, with much heavier bill, proportionately shorter tail; white confined to hindneck in adult, but young bird may show narrow whitish breast band. **STATUS AND DISTRIBUTION**: Fairly common and widespread in open country at up to 3000 m, including grassland, cultivation, riparian woods and lakeshores. Present in all urban areas; in arid n. Kenya largely confined to towns and villages, where sympatric with Brown-necked Raven.

WHITE-NAPED RAVEN *Corvus albicollis* Plate 80
(White-necked Raven)

Length 56 cm (22″). A large corvid with *very deep, ivory-tipped black bill*, and *broad white collar on hindneck*. Head and neck bronzy brown, the face black. Foreparts otherwise mainly blackish brown, with slight purplish gloss. Remainder of plumage black with faint bluish-green sheen, becoming browner with wear. Wings broad, tail quite short. **Juvenile** duller than adult, with some black streaks on the white nape; scattered white-edged or completely white feathers on neck and breast of some birds. **VOICE**: Common calls include a curiously high-pitched, almost falsetto croak, typically repeated: *krerk krerk krerk. . .*; also a short guttural *wuk* or *raak*, and a soft husky *haa*. A short, somewhat metallic clattering *cluk-cluk-cluk* is given with head bowed in presence of presumed mate. **HABITS**: Usually solitary or in pairs, sometimes in small flocks. Nests and roosts on cliffs, foraging over adjacent country and scavenging around camps and settlements or in towns, where frequently tame. Preys extensively on large insects and rodents. Indulges in aerial play, much as other raven species. **SIMILAR SPECIES**: Pied Crow has white breast and belly, smaller bill. **STATUS AND DISTRIBUTION**: Locally common near mountains, scarps and rocky hills from as low as 400 m in e. Kenya (Voi) to above 4000 m on the higher mountains. In n. Tanzania, ranges from Serengeti NP to Mt Meru, Kilimanjaro and the Usambaras, and north in Kenya to the Taita and Chyulu Hills, most scarps in the Rift and Kerio Valleys, Mt Elgon, the Cheranganis, Maralal, the Mathews Range, Mt Nyiru and the Ndotos. Absent from coastal lowlands and the Lake Victoria basin. Sympatric with Fan-tailed Raven in areas north of the Equator.

FAN-TAILED RAVEN *Corvus rhipidurus* Plate 80

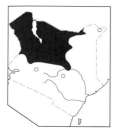

Length 46 cm (18″). A stocky, all-black corvid with an *extremely short tail* and broad wings, providing unique flight silhouette; wing tips extend well beyond tail when perched. Bill heavy. **Adult** plumage shows bronze or blue gloss at close range. **Juvenile** duller and browner. **VOICE**: Varied calls include a guttural *waak*, a high, Pied Crow-like *kwaa-kwaa*, a longer growling *errrraak* or *errrrow* repeated numerous times, a high hollow *WOK*, and a louder, more nasal *YAHNK* or *WHONK*, separate or in series. Some of these and other notes are combined in extended 'songs'. **HABITS**: Pairs or small flocks inhabit broken country, nesting on cliffs. Scavenges near settlements alongside other corvids; usually feeds on the ground. Often soars on thermals and indulges in extensive aerial play. **SIMILAR SPECIES**: Brown-necked Raven has considerably longer tail. **STATUS AND DISTRIBUTION**: Locally common around rocky hillsides and cliffs in arid northern Kenya, mainly below 1500 m. Ranges south to Mt Elgon, the Kerio Valley, and Nakuru, Isiolo, and n. Kitui Districts.

CAPE ROOK *Corvus capensis*
(Black Crow)

Plate 80

Length 43 cm (17"). A lightly built black crow with a *slender bill*. **Adult** plumage mainly black, with purplish and steel-blue gloss. Throat feathers lax, often raised to some degree; head blackish brown with slight gloss, this purplish coppery on crown and nape. Bases of neck feathers dark grey. **Juvenile** browner throughout (as are worn adults). **Voice:** Typically a loud harsh *RRRAK-Raaah* or *Rrraak-aawah*, the second note higher. A liquid *kwer-kaplop* or *gur-lalop* given in display and at other times, in flight or perched, with head and throat feathers erected. Bowing call a low gurgling *gwurrr* followed by a sharp *tik*. Also a guttural cackle. **Habits:** Usually in small groups, sometimes large flocks, foraging in fields and grasslands. Perches on fenceposts, poles and trees. Often bows and puffs out feathers of head and neck as it calls (see above). Nests in trees and shrubs. **Similar Species:** Brown-necked Raven (sympatric in n. Kenya) has much heavier bill. **Status and Distribution:** Locally common on open plains, on farmland and (in n. Kenya) in semi-deserts. Widespread between 1350 and 2500 m in the Kenyan highlands (especially cent. Rift Valley). Small populations in arid n. Kenya from the Lake Turkana basin east to Turbi and Moyale. In n. Tanzania, known only from the eastern Serengeti Plains, Ngorongoro and around Monduli.

STARLINGS AND OXPECKERS, FAMILY STURNIDAE
(World, 110 species; Africa, 48; Kenya, 26; n. Tanzania, 20)

The true starlings (Subfamily Sturninae) are medium-sized, sturdy birds with strong feet and bills. Many are dark or brightly plumaged. In the glossy starlings (*Lamprotornis*) and some others, iridescence is intense, with satiny greens, blues and purples. The sexes may be alike, or the females duller or distinctively patterned. Long graduated tails characterize *Cosmopsarus* and most *Onychognathus*. Forest starlings (e.g. *Cinnyricinclus* and *Poeoptera*) are arboreal, whereas open-country species are as much at home on the ground, where (except for the chestnut-winged starlings) they walk rather than hop. All are omnivorous and, although they can damage citrus fruit, they are great destroyers of insects. None has a really accomplished song, but most utter a variety of whistled, chattering, twittering and squeaking notes. Many are gregarious when not breeding. A few species build domed nests in thorn trees, or a cup of mud and plant material, but the majority nest in tree cavities, rock crevices, and sometimes in buildings. The two to four eggs are usually bluish green, spotted with brown. Incubation is mainly by the female, but both sexes care for the young.

The two oxpeckers (Subfamily Buphaginae) are aberrant starlings endemic to Africa. They accompany large game mammals and livestock in search of ticks.

KENRICK'S STARLING *Poeoptera kenricki*

Plate 79

Length 185–190 mm (7.5"). A slender, *grey-eyed* species of *montane forests* in e. Kenya and ne. Tanzania. **Adult male** glossy black, resembling western Stuhlmann's Starling, but with slight *bronzy* (not blue) gloss; wings and tail dull blackish; no chestnut in the wings. *Eyes slate-grey*; bill and feet black. **Female** slate-grey below and on head, slightly glossy bronzy black on back, wings and tail. *Inner webs of primaries chestnut*, broadly edged and tipped black, obvious only in flight. Bare parts as in male. **Juvenile** duller, sooty grey below; primaries black in male, largely chestnut in female. **Voice:** Call note a loud, monotonous and repetitive *pleep, pleep*. Flocks produce a musical babbling. **Habits:** Gregarious, arboreal and largely confined to forest canopy. Often in mixed flocks with Waller's Starling in fruiting trees. Nests in tree cavities. **Similar Species:** Sympatric Waller's Starling is larger, heavier and broader-tailed. Allopatric Stuhlmann's Starling is blue-black. **Status and Distribution:** The race *bensoni* is a local resident between 1500 and 2500 m in forest on Mt Kenya and in the nearby Meru Forest and Nyambeni Hills. The smaller nominate race is Tanzanian, in Arusha NP, on Mt Meru, Kilimanjaro, and the Pare and Usambara Mountains. Some cold-season movement to as low as 450 m in the East Usambaras.

STUHLMANN'S STARLING *Poeoptera stuhlmanni*

Plate 79

Length 175–180 mm (7"). A slender, *western Kenyan* forest species. **Adult male** *glossy blue-black* on head and underparts, dull brownish black on back, wings and tail; no chestnut in wings. *Eyes brown, the iris with a yellow peripheral ring*; bill and feet black. **Female** *dark grey with faint bluish gloss*; primaries chestnut, with outer edges and tips dark. Eyes brown. **Juvenile** duller, sooty black below; both sexes with chestnut in wings, this lost by male on moulting into adult plumage. **Voice:** From perched birds, songs of clear slurred whistles such as *creep-creep turreep-chlerreep-tleeoo* and *TREEoup, turEEP twilieu, sureep-treep-creep-keew*, or a higher, thinner song, *wiku-swee tuk-see seet-seet treeeee*. Shorter is a loud squealing *werk-REEK* or *tcherp-cherEEP*, or *wee-YEW*, the double note repeated several times after long pauses. Trilling flight call somewhat resembles that of Eurasian Bee-eater. **Habits:** Gregarious; flocks wander extensively in search of fruiting trees, flying high and often perching in

dead emergent treetops above canopy. Quite vocal. **SIMILAR SPECIES**: Kenrick's Starling is eastern, the male bronzy black with grey eyes, female with greenish-bronze gloss. Waller's Starling is larger, stockier and broader-tailed. **STATUS AND DISTRIBUTION**: Locally and irregularly common between 1500 and 2600 m in highland forests of w. Kenya in Nandi, Kakamega, Kericho, Eldama Ravine and Kabarnet Districts. One sight record from Mt Elgon (July 1971).

WALLER'S STARLING *Onychognathus walleri* Plate 79

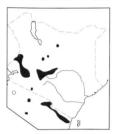

Length 225–230 mm (9"). A dark *highland-forest* starling, both sexes with *black-tipped chestnut primaries. Tail shorter* than in other chestnut-winged starlings and *only slightly graduated*. **Adult male** glossy black with violet sheen (more greenish blue on head). **Female** *O. w. walleri* duller and less glossy than male; head and throat dark grey, the nape and hindcrown densely to almost solidly streaked with shiny greenish blue-black; similar streaks on lower throat merge with faintly glossed breast. *O. w. elgonensis* grey only on chin and throat, with some glossy blue streaks. Eyes red and bill and feet black in both sexes. **Juvenile** dull black. **VOICE**: Common calls are a repeated clear two or three-note whistle: *cheer-whew* and a repetitious *tee, pew-pew* or *pee tee-tee*, the stressed first note higher-pitched. Longer song is a series of high slurred whistles, *weer-tew t'wee* or *wee-turr-tree-wureet*. Call notes include *errack, yak yak* and a low *werk*.

HABITS: Feeds on fruits of forest trees. Males call from canopy or emergent trees. Forms large noisy flocks outside breeding season, sometimes joining other starlings. **SIMILAR SPECIES**: Female Kenrick's Starling, sympatric with Waller's in places, is smaller, slimmer and longer-tailed. Slender-billed Starling is larger, with still longer, more steeply graduated tail. **STATUS AND DISTRIBUTION**: *O. w. elgonensis* is local *west* of the Rift Valley, from Mt Elgon and Saiwa NP south to the Mau, Trans-Mara and Nguruman Forests; in n. Tanzania, known only from a flock near the Grumeti River, w. Serengeti NP (July 1967), locally in the Crater Highlands and the Nou Forest in the Mbulu Highlands. *O. w. walleri* is locally common between 1600 and 3000 m in forests *east* of the Rift, from the Karissia Hills near Maralal, Marsabit and the Mathews Range south to the Aberdares, Mt Kenya, Meru Forest and the Nyambenis; in n. Tanzania on Mt Meru and Kilimanjaro, Arusha NP, and the Pare and Usambara Mountains, with some movement to lower elevations (300 m) in the East Usambaras.

RED-WINGED STARLING *Onychognathus morio* Plate 79

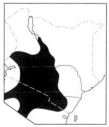

Length 280–310 mm (11–12"). Commonest of the chestnut-winged starlings; a robust dark bird with a long pointed tail. **Adult male** *glossy black* with slight violet-blue gloss, *primaries rich chestnut* with dark tips. **Female** has head and neck grey with narrow glossy violet streaks, these broadening on upper breast. Eyes brown or reddish brown; bill and feet black. **Juvenile** sooty black with slight gloss; primaries as in adult. Mt Elgon birds (sometimes separated as the race *montanus*) are more slender-billed. **VOICE**: When perched, various drawn-out loud, melodious oriole-like whistles: *tu-whee, peeeo, pee-teeeo, p'tew*, or a simple soft *tew*. Song a series of these whistles: *tuwhee tuwer teweedle tuwurtelee turdilee . . ..* In flight, utters a high-pitched twittering. **HABITS**: Forages in pairs or small groups in open country, far from its breeding sites on rock outcrops and urban buildings. Avoids heavy forest. Flies rapidly, calling repeatedly.

SIMILAR SPECIES: Bristle-crowned Starling is more slender, with a much longer tail. Slender-billed Starling typically associated with montane forests and waterfalls, has longer, more graduated tail and much narrower bill; male glossed green on head, female with grey-tipped body feathers. Waller's Starling has short tail, smaller bill. **STATUS AND DISTRIBUTION**: Widespread in cities, rocky hills and gorges from 1000 to 2400 m (600 m near Voi, and to 3000 m on Mt Elgon). Common around Rift Valley scarps, ranging north to the Ndotos and Mt Kulal. In n. Tanzania, locally around kopjes in Serengeti NP and from the Crater and Mbulu Highlands, and Lake Manyara and Tarangire NPs east to Arusha and Moshi Districts, the Pare Mts and Mkomazi GR. Scarce in Usambara foothills.

SLENDER-BILLED STARLING *Onychognathus tenuirostris theresae* Plate 79
(Slender-billed Chestnut-winged Starling)

Length 295–330 mm (11.5–13"). A chestnut-winged starling of *high elevations*. Resembles the preceding species, but *tail much longer* (7–7.5") and more graduated and bill more slender. **Adult male** black with green-glossed head, the feathers black-tipped; back and rump tinged violet; throat glossy blue, darkening to violet on belly. Eyes brown (sometimes narrowly red peripherally); bill and feet black. **Female** duller blue-black, many head and body feathers tipped with dull buff and grey. **Juvenile** uniformly dull black. **VOICE**: Common call note a clear *teeo*. Song a prolonged series of soft and semi-harsh notes mixed with short whistles and other sounds, many of the notes

repeated: *quek-quek-quek-quek*, *tchuEK-tchuEK-tchuEK*, *seeWEEowee*, *cur-cur-cur-cur-cur-SWEEo-sqeeik*. . .. Sings in chorus. **HABITS:** Nests and roosts, sometimes colonially, behind waterfalls. Nest a cup of mud, grasses and moss on ledge or in crevice. Noisy flocks congregate at water and in fruiting trees. Extracts snails from giant lobelias. **SIMILAR SPECIES:** Red-winged Starling, rarely above 2400 m except on Mt Elgon, has heavier and larger bill. Bristle-crowned Starling has much longer, narrower tail and velvety cushion on forecrown. **STATUS AND DISTRIBUTION:** Locally common in cent. Kenyan highlands, at 2400–4500 m, typically in or near forests, but forages on alpine moorlands and in open country at lower elevations. In Kenya, most numerous on Mt Kenya and the Aberdares; small resident populations behind Thomson's Falls at Nyahururu and at smaller waterfalls on the Mau, Elgeyu and Kongelai Escarpments. Reports from Mt Elgon require confirmation. Some northern birds said to be intermediate between *theresae* and the nominate Ethiopian race. In n. Tanzania, one record from the West Usambaras (Aug. 1978); otherwise only in highlands south of our area.

BRISTLE-CROWNED STARLING *Onychognathus salvadorii* Plate 79

Length 395–420 mm (15.5–16.5"). A *very long-tailed*, chestnut-winged starling with prominent *'cushion' of erect velvety black feathers on forecrown.* **Adult** plumage generally black, with violet gloss on head, bluish reflections on body and greenish tinge to tail; chestnut primaries have black tips. Eyes ruby-red; bill and feet black. Sexes similar; **female** has greyer head, smaller 'cushion.' **Juvenile** much duller, with faint gloss. **VOICE:** Characteristic staccato whistles, *suk-SWEEK* or *su-WEER*, and a high two-syllabled whistling *chreep-rr* often given in flight. Annoyance call a harsh scolding *schwaah*. **HABITS:** Similar to those of Red-winged Starling. Arboreal, but comes to ground to feed on fallen fruits. Flocks wander far to fruiting trees. Nests in holes in trees or cliffs. **SIMILAR SPECIES:** Other chestnut-winged starlings are smaller, with less extreme tail and no crown cushion. **STATUS AND DISTRIBUTION:** Locally common below 1300 m around cliffs and rocky gorges in dry bush country, from Baringo and Isiolo Districts north to Sudanese and Ethiopian border areas.

BLACK-BELLIED STARLING *Lamprotornis corruscus* Plate 77
(Black-breasted Starling)

Length 185–195 mm (c. 7.5"). A glossy black starling, metallic blue-green on head, upper breast, wings and back; ear-coverts, shoulders, rump and tail glossed with violet; *no black spots on wing-coverts;* lower breast bluish purple; *belly and crissum black* (with faint bronze or purple sheen) in male, dark sooty in female. Eyes golden yellow; bill and feet black. *L. c. vaughani* (Pemba Island) has violet instead of blue-green crown. **Juvenile** duller, less glossy, sooty black below with little iridescence. **VOICE:** Single bird gives a varied song, including squawks, trills, warbling and fluty whistles; sometimes a short phrase, *tcherk WHEEO* or *tchuk WEEO WEEO*, repeated many times. Groups and flocks produce a continuous babbling chorus, often including imitations of other bird species. Voice of slightly larger inland race *jombeni* may differ somewhat from that of coastal *mandanus*. **HABITS:** Arboreal. Noisy flocks travel widely, seeking fruiting trees. Sometimes in pairs. Nests in tree cavities. **SIMILAR SPECIES:** Most glossy starlings are larger. Lesser Blue-eared has violet-purple belly and black spots on wing-coverts. Immature Blue-eared Starling, also black-bellied, is longer-tailed, dark-eyed, and mainly a ground feeder. **STATUS AND DISTRIBUTION:** *L. c. mandanus* is locally common in coastal lowland forests, mangroves and bush north to the Boni Forest, inland along the Tana River to Garissa and Kora NR, in Shimba Hills NP and up to 1000 m in the East Usambaras. *L. c. jombeni* is uncommon from 1500 to over 2000 m in the Meru and Nyambeni Forests northeast of Mt Kenya. Presumed wanderers recorded in Samburu GR, Meru NP, Kibwezi and southern slopes of Kilimanjaro not assigned racially. *L. c. vaughani* is restricted to Pemba Island.

SPLENDID STARLING *Lamprotornis s. splendidus* Plate 77
(Splendid Glossy Starling)

Length 240–280 mm (9.5–11"). Well named. A *large, broad-tailed, brilliantly iridescent* starling, in flight producing *loud swishing sound with wings.* **Adult male** metallic golden green above, with lower back, scapulars and rump glossed blue; upper tail-coverts greenish blue; *small metallic coppery patch on side of neck; velvety-black band across wing,* below the lower row of black covert spots; *throat and breast mainly brilliant metallic violet,* with brassy or coppery reflections on lower breast; belly and crissum metallic blue. Eyes pale creamy yellow; bill and feet black. **Female** smaller, *bluer below* with reduced brassy/coppery iridescence. **Juvenile** duller, blackish brown (female) or blue-black (male) below with no brassy sheen. **VOICE:** Distinctive nasal, metallic and grating notes such as *nya-au, spi-yonk, kahn* and *kua-kuonk* mixed with whistles, in various combinations. **HABITS:** Mostly arboreal. Shy and elusive. In non-breeding season forms flocks and is distinctly migratory. Nests in tree cavities. **SIMILAR SPECIES:** Purple Starling is smaller with large, bright yellow eyes and purple belly. Blue-eared

Starling is more blue and green, with bright orange-yellow eyes. **Status and Distribution**: Western. Scarce and local in riverine or gallery forest. Has drastically declined in Kenya in wake of extensive deforestation; now in only small numbers in Mt Elgon and Saiwa NPs, October–May; apparently absent June–September. Tanzanian birds (Lake Victoria basin, including Ukerewe Island) perhaps referable to the race *bailundensis*.

PURPLE STARLING *Lamprotornis purpureus amethystinus*   Plate 77
(Purple Glossy Starling)

Length *c.* 260 mm (10.5"). A large western glossy starling with *rich metallic purple head and underparts*. Appears *longer-billed, longer-necked and shorter-tailed than its relatives*. **Adult** glossy green on back and wings, shading to blue on rump and tail. *Bright yellow eyes appear unusually large* (edge of the sclerotic coat, as well as the irides, yellow); bill and feet black. Sexes alike. **Juvenile** iridescent but duller than adult: head, rump and tail blue or violet, mantle golden green or blue; underparts black with violet sheen. **Voice**: A variety of squeaky whistles and chattering calls, sometimes in chorus. **Habits**: Solitary or in small groups. Feeds in fruiting trees or on ground, often alongside Blue-eared Starling. Nests in tree cavities. **Similar Species**: Blue-eared Starling is more blue and green, less purple, and has longer tail. Splendid Starling is larger, broad-tailed, with pale creamy-yellow eyes and noisy flight. **Status and Distribution**: In w. Kenya, an uncommon and local resident in cultivation and other open habitats from Maseno, Akala and Ng'iya west to Ukwala and Busia and north to the slopes of Mt Elgon, Saiwa NP and Kapenguria. Formerly more widespread.

BLUE-EARED STARLING *Lamprotornis chalybaeus*   Plate 77
(Blue-eared Glossy Starling; Greater Blue-eared Starling)

Length of *L. c. cyaniventris* 230–240 mm (9–9.5"), of *L. c. sycobius* 215–235 mm (8.5–9.25"). A brilliantly glossy blue or blue-green starling with dark purplish-blue ear-coverts (often appearing black). Size and colour vary racially. **Adult** *L. c. cyaniventris* is dark metallic green, with blue sheen on head and back, metallic blue rump and upper tail-coverts and greenish-blue tail; lower breast shining blue-green, becoming blue-violet on belly; two rows (only one may show) of black spots on wing-coverts. *Eyes orange-yellow*; bill and feet black. Sexes alike. Smaller *L. c. sycobius* is brighter, *much greener* on head and neck, with well-developed (but normally concealed) bright violet patch near bend of wing, and a sharply defined dark purplish-blue ear-covert patch, *bright magenta-violet on flanks and belly; easily mistaken for Lesser Blue-eared Starling*, but note tail length, narrower ear-covert patch, different voice. **Juvenile** sooty brown, heavily washed with bottle-green or greenish blue, on upperparts; belly dull black; eyes grey-brown. **Voice**: Calls include a nasal, somewhat querulous *chweer* or *chwee-weer*, and a rough *yeeeah* or *wreeeak*. Song a succession of harsh chatterings, high-pitched whistles and nasal or guttural notes: *squeer-weer, tsuck-tsick, cher-rrk-skwiiiiii, squirk . . ..* **Habits**: *L. c. cyaniventris* usually sociable except when breeding, often in large noisy flocks, but *sycobius* often encountered singly or in small numbers. Mainly a ground feeder, but visits fruiting trees; associates with other starlings. Nests in tree cavities. **Similar Species**: Lesser Blue-eared and Bronze-tailed Starlings have shorter tails. Juvenile of southeastern race of Lesser Blue-eared has rufous-brown underparts. Bronze-tailed Starling shows purple/bronze iridescence on tail. **Status and Distribution**: Widespread in open bush, woodland and cultivation, often around towns and villages. *L. c. cyaniventris* is common in the w. and cent. Kenyan highlands north to Mt Elgon and the Mathews Range; also around Moyale; south to Lolgorien, Mara GR, Loliondo and the Crater Highlands above 2000 m. Wanders lower in non-breeding season, to the Lake Victoria basin, northwestern border areas and Lake Turkana. *L. c. sycobius* ranges widely in Tanzania north to Serengeti and Tarangire NPs; also from Arusha and Moshi Districts and Mkomazi GR uncommonly but regularly into s. and se. Kenya, including the coastal lowlands north to Malindi.

LESSER BLUE-EARED STARLING *Lamprotornis chloropterus*   Plate 77
(Lesser Blue-eared Glossy Starling)

Length 180–200 mm (7–8"). **Adults** distinguished from widespread Blue-eared Starling by *shorter tail, greener* iridescence and *narrower dark ear-covert patch; show little or no blue or purple, except on rump and belly*. Eyes orange-yellow; bill and feet black. (*Caution*: in se. and coastal Kenya, race *sycobius* of Blue-eared is frequently mistaken for Lesser Blue-eared.) **Juvenile** has green gloss on back and wings, dark brownish head and dull brown or brownish grey underparts, these rufous-brown in Tanzanian race *elisabeth*. **Voice**: Perched birds give a rising *cherwee* and other short calls, *chirrriree-ree* and *we-wuREET* or *quur-urri*. Song a succession of short squeaks,

squawks and throaty whistles, higher-pitched than those of Blue-eared Starling, and with fewer guttural sounds. In flight, a clear *wirri-wirri* or *wi-WIri*. **HABITS:** Similar to those of Blue-eared Starling. **SIMILAR SPECIES:** Blue-eared Starling compared above. Bronze-tailed Starling is bluer (less green) above, with purple lower breast and belly; tail purple or bronze. **STATUS AND DISTRIBUTION:** In w. Kenya, *L. c. chloropterus* is locally common in bush and wooded habitats on the Kongelai Escarpment and wanderers have been recorded northeast to South Horr. Sight records from Baringo and Isiolo Districts and Ol Doinyo Sapuk are unsubstantiated, but may refer to *L. chalybaeus sycobius*. *L. chloropterus elisabeth* is a miombo-woodland bird in interior Tanzania, but there are records of wanderers (early in 20th century) north to Tanga, Vanga, Mombasa and edge of the Arabuko–Sokoke Forest near Malindi.

BRONZE-TAILED STARLING *Lamprotornis chalcurus emini*   Plate 77
(Bronze-tailed Glossy Starling)

Length 195–230 mm (8–9"). A northwestern glossy starling resembling Blue-eared, but **adult** smaller than sympatric race of that species, bluer above and *rich purple on belly*. Rather short iridescent *tail usually appears purple* (bluer at sides and tip), but shows bronze or bronzy-purple reflections at some angles, especially when bird flies against the light; *upper tail-coverts and rump purplish blue to bronzy purple, contrasting with blue-green back.* Eyes deep yellow or orange; bill and feet black. **Juvenile** blackish with blue tinge above; otherwise dull sooty black, with greenish-blue sheen on breast; tail greenish blue; eyes presumably brown. **VOICE:** Loud nasal and throaty chattering like that of Blue-eared Starling, but somewhat harsher. **HABITS:** Feeds on the ground, often with Blue-eared Starling. Wings make considerable noise in flight, like those of Splendid Starling. **SIMILAR SPECIES:** The two blue-eared starlings have greenish-blue tails, that of *L. chalybaeus* quite long (rump of that species may appear purplish). Purple Starling has blue rump and tail, much purple on head and breast. **STATUS AND DISTRIBUTION:** Uncommon local resident of dry bush and bushed grassland in nw. Kenya, with small populations around Lokichokio, Kapenguria and parts of the Kerio Valley. Formerly at Kitale and Kakamega.

RÜPPELL'S LONG-TAILED STARLING *Lamprotornis purpuropterus*   Plate 77
(Rüppell's Long-tailed Glossy Starling)

Length 270–315 mm (10.5–12.5"). A dark glossy starling with *long (6-inch), graduated purple or bronzy tail* and *creamy- white eyes*. Plumage generally *blue-black with violet and purple reflections*; belly and under tail-coverts black; *no spots on wing-coverts*. Sexes similar (female slightly smaller). Bill and feet black. **Juvenile** duller, with shorter tail; head sooty with some violet gloss; underparts dull black, except for some metallic blue on breast. Eyes dark. **VOICE:** Commonly uttered call *kewo KWEERR KWEWEERR*. Song a great variety of rolling whistles, high squeaks, harsh grating sounds, nasal metallic notes and short warbles, each note or phrase distinct but part of a complex prolonged utterance, neither musical nor unpleasant: *chawaaa chwaa chuweeer-rrrrrrooo, wha-cheeer chiWEEEK, whaaaah, kwa-kwa QUEEEEEEEERRRR, tsuck-wiiiiiii-iiiiiiiii, tsickWEEEEEO, whu-CHIIIII.* **HABITS:** Feeds on the ground in pairs or small groups, often with other starlings. Sings from shaded perch for extended periods during heat of day. Nests in tree cavity or abandoned nest of other species. **SIMILAR SPECIES:** Splendid Starling is also pale-eyed, but much stockier, with broad tail and more greenish iridescence. Purple Starling is shorter-tailed, iridescent green on back, with large bright yellow eyes. **STATUS AND DISTRIBUTION:** Widespread in open or lightly wooded country, often around villages and in cultivation. Common in and *west* of the Rift Valley, from Lokichokio and s. Turkana District to Trans-Nzoia and the Lake Victoria basin, Mara GR, Serengeti NP, Loliondo and Olduvai. *East* of the Rift Valley generally uncommon and local around the Athi, Galana, Tiva and Tana Rivers; also locally on the Laikipia Plateau and from Meru NP south to Tsavo, and in coastal lowlands from Garsen to the Boni Forest.

HILDEBRANDT'S STARLING *Lamprotornis hildebrandti*   Plate 77

Length 190–200 mm (7.5–8"). A *rufous-bellied* starling with *no white breast band*. **Adult** iridescent *dark violet-blue on upperparts*, head and breast; greenish wash on wings and hindneck; lower breast pale rufous, darker from belly to under tail-coverts. *Eyes red;* bill and feet black. **Juvenile** duller, with shiny *blue-green wings, bluer on back, rump and tail.* Head at first brown, with some rufous on face; underparts generally dull rufous, the upper breast browner, lower breast obscurely spotted. Eyes brown. Some (older?) individuals blackish from crown to malar region. **VOICE:** Song of harsh creaky notes interspersed with whistles, slowly uttered, with many elements separated by distinct pauses: (1) *cherraah-cherrah, squirk, kwerra-kwerra, eeeeek querk. . .*, (2) *errraaa-errraaa, turlewp, queeleree, cherrrah, eeeep. . .*, the clearer notes much higher-pitched than the others. Lower-pitched are a guttural subsong, *kwa-aa kw-kweeo, kwer-kwee-er*, and a frequently repeated *chiweh-chiweh-chiweh.* **HABITS:** A ground feeder, in pairs or family groups, often with Superb Starlings. Less confiding than that species.

Nests in tree cavities. **SIMILAR SPECIES**: Adult Superb Starling has white breast band and under tail-coverts, creamy-white eyes; juvenile is dull black on breast, lacks well-defined breast band and is brown-eyed. Shelley's Starling is uniformly dark chestnut below, breast no paler than belly; has orange eyes. **STATUS AND DISTRIBUTION**: Locally common resident of bush country between 700 and 1700 m. In Kenya from Maralal and the Laikipia Plateau, east to Isiolo District and Meru NP, south from the upper Tana River, Thika and Nairobi NP to Sultan Hamud and Kibwezi Districts, the Tsavo and Amboseli NPs, Loita Plains and Mara GR. Ranges across n. Tanzania from Serengeti NP and Maswa GR east to Lake Manyara and Tarangire NPs, Masailand and Mkomazi GR.

SHELLEY'S STARLING *Lamprotornis shelleyi*   **Plate 77**

Length 180–190 mm (7–7.5"). A dark glossy starling of open bush country. Sexes alike. **Adult** recalls Hildebrandt's Starling, but differs in its *deep chestnut belly;* upperparts and breast rich violet-blue; wings more greenish; ear-coverts violet. Eyes orange; bill and feet black. **Juvenile** differs from young Hildebrandt's in its greyer-brown head and back, the latter without gloss; in the hand, separated by smaller bill, shorter outermost primary and greyish (not blackish) undersides of flight feathers. **VOICE**: A strident call, likened to those of Superb Starling and White-browed Sparrow-Weaver (Benson 1946). **HABITS**: Individuals or small groups commonly perch in tops of *Commiphora* trees; sometimes in flocks with Magpie Starlings. Appears to feed less on the ground than Hildebrandt's or Superb Starlings. Not shy, but less bold than those species. **SIMILAR SPECIES**: Hildebrandt's Starling compared above. **STATUS AND DISTRIBUTION**: Scarce and local in *Acacia* and *Commiphora* thorn-scrub in n. and e. Kenya, largely below 1300 m. Northern populations around Lokichokio, Mandera, El Wak and Wajir may be resident all year, but in e. and se. Kenya it is a non-breeding visitor August–March, recorded south to Meru and Tsavo East NPs, Maungu, Mt Kasigau and Taru, also in Tana River District from Garissa south to Karawa, and once to Bamburi near Mombasa (Sept. 1978). Once reported feeding large young near Simba (van Someren 1932), otherwise no Kenyan breeding records.

SUPERB STARLING *Lamprotornis superbus*   **Plate 77**

Length 180–190 mm (7–7.5"). A familiar glossy starling with *rufous-orange belly* and *creamy-white eyes.* **Adults** iridescent blue above, on throat and on breast, greener on wings; head and spots on wing-coverts velvety black. *Lower breast and belly rich rufous-orange,* separated from blue upper breast by a *narrow white band; under tail-coverts and wing-linings white;* bill and feet black. Sexes alike. **Juvenile** has duller iridescence above, head and breast dull black, with little or no suggestion of adult's white band separating dark breast from rufous-orange belly. Eyes brown, soon becoming greyish white. **VOICE**: A sustained loud warbling composed of trilling and chattering notes, often in chorus. Mimics other birds. Subsong when loafing in midday of slower, softer phrases, e.g. *cheeerit tsweee-eur, sweeshi-ee swee-eee, chwee-eu chwee-eu, weeeeeeu* and *whicher-which*, etc., in varying patterns. Alarm call an extended *chii-irrrr*; also in excitement a repeated *whit-chor-chi-vii* (van Someren 1956). When feeding, a rasping *cherrah-cher-rreet.* In flight, a similar screeching trilled call, *cherrah-cherrreek* or *skerrrreeee-cherrrrroo-tcherreeeeeet,* shrill and higher-pitched at end. **HABITS**: Cheeky, noisy, gregarious and often very confiding. Feeds largely on the ground. Spends hot hours resting, preening and singing softly in leafy tree. In alarm or excitement, assumes upright stance. Constructs untidy bulky nest in thorn tree and, if in less well-armed tree, adds extensive barricade of thorny twigs near and around nest. **SIMILAR SPECIES**: Hildebrandt's and Shelley's Starlings have no white on underparts. **STATUS AND DISTRIBUTION**: Common and widespread resident below 2200 m, sometimes higher. Ranges throughout Kenya and n. Tanzania in arid, semi-arid and semi-humid areas, occupying open shrubby or wooded habitats, cultivation and gardens. Absent only from the Lake Victoria basin (except around Ahero and Ruma NP), coastal lowlands south of Ngomeni, and the Usambara Mountains.

GOLDEN-BREASTED STARLING *Cosmopsarus regius*   **Plate 77**

Length 340–355 mm (13.5–14"). A resplendent *long-tailed* starling. Sexes similar. **Adult** highly coloured: iridescent blue above, more purple on wings, with rich coppery red-violet on flight feathers; *head and throat shining satiny green;* ear-coverts blue; *upper breast with semicircular patch of iridescent reddish violet,* rest of *underparts rich golden yellow;* tail slender and strongly graduated, black with bronze or old-gold reflections. Eyes creamy white; bill and feet black. **Juvenile** much duller: head and upperparts brownish, with some iridescent green; sides of head, throat and breast grey-brown; otherwise dull yellow below. Eyes greyish. **VOICE**: In flight, a whistling, chattering *cherrrreeeeeeter-cherrrree.* **HABITS**: Typically in small restless groups, wild and unapproachable, although confiding at some safari lodges, where it may feed with other starlings and buffalo-weavers. Flies rapidly and low. Nests in tree cavities. **STATUS AND DISTRIBUTION**: Fairly common and widespread resident of arid and semi-arid bushed grasslands between 50 and 1200 m, in n. and e. Kenya from Mandera, Moyale and

North Horr south (almost entirely east of the Rift Valley) to Samburu and Shaba GRs, Meru and the Tsavo NPs, and along the Tana River to coastal lowlands north of Malindi. In ne. Tanzania, ranges from Mkomazi GR west to Naberera on the Masai Steppe.

ASHY STARLING *Cosmopsarus unicolor*   Plate 122

Length 280–300 mm (11–12"). A *plain, brownish-grey, long-tailed* starling of dry country in *interior Tanzania*. **Adults** paler, more pure grey, on top of head, ear-coverts and breast, and with faint greenish gloss on wings and tail. Eyes pale yellowish cream, contrast with black lores. Sexes alike. **Juvenile** dull ashy grey, with pale horn-coloured bill and prominent pale eye-ring; eyes darker. **Voice:** Not very vocal. Call a plaintive *kuri-kiwera*, second note higher; song *koora tcheeo chink chink* (Fuggles-Couchman 1984.) **Habits:** Pairs or small flocks perch in low treetops and feed on the ground. **Status and Distribution:** A Tanzanian endemic, locally common in bush, savanna and acacia woodland between 1000 and 1850 m, ranging north to Tarangire NP and Mangola Springs. Formerly in lowlands near Kilimanjaro. Formerly attributed to Kenya on the basis of a specimen taken in 1917 at Lake Jipe, but there is no evidence that it was secured in Kenyan territory.

VIOLET-BACKED STARLING *Cinnyricinclus leucogaster*   Plate 78
(Plum-coloured Starling)

Length 154–172 mm (6–7"). Sexually dimorphic. **Male** *shining metallic violet or plum colour above* (blue or bronze reflections in certain lights, more pinkish when worn) and on throat and breast, with rest of underparts white. Outer tail feathers partly white on outer webs in *C. l. verreauxi*. **Female** and **juvenile** brown above, with pale tawny feather edges; crown and nape rufous-brown with dark streaks; *underparts white, heavily brown-streaked.* Irides of both sexes dark brown, with narrow yellow outer rim. Bill short and black, skin at gape often conspicuously yellow. **Voice:** A series of rapidly delivered metallic squawks and trills, often in chorus. **Habits:** Arboreal and highly gregarious. Undertakes major local movements related to fruiting of trees. Shy and restless, seldom remaining long in one place. Flight fast and direct. **Status and Distribution:** Locally and seasonally common non-breeding visitor in wooded areas, including suburban gardens. *C. l. leucogaster* is a vagrant from the northern tropics, recorded south to Lake Turkana. Widespread *C. l. verreauxi*, from the southern tropics (mainly March–Sept.), is common north to Mt Elgon, Maralal and Meru NP, often in large flocks in coastal lowlands north to Lamu. Sporadic breeding recorded in Saiwa NP, Eldama Ravine, Laikipia, Nairobi and Mara GR, March–September. Some birds present throughout the year.

ABBOTT'S STARLING *Cinnyricinclus femoralis*   Plate 78

Length 165–180 mm (6.5–7"). A little-known *highland-forest* species. **Adult male** glossy *blue-black above and on head, throat and breast; belly and crissum white.* Eyes pale creamy yellow; bill and feet black. **Female** brown on upperparts, head, throat and breast; chin whitish and streaked, belly and crissum buffy white, uniformly streaked with brown. Eyes yellow; bill and feet black. **Juvenile** similar to female, but centre of belly creamy white, with streaking limited to sides and flanks; eyes brown. Presumed immature male streaked below, but grey above and dusky brown on breast, with posterior underparts buffy white with broad dark streaks; eyes yellow. **Voice:** Territorial song short, high-pitched and squeaky, sometimes including 'twangy' metallic elements recalling those of Violet-backed Starling or the 'squeaking-hinge' notes of Dark-backed Weaver; usually short: (1) *skeek seeu wee-seek-useek*, (2) *sklieu sqew-iuwee, tsiueek seeuseet*, (3) *skeek swuiu-weenk seekuweenk*. Often a few widely spaced soft, thin *tseet* or *tsuik* notes separate the louder main song phrases. **Habits:** Gregarious except when breeding; flocks wander widely in search of fruiting trees. Male sings from exposed perches in or near canopy. Nests in tree cavities. **Similar Species:** Sharpe's Starling is entirely pale below. Magpie Starling occupies dry bush country, has white wing patches and red eyes. **Status and Distribution:** Endemic to East Africa. Generally scarce and local in forests between 1800 and 2500 m on Mt Kenya (especially above Naro Moru and Embu), the Aberdares, and (at least formerly) Limuru Escarpment and the Chyulu Hills. In n. Tanzania, known only from Mt Meru and the Ngurdoto Forest in Arusha NP, Kilimanjaro and the North Pare Mountains.

SHARPE'S STARLING *Cinnyricinclus sharpii* Plate 78

Length 155–175 mm (6–7"). A short-billed, bicoloured starling of highland forest. Sexes alike. **Adult** shiny blue-black above, including sides of head, with some violet reflections; *underparts pale buff, with tawny wash on belly, flanks and under tail-coverts*; wing-linings black. *Eyes golden yellow*; bill black, rather broad at base. **Juvenile** duller (more brown) above than adult, with dusky arrowhead-shaped spots on underparts and orange-brown eyes. **VOICE**: High-pitched, squeaky, metallic song is reminiscent of Dark-backed Weaver's: *speenk spee-spee tsink-seresee-see cheenk seekserawn speek-speek-speek-speek* and variations. Call note a sharp *speek, spink* or *cheenk*. **HABITS**: Pairs or small flocks often rest on bare emergent branches above forest canopy or in isolated trees in clearings. Subject to local movements in response to fruiting of trees. Nests in tree cavities. **SIMILAR SPECIES**: Adult male Abbott's Starling has dark throat and breast. Female Violet-backed Starling slightly resembles juvenile Sharpe's. **STATUS AND DISTRIBUTION**: Uncommon local resident and wanderer between 1400 and 3000 m, from Mt Elgon, Cheranganis, Mt Marsabit and the Mathews Range, south to the Tugen Hills, the Nandi, Kakamega, Mau, Trans-Mara and Lolgorien Forests, Olololoo escarpment, nw. Mara GR, the Aberdares, Mt Kenya, and Meru Forest. Also recorded from Ol Doinyo Sapuk (near Thika), Nairobi, and the Nguruman, Namanga, Chyulu and Taita Hills. In n. Tanzania, a common resident in Arusha NP, on Mt Meru, Kilimanjaro and the North Pare Mts; elsewhere known only from two records in the West Usambaras (Oct. 1931 and March 1979).

FISCHER'S STARLING *Spreo fischeri* Plate 78

Length 175–190 mm (7–7.5"). An *ashy-grey and white* starling of dry country. Sexes alike. **Adult** pale brownish grey above with faint greenish-blue gloss; *head pale grey, shading to dark brownish grey on breast*; belly white; dark grey patch on sides. *White eyes* contrast with black lores and small black subocular area; bill and feet black. **Juvenile** browner on back, with tawny-rufous feather edges. *Bill yellow below; eyes brown.* **VOICE**: A sequence of rather high strident trills and short notes, e.g. *prrrreeeo-prrrreee, squirrreee-squew sri-sri-sri-sri-shiaaa skew. . .* Flocks indulge in prolonged chattering. **HABITS**: Usually in small flocks. Feeds largely on the ground, often with other starlings or buffalo-weavers. **SIMILAR SPECIES**: Wattled Starling lacks pale grey head, shows conspicuous whitish rump patch in flight, has brown eyes. **STATUS AND DISTRIBUTION**: Locally common resident of dry open bush below 1400 m in n. and e. Kenya, from Moyale, Mandera and South Horr south through the eastern lowlands to Namanga, Amboseli and the Tsavo NPs, the lower Tana River and lowlands around Garsen and Ijara. In ne. Tanzania, ranges from the Mkomazi GR, lowlands southeast of Kilimanjaro and the Masai Steppe west to Tarangire NP; also in lowlands around Longido.

WHITE-CROWNED STARLING *Spreo albicapillus* Plate 78

Length 260–280 mm (10–11"). A unique *large northern* starling with *white-streaked brown underparts, whitish crown and long buffy-white patch in secondaries*; wing-linings, belly and under tail-coverts also white (often earth-stained). Sexes alike or similar. **Adults** shiny olive-green above, shading to greenish blue on wings, upper tail-coverts and tail; lores blackish; sides of face dark brown. *Eyes white*; bill and feet black. Much variation in amount of white on throat and breast. The more western race *horrensis* is considerably smaller than nominate *albicapillus*. Dark-eyed **juvenile** has pale tawny-white crown, yellow bill with brown tip, and reduced streaking on underparts. **VOICE**: A shrill rising *tschurreeeet* or *tchu-tchu tsureeeeet*. **HABITS**: Gregarious; a communal breeder, building numerous bulky, untidy grass-and-stick nests together in outer branches of thorn trees. Small flocks feed on ground in dry, stony bush country, often in and around villages; numbers gather seasonally at fruiting *Salvadora* shrubs. **STATUS AND DISTRIBUTION**: Locally common in arid and semi-arid bush between 300 and 1000 m, *S. a. horrensis* ranges along the northern edge of the Dida Galgalu Desert from North Horr east to Maikona and Turbi, north to the Ethiopian border. *S. a. albicapillus* of Ethiopia and Somalia reaches ne. Kenya at Mandera and Ramu.

MAGPIE-STARLING *Speculipastor bicolor* Plate 78, Figure p. 636

Length 170–190 mm (6.5–7.5"). A pied starling of dry country in n. and e. Kenya. *White patches at base of primaries conspicuous in flight*. **Adult male** *shiny blue-black on upperparts, head and upper breast*, less glossy on wings and tail; lower breast, belly and under tail-coverts white. *Eyes blood-red*. **Female** dull blackish above, with dark grey crown; dark grey throat separated from white belly by a glossy black breast band; wings as in male. *Eyes red* or *orange-red*; bill and feet black in both sexes. **Juvenile** dark brown or grey-brown, with contrasting white belly. Eyes brown, becoming orange-red in immature. Moulting individuals show scattered glossy black feathers as adult plumage develops. Exceptional young birds are entirely whitish below, including chin and throat. **VOICE**: Perched, a prolonged soft, babbling *quereeeh quaaa kereek quak-quak, quereek suaaaa, cherak-*

chak-chak. . . with interspersed higher, harsher notes, but lacks strident trills of Fischer's Starling. Also has a shrill whistling flight call. **HABITS**: Nomadic or irregularly migratory, wandering in flocks. Feeds in trees and on ground. Nests in holes in cliffs, river banks and termitaria. **SIMILAR SPECIES**: Abbott's Starling of highland forest lacks white wing patches, has yellow eyes. **STATUS AND DISTRIBUTION**: Locally common below 1200 m in thorn-bush throughout n. Kenya, breeding opportunistically May–June, followed by post-breeding dispersal south to the Kerio Valley, and Baringo and Isiolo Districts. Flocks regular August–November south to Garissa, Bura and Garsen on the Tana River, the coastal lowlands north of Malindi, and in Tsavo East NP. A few old specimen records from Nairobi and Lake Magadi. In n. Tanzania, known from two records near the Pare Mts (Jan. 1957 and Oct. 1962).

Immature male Magpie-Starling.

WATTLED STARLING *Creatophora cinerea*   **Plate 78**

Length 190–200 mm (7.5–8"). A highly gregarious grey or grey-brown starling with a *pale rump*. **Non-breeding adult** *pale grey* or brownish grey, the *almost white rump contrasting with black flight feathers and tail*; greater coverts black in female, whitish in male; primary coverts white in adult male. Head feathered, but with streak of bare blue-grey skin on each side of throat. **Breeding male** loses feathers on top of head, exposing bare skin: *bright yellow from eyes to hindcrown*, black on front part of head and throat; at same time develops pendent black wattles on forehead and chin, and small ones in middle of crown; much individual variation. Eyes brown; bill pinkish white, blackish at base; feet dark flesh-brown, flesh-pink or grey. **Breeding female** much like non-breeding male, but primary coverts blackish or brown, and wings of worn birds entirely brown. **Juvenile** browner above (especially female), sometimes with suggestion of streaks below; *bill dusky or brown; bare streak on each side of throat yellow, greenish yellow or dusky*. **VOICE**: High-pitched thin, squeaky notes, *tsirrit-tsirrit tseep, seeet-seeereeet*; also a harsh three-syllabled flight call; alarm note a rasping nasal *graaaah*. Flocks maintain a babbling of varied squeaks, squawks and squeals. **HABITS**: Travels in dense flocks, often associating with large wild or domestic mammals, feeding on disturbed insects. Breeding is irregular and opportunistic, dependent on green conditions and presence of insects following heavy rains. Random-appearing non-breeding wandering doubtless governed also by availability of insect food. Builds clusters of large, untidy domed nests of sticks in trees and shrubs. **SIMILAR SPECIES**: Fischer's Starling has dark rump and grey breast; adults have white eyes. **STATUS AND DISTRIBUTION**: Widespread from sea level to over 2000 m, especially in bushed and wooded grassland and cultivation; common in most national parks and game reserves. Breeds mainly in and east of the Rift Valley.

RED-BILLED OXPECKER *Buphagus erythrorhynchus*   **Plate 78**

Length 190–200 mm (7.5–8"). A slender, *red-billed* brown bird invariably *associated with large mammals*. Sexes alike. **Adult** *uniformly brown above, the rump little or no paler than the back*. Eyes vermilion, with *broad yellow orbital ring*; feet dark brown. **Juvenile** sooty brown above and on breast, darker than in adult; at fledging, bill yellow with dark line along culmen, but gradually darkens and in two months is entirely dusky brown; bare orbital skin dark brown. In a further two months bill shows red at base, and at six to seven months bird has all-red bill and orange-red eyes. **VOICE**: Usually silent when on animals. Flying or in trees, gives a hissing *krissss, krissss. . .*, or a more buzzing *zhhhhhhhh*; also *tsee-tsee-tsee-tsee-tsee* and a harsh *tsik-tsik-tsik*. **HABITS**: Spends

most of day actively clambering about on mammals, wild or domestic; clings with sharp claws, supported by pointed tail. Inserts its head well into host's nostrils and ears. Feeds on bits of mammalian tissue as well as on ticks, enlarging small abrasions; perhaps eats leeches when on hippopotami. Flies to tree branches when disturbed from animals, perching in upright attitude. Builds nest of grass or hair in tree cavity, among rocks or in buildings. A co-operative breeder. **SIMILAR SPECIES**: Adult Yellow-billed Oxpecker has two-toned bill, the basal part swollen and bright yellow; rump much paler than back. **STATUS AND DISTRIBUTION**: Apart from coastal areas where scarce and local, widespread and common at up to 2500 m in Kenya and n. Tanzania, wherever large wild mammals and undipped livestock are present.

YELLOW-BILLED OXPECKER *Buphagus a. africanus*   Plate 78

Length 205–215 mm (8–8.5"). **Adult** resembles Red-billed Oxpecker, but *basal half of bill bright yellow*, and *rump and upper tail-coverts pale creamy buff*, noticeably paler than the brownish back; throat and upper breast dark brown, rest of underparts creamy buff. Eyes scarlet (fading to yellow soon after death), with no yellow orbital ring; bill *with broad, bright yellow mandibular rami* and *bright red tip*; feet dark brown. Sexes alike. At fledging, bill of **juvenile** yellow, without dark culmen of preceding species, but soon becomes entirely brown or blackish; eyes brown. Older **immature** has scarlet-tipped yellow bill, blackish at base of maxilla; eyes brownish grey. **VOICE**: A hissing, churring alarm call similar to that of preceding species. Also a reedy rattling. **HABITS**: Similar to those of Red-billed Oxpecker. Shows marked preference for buffalo. Eats blood-sucking flies, as well as ticks. **SIMILAR SPECIES**: See Red-billed Oxpecker. **STATUS AND DISTRIBUTION**: Much less numerous than Red-billed Oxpecker. Apart from the Laikipia Plateau, now largely absent outside NPs and GRs. Fairly common in Nairobi, Amboseli and the Tsavo NPs, and from Mara GR south to Serengeti NP, Maswa GR, Ngorongoro Crater, Lake Manyara, Tarangire and Arusha NPs and the Mkomazi GR.

Yellow-billed Oxpeckers on African Buffalo.

SUNBIRDS, FAMILY NECTARINIIDAE
(World, 120 species; Africa, 74; Kenya, 34; n. Tanzania, 26)

These small, flower-probing passerines superficially resemble the unrelated New World hummingbirds (Trochilidae) in their highly developed iridescence, and they occupy a similar ecological niche in Africa. However, they have short, rounded wings, and although extremely active and restless they do not have the extraordinary specialized flight of hummers and normally feed from a perch. *Nectarinia* species have long, often deeply curved bills, with which they probe open blossoms or pierce the bases of deep tubular corollas to reach otherwise inaccessible nectaries. The more warbler-like *Anthreptes* have relatively short, straight bills and usually glean foliage for insects, although they visit flowers and also eat small fruits. Some males have narrow elongated central tail feathers. Most male plumages display glittering green, blue, purple or bronze reflections, often in combination with bright non-metallic yellow, red or orange. With some exceptions, females are dull, with little or no iridescence. Some males (and a few females) have yellow, orange or red erectile pectoral tufts, usually more or less concealed at the sides of the breast, but conspicuous during display. After breeding, certain male sunbirds moult into a duller eclipse plumage, which varies greatly among related forms.

Although many species are flower-dependent, sunbirds occupy habitats ranging from coastal forest to alpine moorland. They tend to be solitary or in pairs, but regular seasonal movements in response to flowering can result in concentrations at such favoured plants as *Aloe*, the orange-flowered mint *Leonotis*, *Erythrina* (coral-bean) trees, and parasitic mistletoes. Males are especially pugnacious, more so during the breeding season. Vocalizations include insistent sharp feeding and flight calls. Some species have well-developed distinctive songs, typically rapid, high-pitched and not easily described. The nest is a domed pouch, often with a porch-like projection above the side entrance, and usually suspended from the branch of a tree or shrub. The one or two, often heavily marked eggs are incubated only by the female, but young are tended by both sexes.

Some female and juvenile sunbirds are difficult to identify, owing in part to considerable variation within species. Juvenile males may have a dusky or black throat patch; their plumage otherwise resembles that of adult females (a few of which are also black-throated). Immature males in moult may show a broad black mid-ventral line as incoming dark belly and breast feathers replace the paler juvenile plumage. Patchy adult males moulting in and out of breeding dress usually show sufficient iridescence to provide identification clues. Colours of bare parts, mentioned in only a few of the species accounts, are similar in most sunbirds.

PLAIN-BACKED SUNBIRD *Anthreptes reichenowi yokanae* Plate 106
(Blue-throated Sunbird)

Length 100–115 mm (4–4.5"). A small, arboreal, *coastal* species. **Adult male** has black *forehead, face and throat* with some metallic blue reflections; plumage otherwise pale olive, more yellow in centre of breast and belly, and with yellow pectoral tufts. **Female** olive above, with faint whitish superciliary stripes and eyelids; underparts yellowish white. **Juvenile** resembles adult female, but upperparts olive-brown. **VOICE**: Song *tee-tee-tee-tee* followed by a lower, often descending *tew-tew-tew-tew-tew. . .*, and at times ending with some higher warbling notes. Also *tsee-tsee-tsee-tsee su-seeu seeu seeu seeu seeu tsu*, or *tsi-tsi tsee-su see-su see-su tse tew-yew*, the last two or three notes lower. In alarm, a prolonged *wee-wee-wee. . .* or *tew-tew-tew. . .*, or a complaining *eea-eeea-eeea*, which may change to a chatter. **HABITS**: Pairs often accompany mixed-species flocks or feed alone in the forest canopy, gleaning foliage for insects and sometimes visiting flowers. **SIMILAR SPECIES**: Amani Sunbird, in same habitat, is white below. **STATUS AND DISTRIBUTION**: Uncommon local resident of lowland forest from Tanga north to the lower Tana River, inland to the Shimba Hills and to 1000 m in the East Usambaras. In Kenya, most numerous in the Arabuko–Sokoke Forest near Malindi.

WESTERN VIOLET-BACKED SUNBIRD *Anthreptes l. longuemarei* Plate 106

Length 125–130 mm (5"). A *western* species of *high-rainfall areas*, slightly larger than the common *Eastern Violet-backed Sunbird*. **Adult male** *uniformly iridescent violet above*, including rump (may be slightly bluer) and tail; *throat violet*, otherwise white below, with yellow pectoral tufts. **Female** greyish brown above, with white superciliary stripes, dark metallic violet tail and upper tail-coverts. White throat and upper breast contrast with *yellow belly, flanks and crissum*. **Juvenile** olive-brown above and *entirely pale yellow below*; feet dark olive, bill greenish black above, greenish grey below. **VOICE**: A rapid twittering song, not described in detail. Call note a hard *tit*. **HABITS**: In pairs or with mixed-species flocks. Probes flowers and gleans foliage; visits garden flowers, including those of introduced bottle-brush trees (*Callistemon*). **SIMILAR SPECIES**: Male Eastern Violet-backed Sunbird of drier habitats has greenish-blue rump, female lacks yellow below. Uluguru Violet-backed Sunbird is restricted to eastern forests. Juvenile Eastern Violet-backed is only faintly tinged with yellowish on underparts. **STATUS AND DISTRIBUTION**: Scarce and local in Muhoroni and Kapenguria Districts of w. Kenya, where present in gardens, cultivation and along forest borders. Formerly near Bungoma.

EASTERN VIOLET-BACKED SUNBIRD *Anthreptes orientalis*   **Plate 106**
(Kenya Violet-backed Sunbird)

Length 115–125 mm (4.5–5"). The common violet-backed sunbird; a species of *dry habitats*. Bill short, relatively stout. **Adult male** *snowy white* below, except for violet chin and yellow pectoral tufts; upperparts mostly shining violet, the *rump greenish or blue-green*, and a patch of iridescent turquoise on bend of wing; tail violet-blue, narrowly edged with white. **Female** mostly brown above, with grey rump, *dark blue tail* and bold white superciliary stripes; *underparts entirely white*. **Juvenile** grey-brown above, with long whitish superciliaries, iridescent blue tail (narrowly pale-edged), and dull white underparts faintly yellowish-tinged on belly. **Voice**: Note of male a nasal *chwee* or *tswee-tswee*. **Habits**: Usually solitary. Visits flowers, but also forages warbler-like in foliage. Male frequently sings from top of low tree or shrub. Often places nest near wasp's nest. **Similar Species**: Male Western Violet-backed Sunbird has no blue-green on rump. Male Uluguru Violet-backed also has blue-green rump, is slightly more bluish-violet above, but best separated from Eastern Violet-backed by habitat. Females and young of both Western and Uluguru are yellow-bellied; Uluguru female is violet above. **Status and Distribution**: Fairly common and widespread resident of dry bush and savanna below 1300 m. Ranges throughout n. Kenya south to the Kerio Valley and Baringo District, and in eastern lowlands to the lower Tana River, Galana Ranch, Tsavo and Amboseli NPs, into n. Tanzania in the Mkomazi GR, lowlands north of Arusha, the Masai Steppe west to Tarangire and Lake Manyara NPs. Absent from the Lake Victoria basin and adjacent highlands, and from much of the coastal lowlands (where replaced by *A. longuemarei* and *A. neglectus*, respectively).

ULUGURU VIOLET-BACKED SUNBIRD *Anthreptes neglectus*   **Plate 106**

Length 118–122 mm (4.75"). An eastern *forest* sunbird, *violet-backed in both sexes*. **Adult male** decidedly *greyish below*, usually with brownish wash, especially on lower belly and crissum, purplish and brown on chin/upper throat and with yellow (rarely orange) pectoral tufts. Sides of face, ear-coverts and broad collar around back of neck dark dull brown, separating iridescence of crown and back; the latter slightly more bluish violet than in *A. orientalis*, becoming bright greenish blue on rump; tail bluish purple. Greater wing-coverts brown and flight feathers edged with dull mustard-yellow (edges pale tawny or tan in other violet-backed species); iridescent turquoise patch on lesser coverts. Bill blackish horn. **Female** iridescent violet on crown, upper back and upper tail-coverts, with some brassy-green iridescence on bend of wing; tail duller bluish purple; lower back dull brown, with bright turquoise-green iridescence on rump; sides of face and ear-coverts grey-brown, extending as a broad dull collar around back of neck. *Underparts pale grey* (sometimes obscurely streaked on breast), with *olive-yellow belly and crissum*; wings brown, with olive-yellowish feather edging. **Juvenile female** shows less iridescence above, only a trace of violet on wing and upper back, and duller gloss on crown and tail than in adult; much more yellow on belly. **Voice**: A loud *sweep, sweep, sweep* or *seep-sureep, sureep . . .*, persistently uttered. **Habits**: Pairs or small groups forage in forest or forest-edge trees; also visits garden flowers. Builds nest like that of Olive Sunbird, but with shorter attachment and streamers (Sclater and Moreau 1933). **Similar Species**: Males of other violet-backed sunbirds have white underparts. Eastern Violet-backed inhabits drier non-forest areas; male also has iridescent blue-green rump, but female is all white below and has prominent whitish superciliary stripes. **Status and Distribution**: In Kenya, rare and local in coastal and riverine forest; known from the lower Tana River, Shimba Hills NP and Diani Forest. In ne. Tanzania, throughout the East Usambaras and at Ambangulu (1200 m) in the West Usambaras.

AMANI SUNBIRD *Anthreptes pallidigaster*   **Plate 106**

Length 84–90 mm (3.25–3.5"). A small, white-bellied coastal-woodland species. **Adult male** *dark iridescent bottle-green*, sometimes with violet reflections, on head, throat and breast; tail glossy blue-black; underparts white, with *orange pectoral tufts*. **Female** grey above with faint violet reflections; tail blue-black; underparts creamy white. **Juvenile** resembles adult female but is paler grey. **Voice**: Song a colourless high-pitched series of notes: *su-su-suweet sususuweet-schweeeeet*. Also a disyllabic *seeeet-seeeet*. **Habits**: Pairs or family groups sometimes join mixed-species flocks in treetops. Actions warbler-like. **Similar Species**: Female Plain-backed Sunbird is tinged yellowish below, has olive tail. **Status and Distribution**: Scarce and local East African endemic, in Kenya confined to *Brachystegia* stands in the Arabuko–Sokoke and Marafa forest areas near Malindi. In ne. Tanzania, ranges up to 900 m in the East Usambaras; also in the Uzungwa Mts south of our region.

GREEN SUNBIRD *Anthreptes rectirostris tephrolaemus* (Grey-chinned Sunbird)

Plates 106, 107

Length 90–98 mm (3.5–4"). A canopy species of west Kenyan forests. **Adult male** iridescent golden green above, the wings and short dusky tail edged with yellow-olive; *underparts grey, with broad green band across lower throat and upper breast, this bordered below by a narrow dull ochre band*; chin greyish white, pectoral tufts bright yellow. **Female** olive above and mostly olive below, more yellowish on belly, grey on the chin; shows yellowish superciliary stripes and some dull green iridescence on bend of wing and green-edged back feathers, but bird appears plain in treetops. In the hand, note *brownish-red eyes.* **Juvenile** olive above, sometimes with a few scattered metallic green feathers; paler olive below, sides and flanks darker, and throat and breast faintly mottled with dark olive; centre of belly dull yellow. Eyes brown. **Voice:** Not reliably described. **Habits:** Warbler-like. Usually remains high, in pairs or small groups. Feeds on small fruits and insects, but numbers gather at flowering trees in forest and adjacent gardens. Nests in clump of moss or orchids on side of tree trunk. **Similar Species:** Collared Sunbird is bright yellow below. **Status and Distribution:** Uncommon resident of the Kakamega, Nandi and Kericho Forests. Formerly on Mt Elgon and along the Yala and Sio Rivers.

BANDED GREEN SUNBIRD *Anthreptes rubritorques*

Plate 123

Length 85–90 mm (*c.* 3.5"). A short-tailed, *canopy-inhabiting* sunbird of Tanzania's Usambara Mts. **Adult male** shining green above, mainly grey below, with *narrow scarlet band across upper breast*; centre of lower breast, belly and under tail-coverts pale yellow; pectoral tufts bright yellow (or yellow and orange). **Female** lacks breast band, is green above and pale greyish yellow below with indistinct yellowish streaks. **Juvenile** dark olive-green above, yellowish olive below. **Voice:** Male utters a repeated chirp of remarkable carrying power, the same note repeated several times, sometimes accelerating into a song. Also a disyllabic *thk-eer.* Female generally silent (Moreau and Moreau 1937). **Habits:** Gregarious yet unobtrusive. Gleans foliage in forest canopy, always high. **Similar Species:** Eastern Double-collared Sunbird, a conspicuous bird of gardens and forest edge, has more curved bill: male has green throat and broader red breast band; female paler above, with dark tail and more yellowish underparts. Green Sunbird is only in w. Kenya. **Status and Distribution:** Fairly common resident between 250 and 1500 m in Usambara forests.

COLLARED SUNBIRD *Anthreptes collaris*

Plate 105

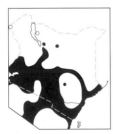

Length 100–105 mm (4–4.5"). A small, *green-and-yellow* forest sunbird with a short bill. **Adult male** *brilliant iridescent green on upperparts, head and upper breast*, the latter separated from otherwise *yellow underparts* by narrow violet band; flanks washed with olive. **Female** similar to male, but entirely yellow below, tinged olive on throat (more so in western *A. c. garguensis*). **Juvenile** resembles female, except for dusky yellow chin and neck. **Voice:** Song variable but usually with most notes distinct, not run together: (1) *tsit-tsit-chuweet chuweet chuet chuet chuet chueeet eet*; (2) a short twittering, *ch-ch-ch-chwee chwee*; (3) *tschu-er-tschee wer tchwer chee* (van Someren 1956); (4) a faster *spit-spit-spit-suweet*; (5) a more ringing *chwer-chwer-chwer-chwer. . .*, not sunbird-like. Call notes include a thin nasal *tuwee, tuwee* or *tchee tchee*, and a low hard *tik.* **Habits:** Usually in pairs, but numbers gather at flowering trees. Often in mixed bird flocks. Restlessly gleans foliage and darts after insects; visits garden flowers. Confiding and less pugnacious than many sunbirds. Builds compact pendent pouch-like nest with side-top entrance protected by a porch, placed low or high in thorny shrub or sapling or built near wasps' nest in thornless plant. **Similar Species:** Yellow-bellied race of Variable Sunbird is longer- billed, has darker throat and breast with much blue and purple; orange or yellow pectoral tufts. See Green Sunbird. **Status and Distribution:** Common and widespread resident from sea level to above 2200 m in varied wooded habitats, including gardens. Absent only from arid regions. *A. c. elachior* ranges throughout coastal lowlands north to the Boni Forest and inland to the eastern Kenyan plateau; in n. Tanzania to the Usambara and Pare Mts and Kilimanjaro lowlands. *A. c. garguensis* occupies Tanzanian highlands from Arusha, Tarangire and Lake Manyara NPs and the Mbulu and Crater Highlands, north through the w. and cent. Kenyan highlands to the Mathews Range, Ndotos, Mt Marsabit, Mt Kulal and Lokichokio.

PYGMY SUNBIRD *Anthreptes p. platurus*

Plates 105, 107

Length of breeding male, 170–175 mm (7"), of female 90 mm (3.5"). A tiny, short-billed, *yellow-bellied* sunbird of *arid nw. Kenya.* **Breeding male** bright metallic green, with rich yellow lower breast and belly; upper tail-coverts violet; wings and tail black; *two central rectrices narrow and greatly elongated,* at times exceeding bird's body length. **Female** *pale ash-brown above; tail blue-black with whitish corners; underparts plain*: chin whitish, throat yellowish white, shading to lemon-yellow on breast and belly. Faint yellowish superciliary stripes usually

evident. **Non-breeding male** (April–Oct.) resembles female, but slightly greyer on back. **VOICE**: Song a soft trill. Call note *twee* or *twee-weet.* **HABITS**: Nomadic; often travels in flocks of ten or more, foraging low in dry scrub. Attracted to flowering acacias and aloes. Rather shy; may fly far if disturbed. **SIMILAR SPECIES**: Collared Sunbird, a forest species, resembles male Pygmy which has moulted its long tail feathers, but shows purple band between the green and yellow of underparts, and blue-green upper tail-coverts. Female Beautiful Sunbird has yellowish chin, and longer, moderately curved bill. **STATUS AND DISTRIBUTION**: Irregular vagrant to dry bush country in nw. Kenya. Records (some involving numerous individuals) from s. Turkana (July 1926), Lodwar (Sept–Oct. 1953), Baringo (Nov. 1976 and 1977), Kapedo (Nov. 1979) and the Kerio Valley (Oct. 1990).

OLIVE SUNBIRD *Nectarinia olivacea*   Plates 106, 107

Length 105–130 mm (4–5″). *Plain olive* with no iridescence, both sexes could be mistaken for females of other species, but *large bill* a good field character, as are the *bright yellow pectoral tufts* (absent in females of the large, dark western race). Coastal birds noticeably small, both sexes with yellow tufts. **Adult male** olive, the wings and tail browner and edged with light olive; crown and face more dusky; underparts pale olive or olive-grey, with greenish wash on flanks and crissum; *bill black, long, well curved;* eyes *large* and dark. **Female** similar to male but smaller. **Juvenile** resembles female but more yellow. **VOICE**: Song of coastal *N. o. changamwensis* a deliberate series of short, loud, sharp, clear notes, *tew-tew-twit-twit,* or longer, often accelerating and falling slightly in pitch near end: *teu. . . teu . . . twit-twit-twit-twit-tit-tit-tit;* sometimes *tsee-tseep tsee-tseep tsep-turp.* Western *vincenti* has a brief *weet-tur-weet* which can lead to a longer *tee tee-tew-tu-tur-TEE TEE-tee-tee-tew-tew-tew tu-weet.* Usual call a staccato *tuc...tuc...* or *t-tuc-tuc,* often in flight. Also gives a persistent high-pitched squeak and a scolding *dya-dya.* **HABITS**: Usually solitary or in pairs, gleaning foliage in forest, but 20–30 may feed together at flowers of forest trees or planted jacarandas. Quite vocal. Builds untidy nest resembling a collection of rubbish and with dangling streamers of plant fibre up to 0.5 m long, low or high in forest tree, shrub or fern. **SIMILAR SPECIES**: Largely olive females of other sunbirds have no yellow pectoral tufts. In w. Kenya, where female Olive lacks tufts, rely on large bill, voice and plain plumage. **STATUS AND DISTRIBUTION**: Fairly common and widespread resident below 2300 m in forest, woodland and wooded gardens, favouring cool, damp places. Four races: *changamwensis* in coastal lowlands north to the Boni Forest, inland along the lower Tana River to Bura and Garissa, also to Mt Kasigau and the Taita Hills, and in ne. Tanzania to the Usambara and South Pare Mts; *neglecta* from the cent. Kenyan highlands, Mt Endau and the Chyulu Hills south to Taveta, North Pare Mts, Kilimanjaro, mts Meru and Monduli and Arusha NP; *vincenti* (sometimes merged with Ethiopian *ragazzii*) in Kenya west of the Rift Valley, from Mt Elgon and the Cheranganis south to Lolgorien and the Migori River; *granti* is restricted to Pemba and Zanzibar.

MOUSE-COLOURED SUNBIRD *Nectarinia veroxii fischeri*   Plate 106
(Grey Sunbird)

Length 120–125 mm (5″). A *grey*-plumaged, *coastal sunbird*, both sexes with *scarlet pectoral tufts.* Upperparts slaty, slightly darker on wings and tail; light glossy blue wash sometimes visible on crown, back and wing-coverts; underparts pale grey; bill and feet black. Female slightly smaller. **VOICE**: Song a fairly loud series of short, well-separated phrases, *ee-sew. . . tsu-ee-see. . . ee-see. . . tsu, ee-su ee-chew. . .,* or longer phrases such as *tsee tsee tsee tseu-wee* or *tchew-wee-tsi-see-chew,* repeated frequently. Sharp call notes include *tsip* and *cheep-chew.* **HABITS**: Solitary or in pairs; more deliberate in its movements than other sunbirds. Often associated with buildings and other man-made structures, on which most nests are built. **SIMILAR SPECIES**: Olive Sunbird is more olive in all plumages, and has yellow pectoral tufts. **STATUS AND DISTRIBUTION**: Uncommon resident of coastal bush, thickets, forest edge and mangroves from Tanga north to Lamu and Manda Islands and Somali border areas, inland along the lower Tana River to Baomo; most numerous south of Malindi.

GREEN-HEADED SUNBIRD *Nectarinia verticalis viridisplendens*   Plate 105

Length 140 mm (5.5″). Often appears *blue*-headed (and therefore misidentified as extralimital Blue-headed Sunbird). A sturdy bird, *golden olive above* and *grey below;* head of **adult male** entirely iridescent green, bluer *on chin and throat;* rest of underparts ash-grey. Viewed from underneath, easily mistaken for extralimital Blue-throated Brown Sunbird (see note below). **Female** green only on top and sides of head; entirely grey below. Pectoral tufts yellowish cream in male, smaller and whitish in female. Distinctive **juvenile** olive above, with *black forehead, crown, chin and throat;* olive breast and belly separated from black throat by narrow yellow band. **VOICE**: Song a prolonged twittering preceded by rapid *chip* notes. Calls include a soft, high-pitched *chip, whew, tsit, tzit,* the notes in assorted order, and a plaintive mewing *chiuwee* or *tseea-wee, cheea-weu.* Alarm note a

harsh *chee*. **HABITS**: Visits flowers, often piercing tubular corollas, but more often gleans foliage and bark for insects and spiders. Usually in pairs. Builds bulky nest with long dangling streamers. **SIMILAR SPECIES**: Blue-headed Sunbird, *N. alinae*, is confined to montane forests of the Albertine Rift, well west of our area. Also Ugandan is Blue-throated Brown Sunbird, *N. cyanolaema*, several times reported from Kakamega Forest, but without substantiation: male is mostly dark brown above and on sides of face, usually shows *steel-blue* iridescence on forecrown, chin, throat and upper breast, and rest of underparts are sooty grey with cream pectoral tufts; brownish-backed female has distinctive facial pattern, with *prominent white stripe above and another below the eye*, underparts mottled whitish and dark grey, olive-tinged on flanks and under tail-coverts. **STATUS AND DISTRIBUTION**: Fairly common and widely distributed throughout the cent. and w. Kenyan highlands between 1500 and 2400 m in forest, riverine woods and gardens. In n. Tanzania, known in our area only from two records along the Grumeti River, Serengeti NP.

GREEN-THROATED SUNBIRD *Nectarinia rubescens kakamegae*   Plates 105, 107

Length 130–140 mm (*c*. 5.5"). A dark sunbird of west Kenyan forests. **Adult male** *velvety brownish black*, with *metallic blue-green forecrown* (bordered posteriorly by violet) and malar streaks, and paler *green throat and upper breast*; a thin line of violet bordering the breast patch is seldom visible in the field. **Female** dusky brown above, with olivaceous wash on back, wings and tail; underparts yellowish, *broadly streaked with dusky brown*; faint yellowish superciliary stripes. **Juvenile** less streaked, more mottled, below, male (always?) with blackish chin and throat; crown, lores, cheeks and ear-coverts darker brown than back, contrasting with pale dull yellow malar streaks and thin short pale superciliaries. **Immature male** similar to adult female, but with iridescent green chin and throat. Some immatures are less brown (more olive) above, more yellowish below. **VOICE**: Songs include *seet-seet-seet-seet* and *chereet, see-seet*; also a loud *sweeu-sweeu-sweeu*. Call note a hard *tsick*. **HABITS**: Usually in pairs or small family groups in the canopy, and often with mixed-species flocks in flowering trees. Hovers at tree trunks to capture spiders and insects. **SIMILAR SPECIES**: Amethyst Sunbird unlikely in forest interior: male has rose-purple throat; female closely resembles female Green-throated, but is generally paler olive-brown or olive-grey above, less heavily streaked below. **STATUS AND DISTRIBUTION**: Locally common resident of the Nandi and Kakamega Forests. Formerly along the upper Yala River.

AMETHYST SUNBIRD *Nectarinia amethystina*   Plates 105, 107
(Black Sunbird)

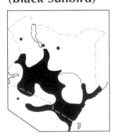

Length 135–140 mm (5.5"). **Adult male** non-reflective *velvety black*, more brownish on back, with *glittering green crown which often appears turquoise*; throat and patch on bend of wing metallic ruby or rose-purple. Male of coastal *N. a. kalckreuthi* may show metallic purple on upper tail-coverts. **Female** pale brown or olive-grey above, with dark lores, *whitish superciliary stripes* (short in *N. a. kirkii*); *pale yellowish below streaked with dusky brown*. At least some coastal females are much paler and more lightly streaked below, than inland birds. **Juvenile** resembles adult female, but throat dusky or blackish, upperparts with yellowish wash, and flight feathers with yellow edges. **Immature male** similar, but has some rose-purple iridescence on throat; older birds show scattered black feathers. **VOICE**: A loud, sustained twittering song. Usual call a succession of clear, sharp penetrating notes, *chip chip-tew, chewit*, or *chewit-chewit*, or *tyi-tyi-tyi-tyi*. **HABITS**: Usually solitary or in pairs, but numbers concentrate at favourite flowering trees (*Erythrina, Markhamia, Bombax, Jacaranda*). Aggressive towards other sunbirds. Often decorates nest with lichens. **SIMILAR SPECIES**: Male Green-throated Sunbird has more golden-green forecrown with violet rear edge, and bright green throat; female darker brown above, more heavily streaked below, but not always distinguishable in the field. Female Scarlet-chested Sunbird lacks superciliary stripes, has barred throat and white edging on primary coverts. **STATUS AND DISTRIBUTION**: Fairly common and widespread resident of woodland, forest edge and suburban gardens below 2000 m. *N. a. kalckreuthi* ranges in coastal lowlands north to the Boni Forest; *kirkii* in the w. and cent. Kenyan highlands north to mts Marsabit, Kulal, Nyiru and Loima, and in n. Tanzania from Loliondo and the Crater Highlands east to Arusha NP, Mt Meru, Kilimanjaro, the Pare Mts, Mkomazi GR and (sparingly) the Usambaras. In low dry regions, confined to riverine woods or other richer habitats.

SCARLET-CHESTED SUNBIRD *Nectarinia senegalensis*   Plates 105, 107

Length 145–150 mm (6"). A sturdy, *dark* sunbird with a long, well-curved bill. **Adult male** dark blackish brown, slightly paler on wings and tail, with iridescent green crown, chin and upper throat; many feathers of *scarlet lower throat and breast* with minute blue bands (visible only at close range). Small violet 'shoulder' patch present in coastal race. **Female** greyish brown above, with white-edged outer wing-coverts and *no superciliary stripes*; *underparts heavily marked*, the dull yellow ground-colour obscured by brown except on belly; *dark brown chin*

and throat narrowly barred with lighter brown and with yellowish-white tips, giving a somewhat mottled appearance; breast and belly dull yellow or yellowish white, streaked with dark brown; under tail-coverts yellowish white with dark bases. **Juvenile** resembles adult female, but *throat uniform dusky or greyish black* and the *yellow breast and belly heavily mottled and barred with black*. **Immature male** has scarlet breast patch (with numerous minute iridescent blue feather bands), but otherwise resembles female or juvenile. Adult plumage assumed gradually by prolonged moult. **VOICE**: Male commonly gives a simple, loud, clear prolonged *tew tew tew. . .* or *tee-tee tew-tew*, and an equally loud, penetrating *cheet cheet chueet sweet-seechu-sweet sweet-seechu-seet seechu-sheechu-seechu. . .*, the notes distinct, not run together. Another song begins with a few *tchik* or *chewit* notes and continues as an extended weak series, *see tsee tsewit, tsick, tsetsee tsick chewik. . .*, this at times more variable, almost warbling and long-continued. **HABITS**: Feeds low in garden flowers or at tall flowering trees, in pairs, family groups or larger concentrations. Active and restless. Singing male perches prominently, either twisting about and posturing or remaining almost motionless. Builds conspicuous neat or untidy nest, usually suspended from outer part of low or high branch, sometimes near hornets' nest. **SIMILAR SPECIES**: Male Hunter's Sunbird has violet rump, black throat, brighter scarlet breast with few blue-banded feathers; female Hunter's, mainly in dry areas, is paler than female Scarlet-chested, mottled on throat. Female Amethyst and Green-throated Sunbirds have prominent superciliary stripes. **STATUS AND DISTRIBUTION**: Absent from arid n. and e. Kenya, but otherwise widespread and fairly common in forest edge, woodland, savanna, cultivation and gardens in areas of medium to high rainfall. *N. s. lamperti* ranges up to 2000 m from Mt Elgon and Saiwa NPs east to the Laikipia Plateau, Mt Kenya and the Nyambenis, south through w. and cent. Kenya to the Lake Victoria basin, Mara GR, Loita and Chyulu Hills, and into n. Tanzania at Loliondo, Serengeti NP and the Crater Highlands. *N. s. gutturalis* occupies much of Tanzania north to Lake Manyara, Tarangire and Arusha NPs, and coastal lowlands north to Malindi, inland to the Usambaras and Shimba Hills. Reports from the lower Tana River require confirmation.

HUNTER'S SUNBIRD *Nectarinia hunteri*   Plates 105, 107

Length 128–145 mm (5–5.75"). The *dry-country* counterpart of Scarlet-chested Sunbird. **Adult male** similar to that species, but velvety black, with *lower rump, upper tail-coverts and 'shoulder' patch iridescent violet* and the *black throat bordered on each side by a thin metallic green streak*; breast pure vivid scarlet (most feathers lacking the narrow iridescent blue bands of Scarlet-chested Sunbird, but edges of the red patch may show some blue). **Female** grey-brown above, paler than Scarlet-chested; primary coverts edged with white. Underparts dull white, *strongly mottled with sepia-brown on throat and breast*, more faintly on belly, and flanks washed with brown. Chin and throat become much darker as pale feather edges wear off; worn birds easily mistaken for Scarlet-chested. **Juvenile** variable; resembles young Scarlet-chested, but often pale-throated and lacks blackish appearance of that species; dark-throated young birds best distinguished by habitat. **Immature male** shows scarlet breast patch contrasting with black throat, these areas separated by a narrow metallic violet border, but almost no iridescent feather bands within the red. (Comparable plumage of Scarlet-chested Sunbird has a duller red patch including many tiny metallic blue-violet feather bands, and a metallic green chin and throat.) **VOICE**: Usual note a loud *TEW*, repeated frequently; also a harsher scolding *tchew-tchew-tchew* or *tchi-tchi-tchi-tchi*, much like calls of Scarlet-chested Sunbird. More song-like is a series of clear distinct notes, *tew-tew-tew-tew-tew-tee-tee-tee-tee*. **HABITS**: Solitary; restless and rather shy. Particularly attracted to flowering *Delonix* trees and *Aloe*; also feeds in *Acacia* blossoms. **SIMILAR SPECIES**: Scarlet-chested Sunbird compared above. **STATUS AND DISTRIBUTION**: Locally common resident of dry areas, especially *Acacia* and *Commiphora* scrub below 1000 m. Ranges from Mt Kulal south to the Kerio Valley, lakes Baringo and Bogoria, Samburu and Shaba GRs and, except coastally, through eastern lowlands and the Tsavo NPs into ne. Tanzania in the Mkomazi GR and eastern edge of the Masai Steppe at Lembeni, Same and Mkomazi. Largely allopatric and ecologically separated from Scarlet-chested Sunbird.

VARIABLE SUNBIRD *Nectarinia venusta*   Plates 105, 107
(Yellow-bellied Sunbird)

Length 105–115 mm (4–4.5"). A small, *blue-backed, usually yellow-bellied* sunbird. **Breeding male** iridescent blue above, often washed violet on the crown, the black tail with a trace of blue; chin to upper breast iridescent blue-violet; rest of underparts yellow to orange-yellow in *N. v. falkensteini*, white in the race *albiventris*; pectoral tufts orange or yellow. **Non-breeding male** resembles female, but some blue feathers retained on wings and upper tail-coverts, occasionally on body. **Female** *falkensteini* brownish olive or olive-brown above, with *blue-black tail* and upper coverts; buffy white to yellow below, breast clouded with olive. Female *albiventris* grey-brown above, white below, somewhat greyer on breast. **Juvenile male** similar to adult female of same race, but with blackish or dusky throat patch. **VOICE**: Song a fairly loud short *tsip-tsip-tsip chuchuchuchuchu*. Alarm call an insistent *tcheer-tcheer* or *chiu-chee-cheer*. Other

calls include a scolding *tschew-TSEEP* or *chew-tsew-EEP*. **HABITS**: Usually in pairs, except for occasional gatherings at favoured food plants. Typically feeds low, in *Leonotis* or garden flowers. Less aggressive than many sunbirds. Active and restless; sometimes hovers at flowers. Builds ovoid nest in low herb or shrub. **SIMILAR SPECIES**: Collared Sunbird is iridescent green, not blue. Female Olive-bellied Sunbird has pale superciliary stripes and is more streaked below. Females of both double-collared sunbirds have darker olive underparts, lacking clear yellow on the belly. **STATUS AND DISTRIBUTION**: *N. v. falkensteini* is common and widespread in bush, savanna, open woodland, forest edge, cultivation and gardens below 3000 m, especially in the cent. and w. Kenyan highlands and in n. Tanzania east to Kilimanjaro, the Pare Mts and West Usambaras; in some areas, moves from breeding places to higher elevations as males assume eclipse plumage. *N. v. albiventris* of arid e. and ne. Kenya ranges from northern border areas east of Lake Turkana, south to Marsabit and Isiolo Districts and through eastern border areas to the lower Tana River; also in coastal lowlands from the Somali border south to Lamu District.

OLIVE-BELLIED SUNBIRD *Nectarinia chloropygia orphogaster*   Plates 106, 107

Length 105–110 mm (4–4.5"). Resembles both double-collared sunbirds. **Adult male** iridescent green above and on head, with upper tail-coverts more bluish green; long pectoral tufts yellow. *No blue or violet iridescence separating green throat from scarlet breast band.* Belly and crissum dark olive-brown. **Female** *dark olive above*, with narrow pale superciliary stripes; underparts pale olive-yellow, grading to whitish on chin, with soft olive streaking on breast and flanks. **Juvenile** grey-brown above (acquiring green iridescence as moult progresses); head, throat and upper breast dusky; rest of underparts yellowish. **VOICE**: Main song an ascending, rapid, scratchy trill with one to three introductory notes and a terminal phrase, *ski ski-skirrrrrrrrrrr su-skitsue-skitsu-sit.* A simpler slower song, *tsureep-seep-seep seep seep.* Call note a thin squeaky *chwee.* **HABITS**: Solitary or in groups. Usually feeds low in flowering herbs or shrubs; pierces large tubular corollas at their bases to reach the nectaries. **SIMILAR SPECIES**: Male Eastern Double-collared Sunbird, of much higher elevations, has paler belly and blue upper tail-coverts, while male Northern Double-collared is blue-green above, with violet-purple upper tail-coverts and broad red breast band; females are best separated by elevation and range. Female Variable Sunbird is yellow or white below and may show suggestion of streaking, but lacks pale superciliary stripes. **STATUS AND DISTRIBUTION**: Locally common resident of forest edge, moist thickets, riverine bush and cultivation between 1150 and 1550 m in w. Kenya from Kakamega, Mumias and Busia Districts south to Ukwala, Yala, Ng'iya and Rapogi. Formerly at Sotik.

NORTHERN DOUBLE-COLLARED SUNBIRD *Nectarinia preussi kikuyuensis*
Plates 106, 107

Length 110–115 mm (4–4.5"). The two double-collared sunbird species can be difficult to separate. **Adult male** Northern is dark iridescent *blue-green* above, with *violet or bluish-purple upper tail-coverts* (difficult to see). The *scarlet breast band, usually noticeably wider than in Eastern Double-collared,* is separated from green throat by line of iridescent *violet* feathers; pectoral tufts yellow; belly olive-brown, darker in Mt Kenya birds; *tail relatively short; bill short and black.* **Female** and **juvenile** olive-brown above, greenish yellow below, with olive wash on flanks; throat slightly greyer. **VOICE**: Call note a hard *chick* or *chip-chip.* Song of two well-separated notes followed by a short, fast sizzling twitter and ending with more distinct lower notes: *tsip. . . . . sweet. . . sususususrisrisri-tsew-tsutsu tsu.* **HABITS**: Forages both in treetops and in lower growth; frequently feeds at garden flowers with other sunbirds. **SIMILAR SPECIES**: Eastern Double-collared Sunbird appears longer-tailed and longer billed; male is more golden green above, and in nominate *N. m. mediocris* has contrasting blue (not violet) upper tail-coverts; scarlet breast band is narrower; also vocally distinct. Female difficult to separate except by bill size and relative tail length, though Eastern usually has darker throat. At lower elevations in w. Kenya, see Olive-bellied Sunbird. **STATUS AND DISTRIBUTION**: Locally common resident between 1700 and 2800 m in forest edge, riverine woods and gardens in the w. and cent. Kenyan highlands from Mt Elgon, Maralal and the Mathews Range south to Lolgorien and Nairobi. Most numerous at Mt Elgon, Kapenguria, North Nandi, Naro Moru, Limuru and in Nairobi suburbs. Although range overlaps with that of Eastern Double-collared above 1800 m, only rarely (Kieni Forest, s. Aberdares) are the two species found together.

EASTERN DOUBLE-COLLARED SUNBIRD *Nectarinia mediocris*   Plates 106, 107

Length 115 mm (4.5"). *Longer-billed, longer-tailed* and with *narrower scarlet breast band* than the preceding species, and generally at *higher elevations.* **Adult male** has brilliant golden-green head and upperparts, with contrasting steel-blue upper tail-coverts (violet in Tanzanian *usambarica*). The scarlet breast band (especially narrow in *usambarica*) is separated from green throat by line of iridescent *blue* feathers; pectoral tufts bright yellow; belly and crissum pale yellowish olive. **Female** and **juvenile** resemble those of Northern Double-collared, but *bill and tail somewhat longer.* Female *usambarica* is greener above and has a more distinctly streaked throat than nominate *mediocris.* **VOICE**: Song high-pitched and thin, the introductory notes higher (not

distinct and well separated as in song of preceding species): *tsit-tsit-tsit, see-see-see-see-see-see*, or *tsip tsip tsee-see-ch-tsitsitsi-su-see-see-tsip-su-sisisi*. Also gives isolated *tsip* notes. **HABITS:** Like those of preceding species. Typically favours areas with numerous *Kniphofia* (red-hot poker) plants. **SIMILAR SPECIES:** Northern Double-collared Sunbird compared above. In w. Kenya see Olive-bellied Sunbird. **STATUS AND DISTRIBUTION:** *N. m. mediocris* is resident between 1850 and 3700 m in forest, adjacent bamboo and giant heath and gardens in the w. and cent. Kenyan highlands; common on the Cheranganis, Mau, Aberdares and Mt Kenya; present also on Mt Kulal, Mt Nyiru and the Ndotos, and recorded once from Mt Elgon. Descends to lower elevations in cool weather, but seasonal movements poorly understood. In n. Tanzania, common from Kenyan border at the Ngurumans and Loliondo south through the Crater and Mbulu Highlands to Mt Hanang; east to Arusha NP, Mt Meru and Kilimanjaro. Also attributed to the North Pare Mts and the Taita and Chyulu Hills (Britton 1980), but replaced by *N. m. usambarica* in the South Pares and West Usambaras. Van Someren (1939) believed that Chyulu birds were distinct from *mediocris*, and a breeding pair in the Taita Hills, March 1993, appeared to be *usambarica*, not otherwise reported from Kenya.

MARICO SUNBIRD *Nectarinia mariquensis*   Plates 105, 107
(Mariqua Sunbird)

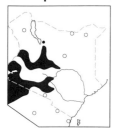

Length 112–128 mm (4.25–5"). A dark, rather stocky sunbird. **Adult male** with head, throat and upperparts glittering golden green; wings and tail black; a narrow blue band below the green throat, and below this a *broader band of deep maroon*; rest of underparts black (*osiris*) or greyish black (*suahelica*). In the hand, readily distinguished from Purple-banded Sunbird by longer wing (over 60 mm; under 60 mm in Purple-banded). **Female** ashy brown above, darker on wings and tail, the latter with white tips and edges; indistinct pale superciliary stripes; throat pale yellow; *breast and belly yellow with dark streaking.* **Juvenile** grey-brown or olive-brown above, yellowish below, with blackish chin/throat patch and much coarse, dark, diffuse mottling on breast; white on outer and inner webs of outer rectrices near tips. **VOICE:** Sharp *chic-chip* call notes. Song distinctive, much louder than that of Purple-banded Sunbird, usually with a few high notes leading into a loud long squeaky chatter; frequent sharp *chip, chick* or *tsick* notes, sometimes doubled, are interspersed throughout: *tse-tse-tseetsee chip-chip-chip tsitsitsitsee chick-che-chee-chu, tsee-che tseeu, tsik-tsik-tsik-cheeeeu tseu, chwee-chwee* . . .. **HABITS:** Solitary or in pairs, but several may feed together in blooming *Kigelia* and *Erythrina* trees; also favours flowers of *Aloe, Leonotis,* and introduced *Jacaranda* and bottle-brush (*Callistemon*) trees; feeds on insects among non-flowering plants. Not so restless as Purple-banded Sunbird. **SIMILAR SPECIES:** Male Purple-banded Sunbird is smaller and shorter-billed, with a more violet and less maroon breast band than male Marico; female Purple-banded is paler yellow below and often has a dusky throat. Juvenile male Red-chested Sunbird is paler yellow below, the pale portions of outer tail feathers grey, not white. Juvenile Green-throated Sunbird, of the forest canopy, is much longer-billed. **STATUS AND DISTRIBUTION:** *N. m. osiris* is thinly distributed in northern open bush and savanna at Moyale, Mt Kulal, Mt Nyiru and in the Ndoto foothills; also from Kapenguria and the Kerio Valley east to Maralal, Laikipia Plateau, Samburu GR and Meru NP. *N. m. suahelica* is common and widespread from Busia, Mumias and Kakamega Districts, higher parts of the Lake Victoria basin, Lolgorien and Mara GR east to Nairobi, Thika, Athi River, Machakos and Sultan Hamud Districts, south into n. Tanzania at Serengeti NP and Maswa GR. Status uncertain in the east, but reported from Tarangire NP and Mkomazi GR. Early sight records from Tsavo East NP and the lower Tana River require substantiation.

PURPLE-BANDED SUNBIRD *Nectarinia bifasciata*   Plates 105, 107
(Little Purple-banded Sunbird)

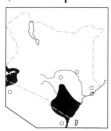

Length 95–100 mm (3.75–4"). The dark-plumaged **breeding male** appears metallic blue-green and black at a distance, the race *microrhyncha almost identical in plumage to the larger Marico Sunbird,* but with a *shorter* (14 mm), *less strongly decurved bill;* upperparts also more blue-green (less golden green), the breast band more violet and less maroon, but colour differences subtle and unreliable. Maroon breast band 7–10 mm wide in *microrhyncha,* suffused with violet and bordered above and below with blue or violet; only 3–5 mm of maroon in *tsavoensis,* sometimes lacking or evident only at sides. Lower breast and belly jet-black (not greyish black as in *suahelica* race of Marico); under tail-coverts sometimes tipped with metallic blue or green. **Non-breeding male** *microrhyncha* resembles a 'black-throated' female, but has dark wings and iridescent green wing- and upper tail-coverts. *N. b. tsavoensis* apparently has no eclipse plumage (specimens show moult progressing from one metallic plumage to another). **Females** of both forms pale *yellowish below, lightly but sharply dusky-streaked on breast;* throat white, or dusky with contrasting long white malar stripes. Upperparts grey-brown; faint whitish superciliary stripes, black lores and some white on lower eyelids; primaries edged whitish; tail blue-black, the feathers narrowly tipped grey or dull white, and with narrow grey outer edges. **Juvenile male** resembles dark-throated female. **Immature male** has metallic green feathers mixed with black on throat and wing-coverts, and often a broad black mid-ventral line. **VOICE:** Call a high *tsik-*

tsiki-tsik or *brrrzi*. Typical song of *N. b. microrhyncha* high-pitched, softer, thinner and much less emphatic than that of Marico Sunbird, often with distinct short introductory notes leading into a high twittering: *tsi tsi tsi tsee-tsee-tsee-tsee-tsee seeseetsew seesueet tseet tseu cheet sitisitisitisreeee*. A simpler song is *chitisee-see-see-see-see-see*. *N. b. tsavoensis* has a rapid sputtering *tsusitiseesee, chuchiti-tsi-tsi-tsi-tsi sitisee-see-see-see chitisee . . .*, and *sitisee-see-see tseu-tseu-tseu chiti-tisiti-see-swee*, sometimes shortened to only the last few notes. Loud annoyance chatter *chi-chi-chi-chi . . .*. Immature males regularly sing. **HABITS**: Forages alone or in small groups, especially in blooming acacias; also attracted to mistletoe flowers. Seldom feeds in herbaceous plants. Active and restless, flitting quickly and often erratically; hovers, sometimes flycatches. Immature and eclipse males sing enthusiastically. Nest neat or scruffy, sometimes decorated with lichens. **SIMILAR SPECIES**: Male Marico Sunbird is best separated by longer, more strongly curved bill, by voice, and in the hand by larger size (wing over 60 mm); female by bill differences and more heavily streaked underparts. Violet-breasted Sunbird is larger, longer-billed, and male has broad shining violet breast band extending almost to the throat (which is slightly bluer green, less brassy, than in Purple-banded); female has greyer throat and is almost unstreaked below. Female Black-bellied Sunbird has fainter ventral streaking, and may show a trace of red; otherwise nearly identical to Purple-banded. **STATUS AND DISTRIBUTION**: Locally common. *N. b. tsavoensis* occupies dry eastern *Commiphora* and *Acacia* bush and scrub from inland Somali border areas, southeast through the Tsavo parks to Mkomazi GR, Same and Korogwe in ne. Tanzania. *N. b. microrhyncha* inhabits moist coastal bush and thickets, mangroves and suburban gardens north to Malindi (rarely to Manda Island and Boni Forest), also disjunctly in the Lake Victoria basin east to Ahero, Migori and Lolgorien, with some seasonal wandering to nw. Mara GR, and south to the Grumeti River and w. Serengeti NP. We know of no specimens or sight records from the Karasuk–Kerio Valley area where reported by Short *et al.* (1990). **NOTE**: The two forms here considered conspecific have at times been treated as separate species. The range of *tsavoensis* bisects that of *microrhyncha*, but we are aware of no specimens or other evidence to support the claim (Clancey and Williams 1957) of partial overlap in ranges.

VIOLET-BREASTED SUNBIRD *Nectarinia chalcomelas* Plates 105, 107

Length 110 mm (4.25"). A stunning eastern species superficially like Purple-banded Sunbird, but larger, *longer-billed* and somewhat *shorter-tailed*. **Adult male** iridescent green above, with glossy blue-black wings, tail and belly; *wide breast band brilliant iridescent violet, not bordered below with maroon,* and *extending nearly to the blue-green throat*. (*Caution*: race *tsavoensis* of Purple-banded shows little or no maroon, and the blue-violet breast band is narrow.) No pectoral tufts. **Female** dull brownish *grey* above, with faint whitish superciliary stripes, prominent whitish primary edges and inconspicuous dull white tail-feather tips; *grey underparts, immaculate or with only a suggestion of streaks* or mottling on breast; more yellowish or creamy on belly. **Juvenile** male has black throat; female similar to adult, perhaps more streaked below. **Immature male** has green or green-and-black throat, may show broad black mid-ventral line. **VOICE**: A thin, high, hurried *tsewtsi-tse-tseep-sisisisi-tsewtsi-tsi-tsi . . .*, sometimes with a short trilled *trrrreeee* near the end; also *whichichee-see-tsiseesee*. Calls include *tsik* and *chiew-chiew-chiew . . .*, and a rapid, loud monotonous chatter, *chee-chee-chee-chee-chee . . .*. **HABITS**: Forages somewhat less actively, more deliberately, than *N. b. tsavoensis*, in low flowering trees and shrubs. Sometimes perches quietly for long periods. **SIMILAR SPECIES**: Purple-banded Sunbird compared above. Allopatric Marico Sunbird has broad maroon (not violet) breast band, the *female distinctly streaked and yellowish below*. Female Shining Sunbird (n. Kenya) has longer whitish superciliary stripes extending from bill to behind eyes; also more white in tail. Pemba Sunbird is restricted to Pemba Island (where Violet-breasted absent). **STATUS AND DISTRIBUTION**: Local and uncommon in moist coastal shrub-savanna and grassy thickets from the Somali border and Kiunga south to the Tana River delta, occasionally wandering to Watamu and Kilifi; also inland to Ijara, along the Tana to Bura, and periodically to Galana Ranch, where sympatric with *N. b. tsavoensis*. Status inland unclear, perhaps seasonal. A specimen reportedly from Moyale, not seen by us, was probably misidentified.

PEMBA SUNBIRD *Nectarinia pembae* Plate 124

Length 95–100 mm (c. 4"). Restricted to Pemba Island off ne. Tanzania. **Adult male** closely resembles Violet-breasted Sunbird, but much smaller and with *iridescent violet-and-green lesser coverts*, green iridescence over entire head and neck (slightly bluer on head), and an equally brilliant purple breast band. Wings and tail deep blue-black, faintly glossy; greater coverts edged with iridescent green, the primaries with violet. No eclipse plumage. **Female** warm olive-brown to greyish mouse-brown above, with narrow whitish superciliary stripes; darker and more blue-black on tail; whitish from chin to breast, but posterior underparts pale yellow; sometimes a faint suggestion of streaks at sides of breast. Young females are somewhat more yellowish. **Immature male** resembles female, but has blackish throat, sometimes hint of green and purple iridescence. **VOICE**: Call note, a frequently repeated *tslink* or high-pitched *ssweek* (distinct from notes of Violet-breasted Sunbird), repeated continuously, sometimes for several minutes. Song unrecorded. **HABITS**: Males very pugnacious; spend much time calling from high bare tree branches. **SIMILAR SPECIES**: No

similar sunbird is present on Pemba Island. **STATUS AND DISTRIBUTION**: Endemic to Pemba Island, where common and widespread, occupying all habitats, including towns and small offshore coral islets.

ORANGE-TUFTED SUNBIRD *Nectarinia bouvieri* Plates 105, 107

Length 115 mm (4.5"). A scarce western species with long (18–19 mm), slightly curved bill. **Adult male** resembles Marico and Violet-breasted Sunbirds, but has *purple-and-blue forecrown, blue chin* and often shows *conspicuous bright orange, yellow-tipped pectoral tufts*; narrow iridescent breast band of blue and violet bordered below by a non-metallic maroon band (difficult to see); belly deep dusky sepia. *Upperparts shiny brassy green*, much less blue-green (especially on lower back and rump) than in Marico Sunbird. **Female** recalls female double-collared sunbirds, but more brownish olive above, with variable buff or whitish superciliary stripes extending behind eyes; tail blue-black with narrow white outer edges; underparts olive-yellowish, clearer yellow on belly, with *indistinct dusky streaks or mottling, these often coalescing on throat and chin, which appear dark.* **Juvenile** similar to adult female, but young male has dark throat. **Immature male** greyish brown above, with extensive dull pinkish-copper iridescence on back, wing-coverts and on the black throat, this appearing brassy green in some lights; broad blackish mid-ventral line from throat to belly. May show blue-green and violet iridescence on breast; sides and flanks pale dull yellow. Tail shiny blue-black, the feathers edged metallic blue-green. **VOICE**: Song short, rapid, not very high-pitched: *tsitsip-chip*, or *ch-ch-sirrrip*, rising at end; sometimes a longer *sit-sit-sit-tsewtsewtsew*. Call note a low *cheep* or *chip-ip* and a loud *tchew*. **HABITS**: Solitary or with other sunbirds in shrubs or low trees at forest border; tends to feed low, often favouring thistle-like *Acanthus* flowers. **SIMILAR SPECIES**: Male Marico Sunbird lacks pectoral tufts, as does larger Violet-breasted Sunbird (eastern only). Females: both double-collared sunbirds lack brownish cast, are more pure olive above, lack noticeable superciliary stripes, and have much shorter bills, and Eastern Double-collared is at higher elevations; Marico Sunbird is more heavily streaked below; Olive-bellied is faintly streaked, but with whitish chin and pale yellow throat, brighter and paler yellow belly; Copper is diffusely streaked, with yellowish chin and throat; and Variable is bright yellow on belly and crissum, lacks superciliary stripes. All but the double-collareds are pale (not dusky olive) on chin and upper throat. **STATUS AND DISTRIBUTION**: Rather scarce and local, known only from riverine-forest margins in Busia District (Sept. 1988) and glades and edges of the Kakamega Forest in w. Kenya. Possibly resident.

SUPERB SUNBIRD *Nectarinia superba buvuma* Plate 106

Length 160–170 mm (6.5–7"). A *large-billed* sunbird of Ugandan border areas. **Adult male** dark metallic golden green above, the *crown blue* with greenish and violet reflections; wings and tail black; throat and upper breast shining ruby-red to violet-blue; *lower breast and belly deep non-iridescent maroon; bill black.* No eclipse plumage. **Female** olive above, with pale superciliary stripes; yellowish olive below, sometimes more orange on belly and crissum. **Juvenile** resembles female, but posterior underparts olive-yellow. **Immature male** moults very gradually from juvenile to adult plumage, the flank feathers replaced last. West of our area, some individuals breed in this patchy intermediate dress. **VOICE**: Call note a sharp *tsirp*, seldom heard. **HABITS**: A solitary species of riverine and forest-edge trees; attracted to flowering banana plants. **STATUS AND DISTRIBUTION**: Rare and local; possibly resident. Four acceptable Kenyan records, including a single early specimen from Mumias (now lost); recent sight records near Mumias (Dec. 1990) and Busia District (Sept. 1991, July 1993).

COPPER SUNBIRD *Nectarinia cuprea* Plates 106, 107

Length 130 mm (5.25"). A dark western species. **Breeding male** shining *burnished copper* with ruby and pink reflections on head and breast, purple on rump and upper tail-coverts, blue-black on wings and tail; belly and crissum black. **Non-breeding (and immature?) male** similar to female, but iridescent wing-coverts and tail of breeding plumage are retained, as are the upper tail-coverts (and sometimes a few shiny back feathers); may show black mid-ventral line or blotching. **Female** brownish olive above, with *dusky or blackish lores*, some dark postocular feathers and indistinct buff superciliary stripes; underparts dull olive-yellow, more yellow on belly; breast obscurely and diffusely streaked brownish olive; tail blue-black, with obscure pale tips and sides. **Juvenile** resembles female, but male has dusky throat. **VOICE**: Song distinctive, several thin notes followed by an accelerating 'bouncing-ball' trill: *tsip, tsip, tsip, tsip, tsee-see-see-see-see-seeseesee.* Also gives a repetitive *chip-chip-chip. . .* when feeding, and a hoarse *tsit-chit* in flight between flowers. **HABITS**: Solitary or gregarious, congregating at favourite plants, including the introduced *Lantana camara*. Often forages in low vegetation. Regularly pierces corolla bases. Nest has long pendent streamers. **SIMILAR SPECIES**: Male Tacazze Sunbird is much larger, longer-tailed, and at high elevations. Females: Olive-bellied is much darker above, more distinctly (but faintly) streaked below, with whitish (not yellowish) chin;

Variable has clear yellow belly, no superciliary stripes; Orange-tufted is darker, longer-billed, with dusky or olive chin; Northern Double-collared is much darker above, more olive throughout, lacks superciliary stripes and is shorter-billed. **STATUS AND DISTRIBUTION:** Fairly common resident of bush, thickets, shrubby swamp margins, forest borders and cultivation throughout the Lake Victoria basin, north to Kakamega and Kitale, east to Muhoroni and south in n. Tanzania to Musoma.

TACAZZE SUNBIRD *Nectarinia tacazze jacksoni* Plates 104, 107

Length of male 230 mm (9"), of female 140–150 mm (5.5–6"). A large, dark, highland sunbird with elongated central tail-feathers. **Breeding male** blackish, with head, throat and neck burnished bronzy green (inviting confusion with Bronze Sunbird in poor light); back purple, sometimes mixed with bronze-green; *wing- and upper tail-coverts shining purple, as is rump; breast ruby-red and violet;* rest of underparts, flight feathers and tail black. No pectoral tufts. **Non-breeding male** brownish grey, with black belly, wings and tail (including long central feathers); black mask bordered below by whitish streak; bend of wing, lower back, rump and upper tail-coverts shining purple; iridescent body feathers gradually appear elsewhere, producing mottled effect. **Female** duller and greyer than female Bronze Sunbird, dusky olive above, with dull *whitish superciliary and malar stripes outlining black lores and dusky ear-coverts; underparts greyish olive, pale yellow in centre of belly.* Pointed central tail feathers 5 mm longer than the others, dusky black with faint bluish gloss; outer rectrices conspicuously edged and tipped with white. **Juvenile** resembles female, but usually yellower. **VOICE:** Song a sibilant sputtering twitter, often long-extended, interspersed with occasional louder single notes, but otherwise little fluctuation in pitch, *sweetsiuswitter TSEU seet-swirursittii, tsit-tsit-tsit-chitichiti-chiti . . ..* Less frequent is a slower *tew tew tew tew tew. . ..* **HABITS:** Quarrelsome with smaller sunbirds. Usually solitary, although several may gather at flowering *Leonotis, Kniphofia* (red-hot poker) and introduced *Eucalyptus* and *Callistemon* (bottle-brush) trees. Also visits sugar-water feeders. **SIMILAR SPECIES:** Male Bronze Sunbird lacks reddish and purple reflections. Female Bronze is much brighter yellow below than Tacazze, with olive streaking; light facial streaks less contrasting. Female Malachite Sunbird is more yellow than female Tacazze, but resembles young of latter. **STATUS AND DISTRIBUTION:** Fairly common resident of forest, bamboo and giant heath between 1800 and 4000 m in Kenyan highlands from Mt Elgon and the Cheranganis southeast to the Mau, Aberdares and Mt Kenya; also in the north on Mt Nyiru and the Ndotos. Descends to flowering gardens at lower elevations during cold, wet months. In n. Tanzania, common on Mt Meru and Kilimanjaro, above 2150 m in the Crater Highlands and at 2900 m on Mt Hanang.

BRONZE SUNBIRD *Nectarinia k. kilimensis* Plates 104, 107

Length of male 220 mm (8.5–9"), of female 125 mm (5"). A familiar long-tailed sunbird. **Adult male** generally black, with *gold, bronze, and green reflections* on head, throat and back; lower breast, belly, wings and tail non-metallic black with slight purplish wash. No pectoral tufts. Bill shorter but more *deeply curved* than in Tacazze Sunbird. **Female** brownish olive above, with *dusky mask* and *narrow creamy-white superciliary stripes; underparts yellow, with diffuse greyish-olive streaks;* throat paler, more whitish, with ill-defined streaks; most tail feathers white-tipped, the outermost also white-edged and the *central pair slightly elongated* (5–6 mm longer than others). **Juvenile** resembles female but is more greenish olive above, with dusky forehead; short superciliary stripes yellowish, underparts more mottled than streaked; bill shorter and straighter than adult's; male has brown sides of face, dusky throat fading into olive breast and greenish-yellow belly. **VOICE:** Male calls *chee-wit-chee, chee-wit-wit* in pursuit of other sunbirds. Song an extended rapid sputtering with occasional louder harsher notes: *spitisew-spit-spit-spit-spit-chitisewsi-sweet-chirwee, chiwee, tsip-tsip-tsip-tsip, tsi-WHEW, tsip tsuweep, sitisitisew. . ..* Territorial female has an insistent *psew-psew-seep* or *tsew-EEP.* **HABITS:** Favours tubular flowers of *Erythrina, Kniphofia* (red-hot poker) and cultivated *Aloe* species. Frequent in highland gardens, where quarrelsome with other species and dominant at sugar-water feeders. Builds rather untidy nest, often with projecting porch above the entrance hole, low or high in tree. **SIMILAR SPECIES:** Male Tacazze Sunbird easily mistaken for Bronze in dull light, when both show bronzy-green head reflections. Look for Tacazze's purple or red-violet on wing- and upper tail-coverts; female Tacazze is duller below, unstreaked, with prominent whitish malar stripes. Female Malachite Sunbird is much duller: browner above, unstreaked on throat and breast, less yellow below. **STATUS AND DISTRIBUTION:** Common and widespread at forest edge, in clearings, cultivation and suburban gardens between 1200 and 2800 m in the cent. and w. Kenyan highlands, from Mt Elgon, Trans-Nzoia and Maralal south to the Chyulu Hills, Narok and the Ngurumans, and in n.Tanzania at Loliondo, throughout the Crater and Mbulu Highlands, Kilimanjaro and Mt Meru, Arusha and Moshi Districts. Some post-breeding dispersal to lower, drier areas (e.g. Lake Baringo, April 1980; Mwingi, April 1972; n. Serengeti NP, Nov. 1986).

GOLDEN-WINGED SUNBIRD *Nectarinia reichenowi*   **Plate 104**

Length of male 240 mm (9.5"), of female, 130 mm (5"). Unmistakable. A *long-tailed* highland sunbird with *bright yellow wing patches* and strongly decurved bill in *both* sexes. **Breeding male** iridescent bronzy gold on head, neck, back and lesser wing-coverts; most wing and tail feathers black with broad yellow edges, these forming a patch on the closed wing; *central tail feathers elongated*; throat and upper breast metallic copper, grading to black on lower breast and belly. **Non-breeding male** has head, back and entire underparts velvety black; wings and tail as in breeding dress. **Female** olive above, with forehead, crown and ear-coverts dark olive-brown, shading to black on lores and under eyes; underparts yellowish with olive mottling, belly and flanks olive. **Juvenile female** resembles adult; **juvenile male** dull blackish below, with some olive, and with yellow plumage duller, less golden, than in adult. **VOICE**: Calls include a rapid *chuk-chi-chi-chek*, an insistent *cher-cher-cher* and a single *tweep*. Song a prolonged twittering warble interspersed with high *chi-chi-chi. . .* phrases. **HABITS**: Particularly attracted to flowering *Leonotis* and *Crotalaria* (lion's claw) plants. Usually solitary, but several may gather at flowering shrubs. **STATUS AND DISTRIBUTION**: Locally common along forest borders, extending into cultivation and gardens in all highland areas. The smaller race *lathburyi* is endemic to the Mathews Range and mts Uraguess, Nyiru and Kulal between 1850 and 2400 m. Nominate birds range between 1800 and 3000 m in the w. and cent. Kenyan highlands from Mt Elgon and the Cheranganis to the Mau, Aberdares, Mt Kenya, Nairobi and the Chyulu Hills; in n. Tanzania from the Ngurumans and Loliondo, south through the Crater and Mbulu Highlands east to Arusha NP, Mt Meru and Kilimanjaro, sparingly in the South Pare and West Usambara Mts. In cool, wet months moves lower (Baringo, Machakos, Olorgesailie, Ngulia, Lake Victoria basin, Lolgorien, Serengeti and Lake Manyara).

MALACHITE SUNBIRD *Nectarinia famosa cupreonitens*   **Plates 104, 107**

Length of breeding male 220–240 mm (9-9.5"), of female, 150 mm (6"). **Breeding male** *brilliant emerald-green*, with *bright yellow pectoral tufts* and *long central tail feathers*; some golden reflections on back and throat; may appear bluer on belly; flight feathers and tail black. **Non-breeding male** (late Aug.–Oct.) similar to female, but wing feathers, tail-coverts and rectrices retained from breeding plumage. Moulting birds may show dark mid-ventral line. **Female** grey-brown above, with faint yellowish superciliary stripes above dark lores and ear-coverts; tail blackish, narrowly edged and tipped with white, the central feathers 2–3 mm longer than the others. *Underparts yellowish, heavily mottled* with olive-brown on sides, breast and throat, the latter contrasting with yellowish moustachial stripes. **Juvenile** resembles female, but upperparts more olive-green, underparts yellower, becoming dusky olive on breast and throat; young male can have blackish throat. **VOICE**: Call note a sharp *chip-chip* or *chi-cheer*. Song a series of short notes, *chip. . . chi. . . chew-chew-chew. . .*, accelerating into a sputtering warble, repeated at short intervals. **HABITS**: Usually in pairs, but numbers attracted to stands of flowering *Aloe*, *Leonotis* and *Kniphofia*, and wanders far into open grassland whenever these in bloom. Moves to lower levels in cool, wet months. **SIMILAR SPECIES**: Male Scarlet-tufted Malachite Sunbird has red pectoral tufts, still longer bluish-black central tail feathers; female has orange-red tufts, square-tipped tail (Malachite's slightly pointed), is duskier below. Female Tacazze is greyer, less yellow on face and underparts, with more curved bill. **STATUS AND DISTRIBUTION**: Locally common along forest edges and in grassland between 1850 and 3000 m in the w. and cent. Kenyan highlands, reaching 3400 m on Mt Elgon (where Scarlet-tufted Malachite Sunbird absent). Common on the Cheranganis, lower slopes of the Aberdares, Mt Kenya and the Mau; also on Mt. Nyiru and the Chyulu Hills. In n. Tanzania, common in the Crater Highlands, on Mt Meru and Kilimanjaro, and down to 1650 m in the West Usambaras.

SCARLET-TUFTED MALACHITE SUNBIRD *Nectarinia j. johnstoni*   **Plates 104, 107**

Length of male *c.* 270 mm (10.5"), of female 140 mm (5.5"). A large, long-billed, *moorland* species. **Breeding male** metallic green, with bluish reflections on rump and upper tail-coverts; wings and tail blue-black, the much elongated central tail feathers edged with metallic green; lower belly and crissum black; *pectoral tufts bright scarlet*. **Non-breeding male** brownish, with wings and tail as in breeding plumage. **Female** sepia-*brown* above, somewhat paler below, with paler edges to throat feathers, faint whitish moustachial streaks; *orange-red pectoral tufts*; tail black, square-tipped, with no white. **Juvenile** resembles female, but lacks pectoral tufts. **VOICE**: A harsh rasping *chk-k* or *chaa-chaa*. Song a rather mellow *sreep-sreep cheeureeeeep-reep*. **HABITS**: Fearless of man. Feeds extensively on insects in flowering giant *Lobelia* and *Senecio* plants. On Mt Kenya nests in tussock grass above 4100 m, at lower elevations in *Erica* shrubs or in *Lobelia* and *Senecio* inflorescences (Young and Evans 1993). **SIMILAR SPECIES**: Male Malachite Sunbird is smaller, brighter green, and has yellow pectoral tufts. Young Tacazze Sunbird most similar to female and juvenile *johnstoni*, but paler below, with pointed white-edged tail. **STATUS AND DISTRIBUTION**: A common resident between 3000 and 4500 m on moorlands of Mt Kenya, the Aberdares, Mt Meru, Kilimanjaro, and at 3400 m on Olosirwa in the Crater Highlands. A specimen (1 June 1934) from 2150 m on the North Pare Mts represents the only evidence of wandering.

RED-CHESTED SUNBIRD *Nectarinia erythrocerca* Plates 104, 107

Length of male 135–150 mm (5.25–6"), of female 104-112 mm (4-4.5"). A *western lakeshore* sunbird. **Adult male** brilliant iridescent blue-green above; green throat separated from broad non-iridescent *crimson or deep red (not scarlet) breast band* by narrow line of shining violet; posterior underparts black; *central rectrices extend an inch beyond rest of tail.* **Female** brownish olive above; *graduated tail blue-black, tipped whitish.* Pale yellowish feathers on upper and lower eyelids; primary edges pale yellowish, forming conspicuous wing panel in fresh plumage. Chin and throat more or less dusky; rest of underparts pale yellow, with extensive dusky mottling on breast and belly. **Juvenile male** brownish olive above, yellowish below, with dark mottling on breast and belly; chin and throat black; long pale yellowish moustachial streaks. **Voice:** Call note a sharp repeated *spink* or *spink-spink.* Song a short thin twitter on the same pitch, *tsi-si-sip-see-see-swee* or *tsi-tsi-tsi-tsi-tsi-tsi-tsi-tsip.* **Habits:** Feeds low in flowering shrubs and garden plants, usually in pairs. Pugnacious. Often nests over water. **Similar Species:** Male Beautiful Sunbird is yellow on sides of breast; female has narrow yellowish superciliary stripes and is brighter yellow below. All populations of Black-bellied Sunbird are geographically distant. Female Copper Sunbird has yellowish chin and throat (not dusky). Black-throated juvenile Amethyst Sunbird shows no yellowish wing panel, is more streaked than mottled below; it also has short pale superciliary stripes, as does juvenile Marico Sunbird (which is brighter yellow on belly). **Status and Distribution:** A fairly common resident in the Lake Victoria basin, particularly on shores and islands; also in adjacent Mara Region of n. Tanzania. Rarely far from the lakeshore, although east to Ahero, Ruma NP and Migori. **Note:** Spelling of the specific name follows Rand (1967).

BLACK-BELLIED SUNBIRD *Nectarinia nectarinioides* Plates 104, 107

Length 120–135 mm (4.75–5.5"). Smallest of the long-tailed sunbirds. **Adult male** bright iridescent green above and on throat; wings and tail black. *N. n. nectarinioides* has a broad *orange-red breast band and yellow pectoral tufts,* rest of underparts black. Northern *erlangeri* has breast more pure red, less orange, and *no pectoral tufts.* In both races, central rectrices extend 2 cm beyond others (some worn birds lack these, and belly brown instead of black). Close to, in bright light, green head shows faint brassy-pink iridescence. **Female** pale greyish olive-brown above, with suggestion of superciliary stripes. Underparts pale yellowish, *faintly streaked with dusky brown on breast and sides;* throat greyish, *sometimes with a trace of red or orange on the breast.* Tail bluish, tipped with white. **Juvenile** olive above, with short pale superciliary stripes, yellowish malar streaks, and blackish chin/throat patch joining mottled dusky and olive-yellowish upper breast; rest of underparts pale yellow, with faint brown mottling on lower breast and sides. **Voice:** Song a two-parted, thin *tsit-tsit-tsit-tsit-tsitsereetsereet* or *tsit-tsit, sit-sreet sit-sreet.* **Habits:** Solitary or in small family groups. Forages high in crowns of riverine trees, flowering baobabs and blooming *Loranthus.* Builds nest with characteristic hanging 'tail' in low tree or shrub. **Similar Species:** Male Beautiful Sunbird has red breast patch bordered laterally by yellow, and green iridescence of head lacks brassy-pink sheen of Black-bellied; female unmarked creamy yellow on underparts. Male Red-chested Sunbird of western lakesides is larger, more blue-green, with crimson (not orange-red or scarlet) breast band bordered below by violet line. Female Purple-banded Sunbird is more heavily streaked than female Black-bellied. **Status and Distribution:** *N. n. erlangeri* ranges in ne. Kenya from the Daua River south through Wajir to the Northern Uaso Nyiro River, there intergrading with nominate *nectarinioides.* The latter is locally common below 1300 m in eastern riverine acacias and dry thornbush from the Northern Uaso Nyiro and Tana Rivers, south through the Tsavo parks (common along the Tiva and Galana Rivers) to the Mkomazi GR in ne. Tanzania.

BEAUTIFUL SUNBIRD *Nectarinia pulchella* Plates 104, 107

Length of male 140–150 mm (5.5–6"), of female, 85–90 mm (3.5"). Another small, long-tailed species. **Breeding male** glittering green above and on throat, with coppery reflections on back; wings and tail black; *longitudinal strip of scarlet in centre of yellow breast;* rest of underparts metallic green in nominate *pulchella,* black in *N. p. melanogastra.* Central tail feathers extend 4–5 cm beyond others. **Non-breeding male** resembles adult female, but has black flight feathers, long central rectrices and sometimes scattered metallic feathers (especially green wing-coverts). **Female** *N. p. pulchella* pale greyish olive or brownish olive above, with narrow yellowish superciliary stripes beginning over eyes; lores blackish; sides of face dark olive-brown. Underparts creamy yellow, more whitish on upper throat and chin; tail dusky, tipped white. *N. p. melanogastra* said to show dusky streaking below. **Juvenile** resembles adult female, but male black on chin and throat. **Immature male** shows green iridescence in black throat. **Voice:** Foraging call a weak *chip. . . chip.* Annoyance call a loud *tseu-tseu-tseu-tseu . . ..* Song a variable high-pitched *shrrrr-tsit-tsit-sitsit-cheet-tsitsiseet-seet. . ..* **Habits:** Singles or small groups feed in dry bush, often in acacias. Also visits garden flowers. **Similar Species:** Male Black-bellied Sunbird has no yellow on breast. Male Red-chested Sunbird is larger, lacks yellow below, and has violet-bordered crimson or deep red breast band. Female Pygmy Sunbird is brighter yellow below and has shorter bill. **STATUS AND DISTRIBUTION**: Widespread in low dry thorn-bush. Nominate *pulchella* is common below 1300 m in nw. Kenya, from Lokichokio and Turkana District south to the Kongelai Escarpment, Kerio Valley and lakes Baringo and Bogoria. *N. p. melanogastra* ranges east and south of the cent. Kenyan highlands from the upper Tana River, Kitui and the Tsavo parks, west through Amboseli NP, Kajiado and Magadi Districts to the Southern Uaso Nyiro River; also in low dry parts of Nyanza and the Lake Victoria basin north to Siaya and Bondo; ranges south into n. Tanzania in the Mara Region, Serengeti, Lake Manyara and Tarangire NPs, lowlands around Lake Natron, Longido, Arusha and Moshi Districts, the Masai Steppe and Mkomazi GR. During periods of severe drought moves to higher elevations (e.g. Nairobi suburbs and cent. Rift Valley).

SHINING SUNBIRD *Nectarinia habessinica turkanae*   Plates 106, 107

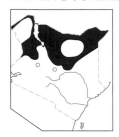

Length *c.* 130 mm (5.25"). A dry-country species of *northern* Kenya. **Adult male** the *only far-northern sunbird with broad scarlet breast band*. Iridescent green above, including head and some wing-coverts; coppery reflections on back, coppery and violet on crown, bluish on rump and upper tail-coverts. Wings and tail black. *Orange-scarlet breast band* sometimes bordered above and below by faint narrow lines of metallic blue; *rest of underparts black*; pectoral tufts yellow. **Female** *pale ashy brown or brownish grey above*, with blackish loral spots and faint *long whitish superciliary stripes* from bill to behind eyes. Underparts pale brownish grey, almost white on throat, obscurely streaked on breast and sides; under tail-coverts whitish, with bold dusky brown feather centres; tail black, the outer feathers narrowly tipped and edged white. **Juvenile** similar to female, but chin and upper breast black. **VOICE**: Usual note a sharp *spik-spik* or *speek-speek*. Song of Kenyan birds not recorded; in Yemen, a rather low-pitched *skieu-ek-ek, skieu-tsek-tsek-tsek . . ..* **HABITS**: Partial to flowering aloes and acacias; sometimes hovers when feeding. **SIMILAR SPECIES**: Male double-collared sunbirds and Olive-bellied Sunbird are smaller and in different habitats; none is black-bellied. Female Marico Sunbird has faint yellow wash on lower breast and belly, dusky streaks which coalesce on throat. Other similar species are allopatric. **STATUS AND DISTRIBUTION**: Local and uncommon in northern arid/semi-arid thorn-bush below 1000 m, from Lokichokio east to Mandera and south to base of the Kongelai Escarpment, Kapedo, Lake Baringo, Isiolo and Meru NP.

SPARROWS AND PETRONIAS, FAMILY PASSERIDAE
(World, *c.* 30 species; Africa, 18; Kenya, 6; n. Tanzania, 6)

These birds are sometimes included with the weavers in the family Ploceidae (Moreau and Greenway 1962), the two groups being similar in palate structure, nesting habits and social behaviour. The main external feature distinguishing them from weavers is their dorsally positioned and greatly reduced outer (10th) primary, its tip projecting only slightly from under the outermost upper primary covert. On the basis of studies of egg-white proteins, Sibley (1970) suggested recognition of family status until more information is available. Sparrows are allied to fringillids, but differ in their complete post-juvenile moult, and in building a bulky domed nest with a side entrance (in tree branches, cavities, under eaves of buildings or in thatched roofs). They are granivorous, ground-feeding, open-country birds, some species remarkably adaptable and closely associating with humans. They may appropriate nests of other birds, especially weavers and swallows. All species lay speckled eggs. The sexes are often alike or similar; plumage coloration is largely of rufous, brown and grey tones, and some species have prominent black throat patches. Vocally, sparrows rank low, most species having only simple chirps, sometimes run together to serve as a song.

GREY-HEADED SPARROW *Passer griseus*   Plate 108
(including Parrot-billed, Swahili and Swainson's Sparrows)

Length 140–180 mm (5–7"). A widespread grey-headed sparrow, represented by four races within our area: *P. g. ugandae*, with relatively small bill, *rich tawny-rufous upperparts* and generally *pale greyish-white underparts*; larger *P. g. gongonensis*, with stouter, more swollen bill, and typically with uniform dark grey underparts (usually no white on throat, but under tail-coverts sometimes whitish); *P. g. suahelicus*, similar in size and in colour of underparts to *ugandae*, but duller above, the dusky brown back almost uniform in tone with the crown; *P. g. swainsonii*, similar to *gongonensis* but smaller, with *smaller bill, darker and duskier head and face*, grey underparts, and *dull brownish back contrasting with tawny-rufous rump and upper tail-coverts*. In all forms, bill black when breeding, horn-brown at other times. Sexes alike. **Juveniles** resemble adults, but bill buffy horn and back with dusky streaks. **VOICE**: Chirping and chattering much like those of House Sparrow. *P. g. ugandae* often gives a single *chirp* or *cheep*, and a short rapid *chchchchch* and *ch-ch-ch-chiwirp*, slightly rising in pitch; also a series of thin notes, often four in number, *tseup seep chirp tseep*, the group frequently repeated. Song of *ugandae* and *gongonensis* a prolonged monotonous series of loud sharp

notes, *TCHEW TCHEW TCHEW . . .*, with little variation. *P. g. gongonensis* also gives a series of alternating notes, *chew chur chew chur chew chur. . .*, at times each note slightly longer and more slurred, *tcheew chirrup tchewew tchewer tchwe tchwer. . .*; comparable song of *ugandae*, is *dzreep dzhirp dzreep dshirp dzhreep . . .* *P .g. gongonensis* has isolated churring notes, *chrrrrrrryek* or *wurrrrrrk*, and a longer *tserkisee-chirrrr*. Other races give similar calls, but voice of *swainsonii* not well described. **HABITS**: In pairs or small flocks, often feeding with other sparrows and weavers. Bold and fearless in towns and villages. Male 'sings' from prominent perch for extended periods. **STATUS AND DISTRIBUTION**: Except in arid parts of the north and northeast, ranges widely from sea level to over 2500 m, in varied habitats from bushed grassland, savanna and forest edge to towns and villages. *P. g. ugandae* is common west of the Rift Valley, meeting and intergrading with *gongonensis* in several Rift localities, and apparently with *suahelicus* in Tanzania (White 1963). May reach coastal Tanzanian lowlands at Tanga. *P. g. gongonensis* is common east of the Rift, ranging north to Lake Turkana, south to n. and ne. Tanzania, and throughout coastal Kenyan lowlands, intergrading with *ugandae* and possibly with *suahelicus*, whose range is centred in sw. Kenya and n. Tanzania from Narok District south through the Mara GR, Loita Plains/Hills to Serengeti NP and the Crater Highlands; *suahelicus* also present (regularly?) with *gongonensis* and *ugandae* at Lake Elmenteita in the Rift Valley. *P. g. swainsonii* known from Ethiopian border highlands at Moyale, intergrades with *gongonensis* in Turkana and Marsabit Districts, also with *ugandae* in Eritrea and Sudan (White, *op. cit*). **NOTE**: Certain of the above forms seem in places to behave as separate species, occupying the same or adjacent areas and appearing to remain distinct. Elsewhere, two, and rarely three, of these same forms mingle with one another and with birds of intermediate phenotypes. How these may segregate for breeding is unknown; none of the East African populations has received detailed study. At present, the frequency of intermediate birds and lack of obvious vocal or behavioural distinctions suggest that most forms should be considered conspecific. With some misgivings, we treat the Southern Grey-headed Sparrow as a separate species, *P. diffusus*, following Dowsett and Dowsett-Lemaire (1980, 1993), Dowsett and Forbes-Watson (1993) and Short *et al.* (1990). This bird apparently hybridizes only infrequently with northern birds in contact zones.

SOUTHERN GREY-HEADED SPARROW *Passer diffusus mosambicus*   Plate 124

Length 130–160 mm (5–6.25"). In our region, restricted to Pemba Island. Resembles a small, *pale* Grey-headed Sparrow with a *noticeably small bill*. Upperparts pale brown, with dull cinnamon rump and 'shoulders'; large white bar across median coverts; remiges and tail dull brown with pale feather edges. Head pale brownish grey, contrasting with back; crown and forehead almost pure grey. Underparts pale ashy grey, almost white on throat. **VOICE AND HABITS**: Not known to differ significantly from those of *P. griseus*. **SIMILAR SPECIES**: See Grey-headed Sparrow. **STATUS AND DISTRIBUTION**: Fairly common on Pemba Island, Tanzania. See **NOTE** under the preceding species.

RUFOUS SPARROW *Passer rufocinctus*   Plate 108

Length 130–140 mm (5–5.5"). A brightly coloured, *pale-eyed*, highland sparrow. **Adult male** has top and sides of head grey, bordered by *rufous streak from eyes back and around ear-coverts* to side of breast; moustachial and supraloral streaks pale buff; lores dusky; *chin and throat black. Back rufous with black streaks; rump and upper tail-coverts plain bright rufous.* Wings dusky brown with two pale buff wing-bars. Eyes cream-coloured or creamy tan; bill black; feet dull brown. *P. r. shelleyi* has black postocular lines and a smaller black bib than in nominate birds. **Female** resembles male, but throat patch dusky grey. **Juvenile** dull tawny instead of rufous above, male's throat black, female's grey; eyes brown. **VOICE**: Notes include a sharp *tsui* or *tseuPEE*, a high-pitched squeaky *tsweet*, a louder rolling *tchweep*, and a loud *CHEWP* recalling Grey-headed Sparrow. Song consists of thin sharp metallic notes, often alternating with a few lower chirps: *tseup CHREE, tseup CHREE, tsweet SHREEP. . ..* A repeated *chiREET* note also may serve as a song. **HABITS**: Much like those of House Sparrow. Typically in pairs. Builds large, untidy globular grass nests in trees, huts and buildings. **SIMILAR SPECIES**: Other *Passer* species are dark-eyed and lack rufous stripes on head. **STATUS AND DISTRIBUTION**: The nominate race is common in various non-forested habitats, including cultivation, in and near the Rift Valley highlands, from Eldoret, Maralal, Laikipia and Meru Districts south to the Mara GR, Narok, Kajiado and Machakos; in n. Tanzania, widespread around human habitation from Serengeti NP east through the Crater Highlands to Arusha District and western slopes of Kilimanjaro at Ngare Nairobi. *P. r. shelleyi* reaches our region in Ugandan border areas at the base of the Kongelai Escarpment and around Kunyao; also an early record from the North Kerio River. **NOTE**: Treated as a race of *P. iagoensis* by White (1963) and Hall and Moreau (1970), and as a race of the southern African *motitensis* by Britton (1980) and Dowsett and Forbes-Watson (1993).

SOMALI SPARROW *Passer castanopterus fulgens*   **Plate 108**

Length 115 mm (4.5"). A small, brightly coloured sparrow of arid n. Kenya. **Breeding male** *yellow* below and on face, with prominent yellow cheeks and black bib. *Crown, nape and wing-coverts rich rufous-brown*; back streaked grey and black. Bill black; eyes brown. **Non-breeding male** less yellow, greyer on crown, has smaller bib with pale feather edges; bill yellowish brown. **Female** much like female House Sparrow, but *pale lemon yellow below*, buffier on breast, sides and flanks. **Juvenile** similar, but dingier below. **VOICE**: Chirping notes similar to those of House Sparrow. **HABITS**: Gregarious except when breeding, becoming locally abundant around artificial food sources (e.g. famine-relief centres). Nests away from human habitation in tree cavities along dry watercourses. **SIMILAR SPECIES**: Female House Sparrow compared above. **STATUS AND DISTRIBUTION**: A locally common resident of tree-lined watercourses and villages in arid/semi-arid areas of n. Kenya, from Lake Turkana and Ethiopian border areas south to Marsabit, Laisamis, the base of the Ndotos and Kapedo.

HOUSE SPARROW *Passer domesticus indicus*   **Plate 108**

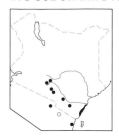

Length 140 mm (5.5"). A familiar species. East African birds are smaller, paler and with brighter white cheeks than the European subspecies. **Adult male** streaked tawny-rufous and black on back, with crown, rump and upper tail-coverts grey; dark chestnut band on side of head, and below this a black band connecting with the *large black bib*. Bill black in breeding season, otherwise horn-brown. **Female** and **juvenile** buffy brown, with broad pale buff superciliary stripes, yellowish-horn bill and white wing-bars. **VOICE**: Chirping notes like those of northern races. **HABITS**: Bold and confiding. Nests under eaves, in gutter pipes, and in holes in rock walls. Probably competes with Grey-headed Sparrow for nest sites and food. **SIMILAR SPECIES**: See female Somali Sparrow. **STATUS AND DISTRIBUTION**: Introduced at Mombasa early this century, but not becoming well established until the mid-1980s or later. Remains local and rather uncommon in coastal towns from Dar es Salaam north to Malindi. Has spread along highways and railroad lines inland to Voi, Mtito Andei, Sultan Hamud, Nairobi and Thika, breeding in villages, petrol stations, and in some national park lodges (e.g. Tsavo East NP, nesting near Voi in 1986, at Aruba Lodge in 1988). First reported in Nairobi in October 1992, and now thriving on garbage in many parts of the city. Recent (1993) sight records at Same and Kılımanjaro International Airport near Moshi suggest similar truck-assisted passage out of coastal ports to interior n. Tanzania. (Present on Zanzibar, but not recorded on nearby Pemba Island.)

CHESTNUT SPARROW *Passer eminibey*   **Plates 108, 115**

Length 105–112 mm (*c.* 4.25"). A small *Passer* with some chestnut feathers in all plumages. **Adult male** *largely rich chestnut-rufous*, darker on head and face; wings and tail blackish, with pale rufous feather edges. *Effectively resembles a miniature Chestnut Weaver.* **Female** chestnut only on lower back and rump, with variable amounts on throat and above eyes; head greyish, back grey-brown with blackish streaks. **Juvenile** male resembles a dull female, becoming mottled as the chestnut adult feathers appear. **VOICE**: Song thin and high-pitched, *tchiweeza tchiweeza tchi-tchi-tchi-tchi see-see-see-see-serichi*. Flight call a ringing *chew chew*. **HABITS**: Gregarious. Builds spherical nest of grass with side entrance, but will also use old weaver nests. **SIMILAR SPECIES**: Chestnut Weaver is much larger, with longer, heavier bill. **STATUS AND DISTRIBUTION**: Locally common resident of open thorn-bush, savanna, open woodland and gardens below 2200 m, mainly in the Rift Valley and adjacent plateau country. Ranges from the Karasuk Hills and below the Kongelai Escarpment to Baringo and Maralal Districts, Samburu and Shaba GRs and Meru NP; also locally in the cent. Rift Valley south to Narok, Kajiado and Namanga and southeast to Amboseli and Tsavo West NPs. In n. Tanzania, locally common from se. Serengeti NP, lowlands around Lake Natron and Longido south to Tarangire NP and the Masai Steppe. Continued presence around Marsabit and Wajir requires confirmation.

YELLOW-SPOTTED PETRONIA *Petronia pyrgita*   **Plate 108**

Length 150 mm (6"). A drab brownish-grey sparrow with *narrow broken white eye-ring and indistinct pale superciliary stripes*. A small yellow spot in centre of throat, below the white chin, is seldom visible in the field but is conspicuous in calling birds, 'flashing' with each chirp; not present in all individuals. Breast brownish, throat and belly white; wing-bars and flight-feather edges whitish. Eyes brown; bill and feet pale horn-pink. Sexes alike. **Juvenile** much browner, with buff wing-bars and flight-feather edgings; superciliary stripes buff, more pronounced than in adult. **VOICE**: Song a simple *chiew-chiew-chiew-chiew-chiew-tcheep*. Call is a double *Passer*-like *cherp-cherp*. **HABITS**: Quiet and inconspicuous. Feeds on the ground in pairs or small groups. Sings from elevated perches, and nests in tree cavities. **SIMILAR SPECIES**: Juvenile *Passer* sparrows lack the eye-ring and have darker bills. **STATUS AND DISTRIBUTION**: A widespread but rather uncommon resident between 500 and 1500 m in open dry woodland, savanna, and bush, ranging across much of n. and e. Kenya south to Tsavo and Amboseli NPs, Mkomazi GR and the Masai Steppe, Tarangire, Lake Manyara and Serengeti NPs. Absent from coastal lowlands south of the Sabaki River, the Lake Victoria basin, w. and cent. Kenyan highlands, the Crater and Mbulu Highlands and the Usambara Mts.

WEAVERS AND RELATIVES, FAMILY PLOCEIDAE
(World, 113 species; Africa, 101; Kenya, 60; n. Tanzania, 42)

Although a diverse group, ploceids typically are thick-billed birds with strong legs and feet. Plumage is highly variable, and there are pronounced seasonal changes in some species. The sexes are alike in *Sporopipes*, the Plocepasserinae and some Bubalornithinae. The 10th (outermost) primary is moderately long in *Bubalornis*, quite small in some other genera (but reduction never as pronounced as in Passeridae). Bill structure varies considerably. The most highly specialized subfamily presumably is Ploceinae; the most primitive Bubalornithinae. *Bubalornis* apparently is unique among passerine birds in its well-developed, sometimes visible penis.

Ploceids occupy varied habitats, ranging from dry bush to marshes, swamps and heavy forest. Their breeding habits are particularly diverse; some species are solitary, others highly colonial, but all construct covered nests. The buffalo-weavers (Bubalornithinae) build bulky arboreal communal structures of sticks, with separate internal nest chambers. Social weavers, sparrow-weavers and the Rufous-tailed Weaver (Plocepasserinae) build rounded or ovoid nests of dry grass or leaves with an entrance near the bottom. The feather-lined grass nest of the Speckle-fronted Weaver (Sporopipinae) has a porch-like extension over the lateral entrance. True weavers (Ploceinae: see p. 659) intricately weave elaborate nests of green grasses, palm-leaf strips or other plant material; some are remarkably compact, with downward-pointing entrance tubes. Most *Ploceus* species and their near relatives build in trees or shrubs. The thick-billed Compact Weaver and Grosbeak-Weaver, queleas, bishops and widowbirds all weave a ball of dry grasses, with a side entrance hole, attached to reeds, low shrubs or grass stems. Ploceid eggs are spotted, unlike those of estrildids.

The family as treated here excludes the sparrows (Passeridae) and waxbills, whydahs and indigobirds (Estrildidae). Some DNA studies (Sibley and Ahlquist 1981) suggest that wagtails and pipits may be closely related to ploceids, but pending confirmation we retain them in Motacillidae.

WHITE-HEADED BUFFALO-WEAVER *Dinemellia dinemelli*   Plate 109

Length 180–185 mm (*c.* 7"). Sexes alike. A striking bird, with *white head* and underparts, *bright orange-red upper and under tail-coverts and white wing patches* (primary bases); small patch at bend of wing also red or orange; back, wings and tail dusky brown in northern birds, black in southern *boehmi*. Eyes dark brown; bill and feet black. **Juvenile** resembles adults, but orange-red replaced by orange. **VOICE**: Calls include a shrill, strident, somewhat parrot-like *skwieeeer*, a more rasping metallic *errrrrrrh*, a thinner *kiiyerrr*, and a loud ringing *TEW* repeated at intervals of several seconds. **HABITS**: Noisy and gregarious, but lone males call from treetops. Forages on ground, often with starlings, feeding on insects. Nests in colonies in thorn trees, alone or in small groups, building large (to 0.5 m in length) ovoid structures lined with grass and feathers, the nest somewhat flattened (not high and rounded like those of *Bubalornis*), with short entrance tube at same level as nest chamber, opening downwards. Nest may be suspended from long branch or closely attached to underside; often surrounded with extra thorny twigs. **STATUS AND DISTRIBUTION**: *D. d. dinemelli* is common and widespread in n. and e. Kenya, mainly in dry bush and savanna below 1400 m; scarce in the highlands; absent from Lake Victoria basin and coastal lowlands south of Ngomeni. *D. d. boehmi* ranges through much of interior Tanzania north to Serengeti, Lake Manyara and Tarangire NPs, the Masai Steppe and Mkomazi GR, intergrading with the nominate race in se. Kenya.

RED-BILLED BUFFALO-WEAVER *Bubalornis niger intermedius*   Plate 109

Length 215–230 mm (8.5–9"). Starling-sized and sturdy. Sexes distinct. **Adult male** mostly black, with *stout reddish bill* (dusky at tip) and white-edged primaries; irregular white patches from sides of breast to flanks. Eyes brown; tarsi and toes reddish brown. **Female** dark brown above, white below, with *heavy dark mottling* on breast, sides and flanks; heavily streaked on lower breast, lightly so on belly. *Bill horn-brown, pinkish at base below.* **Juvenile** pale brown above, with grey cheeks; *bill largely yellow-orange or pinkish;* underparts spotted and barred; some black-and-white blotches on sides. **VOICE**: Male gives a strident chattering *chi-chi-chi-skwi-chiree-chiree-skwiree-skirrow*, and a drier *chyerr chyerr cherk-cherk-cherk-cherk;* the loud rapid chatter may be followed by a skirling or squealing *skeekia-skeekia-skeekia.* Female has a more musical *chwee.* **HABITS**: Noisy and gregarious. Groups feed on the ground, often with starlings; adept at running. Builds massive thorny stick nest (to 1 m or more in length), usually in acacia or baobab tree, each containing up to 10 chambers with small entrances; used for communal roosting as well as breeding.

SIMILAR SPECIES: White-billed Buffalo-Weaver has ivory or blackish bill; young much darker below than young Red-billed. **STATUS AND DISTRIBUTION**: Common and widespread in bush and savanna with large trees, mainly east of the Rift Valley and below 1500 m; widely sympatric with the preceding species. Ranges south into Tanzania in the Mkomazi GR, and from Tarangire and Lake Manyara NPs to the Serengeti and Maswa GR. Isolated small populations in w. Kenya at Ahero and Ruma NP. Report of sympatry with *B. albirostris* in the Kerio Valley erroneous.

WHITE-BILLED BUFFALO-WEAVER *Bubalornis albirostris* Plate 109

Length 215–230 mm (8.5–9"). **Breeding male** similar to preceding species, but *bill ivory-white* (dusky at tip), rough and somewhat swollen at base, becoming largely or entirely black in **non-breeding male**; bill of **female** similar, but lacks basal swelling. Plumage of both sexes black or brownish black, often with white feather bases showing along sides. Eyes dark brown; feet black. **Juvenile** dusky brown above, mottled or streaked with dusky and white below; throat white; bill blackish. **VOICE**: Near nest male gives a harsh dry rattle, *tshutchutchutchu*, leading into a rapid, strident, squealing *skwee-skwee-skwee-kerEEkerilli-kerilli-kerEE*, or a rapid *chuka-chuka-wurki skwiya-queeyanh-queeyanh, wik-wik-wik-wik-wik*; also a rollicking mechanical *cue-cue-cue-cue-cue . . .*, rapidly delivered. **HABITS**: Similar to those of preceding species. Noisy at nesting colonies. Builds large multi-chambered nest of dry sticks like that of preceding species, sometimes with long extensions of thorny twigs along approaches. **SIMILAR SPECIES**: See Red-billed Buffalo-Weaver. **STATUS AND DISTRIBUTION**: Locally common resident from nw. Kenyan border areas and Turkana District south to the Turkwell and Kerio Valleys, lakes Baringo and Bogoria.

DONALDSON-SMITH'S SPARROW-WEAVER *Plocepasser donaldsoni* Plate 109

Length 165 mm (6.5"). A northern weaver with *scaly crown, dark malar lines*, and white lower rump and upper tail-coverts; upperparts generally pale brown; cheeks and underparts pale buff, mottled with brown on breast, sides and flanks. Bill large, blackish. **Juvenile** browner above, with tawny-buff feather edges. **VOICE**: A prolonged varied song of harsh and soft notes interspersed with whistles and short warbling notes, somewhat starling-like: *tsick-tsurr-sweeet, chirrrrr, tsurr-suweep, chuWEE. . .* and *chwee, tchur, skwee, teeee, wueeet-tweer-skweee-churrr. . .* **HABITS**: Much like those of White-browed Sparrow-Weaver. **SIMILAR SPECIES**: White-browed Sparrow-Weaver has bold white superciliary stripes and much white in wings. **STATUS AND DISTRIBUTION**: Locally common in n. Kenya, below 1500 m in dry bush and open short-grass country with scattered acacias. Ranges from east side of Lake Turkana and adjacent Ethiopian border areas south and southeast to Wajir, Mado Gashi and Isiolo Districts. Sympatric with the following species in Samburu, Buffalo Springs and Shaba GRs.

WHITE-BROWED SPARROW-WEAVER *Plocepasser mahali melanorhynchus* Plate 109

Length 165 mm (6.5"). A common dry-country bird with *white rump and upper tail-coverts, broad white superciliary stripes* (not extending to bill), and *broadly white-edged wing feathers*. Back and sides of face brown; crown and forehead blackish brown; underparts largely white; some black marks at sides of breast continuous with black malar region. Eyes brown; bill black; feet pinkish. **Juvenile** resembles adult, but has paler bill. **VOICE**: A chattering, squealing song, often prolonged and given in chorus, the shrill notes distinct or rapidly run together, e.g. *chiwerp skiweep tsweee skeeep skeweeerk cheerp; chirrup-chirru, squeek squew-weechiew chiwew ski-skiwee wichew chuwiew. . .*; or a strident *squa-ee-ch-ch-cheeeah-squaeeek*. Has various other squealing and chirping calls. **HABITS**: Highly social, in noisy flocks of 20 or more, breeding in small colonies in thorn trees. Builds untidy rounded or ovoid nest with short entrance tube sometimes projecting downwards. When young partly grown, a second entrance is opened, as in *Pseudonigrita* nests (Granvik 1934). Feeds on the ground, at times with starlings and buffalo-weavers, mainly on insects and seeds; also visits grain fields. **SIMILAR SPECIES**: Donaldson-Smith's Sparrow-Weaver has white rump, but is less boldly patterned, mottled below, with white cheeks and throat separated by narrow dark line from bill to side of neck. **STATUS AND DISTRIBUTION**: Common to abundant in bush, savanna and dry woodland (mainly among acacias below 1400 m) through much of Kenya south to Namanga, Longido and the Mkomazi GR, but largely absent from the Lake Victoria basin, coastal lowlands and the more arid northern and eastern areas.

Kenyan Weaver Nests (*Malimbus, Anaplectes, Amblyospiza, Plocepasser, Pseudonigrita, Bubalornis* and *Dinemellia*)

1 Red-headed Malimbe, *Malimbus rubricollis*. Solitary. Western forest trees only. Similar nests of *Anaplectes* not in forest.

2 Red-headed Weaver, *Anaplectes rubriceps*. Solitary or two or three nests in close proximity. Typically of firm materials; many projecting ends. Length of entrance tube varies. Conspicuous, often near buildings. Uncommon but widespread in savanna, riverine trees, gardens.

3 Black-capped Social Weaver, *Pseudonigrita cabanisi*. Colonial in isolated trees in dry areas of north and east. Often of inverted-cone shape, but may be more spherical. Typically with two entrance holes. Sometimes compound (3c). Often on thin dangling twig stripped of its leaves.

4 Grosbeak-Weaver, *Amblyospiza albifrons*. Solitary or in small groups in marshes. Compact and tightly woven between upright reed stems or *Typha* leaves. Roosting nest (4a) with larger entrance than those used for breeding (4b).

5 Grey-capped Social Weaver, *Pseudonigrita darnaudi*. Colonial in acacias (especially *A. drepanolobium*) or tall spindly saplings. Variable in shape; rather large for size of bird; may show two entrances after eggs hatch. Two nests sometimes attached to one another.

6 White-browed Sparrow-Weaver, *Plocepasser mahali*. Colonial. Locally common in acacias, often on safari-lodge grounds and in campsites. Bulky, untidy, rounded or ovoid, sometimes curved downwards. One entrance when containing eggs, two after hatching.

7 Chestnut-crowned Sparrow-Weaver, *Plocepasser superciliosus*. Northwestern. Solitary or a few nests in small leafy tree. Loosely constructed with long projecting grass stems.

8 Donaldson-Smith's Sparrow-Weaver, *Plocepasser donaldsoni*. Local south to Isiolo District. Colonial, usually in acacias, often low. Resembles nest of partly sympatric *P. mahali*, but sometimes more elongate.

9 White-headed Buffalo-Weaver, *Dinemellia dinemelli*. Northern and eastern. Solitary or a few together in a tree. Large, of twigs, stems or coarse grasses.

10 Red-billed Buffalo-Weaver, *Bubalornis niger*. Common, widespread. Bulky masses of dry, often thorny twigs, typically several in one large tree (10a). Old nests frequently used as supports for colonies of Chestnut Weaver nests.

11 White-billed Buffalo-Weaver, *Bubalornis albirostris*. Northwestern, south to Lake Bogoria. Resembles nest of *B. niger*. Variable. May have long tunnel of thorny twigs as shown.

Ring stage of nest of Red-headed Weaver.

CHESTNUT-CROWNED SPARROW-WEAVER *Plocepasser superciliosus* **Plate 109**

Length 150–160 mm (*c.* 6"). Unique. *Sparrow-like, with a pronounced head pattern*: long white superciliary stripes, subocular marks and sub-moustachial stripes, plus black malar lines; crown and ear-coverts chestnut. Upperparts mainly rufous-brown, with *two white wing-bars and conspicuous whitish flight-feather edges*. Underparts greyish white. **Juvenile** slightly paler than adult. **Voice**: A short undistinguished song, *wit SEEU witiseet-seet-seet*, often ending in a dry metallic trill, *triiiiiiii*. **Habits**: Quiet and unobtrusive. Pairs and small groups feed on ground, in undergrowth or low trees. One or more pairs build untidy globular nests of dry grass and leaves in leafy tree. **Status and Distribution**: A local and uncommon resident of w. Kenyan bush and lightly wooded slopes between 1200 and 1800 m, from the Karasuk Hills south to the Kongelai Escarpment, in the Kerio Valley and the Tugen Hills. Several pairs reportedly bred east of Lake Turkana in October 1984, but substantiation lacking.

RUFOUS-TAILED WEAVER *Histurgops ruficaudus* **Plate 122**

Length 200–220 mm (8–8.5"). A *scaly-looking Tanzanian* weaver with much *tawny-rufous in tail and wings*. **Adult** *pale-eyed*. Body generally mottled with grey-brown, wings darker with inner webs of flight-feathers pale tawny-rufous; central rectrices dark brown. Underparts pale greyish white, mottled with brownish grey. Bill and feet brownish; eyes bluish white. **Juvenile** darker brown, with extensive scaly mottling on underparts, *yellowish-horn* bill and *brown eyes*. **Voice**: A bleating *pchweezzee* (Fuggles-Couchman and Elliott 1946) and a squealing *skwee-ur* (Moreau). **Habits**: Gregarious and noisy. Feeds on the ground, alone or in company with starlings and buffalo-weavers. Tame and confiding around some national park lodges and camps. Builds large untidy grass nest with short but wide lateral entrance tube, in loose scattered colonies among acacia trees. **Similar Species**: Female and juvenile Red-billed Buffalo-Weavers are darker above and have no rufous in wings or tail. **Status and Distribution**: Endemic to n. Tanzania, where locally common in acacia savanna from Tarangire and Lake Manyara NPs west through the Ngorongoro Conservation Area, and from Lake Eyasi to Serengeti NP, Maswa GR and the Wembere Steppe. Particularly numerous around lakes Lygarja and Masek.

GREY-CAPPED SOCIAL WEAVER *Pseudonigrita arnaudi* **Plate 109**

Length 110–120 mm (4.5"). A small, *grey-crowned* bird with a *short, pale-tipped tail*. **Adult** *P. a. arnaudi* mostly grey-brown, with primaries and most of tail black; entire top of head pale grey, appearing whitish in strong light; narrow white eye-ring prominent. Eyes brown; bill black; feet pinkish brown. *P. a. dorsalis* has centre of back conspicuously grey. **Juvenile** buffier brown, crown grey-brown and contrasting little with back; cheeks darker brown, a little black around eyes. Bill brownish horn, yellowish at base. **Voice**: Among the varied calls are a sharp, high-pitched *tew tew tew*, *tu-tew*, *tu-tew*, or *SPI-chew-SPI-chew*, *spik-spik*, *PI-tsew-PI-tsew*. When going to roost, a shrill trilling *che-cheh sireeeee*, a trilled *rreet-rreeee-rreeee* and a loud, strident *sreet-sreet-sreet . . . .* Other calls are a rolling *chew* and a repeated *chreet-chewt*, the quality reminiscent of a House Sparrow's chirp. **Habits**: Gregarious. Breeds in small, dense colonies in thorn trees. Builds relatively large, compact grass nest, large for size of bird, and may have two entrance holes on underside, especially when used for roosting in non-breeding season; before egg-laying, one entrance is closed. Nest firmly woven to several branchlets, usually in tall spindly saplings or ant-gall acacias. Also roosts in old nests of other weavers. **Similar Species**: Juvenile Black-capped Social Weaver resembles young Grey-capped, but entire upper half of head is brown, bill larger and tail longer. **Status and Distribution**: *P. a. arnaudi* is a locally common resident of bush and light acacia woodland in dry country, mainly below 1400 m, largely in and east of the Rift Valley; ranges from the Karasuk Hills south to the base of the Kongelai Escarpment, and from the southern Kerio Valley east to the Laikipia Plateau, south to lakes Magadi and Natron; also from Nairobi and Amboseli NPs to Mt Meru and Tarangire NP in n. Tanzania. *P. a. dorsalis* ranges from se. Mara GR, south through Serengeti NP to Lake Eyasi and beyond.

BLACK-CAPPED SOCIAL WEAVER *Pseudonigrita cabanisi* **Plate 109**

Length *c.* 130 mm (5"). Sparrow-sized, with *tail and top half of head black*; otherwise pale brown above; underparts white, with black streak along each side of breast (sometimes concealed by wings) and another from centre of lower breast to mid-belly. Eyes red; *bill ivory*, the mandible tinged yellow-green; feet brownish. **Juvenile** has upper half of head dark brown, bill dull horn-coloured. **Voice**: High-pitched squealing chatter in nesting colony indulged in by numerous birds, *sk'peee chwee-cher skiieer chir-chir squirrrrrr chirr-chrii-chirr. . .*; more wiry, less coarse, than chattering of Donaldson-Smith's Sparrow-Weaver, often vocal in same areas. **Habits**: Gregarious. Feeds on the ground. Nests in colonies in isolated acacia trees, the variable but often somewhat cone-shaped grass nest frequently on pendent slender branchlets; two entrances underneath, as in preceding species; a few

nests sometimes clustered together. Non-breeding flocks partially nomadic. **SIMILAR SPECIES**: Juvenile Grey-capped Social Weaver has short, pale-tipped tail. **STATUS AND DISTRIBUTION**: Locally common in dry open savanna and grassy bush below 1300 m. Ranges from ne. Kenyan border areas southwest to Barsaloi, Samburu, Buffalo Springs and Shaba GRs and south through Wajir to Meru, both Tsavo NPs and Galana Ranch. Wanderers reported from Tanzania's Pare Mts and lowlands south of Kilimanjaro at Naberera.

SPECKLE-FRONTED WEAVER *Sporopipes frontalis emini* Plate 108

Length 115 mm (4.5"). Small and *sparrow-like*, with *black-and-white-speckled forecrown and moustachial stripes*. **Adult** ashy brown above, with *rufous nape and band behind ear-coverts*; underparts greyish white. Eyes brown; bill horn-brown; feet pinkish brown. **Juvenile** resembles adult, but hindneck pale tawny. **VOICE**: Upon taking flight, *tsip-tsip-tsip-tsip*. Song thin, silvery and slightly accelerating, *tsitsitsi tee-tee-tee-teetee-teee*. **HABITS**: Feeds on the ground. Breeds singly or in small groups. Builds large, untidy feather-lined grass nest with porch-like extension over entrance, usually in low acacia. Somewhat gregarious in non-breeding season. **STATUS AND DISTRIBUTION**: Local and generally uncommon in bush and open savanna between 400 and 2000 m, typically in dry areas. Found from nw. Kenya and southern Turkana District south through the Kerio and Rift Valleys and Laikipia Plateau to Meru and the Tsavo NPs, also from Narok District south to Namanga and Amboseli NP. In n. Tanzania, to Lake Natron, Serengeti NP, lowlands north of Arusha, the Masai Steppe and Tarangire NP. Absent from more arid areas of n. and e. Kenya, the Lake Victoria basin and coastal lowlands.

GROSBEAK-WEAVER *Amblyospiza albifrons* Plate 109
(Thick-billed Weaver)

Length 150–165 mm (6–6.5"). Thickset, with a *heavy grosbeak-like bill*. Sexually dimorphic. **Adult male** slaty black or brownish black, with the head either black (*A. a. unicolor* and *montana*) or contrastingly rusty brown (*melanota*). Forehead varies from white in breeding dress to brownish or black in eclipse plumage; *white patch at base of primaries conspicuous in flight* and display; whitish feather edges on underparts disappear with wear. Eyes brown; bill and feet black. **Female** brown above, with some rufous feather edges; *boldly streaked dark brown on white below*; bill yellowish horn. **Juvenile** resembles adult female, but is more rufous above, buffy below. **VOICE**: Song a pleasing medley of chirps, high squeaky notes and buzzy sounds: *khhzz, sip-sip-sip, tip-tip seet. . .*, interspersed with a twangy musical *tur-treee* or *twaa-weee. . .* Also gives a chattering or twittering call in flight. **HABITS**: In breeding season, small groups gather in reeds or sedges. Comes to ground for seeds and visits bird feeders in Nairobi suburbs; flocks or individuals commonly feed in fruiting trees. Displaying male raises and fans wings, swaying from side to side. Flight undulating, often high. Weaves a neat, compact ovoid nest of leaf fibres with side entrance hole, this larger in nests used solely for roosting. **SIMILAR SPECIES**: Flying female Violet-backed Starling might be mistaken for female Grosbeak-Weaver if bill not visible. **STATUS AND DISTRIBUTION**: Locally common resident and wanderer below 3000 m in marshes and swamps; also in forest canopy and edge, and in woodland. *A. a. melanota* occupies w. Kenya from Mt Elgon and Kapenguria south to Nandi, Kakamega, Mumias and Busia Districts and the Lake Victoria basin. *A. a. montana* ranges from the cent. Kenyan highlands south to Thika, Nairobi, Narok, Mara GR and the Loita Hills; locally in n. Tanzania at Karatu, Mbulumbulu and Lake Manyara NP. The race *unicolor* is locally fairly common in coastal lowlands from the lower Tana River south to Pemba Island and Tanga, inland to Kibwezi, Lake Jipe, Taveta, Rombo, Moshi and Arusha Districts; scarce in the Usambara Mountains. Formerly in the Voi swamp, but no recent records.

PLOCEUS WEAVERS are widely distributed birds, some noisy and obtrusive, breeding colonially; others are relatively inconspicuous, and solitary breeders. The remarkable woven nests of numerous species are noticeable features of the landscape: some are spherical, others onion-shaped or with spout-like entrance tubes of varying lengths; they may be tightly and neatly woven or coarse and untidy. Certain species build only over water. Males typically weave the nests, which are then lined by females; construction may be quite protracted. Some species have a mania for building, often repairing old nests or starting several new ones. Most weavers breed during the rains, although forest species have less well-defined nesting periods. Several are solitary or accompany mixed bird parties. Adults are both insectivorous and granivorous, and the young are fed largely on insects.

Males are readily identified in breeding dress, but those of several species assume a duller, female-like eclipse plumage after nesting. Some females also undergo a seasonal plumage change. Young birds are generally female-like in plumage, but tend to be browner above, buffier below and paler-billed. During much of the year these dull-plumaged weavers that wander through the countryside in great numbers pose decided identification problems. Naming them requires careful attention to size, proportions, bare-part colours and plumage details. Distribution, habitat and nest type are useful in identifying breeding birds. Remarks under **SIMILAR SPECIES** in the following accounts do not attempt to cover all confusing juveniles and immatures.

All species are presumably year-round residents in our region, but many are subject to wandering, and flocks suddenly appear in nesting areas when conditions are satisfactory. There is considerable post-breeding dispersal, and birds may undertake long flights to favoured food sources.

COMPACT WEAVER *Ploceus superciliosus*   Plates 114, 116

Length 112–120 mm (4.5–5″). A *stocky, short-tailed, west Kenyan* weaver with a *thick conical bill*. **Breeding male** dusky olive, with yellow crown and underparts grading to chestnut on forehead; sides of face, chin and throat black. Bill black above, pale grey-blue below; eyes brown; feet brownish pink or pinkish buff. **Breeding female** similar to male, but with dark brown crown and yellow superciliary stripes. **Non-breeding adult** *largely brown* (*darker and streaked with dusky above*; *paler, more tawny below*), with buff superciliary stripes and cheeks, blackish-brown crown and eye-lines; inner secondaries have pale margins; bill slate. **Juvenile** resembles non-breeding adult, but superciliaries and underparts are pale yellow, and the bill brown above, and buff below. **VOICE**: A short, harsh *cheee*, producing chattering effect from a flock; song a melodious *cheewery-cheewery-cheewery* (Marchant in Bannerman 1949). **HABITS**: Forages in small flocks or pairs in tall moist grassland and grassy bush. Not colonial. Builds small ovoid nest with circular entrance hole high on one side, much like small Grosbeak-Weaver's nest, and attached to tall stems in wet grassland or marsh. **SIMILAR SPECIES**: Smaller juvenile Pin-tailed Whydah is almost plain brown above and unmarked buff below, but has much smaller black or reddish bill. **STATUS AND DISTRIBUTION**: A local and uncommon resident of moist bush, grassy riverine borders, cultivation, marshes and inundated grassland, from around Mt Elgon and Bungoma, Busia, Mumias and Kakamega Districts south to the Lake Victoria basin, Kisii and Lolgorien.

BAGLAFECHT or REICHENOW'S WEAVER *Ploceus baglafecht*   Plates 113, 114, 116
(includes Emin's Weaver and Stuhlmann's Weaver)

Length 140–150 mm (5.5–6″). Most Kenyan birds are *P. b. reichenowi*, **adults** of which are *black above and bright yellow below*, the **male** with *yellow forehead and forecrown* and with a *long black mask* enclosing *bright yellow eyes*; **female** has *entire top and sides of head black*. Both sexes show bright yellow wing edgings. No discrete non-breeding plumage (unlike *P. b. emini* and extralimital *P. b. baglafecht*). Confusing birds in w. and nw. Kenya, treated in the literature as *reichenowi-baglafecht* intergrades (but see below), include breeding females from the Mt Elgon area which have the olive-green upper back heavily mottled or striped with black. Nearly identical are females from the Kerio River, but males from the latter locality appear to be typical *reichenowi*. **Juvenile** *reichenowi* is uniformly *deep buffy yellow below*, with much yellow on the wings; *olive-brown upperparts* are *heavily streaked*, and face and crown dark olive; bill *buffy horn*; *eyes brown*. **Immature male** *reichenowi* resembles adult female, but upperparts streaked and mottled olive and black; *bill blackish above, buffy horn below*; eyes brown, gradually becoming yellowish. **Adults** of distinct northwestern *emini* have *white lower breast and belly*, the **breeding male** with *yellow forehead/forecrown and wing edgings, black sides of face, hindcrown and back contrasting with grey rump and olive-green tail*. **Non-breeding male** *emini* has *hindcrown, upper back and scapulars light grey, streaked with black*. **Breeding female** resembles breeding male, but *entire top and sides of head black*; **non-breeding female** has black-streaked grey back and scapulars. **Juvenile** *emini* has bright yellowish-green head (including sides of face), contrasting with buffy-brown, dusky-streaked back and plain brown rump; anterior underparts yellow, fading to creamy white on lower breast and belly; bill buffy horn. **Immature** *emini* (both sexes) has black forehead/forecrown, grey upperparts with black streaks on back, generally creamy-white underparts with pale buff upper breast and some yellow on the chin; bill black. **Intergrades** between *reichenowi* and *emini* (Elgon area and nw. Kenya) are variable, but have prominent white belly; those between *reichenowi* and Ugandan *stuhlmanni* (w. Kenya south of Elgon) are mostly black-headed, olive and black on the back and entirely yellow below. **VOICE** (*reichenowi*): Varied calls, including a dry *rink* or *errink*, a chirping *chweeeup*, a chattering *chwi, chi-chi-chichit*, and a sharp *spi! spi! spi!* near nest, and a longer *sweeeeee.....tchit*. Nondescript song infrequent. **HABITS**: Not gregarious. Pairs or family groups tame and confiding in towns and suburban gardens, where belligerent and domineering at bird feeders, even killing smaller birds. Omnivorous. Builds small, rather coarse nest with short entrance porch, the roof often well attached to leaf and twig support; low or high in tree or shrub. Males build extra, sometimes incomplete, nests. **SIMILAR SPECIES**: Black-necked Weaver lacks yellow wing edgings, male has short black eye-lines and a black throat patch; female's black crown is separated from connecting long eye-lines by yellow superciliary stripes. **STATUS AND DISTRIBUTION**: *P. b. reichenowi* is common in cultivation, clearings, towns, open woods and forest edges throughout the Kenyan highlands, including most isolated northern mountains and the Nguruman, Chyulu and Taita Hills; it ranges south to the Crater and Mbulu Highlands, Arusha NP,

Mt Meru, Kilimanjaro, and the Pare and Usambara Mts. *P. b. emini* is locally and mainly extralimitally distributed on Mt Loima, extending south to the Kongelai Escarpment (where observed feeding fledged young, July 1994). Apparent intergrades between *emini* and *reichenowi* known between Kitale and Kapenguria. White (1963) treats black-and-green-backed birds from the northwest as intergrades between *reichenowi* and nominate *baglafecht* of w. Ethiopia and s. Sudan; birds from Elgon and the Kerio Valley were considered the same by van Someren (1922) and Friedmann (1937), but at least some of those specimens (not seen by us) may be *P. b. reichenowi-stuhlmanni* intergrades such as those now known from Malaba, Bungoma and Siaya Districts.

SLENDER-BILLED WEAVER *Ploceus p. pelzelni*   Plates 113, 115

Length 115 mm (4.5"). A *small*, western swamp species with *very slender bill*. No distinct non-breeding plumage. **Male** yellow below and olive above, with black of forehead, face and throat extending to a point on upper breast; wings dusky, edged with yellow. Eyes light yellowish brown to dark brown; bill black; feet pale blue-grey. **Female** plain yellowish olive above, with yellow face, forecrown and underparts. **Juvenile** olive above, with dusky back streaks, pale yellow superciliary stripes, yellow and buff wing edgings; underparts buffy yellow; bill pale horn-brown. **Voice**: Call a buzzing *bzzzzzt*, reminiscent of Sedge Warbler's call. Song unrecorded. **Habits**: Roosts and usually nests over water; feeds in cultivation and moist thickets. Builds small spherical and loosely woven nest of grasses, with short entrance tube, in papyrus, occasionally in trees. **Similar Species**: Little Weaver has smaller bill, avoids lakeshore swamps, preferring acacia bush or woodland. Spectacled Weaver also slender-billed, but adult has narrow black mask and pale eyes. **Status and Distribution**: Fairly common in the Lake Victoria basin, mainly in papyrus swamps, marshes and waterside trees, from Port Victoria, Lake Kanyaboli and Usengi east and south to Kisumu, Kendu Bay, Ruma NP, Muhoro Bay and Tanzania's Musoma and Mwanza Districts.

LITTLE WEAVER *Ploceus luteolus*   Plates 115, 116

Length 110–112 mm (4.25"). A *diminutive, small-billed* weaver of *dry acacia bush and woodland*. **Breeding male** has black forehead, face and throat, and dusky wings and tail with yellow feather edgings; back olive; underparts mostly yellow. *Eyes bright hazel-brown*; bill black; feet blue-grey. **Breeding female** yellow below and on face; olive above from forehead to tail. Bill black. **Non-breeding male** has olive crown, is streaked black and buff on back; face, throat and breast are buff, the belly white. Bill pale brown. **Non-breeding female** and **juvenile** greyish above, yellowish on face and under tail-coverts, buff on breast and flanks, whitish on belly; bill pale brown. **Voice**: Call note a soft *tsip*. Song varied, of typical harsh weaver quality but containing numerous clear notes. **Habits**: Comparatively silent and unobtrusive. Does not tremble wings when singing. Solitary or in small groups. Builds well-made, small, spherical nest (usually one to three per tree) with short to fairly long entrance tube (lacking in new nests), typically on low acacia branches. Some nests of *P. l. kavirondensis* looser and rougher than those of nominate *luteolus*. **Similar Species**: Slender-billed Weaver, also small, prefers swamps and has longer, thinner bill. Northern Masked Weaver is larger, bigger-billed, the male with rufous around black facial mask. Lesser Masked Weaver is also larger-billed and has pale eyes. **Status and Distribution**: *P. l. luteolus* is a fairly common resident of acacia bush and woodland in nw. Kenya from Lokichokio and Turkana District south to Kacheliba and Kongelai, the Turkwell and Kerio Valleys, lakes Baringo and Bogoria. *P. l. kavirondensis* is scarce and local, from s. Uganda to our area at Lake Kanyaboli (where sympatric with Slender-billed Weaver), Muhoroni, Rapogi and Mara GR.

SPECTACLED WEAVER *Ploceus ocularis*   Plate 115

Length 140 mm (5.5"). *Slender-billed* and *greenish-backed*, with a *narrow black mask extending from bill to behind the pale eyes*. No seasonal plumage change. **Adult male** has *black throat patch*. Eyes greyish white to pale yellow; bill black; feet bluish. **Female** all yellow below, shading to saffron and washed with orange-rufous on face and throat. Eyes grey to yellowish buff; bill and feet as in male. Western *P. o. crocatus* has less rufous. **Juvenile** resembles adult female, but bill pale buffy brown. **Voice**: Calls include a liquid chirp which may develop into chattering (Sclater and Moreau 1933), a distinctive resonant, descending *chirr-r-r* and a loud metallic rattling on one pitch: *CHEE-CHEE-CHEE-CHEE-CHEE-CHEE*. Foraging call *peeit*. Song a rapid trilling *pi-sir-see-sir-sit* (van Someren 1956). **Habits**: A shy, often skulking bird, usually in pairs. Forages like a warbler or tit in tangled shrubs and creepers, especially in damp places; acrobatic and agile. Insectivorous and frugivorous. Weaves compact nest of fine palm, banana, or grass leaf strips, with *long spout 7–8 cm wide*, usually conspicuous at end of drooping acacia branch or palm frond, often over water. **Similar Species**: Female Northern Brown-throated Weaver, typically in papyrus, has streaked olive-brown upperparts, not plain olive-green as in female Spectacled, but otherwise similar, including eye colour. Western Slender-billed Weaver is smaller, has still slimmer bill, and male has entire front of head black. **Status and**

DISTRIBUTION: Uncommon but widespread resident of tangled growth in woodland, forest or swamp edges and dense bush, from sea level to over 2000 m. *P. o. suahelicus* ranges in and east of the Rift Valley from the Northern Uaso Nyiro River south through cent. Kenya to Nairobi, the Chyulu Hills and into Tanzania on Kilimanjaro and in Moshi District; also in coastal lowlands from the lower Tana River south to Tanga and Dar es Salaam, inland in the Shimba Hills, and the Usambara and Pare Mts. *P. o. crocatus* ranges in w. Kenya from Mt Elgon and Saiwa NPs, the Kongelai Escarpment and the Kerio Valley, south through the western highlands to the Lake Victoria basin, Mara GR, and Loita and Nguruman Hills; in n. Tanzania at Serengeti NP (in riverine woods), Loliondo, the Crater and Mbulu Highlands, Mt Hanang, and Lake Manyara, Tarangire and Arusha NPs.

BLACK-BILLED WEAVER *Ploceus melanogaster stephanophorus*   Plate 114

Length 130–140 mm (5–5.5"). A solitary *black forest weaver with a yellow face*. No seasonal plumage change. **Adult male** has golden-yellow forecrown and sides of face, with black throat and narrow line through eyes. **Female** has entire head yellow, apart from dark eye-lines. Eyes dark red, bill black and feet grey in both sexes. **Juvenile** dull sooty black above, greenish olive-yellow from forehead to throat, merging into greenish brown on breast and belly; bill pale grey-brown. **Immature** dull sooty black above, sooty brown below (brighter on breast), yellow forehead, face and throat washed with chestnut; bill blackish. **VOICE**: Apparently not recorded. **HABITS**: Solitary or in pairs, usually in forest undergrowth and mid-level trees, often near ground. Forages noisily in hanging creepers, vines and clumps of dry dead leaves. Nest of grass, three to four metres above ground in shrub or tree. **STATUS AND DISTRIBUTION**: Uncommon in many w. Kenyan forests and second-growth woods from Mt Elgon and Saiwa NP south to the Nandi, Kakamega, Mau and Trans-Mara Forests, east to the Cherangani, Karissia and Tugen Hills, with isolated records at Subukia and in Aberdare NP (The Ark, Nov.–Dec. 1992).

BLACK-NECKED WEAVER *Ploceus nigricollis*   Plate 114

Length 140–150 mm (5.5–6"). **Adult** *black or dark sepia-brown above* and *bright yellow below*. **Male** has deep golden-yellow head with black eye-lines; throat patch and nape also black. Eyes brown or red-brown (not whitish or pale yellow as in central African birds); bill black; feet grey. **Female** has *prominent yellow superciliary stripes* and no throat patch. Eastern *P. n. melanoxanthus* is black above, western *nigricollis* dark sepia with greenish wash on rump. **Subadult** less blackish above, with yellow-olive wash, and tail feathers edged with yellowish. **Juvenile** and **immature males** resemble adult female, but are dull olive-brown or dusky olive above and pale-billed. **VOICE**: Usually silent; infrequent calls include a semi-metallic *trreeng-trreeng* with a trilling or quavering quality, a dry *tswick-tswick-tswick-tswick* and a single *chwick*. **HABITS**: Shy and retiring. Pairs or small groups often join mixed-species flocks in undergrowth or low trees, foraging like a Spectacled Weaver. Insectivorous. Builds neat, firm nest of wiry grasses, with downward-projecting entrance tube *c*. 20 cm long and usually under 5 cm in diameter (narrower than Spectacled Weaver's). Nest usually solitary, rarely two or three together, well concealed in shrub or low tree. **SIMILAR SPECIES**: See Dark-backed and Baglafecht Weavers. **STATUS AND DISTRIBUTION**: Western *P. n. nigricollis* is locally fairly common in moist secondary growth, riverine bush and forest edges from Bungoma, Busia, Mumias and Kakamega Districts south to the Lake Victoria basin, South Nyanza, Lolgorien and the western Mara GR; in n. Tanzania along riverine woods in the Mara Region and w. Serengeti NP. *P. n. melanoxanthus* is an uncommon local resident of *dry* bush and woodland between sea level and 1300 m; ranges from Baragoi, the Ndotos, Wamba and the Lorian Swamp south along the edge of the cent. Kenyan highlands through Meru and Kitui Districts to the Tsavo and Amboseli NPs, west to Kajiado, Olorgesailie and Magadi, into n. Tanzania at Lake Natron, lowlands north of Arusha, Tarangire NP, the Masai Steppe and Mkomazi GR; local in coastal lowlands from Ijara and Kiunga south to the Mombasa area.

BROWN-CAPPED WEAVER *Ploceus insignis*   Plate 114

Length 125–130 mm (5"). An arboreal *forest* weaver with *yellow back* and underparts contrasting with black scapulars, wings and tail. No seasonal plumage change. **Adult male** has black face and throat and *chestnut crown*. **Female** is entirely *black-headed*. Eyes dark red, bill black, feet light greyish or purplish brown in both sexes. **Juvenile male** has olive-green crown and face speckled with black, throat yellow, bill pale horn-brown; **juvenile female** has yellow flecks on black crown. **VOICE**: Usually silent, but in West Africa infrequently sings a nasal whistling song, *twit chirr, chirr, chirr, chitt, twit chirr* (Newton, in Bannerman 1949). **HABITS**: Solitary or in pairs, sometimes with mixed-species flocks; gleans insects from foliage and works nuthatch-like along large tree branches or trunks. Nest has long pendent entrance tunnel, and is woven to underside of branch (Jackson 1938). **SIMILAR SPECIES**: Dark-backed and Baglafecht Weavers lack yellow on back. **STATUS AND DISTRIBUTION**: Uncommon to fairly common in montane forest between 1600

and 3000 m, from Marsabit, the Mathews Range, Maralal, the Cheranganis and Mt Elgon south through the w. and cent. Kenyan highlands to Mt Kenya, the Aberdares, Mau, Trans-Mara and Nguruman Forests and into n. Tanzania at Loliondo.

HOLUB'S GOLDEN WEAVER *Ploceus xanthops*   Plate 113
(Golden Weaver)

Length 160–167 mm (*c.* 6.5"). A *large greenish-yellow* weaver with *pale yellow eyes.* No seasonal plumage change. **Adult male** has orange wash on throat and upper breast, largely or entirely lacking in duller female. Bill black; feet brownish pink. **Juvenile** resembles adult female, but greener and indistinctly streaked; bill brownish above and dull yellow below; feet pale pinkish brown. **Voice:** Short chattering song ends with a dry trill followed by various squeaky notes, *chichi-chichi-chi-squirrrrrrrrrrrr ski-wee,* and sometimes a final descending rail-like whinny, *qui-ee-ee-eh-er.* Call note a loud sparrow-like *chirp.* **Habits:** Solitary or in family groups, although two to three pairs may nest close together. Builds rounded, loosely woven, untidy nest near or over water, in trees, reeds or cultivated bamboo. **Similar Species:** Other 'golden' weavers are smaller, the males with brighter orange on head, and with red, pink or brown eyes. **Status and Distribution:** Widespread and fairly common in gardens, cultivation, moist secondary woods, swamp edges and along waterways between 1200 and 2300 m. Ranges throughout the w. and cent. Kenyan highlands from Mt Elgon and Saiwa NPs south to the Lake Victoria basin, South Nyanza, Mara GR, Loita Hills, cent. Rift Valley, and Nyeri, Nanyuki, Meru, Murang'a, Thika, Nairobi and Machakos Districts. In n. Tanzania, local and generally uncommon in Serengeti NP and in the Crater and Mbulu Highlands.

AFRICAN GOLDEN WEAVER *Ploceus subaureus aureoflavus*   Plate 113
(Yellow Weaver)

Length 115–140 mm (4.5–5.5"). *Brilliant yellow,* olive-tinged on upperparts; tail-and wing-feather edgings bright yellow. *Eyes of* **adults** *pink, red or orange* (never dark brown). **Breeding male** has orange-rufous crown, face and throat, and black bill. **Non-breeding male** olive on crown and face, with a touch of rufous on the throat below pale brown bill. **Breeding female** *black-billed,* with *indistinctly streaked olive upperparts,* and yellow below except for white in centre of belly. **Non-breeding female** more greenish olive with *distinct blackish streaks on back*; belly white, or yellow and white; bill pale buffy brown. **Juvenile** and **immature** also heavily streaked above, the **male** pale yellow below with white belly centre; **female** pale yellow from chin to breast, otherwise mostly white below. **Voice:** Noisy, prolonged and rather featureless chattering at nest colony. **Habits:** Highly gregarious, nesting (sometimes with Golden Palm Weaver) in trees, shrub, or reeds, usually near or over water, occasionally in drier sites. Builds spherical nest of grass or palm-leaf strips with bottom entrance. **Similar Species:** Golden Palm Weaver has dark brown eyes (appearing black), shows no white on underparts in any plumage; adult male's head bright orange, with rufous on the throat. **Status and Distribution:** Fairly common in coastal lowlands from the Tana delta south to Tanga and Dar es Salaam; local inland along the Galana, Tsavo and Athi Rivers, also on the upper Tana River around Mwea NR. Scattered populations in Sultan Hamud, Kibwezi and Taveta Districts. In n. Tanzania, ranges from the Usambara foothills to the Mkomazi Valley and base of the South Pare Mts.

ORANGE WEAVER *Ploceus aurantius rex*   Plates 113, 116

Length 140 mm (5.5"). A western weaver with no seasonal plumage change. **Male** *orange-yellow,* except for yellowish-olive back, dusky wings with yellow feather edgings, and sometimes a small black loral spot. *Eyes pale grey;* bill pale brown, lighter below; feet dull pinkish. **Female** and **juvenile** dull olive above with faint dark streaking, the rump brighter; superciliary stripes greenish yellow, wings as in male. Underparts whitish, greyer on breast and flanks, sometimes with trace of pale yellow on throat and breast; bill as in male. **Voice:** Noisy chattering in nesting colonies, otherwise largely silent. **Habits:** In Uganda, breeds in colonies, often with other weavers, in trees or shrubs at water's edge or in reeds over water. Builds compact ovoid or globular nest of grass or palm leaf strips; entrance opens downwards under slight portico or lip. **Similar Species:** Holub's Golden Weaver is larger, with black bill, and orange is confined to throat and upper breast in male. Golden Palm Weaver is entirely allopatric. Male Northern Brown-throated Weaver has rufous-brown throat; female much browner and buffier (less grey) below, more heavily streaked above, with black bill and dark eye-lines. Female Spectacled Weaver, with similar eye colour, is olive-green above, yellow below, with *black* bill. **Status and Distribution:** Endemic to islands and shores of Lake Victoria. Breeds locally in Uganda and nw. Tanzania; only a vagrant to our area, recorded three times near Kisumu (Aug. 1961, Nov. 1981 and Nov. 1984).

Kenyan Weaver Nests (*Ploceus* spp.)

(Nests may vary geographically, individually and even locally depending on available nest materials.)

1 African Golden Weaver, *P. subaureus aureoflavus*. Eastern. Spherical, neat and strong, of grass or palm-leaf strips; often near or over water in reeds, shrubs, palms or other trees; usually attached from a single support point. May be in mixed colony with Golden Palm Weaver.

2 Golden Palm Weaver, *P. bojeri*. Similar to No. 1, typically in palms or reeds, but may be in *Typha*, ornamental vines or shrubs. Nest of Taveta Golden Weaver, *P. castaneiceps* (not figured), similar but less neat and typically attached to several stems.

3 Vitelline Masked Weaver, *P. velatus uluensis*. Solitary or a few together.
Suspended from branch tip, usually in acacia; very short entrance tube or none.

4 Northern Masked Weaver, *P. taeniopterus*. Colonial. In trees, shrubs or reeds near water, often with other weavers. More or less spherical, with no tube. In our area only in vicinity of lakes Baringo and Bogoria.

5 Holub's Golden Weaver, *P. xanthops*. Solitary or in small groups, in trees, shrubs, cultivated bamboo, low or high. Often in towns and gardens.

6 Baglafecht (Reichenow's) Weaver, *P. baglafecht reichenowi*. Solitary or a few together. Coarse, spherical to ovoid, with entrance tube short or vestigial; roof often well attached to leaf and twig support; among foliage of tree or shrub, low or high.

7 Lesser Masked Weaver, *P. intermedius*. Usually in colony in acacia. Untidy, often rough, with short but variable entrance tube. Two extremes shown.

8 Black-necked Weaver, *P. n. nigricollis*. Well woven, often concealed in foliage of tree or shrub; long tube narrower (to *c*. 6 cm wide) than in Spectacled Weaver's nest.

9 Dark-backed Weaver, *P. bicolor kersteni*. Woven of coarser materials (creeper tendrils, rootlets) than smoother nest of Black-necked Weaver. Often conspicuous.

10 Spectacled Weaver, *P. ocularis crocatus*. Woven of fine grasses, typically conspicuous on drooping branch tip or palm frond. Wide tube (7–8 cm) characteristic; length variable (two extremes shown).

11 Black-headed (Village) Weaver, *P. cucullatus paroptus*. Eastern. Large colonies, in low shrub or high in tree; often near or in villages. Entrance tube typically short, sometimes lacking, occasionally conspicuous (two extremes shown).

12 Black-headed (Village) Weaver, *P. c. bohndorfii*. Western. Large colonies in trees or shrubs. Spherical, with short tube.

13 Northern Brown-throated Weaver, *P. castanops*. Solitary or colonial. Small with short tube, often loosely woven; in papyrus, shrubs or trees near Lake Victoria.

14 Jackson's Golden-backed Weaver, *P. jacksoni*. Colonial in reeds, tall grass or on branch tips over water. (Nest of Yellow-backed Weaver, *P. melanocephalus*, is similar.)

15 Heuglin's Masked Weaver, *P. heuglini*. Western. Small colonies in trees. Globular, with short tube or none. Scarce.

16 Vieillot's Black Weaver, *P. nigerrimus*. Western. Large colonies, usually at forest edge. Spherical, with no tube or mere vestige of one.

17 Little Weaver, *P. l. luteolus*. Solitary in low acacia. Small size diagnostic for species. Compact and firm; tube may be shorter than shown.

18 Little Weaver, *P. l. kavirondensis*. Lake Victoria basin/Mara GR. Solitary. Small, well woven but rough if made of coarse grasses.

19 Compact Weaver, *P. superciliosus*. Solitary in tall grass or reeds. Resembles small nest of Grosbeak-Weaver (p. 657).

20 Chestnut Weaver, *P. rubiginosus*. Coarse, unkempt, typically few to several nests clustered together, usually in huge colonies in low trees, shrubs or tall grass.

21 Speke's Weaver, *P. spekei*. Coarse, bulky and untidy, generally rounded, with short entrance tunnel opening laterally or downwards, but bristly projecting grass stems may obscure basic structure. Close together or in clusters, commonly in acacia.

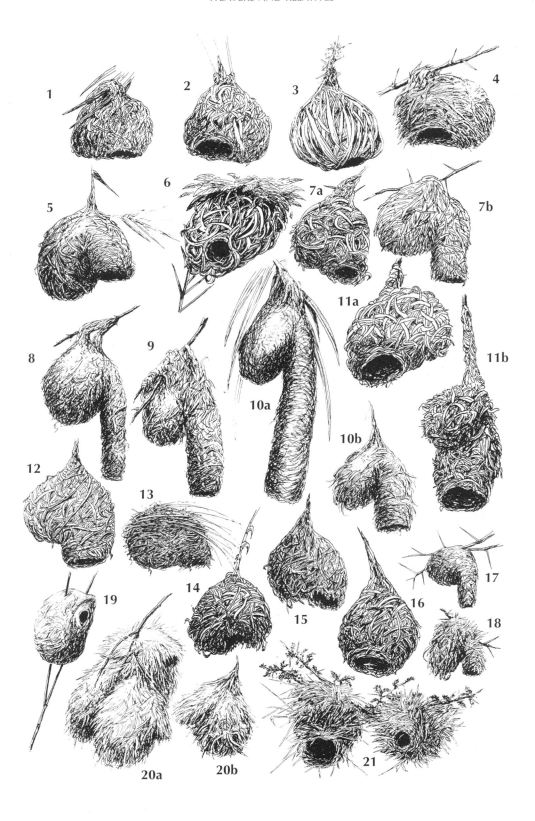

GOLDEN PALM WEAVER *Ploceus bojeri*   Plate 113

Length 140 mm (5.5"). Brilliant yellow, with *dark brown eyes* (*appearing black* in the field). Often associated with palms. **Adult male** has *bright orange head, shading to orange-rufous on the lower throat.* Back slightly darker; wings and tail tinged with dusky. No seasonal plumage change. Yellow-headed subadult males developing orange on nape and showing some orange-rufous on the lower throat are easily mistaken for Taveta Golden Weaver, but lack both the *well-defined* rufous occipital crescent and rufous patch on the *upper breast* of that species. **Female** mustard-yellow above, with indistinct back streaking; underparts entirely yellow (unlike African Golden Weaver). Bill of both sexes blackish above and yellowish below; feet pink. **Juvenile** and **immature** resemble female, but underparts paler yellow; possibly more heavily streaked above than adults. **Voice:** Largely silent away from nesting colonies, where high-pitched chattering is characteristic. **Habits:** Gregarious and noisy, sometimes nesting in colonies alongside African Golden Weaver. Nest spherical, with no entrance tube, typically suspended under palm leaves. **Similar Species:** Breeding male African Golden Weaver has red or pink eyes and rufous-orange is confined to face and throat; non-breeding male, female and young are white or yellow and white on the belly. Male Taveta Golden Weaver has well-defined rufous crescent on occiput and rufous on breast; female is darker, more yellowish olive, and prominently streaked above. **Status and Distribution:** Fairly common coastal resident from Lamu south to Moa, inland locally along the Tana River to Meru NP and on the Northern Uaso Nyiro River from Shaba and Samburu GRs east to the Lorian Swamp. Also locally along the Athi River, and breeds alongside African Golden Weaver at Hunter's Lodge (near Kibwezi).

TAVETA GOLDEN WEAVER *Ploceus castaneiceps*   Plates 113, 116

Length 145 mm (5.75"). A *bright yellow, southeastern* weaver with no seasonal plumage change. **Adult male** has yellow-olive back, wings and tail, *well-defined rufous crescent on back of head* and *rufous patch on breast.* Eyes brown; bill black; feet pinkish brown. **Female** *bright yellow below,* with yellow superciliary streaks and wing edgings; back yellowish olive with *dark stripes. Eyes brown; bill dusky above, yellow below.* **Juvenile** dull *brownish* olive above, heavily streaked with dusky; noticeable yellowish superciliary stripes and dark eye-lines; pale yellow on face and throat, becoming buff on breast and flanks; lower belly white; bill dark above, yellowish white below. **Voice:** Male's song a twittering *creee-er-curee-twee-twee.* The chattering is low-pitched. **Habits:** Gregarious, often nesting in large colonies. Builds spherical or ovoid nest with no entrance tube, usually of green grass and suspended over water. Disperses into dry bush following breeding. **Similar Species:** Adult male of allopatric Golden Palm Weaver usually has entire head orange, deepening to rufous on lower throat; subadults confusing (see above). African Golden Weaver has pink, red or orange eyes. **Status and Distribution:** Endemic to lowlands around the base of Mt Kilimanjaro, where largely confined to swamps and inundated bush, often breeding in *Typha* (cattail) stands. In Kenya, locally common in Amboseli–Taveta area and at Lake Jipe. Other Kenyan reports (including misidentified Tsavo specimens) reflect confusion with related species. Also in Himo, Moshi and Usa River Districts of n. Tanzania, including Arusha NP, and at least formerly in reedbeds in the Mkomazi Valley.

NORTHERN BROWN-THROATED WEAVER *Ploceus castanops*   Plates 113, 115, 116

Length 140 mm (5.5"). A western *lakeside* weaver with *dark face, pale eyes* and *rather slender bill.* **Adult male** golden yellow, with faintly streaked olive back and with deep chestnut face and throat which appear black at a distance. No seasonal plumage change. *Eyes whitish or pale straw colour; bill black; feet pink.* **Female** olive-brown or olive-buff with dusky streaking above; underparts pale tawny-buff; *lores and small patch around eyes blackish.* Eyes cream or creamy buff; bill black; feet brownish pink. **Juvenile** streaked buff and brown above, with yellow wing-feather edgings; underparts pinkish buff, except for white belly. Bill dark brown above, dull yellow below; feet pale brown; eyes brown. **Immature male** shows adult's pattern, but has little or no chestnut on lores and forehead, and that on throat dull; yellow head feathers are veiled with grey; dusky streaks on back; eye colour variable, often pale tan. **Voice:** Only a soft chattering reported. **Habits:** Typically a waterside bird in small flocks, often with other weavers; forages on ground, in vegetation over water, and on floating aquatic plants. Nests alone or colonially in reeds, shrubs or trees, sometimes with other weavers. **Similar Species:** See Orange Weaver. Males of all 'masked' weavers are larger-billed and have black on the face. Female Spectacled Weaver (also pale-eyed) is plain olive-green above. Female Yellow-backed Weaver closely resembles female *castanops,* but is dark-eyed and heavier-billed. **Status and Distribution:** Local and uncommon resident of papyrus stands and ambatch (*Aeschynomene*) in the Lake Victoria basin, from Port Victoria, Lake Kanyaboli, Usengi and Rusinga Island east to Kisumu and Kendu Bay.

RÜPPELL'S WEAVER *Ploceus galbula*   Plates 115, 116

Length 125–140 mm (5–5.5"). A 'golden' weaver of *northeastern* Kenyan border areas. **Breeding male** *deep golden yellow, with chestnut forehead, face* and *lower chin*; lores and upper chin black; *back olive-yellow*, slightly mottled with dusky; lower back, rump, and upper tail-coverts purer yellow; wings more dusky. Eyes orange-red; bill black; feet red-brown. **Non-breeding male** has yellowish-olive crown, nape and back and brown bill. **Female** pale grey-brown to olive-grey above, with dark streaks on back; rump and tail olivaceous, the rectrices and most wing feathers edged with yellow; may show *trace of chestnut on face*. Underparts white, shading to buffy yellow on throat and breast; flanks greyish buff. *Eyes dark red-brown*; bill pale horn. **Immature male** has pale brownish bill, with paler and less extensive chestnut than in adult, none on chin. **Juvenile** resembles adult female but breast deeper buffy yellow. **VOICE**: Song a wheezy chatter ending in insect-like hissing sounds. Call a dry *cheee-cheee* (Hollom *et al.* 1988). **HABITS**: In Somalia, forms enormous flocks and breeds in colonies around water holes. Builds spherical nest with or without short entrance tube. **SIMILAR SPECIES**: Female Vitelline Masked Weaver, nearly identical in plumage, has red or orange-red eyes. **STATUS AND DISTRIBUTION**: Abundant in Somalia and Ethiopia, but only one Kenyan record to date: an adult collected at Karo-Lola, a few miles west of Mandera, May 1901. Probably overlooked.

JUBA WEAVER *Ploceus dichrocephalus*   Plates 115, 116
(Jubaland Weaver)

Length 115–130 mm (*c.* 5"). A dark-headed weaver of extreme northeastern Kenya. **Male** yellow above, often with *rich chestnut head*, darker on crown and more dusky on throat; breast and sides paler rufous. Some males have *black crown and cheeks* and *chestnut throat*. **Female** brownish above, more olive on head, with broad dusky streaking on back; upper tail-coverts dull olive-yellow; face and superciliary stripes dull yellow, throat yellowish white, diffuse pale yellowish-buff band across breast; sides and flanks pinkish buff; rest of underparts whitish; wing-coverts and flight feathers edged with dull yellow. Eyes dark brown; *bill blackish above, yellow to orange-yellow below*; feet flesh-pink. **Juvenile** said to resemble young Yellow-backed Weaver, but upper tail-coverts olivaceous, not buff. **VOICE**: Undescribed. **HABITS**: Gregarious; nests in small colonies in trees near water. **SIMILAR SPECIES**: Male of allopatric Yellow-backed Weaver has slimmer bill, bright yellow collar between dark nape and olive-yellow back, a black head, and more extensive rufous on underparts. **STATUS AND DISTRIBUTION**: Locally common in lush riverine bush in the Daua River Valley immediately west of Mandera.

YELLOW-BACKED WEAVER *Ploceus melanocephalus fischeri*   Plates 115, 116
(Yellow-collared Weaver)

Length 135–145 mm (*c.* 5.5"). Confined to wetlands of the Nile watershed. **Breeding male** has *black head separated from olive-yellow back by bright yellow nuchal collar*; underparts orange-chestnut, with yellow belly. Eyes brown; bill largely black, the culmen distinctly curved; feet light brown or brownish pink. **Breeding female** *buffy brown above, with blackish streaks on back and scapulars*, and *yellow superciliary stripes. Upper tail-coverts brownish or buff*; head olive-yellow, contrasting with back; sides of face buffy. *Buffy-yellow to tawny-buff wash on breast and flanks; rest of underparts whitish. Eyes brown*; bill blackish above, dull yellowish white below. **Non-breeding adults** similar, but with broader black dorsal streaks; bill blackish above, pale brownish below. **Juvenile** resembles female, but only faintly washed with tawny-buff below. **VOICE**: Male produces a wheezy chatter and a nasal *chaa*. **HABITS**: Gregarious. Always associated with water, but wanders seasonally. Builds spherical nest, with or without small spout, usually 2–3 m above water in reeds, grass or shrubs. **SIMILAR SPECIES**: The largely allopatric but very similar Jackson's Golden-backed Weaver has an almost straight culmen: male has entire back yellow, and black of head continues onto nape; eyes crimson (not brown); female more reddish brown, upper tail-coverts bright olive, underparts pale yellow, sometimes with buff flanks. **STATUS AND DISTRIBUTION**: Locally common in reedbeds, swamps and marshes around Lake Victoria, including Lake Kanyaboli, and along the Nzoia River upstream to Mumias. Does not extend east of 35°E.

JACKSON'S GOLDEN-BACKED WEAVER *Ploceus jacksoni*   Plates 113, 115

Length 125 mm (5"). The acacia/ambatch counterpart of the preceding species. **Breeding male** *plain golden yellow on back*, with black head and nape; underparts bright chestnut, except for yellow belly. *Eyes crimson*; bill black, the culmen nearly straight. **Breeding female** and **non-breeding male** much like preceding species, but *olivaceous above from head to upper tail-coverts*, the back with dusky streaks. Superciliary stripes and underparts pale bright *yellow*, with some buff or orange-buff on breast and white in centre of belly. *Eyes red-brown (male)* or *dark brown (female)*; bill brown, paler below in male. **Juvenile** resembles female, but is more extensively buffy on breast and sides; bill buffy brown, paler below. **VOICE**: Male utters a sizzling wheezing chatter at nest. **HABITS**: Gregarious. Nests in small colonies in acacia, ambatch (*Aeschynomene*) or reeds, often beside or

over water. Builds compact, ovoid or spherical nest of fine grass or palm-leaf fibres. May wander to drier areas after breeding. **Similar Species**: See Yellow-backed Weaver. **Status and Distribution**: Locally common in acacia scrub and woodland, generally near water; also in swamps and cultivation. Two disjunct populations: one in w. Kenya from the Turkwell and Kerio Valleys to lakes Baringo and Bogoria, and near Rongai, also in the Lake Victoria basin from Busia, Lake Kanyaboli, Ahero and Kendu Bay south in Tanzania to riverine woods along the Tarina, Grumeti and Mbalageti Rivers (w. Serengeti NP). In s. Kenya locally from Namanga, Amboseli NP, Kimana, Oloitokitok, Rombo, Taveta, Lake Jipe and Mzima Springs in Tsavo West NP to adjacent ne. Tanzania, where known from Arusha, Lake Manyara and Tarangire NPs and the Masai Steppe.

HEUGLIN'S MASKED WEAVER *Ploceus heuglini*   Plates 115, 116

Length 116–124 mm (4.5–5"). A small 'masked' weaver distinguished by pale *yellow-ish-buff eyes* in both sexes. **Breeding male** *yellow from bill to nape*, with *black face, ear-coverts and throat patch extending in a long point to the upper breast*. Back olive-yellow, faintly streaked; rump and underparts rather pale lemon-yellow. Bill black; feet pinkish. **Non-breeding male** more greenish above, including crown and sides of face; entire underparts yellow; bill pale buffy brown. **Breeding female** olive above, streaked dusky; yellow breast and under tail-coverts separated by whitish belly; bill brown to blackish; feet brownish pink. **Non-breeding female** and **juvenile** differ from breeding female in duller upperparts, paler underparts with ochre wash on breast, and pale buffy-brown bill. **Voice**: Male sings a wheezy chattering *tsureet tsureet wichichichi tseet-tseet tzwee-tzwee-tzwee. . .* and a shorter *tsuree-tsee-tsee-tsee-tsee*. Breeding female sings *seet seet seet sueet sureet chree chree chree chroo*. **Habits**: Usually in pairs, but nests in small colonies. Builds ovoid, rather coarse nest with short entrance tube, in tree. **Similar Species**: Most male 'masked' weavers have black or chestnut forehead and are brighter yellow below. Larger male Speke's Weaver (allopatric) has yellow forehead, but back is heavily streaked. Female Speke's is yellowish-eyed but larger, greyer (not bright olive) above, and buffy or pale yellow below. Female Vitelline Masked has dark eyes. Female Lesser Masked is pale-eyed, but has grey (not pinkish) feet. **Status and Distribution**: Scarce and local in w. Kenya where at the eastern limits of its range. Sporadic records from Lokitaung, Kerio River, Kapenguria, Soy and Bungoma, in acacia savanna and cultivation. Has bred regularly in recent years at Kiminini near Kitale, nesting in isolated trees near buildings.

VITELLINE MASKED WEAVER *Ploceus velatus uluensis*   Plates 115, 116

Length 117–135 mm (4.5–5.25"). A small, *dry-country* weaver with *reddish eyes* and pale *pinkish feet*. **Breeding male** black-masked, but with *limited black on throat and forehead* (chin, upper throat and feathers at base of culmen only; most of forehead chestnut). Bill black. **Non-breeding male** and **breeding female** olive or yellowish olive above with blackish streaks, and with yellow-olive tail; underparts pale yellow, with greyish-olive flanks and white belly. Eyes red or red-brown; feet pinkish; bill grey-brown, with base of mandible pale brown or yellowish horn. **Non-breeding female** *largely white below*, with yellowish-buff upper breast and pinkish-buff flanks; *streaked grey-brown and black on back*; head more olive, superciliary stripes not prominent; tail yellow-olive; *eyes red or orange-red*. **Juvenile** and **immature** resemble non-breeding female but still browner, with sides of throat and breast buffy. Eyes brown in juvenile, becoming reddish; feet pinkish. **Voice**: A dry sputtering leading into a squeaky trill, *tsuk, tsik-skikit-sker skeeeeerrrrrrrr*. **Habits**: Less gregarious than other 'masked' weavers; usually in pairs, but nests in small colonies in trees. Builds distinctive onion-shaped nest of green grasses, lacking entrance tube. **Similar Species**: Other 'masked' weavers are larger-billed, the breeding males more extensively black on the throat; male Heuglin's Masked and Speke's have yellow foreheads and yellowish (not red) eyes. Lesser Masked has black face mask surrounding white or cream eyes. Other olive-backed female weavers include Heuglin's Masked, entirely yellow below, with yellowish-buff eyes; Black-headed, larger, heavy-billed and with orange-red eyes; Northern Masked, buff or buffy white below, its yellowish superciliaries contrasting with dark crown and brown eyes; Lesser Masked, pale-eyed, grey-footed and mostly yellow below. Immature male Chestnut Weaver is brownish-backed and red-eyed, but with larger bill, bold superciliary stripes and cinnamon breast band. *Caution*: brown-eyed juvenile Lesser and Vitelline Masked Weavers may be indistinguishable if adult bill shape not yet obvious. **Status and Distribution:** Widespread and fairly common below 1750 m in dry savanna and thorn-bush, more numerous or noticeable following periods of heavy rain. Ranges in Kenya north, east and south of the highlands, but absent from the Lake Victoria basin, coastal lowlands and much of the northeast. In n. Tanzania, an uncommon resident in Serengeti NP, the Crater and Mbulu Highlands, Lake Manyara and Tarangire NPs, in lowlands north of Arusha, the Masai Steppe and Mkomazi GR.

LESSER MASKED WEAVER *Ploceus intermedius*   **Plates 115, 116**
(Masked Weaver)

Length 125 mm (5"). Easily identified by *blue-grey tarsi and toes and cream or pale yellow eyes in all adult plumages*. Black-masked **breeding male** *P. i. intermedius* has *black forehead* and *black of throat extending to the breast*. Coastal birds are plain bright yellow below; those inland have darker, more saffron underparts. Bill black. Tanzanian *P. i. cabanisii* has crown and breast clearer yellow. **Breeding female** and **non-breeding male** yellowish olive above, superciliary stripes and underparts pale yellow, becoming white on belly; female's bill dark slate-grey above, pale grey below. **Juvenile** (and **immature**?) similar, but eyes dark brown; back yellowish olive (perhaps olivaceous brown in some juveniles); face and breast buffy yellow, flanks pale buffy grey, sometimes the throat and lower breast almost white like remaining underparts; bill pale tan; feet brownish pink, becoming grey; probably indistinguishable from young Vitelline Masked Weaver, except by more slender bill and, in older birds, the grey feet. **Voice:** A rapid wheezy chattering or babbling, somewhat squeaky and metallic. **Habits:** Gregarious; breeds in large colonies or isolated pairs, typically in trees or bushes over or beside water. Builds distinctive nest of dry, straw-coloured material, untidy, more or less spherical, with short (6 cm) entrance tube. **Similar Species:** Breeding male Northern Masked Weaver is dark-eyed. Adult Black-headed Weaver has orange-red or red-brown eyes and black scapulars. Breeding male Speke's and Heuglin's Masked have yellow foreheads. Bills of Little and Slender-billed are much smaller. Vitelline Masked has deeper, shorter bill, adults reddish-eyed; male has very little black at base of maxilla, rest of forehead chestnut, and black of throat much restricted. Some non-breeding male and female Vitelline Masked nearly identical in plumage to *intermedius*, but red-brown or red-orange eyes and pinkish feet readily separate them (dark-eyed young perhaps indistinguishable). Some individual Vitelline Masked have duller, less contrasting superciliary stripes. Female Northern Masked has brown eyes and pinkish-brown feet; immature Northern Masked whitish-eyed, but has much heavier bill than Lesser Masked. **Status and Distribution:** *P. i. intermedius* is widespread, except in highlands and much of arid ne. Kenya; locally common in savanna, bush and cultivation, usually below 1500 m, in both humid and dry areas, in the latter mainly as a migrant, breeding during the rains. Sympatric in many areas with other 'masked' weavers. *P. i. cabanisii* is known in our territory only in the Arusha–Moshi area of ne. Tanzania.

NORTHERN MASKED WEAVER *Ploceus t. taeniopterus*   **Plates 115, 116**

Length 120–135 mm (4.75–5.25"). Local in the *Lake Baringo area*. Resembles Lesser Masked Weaver, but *thicker-billed* and *brown-eyed*. **Breeding male** has *chestnut forehead and forecrown*, with *black of face and throat extending to breast*. Upperparts largely unstreaked yellow-olive, the rump bright yellow as are the underparts; wing edgings more buffy yellow. Bill black; feet dull brownish or pinkish. Back of **non-breeding male** streaked buff and black, the rump unmarked brownish buff; olive-tinged head has fine dark streaking and *prominent yellow superciliary stripes*. Black wings marked with two white bars and pale yellow or white flight-feather edges; tail dusky, the feathers broadly edged with olive-yellow. Underparts buffy white, to pure white on belly; bill dark brown. **Female** resembles non-breeding male, but smaller, paler buff below; tail grey-brown, most rectrices with narrow pale tips. Eyes brown; bill largely blackish; feet pinkish brown. **Juvenile** and **immature** similar, but buff from head to upper breast. Eyes of juvenile *greyish white to cream*, but confusing Lesser Masked Weaver has much thicker bill and buffier plumage. **Voice:** At nest, a wheezy chattering not unlike that of Lesser Masked Weaver. Also a harsh, grating alarm call. **Habits:** Gregarious, typically nesting during the rains in loose colonies of 30–100 pairs, low in lakeside sedges, shrubs and low tree branches over water, often close to colonies of other weavers and bishops. Builds spherical nest with downward-opening entrance but no prolonged tube. **Similar Species:** Lesser Masked Weaver compared above. Male Heuglin's Masked has pale eyes, is yellow from forehead to nape. Male Vitelline Masked has red eyes, and black of underparts is confined to chin and upper throat. Female and non-breeding male Heuglin's are yellow below (sometimes with whitish belly), not buffy, and dorsal ground-colour is greenish or olive, not buff or tan. Females of Heuglin's and Lesser Masked are pale-eyed. Female Speke's is olive-grey (not olive-yellow) above, without well-defined superciliaries, and eyes of adults are pale buffy tan. Female and non-breeding male Vitelline Masked olive-green or yellow-green on back, more whitish below, with buff only on breast and flanks; eyes red-brown or reddish orange. **Status and Distribution:** In Kenya, apparently restricted to Lake Baringo and swamps north of Lake Bogoria, where a common resident, breeding in low lakeside vegetation. As no early records, possibly a recent colonist. Collected in cattails (*Typha*) near Fort Ileret on eastern Lake Turkana in January 1959, when also present in marshes of Omo River delta in Ethiopian territory.

SPEKE'S WEAVER *Ploceus spekei*   **Plates 115, 116**

Length 142–152 mm (c. 5.75"). A heavy, *big-billed, pale-eyed* weaver with no seasonal plumage change. **Adult male** bright *yellow from nape to forehead*, on rump and on underparts; *back mottled black and yellow* (sometimes largely black); face and throat also black, the latter edged rufous. *Eyes creamy white; bill heavy, long and black*; feet dusky pink. **Female** dull greyish olive above, back heavily streaked with dusky brown; *superciliaries*

indistinct; lores and short postocular line dusky; wing edgings pale buffy yellow; underparts pale yellow from chin to lower breast, white on belly, darker and greyer on flanks; *eyes pale buff or creamy tan;* bill blackish at tip and broadly along culmen; feet pinkish. **Juvenile** and **immature male** similar, but duller brownish grey or greyish olive-brown above, more olive on crown, rump and upper tail-coverts; duller pale yellowish buff on throat and breast; *eyes brown; bill largely pale pinkish buff* or fleshy-horn colour. **Immature male moulting to adult plumage** mottled yellow and grey on crown, cheeks light greyish buff, with black feathers on lores, auriculars, chin and throat; breast mottled orange-rufous, underparts otherwise yellow and white; *eyes yellowish; bill pale horn-brown above, whitish below,* becoming black. **VOICE**: Harsh chattering at nests; also a single sharp *tseep!* Male's song *pew. . . pew . . . tew, chinkichi-chewchew-skerinkitsitew . . .*, with variations. **HABITS**: Gregarious, usually nesting in large colonies, occasionally as isolated pairs. Wanders widely after breeding. Attracted to bird feeders. Builds untidy nest of grass with many projecting stems, bulky and globular with short entrance tube, typically attached laterally to acacia branches. **SIMILAR SPECIES**: Male of allopatric Heuglin's Masked Weaver has similar head pattern, but is smaller, lightly marked above, and black throat patch narrows to point on breast. Female Black-headed Weaver is red-eyed, with distinct yellow superciliary stripes and yellowish-olive head contrasting with back; in breeding plumage, bright yellow (not dull yellowish buff) from cheeks to lower breast. **STATUS AND DISTRIBUTION**: Common resident of savanna, bushed grassland, cultivation, towns, villages and suburban gardens, typically between 1400 and 2200 m in the cent. Kenyan highlands. Ranges from Maralal, the central Rift Valley and Laikipia south to Narok, Ngong, Nairobi, Athi RIver and Machakos Districts; locally abundant in the Rift Valley from Naivasha to Kedong, and occasional in the Lake Victoria basin. A single male at Moyale (March 1984) represents southern limit of Ethiopian population. In n. Tanzania, local in the Crater and Mbulu Highlands and Arusha District.

BLACK-HEADED or VILLAGE WEAVER *Ploceus cucullatus*   Plates 115, 116
(Layard's Black-headed Weaver; Spotted-backed Weaver)

Length 135–155 mm (5.25–6"). A large, heavy-billed weaver represented in Kenya by two very distinct races perhaps better regarded as incipient species. **Breeding male** of *P. c. bohndorffi* (150–155 mm) has black of head and throat terminating in a point on the breast, where bordered by chestnut; *bright yellow from hindcrown to rump, except for black scapulars* flanking the upper back; underparts bright yellow. Eyes orange-red to red-brown; bill black; feet brownish grey or light brown. **Breeding female** *entirely yellow below, on face and on superciliaries,* or fading to mixed yellow and white on belly; under tail-coverts mottled yellow and white. *Yellowish-olive head contrasts with dusky-striped, olive-brown back;* rump lighter brown; upper tail-coverts yellow-olive; wing edgings pale yellow or whitish; eyes pale orange-red, bill black, feet pinkish brown. **Non-breeding birds** of both sexes have *back and rump ashy grey or grey-brown, streaked with dusky*: **male** *mostly pinkish buff below, with yellow throat and upper breast* and with bill pale buffy brown, lighter below; **female** whiter below than male, with yellow throat. **Juvenile** similar to non-breeding adult, but *brownish* above and brown-eyed. **Immature** has orange-red eyes. *P. c. paroptus* is smaller (135–140 mm), **breeding male** with *entirely black head* and with *yellow back densely spotted with black, scapulars with much yellow,* and bill smaller than in *bohndorffi*; other plumages similar to those of *bohndorffi*. Xanthochroic individuals, with little black, are known in both races. **VOICE**: At nests, a featureless wheezy chattering interspersed with squeaking and various sibilant notes, usually by numerous males in unison. Large colonies produce a continuous roar. **HABITS**: Gregarious, nesting in crowded colonies and using favoured sites (often in villages or towns) for years. Builds coarse, spherical nest, adding short (3–10 cm) entrance tube during incubation; weaving mostly by male, lining added by female. Western birds may nest in mixed colonies with Vieillot's Black Weaver. **SIMILAR SPECIES**: Male Lesser Masked and Heuglin's Masked Weavers are smaller and pale-eyed; Lesser Masked has blue-grey tarsi. Northern Masked has dark brown eyes, and a chestnut forehead with no black. Speke's and Heuglin's Masked are yellow from forehead to nape. Female Yellow-backed resembles female Black-headed, but is smaller (wing 68–82 mm, compared with 80–98 mm in *cucullatus*). **STATUS AND DISTRIBUTION**: Locally common to abundant in bushed and wooded grassland, cultivation, villages and gardens. Western *P. c. bohndorffi* ranges from Mt Elgon, Kapenguria, Kitale and Trans-Nzoia Districts south to the Lake Victoria basin, South Nyanza, and into n. Tanzania in the Mara Region and w. Serengeti NP. *P. c. paroptus* (formerly *nigriceps*) is widespread from the Northern Uaso Nyiro River and Meru NP south through cent. and e. Kenya, including the coastal lowlands, to the Mkomazi GR, Usambara foothills and Tanga Region in Tanzania. Records from Moyale and the Daua River Valley represent the southern limit of Ethiopian birds.

VIEILLOT'S BLACK WEAVER *Ploceus n. nigerrimus*   Plate 114

Length 135–155 mm (5.25–6"). A dark, west Kenyan weaver with no seasonal plumage change. **Adult male** *black, with bright yellow eyes.* Bill black; feet light brown or grey-brown. **Female** *dark dusky olive* above, with darker head and heavily streaked back; *dull yellowish on throat and centre of belly;* upper breast, sides and flanks dark brownish olive. *Eyes tan or yellow;* bill brownish grey or horn-brown, pale at base; feet pale greyish pink to brownish pink. **Juvenile** resembles adult female, but eyes at first dark grey. Yellow-eyed **immature male** simi-

lar to adult female, but central crown feathers and underparts more blackish; **immature female** is brown-eyed. Black **subadult male** retains dull yellow feathers on lower belly for some months. **VOICE**: Insistent sputtering and chattering at nesting colonies. **HABITS**: Highly gregarious and otherwise much as Black-headed Weaver, the two sometimes nesting in mixed colonies (and known to hybridize outside our area). Builds rough-looking nest of long coarse leaf blades or strips; shape resembles that of Black-headed, but short entrance tube does not extend below bottom of nest; entrance unusually large and semicircular. **SIMILAR SPECIES**: Female Black-headed Weaver is bright yellow below. **STATUS AND DISTRIBUTION**: Local and generally uncommon resident in w. Kenya, around edges and clearings of the Nandi, Kakamega and Kaimosi Forests. Wanders occasionally to Nambale, Ng'iya and Kisumu Districts.

CHESTNUT WEAVER *Ploceus r. rubiginosus* **Plate 115**

Length 140 mm (5.5"). **Breeding male** *bright chestnut, with black head*; wings and tail black with buff edgings; eyes red or orange-red; bill black to slate-grey; feet greyish. **Non-breeding male** *buffy brown, broadly streaked with black above* except on rump; wing edgings buffy white; *superciliaries and sides of face buff; breast, sides and flanks pale tawny or cinnamon-buff, contrasting with white throat and belly*; eyes red, bill dark buffy brown. **Female** similar, but breast and sides buff; eyes brown (always?), bill black, feet dusky pink. **Immature male** resembles female, but rufous-tinged, especially on wing edgings, and with brownish postocular and malar streaks. Eyes red; bill dusky above, greyish or buffy brown below; feet pinkish brown. Some (older?) individuals have entire head, throat, breast and back pale chestnut, the back streaked with black. **Juvenile** resembles non-breeding male, but eyes brown, bill paler. **VOICE**: Flocks produce a loud quelea-like sizzling, the volume of sound from a large nesting colony far-carrying. Individuals have unique emphatic call notes, *squip* or *tseup*, also chattering sounds. **HABITS**: Highly gregarious, breeding in hundreds or thousands among thorn trees and shrubs. Builds a rounded, rather bulky and untidy nest. **SIMILAR SPECIES**: Male Chestnut Sparrow is much smaller and has a short bill. **STATUS AND DISTRIBUTION**: Common to abundant seasonal breeder and wanderer, usually above 1500 m in bush, savanna, open woodland and cultivation, typically in drier areas. Widespread, but largely absent from most highland areas above 1650 m, much of ne. Kenya, the Lake Victoria basin, Mara GR, Serengeti NP and the coastal lowlands. A 'rains migrant' to many parts of n. and e. Kenya, numbers varying greatly from year to year.

CLARKE'S WEAVER *Ploceus golandi* **Plate 114**

Length 130–132 mm (5"). Endemic to *Brachystegia* woods at and near the Kenyan coast. Small and slender-billed. **Adult male** *black on head, back, throat, breast and wings; 'shoulders', larger wing-coverts and flight-feather edges bright greenish yellow; two prominent yellow wing-bars*; rump and upper tail-coverts olive; lower breast bright yellow, merging with white lower belly; under tail-coverts yellow and white; leg feathers black; tail feathers greenish black with yellowish-olive edges. Eyes brown; bill black, with light pinkish-brown patch on mandible; feet pale flesh-pink to bright orange-pink. No seasonal plumage change known. **Female** olive above, with dark back streaks and bold yellow wing edgings; underparts largely bright yellow, the colour extending posteriorly as streaks on the white belly; bill grey, paler at base; feet pink to orange-pink. **Juvenile** (no specimen known) olive, with indistinct dark streaks on back; underparts generally pale yellow, becoming white on belly; bill pale flesh-pink below. **VOICE**: Various loud chattering, chirping, and sizzling sounds from foraging flocks, *ch-ch-sss-sss-sss* or *zsss-zss-zss-zss*, audible for some distance. **HABITS**: Gregarious, in flocks of 30 to over 100, often with helmet-shrikes. Occasionally five to ten birds accompany mixed-species flocks in canopy. Shy and restless. Insectivorous. Nest undescribed. **SIMILAR SPECIES**: Dark-backed Weaver (only other forest weaver within known range of Clarke's) is more golden yellow below, with no yellow wing edgings and no white on belly. **STATUS AND DISTRIBUTION**: Confined to *Brachystegia* woodland from near Malindi (formerly near Kilifi) to north of the Sabaki River, and from the eastern edge of Galana Ranch east to Marafa and Hadu. Most records are from the Arabuko–Sokoke Forest, where largely absent April–July, usually reappearing with young in August, thence regular into November; few records December–February. Flying juveniles begging from females near Sokoke in early April 1982 suggested breeding in March with onset of the rains. Believed to have bred north of the Sabaki in 1994, when many juveniles observed near Dakacha in mid-July.

YELLOW-MANTLED WEAVER *Ploceus tricolor interscapularis* **Plate 114**

Length 130–150 mm (5–6"). A rare dark weaver of the *Kakamega Forest canopy*. **Adult male** black, with *chestnut breast and belly*, and *bright yellow crescent between nape and back*. **Female** dark brownish black below, the bird appearing *all black with a yellow band on upper back*. Eyes of both sexes dark red; bill black; feet brown or grey-brown. **Juvenile** paler dusky brown from cheeks to under tail-coverts; face and throat tinged rufous; *forehead to upper back dull orange-rufous*; rest of upperparts black. **VOICE**: A sharp *tsst* or *chirr-it* (Williams and Arlott 1980). Not very vocal. **HABITS**: Forages nuthatch- or tit-like on branches and tree limbs. Usually in pairs. **SIMILAR SPECIES**: Male Vieillot's Black Weaver has yellow eyes and all-black plumage. **STATUS AND DISTRIBUTION**: Very rare resident of the Kakamega Forest, and formerly the upper Yala River forests. Last recorded July 1972, and perhaps now extirpated.

DARK-BACKED WEAVER *Ploceus bicolor*   Plate 114

Length 130–140 mm (5–5.5"). A stocky, black-headed forest weaver with bright yellow underparts and a *greenish-white bill*. Eyes red; feet pinkish or dusky pink. Sexes alike. No seasonal plumage change. Two distinct races: *P. b. mentalis* has *dark grey back*, and the throat black or occasionally yellow and black; *P. b. kersteni entirely black above and on throat, rest of underparts bright golden yellow or saffron-yellow*. **Juvenile** resembles adult, but chin and throat yellow, flecked with black. **VOICE**: Song (*kersteni*) a pleasing reedy arpeggio of five notes, *ronh roonh raank rernh reenh*, punctuated by rapid clicks (audible only at close range), wheezy squeaks and whistles, producing a unique semi-musical sound reminiscent of a gate swinging on rusty hinges. The basic reedy notes are delivered with bill closed, the clicks with neck upstretched, head flung back, and bill open (Sclater and Moreau 1933). Other sounds include a loud *wheet-wheet* and a soft inhaled *heeew*. **HABITS**: Usually in pairs, sometimes in small groups or with mixed bird parties. Insectivorous. Feeds tit-like, often upside-down, and clings to tree trunks. Conspicuous and approachable. Builds distinctive nest of hard vine tendrils, compact, smooth and with long entrance tube. **SIMILAR SPECIES**: Male Clarke's Weaver has yellow wing-bars and flight-feather edges, olive patch on rump and upper tail-coverts. See Black-necked Weaver. **STATUS AND DISTRIBUTION:** Fairly common resident of forest and moist riverine woodland. *P. b. mentalis* is confined to the Nandi and Kakamega Forests in w. Kenya; *kersteni* ranges locally in coastal lowlands north to the Boni Forest, inland along the lower Tana River to Bura and Garissa, in Shimba Hills NP and the Usambara Mts.

USAMBARA WEAVER *Ploceus n. nicolli*   Plate 123

Length 132–140 mm (c. 5.5"). Endemic to Tanzania's Usambara Mts. **Adult male** dull black above, largely brown-headed, with dull yellow forehead and brownish-yellow wash on nape; sides of face and entire throat dusky olive-brown; *breast rich rufous-chestnut*, underparts otherwise yellow. Bill black; eyes yellow. **Female** similar, but entire head brownish black. **Juvenile** resembles adult, except for slate-grey crown with some yellowish feathers in male. **VOICE**: Generally silent; occasionally utters a soft *swi-swee-ee* (Sclater and Moreau 1933). **HABITS**: Singles or pairs forage alone or in mixed-species flocks. Actions tit-like, the birds often hanging upside-down while probing for insects among lichens. Nest undescribed. **SIMILAR SPECIES**: Dark-backed Weaver, with which this species frequently associates, lacks chestnut on breast and has all-black head and throat in both sexes. **STATUS AND DISTRIBUTION**: Rare and little-known endemic, confined to forest and forest edge between 900 and 2200 m in the Usambara Mts. No recent records below 1350 m. Small numbers present at Mazumbai (1525 m) in the West Usambaras, but total population of both ranges probably fewer than 100.

RED-HEADED MALIMBE *Malimbus r. rubricollis*   Plate 114

Length 160–165 mm (6.5"). A *jet-black forest weaver with bright scarlet hood*. **Adult male** has the red extending from forehead to nape and down each side of the neck as a partial collar; eyes red-brown or red-orange; bill and feet black. **Female** similar, but forehead and forecrown velvety black. **Juvenile** duller black, the coloured parts of head orange or red-orange; bill horn-brown. **VOICE**: Call note a wheezing, squeaking chatter reminiscent of calls of Dark-backed Weaver. Note a harsh *tsirp*. **HABITS**: Usually in pairs high in canopy. Climbs nuthatch-like on large limbs, frequently foraging underneath horizontal boughs; sometimes hawks insects. Suspends its untidy, retort-shaped nest from high outer tree branch; nest resembles that of Spectacled Weaver, but spout shorter and much broader. **STATUS AND DISTRIBUTION**: Uncommon resident of the Kakamega Forest, w. Kenya; formerly at Nyarondo.

RED-HEADED WEAVER *Anaplectes rubriceps*   Plates 109, 114

Length 130–140 mm (5–5.5"). A unique colourful weaver with *bright orange or orange-red bill*. **Breeding male** *A. r. leuconotus* has *scarlet head, throat and breast* and a *black mask*; back blackish with some red feathers; wings more brown; flight feathers and rectrices edged pale scarlet; belly white; **non-breeding male** grey or brownish grey above. Striking **breeding male** *A. r. jubaensis* almost *entirely bright scarlet, with some blackish feathers on wings and tail, and blackish scapular edges forming a narrow V*; non-breeding male undescribed.

Females of both races grey above, white below, with greyish wash on breast; wings and tail edged with pale scarlet or yellow; bill orange or pinkish orange. **Juvenile** *leuconotus* olive or yellowish on head, throat and breast; wings and tail edged with orange or scarlet; bill pale brown, dusky on mandible and tip. **VOICE:** Song of *A. r. leuconotus* a high-pitched squeaky *sizzi-sizzi-sizzi-sizzi, tsrrrrrr, siss-siss-siss-siss tsik-tsiksizzisizzi-sizzisizzi . . ..* Call note a sharp *spik* or *tswik*. **HABITS:** Quiet and unobtrusive. Forages tit-like, usually in pairs, sometimes alone or with mixed bird parties. Builds coarse but well-woven nest of thin twigs, leaf midribs, and grass stems, the long spout with numerous straggling ends projecting, suspended by woven stalk from branch or wire, at times near buildings, high or low; solitary or (*jubaensis*) in small colonies. **STATUS AND DISTRIBUTION:** *A. r. leuconotus* is a local and uncommon resident of savanna, bush, woodland, riverine trees and gardens, generally below 2000 m. Sparsely distributed over much of n. and e. Kenya, including Ethiopian border areas between Moyale and Lake Turkana; widespread from Mt Elgon, Kapenguria, Maralal, Mt Nyiru and the Mathews Range south through w. and cent. Kenya to n. Tanzania, where ranging from the Lake Victoria basin east to the Masai Steppe and Mkomazi GR; absent from coastal lowlands. Little-known *A. r. jubaensis* is localized in moist coastal bush from the Somali border at Kiunga south to Kiwayu. **NOTE:** Placed in the genus *Malimbus* by some authorities.

RED-BILLED QUELEA *Quelea quelea aethiopica*   Plates 110, 112

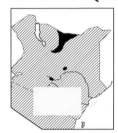

Length 110–130 mm (4.5–5"). A small weaver with a *large rosy-red bill* in most plumages. **Breeding males** variable: face and throat black, pinkish buff or whitish; crown and nape buff; back streaked buff and black; breast rosy or tawny, more whitish towards belly, where sometimes darkly mottled; flight feathers edged yellow. Eyes brown; bill and feet pinkish red. **Non-beeding male and adult female** also *red-billed*; crown and nape grey-brown, *finely* streaked dusky or nearly plain; face and superciliary stripes *whitish,* auriculars *dusky grey*; chin and throat white or buffy white; breast grey-mottled. **Juvenile** resembles female, but bill grey-brown. **Immature** has pinkish-brown bill. **VOICE:** Flocks produce a noisy chatter. Song a nondescript combination of wheezing and chattering notes. Alarm call a sharp *chak-chak*. **HABITS:** Extremely gregarious. Flying flocks dense and highly synchronized, at a distance resembling smoke clouds and containing thousands or millions of birds; these congregate at water holes and at roosts, where their combined weight may break large tree branches. Migratory or nomadic, breeding (stimulated by appearance of green grass) in extensive colonies in trees or reeds. Weaves small, spherical nest of grasses; large entrance at side. **SIMILAR SPECIES:** Female-plumaged Cardinal and Red-headed Queleas have yellow superciliary stripes; Cardinal also has yellow throat. Female-plumaged *Euplectes* are never red-billed. Some female and eclipse whydahs have *small* red bills and bold black head stripes. **STATUS AND DISTRIBUTION:** Common to abundant in drier bushed grassland, savanna and cultivation. Greatest concentrations are south and east of the Kenyan highlands and in n. and ne. Tanzania. Numbers fluctuate seasonally, breeding in e. Kenya during November and in n. Tanzania in December. Apparently three major East African breeding populations: (1) s. Ethiopia–Moyale–Marsabit, (2) s. Somalia–e. Kenya, (3) s. Kenya–ne. Tanzania. Birds from areas 2 and 3 overlap in se. Kenya.

CARDINAL QUELEA *Quelea cardinalis*   Plates 110, 112

Length 100–110 mm (4–4.5"). *Smaller-billed* than preceding species. **Breeding male** *bright red on head and breast;* occiput and nape brownish, streaked buff and black, washed with crimson in nominate race but not in *Q. c. rhodesiae;* back streaked buff and black. **Non-breeding male** similar to female, but usually shows some red on head and throat. **Female** best distinguished from scarce Red-headed Quelea by *smaller, dark brown bill* and by *yellow or buffy-yellow throat.* **Juvenile** has no yellow on throat, shows some dark flecks on brownish breast band. **VOICE:** Male's song a sputtering buzzy *dzeee-dzeee-dzeeee-tsiki-dzee-dzee,* and a rapid sizzling *chhhz-chhhz-chhhz;* at times a simple thin chatter, *chitichititititi.* **HABITS:** Highly gregarious. Displaying male perches on grasstop or bushtop, singing, fluffing out plumage, quivering wings, and jerking the fanned tail. Nomadic. Breeds in tall grass and rank herbage; nest semi-domed, with large side entrance, suspended between stems. **SIMILAR SPECIES:** Male Red-headed Quelea has entire head scarlet, the red throat barred with blackish; female has yellow superciliary stripes and face, but whitish throat. Young Red-billed Quelea is less heavily streaked on head. **STATUS AND DISTRIBUTION:** Common to abundant in tall grassland and moist places (including low sites in generally arid regions during or after heavy rains). *Q. c. cardinalis* ranges from Ugandan border areas and Kerio Valley, south and east through w. and cent. Kenya to the Lake Victoria basin and Nairobi NP. Tanzanian *rhodesiae* extends north to Amboseli and Tsavo NPs, the southern Rift Valley, Mara GR and South Nyanza.

RED-HEADED QUELEA *Quelea erythrops*   Plates 110, 112

Length 110–120 mm (*c.* 4.5"). **Breeding male** has entire *head and throat scarlet;* usually densely to finely *barred blackish on throat.* Bill black; eyes brown; feet pinkish. **Female** has *yellow superciliary stripes and face,* especially in breeding season; breast washed orange-buff or tawny; bill brownish. Perhaps not safely distinguished from female Cardinal Quelea in the field, but short dark moustachial marks more pronounced, and *throat white or buffy white,* not yellowish. **Non-breeding male** similar, but may show red wash on face. **Juvenile** resembles female; upperparts have broad, pale buff feather edges. **Voice:** Male said to have a churring song (Mackworth-Praed and Grant, 1973). Flocks utter a wheezy chatter similar to that of other queleas. **Habits:** Those of the genus. Noisy, highly gregarious, and nomadic. **Similar Species:** Male Cardinal Quelea lacks black on throat; female has more yellow on wings and a yellowish throat. Red-billed Quelea distinguished by bill colour. **Status and Distribution:** Few valid recent records in our region. Small non-breeding flocks (including breeding-plumaged males) fairly regular near Kisumu in w. Kenya, April–July. Sporadic records from the coastal lowlands north to Mombasa, including an exceptional report of flocks totalling 1,000+ in Ramisi District, on the s. Kenyan coast, October 1981.

BISHOPS AND WIDOWBIRDS, GENUS *EUPLECTES*

Finch-like or weaver-like grass-nesting birds with interesting courtship displays. Breeding male widowbirds are black, with brightly coloured 'shoulders' (lesser and median wing-coverts) and prominent tails. Bishops are short-tailed, the breeding males handsomely patterned in orange-red and black, or yellow and black. Most *Euplectes* are polygamous. A male defends a territory, but he mates with several females and builds a nest for each (females may complete the construction). The nest is spherical, with a side entrance, woven of grass strips and lined with flowering or fruiting grass tops, and placed low in grass or shrubs. Breeding is correlated with prolonged rains and verdant grass development. After nesting, males moult into a streaky female-like eclipse plumage. Adults and young form small to huge post-breeding flocks, frequently of mixed species, which wander over large areas, foraging in grasslands and cultivation for seeds, grain and insects. Night roosts are in reedbeds and marshes, and may contain large numbers of birds.

Most female and young *Euplectes* provide identification problems, as do eclipse-plumaged male bishops. Non-breeding widowbirds retain their bright wing patches (often concealed in perched birds). In the hand, wing-lining colour aids in determination. Knowledge of geographic range is useful in identifying several of the most confusing species.

YELLOW-CROWNED BISHOP *Euplectes afer ladoensis*   Plates 111, 112
(Golden Bishop)

Length 95–100 mm (4"). **Breeding male** black, with *bright yellow crown,* back, rump, upper and under tail-coverts and flanks. Face, breast to belly, wings, short tail and bill black. **Breeding female** streaked buff and black above, with broad whitish or pale yellow superciliary stripes; *blackish auriculars contrast with otherwise pale face;* underparts yellowish white, with dark streaks on breast and sides; bill brownish. **Non-breeding female** similar, but underparts buff and more distinctly streaked. **Non-breeding male** resembles female, but is more heavily streaked above. **Juvenile** similar to breeding female, but browner above, with broad buff wing edgings; chin to breast buff; ventral streaks narrow. **Voice:** High-pitched sizzling or buzzing in flight display. Call note a sharp *tsip tsip.* **Habits:** Gregarious at all times. Nomadic; moves to breeding areas in response to rainfall. Presumably polygamous. Breeding male fluffs plumage and performs slow display flights on rapidly beating wings. **Similar Species:** Breeding male Fire-fronted Bishop has black crown, orange-red forehead. Yellow Bishop is much larger, with the entire head and upper back black. All other small female bishops have brown or tan postocular/postauricular areas, lacking the contrast of Yellow-crowned; female Black Bishop is larger and darker, has dark, less contrasting face pattern. **Status and Distribution:** In Kenya, local and uncommon in marshes and inundated grassland, mainly in and near the w. and cent. highlands. Breeds regularly in Baringo, Mwea, Thika and Nairobi Districts; also recorded from the Turkwell delta and Kerio Valley, Lake Victoria basin and Southern Uaso Nyiro swamps. In n. Tanzania, locally common in Arusha District and Masailand.

FIRE-FRONTED BISHOP *Euplectes diadematus*   Plates 111, 112

Length 100 mm (4"). **Breeding male** a *small,* largely black bishop with *orange or red-orange forehead patch* and *bright yellow lower back, rump and under tail-coverts;* upper back streaked yellow and black; wing-coverts and secondaries edged buff, primaries edged yellow. **Non-breeding male, female** and **juvenile** streaked black and buff above; throat and breast are buff with a few narrow streaks, mainly at the sides; belly and under tail-coverts white; *the only 'sparrowy' bishop with yellow-edged flight feathers.* **Voice:** A sizzling song, not particularly

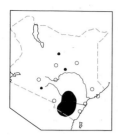

described. Call note a sharp *ze-ze* (Moreau). **HABITS**: Gregarious; often with weavers and queleas. Makes extensive movements in response to rainfall; nests in small scattered colonies. Display apparently not recorded. **SIMILAR SPECIES**: Dull-plumaged bishops of other species lack yellow flight-feather edging. Similarly marked female Cardinal Quelea has heavier bill, is more boldly marked above, has yellowish throat. Female and non-breeding male Red-headed Quelea also have yellow on wings, but are larger-billed, with prominent dark moustachial marks and yellow superciliaries. **STATUS AND DISTRIBUTION**: Locally common nomad, appearing in freshly greened *Acacia* and *Commiphora* bush following heavy rains. Ranges from Laisamis, Habaswein and Meru NP, south through Embu and Kitui Districts to Galana Ranch, the Tsavo NPs, and into n. Tanzania's Mkomazi GR. Also in coastal lowlands from Ijara and Lamu District south to the Sabaki River, occasionally wandering to Mombasa. Several records after heavy rains in the Olorgesailie–Magadi area of the Rift Valley. One sight record from Lake Naivasha (26 April 1981).

BLACK BISHOP *Euplectes gierowii* Plates 111, 112

Length 140–150 mm (5.5–6"). A *large* bishop. **Breeding male** *black, with orange or orange-red hindcrown, nape and breast band* (narrow in w. Kenyan *ansorgei*, broader in smaller and smaller-billed *friederichseni*); *under tail-coverts pale buff, black centrally. Upper back yellow or orange-yellow in ansorgei, orange (extending to upper rump) in friederichseni*. **Female** dark, heavily streaked buff and black above; sides of face dark; wings and tail blackish, buff-edged when fresh; upper tail-coverts black; underparts yellowish buff, with *dark spots on breast. Wing-linings black* (separating it from all except Black-winged Red Bishop). Bill brownish. **Non-breeding male** *black on head, back, wings and rump*, with yellowish chin and superciliary stripes; sides of face and breast rich buff. **Juvenile** resembles female, but has smaller breast spots. **VOICE**: In aerial display, male sings rapid thin, silvery notes followed by a clearer *tee-ee-ee-ee-eee* and then a sizzling *see-zee see-zee see-zhe see-zhe SEE-ZHEE*, accelerating as volume increases. Another aerial song is a buzzing *zee-zee-zee-zee-zee*, often combined with a wheezy *hishaah, hishaah, SHAAAAAAH, tsee-tseet-tseet-tseet*. **HABITS**: Solitary or in pairs. Joins mixed *Euplectes* flocks after breeding. **SIMILAR SPECIES**: All red bishops are smaller, the females paler, not spotted below. **STATUS AND DISTRIBUTION**: *E. g. ansorgei* is a local and uncommon resident in tall moist grassland, scrub and sugarcane in the Lake Victoria basin and Kakamega District, often alongside Black-winged Red Bishop. Primarily Tanzanian *E. g. friederichseni* is locally common in low bush and tall grass around Babati in the Mbulu Highlands, ranging north to Lake Manyara NP, the Grumeti and Seronera Rivers (Serengeti NP), and (at least formerly) to s. Kenya along the Southern Uaso Nyiro River near the Nguruman Hills.

BLACK-WINGED RED BISHOP *Euplectes hordeaceus* Plates 111, 112
(Fire-crowned Bishop)

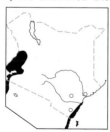

Length 120 mm (5"). Larger than other red bishops, the **breeding male** distinguished by its *black wings* and wing-linings, and *black tail projecting well beyond the orange-red upper coverts*. The back is duller red than rump and hindneck; black on face and chin, and from lower breast to belly. Under tail-coverts buff in nominate *hordeaceus*, white in the western *craspedopterus*. **Non-breeding male, female** and **juvenile** show a *rich tawny-buff breast band* and necklace of short pale brown streaks; sides and flanks buffy brown, *dimly streaked*; superciliary stripes pale yellow. **VOICE AND HABITS**: Courting male performs slow horizontal display flights with flapping wings, flying slowly between perches with body feathers fluffed out and uttering weak 'tsipping' and sizzling notes. **SIMILAR SPECIES**: Other breeding male red bishops have paler wings. Female and non-breeding male Black Bishop in w. Kenya (only other species with black wing-linings) are larger, heavier and darker, with darker ear-coverts. Female and non-breeding Northern and Southern Red Bishops are paler below, usually with little or no streaking, and the buff breast band is much paler and duller. Female Yellow-crowned Bishop lacks bright buff breast band, has more sharply defined blackish streaks on sides and blackish auriculars. All non-breeding male widowbirds have longer tails. **STATUS AND DISTRIBUTION**: Widespread and locally common in cultivation and moist bushed grassland, *E. h. hordeaceus* in the coastal lowlands, including Pemba Island, inland to Taru (exceptionally to Galana Ranch and Tiva River after floods); also Tsavo West NP (Lake Jipe) and lowlands around the Usambara Mts. *E. h. craspedopterus* is widespread in w. Kenya from Mt Elgon and Kapenguria south to the Lake Victoria basin, and local in n. Tanzania's Mara Region and Serengeti NP.

ZANZIBAR RED BISHOP *Euplectes nigroventris* Plates 111, 112

Length 100 mm (4"). A *small* southeastern red bishop. **Breeding male** *all black below, except for orange-red under tail-coverts; orange-scarlet from forehead to nape*. (Some birds, especially inland, have variable amounts of red on the throat). All **other plumages** striped black and buff above; wing-linings pale buff. **VOICE:** Noisy when

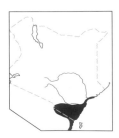

breeding, but calls not particularly described. **HABITS**: In pairs or loose aggregations during nesting season, later joining post-breeding flocks with other *Euplectes* and queleas. **SIMILAR SPECIES**: Southern Red Bishop and noticeably larger Black-winged Red Bishop are scarlet-crowned, with orange-red lower throat and upper breast. Females of Northern and Southern Red Bishops (unlikely in Zanzibar's range) are somewhat larger and with paler ear-coverts. **STATUS AND DISTRIBUTION**: Locally fairly common in coastal lowlands from our southern limit north to Lamu and Manda Islands, inland to the Tsavo NPs, Rombo, Taveta, Lake Jipe and Mkomazi GR. In many coastal areas, sympatric with the preceding species.

SOUTHERN RED BISHOP *Euplectes orix nigrifrons*   Plates 111, (112)

Length 105–110 mm (4–4.25"). **Breeding male** *vivid orange-red or scarlet, with black forehead, face and chin; lower breast to belly also black; wings and tail dusky, broadly edged with pale brown or greyish*; upper back cinnamon-brown; *orange or scarlet under tail-coverts shorter than tail*. Bill black; eyes brown; feet pinkish brown. **Non-breeding male** and **female** streaked brownish buff and dark brown above, with yellowish-buff superciliary stripes; underparts whitish buff, nearly plain or faintly streaked with dark brown on breast, sides and flanks; primaries edged pale brown. Bill pinkish brown with dusky culmen. **Juvenile** resembles female, but has broader and paler feather edges. **VOICE**: When breeding, a variable, rather patternless sizzling or wheezy *tssssssss, zeeeeeeeee tsipitsiptsipi tsip-tsip-tsip-ts-ts-tsip*. Call note a sharp *bzzz-bzzz* or *chiz-chiz*. **HABITS**: Gregarious. Feeds on ground. Male displays from perch or in low whirring flight with rump and back feathers erected, resembling a red-and-black ball. **SIMILAR SPECIES**: Males: Southeastern Zanzibar Red Bishop is smaller, with entire crown orange-red, underparts black, with orange-red crissum; Black-winged Red Bishop has black wings and relatively long black tail; Northern Red Bishop has entire top of head black, long upper and under tail-coverts concealing the tail; Black Bishop is larger, with narrow orange breast band and yellow or orange upper back. Females: Fire-fronted Bishop has yellow-edged primaries; Zanzibar Red Bishop is smaller and less streaked below. Northern Red Bishop is virtually identical; Black-winged Red Bishop is more richly coloured, with yellow supraloral areas, a brown-streaked, bright buff breast band and buffy-brown sides and flanks. **STATUS AND DISTRIBUTION**: Locally and generally uncommon in tall grassland and cultivation, typically in open country near water, including edges of rice paddies. Ranges from interior Tanzania north to Serengeti NP, the Mbulu and Crater Highlands, Lake Manyara NP and Kenyan border areas north of Lake Natron at the Southern Uaso Nyiro River and adjacent swamps. Also locally in the Lake Victoria basin, particularly around Ahero. Occasional wanderers recorded north to Lake Naivasha. Largely allopatric with other red bishops.

NORTHERN RED BISHOP *Euplectes franciscanus*   Plates 111, 112

Length 105–110 mm (4–4.25"). The red bishop of *cent.* and *northern* Kenya. **Breeding male** like Southern Red Bishop, but *entire top of head black* and both *upper and under tail-coverts longer, effectively concealing the tail*. **Female** apparently indistinguishable from Southern Red Bishop. **VOICE AND HABITS:** Similar to those of preceding species. **SIMILAR SPECIES**: See Southern Red Bishop. **STATUS AND DISTRIBUTION**: *E. f. franciscanus* is localized in the Rift Valley around lakes Baringo and Bogoria, where common in areas of seasonally inundated grassland. A sight record from the edge of the Dida Galgalu Desert 40 km north of Marsabit, March 1978, may represent the Ethiopian race *pusillus*. Formerly known from Eldama Ravine and the Northern Uaso Nyiro River.

YELLOW BISHOP *Euplectes capensis crassirostris*   Plates 111, 112
(Yellow-rumped Bishop)

Length 150 mm (6"). A large bishop with diagnostic *large yellow patches on 'shoulders' and rump/lower back*. **Breeding male** rather short-tailed, black, with bright yellow on bend of wing, lower back and rump; often a white mid-ventral line; wing-linings tawny or buff. Bill light blue-grey, black below and at base of maxilla; eyes brown; feet pale pinkish brown. Occasional all-black males lack yellow in plumage. **Non-breeding male** mostly streaky brown, but some yellow areas are conspicuous in flight; bill greyish or bluish horn, pinkish at base. **Female** boldly streaked buff and black above, except for *plain yellowish rump*; has short dark moustachial marks, buffy-white underparts with a breast band of fine brown streaks, and heavy dark brown streaks on sides and flanks. Bill horn-brown, pinkish at base; feet horn-brown. **Juvenile** much less heavily streaked below; dorsal streaks dark brown, not black; *buffy-brown rump streaked like back*. **VOICE**: Song a series of rather weak nasal notes with occasional louder sizzling, *tzeemp tzeemp zziiiiiiiiiiiiiiiit*

zeemp-zeemp-zeemp. Call note a thin *tseep* or *tsip*. HABITS: Generally solitary. Singing male perches on small bush, the yellow back/rump feathers erected to cover the secondaries, and the black flank feathers and neck ruff also raised; when flying from perch, audible wing-rattling alternates with sizzling song, the body plumage remaining fluffed and tail feathers spread. Wanders in small flocks after breeding, often with other *Euplectes*. SIMILAR SPECIES: Male Yellow-mantled Widowbird has long tail and black rump. Female Jackson's Widowbird is richer buff and more heavily streaked on the breast; supraloral areas yellow-buff or orange-buff, and bill smaller. STATUS AND DISTRIBUTION: Widespread and fairly common resident of bushed and wooded grassland and brushy cultivation in and near the w. and cent. Kenyan highlands, mainly above 1400 m. Ranges from Mt Elgon, the Cheranganis, Maralal, and Laikipia, Nanyuki and Meru Districts south to Kisii, Lolgorien, Mara GR, the Loita and Nguruman Hills, Narok, Nairobi, and Machakos and Kitui Districts; also in the Chyulu Hills. In n. Tanzania, from n. Serengeti NP, Loliondo, and the Crater and Mbulu Highlands east to Arusha District.

FAN-TAILED WIDOWBIRD *Euplectes axillaris* Plates 111, 112
(Red-shouldered Widow)

Length 150 mm (6"). A *broad-winged*, rather *short-tailed widowbird* of marshy sites. **Breeding male** largely black, with *buff-bordered, orange-red epaulettes* conspicuous in flight but sometimes concealed when perched. Bill pale blue-grey; eyes brown; feet black. Coastal race *zanzibaricus* is larger-billed, with the wing-coverts often black-tipped. **Non-breeding male** retains *scarlet epaulettes*; otherwise streaked black and buff above, with prominent pale buff superciliary stripes; underparts buffy white with brown streaks. **Female** and **juvenile** similar to non-breeding male, but smaller, with ochre, orange-yellow or russet 'shoulders'. VOICE: A weak, high-pitched, scratchy song, *shreep skrik skrik wirra skreek skreek wirrily wirrily wirrily chink chink chink* (MacLean 1984). HABITS: Gregarious; breeds in small loose groups in moist places. Displaying male perches with scarlet epaulettes prominent, tail spread, hindneck ruff erected; sings in undulating flight with slow exaggerated flaps, the wings appearing very broad. Gathers in large post-breeding flocks. SIMILAR SPECIES: Male Hartlaub's Marsh Widowbird has much longer tail; other female-plumaged *Euplectes* lack orange or russet on wing-coverts. STATUS AND DISTRIBUTION: *E. a. phoeniceus* is a locally common resident of tall inundated grassland and marshes in w. Kenya, from Mt Elgon, Kapenguria, Saiwa NP and Iten south to the Lake Victoria basin and w. Mara GR, mainly west of the Rift and Kerio Valleys, but wanders occasional in some cent. Rift Valley wetlands; in n. Tanzania, local in the Mara Region, Serengeti NP, the Crater and Mbulu Highlands and Lake Manyara NP. *E. a. zanzibaricus* is locally fairly common in coastal lowlands from Lamu south to Tanga and Dar es Salaam, and inland along the lower Tana to Wenje; a sight record from near Lake Jipe (1970) presumably represents this race.

YELLOW-MANTLED WIDOWBIRD *Euplectes macrourus* Plates 111, 112
(Yellow-backed Widow; includes Yellow-shouldered Widowbird)

Length of male, 190 mm (7.5"), of female, 125–135 mm (5–5.5"). Two distinct populations. **Breeding male** of nominate *macrourus* is black, with *yellow back and 'shoulders'*; male *macrocercus* (widespread at lower elevations in w. Kenya) has *yellow only on 'shoulders'*. In both forms, a nearly concealed patch of white on centre of breast, and nuchal ruff may be evident. Bill blue-black; eyes brown; feet black. **Female** and **juvenile** striped buff and black above; *lesser and median wing-coverts yellow-margined*; underparts often washed with yellow; breast faintly streaked. **Non-breeding male** like female, but with yellow wing-coverts of breeding plumage; bill and feet brownish. VOICE: A buzzing or sizzling *zeeeeee*, and thin *tseep* or *tsweep* call notes. HABITS: Generally solitary and shy when breeding. Displaying male has low erratic flight, moving spread tail up and down; when perched, flicks wings and tail, expands nuchal ruff and exposes the usually hidden white breast patch. Yellow-backed *E. m. macrourus* forms sizeable flocks after nesting (not reported for *macrocercus*). SIMILAR SPECIES: Yellow Bishop has short tail, black upper back in breeding male, unstreaked yellow or yellowish rump in most plumages. Female Fan-tailed Widowbird has orange-brown, ochre or russet-edged wing-coverts. STATUS AND DISTRIBUTION: Yellow-backed nominate *macrourus* is local and generally uncommon in moist lush grassland from the Mara GR and Loita Plains/Hills south to n. Serengeti NP and Loliondo District of n. Tanzania. Yellow-shouldered *macrocercus* is locally common in bushed grassland and cultivation in w. Kenya from Kapenguria, Kitale, Malaba, Bungoma and Webuye Districts south to Busia, Mumias, Ng'iya, Maseno and Ahero. The two races are not sympatric within our area.

WHITE-WINGED WIDOWBIRD *Euplectes albonotatus eques* Plates 111, 112

Length of male, 165 mm (6.5"), of female, 130 mm (5"). **Breeding male** mostly black, with cinnamon-rufous 'shoulders' and *white wing patches* (on primary and secondary coverts); wing-linings and primary bases also white. **Non-breeding male** retains rufous and white wing patches and has yellowish superciliary stripes; upperparts broadly streaked yellowish buff and black; *breast faintly streaked with brown*. **Female** and **juvenile** resemble non-

breeding male, but lack white in wings, and the epaulettes (often concealed) are dark ochre-orange or rufous; leading edge of wings, supraloral and submalar areas yellow; throat and breast slightly yellowish. Bill of female brownish above, flesh-white below. Juvenile male may show whitish-buff patch on wing formed by greater-covert edges. **Voice**: A rustling *shwrrrrr* followed by two throaty chirps. **Habits**: Gregarious. Polygamous breeding male perches conspicuously, lowering and spreading tail; in display flight progresses slowly, but flaps wings rapidly and spreads the slightly keeled tail. Normal flight rapid, flocks often flying high. **Similar Species**: Female Yellow-mantled Widowbird is duller, less yellowish, with no rufous at bend of wing. **Status and Distribution**: Locally common in bushed grassland and cultivation below 2000 m. Widespread in the cent. Kenyan highlands and on adjacent eastern plateau. Seasonal in many dry areas following heavy rains, notably from Kibwezi and the Tsavo NPs south to Mkomazi GR, occasionally wandering east to the Shimba Hills. Elsewhere, local and uncommon during or after local rains (e.g. in the west around Saiwa NP and Kitale, w. Mara GR and n. Serengeti NP).

RED-COLLARED WIDOWBIRD *Euplectes ardens*   Plates 111, 112
(Red-naped Widowbird)

Length of male 255 mm (10″), of female 130 mm (5″). A small-bodied, slender-tailed widowbird. **Breeding male** black, with a long flexible tail and, in *E. a. suahelica*, a scarlet crown, nape and *collar*. The Tanzanian race *tropicus* lacks red on the head, and has a red, orange or yellow band across throat only. (Most birds in interior Tanzania and Uganda are similar, but some there are entirely black.) **Non-breeding male, female** and **juvenile** buff with black streaks above, have at least partly *yellow superciliary stripes*, and are unstreaked below. From February to April, males are in mottled intermediate plumage, with some black body feathers and rectrices. **Voice and Habits**: Gregarious and at least partly polygamous. Breeding male makes long low flights with exaggerated wingbeats, long tail curved downwards, and head feathers erected in a hood. Perched, he contorts with quivering wings, fluffs body feathers, and utters a rapid, insect-like *chisisisi chisisisi chisisisi* which, as he flies around, changes to a curious hissing sound. Between flights he flops on to bushtop as if exhausted, tail feathers askew, wings outspread. Normal flight is rapid, with compressed tail straight out behind. Flocks of restless non-breeding birds fly high, descending here and there to feed. Largely granivorous. **Similar Species**: Female-plumaged White-winged Widowbird also has yellowish superciliaries, but is faintly streaked on the breast. **Status and Distribution**: Locally common in open grassland, cultivation, rank herbaceous growth and grassy bush. *E. a. suahelica* occupies the w. and cent. Kenyan highlands between 1500 and 3000 m, ranging from Mt Elgon, the Cheranganis and Mt Kenya south to the Mau, Mara GR, cent. Rift Valley, Aberdare Range, and Nairobi and Machakos Districts; in n. Tanzania at Loliondo, the Crater Highlands, Arusha NP, on Mt Meru and at Kilimanjaro. *E. a. tropicus* is widespread in e. Tanzania, but within our area known only from old records at Amani in the East Usambara Mts, in se. Kenya's Taita District and the lower Tana River floodplain. A sight record from Mt Hanang at 2600 m (Feb. 1946) not racially assigned.

HARTLAUB'S MARSH WIDOWBIRD *Euplectes hartlaubi humeralis*   Plates 111, 112

Length of breeding male 200 mm (8″), of female 150 mm (6″). A bird of *marshes* or tall moist grassland in *western Kenya*. **Breeding male** has *moderately long tail* (unlike Fan-tailed Widowbird) and *buffy orange epaulettes*; most wing feathers buff-edged; bill bluish white; feet dark horn-brown. **Female** and **juvenile** streaked pale brown and black above; underparts buff throughout, with short dark moustachial marks, and dark streaks on breast, sides and flanks; bill pinkish tan or pale brown. **Non-breeding male** female-like but larger, with wings as in breeding plumage. **Voice**: Common call of male perched on shrub, grass stem or sedge a short dry *drrrt*, like that produced by running fingernail along teeth of comb. Song a short, abruptly rising metallic *turrrreeek* or a loud abbreviated *yecck*, immediately followed by a high-pitched faint *su-sitisit* or *see-seepeu*. The *yecck* or *yerrk* notes may also lead into a rising buzzy, yet semi-musical trill with a prolonged ending: *chrrrrrrrittterweeeeeeeeeeeee*. **Habits**: Displaying male flies low, calling, and with orange epaulettes conspicuous. Usually rather wary. May pursue male Fan-tailed Widowbirds that venture into his territory. **Similar Species**: Sympatric Fan-tailed Widowbird has different calls; male is shorter-tailed and with *red* epaulettes; female is smaller, more richly coloured, with russet or orange-brown on 'shoulders'. Long-tailed Widowbird is allopatric. **Status and Distribution**: Local and uncommon resident of wet grasslands and marshes in Busia, Mumias, Kakamega, Webuye and Bungoma Districts.

LONG-TAILED WIDOWBIRD *Euplectes progne delamerei*   Plates 111, 112

Length of breeding male 610–710 mm (24–28″), of non-breeding male 190 mm (7.5″), of female 150 mm (6″). **Breeding male** unmistakable, with *extraordinary long floppy tail*; plumage mainly black, with *white-bordered scarlet epaulettes*. Bill pale blue-grey, almost white. Wings noticeably broad in flight. **Female** and **juvenile** much

smaller, streaked buff and black, with buff patch formed by broad wing-covert margins; no red 'shoulders'; underparts whitish, with buff wash on streaked breast and flanks. **Non-breeding male** *heavy-looking*, boldly streaked black and buff above; '*shoulders*' *orange-red, bordered below by broad buffy band; tail somewhat elongated, pointed*; wings broad and floppy in flight. **VOICE**: Displaying male sings repeated *twi-twi-twi-twi-zizizizizi*, and gives a sharp *zik zik zik* in slow erratic flight with the tail vertically fanned and depressed like a large bustle. If alarmed, he compresses feathers and flies off with great speed, tail streaming out behind. **HABITS**: Often solitary and rather wary. Breeding males roost communally, flying high in late afternoon/evening to marshes or reedbeds. Individuals perch in tall grass, uttering harsh grating calls and displays (as under VOICE). Feeds largely on the ground. Nests in marshy spots in open grassland. **SIMILAR SPECIES**: Female Jackson's Widowbird has larger bill and more boldly marked underparts. Allopatric Hartlaub's Marsh Widowbird female is entirely buff below. **STATUS AND DISTRIBUTION**: Fairly common local resident of montane grasslands, marshes and adjacent grain fields above 1800 m, centred around the Aberdares and Mt Kenya. Ranges from Timau, Nanyuki, Naro Moru, Laikipia and Nyahururu south to Lake Nakuru NP, Elmenteita, Naivasha and the Kinangop Plateau. A small disjunct population is localized on the Uasin Gishu Plateau around Eldoret and Kaptagat.

JACKSON'S WIDOWBIRD *Euplectes jacksoni*   Plates 111, 112

Length of breeding male, 280–300 mm (11–12"), of female, 140 mm (5.5"). **Breeding male** black, with long, *broad decurved tail* and light brown, tawny or buffy-tan 'shoulders'; bill pale bluish white or greenish. **Female** and **juvenile** streaked buff and black above; *underparts pale buff to bright orange-buff*, with variable dark streaking on breast and sides; wing-linings buff. Bill horn-brown to pinkish brown above, flesh-pink below. **Non-breeding male** larger, darker and browner than female, breast almost unstreaked except at sides; wings as in breeding plumage, but with broad tawny or tan feather edges. **VOICE**: Flight note a soft *tu*. Display songs mentioned below. **HABITS**: Always gregarious. Apparently not polygamous. Each male in a loose colony tramples down a circular dancing ring in open grass. In display he sways sideways, jumps forwards giving wheezing, sizzling song, and producing a rattling sound perhaps from the rapidly vibrating wings. Arched tail is elevated except for two feathers held horizontally. He jumps upwards several times, to almost 1 m above ground, with all but the horizontal rectrices cocked forwards over his back, nearly touching the raised neck feathers. As he sings, half-open wings continue shivering, and thrashing feet claw the air. (See Fig. below.) **SIMILAR SPECIES**: Long-tailed Widowbird is smaller-billed; non-breeding male and female whitish (not buff) and more streaked below, with blackish wing-linings. Female Hartlaub's Marsh Widowbird (western only) has dusky wing-linings. **STATUS AND DISTRIBUTION**: Endemic resident of highland grasslands in Kenya and n. Tanzania, often sympatric with the preceding species. Locally common from Eldoret and Nandi east to Laikipia and Mt Kenya, south to the Aberdares, Nairobi NP and Ngong Hills, the Mau, Mara GR, Loita and Nguruman Hills, n. Serengeti NP, Loliondo and the Crater Highlands.

Displaying Jackson's Widowbird.

PARASITIC WEAVER *Anomalospiza imberbis*   Plates 112, 113
(Cuckoo Finch)

Length 110–115 mm (4.5"). *Suggests a short-tailed canary with a dark, deep-based bill.*
Freshly plumaged non-breeding male olive above, the head more yellowish and
contrasting with *black-streaked back*; underparts yellow with pale feather tips; wings
and tail dusky, edged olive-yellow; *bill dusky brown*. **Breeding male** brighter yellow,
with orange tinge to crown, back more heavily streaked, and flank feathers may show
dark shaft streaks. *Bill black, pinkish white at base of mandible*; feet slate-grey to pale
horn-brown. **Female in fresh plumage** tawny-buff, *broadly streaked black above*; face
yellowish buff, with dusky eye-lines; throat buffy white, breast buffy brown, flanks
faintly streaked and washed with brown; **worn female** generally paler, less tawny, with
sharper streaks. **Nestling** pale golden buff, heavily streaked black on head and back;
underparts golden sandy buff, paler on belly; face and throat more tawny. Bill yellowish, with dark brown culmen (van Someren 1922). **Immature male** duller and darker than adult, olive above,
with streaked back; head and neck streaked or plain; underparts dull yellowish, variably streaked on sides. Bill
dusky or dull brownish horn. **Voice**: Usual notes a high, thin, sibilant *tissiwick* (rising) and *tissiway* (falling), often
followed by *djzing-ji-ji*; also a separate *dzi-bee-chew*. Flight call a thin, high, hard *jit jit*. Displaying male gives
a nasal *chi-wee, chi-wee, chi-wee* (Williams and Keith 1962). Song in s. Africa a scratchy *tseep krrik krrik krrik
krrik* or *seedle-eedle-thrush-thrush* (MacLean 1984). **Habits**: Solitary or in small flocks. Often wary. Feeds in
grass and herbage, but perches in shrubs and low trees. Flight rapid, direct and weaver-like. A brood parasite,
laying its eggs in nests of cisticolas and Tawny-flanked Prinia. **Similar Species**: Other weavers (except differently
patterned Grosbeak-Weaver) have longer, thinner bills. Canaries are longer-tailed, have undulating flight. See
female and young queleas. **Status and Distribution**: Uncommon to locally fairly common in moist grassland
and at edges of cultivation below 2000 m. Most numerous after heavy rains, particularly around Mt Elgon, in
Busia, Siaya, Mumias and Kakamega Districts and in the Lake Victoria basin. Also near Thika, Nairobi and Ngong
Districts, the Mara GR and Serengeti NP, but scarce in recent years. Small numbers on Pemba Island. Reports
from the lower Tana River floodplain require confirmation.

WAXBILLS, FAMILY ESTRILDIDAE, SUBFAMILY ESTRILDINAE
(World, *c.* 130 species; Africa, 68; Kenya, 36; n. Tanzania, 27)

Small birds typical of open savanna, bush and forest clearings, several now adapted to cultivation and suburban
environments. Most are granivorous, feeding mainly on grass seeds, but the *Nigrita* species are both insectivorous and frugivorous forest birds. Plumage is often brightly coloured, sometimes barred or spotted; the bill is
bright pink or red in several species. Many are gregarious, especially during the non-breeding season. Most build
rather untidy domed nests with a side entrance, and although waxbills are sometimes called weaver-finches their
nests are not woven. Both sexes incubate the four to seven pure white eggs. Waxbills do not remove their
nestlings' excrement from the nest, which becomes increasingly fouled by fledging time. Both parents feed the
nestlings by regurgitation. Unlike ploceids, nestling waxbills display characteristic patterns of conspicuous spots
or patches at the gape and in the mouth. Most estrildine songs tend to be soft and toneless, often high-pitched
and unimpressive. Numerous species are regularly parasitized by their relatives, the whydahs and indigobirds of
the subfamily Viduinae (p. 692).

GREY-HEADED NEGROFINCH *Nigrita canicapilla*   Plate 119

Length 125 mm (5"). A dark forest finch of canopy, mid-level and undergrowth vegetation. **Adult** grey above and black below, with *white-dotted wing-coverts*; *whitish line
separates grey crown from black face and forehead*. Rump pale grey. Eyes red (quickly
fading to yellow after death); bill and feet black. Western birds are slightly paler above
than those in the cent. Kenyan highlands. Sexes alike. **Juvenile** uniform dark grey with
faint suggestion of head pattern, sometimes a few whitish wing spots; nestlings are grey-
eyed, as, probably, are recently fledged birds. **Voice**: A sweet, plaintive three- or four-
note whistle, *eeee-ti-WEE tew* or *eeee-teuWEEE-weu*. Largely silent in our region
(although highly vocal in West Africa). **Habits**: Solitary or in pairs. Feeds largely on
insects and fruit. Builds bulky untidy nest of leaves and leaf strips with side entrance,
usually in a tree. **Status and Distribution**: Fairly common resident of highland forest
and forest edge between 1550 and 3000 m. *N. c. diabolica* ranges from Mt Kenya, the Nyambenis and Aberdares
south to Nairobi, and in n. Tanzania on Kilimanjaro and Mt Meru, in Arusha NP and in the Crater and Mbulu
Highlands. In w. Kenya, *N. c. schistacea* ranges from Mt Elgon and the Cheranganis, south through the Nandi,
Kakamega, Mau and Trans-Mara Forests to Kilgoris and Lolgorien. Birds in the Ngurumans not racially assigned.

WHITE-BREASTED NEGROFINCH *Nigrita f. fusconota*   **Plate 119**

Length 115 mm (4.5"). A *slender-billed, black-capped* finch of western forests. **Adults** blue-black from forehead to nape, on sides of face, lower rump, upper tail-coverts and tail; otherwise pale brown above, white below; eyes dark brown or dark red; bill black; feet slate-grey. Sexes alike. In **juvenile**, blue-black replaced by dark brown; throat and flanks grey. **VOICE**: Song a prolonged sizzling *tz-tz-tz-tz-tzeeeeeeee*. The high trill may slow down and end with a few separate *tsip* notes. **HABITS**: Arboreal. Solitary or in pairs at forest edge. Forages warbler-like for insects; also eats small fruits. Nest spherical, of bark strips and leaf fibres, with side entrance, in tree. **SIMILAR SPECIES**: Plumage pattern reminiscent of Black-capped Social Weaver, a larger-billed bird of dry acacia country. **STATUS AND DISTRIBUTION**: Local and uncommon resident of the Kakamega Forest, w. Kenya. Formerly on Mt Elgon. **NOTE**: The extralimital Chestnut-breasted Negrofinch, *N. bicolor*, ranging east to w. Uganda, has been attributed to Kenya on the basis of sight reports from Kakamega Forest, several of which have referred to juvenile Red-headed Bluebills. There is no credible Kenyan record.

GREEN-WINGED PYTILIA *Pytilia melba*   **Plate 118**
(Melba Finch)

Length 135 mm (5.5"). An undergrowth skulker with *red rump and red-edged tail* conspicuous as bird flits into cover. **Adult male** *scarlet from forehead to upper breast,* including bill; crown and sides of face dove-grey; lower breast golden yellow, rest of underparts barred dusky and white (under tail-coverts faintly marked); back and *wings golden olive*. Eyes orange-red; bright red bill has brownish culmen except in breeding season; feet pinkish or grey-brown. **Female** similar, but *entire head grey and underparts barred*; rump and tail duller than in male. Bill red, dark brown along culmen. **Juvenile** rather plain grey or olive-brown, with dull reddish upper tail-coverts and tail edges, primaries narrowly edged with olive; flanks of some birds faintly barred. **VOICE**: A soft insect-like *kwik-kweek*. Song a variable plaintive trilled whistle, intermixed with *kwik* and *plink* notes. Contact note a loud sharp *tsip*. **HABITS**: Retiring, rather shy and usually silent. Pairs or small family groups forage in low undergrowth or on the ground, rarely flying more than a few metres. Builds loose ovoid grass nest with roofed side entrance, in low shrub. **SIMILAR SPECIES**: Rare Orange-winged Pytilia is smaller, shows bright orange on wings, and adult male has grey-bordered red face. **STATUS AND DISTRIBUTION**: The race *soudanensis* is a widespread resident of thickets, dense bush, scrub and overgrown cultivation in semi-arid areas (up to 1400 m) north, east and south of the Kenyan highlands, including coastal areas north of Malindi, south into ne. Tanzania in Mkomazi GR, lowlands south of Kilimanjaro, the Masai Steppe and Tarangire NP. *P. m. belli* ranges from the Lake Victoria basin to Mara GR, and from Serengeti NP east to Olduvai Gorge, Lake Eyasi and Lake Manyara NP.

ORANGE-WINGED PYTILIA *Pytilia afra*   **Plate 118**
(Golden-backed Pytilia)

Length 110 mm (4.5"). A rare waxbill, with *orange on the wings*. Noticeably smaller than Green-winged Pytilia. **Adult male** has vermilion face *bordered by a band of grey*. Upperparts golden olive-green; edges of flight feathers and greater coverts bright orange; rump and upper tail-coverts red; tail dusky, washed with crimson; breast olive with orange tinge, otherwise barred whitish and golden olive below, with centre of belly white. Eyes reddish; bill vermilion, browner at base; feet brownish-flesh colour. **Female** duller, with olive-grey head, underparts barred olive-grey and white; belly buffy white; bill brown with some orange-red on lower mandible; wings as in male. **Juvenile** resembles female, but rump more orange. **VOICE**: Call notes a sharp *tsip* and a higher-pitched *tseemp*. Song in s. Africa begins with two or three rattling notes followed by a soft fluty series, ending with a short crackling *kay* (Maclean 1984). **HABITS**: Generally similar to those of preceding species, but little known in our region. Feeds on the ground, mostly on small seeds. **SIMILAR SPECIES**: See Green-winged Pytilia. **STATUS AND DISTRIBUTION**: Formerly an uncommon and local Kenyan resident. Now rare, perhaps largely extirpated by habitat change. Early specimens from the coastal lowlands at Lamu, Sokoke Forest, Mombasa, and inland near Voi, Kikuyu, Fort Hall (Murang'a), Ngong Escarpment, and Mt Kenya. Unknown in cent. Kenyan highlands for the past 50–75 years. Four post-1960 records from Kilifi District (Jan. 1968), Shimba Hills (Jan.–Feb. 1990), Kongelai Escarpment (Nov. 1989) and ne. Elgon (April 1994). All Tanzanian localities are well south of our area.

GREEN-BACKED TWINSPOT *Mandingoa nitidula chubbi*   **Plate 119**
(Green Twinspot)

Length 100 mm (4"). A *small, greenish-backed bird with white-spotted underparts*. **Adult male** dark olive-green above, with faint orange wash on rump and upper tail-coverts; *sides of face, lores and chin vermilion*; throat and breast golden olive-green; rest of underparts black, *boldly marked with round white spots*; eyes brown, eyelids

pink; bill black, with tip and sides and often most of the mandible scarlet; feet brownish pink. **Female** similar, but *face and chin pale orange-tawny*, breast duller olive, eyelids black, bill mostly black. **Juvenile** dull greenish olive above; fore part of face tawny-buff, paler on chin; underparts plain brownish grey, more olive-brown on sides; breast may be obscurely mottled. **VOICE:** Contact call a sharp *tik-tik*; alarm note a low *tirrrr*. Song in s. Africa described as a mixed series of *tick* notes and whistles, *chrrr tik tik tik cheer weet weet weet teeu wooee tseeeu* (Maclean 1984). **HABITS:** Pairs or small family groups forage low or on ground in dense cover. Furtive and inconspicuous. Untidy spherical grass nest in tree lacks entrance tunnel. **SIMILAR SPECIES:** Peters's Twinspot is tawny-russet above. **STATUS AND DISTRIBUTION:** Uncommon and local resident of damp forest undergrowth and borders and dense moist thickets. In the coastal lowlands, ranges from Pemba Island north to the lower Tana River. Inland localities include the Shimba Hills, the Usambara and North Pare Mountains, Taita and Ngulia Hills, Kitovu Forest in Taveta District and Arusha NP. In the cent. Kenyan highlands, small populations remain in n. Nairobi, s. Aberdare and Meru Forests. Periodic reports from around Mt Elgon, Kakamega Forest, s. Kerio Valley, Lolgorien and the Mara GR may in part represent wandering or displaced birds. Formerly recorded from Mt Marsabit.

PETERS'S TWINSPOT *Hypargos niveoguttatus macrospilotus*   Plate 119
(Red-throated Twinspot)

Length 125 mm (5"). A handsome 'polka-dotted' waxbill, *tawny-russet above, with dull red rump and tail*. **Adult male** has greyish-brown crown and nape, dark *red face, throat and breast*; rest of underparts dull black, with *bold white spots on sides and flanks*. Eyes red-brown, bare orbital skin vivid electric blue; bill darker metallic blue, with black tip and culmen; feet slate-grey. **Female** similar, with white-spotted flanks, but *face grey, throat tawny-buff* and red areas duller; lower breast, belly, sides, flanks and under tail-coverts dark grey; bare parts as in male. **Juvenile** plain russet-brown above and on breast; throat paler, sometimes pale buff; lower breast and belly dull brown, the feathers obscurely edged with russet. Bill dull bluish, blackish-tipped. Some birds show a trace of reddish on breast and a few tiny white spots at sides. **VOICE:** Song a thin, wispy, insect-like trill, at times with 'bouncing-ball' rhythm: *tsit, tsit, tsit-tsit-tsit-tsisitsitsitsit*; or a single chip followed by a rattling trill, *spit cheeeeeeeeeeeeee*. **HABITS:** Terrestrial; shy and secretive. Pairs or family groups feed on grass seeds at forest borders and along overgrown trails. Usually silent. Builds large spherical grass nest in shrub or on ground. **SIMILAR SPECIES:** See Green-backed Twinspot. **STATUS AND DISTRIBUTION:** A fairly common resident of dense coastal bush, thickets and forest edge north to the Boni Forest. Locally common inland from the Shimba Hills to Mkomazi GR and the North Pare Mts; also in Kibwezi, Rombo, Taveta and Moshi Districts. Smaller populations (or wanderers) reported from Voi, Ngulia and Mt Endau. Its continued presence in the ground-water forest at Lake Manyara NP and in Arusha District requires confirmation.

ABYSSINIAN CRIMSONWING *Cryptospiza salvadorii*   Plate 119

Length 100–110 mm (4–4.25"). A crimson-backed, dull olive bird of highland-forest areas. **Adult male** greyish olive on head and underparts, throat lighter olive-buff; crimson on back, scapulars, some wing-coverts, parts of secondaries, rump, upper tail-coverts and flanks. Brown eyes rimmed by conspicuous *red or pink eyelids*; bill black; feet dark brown. **Female** similar, slightly less red on back, only a trace on flanks, but *lacks red eyelids*. **Juvenile** has olive-brown upper back, with crimson confined to lower back, rump and upper tail-coverts and a trace on flanks; eyelids (of male) yellowish grey. **VOICE:** A soft *tsip-tsip* when flushed. **HABITS:** Shy and secretive. Generally in pairs or small groups feeding in low grasses on fallen seeds, often along forest tracks. Builds ovoid nest of grass and twigs, covered with moss, in forest tree or vine cluster. Wanders to lower elevations as grass seeds ripen. **SIMILAR SPECIES:** Male Red-faced Crimsonwing (n. Tanzanian mountains) has prominent red lores and broad red area around eyes. Females and young generally indistinguishable. **STATUS AND DISTRIBUTION:** In Kenya, a fairly common but local resident of forest edges and clearings between 1750 and 3000 m. Ranges from Mt Nyiru, the Ndotos, Maralal and Mt Uraguess, south through the w. and cent. highlands to the Nguruman, Namanga and Chyulu Hills; formerly in Nairobi. In n. Tanzania, a common resident of forest interior on Kilimanjaro and Mt Meru, also at Loliondo and Longido, but replaced by the following species in the Crater Highlands, North and South Pare Mts and the Usambaras. Most Kenyan and n. Tanzanian birds represent *C. s. kilimensis*, whereas those from the Ndotos northwards show evidence of intergradation with the nominate Ethiopian race, to which they seem nearer.

RED-FACED CRIMSONWING *Cryptospiza reichenovii australis*   Plate 124

Length 100–110 mm (4–4.25"). A Tanzanian crimsonwing, the **adult male** with *bright red on lores and around eyes*. Otherwise much like preceding species, but somewhat darker. **Female** has no red on face, reduced crimson on body, and eyes are more or less ringed by broad, diffuse pale area extending to the lores. **VOICE:** Call a

high-pitched *tseet*. Song of four descending notes followed by a chirp (Mackworth-Praed and Grant 1955). **HABITS:** Shy and secretive. Pairs or small groups feed on grass seeds along forest tracks or other openings. **SIMILAR SPECIES:** Abyssinian Crimsonwing (sympatric with this species on Mt Meru and Kilimanjaro) has red on face restricted to eyelids. **STATUS AND DISTRIBUTION:** Fairly common resident of highland-forest undergrowth and forest-edge habitats (including tea plantations) below 2500 m in the Crater Highlands, Kilimanjaro, Mt Meru, and the Pare and Usambara Mountains. Recorded as low as 300 m in the East Usambara foothills.

RED-HEADED BLUEBILL *Spermophaga ruficapilla* Plate 119

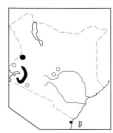

Length 128–140 mm (5–5.5"). A stocky *red-and-black* forest finch with a *heavy metallic blue-and-red bill*. **Adult male** black, with red head, throat, breast, sides and upper tail-coverts; upper back and belly black in widespread nominate race, slate-grey in Tanzanian *cana*. Eyes brown; *eyelids bluish white*; *bill iridescent blue, with red cutting edges and tip*; feet dark brownish olive. **Female** more slaty black and duller red, the *blackish belly densely spotted with white*; bill as in male. **Juvenile** *uniformly dark*; blackish above, sooty brown below; *head, throat and breast rich brown*, often with scattered crimson feathers; upper tail-coverts tinged crimson; bill mostly bright blue. **VOICE:** A thin, squeaking *spit-spit-spit-spit . . .*, often barely audible. Call note a brief *skwee* or *speek*. **HABITS:** Shy; solitary or in pairs. Usually in deep shade, but at times in sunlit foliage at forest edge or along trails. Frequently flicks wings and tail; assumes crouching position while foraging, seldom perching upright for long. Builds large, untidy, spherical nest of grass and leaves in tree or shrub. **SIMILAR SPECIES:** Rare Black-bellied Seed-cracker has *much red in tail, none on bill*; female brown, with no white spots. Twinspots can be confused with female, but have differently coloured upperparts and smaller bill. The smaller and extralimital Chestnut-breasted Negrofinch resembles juvenile, but is a largely *arboreal* insect-eater, with a black bill. **STATUS AND DISTRIBUTION:** *S. r. ruficapilla* is a fairly common resident of western forests from Mt Elgon and Saiwa NP, Nandi and Kakamega Districts to w. Mau, Trans-Mara, Kilgoris, Lolgorien and Rapogi Districts; also along the Mara River and at Siana Springs. Uncommon in the Meru and Embu Forests. *S. r. cana* is endemic to the East Usambara Mts, where local and scarce in forest interior below 1000 m. Mostly in secondary growth, but also along trails and clearings in primary forest.

*BLACK-BELLIED SEED-CRACKER *Pyrenestes ostrinus* Plate 119

Length 140 mm (5.5"). A rare, large-billed finch of Kenyan/Ugandan border areas. **Adult male** bright red on head, breast, sides, flanks and upper tail-coverts; *central rectrices and outer webs of others crimson*; rest of plumage black. Eyes dark red to dark brown; *widened parts of eyelids above and below eye pale blue*, narrower parts in front and behind blackish; *large bill dark blue or blue-grey*, black at tip; feet yellowish brown or greenish brown. Bill size highly variable. **Female** similar, but black replaced by brown; red of tail often duller. **Juvenile** largely brown, with duller red tail. **VOICE:** Call note a low metallic *peenk* (Chapin 1954). **HABITS:** Singles or pairs feed on or near ground, darting into cover when disturbed. Largely silent. Builds untidy spherical or ovoid nest of grasses in tree fork. **SIMILAR SPECIES:** Male Red-headed Bluebill has red on bill, dark feet, *no red on tail*; female has white-spotted underparts. **STATUS AND DISTRIBUTION:** In our area, known from two sight records (Dec. 1990, Sept. 1991) in brushy riverine clearings with rank growth of grasses and sedges in Busia District. These presumably represent nominate *ostrinus*.

BROWN TWINSPOT *Clytospiza monteiri* Plate 119

Length 105–115 mm (4–4.5"). A western bird of shrubby grassland. **Adults** *cinnamon or rufous below, densely spotted with white*; dark olive-brown above, the head greyer. *Crimson upper tail-coverts* at base of short broad dusky tail conspicuous as bird flits into cover. Eyes red-brown or dark red, eyelids pale blue; bill black with blue at base; feet red-brown. **Male** has dark grey head with triangular red spot in centre of lower throat. **Female** lacks red throat spot, this replaced by dull whitish. **Juvenile** grey-throated, with *no white spots below*; back lighter, more tawny-olive. **VOICE:** Call a sharp and frequently repeated *vay, vay, vay*, often loud. Song a variable series of twittering notes (Clement *et al.* 1993). **HABITS:** Usually in pairs or family groups near ground in low cover. Shy. Said to use old weaver nests for roosting and nesting. **SIMILAR SPECIES:** Female Red-headed Bluebill, a forest bird, is larger and darker, with large red-and-blue bill. **STATUS AND DISTRIBUTION:** A local and uncommon w. Kenyan resident of moist savanna undergrowth, tall grass and overgrown cultivation, from Busia and Mumias Districts south to Siaya, Ng'iya and Akala.

BAR-BREASTED FIREFINCH *Lagonosticta rufopicta*   **Plate 118**

Length 100 mm (4"). Resembles Red-billed Firefinch, but darker brown above and washed with dark vinous red or maroon; upper tail-coverts crimson. Sexes alike. **Adult** *dark vinous red on forehead, face and throat; tiny broken white bars on tips of breast feathers often worn and inconspicuous*; belly and tail blackish, but *under tail-coverts buff*. Eyes dark brownish grey, with light blue-grey eyelids; bill rose-red with dusky brown culmen; feet dark brown. **Juvenile** earth-brown, with crimson wash on upper breast and upper tail-coverts; bill dark brown. **VOICE:** Contact note a soft *cheup* or *tseup*. **HABITS:** Much like those of Red-billed Firefinch. Forages in pairs or small family parties. **SIMILAR SPECIES:** Red-billed Firefinch shows faint white dots, not bars, on sides of breast; male all red below, female brown. In African Firefinch, bill is slate-blue, belly and crissum black. **STATUS AND DISTRIBUTION:** A fairly common and widespread w. Kenyan resident in areas of overgrown cultivation, bushed grassland and edges of riverine thickets, from Busia and Mumias Districts south to the north shore of Lake Victoria.

RED-BILLED FIREFINCH *Lagonosticta senegala ruberrima*   **Plate 118**

Length 90–97 mm (3.5–3.75"). One of East Africa's most familiar birds. **Adult male** reddish brown above, washed with rose-red or pinkish red; face, upper tail-coverts and underparts brighter red, with *pale brown belly and under tail-coverts*; tail black with crimson edges. Eyes red, *eyelids yellow or olive*; bill rose-red below, dark grey above with some rose at sides, *culmen blackish*; feet grey-brown. **Female** brown or dusky brown with red rump and upper tail-coverts; *red lores* and reddish wash on face; small white dots on sides; bill shows less red than in male. **Juvenile** resembles female, but has no white spots below and little or no red on face; bill dusky brown. **VOICE:** A soft *sweet-fsseeet* call; a sharp abrupt *chick* of alarm. Contact call a slurred, usually rising *peee* or *pea*, sometimes repeated. The song combines these two calls into *chick-pea-pea* (Payne 1992). **HABITS:** Confiding and feeding in pairs or family groups on ground around towns and villages. Builds loose ball-like nest of grass, trash and feathers in variety of sites. Heavily parasitized by Village Indigobird. **SIMILAR SPECIES:** Bar-breasted Firefinch has white bars, not dots, below. Bill colour distinguishes other firefinches. **STATUS AND DISTRIBUTION:** Common and widespread resident between 1000 and 2000 m, but generally absent from arid n. and e. Kenya, and scarce in coastal lowlands away from towns and villages. Birds in extreme ne. Kenya may represent the race *somaliensis*, but specimens are lacking.

Wing-tips of firefinches showing differences in shape of 9th primary. Red-billed, (left), African, (centre), and Jameson's, (right).

AFRICAN FIREFINCH *Lagonosticta rubricata hildebrandti*   **Plate 118**
(Blue-billed Firefinch)

Length 95–100 mm (4"). Less familiar than preceding species; not likely around towns and villages; mainly in areas of higher rainfall. A *darker* bird than Red-billed Firefinch, *both sexes with black belly and under tail-coverts*, and *slate-blue bill* shading to black at tip. In the hand, a sure distinction from Jameson's Firefinch is the attenuate, somewhat emarginate 9th primary (See Fig above). **Adult male** dark *brown above, washed with vinous maroon* with upper tail-coverts red; tail black, with red edges at base. Face, throat and breast pinkish claret, with a few white spots on sides. Eyes dark brown, eyelids pinkish; feet dusky or dark blue-grey. **Female** paler brown above than male, with *no red on face*; throat pale; breast tawny-brown, sides white-dotted. **Juvenile** resembles female, but buffy brown below, black on under tail-coverts; bill blue-grey. **VOICE:** Alarm call a sharp *pit* or *pit-pit*, or *chit-chit-chit-chit*, the short notes given in irregular series. These notes often included in songs, along with trills. **HABITS:** More wary, less confiding, than Red-billed Firefinch. Feeds on ground. Builds spherical to somewhat flattened nest with side entrance, in grass clump or low shrub among grasses. **SIMILAR SPECIES:** Red-billed and Bar-breasted Firefinches have partly red bills. Jameson's

Firefinch of lower elevations is much paler, the juvenile perhaps not safely separable in the field, although brighter tawny; in the hand, note broadly rounded outermost long (9th) primary. Black-bellied Firefinch (w. Kenya) has black bill, with pinkish patch at sides of mandible. **STATUS AND DISTRIBUTION**: Rather uncommon but widespread resident, between 1500 and 2000 m, in the w. and cent. Kenyan highlands, typically at brushy edges of highland forest, in tall grass, moist thickets and cultivation. Ranges from Mt Elgon and Saiwa NP east to Maralal, Laikipia, the Aberdares, Mt Kenya and the Nyambenis, south to South Nyanza, Lolgorien, the Mau, Nairobi and the Chyulu Hills. In n. Tanzania, resident in Arusha NP, on Kilimanjaro and reported at 925 m in the East Usambara Mts (Aug. 1978). Birds above 3000 m on Mt Hanang reportedly belong to the e. Tanzanian race *haematocephala*.

JAMESON'S FIREFINCH *Lagonosticta rhodopareia*   Plate 118

Length *c.* 100 mm (4"). A *paler, more rosy version of the African Firefinch*, often in lower, drier country (but northern birds at higher elevations). **Adult male** of *L. r. taruensis washed with rose-pink above* (paler, brighter red, not vinous maroon as in African Firefinch); *upper tail-coverts bright red, contrasting with jet-black tail*. Underparts rose-pink, with black lower belly and under tail-coverts; some white dots on sides. Eyes brown; bill bluish slate with black tip; feet dark bluish. In the north, nominate *rhodopareia* is cinnamon-brown above, lacking pink wash on head and back. **Female** orangey brick-red below, southern birds pinker than female African Firefinch. Note the *buff lower belly and black-barred under tail-coverts; red loral spot* often conspicuous. Sides and flanks sparsely white-dotted. Bill as in male. **Juvenile** brown above, tawny russet-brown below. **VOICE**: Song of southern birds a melodious trilled *teu-uuuuuuu-uuu*, or a slower *tew-eu-eu-eu-eu-eu*. A musical *we-twe-twe-twe* or *dee-dee-dee-dee*, and a thin *eet-eeeeet-eet* serve as contact calls. Alarm call a rapid cat-like purring trill (in contrast to separate *pit* notes of African Firefinch). **HABITS**: Avoids towns and villages, but pairs or family groups inhabit edges of shambas or grassy clearings in thorn-scrub and on dry shrubby hillsides. Feeds on ground, but perches in trees. Builds loose spherical grass nest with side entrance near top, low in small shrubs among grass. Parasitized by Purple Indigobird. **SIMILAR SPECIES**: African Firefinch compared above. Bill colour distinguishes other *Lagonosticta* species. **STATUS AND DISTRIBUTION**: The race *taruensis* is local and uncommon in low thorn-scrub below 1400 m. Scattered records in coastal lowlands south to Shimoni and the Tanzanian border, inland along the lower Tana River to Bura, but more common in the Tsavo region around Voi, the Sagala and Ngulia Hills and south to Mkomazi GR. Nominate *rhodopareia* is known in n. and w. Kenya from the Kongelai Escarpment, Kapenguria, Sigor and the Kerio Valley, with old records from Wamba and Isiolo Districts.

BLACK-BELLIED FIREFINCH *Lagonosticta r. rara*   Plate 118

Length 115–130 mm (4.5–5"). A large *western* firefinch. **Adult male** resembles Red-billed Firefinch, but is brighter, more scarlet red, and *black of underparts extends up to the breast; no white dots on sides; bill black, with large purplish-pink patch on each side of mandible*. Eyes dark brown, with light grey eyelids; feet dark brown. **Female** dark ashy brown above, pinkish *red only on lores and rump*; throat grey, underparts rosy pink, with *blackish lower belly and crissum*; bill as in male. **Juvenile** shows red upper tail-coverts, otherwise uniformly sooty brown, male washed with pinkish red; belly soon becomes black. **VOICE**: Song said to be variable, usually three-parted, ending with long chippering trills. Alarm call a sharp nasal *chek*, given singly or repeatedly; also a harsh rising-and-falling call when bird is flushed (Payne 1973). **HABITS**: Pairs or small flocks feed mainly on the ground. Builds loosely woven spherical grass nest in shrub or low tree. **SIMILAR SPECIES**: Red-billed and Bar-breasted Firefinches have no black on underparts; both show white dots at sides of breast. **STATUS AND DISTRIBUTION**: Uncommon and local resident of tall moist grassland and overgrown cultivation between 1150 and 1500 m in the Malaba, Bungoma, Busia, Mumias, Kakamega and Siaya Districts of w. Kenya.

RED-CHEEKED CORDON-BLEU *Uraeginthus bengalus*   Plate 118

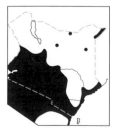

Length 115–120 mm (4.5"). A common 'blue waxbill'. **Adult male** brownish tan above, with azure-blue rump, upper tail-coverts and tail; face and underparts brighter paler azure, the belly centre and crissum buff; *dark red patch on ear-coverts*; bill dull red with blackish tip; eyes dark red; feet pale pinkish brown. *U. b. ugogoensis* is greyer brown above. **Female** lacks red patch. Nominate western race has *face and throat blue, uniform with breast and flanks*; in *brunneigularis, entire head (including cheeks) pale brown; littoralis* and *ugogoensis* similar but paler. **Juvenile** resembles female, but largely buffy brown below; male has blue throat, that of female brown; bill dark slate. **VOICE**: Call note a thin *tseek*. Song, a thin three-note *tse tse tseee*, frequently repeated. **HABITS**: Familiar and tame about habitation, where pairs or small groups feed on the ground. Builds ball-shaped nest of grass with low side entrance hole, in tree or shrub;

often uses old *Ploceus* nests. **SIMILAR SPECIES**: Blue-capped Cordon-bleu is paler, brighter and *longer-tailed*; bill bright pink. Female Southern Cordon-bleu (Tanzania) closely resembles nominate female, but blue is continuous from ear-coverts to sides of neck (females of *littoralis* and *ugogoensis* both show more brown on neck). **STATUS AND DISTRIBUTION**: Common and widespread resident of wooded and bushed habitats, including suburban gardens, from sea level to over 2200 m. Absent from the most arid treeless areas of n. and ne. Kenya. Four intergrading races: nominate *bengalus* west of the Rift Valley, from Mt Elgon and the Cheranganis south to the Lake Victoria basin, Lolgorien and Narok District; *brunneigularis* in the cent. Kenyan highlands, from Kajiado north to Baringo, Maralal, Laikipia and Meru Districts; *littoralis* in coastal Kenyan lowlands south to Tanga, and inland along the lower Tana River to Garsen and to the Tsavo and Amboseli NPs, Mkomazi GR and the North Pare Mts; *ugogoensis* in interior Tanzania north to Serengeti NP and Loliondo, including adjacent areas of the Mara GR, also to Lake Manyara, Tarangire and Arusha NPs, and Kilimanjaro and Moshi Districts.

BLUE-CAPPED CORDON-BLEU *Uraeginthus cyanocephalus*   **Plate 118**

Length 130–135 mm (5.25"). A *pale, long-tailed* 'blue waxbill' of *dry country*. **Adult male** has *entire head azure-blue, uniform with throat and breast*; rump and upper tail-coverts blue, tail dusky blue; belly and under tail-coverts pale tan. Eyes dull red; bill bright pink, with black cutting edges and tip; feet pale brown or buff. **Female** paler throughout and with less blue than Red-cheeked Cordon-bleu. **Juvenile** resembles female, but breast buffy tan. **VOICE**: A high-pitched *see-pee-see-see-pee*. Call note *seeee* or *see-see*. **HABITS**: In pairs, small groups, or mixed-species flocks feeding on the ground. Less confiding than preceding species. Nest like that of preceding species, but often in acacias and in association with hornets. **SIMILAR SPECIES**: Female Red-cheeked Cordon-bleu is darker. Southern Cordon-bleu (Tanzania) resembles female but is darker, and bill colour varies from blackish or bluish slate (paler at base of mandible) to pink or purplish pink with black tip and cutting edges. **STATUS AND DISTRIBUTION**: Widespread and locally common resident of semi-arid habitats, mainly north, east and south of the Kenyan highlands. Present at Lokichokio, and in West Pokot, Kerio Valley, Baringo and Isiolo Districts, Meru and Tsavo NPs, the Olorgesailie–Magadi–Natron area, se. Serengeti NP, Lake Eyasi, Mangola Springs, Tarangire NP and the Masai Steppe.

SOUTHERN CORDON-BLEU *Uraeginthus angolensis niassensis*   **Plate 122**
(Blue Waxbill)

Length 130–135 mm (5.25"). A southern African species, barely reaching our limits in n. Tanzania. **Adults** of both sexes *pale brown from forehead to lower back*; cheeks and anterior underparts pale blue, belly to under tail-coverts pale buffy brown. Bill slate-grey or pinkish, with black cutting edges and tip. Eyes dull red; feet light brown. **Female** paler below than male, with less blue on sides and flanks. **Juvenile** still paler, with no blue on sides, but *face and breast pale blue*; bill dark. **VOICE**: Call note a thin *tseep*. Songs are a mixture of stuttering phrases, *chrrrrrr, chit chit* or *cht cht cht chyeeeeee*, a high-pitched sibilant *seet seet seet seet* and a semi-musical weaver-like series, *skwee-kwee q'wurr yur spee qyur-qyur*. **HABITS**: Similar to those of preceding species. **SIMILAR SPECIES**: Female Red-cheeked Cordon-bleu has less blue on sides of head and neck. Female Blue-capped Cordon-bleu is paler; adult male blue from forehead to nape; juvenile has tan breast. **STATUS AND DISTRIBUTION**: A vagrant to our area. Reportedly sympatric with Blue-capped Cordon-bleu in lowlands south of Arusha, and ranging north to Handeni and Naberera on the Masai Steppe, but habitat differences, if any, are undetermined, and there are no dated records. Attributed to Kenya on the basis of a specimen allegedly collected at Lake Jipe, 12 March 1919, but no evidence that it was taken on the Kenyan side of the lake. Some more recent, but relabelled, skins with erroneous data exist. There are no valid records of this species from Kenya.

PURPLE GRENADIER *Uraeginthus ianthinogaster*   **Plate 118**

Length 135 mm (5.25"). A bright *cinnamon and violet-blue bird with a red bill*. **Adult male** cinnamon-rufous on head, neck and throat, browner on back and wings; *rump and upper tail-coverts purplish blue*; tail black; *pale blue patch around eyes; largely violet-blue below*, sometimes with rufous patches. Eyes red; bill red, dusky at base of maxilla; feet blackish brown. **Female** resembles male above, but silvery-blue eye patches smaller, *underparts cinnamon-brown, spotted and barred with white*. **Juvenile** similar to female, but with uniformly tawny head, throat and breast, and reddish-brown bill. **VOICE**: Song a high, thin *chit-cheet tsereea-ee-ee tsit-tsit*, or *cheerer cheet tsee-tsee sur-chit*. **HABITS**: Rather secretive, foraging on or close to ground in undergrowth and thickets in pairs, family groups or with mixed flocks of other seed-eaters. Builds loose spherical nest of grasses in low shrub. **STATUS AND DISTRIBUTION**: Fairly common and widespread resident of bush and thickets below 2200 m. Absent from many arid areas in n. and e. Kenya, the coastal lowlands (one Lamu record) and much of the Masai Steppe in ne. Tanzania.

YELLOW-BELLIED WAXBILL *Estrilda quartinia kilimensis* **Plate 117**
(East African Swee)

Length 90–100 mm (3.5–4"). A small, plump highland waxbill with pale *olive-green back and wings*. **Adult** has pale grey head and breast, red rump and upper tail-coverts and black tail; yellow from lower breast to under tail-coverts. Eyes brown; *bill black above, scarlet below*; feet black. **Juvenile** resembles adult, but rump and upper tail-coverts orange; bill black. **VOICE**: Usual note a weak *swee* or *sree*. Song *tsee-tsee-tsee-tsueeeee*. **HABITS**: Forages in pairs or small flocks, often with other estrildines, on ground or in low vegetation. Builds flimsy elongate ovoid nest of grass in tree or shrub. **SIMILAR SPECIES**: Fawn-breasted Waxbill has tawny-brown back and all-red bill. **STATUS AND DISTRIBUTION**: Fairly common resident of forest edge, grassy clearings, fallow fields and gardens. Widespread in the w. and cent. Kenyan highlands, with smaller populations on Mt Kulal, Mt Nyiru, the Ndotos, Mathews Range, Mt Marsabit, and the Nguruman, Chyulu and Taita Hills. In n. Tanzania, not uncommon from Loliondo and the Crater Highlands south to Mt Hanang; also in Arusha NP, on Mt Meru, Kilimanjaro, and in the Pare and Usambara Mountains. **NOTE**: Formerly considered conspecific with South African *E. melanotis*.

FAWN-BREASTED WAXBILL *Estrilda p. paludicola* **Plate 117**

Length 90–100 mm (3.5–4"). A *pale* western waxbill of moist grassy areas. **Adult** *tawny-brown above*, with indistinct narrow barring; red on rump and upper tail-coverts; black tail with narrow white feather edges. Ash-grey head blends into creamy white on throat and upper breast; often a pale fawn wash on lower breast and belly, deep pink wash in centre of lower belly (male only?); crissum whitish. Eyes dull red; *bill scarlet.* **Juvenile** resembles adult, but has dark bill and no pink on belly. **VOICE**: Contact call a nasal *tyeek, tyeep* or *tsyee*. Song a harsh *tek, tek, tek, teketree, teketree* (Clement *et al.* 1993). **HABITS**: In pairs or small flocks. Builds compact grass nest, sometimes with short entrance tube, on or just above ground in grass. **SIMILAR SPECIES**: Yellow-bellied Waxbill has pale olive-green upperparts and a scarlet-and-black bill. **STATUS AND DISTRIBUTION**: Local and generally uncommon in w. Kenya, where resident in and near inundated grassland and grassy margins of streams and swamps. Ranges from Mt Elgon and Saiwa NP south through Busia, Mumias and Kakamega Districts to Kisii and Kilgoris, wandering to nw. Mara GR.

CRIMSON-RUMPED WAXBILL *Estrilda rhodopyga centralis* **Plate 117**

Length 107 mm (4.25"). A *red-rumped* waxbill with a *slate-grey or black bill*. Sexes alike. **Adult** warm brown above, with indistinct fine barring; rump and upper tail-coverts red; tail dusky brown, with central feathers tinged crimson, as are the wing-coverts. Broad red streak from bill through eye. Underparts pale tawny-buff, faintly barred on flanks; chin and throat whitish. Eyes brown; bill and feet blackish or slate. **Juvenile** similar, but lacks red streak through eyes. **VOICE**: Contact call a soft *sspt-sspt-sspt*. Also has a soft *tyeek* and a harsh nasal *tchair* or *cheee*, sometimes double (Clement *et al.* 1993). **HABITS**: Generally in small flocks, often with other estrildines. Subject to local movements in response to fruiting grasses. **SIMILAR SPECIES**: Common and Black-rumped Waxbills are distinguished by rump colour. See Fawn-breasted Waxbill. **STATUS AND DISTRIBUTION**: Fairly common and widespread in dense bush, tangles and thickets below 1800 m, usually in grassy sites near water and in overgrown cultivation around villages. Ranges through w., cent., and s. Kenya to n. Tanzania, where present from Serengeti NP and Loliondo east to Lake Manyara, Tarangire and Arusha NPs and Mkomazi GR; also in coastal lowlands from Mombasa south to Moa. Although generally scarce and local in arid n. Kenya, periodic influxes occur following periods of high rainfall. Widely sympatric with Common Waxbill.

BLACK-RUMPED WAXBILL *Estrilda troglodytes* **Plate 117**

Length 95–105 mm (*c.* 4"). A west Kenyan species. Resembles a *pale* Common Waxbill with *black rump and tail* (*outer rectrices narrowly edged white*) and *dark carmine bill*. Sexes similar. **Adult** light grey-brown above, with almost obsolete barring. Eye streaks red; cheeks and throat whitish; underparts otherwise pale greyish buff with faint pinkish tinge below (male brighter on lower belly), and virtually no barring evident; under tail-coverts buffy white. Eyes red-brown; bill dark carmine; feet dark brown. **Juvenile** lacks red eye-streaks, has black bill. **VOICE**: Call a loud repeated *cheu-cheu* or *chit-chit*; in flight, flocks give a continuous *tiup-tiup-tiup* or a soft lisping twittering like that of Common Waxbill. Song a loud explosive *tche-tcheer, chee-eeer* (Clement *et al.* 1993). **HABITS**: Usually in small wandering flocks, but sometimes as many as 100 birds. May feed with other estrildines. **SIMILAR SPECIES**: Common Waxbill is darker and browner, has brown rump and tail; male shows more red below than Black-rumped Waxbill. Crimson-rumped Waxbill

has red rump. **Status and Distribution**: Local and uncommon in dry scrub, thickets and cultivation. Known only from a few localities in Ukwala, Siaya, Mumias and Kisumu Districts. Small numbers possibly resident around rice fields near Ahero.

COMMON WAXBILL *Estrilda astrild*   **Plate 117**

Length 95–105 mm (*c*. 4"). A *brown-rumped* waxbill with a *bright red bill*. **Adult male** warm brown with narrow blackish barring above, including tail; side of face white, with contrasting broad red eye-streak; throat pinkish or pale tan; variably pink breast and sides barred with dusky and white; centre of belly red, under tail-coverts black. Western *E. a. peasei* much pinker than interior *massaica*; coastal *minor* smaller, browner below with white throat. Eyes brown; feet blackish. **Female** paler than male, with fainter pink wash. **Juvenile** has *black bill, orange eye-streaks*, and more suffused barring below. **Voice**: Song a variable, somewhat hesitant sputtering joined with a few semi-musical notes, *skwitchi tsitsi-chwee qyurr . . . tweep . . .qyurr . . . tsip-tsip . . .chwee-chirree cheee skurrrrrrrreee. . . .* Flock utters a soft buzzy twitter. **Habits**: In large flocks except when breeding, wandering in response to fruiting of grasses. Roosts communally in swamps and marshes, many birds perching close together. Builds large, pear-shaped grass nest with entrance tube 7–10 cm long, and often with a canopy over the top, in low shrub or grass. Parasitized by Pin-tailed Whydah. **Similar Species**: Fawn-breasted, Crimson-rumped and Black-rumped Waxbills are all distinguished by rump colour. **Status and Distribution**: Except in arid n. and ne. Kenya, common and widespread in open grassy country, overgrown cultivation, swamp margins, forest borders and thickets between sea level and 3000 m. Three races: *minor* in coastal lowlands south to Tanga and Dar es Salaam, inland to the Usambara and Pare Mountains, Mkomazi GR, Taveta and Moshi Districts, and Tsavo West and Amboseli NPs; *peasei* in w. Kenya from Mt Elgon and the Cheranganis south to the Lake Victoria basin; *massaica* in interior Kenya and n. Tanzania between *minor* and *peasei*.

BLACK-CROWNED WAXBILL *Estrilda n. nonnula*   **Plate 117**

Length 100–105 mm (4"). A black-capped bird with *whitish belly*; *black of head confined to forehead and crown*. **Adult male** has grey back and wings finely barred dusky, appearing uniform grey in the field; rump and upper tail-coverts deep red; tail black; sides of face and underparts white, with slight grey wash from chin to breast and on under tail-coverts; *flanks washed with red*. Eyes brown; bill black, with long rosy-red patch on each side of maxilla, another at each side of mandible near base; feet black. **Female** resembles male, but has less red on flanks, is paler grey on back. **Juvenile** similar, but underparts tinged buffy brown. **Voice**: Songs high-pitched and usually short: (1) *speet-speet, p'seet-seet-seet*, (2) *speet, speet, speet speet-speet-speet*, (3) *sureeeaseet seet-seet-seet*. **Habits**: In pairs or family groups, at times in large flocks with other estrildines. Feeds on ground and in grasses or grain crops (especially millet and sorghum). Builds ovoid grass nest with side entrance, and with apparent roost cavity for male on the top, in tree or shrub. **Similar Species**: Allopatric Black-headed Waxbill is black from crown to nape, on belly and on under tail-coverts. **Status and Distribution**: Local and generally uncommon w. Kenyan resident at forest borders and in adjacent cultivation between 1500 and 2000 m. Ranges from Kapenguria and Saiwa NP, south through the Nandi, Kakamega, Mau and Trans-Mara Forests to Lolgorien and the Migori River. At lower elevations than Black-headed Waxbill, with no apparent overlap.

BLACK-HEADED WAXBILL *Estrilda atricapilla graueri*   **Plate 117**

Length 100–105 mm (4"). A *dark-bellied* montane waxbill with *entire top of head and nape black*. Sexes similar. **Adult's** back and wings finely barred dusky and grey in male, back browner in female; rump and upper tail-coverts red; tail black; sides of face, neck, and chin to breast greyish white, *remaining underparts black, except for bright crimson flanks*. Eyes dark brown; bill all black or with triangular crimson patch on each side of mandible; feet dusky. **Juvenile** dusky brown on back; blackish from breast to under tail-coverts; no red on flanks. **Voice**: Contact call a thin, high-pitched *tee-tee-tee*, similar to that of preceding species. Song a chippering warble, louder and slightly longer than that of Black-crowned Waxbill: *chureeecheet cher-wee-wee-wee chit-chit*. Foraging flocks also utter lisping twittering notes. **Habits**: Forages in small flocks in montane-forest glades and clearings, often with Yellow-bellied Waxbills, usually on the ground or picking seeds from grasses. Builds ovoid grass nest with side entrance in shrubs. **Similar Species**: Allopatric Black-crowned Waxbill has whitish belly, and black is confined to forehead and crown. **Status and Distribution**: Fairly common resident of grassy areas between 2500 and 3300 m in w. and cent. Kenyan forests on Mt Elgon, Mt Kenya and the Aberdares.

BLACK-FACED WAXBILL *Estrilda erythronotus delamerei* **Plate 117**

Length 110–115 mm (*c.* 4.25"). A *red-rumped* waxbill with *black of face extending to chin and upper throat.* Crown, back and wings pale vinaceous grey with narrow black barring; wing-coverts barred dusky and white; rump and upper tail-coverts dark red; tail black; underparts pinkish grey, shading to dull red on flanks, *black on belly and crissum.* Eyes dark brown; bill and feet black. Sexes similar, but female has no black below. **Juvenile** resembles adult female, but young male blackish on belly and under tail-coverts. **VOICE:** A repeated musical whistle, *tyur-ee* or *pee-tyee,* the second note rising in pitch, somewhat resembling song of Rufous-naped Lark. This usually combined with various *cht, tst-tst* and *seet-seet-seet* notes in an extended series. Captives give a single *tink* note (Payne, pers. comm.). **HABITS:** In pairs or small flocks, often with other species. At times decidedly arboreal. Builds large grass nest with roofed side entrance hole, in tree. **SIMILAR SPECIES:** See Black-cheeked Waxbill. **STATUS AND DISTRIBUTION:** Locally common above 1150 m in acacia woodland, bushed grassland, savanna and cultivation from the Lake Victoria basin east to the Loita Hills, and from Thika and Nairobi Districts, south into n. Tanzania; there widespread from Serengeti NP east to Oldeani, Lake Manyara, Tarangire and Arusha NPs, Mkomazi GR and moister parts of the Masai Steppe. **Note:** Often considered conspecific with Black-cheeked Waxbill. We follow Wolters (1985) in treating the two as separate species.

BLACK-CHEEKED WAXBILL *Estrilda charmosyna* **Plate 117**

Length 110–115 mm (*c.* 4.25"). Closely resembles Black-faced Waxbill, but *posterior underparts usually pale pink,* and *black of head confined to sides of face and narrow strip on upper chin adjacent to the bill; rest of chin and throat pinkish white,* shading to dull greyish pink on breast and sides. Female and juvenile duller, less vinaceous above than adult male and less pink below. Birds in the Olorgesailie–Magadi area, and occasional specimens from elsewhere in the species' range (e.g. Bura), are somewhat darker, noticeably greyish-tinged, on the belly. **VOICE:** Apparently similar to that of Black-cheeked Waxbill, but past confusion between the two species may have concealed differences. **HABITS:** Similar to those of the preceding species. **SIMILAR SPECIES:** Black-faced Waxbill has chin and upper throat black; male has black belly and crissum. **STATUS AND DISTRIBUTION:** Local in dry thorn-scrub *below 1000 m* in n. and e. Kenya, from Lokichokio east to s. Turkana and the Huri Hills, south to the Nasolot NR, Turkwell and Kerio Valleys, Baringo District, Samburu and Shaba GRs, and from Meru NP and Kora NR south to Tsavo East NP and the lower Tana River at Bura. Wanderers recorded west to Yatta and Thika Districts during periods of extreme drought. A disjunct 'dark greyish-pink-bellied' population ('*kiwanukae*') occupies the arid Olorgesailie–Magadi area of the s. Kenyan Rift Valley.

ZEBRA WAXBILL *Amandava subflava* **Plate 117**
(Orange-breasted Waxbill)

Length 85–90 mm (3.5"). A tiny waxbill, *yellow or orange below.* **Adult male** olive-brown above, with *bright red upper tail-coverts* and blackish tail, latter with traces of white on outer feathers. Red superciliary stripes; chin and *throat yellow; rest of under-parts orange in western birds* (intensity varying individually); *eastern birds largely yellow below, orange only on breast and under tail-coverts;* sides barred olive-green and pale yellow. Eyes red; bill scarlet, black on culmen and gonys; feet pale pinkish. **Female** lacks red superciliary stripes, is paler below, some birds almost white on throat; breast pale yellow; orange only on under tail-coverts. **Juvenile** brown above, with no red or orange, no bars on flanks. Eyes brown; bill black. **VOICE:** A rapid *trip-trp-trp-trp* when taking wing, and a soft *chit-chit* contact call. Song in s. Africa described as a series of high-pitched notes, often sustained for several minutes (Maclean 1984). **HABITS:** Usually in small flocks, sometimes with other estrildines. Has distinctive habit of sliding down grass stems, seeking fallen seeds. Nests in old nests of weavers, cisticolas or bishops, or builds barrel-shaped grass nest in low herbage. **STATUS AND DISTRIBUTION:** Local and usually uncommon in moist grassland, marsh edges and cultivation between sea level and 2200 m. Nominate *subflava* in w. Kenya, from ne. Mt Elgon south to Busia, Mumias, Kakamega and the Lake Victoria basin, where at times common to abundant in Ahero rice fields. *A. s. clarkei* ranges sparingly in coastal lowlands south to Pemba and Zanzibar, locally inland on grassy lakeshores to Lake Jipe, Arusha NP and Ngorongoro Crater; also locally from Nairobi NP north to Thika and Murang'a Districts.

QUAIL-FINCH *Ortygospiza atricollis muelleri* **Plate 117**

Length 90 mm (3.5"). A *tiny, short-tailed, heavily barred* ground bird of open grasslands. **Adult male** dusky grey above, mottled darker; *distinctive pied facial pattern, white chin patch and black throat;* breast, sides and flanks barred grey, black and white; rich tawny-buff patch in centre of lower breast; belly buffy white. Tail black,

narrowly edged white and with white corners. Bill red or reddish; eyes light brown; feet pinkish flesh. **Female** paler throughout; throat grey. **Juvenile** still paler, with many pale feather margins and unbarred breast; flanks barred grey and white. **VOICE**: Contact and take-off call a sharp *djink* or *tink-tink*, also a lower-pitched *djew*, often in series, in flight. On the ground or in flight, male gives a rambling, rising-and-falling series of notes described as *riek roek riek rieek roek rieek roek . . .*, sometimes extended (Nuttall 1993). Foraging pairs utter various soft notes, and courting male gives an equally soft series of husky or squeaky staccato notes, e.g. *chick-suwit-siksuiWE . . .*, repeated over and over. **HABITS**: Wanders in pairs or small flocks. Flying birds drop to earth suddenly, scampering out of sight in grass; when flushed, they rise quickly with metallic ticking calls, flying a short distance and plummeting back into cover. Frequently drinks at margins of rainpools and lakes. Shy. Builds ovoid or pear-shaped nest with side entrance on or near ground in grass clump. **STATUS AND DISTRIBUTION**: Fairly common but local in grasslands, generally above 1500 m and especially in low, wet places on black 'cotton' soils (e.g. Laikipia Plateau, Nairobi NP, Mara GR). Ranges from w., cent. and s. Kenya south in n. Tanzania to Serengeti, Arusha and Tarangire NPs.

*LOCUST-FINCH *Ortygospiza locustella uelensis* Plate 117

Length 90–100 mm (3.5–4"). A *tiny, short-tailed grassland bird* with *much orange-rufous in the wings*. **Adult male** distinctive, with *bright red face, throat and upper breast*. Tail edged red. Upperparts generally dark brown, forecrown to nape streaked black; innermost wing feathers black, spotted with white, wing-coverts pale crimson with whitish tips. Underparts black. Upper half of maxilla black, rest of bill red; eyes yellow; feet brown. **Female** similar to male above, including wings; face black; *underparts whitish, heavily barred with black on sides and flanks*. Bare parts as in male. Both sexes of *O. l. uelensis* lack the conspicuous white speckling of nominate southern African birds, except for a trace on some females. **VOICE**: Rather silent. Southern African birds give a distinctive *pink-pink*. **HABITS**: Much like those of Quail-Finch. Feeds on open grassy ground, favouring burned areas, the flock rising with audible whir of wings. **SIMILAR SPECIES**: See Quail-Finch. **STATUS AND DISTRIBUTION**: A vagrant in w. Kenyan border areas, seen near Alupe (Aug. 1990) and Mungatsi, Mumias District (Nov. 1991, July 1993 and Nov. 1994).

AFRICAN SILVERBILL *Lonchura cantans orientalis* Plate 117
(Warbling Silverbill)

Length 115 mm (4.5"). A black-tailed, black-rumped finch of dry country. Sexes alike. **Adult** pale earth-brown above, with darker feather centres on crown and nape producing mottled appearance. *Primaries, rump, upper tail-coverts and graduated tail black; central rectrices pointed.* Throat and breast buff, otherwise white below; some individuals have the throat mottled. Eyes brown, narrow bare orbital ring bluish; bill and feet blue-grey. **Juvenile** similar, but many body-feather edges buff, tail feathers edged brown. **VOICE**: A twittering or sizzling song, some notes barely audible; often prolonged (van Someren 1956). **HABITS**: Confiding and sociable, usually in small flocks and often perching tightly together in rows on tree branches. On ground, gives short upward hops to pick seeds from low grasses. Usually uses old weaver nests for breeding, but at times builds an ovoid nest with partially roofed entrance hole at side. **SIMILAR SPECIES**: Grey-headed Silverbill is more brightly coloured, has brown wings and white rump. **STATUS AND DISTRIBUTION**: A rather uncommon but widespread resident and wanderer, usually in acacia scrub and open bush, and mainly below 1500 m. Present in arid/semi-arid n. Kenya south to the edge of the highlands, and across the dry southern areas from lakes Magadi and Natron, east to Amboseli and the Tsavo NPs, Arusha District, n. Masailand and the Mkomazi GR in n. Tanzania. **NOTE**: Formerly considered conspecific with Asian *L. malabarica*.

GREY-HEADED SILVERBILL *Lonchura griseicapilla* Plate 117

Length 110–115 mm (4.5"). The only finch-like bird showing a *prominent white rump in flight*. Sexes alike. **Adults** have *blue-grey head speckled with white and black* on ear-coverts, cheeks and throat; back rich pinkish cinnamon-brown; rump and upper tail-coverts white; wings largely brown, primaries and tail black; eyes brown; bill bluish slate, paler at base of mandible; feet dusky. **Juvenile** duller than adult and with no facial speckling. **VOICE**: Contact call a weak high-pitched trill. Song similar, starting with soft notes and becoming louder near end (Clement *et al.* 1993). **HABITS**: Pairs or small flocks congregate at water holes. Feeds on grass seeds, often with preceding species. Builds large untidy grass nest, with side entrance hole, in tree. **SIMILAR SPECIES**: African Silverbill has black rump and black primaries; lacks facial speckling. **STATUS AND DISTRIBUTION**: Local and uncommon in dry n. Kenya south to West Pokot, lakes

Baringo and Bogoria, Samburu and Shaba GRs, Meru NP and Garissa; more common south of the highlands, from the Loita Hills and Magadi and Kajiado Districts to Amboseli and the Tsavo NPs. In n. Tanzania, from Serengeti NP and Olduvai Gorge east across the Masai Steppe to Mkomazi GR. Prefers less arid country than African Silverbill.

BRONZE MANNIKIN *Lonchura cucullata*   **Plate 119**

Length 85–95 mm (c. 3.5"). A tiny dark bird with a *blackish head, black tail* and a *large, two-toned black-and-blue-grey bill*. Sexes alike. **Adult** grey-brown above, with *iridescent green 'shoulder' patch*, grey-and-brown-barred rump and upper tail-coverts. Crown glossy greenish black; sides of face, throat, and breast glossy bronzy black; *flanks barred brown and white*; glossy green patch on sides in western *L. c. cucullata*, lacking in race *scutata*. **Juvenile** *plain dull brown* above, paler brown below, with whitish or pale buff lower breast and belly centre contrasting with darker brown throat, breast and sides, these areas sometimes faintly barred; *under tail-coverts barred*. Bill black, with pale yellow gape. **VOICE**: Frequent soft buzzy or wheezy twittering, the notes from a flock or group recalling those of white-eyes. **HABITS**: Gregarious except when breeding, in compact flocks of up to 30 birds. Roosts and rests during day in tight clusters of several individuals. Feeds on ground. Tame and familiar around dwellings. Flicks wings and tail when alarmed. Builds small, rather untidy, globular nest with rough roof over side entrance, sometimes near wasp's nest in tree or shrub; more ball-shaped than somewhat flattened nest of Red-billed Firefinch. **SIMILAR SPECIES**: Adult Black-and-white Mannikin is more contrastingly patterned, blackish or rufous above; juvenile paler on underparts than young Bronze, throat and breast little darker than belly, and under tail-coverts unmarked. **STATUS AND DISTRIBUTION**: Common and widespread except in arid areas, including n. and e. Kenya. Most numerous around towns and villages, occupying a variety of open habitats with grass and shrubs. Western nominate race extends from the Lake Victoria basin east to the Rift Valley, there intergrading with *scutata*, which ranges east to Mt Kenya, Thika, Nairobi and Machakos Districts, and throughout the coastal lowlands, including Pemba Island. In n. Tanzania, common in Arusha and Moshi Districts and locally around Lake Manyara. Sympatric with Black-and-white Mannikin in many areas, often flocking with that species.

BLACK-AND-WHITE MANNIKIN *Lonchura bicolor*   **Plate 119**

Length 82–86 mm (3.25"). More sharply patterned than Bronze Mannikin. Two distinct races. **Adult** *poensis glossy black on head, throat and breast*; back dark blackish brown, richer brown on wing-coverts. Outer webs of flight feathers, rump and upper tail-coverts barred black and white; flanks spotted and barred black and white. Bill blue-grey; eyes dark brown; feet black. **Juvenile** *poensis* dark sepia above, including crown and cheeks. Underparts greyish buff, lightly barred on sides; flanks rich dusky brown; *under tail-coverts plain, unbarred*; bill black. **Adult** *nigriceps* ('Rufous-backed Mannikin') like *poensis*, but back and innermost wing feathers rufous. **Juvenile** rich brown above, with rufous wash on back. **VOICE**: A low buzzy twittering like that of Bronze Mannikin. Call note a soft *kip* or *tik*. **HABITS**: Similar to those of Bronze Mannikin, but more of a forest and forest-edge bird, often in damp places. Seldom forms large flocks. Builds large, loose grass nest with side entrance, low or high in tree, sometimes over water. Up to 11 adults may roost together in old mannikin or weaver nest. **SIMILAR SPECIES**: Bronze Mannikin is paler above, with iridescent green on bend of wing, sometimes on sides. Juvenile Bronze resembles young Black-and-white Mannikin, but is paler above, browner and buffier below, with much less contrast between crown/cheeks and throat/breast; belly pale, under tail-coverts barred. **STATUS AND DISTRIBUTION**: *L. b. poensis* is a widespread and locally common resident below 2000 m west of the Rift Valley in forest clearings and borders, grassy riverine thickets and cultivation, from Mt Elgon and Saiwa NP, south through the Nandi and Kakamega Forests to the Lake Victoria basin, Lolgorien and nw. Mara GR. *L. b. nigriceps* is locally distributed in the cent. Kenyan highlands, the Mathews Range, Mt Endau and the Taita Hills, also widespread in coastal lowlands from the lower Tana River and Lamu south to Pemba Island, Tanga and beyond our limits. Inland it ranges to the Usambara and Pare Mountains, and to Taveta, Moshi and Arusha Districts; also locally at Karatu, Oldeani, Loliondo and in the Nguruman Hills. Early specimens from Moyale and Marsabit. **NOTE**: Some authors consider the two forms specifically distinct, but see Dowsett and Dowsett-Lemaire (1993).

MAGPIE-MANNIKIN *Lonchura fringilloides*   **Plate 119**
(Pied Mannikin)

Length 110–120 mm (c. 4.5"). A *large-billed, brown-backed* mannikin. Sexes alike. **Adult** glossy blue-black on head, pectoral patches, tail and upper tail-coverts; scapulars and wings mostly dark brown, centre of back pale brown; a few short white streaks on wing-coverts and back. *Sides and flanks blotched with black around a large buffy-tan patch*; underparts otherwise white, tinged buff on crissum. Eyes dark brown; bill black above, grey-blue below; feet black. **Juvenile** dusky brown above, with blue-black rump and tail; underparts pale buff; bill brownish black. **VOICE**: Contact call a loud *pee-oo-pee-oo*. Alarm call a thin *cheep*. **HABITS**: Similar to those of other

mannikins, with which it often associates, generally in small flocks. Builds untidy grass nest with some leaves, in tall shrub or sapling. **SIMILAR SPECIES**: Black-and-white Mannikin is smaller, with much smaller bill, has glossy black or rufous back; lacks prominent blue-black pectoral patches. **STATUS AND DISTRIBUTION**: Rare and very local in moist bush, forest edge and overgrown cultivation. East African populations appear to have declined considerably in the last 50 years. Currently known only from Amani, East Usambaras (Aug.–Sept. 1977, April 1981), Kitovu Forest near Taveta (Dec. 1989), and at Alupe on Kenyan/Ugandan border (Sept. 1991), the latter sight record unique in w. Kenya and representing a considerable range extension. Formerly in the Ganda Forest near Shimoni.

CUT-THROAT FINCH *Amadina fasciata* Plate 117

Length 100–105 mm (4"). A *pale, scaly-looking finch.* **Adult male** has long *red band extending from the ear-coverts across the throat* and a *dull cinnamon patch on the belly.* Upperparts mainly pale greyish tan, heavily marked with short black bars and flecks, and pale buff spots on back, scapulars and wings; short tail brownish black, narrowly edged and broadly tipped with white. Underparts buffy white with dark wavy bars and chevrons. Eyes brown; bill dull blue-grey or greyish-horn colour; feet pink. **Female** similar, but lacks red, sides of face barred, and with little or no cinnamon on belly. **VOICE**: A sparrow-like chirp, and a loud plaintive *kee-air* note. Song a low buzzing broken by toneless warbling notes (Clement *et al.* 1993). **HABITS**: In pairs when breeding, otherwise forms large flocks around villages and water holes, often in association with other estrildines. Builds spherical nest of dry grass in shrub or tree cavity, but also uses old weaver nests. **STATUS AND DISTRIBUTION**: Fairly common and widespread below 1300 m in dry thorn-scrub, bush and savanna. Subject to local movements, which result in sporadic occurrences in the Lake Victoria basin and coastal lowlands. Although recorded from most low, dry parts of Kenya, restricted in n. Tanzania to the se. Serengeti–Olduvai area, and from Lake Natron and Tarangire NP east across the Masai Steppe to Mkomazi GR. Birds in nw. Kenya (Lokichokio to Lake Turkana) appear closest to the nominate race; all others are referable to *alexanderi.*

JAVA SPARROW *Padda oryzivora* Plate 124

Length 150–160 mm (6–6.5"). An introduced finch with *massive pinkish-red bill* and *large white patch on sides of the black head.* **Adult** otherwise pale grey, with blackish tail and upper tail-coverts; lower belly pinkish-cinnamon, under tail-coverts white. Bill pink or red, with white tip and broad white line along commissure; orbital ring and feet pink. **Juvenile** pale buffy grey above, with darker grey crown; throat and belly buffy white; bill blackish brown with pale pink base; orbital ring pink; feet brownish. **VOICE**: Contact call a liquid *t'luk* or *t'lup.* **HABITS**: Rather like those of House Sparrow (which it appears to replace on Pemba Island). Feeds on the ground, in pairs or small flocks. **STATUS AND DISTRIBUTION**: Introduced to Pemba and Zanzibar Islands. Small numbers on Pemba, mainly in Chake-Chake and nearby cultivated areas.

WHYDAHS AND INDIGOBIRDS, FAMILY ESTRILDIDAE, SUBFAMILY VIDUINAE
(World and Africa, 14 species; Kenya, 8; n. Tanzania, 6)

Small, uniquely African seed-eaters, all host-specific brood parasites on their estrildine relatives. They lay white or cream-coloured eggs, slightly larger and rounder than those of their hosts. Pattern and colour of palate and gape markings of the host species' nestlings are matched by those of the young whydah or indigobird. Unlike some brood parasites, nestling viduines do not evict the host's own offspring, and their close association with the foster family continues for some time after fledging.

Structurally and behaviourally, viduines display features of both ploceids and waxbills, but they seem closer to the latter on the basis of studies of myology (Bentz 1979), egg-white proteins (Sibley 1970) and DNA–DNA hybridization (Sibley and Ahlquist 1990). Following these and other recent workers, we consider them a subfamily of the latter and place all species in the genus *Vidua.* The most striking viduines are the male whydahs, whose breeding plumage is marked by exceptionally elongated central tail feathers. Females and non-breeding males have 'sparrowy' patterns dominated by buff-and-brown streaking. Although viduines have calls of their own, all except Pin-tailed and Steel-blue Whydahs regularly mimic songs of their host species. Indigobirds have short tails and lack elaborate plumes; the males are largely plain glossy black. They parasitize firefinches (*Lagonosticta*), and each male generally mimics the voice of a single firefinch species. Females appear to select a male on the basis of his mimetic songs (probably learned when young from the foster parents). A male uses traditional singing stations year after year, and females visit these sites for mating. No pair bonds are formed. See Payne (1973) for details.

More important than morphology for delimiting indigobird species are mating behaviour and song type. Different forms may share an area without interbreeding, although this is not always true. The young bird's early experience evidently determines its eventual mating preferences; different populations learn different mimetic (firefinch) songs, and such populations are regarded by R. B. Payne as constituting 'cultural species'. The frequent references in the following text to Payne reflect his extensive contributions (personal communications where not specifically referenced) to our species accounts, especially to the sections on voice.

VILLAGE INDIGOBIRD *Vidua chalybeata*   Plate 110
(Common Indigobird; Steelblue Widowfinch; Red-billed Firefinch Indigobird)

Length 105 mm (4"). **Breeding male** largely black with bluish gloss, slightly more blue-green in the red-billed coastal race *amauropteryx*, more indigo-blue in white-billed *centralis*; wings brownish; white patch (usually concealed) on each side of rump. Both races have red-orange, orange or salmon-pink feet (whitish pink in some southern birds). **Non-breeding adults** of both sexes are patterned much like female Pin-tailed Whydah, streaked brown above, with prominent pale buff and dark brown head stripes; underparts mostly grey-brown to buffy brown, white on belly. Bill greyish pink above, paler below. **Juvenile** resembles small female House Sparrow: crown evenly dull grey-brown with *no central stripe*; *buff superciliaries* most noticeable behind eyes; back brownish buff with dusky stripes; wing feathers edged with rufous-buff; breast and sides browner buff. Bill colour varies: in *amauropteryx*, at time of independence from foster

parents, it is pinkish below and at base of the grey or brown maxilla, and at post-juvenile moult (six weeks) the pale areas turn orangish; young *centralis* at first has a dark grey bill, which becomes paler below, the maxilla remaining dark until the first breeding season. **VOICE**: Song a sputtering chatter, e.g. *tsi-tsi-tsi-tsi chchchchchch tswee-ur swee* . . ., typically including the *chick-pea-pea* song of Red-billed Firefinch. Complex non-mimetic songs differ from one population to another; each male has 20 or more song types. Mimicry songs make up about 25 per cent of a male's total song repertoire (Payne). Call note a clear *swee*. **HABITS**: Male sings conspicuously from wire, bushtop or tree; female is more retiring. A ground feeder on fields, lawns, roadsides, often with fire-finches or other estrildids. Polygynous, 10–20 males and numerous females occupying a 'dispersed lek'. Parasitizes Red-billed Firefinch. **SIMILAR SPECIES**: See male Purple Indigobird. Female Paradise Whydah is larger, with darker, heavier bill. Female Pin-tailed Whydah is often red-billed and warm buffy brown below. Female Steel-blue Whydah, stubbier-billed than the indigobirds, is largely white below, with faint buff tinge to breast. **STATUS AND DISTRIBUTION**: *V. c. centralis* is rather uncommon but widespread in moister areas, usually below 1800 m, in gardens, cultivation, woodland edges, and other habitats occupied by its host; local along perma-nent rivers in dry country. Some seasonal movement in places. *V. c. amauropteryx* is coastal, from Kwale north to Lamu District, isolated from interior *centralis* by arid country.

PURPLE INDIGOBIRD *Vidua purpurascens*   Plate 110
(Purple Widowfinch; Jameson's Firefinch Indigobird)

Length 105 mm (4"). **Breeding male** black with dull purplish or purplish-blue gloss, *bill and feet white* or pinkish white, thus identical with Variable Indigobird in appearance. Darker-bodied but wings *paler* brown than in Village Indigobird. **Female** not so red-legged as *chalybeata*, but colour varies seasonally, brighter when breeding, paler when in moult (Payne). Probably indistinguishable from other indigobirds in the field. **VOICE**: Most songs harsh and chattering, not distinguishable from other species in our region, except for the mimetic rapid alarm *purr* of Jameson's Firefinch in which the individual notes are delivered at more than 22 per second. The almost cat-like purring calls to mind the species 'pur-pur-ascens', a good way to match the song with the indigobird's name (Payne). **HABITS**: Poorly known in our region. Parasitizes Jameson's Firefinch. **SIMILAR SPECIES**: Village Indigobird has red, orange or pink feet, sometimes red bill. Variable Indigobird indistinguishable except by voice (see below). **STATUS AND DISTRIBUTION**: Uncommon and local in bush and shrubby woodland occupied by its host. Scattered records from the Kongelai Escarpment, Sigor, west side of Kerio Valley (tape-recorded, 1988), probably Lake Baringo (one sight record); also reported from Kibwezi, Ngulia (Tsavo West NP) and Taita District.

VARIABLE INDIGOBIRD *Vidua funerea nigerrima*   (not illustrated)
(African Firefinch Indigobird; Dusky Indigobird)

Length 105 mm (4"). Morphologically indistinguishable from the preceding species, the **male** with purplish sheen, white bill and whitish feet, but vocally mimics its host species, African Firefinch. Young *nigerrima* differs from *purpurascens* in mouth colour. **VOICE**: A 'trill' of *pit* notes of the African Firefinch, given no faster than 20 per second, thus a sharp *pit-pitpitpitpit*. . . (not always distinguishable from faster purring trill of Jameson's Firefinch). The indigobird also mimics the slurred whistled *bzz-tu* and repeated *too-too* notes of the firefinch

(Payne *et al.* 1992). **Status and Distribution**: In our region, known in Tanzania from Dar es Salaam, Tanga, the North Pare Mts and Moshi District; in Kenya, recently tape-recorded and collected in the Kerio Valley alongside *V. purpurascens* and *V. chalybeata* in brushy riverine woodland (Payne *et al., op. cit.*). Perhaps overlooked elsewhere.

STEEL-BLUE WHYDAH *Vidua hypocherina*   Plate 110

Length of breeding male 280 mm (11"), of female 100–105 mm (4"). **Breeding male** shiny blue-black, with four long, thin central tail feathers. White patch on each side of rump usually concealed. Has white wing-linings, unlike indigobirds. Eyes brown; bill and feet horn-brown. **Adult female and non-breeding male** distinguished from female indigobirds and Pin-tailed Whydah by *tiny whitish, light grey or pale horn bill*, from Paradise Whydah by bill colour and brighter pattern; underparts white, with only faint tinge of buff on sides of breast, and a few short streaks. In the hand, note sharply defined, bright white inner webs of primaries. *Each rectrix has a narrow white inner edge* (and a narrower white outer edge, but not useful in the field). **Juvenile** has dark grey face that contrasts with rest of head (unlike indigobirds), and bill greyish white, not red-brown. **Voice**: One song is a series of simple *chiff, chuff, tik* or *wheez* notes, one to four per second, repeated for several minutes. Said not to mimic the calls of Black-faced Waxbill, the presumed host (Nicolai 1964), but Payne suggests that *hypocherina* may mimic other songs it hears. In an area where Red-cheeked Cordon-bleu was very common, he recorded the whydah singing (1) a rapid *jejejejejeje* like the begging call of the fledged cordon-bleu, (2) a distinctive alarm chatter like that of the adult, and (3) mimicry of incomplete songs of that species; the whydah in that area also uttered (4) a soft chatter, and (5) the *chiff* repetitions mentioned above with "variations that drop in pitch and sound plaintive, like swallow or canary calls". **Habits**: Male often solitary or with inconspicuous female. Joins flocks of other viduines at food concentrations and water holes. Parasitizes Black-cheeked and possibly Black-faced Waxbills, and perhaps other estrildines. **Similar Species**: Male indigobirds (also with lateral white rump patches) resemble Steel-blue Whydah which has moulted its long rectrices, but feet (and sometimes bill) red or pink, and wing-linings dark. Female and immature Pin-tailed Whydah much like comparable Steel-blue Whydah, but are buffy brown on breast and have a *wide* strip of white (half the width of the feather) on the rectrices; also red or brownish-red bills. Female indigobirds are grey-brown on breast. **Status and Distribution**: Uncommon and local in dry bush, bushed grassland and low acacia savanna. In w. Kenya below the Kongelai Escarpment and in the Lake Victoria basin; in the Rift Valley from Lokori south to lakes Baringo and Bogoria, and the Olorgesailie–Magadi area; in n. and e. Kenya at Wamba, in Samburu and Shaba GRs, Meru NP and Kitui District from Mwingi south to Mutha. Sporadic in Tsavo East, se. Serengeti, Lake Manyara and Tarangire NPs.

PIN-TAILED WHYDAH *Vidua macroura*   Plate 110

Length of breeding male 310 mm (12"), of female 100–105 mm (4"). **Breeding male** *black and white, with four long floppy central tail feathers* and a *red or orange bill*; may moult long rectrices, but remains largely black above, with white collar and with much white on wings, lower back and on edges of the tail-coverts, before acquiring non-breeding plumage. **Adult female** streaked rufous-buff and black above, with pale sandy-rufous central crown stripe bordered below by broad black stripe from bill to nape; superciliary stripes buff to above eyes, tinted rufous posteriorly; a broad black mark through each eye joins a narrow black cheek stripe; throat and sides buff or pale rufous-buff, the flanks streaked with dark brown. Bill coral-red in non-breeding season, changing to nearly all black when breeding, back to red following breeding. Female and **non-breeding male** have *inner half of each rectrix white*, obvious in the field. Non-breeding and immature males are whiter below than females, more boldly streaked above, and the black central tail feathers sometimes project slightly; young birds assume adult plumage in their third year. **Juvenile** plain dull grey-brown, paler below, buff on belly; *bill blackish* at first, soon *becoming dull light red*. **Voice**: A repetitive high-pitched song, *tseet tseet tsuweet* or *si-swirt-sweeu-see*. Calls include a low *peeee* (Chapin 1954) and a thin double or triple *chip* in flight. **Habits**: Conspicuous, active and pugnacious. Feeds on ground, scratching for seeds by jumping backwards with both feet together. Flirts long tail when perched and bobs it up and down in fluttery erratic flight. Courting male circles or hovers, singing, above female. Parasitizes Common, Black-rumped and Fawn-breasted Waxbills. Reportedly polygamous. Post-breeding flocks may contain 100 or more birds. Plain brown juveniles usually accompany foster parents, but may join mixed flocks of other finches before moulting. **Similar Species**: Most other female/young whydahs are distinguished by bill colour. Female and young Straw-tailed have rusty on head; female Steel-blue is pale-billed and has whiter underparts. Juvenile Paradise Whydah closely resembles young Pin-tailed, but is larger, bigger-billed, has darker breast (at times with necklace of short streaks) and darker face, with superciliaries little paler than the ear coverts. Female indigobirds have duller, grey-brown or buffy brown underparts. **STATUS AND DISTRIBUTION**: Widespread and common in a variety of mesic habitats including cultivation and gardens, usually below 2500 m. Isolated northern populations at Lokichokio and Mandera. Occasionally recorded at Marsabit and around Lake Turkana.

STRAW-TAILED WHYDAH *Vidua fischeri* Plate 110
(Fischer's Whydah)

Length of breeding male 280 mm (11"), of female 105 mm (4"). **Breeding male** mostly black above, with sandy-buff forehead and crown, and four long, slender, straw-coloured central tail feathers. Bill and feet coral-red. **Adult female** and **non-breeding male** streaked buffy brown and sepia above, the *head unstreaked* rufous-buff, darker rufous on crown; whitish underparts washed with sandy buff on breast and sides; bill pink; feet pale dusky pink. **Juvenile** *dull rusty brown*, paler below; *feet and bill pinkish brown*. **Immature male** resembles adult female, occasionally has short straw-like central rectrices; bill salmon-pink or coral-red. **VOICE**: Song of four or five thin notes followed by a short trill, *p'tchewi-tchui-chitisee-tseeeeeeeeee*, or *tsu-tsutsewit cheeeeee*, frequently repeated. Call note a sharp *tseep*. **HABITS**: Much like those of Pin-tailed Whydah. Breeding males perch conspicuously on trees or wires; females unobtrusive. Parasitizes Purple Grenadier. **SIMILAR SPECIES**: Other female whydahs have streaked crowns. **STATUS AND DISTRIBUTION**: Uncommon to fairly common in bush (especially *Commiphora* and *Acacia*), shrubby grassland and cultivation, particularly in dry areas below 2000 m. In Kenya, in extreme northeast and from Lokichokio, Karasuk Hills and the Kongelai Escarpment to the Kerio and Rift Valleys, Laikipia Plateau, and from Isiolo and Meru Districts south through Kitui to the Tsavo and Amboseli NPs, Namanga, Olorgesailie, Magadi and the Loita Hills. In n. Tanzania, from Lake Natron and lowlands north of Arusha south through the Masai Steppe to Dodoma.

PARADISE WHYDAH *Vidua paradisaea* Plate 110

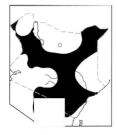

Length of breeding male 335 mm (13"), of female 125 mm (5"). **Breeding male** unmistakable, with black body plumage, broad golden-buff nape band, chestnut breast, and remarkable tail with the two central feathers broad and short, their bare shafts projecting; adjacent pair narrower (25–30 mm at widest point), but greatly elongated and tapering. Bill black; eyes brown. In flight, has distinctive 'hunchbacked' appearance. **Non-breeding male** has head and face streaked black and cream, back streaked tawny and black, wing-coverts broadly edged with tawny-buff, deep tawny breast and flanks streaked with black; belly and crissum white. **Female** patterned like non-breeding male, but much duller, sometimes with short breast streaks. Female has C-shaped mark on side of face, lacking in *V. obtusa* (Payne 1971). Bill colour of breeding females distinctive (see under the following species). **Juvenile** *plain* like young Pin-tailed Whydah, grey-brown above, pale dull brown on throat and breast; rest of underparts white; *bill dull horn-brown*. **VOICE**: Call note a sharp *chip* or *chip-chip*. Flight call a long thin whistle. Songs include mimicry of Green-winged Pytilia. One Kenyan example: *shree-shree sreeeeeeeeeee chrrrrr sreeeeee sreet sreet surreeet sreet skirrreet skeeeeew chree . . ..* Songs recorded in Zambia by Payne (1980) have long introductory whistles followed by a complex downslurred whistle, then a rising shorter whistle; later, a series of short notes and a terminal pair of downslurred whistles or modulated notes. Songs are individually variable. **HABITS**: Somewhat gregarious, even in early breeding season, but the small flocks later separate into pairs. Displaying male makes erratic bounding flights between widely separated treetop perches, the broad central rectrices raised, the longer ones more horizontal, flopping up and down as the bird progresses. Often feeds with other viduines. Parasitizes Green-winged Pytilia. **SIMILAR SPECIES**: See Broad-tailed Paradise Whydah. Immature and adult female Pin-tailed Whydah usually red-billed, have less patterned face, no black streaks within pale central crown stripe. Juvenile Pin-tailed Whydah has smaller bill. Female and immature Steel-blue Whydah are smaller, mostly white below, with whitish bill. Female indigobirds are smaller, duller and smaller-billed. **STATUS AND DISTRIBUTION**: Fairly common resident and wanderer, typically below 1400 m in drier areas (but usually near water and appearing in many places after the rains). Range closely parallels that of its host, from Lokichokio, Turkana and Mandera Districts south to the Kerio and Rift Valleys, Laikipia, Samburu and Shaba GRs, Meru, Tsavo and Amboseli NPs, and in n. Tanzania from Lake Natron, Lake Manyara and Tarangire NPs east across the Masai Steppe to Mkomazi GR. Occasionally wanders to 2000 m and above, and reaches the coastal lowlands in the Tana River delta.

BROAD-TAILED PARADISE WHYDAH *Vidua obtusa* Plate 110

Length of breeding male 300 mm (12"), of female 130 mm (5"). **Breeding male** resembles the more common and widespread Paradise Whydah, but elongated tail feathers shorter, much wider (*c.* 40 mm), and, except at tip, *equally broad throughout*; hindneck coppery rufous, darker than in *V. paradisaea*, and breast deeper chestnut. **Female** lacks the distinctive C-mark on side of face present in *V. paradisaea*, and *in breeding condition* the *paler* *bill* is pinkish grey, whitish grey or blackish above and pinkish, whitish grey or horn below, not all blackish as in *paradisaea*. However, bill colours appear to undergo seasonal changes, as a collected *paradisaea* in early post-nuptial moult was pale-billed, and captive birds of that species regularly become pale-billed during moult, regaining the dark colour following completion of moult (Payne 1971). Female, **non-breeding male** and **immature** paler and more finely streaked than *V. paradisaea*, but in latter plumages the two species probably are inseparable in the field. **Juvenile** apparently indistinguishable in the field, but nestling lacks the black palate spot of young *paradisaea*. **VOICE:** Song a mixture of whistling, chattering and churring notes, *skew chwew sreet skew chrrrrrr chk-chk-chk-chk-tweeeeu chk-chk skweeeeu sweet-sweet sweeeeo*. **HABITS:** Parasitizes Orange-winged Pytilia. In s. Africa, prefers more wooded areas than Paradise Whydah. **STATUS AND DISTRIBUTION:** Probably now extirpated from Kenya, where, presumably, once a scarce resident in Meru District. A male in breeding plumage was taken near Meru in December 1945. Another male collected at Chuka (Feb. 1947) seems somewhat atypical. The Tanzanian range of *V. obtusa* is well south of our region.

SEEDEATERS, CANARIES AND RELATIVES, FAMILY FRINGILLIDAE
(World, *c.* 163 species; Africa, 44; Kenya, 15; n. Tanzania, 10)

These often familiar East African birds are relatives of the holarctic siskins and goldfinches. Although they consume many insects, the short, thick, conical bill is designed for cracking seeds. It has a strongly angled commissure and the mandible edges fit closely together throughout their length (unlike in buntings, Emberizidae). Also characteristic of fringillids is the minute outermost primary, entirely concealed by its upper coverts. Seedeaters typically are streaked and brown-backed, whereas most canaries and African Citril are olive and yellow, often brightly plumaged. The anomalous Oriole-Finch is unique in its *Oriolus*-like plumage and bright orange bill. Fringillid vocalizations vary from thin colourless efforts to loud warbling and often melodious songs. The nest, usually in tree or shrub, is a shallow compact cup of plant materials; the two to five eggs, are white, pale greenish or bluish, and variously marked with black, brown, russet or pale purple. Our species are non-migratory, but significant wandering occurs in some.

STREAKY-HEADED SEEDEATER *Serinus (gularis) elgonensis*   Plate 121
(Streaky-headed Canary)

Length 125–130 mm (5"). A rare, *largely unstreaked* finch with *bold white superciliary stripes* and *dark brown ear-coverts*. **Adult** has *fine whitish lines on crown and nape*, and a *nearly plain grey-brown back*; underparts mostly pale brownish grey, with *contrasting white throat* and *suggestion of short streaks on upper breast* (occasionally obsolete). Bill pale buff; eyes brown; feet light brown. **Juvenile** presumably boldly streaked below (as in southern African races), doubtfully distinguishable from young of the following species. **VOICE:** A variable prolonged medley of twittering, whistles and buzzy notes, *sweet surra seet-seet-seet skuer sweet sewer cheet . . .*, sometimes with long trills added, from a perch. In Zaïre, a sweet canary-like song is given on the wing in circling flight (Chapin 1954). Distinct song of a faintly streaked individual recorded on Kongelai Escarpment consisted of prolonged, monotonous repetition of one phrase, *we see-sew SLIP* or *wee sieu TSIP*, with no embellishment. **HABITS:** Unobtrusive. Flight strongly undulating. Feeds on flowers and fruits, as well as seeds. **SIMILAR SPECIES:** Typical Stripe-breasted Seedeater is heavily and broadly streaked below. Streaky Seedeater is boldly and sharply streaked both above and below, and has well-developed submoustachial stripes. **STATUS AND DISTRIBUTION:** Rare in shrubs and low trees on slopes. An adult male collected 14 June 1900, at 1850 m on southern slope of Mt Elgon, remains the only Kenyan specimen. Reported from Nakuijit on the Suam River in July 1973 (C. F. Mann, pers. comm.) and from the Elgon–Kongelai area in 1994, both near a locality where *S. (r.) striatipectus* has been collected. White (1963) includes North Kavirondo (=Nyanza) within the range, but the basis for this is unclear. **NOTE:** Possibly conspecific with the form *striatipectus* of similar habitats. See note under that species.

STRIPE-BREASTED SEEDEATER *Serinus (reichardi) striatipectus*   Plate 121

Length 125–130 mm (5"). A *heavily streaked*, 'dark-cheeked' finch of escarpments and shrub-covered hills. **Adult** grey-brown or dark brown above, the *upper back obscurely to boldly streaked* with darker brown. *Crown and nape more finely streaked with dark brown and white; bold white superciliary stripes* contrast with dark brown sides of face and ear-coverts. Buff-tinged whitish *underparts broadly streaked with brown*, in fresh plumage the markings soft and diffuse, more obscure on sides and flanks. Worn birds may appear only faintly streaked. Eyes light brown; bill pale horn, the mandible browner. **Juvenile** warmer brown, the streaks somewhat sharper than in adult. **VOICE** (Kongelai Escarpment, Kenya): Variable song (of heavily streaked individuals) a series of buzzy trills, at times sweet and melodious, interspersed with unmusical twittering and much repetition of single notes and phrases, e.g. *djee djee djee djee tchueee tchueee*

tchueee titititititit tsitsi tsuee tsuee tsuit-tsuiti. . . or *twe-twe-twe teedle-ew teedle-ew, weet-weet-weet-weet, queedle-queedle-queedle whicher-whicher chrrrrrrrrrrrrrr, teu, teu-teu. . .,* often mingled with extensive imitations of other bird species. **HABITS**: Shy. Inconspicuous, except when breeding males sing on the wing or from treetops. Territories apparently large, as a given male sings over a considerable area. Nests in low shrubs. **SIMILAR SPECIES**: Streaky Seedeater is larger, more stoutly built, sharply and more darkly streaked below, with bold dark mousachial stripes. Adult Streaky-headed Seedeater is nearly plain below, with only short fine streaks on breast. **STATUS AND DISTRIBUTION**: Uncommon and local on shrubby escarpments with scattered trees between 1600 and 2000 m. Known from Mt Nyiru, Mt Ololokwe, northern slopes of Mt Kenya (near Timau), Don Dol and the Laikipia Plateau, Eldama Ravine, Tugen Hills, the Tambach and Kongelai Escarpments, near Kacheliba and s. Mt Elgon (Mangiki). Unconfirmed reports from Muhoroni and Lake Nakuru NP. Nominate *reichardi* (underparts less buffy and breast streaking darker brown than in *striatipectus*), endemic to *Brachystegia* woodland, ranges north in Tanzania to cent. Tabora District and Kibondo. **NOTE**: The form *striatipectus* has been attributed to either *S. reichardi* or *S. gularis*, and is possibly distinct from both. Few Kenyan specimens are available. Although field observations and photographs indicate considerable variation in ventral streaking, all birds seem to be assignable to either *striatipectus* or *elgonensis*, and we follow White (1963) in maintaining two species. However, birds on the Kongelai Escarpment do not respond to playback of taped songs of southern African *gularis*. The northern forms may be specifically distinct from those in the southern tropics.

STREAKY SEEDEATER *Serinus s. striolatus* **Plate 121**

Length 135–140 mm (5.25–5.5"). A *heavily streaked* terrestrial finch of the highlands. Tan upperparts and variable tawny-buff to whitish underparts *boldly and sharply streaked throughout with dark brown* in **adult**. Broad whitish or pale buff superciliary stripes and dark jaw line complete the overall streaky effect. Some birds show noticeable yellowish-green flight-feather edges. **Juvenile** resembles adult but is duller, with more diffuse streaking. **VOICE**: Short song *chididi see-leep,* high and thin at end. A longer song is composed of *see-leep* notes combined with thin, clear whistles and 'sizzles'; recalls canary or goldfinch. Still longer warbling song is composed of *distinctly separated phrases,* the entire performance lasting several seconds. Call notes include a high-pitched, long-drawn *seeeeeit* and a trio of soft notes, the first highest. **HABITS**: Confiding, especially near habitation (where it forages extensively in suburban gardens) and other openings in wooded country. Nests low in shrubs. Usually in pairs or small family parties. **SIMILAR SPECIES**: Stripe-breasted and Streaky-headed Seedeaters have prominent dark sides of face and no malar/moustachial stripes. **STATUS AND DISTRIBUTION**: Common and widespread above 1300 m, typically in gardens, cultivation, woodland edges, heath and scrub. Ranges from Mt Elgon, the Cheranganis, Maralal, Mt Nyiru and the Ndotos, south through the highlands to the Mau, Trans-Mara, Lolgorien, Nairobi and the Nguruman Hills; in n. Tanzania, from Loliondo and the Crater Highlands east to Mt Meru and Kilimanjaro, Arusha NP and the West Usambara Mts.

YELLOW-RUMPED SEEDEATER *Serinus reichenowi* **Plate 121**

Length 104–113 mm (4–4.5"). Small, dull and streaky, except for *bright yellow rump conspicuous in flight* (but concealed on perched bird). Tail rather short. Upperparts streaked greyish tan and dark brown, sides of face below the whitish superciliary stripes dull brown and with prominent brown moustachial/malar stripes; underparts whitish, with dull brown streaks on breast and flanks; sometimes shows a necklace of short dark streaks on upper breast, contrasting with *pure white throat.* Coastal birds smaller, greyer above and whiter below, and sometimes separated as the race *hilgerti.* **Juvenile** more diffusely streaked, often with some yellow on lower breast and belly. **VOICE**: Song a *continuous,* rapid, finch-like warbling with rich trills and whistles, sweet and canarylike: *chipiti-seeu-tisipitisiew-tisipitispit-tsisew-sipichew-chew-chew-tsip-tsip-tsip. . .,* not divided into short phrases like Streaky Seedeater's song. Call note a clear rising *tweee.* **HABITS**: Excepting singing males, unobtrusive and easily overlooked until flock takes wing. Small to large groups feed in roadside weeds or congregate at water sources. Flocks break up into pairs at approach of breeding season. Flight fast and undulating. **SIMILAR SPECIES**: Darker Black-throated Seedeater has indistinct or obsolete superciliary stripes, is lightly streaked below, but with dark face and throat. Other brown seedeaters lack yellow on rump. **STATUS AND DISTRIBUTION**: Fairly common from sea level to 2000 m, mostly in low, dry areas with scrub, bush, open woodland and cultivation; largely absent from the more arid parts of n. and ne. Kenya, but recorded at Marsabit, Moyale and Wajir. Ranges over much of our area south of 1° N, including the coastal lowlands. Most populations probably resident, but some wandering occurs.

BLACK-THROATED SEEDEATER *Serinus atrogularis somereni* **Plate 121**

Length 105–110 mm (4.5"). A scarce yellow-rumped seedeater of *western Kenya.* Darker above than the preceding species, and darker-faced, with *indistinct superciliary stripes* often evident only behind the eyes; appears *black-throated* owing to dense spotting; underparts otherwise dingy, often tinged with brown or dusky, and much

less streaked than in *reichenowi*. **VOICE AND HABITS:** Not distinguished from those of Yellow-rumped Seedeater. **SIMILAR SPECIES:** Yellow-rumped Seedeater compared above. **STATUS AND DISTRIBUTION:** In Kenya, known only from Kakamega, Siaya and Sioport, where now scarce or overlooked. **NOTE:** *Often* considered a race of *S. reichenowi*, but we follow van den Elzen (1985) in treating the two as separate species.

THICK-BILLED SEEDEATER *Serinus burtoni*   Plate 121

Length 154–162 mm (6–6.5"). A *heavy-looking*, dull-plumaged, stolid seedeater of the highlands, *stout-billed, dark-faced*, with narrow white forehead patch in *S. b. albifrons*, lacking in *kilimensis*. Nearly unmarked dark brown above and rather faintly streaked pale buff below (darker and brighter buff in *tanganjicae*); throat variably mottled with dusky and white; poorly defined whitish wing-bars; *wing-coverts, primaries and tail feathers* all edged with olive-yellow. **Juvenile** resembles adult. **VOICE:** Usual call note a thin, high-pitched *seeeeeeet* or *sweet-seeut*; may be followed (especially at dawn) by a short song of rather loud sharp notes: *tsi-tsi-tsi-tsi-tsi* or *tsi-tsi-tsi-tsi tsew chureet tseweet-tseet, tswi-tswi-tswi* or similar variation. More frequent, and given later in the day, are thin featureless songs varying from a shorter, barely audible *sss, sss, sss* or *tsee-tsee-tsew* to a longer *seee-sew, seweeee-see-see sewit-sit, tsee-tsee-tsew*. **HABITS:** Sluggish and inconspicuous. Confiding. Feeds on fruits and seeds in undergrowth of open forest and in low trees around clearings and edges, usually in small groups. **SIMILAR SPECIES:** Other seedeaters are more sharply patterned and have different habits. **STATUS AND DISTRIBUTION:** Fairly common in highland forest between 1700 and 3000 m, occasionally lower, typically in partially cleared tracts and wooded riverine strips. *S. b. albifrons* occupies highlands east of the Rift Valley, from Nairobi, the Aberdares, Mt Kenya and the Nyambenis north to the Karissia Hills, Maralal, the Mathews Range and the Ndotos. *S. b. tanganjicae* ranges west of the Rift Valley, from Mt Elgon and the Cheranganis, south through the Nandi, Kakamega and Mau Forests to Mau Narok; *kilimensis* extends from Lolgorien, the Mara River forests and Nguruman Hills, south in n. Tanzania to Loliondo, the Crater and Mbulu Highlands, Arusha NP, Kilimanjaro and the North Pare Mts.

YELLOW-CROWNED CANARY *Serinus canicollis flavivertex*   Plate 120
(Cape Canary)

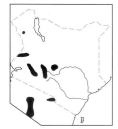

Length 115–125 mm (4.5–5"). A small canary of *high elevations. Yellow-edged tail quite long and distinctly forked.* **Male** has *bright yellow crown*, black-streaked olive-green back, and yellowish-olive rump. Well-patterned wings show two *bright yellow wing-bars* and a *yellow patch* across middle of primaries. Underparts largely yellow, but centre of lower belly white. **Female** duller throughout, more distinctly streaked above, heavily streaked on underparts. **Juvenile** buffy brown above with black streaks, the wing-bars buffy yellow or olive-yellow; underparts pale yellow to yellowish buff, and heavily streaked. **VOICE:** A bright, rapidly delivered and prolonged jumble of canary-like trills, twittering and warbling phrases, sometimes given in chorus by several males. Longer than other canary songs, with jingling quality reminiscent of European Goldfinch, *Carduelis carduelis*. Call a rising, double- or triple-noted *sweet pea* or *peet, swee-ee,* or *pee-eee*. **HABITS:** Forages on ground, usually in pairs, but may form large flocks. Male sings from tops of highland conifers and performs slow 'butterfly' courtship flight. Usual flight less undulating than that of some canaries. **SIMILAR SPECIES:** Differently patterned Yellow-fronted and White-bellied Canaries are species of lower elevations. **STATUS AND DISTRIBUTION:** Common in the highlands, typically from 2200 to over 4000 m, along forest edges and in clearings, cultivation, pastures, gardens and moorlands; descends to lower elevations in cool rainy periods. Ranges widely from Mt Elgon and the Cheranganis southeast to the Mau, Aberdares and Mt Kenya. Small disjunct population on the forest island of Mt Loima (west of Lodwar). In n. Tanzania confined to higher parts of the Crater and Mbulu Highlands, and mts Hanang, Meru and Kilimanjaro.

AFRICAN CITRIL *Serinus citrinelloides*   Plate 120

Length 110–120 mm (*c.* 4.5"). Siskin-like, streaked olive and black above, more yellow on the rump. **Females** of all races except *frontalis* extensively streaked below. **Males** variable, in *kikuyuensis* black-faced and with distinct yellow superciliary stripes, sometimes meeting in a *narrow* band above the black forehead; underparts plain yellow. Male *frontalis* is similar, but with *broad* yellow forehead band and generally paler upperparts. Males of *hypostictus* and *brittoni* are much like females, grey-faced and with well-streaked underparts; no yellow forehead or superciliaries in *hypostictus*, and these narrow but evident in *brittoni* (more distinct in male), in which race grey of face is reduced to a mere chin spot, the cheeks and auriculars greenish. In both sexes of *hypostic-*

tus, cheeks and chin are grey; *brittoni* differs only in averaging brighter yellowish green above, with finer streaks; *frontalis* is distinct from all other females in its *bright yellow forehead band* (extending back to above eyes) and in its *unstreaked yellow underparts.* **Voice**: Usual song of *kikuyuensis* composed of sweet and unhurried short phrases separated by short pauses, often with a longer complex series following or mixed in: *eee-turr-eeee tsurr. . . seeet tsew eeet. . . seeet tsew eeeet. . . sweet seeeet tsrrrr, chwrrr chwereet tsirrr chireet chirreet . . ..* A high-pitched twittering dawn song is faster and somewhat canary-like. Call note a rising *t'tweee;* also gives a soft chittering in flight. Song of *S. c. brittoni* loud, musical and canary-like. Voice of *hypostictus* not well documented, but apparently little different from that of other races; its alarm note a soft *t't'-tee.* **Habits**: Usual flocks of 15–30 birds break up into pairs for breeding. Often feeds among garden flowers and roadside weeds. Not shy. *S. c. brittoni* frequently forages in banana plants and nests among the fruits. **Similar Species**: Papyrus Canary, usually in or near papyrus stands, separated with care by habitat and by shorter, stubbier bill. **Status and Distribution**: Fairly common in acacias, open secondary growth, gardens and scrub in moist areas above 1100 m. *S. c. kikuyuensis* occupies the Kenyan highlands from Nairobi north to Mt Kenya and Meru District, west to Molo, Kericho, Nandi, Sotik and Rapogi. Near Kakamega and Siaya it meets (without intergradation) the western *brittoni,* which ranges north to Mt Elgon, Kitale, Kapenguria and Kongelai. The Ugandan and nw. Tanzanian *frontalis,* attributed to w. Kenya by Clement *et al.* (1993), is said by Britton (1980) to show "some evidence of intergradation" with *kikuyuensis,* but we have seen neither evidence of this nor any Kenyan specimens of *frontalis* (although *brittoni* is at times rather numerous at edges of the Kakamega Forest). Southern *hypostictus* ranges from Lolgorien, nw. Mara GR, and the Loita, Nguruman and Chyulu Hills into Tanzania; there, from Loliondo south to the Crater and Mbulu Highlands, and east to Arusha NP, Kilimanjaro, and the Pare and Usambara Mountains. Most populations presumed resident, but some seasonal wandering occurs in response to food availability. **Note:** The grey-faced *brittoni* and *hypostictus* may well constitute a species separate from *kikuyuensis.* The form *frontalis,* with its distinctive female plumage, probably is specifically distinct. It is so considered by Prigogine (1985), van den Elzen (1985) and Sibley and Monroe (1990), but it is maintained in *citrinelloides* by Short *et al.* (1990) and Clement *et al.* (1993), whom we prefer to follow until the biology of all forms is better known. Dowsett and Dowsett-Lemaire (1993) find no significant vocal differences between *hypostictus* and *frontalis.*

PAPYRUS CANARY *Serinus koliensis* Plate 120

Length 105–110 mm (c. 4.25"). Similar to some African Citrils (namely *S. c. brittoni* and female *S. c. kikuyuensis),* but *bill slightly shorter and stubbier, with somewhat more curved culmen,* the difference subtle, but typical birds readily distinguished with practice. Both sexes streaked on crown, back and breast; **male** brighter, with more yellow, and much less streaked below. Facial mask dusky, that of the **female** appearing hoary as all grey-brown feathers are edged with pale greyish buff; her mask extends onto forehead, unlike male's. **Immature** resembles adult female, the rich buff throat and breast broadly streaked with dark brown; yellow belly narrowly streaked with dusky; upperparts rich olive-brown with broad dark brown streaks; wing-covert and secondary edgings pale buffy white, lacking olive tone of adult. **Juvenile** undescribed. **Voice**: Songs distinct from those of African Citril, usually a rapid series of short chippering notes ending with (or including) a rising slurred *surrreet.* Also gives a more broken song of highly varied, more or less separated notes, *sweet tsiew chip, tsuweesee, chrrrr, chweet-chweet-chweet-chweet, tsuwiwi, tsuweet-sweet, su-eesee, shiew chiew . . ..* Silent outside breeding season. **Habits**: Haunts papyrus stands but feeds elsewhere, foraging on ground, in weeds, sorghum and maize; also in banana plants. Freely perches on bushes and fence wires, as well as on stems of the papyrus plants in which it nests. Roosts in papyrus even in non-breeding season. Nests March–July, perhaps again in November (when vocal). Usually in pairs or solitary, but 12–15 may forage together. **Similar Species**: African Citril discussed above (*brittoni* and female *kikuyuensis* the only sources of confusion: former is partially sympatric; *kikuyuensis* is allopatric). **Status and Distribution**: Endemic to papyrus swamps and adjacent cultivation in the Lake Victoria basin, where locally fairly common from Port Victoria, Lake Kanyaboli and Usengi east to Kisumu and Kendu Bay.

YELLOW-FRONTED CANARY *Serinus mozambicus* Plate 120
(Yellow-eyed Canary)

Length 100–117 mm (4–4.5"). A small, short-tailed, brightly coloured canary with a *broad yellow forehead band extending back over the eyes and ear-coverts.* **Adult** has side of face sharply patterned: a dusky eye-line separates the superciliary stripe from a *yellow cheek patch,* this separated in turn from the chin by a dark malar stripe. Rump, upper tail-coverts and entire underparts bright yellow. Back bright olive with dusky streaks; nape greyer. Bill dusky horn; eyes brown; feet black. Female slightly duller and paler than male. Western *C. m. barbatus* is larger, greener above, with less pronounced streaking than eastern birds, and underparts are brighter yellow. **Juvenile** paler than adult, with a white throat, obscure face pattern, and dusky streaks on the pale yellow breast. **Voice**: A series of sweet whistled, twittering phrases, repetitive, but shorter than songs of most *Serinus;* suggests domestic canary, but less prolonged. Call notes *tseeu-tseeu* and *tseeup.* **Habits**: Gregarious except when breed-

ing; typically feeds on the ground in small flocks, but visits treetops for buds and flowers. Nests in shrub or low tree. **SIMILAR SPECIES**: White-bellied Canary has white belly and is typical of drier country; southern nominate race, however, easily mistaken for Yellow-fronted. **STATUS AND DISTRIBUTION**: Fairly common resident and wanderer in open bush, moist scrub, cultivation and gardens between sea level and 2200 m. Coastal *S. m. mozambicus* ranges north to Lamu and Manda Islands, extending inland along the lower Tana River to Baomo, in the Shimba Hills and East Usambara foothills. Western *S. m. barbatus* ranges from Mt Elgon and Saiwa NP, south through Busia, Mumias, Nandi and Kakamega Districts to the Lake Victoria basin, Sotik, Lolgorien, Mara GR and into Tanzania's Mara Region and n. Serengeti NP. Largely allopatric with White-bellied Canary.

WHITE-BELLIED CANARY *Serinus dorsostriatus* Plate 120

Length 115–125 mm (4.5–5"). A dry-country counterpart of Yellow-fronted Canary. *White belly* most noticeable in the northern race *maculicollis*, in which entire posterior underparts are white and the flanks streaked with dusky. *S. d. dorsostriatus* has less white on belly and flanks, and the crissum is yellowish. In **male**, yellow rump, forehead and superciliary stripes contrast sharply with the olive back; ear-coverts and moustachial/malar stripes dusky olive. **Female** more heavily streaked on back than male, yellow frontal band less clear; underparts paler, with some white on throat, and *conspicuous short dusky breast streaks*. **Juvenile** more streaked below, with little indication of malar stripes. **VOICE**: Song of variable short phrases, e.g. a reiterated series of high-pitched slurred notes, *sweet suer weet-sip, sweeur-tsee-tsip, chweeur wee-chip, swee tsur-eep*, sometimes with a short trill at or near the end. Another song consists of several emphatic sharp notes, the series ending with a loud rising trill. Call note *zhuree* or *twee*. **HABITS**: Similar to those of Yellow-fronted Canary. **SIMILAR SPECIES**: Yellow-fronted Canary is brighter, shorter-tailed, entirely yellow below. Montane Yellow-crowned Canary shows white on belly, but is otherwise differently patterned. **STATUS AND DISTRIBUTION**: Locally common in dry thorn-bush, savanna and open woodland, mainly below 1600 m. Widespread in nw. Kenya south to edge of the highlands, and in low, dry southern areas from the Loita Plains and Narok District east to Amboseli and the Tsavo NPs; in n. Tanzania from Loliondo, Serengeti NP, the Crater and Mbulu Highlands, Lake Manyara and Tarangire NPs, the Masai Steppe, Arusha and Moshi Districts and Mkomazi GR. The southern nominate race and northern *maculicollis* intergrade extensively in cent. and s. Kenya, although Ripley and Heinrich (1966) extend the range of *maculicollis* south to Same and the base of Mt Meru in n. Tanzania. Birds east of Mwingi not racially assigned.

BRIMSTONE CANARY *Serinus sulphuratus sharpii* Plate 120
(Bully Canary)

Length 135–145 mm (*c.* 5.5"). A sparrow-sized canary with a *large, yellowish-brown bill* and *little contrast between rump and back*, the upperparts evenly greenish yellow, faintly streaked darker on the back. **Adult male** has bright yellow superciliary stripes, cheek, and underparts, and distinct olive-green moustachial/malar streaks. **Female** and **juvenile** similar but duller, facial marks fainter, sometimes obscurely streaked on breast. **VOICE**: A sweet rich song of loud prolonged twittering phrases and trills, *sree srrt tsu srrrrrreeeeee chrt su chrrreeeeee chirweee* or *see-ur chrrrrrrrrr see-sitsitsitsitsit, chirwee*, rising at end. **HABITS**: Usually solitary or in pairs; at times in small groups, but less gregarious than most canaries. Perches conspicuously on bushtops or fence wires. Commonly visits gardens to feed on flowers, new shoots, fruits and seeds. Nests in shrub or low tree. **SIMILAR SPECIES**: The two grosbeak-canaries are duller, often brownish, and broadly streaked on the back, streaked on sides and flanks, paler-billed, and with more rump/back contrast (especially Northern Grosbeak-Canary). Smaller canaries all show bright yellow rumps. **STATUS AND DISTRIBUTION**: Widespread and locally common in moist cultivation and bush, mainly below 2400 m. Ranges throughout the w. and cent. Kenyan highlands from Mt Elgon, the Cheranganis, Maralal, Mt Kenya and the Nyambenis south to the Lake Victoria basin, Mara GR, and Narok, Nairobi and Machakos Districts. In n. Tanzania, extends from the Mara Region and Serengeti NP east to Loliondo, with a disjunct population in the Kilimanjaro area (possibly the source of occasional wanderers to the Taita Hills).

SOUTHERN GROSBEAK-CANARY *Serinus buchanani* Plate 120
(Kenya Grosbeak Canary)

Length 142–150 mm (*c.* 6"). The pale grosbeak-like bill separates this *large dull-coloured canary* from all others south of the equator. **Adults** of *both* sexes yellowish olive-green above, with dark streaks and contrasting yellowish rump; underparts olive-yellow. **Male** brighter yellow on rump and underparts, with a few streaks at sides of breast (and sometimes faintly in centre); bill pale pink or pinkish horn, sometimes rather bright. **Juvenile** duller throughout, the rump less contrasting, lightly streaked on breast and with whitish-horn bill. **VOICE**: Call notes

include a whistled *tuweea* or a slurred *queeuleet*, repeated after a short pause, and a long-drawn *seeeek*. Song a series of low, almost guttural ticking or chipping notes interspersed with much higher-pitched and longer squealing notes of penetrating quality: *chrk chrk chrk chrrrrr seeeeeee, tk-tk chrk chrk chrk chrk tsik tsur squeeeeeeeeeeeeee.* **HABITS:** Solitary or in pairs. Feeds weaver-like in trees. Sings from treetops with greening of bush country following the rains. Partial to *Commiphora* thickets. Builds rather flat nest in low tree. **SIMILAR SPECIES:** Male Northern Grosbeak-Canary is darker on the back, has bolder face pattern, brighter yellow underparts, with white lower belly. Brimstone Canary is much brighter yellow below, brighter greenish yellow above, with noticeable moustachial/malar streaks and yellow-tinged bill, no side streaking and little rump/back contrast. **STATUS AND DISTRIBUTION:** Uncommon local resident and wanderer in dry *Acacia* and *Commiphora* bush and scrub south of the Equator, from Kajiado and Sultan Hamud Districts north to Olorgesailie, and the Ngong and Mua Hills. Disjunct population resident in Taita Hills District from Bura west to Maktau. A few n. Tanzanian records from se. Serengeti NP, Mangola Springs in the Lake Eyasi depression, and north of Arusha. **NOTE:** Sometimes considered a race of *S. donaldsoni,* but striking differences in female plumage and distinct songs suggest otherwise. Reports from Tarangire NP require confirmation.

NORTHERN GROSBEAK-CANARY *Serinus donaldsoni* Plates 120, 121
(Abyssinian Grosbeak Canary)

Length 150–155 mm (6"). The grosbeak-canary of *northern Kenya;* stocky, with a *heavy whitish-pink to salmon-pink bill; sexes markedly different.* **Male** *dull olive above, with dark brown streaks on back, bright yellow superciliaries, rump and underparts,* except for *white lower belly;* sparse black streaks on sides and flanks. **Female** suggests a big seedeater, *brown above,* streaked with darker brown (narrowly so on crown and nape); *rump golden yellow,* blending into olive-brown on upper tail-coverts; wing feathers mostly edged with buffy white in fresh plumage. *Underparts buffy white with broad, diffuse brown streaks.* Dark sides of face outlined above by narrow whitish superciliary stripes; forehead and crown tinged with dull olive-yellow. **VOICE:** Songs include: (1) a rapid *seu-seu-seu-seu-seu-seu . . .,* the same note repeated 10–20 times, the series occasionally separated by a *suWEEEER* or *suWEEEEu;* (2) *srceeet . . . wriseet . . . sew . . .sreet . . . wreet . . .,* separate, sweet yet piercing notes, many upslurred and given in groups at three or four second intervals; (3) a ringing *tri-tri-tri-tri-tri-tri-tri-tri-tri-tri.* Call note a loud *twea,* repeated at intervals, similar to one call of Southern Grosbeak-Canary. **SIMILAR SPECIES:** Southern Grosbeak-Canary, with similar habits, shows less rump/back contrast, is duller yellowish green above in both sexes, entirely yellow below, with no white on lower belly. Brimstone Canary is brighter, shows no side/flank streaking and virtually no contrast between rump and rest of upperparts; bill yellow-tinged. Female Northern Grosbeak-Canary is distinguished from most seedeaters by brown appearance and contrasting yellow rump; from Yellow-rumped Seedeater by much larger size and huge bill. **STATUS AND DISTRIBUTION:** Scarce and local below 1600 m in dry open bush and semi-desert scrub north of the Equator. Ranges from Baringo, Rumuruti and Wamba Districts north to Nasolot NR, the Ndotos, Marsabit, e. Turkana and Ethiopian border areas. **NOTE:** Sometimes considered conspecific with Southern Grosbeak-Canary.

ORIOLE-FINCH *Linurgus olivaceus* Plate 121

Length 120 mm (4.75"). A small forest finch with a *bright orange bill.* **Adult male** brilliant yellow, with black head, and black wings with yellow and white feather edgings. **Female** olive, brighter on tail, more olive-yellow on belly; wing feathers edged olive-yellow; bill dull yellowish orange. Some (immatures?) obscurely streaked below. The southern race *kilimensis* has more greenish upperparts and flanks, contrasting with the bright yellow that borders black of neck and breast. **Juvenile** resembles female, but with pale olive wing-covert tips and yellowish-horn bill. **VOICE:** Usual note an extremely high-pitched *tzit-tzit* or *tseet-tseet,* barely audible to human ears. Songs of *L. o. elgonensis* vary from a short rapid *tsew-tsew-tsew siiiiiiiiiiii,* with variable thin notes added, to several high *seet* notes grading into a rather featureless thin twittering or tinkling, *sheeet-seet, seet-seet-seet-sweeet, suweet sieu-sieu, cheew chew-chew-chew titititititi.* Song of Tanzanian *L. o. kilimensis* is canary-like and with considerable fluctuation in pitch: *cheep cheep cheep cheep tsee tsee tsee tsee chureeeeee swee tsip-tsip-tsip-tsip chereeep,* the *chureeeeee* and final *chereeep* upslurred. **HABITS:** Shy and restless. Solitary, in pairs or in groups of eight to fifteen birds, near ground at edges of forest clearings or openings in bamboo; occasionally ascends into trees. Builds nest of mosses, lichens, rootlets and plant down, in low shrub. **SIMILAR SPECIES:** Orioles are larger, longer-billed, more arboreal and vocally distinct. **STATUS AND DISTRIBUTION:** *L. o. elgonensis* is uncommon and local in highland-forest undergrowth between 1550 and 3000 m on Mt Elgon, the Cheranganis and in the North Nandi, Kakamega, Mt Kenya and Meru Forests (inexplicably absent from the Mau forests and those of the Aberdare Range). *L. o. kilimensis,* primarily Tanzanian, is known from the Crater and Mbulu Highlands, Monduli, Mt Meru, Arusha NP, Kilimanjaro and the West Usambaras, with a small disjunct population on Ol Doinyo Orok at Namanga in s. Kenya.

OLD-WORLD BUNTINGS, FAMILY EMBERIZIDAE, SUBFAMILY EMBERIZINAE
(World, c. 45 species; Africa, 14; Kenya, 6; n. Tanzania, 4)

The only African members of this diverse family, buntings are ground-feeding birds with short, deep, conical bills weaker and narrower than those of canaries and seedeaters, and the commissure is distinctive, with the mandible edges slightly separated centrally, not in contact throughout their length. The sturdy feet and large toes are well suited to scratching. Several species are richly coloured, with black-and-white-striped head patterns and white in the tail. Buntings inhabit a wide range of habitats, from rocky desert to the edges of moist highland forest. They are largely terrestrial, but sing from elevated perches. Solitary breeders, they build a shallow cup nest in a low shrub, in a tree fork or on the ground. The two or three eggs are white, bluish or greenish, with dark scrawls, spots and blotches.

ORTOLAN BUNTING *Emberiza hortulana*   Plate 121

Length *c.* 160 mm (6.5"). A well-patterned ground bird with a *short pinkish bill,* and side of face marked by a *pronounced eye-ring.* Whitish or buff wing-covert tips form two pale wing-bars, and *white outer tail feathers are conspicuous in flight.* **Adult male** in winter generally greyish olive from head to breast, except for sulphur-yellow eye-ring, malar region and throat, the latter with a grey stripe on each side. Tawny upperparts streaked with dark brown, the rump plainer; lower breast to under tail-coverts largely rufous-buff. **Female** similar, but streaked with brown on head and breast; ear-coverts grey-brown, and malar stripes dark brown. Duller **first-winter** (the most likely plumage in East Africa) may suggest lark or pipit, but is readily separated by distinctive bill. Upperparts streaked brown and black; throat yellowish, underparts otherwise rich buff to pinkish rufous, or this colour on belly only; breast and sides with dusky streaks. Side of face marked with *whitish eye-ring, dark malar stripe,* and streaked greyish *ear-coverts bordered below by a dusky line; white wing-bars prominent.* Bill pinkish horn above, yellow or pinkish below; eyes brown; feet pinkish brown. **Voice:** Call notes include a high whistled *tew* and a hard *twick.* Its buzzy song perhaps unlikely in our region, but sings feebly on spring passage in North Africa. **Habits:** Forages on ground, but flies to nearby tree or shrub when disturbed. Rather shy. **Similar Species:** House Bunting has streaked throat and rufous 'shoulders'. Young Cinnamon-breasted Rock Bunting is much darker below. Neither shows white in tail. **Status and Distribution:** Vagrant south of the species' usual North African wintering range. Three Kenyan records: Lake Baringo (Oct. 1910), Taita Hills Lodge (Jan. 1986), and Ngulia, Tsavo West NP (Nov. 1993).

HOUSE BUNTING *Emberiza striolata saturatior*   Plate 121

Length 140 mm (5.5"). A largely rufous-brown bunting of *northern Kenyan deserts.* **Adult male** streaked with dusky above; much rufous in wings and outer tail feathers. Black-and-white-streaked forehead and crown bordered by prominent whitish superciliary stripes; grey ear-coverts margined above and below by broad black stripes; greyish throat and upper breast mottled and streaked with black; rest of underparts rufous-brown or tawny-brown. Bill dusky above, yellow below; eyes brown; feet pinkish or yellowish flesh colour. **Female** similar, but head sandy brown, streaked with dark brown, and no black on ear-coverts or cheeks; throat and breast more lightly marked; wings dull cinnamon, with rufous 'shoulders.' **Juvenile** resembles adult female. **Voice:** Song a short wheezy twitter, *zhwe-zhwe-zhwee-dzu-dzee-dzee-dzee,* frequently repeated, with variations. Calls include a hard *tsick* and a nasal *zwee.* **Habits:** Not shy. Feeds in pairs or small groups, gathering into larger flocks around wells, water holes and concentrated food sources such as spilled grain. **Similar Species:** Cinnamon-breasted Rock Bunting is much darker, with light central crown stripe and black wing-coverts with rufous margins. **Status and Distribution:** Locally common resident and nomad below 800 m in rocky deserts from the eastern shore of Lake Turkana to Turbi and the northern edge of the Dida Galgalu Desert, south to Loiengalani and the base of Mt Marsabit; also common around Kamathia near the Sudanese border.

CINNAMON-BREASTED ROCK BUNTING *Emberiza t. tahapisi*   Plate 121
(Rock Bunting)

Length 150 mm (6"). A dark bunting of rough or rocky terrain. **Adult male** *cinnamon-chestnut below, with black throat and upper breast* (feathers white-tipped in fresh plumage); *black head boldly marked with white crown, superciliary, subocular and moustachial stripes;* russet upperparts streaked with black; wing-coverts and flight feathers cinnamon-edged; black tail has tawny outer edges. Bill brownish above, yellow below; eyes and feet brown. **Female** resembles male, except for black-streaked tawny crown, dusky throat and a faint malar stripe. **Juvenile** has entire head streaked tawny-russet and black. **Voice:** Song a rapid *tserk tser sidisidisi-seet,* with rising inflection at end. **Habits:** Individuals or pairs forage in rocky ravines, on broken stony ground and along roadsides. Sings from low trees and bushes, as well as rocks. **Similar Species:** Largely allopatric House Bunting is

paler, with less contrasting head pattern and plain rufous wing-coverts. **STATUS AND DISTRIBUTION**: Widely but locally distributed resident of rocky ground from Lokichokio and the Lake Turkana basin, south through the w. and cent. Kenyan highlands to Nairobi NP; also in Mara GR, and Amboseli and the Tsavo NPs. In n. Tanzania, wide-ranging from Serengeti NP and the Crater Highlands east to Arusha and Moshi Districts and Mkomazi GR, south to Tarangire NP and Kondoa District. Generally absent from the more arid parts of n. and e. Kenya.

GOLDEN-BREASTED BUNTING *Emberiza flaviventris kalaharica* Plate 121

Length 155–160 mm (*c*. 6.25"). A highland bunting with *black-and-white-striped head, two broad white wing-bars* and white-edged outer tail feathers. **Adult** *golden yellow below, deeper orange-tawny on breast*; rest of underparts whitish, dark grey at sides of breast; back rufous with grey feather edges; *rump and upper tail-coverts grey*. Eyes dark brown; bill dark horn-brown above, pinkish below; feet pinkish flesh. Female slightly smaller and duller than male. **Juvenile** still duller throughout, with dusky streaks across breast. **VOICE**: Song variable, but usually consisting of a single phrase repeated numerous times, e.g. (1) a penetrating *sitsit EEU, sitsit EEU. . .*; (2) a shrill whistled *cheRI cheRI cheRI. . .*; (3) *seesher seesher seesher . . .*; (4) a husky, tit-like *seeDJEERit, seeDJEERit . . .*. **HABITS**: Solitary or in pairs, on ground, but males sing from tops of tall trees. Confiding and tame around dwellings. **SIMILAR SPECIES**: Somali Golden-breasted Bunting is brighter, more extensively white on sides and flanks, and inhabits drier low country. Brown-rumped Bunting lacks white in wings, has rufous rump and yellow flanks. In ne. Tanzania, see Cabanis's Bunting. **STATUS AND DISTRIBUTION**: Fairly common resident of open woodland, forest edges and suburban gardens between 1400 and 2200 m in the w. and cent. Kenyan highlands, ranging south to Mara GR and the Loita and Nguruman Hills. In n. Tanzania at Serengeti NP, Mt Meru and Kilimanjaro, with presumed wanderers also recorded from Mangola Springs, Lake Manyara NP and the base of Mt Hanang.

SOMALI GOLDEN-BREASTED BUNTING *Emberiza poliopleura* Plate 121

Length 150 mm (6"). A *dry-country* bunting, noticeably brighter than the preceding species, the *back feathers edged with whitish and pale tawny*, giving a more mottled appearance; golden yellow from chin to lower breast, but with *broadly whitish sides and flanks*. *Rump paler grey* and *outer tail feathers more extensively white* than in Golden-breasted Bunting. **Juvenile** has brownish head with pale buff stripes and tawny-buff underparts with fewer breast streaks than young Golden-breasted. **VOICE**: Song simple and high-pitched: (1) *tsu weetsu weetsu weetsu*, (2) *tseeper-tseepa-tseepa-tsee*, or (3) *tchew weechu weechu weet*, repeated every few seconds. **HABITS**: Pairs or small groups frequently rest in low bushes, and male sings from high perches. Shy; flushes quickly when approached. **SIMILAR SPECIES**: Golden-breasted Bunting compared above. **STATUS AND DISTRIBUTION**: Fairly common resident of dry *Acacia* and *Commiphora* bush and scrub below 1200 m in n. and e. Kenya, south to the edge of the central highlands, and in the dry eastern plateau from Meru NP south to the Tsavo NPs and Mkomazi GR. Reaches the coast north of Malindi. Recorded sporadically at Olorgesailie in the Rift Valley, and apparent nocturnal migrants occasionally caught at Ngulia, Tsavo West NP.

CABANIS'S BUNTING *Emberiza cabanisi orientalis* Plate 123

Length *c*. 175 mm (7"). A yellow-breasted bunting of Tanzania's Usambara Mountains. *Lacks white stripe below eye* conspicuous in similar buntings. **Adult male** black-headed, with grey or whitish central crown stripe bordered below by long white superciliaries; brown or grey-and-brown back sharply streaked with black; most tail feathers white-tipped; underparts largely bright yellow, but under tail-coverts white and lower flanks washed with grey. Eyes, bill and feet brown. **Female** has less distinct crown stripe, black areas of head replaced by brown, and breast (in some individuals) is tawny-buff. **Juvenile** has pale tawny-brown upperparts and superciliary stripes, pale yellowish underparts, with dark brown streaks on upper breast and sides. **VOICE**: Song a loud, piercing modulated whistle, with much individual variation. Described by Sclater and Moreau (1933) as *wee, chidder-chidder-chidder, we* and *her, ip ip ip her, hee*. **HABITS**: Forages on paths, roadsides and patches of open ground. Often nests in tea and coffee shrubs. Attends columns of safari ants. Highly vocal. **SIMILAR SPECIES**: Allopatric Golden-breasted and Somali Golden-breasted Buntings have white subocular stripe on side of face. Somali Golden-breasted occupies different habitat and is conspicuously whitish on sides and flanks. **STATUS AND DISTRIBUTION**: Fairly common resident of open areas of the East Usambara Mts and at Ambangulu, 1220 m in the West Usambaras, otherwise mainly south of our area. Reported presence in Tarangire NP requires confirmation.

BROWN-RUMPED BUNTING *Emberiza affinis forbesi* **Plate 121**

Length 135 mm (5.5"). A little-known *nw. Kenyan* species similar to Golden-breasted Bunting, but with *no wing-bars,* a *brown rump,* and *yellow of underparts includes belly, sides and flanks.* Sexes alike. **VOICE**: Apparently unrecorded. **HABITS**: Similar to those of Somali Golden-breasted Bunting. **SIMILAR SPECIES**: Golden-breasted and Somali Golden-breasted Buntings are grey on rump and grey or whitish on belly, sides and flanks. **STATUS AND DISTRIBUTION**: Rare in nw. Kenya, where known only from the north Kerio River (early specimen) and the base of the Kongelai Escarpment.

APPENDIX 1: TANZANIAN SPECIES NOT INCLUDED IN THIS BOOK

Cape Gannet	*Morus capensis*
Great Bittern	*Botaurus stellaris*
Forest Francolin	*Francolinus lathami*
Udzungwa Forest Partridge	*Xenoperdix udzungwensis*
Chestnut-headed Flufftail	*Sarothrura lugens*
Wattled Crane	*Bugeranus carunculatus*
Forbes's Plover	*Charadrius forbesi*
White-crowned Plover	*Vanellus albiceps*
Black-naped Tern	*Sterna sumatrana*
Afep Pigeon	*Columba unicincta*
Brown-necked Parrot	*Poicephalus suahelicus*
Lilian's Lovebird	*Agapornis lilianae*
Livingstone's Turaco	*Tauraco livingstonii*
Grey Go-away-bird	*Corythaixoides concolor*
Dusky Long-tailed Cuckoo	*Cercococcyx mechowi*
Coppery-tailed Coucal	*Centropus cupreicaudus*
Burchell's Coucal	*Centropus burchelli*
Red-faced Mousebird	*Urocolius indicus*
White-bellied Kingfisher	*Alcedo leucogaster*
Blue-breasted Kingfisher	*Halcyon malimbica*
Böhm's Bee-eater	*Merops boehmi*
Racket-tailed Roller	*Coracias spatulata*
Pale-billed Hornbill	*Tockus pallidirostris*
Whyte's Barbet	*Stactolaema whytii*
Miombo Pied Barbet	*Tricholaema frontata*
Red-faced Barbet	*Lybius rubrifacies*
Black-backed Barbet	*Lybius minor*
Stierling's Woodpecker	*Dendropicos stierlingi*
Angola Lark	*Mirafra angolensis*
Pearl-breasted Swallow	*Hirundo dimidiata*
Greater Striped Swallow	*Hirundo cucullata*
Eastern Saw-wing	*Psalidoprocne orientalis*
Woodland Pipit	*Anthus nyassae*
Short-tailed Pipit	*Anthus brachyurus*
Buffy Pipit	*Anthus vaalensis*
Fülleborn's Longclaw	*Macronyx fuellebornii*
Green-throated Greenbul	*Andropadus chlorigula*
Spotted Greenbul	*Ixonotus guttatus*
Leaf-love	*Pyrrhurus scandens*
Icterine Greenbul	*Phyllastrephus icterinus*
Xavier's Greenbul	*Phyllastrephus xavieri*
Green-tailed Bristlebill	*Bleda eximia*
Western Nicator	*Nicator chloris*
White-rumped Babbler	*Turdoides hartlaubii*
Fire-crested Alethe	*Alethe diademata*
Bearded Scrub Robin	*Cercotrichas barbata*
Bocage's Ground Robin	*Sheppardia bocagei*
Iringa Ground Robin	*Sheppardia lowei*
Lowland Akalat	*Sheppardia cyornithopsis*
Miombo Rock Thrush	*Monticola angolensis*
Rufous Thrush	*Stizorhina fraseri*
Arnott's White-headed Chat	*Myrmecocichla arnotti*
Groundscraper Thrush	*Psophocichla litsipsirupa*
Böhm's Flycatcher	*Muscicapa boehmi*
Grey-throated Flycatcher	*Myioparus griseigularis*
Kungwe Apalis	*Apalis argentea*
Masked Apalis	*Apalis binotata*
Karamoja Apalis	*Apalis karamojae*
Chapin's Apalis	*Apalis chapini*
Mrs Moreau's Warbler	*Bathmocercus winifredae*
Bamboo Warbler	*Bradypterus alfredi*

Barred Wren-Warbler	*Calamonastes stierlingi*
Black-lored Cisticola	*Cisticola nigriloris*
Chirping Cisticola	*Cisticola pipiens*
Churring Cisticola	*Cisticola njombe*
Yellow Longbill	*Macrosphenus flavicans*
Laura's Warbler	*Phylloscopus laurae*
Red-capped Crombec	*Sylvietta ruficapilla*
Long-billed Crombec	*Sylvietta rufescens*
Rufous-bellied Tit	*Parus rufiventris*
Miombo Grey Tit	*Parus griseiventris*
Livingstone's Flycatcher	*Erythrocercus livingstonei*
Souza's Shrike	*Lanius souzae*
Uluguru Bush-shrike	*Malaconotus alius*
Sharp-tailed Glossy Starling	*Lamprotornis acuticaudus*
White-winged Starling	*Neocichla gutturalis*
Anchieta's Sunbird	*Anthreptes anchietae*
Grey-headed Sunbird	*Anthreptes fraseri*
Blue-throated Brown Sunbird	*Nectarinia cyanolaema*
Loveridge's Sunbird	*Nectarinia loveridgei*
Miombo Double-collared Sunbird	*Nectarinia manoensis*
Shelley's Double-collared Sunbird	*Nectarinia shelleyi*
Angola White-bellied Sunbird	*Nectarinia oustaleti*
Rufous-winged Sunbird	*Nectarinia rufipennis*
Regal Sunbird	*Nectarinia regia*
White-bellied Sunbird	*Nectarinia talatala*
Little Green Sunbird	*Nectarinia seimundi*
Montane Marsh Widowbird	*Euplectes psammocromius*
Kilombero Weaver	*Ploceus burnieri*
Bertram's Weaver	*Ploceus bertrandi*
Tanganyika Masked Weaver	*Ploceus reichardi*
Olive-headed Golden Weaver	*Ploceus olivaceiceps*
Weyns's Weaver	*Ploceus weynsi*
Southern Brown-throated Weaver	*Ploceus xanthopterus*
Yellow-throated Petronia	*Petronia superciliaris*
Lavender Waxbill	*Estrilda perreini*
Brown Firefinch	*Lagonosticta nitidula*
White-collared Oliveback	*Nesocharis ansorgei*
Black-chinned Quail-Finch	*Ortygospiza gabonensis*
Red-fronted Antpecker	*Parmoptila woodhousei*
Lesser Seed-cracker	*Pyrenestes minor*
Green Indigobird	*Vidua codringtoni*
Black-eared Seedeater	*Serinus mennelli*
Kipengere Seedeater	*Serinus melanochrous*
Southern Rock Bunting	*Emberiza capensis*

APPENDIX 2: UGANDAN SPECIES NOT COVERED IN THIS BOOK

Spot-breasted Ibis	*Bostrychia rara*
Hartlaub's Duck	*Pteronetta hartlaubii*
Chestnut-flanked Goshawk	*Accipiter castanilius*
Red-thighed Sparrowhawk	*Accipiter erythropus*
Long-tailed Hawk	*Urotriorchis macrourus*
Red-necked Buzzard	*Buteo auguralis*
Cassin's Hawk-Eagle	*Hieraaetus africanus*
Forest Francolin	*Francolinus lathami*
Nahan's Francolin	*Francolinus nahani*
Clapperton's Francolin	*Francolinus clappertoni*
Heuglin's Francolin	*Francolinus icterorhynchus*
Handsome Francolin	*Francolinus nobilis*
Nkulengu Rail	*Himantornis haematopus*
Little Crake	*Porzana parva*
Forbes's Plover	*Charadrius forbesi*
Afep Pigeon	*Columba unicincta*
White-naped Pigeon	*Columba albinucha*
Western Bronze-naped Pigeon	*Columba iriditorques*
Vinaceous Dove	*Streptopelia vinacea*
Black-billed Wood Dove	*Turtur abyssinicus*
Brown-necked Parrot	*Poicephalus suahelicus*
Black-collared Lovebird	*Agapornis swindernianus*
Rose-ringed Parakeet	*Psittacula krameri*
Ruwenzori Turaco	*Tauraco johnstoni*
Dusky Long-tailed Cuckoo	*Cercococcyx mechowi*
Olive Long-tailed Cuckoo	*Cercococcyx olivinus*
Yellow-throated Cuckoo	*Chrysococcyx flavigularis*
Fraser's Eagle-Owl	*Bubo poensis*
Chestnut Owlet	*Glaucidium castaneum*
Bates's Nightjar	*Caprimulgus batesi*
Cassin's Spinetail	*Neafrapus cassini*
Pallid Swift	*Apus pallidus*
White-bellied Kingfisher	*Alcedo leucogaster*
African Dwarf Kingfisher	*Ispidina lecontei*
Chocolate-backed Kingfisher	*Halcyon badia*
Blue-breasted Kingfisher	*Halcyon malimbica*
Black Bee-eater	*Merops gularis*
Red-throated Bee-eater	*Merops bullocki*
Little Green Bee-eater	*Merops orientalis*
Blue-throated Roller	*Eurystomus gularis*
Black Scimitarbill	*Rhinopomastus aterrimus*
White-crested Hornbill	*Tropicranus albocristatus*
Black Dwarf Hornbill	*Tockus hartlaubi*
Red-billed Dwarf Hornbill	*Tockus camurus*
African Pied Hornbill	*Tockus fasciatus*
Piping Hornbill	*Bycanistes fistulator*
White-thighed Hornbill	*Bycanistes cylindricus*
Black-wattled Hornbill	*Ceratogymna atrata*
Western Green Tinkerbird	*Pogoniulus coryphaeus*
Red-rumped Tinkerbird	*Pogoniulus atroflavus*
Yellow-throated Tinkerbird	*Pogoniulus subsulphureus*
Red-faced Barbet	*Lybius rubrifacies*
Black-breasted Barbet	*Lybius rolleti*
Spotted Honeyguide	*Indicator maculatus*
Willcocks's Honeyguide	*Indicator willcocksi*
Dwarf Honeyguide	*Indicator pumilio*
Zenker's Honeyguide	*Melignomon zenkeri*
African Piculet	*Sasia africana*
Gabon Woodpecker	*Dendropicos gabonensis*
Elliot's Woodpecker	*Dendropicos elliotii*

Red-sided Broadbill	*Smithornis rufolateralis*
African Green Broadbill	*Pseudocalyptomena graueri*
Green-breasted Pitta	*Pitta reichenowi*
Rufous-rumped Lark	*Pinarocorys erythropygia*
Sun Lark	*Galerida modesta*
White-throated Blue Swallow	*Hirundo nigrita*
Short-tailed Pipit	*Anthus brachyurus*
Spotted Greenbul	*Ixonotus guttatus*
Simple Greenbul	*Chlorocichla simplex*
Swamp Greenbul	*Thescelocichla leucopleura*
Leaf-love	*Pyrrhurus scandens*
Sassi's Olive Greenbul	*Phyllastrephus lorenzi*
Icterine Greenbul	*Phyllastrephus icterinus*
Xavier's Greenbul	*Phyllastrephus xavieri*
White-throated Greenbul	*Phyllastrephus albigularis*
Green-tailed Bristlebill	*Bleda eximia*
Eastern Bearded Greenbul	*Criniger chloronotus*
Red-tailed Greenbul	*Criniger calurus*
Western Nicator	*Nicator chloris*
Yellow-throated Nicator	*Nicator vireo*
Capuchin Babbler	*Phyllanthus atripennis*
Dusky Babbler	*Turdoides tenebrosus*
Fire-crested Alethe	*Alethe diademata*
Red-throated Alethe	*Alethe poliophrys*
Northern Bearded Scrub Robin	*Cercotrichas leucosticta*
White-bellied Robin-Chat	*Cossyphicula roberti*
Archer's Robin-Chat	*Cossypha archeri*
Lowland Akalat	*Sheppardia cyornithopsis*
Rufous Thrush	*Stizorhina fraseri*
White-fronted Black Chat	*Myrmecocichla albifrons*
Arnott's White-headed Chat	*Myrmecocichla arnotti*
Black-eared Ground Thrush	*Zoothera camaronensis*
Grey Ground Thrush	*Zoothera princei*
Forest Ground Thrush	*Zoothera oberlaenderi*
Kivu Ground Thrush	*Zoothera tanganjicae*
Yellow-eyed Black Flycatcher	*Melaenornis ardesiacus*
Forest Flycatcher	*Fraseria ocreata*
Cassin's Grey Flycatcher	*Muscicapa cassini*
Yellow-footed Flycatcher	*Muscicapa sethsmithi*
Dusky Blue Flycatcher	*Muscicapa comitata*
Sooty Flycatcher	*Muscicapa infuscata*
Grey-throated Flycatcher	*Myioparus griseigularis*
Masked Apalis	*Apalis binotata*
Montane Masked Apalis	*Apalis personata*
Karamoja Apalis	*Apalis karamojae*
Black-capped Apalis	*Apalis nigriceps*
Collared Apalis	*Apalis ruwenzori*
Bamboo Warbler	*Bradypterus alfredi*
Grauer's Rush Warbler	*Bradypterus graueri*
Yellow-browed Camaroptera	*Camaroptera superciliaris*
Red-winged Grey Warbler	*Drymocichla incana*
Brown-crowned Eremomela	*Eremomela badiceps*
Grauer's Warbler	*Graueria vittata*
Short-tailed Warbler	*Hemitesia neumanni*
Grey Longbill	*Macrosphenus concolor*
Yellow Longbill	*Macrosphenus flavicans*
Red-faced Woodland Warbler	*Phylloscopus laetus*
Lemon-bellied Crombec	*Sylvietta denti*
Tit-Hylia	*Pholidornis rushiae*
Stripe-breasted Tit	*Parus fasciiventer*
Ituri Batis	*Batis ituriensis*
Ruwenzori Batis	*Batis diops*
Chestnut-capped Flycatcher	*Erythrocercus mccallii*
White-bellied Crested Flycatcher	*Trochocercus albiventris*
Blue-headed Crested Flycatcher	*Trochocercus nitens*
Red-billed Helmet-shrike	*Prionops caniceps*

Emin's Shrike	*Lanius gubernator*
Red-eyed Puffback	*Dryoscopus senegalensis*
Fiery-breasted Bush-shrike	*Malaconotus cruentus*
Lagden's Bush-shrike	*Malaconotus lagdeni*
Many-coloured Bush-shrike	*Malaconotus multicolor*
Montane Sooty Boubou	*Laniarius poensis*
Black-winged Oriole	*Oriolus nigripennis*
Purple-headed Glossy Starling	*Lamprotornis purpureiceps*
Chestnut-winged Starling	*Onychognathus fulgidus*
Narrow-tailed Starling	*Poeoptera lugubris*
Grey-headed Sunbird	*Anthreptes fraseri*
Blue-headed Sunbird	*Nectarinia alinae*
Splendid Sunbird	*Nectarinia coccinigaster*
Blue-throated Brown Sunbird	*Nectarinia cyanolaema*
Greater Double-collared Sunbird	*Nectarinia afra*
Tiny Sunbird	*Nectarinia minulla*
Purple-breasted Sunbird	*Nectarinia purpureiventris*
Regal Sunbird	*Nectarinia regia*
Palestine Sunbird	*Nectarinia osea*
Little Green Sunbird	*Nectarinia seimundi*
Red-bellied Malimbe	*Malimbus erythrogaster*
Crested Malimbe	*Malimbus malimbicus*
Blue-billed Malimbe	*Malimbus nitens*
Maxwell's Black Weaver	*Ploceus albinucha*
Strange Weaver	*Ploceus alienus*
Fox's Weaver	*Ploceus spekeoides*
Weyns's Weaver	*Ploceus weynsi*
Bush Petronia	*Petronia dentata*
Dusky Twinspot	*Clytospiza cinereovinacea*
Dybowski's Twinspot	*Euschistospiza dybowskii*
Dusky Crimsonwing	*Cryptospiza jacksoni*
Shelley's Crimsonwing	*Cryptospiza shelleyi*
Black-faced Firefinch	*Lagonosticta larvata*
White-collared Oliveback	*Nesocharis ansorgei*
Grey-headed Oliveback	*Nesocharis capistrata*
Chestnut-breasted Negrofinch	*Nigrita bicolor*
Pale-breasted Negrofinch	*Nigrita luteifrons*
Black-chinned Quail-Finch	*Ortygospiza gabonensis*
Red-fronted Antpecker	*Parmoptila woodhousei*
Red-winged Pytilia	*Pytilia phoenicoptera*
Grant's Bluebill	*Spermophaga poliogenys*
White-rumped Seedeater	*Serinus leucopygius*

GAZETTEER

(Tanzanian localities are indicated by Tz)

Aberdare NP, 0°25'S, 36°40'E
Aberdare [Mts], 0°25'S, 36°38'E
Ahero, 0°11'S, 34°50'E
Aitong, 1°11'S, 35°15'E
Akala, 0°04'S, 34°26'E
Allia Bay, 3°45'N, 36°15'E
Alupe, 0°30'N, 34°08'E
Amani (Tz), 5°06'S, 38°38'E
Ambangulu (Tz), 5°05'S, 38°26'E
Amboseli NP, 2°30'S, 37°00'E
Arabuko–Sokoke Forest, 3°20'S, 39°52'E
Archer's Post, 0°39'N, 37°41'E
Ardai Plains (Tz), 3°23'S, 36°20'E
Ark [The], 0°20'S, 36°48'E
Aruba Dam, 3°21'S, 38°49'E
Arusha [Town] (Tz), 3°20'S, 36°45'E
Arusha Chini (Tz), 3°35'S, 37°20'E
Arusha NP (Tz), 3°15'S. 37°00'E
Athi Plains, 1°25'S, 36°53'E
Athi River, 1°19'S, 36°39'E to 2°59'S, 38°30'E
Athi River [Town], 1°27'S, 36°59'E

Babati (Tz), 4°13'S, 35°45'E
Bamburi, 4°00'S, 39°43'E
Baomo, 1°55'S, 40°08'E
Baragoi, 1°47'N, 36°47'E
Baricho, 3°06'S, 39°47'E
Baringo [Lake], 0°38'N, 36°05'E
Bar Olengo, 0°00', 34°12'E
Barsaloi, 1°20'N, 36°52'E
Bogoria [Lake], 0°15'N, 36°06'E
Bondo, 0°06'S, 34°16'E
Boni Forest, 1°40'S, 41°15'E
Buffalo Springs GR, 0°37'N, 37°39'E
Bungoma [Town], 0°34'N, 37°34'E
Bura [Taita District], 3°30'S, 38°18'E
Bura [Tana River District], 1°06'S, 39°57'E
Burungi [Lake] (Tz), 3°53'S, 35°52'E
Busia [Town], 0°25'N, 34°15'E

Chake-Chake (Tz), 5°15'S, 39°45'E
Chalbi Desert, 3°00'N, 37°20'E
Chemelil, 0°05'S, 35°05'E
Chemoni Forest, 0°07'N, 35°08'E
Cherangani Hills, 1°15'N, 35°27'E
Chuka Forest, 0°20'S, 37°39'E
Chyulu Hills, 2°35'S, 37°50'E
Crater Highlands (Tz), 2°43'S to 3°22'S, 35°26'E to 35°56'E

Dakacha, 3°01'S, 39°48'E
Dar es Salaam (Tz), 6°48'S, 39°17'E
Daua River Valley, 4°16'N, 40°46'E to 3°56'N, 41°52'E
Diani Forest, 4°18'S, 39°35'E
Dida Galgalu Desert, 3°00'N, 38°00'E
Dodoma [Town] (Tz), 6°11'S, 35°45'E
Don Dol, 0°24'N, 37°10'E

Eldama Ravine, 0°03'N, 35°43'E
Eldoret, 0°31'N, 35°17'E
Elgeyu–Maraquet [Escarpment], 0°55'N, 35°35'E
Elgon [Mt], 1°08'N, 34°33'E
Elmenteita [Lake], 0°27'S, 36°15'E
El Molo Bay, 2°51'N, 36°42'E
El Wak, 2°49'N, 40°56'E
Emali Plains, 2°05'S, 37°28'E
Embu [Town], 0°35'S, 37°40'E
Embulul (Tz), 3°00'S, 35°46'E
Endau [Mt], 1°16'S, 38°35'E
Endebess, 1°04' N, 34°51'E

Endulen (Tz), 3°11'S, 35°10'E
Engamat (Tz), 3°00'S, 35°48'E
Engaruka (Tz), 2°59'S, 35°57'E
Essimingor [Mt] (Tz), 3°24'S, 36°06'E
Ewaso Ng'iro River, see Uaso Nyiro
Eyasi [Lake] (Tz), 3°40'S, 35°05'E

Fort Hall, see Murang'a.
Fort Ternan, 0°12'S, 35°21'E

Galana Ranch, 3°20'S, 39°20'E
Galana River (see Sabaki), 2°59'S, 38°30'E to 3°05'S, 39°30'E
Ganda Forest, 4°38'S, 39°10'E
Garba Tula, 0°32'N, 38°31'E
Garissa [Town], 0°28'S, 39°38'E
Garsen, 2°16'S, 40°07'E
Gatamayu Forest, 0°59'S, 36°43'E
Gazi, 4°26'S, 39°30'E
Gedi (Gede) Forest, 3°18'S, 40°01'E
Gilgil, 0°29'S, 36°18'E
Gol Mts (Tz), 2°42'S, 35°26'E
Grumeti River (Tz), 2°05'S, 33°57'E to 2°00'S, 34°55'E

Habaswein, 1°01'N, 39°29'E
Hadu, 2°51'S, 39°58'E
Hanang [Mt] (Tz), 4°26'S, 35°24'E
Handeni (Tz), 5°30'S, 38°00'E
Hell's Gate NP, 0°55'S, 36°19'E
Himo (Tz), 3°23'S, 37°33'E
Hola, 1°29'S, 40°02'E
Homa Bay, 0°28'S, 34°27'E
Horr Valley, 2°10'N, 36°55'E
Hunter's Lodge, 2°11'S, 37°43'E
Huri Hills, 3°30'N, 37°47'E

Ijara, 1°36'S, 40°31'E
Ilemi Triangle, 5°20'N, 35°30'E
Ileret, 4°19'N, 36°14'E
Iltalal, 2°51'S, 37°52'E
Irangi Forest, 0°21'S, 37°30'E
Iringa [Town] (Tz), 7°47'S, 35°42'E
Iruru Forest, 0°11'N, 35°05'E
Isiolo [Town], 0°21'N, 37°35'E
Iten [Escarpment], 0°40'N, 35°30'E

Jipe [Lake], 3°35'S, 37°45'E
Juba River (Somalia), 4°10'N, 42°05'E to 0°20'S, 42°30'E

Kabarnet [Town], 0°30'N, 35°45'E
Kabras (Malaba) Forest, 0°26'N, 34°48'E
Kacheliba, 1°29'N, 35°01'E
Kahe (Tz), 3°30'S, 37°26'E
Kaibibich, 1°12'N, 35°17'E
Kaimosi, 0°11'N, 34°57'E
Kaisut Desert, 1°53'N, 37°47'E
Kajiado [Town], 1°51'S, 36°47'E
Kakamega [Town], 0°17'N, 34°45'E
Kakamega Forest, 0°16'N, 34°53'E
Kamathia, 4°56'N, 35°19'E
Kamburu, 0°48'S, 37°42'E
Kanyaboli [Lake], 0°03'N, 34°10'E
Kanyakwat, 1°15'N, 34°55'E
Kapedo, 1°10'N, 36°06'E
Kapenguria [Town], 1°15'N, 35°08'E
Kapiti Plains, 1°38'S, 37°00'E
Kapsabet [Town], 0°12'N, 35°06'E
Kapsarok, 0°18'S, 35°03'E
Kapsoit, 0°20'S, 35°13'E
Kaptagat, 0°28'N, 35°29'E
Karasuk Hills, 2°10'N, 35°08'E
Karatu (Tz), 3°20'S, 35°42'E

Karawa, 2°38'S, 40°12'E
Karissia Hills, 1°03'N, 36°51'E
Karo-Lola, 3°53'N, 41°41'E
Kasigau [Mt], 3°50'S, 38°50'E
Kavirondo Gulf, 0°15'S, 34°35'E
Kedong Valley, 1°10'S, 36°30'E
Kendu Bay, 0°21'S, 34°38'E
Kenya [Mt], 0°10' S, 37°20' E
Kericho [Town], 0°22'S, 35°17'E
Kerio River, 0°53'N, 35°43'E to 2°56'N, 36°11'E
Kerio Valley, 0°18'N, 35°39'E to 1°24'N, 35°39'E
Ketumbeine [Mt] (Tz), 2°44'S, 36°16'E
Kiambere, 0°42'S, 37°47'E
Kiambu, 1°10'S, 36°50'E
Kibaya (Tz), 5°18'S, 36°34'E
Kibigori, 0°04'S, 35°03'E
Kibish (Ilemi Triangle), 5°20'N, 35°40'E
Kiboko, 2°11'S, 37°43'E
Kibondo (Tz), 3°33'S, 30°30'E
Kibwezi Forest, 2°26'S, 37°53'E
Kichwa Tembo (Mara GR), 1°15'S, 35°01'E
Kieni Forest, 0°51'S, 36°44'E
Kiganjo, 0°24'S, 37°00'E
Kijabe, 0°55'S, 36°35'E
Kikuyu, 1°15'S, 36°40'E
Kilgoris, 1°00'S, 34°53'E
Kilifi [Town], 3°38'S, 39°51'E
Kilimanjaro [Mt] (Tz), 3°04'S, 37°22'E
Kilimanjaro [Region HQ] (Tz), see Moshi
Kilosa (Tz), 6°50'S, 36°59'E
Kimana, 2°48'S, 37°32'E
Kiminini, 0°51'N, 34°58'E
Kinangop [Plateau], 0°42'S, 36°34'E
Kipini, 2°32'S, 40°31'E
Kipkabus, 0°18'N, 35°30'E
Kisii [Town], 0°41'S, 34°46'E
Kisite Island, 4°43'S, 39°22'E
Kisumu [Town], 0°06'S, 34°45'E
Kitale [Town], 1°01'N, 35°00'E
Kito Pass, 1°06'N, 35°55'E
Kitovu Forest, 3°27'S, 37°37'E
Kitui [Town], 1°22'S, 38°01'E
Kiunga, 1°45'S, 41°29'E
Kiwayu, 1°59'S, 41°21'E
Kodich, 1°38'N, 35°03'E
Kondoa (Tz), 4°54'S, 35°47'E
Kongelai [Escarpment], 1°25'N, 35°03'E
Konza, 1°45'S, 37°07'E
Koobi Fora, 3°57'N, 36°13'E
Kora NR, 0°05'S, 38°40'E
Korogwe (Tz), 5°09'S, 38°29'E
Koru, 0°11'S, 35°16'E
Kulal [Mt], 2°43'N, 36°56'E
Kunyao, 1°47'N, 35°03'E
Kwale, 4°11'S, 39°27'E

Laikipia [Plateau], 0°25'N, 36°45'E
Laisamis, 1°36'N, 37°48'E
Lali Hills, 3°00'S, 39°15'E
Lambwe Valley GR, see Ruma NP
Lamu [Town, Island], 2°17'S, 40°55'E
Latham Island (Tz), 6°54'S, 39°56'E
Lembeni (Tz), 3°47'S, 37°37'E
Lemek, 1°06'S, 35°23'E
Leroghi [Plateau], 1°00'N, 36°35'E
Lerundo, 0°09'N, 34°51'E
Lessos, 0°13'N, 35°18'E
Lewa Downs, 0°21'N, 37°33'E
Limuru, 1°06'S, 36°39'E
Lobo Lodge (Tz), 1°58'S, 35°13'E
Lodwar [Town], 3°07'N, 35°36'E
Logipi [Lake], 2°14'N, 36°34'E
Loima [Mt], 3°09'N, 35°02'E
Loita [Hills, Plains], 1°30'S, 35°40'E

Loitokitok, see Oloitokitok
Lokichokio, 4°12'N, 34°21'E
Lokitaung, 4°16'N, 35°45'E
Lokori, 1°56'N, 36°02'E
Loldaiga Hills, 0°12'N, 37°07'E
Lolgorien, 1°14'S, 34°38'E
Loliondo (Tz), 2°03'S, 35°37'E
Lolkissale [Mt] (Tz), 3°46'S, 36°24'E
Londiani, 0°10'S, 35°36'E
Longido (Tz), 2°41'S, 36°44'E
Longonot, 0°55'S, 36°27'E
Lorian Swamp, 0°40'N, 39°35'E
Lorugumu [River], 2°53'N, 35°15'E
Lossogonoi [Mt] (Tz), 4°00'S, 37°20'E
Lotakipi (Lotikipi) Plains, 4°33'N, 34°45'E
Lotonok (Lotongot), 1°44'N, 35°38'E
Loyangalani (Loiyengalani), 2°46'N, 36°43'E
Lukenya Hill, 1°28'S, 37°03'E
Lumbwa, 0°12'S, 35°28'E
Lygarja [Lake] (Tz), 3°00'S, 35°02'E

Machakos [Town], 1°31'S, 37°16'E
Mackinnon Road, 3°44'S, 39°03'E
Mado Gashi, 0°44'N, 39°10'E
Magadi [Lake, Town], 1°52'S, 36°17'E
Magaidu Forest (Tz), 2°05'S, 35°37'E
Maikona, 2°56'N, 37°38'E
Maji ya Chumvi, 3°47'S, 39°22'E
Maktau, 3°22'S, 38°08'E
Makuyu, 0°54'S, 37°11'E
Malaba, 0°40'N, 34°18'E
Malaba (Kabras) Forest, 0°22'N, 34°31'E
Malawa River, 0°35'N, 34°17'E
Malikisi, 0°41'N, 34°25'E
Malindi [Town], 3°13'S, 40°07'E
Malka Mari, 4°16'N, 40°46'E
Manda Island, 2°17'S, 40°57'E
Mandera [Town], 3°56'N, 41°52'E
Mangiki, 0°53'N, 34°36'E
Mangola Springs (Tz), 3°25'S, 35°26'E
Manyara [Lake] NP (Tz), 3°35'S, 35°50'E
Mara GR, 1°30'S, 35°00'E
Mara [Region HQ] (Tz), see Mwanza
Mara River, 0°28'S, 35°46'E to 1°31'S, 33°56'E
Marafa Forest, 3°02'S, 39°55'E
Maragoli [Escarpment], 0°00', 34°40'E
Maralal [Town], 1°06'N, 36°42'E
Marang Forest (Tz), 3°15'S, 35°45'E
Mariakani, 3°52'S, 39°28'E
Marich Pass, 1°20'N, 35°10'E
Marigat, 0°28' N, 35°59'E
Marsabit [Mt], 2°17'N, 37°57'E
Masai Steppe (Tz), 4°30'S, 36°30'E to 5°10'S, 37°30'E
Masek [Lake] (Tz), 3°05'S, 35°05'E
Maseno, 0°01'S, 34°36'E
Masinga Dam, 0°56'S, 37°37'E
Maswa GR (Tz), 3°00'S, 34°30'E
Mathews Range, 1°15'N, 37°15'E
Mau [Escarpment], 0°06'S, 35°44'E to 0°55'S, 36°07'E
Mau Forest, 0°30'S, 35°20'E
Mau [Plateau], 0°05'S, 35°27'E to 1°10'S, 36°12'E
Mau Narok, 0°41'S, 35°57'E
Maungu, 3°33'S, 38°45'E
Mazumbai (Tz), 4°48'S, 38°30'E
Mbagathi RIver, 1°25'S, 36°35'E to 1°19'S, 36°39'E
Mbalageti RIver (Tz), 2°12'S, 33°49'E to 2°30'S, 34°48'E
Mbeya [Town] (Tz), 8°54'S, 33°27'E
Mbololo Forest, 3°20'S, 38°26'E
Mbulu [Town] (Tz), 3°51'S, 35°32'E
Mbulu [Escarpment] (Tz), 3°30'S, 35°45'E
Mbulu Highlands (Tz), 3°45'S, 35°40'E to 4°20'S, 35°45'E
Mbulumbulu (Tz), 3°15'S, 35°48'E
Menengai Crater, 0°12'S, 36°04'E

Merti, 1°04'N, 38°40'E
Meru [Town], 0°03'N, 37°39'E
Meru [Mt] (Tz), 3°14'S, 36°45'E
Meru NP, 0°05'N, 38°20'E
Mgeta (Tz), 7°02'S, 37°34'E
Mida Creek, 3°22'S, 39°58'E
Migori [Town], 1°04'S, 34°28'E
Migori River, 0°55'S, 35°10'E to 0°55'S, 34°10'E
Mitole, 2°08'S, 40°11'E
Mkomazi GR (Tz), 4°00'S, 38°00'E
Mnazini, 2°00'S, 40°09'E
Moa (Tz), 4°46'S, 39°10'E
Mogotio, 0°01'S, 35°58'E
Molo, 0°15'S, 35°44'E
Mombasa [Town], 4°03'S, 39°40'E
Mombo (Tz), 4°53'S, 38°17'E
Monduli [Mt] (Tz), 3°18'S, 36°27'E
Moroto [Mt] (Uganda), 2°32'N, 34°46'E
Moshi [Town] (Tz), 3°21'S, 37°20'E
Moshi River (Tz), 3°10'S, 37°22'E to 3°35'S, 37°28'E
Mosiro, 1°30'S, 36°06'E
Mountain Lodge, 0°15'S, 37°10'E
Moyale [Town], 3°32'S, 39°03'E
Mrima Hill, 4°29'S, 39°16'E
Msambweni, 4°28'S, 39°29'E
Mtai Forest (Tz), 4°50'S, 38°46'E
Mtito Andei, 2°41'S, 38°10'E
Mtwapa, 3°57'S, 39°45'E
Mua Hills, 1°28'S, 37°11'E
Mugie (Muge), 0°42'N, 36°36'E
Muhoro Bay, 1°01'S, 34°05'E
Muhoroni, 0°09'S, 35°12'E
Mumias [Town], 0°20'N, 34°29'E
Mungatsi, 0°28'N, 34°19'E
Murang'a (formerly Fort Hall) [Town], 0°43'S, 37°09'E
Musiara Swamp, 1°18'S, 35°04'E
Musoma (Tz), 1°30'S, 33°48'E
Mutha, 1°48'S, 38°26'E
Mwachi River, 4°00'S, 39°30'E
Mwanza [Town] (Tz), 2°31'S, 34°54'E
Mwea NR, 0°50'S, 37°40'E
Mweiga, 0°19'S, 36°54'E
Mwingi, 0°56'S, 38°04'E

Naberera (Tz), 4°12'S, 36°56'E
Nadapal, 4°26'N, 34°16'E
Nairobi, 1°17'S, 36°49'E
Naivasha, [Lake, Town], 0°46'S, 36°21'E
Nakuijit, 1°39'N, 35°08'E
Nakuru [Lake, Town, NP], 0°22'S, 36°05'E
Namanga, 2°33'S, 36°47'E
Nambale, 0°27'N, 34°15'E
Nandi [District HQ], See Kapsabet
Nandi Forest, North, 0°20'N, 35°00'E
Nandi Forest, South, 0°05'N, 35°00'E
Nandi Hills, 0°07'S, 35°11'E
Nanyuki [Town], 0°01'N, 37°04'E
Narok [Town], 1°05'S, 35°52'E
Naro Moru, 0°10'S, 37°01'E
Nasolot NR, 1°50'N, 35°24'E
Natron [Lake] (Tz), 2°25'S, 36°00'E
Ndaragwa, 0°04'S, 36°31'E
Ndotos [Mts], 1°45'N, 37°07'E
Ngaia Forest, 0°22'N, 38°02'E
Ngangao Forest, 3°22'S, 38°20'E
Ngare Nairobi (Tz), 3°03'S, 37°01'E
Ng'iya, 0°03'N, 34°23'E
Ngobit, 0°04'S, 36°47'E
Ngomeni, 3°01'S, 40°11'E
Ngong [Escarpment, Hills, Town], 1°22'S, 36°39'E
Ngorongoro Crater (Tz), 3°10'S, 35°35'E
Ngulia [Hills], 3°00'S, 38°13'E
Ngurdoto Forest (Tz), 3°18'S, 36°55'E
Nguruman Hills, 1°50'S, 35°50'E

Nguuni, 3°59'S, 39°42'E
Njoro, 0°20'S, 35°56'E
North Horr, 3°19'N, 37°04'E
Nou Forest (Tz), 4°05'S, 35°30'E
Nyahururu, 0°02'N, 36°22'E
Nyambeni Hills, 0°20'N, 38°00'E
Nyando Valley, 0°07'S, 35°05'E
Nyanza [Province HQ], see Kisumu
Nyarondo, 0°07'S, 35°08'E
Nyeri, 0°25'S, 36°57'E
Nyiru [Mt], 2°08'N, 36°51'E
Nzoia River, 0°53'N, 37°07'E to 0°03'N, 33°57'E

Ol Bolossat [Lake], 0°09'S, 36°26'E
Oldeani (Tz), 3°16'S, 35°26'E
Ol Doinyo Orok (Namanga), 2°32'S, 36°47'E
Ol Doinyo Sabachi, see Ololokwe
Ol Doinyo Sapuk, 1°08'S, 37°15'E
Olduvai Gorge (Tz), 2°58'S, 35°22'E
Ol Kalou, 0°16'S, 36°23'E
Ol Olmoti (Tz), 3°00'S, 35°38'E
Oloitokitok, 2°56'S, 37°30'E
Ololokwe (Ol Doinyo Sabachi) [Mt], 0°50'N, 37°32'E
Olololoo [Escarpment], 1°05'S, 35°08'E to 1°25'S, 34°48'E
Olorgesailie, 1°34'S, 36°27'E
Olosirwa [Mt] (Tz), 3°04'S, 35°48'E
Omo River, 8°30'N, 38°20'E to 4°30'N, 36°10'E

Pare Mts, North (Tz), 3°45'S, 37°45'E
Pare Mts, South (Tz), 4°30'S, 38°00'E
Pemba Channel, 5°00'S, 39°30'E
Pemba Island (Tz), 5°10'S, 39°48'E
Pokot [District HQ], see Kapenguria
Port Victoria, 0°06'N, 33°58'E
Pugu Hills (Tz), 6°53'S, 39°05'E

Rabai, 3°56'S, 39°34'E
Raboor Island, 0°11'S, 34°32'E
Ramisi, 4°32'S, 39°23'E
Ramu, 3°56'N, 41°13'E
Rapogi, 0°54'S, 34°28'E
Ras Ngomeni, 2°59'S, 40°14'E
Rombo, 3°03'S, 37°42'E
Rongai, 0°10'S, 35°51'E
Ruiru, 1°09'S, 36°58'E
Ruma NP, 0°40'S, 34°15'E
Rumuruti, 0°16'N, 36°32'E
Rusinga Island, 0°24'S, 34°10'E

Sabaki Estuary, 3°09'S, 40°08'E
Sabaki River, 3°05'S, 39°30'E to 3°09'S, 40°08'E
Sagala Hills, 3°27'S, 38°35'E
Sagana, 0°40'S, 37°12'E
Saiwa Swamp NP, 1°06'N, 35°07'E
Samburu (se. Kenya), 3°46'S, 39°17'E
Samburu GR, 0°40'N, 37°30'E
Same (Tz), 4°04'S, 37°44'E
Samia Hills, 0°18'N, 34°09'E
Sand River, 1°33'S, 35°01'E
Sangole, 1°30'S, 40°36'E
Sanya Juu (Tz), 3°11'S, 37°04'E
Sanya Plains (Tz), 3°25'S, 37°10'E
Satima Peak, 0°19'S, 36°37'E
Selengai, 2°11'S, 37°10'E
Serengeti NP (Tz), 2°20'S, 34°50'E
Seronera [River, Valley] (Tz), 2°16'S, 34°47'E
Shaba GR, 0°34'N, 37°50'E
Shimba Hills NP, 4°13'S, 39°25'E
Shimoni, 4°39'S, 39°23'E
Shombole, 2°05'S, 36°07'E
Siana Springs, 1°30'S, 35°24'E
Siaya, 0°04'N, 34°19'E
Sigi Valley (Tz), 5°03'S, 39°00'E
Sigor, 1°29'S, 35°28'E

Simba, 2°10'S, 37°36'E
Simba Plains, 2°20'S, 37°35'E
Sioport, 0°13'N, 34°01'E
Sio River, 1°09'N, 34°33'E to 0°14'N, 34°01'E
Sokoke, see Arabuko–Sokoke Forest
Solai [Lake, Town], 0°03'N, 36°09'E
Sololo, 3°33'N, 38°39'E
Songhor, 0°03'S, 35°13'E
Sotik, 0°41'S, 35°07'E
South Horr, 2°06'N, 36°55'E
Soy, 0°40'N, 35°09'E
Suam [Escarpment, Gorge], 1°10'N, 34°37'E
Suam River = Upper course of Turkwell River
Subukia, 0°01'S, 36°11'E
Suguta Valley, 2°10'N, 36°31'E
Suk District, see Karasuk Hills
Sultan Hamud, 2°01'S, 37°22'E
Suswa [Mt], 1°09'S, 36°21'E

Tabora (Tz), 5°01'S, 32°48'E
Taita Hills [District HQ], see Wundanyi
Taita Hills Lodge, 3°30'S, 38°16'E
Taita Hills, 3°25'S, 38°20'E
Talek River, 1°26'S, 35°12'E
Tambach, 0°36'N, 35°31'E
Tana River, 0°42'S, 37°14'E to 2°33'S, 40°31'E
Tana River delta, 2°32'S, 40°30'E
Tana River Primate Reserve, 1°55'S, 40°12'E
Tanga [Region, Town] (Tz), 5°03'S, 39°06'E
Tarangire NP (Tz), 4°00'S, 36°00'E
Tarina River (Tz), 1°47'S, 34°26'E to 2°02'S, 34°14'E
Taru, 3°44'S, 39°09'E
Taveta, 3°25'S, 37°42'E
Tenewe Island, 2°28'S, 40°47'E
Thika, 1°03'S, 37°05'E
Thika River, 0°44'S, 36°47'E to 0°54'S, 37°28'E
Thomson's Falls (at Nyahururu), 0°02'N, 36°22'E
Thura River, 0°35'S, 37°53'E
Tigoni, 1°08'S, 36°40'E
Timau, 0°05'N, 37°14'E
Timboroa, 0°04'N, 35°32'E
Tiva River, 1°34'S, 37°50'E to 2°06'S, 39°19'E
Todenyang, 4°32'N, 35°56'E
Trans-Mara Forest, 0°40'S, 35°32'E
Trans-Nzoia [District HQ], see Kitale
Tsavo East NP [HQ], 3°22'S, 38°35'E
Tsavo River, 3°11'S, 37°43'E to 2°59'S, 38°31'E
Tsavo West NP [HQ], 2°50'S, 38°10'E
Tugen HIlls, 0°30'N, 35°48'E
Turbi, 3°20'N, 38°23'E

Turbo, 0°38'N, 35°03'E
Turkana, [Lake] (formerly Lake Rudolph), 3°30'N, 36°00'E
Turkwell Delta, 3°04' N, 36°09'E
Turkwell River, 1°09'N, 34°35'E to 3°07'N, 36°04'E
Turkwell Valley, 2°00'N, 35°27'E to 3°07'N, 35°36'E

Uasin Gishu [District HQ], see Eldoret
Uasin Gishu [Plateau], 0°31'N, 35°17'E
Uaso Nyiro River, Northern, 0°20'N, 36°33'E to 1°11'N, 39°34'E
Uaso Nyiro River, Southern, 0°29'S, 35°49'E to 2°08'S, 36°02'E
Uaso Nyiro Swamp, 2°05'S, 36°07'E
Udzungwa Mts (Tz), 8°20'S, 35°50'E
Ukerere Island (Tz), 2°03'S, 33°00'E
Ukwala, 0°12'N, 34°11'E
Ulu Hills, 1°49'S, 37°15'E
Uluguru Mts (Tz), 7°10'S, 37°40'E
Uraguess [Mt], 0°56'N, 37°24'E
Usa River (Tz), 3°22'S, 36°52'E
Usambara Mts, East (Tz), 5°00'S, 38°40'E
Usambara Mts, West (Tz), 4°40'S, 38°20'E
Usengi, 0°04'S, 34°04'E

Vanga, 4°39'S, 39°13'E
Victoria [Lake], 0°00', 33°00'E
Voi, 3°23'S, 38°34'E
Voi River, 3°22'S, 38°23'E to 3°37'S, 39°48'E

Wajir, 1°45'N, 40°04'E
Wamba, 0°59'N, 37°19'E
Watamu, 3°21'S, 40°01'E
Webuye, 0°36'N, 34°46'E
Wei-Wei River, 1°16'N, 35°27'E to 1°35'N, 35°31'E
Wembere Steppe (Tz), 3°50'S, 34°20'E to 5°10'S, 33°55'E
Wenje, 1°47'S, 40°06'E
Whale Island, 3°24'S, 39°59'E
Winan Gulf, 0°15'S, 34°35'E
Witu, 2°22'S, 40°30'E
Wundanyi, 3°24'S, 38°22'E

Yala, 0°06'N, 34°32'E
Yala River, 0°07'N, 35°02'E to 0°02'N, 33°59'E
Yala River Forest, 0°10'N, 34°45'E
Yala Swamp, 0°03'N, 34°05'E
Yatta, 1°10'S, 37°26'E
Yatta Plateau, 2°00'S, 38°00'E

Zanzibar [Island] (Tz), 6°10'S, 39°20'E

LITERATURE CITED

Andrews, P., C. P. Groves and J. F. M. Horne. 1975. *Ecology of the lower Tana River floodplain (Kenya). Journ. E. Afr. Nat. Hist. Soc. and Natl. Mus.* 151: 1–31.

Archer, G. F., and E. M. Godman, 1961. *The Birds of British Somaliland and the Gulf of Aden.* Oliver and Boyd, Edinburgh and London. Vols. 3–4.

Ash, J. S. 1978. Ethiopia as a presumed wintering area for the eastern Grasshopper Warbler *Locustella naevia straminea. Bull. Brit. Orn. Club* 98: 22–24.

Ash, J. S. 1981. A new race of the Scaly Babbler *Turdoides squamulatus* from Somalia. *Bull. Brit. Orn. Club* 101: 399–403.

Ash, J. S. 1983. Over fifty additions of birds to the Somalia list including two hybrids, together with notes from Ethiopia and Kenya. *Scopus* 7: 54–79.

Ash, J. S., and J. E. Miskell. 1983. Birds of Somalia, their habitat, status and distribution. *Scopus* Special Suppl. No. 1. Nairobi. 95 pp.

Bannerman, D. A. 1949. *The Birds of Tropical West Africa.* Vol. 7. Oliver and Boyd, London.

Bannerman, D. A. 1953. *The Birds of West and Equatorial Africa.* Vol. 1. Oliver and Boyd, London.

Beaman, Mark. 1994. *Palearctic birds: a checklist of the birds of Europe, North Africa and Asia north of the foothills of the Himalayas.* Harrier Publ., Stonyhurst, England.

Bednall, D. K., and J. G. Williams. 1989. Range retraction of the White-eyed Gull *Larus leucophthalmus* from the eastern coast of Africa. *Scopus* 13: 122–123.

Beesley, J. S. 1972. Birds of the Arusha National Park, Tanzania. *Journ. E. Afr. Nat. Hist. Soc. and Natl. Mus.* 132: 1–30.

Bennun, L. A. 1991. An avifaunal survey of the Trans-Mara Forest, Kenya. *Scopus* 14: 61–71.

Bennun, L. A., C. Gichuki, J. Darlington and F. Ng'weno. 1986. The avifauna of Ol Doinyo Orok, a forest island: initial findings. *Scopus* 10: 83–86.

Benson, C. W. 1946. Notes on the birds of southern Abyssinia. *Ibis* 88: 287–306, 444–461.

Benson, C. W. 1952. Notes from Nyasaland. *Ostrich*: 23: 144-159.

Benson, C. W., and F. M. Benson. 1947. Breeding and other records from Nyasaland, *Ibis* 89: 279-290.

Benson, C. W., and F. M. Benson. 1977. *The Birds of Malawi.* Montfort Press, Limbe, Malawi.

Bentz, G. D. 1979. The appendicular myology and phylogenetic relationships of the Ploceidae and Estrildidae (Aves: Passeriformes). *Bull. Carnegie Museum Nat. Hist.* No. 15: 1–25. Pittsburgh, Pennsylvania.

Britton, P. L. (ed.) 1980. *Birds of East Africa: their habitat, status and distribution.* East Africa Natural History Society, Nairobi.

Britton, P. L. and H. 1985. Shoebill *Balaeniceps rex*: a deletion from the Kenya avifauna. *Scopus* 9: 50.

Brown, L. H. 1974. The races of the European Snake Eagle *Circaetus gallicus. Bull. Brit. Orn. Club* 94: 126–128.

Brown, L. H. 1977. The White-winged Dove *Streptopelia reichenowi* in SE Ethiopia, comparisons with other species, and a field key for identification. *Scopus* 1: 107–109.

Brown, L. H., and P. L. Britton. 1980. *The Breeding Seasons of East African Birds.* East Africa Natural History Society, Nairobi.

Brown, L. H., E. K. Urban and K. Newman. 1982. *The Birds of Africa.* Vol. 1. Academic Press, London.

Browning, M. R., 1992. Comments on the nomenclature and dates of publication of some taxa in Bucerotidae. *Bull. Brit. Orn. Club* 112: 22–25.

Campbell, B., and E. Lack. 1985. *A Dictionary of Birds.* British Ornithologists' Union. T. and A. D. Poyser, Calton.

Carter, C. 1978. Eastern Least Honeyguide (*Indicator meliphilus*) at Ndola. *Bull. Zamb. Orn. Soc.* 10: 30–31.

Chandler, R. J., and C. Wilds. 1994. Little, Least and Saunders's Terns. *British Birds* 87: 60–66.

Chapin, J. P. 1932. The Birds of the Belgian Congo, Part 1. *Bull. Amer. Mus. Nat. Hist.* 65. New York.

Chapin, J. P. 1939. The Birds of the Belgian Congo, Part 2. *Bull. Amer. Mus. Nat. Hist.* 75. New York.

Chapin, J. P. 1953. The Birds of the Belgian Congo, Part 3. *Bull. Amer. Mus. Nat. Hist.* 75A. New York.

Chapin, J. P. 1954. The Birds of the Belgian Congo, Part 4. *Bull. Amer. Mus. Nat. Hist.* 75B. New York.

Chappuis, C. 1975. Les Oiseaux de l'Ouest Africain. Discs 5 and 6. *Alauda* 43: 450–474.

Clancey, P. A. 1982. The Little Tern in southern Africa. *Ostrich* 53: 102–106.

Clancey, P. A. 1984. Further on the status of *Anthus latistriatus* Jackson, 1899. *Le Gerfaut* 74: 375–382.

Clancey, P. A. 1990. A review of the indigenous pipits (genus *Anthus* Bechstein: Motacillidae) of the Afrotropics. *Durban Mus. Novitates* 15: 42–72.

Clancey, P. A., and J. G. Williams. 1957. The systematics of the Little Purple-banded Sunbird *Cinnyris bifasciatus* (Shaw), with notes on its allies. *Durban Mus. Novitates* 5: 27–41.

Clancey, P. A., W. J. Lawson and M. P. S. Irwin. 1969. The Mascarene Martin *Phedina borbonica* (Gmelin) in Mozambique: a new species to the South African list. *Ostrich* 40: 5–8.

Cleere, N. 1995. The identification, taxonomy and distribution of the Mountain Nightjar *Caprimulgus poliocephalus*/Fiery-necked Nightjar *C. pectoralis* complex. *Bull. Afr. Bird Club* 2: 86–97.

Clement, P., A. Harris and J. Davis. 1993. *Finches and Sparrows.* A & C Black, London.

Cottam, P. 1957. The pelecaniform characters of the skeleton of the shoe-bill stork, *Balaeniceps rex. Zool. Bull.*

Brit. Mus. (Nat. Hist.) 5: 51–72.

Cox, J. B. 1980. Some remarks on the breeding distribution and taxomy of the prions (Procellariidae: *Pachyptila*). *Rec. S. Austr. Museum* 18: 91–121.

Cramp, S., and K. E. L. Simmons (eds.) 1977. *The Birds of the Western Palearctic.* Vol. 1. Oxford Univ. Press, Oxford.

Cramp, S., and K. E. L. Simmons (eds.) 1983. *The Birds of the Western Palearctic.* Vol. 3. Oxford Univ. Press, Oxford.

Cramp, S. (ed.) 1985. *The Birds of the Western Palearctic.* Vol. 4. Oxford Univ. Press, Oxford.

Cramp, S., and C. M. Perrins (eds.) 1993. *The Birds of the Western Palearctic.* Vol. 7. Oxford Univ. Press. Oxford.

Crowe, T. M. 1978. The evolution of guinea-fowl (Galliformes, Phasianidae, Numidinae): taxonomy, phylogeny, speciation and biogeography. *Ann. S. Afr. Mus.* 76: 43–136.

Dittami, J., and V. Haas. 1982. A family of White Storks *Ciconia ciconia* at Lake Nakuru: the first breeding record for Kenya? *Scopus* 6: 70.

Dowsett, R. J. 1972. Geographical variation in *Pseudhirundo griseopyga*. *Bull. Brit. Orn. Club* 92: 97–100.

Dowsett, R. J. 1974. Geographical variation in iris colour in the bulbul *Andropadus milanjensis*. *Bull. Brit. Orn. Club* 94: 102–104.

Dowsett, R. J., and F. Dowsett-Lemaire. 1980. The systematic status of some Zambian birds. *Le Gerfaut* 70: 151–199.

Dowsett, R. J., and F. Dowsett-Lemaire. 1993. Comments on the taxonomy of some Afrotropical bird species. *Tauraco Research Report* 5: 323–389. Tauraco Press, Jupille, Li¡ege, Belgium.

Dowsett, R. J., and A. D. Forbes-Watson. 1993. *Checklist of Birds of the Afrotropical and Malagasy Regions.* Tauraco Press, Liège, Belgium.

Dowsett-Lemaire, F. 1990. Eco-ethology, distribution and status of Nyungwe Forest birds (Rwanda). *Tauraco Res. Report* 3: 31–85.

Elliott, H. F. I., and N. R. Fuggles-Couchman. 1948. An ecological survey of the birds of the Crater Highlands and Rift Lakes, northern Tanganyika Territory. *Ibis* 90: 394–425.

Erasmus, R. P. B. 1992. Notes on the call of the Grass Owl *Tyto capensis*. *Ostrich* 63: 184–185.

Evans, T. D., L. G. Watson, A. J. Hipkiss, J. Kiure, R. J. Timmins and A. W. Perkin. 1994. New records of Sokoke Scops Owl *Otus ireneae*, Usambara Eagle Owl *Bubo vosseleri* and East Coast Akalat *Sheppardia gunningi* from Tanzania. *Scopus* 18: 40–47.

Ferguson-Lees, I. J. (in prep.) *Raptors. An identification guide to the birds of prey of the world.* A & C Black, London.

Finch, B. W. 1987. Rock-loving Cisticola *Cisticola aberrans* near Kichwa Tembo, Maasai Mara, sw. Kenya. *Scopus* 11: 44–46.

Fishpool, L. D. C., R. Demey, G. Allport and P. V. Hayman. 1994. Notes on the field identification of the bulbuls (Pycnonotidae) of Upper Guinea. *Bull. Afr. Bird Club* 1: 32–38.

Freitag, S., and T. J. Robinson. 1993. Phylogeographic patterns in mitochondrial DNA of the Ostrich (*Struthio camelus*). *Auk* 110: 614–622.

Friedmann, H. 1937. Birds collected by the Childs Frick Expedition to Ethiopia and Kenya Colony. Part 2, Passeres. U. S. Natl Mus. Bull. 253. Smithsonian Inst, Washington, D.C.

Fry, C. H. 1976. On the systematics of African and Asian Tailor-birds (Sylviinae). *Arnoldia* 8 (No. 6): 1–15.

Fry C. H. 1984. *The Bee-eaters.* T. and A. D. Poyser, Calton.

Fry, C. H., S. Keith and E. K. Urban. 1988. *The Birds of Africa.* Vol. 3. Academic Press, London.

Fry, C. H., K. Fry and A. Harris. 1992. *Kingfishers, Bee-eaters and Rollers.* Christopher Helm/A & C Black, London.

Fuggles-Couchman, N. R. 1984. The distribution of, and other notes on, some birds of Tanzania. Part 2. *Scopus* 8: 81–92.

Fuggles-Couchman, N. R., and H. F. I. Elliott. 1946. Some records and field-notes from north-eastern Tanganyika Territory. *Ibis* 88: 327–347.

Gill, F. B. 1990. *Ornithology.* W. H. Freeman and Co., New York.

Grant, P. J. 1986. *Gulls: a guide to identification.* 2nd Ed. T. and A. D. Poyser, Calton.

Granvik, H. 1934. The ornithology of North Western Kenya Colony with special regard to the Suk and Turkana districts. *Rev. Zool. Bot. Afr.* 25, I: 1–190.

Greenway, P. J. 1968. A Classification of the Vegetation of East Africa. *Kirkia* 9: 1–68.

Griffiths, J. F. 1958. Climatic zones of East Africa. *E. A. Agriculture Journ.* 1958: 178–185.

Grimshaw, J. M. 1995. Birds of prey and owls of the western and northern slopes of Mt Kilimanjaro, Tanzania. *Scopus* 19: 27–37.

Hall, B. P., and R. E. Moreau. 1970. *An Atlas of Speciation in African Passerine Birds.* Brit. Mus. (Nat. Hist.), London.

Hancock, J., and J. Kushlan. 1984. *The Herons Handbook.* Harper and Row, New York.

Harper, P. C. 1980. The field identification and distribution of the Thin-billed Prion (*Pachyptila belcheri*) and the Antarctic Prion (*Pachyptila desolata*). *Notornis* 27: 235–286.

Harrison, P. 1983. *Seabirds: an identification guide*. Croom Helm Ltd, Beckenham.

Hayman, P., J. Marchant and T. Prater. 1986. *Shorebirds: an identification guide to the waders of the world*. Croom Helm Ltd, London.

Hollom, P. A. D., R. F. Porter, S. Christensen and I. Willis. 1988. *Birds of the Middle East and North Africa*. T. and A. D. Poyser, Calton.

Humphrey, P. S. and K. C. Parkes. 1959. An approach to the study of molts and plumages. *Auk* 76: 1–31.

Irwin, M. P. S. 1993. Further remarks on the grasswarblers *Cisticola melanura, angusticauda* and *fulvicapilla*. *Honeyguide* 39: 36–38.

Jackson, Sir Frederick. 1938. *The Birds of Kenya Colony and the Uganda Protectorate* (3 vols). Completed and edited by W. L. Sclater. Gurney and Jackson, London.

Jensen, F. P., and S. Brogger-Jensen. 1992. The forest avifauna of the Uzungwa Mountains, Tanzania. *Scopus* 15: 65–83.

Johnsgard, P. A. 1978. *Ducks, Geese and Swans of the World*. Univ. of Nebraska Press, Lincoln.

Johnston, Sir Harry. 1902. On the occurrence of *Balaeniceps rex* on Lake Victoria. *Ibis*, 8th Ser. (6): 334–336.

Keith, G. S., and W. W. H. Gunn. 1971. Birds of the African rain forests. Sounds of nature No. 9. Federation of Ontario Naturalists. Ontario, and Am. Mus. Nat. Hist. New York.

Keith, G. S., E. K. Urban and C. H. Fry. 1992. *The Birds of Africa*. Vol. 4. Academic Press, London.

Lawson, W. J. 1964. Geographical variation in the Cape Batis *Batis capensis* (Linnaeus). *Durban Mus. Novitates* 7, Part 8: 189–200.

Lewis, A., and D. Pomeroy, 1989. *A Bird Atlas of Kenya*. A. A. Balkema, Rotterdam and Brookfield.

Ligon, D., and N. C. Davidson. 1988. Phoeniculidae, in C. H. Fry *et al.* (eds.), *The Birds of Africa*. Vol. 3. Academic Press, London.

Livezey, B. C. 1986. A phylogenetic analysis of recent Anseriform genera using morphological characters. *Auk* 103: 737–754.

Louette, M. 1990. The nightjars of Zaïre. *Bull. Brit. Orn. Club* 110: 71–77.

Lynes, H. 1930. Review of the genus *Cisticola*. *Ibis*, 12 Ser., Vol. 6., *Cisticola* Suppl: 1–673.

McLachlan, G. R., and R. Liversidge. 1978. *Roberts' Birds of South Africa*, 4th Ed. John Voelcker Bird Book Fund, Cape Town.

Mackworth-Praed, C. W., and C. H. B. Grant. 1952. *Birds of Eastern and Northeastern Africa. African handbook of birds, Ser. 1*. Vol. 1. Longmans, London.

Mackworth-Praed, C. W., and C. H. B. Grant. 1955. *Birds of Eastern and Northeastern Africa. African handbook of birds. Ser.1,* Vol. 2. Longmans, London.

Mackworth-Praed, C. W., and C. H. B. Grant. 1973. *Birds of West Central and Western Africa. African handbook of birds. Ser. 3*. Vol. 2. Longmans, London.

Maclean, G. L. 1984. *Roberts' Birds of Southern Africa*, 5th ed. John Voelcker Bird Book Fund, Cape Town.

Madge, S., and H. Burn. 1988. *Wildfowl: an identification guide to the ducks, geese and swans of the world*. Croom Helm Ltd., London.

Mann, C. F. 1986. Christmas Island Frigatebirds *Fregata andrewsi* on the Kenya coast. *Bull. Brit. Orn. Club* 106: 89–90.

Mann, C. F., P. J. Burton and I. Lennerstedt. 1978. A re-appraisal of the systematic position of *Trichastoma poliothorax* (Timaliinae, Muscicapidae). *Bull. Brit. Orn. Club* 98: 131–140

Mayr, Ernst. 1942. *Systematics and the Origin of Species*. Columbia Univ. Press, New York.

Miskell, J. E., and J. S. Ash. 1985. Gillett's Lark *Mirafra gilletti* new to Kenya. *Scopus* 9: 53–54.

Moreau, R. E. 1935. A synecological study of Usambara, Tanganyika Territory, with particular reference to birds. *J. Ecol.* 23: 1–43.

Moreau, R. E. 1966. *The Bird Faunas of Africa and its Islands*. Academic Press, London and New York.

Moreau, R. E., and J. C. Greenway, Jr. 1962. Family Ploceidae, in E. Mayr and J. C. Greenway, Jr. (eds.), *Checklist of Birds of the World*, Vol. 15. Mus. Comp. Zool., Cambridge, Mass.

Moreau, R. E., and W. M. Moreau. 1937. Biological and other notes on some East African birds. Part 2. *Ibis,* 14 Ser. (2): 321–345.

Nicolai, J. 1964. Der Brutparasitismus der Viduinae als ethologisches Problem. *Z. Tierpsychol.* 21: 129–204.

Nuttall, R. J. 1993. Vocal behaviour of the Quail Finch *Ortygospiza atricollis*. *Ostrich* 64: 97–104.

Nyamweru, Celia. 1986. Climate, vegetation and wildlife in Kenya. *Swara* 9 (no. 6): 14–19.

Owre, O. T., and D. R. Paulson. 1968. Records of falconiformes from the Lake Rudolf area, Kenya. *Bull. Brit. Orn. Club* 88: 151–152.

Pakenham, R. H. W. 1943. Field notes on the birds of Zanzibar and Pemba. *Ibis* 85: 165–189.

Pakenham, R. H. W. 1979. *The Birds of Zanzibar and Pemba*. BOU Check-list No. 2. Brit. Orn. Union, London.

Parker, I. S. C., and A. C. Parker. 1994. *Amaurornis flavirostris*: Plumages. (Unpubl. ms.)

Payne, R. B. 1971. Paradise Whydahs *Vidua paradisaea* and *V. obtusa* of southern and eastern Africa, with notes on differentiation of the females. *Bull. Brit. Orn. Club* 91 (3): 68–76.

Payne, R. B. 1973. Behavior, mimetic songs and song dialects, and relationships of the parasitic indigobirds (*Vidua*) of Africa. *Ornith. Monographs* No. 11. Amer. Ornithologists' Union.

Payne, R. B. 1980. Behavior and songs of hybrid parasitic indigobirds. *Auk* 97 (1): 118–134.

Payne, R. B., L. L. Payne, M. E. D. Nhlane and K. Hustler. 1992. Species status and distribution of the parasitic indigo-birds *Vidua* in east and southern Africa. *Proc. 8th Pan-African Ornith. Congress.* R. T. Wilson, Ed. Bartridge Partners. Umberleigh, North Devon: 40–52.

Pearson, D. J. 1989. The separation of Reed Warblers *Acrocephalus scirpaceus* and Marsh Warblers *A. palustris* in eastern Africa. *Scopus* 13: 81–89.

Pearson, D. J., and J. S. Ash (in press). The taxonomic position of the Somali Courser *Cursorius (cursor) somalensis. Bull. Brit. Orn. Club.*

Pearson, D. J., G. C. Backhurst, B. W. Finch and D. A. Turner. 1989. Barbary Falcons *Falco pelegrinoides* in Tsavo. *Scopus* 13: 117–118.

Pearson, D. J., M. A. C. Coverdale, A. L. Archer and A. D. Forbes-Watson. 1989. Great Grey Shrike *Lanius excubitor* in the Ilemi Triangle. *Scopus* 13: 134.

Peters, J. L. 1948. *Check-list of Birds of the World.* Vol. 6. Mus. Comp. Zool., Cambridge, Mass.

Peterson, R. T. 1980. *A Field Guide to the Birds.* Houghton Mifflin, Boston.

Porter, R. F., Ian Willis, S. Christensen and B. P. Nielsen. 1981. *Flight Identification of European Raptors.* T. and A. D. Poyser, Calton.

Pratt, D. J., and M. D. Gwynne. 1977. *Rangeland Management and Ecology in East Africa.* Hodder and Stoughton, London.

Prigogine, A. 1985. Recently recognized bird species in the afrotropical region [,] a critical review. *Proc. Int. Symp. Afr. Vertebrates*: 91–114. Bonn.

Rand, A. L. 1967. Nectariniidae, in R. A. Paynter, Jr. (ed.), *Check-list of Birds of the World,* Vol. 12. Harvard Univ. Press, Cambridge, Mass.

Ripley, S. D., and G. Heinrich. 1966. Comments on the Avifauna of Tanzania I. *Postilla* No. 96.

Ripley, S. D., and G. Heinrich. 1969. Comments on the Avifauna of Tanzania 2. *Postilla* No. 134.

Sclater, W. L., and R. E. Moreau. 1932. Taxonomic and field notes on some birds of north-eastern Tanganyika Territory, Parts I and II. *Ibis* 2: 487–522, 656–683.

Sclater, W. L., and R. E. Moreau. 1933. Taxonomic and field notes on some birds of north-eastern Tanganyika Territory, Parts III–V. *Ibis* 3: 1–33, 187–219, 399–440.

Shantz, H. L., and C. F. Marbut, 1923. *The Vegetation and Soils of Africa.* Amer. Geog. Soc. Res. Series No. 13. New York.

Sheldon, F. H., and D. W. E. Winkler. 1993. Intergeneric phylogenetic relationships of swallows estimated by DNA-DNA hybridization. *Auk* 110: 798–824.

Shirihai, H., Ian Sinclair and P. R. Colston. 1995. A new species of *Puffinus* shearwater from the western Indian Ocean. *Bull. Brit. Orn. Club* 115: 75–83.

Short, L. L. 1982. *Woodpeckers of the World.* Delaware Mus. Nat. Hist,. Greenville, Delaware.

Short, L. L., and J. F. M. Horne. 1985a. Aspects of duetting in some ground barbets. *Proc. of Vth Pan-African Ornith. Congress*: 729–744.

Short, L. L., and J. F. M. Horne. 1985b. Social behavior and systematics of African barbets (Aves: Capitonidae). *Proc. Int. Symp. African Vertebrates*: 255–278. Bonn.

Short, L. L., and J. F. M. Horne. 1988. Order Piciformes, in C. H. Fry *et al.* (eds.), *The Birds of Africa,* Vol 3. Academic Press, London.

Short, L. L., J. F. M. Horne and C. Muringo-Gichuki. 1990. Annotated Check-list of the birds of East Africa. *Proc. West. Foundation Vert. Zool.* 4, No. 3. 246 pp.

Sibley, C. G. 1970. A comparative study of the egg-white proteins of passerine birds. *Bull. Peabody Mus. Nat. Hist.,* Yale Univ. Press, 32: 1–131.

Sibley, C. G., and Jon E. Ahlquist. 1981. The relationships of wagtails and pipits (Motacillidae) as indicated by DNA-DNA hybridization: *L'Oiseau et R.F.O.* 51: 189–199.

Sibley, C. G., and J. E. Ahlquist. 1985. The relationships of some groups of African birds, based on comparisons of the genetic material, DNA. *Proc. Int. Symp. Afr. Vertebrates*: 115–116. Bonn.

Sibley, C. G., and J. E. Ahlquist. 1990. *Phylogeny and Classification of Birds.* Yale Univ. Press, New Haven, Conn.

Sibley, C. G., J. E. Ahlquist and B. L. Monroe, Jr. 1988. A classification of the living birds of the world based on DNA-DNA hybridization studies. *Auk* 105: 409–423.

Sibley, C. G., and Burt L. Monroe, Jr. 1990. *Distribution and Taxonomy of Birds of the World.* Yale Univ. Press, New Haven, Conn.

Sinclair, I. 1984. *Field Guide to the Birds of Southern Africa.* Struik Publ., Cape Town.

Steyn, P. 1982. *Birds of Prey of Southern Africa.* David Philip Ltd., Cape Town.

Stronach, N. 1990. New information on birds in Serengeti National Park, Tanzania. *Bull. Brit. Orn. Club* 110: 198–202.

Stuart, S. N., and J. M. Hutton. (eds.), 1977. The Avifauna of the East Usambara Mountains, Tanzania. (Unpubl. report compiled by Cambridge East Afr. Ornith. Expedition.)

Survey of Kenya. 1962. *Atlas of Kenya*. Nairobi.

Survey of Kenya. 1978. *Kenya and northern Tanzania route map*. Nairobi.

Svendsen, J. O., and L. Hansen. 1992. Some bird voices from the Udzungwa Mountains, Tanzania. Zool. Mus., Copenhagen.

Tarboton, W. R., and C. H. Fry. 1986. Breeding and other behaviour of the Lesser Jacana. *Ostrich* 57: 233–243.

Tennant, J. R. M. 1964. The birds of Endau Mountain in the Kitui District of Kenya. *Ibis* 106: 1–6.

Thomsett, S. 1989. The Barbary Falcon *Falco pelegrinoides* in Kenya. *Scopus* 13: 116–117.

Thomson, A. L. 1964. *A New Dictionary of Birds*. Thomas Nelson and Sons Ltd, London.

Tomlinson, W. 1950. Some notes chiefly from the Northern Frontier District of Kenya. Part II. *Journ. E. Afr. Nat. Hist. Soc. and Natl Mus.* 19: 225–250.

Traylor, M. A. 1970. East African *Bradornis*. *Ibis* 112: 513–531.

Traylor, M. A. 1986a. [African] Sylviidae, in E. Mayr and G. W. Cottrell (eds.), *Check-list of Birds of the World*, Vol. 11. Harvard Univ. Press, Cambridge, Mass.

Traylor, M.A. 1986b. [African] Muscicapidae, in E. Mayr and G. W. Cottrell (eds.), Check-list of *Birds of the World*, Vol. 11. Harvard Univ. Press, Cambridge, Mass.

Traylor, M. A. 1986c. Platysteiridae, in E. Mayr and G. W. Cottrell (eds.), *Check-list of Birds of the World*, Vol. 11. Harvard Univ. Press, Cambridge, Mass.

Traylor, M. A. 1986d. [African] Monarchidae, in E. Mayr and G. W. Cottrell (eds.), *Check-list of Birds of the World*, Vol. 11. Harvard Univ. Press, Cambridge, Mass.

Urban, E. K., C. H. Fry and S. Keith. 1986. *The Birds of Africa*. Vol. 2. Academic Press, London.

Urban, E. K., C. H. Fry and S. Keith (in prep.). *The Birds of Africa* Vol. 5. Academic Press, London.

van den Berg, A. B., C. Smeenk, C. Bosman, B. Haase, A. van der Niet and G. Cadee. 1991. Barau's Petrel *Pterodroma baraui*, Jouanin's Petrel *Bulweria fallax* and other seabirds in the northern Indian Ocean in June-July 1984 and 1985. *Ardea* 79: 1–13.

van den Elzen, R. 1985. Systematics and evolution of African canaries and seedeaters (Aves: Carduelidae). *Proc. Int. Symp. Afr. Vertebrates*: 435–451. Bonn.

van Someren, V. G. L. 1916. A list of birds collected in Uganda and British East Africa with notes on their nesting and other habits. *Ibis,* 10th Ser., Vol. 4 (2): 193–252.

van Someren, V. G. L. 1922. Notes on the Birds of East Africa. *Novitates Zoologicae* Vol. 29: 1–246.

van Someren, V. G. L. 1925. The birds of Kenya and Uganda. *Journ. E. Afr. and Uganda Nat. Hist. Soc.* Parts 1 and 2.

van Someren, V. G. L. 1932. Notes on the birds of East Africa. *Novitates Zoologicae* Vol. 37: 252–380.

van Someren, V. G. L. 1939. Coryndon Memorial Museum Expedition to the Chyulu Hills, April-July 1938. *Journ. E. Afr. and Uganda Nat. Hist. Soc.* Parts 1 and 2: 1–129.

van Someren, V. G. L. 1956. Days with Birds. *Fieldiana: Zoology*, Vol. 38. Chicago [Field] Natural History Museum Press, Chicago, Ill.

Vaurie, C. 1959. *The Birds of the Palearctic Fauna. Passeriformes.* H. F. & G. Witherby Ltd., London.

Vaurie, C. 1965. *The Birds of the Palearctic Fauna. Non-Passeriformes.* H. F. & G. Witherby Ltd., London.

Veit, R., and L. Jonsson. 1984. Field identification of smaller sandpipers within the genus *Calidris*. *American Birds* 38 (5): 853–876.

Vielliard, J. 1972. Données Biogéographiques sur l'avifaune d'Afrique Centrale. *Alauda* 40: Part 2: 64–92.

Vincent, J. 1935. Birds of northern Portuguese East Africa. List of, and observations on, the collections made during the British Museum expedition of 1931–32. *Ibis*, 13th Ser, Vol. 5: 355–397.

Voous, K. H. 1973. List of recent Holarctic bird species. Non-passerines. *Ibis* 115: 612–638.

Voous, K. H. 1977. List of recent Holarctic bird species. Passerines. *Ibis* 119: 223–250, 376–406.

Voous, K. H. 1985. [Classification] in B. Campbell and E. Lack. *A Dictionary of Birds*

White, C. M. N. 1962. *A revised check list of African shrikes, orioles, drongos, starlings, crows, waxwings, cuckoo-shrikes, bulbuls, accentors, thrushes and babblers*. Govt Printer, Lusaka.

White, C. M. N. 1963. *A revised check list of African flycatchers, tits, tree creepers, sunbirds, white-eyes, honey eaters, buntings, finches, weavers and waxbills*. Govt Printer, Lusaka.

White, C. M. N. 1965. *A revised check list of African non-passerine birds*. Govt Printer, Lusaka.

White, G. B. 1974. Rarest eagle owl in trouble. *Oryx* 12: 484–486.

Williams, J. G., and N. Arlott. 1980. *A Field Guide to the Birds of East Africa*. Collins, London.

Williams, J. G., and G. S. Keith. 1962. A contribution to our knowledge of the Parasitic Weaver, *Anomalospiza imberbis*. *Bull. Brit. Orn. Club* 82: 141–142.

Wolters, H. E. 1985. Species limits in some Afrotropical Estrildidae (Aves Passeriformes). *Proc. Int. Symp. Afr. Vertebrates*: 425–434. Bonn

Young, T. P., and M. R. Evans. 1993. Alpine vertebrates of Mount Kenya, with particular notes on the Rock Hyrax. (Ms.)

Zimmerman, D. A. 1972. The avifauna of the Kakamega Forest, western Kenya, including a bird population study. *Bull. Amer. Mus. Nat. Hist.* 149: Article 3: 259–339.

INDEX TO ENGLISH NAMES

Numbers in **bold** refer to plate numbers, and are followed by the page on which the species appears. Alternative names of species are shown in parentheses.

INDEX TO SCIENTIFIC NAMES

(Numbers refer to the page on which the species appears).